W

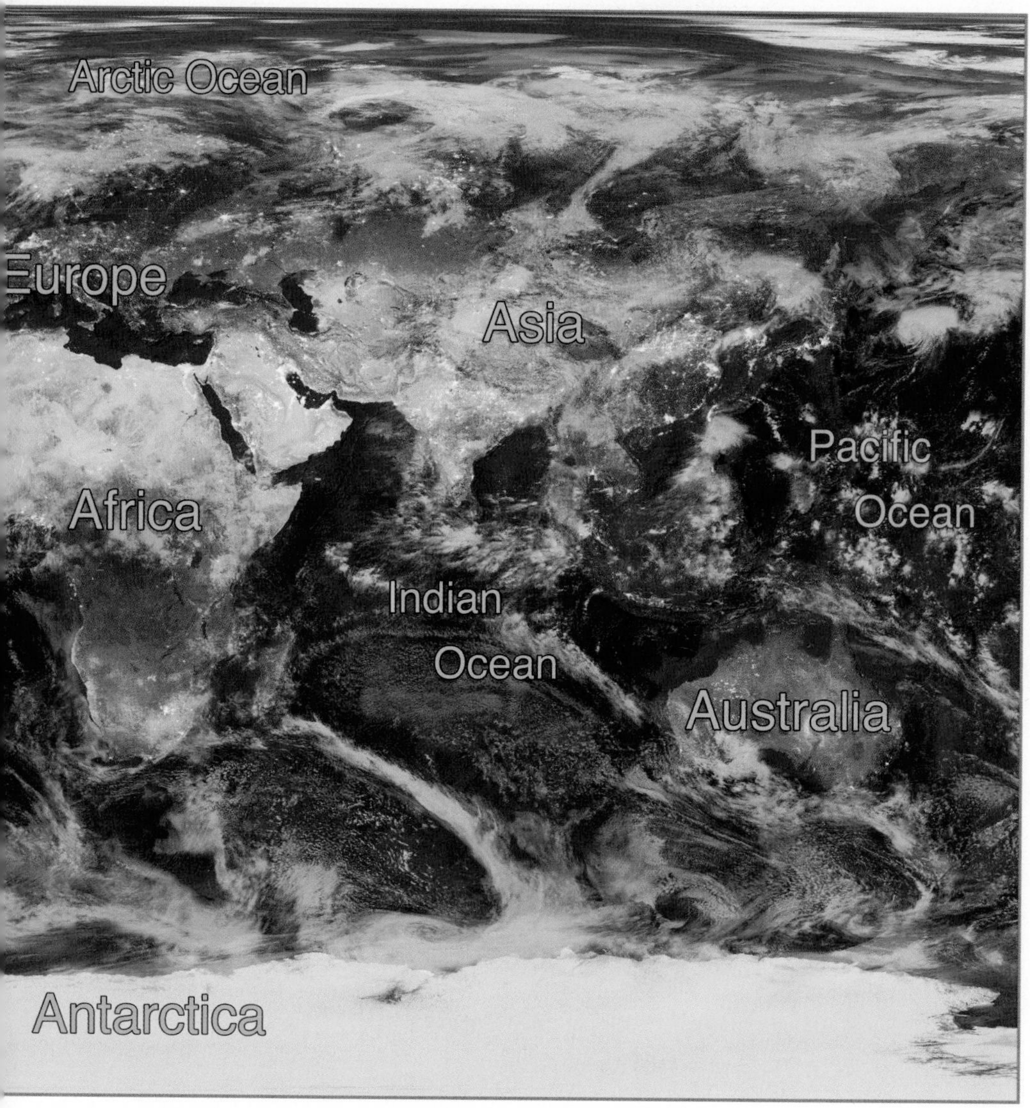
Arctic Ocean
Europe
Asia
Africa
Pacific
Ocean
Indian
Ocean
Australia
Antarctica

THIRD SEAGULL EDITION

Worlds Together, Worlds Apart

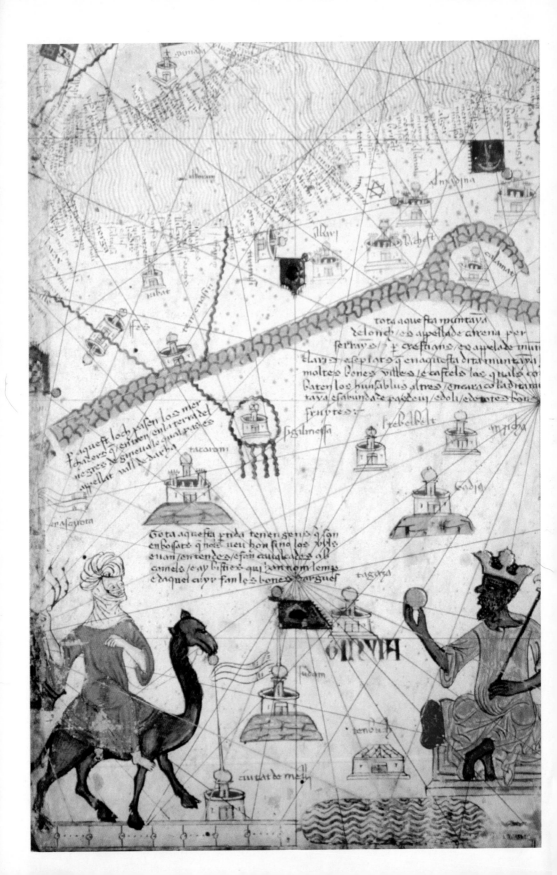

THIRD SEAGULL EDITION

Worlds Together, Worlds Apart

From the Beginnings of Humankind to the Present

Jeremy Adelman
Elizabeth Pollard
Clifford Rosenberg
Robert Tignor

W. W. NORTON & COMPANY
Independent Publishers Since 1923

W. W. Norton & Company has been independent since its founding in 1923, when William Warder Norton and Mary D. Herter Norton first published lectures delivered at the People's Institute, the adult education division of New York City's Cooper Union. The firm soon expanded its program beyond the Institute, publishing books by celebrated academics from America and abroad. By midcentury, the two major pillars of Norton's publishing program—trade books and college texts—were firmly established. In the 1950s, the Norton family transferred control of the company to its employees, and today—with a staff of five hundred and hundreds of trade, college, and professional titles published each year—W. W. Norton & Company stands as the largest and oldest publishing house owned wholly by its employees.

Editor: Jon Durbin
Project Editor: David Bradley
Assistant Editor: Lily Gellman
Managing Editor, College: Marian Johnson
Managing Editor, College Digital Media: Kim Yi
Production Manager: Jane Searle
Media Editor: Carson Russell
Media Project Editor: Rachel Mayer
Associate Media Editor: Alexander Lee
Assistant Media Editor: Alexandra Malakhoff
Marketing Manager, History: Sarah England Bartley
Design Director: Rubina Yeh
Designer: Lissi Sigillo
Director of College Permissions: Megan Schindel
Permissions Specialist: Elizabeth Trammell
Photo Editor: Mike Cullen
Composition: KnowledgeWorks Global Ltd.
Illustrations: Mapping Specialists, Ltd.
Manufacturing: Transcontinental Printing–Beauceville

Permission to use copyrighted material is included in the credits section of this book, which begins on page C-1.

ISBN: 978-0-393-44271-7

W. W. Norton & Company, Inc., 500 Fifth Avenue, New York, NY 10110-0017
wwnorton.com

W. W. Norton & Company Ltd., 15 Carlisle Street, London W1D 3BS

2 3 4 5 6 7 8 9 0

BRIEF CONTENTS

CONTENTS

1

Becoming Human   2

STORYLINE: Prehistory and the Peopling of the Earth

2

Rivers, Cities, and First States, 3500–2000 BCE   46

STORYLINE: Comparing First Cities

3

Nomads, Territorial States, and Microsocieties, 2000–1200 BCE   88

STORYLINE: Comparing First States

4

First Empires and Common Cultures in Afro-Eurasia, 1250–325 BCE 126

STORYLINE: Comparing First Empires and the Beginnings of Judaism

5

Worlds Turned Inside Out, 1000–350 BCE   164

6

Shrinking the Afro-Eurasian World, 350–100 BCE   202

7

Han Dynasty China and Imperial Rome, 300 BCE–300 CE   242

STORYLINE: Comparing the Han and Roman Empires

8

The Rise of Universalizing Religions, 300–600 CE   280

STORYLINE: The Rise of Christianity, the Spread of Buddhism, and the Beginnings of Common Cultures

9

New Empires and Common
Cultures, 600–1000 CE   318

STORYLINE: Religion and Empires: Islam, the Tang Dynasty, Christendom, and Common Cultures

10

Becoming "The World," 1000–1300 CE   358

STORYLINE: The Emergence of the World We Know Today

11

Crises and Recovery in Afro-Eurasia, 1300–1500   404

STORYLINE: The Black Death, Recovery, and Conquest

12

Contact, Commerce, and Colonization, 1450–1600   442

STORYLINE: The Age of Global Exploration and Colonization

13

Worlds Entangled, 1600–1750   482

STORYLINE: The Emergence of Global Trade

14

Cultures of Splendor and Power, 1500–1780   530

STORYLINE: The Creation of Global Cultures

15

Reordering the World, 1750–1850   570

STORYLINE: The Global Impact of the Atlantic and Industrial Revolutions

16

Alternative Visions of the Nineteenth Century   612

STORYLINE: Global Challenges to Western Expansion

17

Nations and Empires, 1850–1914   650

STORYLINE: How Nation-States Became Global Empires

18

An Unsettled World, 1890–1914   692

STORYLINE: The Global Impact of Modernity

19

Global Crisis, 1910–1939   730

STORYLINE: World War I and the Growth of Mass Societies

20

The Three-World Order, 1940–1975   770

STORYLINE: World War II and the Emergence of the First, Second, and Third Worlds during the Cold War

21

Globalization, 1970–2000   814

STORYLINE: The Emergence of Modern Globalization

22

Twenty-First-Century Global Challenges, 2001–The Present   858

STORYLINE: The Impact of Modern Globalization Today

MAPS

PREFACE

Worlds Together, Worlds Apart sets the standard for those who want to teach a globally integrated and comparative world history survey course. Building on the success of earlier editions, co-authors Jeremy Adelman (Princeton University), Elizabeth Pollard (San Diego State University), Clifford Rosenberg (City University of New York), and Robert Tignor (Princeton University) have created this dynamic and highly accessible new Third Seagull Edition of *Worlds Together, Worlds Apart*.

The new Third Seagull Edition is written with clear, accessible prose and explanations, with a narrative that is twenty percent shorter than the Full Edition. It is a coherent, concise, cutting-edge survey of the field built around world history stories of significance, which we call **"Global Storylines."** These Global Storylines have the dual benefit of making the material more focused and more manageable for students. They also allow students to more readily make connections and comparisons across time and place since most, if not all, regions of the world are discussed in many of the chapters. Some of our favorite examples of Global Storylines include the creation of the Silk Roads and comparing the Han dynasty and the Roman Empire in the first volume, and in the second volume the global impact of the Atlantic and industrial revolutions and the alternative visions for organizing societies in response to the rise of nineteenth-century capitalism, and the impact of modern globalization today.

The New Third Seagull Edition

New Authorial Leadership

The publication of the new editions of the *Worlds Together, Worlds Apart* book family (Third Seagull, Concise Third, and Full Sixth Editions) brings a number of significant changes, most visibly with the authorial team. Out of that initial team of authors, the authors of *Worlds Together, Worlds Apart* agreed to reconstitute into a smaller team of four. **Elizabeth Pollard,** a Roman historian at San Diego State University, becomes the lead author of the first volume, cutting across all versions. For nearly two decades, she has taught the pre-1500 CE world history survey to classes of 30 to 500 students both in person and remotely. **Jeremy Adelman,** a historian of Latin America and the Atlantic world and the director of the Global History Lab at Princeton University, becomes lead author of the second volume. Adelman teaches a survey in global history from 1300 to the present both at Princeton and online. Tens of thousands of students worldwide have taken his course. In addition to these new lead authors for each volume,

Clifford Rosenberg (City University of New York), a distinguished historian of modern France and its empire, continues to bring his diverse teaching experiences and pedagogical insights to the modern volumes in the Concise and Seagull Editions. And **Robert Tignor,** a distinguished Africanist and the original general editor and the soul behind this book, remains an author in both volumes bringing his experience and eye for the big picture to bear on the book's prose. The changes in our authorial team have also brought departures. We started *Worlds Together, Worlds Apart* in its first edition as a much larger group, which included Steve Aron, Peter Brown, Ben Elman, Steve Kotkin, Xinru Liu, Sue Marchand, Holly Pittman, Gyan Prakash, Brent Shaw, and Michael Tsin. They were vital to mobilizing the latest specialist scholarship and to integrating a wide range of perspectives into one narrative, and this edition is indebted to their contributions. Our team of four allows us to strengthen the core themes with a unity of voice while remaining committed to the original principles of diversity of perspective.

A Strong Focus on Teaching with Primary Sources

From teaching a diverse array of students, we have learned about the challenge of teaching complex global processes—how societies converge, connect, and come together and how global orders fall apart. In addition to teaching a varied set of students, we have also taught world history in multiple formats and settings, including **hybrid, fully on-line, and large lecture classes.** In each of these modalities, we have developed extensive experience teaching with primary sources, which the new Third Seagull Edition of *Worlds Together, Worlds Apart* reflects in its **new online Primary Source Exercises.** These new online Primary Source Exercises are based largely on the documents and images found in the Concise and Full Edition's unique built-in reader, and they are designed to help students learn how to analyze and interpret both textual and visual primary sources, while developing their historical thinking skills like causation, continuity and change, comparison, and context. These Primary Source Exercises also bring a range of important themes to life, from gender to the environment, as for example in Chapter 9, "New Empires and Common Cultures, 600–1000 CE," has a number of sources on gender and new empires, and the new Chapter 22, "Twenty-First-Century Global Challenges, 2001–the Present," focuses on global climate change and features selections from Donald Trump and Greta Thunberg.

New Scholarship on Compelling Topics for Students

Our diverse teaching experience has also made us fully aware that most students taking world history survey courses come from majors cutting across the undergraduate curriculum. As a result, we have purposefully highlighted cutting-edge world history research on a wide range of topics that appeal highly to students, such as gender, race, the environment, migrations, trade, and technological changes.

The new Third Seagull Edition pays considerable attention to looking at world history through the lens of **gender.** In Chapter 4, covering parts of the second and first millennia BCE, we encounter the brilliant leader and military strategist Sammuramat, who wore clothes that disguised her gender, built a massive city at Babylon, and undertook daring and far-reaching military campaigns stretching from Egypt to India. Al-Khayzurān Bint Atta and her daughter-in-law Zubaidah in the Abbasid court of the late eighth and early ninth centuries CE provide insight into exceptional women's power in increasingly patriarchal contexts. In Chapter 10, a fascinating discussion on Mongol women shows the powerful role that women could play in cultures regarded as male dominant. We see a similar phenomenon in the early modern period in West Africa in Chapter 13, where we highlight strong women leaders who fought for their visions for the Kongo kingdom as it endured civil wars and the future of its lucrative slave trade hung in the balance. In Chapter 18, as part of the discussions on cultural modernity, we provide insights into the global nature of the women's suffrage movement in the early part of the twentieth century. And in the era of decolonization, covered in Chapter 20, we draw attention to women's mobilization in struggles to decolonize colonial Africa, and to women's roles in decolonization movements all over the world.

A second major focus is climate and the role it has played in producing radical changes in the lives of humans and **our environment**. For example, a long-term warming of the globe facilitated the domestication of plants and animals and led to an agricultural revolution and the emergence of settled societies. In the seventeenth century, the dramatic drop in global temperatures, now known as the Little Ice Age, produced political and social havoc and led to civil wars, population decline, and regime change all around the globe. These are the new focuses of Chapters 1 and 13. Likewise, the rise of modern empires significantly altered the balance of commercial ties between societies, while the later turn to industrialism turned an interconnected world into an interdependent and even more fragile one. These are the subjects of major revisions in Chapters 12, 15, and 19. Indeed, all chapters have been substantially revised, and the new Chapter 22, "Twenty-First-Century Global Challenges, 2001–the Present," focuses on four major challenges of the twenty-first century—global terror, global inequality, global climate change, and pandemics—and provides major new discussions on the expansion of state violence, racial justice protests, and new LGBTQ rights.

New Media for In-Person, Hybrid, and Remote Learning Experiences

The new Third Seagull Edition is also the most innovative to date when it comes to learning with digital materials, exercises, and activities. **Lead media author Alan Karras** (University of California, Berkeley) has brought together an outstanding team of media authors to develop the comprehensive ancillary package for the Third Seagull Edition, substantially increasing the learning and teaching support available to students and instructors for in-person, hybrid, remote, and "flipped classroom" learning modalities.

- **NEW online: Primary Source Exercises** and **Map Exercises** exist for each chapter in the book and are based on the maps and readings that go beyond what is in the Seagull Edition. These assignable, interactive learning tools provide the opportunity for critical analysis practice every week of the semester.
- **InQuizitive**, Norton's award-winning adaptive learning tool, is constructed around the Core Objectives and global comparisons in each chapter. InQuizitive offers an interactive game-like platform that strengthens student comprehension, allowing students to arrive at class better prepared to engage in meaningful discussion.
- **History Skills Tutorials** give students the necessary framework to analyze primary source documents, images, and maps. Guided by videos with author Elizabeth Pollard and supported by interactive assessments, these tutorials help students learn and practice the ways historians think.

Worlds Together, Worlds Apart's Guiding Principles

Five principles inform this book, guiding its framework and the organization of its individual chapters. The first is that **world history is global history**. We have chosen not to deal with the great regions and cultures of the world as separate units, devoting individual chapters to East Asia, South Asia, Southwest Asia, Europe, Africa, and the Americas. Instead, our goal is to place each of these regions in its largest geographical context. Accordingly, we have written chapters that are truly global in that most major regions of the world are discussed in each chapter. We achieved these globally integrated chapters by building each around a significant world history story—a **"Global Storyline."** It would be misleading, of course, to assert that the context is always "the world," because none of these regions, even the most highly developed commercially, enjoyed prolonged commercial or cultural contact with peoples all over the globe before Columbus's voyage to the Americas and the later expeditions of the sixteenth century. Yet, surprisingly, a global storyline can be told even from the earliest history of humanity. Humans were on the move more than 100,000 years ago and migrated across the planet more than 10,000 years ago. Long after these initial large-scale migrations, the peoples living on the Afro-Eurasian landmass, an important building block for our study, deeply influenced one another, as did the more scattered peoples living in the Americas and in Africa below the Sahara. Products, ideas, and persons traveled widely across the large land units of Eurasia, Africa, and the Americas. Our Global Storylines—sometimes traced across connected regions and sometimes told as comparative narratives—give meaning to these exchanges of goods and ideas and movements of people.

The second principle informing this work is **the importance of chronology in framing world history**. We have framed the chapters around significant world history stories and periods that transcended regional and cultural boundaries—moments or periods of meaningful change in the way that human beings organized their lives. Some of these changes were dramatic and affected many people, sweeping across large landmasses. They affected peoples living in widely dispersed societies, and they often led to radically varied cultural responses in different regions of the world. In other cases, changes occurred in only one locality while other places retained their traditions or took alternative routes. Chronology helps us understand the ways in which the world has, and has not, shared a common history. It also provides a continual forward momentum toward the present for students and makes it easier for them to see connections and make comparisons.

The third principle is **historical and geographical balance**. Ours is not a history focused on the rise of the west. We pay attention to the histories of all peoples and take care not to privilege the developments that led directly into European history, as if the history of the rest of the world were but a prelude to the rise of the west. We engage peoples living outside Europe on their own terms and try to see world history from their perspectives. Our presentation of Europe in the period leading up to and including the founding of the Roman Empire is different from many of the standard treatments. The Europeans we describe are rather rough, wild-living, warring peoples living on the fringes of the settled parts of the world and looked down on by more politically stable communities. They hardly seem to be the ilk that will catapult Europeans to world leadership a millennium later—indeed, they were very different people from those who, as the result of myriad intervening and contingent events, founded the nineteenth- and twentieth-century empires whose ruins are still all around us.

Our fourth principle is **an emphasis on connections and disconnections across societal and cultural boundaries**. World history is the history of the connections among peoples often living at great distances from one another, and it is also the history of the resistance of peoples living within and outside societies to connections that threatened to rob them of their independence. A stress on connections inevitably foregrounds the elements within societies that promoted long-distance ties. *Worlds Together, Worlds Apart*, as a title, is not intended to convey the message that the history of the world is a story of increasing integration. What for one ruling group brought benefits in the form of increased workforces, material prosperity, and political stability often meant enslavement, political subordination, and loss of territory for other groups. The historian's task, then, is not only to represent the different experiences of increased connectedness, describing worlds that came together, but also to trace the opposite trends, describing peoples and communities that remained, or intentionally grew, apart.

The fifth and final principle is that **world history is a narrative of big stories and broad comparisons**. *Worlds Together, Worlds Apart* is not a book of record or a history of the world. Indeed, in a work that traces global storylines from the beginnings to the present, the notion that no event or individual worthy of attention would be excluded is folly. We have sought to offer clear stories and interpretations that synthesize the vast body of data that often overwhelms histories of the world. Our aspiration is to identify the main historical forces that have shaped human experience and to highlight the monumental innovations that have changed the way humans lived. Cross-cultural comparisons of developments, institutions, and even founding figures receive attention to make students aware that some common institutions, such as family or the economy, did not have the same features in every society. But conversely, the seemingly diverse terms that were used, say, to describe learned and religious people in different parts of the world—monastics in Europe, *ulama* in the Islamic world, Brahmans in India, and scholar-gentries in China—often meant much the same thing in very different settings. We have constructed *Worlds Together, Worlds Apart* around big ideas and stories rather than filling the book with names and dates that encourage students to memorize rather than understand world history concepts.

Overview of Volume One

Volume One of *Worlds Together, Worlds Apart* deals with the period from the beginnings of human history through the development of new political structures like cities, territorial states, and empires and the rise of the world's universalizing religions, all leading toward the emergence of the regions of the world that we recognize today, which then immediately face the major disruptions of the Mongol invasions of the thirteenth century and the spread and destruction of the Black Death across Afro-Eurasia in the fourteenth century. It is divided into eleven chronological chapters, each of which marks a distinct global historical period.

Chapter 1 Becoming Human

Global Storyline: Prehistory and the Peopling of the Earth

Chapter 2 Rivers, Cities, and First States, 3500–2000 BCE

Global Storyline: Comparing First Cities

Chapter 3 Nomads, Territorial States, and Microsocieties, 2000–1200 BCE

Global Storyline: Comparing First States

Chapter 4 First Empires and Common Cultures in Afro-Eurasia, 1250–325 BCE

Global Storyline: Comparing First Empires and the Beginnings of Judaism

Chapter 5 Worlds Turned Inside Out, 1000–350 BCE

Global Storyline: The Axial Age

Overview of Volume Two

The chronological organizational structure for Volume Two reaffirms the commitment to write a decentered, global history of the world that is not moving inevitably toward a "rise of the west" story. Christopher Columbus is not the starting point, as he is in so many modern world histories. Rather, we begin in the eleventh and twelfth centuries with two major developments in world history: the Mongol invasions and the destruction and recovery from the Black Death. From there we describe how major historical processes changed the modern world in significant ways, including the rise of global exploration, the creation of global cultures, the expansion of global trade, alternative visions in the nineteenth century of western expansions, the transformation of nation-states into global empires, the uncertainty and disruption of modernism, World War I and the growth of mass societies, World War II and the emergence of a three-world order during the Cold War, and the emergence and impact of modern globalism today. We are excited that the epilogue from previous editions has now been rewritten and expanded to become the new standalone Chapter 22, "Twenty-First-Century Global Challenges, 2001–the Present."

Media & Print Ancillaries

The new Third Seagull Edition of *Worlds Together, Worlds Apart* is supported by a collection of digital resources proven to help faculty meet their course goals—in the classroom and online—and activities for students to develop core skills in reading comprehension, critical thinking, and historical analysis.

For Students

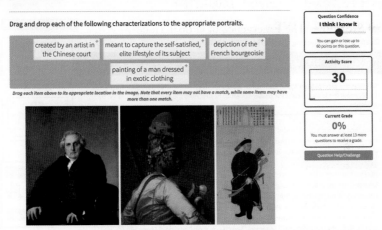

- To support the continued growth of students' historical skills, *Worlds Together, Worlds Apart* offers a series of brief, assignable **Primary Source Exercises** to accompany every chapter of the book. These exercises draw largely on the 100+ primary source documents from the Global Themes and Sources feature and the primary source images from the Interpreting Visual Evidence feature found at the end of each chapter in the Full and Concise Editions. Students are asked a series of interactive questions through which they practice analyzing the building blocks of the world history course.

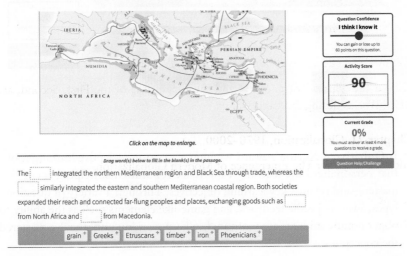

- To provide the opportunity for map-reading practice each week of the semester, *Worlds Together, Worlds Apart* offers stand-alone **Map Exercises** for every chapter of the book. Each exercise extracts the key maps from the chapter and presents students with interactive questions designed to assess their ability to read, dissect, interpret, and draw historical conclusions from the information depicted. Answer-specific feedback helps guide students through the maps, and connect the information back to the chapter reading.

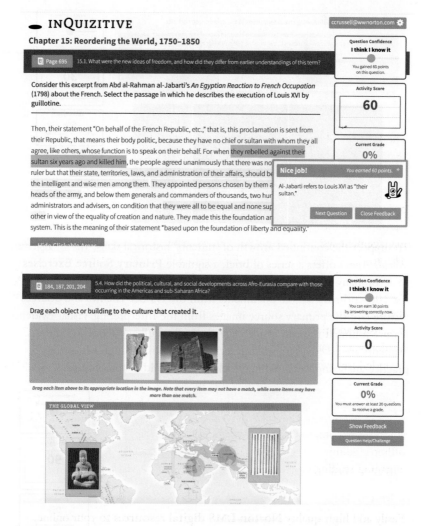

- **InQuizitive** is Norton's award-winning, easy-to-use adaptive learning tool that personalizes the learning experience for students, helping them master—and retain—key learning objectives. Through a variety of question types, answer-specific feedback, and game-like elements such as the ability to wager points, students are motivated to keep working until they've mastered the concepts.

Framework for Analyzing Documents

Historians keep important questions in mind while analyzing documents for clues to the past. Watch author and historian Elizabeth Pollard demonstrate how she analyzes documents.

Watch the video featuring Elizabeth Pollard analyzing an excerpt from Rabban Bar Sãwmã, *Pilgrimage to Jerusalem.*

- The **History Skills Tutorials** feature three online modules—"Analyzing Images," "Analyzing Primary Source Documents," and "Analyzing Maps"—to support students' development of the key skills needed for the history course. Each module features author videos modeling the analysis process, followed by interactive questions that will challenge students to apply what they have learned. The tutorials can be integrated directly into an existing learning management system, making for easy assignability and easy student access.
- The **student website** offers additional study and review materials for students to use outside class. The website is available via the *Worlds Together, Worlds Apart* digital landing page and includes author videos, interactive maps from the text, flashcards, detailed chapter outlines, and an online reader with dozens of additional primary source documents and images, each with a brief headnote and sample analysis questions.
- Included free with new copies of the text, the **Norton Ebook** offers an active reading experience, enabling students to take notes, bookmark, search, highlight, and even read offline. Instructors can add notes that students see when they read the text. Norton Ebooks can be viewed on—and synced among—all computers and mobile devices, and can be made available for offline reading. Author videos are embedded throughout to create an engaging reading environment.

For Instructors

- Easily add high-quality **Norton LMS digital resources** to your online, hybrid, or lecture courses. Get started building your course with our easy-to-use integrated resources; all activities can be accessed right within your existing learning management system. The downloadable file includes integration links to the following resources, organized by chapter: the Norton Ebook, InQuizitive, History Skills Tutorials, Primary Source Exercises, Map Exercises, and student website resources.

- The **Instructor's Manual** has everything instructors need to prepare lectures and classroom activities: lecture outlines; lecture ideas; classroom activities; image activities; lists of recommended books, films, and websites; and more. All resources from the Instructor's Manual are also available online through Norton's **Interactive Instructor's Guide** (IIG). The IIG includes searchable, filterable Instructor's Manual content plus instructor-facing videos with the book authors—great source material for instructors embarking on their first world history course.
- The **Test Bank** contains well over 1,000 multiple-choice, true/false, and short-answer questions. Questions are classified according to level of difficulty and Bloom's Taxonomy, providing multiple avenues for comprehension and skill assessment, and making it easy to construct tests that are meaningful and diagnostic. The Test Bank is available through the new **Norton Testmaker**, which allows you to create assessments for your course from anywhere with an Internet connection, without downloading files or installing specialized software.
- **Lecture PowerPoints and Art PowerPoints** feature lecture outlines, key talking points, and the photographs and maps from the book to support in-class presentations. **StoryMaps PowerPoints** break complex maps from the text into a sequence of annotated slides that address topics such as the Silk Roads, the spread of the Black Death, and population growth and the economy.

Acknowledgments

Worlds Together, Worlds Apart got its start with financial support from Princeton University's 250th Anniversary Fund for undergraduate teaching and, as such, it drew heavily on the expertise of the Princeton history department, in particular, Mariana Candido, Robert Darnton, Natalie Z. Davis, Sheldon Garon, Anthony Grafton, Molly Greene, David Howell, Harold James, William Jordan, Emmanuel Kreike, Elizabeth Lunbeck, Michael Mahoney, Arno Mayer, Kenneth Mills, John Murrin, Susan Naquin, Willard Peterson, Theodore Rabb, Bhavani Raman, Stanley Stein, and Richard Turits. When necessary, the authors of the initial iterations of the book reached outside the history department, getting help from Michael L. Bender, L. Carl Brown, Michael Cook, Norman Itzkowitz, Martin Kern, Thomas Leisten, Heath Lowry, and Peter Schaefer. David Gordon and Shamil Jeppie, graduates of the Princeton history department, offered input as the early editions developed.

The early iterations of *Worlds Together, Worlds Apart* relied on the above-and-beyond administrative support of Judith Hanson, Pamela Long, and Eileen Kane, all at Princeton University. More recent editions owe a debt of gratitude to Emily Pace and Leah Gregory, graduate students at San Diego State University who helped track down sources, images, and permissions.

Beyond Princeton, the authorial team benefited from exceptionally gifted and giving colleagues who have assisted this book in many ways. Colleagues at

Louisiana State University, the University of North Carolina, the University of Pennsylvania, and the University of California at Los Angeles, where Suzanne Marchand, Michael Tsin, Holly Pittman, and Stephen Aron, respectively, are now teaching, pitched in whenever we turned to them. Especially helpful have been the contributions of Joyce Appleby, James Gelvin, Naomi Lamoreaux, and Gary Nash at UCLA; Michael Bernstein at Tulane University; and Maribel Dietz, John Henderson, Christine Kooi, David Lindenfeld, Reza Pirbhai, and Victor Stater at Louisiana State University. It goes without saying that none of these individuals bear any responsibility for factual or interpretive errors that the text may contain. Xinru Liu would like to thank her Indian mentor, Romila Thapar, who changed the way we think about Indian history.

Reviewers

The quality and range of reviews on this project were truly exceptional. The final version of the manuscript and the media package were greatly influenced by the thoughts and ideas of numerous instructors, including

Saad Abi-Hamad, Florida International University
Hugh Agnew, Columbian College of Arts and Sciences
Andreas Agocs, University of the Pacific
Stewart Anderson, Brigham Young University
Anthony Barbieri-Low, University of California, Santa Barbara
Michelle Benson-Saxton, University at Buffalo
Brett Berliner, Morgan State University
Carolyn Noelle Biltoft, Georgia State University
Edward Bond, Alabama A&M University
Liam Brockey, Michigan State University
Spencer Brown, Sierra College
Gayle Brunelle, California State University, Fullerton
Kate Burlingham, California State University, Fullerton
Daniel Burton-Rose, Northern Arizona University
Grace Chee, West Los Angeles College
Stephen Colston, San Diego State University
Matthew Conn, Michigan State University
John Corbally, Diablo Valley College
Christian Davis, James Madison University
Paula Devos, San Diego State University
Robert Dietle, Western Kentucky University
Eric Dursteler, Brigham Young University
Beth Fickling, Coastal Carolina Community College
Gerleman, George Mason University
Norah Gharala, University of Houston
Julie Gibbings, University of Edinburgh

Laura Hilton, Muskingum University
Paul Hudson, Georgia Perimeter College
Holly Hulburt, Southern Illinois University
Bonny Ibhawoh, McMaster University
Stefan Kamola, Eastern Connecticut State University
Alan Karras, University of California, Berkeley
David Kiracofe, Tidewater Community College
Jeremy LaBuff, Northern Arizona University
Senya Lubisich, Citrus College
Elaine MacKinnon, University of West Georgia
Anthony Makowski, Delaware County Community College
Harold Marcuse, University of California, Santa Barbara
Lindsey B. Maxwell, Gulliver Preparatory School
Jamie McCandless, Kennesaw State University
Anthonette McDaniel, Pellissippi State Community College
Jeff McEwen, Chattanooga State Community College
Thomas McKenna, Concord University
Eva Moe, Modesto Junior College
April Najjaj, Texas A&M University
Alice Pate, Kennesaw State University
Chandrika Paul, Shippensburg University
Sandra Peterson, Durham Technical Community College
David Pigott, BYU–Idaho
Jared Poley, Georgia State University
Sara Pulliam, United States Naval Academy
Dana Rabin, University of Illinois, Urbana-Champaign
Masako Racel, Kennesaw State University
Charles Reed, Elizabeth City State University
Alice Roberti, Santa Rosa Junior College
Steven Rowe, Chicago State University
Ariel Salzmann, Queen's University
Lynn Sargeant, California State University, Fullerton
Robert Saunders, Farmingdale State College
Sharlene Sayegh-Canada, California State University, Long Beach
Claire Schen, University at Buffalo
Ethan Segal, Michigan State University
Jason Sharples, Florida Atlantic University
Jeffrey Shumway, Brigham Young University
Greg Smay, University of California, Berkeley
Kristin Stapleton, University at Buffalo
Margaret Stevens, Essex County College
Pamela Stewart, Arizona State University
David Terry, Grand Valley State University

Lisa Tran, California State University, Fullerton
Michael Vann, California State University, Sacramento
Theodore Weeks, Southern Illinois University
Jason Wolfe, Louisiana State University
Reza Yeganehshakib, Saddleback College
Krzysztof Ziarek, University at Buffalo

Publishing a special book like *Worlds Together, Worlds Apart* involves many talented people. We feel the *Worlds Together, Worlds Apart* media package is the best in the marketplace. We'd particularly like to thank our team of media authors for their extraordinary efforts, including Alan Karras, the lead media author, and his terrific team of media authors—Shane Carter, Ryba Epstein, Andrew Hardy, Emily Gottreich, and Erik Vincent. We also want to thank our digital primary source exercise team: Annette Chamberlin, Stephanie Ballenger, and Derek O'Leary.

And an equally big thanks to our extraordinary book and media team partners at W. W. Norton: Jon Durbin, our print editor for all six editions; Carson Russell, our media editor; Rachel Mayer, Alexander Lee, and Lexi Malakhoff, our media team; Sarah England Bartley, Janise Turso, Courtney Brandt, and Lib Triplett, our marketing and sales specialist team; Harry Haskell, David Bradley, Jennifer Greenstein, Gerra Goff, and Lily Gellman, our manuscript and project editing teams; Jane Searle, Ben Reynolds, and Ashley Horna, our production team; Lissi Sigillo, the Seagull Edition's extraordinary designer; Mike Cullen, our terrific photo researcher; and Elizabeth Trammell, our diligent permissions manager.

While the new Third Seagull Edition of *Worlds Together, Worlds Apart* marks the handoff to a new leadership team, we want to pause for a moment and send special thanks to all our original co-authors for making this a wonderful journey. The journey began with a year of regular lunch and dinner meetings, with shared readings and fascinating debates about how to remap world history in what was then the dawning of a global age. We would not be where we are today without your amazing collaboration, creative insights, hard work, and collegiality. Thank you, thank you, thank you—Steve Aron, Peter Brown, Ben Elman, Steve Kotkin, Xinru Liu, Sue Marchand, Holly Pittman, Gyan Prakash, Brent Shaw, and Michael Tsin. Just as your voices have shaped the way we came to think about the global past, they live on in this book.

Finally, much of the new Third Seagull Edition was written during the pandemic. We are grateful for the support and understanding of our family members, also working from home, in some cases in another room of the house, and in the case of a homeschooling third-grader, at a makeshift desk 3 feet away. As the world seemed to be coming apart, we took joy in working together with you nearby.

ABOUT THE AUTHORS

Jeremy Adelman (*D.Phil. Oxford University*) has lived and worked in seven countries and on four continents. A graduate of the University of Toronto, he earned a master's degree in economic history at the London School of Economics (1985) and a doctorate in modern history at Oxford University (1989). He is the author or editor of ten books, including *Sovereignty and Revolution in the Iberian Atlantic* (2006) and *Worldly Philosopher: The Odyssey of Albert O. Hirschman* (2013), a chronicle of one of the twentieth century's most original thinkers. He has been awarded fellowships by the British Council, the Social Science and Humanities Research Council of Canada, the Guggenheim Memorial Foundation, and the American Council of Learned Societies (the Frederick Burkhardt Fellowship). He is currently the Henry Charles Lea Professor of History and the director of the Global History Lab at Princeton University. His next book is called *Earth Hunger: Global Integration and the Need for Strangers.*

Elizabeth Pollard (*Ph.D. University of Pennsylvania*) is professor of history at San Diego State University. Her research investigates women accused of witchcraft in the Roman world and explores the exchange of goods and ideas between the Mediterranean and the Indian Ocean in the early centuries of the Common Era. Her pedagogical interests include digital humanities approaches to Roman history and witchcraft studies as well as the impact of global perspectives on teaching, learning, and writing about the ancient Mediterranean. Pollard was named SDSU Distinguished Professor for Teaching Excellence in 2013 and was awarded the Faculty Innovation and Leadership Award by the California State University chancellor in 2020. In summer 2020, she co-designed and led the training program that will enable nearly 1,000 SDSU faculty to teach their courses entirely online in 2020–2021.

Clifford Rosenberg (*Ph.D. Princeton University*) is associate professor of European history at City College and the Graduate Center, CUNY. He specializes in the history of modern France and its empire and is the author of *Policing Paris: The Origins of Modern Immigration Control between the Wars*. He is now working on a book about the spread of tuberculosis between France and Algeria since the mid-nineteenth century.

Robert Tignor (*Ph.D. Yale University*) is professor emeritus and the Rosengarten Professor of Modern and Contemporary History at Princeton University and the three-time chair of the history department. With Gyan Prakash, he introduced Princeton's first course in world history thirty years ago. Professor

Tignor has taught graduate and undergraduate courses in African history and world history and has written extensively on the history of twentieth-century Egypt, Nigeria, and Kenya. Besides his many research trips to Africa, Professor Tignor has taught at the University of Ibadan in Nigeria and the University of Nairobi in Kenya.

Alan Karras (*Ph.D. University of Pennsylvania*) is the associate director of International & Area Studies at the University of California, Berkeley, and has previously served as chair of the College Board's test development committee for world history and as co-chair of the College Board's commission on AP history course revisions. The author and editor of several books, he has written about the eighteenth-century Atlantic world and, more broadly, global interactions that focus on illicit activities like smuggling and corruption. An advocate of linking the past to the present, he is now working on a history of corruption in empires, focusing on the East India Company.

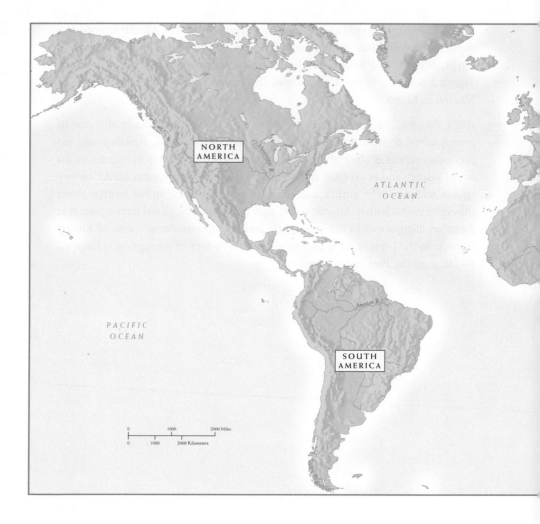

NORTH AMERICA

ATLANTIC OCEAN

PACIFIC OCEAN

SOUTH AMERICA

0   1000   2000 Miles
0   1000   2000 Kilometers

Geography in the Ancient and Modern Worlds

Today, geographers usually identify six inhabited continents: Africa, Asia, Australia, Europe, North America, and South America. Inside these continents they locate a vast number of subcontinental units, such as East Asia, South Asia, Southeast Asia, the Middle East, North Africa, and sub-Saharan Africa. Yet this geographic understanding would have been alien to premodern people, who did not think of themselves as inhabiting continents bounded by large bodies of water. Lacking a firm command of the seas, they saw themselves as living on contiguous landmasses. Hence, in this textbook, we have chosen to use a set of geographic terms that more accurately reflect the world of the premoderns.

The most interconnected and populous landmass of premodern times was Afro-Eurasia. The term *Eurasia* is widely used in general histories, but we find it inadequate. The preferred term, from our perspective, must be *Afro-Eurasia*, for the interconnected landmass of premodern—and, indeed, much of modern—times

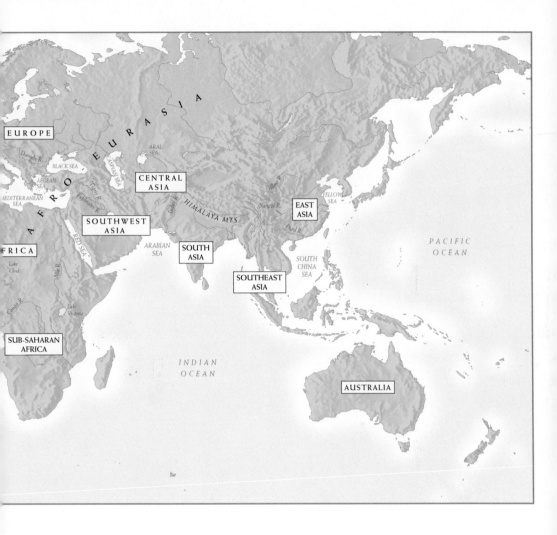

included large parts of Europe and Asia and significant regions in Africa—particularly Egypt, North Africa, and even parts of sub-Saharan Africa.

It was only in the period from 1000 to 1300 CE that the divisions of the world that we take for granted today began to take shape. The peoples of the northwestern part of Afro-Eurasia did not see themselves as European Christians, and hence as a distinct cultural entity, until the end of the Middle Ages. Islam did not arise and extend its influence throughout the middle zone of Afro-Eurasia until the eighth and ninth centuries CE. Nor did the peoples living in what we today term the Indian subcontinent feel a strong sense of their own cultural and political unity until the Delhi Sultanate and the Mughal Empire brought political unity to that vast region. As a result, we use the terms *South Asia*, *Vedic society*, and *India* in place of *Indian subcontinent* for the premodern part of our narrative, and we use *Southwest Asia* and *North Africa* to refer to what today is designated as the *Middle East*.

Worlds Together, Worlds Apart

1

Becoming Human

Core Objectives

- **DESCRIBE** various creation narratives traced in this chapter, including the modern scientific narrative of human evolution, and **EXPLAIN** why they differ.

- **TRACE** the major developments in hominin evolution that resulted in the traits that make *Homo sapiens* "human."

- **DESCRIBE** human ways of life and cultural developments from 300,000 to 12,000 years ago.

- **COMPARE** the ways communities around the world shifted to settled agriculture, and **ANALYZE** the significance this shift had for social organization.

In summer 2017, the story of human origins was rocked by findings that may well push back, and relocate to a different region of Africa, the earliest evidence for *Homo sapiens*. The new arguments about the time and place of our origins were grounded in the work of a team of paleoanthropologists who traveled to Jebel Irhoud in Morocco to establish a more precise date for hominin remains that had been unearthed by miners in the 1960s. What the team found were stone tools and fossilized skull fragments (including a jaw) belonging to five individuals. Thermo-luminescence dating of objects found with the bones, as well as uranium series dating of a tooth, showed that the possible *Homo sapiens* at Jebel Irhoud lived as early as 315,000 years ago—more than 100,000 years earlier than the previously accepted date of 200,000 years ago based on finds in East Africa.

Research on ancient DNA (aDNA) is also rewriting long-standing theories of human evolution and hominin migration out of Africa. For instance, DNA analysis of a 2,000-year-old skeleton from sub-Saharan Africa has pointed to a split in the branches of *Homo sapiens* lineage more than 250,000 years ago. And some paleogenomic researchers, using aDNA analyses together with statistical models, would push back the date for *Homo sapiens* long before that. As a result of these exciting new findings based on a diverse range of research methodologies, the genetic split indicated by the 2,000-year-old sub-Saharan skeleton supports the idea that the spread of *Homo sapiens* in Africa occurred longer ago and is more complicated than the 200,000-years-ago origin for *Homo sapiens* that scholars accepted just a decade ago. The modern scientific creation narrative evolves as new evidence unearthed through excavation adds more data to the story that scholars work to piece together.

Most of the common traits of human beings—the abilities to make tools, engage in family life, use language, and refine cognitive abilities—evolved over many millennia and crystallized around the time *Homo sapiens* migrated out of Africa more than 100,000 years ago. Only with the beginning of settled agriculture did significant cultural differences develop between groups of humans, as artifacts such as tools, cooking devices, and storage containers reveal. Put simply, the differences we think of as separating humankind's cultures today are less than 15,000 or 20,000 years old.

This chapter lays out the origins of humanity from its common source. It shows that many different hominins preceded modern humans and that humans came from a recent stock of migrants traveling out of Africa and across Eurasia in waves. Flowing across the world, our ancestors adapted to environmental constraints and opportunities. They created languages, families, and clan systems, often innovating to defend themselves against predators. One of the biggest breakthroughs was the domestication of plants and animals and the creation of settled agriculture. With this development, humans could stop following food and begin producing it where they desired.

Global Storyline

Prehistory and the Peopling of the Earth

- Communities, from long ago to today, produce varied creation narratives in order to make sense of how humans came into being.

- Hominin development across millions of years results in modern humans (*Homo sapiens*) and the traits that make us "human."

- During the period from 300,000 to 12,000 years ago, humans live as hunters and gatherers and achieve major breakthroughs in language and art.

- Global revolution in domesticating crops and animals leads to settled agriculture-based communities, while other communities develop pastoral ways of life.

Creation Narratives

For thousands of years, humans have constructed narratives of how the world, and humans, came to be. These **creation narratives** have varied over time and across cultures, depending on a society's values and the evidence available. To understand the origins of modern humans, we must come to terms with scales of time: the billions, millions, and hundreds of thousands of years through which the universe, earth, and life on it developed into what they are today. Though the hominin ancestors of modern humans lived millions of years ago, our tools for telling the modern creation narrative are relatively new.

Only 350 years ago, English clerics claimed on the basis of biblical calculations and Christian tradition that the first day of creation was Sunday, October 23, 4004 BCE. These seventeenth-century clerics were not the first to engage critically with the biblical story of creation. Rabbi Yose ben Halafta, a second-century CE rabbinic sage some 1,500 years earlier, used Genesis to calculate his own date for the beginning of creation (October 7, 3761 BCE). And the first-century CE writer Philo, an Alexandrian Jew who opined that "no one, whether poet or historian, could ever give expression in an adequate manner to the beauty of [Moses's] ideas respecting the creation of the world," wrote an extended philosophical treatise that set out to do just that.

Modern science, however, indicates that the origin of the universe dates back 13.8 billion years and that hominins began to separate from apes some 7 million years ago. These new discoveries have proved as mind-boggling to Hindus and Muslims as to Christians and Jews—all of whom believed, in different ways, that the universe was not so old and that divine beings had a role in creating it and all life, including the first humans. For millennia, human communities across the globe have constructed narratives that extend back differing lengths of time and suggest various roles for humans and gods in the process of universal creation. For instance, the Judeo-Christian narrative debated by English clerics and turn-of-the-first-millennium Jewish scholars portrays a single God creating a universe out of nothingness, populating it with plants, animals, and humans, in a span of six days. The centuries-old creation story of the Yoruba peoples of West Africa depicts a divine being descending from the heavens in human form and becoming the godlike king Oduduwa, who established the Yoruba kingdom and the rules by which his subjects were to live. The foundational texts of Hinduism, which date to the seventh or sixth century BCE, account that the world is millions, not billions, of years old. Chinese Han dynasty (206 BCE–220 CE) astronomers believed that at the world's beginning the planets were conjoined and that they would merge again at the end of time. The Buddhists' cosmos comprised millions of worlds, each consisting of a mountain encircled by four continents, its seas surrounded by a wall of iron.

Yet even the million-year time frames and multiple planetary systems that ancient Asian thinkers endorsed did not prepare their communities for the idea that humans are related to apes. In all traditional cosmologies, humans came into existence fully formed, at a single moment, as did the other beings that populated the world. Modern discoveries about humanity's origins have challenged these traditions, because no tradition conceived that creatures evolved into new kinds of life; that apes, humans, and other hominins branched from one another in a long evolutionary process; and that all of humanity originated in Africa.

Hominins to Modern Humans

The modern scientific creation narrative of human evolution would have been unimaginable even just over a century ago, when Charles Darwin was formulating his ideas about human origins. As we will see in this section, scientific discoveries have shown that modern humans evolved from earlier hominins. Through adaptation to their environment, various species of hominins developed new physical characteristics and distinctive skills. Millions of years after the first hominins appeared, the first modern humans—*Homo sapiens*—emerged and spread out across the globe.

EVOLUTIONARY FINDINGS AND RESEARCH METHODS

New insights into the time frame of the universe and human existence have occurred over a long period of time. Geologists made early breakthroughs in the eighteenth century when their research into the layers of the earth's surface revealed a world much older than biblical time implied. Evolutionary biologists, most notably Charles Darwin (1809–1882), concluded that all life had evolved over long periods from simple forms of matter. In the twentieth century, astronomers, evolutionary biologists, and archaeologists developed sophisticated dating techniques to pinpoint the chronology of the universe's creation and the evolution of all forms of life on earth. And in the early twenty-first century, paleogenomic researchers are recovering full genomic sequences of extinct hominins (such as the Neanderthals) and using ancient DNA to reconstruct the full skeletons of human ancestors (such as the Denisovans) of whom only a few bones have survived. Their discoveries have radically transformed humanity's understanding of its own history. A mere century ago, who would have accepted the idea that the universe came into being 13.8 billion years ago, that the earth appeared about 4.5 billion years ago, and that the earliest life forms began to exist about 3.8 billion years ago?

Yet, modern science suggests that human beings are part of a long evolutionary chain stretching from microscopic bacteria to African apes that appeared about 23 million years ago, and that Africa's "Great Ape" population separated into several distinct groups of **hominids**: one becoming present-day gorillas; the second becoming chimpanzees; and the third becoming modern humans only after following a long and complicated evolutionary process. Our focus will be on the third group of hominids, namely the **hominins** who became modern humans. A combination of traits, evolving over several million years, distinguished humans from other hominids, including (1) lifting the torso and walking on two legs (bipedalism), thereby freeing hands and arms to carry objects and hurl weapons; (2) controlling and then making fire; (3) fashioning and using tools; (4) developing cognitive skills and an enlarged brain and therefore the capacity for language; and (5) acquiring a consciousness of "self." All these traits were in place at least 150,000 years ago.

Two terms central to understanding any discussion of hominin development are *evolution* and *natural selection*. **Evolution** is the process by which species of plants and animals change and develop over generations, as certain traits are favored in reproduction. The process of evolution is driven by a mechanism called *natural selection*, in which members of a species with certain randomly occurring traits that are useful for environmental or other reasons survive and reproduce with greater success than those without the traits. Thus, biological evolution (human or otherwise) does not imply progress to higher forms of life, but instead implies successful adaptation to environmental surroundings.

EARLY HOMININS, ADAPTATION, AND CLIMATE CHANGE

It was once thought that evolution is a gradual and steady process. The consensus now is that evolutionary changes occur in punctuated bursts after long periods of stasis, or non-change. These transformative changes were often brought on, especially during early human development, by dramatic alterations in climate and by ruptures of the earth's crust caused by the movement of tectonic plates below the earth's surface. The heaving and decline of the earth's surface led to significant changes in climate and in animal and plant life. Also, across millions of years, the earth's climate was affected by slight variations in the earth's orbit, the tilt of the earth's axis, and the earth's wobbling on its axis.

Australopithecines As the earth experienced these immense changes, what was it like to be a hominin in the millions of years before the emergence of modern humans? An early clue came from a discovery made in 1924 at Taung, not far from the present-day city of Johannesburg, South Africa. A twenty-nine-year-old scientist named Raymond Dart identified the pint-sized skull and bones of a creature, nicknamed "Taung child," that had both ape-like and humanoid features. Dart officially labeled his bipedal find *Australopithecus africanus*. **Australopithecines** existed not only in southern Africa but in the north as well. In 1974, an archaeological team under the leadership of Donald Johanson unearthed a relatively intact skeleton of a young adult female australopithecine near the Awash River in present-day Ethiopia. While the technical name for the find became *Australopithecus afarensis*, the researchers

Table 1.1 The Age of the Universe and Human Evolution

Development	Time
Big-bang moment in the creation of the universe	13.8 BILLION YEARS AGO (BYA)
Formation of the sun, earth, and solar system	4.5 BYA
Earliest life forms appear	3.8 BYA
Multicellular organisms appear	1.5 BYA
First hominids appear	7 MILLION YEARS AGO (MYA)
Australopithecus afarensis appear (including Lucy)	3.9 MYA
Homo habilis appear (including Dear Boy)	2.5 MYA
Homo erectus appear (including Java and Peking Man)	1.8 MYA
Homo erectus leave Africa	1.5 MYA
Neanderthals appear	400,000 YEARS AGO
Homo sapiens appear	300,000 YEARS AGO
Homo sapiens leave Africa	180,000 YEARS AGO
Homo sapiens migrate into Asia	120,000 YEARS AGO
Homo sapiens migrate into Australia	60,000 YEARS AGO
Homo sapiens migrate into Europe	50,000 YEARS AGO
Homo sapiens migrate into the Americas	16,000 YEARS AGO
Homo sapiens sapiens appear (modern humans)	35,000 YEARS AGO

(A bracket spanning from "First hominids appear" to the bottom row is labeled: <1% of Earth's Existence)

Before the agricultural revolution, dates are usually marked as BP, which counts the number of years before the present. These BP (or "before the present") dates might also be assigned units such as BYA (billions of years ago), MYA (millions of years ago), or KA (thousands of years ago), depending on what scale is most appropriate for the development being described. More recent dates, beginning around 12,000 years ago, are marked with BCE (before [the] Common Era) as the unit of time. To render a BP date into a BCE date, simply subtract 2,000 years to account for the 2,000 years of the Common Era (CE). So 12,000 BP = 10,000 BCE (plus the 2,000 years of the Common Era since the year 1).

who found the skeleton gave it the nickname Lucy, based on the then-popular Beatles song "Lucy in the Sky with Diamonds."

Lucy was remarkable. She stood a little over 3 feet tall, she walked upright, her skull contained a brain within the ape size range (that is, one-third human size), and her jaw and teeth were human-like. Her arms were long, hanging halfway from her hips to her knees—suggesting that she might not have been bipedal at all

Table 1.2 Human Evolution

Species	Time*
Sahelanthropus tchadensis (including Toumai skull)	7 MILLION YEARS AGO (MYA)
Orrorin tugenensis	6 MYA
Ardipithecus ramidus (including Ardi)	4.4 MYA
Australopithecus anamensis	4.2 MYA
Australopithecus afarensis (including Lucy)	3.9 MYA
Australopithecus africanus (including Taung child)	3.0 MYA
Homo habilis (including Dear Boy)	2.5 MYA
Homo erectus and *Homo ergaster* (including Java and Peking Man)	1.8 MYA
Homo heidelbergensis (common ancestor of *Homo neanderthalensis* and *Homo sapiens*)	600,000 YEARS AGO
Homo neanderthalensis	400,000 YEARS AGO
Homo sapiens	300,000 YEARS AGO
Homo naledi	c. 280,000 YEARS AGO
Homo sapiens sapiens (modern humans)	35,000 YEARS AGO

*Dates are approximate (midpoint on a range), based on multiple finds. Some species are represented with hundreds of examples (more than 300 examples of *Australopithecus afarensis*, of which "Lucy" is the most famous, date across a span of almost 1 million years), while the evidence for other species is more limited (*Sahelanthropus tchadensis* is represented by a single skull).

Source: Smithsonian Institute Human Origins Program.

times and sometimes resorted to arms for locomotion, in the fashion of a modern baboon. Above all, Lucy's skeleton was relatively complete and showed us that hominins were walking around more than 3 million years ago. It is important to emphasize that australopithecines were not humans but they carried the genetic and biological material out of which modern humans would later emerge. These precursors to modern humans had a key trait for evolutionary survival: they were remarkably good adapters. They could deal with dynamic environmental shifts, and they were intelligent.

Adaptation For hominins, like the rest of the plant and animal world, survival required constant adaptation (the ability to alter behavior and to innovate, finding new ways of doing things). During the first millions of years of hominin existence, these slow changes involved primarily physical adaptations to the environment. The places where researchers have found early hominin remains in southern and eastern Africa had environments that changed from being heavily forested and well watered to being arid and desertlike, and then back again. (See Map 1.1.) Hominins had to keep pace with these changing physical environments or else risk extinction. In fact, many of the early hominin groups did die out.

In adapting, early hominins began to distinguish themselves from other mammals that were physically similar to themselves. It was not their hunting prowess that made the hominins stand out, because plenty of other species chased their prey with skill and dexterity. The single trait that gave early hominins a real advantage for survival was bipedalism: they became "two-footed" creatures that stood upright. At some point, the first hominins were able to remain upright and move about, leaving their arms and hands free for other useful tasks, like carrying food over long distances. Once they ventured into open savannas (grassy plains with a few scattered trees), about 1.7 million years ago, hominins had a tremendous advantage. They were the only primates (an order of mammals consisting of man, apes, and monkeys) to move consistently on two legs. Because they could move continuously and over great distances, they were able to migrate out of hostile environments and into more hospitable locations.

Climate Changes The climate in eastern and southern Africa, where hominin development began, was conducive to the development of diverse plant and animal species. When the world entered its fourth great ice age approximately 40 million years ago, the earth's temperatures dropped and its continental ice sheets, polar ice sheets, and mountain glaciers expanded. We know this because during the last several decades paleoclimatologists have used measurements of ice cores and oxygen isotopes in the ocean to chart the often-radical

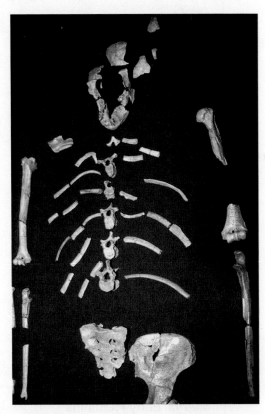

Fossil Bones of Lucy Archaeologist Donald Johanson discovered the fossilized bones of this young female in the Afar region of Ethiopia. Representative of *Australopithecus afarensis*, which lived from 3.9 to 2.9 million years ago, Lucy's bones are believed to date from approximately 3.2 million years ago and provide evidence of some of the first hominins to appear in Africa. This find was of great importance because the bones were so fully and completely preserved.

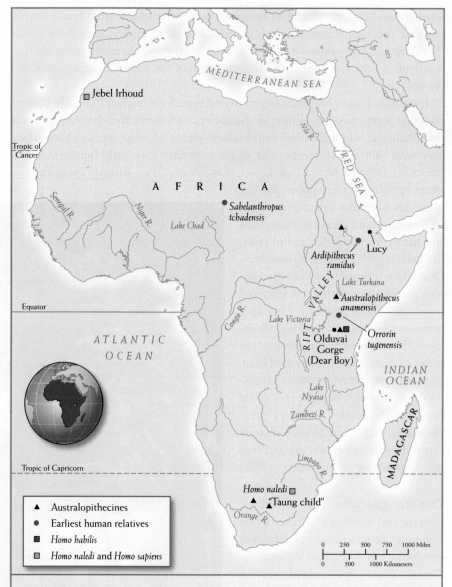

Map 1.1 Early Hominins

....

The earliest hominin species evolved in Africa millions of years ago.

- Judging from this map, in which parts of Africa has evidence for hominin species been excavated?
- Use Table 1.2 to assign dates to these hominin finds. What, if any, hypotheses might you suggest to correlate the geographic spread of the finds with the evolution of hominin species over time?
- According to this chapter, how did the changing environment of eastern and southern Africa shape the evolution of these modern human ancestors?

changes in the world's climate. The fourth great ice age lasted until 12,000 years ago. Like all ice ages, it had alternating warming and cooling phases that lasted between 40,000 and 100,000 years each. Between 10 and 12 million years ago, the climate in Africa went through one such cooling and drying phase. To the east of Africa's Rift Valley, stretching from South Africa north to the Ethiopian highlands, the cooling and drying forced forests to contract and savannas to spread. It was in this region that some apes left the shelter of the trees, stood up, and learned to walk, to run, and to live in savanna lands—thus becoming the precursors to humans and distinctive as a new species.

Using two feet for locomotion augmented the means for obtaining food and avoiding predators and improved the chances these creatures had to survive in constantly changing environments. In addition to being bipedal, hominins had opposable thumbs. This trait, shared with other primates, gave hominins great physical dexterity, enhancing their ability to explore and to alter materials found in nature. Manual dexterity and standing upright also enabled them to carry young family members if they needed to relocate, or to throw missiles (such as rocks and sticks) with deadly accuracy to protect themselves or to obtain food.

Hominins used their increased powers of observation and memory, what we call cognitive skills, to gather wild berries and grains and to scavenge the meat and marrow of animals that had died of natural causes or as the prey of predators. All primates are good at these activities, but hominins came to excel at them. Cognitive skills, which also included problem solving and—eventually—language, were destined to become the basis for further developments. Early hominins were highly social. They lived in bands of about twenty-five individuals, trying to survive by hunting small game and gathering wild plants. Not yet a match for large predators, they had to find safe hiding places. They thrived in places where a diverse supply of wild grains and fruits and abundant wildlife ensured a secure, comfortable existence. In such locations, small hunting bands of twenty-five could swell through alliances with others to as many as 500 individuals. Like other primates, hominins communicated through gestures, but they also may have developed a very basic form of spoken language that led (among other things) to the establishment of rudimentary cultural codes such as common rules, customs, and identities.

Early hominins lived in this manner for more than 4 million years, changing their way of life very little except for moving around the African landmass in their never-ending search for more favorable environments. Even so, their survival is surprising. There were not many of them, and they struggled in hostile environments surrounded by a diversity of large mammals, including predators such as lions.

As the environment changed over the millennia, these early hominins gradually changed as well. Over this 4-million-year period, their brains more than doubled in size; their foreheads became more elongated; their jaws became less massive; and they began to look much more like modern humans. Adaptation to environmental changes also created new skills and aptitudes, which expanded the ability to store and analyze information. With larger brains, hominins could form mental maps of their worlds—they could learn, remember what they learned, and convey these lessons to their neighbors and offspring. In this fashion, larger groups of hominins created communities with shared understandings of their environments.

Diversity Recent discoveries in Kenya, Chad, and Ethiopia suggest that hominins were both older and more diverse than early australopithecine finds (both *afarensis* and *africanus*) had suggested. In southern Kenya in 2000, researchers excavated bone remains, at least 6 million years old, of a chimpanzee-sized hominid (named *Orrorin tugenensis*) that walked upright on two feet. In Chad in 2001, another team unearthed the 7-million-year-old "Toumai skull," with a mix of attributes (small cranial capacity like a chimp's but more human-like teeth and spinal column placement at the base of the skull) that perplexed researchers but led them to place this new find, technically named *Sahelanthropus tchadensis*, in the story of human evolution. These finds indicate that bipedalism must be millions of years older than scientists thought based on discoveries like Lucy (*Australopithecus afarensis*) and "Taung child" (*Australopithecus africanus*). Moreover, *Orrorin* and *Sahelanthropus* teeth indicate that they were closer to modern humans than to australopithecines. In their arms and hands, though, which show characteristics needed for tree climbing, the *Orrorin* hominins seemed more ape-like than the australopithecines. So *Orrorin* hominins were still somewhat tied to an environment in the trees. Only the chimp-sized skull fragments of *Sahelanthropus* have been found, so no conclusions about their bodies, other than that they walked upright, can be drawn.

The story of hominin evolution continues to unfold and demonstrates that hominin diversity continued to thrive in Africa even as other hominins, like *Homo erectus*, migrated out of the continent. Far inside a cave near Johannesburg, South Africa, spelunkers recently made a discovery that led to the excavation of more than 1,550 fossil remains (now named *Homo naledi*, for the cave in which they were found). Researchers have been able to assemble a composite skeleton that revealed that the upper body parts resembled some of the much earlier pre-*Homo* finds, while the hands (both the palms and curved fingers), the wrists, the long legs, and the feet are close to those of modern humans. The males were around 5 feet tall and weighed 100 pounds, while the females were shorter and lighter. Recent publications have suggested a surprisingly late date range of 335,000 to 236,000 years ago, and therefore much research remains to be done to determine how these fossils fit the story of human evolution.

The fact that different kinds of early hominins were living in isolated societies and evolving separately, though in close proximity to one another, in eastern Africa between 4 and 3 million years ago until as recently as 300,000 years ago indicates much greater diversity among their populations than scholars previously imagined. The environment in eastern Africa generated a fair number of different hominin populations, a few of which would provide our genetic base, but most of which would not survive in the long run.

Tool Use by *Homo habilis*

One million years after Lucy, the first beings whom we assign to the genus *Homo*, or "true human," appeared. Like early hominins, *Homo habilis* was bipedal, possessing a smooth walk based on upright posture. *Homo habilis* had an even more import-ant advantage over other hominins: brains that were growing larger. Big brains are the site of innovation: learning and storing lessons so that humans could pass those lessons on to later generations, especially in the making of tools and the efficient use of resources (and, we suspect, in defending themselves). Mary and Louis Leakey, who made astonish-ing fossil discoveries in the 1950s at Olduvai Gorge in present-day north-

The Leakeys Louis Leakey and his wife, Mary, were dedicated archaeologists whose work in East Africa established the area as one of the starting points of human development. Mary Leakey was among the most successful archaeologists studying hominins in Africa. Her finds, including the one in this photograph from Laetoli, Tanzania, highlight the activities of early men and women in Africa. The footprints, believed to be those of an *Australopithecus afarensis*, date from 3.7 to 3 million years ago.

ern Tanzania, identified these important traits. The Leakeys' finds included an intact skull that was 1.8 million years old. They nicknamed the creature whose skull they had unearthed Dear Boy.

Objects discovered with Dear Boy demonstrated that by this time early humans had begun to make tools for butchering animals and, possibly, for hunting and killing smaller animals. The tools were flaked stones with sharpened edges for cutting apart animal flesh and scooping out the marrow from bones. To mimic the slicing teeth of lions, leopards, and other carnivores, these early humans had devised these tools through careful chipping. Dear Boy and his companions had carried usable rocks to distant places, where they made their implements with special hammer stones—tools to make tools. Unlike other tool-using animals (for example, chimpanzees), early humans were now intentionally fashioning implements, not simply finding them when needed. More important, they were passing on knowledge of these tools to their offspring and, in the process, grad-ually improving the tools. The Leakeys, believing that making and using tools represented a new stage in the evolution of human beings, gave Dear Boy and his companions the name ***Homo habilis***, or "skillful human." While scholars today may debate whether toolmaking (rather than walking upright or having a large

Olduvai Gorge, Tanzania Olduvai Gorge is probably the most famous archaeological site containing hominin finds. Mary and Louis Leakey, convinced that early humans originated in Africa, discovered the fossil remains of *Homo habilis* (skillful man) in this area between 1960 and 1963. They argued that these findings represent a direct link to *Homo erectus*.

brain) is the key trait that distinguishes the first humans from earlier hominins, *Homo habilis*'s skills made them the forerunners, though very distant ones, of modern men and women.

MIGRATIONS OF *HOMO ERECTUS*

By 1 million years ago, many of the hominin species that flourished together in Africa had died out. One surviving species, which emerged about 1.8 million years ago, had a large brain capacity and walked truly upright; it therefore gained the name **Homo erectus**, or "standing human." Three important features distinguished *Homo erectus* from their competitors and made them more able to cope with environmental changes: their family dynamics, use of fire, and ability to travel long distances. Discoveries in Asia and Europe show that *Homo erectus* migrated out of Africa in some of the earliest waves of hominin migration around the globe.

Family Dynamics One of the traits that contributed to the survival of *Homo erectus* was the development of extended periods of caring for their young. Although their enlarged brain gave these hominins advantages over the rest of the animal world, it also brought one significant problem: their heads were too large to pass through the females' pelvises at birth. Their pelvises were only big enough to deliver an infant with a cranial capacity that was about a third an adult's size. As a result, offspring required a long period of protection by adults as they matured and their brain size tripled.

This difference from other species also affected family dynamics. For example, the long maturation process gave adult members of hunting and gathering bands time to train their children in those activities. In addition, maturation and brain growth required mothers to spend years breast-feeding and then preparing food for children after their weaning. In order to share the responsibilities of child-rearing, mothers relied on other women (their own mothers, sisters, and friends) and girls (often their own daughters) to help with nurturing and protecting, a process known as *allomothering* (literally, "other mothering").

Use of Fire *Homo erectus* began to make rudimentary attempts to control their environment by means of fire. It is hard to tell from fossils when hominins— *Homo erectus* or *Homo sapiens* (modern humans)—learned to use fire. The most reliable evidence comes from cave sites less than 250,000 years old, where early humans apparently cooked some of their food, but some archaeologists have suggested that hominin mastery of fire occurred as early as 500,000 years ago, by *Homo erectus*. Fire provided heat, protection, a gathering point for small communities, and a way to cook food. It was also symbolically powerful: here was a source of energy that humans could extinguish and revive at will. The uses of fire had enormous long-term effects on human evolution. Because they were able to boil, steam, and fry wild plants, as well as otherwise undigestible foods (especially raw muscle fiber), hominins who mastered this technology could expand their diets. Because cooked foods yield more energy than raw foods and because the brain, while only 2 percent of human body weight, uses between 20 and 25 percent of all the energy that humans take in, cooking was decisive in the evolution of brain size and functioning.

Early Migrations Being bipedal, *Homo erectus* could move with a smooth and rapid gait, so they could cover large distances quickly. They were the world's first long-distance travelers, forming the first mobile human communities. (See Table 1.3.) Around 1.5 million years ago, *Homo erectus* individuals began migrating out of Africa, first into the lands of Southwest Asia. From there, they traveled along the Indian Ocean shoreline, moving into South Asia and Southeast Asia and later northward into what is now China. Their migration was a response in part to the environmental changes that were transforming the world. The Northern Hemisphere experienced thirty major cold phases during this period, marked by glaciers spreading over vast expanses of the northern parts of Eurasia and the Americas. The glaciers formed as a result of intense cold that froze much of the world's oceans, lowering them some 325 feet below present-day levels. These lower ocean levels made it possible for the migrants to travel across land bridges into Southeast Asia and from East Asia to Japan, as well

Table 1.3 Migrations of *Homo sapiens*	
Species	**Time**
Homo erectus leave Africa	c. 1.5 MILLION YEARS AGO
Homo sapiens leave Africa	c. 180,000 YEARS AGO
Homo sapiens migrate into Asia	c. 120,000 YEARS AGO
migrate into Australia	c. 60,000 YEARS AGO
migrate into Europe	c. 50,000 YEARS AGO
migrate into the Americas	c. 16,000 YEARS AGO

as from New Guinea to Australia. The last parts of the Afro-Eurasian landmass to be occupied were in Europe.

Discoveries of the bone remains of "Java Man" and "Peking Man" (named according to the places where archaeologists first unearthed their remains) confirmed early settlements of *Homo erectus* in Southeast and East Asia. The remains of Java Man, found in 1891 on the island of Java, turned out to be those of an early *Homo erectus* that had dispersed into Asia nearly 2 million years ago. Peking Man, found near Beijing in the 1920s, was a cave dweller, toolmaker, and hunter and gatherer who settled in northern China. Originally believing that Peking Man dated to around 400,000 years ago, archaeologists thought that warmer climate might have made the region more hospitable to migrating *Homo erectus*. But recent application of the aluminum-beryllium technique to analyze the fossils has suggested they date to 770,000 years ago, a time when China's climate would have been much colder. Peking Man's brain was larger than that of his Javan cousins, and there is evidence that he controlled fire and cooked meat

Skulls of Ancestors of *Homo sapiens* Shown here are seven skulls of ancestors of modern-day men and women, arranged to highlight brain growth over time. The larger the brain, the more developed the regions of the brain that process vision, different kinds of cognition, and communication can be. The skulls represent (*left to right*): *Adapis*, a lemur-like animal that lived 50 million years ago; *Proconsul*, a primate that lived about 23 million years ago; *Australopithecus africanus*; *Homo habilis*; *Homo erectus*; *Homo sapiens* from the Qafzeh site in Israel, about 90,000 years old; and *Homo sapiens sapiens* from France, about 22,000 years old.

in addition to hunting large animals. He made tools of vein quartz, quartz crystals, flint, and sandstone. A major innovation was the double-faced axe, a stone instrument whittled down to sharp edges on both sides to serve as a hand axe, a cleaver, a pick, and probably a weapon to hurl against foes or animals. Even so, these early predecessors still lacked the intelligence, language skills, and ability to create culture that would distinguish the first modern humans from their hominin relatives.

HOMO SAPIENS: THE FIRST MODERN HUMANS

The first traces that we have of **Homo sapiens** come from modern-day Morocco and suggest that the first modern humans emerged sometime around 315,000 years ago. This bigger-brained, more dexterous, and more agile species of humans differed from their precursors, including *Homo habilis* and *Homo erectus*. Their distinctive traits, including greater cognitive skills, made *Homo sapiens* the first modern humans and enabled

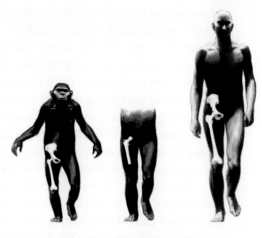

The Physical Evolution of Hominins These three figures show the femur bones of Lucy, *Orrorin tugenensis* (one of the earliest of the hominins, who may have existed around 6 million years ago), and *Homo sapiens*. *Homo sapiens* have a larger femur bone and were bigger than Lucy—a representative of the hominin species *Australopithecus afarensis*—but have the same bone structure. Particularly useful indicators for determining differences among human ancestors are skull size (which can indicate the size of the brain and thus cognitive ability), the position at the base of the skull where the spine enters the cranium (which can indicate bipedalism), jawbones and teeth (which can indicate the kind of food they could have chewed), femur bones (which can indicate overall size and manner of walking), and foot and hand structure (which can indicate the kind of activities they performed).

them to spread out from Africa by 100,000 years ago and flourish in even more diverse regions across the globe than *Homo erectus* did.

Large-scale shifts in Africa's climate and environment several hundred thousand years ago put huge pressures on all types of mammals, including hominins. In these extremely warm and dry environments, the smaller, quicker, and more adaptable mammals survived. What counted now was no longer large size and brute strength, but the ability to respond quickly, with agility, and with great speed. The eclipse of *Homo erectus* by *Homo sapiens* was not inevitable. After all, *Homo erectus* was already scattered around Africa and Eurasia by the time *Homo sapiens* emerged; in contrast, even as late as 100,000 years ago there were only about 10,000 *Homo sapiens* adults living primarily in a small part of the African landmass. When *Homo sapiens* began moving in large numbers out of Africa and the two species encountered each other in the same places across the globe,

Homo sapiens individuals were better suited to survive—in part because of their greater cognitive and language skills.

The *Homo sapiens* newcomers followed the trails blazed by earlier migrants when they moved out of Africa. (See Map 1.2.) Evidence, including part of a fossilized jaw with teeth, from a cave on Mount Carmel in Israel indicates that *Homo sapiens* were living there as early as 180,000 years ago. Whether that evidence suggests significant migrations or more limited forays by *Homo sapiens* is still unclear. Nevertheless, it is clear that from 120,000 to 50,000 years ago, *Homo sapiens* were moving in ever increasing numbers into the same areas as their genetic cousins, reaching across Southwest Asia and from there into central Asia—but not into Europe. They flourished and reproduced. By 30,000 years ago, the population of *Homo sapiens* had grown to about 300,000. Between 60,000 and 12,000 years ago, these modern humans were surging into areas tens of thousands of miles from the Rift Valley and the Ethiopian highlands of Africa.

In the area of present-day China, *Homo sapiens* were thriving and creating distinct regional cultures. Consider Shandingdong Man, a *Homo sapiens* who dates to about 18,000 years ago. His physical characteristics were closer to those of modern humans, and he had a similar brain size. His stone tools, which included choppers and scrapers for preparing food, were similar to those of the *Homo erectus* Peking Man. His bone needles, however, were the first stitching tools of their kind found in China, and they indicated the making of garments. Some of the needles measured a little over an inch in length and had small holes drilled in them. Shandingdong Man also buried his dead. In fact, a tomb of grave goods includes ornaments suggesting the development of aesthetic tastes and religious beliefs.

Homo sapiens were also migrating into the northeastern fringe of East Asia. In the frigid climate there, they learned to follow herds of large Siberian grazing animals. The bones and dung of mastodons made decent fuel and good building material. Pursuing their prey eastward as the large-tusked herds sought pastures in the steppes (treeless grasslands) and marshes, these groups migrated across the ice to Japan. Archaeologists have discovered a woolly mammoth fossil in the colder north of Japan, for example, and an elephant fossil in the warmer south. Elephants in particular roamed the warmer parts of Inner Eurasia. The hunters and gatherers who moved into Japan gathered wild plants for sustenance, and they dried, smoked, or broiled meat by using fire.

About 30,000 years ago, *Homo sapiens* began edging into the weedy landmass that linked Siberia and North America (which hominins had not populated). This thousand-mile-long land bridge, later called Beringia, must have seemed like an extension of familiar steppe-land terrain, and these individuals lived isolated lives there on a broad and (at the time) warm plain for thousands of years before beginning to migrate into North America. The first migrations occurred around 16,000 years ago, by foot and by boat. Modern humans poured eastward and southward into North America. A final migration occurred about

8,000 years ago by boat, since by then the land bridge had disappeared under the sea. (See Map 1.2 for evidence that demonstrates the complex picture of the peopling of the Americas, both along the western coastline and to the east.)

Using their cognitive abilities to adapt to new environments and to innovate, these migrants, who were the first discoverers of America, began to fill up the landmasses. They found ample prey in the herds of woolly mammoths, caribou, 3-ton giant sloths, and 200-pound beavers. But the explorers could also themselves be prey—for they encountered saber-toothed tigers, long-legged eagles, and giant bears that moved faster than horses. The melting of the glaciers about 8,000 years ago and the resulting disappearance of the land bridge eventually cut off the first Americans from their Afro-Eurasian origins. Thereafter, the Americas became a world apart from Afro-Eurasia.

Although modern humans evolved from earlier hominins, no straight-line descent tree exists from the first hominins to *Homo sapiens*. Increasingly, scientists view our origins as shaped by a series of progressions and regressions as hominin species adapted or failed to adapt and died out. The remains of now-extinct hominin species, such as *Homo ergaster, Homo heidelbergensis, Homo neanderthalensis*, and now *Homo naledi* (see Table 1.2), offer intriguing glimpses of ultimately unsuccessful branches of the complex human evolutionary tree. Spreading into Europe and parts of Southwest Asia along with other hominins, Neanderthals, for example, had big brains, used tools, wore clothes, buried their dead, hunted, lived in rock shelters, and even interacted with *Homo sapiens*. Yet when faced with environmental challenges, *Homo sapiens* survived, while Neanderthals died out sometime between 45,000 and 35,000 years ago, although recent genetic evidence suggests that some interbreeding occurred between Neanderthals and *Homo sapiens*.

Indeed, several species could exist simultaneously, but some were more suited to changing environmental conditions—and thus more likely to survive—than others. Evidence that interbreeding between these different species may have given some *Homo sapiens* a survival advantage emerged in 2008, when Russian archaeologists dug up a pinky bone at the Denisova Cave in the Altai Mountains of southern Siberia and thereby discovered another hominin group that had many of the characteristics of *Homo sapiens*. These hominins, who looked different from *Homo sapiens*, had lived in this cave off and on from 287,000 years ago. They even shared a common ancestor with the Neanderthals about 400,000 years ago and interbred with the Neanderthals and our own species, as indicated by DNA drawn from living peoples in East Asia, Australia, the Pacific Islands, and the Americas. Some scientists have suggested that the interbreeding of *Homo sapiens* with the Denisovans enabled modern humans to survive in the Tibetan highlands at altitudes of close to 11,000 feet and as early as 15,000 years ago. Using aDNA drawn from Denisovan remains, scientists have reconstructed their body types, noting that they had massive brain cases and giant molars as well as larger neck vertebrae, thicker ribs, and a higher bone density

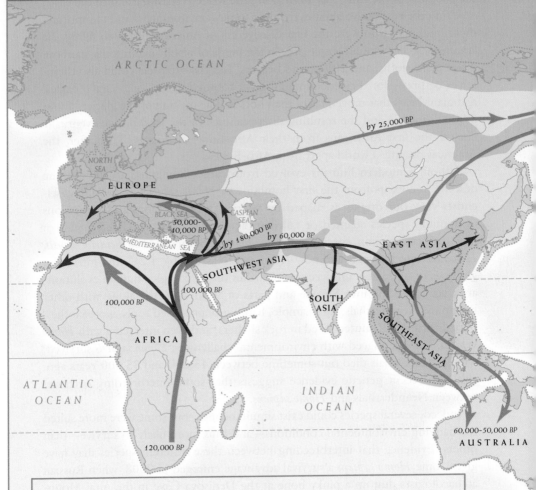

ARCTIC OCEAN

by 25,000 BP

NORTH
SEA

EUROPE

BLACK SEA
50,000–
40,000 BP

CASPIAN
SEA

MEDITERRANEAN SEA

by 180,000 BP

by 60,000 BP

EAST ASIA

SOUTHWEST ASIA

100,000 BP

SOUTH
ASIA

SOUTHEAST ASIA

100,000 BP

AFRICA

ATLANTIC
OCEAN

INDIAN
OCEAN

60,000–50,000 BP

AUSTRALIA

120,000 BP

Map 1.2 Early Migrations: Out of Africa

Hominin species, like *Homo erectus*, began migrating out of Africa hundreds of thousands of years before the present (BP), but only *Homo sapiens* went to all major inhabitable regions.

- According to this map, when and to what regions did *Homo erectus* migrate? *Homo neanderthalensis*? *Homo sapiens*? Compare the location, extent, and dates of each species' migration.

- Locate the extent of ice sheets and identify the differences in exposed landmasses, as compared to modern shorelines. How did ice sheets and exposed land shape each species' migration patterns?

- Examine the dates for human settlement of the Americas. What do these dates suggest about human migration in the Americas?

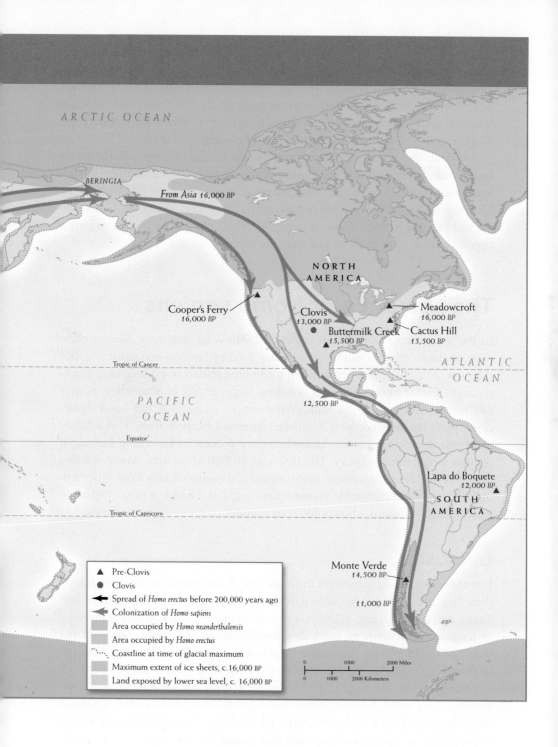

BERINGIA

From Asia *16,000 BP*

NORTH AMERICA

Cooper's Ferry
16,000 BP

Clovis
13,000 BP

Buttermilk Creek
15,500 BP

Meadowcroft
16,000 BP

Cactus Hill
15,500 BP

Tropic of Cancer

PACIFIC OCEAN

ATLANTIC OCEAN

Equator

12,500 BP

Lapa do Boquete
12,000 BP

SOUTH AMERICA

Tropic of Capricorn

Monte Verde
14,500 BP

11,000 BP

ARCTIC OCEAN

▲ Pre-Clovis
● Clovis
← Spread of *Homo erectus* before 200,000 years ago
← Colonization of *Homo sapiens*
Area occupied by *Homo neanderthalensis*
Area occupied by *Homo erectus*
Coastline at time of glacial maximum
Maximum extent of ice sheets, c. 16,000 BP
Land exposed by lower sea level, c. 16,000 BP

0   1000   2000 Miles
0   1000   2000 Kilometers

than modern humans. They may have weighed well over 200 pounds and were robust and very large individuals. One investigator observed that they would have done well as modern-day football players. Advances in aDNA technology may allow researchers to identify previously unclassified remains as Denisovans. Scholars' understanding of this recent hominin relative, genetically distinct from Neanderthals and modern humans, is only beginning to take form.

Although the primary examples emphasized in this chapter—*Homo habilis* and *Homo erectus*—were among some of the world's first human-like inhabitants, they probably were not direct ancestors of modern men and women. By 25,000 years ago, DNA analysis reveals, nearly all genetic cousins to *Homo sapiens* had become extinct. *Homo sapiens*, with their physical agility and superior cognitive skills, were ready to populate the world.

The Life of Early *Homo sapiens*

In the period from 300,000 to around 12,000 years ago, early *Homo sapiens* were similar to other hominins in that they lived by hunting and gathering, but their use of language and new cultural forms represented an evolutionary breakthrough. Earlier hominins could not form large, lasting communities, as they had limited communication skills. While simple commands and hand signals developed over time, complex linguistic expression escaped them. This achievement was one of the last in the evolutionary process of becoming human; it did not occur until between 100,000 and 50,000 years ago. Many scholars view it as the critical ingredient in distinguishing human beings from other animals. It is this skill that made *Homo sapiens* "sapiens," which is to say "wise" or "intelligent"—humans who could create culture.

LANGUAGE

Few things set *Homo sapiens* off from the rest of the animal world more starkly than their use of language. Although the beginnings and development of language are controversial, scholars agree that the cognitive abilities involved in language development marked an evolutionary milestone. Some earlier hominins could express themselves by grunting, but natural language (the use of sounds to make words that convey meaning to others) is unique to modern humans. The development of language required a large brain and complex cognitive organization to create word groups that would convey symbolic meaning. Verbal communication required an ability to think abstractly and to communicate abstractions. Language was a huge breakthrough, because individuals could teach words and ideas to neighbors and offspring. Language thus enhanced the ability to accumulate knowledge that could be transmitted across both space and time.

Biological research has demonstrated that humans can make and process many more primary and distinctive sounds, called phonemes, than other animals can. Whereas a human being can utter fifty phonemes, an ape can form only twelve. Also, humans can process sounds more quickly than other primates can. With fifty phonemes it is possible to create more than 100,000 words; by arranging those words in different sequences and developing rules in language, individuals can express countless subtle and complex meanings. Recent research suggests that use of complex languages occurred about 100,000 years ago and that the nearest approximation to humanity's earliest language existing today belongs to two African peoples, the !Kung of southern Africa and the Hadza of Tanzania. These peoples make a clicking sound by dropping the tongue down from the roof of the mouth and exhaling. As humans moved out of Africa and spread around the globe, they expanded their original language into nineteen language families, from which all of the world's languages then evolved. (See Map 1.3.) It was the

Map 1.3 Original Language Family Groups

The use of complex language developed 100,000 years ago among *Homo sapiens* in Africa. As humans dispersed throughout the globe, nineteen language families evolved from which all modern languages originate.

- How many different landmasses did language evolve on? Which landmasses have a greater number of language families, and why might that be?
- On the basis of this map, what geographic features had an impact on the evolution of language groups?
- Why do you think separate languages emerged over time?

development of language and the cultural forms discussed later in this section that allowed *Homo sapiens* to engage dynamically with their environments.

HUNTING AND GATHERING

Although these early humans were developing language skills that distinguished them from their hominin relatives, like their predecessors they remained hunters and gatherers until around 12,000 years ago (for almost 95 percent of our existence). As late as 1500 CE, as much as 15 percent of the world's population still lived by **hunting and gathering.** Early *Homo sapiens* hunted animals, fished, and foraged for wild berries, nuts, fruit, and grains, rather than planting crops, vines, or trees. Even today hunting and gathering societies endure, although only in the most marginal locations—often at the edge of deserts. Researchers consider the present-day San peoples of southern Africa as an isolated remnant continuing their traditional hunting and gathering modes of life. Modern scholars use the San to reveal how men and women must have lived hundreds of thousands of years ago. The fact that hominin men and women (going back to *Homo erectus* and *habilis* and beyond) survived as hunters and gatherers for millions of years, that early *Homo sapiens* also lived this way, and that a few contemporary communities still forage for food suggests the powerful attractions of this way of life. Hunters and gatherers could find enough food in about three hours of foraging each day, thus affording time for other pursuits such as relaxation, interaction, and friendly competitions with other members of their bands. Scholars believe that these small bands were relatively egalitarian compared with the more male-dominated societies that arose later. They speculate that men specialized in hunting and women specialized in gathering and child-rearing. Some scholars believe that women even made a larger contribution and had high status because the dietary staples of the community were cereals and fruits, whose harvesting and preparation were likely women's responsibility.

PAINTINGS, SCULPTURE, AND MUSIC

The ability to draw allowed *Homo sapiens* to understand their environment, to bond among their kin groups (groups related by blood ties), and to articulate important mythologies. Accomplished artwork from this era has been found across Afro-Eurasia. For instance, in a deep cave at Altamira in Spain more than two dozen life-size figures of bison, horses, and wild bulls, all painted in vivid red, black, yellow, and brown, are arranged across the ceiling of the huge chamber. More than 50,000 similarly stunning works of art have been found in caves across Europe and elsewhere. The images on cave walls accumulated in some instances over a period of 25,000 years, and they changed little in that time. The earliest figurative art now would appear to be found in a cave in Borneo. It features a spindly-legged, thick-bodied wild cow, drawn in reddish ocher, and is

Hadza of Modern Tanzania Hunting and gathering was the way that most humans lived for hundreds of thousands of years. Although their way of life is dying out, modern hunters and gatherers offer useful ethnographic comparisons for understanding how humans lived in the millennia prior to sedentary agriculture. These Hadza, from modern Tanzania, dig up edible roots that offer a reliable and high-calorie food source for their community.

at least 40,000 years old. Like this wild cow, the subjects of most ancient art are large game—animals that early humans would have considered powerful symbols. The artists rendered these animals in such a way that the natural contours of the cave wall defined a bulging belly or an eye socket. Many images appear more than once, suggesting that they are works from several occasions or by several artists. And some, like the horses and lions of Chauvet cave in France from 35,000 years ago, appear in overlapping, layered images that might have evoked a sense of motion, especially when viewed by flickering torchlight in the dark of a cave. The remarkably few human images show hunters, naked females, or dancing males. There are also many handprints made by blowing paint around a hand placed on the cave wall, or by dipping hands in paint and then pressing them to the wall. There are even abstract symbols such as circles, wavy lines, and checkerboards; often these appear at places of transition in the caves.

Scholars have rejected an initial theory that these paintings were decorative, for the deep caves were not homes and had no natural light to render the images visible. Perhaps the images helped the early humans define themselves as separate from other parts of nature. Alternatively, they might have been the work of powerful shamans, individuals believed to hold special powers to understand and control the forces of the cosmos. The subjects and the style of the paintings are similar to images engraved or painted on rocks by some hunting and

Bone Flute Paleolithic flutes have been found at sites in Germany, France, and Slovenia. Made of animal bone (bird and bear) and mammoth ivory, these flutes date back to 35,000 years ago and perhaps even as long ago as 43,000 years ago.

gathering societies living today, especially the San and the !Kung peoples of southern Africa. In those societies, paintings mark important places of ritual: shamans make them during trances while mediating with the spirit world on behalf of their communities.

Paintings were not the only form of artistic expression for early humans. Archaeologists also have unearthed small sculptures of animals shaped out of bone and stone that are even older than the paintings. Most famous are figurines of rotund, and perhaps pregnant, females. Statuettes like the so-called Venus of Willendorf, found in Austria, demonstrate that successful reproduction was a very important theme. Other sculptures represent animals in postures of movement or at rest.

The caves of early men and women also resounded to the strains of music. In 2008, archaeologists working in southwestern Germany discovered a hollowed-out bone flute with five openings that they dated to approximately 35,000 years ago, roughly the same time that humans began to occupy this region. When researchers put the flute to musical tests, they also concluded that the instrument was capable of making harmonic sounds comparable to those of modern-day flutes.

Only *Homo sapiens* had the cognitive abilities to produce the abundant sculptures and drawings of this era, thus leaving a permanent mark on the symbolic landscape of human development. Such visual expressions marked the dawn of human culture and a consciousness of men's and women's place in the world. Symbolic activity of this sort enabled humans to make sense of themselves, nature, and the relationship between humanity and nature. That relationship with nature—which had remained static for hundreds of thousands of years of hunting and gathering—would change with the agricultural revolution.

Global Agricultural Revolution

About 12,000 years ago (around 10,000 BCE), a fundamental shift occurred in the way humans produced food for themselves—what some scholars have called an agricultural, or ecological, revolution. Around the same time, a significant warming trend that had begun around 11,000 BCE resulted in a profusion of plants and animals, large numbers of which began to exist closer to humans. In this era of major change, humans established greater control over nature.

The transformation consisted of the **domestication** of wild plants and animals. Population pressure was one factor that triggered the move to settled agriculture, as hunting and gathering alone could not sustain the growth in numbers of people. A revolution in agriculture, in turn, led to a vast population expansion because men and women could now produce more calories per unit of land. As various plants and animals were domesticated around the world, people settled in villages and social relationships changed.

THE BEGINNINGS OF SETTLED AGRICULTURE AND PASTORALISM

Learning to control environments through the domestication of plants and animals was a gradual process. Communities shifted from a hunting and gathering lifestyle (which requires moving around in search of food) to one based on agriculture (which requires staying in one place until the soil has been exhausted). **Settled agriculture** refers to the application of human labor and tools to a fixed plot of land for more than one growing cycle. Alternatively, some people adopted a lifestyle based on **pastoralism** (the herding of domesticated animals), which complemented settled farming.

Early Domestication of Plants and Animals The formation of settled communities enabled humans to take advantage of favorable regions and to take risks, spurring agricultural innovation. In areas with abundant wild game and edible plants, people began to observe and experiment with the most adaptable plants. For ages, people gathered grains by collecting seeds that fell freely from their stalks. At some point, observant collectors perceived that they could obtain larger harvests if they pulled grain seeds directly from plants. The process of plant domestication probably began when people noticed that certain edible plants retained their nutritious grains longer than others, so they collected these seeds and scattered them across fertile soils. When ripe, these plants produced bigger and more concentrated crops. Plant domestication occurred when the plant retained its ripe, mature seeds, allowing an easy harvest. People used most seeds for food but saved some for planting in the next growing cycle, to ensure a food supply for the next year.

Dogs were the first animals to be domesticated (although in fact they may have adopted humans, rather than the other way around). At least 33,000 years ago in China and central Asia, including Mongolia and Nepal, humans first domesticated gray wolves and made them an essential part of human society. Dogs did more than comfort humans. They provided an example of how to achieve the domestication of other animals and, with their herding instincts, they helped humans control other domesticated animals, such as sheep. In the central Zagros Mountains region, where wild sheep and wild goats were abundant, they became the next animal domesticates. Perhaps hunters returned home with

Domestication This detail from a wall painting in the Tassili-n-Ajjer mountain range in modern Algeria depicts early domestication of cattle and other animals.

young wild sheep, which then reproduced, and their offspring never returned to the wild. The animals accepted their dependence because the humans fed them. Since controlling animal reproduction was more reliable than hunting, domesticated herds became the primary source of protein in the early humans' diet.

When the number of animals under human control and living close to the settlement outstripped the supply of food needed to feed them, community members could move the animals to grassy steppes for grazing. These pastoralists herded domesticated animals, moving them to new pastures on a seasonal basis. Goats, the other main domesticated animal of Southwest Asia, are smarter than sheep but more difficult to control. The pastoralists may have introduced goats into herds of sheep to better control herd movement. Pigs and cattle also came under human control at this time.

Transhumant Herders and Nomadic Pastoralists Pastoralism appeared as a way of life around 5500 BCE, essentially at the same time that full-time farmers appeared (although the beginnings of plant and animal domestication had begun many millennia earlier). Over time, two different types of pastoralists with different relationships to settled populations developed: transhumant herders and nomadic pastoralists. Transhumant herders were closely affiliated with agricultural villages whose inhabitants grew grains, especially wheat and barley, which required large parcels of land. These herders produced both meat and dairy products, as well as wool for textiles, and exchanged these products with the agriculturalists for grain, pottery, and other staples. Extended families might farm and herd at the same time, growing crops on large estates and grazing their herds in the foothills and mountains nearby. They moved their livestock seasonally, pasturing their flocks in higher lands during summer and in valleys in winter. This movement over short distances is called *transhumance* and did not require herders to vacate their primary living locations, which were generally in the mountain valleys.

In contrast with transhumant pastoralism, *nomadic pastoralism* came to flourish especially in the steppe lands north of the agricultural zone of southern Eurasia. This way of life was characterized by horse-riding herders of cattle and other livestock. Because horses provided decisive advantages in transportation and warfare, they gained more value than other domesticated animals. Thus, horses soon became the measure of household wealth and prestige. Unlike the transhumant herders, the nomadic pastoralists often had no fixed home, though they often returned to their traditional locations. They moved across large distances in response to the size and needs of their herds. Beginning in the second millennium BCE, the northern areas of the Eurasian landmass, stretching from present-day Ukraine across Siberia and Mongolia to the Pacific Ocean, became the preserve of these horse-riding pastoral peoples, living as they did in a region unable to support the extensive agriculture necessary for large settled populations. Historians know much less about these horse-riding pastoral nomads than about the agriculturalists and the transhumant herders, as their numbers were small and they left fewer archaeological traces or historical records. Their role in world history, however, is as important as that of the settled societies. In Afro-Eurasia, they domesticated horses and developed weapons and techniques that at certain points in history enabled them to conquer sedentary societies. As we will see in the next section (and later chapters), they also transmitted ideas, products, and people across long distances, maintaining the linkages that connected east and west.

AGRICULTURAL INNOVATION: AFRO-EURASIA AND THE AMERICAS

The agricultural revolutions that occurred worldwide between 9000 and 2000 BCE had much in common: climatic change; increased knowledge about plants and animals; and the need for more efficient ways to feed, house, and promote the growth of a larger population. These concerns led peoples in Eurasia, the Americas, and Africa to see the advantages of cultivating plants and domesticating wildlife. (See Map 1.4.)

Some communities were independent innovators, developing agricultural techniques based on their specific environments. In Southwest Asia, East Asia, Africa, and the Americas, the distinctive crops and animals that humans first domesticated reflect independent innovation. As we will see in the following section, other communities (such as those in Europe) were borrowers of ideas,

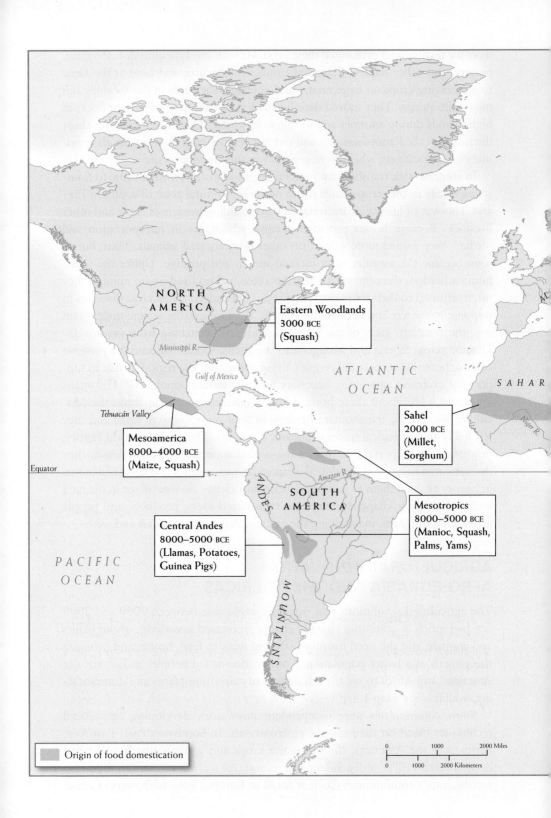

NORTH
AMERICA

Eastern Woodlands
3000 BCE
(Squash)

Mississippi R.

Gulf of Mexico

ATLANTIC
OCEAN

SAHAR

Tehuacán Valley

Niger R.

Sahel
2000 BCE
(Millet,
Sorghum)

Mesoamerica
8000–4000 BCE
(Maize, Squash)

Equator

Amazon R.

ANDES

SOUTH
AMERICA

Mesotropics
8000–5000 BCE
(Manioc, Squash,
Palms, Yams)

Central Andes
8000–5000 BCE
(Llamas, Potatoes,
Guinea Pigs)

PACIFIC
OCEAN

MOUNTAINS

Origin of food domestication

0   1000   2000 Miles

0   1000   2000 Kilometers

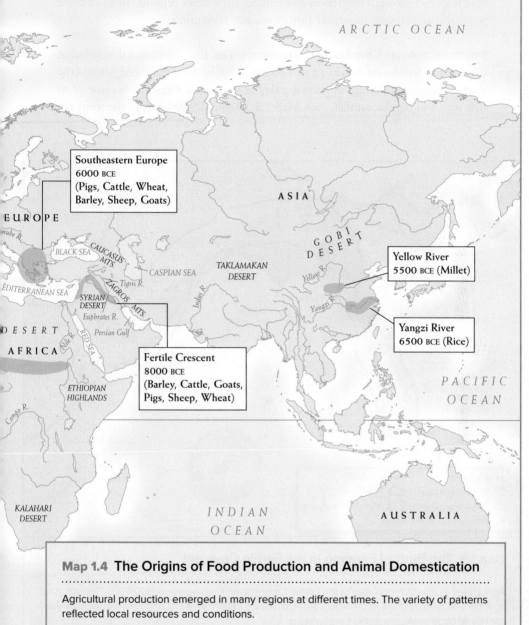

Southeastern Europe
6000 BCE
(Pigs, Cattle, Wheat,
Barley, Sheep, Goats)

ARCTIC OCEAN

ASIA

EUROPE

Danube R.

BLACK SEA

CAUCASUS MTS.

CASPIAN SEA

Tigris R.

MEDITERRANEAN SEA

SYRIAN DESERT

ZAGROS MTS.

Euphrates R.

Persian Gulf

DESERT

AFRICA

Nile

RED SEA

ETHIOPIAN HIGHLANDS

Congo R.

TAKLAMAKAN DESERT

Indus R.

GOBI DESERT

Yellow R.

Yangzi R.

Yellow River
5500 BCE (Millet)

Yangzi River
6500 BCE (Rice)

Fertile Crescent
8000 BCE
(Barley, Cattle, Goats,
Pigs, Sheep, Wheat)

PACIFIC OCEAN

KALAHARI DESERT

INDIAN OCEAN

AUSTRALIA

Map 1.4 The Origins of Food Production and Animal Domestication

Agricultural production emerged in many regions at different times. The variety of patterns reflected local resources and conditions.

- In how many different locations, and at what different times, did agricultural production and animal domestication emerge? What is the range of crops and animals domesticated in each region?

- What specific geographic features (for instance, specific mountains, rivers, or latitudes) are common among these early food-producing areas? Do those geographic features appear to guarantee agricultural production?

- Why do you think agriculture emerged in certain areas and not in others?

which spread through migration and contact with other regions. In all of these populations, the shift to settled agriculture was revolutionary.

Southwest Asia: Cereals and Mammals The first agricultural revolution occurred in Southwest Asia in an area bounded by the Mediterranean Sea and the Zagros Mountains, a region known today as the Fertile Crescent because of its rich soils and regular rainfall. (See Map 1.5.) Around 9000 BCE, in the southern

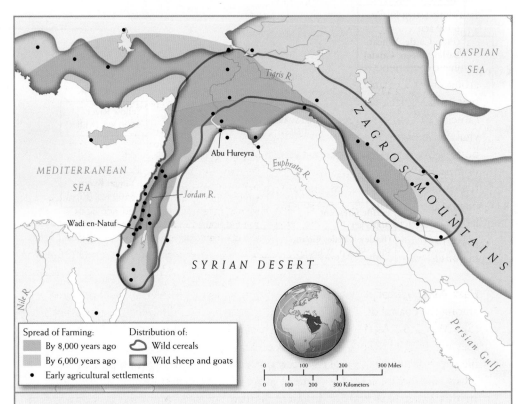

Map 1.5 The Birth of Farming in the Fertile Crescent

Agricultural production occurred in the Fertile Crescent starting roughly in 9000 BCE. Though the process was slow, farmers and herders domesticated a variety of plants and animals, which led to the rise of large-scale, permanent settlements.

- Trace the region where the wild cereals were domesticated as well as the density of agricultural settlements. How does the region you traced relate to the reason this area is called the "Fertile Crescent"?
- What topographical features appear to influence the location of agricultural settlements and farming?
- What relationship existed between cereal cultivators and herders of goats and sheep?

corridor of the Jordan River valley, humans began to domesticate the wild ancestors of barley and wheat, which were the easiest to adapt to settled agriculture and the easiest to transport. Although the changeover from gathering wild cereals to regular cultivation took several centuries and saw failures as well as successes, by 8000 BCE cultivators were selecting and storing seeds and then sowing them in prepared seedbeds. Moreover, in the valleys of the Zagros Mountains on the eastern side of the Fertile Crescent, similar experimentation was occurring with animals around the same time. Of the six large mammals—goats, sheep, pigs, cattle, camels, and horses—that have been vital for meat, milk, skins, and transportation, humans in Southwest Asia domesticated all except horses. With the presence of so many valuable plants and animals, Southwest Asia led the agricultural revolution and gave rise to many of the world's first major city-states (see Chapter 2).

Large Two-Handled Yangshao Pot In the village of Yangshao in Henan Province, remains were first found in 1921 of a people who lived more than 6,000 years ago. This pot comes from those people, who were named Yangshao after the modern village in which the evidence for their culture was first found. The ancient Yangshao lived in small, rammed-earth fortresses and, without the use of pottery wheels, created fine white, red, and black painted pottery with human faces and animal and geometric designs. This jar was found in Gansu Province and dates to around 2500 BCE.

East Asia: Water and Rice A revolution in food production also occurred among the coastal dwellers in East Asia, although under different circumstances. (See Map 1.6.) As the rising sea level created the Japanese islands, hunters in that area tracked a diminishing supply of large animals, such as giant deer. When big game became extinct, men and women sought other ways to support themselves, and before long they settled down and became cultivators of the soil. In this postglacial period, divergent human cultures flourished in northern and southern Japan. Hunters in the south created primitive pebble and flake tools, whereas those in the north used sharper blades about a third of an inch wide. Production of earthenware pottery—a breakthrough that enabled people to store food more easily—also may have begun in this period in the south. Throughout the rest of East Asia, the spread of lakes, marshes, and rivers created habitats for population concentrations and agricultural cultivation. Two newly formed river basins, along the Yellow River in northern China and the Yangzi River in central China, became densely populated areas that were focal points for intensive agricultural development.

What barley and wheat were for Southwest Asia, rice along the Yangzi River and millet along the Yellow River were for East Asia—staples adapted to local

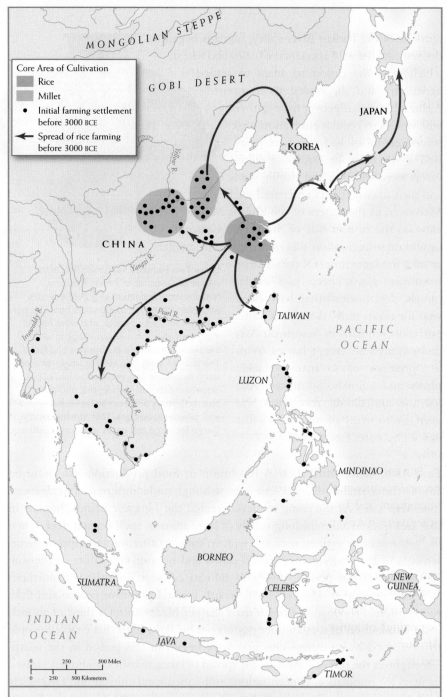

Core Area of Cultivation

- Rice
- Millet
- • Initial farming settlement before 3000 BCE
- ← Spread of rice farming before 3000 BCE

MONGOLIAN STEPPE

GOBI DESERT

Yellow R.

CHINA

Yangzi R.

JAPAN

KOREA

Pearl R.

TAIWAN

PACIFIC OCEAN

LUZON

Irrawaddy R.

Mekong R.

MINDINAO

BORNEO

SUMATRA

CELEBES

NEW GUINEA

INDIAN OCEAN

JAVA

TIMOR

0   250   500 Miles

0   250   500 Kilometers

Map 1.6 The Spread of Farming in East Asia

Agricultural settlements appeared in East Asia between 6500 and 5500 BCE, several thousand years later than they did in the Fertile Crescent.

- According to this map, where did early agricultural settlements appear in East Asia?
- What two main crops were domesticated in East Asia? Where did each crop type originate, and to what regions did each spread?
- How did the physical features of these regions shape agricultural production?

environments that humans could domesticate to support a large, sedentary population. Archaeologists have found evidence of rice cultivation in the Yangzi River valley in 6500 BCE, and of millet cultivation in the Yellow River valley in 5500 BCE. Innovations in grain production, including the introduction of a faster-ripening rice from Southeast Asia, spread through internal migration and wider contacts. Ox plows and water buffalo plowshares were prerequisites for large-scale millet planting in the drier north and the rice-cultivated areas of the wetter south. By domesticating plants and animals, the East Asians, like the Southwest Asians, laid the foundations for more populous societies.

Africa: The Race with the Sahara The evidence for settled agriculture in the various regions of Africa is less clear. Most scholars think that the Sahel area (spanning the African landmass just south of the Sahara Desert) was likely where hunters and gatherers became settled farmers and herders without borrowing from other regions. In this area, an apparent move to settled agriculture, including the domestication of large herd animals, occurred two millennia before it did along the Mediterranean coast in North Africa. From this innovative heartland, Africans carried their agricultural breakthroughs across the landmass.

In the wetter and more temperate locations of the vast Sahel, particularly in mountainous areas and their foothills, villages and towns developed. These regions were lush with grassland vegetation and teeming with animals. Before long, the inhabitants had made sorghum, a cereal grass, their principal food crop. Residents constructed stone dwellings, underground wells, and grain storage areas. In one such population center, fourteen circular houses faced each other to form a main thoroughfare, or a street.

The Sahel was colder and moister in 8000 BCE than it is today. As the world became warmer and the Sahara Desert expanded, around 2000 BCE, this region's inhabitants had to disperse and take their agricultural and herding skills into other parts of Africa. (See Map 1.7.) Some went south to the tropical rain forests of West Africa, while others trekked eastward into the Ethiopian highlands. In their new environments, farmers searched for new crops to domesticate. The rain forests of West Africa yielded root crops, particularly the yam and cocoyam, both of which became the principal life-sustaining foodstuffs. The ensete plant, similar to the banana, played the same role in the Ethiopian highlands. Thus, the beginnings of agriculture in Africa involved both innovation and diffusion, as Africans applied the techniques that first emerged in the Sahel to new plants and animals.

The Americas: A Slower Transition to Agriculture The shift to settled agriculture occurred more slowly in the Americas. When people entered the Americas around 16,000 years ago (14,000 BCE), they set off an ecological transformation but also adapted to unfamiliar habitats. The flora and fauna of the Americas were different enough to induce the early settlers to devise ways of living that distinguished them from their ancestors in Afro-Eurasia. Then, when the glaciers began to melt around 12,500 BCE and water began to cover the land bridge between East Asia and America, the Americas and their peoples truly became a world apart.

Food-producing changes in the Americas were different from those in Afro-Eurasia because the Americas did not undergo the sudden cluster of innovations that revolutionized agriculture in Southwest Asia and elsewhere. Tools ground from stone, rather than chipped implements, appeared in the Tehuacán Valley in present-day eastern central Mexico by 6700 BCE, and evidence of plant domestication there dates back to 5000 BCE. But villages, pottery making, and sustained population growth came later. For many early American inhabitants, the life of hunting, trapping, and fishing went on as it had for millennia.

On the coast of what is now Peru, people found food by fishing and by gathering shellfish from the Pacific. Archaeological remains include the remnants of fishnets, bags, baskets, and textile implements; gourds for carrying water; stone knives, choppers, and scrapers; and bone awls (long, pointed spikes often used for piercing) and thorn needles. Thousands of villages likely dotted the seashores and riverbanks of the Americas. Some communities made breakthroughs in the management of fire, which enabled them to manufacture pottery; others devised irrigation and water sluices in floodplains; and some even began to send their fish catches inland in return for agricultural produce.

Maize (corn), squash, and beans (first found in what is now central Mexico) became dietary staples. The early settlers foraged small seeds of maize, peeled them from ears only a few inches long, and planted them. Maize offered real advantages because it was easy to store, relatively imperishable, nutritious, and easy to cultivate alongside other plants. Nonetheless, it took 5,000 years for farmers to complete its domestication. Over the years, farmers had to mix and breed different strains of maize for the crop to evolve from thin spikes of seeds to cobs rich with kernels, with a single plant yielding big, thick ears to feed a growing permanent population. Thus, the agricultural changes afoot in Mesoamerica were slow and late in maturing. The pace was even more gradual in South America, where early settlers clung to their hunting and gathering traditions.

Across the Americas, the settled, agrarian communities found that legumes (beans), grains (maize), and tubers (potatoes) complemented one another in keeping the soil fertile and offering a balanced diet. Unlike the Afro-Eurasians, however, the settlers did not use domesticated animals as an alternative source of protein. In only a few pockets of the Andean highlands is there evidence of the domestication of tiny guinea pigs, which may have been tasty but unfulfilling meals. Nor did people in the Americas tame animals that could protect villages (as dogs did in Afro-Eurasia) or carry heavy loads over long distances (as cattle and horses did in Afro-Eurasia). Although llamas could haul heavy loads,

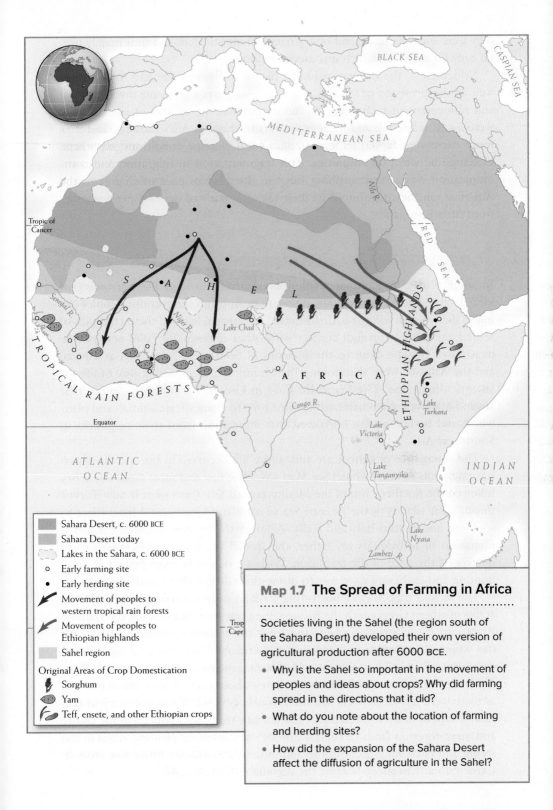

BLACK SEA

CASPIAN SEA

MEDITERRANEAN SEA

Nile R.

RED SEA

Tropic of Cancer

S · A · H · E · L

Senegal R.

Niger R.

Lake Chad

TROPICAL RAIN FORESTS

A F R I C A

ETHIOPIAN HIGHLANDS

Congo R.

Lake Turkana

Equator

Lake Victoria

ATLANTIC OCEAN

Lake Tanganyika

INDIAN OCEAN

Lake Nyasa

Zambezi R.

	Sahara Desert, c. 6000 BCE
	Sahara Desert today
	Lakes in the Sahara, c. 6000 BCE
o	Early farming site
•	Early herding site
➤	Movement of peoples to western tropical rain forests
➤	Movement of peoples to Ethiopian highlands
	Sahel region

Original Areas of Crop Domestication

Sorghum

Yam

Teff, ensete, and other Ethiopian crops

Tropic of Capr

Map 1.7 The Spread of Farming in Africa

Societies living in the Sahel (the region south of the Sahara Desert) developed their own version of agricultural production after 6000 BCE.

- Why is the Sahel so important in the movement of peoples and ideas about crops? Why did farming spread in the directions that it did?

- What do you note about the location of farming and herding sites?

- How did the expansion of the Sahara Desert affect the diffusion of agriculture in the Sahel?

they were uncooperative and only partially domesticated, and thus mainly useful only for their fur, which was used for clothing.

Nonetheless, the domestication of plants and animals in the Americas, as well as the presence of villages and clans, suggests significant diversification and refinement of technique. At the same time, the centers of such activity were many, scattered, and more isolated than those in Afro-Eurasia—and thus more narrowly adapted to local geographical climatic conditions, with little exchange between communities. This fragmentation in migration and communication was a distinguishing force in the gradual pace of change in the Americas, and it contributed to their taking a path of development separate from Afro-Eurasia's.

BORROWING AGRICULTURAL IDEAS: EUROPE

In some places, agricultural revolution occurred through the borrowing of ideas from neighboring regions, rather than through innovation. Peoples living at the western fringe of Afro-Eurasia, in Europe, learned the techniques of settled agriculture through contact with other regions. By 7000 BCE, people in parts of Europe close to the societies of Southwest Asia, such as Greece and the Balkans, were abandoning their hunting and gathering way of life for an agricultural one. The Franchthi Cave in Greece, for instance, reveals that around 6000 BCE the inhabitants learned how to domesticate animals and plant wheat and barley, having borrowed that innovation from their neighbors in Southwest Asia.

The emergence of agriculture and village life occurred in Europe along two separate paths of borrowing. (See Map 1.8.) The first and most rapid trajectory followed the northern rim of the Mediterranean Sea: from what is now Turkey through the islands of the Aegean Sea to mainland Greece, and from there to southern and central Italy and Sicily. Whether the process involved the actual migration of individuals or, rather, the spread of ideas, connections by sea quickened the pace of the transition. Within a relatively short period of time, hunting and gathering gave way to domesticated agriculture and herding.

The second trajectory of borrowing took an overland route: from Anatolia, across northern Greece into the Balkans, then northwestward along the Danube River into the Hungarian plain, and from there farther north and west into the Rhine River valley in modern-day Germany. This route of agricultural development was slower than the Mediterranean route for two reasons. First, domesticated crops, or individuals who knew about them, had to travel by land, as there were few large rivers like the Danube. Second, it was necessary to find new groups of domesticated plants and animals that could flourish in the colder and more forested lands of central Europe, which meant planting crops in the spring and harvesting them in the autumn, rather than the other way around. Cattle rather than sheep became the dominant herd animals.

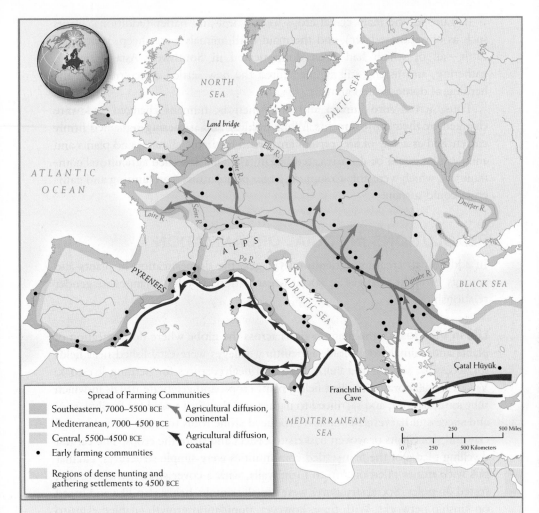

Map 1.8 The Spread of Agriculture in Europe

The spread of agricultural production into Europe after 7000 BCE represents geographic diffusion. Europeans borrowed agricultural techniques and technology from other groups, adapting those innovations to their own situations.

- Trace the two pathways by which agriculture spread across Europe. What shaped the routes by which agriculture diffused?
- How might scholars know that there were two routes of diffusion, and why would the existence of different diffusion routes matter?
- Identify the locations of the early farming communities. What geographical features seem to have influenced where these farming communities sprang up?

In Europe, the main cereal crops were wheat and barley (additional plants such as olives came later), and the main herd animals were sheep, goats, and cattle—all of which had been domesticated in Southwest Asia. Hunting, gathering, and fishing still supplemented the new settled agriculture and the herding of domesticated animals.

Thus, across Afro-Eurasia and the Americas, humans changed and were changed by their environments. While herding and gathering remained firmly entrenched as a way of life, certain areas with favorable climates and plants and animals that could be domesticated began to establish settled agricultural communities, which were able to support larger populations than hunting and gathering could sustain.

REVOLUTIONS IN SOCIAL ORGANIZATION

In addition to creating agricultural villages, the domestication of plants and animals brought changes in social organization, notably changes in gender relationships.

Life in Villages In the many regions across the globe where domestication of plants and animals took hold, agricultural villages were established near fields for accessible sowing and cultivating, and near pastures for herding livestock. Villagers collaborated to clear fields, plant crops, and celebrate rituals in which they sang, danced, and sacrificed to nature and the spirit world for fertility, rain, and successful harvests. They also produced stone tools to work the fields, and clay and stone pots or woven baskets to collect and store the crops. The earliest dwelling places of the first settled communities were simple structures: circular pits with stones piled on top to form walls, with a cover stretched above that rested on poles. Social structures were equally simple, being clan-like and based on kinship networks. With time, however, population growth enabled clans to expand. As the use of natural resources intensified, specialized tasks evolved and divisions of labor arose. Some community members procured and prepared food; others built terraces and defended the settlement. Later, residents built walls with stones or mud bricks and clamped them together with wooden fittings. Some villagers became craftworkers, devoting their time to producing pottery, baskets, textiles, or tools, which they could trade to farmers and pastoralists for food. Craft specialization and the buildup of surpluses contributed to social stratification (the emergence of distinct and hierarchically arranged social classes), as some people accumulated more land and wealth while others led the rituals and sacrifices.

Archaeological sites in Southwest Asia have provided evidence of what life was like in some of the earliest villages. At Wadi en-Natuf, for example, located about 10 miles from present-day Jerusalem, a group of people known historically as Natufians began to dig sunken pit shelters and to chip stone tools around 12,500 BCE. In the highlands of eastern Anatolia, large settlements clustered around monumental public buildings with impressive stone carvings that reflect a complex social organization. In central Anatolia around 7500 BCE, at the site of Çatal Hüyük, a dense honeycomb settlement featured rooms with artwork of a high quality. The walls were covered with paintings, and sculptures of wild bulls, hunters, and pregnant women enlivened many rooms.

As people moved into the river valley in Mesopotamia (in present-day Iraq) along the Tigris and Euphrates Rivers, small villages began to appear after 5500 BCE. They collaborated to build simple irrigation systems to water their fields. Perhaps because of the increased demands for community work to maintain the irrigation systems, the communities in southern Mesopotamia became stratified, with some people having more power than others. We can see from the burial sites and myriad public buildings uncovered by archaeologists that, for the first time, some people had higher status derived from birth rather than from the merits of their work. A class of people who had access to more luxury goods, and who lived in bigger and better houses, now became part of the social organization.

Çatal Hüyük This artist's drawing depicts the settlement at Çatal Hüyük, which offers evidence of a Neolithic community's shift, over a 2,000-year span of time, to settled agriculture and more densely packed living. The one-room houses were entered from the roof (via ladders into the living areas) and included space for daily chores (like food preparation), storage, sleeping, and even the burial of the dead under the floor of the living area.

Men, Women, and Evolving Gender Relations Gender roles became more pronounced during the gradual transition to agriculturally based ways of life. For millions of years, biological differences—the fact that females give birth to offspring and lactate to nourish them, and that males do neither of these—determined female and male behaviors and attitudes toward each other. One can speak of the emergence of gender relations and roles (as distinct from biological differences) only with the appearance of modern humans (*Homo sapiens*). Only when humans began to think in complex symbolic ways and give voice to these perceptions in a spoken language did well-defined gender categories of *man* and *woman* crystallize. At that point, around 150,000 years ago, culture joined biology in governing human interactions.

As human communities became larger, more hierarchical, and more powerful, the rough gender egalitarianism of hunting and gathering societies eroded. Because women had been the primary gatherers, their knowledge of wild plants had contributed to early settled agriculture, but they did not necessarily benefit from that transition. Advances in agrarian tools introduced a harsh working life that undermined women's earlier status as farmers. Men, no longer so involved in hunting and gathering, now took on the heavy work of yoking animals to plows. Women took on the backbreaking and repetitive tasks of planting, weeding, harvesting, and grinding the grain into flour. Thus, although agricultural innovations increased productivity, they also increased the drudgery of work, especially for women. Fossil evidence from Abu Hureyra, Syria, reveals damage to the vertebrae, osteoarthritis in the toes, and curved and arched femurs, all suggesting that the work of bending over and kneeling in the fields took its toll on female agriculturalists. The increasing differentiation of the roles of men and women also affected power relations within households and communities. The senior male figure became dominant in these households, and males dominated females in leadership positions.

The agricultural revolution marked a greater division among men, as well as between men and women. Where the agricultural transformation was most widespread, and where population densities began to grow, the social and political differences created inequalities. As these inequalities affected gender relations, patriarchy (the rule of senior males within households) began to spread around the globe.

Conclusion

Over thousands of generations, African hominins evolved from other primates, leading to new genera such as *Australopithecus* and *Homo*. The latter genus encompassed a range of now-extinct hominins, including the bipedal, toolmaking, fire-using *Homo erectus*, who migrated far from their native habitats to fill other landmasses. They did so in waves, often in response to worldwide cycles of climatic change. *Homo sapiens*, with bigger brains and consequently greater cognition, emerged in Africa about 300,000 years ago and migrated out of Africa beginning 180,000 years ago. With greater adaptive skills, they were better prepared to face the elements when a cooling cycle returned, and eventually they became the only surviving branch of the tree of human ancestors. *Homo sapiens* used language and art to engage in abstract, representational thought and to convey the lessons of experience to their neighbors and descendants. As modern humans stored and shared knowledge, their adaptive abilities increased.

Although modern men and women shared an African heritage, these individuals adapted over many millennia to the environments they encountered as they began to fill the earth's corners and practice hunting and gathering ways of life. Some settled near lakes and took to fishing, while others roamed the northern steppes hunting large mammals. No matter where they went, their dependence on nature yielded broadly similar social and cultural structures.

It took another warming cycle for people ranging from Africa to the Americas to begin putting down their hunting weapons and start domesticating animals and plants.

The changeover to settled agriculture was not uniform worldwide. As communities became more settled, the world's regions began to vary as humans learned to modify nature to fit their needs. The varieties of animals that they could domesticate and the differing climatic conditions and topography that they encountered shaped the ways in which people drifted apart in spite of their common origins. What these settled communities shared, however, was increasing social hierarchy, including the unequal status of men and women.

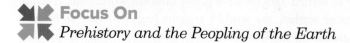

Focus On

Prehistory and the Peopling of the Earth

- **Bipedalism:** Hominins come down from the trees in Africa, become upright, and walk on two legs.
- **Big brains:** Ancestors to modern humans make tools and fire and acquire larger brains.

- **Cognitive skills:** *Homo sapiens* hominins develop the capacity for language and learn to communicate with one another, develop a sense of self, and produce art.
- **Village life:** People domesticate plants and animals and begin to live in more socially complex communities.

Key Terms

australopithecines p. 6
creation narratives p. 4
domestication p. 27
evolution p. 6
hominids p. 5

hominins p. 6
Homo erectus p. 14
Homo habilis p. 13
Homo sapiens p. 17

hunting and gathering p. 24
pastoralism p. 27
settled agriculture p. 27

CHRONOLOGY   5 MYA*   1 MYA

Afro-Eurasia		
Africa		
Europe and the Mediterranean		
Southwest and Inner Asia		
East Asia		
The Americas		

- *Australopithecus africanus* hominid species appears 3 MYA
- *Homo habilis* appears 2.5 MYA

Homo erectus appears and ● migrates 1.8 MYA

Beginnings of Ice Age across the Northern Hemisphere 2.5–1 MYA

*millions of years ago

**years ago

THINKING ABOUT GLOBAL CONNECTIONS

- **Thinking about Exchange Networks and Human Evolution** Across several million years, the hominin ancestors of humans, especially *Homo erectus*, and then *Homo sapiens*, migrated out of Africa. What role did evolution play in making it possible for our hominin ancestors and then *Homo sapiens* to migrate across the globe?

- **Thinking about the Environment and Human Evolution** Climate change and environmental conditions have played a recurring role in the narrative recounted in this chapter. In what specific ways did the climate change, and in what specific ways did the environment help shape the evolution of humans and influence the shift from hunting and gathering to settled agriculture?

- **Thinking about Changing Gender Relationships and the Agricultural Revolution** Some scholars have argued that the hunting and gathering ways of life for both *Homo erectus* and *Homo sapiens* allowed women—biologically, through their lactation and child-rearing, and calorically, through their dominant role as gatherers—to make a larger and more significant contribution to their communities than their male counterparts did. In what ways might the development of settled agriculture have ushered in a shift in these gender roles?

 Go to INQUIZITIVE to see what you've learned—and learn what you've missed—with personalized feedback along the way.

200,000 YA**	150,000 YA	100,000 YA	50,000 YA	10,000 YA	1 CE

Human migration from Afro-Eurasia begins 18,000 YA ●

Ice Age ends 16,000–10,000 BCE

Homo sapiens emerges in Africa 315,000 YA

Homo sapiens migrates out of Africa 180,000–50,000 YA

Cave art develops in Europe 30,000 YA ●

Beginnings of agricultural revolution in Southwest Asia 9000 BCE ●

Agricultural settlements emerge in Southwest Asia 6000–5000 BCE

Pastoralism begins in Inner Asia 3000 BCE ●

Rice cultivation in Yangzi River valley develops 6500 BCE ●

Millet cultivation in Yellow River valley develops 5500 BCE ●

Maize cultivation emerges in central Mexico 2000 BCE ●

2

Rivers, Cities, and First States

3500–2000 BCE

Core Objectives

- **IDENTIFY** the earliest river-basin societies, and **ANALYZE** their shared and distinctive characteristics.

- **EXPLAIN** the religious, social, and political developments that accompany early urbanization from 3500 to 2000 BCE.

- **TRACE** and **EVALUATE** the influence of long-distance connections across Afro-Eurasia during this period.

- **COMPARE** early urbanization with the ways of life in small villages and among pastoralists.

One of the first urban centers in the world was the ancient city of Uruk. Located in southern Mesopotamia on a branch of the Euphrates River, it was home to between 25,000 and 50,000 people by the late fourth millennium BCE and boasted many large public structures and temples. One temple, erected to house and honor the city's patron deity Inanna, had stood there since before 3000 BCE; with plastered mud-brick walls that formed stepped indentations, it perched high above the plain. In another area, administrative buildings and temples adorned with elaborate façades stood in courtyards defined by tall columns. Colored stone cones arranged in elaborate geometric patterns covered parts of these buildings. An epic poem devoted to its later king, Gilgamesh, described Uruk as the "shining city."

Over the years, Uruk became an immense commercial and administrative center. A huge wall with seven massive gates surrounded the metropolis, and down

Uruk Scholars from the Uruk visualization project drew on texts, excavation reports, and topographic data to produce this 2012 computer-generated reconstruction proposal of Uruk, King Gilgamesh's "shining city." The image includes more than 300 buildings and 4,000 human figures to visualize how the center of Uruk would have looked on the day of a religious festival.

the middle ran a canal carrying water from the Euphrates. On one side of the city were gardens, kilns, and textile workshops. On the other was the temple quarter where priests lived, scribes kept records, and the *lugal* ("big man" in the Sumerian language) conferred with the elders. As Uruk grew, many small industries— including pottery crafting, metalworking, stone bowl making, and brickmaking— became centralized in response to the increasing sophistication of construction and manufacturing.

Uruk was the first city of its kind in world history. Earlier humans had settled in small communities scattered over the landscape. As some communities gradually became focal points for trade, a few of these hubs grew into cities with large populations and institutions of economic, religious, and political power. Most inhabitants no longer produced their own food, working instead in specialized professions.

Between 3500 and 2000 BCE, a handful of remarkable societies clustered in a few river basins on the Afro-Eurasian landmass. These regions—in Mesopotamia (between the Tigris and Euphrates Rivers), in northwest India (on the Indus River), in Egypt (along the Nile), and in China (near the Yangzi and Yellow Rivers)—became the heartlands for densely populated settlements with complex cultures. Here the world saw the birth of the first large cities that exhausted surrounding regions of their resources. One of these settings (Mesopotamia) brought forth humankind's first writing system, and all laid the foundations for kingdoms radiating out of opulent cities. This chapter describes how each society evolved, and it explores their similarities and differences. It is important to note how exceptional these large city-states were, and we will see that many smaller societies prevailed elsewhere. The Aegean, Anatolia, western Europe, the Americas, and sub-Saharan Africa offer reminders that most of the world's people dwelt in small communities, far removed culturally from the monumental architecture and accomplishments of the big new states.

Global Storyline

Comparing First Cities

- Complex societies form around five great river basins.

- Early urbanization brings changes, including new technologies, monumental building, new religions, writing, hierarchical social structures, and specialized labor.

- Long-distance trade connects many of the Afro-Eurasian societies.

- Despite impressive developments in urbanization, most people live in farming villages or in pastoralist communities.

Settlement and Pastoralism

Around 3500 BCE, cultural changes, population growth, and technological innovations gave rise to complex societies. Clustered in cities, these larger communities developed new institutions, and individuals took on a wide range of social roles and occupations, resulting in new hierarchies based on wealth and gender. At the same time, the number of small villages and pastoralist communities grew.

Water was the key to settlement, since predictable flows of water determined where humans settled. Reliable water supplies allowed communities to sow crops adequate to feed large populations. Abundant rainfall allowed the world's first villages to emerge, but the breakthroughs into big cities occurred in drier zones where large rivers formed beds of rich soils deposited by flooding rivers. With irrigation innovations, soils became arable. Equally important, a worldwide warming cycle expanded growing seasons. The **river basins**—with their fertile soil, irrigation, and available domesticated plants and animals—made possible the agricultural surpluses needed to support city dwellers.

EARLY CITIES ALONG RIVER BASINS

The material and social advances of the early cities occurred in a remarkably short period—from 3500 to 2000 BCE—in three locations: the basin of the Tigris and Euphrates Rivers in central Southwest Asia; the northern parts of the Nile River flowing toward the Mediterranean Sea; and the Indus River basin in northwestern South Asia. About a millennium later, a similar process began along the Yellow River and the Yangzi River in China. (See Map 2.1.) In these regions humans farmed and fed themselves by relying on intensive irrigation agriculture. Gathering in cities inhabited by rulers, administrators, priests, and craftworkers, they changed their methods of organizing communities by worshipping new gods in new ways and by obeying divinely inspired monarchs and elaborate bureaucracies. New technologies appeared, ranging from the wheel for pottery production to metalworking and stoneworking for the creation of both luxury objects and utilitarian tools. The technology of writing used the storage of words and meanings to extend human communication and memory.

With cities and new technologies came greater divisions of labor. Dense urban settlement enabled people to specialize in making goods for the consumption of others: weavers made textiles, potters made ceramics, and jewelers made precious ornaments. Soon these goods were traded with outlying areas. As trade expanded over longer distances, raw materials such as wool, metal, timber, and precious stones arrived in the cities and could be fashioned into new, manufactured goods. (See Map 2.2.) One of the most coveted metals was copper: easily smelted and shaped (not to mention shiny and alluring), it became the metal of choice for charms, sculptures, and valued commodities. When combined with arsenic or tin, copper hardens and becomes **bronze**, which is useful for tools and weapons. Consequently, this period marks the beginning of the Bronze Age, even though the use of this alloy extended into and flourished during the second millennium BCE (see Chapter 3).

The dawn of cities and city-states had drawbacks for those who had been hunters and gatherers or had lived in towns. As rulers, scribes, bureaucrats, priests, artisans, and wealthy farmers rose, so did social stratification. Men made gains at the expense of women, for men dominated the prestigious positions and societies became highly patriarchal. All those who lived close to cities had to fashion their own city-states to protect themselves lest they be exploited, or even enslaved.

The emergence of cities as population centers created one of history's most durable worldwide distinctions: the **urban-rural divide**. Where cities appeared alongside rivers, people adopted lifestyles based on specialized labor and the mass production of goods. In contrast, most people continued to live in the countryside, where they remained on their lands, cultivating the land or tending livestock, though they exchanged their grains and animal products for goods from the urban centers. The two ways of life were interdependent and both worlds remained linked through family ties, trade, politics, and religion.

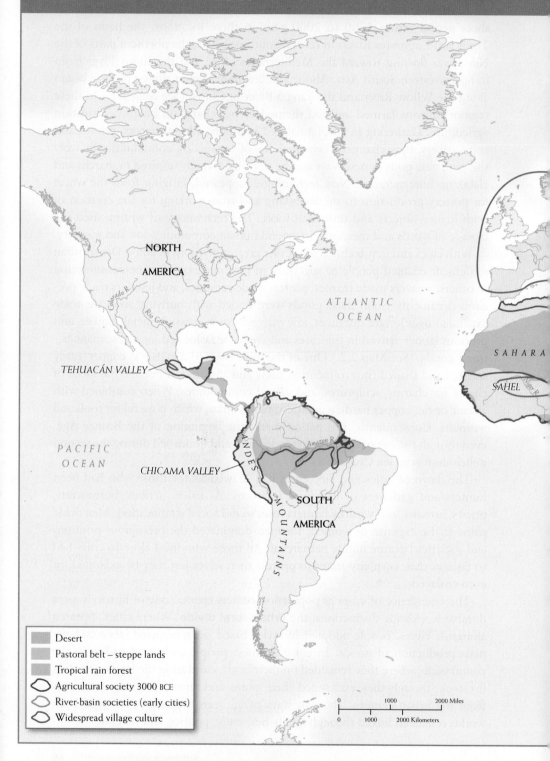

NORTH
AMERICA

Mississippi R.

Colorado R.

Rio Grande

ATLANTIC
OCEAN

SAHARA

SAHEL

Niger R.

TEHUACÁN VALLEY

PACIFIC
OCEAN

Amazon R.

CHICAMA VALLEY

ANDES

SOUTH
AMERICA

MOUNTAINS

Desert
Pastoral belt – steppe lands
Tropical rain forest
Agricultural society 3000 BCE
River-basin societies (early cities)
Widespread village culture

0		1000		2000 Miles
0	1000		2000 Kilometers	

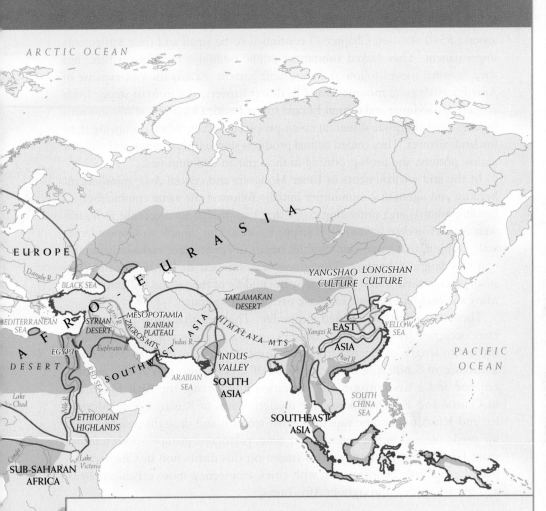

Map 2.1 The World in the Third Millennium BCE

....

Human societies became increasingly diversified as agricultural, urban, and pastoralist communities expanded. While urban communities began to develop in several major river basins in the Eastern Hemisphere, not every river basin produced cities in the third millennium BCE. Pastoralism, village life, agricultural communities, and continued hunting and gathering were by far the norm for most of the peoples of the earth.

- In what different regions did pastoralism and river-basin societies emerge? Where did pastoralism and river-basin societies not emerge? What might account for where these ways of life developed and where they did not?

- Considering the geographic features highlighted on this map, why do you think cities appeared in the regions that they did? What might explain why cities did not appear elsewhere?

- How did geographic and environmental factors promote interaction between pastoralist and sedentary agricultural societies?

PASTORALIST COMMUNITIES

The transhumant herder communities that had appeared in Southwest Asia around 5500 BCE (see Chapter 1) continued to be small and their settlements impermanent. They lacked substantial public buildings or infrastructure, but their seasonal moves followed a consistent pattern. Across the vast expanse of Afro-Eurasia's great mountains and its desert barriers, and from its steppe lands ranging across inner and central Eurasia to the Pacific Ocean, these transhumant herders lived alongside settled agrarian people, especially when occupying their lowland pastures. They traded animal products such as meat, hides, and milk for grains, pottery, and tools produced in the agrarian communities.

In the arid environments of Inner Mongolia and central Asia, transhumant herding and agrarian communities initially followed the same combination of herding animals and cultivating crops that had proved so successful in Southwest Asia. However, it was in this steppe environment, unable to support large-scale farming, that some communities began to concentrate exclusively on animal breeding and herding. Though some continued to fish, hunt, and farm small plots in their winter pastures, by the middle of the second millennium BCE many societies had become full-scale pastoral communities.

These pastoralists dominated steppe life. The area that these pastoral societies occupied lay between 40 degrees and 55 degrees north and extended the entire length of Eurasia from the Great Hungarian Plain to Manchuria, a distance of 5,600 miles. The steppe itself divided into two zones, an eastern one and a western one, the separation point being the Altai Mountains in Central and East Asia where the modern states of Russia, China, Mongolia, and Kazakhstan come together. Frost-tolerant and drought-resistant plant life predominated in the region. Over time, pastoralist groups—both transhumant herders and pastoral nomads (more on this distinction in Chapter 3)—played a vital role by interacting with cities, connecting more urbanized areas, and spreading ideas throughout Afro-Eurasia.

Between the Tigris and Euphrates Rivers: Mesopotamia

The world's first complex society arose in Mesopotamia. Here the river and the first cities changed how people lived. Mesopotamia, whose name is a Greek word meaning "[region] between two rivers," is a landmass including all of modern-day Iraq and parts of Syria and southeastern Turkey. From their headwaters in the mountains to the north and east to their destination in the Persian Gulf, the Tigris and Euphrates Rivers are wild and capricious. Unpredictable floodwaters could wipe out years of hard work, but when managed properly they could transform the landscape into verdant and productive fields.

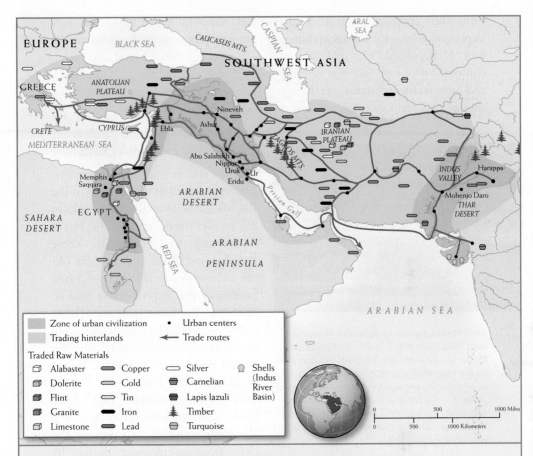

Map 2.2 Trade and Exchange in Southwest Asia and the Eastern Mediterranean, Third Millennium BCE

Extensive commercial networks linked the urban cores of Southwest Asia.

- Of the traded raw materials shown on the map, which ones were used for building materials, and which ones for luxury items?
- Which regions had timber, and which regions did not? How would the needs of river-basin societies have influenced trade with the regions that had timber?
- Using the map, describe the extent and likely routes of trade necessary for the creation of the treasures of Ur in Mesopotamia (with items fashioned from gold, lapis lazuli, and carnelian) and the wealth buried with kings of Egypt in their pyramids (silver, gold, lapis lazuli, and carnelian).

Both rivers provided water for irrigation and, although hardly navigable, were important routes for transportation and communication by pack animal and by foot. Mesopotamia's natural advantages—its rich agricultural land and water, combined with easy access to neighboring regions—favored the growth of cities and later territorial states (see Chapter 3). These cities and states became the sites of important cultural, political, and social innovations.

Early Mesopotamian Waterworks From the sixth millennium BCE, irrigation was necessary for successful farming in southern Mesopotamia. By the first millennium BCE, sophisticated feats of engineering allowed the Assyrians to redirect water through constructed aqueducts, like the one illustrated here on a relief at Nineveh from the palace of the Assyrian king Sennacherib (who will be discussed in Chapter 4).

TAPPING THE WATERS

The first rudimentary advances in irrigation occurred in the foothills of the Zagros Mountains along the banks of the smaller rivers that feed the Tigris. Converting the floodplain—where the river overflows and deposits fertile soil—into a breadbasket required mastering the unpredictable waters. Both the Euphrates and the Tigris, unless controlled by waterworks, were unfavorable to cultivators because the annual floods occurred at the height of the growing season, when crops were most vulnerable. Low water levels occurred when crops required abundant irrigation. To prevent the river from overflowing during its flood stage, farmers built levees along the banks and dug ditches and canals to drain away the floodwaters. Engineers devised an irrigation system whereby the Euphrates, which has a higher riverbed than the Tigris, essentially served as the supply and the Tigris as the drain. Storing and channeling water year after year required constant maintenance and innovation by a corps of engineers.

The Mesopotamians' technological breakthrough was in irrigation, not in agrarian methods. Because the soils were fine, rich, and constantly replenished by the floodwaters' silt, soil tillage was light work. Farmers sowed a combination of wheat, millet, sesame, and barley (the basis for beer, a staple of their diet).

CROSSROADS OF SOUTHWEST ASIA

Though its soil was rich and water was abundant, southern Mesopotamia had few other natural resources apart from the mud, marsh reeds, spindly trees, and low-quality limestone that served as basic building materials. To obtain high-quality stone, metal, dense wood, and other materials for constructing and embellishing their cities with their temples and palaces, Mesopotamians interacted with the inhabitants of surrounding regions. In return for their exports of textiles, oils, and other commodities, Mesopotamians imported cedar wood from Lebanon, copper and stones from Oman, more copper from Turkey and Iran, and the precious blue gemstone called lapis lazuli, as well as ever-useful tin, from faraway Afghanistan. Maintaining trading contacts was easy, given Mesopotamia's open boundaries on all sides. The area became a crossroads for the peoples of Southwest Asia, including Sumerians, who concentrated in the south; Hurrians, who lived in the north; and Akkadians, who populated western and central Mesopotamia. Trade and migration contributed to the growth of cities throughout the river basin, beginning with the Sumerian cities of southern Mesopotamia.

THE WORLD'S FIRST CITIES

During the first half of the fourth millennium BCE, a demographic transformation occurred in the Tigris-Euphrates river basin, especially in the southern area called Sumer. The population expanded as a result of the region's agricultural bounty, and many Mesopotamians migrated from country villages to centers that eventually became cities. (A **city** is a large, well-defined urban area with a dense population.) The earliest Sumerian cities—Uruk, Eridu, and Nippur—developed over about 1,000 years, dominating the southern part of the floodplain by 3500 BCE. Buildings of mud brick show successive layers of urban development, as at Eridu, where more than twenty reconstructed temples were piled atop one another across four millennia, resulting in a final temple that rose from a platform like a mountain, visible for miles in all directions.

As the temple grew skyward, the village expanded outward and became a city. From their homes in temples located at the center of cities, the cities' gods broadcast their powers. In return, urbanites provided luxuries, fine clothes, and enhanced lodgings for the gods and their priests. In Sumerian cosmology, created by ruling elites, humans existed solely to serve the gods, so the urban landscape reflected this fact: a temple at the core, with goods and services flowing to the center and with divine protection and justice flowing outward.

Some thirty-five of these politically equal city-states with religious sanctuaries dotted the southern plain of Mesopotamia. Sumerian ideology glorified a way of life and a territory based on politically equal city-states, each with a guardian deity and sanctuary supported by its inhabitants. (A **city-state** is a political organization based on the authority of a single, large city that controls outlying territories.) Because early Mesopotamian cities served as meeting places for peoples and their deities, they gained status as religious and economic centers. Whether enormous (like Uruk and Nippur) or modest (like Ur and Abu Salabikh), all cities were spiritual, economic, and cultural homes for Mesopotamian subjects.

Simply making a city was therefore not enough: urban design reflected the city's role as a wondrous place to pay homage to the gods and their human intermediary, the king. Within their walls, early cities contained large houses separated by date palm plantations and extensive sheepfolds. As populations

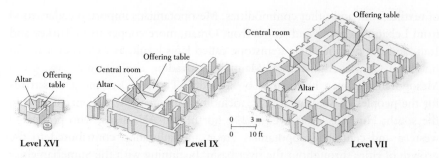

Layout of Eridu Over several millennia, temples of increasing size and complexity were built atop each other at Eridu in southern Iraq. The culmination came with the elaborate structure of level VII.

grew, the Mesopotamian cities became denser, houses became smaller, and new suburbs spilled out beyond the old walls. The typical layout of Mesopotamian cities reflected a common pattern: a central canal surrounded by neighborhoods of specialized occupational groups. The temple marked the city center, with the palace and other official buildings on the periphery. In separate quarters for craft production, families passed down their trades across generations. In this sense, the landscape of the city mirrored the growing **social hierarchies** (distinctions between the privileged and the less privileged).

GODS AND TEMPLES

The worldview of the Sumerians and, later, the Akkadians of Mesopotamia, included a belief in a group of gods that shaped their political institutions and controlled everything—including the weather, fertility, harvests, and the underworld. As depicted in the *Epic of Gilgamesh* (a second-millennium BCE composition based on oral tales about Gilgamesh, a historical but mythologized king of Uruk), the gods could give but could also take away—with droughts, floods, and death. Gods, and the natural forces they controlled, had to be revered and feared. Faithful subjects imagined their gods as immortal beings whose habits were capricious and who had contentious relationships and gloriously work-free lives.

Each major god of the Sumerian pantheon (an officially recognized group of gods and goddesses) dwelled in a lavish temple in a particular city that he or she had created; for instance, Enlil, god of air and storms, dwelled in Nippur; Enki (also called Ea), god of water, in Eridu; Nanna, god of the moon, in Ur; and Inanna (also called Ishtar), goddess of love, fertility, and war, in Uruk. These temples, and the patron deity housed within, gave rise to each city's character, institutions, and relationships with its urban neighbors. Inside these temples, benches lined the walls, with statues of humans standing in perpetual worship of the deity's images. By the end of the third millennium BCE, the temple's platform base had changed to a stepped platform called a *ziggurat*, with the main

Ziggurat The first ziggurat of Mesopotamia, dedicated to the moon god Nanna, was built by the founder of the Neo-Sumerian dynasty, Ur-Nammu (2112–2095 BCE). Although temples had been raised on platforms since early times, the distinctive stepped form of the ziggurat was initially borrowed from the Iranian plateau. It became the most important sacred structure in Mesopotamia.

temple on top. Surrounding the ziggurat were buildings that housed priests, officials, laborers, and servants.

Temples functioned as the god's estate, engaging in all sorts of productive and commercial activities. Temple dependents cultivated cereals, fruits, and vegetables by using extensive irrigation and cared for flocks of livestock. Other temples operated workshops for manufacturing textiles and leather goods, employing craftworkers, metalworkers, masons, and stoneworkers. Enormous labor forces were involved in maintaining this high level of production.

ROYAL POWER, FAMILIES, AND SOCIAL HIERARCHY

Like the temples, royal palaces reflected the power of the ruling elite. Royal palaces appeared around 2500 BCE and served as the official residence of a ruler, his family, and his entourage. As access to palaces and temples over time became limited, gods and kings became inaccessible to all but the most elite. Although located at the edge of cities, palaces were the symbols of permanent secular, military, and administrative authority distinct from the temples' spiritual and economic power.

The Royal Cemetery at Ur shows how Mesopotamian rulers used elaborate burial arrangements to reinforce their religious and socioeconomic hierarchies. Housed in a mud-brick structure, the royal burials held not only the primary remains but also the bodies of more than eighty men and women who had been sacrificed. Huge vats for cooked food, bones of animals, drinking vessels, and musical instruments suggest the lifestyle of those who joined their masters in the graves. Honoring the royal dead by including their followers and possessions in their tombs underscored the social hierarchies—including the vertical ties between humans and gods—that were the cornerstone of these early city-states.

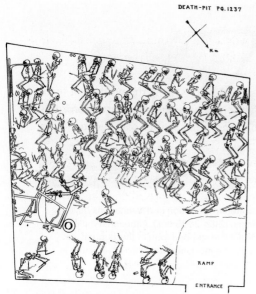

DEATH-PIT PG.1237

RAMP

ENTRANCE

Death Pit 1237 from the Royal Tombs of Ur
The excavation team at Ur produced careful drawings and notes as they uncovered the Royal Tombs of Ur in 1927–28. Their drawing of Death Pit 1237 illustrates the rich grave offerings of gold, silver, lapis lazuli, and shell (including a lyre, on the left-hand side). It also shows the remains of six men (armed and lined up by the door, along the bottom) and sixty-seven well-dressed women who were likely buried alive as a funerary offering to honor and accompany the most elaborately decked-out female (Body 61, top right corner) in the afterlife.

Social hierarchies were an important part of the fabric of Sumerian city-states. Ruling groups secured their privileged access to economic and political resources by erecting systems of bureaucracies, priesthoods, and laws. Priests and bureaucrats served their rulers well, championing rules and norms that legitimized the political leadership. Occupations within the cities were highly specialized, and a list of professions circulated across the land so that everyone could know his or her place in the social order. The king and priest in Sumer were at the top of the list, followed by bureaucrats (scribes and household accountants), supervisors, and craftworkers, such as cooks, jewelers, gardeners, potters, metalsmiths, and traders. There were also independent merchants who risked long-distance trading ventures, hoping for a generous return on their investment. The biggest group, which was at the bottom of the hierarchy, comprised workers who were not enslaved but were dependent on their employers' households. Movement among economic classes was not impossible but, as in many traditional societies, it was rare.

The family and the household provided the bedrock for Sumerian society, and its patriarchal organization, dominated by the senior male, reflected the balance between women and men, children and parents. The family consisted of the husband and wife bound by a contract: she would provide children, preferably male, while he provided support and protection. Monogamy was the norm unless there was no son, in which case a second wife or an enslaved woman would bear male children to serve as the married couple's offspring. Adoption was another way to gain a male heir. Sons would inherit the family's property in equal shares, while daughters would receive dowries necessary for successful marriage into other families. Some women joined the temple staff as priestesses and gained economic autonomy that included ownership of estates and productive enterprises, although their fathers and brothers remained responsible for their well-being.

FIRST WRITING AND EARLY TEXTS

Mesopotamia was the birthplace of the world's first writing system, inscribed to promote the economic power of the temples and kings. Those who wielded new writing tools were **scribes**; from the very beginning they were near the top of the social ladder, under the big man and the priests. As the writing of texts became more important to the social fabric of cities, and facilitated information sharing across wider spans of distance and time, scribes consolidated their elite status.

Mesopotamians were the world's first record keepers and readers. The precursors to writing appeared in Mesopotamian societies when farming peoples and officials who had been using clay tokens and images carved on stones to seal off storage areas began to use them to convey messages. These images, when combined with numbers drawn on clay tablets, could record the distribution of goods and services.

Around 3200 BCE, someone, probably in Uruk, understood that the marks (most were pictures of objects) could also represent words or sounds. Before long, scribes connected visual symbols with sounds, and sounds with meanings, and they discovered they could record messages by using abstract symbols or signs to denote concepts. Such signs later came to represent syllables, the building blocks of words. By impressing signs into wet clay with the cut end of a reed, scribes pioneered a form of wedge-shaped writing that we call *cuneiform*; it filled tablets with information that was intelligible to anyone who could decipher it, even in faraway locations or in future generations. Developing over 800 years, this Sumerian innovation enhanced the urban elites' ability to trade goods, to control property, and to transmit ideas through literature, historical records, and sacred texts. The result was a profound change in human experience, because representing symbols of spoken language facilitated an extension of communication and memory.

Much of what we know about Mesopotamia rests on scholars' ability to decipher cuneiform script. By around 2400 BCE, texts began to describe the political makeup of southern Mesopotamia, giving details of its history and economy. Adaptable to different languages, cuneiform script was borrowed by other peoples in Mesopotamia to write not only Semitic languages such as Akkadian and, much later, Old Persian, but also the languages of the Hurrians and the Hittites.

City life and literacy also gave rise to written narratives, the stories of a "people" and their origins. "The Temple Hymns," written around 2100 BCE, describe thirty-five divine sanctuaries. The Sumerian King List, known from texts written around 2000 BCE, recounts the reigns of kings by city and dynasty and narrates the long reigns of legendary kings before the so-called Great Flood. A crucial event in Sumerian identity, the Great Flood, a pastoral-focused version of which is also found in biblical narrative, explained Uruk's demise as the gods' doing.

Changes in Cuneiform over Time The world's earliest script, cuneiform, changed over time and was used to write many different languages. The first image (*top left*) shows the earliest version of cuneiform being used to write in the Sumerian language (here, a c. 2500 BCE accounting text). The next image (*top right*) shows the more formalized cuneiform script used to write in the Akkadian language more than a millennium after its invention by the Sumerians. The third image (*bottom left*) shows the Hittites' use of cuneiform script to render their language (here, in a letter sealed in a clay envelope). The final image (*bottom right*) demonstrates the use of cuneiform more than 2,000 years after its invention, in this case to record in Assyrian the flood story from the *Epic of Gilgamesh*.

Flooding was the most powerful natural force in the lives of those who lived by rivers, and it helped shape the foundations of Mesopotamian societies.

CITIES BEGIN TO UNIFY INTO "STATES"

No single city-state dominated the whole of Mesopotamia in the fourth and third millennia BCE, but the most powerful and influential were the Sumerian city-states (2850–2334 BCE) and their successor, the Akkadian territorial state (2334–2193 BCE). In the north, Hurrians urbanized their rich agricultural zone around 2600 BCE, including cities at Urkesh and Tell Brak. (See Map 2.3.)

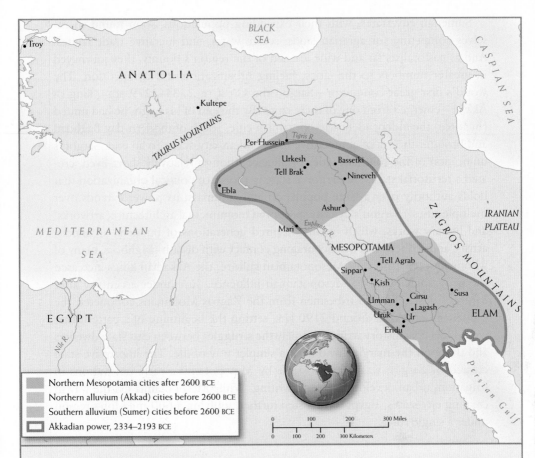

Map 2.3 The Spread of Cities in Mesopotamia and the Akkadian State, 2600–2200 BCE

....

Urbanization began in the southern river basin of Mesopotamia and spread northward. Eventually, the region achieved unification under Akkadian power.

- According to this map, what natural features influenced the location of Mesopotamian cities?
- Where were cities located before 2600 BCE, as opposed to afterward? What does the area under Akkadian power suggest that the Akkadian territorial state was able to do?
- How did the expansion northward reflect the continued influence of geographic and environmental factors on urbanization?

Sumerian city-states, with their expanding populations, soon found themselves competing for agrarian lands, scarce water, and lucrative trade routes. And as pastoralists far and wide learned of the region's bounty, they journeyed in greater numbers to the cities, fueling urbanization and competition. The world's first great conqueror—Sargon the Great (r. 2334–2279 BCE), king of Akkad—emerged from one of these cities. By the end of his reign, he had united (by force) the independent Mesopotamian cities south of modern-day Baghdad and brought the era of competitive independent city-states to an end. Sargon's unification of the southern cities by alliance, though relatively short-lived, created a territorial state. (A territorial state is a form of political organization that holds authority over a large population and landmass; its power extends over multiple cities.) Sargon's dynasty sponsored monumental architecture, artworks, and literary works, which in turn inspired generations of builders, architects, artists, and scribes. And by encouraging contact with distant neighbors, many of whom adopted aspects of Mesopotamian culture, the Akkadian kings increased the geographic reach of Mesopotamian influence. Just under a century after Sargon's death, foreign tribesmen from the Zagros Mountains conquered the capital city of Akkad around 2190 BCE, setting the beginning of a pattern that would fuel epic history writing, namely the struggles between city-state dwellers and those on the margins who lived a simpler way of life. The impressive state created by Sargon was made possible by Mesopotamia's early innovations in irrigation, urban development, and writing. While Mesopotamia led the way in creating city-states, Egypt went a step further, unifying a 600-mile-long region under a single ruler.

"The Gift of the Nile": Egypt

In Egypt, complex societies grew on the banks of the Nile River, and by the third millennium BCE their peoples created a distinctive culture and a powerful, prosperous state. The earliest inhabitants along the banks of the Nile were a mixed people. Some had migrated from the eastern and western deserts in Sinai and Libya as these areas grew barren from climate change. Others came from the Mediterranean. Equally important were peoples who trekked northward from Nubia and central Africa. Ancient Egypt was a melting pot where immigrants blended cultural practices and technologies.

Like Mesopotamia, Egypt had densely populated areas whose inhabitants depended on irrigation, built monumental architecture, gave their rulers immense authority, and created a complex social order based in commercial and devotional centers. Yet the ancient Egyptian culture was profoundly shaped by its geography. The environment and the natural boundaries of deserts, river rapids, and sea dominated the country and its inhabitants. Only about 3 percent of Egypt's land area was cultivable, and almost all of that cultivable land was in the Nile Delta—the rich alluvial land lying between the river's two main branches as it flows north of modern-day Cairo into the Mediterranean Sea. This environment shaped Egyptian society's unique culture.

THE NILE RIVER AND ITS FLOODWATERS

Knowing Egypt requires appreciating the pulses of the Nile. The world's longest river, it stretches 4,238 miles from its sources in the highlands of central Africa to its destination in the Mediterranean Sea. Egypt was deeply attached to sub-Saharan Africa; not only did its waters and rich silt deposits come from the African highlands, but much of its original population had migrated into the Nile Valley from the west and the south many millennia earlier.

The Upper Nile is a sluggish river that cuts through the Sahara Desert. Rising out of central Africa and Ethiopia, its two main branches—the White and Blue Niles—meet at present-day Khartoum and then scour out a single riverbed 1,500 miles long to the Mediterranean. The annual floods gave the basin regular moisture and enriched the soil. Although the Nile's floodwaters did not fertilize or irrigate fields as broad as those in Mesopotamia, they created green belts flanking the broad waterway. These gave rise to a society whose culture stretched along the navigable river and its carefully preserved banks. Away from the riverbanks, on both sides, lay a desert rich in raw materials but largely uninhabited. (See Map 2.4.) Egypt had no fertile hinterland like the sprawling plains of Mesopotamia. In this way, Egypt was arguably the most river focused of the river-basin cultures.

The Nile's predictability as the source of life and abundance shaped the character of the people and their culture. In contrast to the wild and uncertain Euphrates and Tigris Rivers, the Nile was gentle, bountiful, and reliable. During the summer, as the Nile swelled, local villagers built earthen walls that divided the floodplain into basins. By trapping the floodwaters, these basins captured the rich silt washing down from the Ethiopian highlands. Annual flooding meant that the land received a new layer of topsoil every year. The light, fertile soils made planting simple. Peasants cast seeds into the alluvial soil and then had their livestock trample them to the proper depth. The never-failing sun, which the Egyptians worshipped, ensured an abundant harvest. In the early spring, when the Nile's waters were at their lowest and no crops were under cultivation, the sun dried out the soil.

The peculiarities of the Nile region distinguished it from Mesopotamia. The Greek historian and geographer Herodotus noted 2,500 years ago that Egypt was the gift of the Nile and that the entire length of its basin was one of the world's most self-contained geographical entities. Bounded on the north by the Mediterranean Sea, on the east and west by deserts, and on the south by waterfalls, Egypt was destined to achieve a common culture. Due to these geographical features, the region was far less open to outsiders than was Mesopotamia, which was situated at a crossroads. Egypt created a common culture by balancing a struggle of opposing forces: the north or Lower Egypt versus the south or

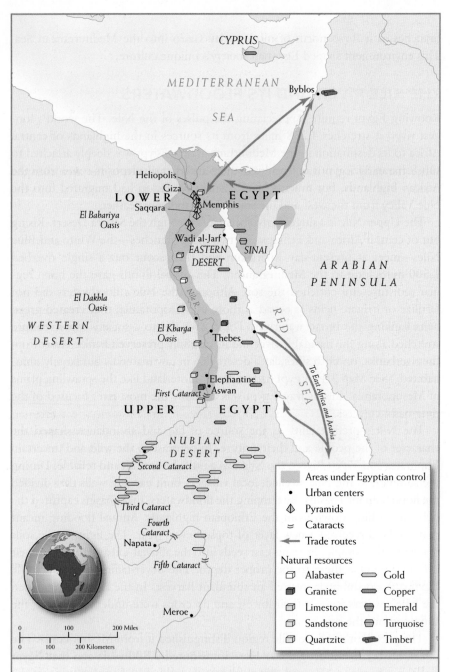

Map 2.4 Old Kingdom Egypt, 2686–2181 BCE

Old Kingdom Egyptian society reflected a strong influence from its geographical location.

- What geographical features contributed to Egypt's isolation from the outside world and the people's sense of their unity?

- What natural resources enabled the Egyptians to build the Great Pyramids? What resources enabled the Egyptians to fill those pyramids with treasures?

- Based on the map, why do you think it was important to the people and their rulers for Upper and Lower Egypt to be united?

Upper Egypt; the black, rich soil versus the red sand; life versus death; heaven versus earth; order versus disorder. For Egypt's rulers the primary task was to bring stability or order, known as *ma'at*, out of these opposites. The Egyptians believed that keeping chaos, personified by the desert and its marauders, at bay through attention to *ma'at* would allow all that was good and right to occur.

THE EGYPTIAN STATE AND DYNASTIES

Once the early Egyptians harnessed the Nile to agriculture, the area changed quickly from scarcely inhabited to socially complex. A king, later called the pharaoh and considered semidivine, was at the center of Egyptian life (Egyptian kings did not use the title *pharaoh* until the mid to late second millennium BCE). He ensured that the forces of nature, in particular the regular flooding of the Nile, continued without interruption. This task had more to do with appeasing the gods than with running a complex hydraulic system. The king protected his people from chaos-threatening invaders from the eastern desert, as well as from Nubians on the southern borders. In wall carvings, artists portrayed early kings carrying the shepherd's crook and the flail, indicating their responsibility for the welfare of their flocks (the people) and of the land. Under the king an elaborate bureaucracy organized labor and produced public works, sustaining both his vast holdings and general order throughout the realm.

The narrative of ancient Egypt's history follows its thirty-one dynasties, spanning nearly three millennia from 3100 BCE down to its conquest by Alexander the Great in 332 BCE. (See Table 2.1.) Since the nineteenth century, scholars have recast the story around three periods of dynastic achievement: the Old Kingdom, the Middle Kingdom, and the New Kingdom. At the end of each era, cultural flourishing suffered a breakdown in central authority, known respectively as the First, Second, and Third Intermediate Periods.

KINGS, PYRAMIDS, AND COSMIC ORDER

The Third Dynasty (2686–2613 BCE) launched the foundational period known as the Old Kingdom, the golden age of ancient Egypt. By the time it began, the basic institutions of the Egyptian state were in place, as were the ideology and ritual life that legitimized the dynastic rulers.

The king presented himself to the population by means of impressive architectural spaces, and the priestly class performed rituals reinforcing his supreme status within the universe's natural order. One of the most important rituals was the Sed festival, which renewed the king's vitality after he had ruled for thirty years and sought to ensure the perpetual presence of water. King Djoser, from the Third Dynasty, celebrated the Sed festival at his tomb complex at Saqqara. This magnificent complex includes the world's oldest stone structure, dating to around 2650 BCE. Here Djoser's architect, Imhotep, designed a step pyramid that ultimately rose some 200 feet above the plain. The whole complex became

Table 2.1 Dynasties of Ancient Egypt

Dynasty*	Date
Predynastic Period dynasties I and II	3100–2686 BCE
Old Kingdom dynasties III–VI	2686–2181 BCE
First Intermediate Period dynasties VII–X	2181–2055 BCE
Middle Kingdom dynasties XI–XIII	2055–1650 BCE
Second Intermediate Period dynasties XIV–XVII	1650–1550 BCE
New Kingdom dynasties XVIII–XX	1550–1070 BCE
Third Intermediate Period dynasties XXI–XXV	1070–747 BCE
Late Period dynasties XXVI–XXXI	747–332 BCE

*The term *dynasty* generally refers to a series of rulers who are related to one another. Intermediate periods mark breaks between the kingdoms (Old, Middle, and New). While scholars make attempts to synchronize the dates with modern chronology and other events in the ancient world, the succession of rulers comes from Egyptian texts. The term *pharaoh*, as a title for the Egyptian king, came into use in the New Kingdom.

Source: Compiled from Ian Shaw and Paul Nicholson, eds., *The Dictionary of Ancient Egypt* (London: British Museum Press, 1995), pp. 310–11.

a stage for state rituals that emphasized the divinity of kingship and the unity of Egypt.

The step pyramid at Djoser's tomb complex was a precursor to the grand pyramids of the Fourth Dynasty (2613–2494 BCE). These kings erected their monumental structures at Giza, just outside modern-day Cairo and not far from the early royal cemetery site of Saqqara, where Djoser's step pyramid stood. The pyramid of Khufu, rising 481 feet above the ground, is the largest stone structure in the world, and its corners are almost perfectly aligned to due north, west, south, and east. The oldest papyrus texts ever found—including a set of records kept by an official named Merer around 2550 BCE, which was excavated recently at the ancient port of Wadi al-Jarf—document a meticulous timetable for the gathering of stone for pyramid construction during Khufu's reign and tabulations of food to feed workers.

Construction of pyramids entailed the backbreaking work of quarrying the massive stones, digging a canal so barges could bring them from the Nile to the base of the Giza plateau, building a harbor there, and then constructing sturdy brick ramps that could withstand the stones' weight as workers hauled them ever higher along the pyramids' faces. Most likely a permanent work-force of up to 21,000 laborers endured 10-hour workdays, 300 days a year, for approximately 14 years just to complete the great pyramid of Khufu. The finished product was a miracle of engineering and planning. Khufu's great pyramid contained 21,300 blocks of stone with an average weight of 2½ tons, though some stones weighed up to 16 tons. Roughly speaking, one stone had to be put in place every 2 minutes during daylight. The stone blocks were planed so precisely that they required no mortar.

Surrounding these royal tombs at Giza were those of high officials, almost all members of the royal family. The enormous amount of labor involved in building these monuments came from peasant-workers as well as enslaved people captured and brought from Nubia and the Mediterranean. Filling these monuments with wealth for the occupants' afterlife similarly required a range of specialized labor (from jewelers to weavers to stone carvers to furniture makers). Long-distance trade was required to bring from far away not only the jewels and precious metals (like lapis lazuli, carnelian, and silver) required for such offerings, but also the materials to construct the ships that helped make that trade possible (like timber from Byblos). Through their majesty and complex construction, the Giza pyramids reflect the degree of centralization and the surpluses in Egyptian society at this time as well as the trade and specialized labor that fueled these undertakings.

The Pyramids of Giza The Pyramid Fields of Giza lie on the western side of the Nile, with the bustling modern city of Cairo in the distance. Old Kingdom kings harnessed massive amounts of resources and human labor to complete these monumental structures over the course of several decades in the twenty-sixth century BCE. In the foreground stand three small pyramids of queens; the mostly collapsed structure belonged to Queen Hetepheres I. Behind them is the pyramid of Menkaure, the penultimate king of the Fourth Dynasty. Beyond Menkaure's pyramid is that of Khafre, which retains some of its casing stones near the top. In the distance, behind Khafre's pyramid, is the pyramid of Khufu, the largest of the three (taller than Khafre's by just under 10 feet).

Kings used their royal tombs, and the ritual of death leading to everlasting life, to embody the state's ideology and the principles of the Egyptian cosmos. They also employed symbols, throne names, and descriptive titles for themselves and their advisers to represent their own power and that of their administrators, the priests, and the landed elite. As in Mesopotamian city-states, the Egyptian cosmic order was one of inequality and stark hierarchy that did not seek balance among people (for it buttressed the inequalities and stark hierarchies of Egyptian society); rather, Egyptian religion sought balance between universal order (*ma'at*) and disorder. It was the job of the king to maintain this cosmic order for eternity.

GODS, PRIESTHOOD, AND MAGICAL POWER

Egyptians understood their world as inhabited by three groups: gods, kings, and the rest of humanity. Official records showed representations of only gods and kings. Yet the people did not confuse their kings with gods—at least during the kings' lifetimes. Mortality was the bar between rulers and deities; after death, kings joined the gods whom they had represented while alive.

As in Mesopotamia, every region in Egypt had its resident god. Some gods, such as Amun (believed to be physically present in Thebes, the political center of Upper Egypt), transcended regional status because of the importance of their hometown. Over the centuries the Egyptian gods evolved, combining often-contradictory aspects into single deities, including Horus, the sky god of kinship; Osiris, the god of regeneration and the underworld; Isis, who represented the ideals of sisterhood and motherhood; Hathor, the goddess of childbirth and love; Ra, the sun god; and Amun, a creator considered to be the hidden god.

Official religious practices took place in the main temples. The king and his agents offered respect, adoration, and thanks to the gods in their temples. In return, the gods maintained order and nurtured the king and—through him—all humanity. In this contractual relationship, the gods were passive while the kings were active, a difference that reflected their unequal relationship.

The tasks of regulating religious rituals and mediating among gods, kings, and society fell to one specialist class: the priesthood. Creating this class required elaborate rules for selecting and training the priests. Only priests could enter the temples' inner sanctuaries, and the gods' statues left the temples only for great festivals. Thus, priests monopolized communication between spiritual powers and their subjects.

Unofficial religion was also important. Ordinary Egyptians matched their elite rulers in faithfulness to the gods, but their distance from temple life caused them to find different ways to fulfill their religious needs and duties. They visited local shrines, where they prayed, made requests, and left offerings to the gods.

Unlike modern sensibilities that might see magic as opposed to, or different from, categories such as religion or medicine, Egyptians saw magic

Egyptian Gods In this image from a thirteenth-century BCE copy of the *Book of the Dead* owned by a scribe named Hunefer (on left, in white), falcon-headed Horus leads Hunefer to Osiris, who wears a white crown with plumes and holds a crook and flail across his chest. Behind Osiris stand Isis (left) and Nephthys (right).

(personified by the god Heka) as a category closely intertwined with, if not indistinguishable from, the other two. Magic, or Heka, was a force that was present at creation and preexisted order and chaos. Magic had a special importance for commoners, who believed that amulets held extraordinary powers, such as preventing illness and guaranteeing safe childbirth. To deal with profound questions, commoners looked to omens and divination. Like the elites, commoners attributed supernatural powers to animals. Chosen animals received special treatment in life and after death: for example, the Egyptians adored cats, whom they kept as pets and whose image they used to represent certain deities. Apis bulls, sacred to the god Ptah, merited special cemeteries and mourning rituals. Ibises, dogs, jackals, baboons, lizards, fish, snakes, crocodiles, and other beasts associated with deities enjoyed similar privileges.

Spiritual expression was central to Egyptian culture at all levels, and religion helped shape other cultural achievements, including the development of a written language.

WRITING AND SCRIBES

Egypt, like Mesopotamia, was a scribal culture. By the middle of the third millennium BCE, literacy was well established among small circles of scribes in Egypt and Mesopotamia. The fact that few individuals were literate heightened the scribes' social status. Most high-ranking Egyptians were also trained as scribes for the king's court, the army, or the priesthood. Some kings and members of the royal family learned to write as well. Although in both cultures writing may

 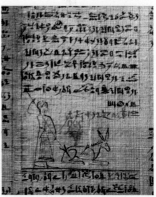

Egyptian Hieroglyphs and "Cursive Script" The Egyptians wrote in two distinctive types of script. The more formal is hieroglyphs, which are based on pictorial images that carry values of either ideas (logograms) or sounds (phonemes). All royal and funerary inscriptions, such as this funerary relief (*left*) from the Old Kingdom (from the tomb of Nefertiabet, c. 2550 BCE), are rendered in hieroglyphic script. Nefertiabet's inscription describes, with a mixture of images and words, the funerary offerings, including food, fabric, and cosmetics. Daily documents, accountings, and literary texts—such as the fragment from the *Book of the Dead* (*right*)—were most often written in a cursive script called hieratic, which was written with ink on papyrus. The form of the cursive signs is based on the hieroglyphs but is more abstract and can be formed more quickly.

have emerged in response to economic needs, people in Egypt soon grasped its utility for commemorative and religious purposes.

Ancient Egyptians used two forms of writing. Elaborate *hieroglyphs* (from the Greek "sacred carving") served in formal temple, royal, or divine contexts. More common, however, was *hieratic* writing, a cursive script written with ink on papyrus or pottery. (*Demotic* writing, from the Greek *demotika*, meaning "popular" or "in common use," developed much later and became the vital transitional key on the Rosetta Stone that ultimately allowed the nineteenth-century decipherment of hieroglyphs.) Used for record keeping, hieratic writing also found uses in letters and works of literature—including narrative fiction, manuals of instruction and philosophy, cult and religious hymns, love poems, medical and mathematical texts, collections of rituals, and mortuary books.

Literacy spread first among upper-class families. Most students started training when they were young. After mastering the copying of standard texts in hieratic cursive or hieroglyphs, students moved on to literary works. The upper classes prized literacy as proof of high intellectual achievement. When elites died, they had their student textbooks placed alongside their corpses as evidence of their talents. The literati produced texts mainly in temples, where these works were also preserved. Writing in hieroglyphs and the composition of texts in hieratic, and later demotic, script continued without break in ancient Egypt for almost 3,000 years.

THE PROSPERITY AND DEMISE OF OLD KINGDOM EGYPT

Cultural achievements, agrarian surpluses, and urbanization ultimately led to higher standards of living and rising populations. Under pharaonic rule, Egypt enjoyed spectacular prosperity. Its population swelled from 350,000 in 4000 BCE to 1 million in 2500 BCE and nearly 5 million by 1500 BCE. However, expansion and decentralization eventually exposed the weaknesses of the Old and Middle Kingdom dynasties.

The state's success depended on administering resources skillfully, especially agricultural production and labor. Everyone, from the most powerful elite to the workers in the field, was part of the system. In principle, no one possessed private property; in practice, Egyptians treated land and tools as their own—but submitted to the intrusions of the state. The state's control over taxation, prices, and the distribution of goods required a large bureaucracy that maintained records, taxed the population, appeased the gods, organized a strong military, and aided local officials in regulating the Nile's floodwaters.

Royal power, along with the Old Kingdom, collapsed in the three years following the death of Pepy II in 2184 BCE. Local magnates assumed hereditary control of the government in the provinces and treated lands previously controlled by the royal family as their personal property. An extended drought strained Egypt's extensive irrigation system, which could no longer water the lands that fed the region's million inhabitants. In this so-called First Inter-mediate Period (2181–2055 BCE), local leaders plunged into bloody regional struggles to keep the irrigation works functioning for their own communities until the century-long drought ended. Although the Old Kingdom declined, it established institutions and beliefs that endured and were revived several cen-turies later.

The Indus River Valley: A Parallel Culture

Cities emerged in the Indus River valley in South Asia in the mid-third millen-nium BCE. The urban culture of the Indus area is called "Harappan" after the urban site of Harappa that arose on the banks of the Ravi River, a tributary of the Indus. Developments in the Indus basin reflected local tradition combined with strong influences from Iranian plateau peoples, as well as indirect influ-ences from distant Mesopotamian cities. Villages appeared around 5000 BCE on the Iranian plateau along the Baluchistan Mountain foothills, to the west of the Indus. By the early third millennium BCE, frontier villages had spread eastward to the fertile banks of the Indus River and its tributaries. (See Map 2.5.) The river-basin settlements soon yielded agrarian surpluses that supported greater wealth, more trade with neighbors, and public works. Urbanites of the Indus region and the Harappan peoples began to fortify their cities and to undertake public works similar in scale to those in Mesopotamia, but strikingly different in function.

The Indus Valley ecology boasted many advantages—especially compared to the area near the Ganges River, the other great waterway of the South Asian landmass. The melting snows in the Himalayas watered the semitropical Indus Valley, ensuring flourishing vegetation, plus the region did not suffer the yearly monsoon downpours that flooded the Ganges plain. The expansion of agricul-ture in the Indus basin, as in Mesopotamia, Egypt, and China, depended on the Indus River's annual floods to replenish the soil and avert droughts. From June to September, the river inundated the plain. New evidence has suggested that the monsoons also brought seasonal flows of water into long-dried-up riverbeds (especially the so-called paleochannel of the Ghaggar-Hakra, a river that had dried up almost three thousand years before Harappan society began to thrive). This evidence poses a unique question about river-fueled society in the third millennium BCE: How did the Harappan settlements clustered along this paleo-channel to the east of the Indus River harness a seasonal flow of water into an otherwise-dried-up riverbed, as compared with a year-round river?

Whether along the year-round-flowing Indus or the seasonal flows of water in the Ghaggar-Hakra paleochannel, farmers planted wheat and barley, harvest-ing the crops the next spring. Harappan villagers also improved their tools of

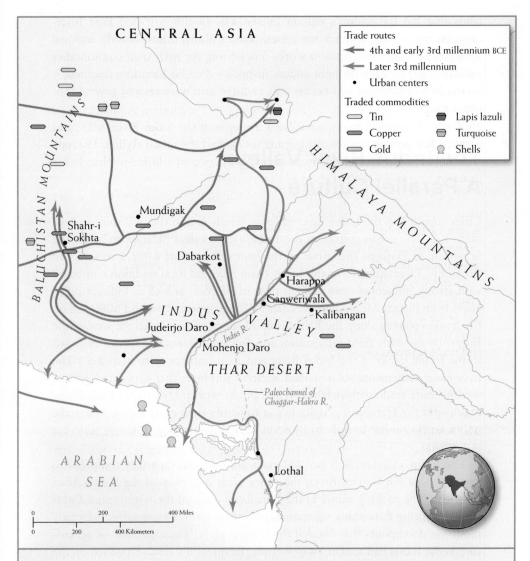

Map 2.5 The Indus River Valley in the Third Millennium BCE

Historians know less about the urban society of the Indus Valley in the third millennium BCE than they do about its contemporaries in Mesopotamia and Egypt, in part because of the absence of a written record. Recent scholarship has suggested the importance of a second seasonal flow (as opposed to a year-round river) in the channel of the long-dried-up Ghaggar-Hakra to the east of the Indus.

- Where were cities concentrated in the Indus Valley? Why do you think the cities were located where they were?
- How do the trade routes of the fourth and early third millennium BCE differ from those of the later third millennium BCE? What might account for those differences?
- What commodities appear on this map? What is their relationship to urban centers and trade routes?

cultivation. Researchers have found evidence of furrows, probably made by plowing, that date to around 2600 BCE. These developments suggest that, as in Mesopotamia and Egypt, farmers were cultivating harvests that yielded a surplus that allowed many inhabitants to specialize in other activities. In time, rural wealth produced urban splendor. More abundant harvests, now stored in large granaries, brought migrants into the area and supported expanding populations. By 2500 BCE cities began to replace villages throughout the Indus River valley, and within a few generations towering granaries marked the urban skyline. Harappa and Mohenjo Daro, the two largest cities, each covered a little less than half a square mile and may have housed 35,000 residents.

Harappan cities sprawled across a vast floodplain covering 500,000 square miles—two or three times the size of the Mesopotamian cultural zone. At the height of their development, the Harappan peoples reached the edge of the Indus ecological system and encountered the cultures of northern Afghanistan, the inhabitants of the desert frontier, the nomadic hunters and gatherers to the east, and the traders to the west. Scholars know less about Harappan society than about Mesopotamia or ancient Egypt, since many of the remains of Harappan culture lie buried under deep silt deposits accumulated over thousands of years of heavy flooding. But what they do know about Harappan urban culture and trade routes is impressive.

HARAPPAN CITY LIFE AND WRITING

The well-planned layout of Harappan cities and towns included a fortified citadel housing public facilities alongside a large residential area. The main street running through the city had covered drainage on both sides, with house gates and doors opening onto back alleys. Citadels were likely centers of political and ritual activities. At the center of the citadel of Mohenjo Daro was the famous great bath. The location, size, and quality of the bath's steps, mortar and bitumen sealing, and drainage channel all suggest that the structure was used for public bathing rituals.

The Harappans used brick extensively—in upper-class houses, city walls, and underground water drainage systems. Workers used large ovens to manufacture the durable construction materials, which the Harappans laid so skillfully that basic structures remain intact to this day. A well-built house of a wealthier family had private bathrooms, showers, and toilets that drained into municipal sewers, also made of bricks. Houses in small towns and villages were made of less durable and less costly sun-baked bricks.

In terms of writing, the peoples of the Indus Valley developed a logographic system of writing made up of about 400 signs (far too many for an alphabetic system, which tends to have closer to thirty symbols). Without a bilingual or trilingual text, like the Behistun inscription for Sumerian cuneiform or the Rosetta Stone for Egyptian hieroglyphs, Indus Valley script has been impossible to decipher. Computer analysis, however, is helping researchers identify some

Mohenjo Daro Mohenjo Daro, the "mound of dead," is a large urban site of the Harappan culture. The view of the city demonstrates a neat layout of houses and civic facilities such as sewer draining.

features of the script and the pre-Indo-European language it might record. Even so, some scholars suggest that the signs might not represent spoken language, but rather might be a non-linguistic symbol system. Although a ten-glyph-long public inscription has been found at the Harappan site of the ancient city of Dholavira, nearly all of what remains of the Indus Valley script is to be found on a thousand or more stamp seals and small plaques excavated from the region. These seals and plaques may represent the names and titles of individuals rather than complete sentences. As of yet, there is no evidence that the Harappans produced historical records such as the King Lists of Mesopotamia and Egypt, thus making it impossible to chart a history of the rise and fall of dynasties and kingdoms. Hence, our knowledge of Harappa comes exclusively from archaeological reconstructions, reminding us that "history" is not what happened but only *what we know about what happened*.

TRADE

The Harappans engaged in trade along the Indus River, through the mountain passes to the Iranian plateau, and along the coast of the Arabian Sea as far as the Persian Gulf and Mesopotamia. They traded copper, flint, shells, and ivory, as well as pottery, flint blades, and jewelry created by their craftworkers, in exchange for gold, silver, gemstones, and textiles. Trade was facilitated by standardized sets of weights and measures. Carnelian, a precious red stone, was a local resource, but lapis lazuli had to come from what is now northern Afghanistan. Some of the Harappan trading towns nestled in remote but strategically important places. Consider Lothal, a well-fortified port at the head of the Gulf of Khambhat (Cambay). Although distant from the center of Harappan society, it provided vital access to the sea and to valuable raw materials. Its many workshops processed precious stones, both local and foreign. Because the demand for gemstones and metals was high on the Iranian plateau and in Mesopotamia, control of their extraction and trade was essential to maintaining the Harappans' economic power. So the Harappans built fortifications and settlements near sources of carnelian and copper mines.

Through a complex and vibrant trading system, the Harappans maintained access to mineral and agrarian resources. To facilitate trade, rulers relied not just on Harappan script but also on a system of weights and measures that they devised and standardized. Archaeologists have found Harappan seals, used to stamp commodities with the names of their owners or the nature of the goods, at sites as far away as the Persian Gulf, Mesopotamia, and the Iranian plateau.

The general uniformity in Harappan sites suggests a centralized and structured state. Unlike the Mesopotamians and the Egyptians, however, the Harappans apparently built neither palaces nor grand royal tombs. What the Indus River people show us is how much the urbanized parts of the world were diverging from one another, even as they borrowed from and imitated their neighbors.

The Yellow and Yangzi River Basins: East Asia

Like the Mesopotamians, Egyptians, and Harappans, East Asian peoples clustered in river basins. Their settlements along the Yellow River in the north and the Yangzi River to the south became the foundation of the future Chinese state. By 5000 BCE, both millet in the north and rice in the south were under widespread cultivation.

Yet in the following three millennia (when Mesopotamia, Egypt, and the Indus Valley were creating complex, city-based cultures), the Chinese moved slowly toward urbanization. (See Map 2.6.) Like the other regions' waterways, the Yellow and Yangzi Rivers had annual floods and extensive floodplains suitable for producing high agricultural yields and supporting dense populations. In China, however, the evolution of hydraulic works, big cities, priestly and bureaucratic classes, and a new writing system took longer. A lack of easily domesticated animals and plants contributed to the different developmental path in China, as did geographic barriers. The Himalaya Mountains and the Taklamakan and Gobi Deserts prevented large-scale migrations between East Asia and central Asia and hindered the diffusion of cultural breakthroughs occurring elsewhere in Afro-Eurasia.

FROM YANGSHAO TO LONGSHAN CULTURE

China's classical histories have claimed that China's cultural traditions originated in the Central Plains of the Yellow River basin and spread outward to less developed regions inside and even beyond mainland China. These histories place the beginnings of Chinese culture at the Xia dynasty, dating from 2200 BCE. Archaeological studies of river-basin environments in East Asia tell a different story, however. Whether or not the Xia existed as a historical dynasty, archaeological evidence suggests our study of the Yellow River basin and Yangzi delta should begin earlier—in the two millennia from 4000 to 2000 BCE.

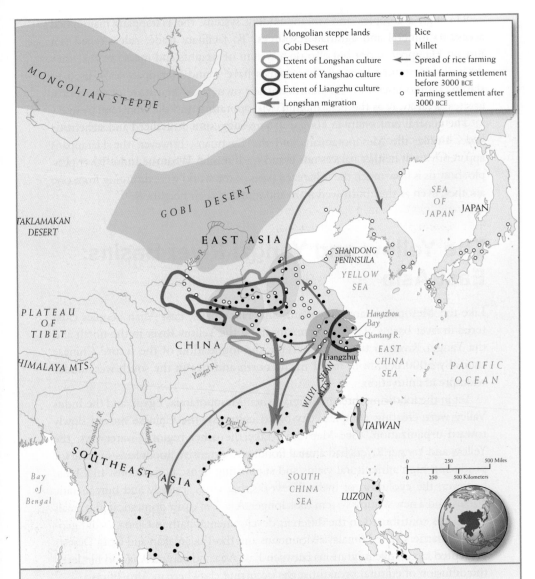

Legend:
- Mongolian steppe lands
- Gobi Desert
- Extent of Longshan culture
- Extent of Yangshao culture
- Extent of Liangzhu culture
- Longshan migration
- Rice
- Millet
- Spread of rice farming
- Initial farming settlement before 3000 BCE
- Farming settlement after 3000 BCE

Map 2.6 River-Basin Peoples in East Asia, 5000–2000 BCE

Complex agricultural societies emerged in East Asia during the third millennium BCE.

- Locate the three distinct cultures on the map. Where is each located, and what major crop was grown in each?
- What topographical features may have shaped the extent and spread of the various cultures represented on the map?
- Locate the dots for farming before 3000 BCE and those for farming after 3000 BCE. What hypotheses might you offer based on the location of farming before and after 3000 BCE?

China in 4000 BCE was very different geographically and culturally from what it is today. A warmer and moister climate divided its vast landmass into distinctive regions. Only after a long cycle of cooler and drier weather did these bodies of water dry up and the landmass become a single geographical unit. Recent archaeological research records that at least eight distinct regional cultures appeared between 4000 and 2000 BCE, and only as these communities interacted did their institutions and ways of life come together to create a unified Chinese culture.

Yet China was a land apart in the Afro-Eurasian landmass, isolated by the mountains of the Tibetan plateau in the west, the deserts of Inner Mongolia in the north, the tropical rain forests in the south, and the ocean in the east. China had only two difficult natural routes to the rest of Asia and Europe. One route led into central Asia by the narrow Gansu Corridor, running between the Qilian Mountains on the northern edge of the Tibetan plateau and the Gobi Desert. The other ran along a narrow band of the steppe north of the Yellow River and around the Gobi Desert, eventually ending up in the Mongolian steppe, the Altai Mountains, and the Kazakh steppe. Though trade with and migration into China were more limited than that which fused together Egypt, Mesopotamia, and the Indus Valley, nomadic cultures and technologies nevertheless filtered from the steppes to settled communities on the rivers.

The major divide in China was between the northern Yellow and more centrally located Yangzi river basins. Not only did inhabitants of these two regions rely on different crops—millet in the north and rice in the south—but they built their houses differently, buried their dead in different ways, and produced distinctive pottery styles. The best known of the early cultures developed along the Yellow River and in the Central Plains area and is known as the Yangshao culture.

Yangshao villages typically covered 10 to 14 acres and were composed of houses erected around a central square. Villagers had to move frequently because they practiced slash-and-burn agriculture. Once residents had exhausted the soil, they picked up their belongings, moved to new lands, and constructed new villages. Their lives were hard. Excavated cemeteries reveal that nearly 20 percent of the burials were of children fifteen years and younger; only a little more than half of those buried lived past the age of forty.

Around 3000 BCE, the Yangshao culture gave way to the Longshan culture, which had an even larger

Yangshao Bowl with Dancing Figures, c. 5000–1700 BCE The Yangshao, also referred to as the "painted pottery" culture, produced gray or red pottery painted with black geometric designs and occasionally with pictures of fish or human faces and figures. Because the potter's wheel was unknown at the time, the vessels were probably fashioned with strips of clay.

geographical scope and would provide some of the cultural foundations for the first strong states that emerged in the Central Plains. Longshan flourished from 3000 BCE to 2000 BCE and had its center in Shandong Province. Although the Longshan way of life first took form in coastal and southern China, outside the Central Plains, it moved quickly into this hub of economic and political activity. Proof of its widespread cultural influence can be seen from the appearance of a unique style of black pottery, stretching all the way from Manchuria in the north through the Central Plains to the coast and beyond to the island of Taiwan.

The Longshan people likely migrated in waves from the peripheries of East Asia to the eastern China seashore. Their achievements, compared to those of the Yangshao, suggest marked development between 5000 and 2000 BCE. Several independent regional cultures in northern and southern China began to produce similar pottery and tools and to plant the same crops, probably reflecting contact. They did not yet produce city-states, but agriculture and small settlements flourished in the increasingly populated Yellow River valley.

Some of the hallmarks of early urban life are evident in the archaeological remains. Longshan communities built defensive walls for protection and dug wells to supply water. They buried their dead in cemeteries outside their villages. Of several thousand graves uncovered in southern Shanxi Province, the largest ones contain ritual pottery vessels, wooden musical instruments, copper bells, and painted murals. Shamans performed rituals using jade axes. Jade quarrying, in particular, indicated technical sophistication, as skilled craftworkers incised jade tablets with powerful expressions of ritual and military authority. The threat of organized violence among Longshan villages was real. Discoveries at one Longshan site revealed a household whose members were scalped. At this same site, attackers filled the water wells with five layers of human skeletons, some decapitated. Clearly, the villages' defensive walls were essential.

Longshan Beaker, c. 2500 BCE
Longshan has been called the "black pottery" culture, and its exquisite black pottery was not painted but rather decorated with rings, either raised or grooved. Longshan culture was more developed than the Yangshao culture, and its distinctive pottery was likely formed on a potter's wheel.

As communities became more centralized, contact between regions increased. Links between northern and southern China arose when Longshan peoples began to migrate along the East Asian coast to Taiwan and the Pearl River delta in the far south. Similarities in artifacts found along the coast and at Longshan sites in northern China, such as the form and decoration of pottery and jade items, also point to a shared sphere of culture and trade.

Archaeologists also have found evidence of short-lived political organizations. Although they were nothing like the dynastic systems in Egypt, Mesopotamia, and the Indus Valley, they were wealthy—if localized—polities. They constituted what scholars call the era of Ten Thousand States. One of them, the Liangzhu, has drawn particular interest for its remarkable jade objects and its sophisticated farming techniques. The Liangzhu grew rice and fruits and domesticated water buffalo, pigs, dogs, and sheep. Archaeologists have discovered the remains of net sinkers, wooden floats, and wooden paddles, which demonstrate a familiarity with watercraft and fishing. Artisans produced a black pottery from soft paste thrown on a wheel, and like the Longshan, they created ritual objects from several varieties of jade. Animal masks and bird designs adorned many pieces, revealing a shared cosmology that informed the rituals of the Liangzhu elite.

In the late third millennium BCE, a long drought hit China (as it did Egypt, Mesopotamia, and India). Although the climate change limited progress and forced migrations to more dependable habitats, the Chinese recovered early in the second millennium BCE. Now they created elaborate agrarian systems along the Yellow and Yangzi Rivers that were similar to earlier irrigation systems along the Euphrates, Indus, and Nile. Extensive trading networks and a stratified social hierarchy emerged; like the other river-basin complexes of Asia and North Africa, China became a centralized polity. Here, too, a powerful monarchy eventually united the independent communities. But what developed in China was a social and political system that emphasized an idealized past and a tradition represented by sage-kings, which later ages emulated. In this and other ways, China diverged from the rest of Afro-Eurasia.

Life Outside the River Basins

In 3500 BCE, the vast majority of humans lived outside the complex cities that emerged in parts of Afro-Eurasia. At the other end of the spectrum, many peoples continued to live as hunters and gatherers, or in small agricultural villages, or as pastoralists tending flocks. In between were worlds such as those in the Aegean, Anatolia, Europe, and parts of China, where towns emerged and agriculture advanced, but not with the leaps and bounds of the great river-basin societies.

Some cultures outside the river basins—in the Aegean, Anatolia, and Europe—had a distinctive warrior-based ethos, such that the top tiers of the social ladder held chiefs and military men instead of priests and scribes. In Europe and Anatolia especially, weaponry rather than writing, forts rather than palaces, and conquest rather than commerce dominated everyday life. Settlements in the Americas and sub-Saharan Africa were smaller and remained based on agriculture. Here, too, the inhabitants moved beyond stone implements and hunting and gathering, but they remained more egalitarian than river-basin peoples.

AEGEAN WORLDS

Contact with Egypt and Mesopotamia affected the worlds of the Aegean Sea (the part of the Mediterranean Sea between the Greek Peloponnese and Anatolia), but it did not transform them. Geography stood in the way of significant urban development on the mountainous islands of the Aegean, on the Anatolian plateau, and in Europe. Even though people from Anatolia, Greece, and the Levant had populated the Aegean islands in the sixth millennium BCE, their small villages, of 100 inhabitants or fewer, endured for 2,000 years before becoming more complex. On mainland Greece and on the Cycladic islands in the Aegean, fortified settlements housed local rulers who controlled a small area of agriculturally productive countryside.

Metallurgy developed both on the island of Crete and in the Cyclades. There is evidence of more formal administration and organizations in some communities by 2500 BCE, but the norm was scattered settlements separated by natural obstacles. One exciting recent find has been reported by scholars excavating a ritual center at Dhaskalio, a small islet off the coast of the Aegean island of Keros that was likely attached by land to Keros in the early Bronze Age. At this site, excavations have revealed mid-third-millennium BCE workshops for working imported metals like copper, as well as elaborate monumental engineering projects, including staircases and drainage tunnels, constructed with imported stone.

By the early third millennium BCE, the seafaring peoples of Crete had made occasional contact with Egypt and the coastal towns of the Levant, encountering new ideas, technologies, and materials as foreigners arrived on its shores. People coming by ship from the coasts of Anatolia and the Levant, as well as from Egypt, traded stone vessels and other luxury objects for the island's abundant copper. Graves of Aegean elites, such as those at Knossos on Crete, with their gold jewelry and other exotic objects, show that the elites did not reject the niceties of cultured life, but they knew that their power rested as much on their rugged landscape's resources as on self-defense and trade with others.

ANATOLIA

The highland plateau of Anatolia (in the region of modern-day Turkey) shows clear evidence of regional cultures focused on the control of trade routes and mining outposts. True cities did not develop here until the third millennium BCE, and even then they were not the sprawling population centers typical of the Mesopotamian plain. Instead, small communities emerged around fortified citadels housing local rulers who competed with one another. Two impressively fortified centers were Horoz Tepe and Alaça Hüyük, which have yielded more than a dozen graves—apparently royal—full of gold jewelry, ceremonial standards, and elaborate weapons. Similarly, the settlement at Troy—which would be the site of the Trojan War of the late second millennium BCE—was characterized by monumental stone gateways, stone-paved ramps, and high-status graves filled with gold and silver objects, vessels, jewelry, and other artifacts. Parallel grave finds on Crete, the Greek mainland, and as far away as Ur indicate that Troy participated in the trading system linking the Aegean and Southwest Asian worlds. At the same time, Troy faced predatory neighbors and pirates who attacked from the sea—an observation that explains its impressive fortifications.

EUROPE: THE WESTERN FRONTIER

At the western reaches of the Eurasian landmass was a region featuring cooler climates with smaller population densities. Its peoples—forerunners of present-day Europeans—began to make objects out of metal, formed permanent settlements, and started to create complex societies. Here, hierarchies began to undermine egalitarian ways. Yet, as in the Aegean worlds, population density and social complexity had limits.

More than in the Mediterranean or Anatolia, warfare dominated social development in Europe. Two contributing factors were the persistent fragmentation of the region's peoples and the type of agrarian development they pursued. (See Map 2.7.) The introduction of the plow and the clearing of woodlands expanded agriculture. Flint mining at an industrial level slashed the cost and increased the availability of raw materials needed to make tools for clearing forested lands and

Stonehenge This spectacular site, located in the Salisbury Plain in Wiltshire in southwestern England, is one of several such megalithic structures found in the region. Constructed by many generations of builders, the arrangement of the large stone uprights enabled people to determine precise times in the year through the position of the sun. Events such as the spring and autumn equinoxes were connected with agricultural and religious activities.

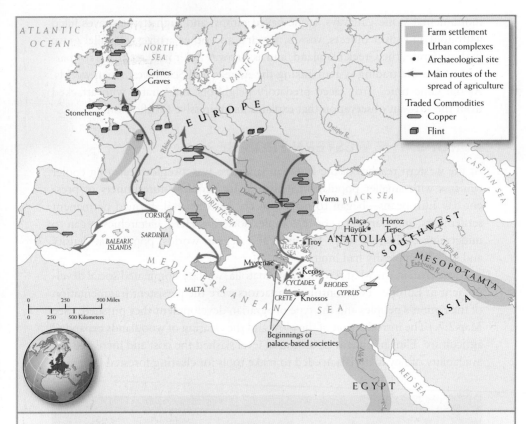

Map 2.7 Settlements outside the River Basins: The Eastern Mediterranean and Europe, 5000–2000 BCE

....

Urban societies in Southwest Asia, like those in Mesopotamia and the Nile Valley, had profound influences on societies in Anatolia, the Aegean, and western Europe.

- Trace the main routes for the spread of agriculture. Based on those routes, how did agriculture spread in this period?
- Locate the icons for copper and flint. Based on your reading of the chapter, how might these commodities have shaped the culture in the regions in which they were located?

tilling them into arable fields. Compared to the river-basin societies, Europe was a wild frontier where violent conflicts over resources were common.

By 3500 BCE, the more developed agrarian peoples had combined into large communities, constructing impressive monuments that remain visible today. In western Europe, large ceremonial centers shared the same model: enormous shaped stones, some weighing several tons each, set in common patterns—in alleyways, troughs, or circles—known as *megalithic* ("great stone") constructions. These daunting projects required cooperative planning and work. In the

British Isles, where such developments occurred later, the famous megalithic complexes at Avebury and Stonehenge probably reached their highest stages of development just before 2000 BCE.

By 2000 BCE, the whole of the northern European plain had come to share a common material culture based on agriculture, the herding of cattle for meat and milk, the use of the plough, and the use of wheeled vehicles and metal tools and weapons, mainly of copper. Increasing communication, exchange, and mobility among the European communities led to increasing wealth but also sparked organized warfare over frontier lands and valuable resources. In an ironic twist, the integration of local communities led to greater friction and produced regional social stratification. The violent men who now protected their communities received ceremonial burials complete with their own drinking cups and weapons. Archaeologists have found these warrior burials in a swath of European lands extending from present-day France and Switzerland to present-day central Russia. Because the agricultural communities now were producing surpluses that they could store, residents had to defend their land and resources from encroaching neighbors.

An aggressive culture was taking shape based on violent confrontations between adult males organized in "tribal" groups. War cultures arose in all western European societies. Armed groups carried bell-shaped drinking cups across Europe, using them to swig beer and mead distilled from grains, honey, herbs, and nuts.

Warfare had the effect of accentuating the borrowing among the region's competing peoples. The violent struggles and emerging kinship groups fueled a massive demand for weapons, alcohol, and horses. Warrior elites borrowed from Anatolia the technique of combining copper with tin to produce harder-edged weapons made of the alloy bronze. Soon smiths were producing them in bulk— as evidenced by hoards of copper and bronze tools and weapons from the period found in central Europe. Traders used the rivers of central and northern Europe to exchange their prized metal products, creating one of the first commercial networks that covered the landmass.

THE AMERICAS

In the Americas, techniques of food production and storage, transportation, and communication restricted the surpluses for feeding those who did not work the land. Thus, these communities did not grow in size and complexity. For example, in the Chicama Valley of Peru, which opens onto the Pacific Ocean, people still nestled in small coastal villages to fish, gather shellfish, hunt, and grow beans, chili peppers, and cotton (to make twined textiles, which they dyed with wild indigo). By around 3500 BCE, these fishermen abandoned their cane and adobe homes for sturdier houses, half underground, on streets lined with cobblestones.

Hundreds, if not thousands, of such villages dotted the seashores and riverbanks of the Americas. Some made the technological breakthroughs required to produce pottery; others devised irrigation systems and water sluices in areas where floods occurred. Some even began to send their fish catches inland in return for agricultural produce. Ceremonial structures highlighted communal devotion and homage to deities, as well as rituals to celebrate birth, death, and the memory of ancestors.

In the Americas, the largest population center was in the valley of Tehuacán (near modern-day Mexico City). Here the domestication of corn created a food source that enabled people to migrate from caves to a cluster of pit-house villages that supported a growing population. By 3500 BCE, the valley held nothing resembling a large city. People lived in clusters of interdependent villages, especially on the lakeshores: here was a case of high population density, but not urbanization.

SUB-SAHARAN AFRICA

The same pattern occurred in sub-Saharan Africa, where the population grew but did not concentrate in urban communities. About 12,000 years ago, when rainfall and temperatures increased, small encampments of hunting, gathering, and fishing communities congregated around the large lakes and rivers flowing through the region that would later become the Sahara Desert. Large game animals roamed, posing a threat but also providing a source of food. Over the millennia, in the wetter and more temperate locations of this vast region—particularly the upland mountains and their foothills—permanent villages emerged.

As the Sahara region became drier, people moved to the desert's edges, to areas along the Niger River and the Sudan. Here they grew yams, oil palms, and plantains. In the savanna lands that stretched all the way from the Atlantic Ocean in West Africa to the Nile River basin in present-day Sudan, settlers grew grains such as millet and sorghum, which spread from their places of origin to areas along the lands surrounding the Niger River basin. Residents constructed stone dwellings and dug underground wells and food storage areas. As an increasing population strained resources, groups migrated south toward the Congo River and east toward Lake Nyanza, where they established new farms and villages. Although population centers were often hundreds or thousands of miles apart and were smaller than the urban centers in Egypt and Mesopotamia, the widespread use of the same pottery style, with rounded bottoms and wavy decoration, suggests that they maintained trading and cultural contacts. In these respects, sub-Saharan Africa matched the ways of life in Europe and the Americas.

Conclusion

Over the fourth and third millennia BCE, the world's social landscape changed in significant ways. In a few key locations, where giant rivers irrigated fertile lands, complex human cultures began to emerge. These areas experienced all the advantages and difficulties of expanding populations: occupational specialization; social hierarchy; rising standards of living; sophisticated systems of art and science; and centralized production and distribution of food, clothing, and other goods. Ceremonial sites and trading crossroads became cities that developed centralized religious and political systems. As scribes, priests, and rulers labored to keep complex societies together, social distinctions within the city (including the roles of men and women) and the differences between country folk and city dwellers sharpened.

Although river-basin cultures shared basic features, each one's evolution followed a distinctive path. Where there was a single river—the Nile or the Indus—the agrarian hinterlands that fed cities lay along the banks of the waterway. In these areas cities were small; thus, the Egyptian and Harappan worlds enjoyed more political stability and less rivalry. In contrast, cities in the immense floodplain of the Tigris and Euphrates needed large hinterlands to sustain their populations. Because of their growing power and need for resources, Mesopotamian cities vied for preeminence, and their competition often became violent.

In most areas of the world, however, people still lived in simple, egalitarian societies based on hunting, gathering, and basic agriculture—as in the Americas and sub-Saharan Africa. In Anatolia, Europe, and parts of China, regional cultures emerged as agriculture advanced and populations grew—but not with the leaps and bounds and fast-paced momentum of the river-basin cultures. Some of them, as in the Aegean and Europe, forged warrior societies. Beyond these frontiers, farmers and nomads survived as they had for many centuries. Thriving trading networks connected many, but not all, of these regions to one another.

Changes in climate affected everyone and could slow or even reverse development. How—and whether—cultures adapted depended on local circumstances. As the next chapter will show, the human agents of change often came from the fringes of larger settlements and urban areas.

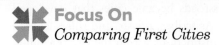

Focus On
Comparing First Cities

Mesopotamia

- Peoples living along the Tigris River and Euphrates River control floodwaters and refine irrigation techniques.

- Mesopotamians establish the world's first large cities, featuring powerful rulers, social hierarchies, and temples (ziggurats) for worship of their gods.

- Mesopotamia is the birthplace of writing.

Egypt

- Peoples of Egypt use Nile River waters to irrigate their lands and create a bountiful agriculture.

- Egyptian kings unify their territory, establish a powerful state, and develop a vibrant economy.

- Egyptians build magnificent burial chambers (pyramids), develop hieroglyphic writing, and worship a pantheon of gods.

Indus Valley

- South Asian peoples harness the Indus River and create cities (like Harappa and Mohenjo Daro), as well as a form of writing called Indus Valley script.

- Harappan cities include residential housing and public structures (like baths) with excellent drainage.

- Indus Valley peoples export copper, shells, and carnelian (as well as lapis lazuli and turquoise, from nearby sources) to peoples of Mesopotamia and Egypt.

East Asia

- Peoples dwelling in the basins of the Yellow River and the Yangzi River control the waters' flow and expand agriculture.

- These people develop elaborate cultures, which scholars later label Yangshao and Longshan.

- While agriculture in East Asia does not produce city-states in this period, Longshan peoples leave behind distinctive pottery and jade artifacts, suggesting evidence of regional trade.

CHRONOLOGY

	4000 BCE	3000 BCE
Southwest Asia and Egypt	Earliest Sumerian cities appear in Mesopotamia 3500 BCE First Dynasty emerges in Egypt 3100 BCE	
South Asia		
East Asia	Yangshao culture thrives along Yellow River 4000–3000 BCE	
Europe and the Mediterranean		
The Americas	Chicama Valley culture thrives on Pacific coast of South America 3500 BCE Tehuacán Valley in Mexico thrives 3500 BCE Dense village life along many lakes and rivers 3500 BCE	
Inner and Central Asia	Spread of nomadic pastoralism begins 3500 BCE	

THINKING ABOUT GLOBAL CONNECTIONS

- **Thinking about River-Basin Societies and the Environment** Human interaction with the environment—including climate, geography, the characteristics of the rivers, and the continued cultivation of crops and herds—played a significant role in shaping each early river-basin community. Describe ways that these environmental factors influenced the unique characteristics of each river-basin society.

- **Thinking about Exchange Networks among Early River-Basin Societies** Carnelian from the Indus region buried in elite tombs of Egypt; lapis lazuli from the region of modern-day Afghanistan on necklaces adorning Harappan necks; shell from the Indus floodplain inlaid on Mesopotamian grave goods—these examples provide evidence of how trade

in raw materials bound river-basin societies together in the third millennium BCE. What routes might such goods have traveled? What does this exchange of commodities suggest about other types of exchange that may have been taking place between these river-basin societies?

- **Thinking about Changing Power Relationships in River-Basin Societies** From 3500 to 2000 BCE, as societies developed in the river basins of Mesopotamia, Egypt, South Asia, and East Asia, more intensive cultivation brought agricultural surpluses that ushered in a wide range of impacts. Explain, with examples from each of the river-basin societies, how food surpluses led to job specialization, wealth accumulation, and the resulting social hierarchies.

Key Terms

bronze p. 49	city-state p. 55	scribes p. 59	urban-rural divide p. 49
city p. 55	river basin p. 48	social hierarchies p. 56	

 Go to INQUIZITIVE to see what you've learned—and learn what you've missed—with personalized feedback along the way.

2000 BCE	**1000** BCE

Old Kingdom Egypt 2686–2181 BCE

Sargon's Akkadian territorial state in Mesopotamia 2334–2200 BCE

Cities appear in Indus Valley 2500 BCE

Longshan culture flourishes in Yellow River valley 3000–2000 BCE

Fortified villages in the Aegean 2500 BCE

Stonehenge constructed 2000 BCE

3

Nomads, Territorial States, and Microsocieties

2000–1200 BCE

Core Objectives

- **EXPLAIN** the relationship between climate change and human settlement patterns in the second millennium BCE.
- **DESCRIBE** the impact of trans-humant herders and pastoral nomads on settled communities.
- **COMPARE** the varied processes by which territorial states formed and interacted with each other across Afro-Eurasia.
- **EXAMINE** the development of microsocieties in the South Pacific and the Aegean, and **EXPLAIN** the role geography played in their development.

Around 2200 BCE, the Old Kingdom of Egypt collapsed. The collapse did not occur because of incompetent rulers, of which there were many, or a decline in the arts and sciences, which is evident in unfinished building projects; the Old Kingdom fell because of radical changes in climate—namely, a powerful warming and drying trend that blanketed Afro-Eurasia between 2200 and 2150 BCE. The Mesopotamians and Harappans were as hard hit as the Egyptians.

In Egypt the environmental disaster yielded a series of low floods of the Nile because the usual monsoon rains did not arrive to feed the river's upper regions. With less water to irrigate crops, farmers could not grow enough food for the river basin's million inhabitants. Documents from this period reveal widespread suffering and despair. Consider the following tomb inscription: "All of Egypt was dying of hunger to such a degree that everyone had come to eating his children." Or another: "The tribes of the desert have become Egyptians everywhere. . . . The plunderer is everywhere, and the servant takes what he finds." Herders and pastoral nomads also felt the pinch. As these outsiders pressed upon permanent settlements in search of food, the governing structures in Egypt—and elsewhere, in Mesopotamia and the Indus Valley—broke down. The pioneering city-states of the third millennium BCE may have created unprecedented differences between elites and commoners, between urbanites and rural folk, but everyone felt the effects of this disaster.

This chapter focuses on two related developments. The first focus is the impact of climate change on the peoples of Afro-Eurasia: famines occurred, followed by political and economic turmoil. The old order gave way as river-basin states in Egypt, Mesopotamia, and the Indus Valley collapsed. Herders and pastoral nomads, driven from grazing areas that were drying up, forced their way into the heartlands of these great states in pursuit of better-watered lands. Once there, they challenged the traditional ruling elites. The nomads also brought with them a new military weapon— the horse-drawn chariot. Nomads and their chariots form the second focus of this chapter, for chariots introduced a type of warfare that would dominate the plains of Afro-Eurasia for a half a millennium. The nomads' advantage proved only temporary, however. Soon the Egyptians, Mesopotamians, Chinese, and many others learned from their chariot-driving conquerors: they assimilated some of their foes into their own societies and drove others away, adopting the invaders' most useful techniques. This chapter also examines worlds apart from the expanding centers of population and politics, where climate change and chariot-driving nomads were shaping world history. The islanders of the Pacific and the Aegean did not interact with one another with such intensity—and therefore their political systems evolved differently. In these locales, microsocieties (small-scale, loosely interconnected communities) were the norm.

Global Storyline

Comparing First States

- Climate change and environmental degradation lead to the collapse of river-basin societies.

- Transhumant migrants (with their animal herds in need of pasturage) and pastoral nomads (with their horse-drawn chariots) interact, in both destructive and constructive ways, with settled agrarian societies.

- A fusion of migratory and settled agricultural peoples produce expanded territorial states—in Egypt, Southwest Asia, the Indus River valley, and Shang China—that supplant earlier river-basin societies.

- Microsocieties emerge in the eastern Mediterranean and South Pacific based on expanding populations and increased trade.

Nomadic Movement, Climate Change, and the Emergence of Territorial States

At the end of the third millennium BCE, a changing climate, drought, and food shortages led to the overthrow of ruling elites throughout central and western Afro-Eurasia. Walled cities could not defend their hinterlands. Trade routes lay open to predators, and pillaging became a lucrative enterprise. Clans of horse-riding **pastoral nomads**—from the relatively sparsely populated and isolated Inner Eurasian steppes—swept across vast distances, eventually threatening settled people in cities. **Transhumant herders**—who lived closer to agricultural settlements and migrated seasonally to pasture their livestock—also advanced on populated areas in search of food and resources. These migrations of pastoral nomads and transhumant herders occurred across Eurasia, in the Arabian Desert and Iranian plateau in the west, and in the Indus River valley and the Yellow River valley in the east. (See Map 3.1.) Many transhumant herders and nomadic pastoralists settled in the agrarian heartlands of Mesopotamia, the Indus River valley, the highlands of Anatolia, Iran, China, and Europe. After the first wave of newcomers, more migrants arrived by foot or in wagons pulled by draft animals. Some sought temporary work; others settled permanently. They brought horses and new technologies that were useful in warfare; religious practices and languages; and new pressures to feed, house, and clothe an ever-growing population. This millennia-long process is sometimes referred to as **Indo-European migrations**.

The term *Indo-European* was created by comparative linguists to trace and explain the similarities within the large language family that includes Sanskrit, Hindi, Persian, Greek, Latin, and what would become German and English. Words and concepts that appear in many languages, such as numbering systems and words like *mother*, *father*, and *god*, suggest these so-called Indo-European languages may have had a common origin. For instance, the number one is *eka* (in Sanskrit), *ek* (in Hindi), *hen* (in Greek), *unus* (in Latin), *un* (in French), and *ein* (in German). The word for mother is *mātṛ* (in Sanskrit), *mātā* (in Hindi), *mêter* (in Greek), *mater* (in Latin), *mère* (in French), and *mutter* (in German). A host of demographic, geographic, and other factors shape the movement and development of languages over time. Nonetheless, migrations of the earliest speakers of the Indo-European language group, who carried not only their language but also their technology and culture, are likely part of the story of the spread of pastoralists from the central Eurasian steppe into Europe, Anatolia, Southwest Asia, and South Asia.

Perhaps the most vital breakthroughs that nomadic pastoralists transmitted to settled societies were the harnessing of horses and the invention of the **chariot**, a horse-drawn vehicle with two spoked and metal-rimmed wheels, used in warfare

War Chariots *Upper right:* A large vase typical of Mycenaean art on the mainland areas of Greece. Note the presence of the horse-drawn chariot. The possession of this more elaborate means of transport and warfare characterized the warrior elites of Mycenaean society and linked them to developments over wide expanses of Afro-Eurasia at the time. *Upper left:* This wooden chest covered with stucco and painted on all sides with images of the Egyptian pharaoh in his war chariot was found in the fabulously wealthy tomb of Tutankhamun in the Valley of the Kings in Egypt. The war chariot was introduced into Egypt by the Hyksos. By the reign of Tutankhamun in the New Kingdom, depictions of the pharaoh single-handedly smiting the enemy from a war chariot drawn by two powerful horses were common. *Bottom left:* Spoke-wheeled chariot, with two horse skeletons. Six chariots were excavated at Yin Xu near Anyang (capital of the Shang dynasty), five of them with a male skeleton behind the carriage. The Shang fought with neighboring pastoral nomads from the central Asian steppes. To do this, they imported horses from central Asia and copied the chariots of nomads they had encountered. This gave Shang warriors devastating range and speed for further conquest.

and later in processions and races. The chariot revolution was made possible, however, only through the interactions of pastoralists and settled communities. On the vast steppe lands north of the Caucasus Mountains, during the late fourth millennium BCE, settled people had domesticated horses in their native habitat. The domestication of horses was a major breakthrough for humans. Horses could forage for themselves, even in snow-covered lands; hence they did not require humans to find food for them. Moreover, they could be ridden up to 30 miles a day. Elsewhere, as on the northern steppes of what is now Russia, horses were a food source. Only during the late third millennium BCE did people harness horses with cheek pieces and mouth bits in order to facilitate the control of horses and their use for transportation. Parts of horse harnesses made from wood, bone, bronze, and iron, found in tombs scattered across the steppe, reveal the evolution of headgear from simple mouth bits to full bridles with headpiece, mouthpiece, and reins.

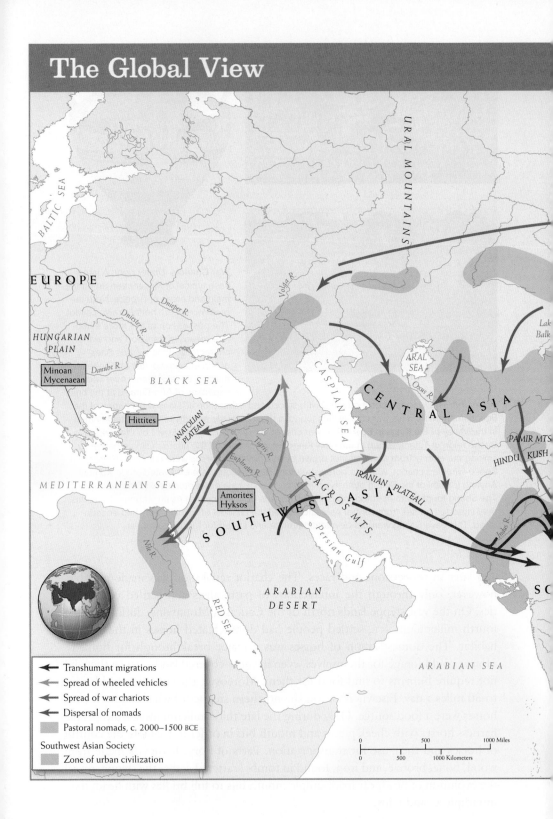

The Global View

Legend:
- Transhumant migrations
- Spread of wheeled vehicles
- Spread of war chariots
- Dispersal of nomads
- Pastoral nomads, c. 2000–1500 BCE

Southwest Asian Society
- Zone of urban civilization

Map labels:

BALTIC SEA

URAL MOUNTAINS

EUROPE

Dnieper R.

Dniester R.

HUNGARIAN PLAIN

Minoan Mycenaean

Danube R.

BLACK SEA

Volga R.

CASPIAN SEA

ARAL SEA

Oxus R.

CENTRAL ASIA

Lake Balk

Hittites

ANATOLIAN PLATEAU

Tigris R.

Euphrates R.

ZAGROS MTS.

IRANIAN PLATEAU

PAMIR MTS.

HINDU KUSH

MEDITERRANEAN SEA

Amorites Hyksos

SOUTHWEST ASIA

Persian Gulf

Indus R.

Nile R.

ARABIAN DESERT

RED SEA

ARABIAN SEA

SO

S

| 0 | 500 | 1000 Miles |
| 0 | 500 | 1000 Kilometers |

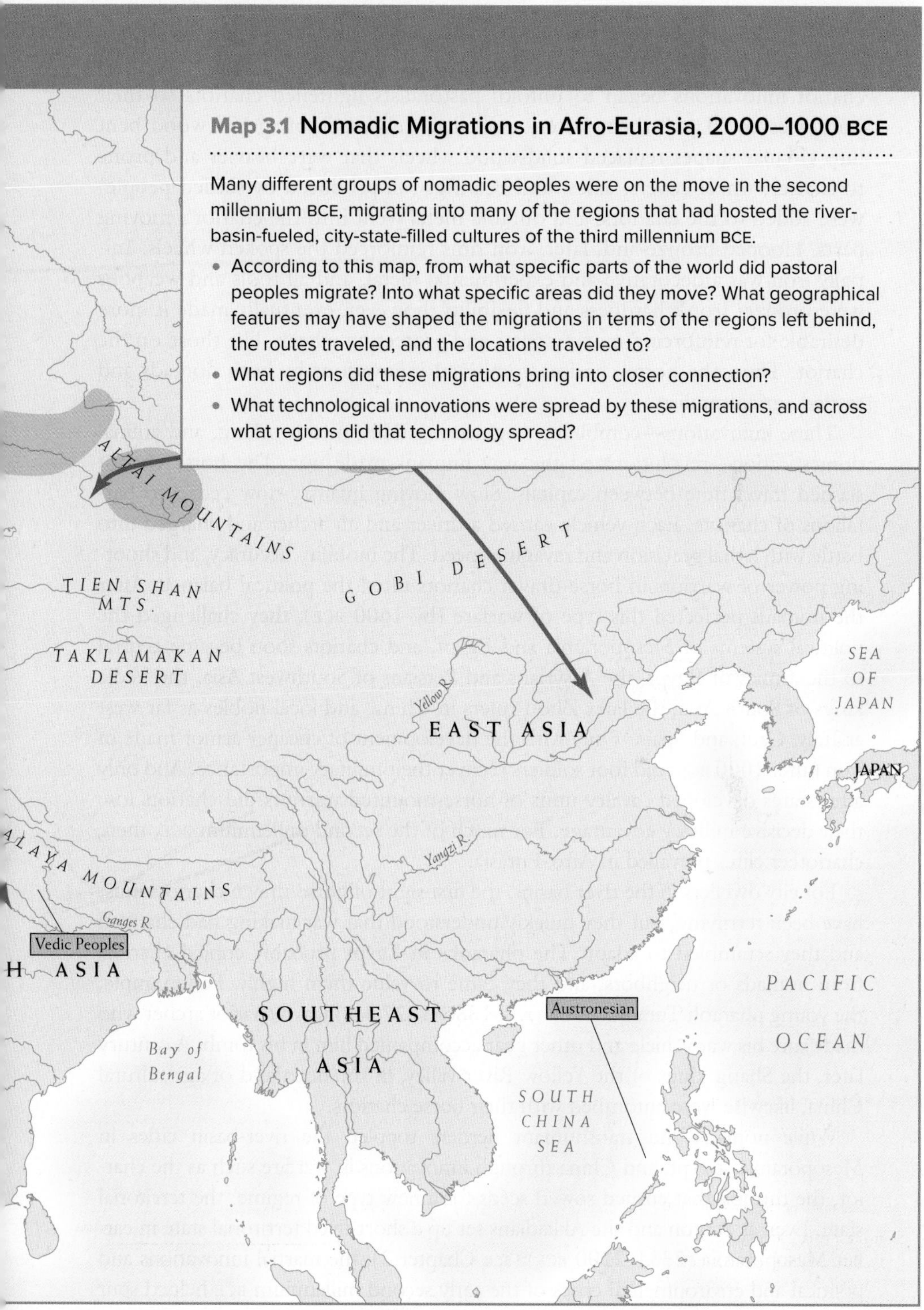

Map 3.1 Nomadic Migrations in Afro-Eurasia, 2000–1000 BCE

Many different groups of nomadic peoples were on the move in the second millennium BCE, migrating into many of the regions that had hosted the river-basin-fueled, city-state-filled cultures of the third millennium BCE.

- According to this map, from what specific parts of the world did pastoral peoples migrate? Into what specific areas did they move? What geographical features may have shaped the migrations in terms of the regions left behind, the routes traveled, and the locations traveled to?
- What regions did these migrations bring into closer connection?
- What technological innovations were spread by these migrations, and across what regions did that technology spread?

ALTAI MOUNTAINS

TIEN SHAN MTS.

GOBI DESERT

TAKLAMAKAN DESERT

Yellow R.

EAST ASIA

SEA OF JAPAN

JAPAN

ALAYA MOUNTAINS

Ganges R.

Vedic Peoples

H ASIA

Yangzi R.

SOUTHEAST ASIA

Bay of Bengal

Austronesian

SOUTH CHINA SEA

PACIFIC OCEAN

Sometime around 2000 BCE, pastoral nomads in the mountains of the Caucasus joined the bit-harnessed horse to the two-wheeled chariot. Various chariot innovations began to unfold: pastoralists lightened chariots so their warhorses could pull them faster; spoked wheels made of special wood bent into circular shapes replaced solid-wood wheels that were heavier and prone to shatter; wheel covers, axles, and bearings (all produced by settled people) were added to the chariots; and durable metal went into the chariot's moving parts. Hooped bronze and, later, iron rims reinforced the spoked wheels. Initially iron was a decorative and experimental metal, and all tools and weapons were bronze. Iron's hardness and flexibility, however, eventually made it more desirable for reinforcing moving parts and protecting wheels, like those on the chariot. Thus, the horse chariots combined innovations by both nomads and settled agriculturalists.

These innovations—combining engineering skills, metalworking, and animal domestication—revolutionized the way humans made war. The horse chariot slashed travel time between capitals. Slow-moving infantry now ceded to battalions of chariots. Each vehicle carried a driver and an archer and charged into battle with lethal precision and ravaging speed. The mobility, accuracy, and shooting power of warriors in horse-drawn chariots tilted the political balance. After the nomads perfected this type of warfare (by 1600 BCE), they challenged the political systems of Mesopotamia and Egypt, and chariots soon became central to the armies of Egypt, the Assyrians and Persians of Southwest Asia, the Vedic kings of South Asia, the later Zhou rulers in China, and local nobles as far west as Italy, Gaul, and Spain. Only with the development of cheaper armor made of iron (after 1000 BCE) did foot soldiers recover their military importance. And only after states developed cavalry units of horse-mounted warriors did chariots lose their decisive military advantage. For much of the second millennium BCE, then, charioteer elites prevailed in Afro-Eurasia.

For city dwellers in the river basins, the first sight of horse-drawn chariots must have been terrifying, but they quickly understood that war making had changed and they scrambled to adapt. The pharaohs in Egypt probably copied chariots from nomads or neighbors, and they came to value them highly. For example, the young pharaoh Tutankhamun (r. c. 1336–1327 BCE) was a chariot archer who made sure his war vehicle and other gear accompanied him in his tomb. A century later, the Shang kings of the Yellow River valley, in the heartland of agricultural China, likewise were entombed with their horse chariots.

While nomads and transhumant herders toppled the river-basin cities in Mesopotamia, Egypt, and China through innovations in warfare such as the chariot, the turmoil that ensued sowed seeds for a new type of regime: the territorial state. Even as Sargon and the Akkadians set up a short-lived territorial state in earlier Mesopotamia (2334–2200 BCE) (see Chapter 2), the martial innovations and political and environmental crises of the early second millennium BCE helped spur more enduring development of territorial states elsewhere. The **territorial state** was a centralized kingdom organized around a charismatic ruler. The new rulers of these territorial states exerted power not only over localized city-states but also over distant hinterlands. They enhanced their stability through rituals for passing the torch of command from one generation to the next. People no longer identified themselves as residents of cities; instead, they felt allegiance to large territories, rulers, and broad linguistic and ethnic communities. These territories for the first time had identifiable borders, and their residents felt a shared identity. Territorial states differed from the city-states that preceded them in that the new territorial states in Egypt, Mesopotamia, and China based their authority on monarchs, widespread bureaucracies, elaborate legal codes, large territorial expanses, definable borders, and ambitions for continuous expansion.

The Territorial State in Egypt

The first of the great territorial states of this period arose from the ashes of chaos in Egypt. The long era of prosperity associated with Old Kingdom Egypt ended when drought brought catastrophe to the area. For several decades the Nile did not overflow its banks, and Egyptian harvests withered. As the pharaohs lost legitimacy and fell prey to feuding among rivals for the throne, regional elites replaced the authority of the centralized state. Egypt, which had been one of the most stable corners of Afro-Eurasia, endured more than a century of tumult before a new order emerged. The pharaohs of the Middle Kingdom and, later, the New Kingdom reunified the river valley and expanded south and north.

RELIGION AND TRADE IN MIDDLE KINGDOM EGYPT (2055–1650 BCE)

Around 2050 BCE, after a century of drought, the Nile's floodwaters returned to normal and crops grew again. In the centuries that followed, pharaohs at Thebes consolidated power in Upper Egypt and began new state-building activity, ushering in a new phase of stability that historians call the Middle Kingdom. The rulers of this era developed Egypt's religious and political institutions in ways that increased state power, creating the conditions for greater prosperity and trade.

Religion and Rule Spiritual and worldly powers once again reinforced each other in Egypt. Gods and rulers together replaced the chaos that people believed had brought drought and despair. Amenemhet I (1985–1955 BCE), first pharaoh of the long-lasting Twelfth Dynasty (1985–1795 BCE), elevated a formerly less significant god, Amun, to prominence. The king capitalized on the god's name, which means "hidden," to convey a sense of his own invisible omnipresence throughout the realm. Because Amun's attributes of air and breath were largely intangible, believers in other gods were able to embrace his cult. Amun's cosmic power appealed to

Hypostyle Hall The precinct of Amun-Re in the Karnak temple complex (near modern-day Luxor) was made up of a series of gates, courts, and temples that were built over time by many pharaohs from the Middle and New Kingdoms. The lofty, inscribed columns of the Great Hypostyle Hall (pictured here), which was built by Ramses II in the thirteenth century BCE, offer stunning evidence of the construction projects that pharaohs built to underscore their power and their relationship to the divine.

people in areas that had recently been impoverished.

The pharaoh's elevation of the cult of Amun unified the kingdom and brought even more power to Amun and the pharaoh. Consequently, Amun eclipsed all the other gods of Thebes. Merging with the formerly omnipotent sun god Re, the deity now was called Amun-Re: the king of the gods. Because the power of the gods and kings was intertwined, the pharaoh as Amun's earthly champion enjoyed enhanced legitimacy as the supreme ruler.

The massive temple complex dedicated to Amun-Re offers evidence of the gods' and the pharaoh's joint power. Middle Kingdom rulers tapped into their kingdom's renewed bounty, their subjects' loyalty, and the work of untold commoners and enslaved peoples to build Amun-Re's temple complex at Thebes (present-day Luxor). For more than 12,000 years, Egyptians and the people they enslaved toiled to erect monumental gates, enormous courtyards, and other structures in what was arguably the largest, longest-lasting public works project ever undertaken. Blending the pastoral ideals of herders into the institutions of their settled and hierarchical territorial state, Middle Kingdom rulers also nurtured a cult of the pharaoh as the good shepherd whose prime responsibility was to care for his human flock. In a building inscription at Heliopolis, a pharaoh named Senusret III from the nineteenth century BCE claims to have been appointed by Amun as "shepherd of the land." And 500 years later, in the fourteenth century BCE, Amenhotep III's building inscription at Karnak describes him as "the good shepherd for all people." By instituting charities, offering homage to gods at the palace to ensure regular floodwaters, and performing ceremonies to honor their own generosity, the pharaohs portrayed themselves as these shepherds. In these inscriptions and in imagery (recall the shepherd's crook as one of the pharaoh's symbols), pharaohs exploited distinctly pastoralist symbolism. As a result, the cult of Amun-Re was both a tool of political power and a source of spiritual meaning for the different peoples of the blended territorial state of Egypt.

Merchants and Expanding Trade Networks Prosperity gave rise to an urban class of merchants and professionals who used their wealth and skills to carve out new opportunities for themselves. They indulged in leisure activities such as formal banquets with professional dancers and singers, and they honed their skills in hunting, fowling, and fishing. In a sign of their upward mobility and autonomy, some members of the middle class constructed tombs filled with representations of the material goods they would use in the afterlife as well as the occupations that would engage them for eternity. This new merchant class did not rely on the king's generosity and took burial privileges formerly reserved for the royal family and a few powerful nobles.

As they centralized power and consolidated their territorial state, Egyptians also expanded their trade networks. (See Map 3.2.) Because the floodplains had long since been deforested, the Egyptians needed to import massive quantities of wood by ship. Most prized were the cedars from Byblos (a city in the land soon known as Phoenicia, roughly present-day Lebanon), which were crafted into furniture and coffins. Commercial networks extended south through the Red Sea to present-day Ethiopia and were used to import precious metals, ivory, livestock, and exotic animals such as panthers and monkeys. They brought enslaved people as well. Expeditions to the Sinai Peninsula searched for copper and turquoise. Egyptians looked south for gold, which they prized for personal and architectural ornamentation. To acquire it, they crossed into Nubia, where they met stiff resistance. One Egyptian official from the reign of Amenemhet II (the third pharaoh of the long-lasting Twelfth Dynasty) bragged about his expeditions into the Sinai and south into Nubia: "I forced the (Nubian) chiefs to wash gold. . . . I went overthrowing by the fear of the Lord of the Two Lands [i.e., the pharaoh]." Eventually, the Egyptians colonized Nubia to broaden their trade routes and secure these coveted resources. As part of Egyptian colonization southward, a series of forts

Luxury Imports This chest amulet from Tutankhamun's fourteenth-century BCE tomb highlights the use of luxury imports in Egyptian religious and visual culture. Lapis lazuli, turquoise, and carnelian from the east and gold from the south were combined to create uniquely Egyptian symbolism, including a falcon flanked with cobras and topped with an eye of Horus, with papyrus and lotus flowers dangling below. Scientists recently determined that the yellow glass that makes up the scarab forming the falcon's body contains reidite, a mineral that can be formed only when a meteorite strikes and melts the desert sand.

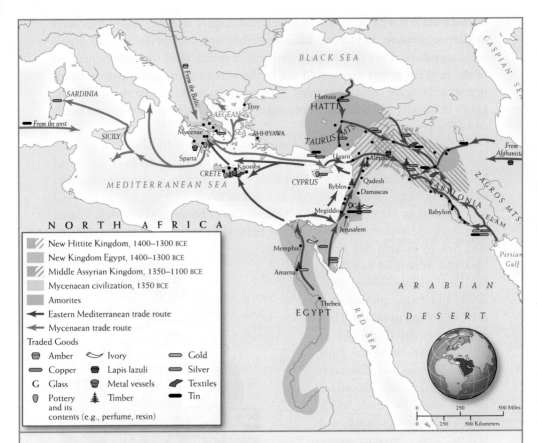

Map 3.2 Territorial States and Trade Routes in Southwest Asia, North Africa, and the Eastern Mediterranean, 1500–1350 BCE

....

Trade in many commodities brought the societies of the Mediterranean Sea and Southwest Asia into increasingly closer contact.

• What were the major trade routes and the major trading states in Southwest Asia, North Africa, and the eastern Mediterranean during this time?

• What were the major trade goods? Which regions appear to have had more, and more unique, resources than the others?

• What did each region need from the others? What did each region have to offer in exchange for the goods it needed?

extended as far south as the second cataract of the Nile River (just south of the modern-day border between Egypt and Sudan).

MIGRATIONS AND EXPANDING FRONTIERS IN NEW KINGDOM EGYPT (1550–1070 BCE)

The success of the new commercial networks lured pastoral nomads who were searching for work. Later, chariot-driving Hyksos invaders from Southwest Asia attacked Egypt, setting in motion the events marking the break between what historians call the Middle and New Kingdoms of Egypt. Although the invaders challenged the Middle Kingdom, they also inspired innovations that enabled the New Kingdom to thrive and expand.

Hyksos Invaders Sometime around 1640 BCE, a western Semitic-speaking people, whom the Egyptians called the **Hyksos** ("Rulers of Foreign Lands"), overthrew the unstable Thirteenth Dynasty (toward the end of Egypt's Middle Kingdom period). The Hyksos had mastered the art of horse chariots. Thundering into battle with their war chariots and their superior bronze axes and composite bows (made of wood, horn, and sinew), they easily defeated the pharaoh's foot soldiers. The victorious Hyksos did not destroy the conquered land, but adopted and reinforced Egyptian ways. Ruling as the Fifteenth Dynasty, the Hyksos asserted control over the northern part of the country and transformed the Egyptian military.

After a century of political conflict, an Egyptian who ruled the southern part of the country, Ahmosis (r. 1550–1525 BCE), successfully used the Hyksos weaponry—horse chariots—against the invaders themselves and became pharaoh. This conquest marked the beginning of what historians call New Kingdom Egypt. Hyksos invasions had taught Egyptian rulers that they must vigilantly monitor their frontiers, for they could no longer rely on deserts as buffers. Ahmosis assembled large, mobile armies and drove the Hyksos "foreigners" back. Diplomats followed in the army's path, as the pharaoh initiated a strategy of interference in the affairs of Southwest Asian states. Such policies laid the groundwork for statecraft and an international diplomatic system that future Egyptian kings used to dominate the eastern Mediterranean world.

Migrations and invasions introduced new techniques that the Egyptians adopted to consolidate their power. These included bronze working (which the Egyptians had not perfected), an improved potter's wheel, and a vertical loom. South Asian animals such as humped zebu cattle, as well as vegetable and fruit crops, now appeared on the banks of the Nile for the first time. Other significant innovations pertained to war, such as the horse and chariot, the composite bow, the scimitar (a sword with a curved blade), and other weapons from western Eurasia. These weapons transformed the Egyptian army from a standing infantry to a high-speed, mobile, and deadly fighting force. Egyptian troops extended the military frontier as far south as the fourth cataract of the Nile River (in northern modern-day Sudan), and the kingdom now stretched from the Mediterranean shores to Ethiopia.

Expanding Frontiers By the beginning of the New Kingdom, the territorial state of Egypt was projecting its interests outward: it defined itself as a superior, cosmopolitan society with an efficient bureaucracy run by competent and socially mobile individuals. Paintings on the walls of Vizier Rekhmire's tomb from the mid-fifteenth century BCE record the wide-ranging tribute from distant lands that he received on behalf of the pharaoh, including a veritable menagerie: cattle, a giraffe, an elephant, a panther, baboons, and monkeys. The collected taxes that are enumerated in the accompanying inscriptions included offerings of gold, silver, linen, bows, grain, and honey. Rekhmire's tomb, with its paintings, tax lists, and instructions for how to rule, offers a prime example of how the bureaucracy managed the expanding Egyptian frontiers. Pushing the transnational connectivity even further, it has been argued that inscriptions and paintings from Rekhmire's tomb, together with other tomb paintings, show that Keftiu (people from Minoan Crete), along with Hittites from Asia Minor, Syrians from the Levant, and Nubians from the south, may have gathered for some major multinational event in Egypt, like a Sed festival.

Exotic Tribute From the sumptuously painted tomb of the vizier Rekhmire (Theban Tomb 110), this scene depicts a range of tribute goods brought to Thutmosis III. Tribute from Nubia included oxen, dogs, and a giraffe (with a monkey clinging to its neck) and, from Syria, a baby elephant, a brown bear, horses, and a chariot. Other gifts not pictured here were gold and silver vessels from the Keftiu (of Minoan Crete) as well as incense and exotic animals from Punt (a region to the south of Egypt that scholars have not yet positively identified, likely located on the African coast of the Red Sea in modern Ethiopia and Somalia).

As mentioned above, Egypt expanded its control southward into Nubia, as a source of gold, exotic raw materials, and manpower. Historians identify this southward expansion most strongly with the reign of Egypt's most powerful woman ruler, Hatshepsut. She served as regent for her young stepson, Thutmosis III, who came to the throne in 1479 BCE when his father—Hatshepsut's half brother and husband—Thutmosis II died. When her stepson was seven years old, Hatshepsut proclaimed herself "king," ruling as co-regent until she died two decades later. During her reign there was little military activity, but trade contacts into the Levant and Mediterranean and southward into Nubia flourished. When he ultimately came to power, Thutmosis III (r. 1479–1425 BCE) launched another

Hatshepsut The only powerful queen of Egyptian pharaonic history was Hatshepsut, seen here in two portraits created during her reign (1479–1458 BCE). In the earlier statue (*left*), a young, feminine Hatshepsut wears a masculine headdress and kilt but is labeled in the accompanying inscription as a "perfect goddess" and "daughter of Re." Because a woman on the throne of Egypt would offend the basic principles of order (*ma'at*), Hatshepsut usually portrayed herself as a man, especially late in her reign, as in the later image here (*right*). This masculine portrayal was reinforced by the use of male determinatives in the hieroglyphic renditions of her name.

expansionist phase, northeastward into the Levant. The famed Battle of Megiddo, the first recorded chariot battle in history, took place twenty-three years into his reign. Thutmosis III's army at Megiddo, including nearly 1,000 war chariots, defeated his adversaries and established an Egyptian presence in Palestine. The growth phase launched by Thutmosis III would continue for 200 years. Having evolved into a strong, expanding territorial state, Egypt was now poised to engage in commercial, political, and cultural exchanges with the rest of the region.

Territorial States in Southwest Asia

Climate change and invasions by migrants also transformed the societies of Southwest Asia, and new territorial kingdoms arose in Mesopotamia and Anatolia (modern-day Iraq and Turkey, respectively). Here, as in Egypt, the drought at the end of the third millennium BCE was devastating. Harvests shrank, the price of basic goods rose, and the social order broke down. In southern Mesopotamia, cities were invaded by transhumant herders (not chariot-driving nomads) who sought grazing lands to replace those swallowed up by expanding deserts. A millennium of intense cultivation, combined with severe drought, brought disastrous consequences: rich soil in the river basin was depleted of nutrients; salt water from the Persian Gulf seeped into the marshy deltas, contaminating the water table; and the main branch of the Euphrates River shifted to the west. Many cities lost access to their fertile agrarian hinterlands and withered away. Mesopotamia's center of political and economic gravity shifted northward, away from the silted, marshy deltas of the southern heartland.

As scarcities mounted, transhumant peoples began to press in upon settled communities more closely. Mesopotamian city dwellers were scornful of the rustic migrants, whom they called **Amorites** ("westerners"), invading their cities. While these transhumant herders may have been western "foreigners" to those living in the urban centers of Mesopotamia, they were not strangers. These rural folk had wintered in villages close to the rivers to water their animals, which grazed on fallow fields. In the scorching summer, they retreated to the cooler highlands. Their flocks provided wools, leather, bones, and tendons to the artisan-based industries of the urban centers of Mesopotamia. In return, the herders purchased crafted products and agricultural goods. They also paid taxes, served as warriors, and labored on public works projects, but had few political rights within city-states.

Around 2000 BCE, Amorites from the western desert joined allies from the Iranian plateau to bring down the Third Dynasty of Ur, which had controlled all of Mesopotamia and southwestern Iran for more than a century. These Amorites and their allies founded the Old Babylonian kingdom, centered on the southern Mesopotamian city of Babylon, near modern-day Baghdad. Other territorial states arose in Mesopotamia in the millennium that followed, sometimes with one dominating the entire floodplain and sometimes with multiple powerful kingdoms vying for territory. As in Egypt, a century of political instability followed the demise of the old city-state models. Here, too, pastoralists played a role in the restoration of order, increasing the wealth of the regions they conquered and helping the cultural realm to flourish. The Old Babylonian kingdom expanded trade and founded territorial states with dynastic ruling families and well-defined frontiers. Pastoralists also played a key role in the development of territorial kingdoms in Anatolia.

MESOPOTAMIAN KINGSHIP

The new rulers of Mesopotamia changed the organization of the state and promoted a distinctive culture, as well as expanding trade. Herders-turned-urbanite-rulers mixed their own nomadic social organization with that of the once-dominant city-states to create the structures necessary to support much larger territorial states. The basic social organization of the Amorites, out of which the territorial states in Mesopotamia evolved, was tribal (dominated by a ruling chief) and clan based (claiming descent from a common ancestor). Over time, chieftains drew on personal charisma and battlefield prowess to become kings; kings allied with the merchant class and nobility for bureaucratic and financial support; and kingship became hereditary.

Over the centuries, powerful Mesopotamian kings expanded their territories and subdued weaker neighbors, inducing them to pay tribute in luxury goods, raw materials, and manpower as part of a broad confederation of city-states under the kings' protection. Control over military resources (metals for weaponry and, later, herds of horses for pulling chariots) was necessary for dominance. The ruler's charisma also mattered. Unlike the more institutionalized Egyptian leadership, Mesopotamian kingdoms could vacillate from strong to weak, depending on the leader's personality.

The most famous Mesopotamian ruler of this period was Hammurabi (r. 1792–1750 BCE). Continuously struggling with powerful neighbors, he sought to centralize state authority and to create a new legal order. Using diplomatic and military skills to become the strongest king in Mesopotamia, he made Babylon his capital. He implemented a new system to consolidate power, appointing regional governors to manage outlying provinces and to deal with local elites. Like the Egyptian pharaohs of the Middle Kingdom, Hammurabi was shepherd and patriarch of his people, responsible for proper preparation of the fields and irrigation canals and for his followers' well-being. Balancing elite privileges with the needs of the lower classes, the king secured his power. **Hammurabi's Code**, with its "eye-for-an-eye," if/then, reciprocity of crime and punishment, is an example of this balancing act. Its compilation of 282 edicts outlines crimes and their punishments. The laws dealt with theft, murder, professional negligence, and many other matters of daily life. The laws make it clear that governing public matters was man's work and upholding a just order was the supreme charge of rulers. Whereas the gods' role in ordering the world was distant, the king was directly in command of ordering relations among people. Accordingly, the code elaborated in exhaustive detail the social rules that would ensure the kingdom's peace through its primary instrument— the family. The code outlined the rights and privileges of fathers, wives, and children. The father's duty was to treat his kin as the ruler would treat his subjects, with strict authority and care. Adultery was harshly punished, resulting in the drowning of the adulterous wife and her lover, unless the husband or king intervened.

The code also divided the people in the Babylonian kingdom into three classes: "free persons," "dependents," and "slaves." Each class had an assigned value and distinct rights and responsibilities. While its eye-for-an-eye, tooth-for-a-tooth reciprocity is remarkable, the code also made it clear that Babylonia was a stratified society, in which some persons (and eyes and teeth!) were more valued than others. Punishments for offenses were determined by the status of the committer and that of the one who suffered. The code itself was inscribed in the last years of Hammurabi's reign, after his conquests had created a larger state, and represented a way to celebrate the king's achievements.

Gilgamesh in Image and Text *Left*: This terra-cotta plaque is one of the few visual depictions of Gilgamesh (on the left wielding the knife) and his sidekick, Enkidu. It illustrates one of the episodes in their shared adventures, the killing of Humwawa, the monster of the Cedar Forest. The style of the plaque indicates that it was made during the Old Babylonian period, between 2000 and 1600 BCE. *Right*: The text of the Gilgamesh epic was preserved on tablets of baked clay, like the now-fragmentary tablets shown here, which were found in the seventh-century BCE library of the Neo-Assyrian king Ashurbanipal. The *Epic of Gilgamesh* had enduring appeal for those in Mesopotamia, who passed the story along for millennia, first orally, then in images like the one here, then in text.

Power and Culture Mesopotamian rulers commissioned public art and works projects and promoted institutions of learning. To dispel their image as rustic foreigners and to demonstrate their familiarity with the region's core values, new Mesopotamian rulers valued the oral tales and written records of the earlier Sumerians and Akkadians. Scribes copied the ancient texts and preserved their tradition. Royal hymns portrayed the king as a legendary hero of quasi-divine status.

Heroic narratives about legendary founders, based on traditional stories about the rulers of ancient Uruk, legitimized the new rulers. The most famous tale was the *Epic of Gilgamesh*, one of the earliest surviving works of literature. Originally composed more than a millennium earlier, in the Sumerian language, this epic narrated the heroism of the legendary king of early Uruk, Gilgamesh. This epic is probably best known for the passage in which Gilgamesh seeks out advice from Utnapishtim, the survivor of a terrible flood, in a story that resonates with that of Noah from Genesis in the Hebrew scriptures. Utnapishtim's flood story, however, is just one part of Gilgamesh's epic, which describes the title character's rivalry and, later, friendship with Enkidu and his quest for immortality after his friend Enkidu's death. Preserved by scribes in royal courts through centuries, the epic offers an example of how the Mesopotamian kings invested in cultural production to explain important political relations, unify their people, and distinguish their subjects from those of other kingdoms.

Trade and the Rise of a Private Economy Another feature of the territorial state in Mesopotamia was its shift away from economic activity dominated by the city-state and toward independent private ventures. Mesopotamian rulers designated private entrepreneurs rather than state bureaucrats to collect taxes.

People paid taxes in the form of commodities such as grain, vegetables, and wool, which the entrepreneurs exchanged for silver. They, in turn, passed on the silver to the state after pocketing a percentage for their profit. This process generated more private economic activity and wealth, and more revenues for the state.

Mesopotamia was a crossroads for caravans leading east and west. Peace and good governance allowed trade to flourish. The ability to move exotic food-stuffs, valuable minerals, textiles, and luxury goods across Southwest Asia won Mesopotamian merchants and entrepreneurs a privileged position as middle-men. Merchants also used sea routes for trade with the Indus Valley. Before 2000 BCE, mariners had charted the waters of the Red Sea, the Gulf of Aden, the Persian Gulf, and much of the Arabian Sea. And during the second millennium BCE, shipbuilders figured out how to construct larger vessels and rig them with towering masts and woven sails—creating seaworthy craft that could carry bulkier loads. Shipbuilding required wood (particularly cedar from Phoenicia) as well as wool and other fibers (from the pastoral hinterlands) for sails. Such reliance on imported materials reflected a growing regional economic special-ization and an expanding sphere of interaction across western Afro-Eurasia. The benefits and risks of trade in Mesopotamia are evident from royal edicts of debt annulment (to help merchants who had overstretched) and formalized commercial rules governing taxes and duties. In trade and other exchanges, Mesopotamia became a crucial link between Egypt, Anatolia, and southwestern Iran. Centralized control of the region facilitated a thriving trade in such pre-cious commodities as horses, chariots, and lapis lazuli, which was exchanged for gold, wood, and ivory.

THE OLD AND NEW HITTITE KINGDOMS (1800–1200 BCE)

Chariot warriors known as the Hittites established territorial kingdoms in Anatolia, to the northwest of Mesopotamia. Anatolia was an overland cross-roads that linked the Black and Mediterranean Seas. Like other plateaus of Afro-Eurasia, it had high tablelands, was easy to traverse, and was hospitable to large herding communities. During the third millennium BCE, Anatolia had become home to numerous communities run by native elites. These societies combined pastoral ways of life, agriculture, and urban commercial centers. Before 2000 BCE, peoples speaking Indo-European languages began to enter the plateau, probably coming from the steppe lands north and west of the Black Sea. The newcomers lived in fortified settlements and often engaged in regional warfare, and their numbers grew. Splintered into competing clans, they fought for regional supremacy. They also borrowed extensively from the cultural developments of the Southwest Asian urban cultures, especially those of Mesopotamia.

In the early second millennium BCE, the chariot warrior groups of Anatolia grew powerful on the commercial activity that passed through their region. Chief among them were the **Hittites**. Hittite lancers and archers rode chariots across vast expanses to plunder their neighbors and demand taxes and tribute. In the seventeenth century BCE, the Hittite leader Hattusilis I unified these chariot aristocracies, secured his base in Anatolia, defeated the kingdom that controlled northern Syria, and then campaigned along the Euphrates River. His grandson and successor, Mursilis I, sacked Babylon in 1595 BCE. The Hittites ultimately built their capital at Hattusa, in central Anatolia, complete with massive walls, a monumental gate with lions carved into it, multiple temples and granaries, and a palace. Near Hattusa, the rock-cut sanctuary of Yazilikaya contains reliefs of gods and goddesses marching in procession, as well as images of Hittite kings.

Two centuries after the successes of Hattusilis I, the Hittites enjoyed another period of political and military success. In 1274 BCE, they fought the Egyptians at the Battle of Qadesh (in modern Syria), the largest and best-documented chariot battle of antiquity. Both sides claimed victory. The treaty that records reciprocal promises of nonaggression by the Egyptians and Hittites nearly fifteen years after

Akhenaten and Aten Akhenaten, one of the correspondents in the Amarna letters that reveal so much about international diplomacy among the community of major powers, also forged a revolutionary, if short-lived, change in Egyptian religion. His elevation of the sun disk, Aten, to supreme authority displaced the long-standing power of the god Amun-Re and his priestly elite. On this relief carving, the sun disk, Aten, beams down on Akhenaten and his family with rays that end in hands holding ankhs, the Egyptian symbol for life. This intimate scene depicts Akhenaten lovingly cradling his young daughter across from his wife, Nefertiti, who holds their other two daughters.

the battle is the oldest surviving peace treaty, and a replica of it is displayed at the United Nations. Soon after Qadesh, the Egyptian forces withdrew from the region. Hittite control—spanning from Anatolia across the region between the Nile and Mesopotamia—was central to balancing power among the territorial states that grew up in the river valleys.

A COMMUNITY OF MAJOR POWERS (1400–1200 BCE)

Between 1400 and 1200 BCE, the major territorial states of Southwest Asia and Egypt perfected instruments of international diplomacy. A cache of 350 letters, referred to by modern scholars as the Amarna letters after the present-day Egyptian village of Amarna, where they were discovered, offers intimate views of the interactions among the powers of Egypt and Southwest Asia. The letters include communications between Egyptian pharaohs and various leaders of Southwest Asia, including Babylonian and Hittite kings. Powerful rulers referred to one another as brothers, suggesting not only a high degree of equality but also a desire to foster friendship among large states. Trade linked the regimes and was so vital to the economic and political well-being of rulers that if a commercial mission was plundered, the ruler of the area in which the robbery occurred assumed responsibility and offered compensation to the injured parties.

Because trade was so important, the leaders of these powers settled their differences through treaties and diplomatic negotiations rather than on the battlefield. Each state knew its place in the political pecking order. It was an order that depended on constant diplomacy, based on communication, treaties, marriages, and the exchange of gifts. As nomadic peoples combined with settled urban polities to create new territorial states in Egypt, Mesopotamia, and Anatolia, and as those territorial states came into contact with one another through trade, this diplomacy was vital to maintaining the interactions in this community of major powers in Southwest Asia.

Nomads and the Indus River Valley

Compared with those in Egypt and Mesopotamia, territorial states emerged more slowly in the Indus River valley. Late in the third millennium BCE, drought ravaged the Indus River valley as it did other regions. By 1700 BCE, the population of the old Harappan heartland had plummeted. Here, too, around 1500 BCE, yet another group of nomadic peoples, calling themselves Aryans ("respected ones"), emerged from their homelands in the steppes of Inner Eurasia. In contrast with developments in Egypt, Anatolia, and Mesopotamia, these pastoral nomads did not immediately establish large territorial states. Crossing the northern highlands of central Asia through the Hindu Kush, they descended into the fertile Indus River basin (see Map 3.3) with large flocks of

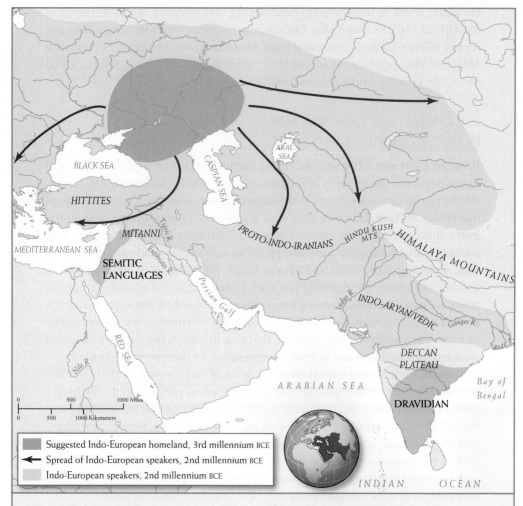

Map 3.3 Indo-European Migrations, Second Millennium BCE

....

One of the most important developments of the second millennium BCE was the movement of Indo-European peoples.

- Where did the Indo-European migration originate?
- Where did Indo-European migrations spread to during this time?
- How do these migrations relate to the Afro-Eurasian developments that are traced in this chapter?

cattle and horses. They sang chants from the Rig-Veda as they sacrificed some of their livestock to their gods. Known collectively as the Vedas ("knowledge"), these hymns served as the most sacred texts for the newcomers, who have been known ever since as the **Vedic peoples**. Sanskrit, the spoken language of the Vedic peoples, is one of the earliest known Indo-European languages and a source for virtually all the European languages, including Greek, Latin, English, French, and German.

Like other nomads from the northern steppe, Vedic peoples brought domesticated animals—especially horses, which pulled their chariots and established their military superiority. Not only were they superb horse charioteers, but they were also masters of copper and bronze metallurgy and wheel making. Their expertise in these areas allowed them to produce the very chariots that transported them into their new lands.

The Vedic peoples were deeply religious. They worshipped a host of deities, the most powerful of which were the sky god and the gods that represented horses. They were confident that their chief god, Indra (the deity of war), was on their side. The Vedic peoples also brought elaborate rituals of worship, which set them apart from the indigenous populations. Perhaps the most striking of these was the year-long Ashvamedha, a ritual that culminated in an elaborate horse sacrifice that reinforced the power and territorial claims of the leader. As with many Afro-Eurasian migrations, the outsiders' arrival led to fusion as well as to conflict. While the native-born peoples eventually adopted the newcomers' language, the newcomers themselves took up the techniques and rhythms of agrarian life. The Vedic peoples used the Indus Valley as a staging area for

Indra The Vedic peoples worshipped their gods by sacrificing and burning cows and horses and by singing hymns and songs, but they never built temples or sculpted idols. Therefore, we do not know how they envisioned Indra and their other gods. However, when Buddhists started to make images of Buddha in the early centuries CE, they also sculpted Indra and other Vedic deities. This image of Indra riding his elephant, Airavata, dates to the second century BCE and was found in Bhaja Cave 19 on the northwest coast of India.

migrations throughout the northern plain of South Asia. As they mixed agrarian and pastoral ways and borrowed technologies (such as ironworking) from farther west, their population expanded and they began to look for new resources. With horses, chariots, and iron tools and weapons, they marched south and east. By 1000 BCE, they reached the southern foothills of the Himalayas and began to settle in the Ganges River valley. Five hundred years later, they had settlements as far south as the Deccan plateau.

Each wave of occupation involved violence, but the invaders did not simply dominate the indigenous peoples. Instead, the confrontations led them to embrace many of the ways of the vanquished. In particular, the Vedic newcomers were impressed with inhabitants' farming skills and knowledge of seasonal weather. These they adapted even as they continued to expand their territory. They moved into huts constructed from mud, bamboo, and reeds. They refined the already sophisticated production of beautiful carnelian stone beads, and they further aided commerce by devising standardized weights. In addition to raising domesticated animals, they sowed wheat and rye on the Indus plain, and they learned to plant rice in the marshy lands of the Ganges River valley. Later they mastered the use of plows with iron blades, an innovation that transformed the agrarian base of South Asia. This turn to settled agriculture was a major shift for the nomadic pastoral Vedic peoples. After all, their staple foods had always been dairy products and meat, and they were used to measuring their wealth in livestock (horses were most valuable, and cows were more valuable than sheep). Moreover, because they could not breed their prized horses in South Asia's semitropical climate, they initiated a brisk import trade from central and Southwest Asia.

As the Vedic peoples filled the relative void left by the collapse of the Harappans and adapted to their new environment, their initial political organization took a somewhat different course from that of Southwest Asia. Whereas competitive kingdoms dominated the landscape in Southwest Asia, competitive and balanced regimes were slower to emerge in South Asia. The result was a slower process of political integration.

The Shang Territorial State in East Asia

China's first major territorial state combined features of earlier Longshan culture with new technologies and religious practices. Climate change affected East Asia much as it had central and Southwest Asia. Stories written on bamboo strips and later collected into what historians call the "Bamboo Annals" tell of a time at the end of the legendary Xia dynasty when the sun dimmed and frost and ice appeared in the summer, followed by heavy rainfall, flooding, and then a long drought. According to Chinese mythology, the first ruler of the Shang dynasty defeated a despotic Xia king and then offered to sacrifice himself so that the drought would end. This leader, Tang, survived to found the territorial state called Shang around 1600 BCE in northeastern China.

The Shang state was built on four elements that the Longshan peoples had already introduced: a metal industry based on copper; pottery making; walled towns; and divination using animal bones. To these Longshan foundations, the Shang dynasty added hereditary rulers whose power derived from their relation to ancestors and gods; written records; large-scale metallurgy (especially in bronze); tribute; and various rituals.

STATE FORMATION

A combination of these preexisting Longshan strengths and Shang innovations produced a strong Shang territorial state and a wealthy and powerful elite, noted for its intellectual achievements and aesthetic sensibilities.

Shang kings used a personalized style of rule, making regular trips around the country to meet, hunt, and conduct military campaigns. With no rival territorial states on its immediate periphery, the Shang state did not create a strongly defended, permanent capital, but rather moved its capital as the frontier expanded and contracted. Bureaucrats used written records to oversee the large and expanding population of the Shang state.

Advanced Shang metalworking—the beginnings of which appeared in northwestern China at pre-Shang sites dating as early as 1800 BCE—was vital to the Shang territorial state. Shang bronze work included weapons, fittings for chariots, and ritual vessels. Because copper and tin were available from the North China plain, only short-distance trade was necessary to obtain the resources that a bronze culture needed. (See Map 3.4.) Shang bronze-working technique involved the use of hollow clay molds to hold the molten metal alloy, which, when removed after the liquid had cooled and solidified, produced firm bronze objects. The casting of modular components that artisans could assemble later promoted increased production and permitted the elite to make extravagant use of bronze vessels for burials. The bronze industry of this period shows the high level not only of material culture (in the practical function of the physical objects) but also of cultural development (in the aesthetic sense of

Bronze At the height of the Shang state, circa 1200 BCE, its rulers erected massive palaces at the capital of Yin, which required bronze foundries for their wine and food vessels. In these foundries, skilled workers produced bronze weapons, ritual objects, and elaborate ceremonial drinking and eating vessels, like the one pictured.

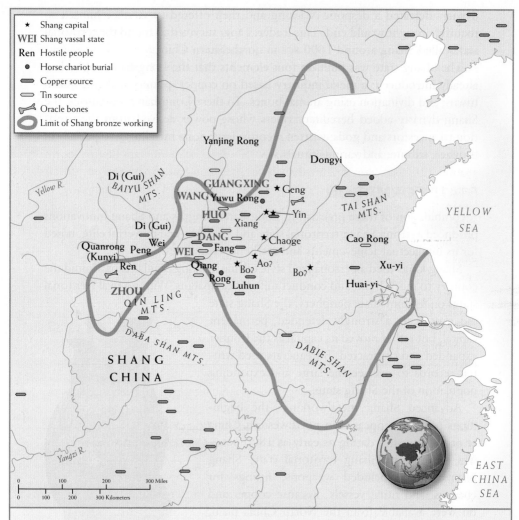

Map 3.4 Shang Dynasty in East Asia

The Shang state was one of the most important and powerful of early Chinese dynasties.

- Based on your analysis of this map, what raw materials were the most important to the Shang state?
- How were the deposits of these raw materials distributed across Shang territory and beyond? How might that distribution have shaped the area marked on the map as the limit of Shang bronze working?
- Locate the various Shang capitals. Why do you think they were located where they were?

beauty and taste conveyed by the choice of form). Since Shang metalworking required extensive mining, it necessitated a large labor force, efficient casting, and a reproducible artistic style. Although the Shang state highly valued its artisans, it treated its copper miners as lowly tribute laborers. By controlling access to tin and copper and to the production of bronze, Shang kings prevented their rivals from forging bronze weapons and thus increased their own power and legitimacy. With their superior weapons, Shang armies by 1300 BCE could easily destroy armies wielding wooden clubs and stone-tipped spears.

Chariots entered the Central Plains of China with nomads of the north around 1200 BCE, much later than their appearance in Egypt and Southwest Asia. They were quickly adopted by the upper classes. Chinese chariots were larger (fitting three men standing in a box mounted on eighteen- or twenty-six-spoke wheels) and much better built than those of their neighbors. As symbols of power and wealth, they were often buried with their owners. Yet, unlike elsewhere in Afro-Eurasia, they were at first little used in warfare during the Shang era, perhaps because of the effectiveness and shock value of large Shang infantry forces, composed mainly of foot soldiers armed with axes, spears, arrowheads, shields, and helmets, all made of bronze. In Shang China, the chariot was used primarily for hunting and as a mark of high status. Shang metalworking and the incorporation of the chariot gave the Shang state a huge advantage and unprecedented power over its neighbors.

AGRICULTURE AND TRIBUTE

The Shang dynastic rulers also understood the importance of agriculture for winning and maintaining power, so they did much to promote its development. The activities of local governors and the masses revolved around agriculture. Rulers controlled their own farms, which supplied food to the royal family, craftworkers, and the army. Farmers drained low-lying fields and cleared forested areas to expand the cultivation of millet, wheat, barley, and possibly rice. Their tools included stone plows, spades, and sickles. Farmers also cultivated silkworms and raised pigs, dogs, sheep, and oxen. Thanks to the twelve-month, 360-day lunar calendar developed by Shang astrologers, farmers were better able to track the growing season. By including leap months, this calendar maintained the proper relationship between months and seasons, and it relieved fears about solar and lunar eclipses by making them predictable.

The ruler's wealth and power depended on tribute from elites and allies. Elites supplied warriors and laborers, horses and cattle. Allies sent foodstuffs, soldiers, and workers and "assisted in the king's affairs"—perhaps by hunting, burning brush, or clearing land—in return for his help in defending against invaders and making predictions about the harvest. Commoners sent their tribute to the elites, who held the land as grants from the king. Farmers transferred their surplus crops to the elite landholders (or to the ruler if they worked on his personal landholdings) on a regular schedule. Tribute could also take the form of turtle shells and cattle scapulas (shoulder blades), which the Shang used for divination by means of oracle bones (see below). Divining the future was a powerful way to legitimate royal power—and then to justify the right to collect more tribute. By placing themselves symbolically and literally at the center of all exchanges, the Shang kings reinforced their power over others.

SOCIETY AND RITUAL PRACTICE

The advances in metalworking and agriculture gave the state the resources to sustain a complex society, in which religion and rituals reinforced the social hierarchy. The core organizing principle of Shang society was familial descent traced back many generations to a common male ancestor. Grandparents, parents, sons, and daughters lived and worked together and held property in common, but male family elders took precedence. Women from other male family lines married into the family and won honor when they became mothers, particularly of sons.

The death ritual, which involved sacrificing humans to join the deceased in the next life, reflected the importance of family, male dominance, and social hierarchy. Members of the royal elite were often buried with their full entourage, including wives, consorts, servants, chariots, horses, and drivers. The inclusion of personal servants and people enslaved by the elite among those sacrificed indicates a belief that the familiar social hierarchy would continue in the afterlife. An impressive example of the burial practices of the Shang elite is the tomb of an exceptional prominent woman, Fu Hao (also known as Fu Zi), who was consort to the king, a military leader in her own right, and a ritual specialist. She was buried with a wide range of objects made from bronze and jade (including weapons), ivory, pottery, cowrie shells that were used as currency, and a large cache of oracle bones, as well as six dogs and sixteen humans who appear to have been sacrificed to accompany her at death.

The Shang state was a full-fledged theocracy: it claimed that the ruler at the top of the hierarchy derived his authority through guidance from ancestors and gods. Shang rulers practiced ancestral worship, which was the major form of religious belief in China during this period. Ancestor worship involved performing rituals in which the rulers offered drink and food to their recently dead ancestors with the hope that they would intervene with their more powerful long-dead ancestors on behalf of the living. Divination was the process by which Shang rulers communicated with ancestors and foretold the future by means of **oracle bones**. Diviners applied intense heat to the shoulder bones of cattle or to turtle shells and interpreted the cracks that appeared on these objects as auspicious or inauspicious signs from the ancestors regarding royal plans and actions. On these so-called oracle bones, scribes subsequently inscribed the queries asked of the ancestors to confirm the diviners' interpretations. Thus, Shang writing began as a dramatic ritual performance in which the living responded to their ancestors' oracular signs.

The oracle bones and tortoise shells offer a window into the concerns and beliefs of the elite groups of these very distant cultures. The questions put to diviners most frequently as they inspected bones and shells involved the weather—hardly surprising in communities so dependent on growing seasons and good harvests—and family health and well-being, especially the prospects of having male children, who would extend the family line.

In Shang theocracy, because the ruler was the head of a unified clergy and embodied both religious and political power, no independent priesthood emerged. Diviners and scribes were subordinate to the ruler and the royal pantheon of ancestors he represented. Ancestor worship sanctified Shang control and legitimized the rulers' lineage, ensuring that the ruling family kept all political and religious power. Because the Shang gods were ancestral deities, the rulers were deified when they died and ranked in descending chronological order. Becoming gods at death, Shang rulers united the world of the living with the world of the dead.

SHANG WRITING

As scribes and priests used their script on oracle bones for the Shang kings, the formal character-based writing of East Asia developed over time. So although Shang scholars did not invent writing in East Asia, they perfected it. Evidence for writing in this era comes entirely from oracle bones, which were central to political and religious authority under the Shang. Other written records may have been on materials that did not survive. This accident of preservation may explain the major differences between the ancient texts in China (primarily divinations on bones) and in the Southwest Asian societies that impressed cuneiform on clay tablets (primarily for economic transactions, literary and religious documents, and historical records). In comparison with the development of writing in Mesopotamia and Egypt, the transition of Shang writing from record keeping (for example, questions to ancestors, lineages of rulers, or economic transactions) to literature (for example, myths about the founding of states) was slower. Shang rulers initially monopolized writing through their scribes, who positioned the royal families at the top of the social and political hierarchy. And priests wrote on the oracle bones to address the otherworld and gain information about the future so that the ruling family would remain at the center of the political system.

As Shang China cultivated developments in agriculture, ornate bronze metalworking, and divinatory writing on oracle bones, the state did not face the repeated waves of pastoral nomadic invaders seen in other parts of Afro-Eurasia. It was nonetheless influenced by the chariot culture that eventually filtered into East Asia. Given that so many of the developments in Shang China bolstered the authority of the dynastic rulers and elite, it is perhaps not surprising that the chariot in China was initially more a marker of elite status than an effective tool for warfare.

Microsocieties in the South Pacific and in the Aegean

As environmental circumstances drove pastoral nomads and transhumant herders toward settled agriculturalists, leading ultimately to the development of powerful and somewhat intertwined territorial states in Egypt, Southwest Asia, the Indus River valley, and Shang China, other pressures drove migrations across the South Pacific and Aegean. These maritime migrations led to the development after 2000 BCE, in such places as Austronesia and the Aegean, of **microsocieties**: small-scale, fragmented, and dispersed communities that had limited interaction with others.

THE SOUTH PACIFIC (2500 BCE–400 CE)

Austronesian-speaking peoples with origins in coastal South China migrated into the South Pacific and formed microsocieties there. While the precise date for the beginning of these migrations is debated among scholars, the proliferation of peoples across the South Pacific was well under way by the third millennium BCE. Using their double-outrigger canoes, which were 60 to 100 feet long and bore huge triangular sails, the early Austronesians crossed

Austronesian Canoe Early Austronesians crossed the Taiwan Straits and colonized key islands in the Pacific using double-outrigger canoes from 60 to 100 feet long equipped with triangular sails. In good weather, such canoes could cover more than 120 miles in a day. This relief, from Borobudur, a later Buddhist temple in Java, shows an eighth-century CE depiction of a double-outrigger canoe.

the Taiwan Straits and colonized key islands in the Pacific. Their vessels were much more advanced than the simple dugout canoes used in inland waterways. In good weather, double-outrigger canoes could cover more than 120 miles in a day. The invention of a stabilization device for deep-sea sailing sometime after 2500 BCE triggered further Austronesian expansion into the Pacific. By 400 CE, these nomads of the sea had reached most of the islands of the South Pacific. Their seafaring skills enabled the Austronesians to monopolize trade wherever they went.

By comparing the vocabularies and grammatical features of languages spoken today by the remaining tribal peoples in Taiwan, the Philippines, and Indonesia, scholars have traced the ancient Austronesian-speaking peoples back to coastal South China in the fourth millennium BCE. Pottery, stone tools, and domesticated crops and pigs also provide markers for tracking Austronesian settlements throughout the coastal islands and in the South Pacific. According to archaeologists, the same cultural features had spread from Taiwan to the Philippines (by 2500 BCE), to Java and Sumatra (by 2000 BCE), and to parts of Australia and New Guinea (by 1600 BCE). The Austronesians then ventured farther eastward into the South Pacific, apparently arriving in Samoa and Fiji in 1200 BCE and on mainland Southeast Asia in 1000 BCE. (See Map 3.5.) The Austronesians reached the Marquesas Islands, strategically located for northern and southern exploration, in the central Pacific around 200 CE. Over the next few centuries, some moved on to Easter Island to the south and Hawaii to the north. The immense 30-ton stone structures on Easter Island represent the monumental Polynesian architecture produced after their arrival.

Equatorial lands in the South Pacific have a tropical or subtropical climate and, in many places, fertile soils containing nutrient-rich volcanic ash. In this environment the Austronesians cultivated dry-land crops (yams and sweet potatoes), irrigated crops (more yams, which grew better in paddy fields or in rainy areas), and harvested tree crops (breadfruit, bananas, and coconuts). In addition, colonized areas beyond the landmass, such as the islands of Indonesia, had labyrinthine coastlines rich in maritime resources, including coral reefs and mangrove swamps teeming with wildlife. Island-hopping led the adventurers to encounter new food sources, but the shallow waters and reefs offered sufficient fish and shellfish for their needs.

In the South Pacific, the Polynesian descendants of the early Austronesians shared a common culture, language, technology, and stores of domesticated plants and animals. These later seafarers came from many different island communities (hence the name *Polynesian*, "belonging to many islands"), and after they settled down, their numbers grew. Their crop surpluses allowed more densely populated communities to support craft specialists and soldiers. Most settlements boasted ceremonial buildings to promote local solidarity and forts to provide defense. On larger islands, communities often cooperated and organized workforces to enclose ponds for fish production and to build and maintain large irrigation works for agriculture. In terms of political structure,

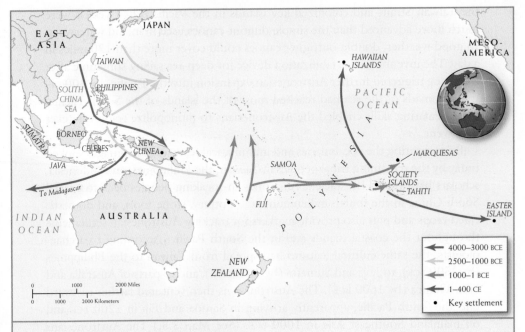

Map 3.5 Austronesian Migrations

....

The Pacific Ocean saw many migrations from East Asia.

- Where did the Austronesian migrants come from? What were the boundaries of their migration? Trace the stages of Austronesian migration over time. Why do you think these migrations took place over such a long time period?

- Why, unlike other migratory people during the second millennium BCE, did Austronesian settlers in Polynesia become a world apart?

Polynesian communities ranged from tribal or village units to multi-island alliances that sometimes invaded other areas.

The expansion of East Asian peoples throughout the South Pacific and their trade back and forth, however, did not integrate the islands into the mainland culture. Expansion could not overcome the tendency of these Austronesian microsocieties, dispersed across a huge ocean, toward fragmentation and isolation.

THE AEGEAN WORLD (2000–1200 BCE)

In the region around the Aegean Sea (the islands and the mainland of present-day Greece), no single power emerged before the second millennium BCE, but island microsocieties (the Minoans and the Mycenaeans) developed an expanding trade network and distinctive cultures. Settled agrarian communities were linked only by trade and culture. Fragmentation was the norm—in part because the landscape had no great river-basin systems or large common plain. In its fragmentation, the island world of the eastern Mediterranean initially resembled that of the South Pacific.

As an unintended benefit of the lack of centralization, there was no single regime to collapse when the droughts arrived. Thus, in the second millennium BCE, peoples of the eastern Mediterranean did not struggle to recover lost grandeur. Rather, they enjoyed a remarkable though gradual development, making advances based on influences they absorbed from Southwest Asia, Egypt, and Europe. Residents of Aegean islands like Crete and Thera enjoyed extensive trade with the Greek mainland, Egypt, Anatolia, Syria, and Palestine. It was also a time of population movements from the Danube region and central Europe into the Mediterranean. Groups of these migrants settled in mainland Greece in the centuries after 1900 BCE; modern archaeologists have named them Mycenaeans after their famous palace at Mycenae. Soon after settling in their new environment, the Mycenaeans turned to the sea to look for resources and interaction with their neighbors.

At the outset, the main influence on the Aegean world came from the east by sea. As the institutions and ideas that had developed in Southwest Asia moved westward, they found a ready reception along the coasts and on the islands of the Mediterranean. Trade was the main source of eastern influences, with vessels carrying cargoes from island to island and up and down the commercial centers along the coast. (See Map 3.6.) Mediterranean trade centered on tin from the east and readily available copper, both essential for making bronze (the primary metal in tools and weapons). Islands such as Cyprus and Crete, located in the midst of the active sea-lanes, flourished. Cyprus had large reserves of copper ore, which started to generate intense activity around 2300 BCE. By 2000 BCE, harbors on the southern and eastern sides of the island were shipping and transshipping goods, along with copper ingots, as far west as Crete, east to the Euphrates River, and south to Egypt.

Minoan Culture Crete, too, was an active trading node in the Mediterranean, and its culture reflected outside influences as well as local traditions. Around 2000 BCE, a large number of independent palace centers began to emerge on Crete, at Knossos (ultimately the most impressive of them) and elsewhere. Scholars have named the people who built these elaborate centers the Minoans, after the legendary King Minos who may have ruled Crete at this time. The Minoans sailed back and forth across the Mediterranean, and by 1600 BCE they were colonizing other Aegean islands as trading and mining centers. The Minoans' wealth soon became a magnet for the Mycenaeans, their mainland competitors, who took over Crete around 1400 BCE.

As the island communities traded with the peoples of Southwest Asia, they borrowed some ideas but also kept their own cultural traditions. In terms of borrowing, the monumental architecture of Southwest Asia found small-scale

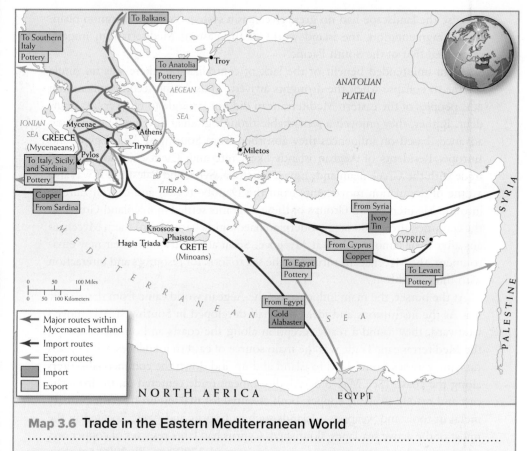

Map 3.6 Trade in the Eastern Mediterranean World

Greece, Egypt, and Cyprus were trade hubs in the eastern Mediterranean.

- What major commodities were traded in the eastern Mediterranean?
- Why did trade originally move from east to west?
- What role did geographic location play in the Mycenaeans' eventual conquest of the Minoans?

echoes in the Aegean world—notably in the palace complexes built on Crete between 1900 and 1600 BCE.

In terms of a distinctive cultural element, worship on the islands focused on a female deity, the "Lady," but there are no traces of large temple complexes similar to those in Mesopotamia, Anatolia, and Egypt. Nor, apparently, was there any priestly class of the type that managed the temple complexes of Southwest Asian societies. Moreover, it is unclear whether these societies had full-time scribes. The so-called Phaistos disk, found in the palace of the city of Phaistos on Crete and measuring just over 6 inches across, is arguably an example of early Minoan writing. Its 242 symbols, spiraling inward from the rim of the disk, were impressed into the clay using 45 different stamps, including a rosette, an ear of grain, olives, fish, and birds. Some have suggested that the text might record a calendar or (most recently) a prayer to a mother goddess; still others insist the text is too limited to be convincingly deciphered.

Perhaps not surprisingly for a fragmented microsociety, there was significant regional diversity within this small Aegean world. On Crete, the large, palace-centered communities controlled centrally organized societies with a high order of refinement. Confident in their wealth and power, the sprawling, airy palaces had no fortifications and no natural defenses. On Thera (modern Santorini), a small island to the north of Crete, a trading city was not centered on a major palace complex but rather featured private houses, with bathrooms including toilets and running water and other rooms decorated with exotic wall paintings. It was this same island of Thera that was the center of a catastrophic volcanic eruption in the mid-second millennium BCE that likely contributed to the decline of the Minoans.

Seaborne Trade Shipwrecks recovered by underwater archaeologists, who work methodically to document their cargo, demonstrate the scale of seaborne trade in the late second millennium BCE. The famous Uluburun shipwreck, which sunk off the southern coast of Turkey around 1325 BCE, was transporting 10 tons of copper and more than 100 amphorae (large two-handled jars) containing all kinds of high-value commodities.

Mycenaean Culture The Mycenaean culture was more war oriented than that of the peaceful, seafaring Minoans. When the Mycenaeans migrated to Greece from central Europe, they brought their Indo-European language, their horse chariots, and their metalworking skills. Their move was gradual, lasting from about 1850 to 1600 BCE, but ultimately they dominated the indigenous population. They maintained their dominance with their powerful weapon, the chariot, until 1200 BCE. The battle chariots and festivities of chariot racing described in the centuries-later epic poetry of Homer's *Iliad* (recounting the legendary Trojan War in which Mycenaean Greeks attacked the city of Troy, in Anatolia) express memories of glorious chariot feats that echo Vedic legends from South Asia. Homer's "Catalog of Greek Ships" (*Iliad* 2.494–759), detailing the many different Greek communities that sent ships of warriors to fight at Troy, also illustrates the diffuse and fragmented political situation, yet common culture and ideals, that bound together the Greek microsociety.

Aegean Fresco This is one of the more striking wall paintings, or frescoes, discovered by archaeologists in the 1970s and 1980s at Akrotiri on the island of Thera (modern Santorini) in the Aegean Sea. Its brilliant colors, especially the blue of the sea, evoke the lively essence of Minoan life on the island. Note the houses of the wealthy along the port and the flotilla of ships that reflects the seaborne commerce that was beginning to flourish in the Mediterranean in this period.

The Mycenaean material culture emphasized displays of weaponry, portraits of armed soldiers, and illustrations of violent conflicts. The main palace centers at Tiryns and Mycenae were the hulking fortresses of warlords surrounded by rough-hewn stone walls and strategically located atop large rock outcroppings. In these fortified urban hubs, a preeminent ruler (*wanax*) stood atop a complex bureaucratic hierarchy. At the heart of the palace society were scribes, who recorded in their Linear B script the goods and services allotted to local farmers, shepherds, and metalworkers, among others. Tombs of the Mycenaean elite contain many gold vessels and ostentatious gold masks. Amber beads in the tombs indicate that the warriors had contacts with inhabitants of northern European coniferous forest regions, whose trees secreted that highly valued resin.

Mycenaean expansion eventually overwhelmed the Minoans on Crete. The Mycenaeans created colonies and trading settlements, reaching as far as Sicily and southern Italy. The trade and language of these early Greek-speaking peoples created a veneer of unity linking the dispersed worlds of the Aegean Sea. Yet, at the close of the second millennium BCE, the eastern Mediterranean faced internal and external convulsions that ended the heyday of these microsocieties. Most notable was a series of migrations of peoples from central Europe who moved through southeastern Europe, Anatolia, and the eastern Mediterranean (see Chapter 4 for more on these Sea Peoples). The invasions, although often destructive, did not extinguish but rather reinforced the creative potential of this frontier area. Because theirs was a closed maritime world—in comparison with the wide-open Pacific—the Greek-speaking peoples around the Aegean quickly reasserted dominance in the eastern Mediterranean that the Austronesians did not match in Southeast Asia or Polynesia.

Conclusion

The second millennium BCE was an era of migrations, warfare, and territorial state building in Afro-Eurasia. Whereas river-basin societies had flourished in the fourth and third millennia BCE in Mesopotamia, Egypt, the Indus Valley, and East Asia, now droughts shook the agrarian foundations of their economies. Old states crumbled; from the steppes and plateaus pastoral nomads and transhumant herders descended in search of food, grazing lands, and other opportunities. As transhumant herders pressed into the river-basin societies, the social and political fabric of these communities changed. Likewise, horse-riding nomads from steppe communities in Inner Eurasia conquered and settled in the agrarian states, bringing key innovations. Foremost were the horse chariots, which became a military catalyst sparking the evolution from smaller states to larger territorial states encompassing crowded cities, vast hinterlands, and broadened trade networks. The nomads and herders also adopted many of the settled peoples' beliefs and customs. On land and sea, migrating peoples created zones of long-distance trade that linked agrarian societies.

Through a range of trade, migrations, and conquest throughout the second millennium BCE, the Nile Delta, the basin of the Tigris and Euphrates Rivers, the Indus Valley, and the Yellow River basin were brought into even closer contact than before. In Southwest Asia and the Nile River basin, the interaction led to an elaborate system of diplomatic relations. The first territorial states appeared in this millennium, composed of multiple communities living under common laws and customs. An alliance of farmers and warriors united agrarian production with political power to create and defend territorial boundaries. The new arrangements overshadowed the nomads' historic role as predators and enabled them to become military elites within these new states. Through taxes and drafted labor, villagers repaid their rulers for local security and state-run diplomacy.

The rhythms of state formation differed where regimes were not closely packed together. In East Asia, for example, the absence of strong rivals allowed the emerging Shang dynasty to develop more gradually. Where landscapes had sharper divisions—as in the island archipelagos of the South Pacific and in the Mediterranean—small-scale, decentralized, and fragmented microsocieties emerged. But fragmentation is not the same as isolation. Even peoples in the worlds apart from the developments across Afro-Eurasia were not entirely secluded from the increasing flows of technologies, languages, goods, and migrants.

Focus On
Comparing First States

Egypt and Southwest Asia

- Invasions by nomads and transhumant herders lead to the creation of larger territorial states: New Kingdom Egypt, the Hittites, and Mesopotamian states.

- Creating a centuries-long peaceful era, a community of major powers emerges among the major states as the result of shrewd statecraft and diplomacy.

Indus River Valley

- Migratory Vedic peoples from the steppes of Inner Eurasia use chariots and rely on domesticated animals to spread out and begin integrating the northern half of South Asia.

Shang State (China)

- Shang dynastic rulers promote improvements in metalworking, agriculture, and the development of writing, leading to the growth of China's first major state.

Microsocieties

- Substantial increases in population, migrations, and trade lead to the emergence of microsocieties among peoples in the South Pacific (Austronesians) and the Aegean world (Minoans and Mycenaeans).

Key Terms

Amorites p. 102	Hittites p. 106	microsocieties p. 116	transhumant herders p. 90
chariot p. 90	Hyksos p. 99	oracle bones p. 114	
Hammurabi's Code p. 103	Indo-European migrations p. 90	pastoral nomads p. 90 territorial state p. 94	Vedic peoples p. 109

CHRONOLOGY

	2500 BCE	2000 BCE
Egypt and Southwest Asia	Middle Kingdom in Egypt 2055–1650 BCE	Hammurabi's Babylonia 1792–1750 BCE
South Asia		
East Asia		
The Mediterranean		
South Pacific	Austronesian migrations 2500 BCE–400 CE	

- **Thinking about Environmental Impacts and Territorial States**
Around 2000 BCE, a series of environmental disasters helped destroy the societies that had thrived in parts of Afro-Eurasia in the third millennium BCE. What were the short-term and long-term impacts of these environmental troubles? How did they influence the movement of peoples and the formation of territorial states in the second millennium BCE?

- **Thinking about Transformation & Conflict and Territorial States** The second millennium BCE witnessed large-scale migrations of nomadic peoples who brought with them their domesticated horses and their chariot technology. These people are referred to by scholars as Indo-Europeans, largely on the basis of their languages.

Contrast the impact of migrations into Southwest Asia (Anatolia and Mesopotamia), Egypt, South Asia, and East Asia. To what extent did conflict play a role in the impact of Indo-European-language speakers on the formation of territorial states?

- **Thinking about Interconnection & Divergence and Territorial States**
While territorial states formed in Egypt, Mesopotamia, South Asia, and East Asia, microsocieties formed in the South Pacific and in the Aegean Sea. What factors influenced whether a region might host a territorial state as opposed to a microsociety? What areas of the planet were still worlds apart? What ways of life continued to predominate in those worlds apart from the territorial states and microsocieties discussed in this chapter?

 Go to INQUIZITIVE to see what you've learned—and learn what you've missed—with personalized feedback along the way.

1500 BCE	1000 BCE	500 BCE

New Kingdom in Egypt 1550–1070 BCE

Community of major powers 1400–1200 BCE

Vedic migration into Indus River valley begins 1500 BCE

Vedic migration into Ganges River valley begins 1000 BCE

Shang state 1600–1046 BCE

Minoan culture in Aegean 2000–1600 BCE

Mycenaean culture in Greece and Aegean 1850–1200 BCE

4

First Empires and Common Cultures in Afro-Eurasia

1250–325 BCE

Core Objectives

- **DESCRIBE** the factors that contributed to the rise of early empires in the centuries after 1200 BCE and the characteristics of these empires.

- **COMPARE** empire formation, or the lack thereof, in Southwest Asia, South Asia, and East Asia in this period.

- **EVALUATE** the connection between empires and war, religion, and trade.

- **ANALYZE** the relationships between empires and the peoples on their peripheries.

Sennacherib—ruler of the Neo-Assyrian Empire early in the seventh century BCE—writes that at the end of one successful campaign he took "200,150 people, great and small, male and female, horses, mules, asses, camels, and sheep without number, I brought away from them and counted them my spoil." The booty about which Sennacherib boasts was unheard of in earlier ages. The immensity of such conquest highlights the arrival of a new era that involved empires with even larger geographical, political, economic, and cultural ambitions and achievements than the territorial states that preceded them (see Chapter 3). Given the nature and process of their formation, these early empires arguably replaced, rather than descended from, the earlier territorial states.

One key factor shaping these developments was warfare spurred by military innovation. Additionally, radical climate change drove many of the warrior/political leaders from the fringes of formerly powerful territorial states to the centers of power. There they established hybrid societies uniting cities and their hinterlands among the Neo-Assyrians and Persians of Southwest Asia, in the Vedic parts of South Asia, and in Zhou China. Imperial ideologies and religious beliefs supported the new empires. Farming yields increased and populations grew. On the fringes of empires, microsocieties arose and made significant contributions to human development: the seafaring Phoenicians developed a simplified alphabet, the Israelites espoused a strict monotheism, and Greek city-states came to the fore and even began to challenge the power of the Persian Empire.

Global Storyline

Comparing First Empires and the Beginnings of Judaism

- Climate change, migrations, technological advances, and administrative innovations contribute to the development of the world's first great empires.

- The Neo-Assyrians and then the Persians employ two different approaches to consolidate and maintain empires in Southwest Asia.

- South Asia becomes more culturally integrated despite the absence of a strong, centralized political authority.

- The Zhou dynasty establishes loose political integration in East Asia.

Forces of Upheaval and the Rise of Early Empires

Four related forces shaped the development of early empires in the first millennium BCE: climate change, migrations, new technologies, and administrative innovations. Migrants driven by climate change mingled with settled peoples. Ambitious leaders used innovations in technology and administration to create new states that went on to conquer other kingdoms. Gradually, a new political organization came into being: the **empire**. An empire is a group of states or different ethnic groups brought together under a single sovereign power. With varying degrees and types of centralization (as we will see in Southwest Asia, South Asia, and East Asia), empires connected distant regions through common languages, unifying political systems, trade, and shared religious beliefs. While most regions of Afro-Eurasia did not experience the rise of empire, those that did, and their neighbors, were profoundly affected by the development.

CLIMATE CHANGE

Beginning around 1200 BCE, another prolonged period of drought gripped Afro-Eurasia, causing social upheavals and migrations and utterly destroying settled societies and long-established governments. Many regions that had enjoyed rapid population growth in the second millennium BCE now found themselves unable to support such large numbers, forcing peoples to leave their homes in search of food and fertile land. (See Map 4.1.)

From the Mediterranean to East Asia, this wave of drought led to dramatic political shifts. In Egypt, low Nile floods forced pharaohs to spend their time securing food supplies and repelling Libyans from the desert and "Sea People" marauders from the coast. In Anatolia, Hittite kings dispatched envoys to the rulers of all the major agricultural areas, pleading for grain shipments to save their starving people. Even the drastic step of moving their capital to northern Syria, where food was more plentiful, did not prevent Hittite collapse. In mainland Greece, Mycenaean culture disintegrated when diminished rains made it impossible for farmers there to export wine, olives, and timber. Likewise in East Asia, radical climate change was a major factor in political developments. Arid conditions on the plains of central Asia resulted in powerful hot and dry winds that carried immense quantities of dust onto the North China plain. The dust storms reduced the soil's ability to retain moisture and led to a sharp decline in soil fertility. Some groups, like the Zhou peoples, went on the move in search of arable land.

MIGRATIONS

The violent movement of peoples, driven in part by climate change, disrupted urban societies and destroyed the administrative centers of kings, priests, and dynasties. Invaders, moving out of loosely organized peripheral societies, assaulted the urban centers and territorial kingdoms of mainland Greece, Crete, Anatolia, Mesopotamia, Egypt, and East Asia, causing the collapse of many of these once powerful states. Marauders from the Mediterranean basin and the Syrian desert upset the diplomatic relations and the elaborate system of international trade that had linked Southwest Asia and North Africa. In East Asia, the Zhou peoples, who by the twelfth century BCE were settled in the valley of the Yellow River's most important tributary, the Wei River in northwestern China, tangled with the Shang authorities and eventually over-whelmed the regime. In the Indus Valley, waves of nomads pressed down from the northwest, drawn by fertile lands to the south. The upheavals caused by these migrations opened the way for new empires to develop, but only after centuries of turmoil and decline.

NEW TECHNOLOGIES

Technological innovations were crucial in reconstructing communities that had been devastated by drought and violent population movements. Advances in the use of pack camels, seaworthy vessels, iron tools for cultivation, and iron weapons for warfare facilitated the rise of empires.

The camel—first the one-humped Saharan dromedary and later the hardier two-humped Bactrian camel—helped open up trade routes across Afro-Eurasia. The fat stored in camels' humps allows them to survive long journeys and harsh desert conditions, and thick pads under their hoofs enable them to walk smoothly over the difficult terrain that had previously hindered such long-distance exchange. Similarly, new shipbuilding technologies made a significant impact. Whereas boats had once been designed for limited transport on rivers and lakes and along shorelines, new ships boasted larger and better-reinforced hulls. Stronger masts and improved rigging allowed billowing sails to harness wind power more effectively. These innovations, along with improvements in ballast and steering, propelled bold mariners to venture out across large bodies of open water like the Mediterranean Sea.

Innovations in metalworking, in which bronze was supplanted by the harder iron, also facilitated the rise of empires. Iron became the most important and widely used metal from this time onward (hence the term *Iron Age*, sometimes used to describe this period). Although far more abundant than the tin and cop-per used to make bronze, iron is more difficult to extract from ore and to fabri-cate into useful shapes. When the technology to smelt and harden iron advanced, iron tools and weapons replaced those made of bronze. This revolution in met-allurgy brought shifts in agrarian techniques, such as forged-iron-edged plows that allowed farmers to cultivate crops far beyond the traditional floodplains of riverbanks. Farmers could now till more difficult terrain to remove weeds, break up sod, and unearth fertile subsoil. These technological innovations supported larger, more integrated societies.

The Global View

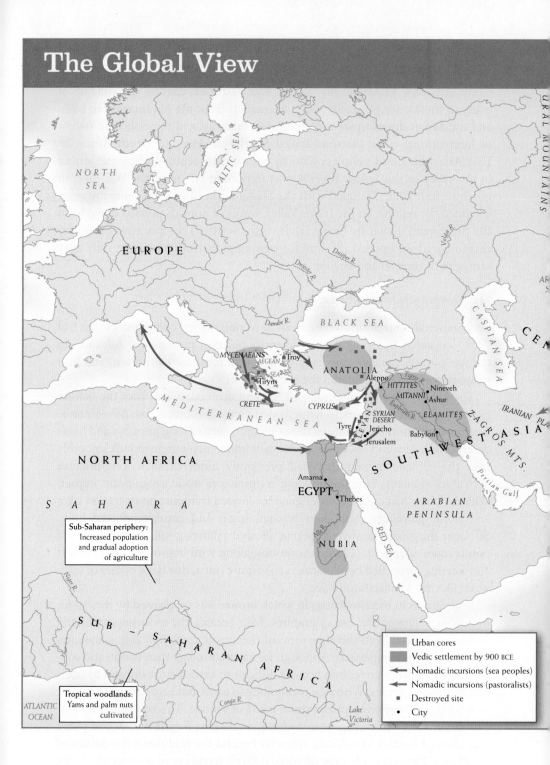

Sub-Saharan periphery:
Increased population
and gradual adoption
of agriculture

Tropical woodlands:
Yams and palm nuts
cultivated

Urban cores

Vedic settlement by 900 BCE

Nomadic incursions (sea peoples)

Nomadic incursions (pastoralists)

Destroyed site

City

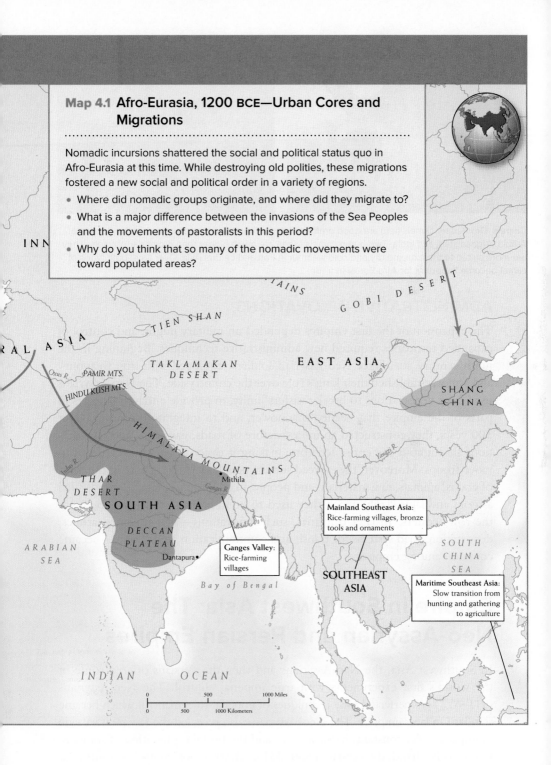

Map 4.1 Afro-Eurasia, 1200 BCE—Urban Cores and Migrations

Nomadic incursions shattered the social and political status quo in Afro-Eurasia at this time. While destroying old polities, these migrations fostered a new social and political order in a variety of regions.

- Where did nomadic groups originate, and where did they migrate to?
- What is a major difference between the invasions of the Sea Peoples and the movements of pastoralists in this period?
- Why do you think that so many of the nomadic movements were toward populated areas?

INN

RAL ASIA

TIEN SHAN

GOBI DESERT

EAST ASIA

Oxus R. PAMIR MTS.

HINDU KUSH MTS.

TAKLAMAKAN DESERT

Yellow R.

SHANG CHINA

HIMALAYA MOUNTAINS

Yangzi R.

THAR DESERT

Indus R.

Mithila
Ganges R.

SOUTH ASIA

DECCAN PLATEAU

Dantapura•

ARABIAN SEA

Ganges Valley: Rice-farming villages

Mainland Southeast Asia: Rice-farming villages, bronze tools and ornaments

SOUTH CHINA SEA

Bay of Bengal

SOUTHEAST ASIA

Maritime Southeast Asia: Slow transition from hunting and gathering to agriculture

INDIAN   OCEAN

| 0 | 500 | 1000 Miles |

| 0 | 500 | 1000 Kilometers |

Camels Dromedary camels (*left*) are good draft animals for travel and domestic work in the deserts of Arabia, Afghanistan, and India. Two-hump camels (*right*) are much bigger than dromedary camels. They are more suited to the extreme dry and cold weather in Iran and central Asia. Over time, both types of camel become important for Afro-Eurasian trade.

ADMINISTRATIVE INNOVATIONS

The expansion of the first empires depended on military might, and control of expanded territories required new administrative techniques. Beginning in the ninth century BCE, fierce Neo-Assyrian soldiers, equipped with iron weaponry and armor, established their king's rule over the countryside. The Neo-Assyrians used mass deportations to break resisters' unity, to provide enslaved laborers in parts of the empire that needed manpower, and to integrate the realm. Over 300 years, they constructed an infrastructure of roads, garrisons, and relay stations throughout the entire territory, making it easier to communicate and to move troops. Moreover, they forced subject peoples to send tribute in the form of grains, animals, raw materials, and people, in addition to precious goods such as gold and lapis lazuli, which they used to build imperial cities and to enrich the royal coffers. In later centuries, such innovations—well-equipped armies, deportation, road systems for transit and communication, and tribute—became common among empires.

Empire in Southwest Asia: The Neo-Assyrian and Persian Empires

In Southwest Asia, the Neo-Assyrians and then the Persians offered some of the world's first experiments with true imperial control. The Neo-Assyrians (911–612 BCE) perfected early techniques of imperial rule, many of which became standard in later empires. The Neo-Assyrians also revealed the raw military side of imperial rule: constant, harsh warfare and the brutal exploitation of subjects. On the other hand, the Persians (560–331 BCE), who took control of Southwest Asia after the Neo-Assyrians, balanced their vast multicultural empire through a gentler combination of centralized administration and imperial ideology.

THE NEO-ASSYRIAN EMPIRE (911–612 BCE)

Defining features of the Neo-Assyrian Empire included deportations, forced labor, and a rigid social hierarchy. Neo-Assyrian rulers divided their empire into two parts and ruled them in different ways. The core of the empire, which the Neo-Assyrians called the "Land of Ashur," included such ancient cities as Ashur and Nineveh on the upper reaches of the Tigris River, and the lands between the Zagros Mountains and the Euphrates River. (See Map 4.2.) The king's appointees governed these interior lands, whose inhabitants had to supply food for the temple of the national god Ashur, manpower for the god's residence in the city of Ashur, and officials to carry out the state's business. Outside the "Land of Ashur" proper lay "the Land under the Yoke of Ashur," whose inhabitants were not considered Neo-Assyrians. In these peripheral territories, local rulers held power as subjects of the Neo-Assyrian Empire. These subordinated states were expected to deliver massive amounts of tribute in the form of gold and silver, as opposed to the manpower or agricultural goods supplied by those in the "Land of Ashur." Tribute went directly to the king, who used it to pay for his extravagant court and ever-increasing military costs.

Forced labor—including serving in the military—and deportations helped integrate the empire and undermine local resistance. The Neo-Assyrian armies were hardened and disciplined professional troops led by officers promoted on the basis of merit, not birth. Their military combined infantry, cavalry, iron weapons, horse-drawn chariots armored with iron plates and carrying expert archers, and siege warfare (complete with massive wheeled siege towers and iron-capped battering rams). The Neo-Assyrian army evolved over time from an all-Neo-Assyrian force that conducted annual summer campaigns to a several-hundred-thousand-strong, year-round force composed of Neo-Assyrians and conquered peoples. By the seventh century BCE, different ethnic groups in the Neo-Assyrian army performed specialized military functions: Phoenicians provided ships and sailors; Medes served as the king's bodyguards; and Israelites supplied charioteers. In addition to a military force, the Neo-Assyrian state needed huge labor forces for agricultural work and for enormous building projects. The Neo-Assyrians recruited most agricultural and construction workers from conquered peoples. Over three centuries, the Neo-Assyrian Empire relocated more than 4 million people, including the whole province of Samaria in present-day Israel and Palestinian territories—a practice that not only supported its stupendous work projects but also undermined local resistance efforts.

Neo-Assyrian Ideology and Propaganda Neo-Assyrian imperial ideology supported and justified its system of expansion, exploitation, and inequality. Even in the early stages of expansion, Neo-Assyrian inscriptions and art expressed a divinely determined destiny that drove the regime to expand westward toward the Mediterranean Sea. The national god Ashur had commanded

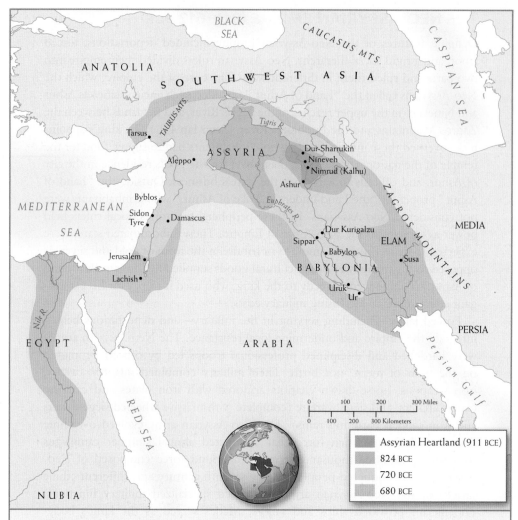

Map 4.2 The Neo-Assyrian Empire

The Neo-Assyrians built the first strong regional empire in Afro-Eurasia. In the process, they faced the challenge of promoting order and stability throughout their diverse realm.

- Where did the Neo-Assyrian Empire expand? How would you compare the various stages of expansion, in terms of timing and geographic reach?
- Which parts of the empire were "the Land of Ashur" and which were "the Land under the Yoke of Ashur"?
- Why do you think expansion after 720 BCE led to the empire's destruction?

all Neo-Assyrians to support the forcible growth of the empire, whose goal was to establish and maintain order and keep an ever-threatening cosmic chaos at bay. Only the god Ashur and his agent, the king, could bring universal order. The king conducted holy war to transform the known world into the well-regulated Land of Ashur, intensifying his campaign of terror and expansion with elaborate propaganda. A three-pronged propaganda program—including elaborate architectural complexes and ceremonies, texts such as inscriptions and year-by-year accounts (annals) of kings' achievements, and vivid images of the army's brutal campaigns—proclaimed that Neo-Assyria's triumph was inevitable.

Tiglath Pileser III The walls of the Neo-Assyrian palaces were lined with stone slabs carved with images of the victories of the king. This fragmentary slab originally decorated the wall of Tiglath Pileser III's palace at Nimrud/Kalhu. It shows the inhabitants and their herds being forced to leave after the defeat of their town by the Neo-Assyrians. Below is Tiglath Pileser III, shaded by his royal umbrella, in his war chariot.

Neo-Assyrian Social Structure

The Neo-Assyrians also exploited a rigid social hierarchy. At the top was the king, who as the sole agent of the god Ashur conducted war to expand the Land of Ashur. Below the king were military elites, rewarded through gifts of land, silver, and exemptions from royal taxes. Over time, these military elites became the noble class and controlled vast estates that included both the land and the local people who worked it. The king and the elites also controlled the most populous part of the society, the peasantry, in which various categories of workers had differing privileges. Many workers were enslaved because they could not pay their debts, but they were allowed to marry partners who were free, conduct financial transactions, and even own property with other enslaved people attached to it. Foreigners enslaved through conquest, however, had no rights and were forced to do hard manual labor on the state's monumental building projects. Those peoples forcibly relocated were not enslaved but they did become attached to the lands that they had to work. Families were small and lived on modest plots of land, where they raised vegetables and planted vineyards.

Neo-Assyrian women were far more restricted than their counterparts in the earlier periods of Sumerian and Old Babylonian Mesopotamia. Under the Neo-Assyrians' patriarchal social system, women had almost no control over their lives. Because all inheritance passed through the male line, it was crucial that a man be certain of the paternity of the children borne by his wives. As a result, all interactions between men and women outside the family were highly restricted.

The so-called Middle Assyrians of the thirteenth century BCE had introduced the practice of veiling, requiring it of all respectable women. Prostitutes who serviced the men of the army and worked in the taverns were forbidden to wear the veil, so that their revealed faces and hair would signal their disreputable status. Any prostitute found wearing the veil would be dragged to the top of the city wall, stripped of her clothing, flogged, and sometimes even killed.

The queens of Neo-Assyria obeyed the same social norms, but their lives were more comfortable and varied than the commoners'. They lived in a separate part of the palace with servants who were either enslaved women or eunuchs (castrated males). Though Neo-Assyrian queens rarely wielded genuine power, they enjoyed respect and recognition, especially in the role of mother of the king. In fact, a queen could serve as regent for her son if the king died while his heir was still a child.

Such was the case with Sammuramat, associated with the quasi-mythical queen Semiramis in Greek sources. Sammuramat served as regent from 810 to 806 BCE, successfully ruling the empire until her son came of age. An early "world historian," the Greek Diodorus Siculus, described the legendary Semiramis as a brilliant military strategist who wore clothes that disguised her gender, beguiled a king through her beauty and intellect into marrying her, built a massive city at Babylon, and undertook daring and far-reaching military campaigns from Egypt to India after her husband's death. The memorial in Ashur to the real Sammuramat, however, in true patriarchal Neo-Assyrian fashion, commemorates her merely by noting her relationship with various male figures: "queen [wife] of Shamshi-Adad, king of the universe, king of Assyria, mother of Adad-nirari, king of the universe, king of Assyria, daughter-in-law of Shalmaneser, king of the four regions."

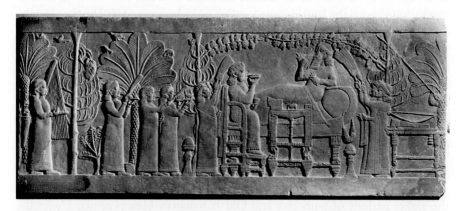

Ashursharrat, Neo-Assyrian Queen While no contemporary images of the exceptional Queen Sammuramat/Semiramis exist, we do get a rare glimpse of a later Neo-Assyrian queen in this relief from Ashurbanipal's palace at Nimrud/Kalhu. Ashursharrat, bedecked in an ornate robe, sits on an elaborately carved chair at the feet of her reclining husband as they celebrate victory in 653 BCE over the Elamite king Te-umman, whose head—in brutal Neo-Assyrian fashion—hangs from the tree on the left.

The Instability of the Neo-Assyrian Empire At their peak, the Neo-Assyrians controlled most of the lands stretching from Persia to Egypt. Yet their empire was unstable, as it required occupying armies to be spread across vast territories and a relentless propaganda machine. Discontent among nobles ultimately led to civil war, which made the Neo-Assyrian Empire vulnerable to external threats as well. The conquest of Nineveh by a combined force of Medes, Neo-Babylonians, and other groups contributed to the collapse of the Neo-Assyrian Empire in 612 BCE.

THE PERSIAN EMPIRE (560–331 BCE)

After a brief interlude of Neo-Babylonian rule—including the reign of Nebuchadnezzar II (r. c. 605–562 BCE) and the creation of his legendary Hanging Gardens of Babylon—the Persians asserted power and created a gentler form of imperial rule in Southwest Asia, based more on persuasion and mutual benefit than on raw power. A nomadic group speaking an Indo-Iranian language, the Persians had arrived on the Iranian plateau from central Asia during the second millennium and gradually spread to the plateau's southwestern part. These expert horsemen shot arrows from horseback with deadly accuracy in the midst of battle. After Cyrus the Great (r. 559–529 BCE) united the Persian tribes, his armies defeated the Lydians in southwestern Anatolia and took over their gold mines, land, and trading routes. He next overpowered the Greek city-states on the Aegean coast of Anatolia. In building their immense empire, the Persians, whose ancestors were pastoralists and had no urban traditions to draw on, adapted the ideologies and institutions of the Neo-Babylonians, the Neo-Assyrians, and indigenous peoples, modifying them to fit their own customs and political aims.

The Integration of a Multicultural Persian Empire From their base on the Iranian plateau, the Persian rulers developed a centralized yet multicultural empire that reached from the Indus Valley to northern Greece and from central Asia to the south of Egypt. (See Map 4.3.) Cyrus, the founder of the Persian Empire, presented himself as a benevolent ruler who had liberated his subjects from the oppression of their own kings. He pointed to his victory in Babylon as a sign that the city's gods had turned against its king as a heretic. Cyrus released the Jews from their captivity in Babylon, to which they had been exiled by the Neo-Babylonian king Nebuchadnezzar II around 587 BCE; they then returned to Jerusalem in 538 BCE to begin rebuilding their temple. Even the Greeks, who later defeated the Persians, saw Cyrus as a model ruler.

In the aftermath of Cyrus's death on the battlefield, Darius I (r. 522–486 BCE) overcame his main rival for power and put the new empire on a solid footing. First, he suppressed revolts across the lands, recording this feat on the Behistun inscription, a monumental rock relief overhanging the road to his capital, Persepolis. Then he conquered territories held by dozens of different ethnic groups, stretching from the Indus River in the east to the Aegean and Mediterranean Seas in the west, and from the Black, Caspian, and Aral Seas in the north to the Nile River in the south. To manage this huge domain, Darius introduced dynamic administrative systems that enabled the empire to flourish for another two centuries. Its new bureaucracy combined central and local administration and made effective use of the strengths of local tradition, economy, and rule—rather than forcing Persian customs on subject people via rigid central control.

This empire was both centralized and multicultural. The Persians believed that all subject peoples were equal; the only requirements were to be loyal to the king and to pay tribute—which was considered an honor, not a burden. Although local Persian administrators used local languages, Aramaic (a dialect of

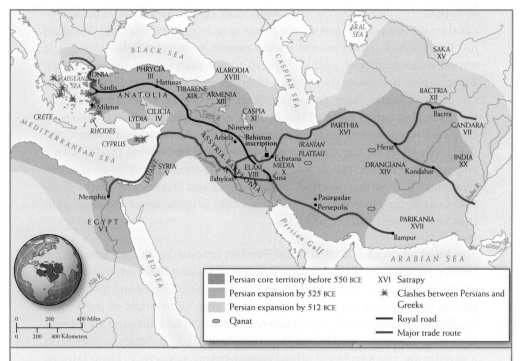

Map 4.3 The Persian Empire, 550–479 BCE

Starting in the sixth century BCE, the Persians succeeded the Neo-Assyrians as rulers of the large regional empire of Southwest Asia and parts of North Africa. Compare the Persian Empire's territorial domains with those of the Neo-Assyrian Empire in Map 4.2.

- Geographically, how did the Persian Empire differ from the Neo-Assyrian state?
- Analyzing the map, how many Persian satrapies existed? What role do you think they played in the success of the Persian Empire?
- How did *qanats* and road systems help the Persians consolidate their imperial power?

a Semitic language long spoken in Southwest Asia) became the empire's official language because many of its literate scribes came from Mesopotamia. Darius brought the wealth of the periphery to the imperial center by establishing a system of provinces, or **satrapies**, each ruled by a governor (called a satrap) who was a relative or a close associate of the king. The local bureaucrats and officials who administered the government worked under close monitoring by military officers, central tax collectors, and spies (the so-called eyes of the king) who enforced the satraps' loyalty. Darius established a system of fixed taxation and formal tribute allocations. Moreover, he promoted trade throughout the empire by building roads, establishing a standardized currency including coinage, and introducing standard weights and measures. These strategies helped integrate and centralize the empire's vast territories.

Zoroastrianism, Ideology, and Social Structure The Persians built their ideology of kingship and their social structure on religious foundations. They drew their religious ideas from their pastoral and tribal roots, and thus their ideology reflected traditions of warrior and priestly classes similar to those preserved in the Vedic texts of the Indus Valley. Zoroaster (also known as Zarathustra), who most likely lived sometime after 1000 BCE in eastern Iran, crystallized the region's traditional beliefs into a formal religious system. The main source for the teachings of Zoroaster is the Avesta, a collection of holy works initially transmitted orally by priests and then, according to legend, written down in the third century BCE. **Zoroastrianism** ultimately became the religion of the empire.

Zoroaster promoted belief in the god Ahura Mazda, who had created the world and all that was good. In dualistic contrast, Ahura Mazda's adversary, Ahriman, was deceitful and wicked. The Persians saw these two forces—light and truth versus darkness and lies—as engaged in a cosmic struggle for control of the universe. Zoroastrianism treated humans as capable of choosing between good and evil. Human choices had consequences: rewards or punishments in the afterlife. Strict rules of behavior determined the fate of each individual. For example, because animals were good, they deserved to be treated well. Intoxicants, widely used in tribal religions, were forbidden. Also, there were strict rules for treatment of the dead. For example, to prevent death from contaminating the sacred elements of earth, fire, and water, it was forbidden to bury, burn, or drown the deceased. Instead, people left corpses out for beasts and birds of prey to devour. The Greek historian Herodotus, who investigated the customs of the Persians in his attempt to explore the background of the Greco-Persian wars in the early fifth century BCE, was perplexed by this practice and reported that Persian corpses were mangled by birds or dogs and then encased in wax before burial.

Persians believed that their kings were appointed by Ahura Mazda as ruler over all peoples and all lands of the earth and charged by him with maintaining perfect order from which all creation would benefit. As such, kings enjoyed absolute authority. In return, they were expected to follow moral and political guidelines that reflected Zoroastrian notions of ethical behavior. Kings also had to show physical superiority that matched their moral standing. They had to be expert horsemen and peerless in wielding bows and spears. These were qualities valued by all Persian nobles, who revered the virtues of their nomadic ancestors. According to the ancient Greek historian Herodotus, Persian boys were taught three things only: "to ride, to shoot with the bow, and to tell the truth."

The Persian social order included four diverse groups with well-defined roles. A ruling class consisted of priests maintaining the ritual fire in temples, nobles administering the state, and warriors protecting and expanding the empire. An administrative and commercial class included scribes and bureaucrats who kept imperial records and merchants who secured goods from distant lands. The other two groups were made up of artisans and, finally, peasants who grew the crops and tended the flocks that fed the imperial machine.

The powerful Persian hereditary nobility surrounded and supported the king. These nobles had vast landholdings and often served the king as satraps or advisers. Also close to the king were wealthy merchants who directed trade across the vast empire. Royal gifts solidified the relations between king and nobles, reinforcing the king's place at the top of the political and social pyramid. In public ceremonies the king presented gold vessels, elaborate textiles, and jewelry to reward each recipient's loyalty and demonstrate dependence on the crown. Any kind of failure would result in the withdrawal of royal favor. Should such failures be serious or treasonous, the offenders faced torture and death. In Persian society, class and royal favor counted for everything.

Public Works and Imperial Identity The Persians undertook significant building projects that helped unify their empire and consolidate imperial identity. For one, the Persians engaged in large-scale road building and constructed a system of rapid and dependable communication. The key element in the system was the Royal Road, which followed age-old trade routes some 1,600 miles from western Anatolia to the heart of the empire in southwestern Iran; trade routes continued eastward across the northern Iranian plateau and into central Asia. Traders used the Royal Road, as did the Persian army; subjects took tribute to the king, and royal couriers carried messages to the satraps and imperial armies over this road. As the Neo-Assyrians had done, the Persians placed way stations with fresh mounts and provisions along the route. Known routes and connections like these helped merchants conduct long-distance trade. Many examples of this trade can be found in the Egibi family's archive of more than 1,700 texts that span more than 120 years, from 606 to 484 BCE. These texts document the Egibis' trade in agricultural goods like barley, dates, onions, and wool across the region controlled by the Neo-Babylonians and then the Persians.

In addition to the Royal Road, the Persians devised other ways to connect the far reaches of the empire with its center. Darius oversaw the construction of a

Persian Water-Moving Technique The Persians perfected the channeling of water over long distances through underground channels called *qanats*. This technique, an efficient way to move water without evaporation, is still used today in hot, arid regions. In this example near Yazd, in central Iran, the domed structure leading to the underground tunnel is flanked by two brick towers called *badgir* (wind towers), an ancient form of air conditioning that cools the water using *bad* (the Persian word for wind).

canal more than 50 miles long linking the Red Sea to the Nile River. Additionally, Persians developed a system of *qanats,* underground tunnels through which water flowed over long distances without evaporating or being contaminated. Laborers from local populations toiled on these feats of engineering as part of their obligations as subjects of the empire.

Until Cyrus's time, the Persians had been pastoral nomads who lacked traditions of monumental architecture, visual arts, or written literature or history. Multiple capitals—at Persepolis, Pasargadae, and Susa—expressed a Persian imperial identity. Skilled craftworkers from all over the empire blended their distinct cultural influences into a new Persian architectural style. The Persians used monumental architecture with grand columned halls and huge open spaces to provide reception rooms for thousands of representatives bringing tribute from all over the empire and to help integrate subject peoples by connecting them to one central, imperial authority. In the royal palace, three of the columned halls stood on raised platforms accessed via processional stairways that were lined with elaborate images of subjects bringing gifts and tribute to the king. This highly refined program of visual propaganda showed the Persian Empire

Persepolis In the highland valley of Fars, the homeland of the Persians, Darius and his successors built a capital city and ceremonial center at the site of Persepolis. On top of a huge platform, there were audience halls, a massive treasury, the harem, and residential spaces. The largest palace, called the Apadana, was constructed of mud brick. The roof was supported by enormous columns projecting the images of bulls.

as a society of diverse but obedient peoples. The carvings on the great stairway of Persepolis demonstrate the range of peoples who visited the palace, each bringing distinctive tribute: the Armenians presenting precious metal vessels, the Lydians carrying gold armlets and bowls, the Egyptians offering exotic animals, and the Sogdians leading proud horses.

While the stream of tribute ebbed and flowed over time, the multicultural Persian Empire was able to hold power in Southwest Asia for more than 200 years. Although the empire was weakened by challenges posed by Greek city-states to its west in the fifth century BCE, it persisted until it fell to the invading army of Alexander the Great in 331 BCE. First the Neo-Assyrians, and then later the Persians, had fashioned their own brands of empire that used a combination of military force, rigid political and social organization, and religious ideology to maintain successive control over Southwest Asia.

Imperial Fringes in Western Afro-Eurasia

A very different world emerged on Afro-Eurasia's western edges. Although their powerful neighbors affected them, western peoples—such as the Sea Peoples, the Greeks, the Phoenicians, and the Israelites—retained their own languages, beliefs, and systems of rule. While their communities were smaller than those in Southwest Asia, each asserted power and had long-lasting influence disproportionate to their size.

SEA PEOPLES

New migrations brought violent change to long-established kingdoms and states in the Mediterranean and Southwest Asia. Beginning around 1200 BCE, as the full effects of drought struck, new waves of Indo-European-speaking peoples left the Danube River basin in central Europe. A rapid rise in population and the development of local natural resources, particularly iron, spurred this group, who came to be known as the **Sea Peoples**, to move down the Danube toward the Black Sea. The invaders, armed with iron weaponry, brought turmoil to the peoples living in southeastern Europe, the Aegean, and the eastern Mediterranean.

The Hittites of Anatolia were the first to fall to the migrants' invasion. Once the invaders reached the Mediterranean, they mainly used boats for transportation, hence the label Sea Peoples (not a name they called themselves but rather one from the perspective of those whom they attacked). The Egyptians knew them as the Peleset, and only with great difficulty did the pharaohs repel them. Ramses III's mortuary temple in Thebes displays a massive relief depicting the so-called Battle of the Delta (c. 1175 BCE), in which he and his Egyptian forces fought off their invasions. Outside Egypt, other states and kingdoms suffered heavily from their ravages. The great trading cities of the Levant, especially Ugarit, an important port city in what is today northern Syria, were destroyed in the tumultuous movement of peoples in the twelfth century BCE. In the remains of the destroyed palace, cuneiform tablets were found that report on the impending disaster in vivid detail. One of the tablets sent to the king warns of the arrival of the *hapiru*, one of the threatening nomad peoples, and asks the ruler to prepare 150 ships for defense. Another, earlier tablet sent by the king of Ugarit to the king of Alashia (Cyprus) describes the threat, saying, "Behold, the enemy's ships came [here]; my cities were burned, and they did evil things to my country. . . . May my father know it: the seven ships of the enemy that came here inflicted much damage to us." All the major centers of the coast and inland were burned to the ground, including Alalakh, Hamath, Qatna, and Kadesh. Many were never reoccupied. The Sea Peoples ultimately settled along the southern coast of Southwest Asia, where they became known as the Philistines.

In the Mediterranean, the Sea Peoples' intrusion shook the social order of the Minoans on the island of Crete (see Chapter 3).

Mycenaean Arms and Armor This Mycenaean vase illustrates the central role of arms and war to the societies on mainland Greece through 1200 BCE. The men bear common suits of armor and weapons—helmets, corsets, spears, and shields—most likely supplied to them by the palace-centered organizations to which they belonged. Despite these advantages, they were not able to mount a successful defense against the land incursions that destroyed the Mycenaean palaces toward the end of the thirteenth century BCE.

Agricultural production in the region declined, and as the palace-centered bureaucracies and priesthoods of the second millennium BCE vanished, more violent societies emerged that relied on the newcomers' iron weapons. These more warlike Mycenaeans, who lived in one of the marginal areas of the Greek mainland and were dependent for their livelihood on exporting olives, wine, and timber, were hard hit by the political, economic, and climate-related problems wracking the eastern Mediterranean at the end of the second millennium BCE. Diminished rains made it impossible for farmers there to export these products and led to the disintegration of their culture. As a result, the Greek mainland experienced a 400-year period of economic decline, vividly captured by the Athenian historian Thucydides, writing in the fifth century BCE. Looking back on a dismal past, he remembered a dark age, "when there was no commerce, when people did not have dealings with each other without fear either on land or sea, when they only cultivated enough of their own land to provide a living for themselves." This was the culture of warrior-heroes described in the *Iliad*, an epic poem about the Trojan War, based on oral tales passed down for centuries before their compilation by Homer in the eighth century BCE. The Greek descendants of these warrior-heroes of the Mycenaean past developed dynamic communities and, as we will see in the next section, offered one of the most significant challenges to the Persians.

THE GREEKS

While the Neo-Assyrians and then the Persians thrived in Southwest Asia, the Greek city-states of the Peloponnese, of the Aegean islands, and along the west coast of Anatolia were experimenting with a range of political systems, from the dual kingship of warlike Sparta to the aristocracy, brief tyranny, and then democracy of Athens. Even with their political differences, the Greeks of the so-called Archaic period (from the eighth through the sixth century BCE) shared a language, religion, and culture that united them. The Olympic Games, celebrated to honor Zeus beginning in 776 BCE, were an example of that shared Panhellenic ideal. The Greek city-states, for all their differences, offer a good example of the energy and dynamism of a comparably small-scale society emerging in the shadow of the Persians. In areas of contact with the Persian Empire, Greek-speaking people in different cities sometimes cooperated with the Persians, even borrowing their ideas, but sometimes strongly resisted them.

In 499 BCE, some Greek city-states and others in the eastern Mediterranean revolted against the Persians, who claimed control over the Greek islands and mainland. During the six-year struggle, some Greek communities sided with the Persians and suffered condemnation by other Greeks for doing so. On the mainland, most Greek cities resisted the Persian king's authority. In 490 BCE, Darius and his vast army invaded mainland Greece but suffered a humiliating defeat at the hands of the much smaller force of Athenians at Marathon, near Athens. The Persians retreated and waited another decade before challenging their western foe again. Meanwhile, however, Athens was becoming a major sea power.

Under the leadership of Themistocles in the 480s BCE, Athens became a naval power whose strength was its fleet of triremes (battleships). When Greek and Persian forces clashed again in 480 BCE, Persian land forces led by Darius's successor Xerxes fought through Leonidas's 300 Spartans (and other Greeks) at Thermopylae only to have their navy lose the pivotal sea battle at Salamis. A year later, the Persians suffered a decisive defeat on land and eventually lost the war. Persian military defeats changed the balance of power. For the next 150 years, Persia lost ground to the Greeks, who gradually regained territory in southeastern Europe and western Anatolia. That expanded territory, and its governance, would become in the fifth century BCE the root of Greek civil discord (see Chapter 5).

THE PHOENICIANS

Another important group on the fringes extended its influence across the Mediterranean through its seafaring and trade: this group was the Chanani (called "Canaanites" in Hebrew scriptures), living in the region of modern-day Lebanon. We know these entrepreneurial people by the name that the Greeks gave them—**Phoenicians** ("purple people")—because of an expensive purple dye that they manufactured and traded. A mixture of the local population and the more recently arrived Sea Peoples, these traders preferred opening up new markets and new ports to subduing frontiers. The Phoenicians maintained their autonomy from Neo-Assyrian kings by supplying them with exotic luxuries. Phoenician coastal cities were ideally situated to develop trade throughout the entire Mediterranean basin. Inland stood an extraordinary forest of massive cedars—perfect timber for making large, seaworthy craft, and a highly desirable export to the treeless heartlands of Egypt and Mesopotamia. (See Map 4.4.)

Innovations in shipbuilding and seafaring enabled Phoenicians to sail as far west as present-day Morocco and Spain, carrying huge cargoes of such goods as timber, dyed cloth, glassware, wines, textiles, copper ingots, and carved ivory. Their trading colonies all around the southern and western rims of the

Greeks at War This fifth-century BCE krater (a 2-foot-tall wine-mixing vessel) illustrates an Amazonomachy. This scene—oft repeated in a variety of media—shows helmeted, shield-carrying, spear-wielding Greek warriors fighting against Amazons who serve as a stand-in for the recently defeated Persian foe. Fifth-century BCE art, including murals and large-scale friezes over the entryways of temples as well as smaller-scale imagery on pottery, focused more on such mythical/legendary events than on recent historical battles.

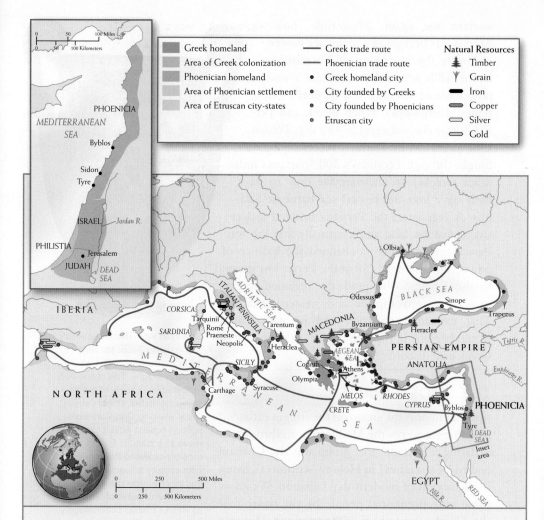

Map 4.4 The Mediterranean World, 1000–400 BCE

Peoples on the fringes of the great regional empires of Southwest Asia and North Africa had strong influences beyond their borders, despite their political marginalization. Though politically dwarfed by the Neo-Assyrian and Persian Empires, various groups in the Mediterranean basin displayed strong cultural and economic power.

- What were the borderland communities, and what did they trade?
- How far did their trading networks and settlement patterns extend?
- Why were such small communities able to flourish in terms of trade and settlement?

Mediterranean (including Carthage in modern-day Tunisia) became major ports that shipped goods from interior regions throughout the Mediterranean. There they competed with Greek colonies that were similarly settling in the western Mediterranean to pursue commerce and relieve population pressures. While the Phoenicians are noteworthy for their seafaring and trade, they are perhaps best known for their revolutionizing of commerce and communication through their development of the **alphabet** in the mid-second millennium BCE. This new method of writing arrived in the west in 800 BCE, probably through Greek traders working in Phoenician centers. The alphabet allowed educated people to communicate directly with one another, dramatically reducing the need for professional scribes. The Phoenicians' trade and their alphabet allowed this "fringe" group to exert influence far beyond the confines of their political borders.

THE ISRAELITES

To the south of the mountains of Lebanon, the homeland of the Phoenicians, another minor region extended to the borderlands of Egypt. In this narrow strip of land between the Mediterranean Sea to the west and the desert to the east, an important microsociety emerged, that of the Israelites. The Israelites' own later stories emphasized their beginnings in Mesopotamia to the east and their patriarch Abraham's origin in the city of Ur on the Euphrates. Later stories stressed their connections with pharaonic Egypt to the west and the mass movement of a captive Israelite population out of Egypt under Moses in the late second millennium BCE. Archaeological evidence suggests that a local culture emerged in the area of present-day Israel between 1200 and 1000 BCE. These developments culminated in a kingdom centered at Jerusalem under King David (r. c. 1000–960 BCE). The kingdom that David and his successor Solomon (r. c. 960–930 BCE) established around Jerusalem, centered on the great temple that Solomon built in the city, did not last long. It fragmented immediately after Solomon's reign, forming the small kingdom of Israel in the north and the smaller Judah in the south.

Within the small kingdom founded by David and Solomon, profound religious and cultural changes took place. Solomon's great temple in Jerusalem outranked all other shrines in the land. The educated upper classes especially, who were linked to the temple, focused on one god, YHWH, over other regional deities in a form of reverence modern scholars call *henotheism* (the recognition of the power of one god over other spirits and deities that still exist). Gradually, however, there was a move to **monotheism** (the acceptance of only one god to the exclusion of all others).

The long transition to monotheism, completed by the seventh century BCE, did not take place without resistance. Challenging the power of kings and priests, prophets like Isaiah (c. 720s BCE), Ezra (c. 600s BCE), and Jeremiah (c. 590s BCE) helped articulate the Israelites' monotheistic religion. Prophets threatened divine annihilation for groups that opposed the new idea of one temple, one god, and one moral system to the exclusion of all others. The Neo-Assyrians to the east figured large in many of the prophets' warnings. Ultimately, the Torah—a series of five books that encapsulated the laws governing all aspects of life, including family and marriage, food, clothing, sex, and worship—became an exclusive "contract" between all these people and their one and only god. As Jewish people scattered over time across Afro-Eurasia, their monotheism would come to have a far-reaching impact.

PHÆNICIAN	ANCIENT GREEK	LATER GREEK	ROMAN
			A
		B	B
		Γ	G
		Δ	D
		E C	E
			F
		Z	Z
			H
		Θ	Th
		I	I
		K	K
		Λ	L
		M	M
		N	N
		Ξ	X
		O	O
		Π	P
			Q
		P	R
		Σ C	S
		T	T

The Phoenician Alphabet *Left:* The first alphabet was written on clay tablets using cuneiform script. It was developed by Phoenician traders who needed a script that was easy to learn so that they could record transactions without specially trained scribes. This tablet was found at the port town of Ugarit (Ras Shamra), in Syria, and is dated to the fourteenth century BCE. *Right:* The forms of the letters in the Phoenician alphabet of the first millennium BCE are based on signs used to represent the Aramaic language. These Phoenician letters were then borrowed by the ancient Greeks. Our alphabet is based on that used by the Romans, who borrowed their letter forms from the later Greek inscriptions.

Foundations of Vedic Culture in South Asia

In South Asia, language and belief systems—rather than a unified political system enforced and enlarged by military conquests—brought people together. Indo-European-speaking peoples, also known as Vedic peoples for the religious traditions they brought with them, entered South Asia through the passes in the Hindu Kush Mountains in the middle of the second millennium BCE and eventually occupied the whole of what are today Pakistan, Bangladesh, and northern India (see Chapter 3). Here the migrant population, together with the indigenous inhabitants, fostered a flourishing culture. Unlike in societies in Southwest Asia, the new rulers in this region did not have previous states on which to found their power. Floods and earthquakes had weakened the earlier Harappan urban centers in the Indus River valley (see Chapter 2), and their urban culture had died out several centuries earlier. Vedic newcomers integrated this territory through a shared culture. Even though the Vedic migrants changed the social and cultural landscape of the region, they did not give it greater political coherence by creating a single, unified regional kingdom.

VEDIC PEOPLES SETTLE DOWN

The men and women who migrated into the northern lands of South Asia were illiterate, chariot-riding, and cattle-keeping pastoral peoples, who lacked experience of cities and urban life. They brought with them much beloved and elaborate rituals, mainly articulated in hymns, called **Vedas** (Sanskrit for "wisdom" or "knowledge"), which they retained as they entered a radically different environment and which they relied on to provide a foundation for assimilating new ways. Transmitted orally, but eventually written down in Sanskrit, Vedic hymns reflected their earlier lives on the plains of central Asia and were infused with images of animals and gods. For example, in some of these Vedic poems storms "gallop" across the heavens, and thunder sounds like the "neigh of horses."

These Indo-European-speaking migrants, equipped with their Vedic traditions, encountered indigenous people who either lived in agricultural settlements or were herders like themselves. They allied themselves with some peoples and made enemies of others. In their interactions with local peoples, the Vedic migrants kept their own language and religious rituals but also absorbed local words and deities. Allies and defeated enemies who became part of their society had to accept Vedic culture. By the middle of the first millennium BCE, the Vedic peoples covered all of what is now northern India, and their language and rituals had become dominant in their new land. (See Map 4.5.)

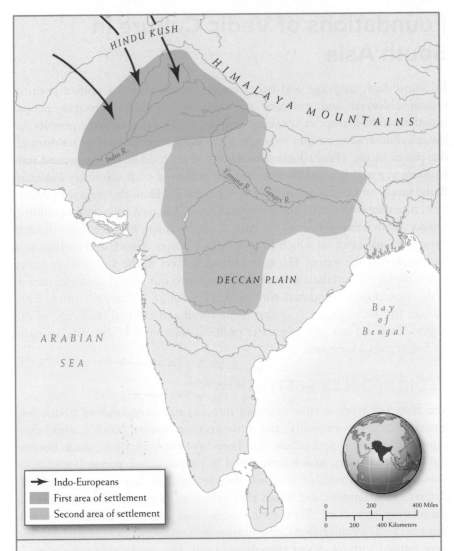

Map 4.5 South Asia, 1500–400 BCE

Indo-European peoples crossed over mountainous areas and entered northern South Asia, bringing with them their nomadic ways. They were, however, quick to learn settled agriculture from the local inhabitants.

- Where did the Indo-Europeans originally come from?
- Where did they settle? What geographical features may have influenced the stages of expansion southward?
- Based on your reading, why did Vedic culture prosper and provide a basis of unity for such large populations?

Vedic elites, with their pastoral nomadic roots, never lost their passion for fine horses, and they created trading routes to the northwest, beyond the Hindu Kush, to maintain a supply of these horses. But as the Vedic peoples entered the fertile river basins, they gradually settled down and turned to agriculture and herding. Indigenous farmers taught the Vedic newcomers farming techniques. For example, the iron plow was crucial for tilling the Ganges plain and transforming the Deccan plateau into croplands. In the drier north, the Vedic peoples grew wheat, barley, millet, and cotton; in the wet lowlands, they cultivated rice paddies. Farmers also produced tropical crops such as sugarcane and spices like pepper, ginger, and cinnamon. With farming success came increased populations and urban settlements across the region, fueled by agricultural surplus and trade in goods, both raw (grain) and manufactured (sugarcane into sugar).

SOCIAL DISTINCTIONS: CLANS AND *VARNA*

Over time, Vedic societies became more complex and less egalitarian than those of their pastoral ancestors. In the process of fanning out across the five tributaries of the Indus River and settling in the plain between the Ganges and Yamuna Rivers, the Vedic peoples created small regional governments and chieftainships. Jockeying for land and resources, they fought fiercely with the indigenous peoples and even more fiercely among themselves.

Vedic chieftainships eventually became small kingdoms with inhabitants bound to each other through lines of descent from a common ancestor. They traced their lineage—identified as either solar or lunar—through blood ties, marriage alliances, and invented family relations. The two lineages, solar and lunar, included many *clans* (groups of households claiming descent from a common ancestor) in which seniority determined one's power and importance. The Vedic peoples absorbed many local clans into their own lineages. Clans that adopted the Vedic culture became part of the lineage (through marriage or made-up ties) and were considered insiders. In contrast, clans that had other languages and rituals were considered to be uncivilized outsiders. These two lineages became less important over time, but were memorialized in the later *Mahabharata*, one of the two major Sanskrit epics of ancient India, which relates the last phase of the lunar lineage, and the *Ramayana*, the second Sanskrit epic, which celebrates a hero of the solar lineage.

As Vedic peoples settled into agrarian communities after 1000 BCE, their social structure became even more complex and hierarchical. Among other distinctions, divisions developed between those who controlled the land and those who worked it. Vedic peoples used the term **varna** to refer to their rigid status distinction and recognized four ranked social groups into which one was born—Brahmans, Kshatriyas, Vaishyas, and Shudras. Since the Sanskrit word *varna* means "color," its use suggests that the four-class system originated in the encounter between clans and communities of different complexions and

Scenes from the *Mahabharata* Reliefs on the walls of the Kailasa Temple in the Ellora Cave complex in northwest India depict scenes from the *Mahabharata* and the *Ramayana*. While these images were carved in the eighth century CE, they illustrate scenes from these epics that recount the distant Vedic past thousands of years earlier, when the lunar and solar lineages struggled against one another and among themselves. Archers, war elephants, chariots, hand-to-hand combat, and diplomatic scenes combine on this relief to narrate the main battle from the *Mahabharata* between two rival factions of the lunar lineage.

cultures. Vedic hymns described the origins of the *varnas* in their creation narrative. When the gods sacrificed Purusha to create the universe, the Brahmans (priests) came from his mouth, his arms produced the Kshatriyas (warriors), the thighs gave birth to the Vaishyas (commoners), and from the feet emerged the Shudras (laborers and servants).

Clan members who had been politically the most powerful and had led their communities into northern India claimed the status of Kshatriyas. It was they who controlled the land. Less powerful clan members, who worked the land and tended livestock, became Vaishyas. Paid and enslaved laborers who served in the households and fields of the Vaishyas came from outside the Vedic lineages and became known as Shudras. Brahmans claimed the highest status, for they performed the rituals and understood the religious principles without which life was believed to be unsustainable. Brahmans and Kshatriyas reinforced each other's high status. Brahmans performed the sacrifices that converted warriors into kings, and kings reciprocated by paying fees and gifts to the Brahmans. Vaishyas and Shudras were left with the tasks of ensuring the sustenance of the elite. The Brahmans guided a society in which the proper relationship with the forces of nature as represented by the deities constituted the basis of prosperity. As agriculture became ever more important, Brahmans acted as agents of Agni, the god of fire, to purify the new land for cultivation. This complex hierarchy, so inextricably connected with Vedic religion, provided the primary unifying structure for society in South Asia.

UNITY THROUGH THE VEDAS AND UPANISHADS

A Vedic culture, transmitted from generation to generation by the Brahmans, unified what political rivalries had divided. A common language (Sanskrit); belief in Agni, Indra, and other gods; and shared cultural symbols linked the dispersed communities and gave Vedic peoples a collective identity. Though Sanskrit was a language imported from central Asia, the people used it to transmit the Vedas orally. By expressing sacred knowledge in the rhythms and rhymes of Sanskrit, the Vedic peoples effectively passed on their culture from one generation to the next.

The Vedas promoted cultural unity and pride through common ritual practices and support for hereditary leaders. As the priests of Vedic society, the Brahmans were responsible for memorizing the Vedic works. These included commentaries on sacred works from early nomadic times as well as new rules and rituals explaining the settled, farming way of life. The main body of Vedic literature includes the four Vedas: Rig-Veda, Sama-Veda, Yajur-Veda, and Atharva-Veda. The Rig-Veda, the earliest text, is a collection of hymns praising the gods, including Indra (god of war), Agni (god of fire), and Varuna (god of water). The Sama-Veda is a textbook of songs for priests to perform when making ritual sacrifices; most of its stanzas also appear in the Rig-Veda. The Yajur-Veda is a prayer book for the priest who conducted rituals for chariot races, horse sacrifices, or the king's coronation. The Atharva-Veda includes charms and remedies; many address problems related to agriculture, a central aspect of life. Although the Vedic period left no impressive buildings and artifacts, the Vedas laid the socioreligious foundations for South Asia.

During the middle of the first millennium BCE, some thinkers (mostly Brahman ascetics dwelling in forests) felt that the Vedic rituals no longer provided satisfactory answers to the many questions of a rapidly changing society. The result was a collection of works known as the **Upanishads**, or "the supreme knowledge," which expanded the Vedic cultural system. Taking the form of dialogues between disciples and a sage, the Upanishads offered insights into the ideal social order. The Upanishads teach that

Gold Coin of Kumaragupta I
Kumaragupta I's coin, dating from the fifth century CE, intentionally drew on much older Vedic concepts (including the Ashvamedha, or horse sacrifice from the Yajur-Veda) and imagery (here, a Hindu goddess).

people are not separate from each other but belong to a cosmic universe called Brahma. While the physical world is always changing and is filled with chaos and illusion, *atman*, the eternal being, exists in all people and all creatures. Atman's presence in each living being makes all creatures part of a universal soul. Although all living beings must die, atman guarantees eternal life, ensuring that souls are reborn and transmigrate into new lives. This cycle continues with humans as they are reborn either as humans or as other living creatures, like cows, insects, or plants.

These unique views of life and the universe, as outlined in the Vedas and Upanishads, were passed along as principles of faith, bringing spiritual unity to the northern half of South Asia because local gods could easily be absorbed into the system. Unlike in Southwest Asia, here in the kingdoms of the Indus Valley and the Ganges plain the common Vedic culture—rather than larger political units—was the unifying bond.

The Early Zhou Empire in East Asia

In China, the Zhou succeeded the Shang state, and Zhou rulers built a powerful tributary empire, claiming the "mandate of heaven." The Zhou had been only a minor state during the Shang's political preeminence; during that period, the Zhou and the Shang had lived side by side, trading and often allying with each other to fend off raiders from the northwest. The appearance of a dynamic leader among the Zhou peoples, King Wu, and the need to find more resources after drought-related dust storms swept across the North China plain, emboldened the Zhou to challenge the Shang. At a battle in 1045 BCE, the Zhou prevailed. King Wu of the Zhou owed his success to his army of 45,000 troops and their superior weaponry, which included dagger axes, bronze armor, and 300 war chariots (small numbers by Southwest Asian standards, but overwhelming in East Asia). (See Map 4.6.) In the centuries that followed, innovations in politics, agriculture, and social structures helped the Zhou integrate their empire.

DYNASTIC INSTITUTIONS AND CONTROL OF THE LAND

When the Zhou took over from the Shang, their new state consisted of more than seventy small states, whose rulers accepted the overarching authority of the Zhou kings. To solidify their power, the Zhou copied the Shang's patrimonial state structure, centered on ancestor worship in which the rulers' power passed down through a lineage of male ancestors reaching back to the gods. Thirty-nine Zhou kings followed one after the other, mostly in an orderly father-to-son succession, over a span of eight centuries.

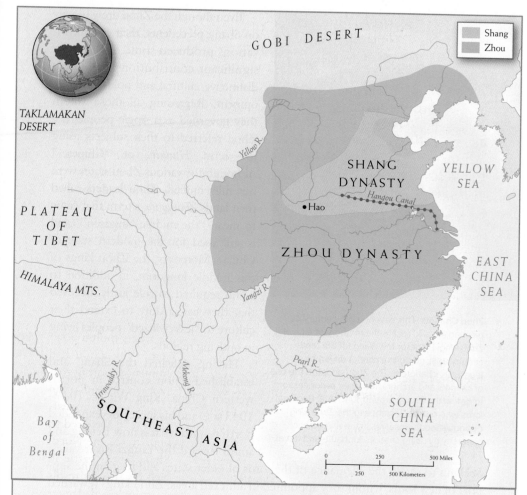

Map 4.6 The Shang and Zhou Dynasties, 2200–256 BCE

Toward the end of the second millennium BCE, the Zhou state supplanted the Shang state as the most powerful political force in East Asia. Using the map, compare and contrast the territorial reach of the Zhou state with that of the Shang.

- In what direction did the Zhou state expand most dramatically?
- As you view the map, why do you think that the Zhou did not expand farther northward and westward?
- Based on your reading, how did the Zhou integrate their geographically large and diverse state?

Zhou Chariots This seventeenth-century CE painting (on silk) recalls the memory of a pivotal Zhou king, Emperor Mu Wang (of the tenth century BCE), riding in a chariot driven by a legendary charioteer. The Zhou adapted the use of chariots and archers from their predecessors to defeat the Shang around 1045 BCE. Regional lords who owed allegiance to the Zhou king distinguished themselves in the aristocratic hierarchy by using chariots for battle and travel.

Even though the Zhou drew heavily on Shang precedents, their own innovations produced some of the most significant contributions to China's distinctive cultural and political development. Regarding all those whom they governed as a single people, the Zhou referred to their subjects using the term *Huaxia*, or "Chinese." Although the various Zhou states were not fully unified, Zhou leaders called their lands *Zhongguo*, a term that came to mean "the middle kingdom" (and is still used for the modern state of China). Moreover, the Zhou kings of this middle kingdom, in addition to being required to rule justly, believed that they had a duty to extend their culture to "less civilized" peoples living in outlying regions.

Having defeated the Shang and established Zhou control in northwestern China, King Wu (r. 1049–1043 BCE) and his successors expanded north toward what is now Beijing and south toward the Yangzi River valley. Seeking to retain the allegiance of the lords of older states and to gain the support of new lords, whom they appointed in annexed areas, Zhou kings rewarded their political supporters with lands that they could pass on to their descendants. As the Zhou expanded their territory, their new colonies often consisted of garrison towns where the Zhou colonizers lived, surrounded by fields (inhabited by local farmers). As under the Shang, Zhou regional lords supplied military forces as needed, paid tribute, and appeared at the imperial court to pledge their continuing allegiance.

The Zhou leaders promoted the integration of China not only through dynastic institutions but also through agricultural advances (including the iron plow, irrigation, and canals). Wooden and, much later, iron plows enabled farmers to break the hard sod of lands beyond the river basins, and over time cultivators learned the practice of field rotation to prevent soil nutrients from being exhausted. In the middle of the first millennium BCE, regional states organized local efforts to regulate the flow of the main rivers. They built long canals to promote communication and trade, and they dug impressive irrigation networks to convert arid lands into fertile belts. This slow agrarian revolution enabled the Chinese population to soar, reaching perhaps 20 million by the late Zhou era.

Under the Zhou, landowners and rulers organized the construction of dikes and irrigation systems to control the floodplain of the Yellow River and Wei River valley surrounding the capital at Hao (present-day Xi'an). For centuries, peasants labored over this floodplain and its tributaries—building dikes, digging canals, and raising levees as the waters flowed to the sea. When their work was done, the bottom of the floodplain was a latticework of rich, well-watered fields, with carefully manicured terraces rising in gradual steps to higher ground. Eventually, irrigation works grew to such a scale that they required management by the Zhou rulers, centered in the Wei River valley, and their skilled engineers. The engineers also designed canals that connected rivers and supported commerce and other internal exchanges. Tens of thousands of workers spent countless days digging these canals, paying tribute in the form of labor.

The canals linked China's two breadbaskets: wheat and millet fields in the north and rice fields in the south. And as with the Yellow River in the north, engineers controlled the Yangzi River in the south. Nomads in mountainous areas or on the Zhou frontiers, who often fought with the Zhou ruler and his regional lords, began to depend on trade with the fertile heartlands. In these ways, the Zhou promoted greater unity within their territory and among the peoples living in and around it.

"MANDATE OF HEAVEN"

In addition to promoting a Chinese ethnic and political identity and cultivating advances in agriculture, Zhou rulers introduced the long-enduring concept of the **mandate of heaven**, which provided a justification for their rule. Attributed by later Chinese intellectuals to King Wu's younger brother Zhou Gong (often referred to as the Duke of Zhou), the mandate asserted that Zhou moral superiority justified taking over Shang wealth and territories and that heaven had imposed a moral mandate on them to replace the Shang, whom they characterized as evil men whose policies

Zhou Wine Vessel Under the Zhou, bronze metallurgy depended on a large labor force. Many workers initially came from Shang labor groups, who were superior to the Zhou in technology. The use of bronze, such as for this wine vessel, exemplified dynastic continuity between the Shang and Zhou.

brought pain to the people through waste and corruption, and return good governance to the people.

At first Zhou leaders presented the mandate of heaven as a religious compact between the Zhou people and their supreme "sky god" in heaven, but over time Zhou kings and the court detached the concept from the sky god and made the mandate into a freestanding Chinese political doctrine. The Zhou argued that since worldly affairs were supposed to align with those of the heavens, heavenly powers conferred legitimate rights to rule only on their chosen representative. In return, the ruler was duty-bound to uphold heaven's principles of harmony and honor. Any ruler who failed in this duty, who let instability creep into earthly affairs, or who let his people suffer, would lose the mandate. Under this system, spiritual authority withdrew support from any wayward dynasts and found other, more worthy, agents. The Zhou rulers had to acknowledge that any group of rulers, even they themselves, could be ousted if they lost the mandate of heaven because of improper practices.

As part of maintaining their mandate and their legitimacy as rulers, Zhou kings created royal calendars, official documents that defined times for undertaking agricultural activities and celebrating rituals. Unexpected events such as solar eclipses or natural calamities could throw into question the ruling house's mandate. Since rulers claimed that their authority came from heaven, the Zhou perfected the astronomical system on which they based their calendar. Zhou astronomers precisely calculated the length of a lunar month (29.53 days) and the solar year. To resolve the discrepancy between a solar year (365.25 days) and a lunar year (354.36 days), the Zhou occasionally inserted a leap month. Scribes dated the reigns of kings by days and years within a repeating sixty-year cycle.

The Zhou's legitimacy was also grounded in their use of bronze ritual vessels, statues, ornaments, and weapons, the large-scale production of which they borrowed from their Shang predecessors. Like the Shang, the Zhou developed an extensive system of bronze metalworking that required a large force of tribute labor. Many of its members were Shang, who were sometimes forcibly transported to new Zhou towns to produce the bronze ritual objects. These objects, sold and distributed across the lands and used in ceremonial rituals, symbolized Zhou legitimacy.

SOCIAL AND ECONOMIC CONTROLS

As the Chinese social order became more integrated, it also became more class based. Directly under the Zhou ruler and his royal ministers were the hereditary nobles, divided into ranks. These regional lords had landholdings of different sizes. They all owed allegiance to the Zhou king, and they supplied warriors to fight in the king's army and laborers to clear land, drain fields, and do other work. The regional lords periodically appeared at court and took part in complex rituals to reaffirm their allegiance to the king. Below the regional lords were high officers at the Zhou court, as well as ministers and administrators who supervised the people's work. Aristocratic warriors stood at the bottom of the noble hierarchy.

Among commoners, an elaborate occupation-based hierarchy developed over time. Early on, most of the population worked as farmers on fields owned by great landholding families, while some commoners were artisans, such as bronze workers or silk weavers. The later occupation-based system, however, divided people more precisely by function—landholders who produced grain, growers of plants and fruit trees, woodsmen, breeders of cattle and chickens, artisans, merchants, weavers, servants, and those with no fixed occupation—and the central government exerted considerable control over how each group did its job. While reports of this control may be overstated, the system does show a unique attempt by the Zhou government to assert power over the empire's diverse peoples.

The Zhou also made political and legal use of family structures. In their patrilineal society, the Zhou established strict hierarchies for both men and women. Both art and literature celebrated the son who honored his parents. Men and women had different roles in family and ceremonial life. On landholdings, men farmed and hunted, while women produced silk and other textiles and fashioned them into clothing. Wealth increasingly trumped other distinctions, however. In particular, rich women high in the Zhou aristocracy enjoyed a greater range of actions than other women did. And wealthy merchants in emerging cities challenged the authority of local lords.

LIMITS AND DECLINE OF ZHOU POWER

The Zhou state relied on culture (its bronzes) and statecraft (the mandate of heaven) to maintain its leadership among competing powers and lesser principalities in its territories. Rather than having absolute control of an empire (like the Neo-Assyrians and Persians had) or a primarily socioreligious unity (like the Vedic peoples of South Asia had), the Zhou state was first among many regional economic and political allies.

The Zhou dynasty was not highly centralized; instead, it expected regional lords to control the provinces. Military campaigns continued to press into new lands or to defend Zhou holdings from enemies. Rulers interacted with neighbors and allies by giving them power, protecting them from aggression, and intermarrying between dynastic family members and local nobles. Consequently, Zhou subordinates had more than autonomy; they had genuine resources that they could turn against the dynasts at opportune moments.

The power of the Zhou royal house over its regional lords declined in the ninth and eighth centuries BCE. In response, the Zhou court at Hao introduced ritual reforms with grandiose ceremonies featuring larger, standardized bronze vessels. Even this move could not reverse the regime's growing political weakness in dealing with its steppe neighbors and internal regional lords. In 771 BCE, northern steppe invaders forced the Zhou to flee their western capital, ushering in the beginning of what would come to be known as the Spring and Autumn period of the Eastern Zhou dynasty centered at Luoyi (modern Luoyang).

The Zhou dynastic period, like the Shang, was later idealized by Chinese historians as a golden age of wise kings and officials. In fact, the Zhou model of government, culture, and society became the standard for later generations. Though the Neo-Assyrian and Persian superpowers were capable of greater expansion during this period, China was sowing the seeds of a more durable state.

Conclusion

Around 1000 BCE, dramatic changes in political and social structures took place across Afro-Eurasia. Consolidations of power, with varying degrees and types of centralization, formed in Southwest Asia (Neo-Assyrians and Persians), Vedic South Asia, and East Asia (among the Zhou). Driving these sociopolitical developments were changes in climate, invasions by nomadic peoples, technological innovations, and new administrative strategies.

A spectrum of power consolidation—from the highly centralized to the more culturally unified—occurred across Afro-Eurasia. The tightly consolidated Neo-Assyrian and Persian Empires differed in fundamental ways from the earlier city-states and territorial states of this area. They created ideologies, political institutions, and economic ties that extended their power across vast regions. Their strong imperial institutions enabled them to exploit human and material resources at great distances from the imperial centers. At the other end of Afro-Eurasia, the Zhou in East Asia established loose integration of diverse peoples and territories through a powerful dynastic arrangement buttressed by a mandate from heaven, but they could not overcome the power of local nobles or fully protect the western frontier from nomadic attacks. In the Vedic world of the Indus Valley and Ganges plain, shared values and revered texts did not lead to a single major state. An unparalleled degree of cultural, as opposed to political or economic, integration bound together northern South Asia. Many centuries would pass before a regime would layer a state over this shared cultural world.

Empire building did not occur everywhere. The majority of the world's people still lived in smaller political groupings. Even within Afro-Eurasia, some areas were completely untouched. And even where the Neo-Assyrian and Persian rulers, soldiers, and traders came into contact with certain groups, they did not necessarily crush them. For example, the nomadic peoples of the northern steppes and the southern desert locations throughout Eurasia continued to be autonomous. But fewer and fewer were untouched by the technological, cultural, and political pulses of empires.

The peoples living in Southwest Asia (under the Neo-Assyrians and then Persians), in the Vedic society of South Asia, and in the Zhou kingdom of East Asia made lasting contributions to the cultural and religious history of humanity. Late Vedic South Asia spun out the concept of cyclic universal time in the form of reincarnation. And in late Zhou China, an ideal of statecraft and social order took shape. On the fringes of these empires, other groups made lasting contributions. The Phoenicians traversed the whole of the Mediterranean basin and spread their simplified alphabet. From the land of Israel, a budding monotheism sprouted. All evolved into powerful cultural forms that in time spread their influences far beyond their sites of origin.

Focus On
Comparing First Empires and the Beginnings of Judaism

Ancient Near East

- Neo-Assyrians use raw military power and massive population relocations to build and maintain the world's first empire.

- Persians rely on tolerance, their system of satrapies, and Zoroastrianism to build a cosmopolitan empire.

Mediterranean World

- Greeks, Phoenicians, and Israelites show the advantages of small-scale states with innovations in writing, trading, and religious thought.

- Sea Peoples migrate into the region, attacking empires in the eastern Mediterranean, including the Hittites and Egyptians, before settling down in the Levant.

South Asia

- Vedic migrants combine with local populations to build a unified but varna-stratified common culture through religious and economic ties.

- Religious texts, like the Vedas and the Upanishads, bring a cultural unity through their rules, rituals, and traditions.

China

- The Zhou dynasty constructs a powerful tributary state through dynastic institutions and agricultural advances.

- Zhou dynasts legitimate their rule through claiming the mandate of heaven (good governance together with upright behavior equates to legitimate rule), a concept that will become a long-lasting political doctrine in China.

Key Terms

alphabet p. 147	monotheism p. 147	Upanishads p. 153
empire p. 128	Phoenicians p. 145	*varna* p. 151
mandate of heaven p. 157	satrapy p. 139	Vedas p. 149
	Sea Peoples p. 143	Zoroastrianism p. 139

CHRONOLOGY

	1500 BCE	1200 BCE
Southwest Asia and North Africa		
The Mediterranean		
South Asia		
East Asia		

THINKING ABOUT GLOBAL CONNECTIONS

- **Thinking about Power Relationships and the Formation of Empires** From 1250 to 325 BCE, several regional empires with centralized rule developed: in Southwest Asia, the Neo-Assyrians and then the Persians established tightly controlled empires; in East Asia, the Zhou achieved loose political unification; and a culturally integrated people thrived in South Asia. Compare the use of military force and its relationship to political centralization in each of these cases. How does religion help bring unification?

- **Thinking about the Environment and the Formation of Empires** Just as climate change around 2000 BCE contributed to the demise of earlier societies, prolonged drought around 1200 BCE again brought dramatic changes to many areas. Compare the environmental crises in Egypt, Southwest Asia, and East Asia in the late second millennium BCE and their results, especially with respect to empire formation.

- **Thinking about Exchange Networks and the Formation of Empires** While this chapter focuses on the formation of empires, the majority of the world's people lived outside or on the fringes of these empires. The Sea Peoples, after disrupting the Hittites, Greeks, and Egyptians, settled down on the coast of Southwest Asia and became the Philistines; the Phoenicians expanded their trade across the Mediterranean; the Greeks effectively resisted Persian authority; and Jewish Israelites founded a kingdom centered on monotheism. Which had the most significant impact on human history: the centralized empires or the peoples on the fringes and beyond? Why?

 Go to INQUIZITIVE to see what you've learned—and learn what you've missed—with personalized feedback along the way.

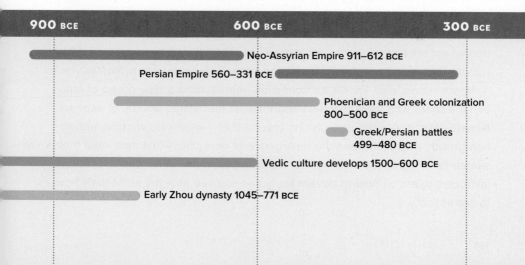

900 BCE | 600 BCE | 300 BCE

Neo-Assyrian Empire 911–612 BCE

Persian Empire 560–331 BCE

Phoenician and Greek colonization 800–500 BCE

Greek/Persian battles 499–480 BCE

Vedic culture develops 1500–600 BCE

Early Zhou dynasty 1045–771 BCE

5

Worlds Turned Inside Out

1000–350 BCE

Core Objectives

- **DESCRIBE** the challenges that Afro-Eurasian empires and states faced in the first millennium BCE, and **COMPARE** the range of solutions they devised.

- **IDENTIFY** Axial Age thinkers and **ANALYZE** their distinctive ideas.

- **EXPLAIN** the relationship between Axial Age thinkers across Afro-Eurasia (East Asia, South Asia, and the Mediterranean) and the political and social situations to which they were responding.

- **COMPARE** the political, cultural, and social developments across Afro-Eurasia with those occurring in the Americas and sub-Saharan Africa.

In the midst of violent struggles for power and territory in China in the sixth century BCE, Master Kong Fuzi instructed his disciples on how to govern, saying: "Guide them by edicts, keep them in line with punishments, and the people will stay out of trouble but will have no sense of shame. Guide them by virtue, keep them in line with the rites, and they will, besides having a sense of shame, reform themselves."

Master Kong, also known as Confucius, represented a new breed of influential leaders who were teachers and thinkers, not kings, priests, or warriors. Nonetheless, it was the convulsions around them—incessant warfare, population growth, migrations, and the emergence of new cities—that motivated their search for insights. By viewing the world in innovative ways, these teachers instructed rulers on how to govern justly and showed ordinary individuals how to live ethically.

The teachers and founders of new ways of thinking from the first millennium BCE, who figure prominently in this chapter, were some of the most influential in history. And their students preserved and passed along their radical new thought. In China, Confucius elaborated a set of principles for ethical living that has guided the Chinese population up to modern times. In South Asia, Siddhartha Gautama (the Buddha) laid out social and spiritual tenets that challenged the traditional social hierarchy based on birth and, with it, the power of the ruling priests and warriors. In Greece, Socrates, Plato, and Aristotle offered ideas that ranged from shaking Greek citizens from their complacency and questioning what they thought they knew about reality to offering a system of logic that conformed to natural and intelligible laws.

The philosophers, theologians, poets, political leaders, and merchants of this era founded literary traditions, articulated new belief systems, and established new political and economic institutions that spread well beyond the places where they began. While wars and havoc raged within their societies and long-distance trade and travel linked societies, these thinkers influenced a world shaped by a search for order and an appetite for new thinking.

Global Storyline

The Axial Age

- A range of challenges—warfare, political upheaval, economic pressures, and social developments—transform the empires and states of Afro-Eurasia.

- "Second-generation" societies arise across Afro-Eurasia in a pivotal period sometimes called the "Axial Age."

- Axial Age thinkers in Afro-Eurasia reshape peoples' views of the world and their place in it.

- Complex new societies develop in the Americas and sub-Saharan Africa.

An "Axial Age"

Some modern thinkers call the mid-first millennium BCE the **Axial Age** to emphasize its pivotal and transitional role between the declining old empires of ancient Egypt, Southwest Asia, northern India, and Zhou China and the later empires of Alexander the Great, Chandragupta's Mauryan Empire in India, Augustus's Rome, and Han Wudi's China (see Chapters 6 and 7). Instrumental to this dynamic period were the ethical, philosophical, and religious innovations taking place in India, China, and Europe.

In this Axial Age, societies on the edges of regional empires or within declining empires of Afro-Eurasia started to follow innovative paths. (See Map 5.1.) These new communities were not just extensions of old ways of life. In each, dramatic innovations in cultural and religious beliefs were expanding people's social, political, and cultural options. Although each of the resulting cultures—in East Asia, South Asia, and the Mediterranean—was distinct from the others, we might call them all **second-generation societies**, given that they built on their predecessors yet represented a departure from ancient legacies.

While Afro-Eurasia experienced an Axial Age and the emergence of second-generation societies, other parts of the world saw complex, urban-based societies emerge for the first time. The first of these in the Americas was established by the Olmecs in Mesoamerica, with artistic and religious reverberations well beyond their homelands. In Africa, distinct regional identities spread in the Upper Nile (in Nubia) and West Africa (among the Nok). One of the most striking features of the first millennium BCE is the long-lasting impact of both the Axial Age second-generation societies that stretched across Afro-Eurasia and the first complex societies isolated from them by oceans and desert.

Eastern Zhou China

Destruction of the old political order paved the way for radical thinkers and cultural flourishing in Eastern Zhou China. Centered at Luoyang, the turbulent Eastern Zhou dynasty was divided by ancient Chinese chroniclers into the Spring and Autumn period (722–481 BCE) and the Warring States period (403–221 BCE). One writer from the Spring and Autumn period described over 500 battles among states and more than 100 civil wars within states, all taking place within 260 years. Fueling this warfare was the spread of cheaper and more lethal weaponry, made possible by new iron-smelting techniques, which in turn shifted influence from the central government to local authorities and allowed warfare to continue unabated into the Warring States period. Regional states became so powerful that they undertook large-scale projects, including dikes and irrigation systems, which had to this point been feasible only for empires. By the beginning of the Warring States period, seven large territorial states dominated the Zhou world. (See Map 5.2.) Their wars and shifting political alliances involved the mobilization of armies and resources on an unprecedented scale. Qin, the most powerful state, which ultimately replaced the Eastern Zhou dynasty in 221 BCE, fielded armies that combined huge infantries in the tens of thousands with lethal cavalries and skilled archers using state-of-the-art crossbows.

The conception of central power changed dramatically during this era. Royal appointees replaced hereditary officeholders. By the middle of the fourth century BCE, power was so concentrated in the major states' rulers that each began to call himself "king" (*wang*). Despite—or perhaps even as a result of—the constant warfare, scholars, soldiers, merchants, peasants, and artisans thrived in the midst of an expanding agrarian economy and interregional trade.

Intricate Jade Carving This small jade plaque, measuring just under 2 inches across, demonstrates the aesthetic sensibility and artistic accomplishment of jade carvers in the Warring States period (403–221 BCE). The intricate design of two facing dragons complete with tiny scales and enclosed within a circular frame carefully etched with a swirling pattern—all on so small an object—required the skilled use of fine rotary tools for carving and polishing jade.

INNOVATIONS IN THOUGHT

Out of this turmoil came new visions that would shape Chinese thinking about the individual's place in society and provide the philosophical underpinnings for the world's most enduring imperial system (lasting from the establishment of the Qin dynasty in 221 BCE until the abdication of China's last monarch in 1912). Often it was the losers among the political elites, seeking to replace their former advantages with new status gained through service, who sparked this intellectual creativity. Many important teachers emerged in China's Axial Age, each with disciples. The philosophies of these "hundred masters," a term mostly used at the time by itinerant scholars, constituted what came to be known as the Hundred Schools of Thought. Among the most influential were Confucianism and Daoism.

Confucius (551–479 BCE) was very much the product of the violent Spring and Autumn period. Serving in minor governmental positions, he believed the founders of the Zhou dynasty had established ideals of good government and principled action. Frustrated, however, by the realities of division and war among rival states all around him, Confucius set out in search of an enlightened ruler. Confucius's teachings stemmed from his belief that human beings behaved ethically not because they wanted to achieve salvation or a heavenly reward but because it was in their human makeup to do so. Humanity's natural

The Global View

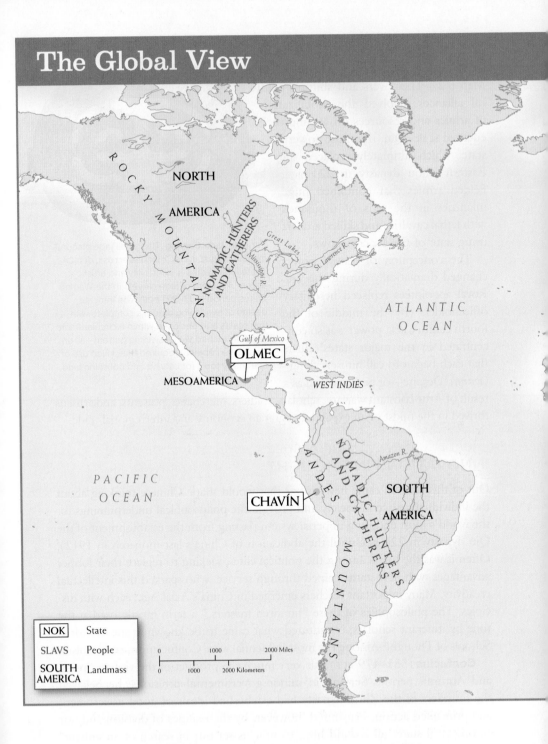

NORTH

AMERICA

ROCKY MOUNTAINS

NOMADIC HUNTERS AND GATHERERS

Great Lakes

St. Lawrence R.

Mississippi R.

Gulf of Mexico

OLMEC

MESOAMERICA

WEST INDIES

ATLANTIC OCEAN

PACIFIC OCEAN

ANDES

NOMADIC HUNTERS AND GATHERERS

Amazon R.

SOUTH

AMERICA

CHAVÍN

MOUNTAINS

NOK	State
SLAVS	People
SOUTH AMERICA	Landmass

0   1000   2000 Miles

0   1000   2000 Kilometers

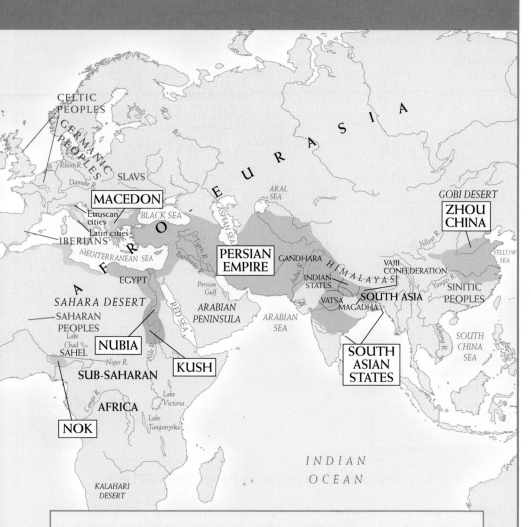

Map 5.1 The World in an Axial Age, c. 500 BCE

By the middle of the first millennium BCE, complex agriculture-based societies beyond the regional empires of Southwest Asia, North Africa, and East Asia contributed to the flowering of new cultural pathways and ideas that reshaped the old empires and territorial states into what we might call second-generation societies.

- According to your reading, where did these second-generation societies appear? What had been located there before?

- Examining the map, how are these second-generation societies influenced by peoples on their margins?

- Which states are in regions closely connected to others? Which appear to be geographically isolated? How might proximity to others or relative isolation have shaped these societies' development?

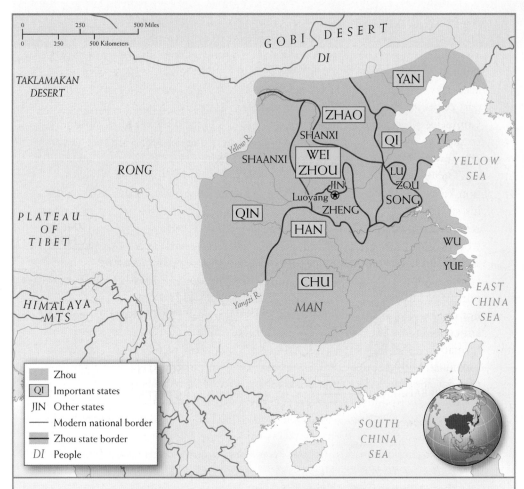

Map 5.2 Zhou China in the Warring States Period, 403–221 BCE

....

The Warring States period witnessed a fracturing of the Zhou dynasty into a myriad of states.

- Find the Zhou capital of Luoyang on the map. Where was it located relative to the other key states?
- Trace the Zhou state borders. How would you compare the boundaries and sizes of the various Zhou states? What does this suggest about the importance of diplomacy during this period?
- How do you think so many smaller polities could survive when they were surrounded first by seven and then by three even larger and more powerful states (Qin, Qi, and Chu)?

tendencies, if left alone, produced harmonious existence. Confucius saw family and filial submission (the duty of children to parents) as the foundation of proper ethical action, including loyalty to the state and rulers. His idea of modeling the state on the patriarchal family—with the ruler respecting heaven as if it were his father and protecting his subjects as if they were his children—became a bedrock principle of Confucian thought. Although he regarded himself as a transmitter of ancient wisdom, Confucius established many of the major guidelines for Chinese thought and action: respect for the pronouncements of scholars, commitment to a broad education, and training for all who were highly intelligent and willing to work, whether noble or humble in birth. This equal access to training for those willing and able offered a dramatic departure from past centuries, when only nobles were believed capable of ruling. Nonetheless, Confucius's distinctions between gentlemen-rulers and commoners continued to support a social hierarchy—although an individual's position in that hierarchy now rested on education rather than on birth.

Confucius's ethical teachings were preserved by his followers in a collection known as *The Analects*. These texts record Confucius's conversations with his students. In his effort to persuade his contemporaries to reclaim what he regarded as the lost ideals of the early Zhou, Confucius proposed a moral framework stressing benevolence (*ren*), correct performance of ritual (*li*), loyalty to the family (*xiao*), and perfection of moral character to become a "superior man" (*junzi*)—that is, a man defined by benevolence and goodness rather than by the pursuit of profit. Confucius believed that a society of such superior men would not need coercive laws and punishment to achieve order. Confucius ultimately left court in 484 BCE, discouraged by the continuing state of warfare. His transformational ideology remained, however, and has shaped Chinese society for millennia, both through its followers and through those who adopted traditions that developed as a distinct counterpoint to Confucian engagement.

Another key philosophy was **Daoism**, which diverged sharply from Confucian thought by scorning rigid rituals and social hierarchies. Its ideas originated with a Master Lao (Laozi, "Old Master"), who—if he actually existed—may have been a contemporary of Confucius. His sayings were collected in *The Daodejing*, or *The Book of the Way and Its Power* (c. third century BCE). Master Lao's book was then elaborated by Master Zhuang (Zhuangzi, c. 369–286 BCE). Master Lao is credited with saying, "The Sage, when he governs, empties [people's] minds and fills their bellies. . . . His constant object is to keep the people without knowledge and without desire, or to prevent those who have knowledge from daring to act." Daoism stressed that the best path (*dao*) for living was to follow the natural order of things. Its main principle was *wuwei*, "doing nothing." Spontaneity, noninterference, and acceptance of the world as it is, rather than attempting to change it through politics and government, were what mattered. In Laozi's vision, the ruler who interfered least in the natural processes of change was the most successful. Zhuangzi focused on the enlightened individual living spontaneously and in harmony with nature, free of society's ethical rules and laws and viewing life and death simply as different stages of existence.

Xunzi and Han Fei Legalism, or Statism, another view of how best to create an orderly life, grew out of the writings of Master Xun (Xunzi, 310–237 BCE) toward the end of the Warring States period. He believed that men and women

Qu Yuan In addition to the innovations of Confucian and Daoist thought, the first millennium BCE also saw an outpouring of poetic work. Qu Yuan (339–278 BCE), shown here in a seventeenth-century painting, is known both from his own writing and from the works of later writers who mention him, such as the famous Chinese historian Sima Qian (145–86 BCE). A disgraced politician, diplomat, and poet, Qu Yuan wrote his famous poem *Li Sao* in the context of the decline of his home state, Chu, over the course of the Warring States period.

are innately bad and therefore require moral education and authoritarian control. In the decades before the Qin victory over the Zhou, the Legalist thinker Han Fei (280–233 BCE) agreed that human nature is primarily evil. He imagined a state with a ruler who followed the Daoist principle of *wuwei*, detaching himself from everyday governance—but only after setting an unbending standard (strict laws, accompanied by harsh punishments) for judging his officials and people. For Han Fei, the establishment and uniform application of these laws would keep people's evil nature in check. As we will see in Chapter 7, the Qin state, before it became the dominant state in China, systematically followed the Legalist philosophy.

Apart from the philosophical discourse of the "hundred masters," with its far-reaching impact across Chinese society, elites and commoners alike tried to maintain stability in their lives through religion, medicine, and statecraft. The elites' rites of divination to predict the future and medical recipes to heal the body found parallels in the commoners' use of ghost stories and astrological almanacs to understand the meaning of their lives and the significance of their deaths. Elites recorded their political discourses on wood and bamboo slips, tied together to form scrolls. They likewise prepared military treatises, ritual texts, geographic works, and poetry. The growing importance of statecraft and philosophical discourse promoted the use of writing, with 9,000 to 10,000 graphs or signs required to convey these elaborate ideas.

What emerged from all this activity was a foundational alliance between scholars and the state. Scholars became state functionaries who were dependent on rulers' patronage. In return, rulers recognized scholars' expertise in matters of punishment, ritual, astronomy, medicine, and divination. Philosophical deliberations focused on the need to maintain order and stability by preserving the state. These bonds that rulers forged with their scholarly elites were a distinguishing feature of governments in Warring States China, as compared with other Afro-Eurasian societies at this time.

INNOVATIONS IN STATE ADMINISTRATION

Regional rulers of the Spring and Autumn period enhanced their ability to obtain natural resources, to recruit men for their armies, and to oversee conquered areas. This trend continued in the Warring States period, as the elites in the major states created administrative districts with stewards, sheriffs, and judges and a system of registering peasant households to facilitate tax collection and army conscription. These officials, who had been knights under the Western Zhou, were now bureaucrats in direct service to the ruler. These administrators were the "superior men" (*junzi*) of Confucian thought. They were paid in grain and sometimes received gifts of gold and silver, as well as titles and seals of office, from the ruler. The most successful of these ministers was the Qin statesman Shang Yang (fourth century BCE). Lord Shang's reforms—including a head tax, administrative districts for closer bureaucratic control of hinterlands, land distribution for individual households to farm, and reward or punishment for military achievement—positioned the Qin to become the dominant state of its time.

INNOVATIONS IN WARFARE

With administrative reforms came reforms in military recruitment and warfare. In earlier periods, nobles had let fly their arrows from chariots while conscripted peasants fought beside them on the bloodstained ground. The Warring States, however, relied on massed infantries of peasants, whose conscription was made easier by the registration of peasant households. Bearing iron lances and unconstrained by their relationships with nobles, these peasants fought fiercely. In addition to this conscripted peasant infantry, armies boasted elite professional troops equipped with iron armor and weapons, and wielding the recently invented crossbow. The crossbow's tremendous power, range, and accuracy enabled archers to kill lightly armored cavalrymen or charioteers at a distance. With improved siege technology, enemy armies assaulted the new defensive walls of towns and frontiers, either digging under them or using counterweighted siege ladders to scale them. Campaigns were no longer limited to an agricultural season and instead might stretch over a year or longer. The huge state armies contained as many as 1 million commoners in the infantry, supported by 1,000 chariots and 10,000 bow-wielding cavalrymen. During the Spring and Autumn period one state's entire army would face another state's, but by the Warring States period armies could divide into separate forces and wage several battles simultaneously.

ECONOMIC, SOCIAL, AND CULTURAL CHANGES

While a growing population presented new challenges, the continuous warfare in these periods spurred economic growth in China. An agricultural revolution on the North China plain along the Yellow River led to rapid population growth,

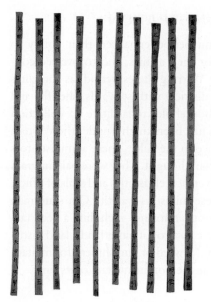

Bamboo-Strip Texts Over the past fifty years, Chinese texts dating to the Warring States (403–221 BCE) and Western Han (206 BCE–9 CE) periods have been unearthed from tombs at various sites, including Jingmen (Guodian tombs) and Changsha (Mawangdui tombs). Written on bamboo strips (as pictured here) and on silk, these texts include philosophical and medical treatises, as well as mathematical and calendrical calculations.

and the inhabitants of the Eastern Zhou reached approximately 20 million. Several factors contributed to increased agricultural productivity beginning in the Spring and Autumn period. Some rulers gave peasants the right to own their land in exchange for taxes and military service, which in turn increased productivity because the farmers were working to benefit themselves. Agricultural productivity was also enhanced by innovations such as crop rotation (millet and wheat in the north, rice and millet in the south) and oxen-pulled iron plowshares to prepare fields.

With this increased agricultural yield came the pressures of accompanying population growth. Ever-attentive peasant farmers tilling the fields of North and South China produced more rice and wheat than anyone else on earth, but that agricultural success was often outpaced by their growing families. As more people required more fuel, deforestation led to erosion of the fields. Many animals were hunted to extinction. Many inhabitants migrated south to domesticate the marshes, lakes, and rivers of the Yangzi River delta; here they created new arable frontiers out of former wetlands. When the expansion into arable land invariably hit its limits, Chinese families faced terrible food shortages and famines. The long-term economic result was a declining standard of living for massive numbers of Chinese peasants.

Despite these long-term cycles of population pressures and famine, larger harvests and advances in bronze and iron casting enabled the beginning of a market economy: trade in surplus grain, pottery, and ritual objects. Peasants continued to barter, but elites and rulers used minted coins. Grain and goods traveled along roads, rivers, and canals. Rulers and officials applied their military and organizational skills for public projects enhancing waterworks.

Economic growth had repercussions at all levels of society. Rulers attained a high level of cultural sophistication, as reflected in their magnificent palaces and burial sites. Archaeological evidence also suggests that commoners could purchase bronze metalwork, whereas previously only Zhou rulers and aristocrats could afford to do so. Social relations became more fluid as commoners gained power and aristocrats lost it. In Qin, for example, peasants who served in the ruler's army could be rewarded with land, houses, enslaved servants, and even status change for killing enemy soldiers. While class relations had a revolutionary fluidity, gender relations became more rigid for elites and nonelites alike as male-centered kinship groups grew. The resulting separation of the sexes and male domination within the family affected women's position. An emphasis on monogamy, or at least the primacy of the first wife over additional wives and concubines, emerged. Relations between the sexes became increasingly ritualized and constrained by moral and legal sanctions against any behavior that appeared to threaten the purity of authoritarian male lineages.

Even with the endless cycles of warfare and chaos—or perhaps because of them—many foundational beliefs, values, and philosophies for later dynasties sprang forth during the Spring and Autumn and Warring States periods. By the middle of the first millennium BCE, China's political activities and institutional and intellectual innovations affected larger numbers of people, over a much broader area, than did comparable developments in South Asia and the Mediterranean.

South Asia

While Chinese scholar-officials were theorizing about how to govern and organize their society, the Vedic peoples who settled in the Ganges Valley were assimilating earlier residents and forging their own new political institutions, economic activities, and belief systems. The heartland of South Asian developments in this period was the mid-Ganges plain, a roughly 70,000-square-mile area in the northeast of present-day India and the southern tip of Nepal. (See Map 5.3.) Waves of Vedic peoples migrated into this region around 600 BCE, clearing land, establishing new cities and trade routes, expanding rice cultivation, and experimenting with new political forms. Abundant monsoon rains made the land suitable for rice farming, as opposed to the wheat and barley farming of the Indus Valley. Vedic migrants cleared land by setting fire to the forests and using iron

Eastern Zhou Coinage Coins in the Eastern Zhou state were made of bronze and were cast in a variety of shapes, some resembling farming tools such as spades and others resembling knives. The variety of shapes might reflect a time when tools were exchanged as a form of currency. In the Warring States period, each region had its own currency.

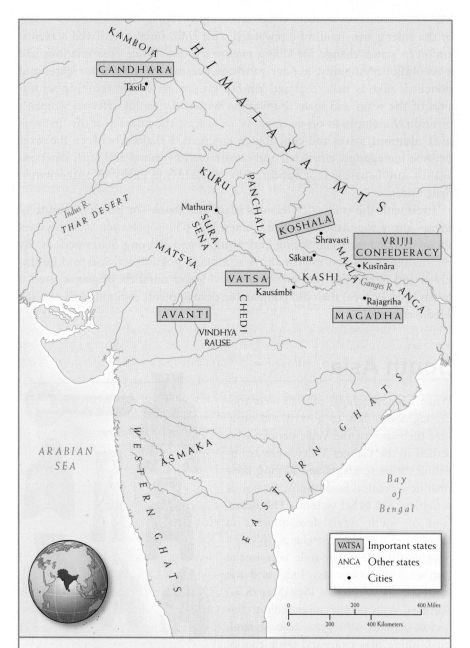

Map 5.3 Major States in the First Millennium BCE in South Asia

· ·

South Asia underwent profound transformations in the first millennium BCE that reflected growing urbanization, increased commerce, and the emergence of two types of states: monarchies and oligarchies.

- Where did the new states and cities appear? How do these compare with the location of the earlier cities of the Harappans (Map 2.5)?

- What geographic and environmental features encouraged or hindered social and cultural integration?

- What other regions had influence on South Asia, and where might South Asian culture spread?

tools—fashioned from ore mined locally—to remove what was left of the jungle. Two major kinds of states appeared in the mid- and lower Ganges plain: those ruled by hereditary monarchs and those ruled by a small elite (oligarchy). South Asian oligarchies were led by the Kshatriya class of warriors and officials. Kshatriya oligarchs controlled the land and other resources, overseeing the enslaved and foreign workers.

In the kingdoms and oligarchic cities of northern India, a new system of hierarchy emerged alongside the old fourfold *varnas* (Brahman priests, Kshatriya warriors, Vaishya commoners, and Shudra laborers). *Varnas* remained the overarching theoretical basis for ranking the social order; however, since booming agriculture allowed for greater variation in professions, occupation and birth received new emphasis. Each occupational group established its own sublevels, called *jatis* (the Sanskrit word for "birth"). *Jatis* were organized not only by kinship and profession but even by product. In the emerging urban centers, for instance, traders were regarded as "purer" than artisans, while those making gold utensils had higher status than those making copper or iron products. Yet members of each group worked together to restrict internal competition, and they closed ranks to preserve their status. *Jatis* banned intermarriage to prevent other groups from accessing their knowledge. Religion buttressed this hierarchical system. Brahmanic texts, some from an earlier period and some from the present, invoked the principle of purity and pollution to rank *varnas* and *jatis* and to hinder movement between them. Occupations were made hereditary, and a taboo was placed on eating together. These injunctions ensured that individuals did not move out of their inherited occupation. Thus, the basis of what would later become the caste system, which still plays an important role in Indian society, was laid at this time.

NEW CITIES AND A CHANGING ECONOMY

Supported by rice agriculture, cities began to emerge on the Ganges plain around 500 BCE and became centers of commercial and intellectual exchange. Some, such as Shravasti and Rajagriha, thrived as artisanal centers, while others, like Taxila, prospered through trade. These cities of the Ganges plain were dominated by men and women whose occupations—bankers, merchants, and teachers—did not fit easily into the old *varnas*. Precisely laid-out streets were crowded with vendors, and wealthy residents employed elephants and horse-drawn chariots to move them about. Alleys leading from the main streets zigzagged between houses built with pebbles and clay. Although city expansion was often haphazard, civic authorities showed great interest in sanitation. The many squares dotting each city had garbage bins, and dirty water drained away in deep sink wells underground. Streets were graded so that rainfall would wash them clean.

Taxila Taxila became the capital of Gandhara, a kingdom located in what is today northern Pakistan and eastern Afghanistan, when it was occupied by the Persian Empire in the fifth century BCE. Dharmarajika was one of the most important monasteries. The walkway around the stupa, a moundlike structure containing Buddhist relics, was covered with glass tiles, and the stupa itself was decorated with jewels.

The new cities offered exciting opportunities and innovations. Rural householders who moved into them prospered by importing rice and sugarcane from villages to sell in the markets; they then transported manufactured goods such as sugar, salt, and utensils back to their villages. The less affluent turned to craftwork, fashioning textiles, needles, fine pottery, copper plates, ivory decorations, and gold and silver utensils. Other professions included physicians, launderers, barbers, cooks, tailors, and entertainers. The elaborate division of labor suggests high degrees of specialization and commercialization. Those with money became bankers who financed trade and industry. As in Greece and China, coins came into use in these cities at about this time. Traders and bankers established municipal bodies that issued the coins and vouched for their worth. Made of silver, the coins had irregular shapes but specific weights, which determined their value; they also were punch-marked, or stamped with symbols of authority on one side.

Yet the opportunities and innovations of the new cities did not ensure success for everyone. Many came to cities in search of work, and some fared better than others. As a whole, city dwellers had more material wealth, but their lives were far more uncertain. In addition, urban life created a new social class: those who did the dirtiest jobs, such as removing garbage and sewage, and were therefore viewed as physically and ritually impure "untouchables." Even though their work kept the cities clean, they were forced to live in shantytowns outside the city limits. These outcasts became receptive audiences for those who would challenge Vedic rituals and Brahman priests.

BRAHMANS, THEIR CHALLENGERS, AND NEW BELIEFS

To the Brahmans, nothing about the cities seemed good, and their efforts to retain their superior status prompted new challenges to traditional beliefs. The Brahmans thought that *varnas* and *jatis* mixing indiscriminately polluted society. Moreover, lowborn persons grasping at higher status by acquiring wealth or skill skewed established hierarchies. When an alphabetic script appeared around 600 BCE, sacred knowledge became more accessible, and thus the Brahmans' ability to control the definition of right and wrong was undermined. Formerly, all of Vedic literature had been memorized, and only the brightest Brahmans could master the tradition (see Chapter 4).

Frightened by these urban threats, Brahmans sought to strengthen their relationships with the kings by establishing the idea of a monarch endowed with divine power. Kingship had been unnecessary in a long-ago golden age, according to Brahmanic scripts; a moral code and priests to uphold it had been enough to keep things in order. Over time, though, the world deteriorated due to rivalry for wealth. According to Brahmanic writings, the gods then decided that people on earth needed a king to maintain order. The gods enticed a reluctant Manu ("Man") with a range of promises, including one-tenth of the grain harvest, one-fiftieth of the cattle, merits for subjects' good behavior, and the most beautiful woman in his domain. The Laws of Manu are associated with this tradition. In the Brahmanic accounts, royal power had a divine origin: the gods chose the king and protected him. Priests and Vedic rituals were essential to royal power, since kingly authority was validated through religious ceremonies carried out by Brahman priests. This emphasis on divine kingship solved some problems but created new ones. The Brahmans' claim to moral authority caused resentment among the Kshatriyas—especially those in the oligarchic republics, whose leaders did not assert divine power. Merchants and artisans also chafed at the Brahmans' claims to superiority. Such resentments provoked challenges to the Brahmans' domination. Some thinkers in South Asia believed that they were in an age of acute crisis because their culture's ancient harmony had been lost. And like many scholars and philosophers elsewhere in this Axial Age, a new group of South Asian scholars and religious leaders developed their own answers to questions about human existence.

Revolutionary South Asian thinkers challenged the Brahmans' worldview by refusing to recognize the gods that populated the Vedic world. Some of these rebels sprang from inside the Vedic tradition; though Brahmans, they rejected the idea that sacrificial rituals pleased the gods. To them, God was a universal concept, not a superhuman creature. Also, they felt that the many cows that priests slaughtered for ritual sacrifices could serve more practical uses, such as plowing the land and producing milk. Their discussions and teachings about the universe and life were later collected in the Upanishads. Other dissidents, such as Mahavira and the Buddha, came from outside the Vedic tradition.

Mahavira and Jainism Vardhamana Mahavira (c. 540–468 BCE) popularized the doctrines of **Jainism**, which had emerged in the seventh century BCE. Born a Kshatriya in an oligarchic republic, Mahavira left home at age thirty to seek the truth about life; he spent twelve years as an ascetic (one who rejects material possessions and physical pleasures) wandering throughout the Ganges Valley before reaching enlightenment. He taught that the universe obeys its own everlasting rules and cannot be affected by any god or other supernatural being. He also believed that the purpose of life is to purify one's soul

through asceticism and to attain a state of permanent bliss. The Jains' religious doctrines emphasized the idea that asceticism, rather than knowledge, would enable one to avoid harming other creatures and thereby purify the soul. Since the doctrine of *ahimsa* ("no hurt") held that every living creature has a soul—killing even an ant would result in an unfavorable rebirth—believers had to watch every step to avoid inadvertently becoming murderers. The extreme nonviolence of Jainism was impossible for peasants, who could not work the land without killing insects. Instead, Jainism became a religion of city dwellers and traders. Mahavira's teachings were transmitted orally for nearly a millennium before being compiled into writing by followers in the fifth century CE.

Brahman Recluse When Buddhists started to tell stories in sculptures and paintings, Brahmans were included when appropriate. This character in Gandharan Buddhist art probably represents a Brahman who lived as a recluse, instead of as a priest. He is not shaved or dressed, but his expression is passionate.

The Buddha and Buddhism The most direct challenge to traditional Brahmanic thinking came from Siddhartha Gautama (c. 563–483 BCE), a contemporary of Mahavira and Confucius. Later known as the **Buddha** (Enlightened One), Gautama objected to Brahmanic beliefs, their rituals and sacrifices, and their preference for kingship that kept the priestly class in power. His Axial Age teachings provided the peoples of South Asia and elsewhere with alternatives to established traditions.

The son of a highly respected Kshatriya warrior, Gautama was born into a comfortable life in a small oligarchic community nestled in the foothills of the Himalayas. Yet, at the age of twenty-nine, he walked away from everything, leaving behind his father, wife, and newborn son. Family and friends wept as he donned a robe and shaved his head and beard, symbols of the ascetic life that he intended to pursue. Gautama struggled with the belief that the life that he and most others were destined to live would consist of little more than endless episodes of suffering, which began with the pain of childbirth, followed by aging, illness, disease, and death, after which reincarnated beings would experience more of the same.

For six years, Gautama lived as an ascetic wanderer before a forty-nine-day meditation led him to the enlightened moment in which he realized that nirvana (spiritual contentment) could be achieved by finding a middle ground between self-indulgence and self-denial. He expressed this new credo as the Four Noble Truths: (1) life, from birth to death, is full of suffering; (2) all suffering is caused by desires; (3) the only way to avoid suffering is to renounce desire; and (4) the only way to rid oneself of desire is through adherence to the Eightfold Path, which includes wisdom (right views and right intentions), ethical behavior (right conduct, right speech, and right livelihood), and mental discipline (right effort, right thought, and right meditation). This teaching represented a dramatic shift in thinking about humanity and correct behavior. Like the Jain teachings of Mahavira, the Buddha's doctrines left no space for Brahmanic deities to dictate human lives. The Buddha's logical explanation of human suffering and his guidelines for renouncing desire appealed to many people for their simplicity, accessibility, and challenge to the Vedic hierarchies.

Like other dissident thinkers of this period, the Buddha delivered his message in a vernacular dialect of Sanskrit that all could understand. His many followers soon formed a community of monks called a *sangha* ("gathering"). The Buddha and his followers wandered from one city to another on the Ganges plain, where they found large audiences as well as the alms needed to sustain the expanding *sangha*. It was these followers who would pass on and eventually compile the Buddha's sayings into the Dhammapada. The Buddha's most influential patrons were urban merchants. In struggles between oligarchs and kings, the Buddha sided with the oligarchs, reflecting his upbringing in an oligarchic republic. He inevitably aroused opposition from the Brahmans, who favored monarchical government. While the Buddha himself did not seek to erase the Vedic hierarchies, Buddhism provided an escape from its oppressive aspects and the prestige that it afforded the Brahmans. Together with Jainism, Buddhism's challenge to Brahmanic thinking appealed particularly in the new urban contexts of South Asia and to those who felt disadvantaged by prevailing Vedic hierarchies in the first millennium BCE.

The Mediterranean World

Political, economic, and social changes also stimulated new thinking in the Mediterranean world. The violent upheavals that tore through the borderland areas of the northern Levant, the coastal lands of Anatolia, the islands of the Aegean and Mediterranean Seas, and mainland Greece in the few centuries after 1000 BCE freed the people in these regions from the domination of the Neo-Assyrians and Persians (see Chapter 4). These borderland communities encircling the Mediterranean basin also created second-generation societies that developed new social and political methods of organization and explored new Axial Age ideas. Phoenicians, Greeks, Cretans, Cypriots, Lydians, Etruscans, and many others exchanged not only trade goods but also ideas about the virtues of self-sufficient cities whose inhabitants shared power more widely than before. (See Map 5.4.)

FORMATION OF NEW CITY-STATES

In the ninth and eighth centuries BCE, as order returned to the eastern Mediterranean and the population rebounded, peoples who were clustered in more concentrated settlements formed city-states. Unlike the city-states of earlier Mesopotamia, which were governed by semidivine monarchs, or the great urban centers of Southwest Asian empires, which were run by elite scribes, high priests, and monarchs, the Mediterranean city-states were governed by their citizens. These self-governing city-states were a new political form that profoundly influenced the Mediterranean region. This new urban entity—known first by the Phoenicians as a *qart*, then by the Greeks as a *polis*, and the Romans as a *civitas*—multiplied throughout the Mediterranean by the sixth century BCE.

The new principles of rulership were revolutionary. Ordinary residents, or "citizens," of these cities—such as Carthage and Gadir (modern-day Cádiz in Spain) among the western Phoenicians; Athens, Thebes, Sparta, and Corinth among the Greeks; and Rome and Praeneste among the early Latins—governed themselves and selected their leaders. Their self-government took various forms, including tyranny (rule by a popularly approved individual), oligarchy (rule by the few), and democracy (rule by all free adult males).

The new cities of the Mediterranean basin included adult male citizens, other free persons (including women, who could not vote or hold office), foreign immigrants, and large numbers of unfree persons (including enslaved people and people tied to the land who could not vote or fight for the polis). The small family unit, or household, was the most important social unit of the city-state, and the city-state was seen as a natural outgrowth of the household. Thus, the free adult male was fully entitled to engage in the city's public affairs. Those enjoying full citizenship rights—the adult freeborn males—in each community decided what tasks, from warfare to public works, the city-state would undertake and what kind of government and laws it would adopt. In contrast, adult women of free birth

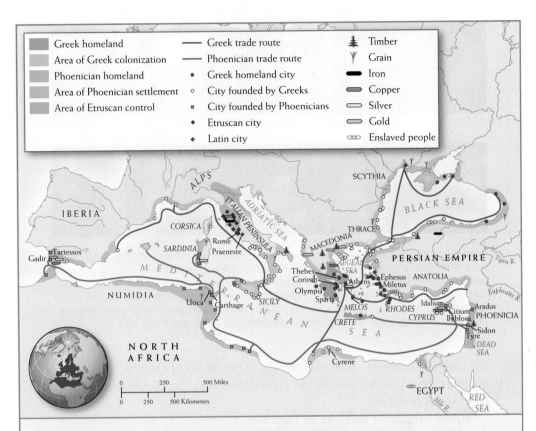

Legend:

- Greek homeland
- Area of Greek colonization
- Phoenician homeland
- Area of Phoenician settlement
- Area of Etruscan control
- Greek trade route
- Phoenician trade route
- Greek homeland city
- City founded by Greeks
- City founded by Phoenicians
- Etruscan city
- Latin city
- Timber
- Grain
- Iron
- Copper
- Silver
- Gold
- Enslaved people

Map 5.4 The Mediterranean World, 1000–350 BCE

Phoenician and Greek city-states, as well as the colonies they founded, dotted the coastline of both the Mediterranean and Black Seas.

- What were the main goods traded in the Mediterranean world in this period? Where were they located?
- To what extent might the concentration of goods in certain regions have driven colonization and fostered trade?
- What areas did the Greeks and Phoenicians control with their homeland cities and their colonies? What was their main settlement pattern?

remained enclosed within the private world of the family and had no standing to debate policy in public, vote, or hold office, although they did go out in public for religious festivals of which there were many. Upper-class women who did carry on intelligent conversations with men in public about public matters were criticized. Families of the lower classes could not afford the luxury of secluding women in such a way, however, when they might be needed to work as agricultural laborers or market vendors or just to do the chores outside the house that wealthy families could employ someone else to do. Spartan women were a particular exception, and

Glimpsing Women's Lives These panels are from two cosmetic containers from fifth-century BCE Greece. While they depict mythological women (Clytemnestra, Cassandra, and Iphigenia in the top scene and the daughters of Nereus in the bottom scene), these women are engaged in activities—such as spinning (*top left*) and marriage preparation (*bottom*)—that would have been meaningful to the women who used these containers to hold their cosmetics and jewelry. The woman on the far right of the marriage scene (*bottom*) uses a device called an *iunx* to cast a love spell.

their unusual behavior—such as exercising in the nude in public (as did men) or holding property in their own right—evoked humor and hostility from men in the other Greek city-states.

Athens developed into one of the most dynamic of these city-states. The Athenian city-state was tiny by the standards of the ancient empires. It covered less than 2,000 square miles, barely big enough to be a Persian satrapy, and its population of roughly 300,000, not counting 60,000 "chattel slaves," was significantly smaller than the population of 35 million who lived under Persian rule. Nonetheless, city-states were competitive places. Their histories relate rivalries between individuals, social classes, and other groups. Competition for honor and prestige was a value that shaped behavior in the city-states. This extreme competitive ethic found an outlet in organized sporting events. Almost from the moment that Greek city-states emerged, athletic contests sprang up. The greatest of these competitions were the Olympic Games, which began in 776 BCE at Olympia in southern Greece.

The competitive spirit among communities also took the destructive form of armed conflicts over borderlands, trade, valuable resources, religious shrines, and prestige. The incessant battles among city-states fueled new developments in military equipment, such as the heavy armor that gave its name to the hoplites, or infantrymen, and in tactics, such as the standard blocklike configuration (which the Greeks called a *phalanx*) in which the regular rank and file fought. These wars were so destructive that they threatened to destabilize the city-states' world. The most famous conflicts were the Peloponnesian War (431–404 BCE) between Athens and Sparta and their respective allies, and the ongoing rivalry

Hoplite Warfare Two lines of helmeted hoplites advance on each other in lockstep, marching shield to shield with spears raised. A pipe player's tune sounds out the pace and maneuvers. The troops in the center offer a view of the inside of the *hoplon* (shield) and how it was grasped by the hoplite, while on the right we see the range of menacing heraldry emblazoned on the shield faces. The scene comes from the Chigi vase, which dates to the seventh century BCE and was found in a tomb in Greek-influenced Etruscan territories on the Italian Peninsula.

between the city-states of Rome and Phoenician Carthage (from c. 500 BCE onward) that led to the Punic Wars. Despite the destabilizing effects of warfare, city-states prospered, and economic innovations facilitated trade and exchange throughout the Mediterranean.

ECONOMIC INNOVATIONS

Without an elaborate top-down bureaucratic and administrative structure, residents of the new cities devised other ways to run their commercial affairs. They developed open trading markets and a system of money that enabled buyers and sellers to know the precise value of commodities so that exchanges were efficient. At their center, the new city-states had a marketplace (*agora* or *forum*), a large open area where individuals bought and sold commodities. These increasingly complex transactions required money, rather than barter or gift exchange. Like the states in Eastern Zhou China and Vedic South Asia, the Greek city-states were issuing a striking variety of coins by the end of the fifth century BCE, and other peoples such as the Phoenicians, Etruscans, and Persians were using them. Each Greek city-state minted coins with distinct features, making them recognizable at a glance. For example, Athens stamped its coins with the image of an owl, Corinth with a Pegasus, Aegina with a turtle, Knossos with a maze, and Akragas with a crab. Coins bought services as well, perhaps at first the services of mercenary soldiers. In the absence of large bureaucracies, Mediterranean cities relied on money to connect the producers and buyers of goods and services, especially as city-states became more far-flung.

The Agora The agora, or central open marketplace, was one of the core defining features of Mediterranean city-states. At its center, each city had one of these open-air plazas, the heart of its commercial, religious, social, and political life. When a new city was founded, the agora was one of the first places that the colonists measured out. The large, rectangular, open area in this picture is the agora of the Greek colonial city of Cyrene (in modern-day Libya).

Indeed, the search for silver, iron, copper, and tin drove traders westward across the Mediterranean. By about 500 BCE, the Phoenicians, Greeks, and others from the eastern Mediterranean had planted new city-states around the shores of the western Mediterranean and the Black Sea. Once established, these colonial communities became completely independent and might even found other colonies. For instance, Corinth founded Syracuse (in Sicily) and then Syracuse went on to settle several Sicilian colonies of its own. Sparta founded Thera (a city-state on the modern island of Santorini in the Aegean), which then went on to found Cyrene (in North Africa). At Cyrene, a foundation inscription hints at the tricky citizenship and property issues involved in creating a new colony, as well as the potential dangers of colonization. One man from each Theran family was required to join the expedition and the expedition had to make a go of it for five years before being allowed to return home. The oath the colonists swore as they set out included burning wax images fashioned in the shape of the would-be colonists and proclaiming that just as these wax images melted away so would the fortunes and lives of the settlers and their descendants should they break their oath to found the Theran colony at Cyrene.

Whether driven by internal competition, population pressures, or economic possibilities, the far-flung colonies of the Greeks and Phoenicians transformed the coastal world. City-based life was common from southern Spain and western Italy to the Crimea on the Black Sea. With amazing speed, seaborne communications spread a Mediterranean-wide urban culture that bolstered the region's wealthy and powerful elites. Among the local elites of Tartessos in southern Spain, the Gallic chiefs in southern France, and the Etruscan and Roman nobles of central Italy, a new aristocratic culture featured similar public displays of wealth: richly decorated chariots, elaborate armor and weapons, fine dining ware, elaborate houses, and public burials. From the western end of the Mediterranean to the Black Sea, the city-state communities developed a culture founded on market-based economies and private property.

In contrast to the privilege enjoyed by these elites was the traffic in human flesh: slavery. Treating men, women, and children as objects of commerce, to be bought and sold in markets, created a new form of commercial slavery called chattel slavery. Slavery—the forced, unfree labor of war captives or of those who sold themselves to pay debt—had existed since the third millennium BCE, but what was new in this Mediterranean context was the commodification of bodies and the scale of the exchange. When dangerous and exhausting tasks such as mining and farming required extra labor, freeborn citizens purchased enslaved laborers. The primary source of enslaved laborers was still mainly war captives. In some city-states, enslaved people may have constituted up to a quarter of the population. In every one of the new city-states, the enslaved provided manual and technical labor of all kinds and produced the agricultural surpluses that supported the urban population.

Encounters with Frontier Communities The forces that transformed the Mediterranean region's mosaic of urban communities and surrounding rural areas also affected those in northern and central Europe. Whether they wished it or not, diverse tribes and ethnic groups—such as the Celts and Germans in western Europe and the Scythians to the north of the Black Sea—who were living in nomadic bands, isolated settlements, and small villages became integrated into the expanding cities' networks of violence, conquest, and trade.

Increasingly drawn to the city-states' manufactured goods—money, wine, ornate clothing, weapons—these tribal peoples became an armed threat to the region's core societies. Seeking to acquire the desired commodities through force rather than trade, frontier peoples convulsed the settled urban societies in wavelike incursions between 2200 and 2000 BCE, 1200 and 1000 BCE, and 400 and 200 BCE. Called "barbarians" (the Greeks' mocking name for foreigners unable to speak their language), the invaders actually were not much different from the Phoenicians or Greeks—who themselves had sought new homes and a better future by migrating. In colonizing the Mediterranean, they, too, had dispossessed the original inhabitants. The Celts, Gauls, Germans, Scythians, and other northerners came to the Mediterranean first as conquerors. Later, when Mediterranean empires grew more powerful and could keep them at bay, they were imported as enslaved laborers. Regarding these outsiders as uncivilized, the Greeks and western Phoenicians seized and colonized their lands—and sold the captives as commodities in their marketplaces.

NEW IDEAS

New ways of thinking about the world emerged from the competitive atmosphere that the Greek city-states fostered. In the absence of monarchical or priestly rule, ideas were free to arise, circulate, and clash. Individuals argued publicly about the nature of the gods, the best state, what is good, and whether to wage war. There was no final authority to give any particular idea a final stamp of approval and force its acceptance. New ideas emerged in science and the arts, and Greek philosophers proposed theories on human society and many other topics.

The Human Form The human body as it appeared naturally, without any adornment, became the ideal set by Greek art. Even gods were portrayed in this nude human form. This statue by Praxiteles is of the god Hermes with the infant Dionysus. Such bold nude portraits of humans and gods were sometimes shocking to other peoples.

Naturalistic Science and Realistic Art In this competitive marketplace of ideas, some daring thinkers developed novel ways of perceiving the cosmos and representing the environment. Rather than seeing everything as the handiwork of all-powerful deities, they took a naturalistic view of humans and their place in the universe. This new thinking was evident in their art, which idealized the natural world. Artists increasingly represented humans, objects, and landscapes not in abstract, idealized, or formal ways but in "natural" ways, as they appeared to the human eye. Even their portrayals of gods became more human-like. Later, these objective and natural views of humans and nature became the new ideals, the highest of which was the unadorned human figure: the nude became the centerpiece of Greek art. Individual artists and writers—such as the vase painter Exekias, the sculptor Praxiteles, and the poet Sappho—began to sign their works in a clear manifestation of the new sense of the individual being freed from the restraints of an autocratic state or a controlling religious system.

New Thinking and Greek Philosophers Axial Age thinkers in city-states such as Miletus and Ephesus in western Anatolia did not accept traditional explanations of how and why the universe worked. Each thinker competed to outdo his peers in offering persuasive and comprehensive explanations of the cosmos, and their theories became ever more radical. For instance, Thales (c. 636–546 BCE) believed that water was the primal substance from which all other things were created. Xenophanes (c. 570–480 BCE) doubted the very existence of gods as they had been portrayed, asserting instead that only one general divine aura suffused all creation but that ethnic groups produced images of gods in their own likeness. Pythagoras (c. 570–495 BCE), who devoted himself to the study of numbers, held that a wide range of physical phenomena, like musical sounds, were in fact based in numbers. Democritus (c. 460–370 BCE) claimed that everything was composed of small and ultimately indivisible particles, which he called *atoma* ("uncuttables"). This rich competition among ideas led to a more aggressive mode of public thinking, which the Greeks called *philosophia* ("love of wisdom").

In the fifth century BCE, **Greek philosophers** ("wisdom lovers") were focusing on humans and their place in society. Some of these professional thinkers tried to describe an ideal state, characterized by harmonious relationships and free from corruption and political decline. One such thinker was Socrates (469–399 BCE), a philosopher who frequented the agora at Athens and encouraged people to reflect on ethics and morality, even as the Peloponnesian War raged on. He stressed the importance of honor and integrity as opposed to wealth and power (just as Confucius had done in Eastern Zhou China and the Buddha had done in Vedic South Asia). Plato (427–347 BCE), a student of Socrates, presented Socrates's philosophy in a series of dialogues (much as Confucius's students had written down his thoughts). In *The Republic*, Plato envisioned a perfect city that philosopher-kings would rule. He thought that if fallible humans could imitate this model city more closely, their states would be less susceptible to the decline that was affecting the Greek city-states of his own day.

Plato's most famous pupil answered the same questions about nature and the acquisition of knowledge differently. Deeply interested in the natural world, Aristotle (384–322 BCE) believed that by collecting and studying all the facts one could about a given thing, one could achieve a better understanding. His main idea was that the interested inquirer can find out more about the world by collecting as much evidence as possible about a given thing and then making deductions from these data about general patterns. This evidence-based inquiry stood in stark contrast to Plato's claim that everything a person observes is in fact only a flawed copy of the "real" thing that exists in a thought-world of abstract patterns accessible only by pure mental meditation—completely the opposite of Aristotle's method.

This competition of ideas raged on for centuries, with the new thinking of these Mediterranean Axial Age philosophers at times fueling the aspirations of the city-states and at other times challenging them.

Common Cultures in the Americas and Sub-Saharan Africa

During what we have termed the Axial Age in Eurasia and North Africa, peoples living in the Americas and most of sub-Saharan Africa built complex, urban-based societies for the first time. These regions did not have the large number of immense cities, the presence of increasingly complex empires, the proliferation of elaborate written texts, the wide variety of load-bearing domesticated animals, and the other ingredients that underlay the radical new ideas of this era in the narrow band above the equator in the Eastern Hemisphere. Nonetheless, among the Chavín of the Andes, the Olmecs of Mesoamerica, the peoples of Nubia, and the West African Nok, exciting new developments were taking place in the first millennium BCE. Since the written record from these communities is limited, however, knowledge of their societies and beliefs is based largely on archaeological remains.

THE CHAVÍN IN THE ANDES

Around 1400 BCE, as the **Chavín** peoples began to share a common belief system, they also began to organize their societies vertically along the steep mountainsides and deep fertile valleys of the Andes. (See Map 5.1.) Valley floors yielded tropical and subtropical produce; the mountains supported maize and other crops; and in the highlands, potatoes became a staple and llamas produced wool and dung (used as fertilizer and fuel) and, eventually, served as beasts of burden. Llamas could not transport humans, however, so the Chavín migratory and political reach remained limited. While most necessities were available nearby thanks to the ecological diversity of the region, the Chavín did undertake some long-distance trade—mainly in dyes and precious stones, such as obsidian. By 900 BCE, the Chavín were erecting elaborate stone carvings, using advanced techniques to weave fine cotton textiles, and making gold, silver, and copper metal goods. Scholars have found evidence that by 400 BCE trade in painted textiles, ceramics, and gold objects spanned the Pacific coast, the Andean highlands, and the watershed eastward to the tropical rain forests of the Amazon basin.

What unified the fragmented Chavín communities was a shared artistic tradition manifested in their devotion to powerful deities. Their spiritual capital was the central temple complex of Chavín de Huántar, in modern Peru's northeastern highlands. The temple boasted a U-shaped platform whose opening to the east surrounded a sunken, circular plaza. From its passageways and underground galleries, priests—whom the Chavín believed were transformed into jaguars through their consumption of hallucinogenic drugs—could make dramatic entrances during ceremonies. Pilgrims brought tribute to Chavín de Huántar, where they worshipped and feasted together. The Chavín drew on influences from as far away as the Amazon and the Pacific coast as they created devotional

Chavín de Huántar Chavín de Huántar is nestled in the Peruvian Andes. The temple complex contains several structures; the so-called Northern Platform is pictured here.

cults that revered wild animals as representatives of spiritual forces. Carved stone jaguars, serpents, and hawks, baring their large fangs and claws to remind believers of nature's powers, dominated the spiritual landscape. The Chavín cult gave way around 400 BCE to local cultural heirs, but some elements of it survived in successor religions adopted by stronger states to the south.

THE OLMECS IN MESOAMERICA

Farther to the north, the first complex society in Mesoamerica emerged about 1500 BCE between the highland plateaus of central Mexico and the Gulf Coast around modern-day Veracruz. (See Map 5.5.) The **Olmecs** are an example of a first-generation community that created new political and economic institutions while contemplating profound questions about the nature of humanity and the world beyond. The culture of the Olmecs—a name meaning "inhabitants in the land of rubber," one of their staples—sprang up from local village roots. The region's peoples formed a loose confederation of villages scattered from the coast to the highlands, mainly nestling in river valleys and along the shores of swampy lakes. Their residents traded with one another, shared a common language, and worshipped the same gods. Around 1500 BCE, the residents of hundreds of hamlets began to develop a single culture and to spread their beliefs, artistic achievements, and social structure far beyond their heartland.

At the core of Olmec culture were its decentralized villages, which housed hundreds—possibly thousands—of households apiece. In these settlements productive subsistence farmers cultivated most of the foodstuffs their communities needed (especially maize, beans, squash, and cacao), while shipping lightweight products including ceramics and precious goods (such as jade, obsidian, or quetzal feathers, used to create masks and ritual figurines) to other villages. Most of the precious

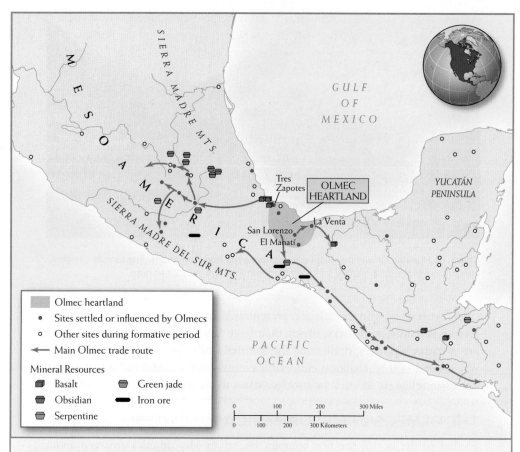

Map 5.5 The Olmec World, 1500–350 BCE

The Olmecs had a strong impact on Mesoamerica's early cultural integration.
- According to this map, how did the Olmecs influence people living beyond the Olmec heartland?
- What geographical factors limited the extent of Olmec influence?
- What is the relationship between resources, trade routes, and Olmec settlements?

objects were for religious purposes rather than everyday consumption. Despite their dispersed social landscape, the Olmec peoples created shared belief systems, a single language, and a priestly class who ensured that villagers and residents of the new urban centers followed highly ritualized practices.

Cities as Sacred Centers The primary Olmec cities, including San Lorenzo, La Venta, and Tres Zapotes, were small compared with the urban centers of Afro-Eurasia, but they served as devotional and secular hubs. The cities featured specialized structures that included massive earthen mounds, platforms, palaces, capacious plazas, and large stone monuments (colossal heads, jaguar sculptures, and basalt thrones). Beneath the mounds of the devotional centers, archaeologists have found axes, knives of sharpened obsidian, other tools, and jade figurines, buried as tokens for those who dwelled in the supernatural world. Olmec devotional art depicted natural and supernatural entities—not just snakes, jaguars, and crocodiles, but also certain humans called shamans, whom the Olmecs believed could commune with the supernatural and transform themselves wholly or partly into beasts. A common figurine is the "were-jaguar," a being that was part man, part animal. Shamans representing jaguars invoked the Olmec rain god, a jaguar-like being, to bring rainfall and secure the land's fertility.

A range of agriculture-linked devotional activity thrived in the Olmecs' major cities. Noble players competed in a complex ball game to honor the rain god, as fans cheered them on. Olmec archaeological sites are filled with the remains of game equipment and trophies, some of which were entombed with dead rulers so they could play ball with the gods in the otherworld. It is likely that athletics and human sacrifice were blended in the same rituals. Many monuments depict a victorious and costumed ballplayer (sporting a jaguar headdress or a feathered serpent helmet) atop a defeated, bound human, though scholars are not sure whether the losers were literally executed. Nevertheless, rainmaking rites did include human sacrifice, which involved executing and dismembering captives. The Olmecs believed that the gods defined calendric passages, and thus controlled the seasons and crucial rainfall patterns. Priests, charting celestial movements, devised a complex calendar that marked the passage of seasons and generations. Indeed, the Olmecs' ceremonial life—from ball games to human sacrifice to calendars—was focused on agricultural and rainfall cycles.

Social Distinctions Unlike many decentralized agrarian cultures that were simple and egalitarian, the Olmecs developed an elaborate cultural system marked by many tiers of social rankings. Daily labor kept village-focused Olmecs busy. The vast majority worked the fertile lands as part of household units, with children and parents toiling in the fields with wooden tools, fishing in streams with nets, and hunting turtles and other small animals. Most Olmecs juggled the needs of their immediate families, those of their village neighbors, and the taxes imposed by rulers.

The priestly class, raised and trained in the palaces at La Venta, San Lorenzo, and Tres Zapotes, directed the exchanges of sacred ritual objects among farming communities. Alongside the priestly elite emerged a secular elite composed of chieftains who supervised agrarian transactions, oversaw artisans, and accepted villagers' tribute. The highest-ranking chieftains commanded villages scattered over a large territory. The chieftains set up workshops, managed by foremen, where craftworkers created pots, painted, sculpted, and wove. Some of their work featured stones and gems imported from surrounding villages.

It is likely that a merchant class also developed to facilitate trade throughout Olmec territories and beyond. As the Olmecs' arts expanded, so did their demand for imported obsidian and jade, seashells, plumes, and other precious goods. The Olmecs exported rubber, cacao, pottery, ceramics, figurines, jaguar pelts, and crocodile skins throughout Mesoamerica. They also conveyed their belief system to neighbors—if not to convert them, at least to influence them and reinforce a sense of superiority.

The Loss of Centers The breakdown of the Olmec culture around the middle of the first millennium is shrouded in mystery. The decline was abrupt in some centers and drawn out in others. At La Venta, the altars and massive basalt heads were defaced and buried, indicating a dramatic shift. Yet there is little evidence of a spasm of war, a peasant uprising, a population shift, or conflict within the ruling classes. Indeed, in many parts of the heartland, the religious centers that had been the hubs of the Olmec world were abandoned but not destroyed. As the bonds between rulers and subjects weakened, so did the exchange of ritual objects that had enlivened the Olmec centers and made them magnets for obedience and piety. Although Olmec hierarchies collapsed, much of the Olmec hinterland remained heavily populated and highly productive. While it lasted, the Olmec combination of an integrated culture, a complex hierarchical social structure, and urban-centered devotional practice offered a degree of cohesion unprecedented in the Americas.

COMMON CULTURES IN SUB-SAHARAN AFRICA

In Africa, too, widespread common cultures emerged in a number of favorable locations. Africa's most significant climate-related historical development in the first millennium BCE was the continued drying up of the northern and central landmass and the sprawl of the great Sahara Desert. (See Map 5.6.) Large areas that had once supported abundant plant and animal life, including human settlements, now became sparsely populated. As a result, the African peoples began to coalesce in a few locations. Most important was the Nile Valley, which may have held more than half of the entire population of Africa at this time.

Climatic change divided Africa from the equator northward to the Sahara Desert into four zones. The first zone was the Sahara itself, which never completely emptied out despite its extreme heat and aridity. Its oases supported pastoral peoples, who raised livestock and promoted contacts between the northern and western parts of the landmass. South of the Sahara was the Sahel, literally the "coast" (Arabic *sahil*) of the great ocean of sand, which saw no city of great size in this period. The next zone was the Sudanic savanna, an area of high grasslands stretching from present-day Senegal along the Atlantic Ocean in the west to the Nile River and the Red Sea in the east. Many of West Africa's kingdoms later emerged there because the area was free of the tsetse fly, which was as lethal to

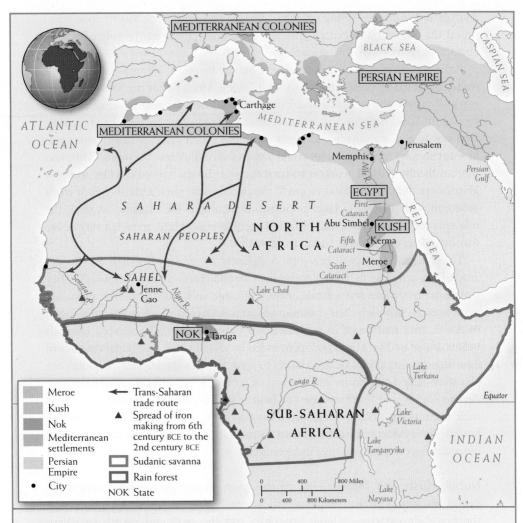

Map 5.6 Africa, 500 BCE

....

The first millennium BCE was a period of cultural, economic, and political integration for North and sub-Saharan Africa.

- According to this map, what effect did the Mediterranean colonies have on Africa?
- What main geographic feature integrated Kush and Egypt? What impact might cataracts have had on integration?
- Where does the map indicate there was a spread of ironworking? What features on the map may have influenced where ironworking spread?

animals as to humans, killing off cattle, horses, and goats. The fourth zone comprised the western and central African rain forests, a sparsely populated region characterized by small-scale societies.

Although there was contact across the Sahara by means of trans-Saharan trade routes traversed by camel and via the Nile Valley, Africa below the Sahara differed markedly from North Africa and Eurasia. It did not develop plow agriculture; instead, its farmers depended on hoes. Also, except in densely populated regions, land was held communally and never carried as much value as labor, which was in short supply. African peoples could always move into new locations. They had more difficulty finding workers to turn the soil. In the savanna, millet and sorghum were the primary food crops; in the rain forests, yams and other root crops predominated. Relatively large populations inhabited the Sudanic savanna, the sole area for which substantial historical records exist. Here, in fact, a way of life that historians call Sudanic began to crystallize.

These Sudanic peoples were not completely dependent on their feet to get around (in contrast to their llama-reliant counterparts in the Americas). They had domesticated several animals, including cattle and goats, and even possessed small horses. Although their communities were scattered widely across this region of Africa, they had much in common. For example, they all possessed religious beliefs dominated by a high god, polities led by sacred kings, and burial customs of interring servants alongside dead rulers to serve them in the afterlife. Sudanic peoples were skilled cultivators and weavers of cotton, which they had domesticated. Archaeologists and historians used to believe that the Sudanic peoples borrowed their institutions, notably their sacred kingships, from their Egyptian neighbors, but linguistic evidence and their burial customs indicate that the Sudanic communities developed these practices independently.

Nubia: Kush and Meroe One of the most highly developed locations of common culture in sub-Saharan Africa was Nubia, a region lying between the first Nile cataract (a large waterfall) and the sixth, just north of where the Blue and White Niles come together. From at least the fourth millennium BCE onward, peoples in this region had contact with both the northern and southern parts of the African landmass. It was one of the few parts of sub-Saharan Africa known to the Eurasian world during this period.

In the second and first millennia BCE, complex societies formed and developed into states in Nubia. The first of the important Nubian states was Kush. A thriving contemporary of Middle Kingdom Egypt, it flourished between 1700 and 1500 BCE between the first and third cataracts and had its capital at Kerma. Because of its proximity to Egypt, it adopted many Egyptian cultural and political practices, even as it was under constant pressure from the northern powerhouse. Its successor states had to move farther south, up the Nile, to keep free from the powerful Egyptians; the kingdom's capitals were repeatedly uprooted and relocated upriver.

Temple of the Lion God at Naqa The small, steep Nubian pyramids of the Meroitic kingdom, reflecting its Egyptian connections up the Nile, are familiar to many. But the kings and queens of Meroe also built other structures that echoed Egyptian themes and architecture. Pictured here is the façade of the temple of the Lion God, Apedemak, at Naqa in the ancient Meroitic kingdom. To the right of the entrance, Queen Amanitore (c. 50 CE) strikes down her enemies in a scene reminiscent of images of Thutmosis III (fifteenth century BCE) or Ramses III (twelfth century BCE) at Luxor.

Nubia was Egypt's corridor to sub-Saharan Africa; a source of ivory, gold, and enslaved men and women; and an area that Egyptian monarchs wanted to dominate. To the Egyptians, the land of Kush and its people were there to be exploited, not conquered, as Egyptians had no desire to live there. Ramses II left his mark with his magnificent monuments at the Nubian site Abu Simbel around 1250 BCE.

Building on the foundations of earlier kings who had ruled the region of Nubia, the **Meroitic kingdom** arose in the fourth century BCE and flourished until 300 CE. This kingdom was centered in the city of Meroe farther south along the Nile, close to its sixth cataract, in the region today known as Sudan. The Meroitic kingdom's rulers were influenced by pharaonic culture, adapting hieroglyphs, erecting pyramids in which to bury their rulers, viewing their kings as divine, and worshipping the Egyptian god Amun. Meroe became a thriving center of production and commerce. Its residents were especially skilled in iron smelting and the manufacture of textiles, and their products circulated widely throughout Africa. However, Meroe was equally a part of the Sudanic savanna way of life—as evidenced by the distinctiveness of its language and the determination of its inhabitants to retain political autonomy, including, if necessary, moving farther south, out of the orbit of Egypt and more into the orbit of Sudanic polities. Although they called their kings pharaohs, the influential leaders of Meroe selected them from among the many members of the royal family, attempting to ensure that their rulers were men of proven talents. In addition, the Nubian states had close commercial contacts with other merchants and commercial hubs in Sudanic Africa.

West African Kingdoms Complex societies also thrived in West Africa. The most spectacular West African culture of the first millennium BCE was the Nok culture, which arose in the sixth century BCE in an area that is today the geographical center of Nigeria. Though slightly south of the savanna lands of West Africa, the area was (and still is) in regular contact with that region. At Taruga, near the present-day village of Nok, early iron smelting occurred in 600 BCE. Taruga may well have been the first place in western Africa where iron ores were smelted. Ironworking was significant for the Nok peoples, who moved from using stone materials directly to iron, bypassing the bronze working that had been a transitional stage in the technology characteristic of other advanced metallurgists in Afro-Eurasia (as in second-millennium BCE Shang China and the Mediterranean). The Nok made iron axes and hoes, iron knives and spears, and luxury items for trade. However, they achieved historical fame not for their iron-smelting prowess but for their magnificent terra-cotta figurines, discovered in the 1940s in the tin-mining region of central Nigeria. These naturalistic figures date to at least 500 BCE. They were likely altarpieces for a cult associated with the land's fertility. Placed next to new lands that were coming into cultivation, they were believed to bless the soil and enhance its productivity.

The Nok were not the only culture developing in this region. Peoples living in the Senegal River basin and Mande peoples around the western branch of the Niger River also began to establish large settlements, in which artisans smelted iron ore and wove textiles and merchants engaged in long-distance trade. West Africa was also home to the Bantu-speaking peoples destined to play a major role in the history of the landmass. Around 300 BCE, small Bantu groups began to migrate southward into the equatorial rain forests, where they cleared land for farming; from there, some moved on to southern Africa. (See Chapter 8 for a discussion of the Bantu peoples.) As impressive as the ironworking, figurines, and trade of West Africa were, these cultures were not yet producing—or at least there is no record of—the type of Axial Age developments that were happening in much of Eurasia.

Conclusion

Afro-Eurasia's great river-basin areas—the Nile, the Tigris-Euphrates, the Indus—were still important in the first millennium BCE, but their time as centers of world cultures was passing. With the development of second-generation societies, these river-basin areas yielded some of their prominence to regions that had been on their fringes, whether the Mediterranean in the west or the Ganges in the east. Within the territorial states in China, the kingdoms and oligarchies in urbanizing South Asia, and the city-states in the Mediterranean world, great social and intellectual dynamism occurred.

During this Axial Age across much of Eurasia, influential thinkers came to the fore with perspectives quite different from those of the earlier river-basin societies and other contemporary developments elsewhere in worlds apart. In China, the political instability of the Warring States period propelled scholars such as Confucius to engage in political debate, in which they stressed respect for social hierarchy. In South Asia, dissident thinkers challenged the Brahmanic spiritual and political order, and the Buddha articulated a religious belief system that was much less hierarchical than its Vedic predecessor. Mediterranean Greek philosophers offered new views about nature, their political world, and human relations and values—based primarily on secular rather than religious ideas.

Even where contacts with other societies were less intense, innovations occurred as the first complex societies began to arise in the Americas and in sub-Saharan Africa. In the Americas, the Olmecs developed a worldview in which mortals had to appease angry gods through human sacrifice, and built elaborate temples where many peoples could pay homage to the same deities. In West Africa, the Nok peoples promoted interregional trade and cultural contact as they expanded their horizons. In sub-Saharan Africa, settled pockets devised complex cultural foundations for community life. One spectacular example of sub-Saharan and Egyptian synthesis was the Nubian culture of the Meroitic kingdom. As the world was coalescing into culturally distinct regions, many of the ideas newly forged in Eurasia, the Americas, and sub-Saharan Africa had a continuing impact on societies that followed.

Focus On
The Axial Age

China
- A multistate system emerges from warfare, revolutionizing society and thought.
- Confucius and Master Lao outline new ideals of governing and living.

South Asia
- Small monarchies and urban oligarchies emerge after the Vedic peoples' migrations and rule over societies organized around the *varna* and *jati* system.
- Dissident thinkers like Mahavira and the Buddha challenge Brahman priests and the *varna* and *jati* system.

The Mediterranean World
- Independent city-states emerge from social destruction and facilitate revolutionary principles in rulership, commerce, and thought.

- Thinkers like Socrates, Plato, and Aristotle challenge conventions and encourage public discourse about the role of the individual in society and the way the universe works.

The Americas
- Chavín peoples and the Olmecs produce increasingly hierarchical, agriculture-based societies and connect villages via trade.
- Large-scale common cultures emerge.

Sub-Saharan Africa
- Expansion of the Sahara Desert and population migrations cause people to coalesce in a few locations.
- Early signs of a common culture appear across the Sudanic savanna.

Key Terms

CHRONOLOGY

	1600 BCE	1400 BCE	1200 BCE
East Asia			
South Asia			
The Mediterranean			
The Americas		Olmec culture emerges and diffuses through Mesoamerica 1500–400 BCE	
Sub-Saharan Africa			Chavín culture flourishes in Central Ande of South America 1400–400 B

THINKING ABOUT GLOBAL CONNECTIONS

- **Thinking about Transformation & Conflict and the Axial Age** In the first millennium BCE across Afro-Eurasia, Axial Age thinkers developed radical new ideas in response to their respective political and cultural situations. In what ways did Axial Age thinkers in East Asia (Confucius and Master Lao), South Asia (Mahavira and the Buddha), and the Mediterranean (naturalist philosophers and Socrates) address the unique transformations and conflicts that were taking place where they lived? How do Zoroaster of Persia and the Jewish prophets of Israel, discussed in Chapter 4, fit this model?

- **Thinking about Worlds Together, Worlds Apart and the Axial Age** From the mid-second through the mid-first millennium BCE, "second-generation" societies developed in Eastern Zhou China, the Ganges plain of South Asia, and the Mediterranean, while parts of South America, Mesoamerica, and sub-Saharan Africa birthed their first complex societies. What are the differences between the second-generation societies of Afro-Eurasia and the first complex societies elsewhere, and what might account for these very different, yet contemporary, developments across the globe?

- **Thinking about Changing Power Relationships and the Axial Age** Axial Age thinkers in East Asia, South Asia, and the Mediterranean offered challenges to both political and social traditions. How did the innovative ideas of thinkers such as Confucius, the Buddha, and Socrates contest and help reshape power relationships ranging from the political to the familial?

 Go to INQUIZITIVE to see what you've learned—and learn what you've missed—with personalized feedback along the way.

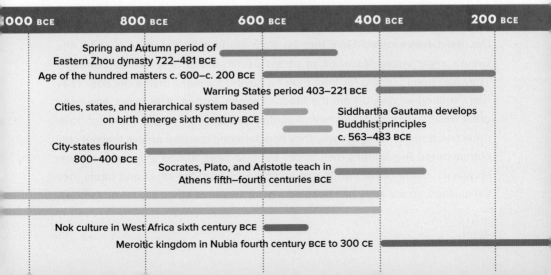

1000 BCE	800 BCE	600 BCE	400 BCE	200 BCE

Spring and Autumn period of Eastern Zhou dynasty 722–481 BCE

Age of the hundred masters c. 600–c. 200 BCE

Warring States period 403–221 BCE

Cities, states, and hierarchical system based on birth emerge sixth century BCE

Siddhartha Gautama develops Buddhist principles c. 563–483 BCE

City-states flourish 800–400 BCE

Socrates, Plato, and Aristotle teach in Athens fifth–fourth centuries BCE

Nok culture in West Africa sixth century BCE

Meroitic kingdom in Nubia fourth century BCE to 300 CE

6

Shrinking the Afro-Eurasian World

350–100 BCE

Core Objectives

- **DESCRIBE** what enabled and motivated Alexander's military pursuits, and **EXPLAIN** why his conquests matter for understanding a connected Afro-Eurasia.

- **DESCRIBE** Hellenism and **EXPLAIN** its impact across Afro-Eurasia.

- **ANALYZE** the political changes that shaped central and South Asia in the aftermath of Alexander's incursion into the region.

- **TRACE** the spread of Buddhism in this period and **EVALUATE** the forces that influenced its spread.

- **TRACE** the early routes of the "Silk Roads" and **ASSESS** their importance in connecting Afro-Eurasia by land and sea.

In the blistering August heat of 324 BCE, at a town on the Euphrates River that the Greeks called Opis (not far from modern Baghdad), Alexander the Great's experienced Macedonian troops declared that they had had enough. They had been fighting far from their homeland for more than a decade. They had marched eastward from the Mediterranean, forded wide rivers, traversed great deserts, trudged over high mountain passes, and slogged through rain-drenched forests. Along the way they had defeated massive armies that not only outnumbered Alexander's own forces but also were armed with fearsome war elephants. Some of his troops had taken wives from the cities and tribes they vanquished, so the army had become a giant swarm of ethnically mixed families.

This was an army like no other. It did more than just defeat neighbors and rivals—it forcefully connected entire worlds, bringing together diverse peoples and lands.

Conquering in the name of building a new world, however, was not what the soldiers had bargained for. They loved their leader, but many thought he had gone too far. They had lost companions and grown weary of war. Some had mutinied at a tributary of the Indus River, halting Alexander's advance into South Asia. Now, at Opis, they threatened to desert him altogether. Summoning up their courage, they voiced these resentments to their supreme commander. Alexander's response was immediate and inspired. In order to persuade his troops not to desert him, he evoked the astounding military triumphs and historic achievement they had accomplished: establishing his rule from Macedonia to the Indus Valley. This far-reaching political vision came to a sudden end with Alexander's death a year later, when he was just thirty-two years old. Even in his short lifetime, though, he had set in motion cultural and economic forces that would transform Afro-Eurasia. As Alexander was expanding eastward, another development was taking form: the Silk Roads. This system of routes constituted the primary commercial network linking East Asia and the Mediterranean world for nearly a thousand years. Many different types of precious commodities were exchanged along its more than 5,000 miles, but the network ultimately took its name from the huge quantities of precious silk that passed along it. At the same time, exchange routes by sea were also taking shape.

As a result of Alexander's conquests and the political developments that followed, as well as the intensifying of trade along land and sea routes, two broad cultural movements came to link diverse populations across wide expanses of the Afro-Eurasian landmass: Hellenism and Buddhism. Hellenism, briefly defined, was a shared Greek identity that spread throughout the lands in which Greeks settled and was expressed in their language, art, architecture, politics, and more. Buddhism, as an Axial Age philosophy, was introduced in the previous chapter. A new form of Buddhism, called Mahayana Buddhism, took shape in the period described in this chapter. New empires—namely Alexander's successor states of the Mediterranean and the Mauryan Empire in South Asia—and newly deepening trade routes created the circuits through which Hellenism and Buddhism flowed.

Imperial conquests and long-distance trade laid the foundations for widespread cultural systems that were far more enduring than the empires themselves. Merchants, monks, and administrators helped connect widespread parts of Afro-Eurasia, as the busy sea-lanes and Silk Roads flourished. Merely a few centuries after the conquests of Alexander and Mauryan kings, the world looked very different from the realms their armies had traversed.

Global Storyline

The Creation of the Silk Roads and the Beginnings of Buddhism

- Conquests by Alexander the Great and the influence of his successor states spread Hellenism across Southwest Asia and into South Asia.

- The Mauryan Empire accelerates the integration of South Asia and helps Buddhism spread throughout that region and beyond.

- "Silk Roads," both overland and by sea, facilitate the movement of commodities (spices, metals, and silks) and ideas (especially Buddhism and Hellenism) across Afro-Eurasia.

Alexander and the Emergence of a Hellenistic World

The armed campaigns of the Macedonians led by Alexander the Great (356–323 BCE) began a drive for empire from the west that connected distant regions and spread a Hellenistic culture throughout the conquered lands. (See Map 6.1.) Alexander came from the frontier state of Macedonia to the north of Greece and commanded a highly mobile force armed with advanced military technologies that had developed during the incessant warfare among Greek city-states in the fifth and fourth centuries BCE. Alexander's novel use of new kinds of armed forces in a series of lightning attacks on the Persian Empire, the nemesis of the Greeks over the previous 200 years, further undermined barriers that separated the Mediterranean world from the rest of Southwest Asia.

Under Alexander's predecessors—especially his father, Philip II—Macedonia had become a large ethnic and territorial state. Philip had unified Macedonia and then gone on to conquer neighboring states. Macedonia boasted gold mines that could finance Philip's new military technology and his disciplined army. Philip's troops included heavily armored infantry that maneuvered in closely arrayed units called phalanxes as well as in large-scale cavalry formations for shock tactics. These infantry and cavalry forces were supported by income not only from Macedonian gold mines but also from the slave trade that passed through Macedonia. By the early 330s BCE, Philip had crushed the Greek city-states to the south, including Athens. After Philip's assassination, his son Alexander steered this new military machine toward the Persian Empire and its king, Darius III.

Historians and biographers have filled libraries with books about Alexander the Great, yet he remains one of the more perplexing figures in world history. Many have explored what motivated Alexander to embark on such an audacious campaign of conquest. To begin with, Alexander was deeply steeped in Greek culture, had absorbed Homer, and hoped to emulate the military exploits of heroic figures like Achilles, Hercules, and Dionysus. Moreover, he had a deep hatred of the Persian Empire; he sought to avenge the Persian invasion of Thrace and the murder of his father, Philip II, which some Macedonian sources attributed to Persian intrigue at Philip's court. Also, the influence of his mother, Olympias, a complex figure much maligned in the historical record, should not be underestimated. Olympias was one of several wives of Philip II (she was also implicated, by some sources, in his assassination), and after Philip's death she may have helped secure Alexander's succession by ordering his rivals killed. For several years after Alexander's death in 323 BCE, she continued to advocate for her son's legacy by advancing the claim of Alexander's son (her grandson) to the throne of Macedonia.

Like many other successful conquerors, Alexander owed much of his success to a readiness to take risks. In his initial forays into Southwest Asia he outpaced, outflanked, and outthought his adversaries, repeatedly taking them by surprise. The Persians had substantial armed forces and an impressive navy. On the battlefield in 331 BCE at Gaugamela (in modern-day northern Iraq), even after having already suffered losses to Alexander in Anatolia (modern Turkey) at the Granicus River in 334 BCE and at Issus in 333 BCE, the Persian king Darius was able to assemble troops from Bactria (modern-day Afghanistan), Scythia (modern-day Ukraine and Kazakhstan), Armenia, and parts of modern-day Turkey that numbered as many as 1,000,000 infantry, 40,000 cavalry, 200 scythed chariots, and 15 war elephants. Even accounting for the tendency of Greek sources to overestimate troop numbers, this assemblage far outnumbered Alexander's infantry of 25,000 and cavalry of 2,000 Macedonians, supported by Greek and mercenary contingents of 10,000. Moreover, the Persians had virtually unlimited financial resources. Yet Alexander's forces were superior in technique, maneuverability, and resourcefulness. Through his military successes he brought under the rule of his

Alexander and Olympias Cameo carved in sardonyx and thought to depict Alexander and his mother, Olympias, in a style used to depict later Hellenistic kings and their queens. A fascinating character in her own right, Olympias exerted a powerful influence on Alexander, helping to strategize his rise to power and working to secure his legacy after his death.

The Global View

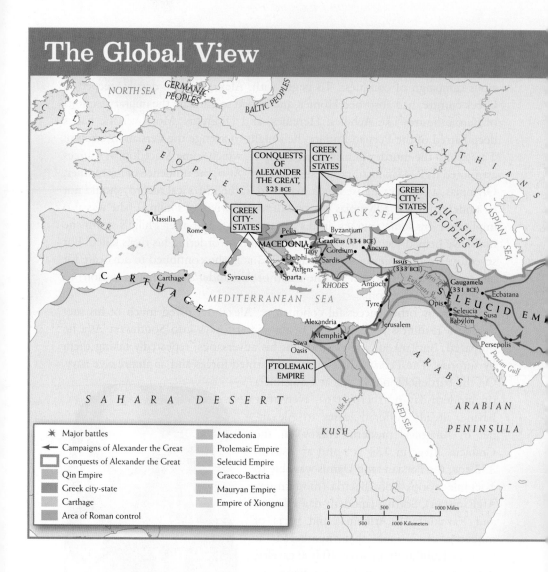

Major battles
Campaigns of Alexander the Great
Conquests of Alexander the Great
Qin Empire
Greek city-state
Carthage
Area of Roman control

Macedonia
Ptolemaic Empire
Seleucid Empire
Graeco-Bactria
Mauryan Empire
Empire of Xiongnu

NORTH SEA
GERMANIC PEOPLES
BALTIC PEOPLES
CELTIC PEOPLES
SCYTHIANS
CAUCASIAN PEOPLES
CASPIAN SEA

CONQUESTS OF ALEXANDER THE GREAT, 323 BCE
GREEK CITY-STATES
GREEK CITY-STATES
GREEK CITY-STATES

Massilia
Rome
Elbo R.
Pella
Byzantium
MACEDONIA
Granicus (334 BCE)
Troy
Gordium
Ancyra
Delphi
Sardis
Athens
Issus (333 BCE)
Sparta
RHODES
Antioch
Gaugamela (331 BCE)
Ecbatana
Tyre
Opis
Seleucia
Susa
SELEUCID EMPIRE
Babylon
Carthage
Syracuse
CARTHAGE
MEDITERRANEAN SEA
Euphrates R.
Tigris R.
Persepolis
Persian Gulf
Alexandria
Jerusalem
Siwa Oasis
Memphis
PTOLEMAIC EMPIRE
SAHARA DESERT
Nile R.
RED SEA
KUSH
ARABS
ARABIAN PENINSULA

0   500   1000 Miles
0   500   1000 Kilometers

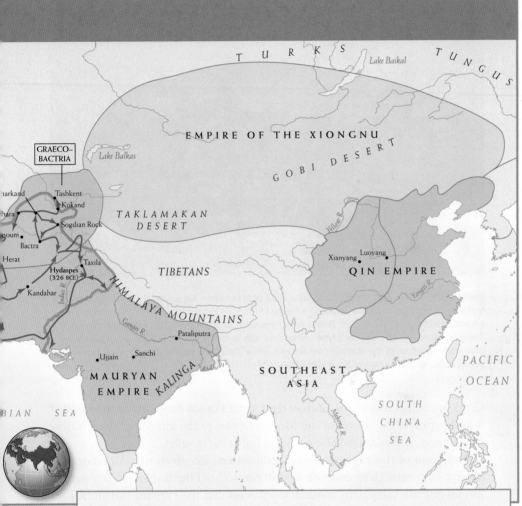

Map 6.1 Afro-Eurasia in 250 BCE, after Alexander's Conquests

Alexander of Macedon did not live long enough or establish the institutions necessary to create one large politically unified empire, but his conquests integrated various Afro-Eurasian worlds culturally and economically. Trace the pathways that Alexander followed on his conquests.

- Locate on the map the Hellenistic successor states. What did these states have in common? How were they different from one another?
- Which areas on the map did Greeks *not* rule? How did the spread of Hellenism affect these areas?
- What features illustrated on the map may have encouraged the spread of Hellenism? What features may have limited the spread of Hellenism?

Battle of Issus Mosaic of the Battle of Issus (333 BCE) between Alexander the Great of Macedon and Darius, the king of Persia (found in a house at Pompeii in southern Italy). Alexander is the bareheaded figure to the far left; Darius is the figure to the right, gesturing with his right hand. The men represent two different types of warfare. On horseback, Alexander leads the cavalry-based shock forces of the Macedonian Greeks, while Darius directs his army from a chariot in the style of the great kings of Southwest Asia.

Greek-speaking elites all the lands of the former Persian Empire, which extended from Egypt and the shores of the Mediterranean to the interior of what is now Afghanistan, and as far to the east as the Indus River valley.

The result of this expansion was hardly an empire, given that Alexander did not live long enough to establish institutions to hold the distant lands together. But his military campaigns continued a process that the Persians had already set in motion of smashing barriers that had separated peoples on the eastern and western ends of Afro-Eurasia. The conqueror saw himself as a new universal figure, a bridge connecting distant cultures. He demonstrated this vision in his adoption of Persian dress and customs; in his marriage to Roxana, the daughter of a chief from Bactria (present-day Afghanistan); and then later in a group wedding at Susa in 324 BCE in which he married Stateira, one of the daughters of the defeated Darius. Eager to create bonds linking west and east at every level, Alexander not only married off many Persian women to his Companions (his elite cavalry force), even if they already had Macedonian wives back at home, but also recognized as many as 10,000 preexisting marriages between rank-and-file Macedonians and Persian women.

Alexander's conquests increased exposure of formerly Persian lands to the commodities of the Mediterranean and to cultural ideas associated with the Greek city-states. Alexander founded dozens of new cities named after himself, not only the famed Alexandria in Egypt but also Iskandariya and Kandahar in modern-day Iraq and Afghanistan. Alexander seized the accumulated wealth that the Persian kings stored in their immense palaces, especially at Persepolis, and dispersed it into the money economies of the Mediterranean city-states. This massive redistribution of wealth fueled a widespread economic expansion in the Mediterranean and beyond.

ALEXANDER'S SUCCESSORS AND THE TERRITORIAL KINGDOMS

Alexander died in Babylon in 323 BCE at age thirty-two. Whether he was struck down by some infectious disease like malaria or by cirrhosis of the liver from his overconsumption of alcohol (which was legendary), Alexander's death brought on the collapse of the regime he had personally held together. The conquered lands fragmented into large territories over which his generals squabbled for control.

Alexander's successors—his generals Seleucus, Antigonus, Ptolemy, Lysimachus, and others—thought of themselves not as citizens of a Greek city-state but rather as absolute rulers over large blocks of territory, modeling themselves on the regional rulers they had defeated. One effect of powerful families' control

Berenice and Ornamental Gorytos *Left:* Portrait head of Berenice, wife and consort of Ptolemy I, the first Macedonian king of Egypt after its conquest by Alexander the Great. Berenice was one of the women who, as queens of huge empires, wielded power and commanded wealth in their own right. *Right:* This ceremonial *gorytos* (bow and arrow case), fashioned from gold and depicting the brutal sacking of a city, was excavated from one of a series of Macedonian royal tombs in Vergina (outside Thessaloniki, in northern Greece). While debates rage over who exactly was buried in these tombs, some argue that this *gorytos* (which is similar to others found in Scythian graves), along with other materials in Tomb II, points to one of the Hellenistic warrior queens, perhaps even Adea Eurydice (the wife of Alexander's half brother Philip III Arrhidaeus).

of whole kingdoms was that some women could now hold great power. Queens in Egypt, Syria, and Macedonia—whether independent or as co-regents with their husbands—established new public roles for women. For example, Berenice I of Egypt (r. c. 320–280 BCE) was the first in a series of powerful women who helped rule the kingdom of the Nile, a line that ended with the famous Cleopatra VII in the 30s BCE. In Macedonia, a series of royal women whose husbands were either dead or incapacitated—Cynane (the widowed half sister of Alexander), Adea Eurydice (the wife of Alexander's half brother Philip III Arrhidaeus, whom sources report to have had some intellectual disability), and Cratesipolis (the widow of one of the generals battling for power in the aftermath of Alexander's death)—not only ruled but also effectively led troops into battle.

Three large territorial states stood out in the new Hellenistic world: the Seleucid Empire (established by Seleucus), stretching from Syria to present-day Afghanistan; Macedonia, ruled by the Antigonids (established by Antigonus); and Egypt, ruled by the Ptolemies (established by Ptolemy). The Seleucid Empire was the largest, comprising much of the territory that had been the Persian Empire, before Alexander's conquest. Macedonia was the smallest but had the distinction of being the homeland of Alexander. The Ptolemaic state, smaller in territory and population than the Seleucid Empire, lasted the longest of Alexander's successor kingdoms, a full 275 years.

The Ptolemies are remarkable for how they effectively merged pharaonic institutions of kingship and priestly power with Hellenistic culture and practices. The Rosetta Stone offers evidence for this cultural hybridity in Hellenistic Egypt. Known for its role in deciphering hieroglyphs, its three scripts record a decree dating to 196 BCE that outlines Ptolemy V's relationship with the Egyptian temples and priesthood. The Ptolemies also united Upper and Lower Egypt, which had been fragmented into as many as eleven political units once the New Kingdom fell, into a centralized state, ruled from Alexandria. The Ptolemies, however, were unwilling to share power with Egyptian nobles. They married within their own royal family; often brothers married sisters or cousins. And despite the trilingualism of the Rosetta Stone, the Ptolemies remained committed to the Greek language and culture. Cleopatra VII, the last of the Ptolemaic line to rule in Egypt, was exceptional in her ability to speak Egyptian, but then again, she was a talented linguist, who also spoke the languages of the Ethiopians, Hebrews, Arabians, Syrians, Medes, and Parthians, according to the later biographer Plutarch.

In areas between these larger Hellenistic kingdoms, middle-sized kingdoms emerged. The old city-states of the Mediterranean, such as Athens and Corinth, still thrived, but now they interacted with a world dominated by these much larger power blocs. On mainland Greece, larger confederations of previously independent city-states formed.

Competition in war remained an unceasing fact of life, but the wars among the kingdoms of Alexander's successors were broader in scope and more complex in organization than ever before. Since the successor kingdoms were nearly equal in strength and employed the same advanced military technology, however, the near-constant state of war between the new kings never achieved much. After battles that killed tens of thousands, and severely injured and wounded hundreds of thousands more, the three major kingdoms—and even the minor ones—remained largely unchanged.

The great powers therefore settled into a centuries-long game of watching one another and balancing threats with alliances. What emerged was a fierce competition that dominated international relations, in which diplomacy and treaty-making sometimes replaced actual fighting. This equilibrium was reminiscent of the first age of international relations in the second millennium BCE (see Chapter 3). Long periods of peace began to grace the intervals between the new kingdoms' violent and destructive wars.

HELLENISTIC CULTURE

The unification of large blocks of territory under Alexander's successors helped spread a common Hellenistic culture. Following existing commercial networks, **Hellenism** was a shared Greek culture that extended across the entire Mediterranean basin and into Southwest Asia. Hellenistic culture included philosophical and political thinking, secular disciplines ranging from history to biology, popular entertainment in theaters, exercising and socializing in gymnasia, competitive public games, and art in many forms. By diffusing well beyond its homeland, it brought worlds together: its influence spread from Greece to all shores of the Mediterranean, into parts of sub-Saharan Africa, across Southwest Asia, and through the Iranian plateau into central and South Asia. It even had echoes in China. Like "Americanization" in the modern world, Hellenism took the attractive elements of one culture—its language, its music, its modes of dress and entertainment—and made these parts of a new global culture. And like "Americanization," in some regions Hellenism was welcomed and in others it was resisted.

Despite pockets of resistance, Hellenism was remarkably successful at taking root across a large swath of Afro-Eurasia and spreading its influence even farther. Archaeologists have found a Greek-style gymnasium and theater in the town of Aï Khanoum in modern Afghanistan and adaptations of Greek sculptures made at the order of the Indian king Chandragupta, of the Mauryan Empire (discussed shortly). We also know of Carthaginians in North Africa who became "Greek" philosophers, and Gallic and Berber chieftains from the far west of France and North Africa had fine Greek-style drinking vessels buried with them.

Common Language The core element of Hellenism was a common language known as *Koine*, or "common," Greek. It replaced the city-states' numerous dialects with an everyday form that people anywhere could understand. *Koine* Greek quickly became the international language of its day. Peoples in Egypt, Judea, Syria, and Sicily, who all had distinct languages and cultures, could now communicate more easily with one another and enjoy the same dramatic comedies and new forms of art and sculpture.

Cosmopolitan Cities Individuals were no longer citizens of a particular city (*polis*); instead they were the first **cosmopolitans**, that is, citizens (*polites*) belonging to the whole world or universe (*kosmos*). Much as Athens had been the model city of the age of the Greek city-state, Alexandria in Egypt became exemplary in the Hellenistic age. Whereas citizens of fifth-century BCE city-states had zealously maintained their exclusive civic identities (as Athenians, Spartans, or Corinthians, for example), Alexandria was a multiethnic city built by immigrants, who rapidly totaled half a million as they streamed in from all over the Mediterranean and Southwest Asia seeking new opportunities. Members of Alexandria's dynamic population, representing dozens of Greek and non-Greek peoples, communicated in the common language that supplanted their original dialects. Soon a new urban culture emerged to meet the needs of so diverse a population.

Hellenistic entertainment in this more connected world had to appeal to broad audiences. Plays were now staged in any city touched by Greek influence and had to translate to any environment. Consequently, the distinctive regional humor and local characters of fifth-century BCE Greek city-state drama gave way to performances populated by the stock characters of standard sitcoms with whom any audience could identify: the greedy miser, the old crone, the jilted lover, the golden-hearted whore, the boastful soldier, the befuddled father, the cheated husband, the rebellious son. Plays were performed in theaters with nearly identical architecture throughout the Mediterranean basin, and laughter

would be just as loud in Syracuse on the island of Sicily as in Scythopolis in the Jordan Valley of Judea.

A new political style of distant, almost godlike kings developed, in part due to the size of the territories over which they ruled. Instead of being accessible, which was not possible when Hellenistic kingdoms and states were so enormous, Hellenistic leaders became larger-than-life figures. Individuals related to political leaders primarily through the personality of the kings and their families. Rulership was personality, and personality could unite large numbers of subjects. For example, Demetrius Poliorcetes, the ruler of Macedonia, stood out in his platform shoes and heavy makeup, and he decorated his elaborate, flowing cape with images of the sun, the stars, and the planets. In the presence of a powerful sun-king like Demetrius, ordinary individuals felt small and inconsequential.

Philosophy and Religion Hellenistic religion and philosophy increasingly focused on the individual and his or her place in the larger world. This growing concern with the individual found expression in many new philosophical schools that proposed a range of ideas, including self-sufficiency (Cynicism), detachment (Epicureanism), and civic involvement (Stoicism). As mentioned in the previous chapter, given the connectedness of Eurasia that was heightened in the late first millennium BCE, echoes with East and South Asian philosophy are not surprising.

For instance, the Athenian Diogenes (c. 412–323 BCE), an early proponent of the Cynic school of philosophy, vividly demonstrates the Hellenistic manifestation of philosophy focused on the self. Diogenes sought freedom from society's laws and customs, rejecting cultural norms as human-made inventions not in tune with nature and therefore false. Similarly turning thoughts to the self, Epicurus (341–270 BCE), the founder of a school in Athens that he called The Garden, envisioned an ideal community of adherents regardless of their gender and social status, centered on his school. Seeking out pleasure and avoiding pain, these Epicureans contemplated the answer to the question "What is the good life?" and struggled to develop a sense of "not caring" (*ataraxia*) about their worries. More widespread than Diogenes's Cynicism and Epicurus's philosophy was Zeno's Stoicism. Zeno (c. 334–262 BCE), from the island of Cyprus, initiated it, and other cosmopolitan figures across the Hellenistic world—from Babylon in Mesopotamia to Sinope on the Black Sea—developed its beliefs. Named after the Stoa Poikilē, the roofed colonnade in the Athenian agora in which Zeno first presented his ideas, Stoicism argued that everything was grounded in nature. Stoicism regarded cities and kingdoms as human-made

◀ **The Theater at Syracuse** The great theater in the city-state of Syracuse, in Sicily, was considerably refurbished and enlarged under the Hellenistic kings. It could seat 15,000 to 20,000 persons. Here the people of Syracuse attended plays written by playwrights who lived on the far side of their world, but whose works they could understand as if the characters were from their own neighborhood. In the common culture of the Hellenistic period, plays deliberately featured typecast characters and situations, thereby broadening their audience.

Dionysus in India While dating to a later period (third century CE), this sarcophagus illustrates the connection of Dionysus with India in stories that reached back to Hellenistic times. In this scene, Dionysus rides in a chariot pulled by two Indian elephants, and even a giraffe and lion join the parade. The presence of this Dionysian scene on a burial container shows the personal value that these Greek cults had for addressing the spiritual concerns of their adherents.

things, important but transient. Being in tune with nature and living a good life required understanding the rules of the natural order and being in control of one's passions, and thus required indifference to pleasure and pain. Stoicism, Epicureanism, and Cynicism offered the individual a range of philosophical responses to the Hellenistic world developing all around.

Long-established religions were also shaped by Hellenism and then re-exported throughout the Mediterranean. For example, Greeks in Egypt drew on the indigenous cult of Osiris and his consort, Isis, to fashion a new narrative about Osiris's death and rebirth that represented personal salvation from death. Isis became a supreme goddess whose "supreme virtues" encompassed the powers of dozens of other Mediterranean gods and goddesses. Believers experienced personal revelations and out-of-body experiences (*exstasis*, "ecstasy"). A ritual of dipping in water (*baptizein*, "to baptize") marked the transition of believers, "born again" into lives devoted to a "personal savior" who delivered an understanding of a new life by direct revelation. These new beliefs, like the worship of Isis, emphasized the spiritual concerns of humans as individuals, rather than the collective worries of kingdoms or city-states. Other Hellenistic adaptations from earlier Greek religion, including cults centered on the Eleusinian Mysteries of Demeter and Bacchic worship of Dionysus, similarly focused on the salvation of the individual as they spread throughout the Hellenistic world.

PLANTATION SLAVERY AND MONEY-BASED ECONOMIES

Ironically, philosophical and religious innovations focused on the self were accompanied by the rise of plantation slavery—the ultimate devaluing of an individual—as an engine of the Hellenistic economy. Large numbers of enslaved people were used in agricultural production, especially in Italy, Sicily, and North African regions close to Carthage. Alexander's conquests and Rome's political rise had produced unprecedented wealth for a small elite. These men and women used their riches to acquire huge tracts of land and to purchase enslaved people (either kidnapped individuals or conquered peoples) on a scale and with a degree of managerial organization never seen before. The slave plantations, wholly devoted to producing surplus crops for profit, helped drive a new Mediterranean economy. The estates created vast wealth for their owners—though at a heavy price to others, as reliance on enslaved laborers now left the free peasants who used to work the fields with no option but to move into overcrowded cities, where employment was hard to find.

The sudden importation of so many enslaved people to work in harsh conditions also had unanticipated outcomes. In 135 BCE, authorities on Sicily faced a massive uprising, led by a Syrian named Eunus, whose followers were amazed at his wonder-working and fortune-telling. A few mistreated enslaved people who resisted their cruel enslavers became a band of 400, whose ranks swelled to tens of thousands of enslaved men, women, and children. The mighty Roman army only with difficulty subdued their revolt. Perhaps more well known is the uprising led by the enslaved gladiator Spartacus on the Italian Peninsula in the late 70s BCE. Again, the superior military force of the Roman state prevailed, but the political repercussions of the slave wars had a fundamental impact in the subsequent political crises that transformed the Roman state.

The circulation of money reinforced the effects of forced labor. With more cash in the economy, wealthy landowners, urban elites, and merchants could more easily do business. The increasing use of Greek-style coins to pay for goods and services (in place of barter) promoted the importation of commodities such as wine from elsewhere in the Mediterranean. As coined money became even more available, even more commercial exchanges occurred. The forced transfer of precious metals to the Mediterranean from Southwest Asia by Alexander's conquests was so large that it actually caused the price of gold to fall.

Roman Slavery One of the most profitable occupations for peoples living beyond the northwestern frontiers of the Roman Empire, in what was called Germania, was providing bodies for sale to Roman merchants. In this relief, we see chained German prisoners whose fate was to become enslaved in the empire. This stone picture supported columns in front of the headquarters of the Roman fortress at Mainz-Kästrich.

In the west, Carthage began to mint its own coins—at first mainly in gold, but later in other metals. Rome moved to a money economy at the same time. By the 270s and 260s BCE, the Romans were issuing coins on a large scale under the pressures of their first war with Carthage (264–241 BCE). By the end of the third century BCE, borderland peoples such as the Gauls had begun to mint coins, imitating the galloping-horse images found on Macedonia's gold coins. So, too, did kingdoms in North Africa, where the coins of Numidian kings bore the same Macedonian royal imagery. By around 100 BCE, inhabitants of the entire Mediterranean basin and surrounding lands were using coins minted by this range of political entities to buy and sell all manner of commodities.

Adaptation and Resistance to Hellenism The new high Greek culture spread far and wide, though it was not fully accepted everywhere in the Mediterranean. It appealed particularly to elites who sought to enhance their position by embracing Hellenistic culture over local values. Syrian, Jewish, and Egyptian elites in the eastern Mediterranean adopted this attitude, as well as Roman, Carthaginian, and African elites in the western Mediterranean.

The Hellenistic influences reached sub-Saharan Africa, where the Meroitic kingdom (see Chapter 5), already influenced by pharaonic forms, now absorbed characteristics of Greek culture as well. It is not surprising that Greek influences were extensive in Meroe, because continuous interaction with the Egyptians also exposed its people to the world of the Mediterranean. Both Meroe and its rival, Axum, located in the Ethiopian highlands, used Greek-style steles (inscribed stone pillars) to boast of their military exploits. Citizens of Meroe worshipped Zeus and Dionysus. The rulers of Meroe, understanding the advantages of the Greek language, employed Greek scribes to record their accomplishments on the walls of Greek-Egyptian temples. In this way, Meroe developed a mix of Greek, Egyptian, and African cultural and political elements.

Not every community succumbed to the allure of Hellenism. The Jews in Judea offer a striking case of resistance and accommodation to its universalizing forces. Having been released from their Babylonian exile by the Persian monarch Cyrus in 538 BCE, the Jews returned to Judea—now a Persian province—and began rebuilding Jerusalem, including a magnificent "second" temple to replace the Temple of Solomon that had been destroyed by the Neo-Babylonians fifty years earlier. While the Persians tolerated local customs and beliefs (see Chapter 4), the Hellenism brought by the Seleucid successor state that took Persia's place after Alexander's conquest brought a shock to Judaism. While some among the Jewish ruling elite began to adopt Greek ways—to wear Greek clothing, to participate in the gymnasium with its cult of male nudity, to produce images of gods as art—others rejected the push. Those who spurned assimilation rebelled against the common elements of Hellenism—its language, music, gymnasia, nudity, public art, and secularism—as being deeply immoral and threatening to their beliefs.

Ultimately, this resistance to Hellenism led to full-scale armed revolt, headed up by the family of the Maccabees. In 167 BCE, the Seleucids provoked the Maccabees by forbidding the practice of Judaism (by outlawing worship and circumcision) and profaning the Jews' temple (by erecting an altar to Zeus in the sanctuary of the temple and sacrificing pigs on it). Though the Maccabees succeeded in establishing an independent Jewish state centered on the temple in Jerusalem, they did not entirely overcome the impact of the new universal culture on Judaism. A huge Jewish community in the Hellenistic city of Alexandria in Egypt embraced the new culture. Scholars there produced a version of the Hebrew scriptures in *Koine* Greek, and historians (such as Jason of Cyrene) and philosophers (such as Philo of Alexandria) wrote in Greek, imitating Greek models.

Similar resistance and accommodation were taking place elsewhere. In the 330s and 320s BCE, when Alexander was uniting the eastern Mediterranean, the city-state of Rome took the first critical military actions to unify Italy. Rather than beginning as a kingdom like Macedonia, Rome went from being a city-state to flourishing as a large territorial state. During this transformation it adopted significant elements of Hellenistic culture: Greek-style temples, elaborately decorated Greek-style pottery and paintings, and an alphabet based on that of the Greeks. Many Roman elites saw immersion in Hellenistic ideals as a way to appear to the rest of the world as "civilized," while others resisted Greek ways as being overly luxurious and contrary to Roman ideals of manliness. The conservative Roman senator Cato the Elder (234–149 BCE) struggled with the tensions that Hellenism introduced to traditional Roman ways. Although he was devoted to the Roman past, the Latin language, and the ideal of small-scale Roman peasant farmers and their families, Cato embraced many Hellenistic influences. He wrote a standard manual for the new economy of slave plantation agriculture, invested in shipping and trading, learned Greek rhetoric (both speaking and writing the language), and added the genre of history to Latin literature. Cato blended

Menorah as Resistance Symbol The menorah—and its miraculous burning for eight days during the rededication of the Jewish temple after it had been profaned by the Hellenistic king Antiochus IV in 167 BCE—became a symbol of Jewish resistance against Hellenistic influence. This image comes from the Roman emperor Titus's triumphal arch (dated to around 81 CE), on which the Romans celebrated their conquest of Judea in the late first century CE.

an extreme devotion to Roman tradition with bold Hellenistic innovations in most aspects of daily life.

Rome's long-time rival, the Phoenician colony of Carthage, also adopted Hellenism but with less internal conflict than in Rome. Carthaginian culture took on important elements of Hellenistic culture. For example, some Carthaginians went to Athens to become philosophers, and innovative ideas on political theory and warfare came from the Greek city-states. The design of sanctuaries, temples, and other public buildings in Carthage reveals a mix of Greek-style pediments and columns, Carthaginian designs and measurements, and local North African motifs and structures. Carthaginian women adorned themselves with jewelry that reflected styles from Egypt, such as ornate necklaces of gold and earrings of lapis lazuli.

Already well integrated into the Mediterranean economy, Carthage welcomed the increased communication and exchange that Hellenism facilitated. Carthaginian merchants traded with other Phoenician colonies in the western Mediterranean, with the towns of the Etruscans and the Romans in Italy, with the Greek trading city of Massilia (modern Marseilles) in southern France, and with Athens in the eastern Mediterranean. In addition, the Carthaginians expanded their commercial interests into the Atlantic, moving north along the coast of Iberia and south along the coast of West Africa, even establishing a trading post at the island of Mogador more than 600 miles down the Atlantic coast of Africa. Profoundly shaped by Alexander's conquests, Hellenism spread even farther across Afro-Eurasia with Alexander's successors.

Converging Influences in Central and South Asia

During this period, tighter political organization in South Asia helped spread new influences, like Hellenism and Buddhism, across the region. The high mountains of modern-day Afghanistan were a major geographical barrier to east-west exchange, but they were not impassable. Mountain passes—pinched like the narrow neck of an hourglass between the high plateau of Iran to the west and the towering ranges of Tibet to the east—offered the shortest route through the formidable Hindu Kush range. By crossing these passes, Alexander's armies expanded the routes between the eastern and western portions of Afro-Eurasia and brought about massive political and cultural changes in central and South Asia. Conquerors moved from west to east (like Alexander), from east to west (like the later nomads from central Asia), and from north to south, through the mountains and into the rich plains of the Indus and Ganges River valleys. At the same time, South Asian trade and religious influences, especially Buddhism, moved northward toward routes running west to east along what became known as the Silk Roads.

CHANDRAGUPTA AND THE MAURYAN EMPIRE

Alexander's brief occupation of the Indus Valley (327–325 BCE) helped pave the way for one of the largest empires in South Asian history, the Mauryan Empire. Before the arrival of Alexander's forces, South Asia had been a conglomerate of small warring states. This political instability came to an abrupt halt when, in 321 BCE, an ambitious young man named Chandragupta Mori (or Maurya), inspired by Alexander, seized the throne of the Magadha kingdom and launched a series of successful military expeditions in what is now northern India. These campaigns would lead to the founding of his new Mauryan Empire.

The Magadha kingdom that Chandragupta overthrew had thrived on the lower Ganges plain since the sixth century BCE and had held great strategic advantages over other states. For one thing, it contained rich iron ores and fertile rice paddies. Moreover, on the northeast Deccan plateau ample woods supported herds of elephants, a mainstay of the powerful Magadha mobile military forces, which used elephants to charge down and terrify the enemy. According to Alexander's contemporary Megasthenes (more on him, shortly), fear of facing those elephants and the large army of Magadha was one of the reasons Alexander's troops refused to cross the Ganges. However, by the time Chandragupta Maurya took over the Magadha kingdom, it was suffering under the heavy taxation and greed of its king.

The Mori family, or Mauryans, did not start out as a distinguished ruling family, but economic strength and military skill elevated them over their rivals. Chandragupta (r. 321–297 BCE), though of lowly origins, probably from the Vaishya *varna*, grew up in the Punjab region of the Indus Valley observing Alexander's onslaught and aspiring to be an equally powerful military and political leader. When Alexander withdrew his forces from northern India, Chandragupta inserted himself into the political vacuum created by the Greek withdrawal.

The **Mauryan Empire** (321–184 BCE), founded by Chandragupta, constituted South Asia's first empire and served as a model for later Indian empire builders. The contemporary Greek world knew this empire as "India," stretching from the Indus River eastward. After supplanting Magadha's Nanda monarchic dynasty, which had been in place for just over a century, Chandragupta used his military resources to reach westward beyond the Ganges plain into the area where four tributaries join the Indus. Here he pushed up to the border with the Seleucid kingdom, the largest successor kingdom of Alexander's empire, based in Mesopotamia.

Alexander's eastern successor, the Seleucid king Seleucus Nicator (358–281 BCE), responded by invading Mauryan territory—only to face Chandragupta's impregnable defenses. Soon thereafter, a treaty between the two powers gave a large portion of Afghanistan to the Mauryan Empire. One of the daughters of Seleucus went to the Mauryan court, accompanied by a group of Greek women. Seleucus also sent to Chandragupta's court an ambassador named Megasthenes— the same Megasthenes who reported on the elephants of Magadha's army.

In return for these gifts and diplomacy, the Mauryans sent Seleucus many South Asian valuables, including hundreds of elephants, which the Greeks soon learned to use in battles.

The Seleucid ambassador Megasthenes lived in South Asia for years and gathered his observations while at the Mauryan court into a book titled *Indica*, after the Greek term for this region. Megasthenes's *Indica* depicted a well-ordered and highly stratified society divided into seven groups: philosophers, farmers, soldiers, herdsmen, artisans, magistrates, and councilors. People respected the boundaries between groups and honored rituals that reinforced their identities: members of different groups did not intermarry or even eat together. Megasthenes also noted the ways in which rulers integrated the region—for example, connecting major cities with extensive tree-lined roads, complete with mile markers. These roads facilitated both trade and the movement of troops. Contrary to Greek expectations of a military closely integrated into civil society, Megasthenes reported that soldiers in India were a profession separate from the rest of the population. Mauryan troops did not pursue any other occupation and stood ready to obey their commander. This military force was huge, boasting cavalry divisions of mounted horses, war elephants, and scores of infantry.

The Regime of Aśoka The Mauryan Empire reached its height during the reign of its third king, Aśoka (r. 268–231 BCE), Chandragupta's grandson. Aśoka's lands included almost all of South Asia; only the southern tip of the subcontinent remained outside his control. In 261 BCE, Aśoka launched the conquest of Kalinga, a kingdom on the east coast of the South Asian subcontinent. The Mauryan army triumphed, but at a high price: about 100,000 soldiers died in battle, many more perished in its aftermath, and some 150,000 people endured forcible relocation. Aśoka was appalled and shamed by the brutal devastation his army had wrought. He vowed to cease inflicting pain on his people and pledged to follow the peaceful doctrines of Buddhism, issuing a famous edict that renounced brutal ways.

In his Kalinga Edict, Aśoka proclaimed his intention to rule according to the Indian concept of *dhamma*, a vernacular form of the Sanskrit word *dharma*, understood widely in Mauryan lands to mean tolerance of others, obedience to the natural order of things, and respect for all of earth's life forms. *Dhamma* was to apply to everyone, including the priestly Brahmans, Buddhists, members of other religious sects, and even Greeks. *Dhamma* became an all-encompassing moral code that all religious sects in South Asia accepted. With *dhamma* as a unifying symbol, Aśoka required all people, whatever their religious practices and cultural customs, to consider themselves his subjects, to respect him as their father, and to conform to his moral code—starting with the precept that people of different religions or sects should get along with one another. He also praised the benefits of agrarian progress and banned large-scale cattle

Stupa and Pillar at Sarnath King Aśoka had stupas built across his domain, each holding relics of the Buddha. The stupa at Sarnath at the Deer Garden (*left*), is one of the few that has remained standing since Aśoka's time and marks the place where the Buddha delivered his first sermon. Also in the Deer Garden stands this edict pillar (*right*). Aśoka had his policies carved on grand pillars like this one, capped by majestic sculptures of animals. This pillar capital has been established as the national emblem of the Republic of India since its independence.

sacrifice as detrimental to agriculture. Meanwhile, he warned the "forest people," the hunters and gatherers living beyond the reach of government, to avoid making trouble.

To disseminate the ideals of *dhamma*, Aśoka regularly issued decrees, which he had chiseled on stone pillars and boulders in every corner of his domain, selecting locations where people were likely to congregate and where they could hear the words as read to them by the few who were literate. Occasionally he also issued edicts to explain his Buddhist faith. All were inscribed in local languages, including Sanskrit, as well as Greek and Aramaic in the Hellenistic- and Persian-influenced northwest.

The Mauryan Empire at its height encompassed 3 million square miles, including all of what is today Pakistan, much of what is Afghanistan, the southeastern part of Iran, and the whole of the Indian subcontinent except for the lands at the southern tip. Its extraordinarily diverse geography consisted of jungles, mountains, deserts, and floodplains, and its equally disparate population of 50 to 60 million inhabitants was made up of pastoralists, farmers, forest dwellers, merchants, artisans, and religious leaders. Yet Aśoka's promotion of the Buddhist tenet of *dhamma* and his elaborate administrative structure were not enough to hold together his empire, which did not last long after his death in 231 BCE.

The proliferation of Buddhism made possible by Aśoka's adoption and whole-hearted sponsorship of the faith, however, was a lasting impact of his reign.

GREEK INFLUENCES IN CENTRAL ASIA

Hellenistic influences shaped politics and culture in the regimes that succeeded direct Greek control in central Asia. Alexander's military had thrust into Asia and reached as far as the Punjab. There he defeated several rulers of Gandhara in 326 BCE. In the course of this campaign he planted many garrison towns—especially in eastern Iran, in northern Afghanistan, and in the Punjab, where he needed to protect his easternmost territorial acquisition. These towns were originally stations for soldiers, but they soon became centers of Hellenistic culture. Many of these outposts displayed the characteristic features of a Greek city-state: a colonnaded main street lined by temples to patron gods or goddesses, a theater, a gymnasium for education, an administrative center, and a marketplace. Following Alexander's death, Seleucus Nicator built more of these Greek garrison towns before he concluded peace with Chandragupta Maurya and withdrew from the region.

The garrison towns founded by Alexander and Seleucus remained and grew into Hellenistic centers. Once the Greek soldiers who had been stationed in them realized they would be spending their lives far from their homeland, they married local women and started families. Bringing their Hellenistic customs to the local populations, the soldiers established institutions familiar to them from the Greek city-states. *Koine* Greek was the official language, but because locals used their own languages in daily life, subsequent generations were bilingual. For centuries, traditional Greek institutions—especially Greek language and writing—survived many political changes and much cultural assimilation, providing a common basis of engagement in a long zone stretching from the Mediterranean to South Asia.

Hellenistic influences were even more pronounced in the regimes that succeeded Seleucid control in central Asia in the late third century BCE. The Seleucid state had taken over the entirety of the former Persian Empire, including its central Asian and South Asian territory. The Hellenistic kingdom of **Bactria** broke away from the Seleucids around 200 BCE to establish a strong state that included the Gandhara region in modern Pakistan. As Mauryan power receded from the northwestern part of India, the Bactrian rulers extended their conquests into this area. Because the cities that the Bactrian Greeks founded included many Indian residents, they have been called "Indo-Greek." Those in Gandhara incorporated familiar features of the Greek polis, but inhabitants still revered Indian gods and goddesses.

Hellenistic Bactria served as a bridge between South Asia and the Greek world of the Mediterranean. Among the goods that the Bactrians sent west were elephants, which were vital to the Greek armies there. Not only did the Bactrian

Greeks revive the cities in India left by Alexander, but they also founded new Hellenistic cities in the Gandhara region. The Greek king Demetrius, who invaded India around 200 BCE, entrusted the extension of his empire in the northern region of India to his generals, many of whom became independent rulers after his death. Sanskrit literature refers to these Greek rulers as the Yavana kings—a word derived from "Ionia," a region whose name applied to all those who spoke Greek or came from the Mediterranean.

Aï Khanoum, on the Oxus River (now the Amu) in present-day Afghanistan, was the site of an administrative center, possibly the capital of the Bactrian state. Unearthed by archaeologists in the 1960s, Aï Khanoum had avoided the devastations that befell so many other Hellenistic cities in this region. Greek-style architecture and inscriptions indicate that the original residents of Aï Khanoum were soldiers from Greece. Following the typical pattern, they married local women and established the basic institutions of a Greek polis. Aï Khanoum's characteristic Greek structures included a palace complex, a gymnasium, a theater, an arsenal, several temples, and elite residences. Featuring marble columns with Corinthian capitals, the palace contained an administrative section, storage rooms, and a library. A main road divided the city into lower and higher parts, with the main religious buildings located in the lower city. Though far from Greece, the elite Greek residents read poetry and philosophy and staged Greek dramas in the theater. Grape cultivation supported a wine festival associated with the god Dionysus. The remains of various statues indicate that the residents not only revered the Greek deity Athena and the demigod Heracles but also paid homage to the Persian Zoroastrian religion.

Perhaps the ruler most adept at mingling Greek and Indian influences was Menander (also known as Milinda), the best-known Yavana/Hellenistic

Three Coins *Top:* Wearing an elephant cap, Demetrius of Bactria titled himself the king of Indians as well as Greeks. On the other side of the coin is Hercules. *Middle:* The king Menander is remembered by Buddhists for his curiosity about their theology. His image appears on one side of the coin with a Greek legend of his name and title. On the other side, Athena is surrounded by Kharosthi script, an Indian type of writing. *Bottom:* The Scythian king Maues used Greek to assert his position as "King of Kings" on one side of his coin. On the other side, the goddess Nike is surrounded by Kharosthi letters.

city-state king of the mid-second century BCE. Using images and legends on coins to promote both traditions among his subjects, Menander claimed legitimacy as an Indian ruler who also cultivated Greek cultural forms. The face of his coins bore his regal image surrounded by the words "King, Savior, Menander," in Greek. The reverse side featured the Greek goddess Athena and the king's title in the local Prakrit language, using Kharosthi script. This mixed Indo-Greek identity was not confined to coins. In his discussions with a Buddhist sage, King Menander debated the nature of the Buddha (was he human or divine?) and showed a keen interest in South Asian religious influences even as he embraced Hellenism. These Indo-Greek legacies persisted long after the Hellenistic regimes collapsed, because they remained essential to communication and trade around the rim of the Indian Ocean.

The Transformation of Buddhism

During this time of political and social change, South Asia also experienced upheavals in the religious sphere, as Hellenism and other east-west connections transformed Buddhism. Impressed by Hellenistic thought, South Asian peoples blended it with their own ethical and religious traditions. Beginning among the Yavana city-states in the northwest, where Buddhism's sway was most pronounced, this blended Buddhism rapidly spread to other regions that were experiencing the same changes. In addition to Hellenism, other layers of influence came together in South Asia through increased seafaring and interactions with nomadic peoples. This cultural fusion profoundly transformed and enriched Buddhism.

INDIA AS A SPIRITUAL CROSSROADS

Many land and sea routes now converged in India, rendering the region a melting pot of ideas and institutions. Improved mastery of the monsoon trade winds in this period opened the Indian Ocean to commerce and made India the hub for long-distance ocean traders and travelers. Another major influence on Buddhism was the Kushans, a horse-riding nomadic group who stabilized east-west connectivity through central Eurasia in the first century CE. With Kushan patronage and the thriving commerce their stability brought to the region, Buddhist communities grew so rich that monks began to live in elegant monastic complexes. (We will discuss the Kushans and their role in Silk Road trade later in this chapter.) The center of each monastic community was a stupa, with its Buddhist relics and sculptures depicting the Buddha's life and teachings. Such monasteries provided generously for the monks, furnishing them with halls where they gathered and worshipped and rooms where they meditated and slept. Buddhist monasteries were also open to the public as places for worship.

THE NEW BUDDHISM: THE MAHAYANA SCHOOL

This mixing of new ways—nomadic, Hellenistic, Mesopotamian, and Persian—with traditional Buddhism produced a spiritual and religious synthesis: **Mahayana** ("Great Vehicle") **Buddhism**. In the first two centuries of the Common Era, Mahayana Buddhists resolved a centuries-long dispute over whether the Buddha was a god or a wise human. They affirmed that the Buddha was indeed a deity. However, Mahayana Buddhism was accommodating; it offered a spiritual pluralism that incorporated outside influences and positioned Indian believers as a cosmopolitan people.

Mahayana Buddhism appealed especially to foreigners and immigrants who traded or settled in India because it made the Buddha easier to understand. The Buddha's preaching had stressed life's suffering and the renunciation of desire to end suffering and achieve nirvana. Newcomers to the region and to Buddhism—such as migrants or traders—saw no attraction in a belief that life consisted of painful cycles of birth, growth, death, and rebirth. This sharp dichotomy between a real world of hardship and the Buddha's abstract world of nirvana gave way to the Mahayana Buddhists' vision that **bodhisattvas**—enlightened demigods, ready to reach nirvana—delayed doing so in order to help others attain it. Early Mahayana texts, like "The Practice of Perfect Wisdom," describe in detail the characteristics of bodhisattvas. These bodhisattvas prepared spiritual halfway points to welcome deceased devotees not yet

Buddhist Cave Temple at Ajanta Buddhists excavated cave temples along the trade routes between ports on the west coast of India and places inland. Paintings and sculptures from Ajanta became the models of Buddhist art in central Asia and China.

ready to release their desires and enter nirvana. The universe of the afterlife in Mahayana Buddhism presented an array of alternatives to the harsh real existence of worldly living. With its bodhisattvas, Mahayana Buddhism enabled all individuals—the poor and powerless as well as the rich and powerful—to move from a life of suffering into a happy existence.

NEW IMAGES OF THE BUDDHA IN LITERATURE AND ART

Just as Buddhism absorbed outside influences and became more appealing, it also inspired literature and art that appealed to diverse peoples. A new genre of literature dealing with the Buddha and the bodhisattvas emerged. Buddhist texts written in Sanskrit disseminated the life of the Buddha and his message far and wide, reaching far corners of Asia. Asvaghosa (c. 80–c. 150 CE), a great Buddhist thinker, wrote a biography of the Buddha, which set the Buddha's life story within the commercial urban environment of the Kushan Empire (instead of in the rural Shakya republic in the Himalaya foothills, where he had actually lived). Asvaghosa's largely fictive version of the Buddha's life story spread rapidly throughout India and beyond, introducing the Buddha and his teachings to many potential converts.

The colorful images of Sanskrit Buddhist texts of the first centuries CE gave rise to a large repertoire of Buddhist sculptural art and drama. On Buddhist stupas and shrines, artisans carved scenes of the Buddha's life, figures of bodhisattvas, and statues of patrons and donors. Fashioned from gray schist rock, these Buddhist sculptures from the Kushan territory (modern Pakistan and northwest region

of India), follow what is called the **Gandharan style**. Those from the central region of India, created mainly from local red sandstone, follow what is called Mathuran style. Gandharan Buddhist art shows strong Greek and Roman influences, whereas the Mathuran style evolved from the carved idols of South Asian folk gods and goddesses.

Stupa Staircase The risers from the staircase of a large stupa in the Gandhara region display scenes from Buddhist stories. The upper one shows men in nomads' clothing playing music, including the Greek-style lyre. On the middle and lower ones, men and women in Greek clothing drink and make merry. The pictures are Buddhist versions of performances in a Greek theater.

Buddhas Greco-Roman influence on the iconography of the Buddha was probably responsible for the Gandharan-style attire and facial expression of Buddhas and bodhisattvas. The seated Buddha (*left*) was crafted from bronze and, with its sun-like crown, looks a lot like Hellenistic images of Helios or Apollo. The Mathuran Buddha of the later Gupta period (*right*), carved from red sandstone, wears a robe so transparent that the artist must have had very fine silk in mind when sculpting it.

Despite their stylistic differences, the schools shared themes and cultural elements. Inspired by Hellenistic art and religious tradition, both took the bold step of sculpting the Buddha and bodhisattvas in realistic human form, rather than symbolic form (such as a bodhi tree, which symbolizes the Buddha's enlightenment). Though the Buddha wore no decorations because he had cut off all links to the world, bodhisattvas were dressed as princes because they were still in this world, generously helping others. What was important was bringing the symbolic world of Buddhism closer to the people.

Buddhist art reflected a spiritual system that appealed to people of diverse cultural backgrounds. Consider the clothes of the patron figures. For male and female figures alike, the garments were simple and well adapted to tropical climates. Those indigenous to the semitropical land had nude upper bodies and a wrapping like the modern *dhoti*, or loincloth, on their lower bodies. Jewelry adorned their headdresses and bodies. By contrast, the nomadic patron figures wore traditional cone-shaped leather hats, knee-length robes, trousers, and boots. Figures with Greek clothing demonstrate continuing Hellenistic influence. The jumble of clothing styles illustrates that Buddhist devotees could share a faith while retaining their ethnic or regional differences.

The Formation of the Silk Roads

Although the Silk Roads were not among human history's more trafficked routes, they thoroughly altered history's course because the travelers along them spread their cultures everywhere they stepped. (See Map 6.2.) The Silk Roads were not straight and paved like the Appian Way in the Roman Empire. They were not human made but entirely natural, traversing mountain passes, valleys, and desert oases—and mapped for the first time only in the twentieth century. Often, they were no more than footpaths. Travelers wishing to journey through remote regions were compelled to hire guides.

In the first century BCE, trade routes along these footpaths and passes stretching from China to central Asia and westward had merged into one big intertwined series of routes famously referred to as the **Silk Roads**, even though caravans transported many other precious commodities, such as incense, gemstones, and metals. The first use of the term by modern Europeans occurred when a German traveler and geographer, Baron Ferdinand von Richthofen, entered the term on a map in 1877. But long before that, Roman writers knew the importance of these routes for bringing silk from the east. Most of the trade along the routes took place over short distances and involved barter. Traders traveled only segments of the routes, passing their goods on to others who took them farther along the road and, in turn, passed them on again. The Silk Roads owed much to earlier overland routes through which merchants exchanged frankincense and myrrh from the Arabian Peninsula for copper, tin, iron, gemstones, and textiles. Even so, silk was the routes' most expensive and prized commodity, and hence they are deserving of their present name. The Silk Roads, in addition, were routes through which Buddhists, Zoroastrians, Syrian Christians, and later on Muslims spread their religions eastward, translating their scriptures and modifying their beliefs as believers moved from one culture to another.

The effects of these long-distance exchanges altered the political geography of Afro-Eurasia. Egypt and Mesopotamia faded as sources of innovation and knowledge, becoming instead crossroads for peoples on either side of them. The former borderlands emerged as new imperial centers. What we now call the Middle East literally became a commercial middle ground between the Mediterranean and India. East Asia, principally China, finally connected indirectly with the Mediterranean via central and South Asia. Through China, whose traders reached Bali and other islands now in Indonesia, connections developed with Japan, Korea, and Southeast Asia. China, insulated from the west by the Himalayas and the Pamir Mountains, remained politically and culturally a mysterious land to those from the Mediterranean. Yet products made from silk revealed to the Greeks and Romans that an advanced society lay far to the east.

NOMADS AND TRADE ROUTES

The horse-riding nomads of Inner Eurasia made long-distance trade possible. For centuries, these scattered nomadic peoples had linked entire regions and facilitated trade and interactions between distant communities. Responding to the drying out of their homelands in the second millennium BCE, they moved southward (see Chapter 3). Moving from place to place and maintaining close contact with their animals, the nomads were exposed to—and acquired resistance to—a greater variety of microbes than settled peoples did. Their relative immunity to disease made them ideal agents for linking distant settled communities. Nomads also raced into political vacuums and installed new regimes that linked northwest China and the Iranian plateau. Among the most important of these nomadic peoples were the Xiongnu (also spelled "Hsiung-nu") pastoralists, originally from the eastern part of the Asian steppe in modern Mongolia. By the third century BCE, their mastery of bronze technology made them the most powerful nomadic community in the area.

When Xiongnu power waned, a new empire, that of the Kushans, arose in their place around 50 CE. The Yuezhi, a nomadic group to the west of the Qin, unified the region's tribes, migrated southwestward, and established this Kushan Empire in Afghanistan and the Indus River basin. The Kushans' empire embraced a large and diverse territory and played a critical role in the formation of the Silk Roads. The Kushans had been an illiterate people, but they adopted Greek as their official language. Kushan coinage, like the Indo-Greek coinage discussed earlier, blended Greek and Indian

Three Kushan Coins The blending of multiple religions into empires that were situated on trade routes is demonstrated on Kushan coinage, which includes a wide variety of deities over time. Kanishka I (r. 127–150 CE), who helped foster the spread of Mahayana Buddhism on the Silk Roads, minted coinage with an image of himself sacrificing at an altar on one side and the Buddha on the reverse (*top*). The same king also minted coins with his image encircled with the words "King of Kings" in Greek script on one side and the Greek sun god, Helios, recognizable by the radiate diadem, on the reverse (*middle*). Kanishka II, who ruled over the Kushans in the early third century CE, minted coins featuring the Hindu god Shiva with his bull, Nandi (horned head peeking out from behind Shiva's right leg), on the reverse (*bottom*). The simultaneous commerce of ideas and goods is easy to imagine given that the imagery on coins that facilitated the exchange reflected a range of gods.

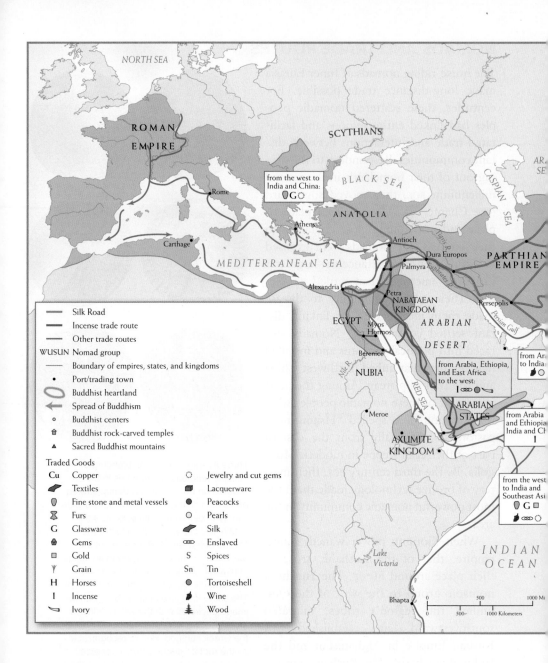

NORTH SEA

ROMAN EMPIRE

SCYTHIANS

BLACK SEA

CASPIAN SEA

ANATOLIA

AR
SE

from the west to India and China:
 G ○

Rome

Athens

Antioch

Dura Europos

PARTHIAN EMPIRE

Palmyra   Euphrates R.

Carthage

MEDITERRANEAN SEA

Alexandria

Petra
NABATAEAN KINGDOM

Persepolis

Tigris R.

EGYPT

Myos Hormos

ARABIAN

DESERT

Persian Gulf

Berenice

from Ar
to India:
 ○

NUBIA

Meroe

RED SEA

from Arabia, Ethiopia, and East Africa to the west:
I ⊂⊃ ●

ARABIAN STATES

from Arabia and Ethiopia
India and Ch
I

AXUMITE KINGDOM

from the west
to India and
Southeast Asi
 G □
 ⊂⊃ ○

Lake Victoria

INDIAN OCEAN

Bhapta

0   500   1000 Mi
0   500—   1000 Kilometers

Silk Road
Incense trade route
Other trade routes
WUSUN Nomad group
Boundary of empires, states, and kingdoms
•   Port/trading town
⬭   Buddhist heartland
⬅   Spread of Buddhism
○   Buddhist centers
⛩   Buddhist rock-carved temples
▲   Sacred Buddhist mountains

Traded Goods

Cu	Copper	○	Jewelry and cut gems
	Textiles	▭	Lacquerware
	Fine stone and metal vessels	●	Peacocks
	Furs	○	Pearls
G	Glassware		Silk
	Gems	⊂⊃	Enslaved
□	Gold	S	Spices
Y	Grain	Sn	Tin
H	Horses	●	Tortoiseshell
I	Incense		Wine
	Ivory	▲	Wood

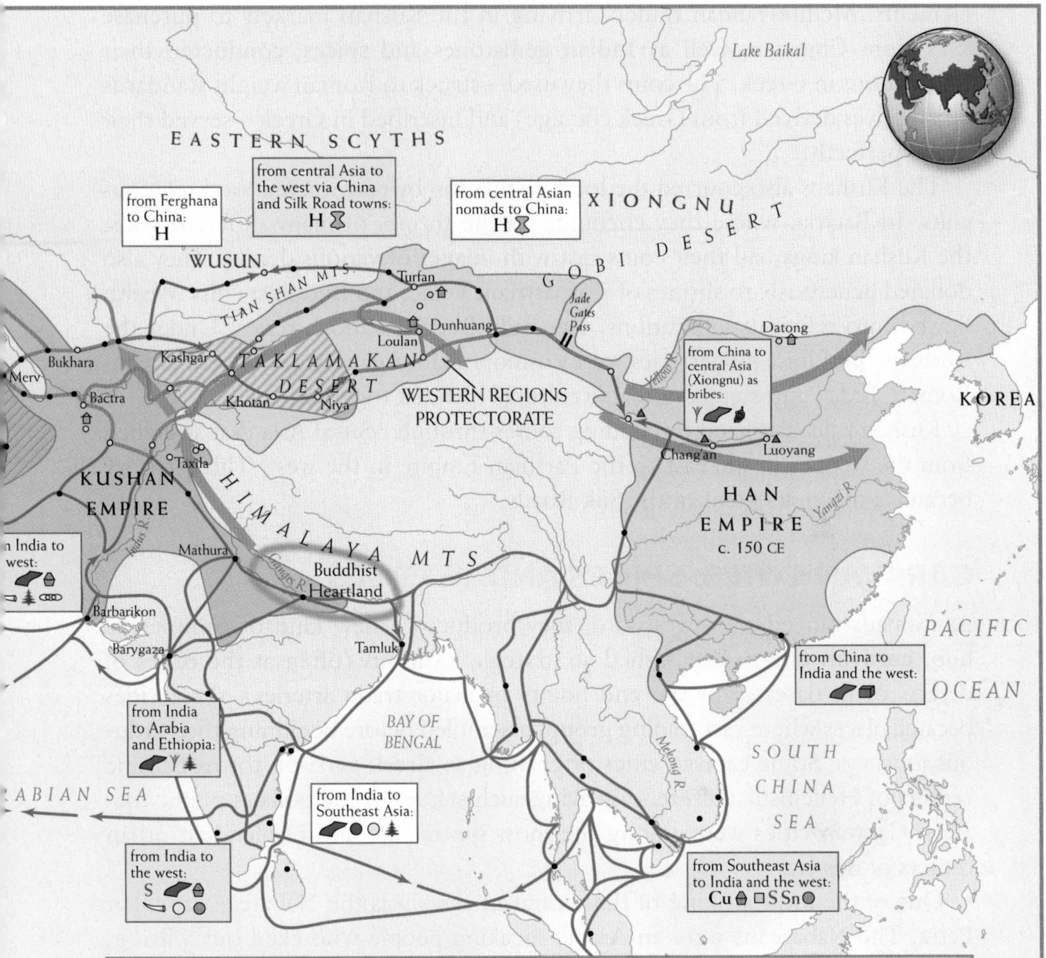

Lake Baikal

EASTERN SCYTHS

from Ferghana
to China:
H

from central Asia to
the west via China
and Silk Road towns:
H ⧗

from central Asian
nomads to China:
H ⧗

XIONGNU

GOBI DESERT

WUSUN

TIAN SHAN MTS

Turfan

Jade
Gates
Pass

Datong

Dunhuang

Loulan

from China to
central Asia
(Xiongnu) as
bribes:

KOREA

Bukhara

Kashgar

TAKLAMAKAN
DESERT

Khotan   Niya

WESTERN REGIONS
PROTECTORATE

Merv

Bactra

Chang'an   Luoyang

KUSHAN
EMPIRE

HIMALAYA MTS

HAN
EMPIRE
c. 150 CE

Yangtze R.

Taxila

n India to
west:

Mathura

Buddhist
Heartland

PACIFIC

Barbarikon

Indus R.
Ganges R.

from China to
India and the west:

OCEAN

Barygaza

Tamluk

from India
to Arabia
and Ethiopia:

BAY OF
BENGAL

Mekong R.

SOUTH
CHINA
SEA

ABIAN SEA

from India to
Southeast Asia:

from India to
the west:
S

from Southeast Asia
to India and the west:
Cu ⬟ □ S Sn ●

Map 6.2 Afro-Eurasian Trade and the Early Spread of Buddhism, c. 150 CE

During the period covered in this chapter, trade along land and sea routes increasingly brought the Afro-Eurasian world together. The early spread of Mahayana Buddhism happened along some of these same routes. This map highlights important commercial routes linking societies and the incredibly wide range of goods traded, as well as the early spread of Buddhism.

- What types of goods were flowing to the east? What goods flowed to the west? What might these flows suggest about the balance of trade in this period?

- Trace the route a trade good might take from Indonesia to Carthage, and from Luoyang to Rome. How do these routes differ? Based on the regions through which each route goes and the various features along the way (ports, Buddhist sites, and so on), what interactions do you imagine might have taken place along either route?

- Based on the location of various Buddhist sites on this map, how were Buddhism and trade interrelated?

elements. Mediterranean traders arriving in the Kushan markets to purchase silks from China, as well as Indian gemstones and spices, conducted their transactions in Greek. The coins they used—struck to Roman weight standards (themselves derived from Greek coinage) and inscribed in Greek—served their needs perfectly.

The Kushans also courted the local population by patronizing local religious cults. In Bactria, where they encountered the shrines of many different gods, the Kushan kings had their coins cast with images of various deities. They also donated generously to shrines of Zoroastrian, Vedic, and Buddhist cults. Wealth flowed into religious institutions, especially Buddhist monasteries. Under the Kushans, Buddhist monasteries were cosmopolitan organizations where Greco-Roman, Indic, and steppe nomadic cultures blended together.

Kushan rule stabilized the trading routes through central Asia that stretched from the steppes in the east to the Parthian Empire in the west. This territory became a major segment of the Silk Roads.

CARAVAN CITIES: SPICES AND TEXTILES

As nomads moved southwestward, they produced a new kind of commercial hub: **caravan cities**. Established at strategic locations (often at the edges of deserts or in oases or at the end points of major trade arteries), these cities became places where vast trading groups assembled before beginning their arduous journeys. Some caravan cities originating as Greek garrison towns became centers of Hellenistic culture, displaying such staples of the polis as public theaters. Caravan cities were among the most spectacular and resplendent urban centers of this era.

One of the most striking of these caravan cities was the Nabatean capital at Petra. The Nabateans were an Arabic-speaking people who eked out a living, primarily as sheepherders, in the Sinai Desert and the northwestern Arabian Peninsula. They also facilitated the movement of frankincense, myrrh, and other spices along the route—sometimes called the Incense or Spice Road—linking the Arabian Peninsula and Indian Ocean with the Mediterranean, where Greeks and Romans used these goods to make perfumes and incense. Because the Greeks and later the Romans needed large quantities of incense to burn in worshipping their gods, the trade passing through this region was extremely lucrative. Although originating in Nabatean herders' practice of carving shelters and cisterns for catching rainwater out of the solid stone of the forbidding landscape, the magnificent "Rock City" of Petra (*petros* in Greek means "rock") was made possible by the wealth accumulated from the spice trade. Houses, shrines, tombs, and even the vast theater—carved entirely from the sandstone terrain to seat 6,000 to 10,000 spectators—reflected Hellenistic influences. Petra's power and wealth lasted from the mid-second century BCE to the early second century CE. The caravan traders, the ruling elite of the rock city, controlled the supply of spices and fragrances from Arabia and India to

Palmyran Tomb Sculpture This tombstone relief sculpture shows a wealthy young Palmyran attended by a servant—probably an enslaved household worker. Palmyra was at the crossroads of the major cultural influences traversing Southwest Asia at the time. The style of the clothing—the flowing pants and top—and the couch and pillows reflect the trading contacts of the Palmyran elite, in this case with India to the east. The hairstyle and mode of self-presentation signal influences from the Mediterranean to the west.

the ever-expanding Roman Empire. Nabatean traders based in Petra traveled throughout the eastern Mediterranean, erecting temples wherever they established trading communities.

With Petra's decline during the Roman period, Palmyra became the most important caravan city at the western end of the Silk Roads. Rich citizens of Rome relied on the Palmyran traders to procure luxury goods for them, importing Chinese silks for women's clothing and incense for religious rituals, as well as gemstones, pearls, and many other precious items. Palmyran traders handled non-silken textiles as well, including cotton from India and cashmere wool from Kashmir or the nearby central Asian highlands. Administered by the chiefs of local tribes, Palmyra maintained considerable autonomy even under formal Roman control. Although the Palmyrans used a Semitic dialect in daily life, for state affairs and business they used Greek, a reminder of the continuing influence of Hellenism. Their merchants had learned Greek when the region came under Seleucid rule, and it remained useful when doing business with caravans from afar, long after the political influences of Hellenism had waned.

Palmyrans built a splendid marble city in the desert. A colonnade, theater, senate house, agora, and major temples formed the metropolitan area.

Complexes of hostels, storage houses, offices, and temples served the needs of traders who passed through. The Palmyrans worshipped many deities, both local and Greek, and seemed concerned about their own afterlife. Like Petra, Palmyra had a cemetery as big as its residential area, with marble sculptures on the tombs depicting city life. Many tombs showed the master or the master and his wife reclining on Greek-style couches, holding drinking goblets. Sculptures of camel caravans and horses tell us that the deceased were caravan traders in this world who anticipated continuing their rewarding occupation in the afterlife.

Caravan cities such as Petra, and later Palmyra, linked the Mediterranean with the silk and incense routes that traversed Afro-Eurasia by land and sea. Goods came into the caravan cities via multiple land routes. One artery stretched from China, then across the Iranian plateau and the Syrian desert to reach the Mediterranean Sea, and another route cut south through modern Afghanistan, into the Indus Valley, then along India's northwest coast and across the Indian Ocean to the Red Sea.

CHINA AND THE SILK ECONOMY

China's flourishing economy owed much to the fact that Chinese silks were the most sought-after commodity in long-distance trade. As thousands of precious silk bales made their way to Indian, central Asian, and Mediterranean markets, silk became the ultimate prestige commodity of the regions' ruling classes. Over time, the exchange between eastern and western portions of the Silk Roads was increasingly mediated by Persian, Xiongnu, Kushan, and other middlemen at the great oases and trading centers that grew up in central Asia. Local communities took profitable advantage of the silk trade from China based on their increased knowledge and contacts.

Not only was silk China's most valuable export, but it also served as a tool in diplomacy with the nomadic kingdoms on China's western frontiers and as a source of funds for the Chinese armies. The country's rulers used silk to pay off neighboring nomads and borderlanders, buying both horses and peaceful borders with the fabric. During the Zhou dynasty, it had served as a precious medium of exchange and trade.

People valued silk as a material for clothing; as a filament made by spinning the protein fibers extracted from the cocoons of silkworms, it is smooth yet strong. Whereas cloth spun from hemp, flax, and other fibers tends to be rough, silk looks and feels rich. Moreover, it is cool against the skin in hot summers and warm in the winter. Silk also has immense tensile strength, making it useful for bows, lute strings, and fishing lines. Artisans even wove silk into a tight fabric to make light body armor or light bags for transporting liquids (particularly useful for traders crossing arid expanses). Before the Chinese invented paper, silk was a popular writing material that was more durable than bamboo or wood.

Texts written on silk often joined other funerary objects in the tombs of aristocratic lords and wealthy individuals.

As the long-distance silk trade grew, commerce within China also expanded. Because of reforms in the Warring States period, economic life in China after 300 BCE centered increasingly on independent farmers producing commercial crops for the marketplaces along land routes as well as rivers, canals, and lakes. As this market economy grew, merchants organized themselves based on family lineages and occupational guilds. Power now shifted away from agrarian elites and into the hands of urban financiers and traders. The traders benefited from the improvement in roads and waterways, which eased the transportation of grain, hides, horses, and silk from the villages to

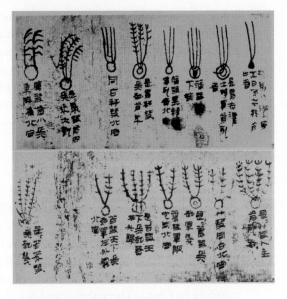

Silk Texts Before the invention of paper, silk was widely used as writing material because it was more mobile and durable than bamboo or wood for correspondence, maps, illustrations, and important texts included as funerary objects in the tombs of aristocrats. The Mawangdui silk texts shown here are from a Hunan tomb that was closed in 168 BCE and opened in 1973.

the new towns and cities. Bronze coins of various sizes and shapes, as well as cloth and silk used in barter, spurred long-distance trade. By the second century BCE, wealthy merchants were ennobled as local magnates and wore clothing that marked their official status. As commerce further expanded, regional lords opened local customs offices along land routes and waterways to extract a share of the money and products for themselves.

Though China still had little intellectual interaction with the rest of Afro-Eurasia, its long-distance commercial exchanges skyrocketed due to the Silk Road trade. Southern silk was only the first of many Chinese commodities that reached the world beyond the Taklamakan Desert. China also became an export center for lacquer, hemp, and linen. From Sichuan came iron, steel, flint, hard stone, silver, and animals, while jade came from the northwest. At the same time, China was importing Mediterranean, Indian, and central Asian commodities.

Despite its early development of commerce, China still had no major ports that could compare to the caravan cities of Petra and Palmyra. Most cities in the landlocked north were administrative centers where farmers and traders gathered under the regional states' political and military protection. The larger cities had gates that closed between sunset and sunrise; during the night, mounted soldiers patrolled the streets. Newer towns along the southeastern seacoast still looked upriver to trade with inland agrarian communities, which also produced silk for export. Facilitating oceanic trade became more of a concern for the state during this period, and merchant ships now enjoyed the protection of military boats. However, internal, interregional trade predominated, and it fed into the Silk Roads through decentralized networks.

THE SPREAD OF BUDDHISM ALONG THE TRADE ROUTES

In addition to silk traders, monks traveled along Afro-Eurasian trade arteries to spread the word of new religions. While Christians would later take advantage of these trade routes to spread their faith (see Chapter 8), Buddhism was the chief expansionist faith in this period. Under Kushan patronage during the first centuries CE, Buddhism reached out from India to China and central Asia, following the Silk Roads. Monks from the Kushan Empire accompanied traders traveling to China. There they translated Buddhist texts into Chinese and other languages, aided by Chinese converts. Buddhist ideas were slow to gain acceptance everywhere the monks proselytized. It took several centuries, and a new wave of nomadic migrations, for Buddhism to take root in China.

Buddhism fared less well when it followed the commercial arteries westward. The religion never became established on the Iranian plateau and made no substantial headway toward the Mediterranean. The main barrier was Zoroastrianism, which had been a state religion in the Persian Empire during the fifth and fourth centuries BCE (see Chapter 4); by the time Buddhism began to spread, Zoroastrianism had long been established in Iran. Iranian Hellenism had done little to weaken the power of Zoroastrianism, whose adherents formed city-based religious communities affiliated primarily with traders. These Zoroastrian traders continued to adhere to their own faith while traveling along the Silk Roads and did nothing to help Buddhism spread westward.

COMMERCE ON THE RED SEA AND INDIAN OCEAN

Using new navigational techniques and larger ships, seafarers eventually expanded the transport of Silk Road commodities via the Red Sea and the Indian Ocean. Although land routes were the tried-and-true avenues for migrants, traders, and wayfarers, they carried only what could be borne on the backs of humans and animals. Travel by land was slow and travelers were vulnerable to marauders. With time, some risk takers found ways of traversing waterways—eventually on an unprecedented scale and with an ease unimaginable to earlier merchants. These risk takers were Arabs, from the commercial middle ground of the Afro-Eurasian trading system.

Arab traders had long carried such spices as frankincense and myrrh to the Egyptians, who used them in religious and funerary rites, and later to the Greeks and Romans. Metals such as bronze, tin, and iron passed along overland routes from Anatolia, as did gold, silver, and chlorite from the Iranian plateau. Gold, ivory, and other goods from the northern part of India passed through Taxila (the capital of Gandhara) and the Hindu Kush Mountains into Persia as early as the sixth century BCE. Following the expansion of the Hellenistic world, however, ships increasingly conducted long-distance trade. Mastering the monsoons over time, they sailed down the Red Sea and across the Indian Ocean as they carried goods between the tip of the Arabian Peninsula and the ports of the Indian landmass.

Arab seafarers led the way into the Indian Ocean, forging links that joined East Africa, the eastern Mediterranean, and the Arabian Peninsula with India, Southeast Asia, and East Asia. Such voyages involved longer stays at sea and were far more dangerous than sailing in the Mediterranean. Yet, by the first century CE, Arab and Indian sailors were transporting Chinese silks, central Asian furs, and fragrances from Himalayan trees across the Indian Ocean. The city of Alexandria in Egypt soon emerged as a key transit point between the Mediterranean Sea and the Indian Ocean. Boats carried Mediterranean exports of olives and olive oil, wine, drinking vessels, glassware, linen and wool textiles, and red coral up the Nile, stopping at Koptos and other port cities, from which camel caravans took the goods to ports on the Red Sea. For centuries, Mediterranean merchants had considered the Arabian Peninsula to be the end of the Spice Roads. But after Alexander's expedition and the establishment of colonies between Egypt and Afghanistan, they began to value the wealth and opportunities that lay along the shores of the Indian Ocean.

Arab sailors who ventured into the Indian Ocean benefited from new navigational techniques, especially celestial bearings (using the position of the stars to determine the position of the ship and the direction to sail). They used large ships called dhows, whose sails were rigged to easily capture the wind; these forerunners of modern cargo vessels were capable of long hauls in rough waters. Beginning about 120 BCE, mariners came to understand the seasonal rain-filled monsoon winds, which blow from the southwest between October and April and then from the northeast between April and October—knowledge that propelled the maritime trade connecting the Mediterranean with the Indian Ocean.

Mariners accumulated the new sailing knowledge in books—each called a **periplus** ("sailing around")—in which sea captains recorded the landing spots and ports between their destinations, as well as their precious cargoes. The *Periplus Maris Erythraei*, or *Periplus of the Red Sea*, was one such first-century BCE handbook. It offered advice to merchants traveling and trading along two major, connected routes: one on the Red Sea along the coastline of Egypt and the other on the Arabian Sea heading eastward to India. The author demonstrates keen observation and navigational skill in cataloguing the navigable routes, the marketable goods at each port, and anthropological insights on the inhabitants of the far-flung regions visited. The revolution in sailing techniques, like celestial bearing and the dhows, combined with practical knowledge, like that contained in the *Periplus Maris Erythraei*, dramatically reduced the cost of long-distance shipping and multiplied the ports of call around large bodies of water. Some historians have argued that there were now two sets of Silk Roads: one by land and one by sea.

Conclusion

Alexander's territorial gains were awesome in their scale, but his empire was as transitory as it was huge. Though it crumbled upon his death, Alexander's conquest had effects more profound than those of any military or political regime before. Alexander's armies ushered in an age of thinking and practices that transformed Greek achievements into a common culture—Hellenism—whose influences, both direct and indirect, touched far-flung societies for centuries thereafter.

Hellenism offered a common language, both literally and figuratively, that linked culture, institutions, and trade. However, many Greek-speaking peoples and their descendants in parts of central and Southwest Asia integrated local cultural practices with their own ways, creating diverse and rich cultures. Thus, the influences of culture flowed both ways. The economic story is equally complex. Following pathways forged by previous empires and kingdoms, Alexander's successors strengthened and expanded existing trade routes and centers of commercial activity, which ultimately led to the creation of the Silk Roads.

Although the effects of this Hellenistic age lasted longer than most cultural systems and had a wider appeal than previous philosophical and spiritual ideas, they did not overwrite everything that came before. Some, like the Jewish people of Judea and Alexandria, either fought against Hellenism with all their might or accommodated to it. Others, like the Romans and Carthaginians, took from the new common culture what they liked and discarded the rest.

In South Asia, the immediate successor to Alexander's military was the Mauryan Empire, which established its dominion over much of South Asia and even some of central Asia for close to a century and a half. Once Mauryan control receded, South Asia was opened up even more than before to currents moving swiftly across Afro-Eurasia, including the institutions and cultures of steppe nomads, seafarers, and Hellenists. The most telling South Asian responses occurred in the realm of spiritual and ethical norms, where Buddhist doctrines began to evolve toward a full-fledged world religious system.

Greater political integration helped fashion highways for commerce and enabled the spread of Buddhism. Nomads, like the Kushans, left their steppe lands and exchanged wares across great distances. As they found greater opportunities for business, their trade routes shifted farther south, radiating out of the oases of central Asia. Eventually merchants, rather than the trading nomads, seized the opportunities provided by new technologies, especially in sailing and navigation, and by thriving caravan cities. These commercial transformations connected distant parts of Afro-Eurasia. The Silk Roads and new sea-lanes connected ports and caravan cities from North Africa to South China, created new social classes, produced new urban settings, supported powerful new polities, and transported Hellenism and Buddhism well beyond their points of origin.

Focus On
The Creation of the Silk Roads and the Beginnings of Buddhism

The Mediterranean World

- The spread of Hellenism around the Mediterranean via Alexander's conquests and his successor kingdoms leads to a common language, cosmopolitan cities, new types of philosophy and religion, plantation slavery, and money-based economies.

Central and South Asia

- The Mauryan Empire, of Chandragupta and his grandson Aśoka, integrates the northern half of India in the aftermath of Alexander's withdrawal from the region.

- The Bactrian kingdom and Kushan Empire further solidify the spread of Hellenism into central Asia.

The Transformation of Buddhism

- The combined influences of Hellenism, Aśoka's adoption of the Buddhist faith, nomadism, and Indian Ocean seafaring transform Buddhism into a world religion.

Formation of Silk Roads

- Nomadic warriors from central Asia complete the final links of the overland Silk Roads, strengthening the ties that join peoples across Afro-Eurasia.

- Overland traders carry spices, transport precious metals, and convey Buddhist thought along the Silk Roads into China.

- Seafaring traders use new navigation techniques and larger ships called dhows to expand the transport of Silk Road commodities to the Mediterranean world via the Indian Ocean.

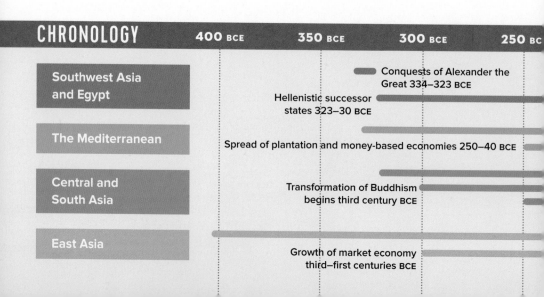

CHRONOLOGY

	400 BCE	350 BCE	300 BCE	250 BC
Southwest Asia and Egypt			Conquests of Alexander the Great 334–323 BCE	
		Hellenistic successor states 323–30 BCE		
The Mediterranean		Spread of plantation and money-based economies 250–40 BCE		
Central and South Asia		Transformation of Buddhism begins third century BCE		
East Asia		Growth of market economy third–first centuries BCE		

- **Thinking about Crossing Borders and Shrinking the Afro-Eurasian World** Alexander's conquests and the resulting Hellenistic kingdoms of his successors brought about a never-before-seen cultural unity across huge swaths of Afro-Eurasia. To what extent was this cultural diffusion—comparable in some ways to the globalization or "Americanization" of culture around the world in modern times—a positive development? In what ways might it have been seen by those living through it as a negative development?

- **Thinking about Transformation & Conflict and Shrinking the Afro-Eurasian World** Alexander and his successors brought about unity initially by brutal conquest, then later through diplomatic strategies and the spread of Hellenistic ideas. Likewise, as the conquest of Kalinga demonstrated, Aśoka brutally conquered territories before his change of heart and promotion of *dhamma*. Compare and contrast the role of military conflict and cultural movements (like Hellenism and *dhamma*) in bringing unity to the Hellenistic world and South Asia.

- **Thinking about Worlds Together, Worlds Apart and Shrinking the Afro-Eurasian World** The long-distance trade routes known as the Silk Roads, and sometimes the Incense Roads, brought intensified interactions among societies across Afro-Eurasia in the last centuries BCE. Which societies were closely involved in this exchange? Which appear to have been less involved? What accounts for these regions' involvement, or lack thereof, in Silk Road exchange?

Key Terms

 Go to **INQUIZITIVE** to see what you've learned—and learn what you've missed—with personalized feedback along the way.

200 BCE	150 BCE	100 BCE	50 BCE

Expansion of Rome and clash with Carthage 330–146 BCE

Mauryan Empire 321–184 BCE

Bactrian kingdom, c. 250–50 BCE

Kushan Empire second century BCE to fourth century CE

Warring States period 403–221 BCE

7

Han Dynasty China and Imperial Rome

300 BCE–300 CE

Core Objectives

- **IDENTIFY** the features that made Han China and imperial Rome globalizing empires.

- **DESCRIBE** the development of the Han dynasty from its beginnings through the third century CE.

- **EXPLAIN** the process by which Rome transitioned from a minor city-state to a dominating Mediterranean power.

- **COMPARE** Han China with imperial Rome in terms of political authority, economy, cultural developments, and military expansion.

In third-century BCE China, the Eastern Zhou state of Qin absorbed the remaining Warring States (see Chapter 5) and set the stage for the Han dynasty. The chief minister of the Qin state, Li Si, urged his king to seize the opportunity presented by the disarray of his opponents: by combining his fearsome armies and his own personal virtues, the king could sweep away his rivals as if dusting ashes from a kitchen hearth. "This is the one moment in ten thousand ages," Li Si whispered to the man who would become Qin Shi Huangdi. The king listened carefully. He followed the advice and laid the foundations for a mighty empire. Although Shi Huangdi's Qin Empire collapsed in 207 BCE after a mere two decades, his political innovations set the stage for the much more powerful and longer-lasting Han Empire (206 BCE–220 CE), which became one of the most successful dynasties in

Chinese history. Following the Qin model, the Han defeated other regional groups and established a Chinese empire that would last for four centuries.

At the other end of Afro-Eurasia, another great state, imperial Rome, also met its rivals in war, emerged victorious, and consolidated its power into a vast empire. The Romans achieved this feat by using violent force on a scale hitherto unseen in their part of the globe. The result was a state of huge size, astonishingly unified and stable. Living in the Roman Empire in the mid-70s CE, Pliny the Elder wrote glowingly about the unity of the imperial Roman state. In his eyes, all the benefits that flowed from Rome's extensive reach derived from the greatness of a peace that joined diverse peoples under one benevolent emperor. In this chapter, we will examine and compare the growth, politics, economies, and societies of the Han and Roman Empires.

Global Storyline

Comparing the Han and Roman Empires

- Flourishing at roughly the same time, Han China and the Roman Empire become powerful and enduring "globalizing empires."

- The Han dynasty, building on Qin foundations, establishes a bureaucratic imperial model and social order in East Asia.

- The Roman Empire becomes a Mediterranean superpower exerting far-reaching political, legal, economic, and cultural influence.

Globalizing Empires: The Han Dynasty and Imperial Rome

The Han and the Roman states became truly **globalizing empires**: they covered immense amounts of territory; included huge, diverse populations; and exerted influence far beyond their own borders. Their major innovation was not that they found new ways to plow resources into big armies and civil bureaucracies or that their rulers gave new justifications for their rule. Rather, what distinguished the Romans and the Han from their predecessors was their commitment to integrating conquered neighbors and rivals into their worlds—by extending laws, offering systems of representation, exporting belief systems, colonizing lands, and promoting trade within and beyond their empires.

Subject peoples became members of empires, not just the vanquished. Those who resisted not only waved away the benefits of living under imperial rule but also became the targets for military retribution.

Even today, geopolitical boundaries bear remarkable resemblances to those defined by these two empires at their peak. These states transcended the limits of previous territorial kingdoms and the first empires by deploying resources in new ways. The leaders of each empire laid out the political and cultural boundaries of regions that we now recognize as "China" and "Christendom."

To be "Han Chinese" meant that elites shared a common written language based on the Confucian classics, which qualified them for public office. It also meant that commoners from all walks of life shared the elites' belief system, which emphasized appropriate decorum and dress for each social level, the view that the agrarian-based Han Empire was a small-scale model of the entire cosmos, and ritual practices associated with ancestor worship. Consistent with Confucian ideals of the previous centuries, the Han practiced filial piety toward their elders, living and dead; for example, family members honored their ancestors with offerings at their tombs. In addition, the Han considered people who lived beyond Han boundaries uncivilized, even if some were ultimately folded into Han rule.

What it meant to be "Roman" changed over time as Rome's imperial reach expanded. In the fifth century BCE, being Roman meant being a citizen of the city of Rome, speaking Latin (the regional language of central Italy), and eating and dressing like Latin-speaking people. Ever important to the Romans was a sense of family, centered on the *domus* (or home), and an ongoing remembering of their ancestors. While wealthy, elite Romans would commission funerary parades to honor their familial dead, Romans of every social class honored their family's dead with graveside offerings of garlands and wine-soaked bread, especially during February's festival of the Parentalia. By the late second century BCE, the concept of Roman citizenship expanded to include not only citizens of the city but also anyone who had formal membership in the larger territorial state that the Romans were building. By the beginning of the third century CE, being Roman meant simply being a subject of the Roman emperors. This Roman identity became so deeply rooted that when the western parts of the empire disintegrated two centuries later, the inhabitants of the surviving eastern parts—who had no connection with Rome, did not speak Latin, and did not dress or eat like the original Romans—still considered themselves "Romans" in this broader sense.

Han Tomb Doors Wealthy Han officials could afford elaborate burials that coincidentally provide much of our evidence for Han material culture, including figurines, vessels of all types, wall paintings, and even silk banners. One feature of these elite Han burials is the ornately carved tomb doors. Close inspection of the detailed imagery reveals robed men (village officials), trees (symbolizing a long-lasting family), flying birds, chariots, and a central monster mask that served as a protective spirit.

The two empires differed in their patterns of development, types of public servants, and ideals for the best kind of government. For example, the civilian magistrate and the bureaucrat were typical of the Han Empire, whereas the citizen, the soldier, and the military governor were at the heart of the Roman Empire. In China, dynastic empires fashioned themselves according to the models of past empires. By contrast, Rome began as a collectively ruled city-state and pursued its road to domination as if creating something new. Nonetheless, like the Chinese, Romans were strongly traditional. Both new empires united huge landmasses and extraordinarily diverse populations.

While both China and Rome participated in Silk Road exchange, both economies were primarily agrarian. Yet free peasants worked the land in China, whereas a huge enslaved population worked the fields of the Roman Empire. At its height, the Han Empire included around 59 million inhabitants and covered 3 million square miles in China proper and, for a while, another 1 million square miles in central Asia. Just over a decade after the Han census and far to the west, the emperor Augustus oversaw a census that counted 4,937,000 Roman citizens (free adult men), which likewise amounted to around 60 million people, when women, children, and enslaved people were accounted for. The Roman Empire governed an area nearly as great as that of Han China, especially when counting the almost 1-million-square-mile area of the Mediterranean Sea, which was like a water highway for the Romans in the lands encircling it. An estimated two out of every three human beings on earth now fell directly under the authority of China or Rome. Their imperial control shaped the destiny and identity of the countless millions living within their respective realms.

Both empires left indelible legacies; following their collapses, both survived as models. Successor states in the Mediterranean sought to become the second Rome, and after the Han dynasty fell, the Chinese people identified themselves and their language simply as "Han." Both empires raised life to a new level of bureaucratic and military complexity and offered a common identity on a grander scale than ever before. It was a vision that would never be lost.

The Han Dynasty (206 BCE–220 CE)

The Han dynasty oversaw an unprecedented blossoming of peace and prosperity in East Asia. Although supporters of the Han dynasty boasted of the regime's imperial uniqueness, in reality it owed much to its predecessor, the Qin state, which contributed vital elements of political unity and economic growth to its more powerful successor regime. (See Map 7.1.) Together, the Qin and Han created the political, social, economic, and cultural foundations that characterized imperial China thereafter.

A CRUCIAL FORERUNNER: THE QIN DYNASTY (221–207 BCE)

Although it lasted only fourteen years, the Qin dynasty integrated much of China and made important administrative and economic innovations. The Qin were but one of many militaristic regimes during the Warring States period (c. 403–221 BCE). What enabled the Qin to prevail over rivals was their expansion into the Sichuan region, which was remarkable for its rich mineral resources and fertile soils. There, a merchant class and the silk trade spurred economic growth, and public works fostered increased food production. These strengths enabled the Qin by 221 BCE to defeat the remaining Warring States and unify an empire that covered roughly two-thirds of modern China.

Supported by able ministers and generals, a large conscripted army, and a system of taxation that financed all-out war, the Qin ruler King Zheng assumed the mandate of heaven from the Zhou. Declaring himself **Shi Huangdi**, or "First August Emperor," in 221 BCE, Zheng harkened back to China's great mythical emperors of antiquity. Forgoing the title of king (*wang*), which had been used by leaders of the Zhou and Warring States, Zheng instead took the title of emperor (*di*), a term that had meant "ancestral ruler" for the Shang and Zhou.

Shi Huangdi centralized the administration of the empire. He forced the defeated rulers of the Warring States and their families to move to Xianyang, the Qin capital—where they would be unable to gather rebel armies. The First August Emperor then parceled out the territory of his massive state into thirty-six provinces, called **commanderies** (*jun*). Each commandery had a civilian and a military governor, as well as an imperial inspector. Regional and

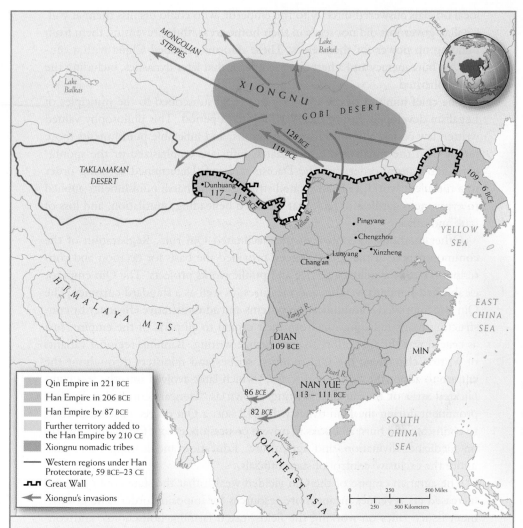

Map 7.1 The Qin and Han Dynasties, 221 BCE–220 CE

The short-lived Qin (221–207 BCE) and the much longer-lasting Han (206 BCE–220 CE) dynasties consolidated much of East Asia into one large regional empire.

- Based on the map, when and where did various phases of expansion take place from the Qin through the Han dynasty? What features shaped that expansion?
- Where was the Great Wall located, and against what was it defending?
- What impact did the pastoral Xiongnu have on the Han dynasty's effort to consolidate a large territorial state?

local officials answered directly to the emperor, who could dismiss them at will. Civilian governors did not serve in their home areas, thus preventing them from building up power for themselves. These reforms provided China with a centralized bureaucracy and a hereditary emperor that later dynasties, including the Han, inherited.

The chief minister of the Qin Empire, Li Si, subscribed to the principles of Legalism developed during the Warring States period. This philosophy valued written law codes, administrative regulations, and inflexible punishments more highly than the rituals and ethics that Confucians emphasized or the spontaneity and natural order that the Daoists stressed. Determined to bring order to a turbulent world, Li Si advocated strict laws and harsh punishments applied to everyone regardless of rank that included beheading, mutilation, and loss of rank and office.

Other methods of control further facilitated Qin rule. Registration of the common people at the age of sixteen provided the basis for taxation and conscription both for military service and public works projects. The Qin emperor established standard weights and measures, as well as a standard currency. The Qin also improved communication systems and administrative efficiency by constructing roads radiating out from their capital to all parts of the empire. Just as crucial was the Qin effort to standardize writing. Banning regional variants of written characters, the Qin required scribes and ministers throughout the empire to adopt the "small seal script," which later evolved into the less complicated style of bureaucratic writing known as "clerical script" that became prominent during the Han dynasty. In 213 BCE, a Qin decree ordered officials to confiscate and burn all books in private possession, except for technical works on medicine, divination, and agriculture. Education and learning were now under the exclusive control of state officials.

The agrarian empire of the Qin yielded wealth that the state could tax, and increased tax revenues meant more resources for imposing order. The government issued rules on working the fields, taxed farming households, and conscripted laborers to build irrigation systems and canals so that even more land could come under cultivation. The Qin and, later, the Han dynasties relied on free farmers and conscripted the farmers' able-bodied sons into their huge armies. Working their own land and paying a portion of their crops in taxes, peasant families were the economic bedrock of the Chinese empire. Long-distance commerce thrived, as well. In the dynamic regional market centers of the cities, merchants peddled foodstuffs as well as weapons, metals, horses, dogs, hides, furs, silk, and salt—all produced in different regions and transported on the improved road system. Taxed both in transit and in the market at a higher rate than agricultural goods, these trade goods yielded even more revenue for the imperial government.

The Qin grappled with the need to expand and defend their borders, extending those boundaries in the northeast to the Korean Peninsula, in the south to present-day Vietnam, and in the west into central Asia. Relations between the settled Chinese and the nomadic Xiongnu to the north and west (see Chapter 6) teetered in a precarious balance until 215 BCE, when the Qin Empire pushed north into the middle of the Yellow River basin, seizing pasturelands from the Xiongnu and opening the region up for settlement. Qin officials built roads into these areas and employed conscripts and criminals to create a massive defensive wall that covered a distance of 3,000 miles along the northern border (the forerunner of the Great Wall of China—though north of the current wall, which was constructed more than a millennium later). In 211 BCE, the Qin settled 30,000 colonists in the steppe lands of Inner Eurasia.

Intellectual Censorship This seventeenth-century painting depicts the infamous "Burning of the Books and Burying of the Scholars" edict enacted by Shi Huangdi at the suggestion of his adviser, Li Si. Unfortunately, even the state-approved texts were destroyed a mere six years later, during the fall of the Qin dynasty and sack of the capital.

Despite its military power, the Qin dynasty collapsed quickly, due to constant warfare and the heavy taxation and exhausting conscription that war required. When conscripted workers mutinied in 209 BCE, they found allies in descendants of Warring States nobles, local military leaders, and influential merchants. The rebels swept up thousands of supporters with their call to arms against the "tyrannical" Qin. Shortly before Shi Huangdi died in 210 BCE, even the educated elite joined former lords and regional vassals in revolt. The second Qin emperor committed suicide in 207 BCE, and his weak successor surrendered to the leader of the Han forces later that year. The resurgent Xiongnu confederacy also reconquered their old pasturelands as the dynasty fell.

BEGINNINGS OF THE WESTERN HAN DYNASTY

The civil war that followed the collapse of Qin rule opened the way for the formation of the Western Han dynasty. A commoner and former policeman named Liu Bang (r. 206–195 BCE) declared himself prince of his home area of Han. In 202 BCE, Liu proclaimed himself the first Han emperor. Claiming the mandate of heaven, the Han portrayed the Qin as evil; yet at the same time they adopted the Qin's bureaucratic system. In reality, Qin laws had been no crueler than those of the Han. Under Han leadership, China's armies swelled with some 50,000 crossbowmen who brandished mass-produced weapons made from

bronze and iron. Armed with the cross-bow, foot soldiers and mounted archers extended Han imperial lands in all directions. Following the Qin practice, the Han also relied on a huge conscripted labor force for special projects such as building canals, roads, and defensive walls.

The first part of the Han dynasty is known as the Western (or Former) Han dynasty (206 BCE–9 CE). The Han brought economic prosperity and the expansion of empire. This was especially the case under **Emperor Wu**, known also as Han Wudi, who presided over one of the longest and most eventful reigns in Chinese history (r. 141–87 BCE). Though he was called the "Martial Emperor" because of the state's many military campaigns, Emperor Wu rarely inspected his military units and never led them in battle. Wu followed the Daoist principle of *wuwei* (noninterference), striving to remain aloof from day-to-day activities and permitting the empire to function on its own if it did not require intervention. Still, he used a stringent penal code to eliminate powerful officials who got in his way. In a single year, his court system prosecuted over a thousand such cases.

HAN POWER AND ADMINISTRATION

Undergirding the Han Empire was the tight-knit alliance between the imperial family and the new elite—the scholar-gentry class—who shared a determination to impose order on the Chinese population. Although the first Han emperors had no choice but to compromise with the aristocratic groups

Qin Archer and Crossbow This kneeling archer was discovered in the tomb of Shi Huangdi, along with the thousands of other bowmen, cavalrymen, and infantry that composed the massive terra-cotta army. Notice his breastplate; its overlapping plates would have enhanced maneuverability. The wooden bow he was holding has disintegrated, but a replica appears above. The bronze arrowhead and trigger mechanism in this reproduction were found with the terra-cotta army.

who had helped overthrow the Qin, in time the Han created the most highly centralized bureaucracy in the world. No fewer than 23,500 individuals staffed the central and local governments. That structure became the source of the Han's enduring power. As under the Qin, the Han bureaucracy touched everyone because all males had to register, pay taxes, and serve in the military.

Qin Coin After centuries of distinctive regional currencies, the Qin created this standardized bronze coin as part of their general unification policy.

The Han court moved quickly to tighten its grip on regional administration. First it removed powerful princes, crushed rebellions, and took over the areas controlled by regional lords. According to arrangements instituted in 106 BCE by Emperor Wu, the empire consisted of thirteen provinces under imperial inspectors. As during the Qin dynasty, commanderies, each administered by a civilian and a military official, covered vast lands inhabited by countless ethnic groups totaling millions of people. These officials maintained political stability and ensured the efficient collection of taxes. However, given the immense numbers under their jurisdiction and the heavy duties they bore, in many respects the local administrative staff was still inadequate to the tasks facing it.

Government schools that promoted the scholar-official ideal became fertile sources for recruiting local officials. In 136 BCE, Emperor Wu founded what became the **Imperial University**, a college for classical scholars that supplied the Han need for well-trained bureaucrats. By the second century CE, the university boasted 30,000 students and faculty. Apart from studying the classics, Han scholars were naturalists and inventors. They made important medical discoveries, dealing with rational explanations of the body's functions and the role of wind and temperature in transmitting diseases. They also invented the magnetic compass and developed high-quality paper. Local elites encouraged their sons to master the classical teachings. This practice could secure future entry into the ruling class and firmly planted the Confucian classics at the heart of the imperial state.

Confucian thought slowly became the ideological buttress of the Han Empire. Under Emperor Wu, the bureaucracy deemed people's welfare to be the essential purpose of legitimate rule. By 50 BCE, *The Analects*, a collection of Confucius's sayings, was widely disseminated, and three Confucian ideals reigned as the official doctrine of the Han Empire: honoring tradition, respecting the lessons of history, and acknowledging the emperor's responsibility to heaven. Scholars used Confucius's words to tutor the princes. By embracing Confucian political ideals, Han rulers established an empire based on the mandate of heaven and crafted a careful balance in which the officials provided a counterweight to the emperor's autocratic strength. When the interests of the court and the bureaucracy clashed, however, the emperor's will was paramount.

THE ECONOMY AND THE NEW SOCIAL ORDER

Part of the Han leaders' genius was their ability to win the support of diverse social groups that had been squabbling for centuries. The basis of their success was their ability to organize daily life, create a stable social order, promote economic growth, and foster a state-centered religion. One important element in promoting political and social stability was that the Han allowed surviving Qin aristocrats to reacquire some of their former power. The Han also urged enterprising peasants who had worked the nobles' lands to become local leaders in the countryside. Successful merchants won permission to extend their influence in cities, and in local areas scholars found themselves in the role of masters when the state removed their lords.

Out of a massive agrarian base flowed a steady stream of tax revenues and labor for military forces and public works. The Han court drew revenues from many sources: state-owned imperial lands, mining, and mints; tribute from outlying domains; household taxes on the nobility; and taxes on surplus grains from wealthy merchants. Emperor Wu established state monopolies in salt, iron, and wine to fund his expensive military campaigns. His policies encouraged silk and iron production—especially iron weapons and everyday tools—and controlled profiteering through price controls. He also minted standardized copper coins and imposed stiff penalties for counterfeiting.

Model of a Han Watchtower Wealthy Han burials contained terra-cotta models of buildings—houses, animal pens, granaries—that would replicate one's life in the afterlife. Shown here is a model of a multistory watchtower standing just over 3 feet tall, the details of which give insight into Han building techniques in the first to third centuries CE. Archers with crossbows stand guard on an upper balcony, while a figure stands in greeting at the front gate.

Han cities were laid out in an orderly grid. Bustling markets served as public areas. Carriages transported rich families up and down wide avenues (and they paid a lot for the privilege: keeping a horse required as much grain as a family of six would consume). Court palaces became forbidden inner cities, off-limits to all but those in the imperial lineage or the government. Monumental architecture in China announced the palaces and tombs of rulers.

Domestic Life Daily life in Han China included new luxuries for the elite and reinforced traditional ideas about gender. Wealthy families lived in several-story homes with richly carved crossbeams and rafters and floors cushioned with embroidered pillows, wool rugs, and mats. Fine embroideries hung as drapes, and screens in the rooms secured privacy. Domestic space reinforced male authority as women and children stayed cloistered in inner quarters, preserving the sense that the patriarch's role was to protect them from a harsh society.

Nonetheless, some elite women, often literate, enjoyed respect as teachers and managers within the family while their husbands served as officials away from home. Ban Zhao, the younger sister of the historian Ban Gu (32–92 CE), was an exceptional woman whose talents reached outside the home. She became the first female Chinese historian and lived relatively unconstrained. After marrying a local resident, Cao Shishu, at the age of fourteen, she was called Madame Cao at court. Subsequently, she completed her elder brother's *History of the Former Han Dynasty* when he was imprisoned and executed. In addition to completing the first full dynastic history in China, Ban Zhao wrote *Lessons for Women*, in which she described the status of elite women and presented the ideal woman in light of her virtue, her type of work, and the words she spoke and wrote. Women who were commoners led less protected lives. Many worked in the fields, and some joined troupes of entertainers to sing and dance for food at open markets.

Silk was abundant and available to all classes, though in winter only the rich wrapped themselves in furs while everyone else stayed warm in woolens and ferret skins. The rich also wore distinctive slippers lined with leather or silk. Wine and cooked meat came to the dinner tables of the wealthy on vessels fashioned with silver inlay or golden handles. Entertainment for those who could afford it included gambling, performing animals, tiger fights, foreign dancing girls, and even live music in private homes, performed by orchestras in the families' private employ. Although events like these had occurred during the Zhou dynasty, they had marked only public ritual occasions.

Social Hierarchy At the base of Han society was a free peasantry of farmers who owned and tilled their own land. The Han court upheld an agrarian ideal— which Confucians and Daoists supported—honoring the peasants' productive labors, while subjecting merchants to a range of controls (including regulations on luxury consumption) and belittling them for not doing physical labor. Confucians envisioned scholar-officials as working hard for the ruler to enhance

Han Entertainment Han entertainment included dancing girls (*left*), musicians (*middle*), and acrobats (*right*).

a moral economy in which profiteering by greedy merchants would be minimal.

In reality, however, the first century of Han rule perpetuated the power of elites. At the apex were the imperial clan and nobles, followed, in order, by high-ranking officials and scholars, great merchants and manufacturers, and a regionally based class of local magnates. Below these elites, lesser clerks, medium and small landowners, free farmers, artisans, small merchants, poor tenant farmers, and hired laborers eked out a living. The more destitute became enslaved government workers and relied on the state for food and clothing. At the bottom were convicts and people who were privately enslaved.

Between 100 BCE and 200 CE, scholar-officials linked the imperial center with local society. At first, their political clout and prestige complemented the power of landlords and large clans, but over time their autonomy grew as they gained wealth by acquiring private property. Following the fall of the Han, they emerged as the dominant aristocratic clans.

In the long run, the imperial court's struggle to limit the power of local lords and magnates failed. Rulers had to rely on local officials to enforce their rule, but those officials could rarely stand up to the powerful men they were supposed to be governing. And when central rule proved too onerous for local elites, they could rebel. Local uprisings against the Han that began in 99 BCE forced the court to relax its measures and left landlords and local magnates as dominant powers in the provinces. Below these privileged groups, powerless agrarian groups turned to Daoist religious organizations that crystallized into potent cells of dissent.

Religion and Omens Under Emperor Wu, Confucianism took on religious overtones. One treatise portrayed Confucius not as a humble teacher but as an uncrowned monarch, and even as a demigod and a giver of laws, which differed from the portrait in *The Analects* of a more modest, accessible, and very human Confucius.

Although Confucians at court championed classical learning, many local communities practiced forms of a remarkably dynamic popular Chinese religion. Imperial cults, magic, and sorcery reinforced the court's interest in astronomical omens—such as the appearance of a supernova, solar halos, meteors, and lunar and solar eclipses. Unpredictable celestial events, as well as earthquakes and famines, could be taken to mean that the emperor had lost the mandate of heaven. Powerful ministers exploited these occurrences to intimidate their ruler. People of high and low social position alike believed that witchcraft could manipulate natural events and interfere with the will of heaven. Religion in its many forms, from philosophy to witchcraft, was an essential feature of Han society from the elite to the poorer classes.

MILITARY EXPANSION AND THE SILK ROADS

The Han military machine was effective at expanding the empire's borders and enforcing stability around the borderlands. Peace was good for business, specifically for creating stable conditions that allowed the safe transit of goods over the Silk Roads. Emperor Wu did much to transform the military forces. Following the Qin precedent, he made military service compulsory, resulting in a huge force: 100,000 crack troops in the Imperial Guard stationed in the capital and more than a million in the standing army.

Expanding Borders Han forces were particularly active along the borders. During the reign of Emperor Wu, Han control extended from southeastern China to northern Vietnam. When pro-Han Koreans appealed for Han help against rulers in their internal squabbles, Emperor Wu's expeditionary force defeated the Korean king and four Han commanderies sprang up in northern Korea. While incursions into Sichuan and the southwestern border areas were less successful due to mountainous terrain and malaria, a commandery nonetheless took root in southern Sichuan in 135 BCE, and soon it opened trading routes to Southeast Asia.

The Han Empire's most serious military threat, however, came from the Xiongnu and other nomadic peoples in the north. The Han inherited from the Qin a symbiotic relationship with these proud, horse-riding nomads: Han merchants brought silk cloth and thread, bronze mirrors, and lacquerware to exchange for furs, horses, and cattle. After humiliating defeats at the hands of the Xiongnu, the Han under Emperor Wu successfully repelled Xiongnu invasions around 120 BCE and ultimately penetrated deep into Xiongnu territory. The Xiongnu tribes were split in two, with the southern tribes surrendering and the northern tribes moving west, ultimately threatening Roman territory.

The Chinese Peace and the Silk Roads The retreat of the Xiongnu and other nomadic peoples introduced a glorious period of internal peace and prosperity some scholars have referred to as a **Pax Sinica** ("Chinese Peace," 149–87 BCE). During this period, long-distance trade flourished, cities ballooned, standards of living rose, and the population surged. As a result of their military campaigns, Emperor Wu and his successors enjoyed tribute from distant subordinate states, intervening in their domestic policy only if they rebelled. The Han instead relied on trade and markets to incorporate outlying lands as prosperous satellite states within the tribute system. The Xiongnu nomads even became key middlemen in Silk Road trade.

When the Xiongnu were no longer a threat from the north, the Han expanded westward. (See Map 7.2.) By 100 BCE, Emperor Wu had extended the northern defensive wall from the Tian Shan Mountains to the Gobi Desert. Along the wall stood signal beacons for sending emergency messages, and its gates opened periodically for trading fairs. The westernmost gate was called the Jade Gate, since jade from the Taklamakan Desert passed through it. Wu also built garrison cities at oases to protect the trade routes. Soldiers at these oasis garrison cities settled with their families on the frontiers. When its military power expanded beyond the Jade Gate, the Han government set up a similar system of oases on the rim of the Taklamakan Desert. With irrigation, oasis agriculture attracted many more settlers. Trade routes passing through deserts and oases now were safer and more reliable—until fierce Tibetan tribes threatened them at the beginning of the Common Era—than the steppe routes, which they gradually replaced.

The Han Empire and Deforestation The Han dynasty had a significant, if unintended, impact on the environment. As the Han peoples moved southward and later westward, filling up empty spaces and driving elephants, rhinoceroses, and other animals into extinction, the farming communities cleared immense tracts of land of shrubs and forests to prepare for farming. The Han were especially fond of oak, pine, ash, and elm, and their artists celebrated them in paintings; farmers, however, saw forests as a challenge to their work. China's grand environmental narrative has been the clearing of old-growth forests that had originally covered the greater part of the territory of China.

But trees prevent erosion, and one of the results of the massive deforestation campaigns during the Han period in the regions surrounding the Yellow River was massive runoffs of soil into the river. In fact, the Yellow River owes its name to the immense quantities of mud that it absorbed from surrounding farmlands. This sediment raised the level of the river above the surrounding plain in many places. In spite of villagers' efforts to build levees along the river's banks, severe flooding occurred, threatening crops, destroying villages, and even undermining the legitimacy of ruling dynasties. During most of the Han Empire, a break in the levees took place every sixteen years. The highest concentration of flooding was between 66 BCE and 34 CE, when severe floods occurred every nine years. As in many empires, the Han's expansion was based on expanded agriculture and brisk trade, but expansion came at a major environmental price: deforestation, flooding, and the destruction of the habitats of many plants and animals.

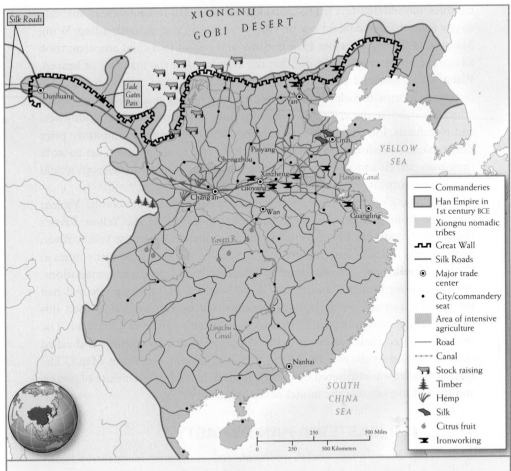

Map 7.2 *Pax Sinica*: The Han Dynasty in the First Century BCE

Agriculture, commerce, and industry flourished in East Asia under Han rule.

- According to the map, what were the main commodities in the Han dynasty, where were they located, and along what routes might they have moved to pass among the empire's regions?
- Locate the lines marking the commanderies into which Han territory was divided. What do you notice about their comparative size, resources, and other features?
- What do you notice about the location of major trade centers and the areas of intensive agriculture?

SOCIAL UPHEAVAL AND NATURAL DISASTER

The strain of military expenses and the tax pressures those expenditures placed on small landholders and peasants were more than the Han Empire could bear. By the end of the first century BCE, heavy financial expenditures had drained the Chinese empire. A devastating chain of events exacerbated the empire's troubles: natural disasters led to crop failures, which led to landowners' inability to pay taxes that were based not on crop yield but on size of landholding. Wang Mang (r. 9–23 CE), a former Han minister and regent to a child emperor, took advantage of the crisis. Believing that the Han had lost the mandate of heaven, Wang Mang assumed the throne in 9 CE and established a new dynasty. He designed reforms to help the poor and to foster economic activity. He made efforts to stabilize the economy by confiscating gold from wealthy landowners and merchants, introducing a new currency, and attempting to minimize price fluctuations. By redistributing excess land, he hoped to allow all families to work their own parcels and share in cultivating a communal plot whose crops would become tax surplus for the state.

Wang Mang's regime, and his idealistic reforms, failed miserably. Violent resistance from peasants and large landholders, as well as the Yellow River's change in its course in 11 CE, contributed to his demise. When the Yellow River, appropriately called "China's Sorrow," changed course—as it has many times in China's long history—tremendous floods caused mass death, vast migrations, peasant impoverishment, and revolt. The floods of 11 CE likely affected half the Chinese population. Rebellious peasants, led by Daoist clerics, used this far-reaching disaster as a pretext to march on Wang's capital at Chang'an. The peasants painted their foreheads red in imitation of demon warriors and called themselves Red Eyebrows. By 23 CE, they had overthrown Wang Mang. The natural disaster was attributed by Wang's rivals to his unbridled misuse of power, and soon Wang became the model of the evil usurper.

THE LATER (EASTERN) HAN DYNASTY

After Wang Mang's fall, social, political, and economic inequalities fatally weakened the power of the emperor and the court. As a result, the Later (or Eastern) Han dynasty (25–220 CE), with its capital at Luoyang on the North China plain, followed a hands-off economic policy under which large landowners and merchants amassed more wealth and more property. Decentralizing the regime was also good for local business and long-distance trade, as the Silk Roads continued to flourish. Chinese silk became popular as far away as the Roman Empire. In return, China received from points west on the Silk Roads commodities including glass, jade, horses, precious stones, tortoiseshells, and fabrics.

By the second century CE, landed elites enjoyed the fruits of their success in manipulating the Later (Eastern) Han tax system. It granted them so many land and labor exemptions that the government never again firmly controlled its human and agricultural resources as Emperor Wu had. As the court refocused on the new capital in Luoyang, local power fell into the hands of great aristocratic families. These elites acquired even more privately owned land and forced free peasants to become their rent-paying tenants, then raised their rents higher and higher.

Such prosperity bred greater social inequity—among large landholders, tenant farmers, and peasants working their small parcels—and a renewed source of turmoil. Simmering tensions between landholders and peasants boiled over in a full-scale rebellion in 184 CE. Popular religious groups championed new ideas among commoners and elites for whom the many-centuries-earlier Daoist sage Master Laozi, the voice of naturalness and spontaneity, was an exemplary model. Daoist masters challenged Confucian ritual conformity, and they advanced their ideas in the name of a divine order that would redeem all people, not just elites. Officials, along with other political outcasts, headed strong dissident groups and eventually formed local movements. Under their leadership, religious groups such as the Yellow Turbans—so called because they wrapped yellow scarves around their heads—championed Daoist upheaval across the empire. The Yellow Turbans drew on Daoist ideas to call for a just and ideal society. Their message received a warm welcome from a population that was increasingly hostile to Han rule.

Proclaiming the Daoist millenarian belief in a future "Great Peace," the Yellow Turbans demanded fairer treatment by the Han state and equal distribution of all farm lands. As agrarian conditions worsened, a widespread famine ensued. It was a catastrophe that, in the rebels' view, demonstrated the emperor's loss of the mandate of heaven. While Han military forces were successful in quashing the rebellion, significant damage had been done to Han rule. The economy disintegrated when people refused to pay taxes and provide forced labor, and internal wars engulfed the dynasty. After the 180s CE, three competing states replaced the Han: the Wei in the northwest, the Shu in the southwest, and the Wu in the south. A long-lasting unified empire did not return for several centuries.

The Roman Empire (C. 300 BCE–C. 300 CE)

At the other end of Afro-Eurasia from Han China, in a centuries-long process, Rome became a great power that ruled over as many as 60 million subjects. The Roman Empire at its height encompassed lands from the highlands of what is now Scotland in Europe to the lower reaches of the Nile River in modern-day Egypt and part of Sudan, and from the borders of the Inner Eurasian steppe in Ukraine and the Caucasus to the Atlantic shores of North Africa. (See Map 7.3.) Whereas the Han Empire dominated an enormous and unbroken landmass, the Roman Empire dominated lands around the Mediterranean Sea. Like the Han Chinese, though, the Romans acquired command over their world through violent military expansion. By the first century CE, almost unceasing wars against their neighbors had enabled the Romans to forge an unparalleled number of ethnic groups and minor states into a single, large political state.

FOUNDATIONS OF THE ROMAN EMPIRE

Three major factors influenced the beginnings of Rome's imperial expansion: migrations of foreign peoples, Rome's military might, and Roman political innovation.

Population Movements Between 450 and 250 BCE, migrations from northern and central Europe brought large numbers of Celts to settle in lands around the Mediterranean Sea. They convulsed the northern rim of the Mediterranean, staging armed forays into lands from what is now Spain in the west to present-day Turkey in the east. One of these migrations involved Gallic peoples from the region of the Alps and beyond who launched a series of violent incursions into northern Italy that ultimately—around 390 BCE—led to the seizure of Rome. The important result for the Romans was not their city's capture, which was temporary yet traumatic, but rather the permanent dislocation that the invaders inflicted on the city-states of the Etruscans. These Etruscans, themselves likely a combination of indigenous people and migrants from Asia Minor centuries before, spoke their own language and were centered in what is now Tuscany. Before the Gallic invasions, the Etruscans had dominated the Italian Peninsula. While the Etruscans with great difficulty drove the invading Gauls back northward, their cities never recovered nor did their ability to dominate other peoples in Italy, including their fledgling rival, the Romans. Thus, the Gallic migrations weakened Etruscan power, one of the most formidable roadblocks to Roman expansion in Italy.

Military Institutions and the War Ethos The Romans achieved unassailable military power by organizing the communities that they conquered in Italy into a system that generated manpower for their army. This

A Loving Etruscan Wife and Husband This lid, dating to around 300 BCE, topped the sarcophagus of Thanchvil Tarnai (wife) and Larth Tetnies (husband). Their intimate pose on the marriage bed—wrapped in an eternal loving embrace with her right hand tenderly tucked behind his neck, their eyes locked and knees touching—suggests a perhaps unexpected degree of equality between husband and wife among the Etruscans of central Italy as Rome expanded to control the entire Italian Peninsula. The image on the side of the coffin that was meant to be seen depicted an Amazonomachy (Greeks fighting Amazons). Scholars have found traces of blue, red, pink, and purple pigments, revealing that the sarcophagus was once richly colored.

development began around 340 BCE, when the Romans faced a concerted attack by their fellow Latin city-states. By then, the other Latins viewed Rome not as an ally in a system of mutual defense but as a growing threat to their own independence. After overcoming these nearby Latins, the Romans charged onward to defeat one community after another in Italy. Demanding from their defeated enemies a supply of men for the Roman army every year, Rome amassed a huge reservoir of military manpower.

In addition to their overwhelming advantage in manpower, the Romans cultivated an unusual war ethos. A heightened sense of honor drove Roman men to push themselves into battle again and again, and never to accept defeat. Guided by the example of great warriors and shaped by a regime of training and discipline, in which minor infractions of duty were punishable by death, the Roman army trooped out to war in annual spring campaigns beginning in the month—still called March today—dedicated to and named for the Roman god of war, Mars.

By 275 BCE, Rome controlled the Italian Peninsula. It next entered into three great **Punic Wars** with Carthage, which had begun as a Phoenician colony and was now the major power centered in the northern parts of present-day Tunisia (see Chapters 4 and 5). The First Punic War (264–241 BCE) was a prolonged naval battle over the island of Sicily. With their victory, the Romans acquired a dominant position in the western Mediterranean. The Second Punic War (218–201 BCE), however, revealed the real strength and might of the Roman army. The Romans drew on their reserve force of nearly 750,000 men to ultimately repulse—with huge casualties and dramatic losses—the Carthaginian general Hannibal's invading force of 20,000 troops and their war elephants. The Romans took the war to enemy soil, winning the decisive battle at Zama near Carthage in late 202 BCE. Despite their ultimate victory, Rome's initial losses in the early years of the Second Punic War were so devastating that a law was passed limiting the wealth that women could display in public, and this *lex Oppia* remained in effect for almost twenty years, until women protested to achieve its repeal. In a final war of extermination, waged between 149 and 146 BCE, the Romans used their overwhelming advantage in manpower, ships, and other resources to bring the five-centuries-long hegemony of Carthage in the western Mediterranean to an end.

With an unrelenting drive to war, the Romans continued to draft, train, and field extraordinary numbers of men for combat. Soldiers, conscripted at age seventeen or eighteen, served for up to ten years at a time or even longer. The Roman historian Livy recorded a speech given in 171 BCE by Spurius Ligustinus, a soldier battle hardened from more than twenty years of service. After recounting his many campaigns in Macedonia, Syria, and Spain, fifty-year-old Ligustinus concluded: "So long as anyone who is calling up an army will judge me to be a suitable soldier, never will I try to be excused." With so many young men devoted to war for such long spans of time, the war ethos became deeply embedded in the ideals of every generation. After 200 BCE, the Romans unleashed this successful

The Global View

NORTH SEA

BALTIC SEA

BRITANNIA

Londinium

0 — 250 — 500 Miles
0 — 250 — 500 Kilometers

GERMANIA INFERIOR

GERMANI

ATLANTIC OCEAN

GALLIA LUGDUNENSIS

BELGICA

DECUMATES

Rhine R. LAURI

IUTHUNGI

GALLIA AQUITANIA

GERMANIA SUPERIOR

RAETIA

NORICUM

Danube R.

PANNONIA

GALLIA NARBONENSIS

ITALIA

ADRIATIC SEA

DALMATIA

LUSITANIA

TARRACONENSIS

CORSICA

Rome

MINORCA

Corduba

BAETIA

MAJORCA

SARDINIA

M E D I T E R R A N E A N   S E A

MAURETANIA TINGITANA

MAURETANIA CAESARIENSIS

Carthage

SICILIA

Syracuse

NUMIDIA

AFRICA

GAETULI

GARAMANTES

Legend:
- Mediterranean Sea current
- Roman expansion to 201 BCE
- Roman expansion, 201–100 BCE
- Roman expansion, 100–44 BCE
- Roman expansion, 44 BCE–14 CE
- Roman expansion, 14–96 CE
- Roman expansion, 96–116 CE
- GALLIA Roman province
- GAETULI Border peoples
- ⊙ Important provincial capitals

Map 7.3 Roman Expansion to 120 CE

Roman expansion continued for several centuries before reaching its peak in the second century CE.

- According to the map, what were Rome's earliest provinces? What provinces were incorporated during the last phase of Rome's expansion? What sense, if any, can you make of the stages of Roman expansion, in terms of where and when the Romans expanded their territory?
- What features—geographical or otherwise—limited Roman expansion farther into Europe, Southwest Asia, and Africa?
- How did the sea current influence the movement of peoples and goods in the Mediterranean?

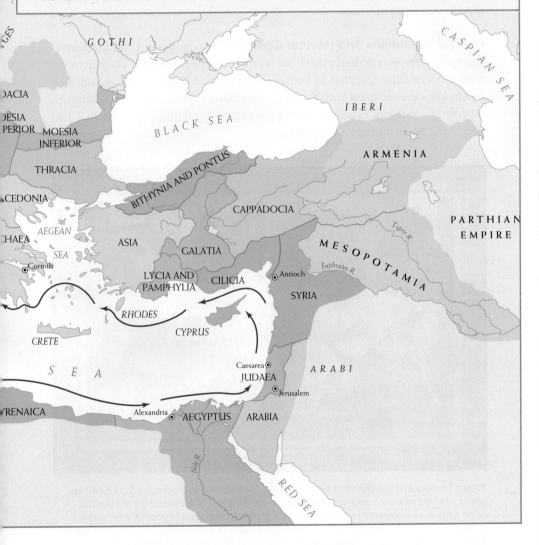

war machine on the kingdoms of the eastern Mediterranean. In 146 BCE, the same year they annihilated what was left of Carthage, the Romans obliterated the great Greek city-state of Corinth, killing all its adult males and selling all its women and children into slavery. Rome's monopoly of power over the entire Mediterranean basin was now unchallenged.

Roman military forces served under men who knew they could win not just glory and territory for the state, but also enormous rewards for themselves. They were talented men driven by burning ambition, from Scipio Africanus in the late 200s BCE, the conqueror of Carthage, to Julius Caesar, the great general of the 50s BCE. Julius Caesar's eight-year-long cycle of Gallic wars resulted in the deaths of more than 1 million Gauls and the enslavement of another million. Western Afro-Eurasia had never witnessed war on this scale; it had no equal anywhere, except in China.

Political Institutions and Internal Conflict The conquest of the Mediterranean placed unprecedented power and wealth into the hands of a few men in the Roman social elite. The rush of battlefield successes had kept Romans and their Italian allies preoccupied with the demands of army service overseas. Once this process of territorial expansion slowed, social and political problems that had been lying dormant began to resurface.

Roman Farmers and Soldiers In the late Republic, most Roman soldiers came from rural Italy, where small farms were being absorbed into the landholdings of the wealthy and powerful. In the empire, soldiers were recruited from rural provincial regions. They sometimes worked small fields of their own and sometimes worked the lands of the wealthy—like the domain in the Roman province of Africa (in modern-day Tunisia) that is depicted in this mosaic.

Following the traditional date of its founding in 509 BCE, the Romans had lived in a state that they called the "public thing," or **res publica** (hence the modern word *republic*). In this state, policy issued from the Senate—a body of permanent members, 300 to 600 of Rome's most powerful and wealthy citizens (by definition, male)—and from popular assemblies of the citizens. Every year the citizens elected the officials of state, principally two consuls who held power for a year and commanded the armies. The people also annually elected ten men who, as tribunes of the plebs ("the common people"), held the task of protecting the common people's interests against those of the rich and powerful. In severe political crises, Romans sometimes chose one man, a dictator, whose words, *dicta*, were law and who held absolute power over the state for no longer than six months. These institutions, originally devised for a city-state, were problematic for ruling a Mediterranean-sized empire.

By the second century BCE, Rome's power elites were exploiting the wealth from its Mediterranean conquests to acquire huge tracts of land in Italy and Sicily. They then imported enormous numbers of enslaved people from all around the Mediterranean to work this land. Free citizen farmers, the backbone of the army, were driven off their lands and into the cities. The result was a severe agrarian and recruiting crisis. In 133 and 123–121 BCE, two tribunes, the brothers Tiberius and Gaius Gracchus, tried—much as Wang Mang would in China more than a century later—to address these inequalities. The Gracchi brothers attempted to institute land reforms guaranteeing to all of Rome's poor citizens a basic amount of land that would qualify them for army service. But political enemies assassinated the elder brother, Tiberius, and orchestrated violent resistance that drove the younger brother, Gaius, to commit suicide while being chased by an angry mob.

Thereafter, poor Roman citizens looked not to state institutions but to army commanders, to whom they gave their loyalty and support, to provide them with land and income. These generals became increasingly powerful and started to compete with one another, ignoring the Senate and the traditional rules of politics. As generals sought control of the state and their supporters took sides, a long series of civil wars began that lasted from 90 BCE to the late 30s BCE. The Romans now turned inward on themselves the tremendous militaristic resources built up during the conquest of the Mediterranean.

EMPERORS, AUTHORITARIAN RULE, AND ADMINISTRATION

Julius Caesar's adopted son, Octavian (63 BCE–14 CE), ultimately reunited the fractured empire and emerged as undisputed master of the Roman world. Octavian's authoritarian one-man rule marked the beginning of the **Pax Romana** ("Roman Peace," 25 BCE–235 CE). This peace depended on the power of one man with enough authority to enforce an orderly competition among Roman aristocrats.

A Roman Town Roman towns featured many of the standard elements of modern towns and cities. Streets and avenues crossed at right angles; roads were paved; sidewalks ran between streets and houses. The houses were often several stories high and had wide windows and open balconies. All these elements can be seen in this street from Herculaneum, eerily preserved by the deadly pyroclastic blast of gas and ash and the volcanic lava flow when nearby Mount Vesuvius erupted in August of 79 CE, burying the town and its inhabitants.

Octavian concentrated immense wealth and the most important official titles and positions of power in his own hands. Signaling the transition to a new political order in which he alone controlled the army, the provinces, and the political processes in Rome, Octavian assumed a new title, **Augustus** ("the Revered One")—much as the Qin emperor Zheng had assumed the new title of Shi Huangdi ("First August Emperor")—as well as the traditional republican roles of *imperator* ("commander in chief," or emperor), *princeps* ("first man"), and *Caesar* (a name connoting his adoptive heritage, but which over time became a title assumed by imperial successors).

Rome's subjects tended to see these emperors as heroic or even semidivine beings in life and to think of the good ones as becoming gods on their death. Yet emperors were always careful to present themselves as civil rulers whose power ultimately depended on the consent of Roman citizens and the might of the army. They contrasted themselves with the image of "king," a role the Romans had learned to detest from the monarchy they themselves had long ago overthrown to establish their Republic in 509 BCE. Nonetheless, the emperors' powers were immense.

Being a Roman emperor required finesse and talent, and few succeeded at it. Of the twenty-two emperors who held power in the most stable period of Roman history (between the first Roman emperor, Augustus, and the early third century CE), fifteen met their end by murder or suicide. As powerful as he might be, no individual emperor alone could govern an empire of such great size and population, encompassing a multitude of languages and cultures. He needed institutions and competent people to help him. In terms of sheer power, the most important institution was the army. Consequently, the emperors systematically transformed the army into a full-time professional force. Men now entered the imperial army not as citizen volunteers but as paid professionals who enlisted for life and swore loyalty to the emperor and his family. It was part of the emperor's image to present himself as a victorious battlefield commander, inflicting defeat on the "barbarians" who threatened the empire's frontiers.

For most emperors, however, governance was largely a daily chore of listening to complaints, answering petitions, deciding court cases, and hearing reports from civil administrators and military commanders. At its largest in the second century CE, the Roman Empire encompassed more than forty administrative units, called provinces. As in Han China, each had a governor appointed or approved by the emperor; but unlike Han China, which had its formal Confucian-trained bureaucracy with ranks of senior and junior officials, the Roman Empire of this period was relatively understaffed in terms of central government officials. The emperor and his provincial governors depended very much on local help, sometimes aided by elite enslaved men and freedmen (formerly enslaved men) serving as government bureaucrats. With a limited staff of full-time assistants and an entourage of friends and acquaintances, each governor was expected to guarantee peace. However, the state relied on private companies for some essential tasks, such as the collection of imperial taxes, in which the profit motives of the publicans (the men in the companies that took up government contracts) were at odds with the expectations of fair government among the empire's subjects.

TOWN AND CITY LIFE

Due to the conditions of peace and the wealth it generated, urban settlements were clustered in core areas of the empire—central Italy, southern Spain, northern Africa, and the western parts of present-day Turkey. The towns, whose

A Roman Municipal Charter These bronze tablets record the charter of Urso (the colony Genetiva Julia), founded in Spain by Julius Caesar in the 40s BCE. Charters like this one, set up for public display in the forum or central open area, displayed regulations for the conduct of public life in a Roman town, including rules governing family inheritance and property transfers, laws on the election of town officials, and definitions of their powers and duties. Of the more than seventy surviving clauses of the Urso charter, only one (number 133) specifically mentions women; this clause proclaims broadly that wives of colonists are bound by the law.

municipal charters echoed Roman forms of government, provided the backbone of local administration for the empire. Towns often were walled, and inside those walls the streets and avenues ran at right angles. A large, open-air, rectangular area called the *forum* dominated the town center. Around it clustered the main public buildings: the markets, the main temples of principal gods and goddesses, and the building that housed city administrators. Residential areas featured regular blocks of houses, close together and fronting on the streets. Larger towns contained large apartment blocks that were not much different from the four- and five-story buildings in any modern city. In the smaller towns, sanitary standards were reasonably good.

The imperial metropolis of Rome was another matter. With well over a million inhabitants, it was larger than any other urban center of its time; Xianyang and Chang'an—the Qin and Han capitals, respectively—each had a population of between 300,000 and 500,000. While Rome's inhabitants were privileged in terms of their access to government doles of wheat and aqueduct-supplied water, their living conditions could be appalling, with people jammed into ramshackle high-rise apartments prone to collapse in a fire. Apart from crime and violence, poor sanitary conditions and the diseases that accompany them were constant threats to the population.

Towns large and small tended to have two major entertainment venues: a theater, adopted from Hellenistic culture and devoted to plays, dances, and other popular events; and an amphitheater, a Roman innovation with a much larger seating capacity that surrounded the oval performance area at its center. In the amphitheaters, Romans could stage exotic beast hunts and gladiatorial matches for the enjoyment of huge crowds of appreciative spectators. These public entertainment facilities of Roman towns stressed the importance of

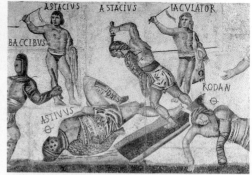

Deadly Roman Entertainment The huge amphitheater (*left*) is in the remains of the Roman city of Thysdrus in North Africa (the town of El Jem in modern-day Tunisia). The wealth of the Africans under the empire enabled them to build colossal entertainment venues that competed with the one in Rome in scale and grandeur. Roman gladiators would fight, sometimes to the death, in such venues. The mosaic from Rome (*right*) shows two gladiators at the end of a full combat in which Astacius has killed Astivus. The Greek letter theta, or "th" (the circle with a crossbar through it), beside the names of Astivus and Rodan indicates that these men are dead—*thanatos* being the Greek word for "death."

gatherings in which citizens participated in civic life, as compared with the largely private entertainment of the Han elite.

SOCIAL AND GENDER RELATIONS

In Rome's civil society, laws and courts governed formal relationships, including those based on patronage and the family. By the last century BCE, the Roman state's complex legal system featured a rich body of written law, courts, and well-trained lawyers. Deeply entrenched throughout the empire, this legal infrastructure long outlasted the Roman Empire. Also firmly embedded in Roman society was a system of personal relationships that linked the rich and powerful with the mass of average citizens. Men and women of wealth and high social status acted as patrons, protecting and supporting dependents or "clients" from the lower classes. From the emperor at the top to the local municipal man at the bottom, the bonds between these groups in each city found formal expression in legal definitions of patrons' responsibilities to clients; at the same time, this informal social code raised expectations that the wealthy would be civic benefactors, sponsoring the construction of public libraries, bathhouses, and theaters.

While patronage was important, the family was at the very foundation of the Roman social order. Legally speaking, the authoritarian *paterfamilias* ("father of

Claudia Antonia Tatiana of Aphrodisias Roman women of the upper class—like Claudia Antonia Tatiana of Aphrodisias (pictured here), Plancia Magna of Perge, Eumachia of Pompeii, Regilla of Athens, and Junia Rustica of Spain—accrued a great deal of money and power in ancient Rome. Such women could own a business, serve in a prominent civic priesthood, or become a major civic donor. Tatiana's clothing and hairstyle are typical of elite women in the Severan period (early third century CE). Just as women in the 1980s adopted the Princess Di haircut and many in the late 2010s sported popstar Ariana Grande's signature high ponytail, elite women across the Roman Empire often styled their hair after the empress's. In this case, Julia Domna's cantaloupe updo.

A Birthday Invitation This thin sheet of wood, one of the many Vindolanda Tablets (named for the fort in Roman Britain where they were found), records a birthday invitation written around 100 CE. It is remarkable not only that this mundane document has survived, but also that it was sent by a woman (Claudia Severa, wife of a garrison commander) to her friend (Sulpicia Lepidina, wife of a military prefect). The note gives an unexpected snapshot of interactions between military wives accompanying their husbands along the Roman frontier.

Coin Hoard Examining batches of coins buried for safekeeping reveals the range of coins in circulation at any one time. This coin hoard was found near Didcot in Oxfordshire, England. Buried around 165 CE, it contained about 125 gold coins minted between the 50s and 160s CE and represents the equivalent of about eleven years' pay for a Roman soldier. Gold coins were used for expensive transactions or to store wealth. Most ordinary purchases or payments were made with silver or brass coins.

the family") had nearly total power over his dependents, including his wife, children, and grandchildren and the people he enslaved. Despite this patriarchal system, Roman women, even those of modest wealth and status, had much greater freedom of action and much greater control of their own wealth and property than did women in most Greek city-states. As in Han China, some women in the Roman world could be well educated, literate, well connected, and in control of their own lives—despite what the laws and ideas of Roman males might suggest.

THE ECONOMY AND NEW SCALES OF PRODUCTION

Rome achieved staggering transformations in agriculture and mining. The area of land surveyed and cultivated rose steadily throughout this period, as Romans spread into arid lands on the periphery of the Sahara Desert to the south and opened up heavily forested regions in present-day France and Germany to the north. Roman agriculture and mining relied on chattel slavery—the use of human beings purchased as private property (see Chapter 6). The massive concentration of wealth and enslaved people at the center of the Roman world led to the first large-scale commercial plantation agriculture and the first technical handbooks on how to run such operations for profit; it also led to dramatic rebellions, such as the Sicilian Revolt (135–132 BCE) and the Spartacus uprising (73–71 BCE), although the latter began among enslaved men in a school for gladiators. Slave-worked estates specialized in products destined for the big urban markets: wheat, grapes, and olives, as well as cattle and sheep. An impressive road system connected the far-flung parts of the empire. Milestones marked most of these roads, and complex ancient maps, called itineraries, charted major roads and distances between towns. (See Map 7.4.)

Rome mined copper, tin, silver, and gold—out of which the Roman state produced the most massive coinage system known in western Afro-Eurasia before early modern times. Public and private demand for metals was so great that traces of the air pollution generated by Roman mining operations remain in ice core samples taken from Greenland today. Rome's standardized currency facilitated taxation and the increased exchange of commodities and services. The economy functioned more efficiently due to this production of

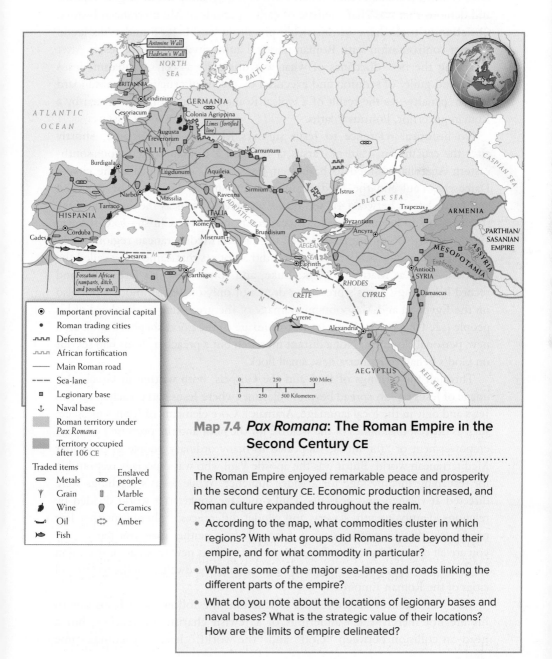

Map 7.4 *Pax Romana*: The Roman Empire in the Second Century CE

The Roman Empire enjoyed remarkable peace and prosperity in the second century CE. Economic production increased, and Roman culture expanded throughout the realm.

- According to the map, what commodities cluster in which regions? With what groups did Romans trade beyond their empire, and for what commodity in particular?

- What are some of the major sea-lanes and roads linking the different parts of the empire?

- What do you note about the locations of legionary bases and naval bases? What is the strategic value of their locations? How are the limits of empire delineated?

coins, which was paralleled only by the coinage output of Han dynasty China and its successors.

THE RISE OF CHRISTIANITY

Over centuries, Roman religion had cultivated a dynamic world of gods, spirits, and demons that was characteristic of earlier periods of Mediterranean history. **Christianity** took shape in this richly pluralistic world. Its foundations lay in a direct confrontation with Roman imperial authority: the trial of Jesus. After preaching the new doctrines of what was originally a sect of Judaism, Jesus was found guilty of sedition and executed by means of crucifixion—a standard Roman penalty—as the result of a typical Roman provincial trial overseen by a Roman governor, Pontius Pilatus.

No historical reference to Jesus survives from his own lifetime. Shortly after the crucifixion, Paul of Tarsus, a Jew and a Roman citizen from southeastern Anatolia, claimed to have seen Jesus in full glory outside the city of Damascus. Paul and the Mediterranean communities to whom he preached and wrote letters between 40 and 60 CE referred to Jesus as the Anointed One (the Messiah, in keeping with Jewish expectations) or the Christ—*ho Christos* in Greek (still the dominant language of the eastern Mediterranean region thanks to Hellenism). Only many decades later did accounts that came to be called the Gospels—such as Matthew, Mark, Luke, and John—describe Jesus's life and record his sayings. Jesus's preaching drew not only on Jewish models but also on the Egyptian and Mesopotamian image of the great king as shepherd of his people (see Chapter 3). With Jesus, this image of the good shepherd took on a new, personal closeness. Not a distant monarch but a preacher, Jesus had set out on God's behalf to gather a new, small flock.

Through the writings of Paul and the Gospels, both written in Greek, this image of Jesus rapidly spread beyond Palestine (where Jesus had preached only to Jews and only in the local language, Aramaic). Core elements of Jesus's message, such as the responsibilities of the well-off for the poor and the promised eventual empowerment of "the meek," appealed to many ordinary people in the wider Mediterranean world. But it was the apostle Paul who was especially responsible for reshaping this message for a wider audience. While Jesus's teachings were directed at villagers and peasants, Paul's message spoke to a world divided by religious identity, wealth, slavery, and gender differences: "There is neither Jew nor Greek, there is neither slave nor free, there is neither male nor female; for you are all one in Christ Jesus" (Galatians 3:28). This new message, universal in its claims and appeal, was immediately accessible to the dwellers of the towns and cities of the Roman Empire.

Just half a century after Jesus's crucifixion, the followers of Jesus saw in his life not merely the wanderings of a Jewish charismatic teacher, but a head-on collision between "God" and "the world." Jesus's teachings came to be understood as the message of a divine being—who for thirty years had moved (largely unrecognized) among human beings. Jesus's followers formed a church: a permanent gathering entrusted to the charge of leaders chosen by God and fellow believers. For these leaders and their followers, death offered a defining testimony for their faith. Early Christians hoped for a Roman trial and the opportunity to offer themselves as witnesses (*martyrs*) for their faith.

Persecutions of Christians were sporadic and were responses to local concerns. Not until the emperor Decius, in the mid-third century CE, did the state direct an empire-wide attack on Christians. But Decius died within a year of launching this assault, and Christians interpreted their persecutor's death as evidence of the hand of God in human affairs. By the last decades of the third century CE, Christian communities of various kinds, reflecting the different strands of their movement through the Mediterranean as well as the local cultures in which they settled, were present in every society in the empire.

THE LIMITS OF EMPIRE

The limitations of Roman force were a pragmatic factor in determining who belonged in, and was subject to, the empire as opposed to who was outside it and therefore excluded. The Romans pushed their authority in the west to the shores of the Atlantic Ocean, and to the south they drove it to the edges of the Sahara Desert. In both cases, there was little additional useful land available to dominate. Roman power was blocked, however, to the east by the Parthians and then the Sasanians and to the north by the Goths and other Germanic peoples. (See Map 7.5.)

The Parthians and Sassanians On Rome's eastern frontiers, powerful Romans, such as Marcus Crassus in the mid-50s BCE, Mark Antony in the early 30s BCE, and the emperor Trajan around 115 CE, wished to imitate the achievements of Alexander the Great and conquer the arid lands lying east of Judea and Syria. Crassus and Antony failed miserably, stopped by the Parthian Empire and its successor, the Sasanian Empire. The Romans, under Trajan, briefly annexed the provinces of Armenia and Mesopotamia but abandoned them soon thereafter. The Parthian people had moved south from present-day Turkmenistan and settled in the region comprising the modern states of Iraq and Iran. Parthian social order was founded on nomadic pastoralism and a war capability based on technical advances in mounted horseback warfare. Reliance on horses made the Parthian style of fighting highly mobile and ideal for warfare on arid plains and deserts. They perfected the so-called Parthian shot: the arrow shot from a bow with great accuracy at long distance and from horseback at a gallop. On the flat, open plains of Iran and Iraq, the Parthians had a decisive advantage over slow-moving, cumbersome mass infantry formations that had been developed for war in the Mediterranean.

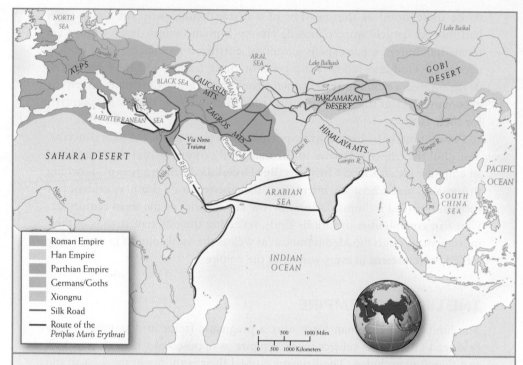

Map 7.5 Imperial Rome and Later (Eastern) Han China, c. 200 CE

....

Imperial Rome and the Later (Eastern) Han dynasty thrived simultaneously for about 200 years at the start of the first millennium CE. Despite their geographic spread and the Silk Roads running across Afro-Eurasia, the two empires did not have as much direct contact as one might expect.

- What major groups lived on the borders of imperial Rome and Han China?
- What were the geographical limits of the Roman Empire? Of Han China?
- Based on the map and your reading, what drew imperial Rome and Han China together? What kept them apart?

Eventually the expansionist states of Parthia and Rome became archenemies: they confronted each other in Mesopotamia for nearly four centuries.

The Sasanians expanded the technical advances in mounted horseback warfare that the Parthians had used so successfully in open-desert warfare against the slow-moving Roman mass infantry formations. King Shapur I (r. 240–270 CE) exploited the weaknesses of the Roman Empire in the mid-third century CE, even capturing the Roman emperor Valerian. One early Christian writer, Lactantius, used Valerian's fate at the hands of the Sasanians—he was forced to serve in captivity as a footstool for the Sasanian king, then flayed and stuffed after death to stand in the Sasanian throne room as a warning to ambassadors—as a lesson for what happens to those who persecute Christians.

As successful as the Parthians and the Sasanians were in fighting the Romans, however, they could never challenge Roman sway over Mediterranean lands. Their decentralized political structure limited their coordination and resources, and their horse-mounted style of warfare was ill suited to fighting in the more rocky and hilly environments of the Mediterranean world. (See Chapter 8 for more on the Sasanians.)

German and Gothic "Barbarians"

In the lands across the Rhine and Danube, to the north, environmental conditions largely determined the limits of empire. The long and harsh winters, combined with excellent soil and growing conditions, produced hardy, dense population clusters scattered across vast distances. These illiterate, kin-based agricultural societies had changed little since the first millennium BCE.

As the Roman Empire fixed its northern frontiers along the Rhine and Danube Rivers, two factors determined its relationship with

Soldier versus Barbarian On the frontiers of the Roman Empire, the legionary soldiers faced the non-Roman "barbarians" from the lands beyond. In this piece of a stone-carved picture from Trajan's Column in Rome, we see a civilized and disciplined Roman soldier, to the left, facing a German "barbarian"—with uncut and unkempt hair, no formal armor, and a thatched hut for a home. Frontier realities were never so clear-cut, of course. Roman soldiers, often recruited from the "barbarian" peoples, were a lot more like them than was convenient to admit, and the "barbarians" were influenced by and closer to Roman cultural models than this picture indicates.

the Germans and Goths on the rivers' other side. First, these small societies had only one big commodity for which the empire was willing to pay: human bodies. So the slave trade out of the land across the Rhine and Danube became immense: gold, silver, coins, wine, arms, and other luxury items flowed across the rivers in one direction in exchange for enslaved people flowing into the empire. Second, the wars between the Romans and these societies were unremitting, as every emperor faced the expectation of dealing harshly with these so-called barbarians. Ironically, internal conflicts within the Roman Empire ultimately prompted increasing use of "barbarians" as soldiers and even as officers who served the empire.

While the Han Empire fell in the early third century CE, the Roman Empire would arguably continue to exist politically for more than two centuries (to at least the "traditional" collapse date of 476 CE), during which its history would become intertwined with the rise of Christianity, one of the world's universalizing religions.

Conclusion

China and Rome both constructed empires of unprecedented scale and duration, yet they differed in fundamental ways. Starting out with a less numerous and less dense population than China, Rome relied on enslaved people and "barbarian" immigrants to expand and diversify its workforce. While less than 1 percent of the Chinese population was enslaved, more than 10 percent of the population in the Roman Empire was enslaved. The Chinese rural economy was built on a huge population of free peasant farmers; this enormous labor pool, together with a remarkable bureaucracy, enabled the Han to achieve great political stability. In contrast, the millions of peasant farmers who formed the backbone of rural society in the Roman Empire were much more loosely integrated into the state structure. They never unified to revolt against their government and overthrow it, as did the mass peasant movements of Later (Eastern) Han China. In comparison with their counterparts in China, the peasants in the Roman Empire were not as well connected because they lived farther apart from one another, and they were not as united in purpose. Here, too, the Mediterranean environment accented separation and difference.

In contrast with the elaborate Confucian bureaucracy in Han China, the Roman Empire was relatively fragmented and underadministered. Moreover, no single philosophy or religion ever underpinned the Roman state in the way that Confucianism buttressed the dynasties of China. Both empires, however, benefited from the spread of a uniform language and imperial culture. The process was more comprehensive in China, which possessed a single language that the elites used, than in Rome, where officially a two-language world existed: Latin in the western Mediterranean, Greek in the east. Both states fostered a common imperial culture across all levels of society. Once entrenched, these cultures and languages lasted well after the end of empire.

Differences in human resources, languages, and ideas led the Roman and Han states to evolve in unique ways. In both places, however, faiths that filtered in from the margins—Christianity and Buddhism—eclipsed the classical and secular traditions that grounded the states' foundational ideals. Expanded communication networks accelerated the transmission of these new faiths. The new religions added to the cultural mix that outlasted the Roman Empire and the Han dynasty.

At their height, both states surpassed their forebears by translating unprecedented military power into the fullest form of state-based organization. Each state's complex organization involved the systematic control, counting, and taxing of its population. In both cases, the general increase of the population, the growth of huge cities, and the success of long-distance trade contributed to the new scales of magnitude, making these states the world's first two long-lasting global empires. The Han were not superseded in East Asia as the model empire until the Tang dynasty in the seventh century CE. In western Afro-Eurasia, the Roman Empire was not surpassed in scale or intensity of development until the rise of powerful European nation-states more than a millennium later.

Focus On
Comparing the Han and Roman Empires

- Han China and imperial Rome assimilate diverse peoples and regard outsiders as uncivilized.

- Both empires develop professional military elites, codify laws, and value the role of the state (not just the ruler) in supporting their societies.

- Both empires serve as models for successor states in their regions.

- The empires differ in their ideals and the officials they value: Han China values civilian bureaucrats and magistrates; Rome values soldiers and military governors.

Key Terms

Augustus p. 266

Christianity p. 272

commanderies p. 246

Emperor Wu p. 250

globalizing empires p. 244

Imperial University p. 251

Pax Romana p. 265

Pax Sinica p. 256

Punic Wars p. 261

res publica p. 265

Shi Huangdi p. 246

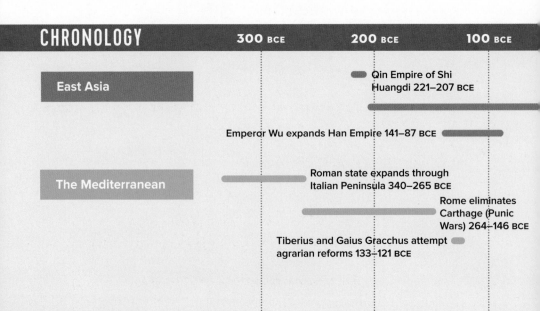

CHRONOLOGY

	300 BCE	200 BCE	100 BCE

East Asia

Qin Empire of Shi Huangdi 221–207 BCE

Emperor Wu expands Han Empire 141–87 BCE

The Mediterranean

Roman state expands through Italian Peninsula 340–265 BCE

Rome eliminates Carthage (Punic Wars) 264–146 BCE

Tiberius and Gaius Gracchus attempt agrarian reforms 133–121 BCE

THINKING ABOUT GLOBAL CONNECTIONS

- **Thinking about Worlds Together, Worlds Apart and Globalizing Empires** In the six centuries between 300 BCE and 300 CE, the Han dynasty and imperial Rome united huge populations and immense swaths of territory not only under their direct control but also under their indirect influence. In what ways did this expansive unity at each end of Afro-Eurasia have an impact on the connections between these two empires? In what ways did these two empires remain worlds apart?

- **Thinking about Changing Power Relationships and Globalizing Empires** Both the Han dynasty and the Roman Empire developed new models for heightened authoritarian control placed in the hands of a single ruler. In what ways did this authoritarian control at the top shape power relationships at all levels of these two societies? What were some potential challenges to this patriarchal, centralized control?

- **Thinking about Transformation & Conflict and Globalizing Empires** Both the Han dynasty and the Roman Empire faced intense threats along their borders. In what ways did Han interactions with nomadic groups like the Xiongnu and Roman interactions with Parthians to the east and Germans and Goths to the north affect these globalizing empires?

Go to INQUIZITIVE to see what you've learned—and learn what you've missed—with personalized feedback along the way.

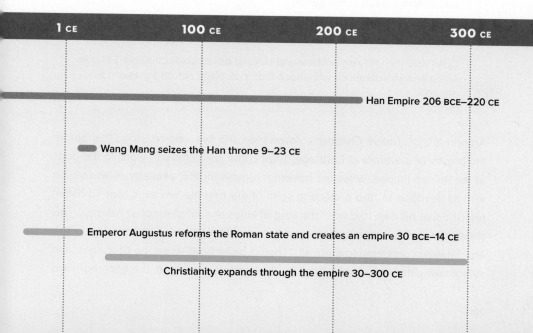

1 CE	100 CE	200 CE	300 CE

Han Empire 206 BCE–220 CE

Wang Mang seizes the Han throne 9–23 CE

Emperor Augustus reforms the Roman state and creates an empire 30 BCE–14 CE

Christianity expands through the empire 30–300 CE

8

The Rise of Universalizing Religions

300–600 CE

Core Objectives

- **DESCRIBE** the characteristics of universalizing religions, and EXPLAIN why universalizing religions developed to varying degrees in Afro-Eurasia but did not develop elsewhere in the world.

- **ANALYZE** the relationship between empires and universalizing religions across Afro-Eurasia in this period.

- **ASSESS** the connections between political unity and religious developments in sub-Saharan Africa and Mesoamerica in the fourth to sixth centuries CE.

- **COMPARE** the unifying political and cultural developments in sub-Saharan Africa and Mesoamerica with those that took place across Eurasia in this period.

Around 180 CE, twelve Christians, seven men and five women, stood trial before the provincial governor at Carthage. Their crime was refusal to worship the gods of the Roman Empire. While the governor argued for the simplicity of his religion with its devotion to "the protecting spirit of our lord the emperor," one Christian retorted that his own lord was "the king of kings and emperor of all nations." This distinction was an unbridgeable gap between the governor and the Christians. The governor condemned them all. "Thanks be to God!" cried the Christians, and straightaway they were beheaded. As the centuries unfolded, the governor's old

Roman ideas of the supremacy of an emperor-lord would give way to the martyrs' devotion to their Lord God as emperor over all. As with Christianity's claim of an "emperor of all nations," a religion's capacity for universalizing—particularly its broad appeal across diverse peoples and cultures—became ever more important to its success.

From 300 to 600 CE, the entire Afro-Eurasian landmass experienced a surge of religious activity. In the west, Christianity became the state faith of the Roman Empire. In India, Vedic religion (Brahmanism) evolved into a more formal spiritual system called Hinduism. Buddhism spread across northern India, central Asia, and China. Around the same time, the peoples living in sub-Saharan Africa reached beyond their local communities, creating common cultures across wider geographical areas. The Bantu-speaking peoples, residing in the southeastern corner of present-day Nigeria, began to spread their way of life throughout the entire southern half of the landmass. Similarly, across the Atlantic Ocean, the Maya established political and cultural institutions over a large portion of Mesoamerica. Across much of the world, spiritual concerns integrated scattered communities through shared faiths. (See Map 8.1.)

This integration was facilitated in Afro-Eurasia in part by the spread of what we might call universalizing religions. Two faiths in this era—Christianity and Buddhism—fit the model for this type of religion particularly well. Six main features characterize **universalizing religions**: their appeal to diverse populations (men and women, freeborn and enslaved, rich and poor); their adaptability as they moved from one cultural and geographical area to another; their promotion of universal rules and principles to guide behavior that transcended place, time, and specific cultural practices; their proselytizing of new believers by energetic and charismatic missionaries; the deep sense of community felt by their converts despite, and perhaps because of, their many demands on followers; and—in the case of Christianity, and to a lesser extent Buddhism—the support given to them by powerful empires. Even as the Roman Empire and the Han dynasty began to crumble, these universalizing traditions continued to flourish.

The peoples living in sub-Saharan Africa and the Americas, too, reached beyond their local communities, creating common cultures across wider geographical areas. As in Eurasia and North Africa, political and cultural transformations undergirded the emergence of these common belief systems. In Africa, the Bantu-speaking peoples, residing in the southeastern corner of present-day Nigeria, began to spread their way of life throughout the entire southern half of the landmass. Similarly, across the Atlantic Ocean, the Maya established political and cultural institutions over a large portion of Mesoamerica and laid the foundations of a common culture. As in Eurasia and North Africa, political and cultural transformations undergirded the emergence of these common belief systems.

Across Afro-Eurasia, universalizing religions were on the move. (See Map 8.2.) Religious leaders carrying written texts (books, scrolls, or tablets of wood or palm leaf) traveled widely. Christians from Persia went to China. Buddhists journeyed from South Asia to Afghanistan and used the caravan routes of central Asia to reach China. Voyages, translations, long-distance pilgrimages, and sweeping conversion campaigns remapped the spiritual landscape of the world. New religious leaders were the brokers of more universal but also more intolerant worldviews, premised on a distinct relationship between gods and their subjects. Religions and their brokers profoundly integrated societies. But they also created new ways to drive them apart.

Global Storyline

The Rise of Christianity, the Spread of Buddhism, and the Beginnings of Common Cultures

- Universalizing religions—notably Christianity and Buddhism—appeal to diverse, widespread populations and challenge the power of secular rulers and thinkers.

- Across Afro-Eurasia, these universalizing religions offer continuity even as powerful empires, specifically the Roman Empire in the west and the Han dynasty in China, are transformed.

- Along the Silk Roads, the merchants and rulers of Sasanian Persia, Sogdiana, and South Asia profoundly influence the exchange of goods, people, and ideas between east and west.

- In the "worlds apart," common cultural beliefs help unify new communities of Bantu speakers in sub-Saharan Africa and newly organized polities in Mesoamerica.

Religious Change and Empire in Western Afro-Eurasia

By the fourth century CE in western Afro-Eurasia, the Roman Empire was hardly the political and military juggernaut it had been 300 years earlier. Surrounded by peoples who coveted its wealth while resisting its power, Rome was fragmenting. So-called barbarians eventually overran the western part of the empire, but in many ways those areas still felt "Roman." Rome's endurance was a boon to the new religious activity that thrived in the turmoil of the immigrations and contracting political authority of the empire. Romans and so-called barbarians alike looked to the new faith of Christianity to maintain continuity with the past, eventually founding a central church in Rome to rule the remnants of empire.

THE APPEAL OF CHRISTIANITY

The spread of new religious ideas, including Christianity, in the Roman Empire changed the way people viewed their existence. Believing implied that an important otherworld loomed beyond the world of physical matter. Feeling contact with that other world gave worshippers a sense of worth; it guided them in this life, and they anticipated someday meeting their guides and spiritual friends there. No longer were the gods understood by believers as local powers to be placated by archaic rituals in sacred places. Many gods became omnipresent figures whom mortals could touch through loving attachment. As ordinary mortals now could hope to meet these divine beings in another, happier world, the sense of an afterlife glowed more brightly.

Christians' emphasis on obedience to their Lord God, rather than to a human ruler, sparked a Mediterranean-wide debate on the nature of religion as well as texts that explored these issues. Christians, like the Jews from whose tradition their sect had sprung, read and followed divinely inspired scriptures that told them what to believe and do, even when those actions went against the empire's laws. Christians spoke of their scriptures as "a divine codex." Bound in a compact volume or set of volumes, which reflected the revolutionary change from scrolls to books for knowledge transmission, this was the definitive code of God's law that outlined proper belief and behavior. By the late fourth century CE, Christians had largely settled on a combination of Jewish scriptures and newly authoritative Christian texts—including history, laws, prophecy, biography, poetry, letters, and ideas about the end of days—that would come to be known as the Bible.

Another central feature of early Christianity was the figure of the **martyr**. Martyrs were women and men whom the Roman authorities executed for persisting in their Christian beliefs instead of submitting to emperor worship, as we saw in this chapter's opening story of the twelve Scillitan martyrs—so-called for the town in North Africa from which they came. While other religions, including Judaism and later Islam, honored martyrs who died for their faith, Christianity claimed to be based directly on "the blood of martyrs," in the words of the North African Christian theologian Tertullian (writing around 200 CE).

The story of Vibia Perpetua, a well-to-do mother in her early twenties, offers a striking example of martyrdom. Perpetua and Felicitas, her maidservant (the Latin word *conserva* is perhaps more accurately translated as "slave," as scholars have recently suggested), refused to sacrifice to the Roman gods. Along with their companions, they were condemned in 203 CE to face wild beasts in the amphitheater of Carthage, a venue small enough that the condemned and the spectators would have had eye contact with one another throughout the fatal encounter. The prison diary that Perpetua dictated before her death offered to Christians and potential converts a powerful religious message that balanced heavenly visions and rewards with her concerns over responsibility to her father, brother, and infant son. The remembered heroism of women martyrs like Perpetua and Felicitas offset the increasingly male leadership—bishops and clergy—of the institutionalized Christian church.

The Global View

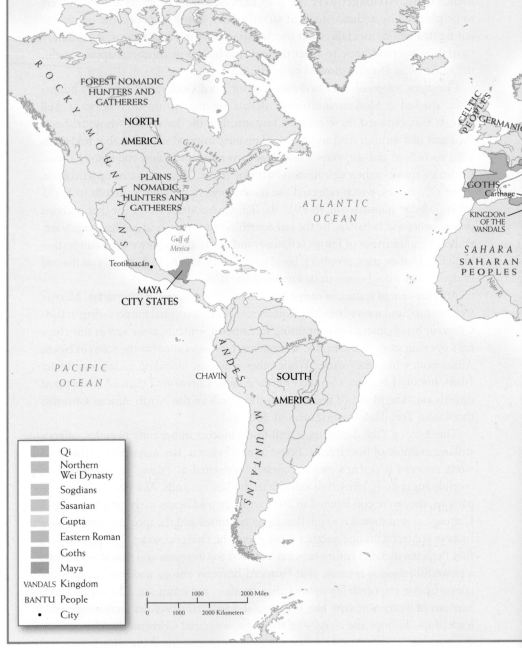

FOREST NOMADIC
HUNTERS AND
GATHERERS

ROCKY MOUNTAINS

NORTH
AMERICA

Great Lakes

Mississippi R.

St. Lawrence R.

PLAINS
NOMADIC
HUNTERS AND
GATHERERS

ATLANTIC
OCEAN

Gulf of
Mexico

Teotihuacán •

MAYA
CITY STATES

CELTIC PEOPLES

GERMANIC

GOTHS
Carthage

KINGDOM
OF THE
VANDALS

SAHARA
SAHARAN
PEOPLES

Niger R.

PACIFIC
OCEAN

ANDES MOUNTAINS

Amazon R.

CHAVIN

SOUTH
AMERICA

Qi

Northern
Wei Dynasty

Sogdians

Sasanian

Gupta

Eastern Roman

Goths

Maya

VANDALS Kingdom

BANTU People

• City

0   1000   2000 Miles

0   1000   2000 Kilometers

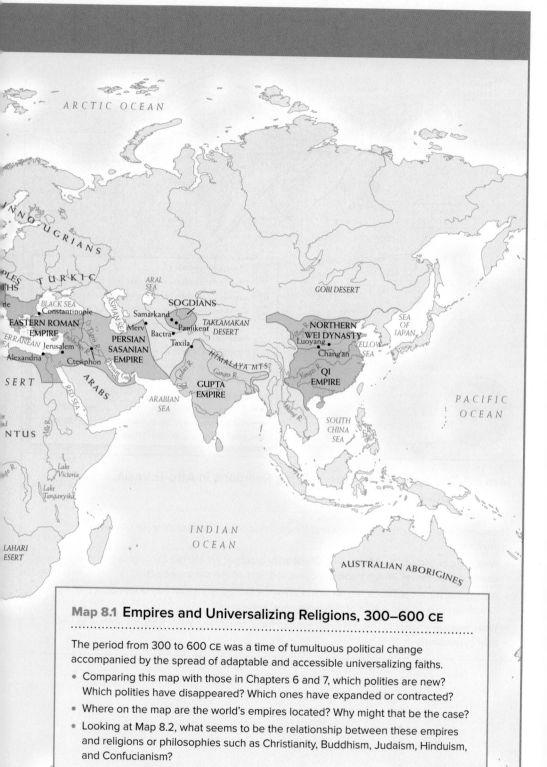

ARCTIC OCEAN

FINNO-UGRIANS

TURKIC

ARAL SEA

GOBI DESERT

SOGDIANS

Samarkand

TAKLAMAKAN DESERT

BLACK SEA
Constantinople

EASTERN ROMAN EMPIRE

Merv · Panjikent
Bactra ·

SEA OF JAPAN

Jerusalem

PERSIAN SASANIAN EMPIRE

Taxila ·

NORTHERN WEI DYNASTY
Luoyang ·

YELLOW SEA

Alexandria

Ctesiphon

HIMALAYA MTS.

Chang'an

QI EMPIRE

Ganges R.

ARABS

GUPTA EMPIRE

RED SEA

ARABIAN SEA

PACIFIC OCEAN

SOUTH CHINA SEA

Lake Victoria

Lake Tanganyika

INDIAN OCEAN

AUSTRALIAN ABORIGINES

KALAHARI DESERT

Map 8.1 Empires and Universalizing Religions, 300–600 CE

The period from 300 to 600 CE was a time of tumultuous political change accompanied by the spread of adaptable and accessible universalizing faiths.

- Comparing this map with those in Chapters 6 and 7, which polities are new? Which polities have disappeared? Which ones have expanded or contracted?

- Where on the map are the world's empires located? Why might that be the case?

- Looking at Map 8.2, what seems to be the relationship between these empires and religions or philosophies such as Christianity, Buddhism, Judaism, Hinduism, and Confucianism?

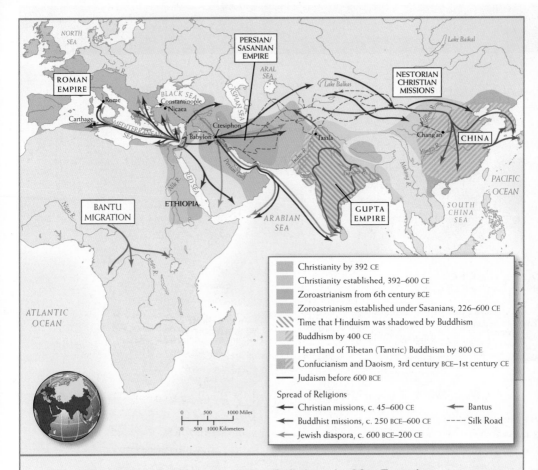

Christianity by 392 CE
Christianity established, 392–600 CE
Zoroastrianism from 6th century BCE
Zoroastrianism established under Sasanians, 226–600 CE
Time that Hinduism was shadowed by Buddhism
Buddhism by 400 CE
Heartland of Tibetan (Tantric) Buddhism by 800 CE
Confucianism and Daoism, 3rd century BCE–1st century CE
Judaism before 600 BCE

Spread of Religions
← Christian missions, c. 45–600 CE   ← Bantus
← Buddhist missions, c. 250 BCE–600 CE   ---- Silk Road
← Jewish diaspora, c. 600 BCE–200 CE

Map 8.2 The Spread of Universalizing Religions in Afro-Eurasia, 300–600 CE

The spread of universalizing religions and the shifting political landscape were intimately connected.

- Where did Hinduism, Buddhism, and Christianity emerge? Where did Zoroastrianism and Confucianism thrive? Which traditions coexisted, and where did they coexist?
- Along what routes did each religion expand? What comparisons can you draw about the directional spread and extent of these religions' expansion?
- What features appear to foster the diffusion of these traditions? What features appear to limit their expansion?

Mosaics of Christian Martyrdom Archaeologists have recently uncovered a sixth-century CE church dedicated to an as-yet-unidentified "glorious martyr" in modern Beit Shemesh, Israel. The inscription (*left*) records a donor's gift of the mosaic floor, marble work, and other elements of a martyrium (a holy site containing the relics of a martyr). A mosaic found in a Roman circus in North Africa (*right*) shows a criminal tied to a stake and being pushed on a cart toward a lunging leopard. Christian martyrs like Perpetua, Felicitas, and perhaps Beit Shemesh's "glorious martyr" were treated like criminals: they were executed, sometimes by being thrown to wild animals.

Constantine: From Conversion to Creed Crucial in spurring Christianity's spread was the transformative experience of Constantine (c. 280–337 CE). Born near the Danubian frontier, he belonged to a class of professional soldiers whose careers took them far from the Mediterranean. Constantine's troops proclaimed him emperor after the death of his father, the emperor Constantius. In the civil war that followed, Constantine looked for signs from the gods. Before the decisive battle for Rome, which took place at a strategic bridge in 312 CE, he supposedly had a dream in which he saw an emblem bearing the words "In this sign you will conquer." The "sign," which he then placed on his soldiers' shields, was the first two letters of the Greek *christos*, a title for Jesus meaning "anointed one." Constantine's troops won the ensuing battle and, thereafter, Constantine's visionary sign became known all over the Roman world. Constantine showered imperial favor on this once-persecuted faith, not only legalizing Christianity (in 313 CE) but also praising the work of Christian bishops and granting them significant tax exemptions.

By the time that Constantine embraced Christianity, it had already made considerable progress within the Roman Empire. It had prevailed in the face of stiff competition and periodically intense persecution from the imperial authorities. Apart from the new imperial endorsement, Christianity's success could be attributed to the sacred aura surrounding its authoritative texts, the charisma of its holy men and women, the fit that existed between its doctrines and popular preexisting religious beliefs and practices, and its broad, universalizing appeal to rich and poor, city dwellers and peasants, enslaved and free people, young and old, and men and women.

In 325 CE, hoping to bring unity to the diversity of belief within Christian communities, Constantine summoned all bishops to Nicaea (modern Iznik in western Turkey) for a council to develop a statement of belief, or **creed** (from the Latin *credo*, "I believe"). The resulting Nicene Creed balanced three separate divine entities—God "the father," "the son," and "the holy spirit"—as facets of one supreme being. Also at Nicaea the bishops agreed to hold Easter, the day on which Christians celebrate Christ's resurrection, on the same day in every church of the Christian world. Constantine's legacy to the Christian church was monumental. His conversion had happened in such a way that Christianity itself became the religion of the Roman Empire. Writing near the end of Constantine's reign, an elderly bishop in Palestine named Eusebius noted that the Roman Empire of his day would have surprised the martyrs of Carthage, who had willingly died rather than recognize any "empire of this world."

Christianity in the Cities and Beyond After 312 CE, the large churches built in every major city, many with imperial funding, signaled Christianity's growing strength. These gigantic meeting halls were called basilicas, from the Greek word *basileus*, meaning "king." They were modeled on Roman law-court buildings and could accommodate over a thousand worshippers. Inside a basilica's vast space, oil lamps shimmered on marble and brought mosaics to life. Rich silk hangings, swaying between rows of columns, increased the sense of mystery and directed the eye to the far end of the building—a splendidly furnished semicircular apse. Under the dome of the apse, which represented the dome of heaven, and surrounded by priests, the bishop sat and preached from his special throne, or *cathedra*. Worshippers had come into a different world. This was heaven on earth.

Basilica Interior The interior of a basilica was dominated by rows of ancient marble columns and was filled with light from upper windows, so that the eye was led directly to the apse of the church, where the bishop and clergy would sit under a dome, close to the altar.

These basilicas became the new urban public forums, ringed with spacious courtyards where the city's poor would gather. In return for the tax exemptions that Constantine had granted them, bishops cared for the metropolitan poor. Bishops also became judges, as Constantine turned their arbitration process for disputes between Christians into a kind of small claims court. Offering the poor shelter, quick justice, and moments of unearthly splendor in grand basilicas, Christian bishops perpetuated "Rome" for centuries after the empire had disappeared.

The spread of Christianity outside the cities and into the hinterlands of Africa and Southwest Asia required the breaking of language barriers. In Egypt, Christian clergy replaced hieroglyphs with Coptic, a more accessible script based on Greek letters, in an effort to bridge the linguistic and cultural gap between town and countryside. In the crucial corridor that joined Antioch to Mesopotamia, Syriac, an offshoot of the Semitic language Aramaic, became a major Christian language. As Christianity spread farther north, to Georgia in the Caucasus and to Armenia, Christian clergy created written languages that are still used in those regions.

THE "FALL" OF ROME IN THE WEST

By the third and fourth centuries CE, the political and economic fabric of the old Roman world was unraveling. (See Map 8.3.) The so-called barbarian invasions of the late fourth and fifth centuries CE further contributed to that demise. These "invasions" were not so much an assault as a violent and chaotic immigration of young fighting men from the frontiers of the empire. Today the term *barbarian* implies uncultivated or savage, but its meaning in antiquity was "foreigner" (with overtones of inferiority). Inhabitants of the empire's western provinces had become accustomed to non-Roman soldiers from across the frontiers, and for them *barbarian* was synonymous with "soldier." The popular image of bloodthirsty barbarian hordes streaming into the empire bears little resemblance to reality.

The Goths It was the Romans' need for soldiers that drew the barbarians in. The process reached a crisis point when tribes of Goths petitioned the emperor Valens (r. 364–378 CE) to let them immigrate into the empire. These Goths were no strangers to Roman influence: in fact, many had been evangelized into an anti-Nicene version of Christianity by the Gothic bishop Ulfilas, who had even translated the Bible into the Gothic language using an alphabet he developed for that purpose.

Desperate for manpower, Valens encouraged the Goths to enter Roman territory but mistreated these new immigrants. A lethal combination of famine and anger at the breakdown of supplies—not innate bloodlust—turned the Goths against Valens. When he marched against them at Adrianople in the hot August of 378 CE, Valens was not seeking to halt a barbarian invasion but rather intending to teach a lesson in obedience to his new recruits. The Gothic cavalry, however, proved too much for Valens's imperial army, and the Romans were trampled to death by the men and horses they had hoped to hire. As the pattern of disgruntled "barbarian" immigrants, civil war, and overextension continued, the Roman Empire in western Europe crumbled.

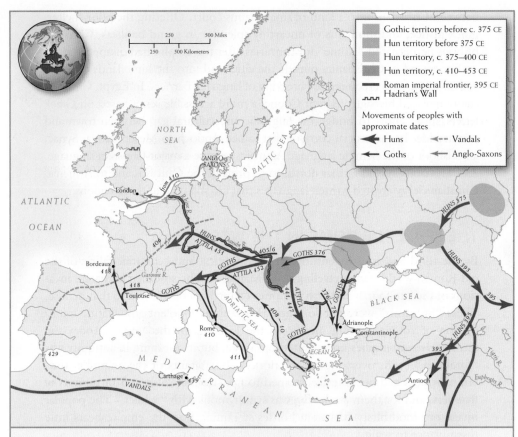

Map 8.3 Western Afro-Eurasia: War, Immigration, and Settlement in the Roman World, 375–450 CE

Invasions and migrations brought about the reconstitution of the Roman Empire at this time.

- Using the map, identify the people who migrated to or invaded the Roman Empire. Where were they from, and where did they go?
- How did these migrations and invasions reshape the political landscape of western Afro-Eurasia?
- Considering these effects, to what extent was the Roman depiction of these groups as "barbarians" a fair assessment?

Rome's maintenance of its northern borders required constant efforts and high taxes. But after 400 CE the western emperors could no longer raise enough taxes to maintain control of the provinces. In 418 CE, the Goths settled in southwest Gaul as a kind of local militia to fill the absence left by the contracting Roman authority. Ruled by their own king, who kept his military in order, the Goths suppressed alarmingly frequent peasant revolts. Roman landowners of Gaul and elsewhere anxiously allied themselves with the new military leaders rather than face social revolution and the raids of even more dangerous armies. Although they practiced a different, "heretical" version of Christianity, the Goths came as Christian allies of the aristocracy, not as godless enemies of Rome.

Hunnish Jewelry This 3½-inch wolf-dragon, in gold embellished with garnets, formed the end of a torque (heavy necklace). Resting on the point of the wearer's collarbone, this symbol blended Roman and Chinese motifs. It was found in the Stavropol territory of modern Russia, in the land between the Black and Caspian Seas.

The Huns Romans and non-Romans also drew together to face a common enemy: the Huns. Led by their king Attila (r. 434–453 CE) for twenty years, the Huns threatened both Romans and Germanic peoples (like the Goths). While the Romans could hide behind their walls, the Hunnish cavalry regularly plundered the scattered villages and open fields in the plains north of the Danube.

Attila intended to be a "real" emperor of a warrior aristocracy. Having adopted (perhaps from the Chinese empire) the notion of a "mandate of heaven"—in his case, a divine right to rule the tribes of the north—he fashioned the first opposing empire that Rome ever had to face in northern Europe. Rather than selling his people's services to Rome, Attila extracted thousands of pounds of gold coins in tribute from the Roman emperors who hoped to stave off assaults by his brutal forces. Drained both militarily and economically by this Hunnish threat, the Roman Empire in the west disintegrated only twenty years after Attila's death.

In the last analysis, barbarians did not destroy the empire. They were only the last straw. The "fall" of the empire in western Europe was the result of a long process of overextension. Rome could never be as strong along its frontiers as it was around the Mediterranean, because those frontiers were too far away. Despite the famous Roman roads, travel time between the Rhine border and Rome was more than thirty days. Lacking the vast network of canals that enabled Chinese emperors to move goods and soldiers by water, Roman power could survive in the north only at the cost of constant effort and high taxes. But after 400 CE, the western emperors could no longer raise enough taxes to maintain control of the northern provinces, and invaders simply moved into the vacuum. In 476 CE, the last Roman emperor of the west, a young boy named Romulus Augustulus (namesake of both Rome's legendary founder and its first emperor), resigned to make way for a so-called barbarian king in Italy.

The political unity of the Roman Empire in the west now gave way to a sense of unity through the church. The Catholic Church (*Catholic* meaning "universal," centered in the bishops' authority) became the one institution to which all Christians in western Europe, Romans and non-Romans alike, felt that they belonged. The bishop of Rome became the symbolic head of the western churches. Rome became a spiritual capital instead of an imperial one. By 700 CE, the great Roman landowning families of the Republic and early empire had vanished, replaced by religious leaders with vast moral authority.

CONTINUITY OF ROME IN THE EAST: BYZANTIUM

Elsewhere the Roman Empire was alive and well. From the borders of Greece to the borders of modern Iraq, and from the Danube River to Egypt and the borders of Saudi Arabia, the empire survived undamaged. The new Roman Empire of the east—to which historians gave the name **Byzantium**—had its own "New Rome," Constantinople. Founded in 324 CE by its namesake, Constantine, on the Bosporus straits separating Europe from Asia, this strategically located city was well situated to receive taxes in gold and to control the sea-lanes of the eastern Mediterranean.

Constantinople was one of the most spectacularly successful cities in Afro-Eurasia, soon boasting a population of over half a million and 4,000 new palaces. Every year, more than 20,000 tons of grain arrived from Egypt, unloaded on a dockside over a mile long. A gigantic hippodrome echoing Rome's Circus Maximus straddled the city's central ridge, flanking an imperial palace whose opulent enclosed spaces stretched down to the busy shore. As they had for centuries before in Rome, emperors would sit in the imperial box, witnessing chariot races as rival teams careened around the stadium. The hippodrome also featured displays of eastern imperial might, as ambassadors came from as far away as central Asia, northern India, and Nubia.

Hagia Sophia The domed ceiling of Justinian's Hagia Sophia in Constantinople soared high above worshippers. Intricate mosaics decorated many of the walls and ceilings. The mosaic adorning the southwestern entryway, shown here, depicts Jesus sitting in the lap of the Virgin Mary. On the right, Constantine presents to Jesus and Mary his new city of Constantinople; on the left, Justinian offers his Hagia Sophia.

Similarly, the future emperor Justinian came to Constantinople as a young man from an obscure Balkan village, to seek his fortune. When he became emperor in 527 CE, he considered himself the successor of a long line of forceful Roman emperors—and he was determined to outdo them. Most important, Justinian reformed Roman laws. Within six years a commission of lawyers had created the *Digest*, a massive condensation and organization of the preexisting body of Roman law. Its companion volume was the *Institutes*, a teacher's manual for schools of Roman law. These works were the foundation of what later ages came to know as "Roman law," followed in both eastern and western Europe for more than a millennium.

Reflecting the marriage of Christianity with empire was Hagia Sophia, a church grandly rebuilt by Justinian on the site of two earlier basilicas. The basilica of Saint Peter in Rome, the largest church built by Constantine two centuries earlier, would have reached only as high as the lower galleries of Hagia Sophia. Walls of multicolored marble, gigantic columns of green and purple granite, audaciously curved semicircular niches placed at every corner, and a spectacular dome lined with gleaming gold mosaics inspired awe in those who entered its doors. Hagia Sophia represented the flowing together of Christianity and imperial culture that for another 1,000 years would mark the Eastern Roman Empire centered in Constantinople.

Internal discord, as well as contacts between east and west, intensified during Justinian's reign. Justinian quelled riots at the heart of Byzantium, like the weeklong Nika riots in 532 CE in which thousands died when a group of senators used the unrest and high emotions of the chariot races as a cover for revolt. He also undertook wars to reclaim parts of the western Mediterranean and to hold off the threat from Sasanian Persia in the east (see next section). Perhaps the grisliest reminder of this increased connectivity was a sudden onslaught in 541–542 CE of the bubonic plague from the east. One-third of the population of Constantinople died within weeks. Justinian himself survived, but thereafter he ruled an empire whose heartland was decimated. Nonetheless, Justinian's contributions—to the law, to Christianity, to the maintenance of imperial order—helped Byzantium last almost a millennium after Rome in the west had fallen away.

The Silk Roads

Although exchange along the Silk Roads had been taking place for centuries (see Chapter 6), the sharing of knowledge between the Mediterranean world and China began in earnest during this period. Wending their way across the difficult terrains of central Asia, a steady parade of merchants, scholars, ambassadors, missionaries, and other travelers transmitted commodities, technologies, and ideas between the Mediterranean worlds and China, and across the Himalayas into northern India, exploiting the commercial routes of the Silk Roads. Ideas, including the beliefs of the universalizing religions described in this chapter, traveled along with goods on these exchange routes. Christianity spread through the Mediterranean and beyond, and as we shall see later in this chapter, Buddhism and the Vedic religion (Brahmanism) also continued to spread.

The great oasis cities of central Asia played a crucial role in the effective functioning of the Silk Roads. While the Sasanians controlled the city of Merv in the

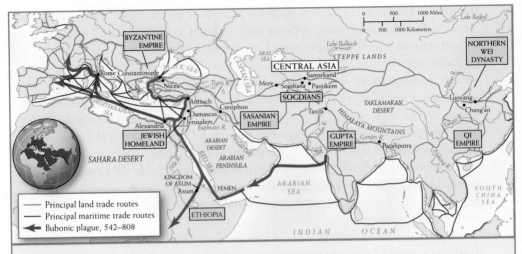

Map 8.4 Exchanges across Afro-Eurasia, 300–600 CE

Southwest Asia remained the crossroads of Afro-Eurasia in a variety of ways. Trade goods flowing between west and east passed through this region, as did universalizing religions.

- Trace the principal trade routes and maritime routes. Locate the cities of Merv, Samarkand, and Panjikent. How do the locations of these cities compare with the locations of some of the major cities of the west in the Mediterranean and the east in India and China?
- Based on your reading of the chapter and their location on the map, what role did the kingdom of Sogdiana and the Sasanian Empire play in trade in this era?
- What was the relationship between trade routes and the spread of the bubonic plague?

west, nomadic rulers became the overlords of Sogdiana and extracted tribute from the cities of Samarkand and Panjikent in the east. The tribal confederacies in this region maintained the links between west and east by patrolling the Silk Roads between Iran and China. They also joined north to south as they passed through the mountains of Afghanistan into the plains of northern India. As a result, central Asia between 300 and 600 CE was the hub of a vibrant system of religious and cultural contacts covering the whole of Afro-Eurasia. (See Map 8.4.)

SASANIAN PERSIA

Beginning at the Euphrates River and stretching for eighty days of slow travel across the modern territories of Iraq, Iran, Afghanistan, and much of central Asia, the Sasanian Empire of Persia (224–651 CE) encompassed all the land routes of western Asia that connected the Mediterranean world with East Asia. In the early third century CE, the Sasanians had replaced the Parthians as rulers of the Iranian plateau and Mesopotamia. The Sasanian ruler called himself the "King of Kings of Iranian and non-Iranian lands," a title suggestive of the

Sasanians' aspirations to universalism. The ancient irrigated fields of what is modern Iraq became the economic heart of this empire. Its capital, Ctesiphon, arose where the Tigris and the Euphrates rivers come close to each other, only 20 miles south of modern Baghdad.

Symbolizing the king's presence at Ctesiphon was the 110-foot-high vaulted Great Arch of Khusro, named after Justinian's rival, Khusro I Anoshirwan (Khusro of the Righteous Soul). As his name implied, Khusro Anoshirwan (r. 531–579 CE) exemplified the model ruler: strong and just. His image in the east as an ideal monarch was as glorious as that of Justinian in the west as an ideal Christian Roman emperor. For both Persians and Arab Muslims of later ages, the Arch of Khusro was as awe-inspiring as Justinian's Hagia Sophia was to Christians.

The Sasanian Empire controlled the trade crossroads of Afro-Eurasia and posed a military threat to Byzantium. Its Iranian armored cavalry was a fighting machine adapted from years of competition with the nomads of central Asia. These fearless horsemen fought covered from head to foot in flexible armor (small plates of iron sewn onto leather) and chain mail, riding "blood-sweating horses" draped in thickly padded cloth. Their lethal swords were light and flexible owing to steel-making techniques imported from northern India. With such cavalry, Khusro in 540 CE sacked Antioch, a city of great significance to early Christianity. The campaign was a warning, at the height of Justinian's glory, that Mesopotamia could reach out once again to conquer the eastern Mediterranean shoreline. Under Khusro II the confrontation between Persia and Rome escalated into the greatest war that had been seen for centuries. Between 604 and 628 CE, Persian forces under Khusro II conquered Egypt and Syria and even reached Constantinople before being defeated in northern Mesopotamia.

Politically united by Sasanian control, Southwest Asia also possessed a cultural unity. Syriac was the dominant language. While the Sasanians them-selves were devout Zoroastrians (see Chapter 4), Christianity and Judaism enjoyed tolerance in Mesopotamia. Nestorian Christians—so named by their opponents for their acceptance of a hotly contested understanding of Jesus's divine and human nature, promoted by a former bishop of Constantinople named Nestorius—exploited Sasanian trade and diplomacy to spread their faith as far as Chang'an in China and the western coast of southern India. Protected by the Sasanian King of Kings, the Jewish rabbis of Mesopotamia compiled the monumental Babylonian Talmud at a time when their western peers, in Roman Palestine, were feeling cramped under the Christian state. The Sasanian court also embraced offerings from northern India, including the *Panchatantra* stories (moral tales played out in a legendary kingdom of the animals), polo, and the game of chess. In this regard Khusro's was truly an empire of crossroads, where the cultures of central Asia and India met those of the eastern Mediterranean.

THE SOGDIANS AS LORDS OF THE SILK ROADS

The Sogdians, who controlled the oasis cities of Samarkand and Panjikent, served as human links between the two ends of Afro-Eurasia. Their religion was a blend of Zoroastrian and Mesopotamian beliefs, touched with Brahmanic influences. Their language was the common tongue of the early Silk Roads, and their shaggy camels bore the commodities that passed through their entrepôts (transshipment centers). Moreover, their mansions, such as those excavated at Panjikent, show strong influences from the warrior aristocracy culture of Iran. The palace walls display gripping frescoes of armored riders, reflecting the revolutionary change to cavalry warfare from Rome to China. The Sogdians were known as merchants as far away as China. Their commercial skills enabled them to become the richest country in central Asia, building large houses and decorating the walls of their homes with elaborate paintings.

Through the Sogdians, products from Southwest Asia and North Africa found their way to the eastern end of the landmass. Carefully packed for the long trek on jostling camel caravans, Persian and Roman goods rode side by side. Along with Sasanian silver coins and gold pieces minted in Constantinople, these exotic products found eager buyers as far east as China and Japan.

BUDDHISM ON THE SILK ROADS

South of the Hindu Kush Mountains, in northern India, nomadic groups made the roads into central Asia safe to travel, enabling Buddhism to spread northward and eastward via the mountainous corridor of Afghanistan into China. Buddhist monks were the primary missionary agents, the bearers of a universal message who traveled across the roads of central Asia, carrying holy books, offering salvation to commoners, and establishing themselves more securely in host communities than did armies, diplomats, or merchants.

At Bamiyan, a valley of the Hindu Kush—two gigantic statues of the Buddha, 121 and 180 feet in height, were carved from a cliffside during the fourth and fifth centuries CE (and stood there for 1,500 years until dynamited by the Taliban in 2001). Travelers found

Multicultural Celebration in Afrasiab This seventh-century CE wall painting was found in what archaeologists have described as an aristocratic house in Afrasiab (modern Samarkand, Uzbekistan), centrally located along the Silk Roads. The procession on the south wall (pictured here) depicts riders on elephants, horses, and camels. The full set of nearly life-size frescoes stretches almost 38 feet in length in what has been called the "Hall of Ambassadors" because it includes groups from China, central Asia, and Korea.

Bamiyan and Yungang Buddhas Compare the Buddhas at Bamiyan (*left*) and Yungang (*right*). Note the Gandharan dress and standing pose of the Bamiyan Buddha, whose majesty and ornamentation the pilgrim Xuanzang described in the mid-seventh century CE. The Buddha in Yungang, one of five created under the emperors of the Northern Wei, sits at the foothills of the Great Wall, marking the eastern destination of the central Asian Silk Roads.

welcoming cave monasteries here and at oases all along the way from the Taklamakan Desert to northern China, where—2,500 miles from Bamiyan—travelers also encountered five huge Buddhas carved from cliffs in Yungang, China. While those at Bamiyan stood tall with royal majesty, the Buddhas of Yungang sat in postures of meditation. In the cliff face and clustered around the feet of the Bamiyan Buddhas various elaborately carved cave chapels housed intricate paintings with Buddhist imagery. Surrounding the Yungang Buddhas, over fifty caves sheltered more than 50,000 statues representing Buddhist deities and patrons. The Yungang Buddhas, seated just inside the Great Wall, welcomed travelers to the market in China and marked the eastern end of the central Asian Silk Road system. (See Map 8.5.) The Bamiyan and Yungang Buddhas are a reminder that by the fourth century CE religious ideas were creating world empires of the mind, transcending kingdoms of this world and bringing a universal message contained in their holy scriptures.

Political and Religious Change in South Asia

South Asia, especially the area of modern India, enjoyed a surge of religious enthusiasm during the Gupta dynasty, the largest political entity in South Asia from the early fourth to the mid-sixth century CE. Its kings facilitated commercial and cultural exchange, much as the Roman Empire had done in the west. Chandragupta I (r. c. 320–335 CE, not to be confused with Chandragupta Maurya from Chapter 6), calling himself "King of Kings, Great King," together with his son,

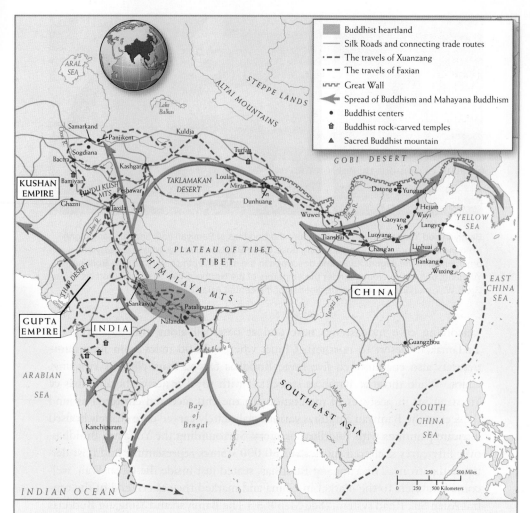

Map 8.5 Buddhist Landscapes, 300–600 CE

Buddhism spread from its heartland in northern India to central and East Asia at this time. Trade routes, along with the merchants and pilgrims who traveled along them, fostered that spread.

- Trace the trade routes and the routes showing the spread of Buddhism. According to the map, what role did increasingly extensive trade routes play in spreading Buddhism?

- Locate the Buddhist centers and rock-carved temples, especially at Bamiyan, Dunhuang, and Yungang. How might their location on trade routes have influenced the spread of this universalizing faith?

- Trace the travels of Faxian and Xuanzang. How are their routes similar and different, and what do they suggest about growing connections between East Asia and South Asia?

Gold Coin of Chandragupta II The Gupta dynasty, based in the Middle and Lower Ganges plains, was known for its promotion of indigenous Indian culture. Here, Chandragupta II, the most famous king of the dynasty, is shown riding a horse in the style of the invaders from the central Asian steppes.

expanded Gupta territory to the entire northern Indian plain and made a long expedition to southern India. The development of Hinduism out of the *varna*-bound Vedic Brahmanic religion and the continued spread of Buddhism helped unify a diverse region and the diverse peoples who lived there.

THE HINDU TRANSFORMATION

During this period, the ancient Brahmanic Vedic religion spread widely in South Asia. Because Buddhism and Jainism had many devotees in cities and commercial communities (see Chapter 5), conservative Brahmans turned their attention to rural India and brought their religion into accord with rural life and agrarian values. This refashioned Brahmanic religion emerged as the dominant faith in Indian society in the form of what we today call **Hinduism**.

In the religion's new, more accessible form, believers became vegetarians, abandoning the animal sacrifices that had been important to their earlier rituals. Their new rituals were linked to self-sacrifice—denying themselves meat rather than offering up slaughtered animals to the gods, as they had done previously. Three major deities—Brahma, Vishnu, and Shiva—formed a trinity representing the three phases of the universe—birth, existence, and destruction, respectively—and the three expressions of the eternal self, or *atma*. Vishnu was the most popular of the three and was thought by believers to reveal himself through various avatars (or incarnations).

Poets during the reign of Chandragupta II (r. c. 380–415 CE), grandson of Chandragupta I and a generous patron of the arts, expressed the religious sentiments of the age. Working with the motifs and episodes from two early epics, the *Mahabharata* and the *Ramayana* (see Chapter 4), these poets addressed new problems and praised new virtues. What had once been lyric dramas and narrative poems written to provide entertainment now served as collective memories of the past and underscored Brahmanic religious beliefs about ideal behavior. The heroes and deeds that the poets praised in classical Sanskrit served as models for kings and their subjects.

A central part of the *Mahabharata* revolves around the final battle between two warring confederations of Vedic tribes. The hero Arjuna, the best warrior of one of these confederations, is unwilling to fight against his enemies because many of them

Hindu Statue This huge statue of a three-headed god, located in a cave on a small island near Mumbai, represents the monotheistic theology of Hinduism. Brahma, the creator; Vishnu, the keeper; and Shiva, the destroyer, are all from one *atma*, the single soul of the universe.

are his cousins. At a crucial moment on the battlefield, Krishna—an avatar of Vishnu, who was Arjuna's charioteer and religious teacher—intervenes, commanding Arjuna to slay his foes, even those related to him. Krishna reminds Arjuna that he belongs to the Kshatriya *varna*, the warriors put on earth to govern and to fight against the community's enemies. The *Bhagavad Gita*, which preserves this tale of Krishna and Arjuna, became part of the authoritative literature of Hindu spirituality. It prescribed religious and ethical teachings and behaviors, called *dharma* in Hinduism, for people at every level of society.

Hindus also adopted the deities of other religions, even regarding the Buddha as an avatar of Vishnu. Thus, the Hindu world of gods became larger and more accessible than the earlier Vedic one, enabling more believers to share a single faith. Hindus did not wish to approach the gods only through the sacrificial rituals at which Brahmans alone could officiate. Individuals, therefore, also developed an active relationship with particular gods through personal devotion, in a practice called *bhakti*. This individualized, personal *bhakti* devotion attracted Hindus of all social strata, while the mythological literature wove the deities into a heavenly order presided over by the trinity of Brahma, Vishnu, and Shiva as universal gods. During this period Hindus lived side by side with Buddhists, competing for followers by building ornate temples and sculptures of gods and by holding elaborate rituals and festivals.

While the stories of human-divine interaction, the larger number of gods, and the development of *bhakti* devotion made Hinduism more personal than the old Vedic Brahmanism had been, Hinduism was still very much rooted in the hierarchical *varna* system. Although Hinduism was more accessible to a wider audience than Brahmanism had been, there were limits to how universalizing this tradition could be since the *varna* system, with which it was closely intertwined, did not extend outside South Asia.

THE TRANSFORMATION OF THE BUDDHA

During the Gupta period, the two main schools of Buddhism—the newer Mahayana (Greater Vehicle) school and the older Hinayana (Lesser Vehicle) school—acquired universalizing features that were different from what the Buddha had preached centuries earlier. The historical Buddha was a sage who was believed to enter *nirvana*, ending the pain of consciousness. In the earliest

Buddhist doctrine, god and supernatural powers were not a factor (see Chapter 5). But by 200 CE, a crucial transformation had occurred: the Buddha's followers started to view him as a god. Mahayana Buddhism not only recognized the Buddha as a god but extended worship to the many bodhisattvas who bridged the gulf between the Buddha's perfection and the world's sadly imperfect peoples (see Chapter 6). It was especially in the Mahayana school that Buddhism became a universalizing religion, whose adherents worshipped divinities, namely the Buddha and the bodhisattvas, rather than recognizing them merely as great men.

Some Buddhists fully accepted the Buddha as god but could not accept the divinity of bodhisattvas; these adherents belonged to the more monkish school of **Hinayana Buddhism**, later called Theraveda in Sri Lanka and Southeast Asia. Rejecting Sanskrit authoritative scripture on the supernatural power of bodhisattvas, they remained loyal to the early Buddhist texts, which were probably based on the words of the Buddha himself. Hinayana temples barred all colorful idols of the bodhisattvas and other heavenly beings; they contained images of only the Buddha. Buddhism, with its vibrant competing Mahayana and Hinayana schools, spread along the Silk Roads far beyond its South Asian point of origin.

CULTURE AND IDEOLOGY INSTEAD OF AN EMPIRE

Unlike China and Rome, India during the Gupta period did not have a centralized empire that could establish a code of laws and an overarching administration. Instead, what emerged to unify South Asia was a distinctive form of cultural synthesis—called by scholars the **Sanskrit cosmopolis**—based on Hindu spiritual beliefs and articulated in the Sanskrit language.

Spearheading this development from 300 to 1300 CE were priests and intellectuals well versed in the Sanskrit language and literary and religious texts. As Sanskrit spread, it stepped beyond religious scriptures and became the public language of politics, although local languages retained their prominence in day-to-day administration and everyday life. Kings and emperors used Sanskrit to express the ideals of royal power and responsibility. Rulers issued inscriptions in it, recording their genealogies and their prestigious acts. Poets celebrated ruling dynasties and recorded important moments in the language.

The emergence of Sanskrit as the common language of the elites in South and Southeast Asian societies also facilitated the spread of Brahmanism. Possessing an unparalleled knowledge of the language, Brahmans circulated their ideals on morality and society in Sanskrit texts, the most influential of which was the **Code of Manu**. This document records a discourse given by a sage, Manu, to a gathering of wise men seeking answers on how to organize their communities after the destruction wrought by a series of floods. The text lays out a set of laws designed to address the problems of assimilating strangers into expanding towns and refining the hierarchical Brahmanic order as the agricultural frontier expanded. Above all, the Code of Manu offered guidance for living within the *varna* and *jati* system, including whom to marry, which profession to follow,

***Varna* Hierarchies** The dazzlingly diverse population of India, as depicted in this palace scene from a Gupta dynasty fresco, from Cave 17 at Ajanta, depended on the ancient system of *varnas* and *jatis* to lend it law and order.

and even what to eat. The Code of Manu provided mechanisms for absorbing new groups into the system of *varnas* and *jatis*, thus propelling Hinduism into every aspect of life, far beyond the boundaries of imperial control.

During this period, settlers from northern India pushed southward into lands formerly outside the domain of the Brahmans. In these territories Brahmans encountered Buddhists and competed with them to win followers. The mixing of these two groups and the intertwining of their ideas and institutions ultimately created a common "Indic" culture organized around a shared vocabulary addressing concepts such as the nature of the universe and the cyclical pattern of life and death. Much of this mixing of ideas took place in schools, universities, and monasteries. The Buddhists already possessed large monasteries, such as Nalanda in northeast India, where 10,000 residential faculty and students assembled, and more than 100 smaller establishments in southeast India housing at least 10,000 monks. In these settings Buddhist teachers debated theology, cosmology, mathematics, logic, and botany. Brahmans also established schools where similar intellectual topics were discussed and where Buddhist and Brahmanic Hindu ideas were fused.

The resulting Indic cultural unity covered around 1 million square miles and a highly diverse population. Although India did not have a single governing entity like China and did not adhere to one religious system as in the Christian Roman Empire, it was developing a distinctive culture based on the intertwining of two shared, accessible, and—to varying degrees—universalizing religious traditions.

Political and Religious Change in East Asia

With the fall of the Han dynasty, China experienced a period of political disunity and a surge of new religious and cultural influences. In the first century CE, Han China was the largest state in the world, with as great a population as the Roman Empire had at its height. Its emperor extracted an annual income of millions of pounds of rice and bolts of cloth and conscripted millions of workers whose families paid tribute through their labor. Later Chinese regarded the end of the Han Empire as a disaster just as great as western Europeans regarded the end of the Roman Empire. In post-Han China, new influences arrived via the Silk Roads through contact with nomadic "barbarians" and the proselytizing of Buddhist monks, and new forms of Daoism responded to a changing society.

THE WEI DYNASTY IN NORTHERN CHINA

After the fall of the Han in 220 CE, several small kingdoms—at times as many as sixteen of them—competed for control. Civil wars raged for roughly three centuries, a time called the Six Dynasties period (220–589 CE), when no single state was able to conquer more than half of China's territory. The most successful regime was that of the Tuoba, a people originally from Inner Mongolia. In 386 CE, the Tuoba founded the Northern Wei dynasty, which lasted 150 years and administered part of the Han territory. Although technically Mongolian "barbarians," the Northern Wei had lived for generations within the Chinese orbit as tributary states.

The Northern Wei maintained many Chinese traditions of statecraft and court life: they taxed land and labor on the basis of a census, conferred official ranks and titles, practiced court rituals, preserved historical archives, and promoted classical learning and the use of classical Chinese for record keeping and political discourse. Though they were nomadic warriors, they adapted their large standing armies to city-based military technology, which required drafting huge numbers of workers to construct dikes, fortifications, canals, and walls.

Among the challenges facing the Northern Wei rulers was the need to consolidate authority over their own highly competitive nomadic people. One strategy was to make their own government more "Chinese." Under Emperor Xiaowen (r. 471–499 CE), for example, the Tuoba royal family adopted the Chinese family name of Yuan and required all court officials to speak Chinese and wear Chinese clothing. However, the Tuoba warrior families resisted these policies. Xiaowen also rebuilt the old Han imperial capital of Luoyang based on classical architectural models dating from the Han dynasty and made it the seat of his government.

Wei rulers sought stronger relationships with the Han Chinese families of Luoyang that had not fled south. The Wei offered them political power as officials in the Wei bureaucracy and more land. For example, the Dowager Empress Fang (regent for Xiaowen 476–490 CE) attempted progressive land

Emperor Xiaowen in Buddhist Procession Emperor Xiaowen's son dutifully commissioned this massive carving (nearly 7 feet by 12 feet) of his father with his retinue in the Longmen Caves in Luoyang. This relief showing Xiaowen (fourth figure from the right) in procession to honor the Buddha was accompanied by another that depicted the empress in procession. Displayed at the entrance to a magnificent Buddhist cave temple, the reliefs are a testament to the Northern Wei's adoption of Chinese aesthetics and their devotion to Buddhism in the early sixth century CE.

reforms that offered land to all young men—whether Han or Wei—who agreed to cultivate it. But even this plan failed to bridge the cultural divides between the "civilized" Han Chinese of Luoyang and the "barbarian" Tuoba Wei, because the latter showed no interest in farming.

Members of the Wei court supported Buddhist temples and monumental cave sites in an appeal to their Tuoba roots while also honoring Confucian traditions dating to the ancient Zhou period. But Emperor Xiaowen's bid for unification was unsuccessful; his death cut short his efforts. Several decades of intense fighting among military rulers in the north followed, ultimately leading to the downfall of the Northern Wei dynasty.

CHANGING DAOIST TRADITIONS

Daoism, a popular Chinese religion under the Han and a challenge to the Confucian state and its scholar-officials, lost its political edge and adapted to the new realities in this period of disunity. Two new traditions of Daoist thought flourished in this era of self-doubt. The first was organized and community oriented, and involved heavenly masters who as mortals guided local religious groups or parishes. Followers sought salvation through virtue, confession, and ceremonies, including a mystical initiation rite. A second Daoist tradition was more individualistic, attempting to reconcile Confucian classical learning with Daoist religious beliefs in the occult and magic. It used trance and meditation to control human physiology. Through such mental and physical efforts, a skilled practitioner could accumulate enough religious merit to prolong his life. The concept of religious merit and demerit in Daoist circles echoed the Buddhist notion of karmic retribution (the cosmic assessment of one's acts in this life that determines one's rebirth into a better or worse next life). For the Daoists, however, eternal life was the ultimate goal, and not the Buddhists' ideal of release from the cycle of life, death, and rebirth.

BUDDHISM IN CHINA

Buddhism's universalizing message appealed to many people living in the fragmented Chinese empire. By the third and fourth centuries CE, travelers from central Asia who had converted to Buddhism had become frequent visitors in the streets and temples of the competing capitals: Chang'an, Luoyang, and Nanjing. Spreading the faith required intermediaries, endowed with texts and explanations, to convey its message. Kumarajiva (344–413 CE), a renowned Buddhist scholar and missionary, was the right man, in the right place, at the right time to spread Buddhism in China—where it already coexisted with other faiths.

Kumarajiva's influence on Chinese Buddhist thought was critical. Not only did he translate previously unknown Buddhist texts into Chinese, but he also clarified Buddhist terms and philosophical concepts. He and his disciples established a Mahayana branch known as Madhyamika (Middle Way) Buddhism, which used irony and paradox to show that reason was limited. For example, they contended that all reality was transient because nothing remained unchanged over time. They sought enlightenment by means of transcendental visions and spurned experiences in the material world of sights and sounds.

Kumarajiva represented the beginning of a profound cultural shift. After 300 CE, Buddhism began to expand in northwestern China, taking advantage of imperial disintegration and the decline of Daoism and state-sponsored Confucian classical learning. The Buddhists stressed devotional acts, such as daily prayers and mantras, which included seated meditations in solitude requiring mind and breath control, as well as the saving power of the Buddha and the saintly bodhisattvas who postponed their own salvation for the sake of others. They even encouraged the Chinese

Xuanzang This painting portrays the Chinese pilgrim Xuanzang accompanied by a tiger on his epic travels in South Asia to collect important Buddhist scriptures.

to join a new class—the clergy. The idea that persons could be defined by faith rather than kinship was not new in Chinese society, but it had special appeal in a time of serious crisis like that of the turbulent Six Dynasties period. In the south, the immigrants from the north found that membership in the Buddhist clergy and monastic orders offered a way to restore their lost prestige.

Even more important, in the northern states—now part Chinese, part "barbarian"—Buddhism provided legitimacy. With Buddhists holding prominent positions in government, medicine, and astronomy, the Wei ruling houses could espouse a philosophy that was just as legitimate as that of the Han Chinese. As a Tuoba who ruled at the height of the Northern Wei in the early sixth century CE, Emperor Xuanwu was an avid Buddhist who made Mahayana Buddhism the state religion during his reign.

In 643 CE, the Chinese Buddhist Xuanzang brought back to Chang'an (then the world's largest city) an entire library of Buddhist scriptures—527 boxes of writings and 192 birch-bark tablets—that he had collected on a pilgrimage to Buddhist holy sites in South Asia. He lodged them in the Great Wild Goose Pagoda and immediately began to translate every line into Chinese. Although the importation of these texts from India was profoundly important, Buddhism did not seek to be the same in all places and at all times. On the contrary, as the expression of a cosmic truth as timeless and varied as the world itself, Buddhism showed a high level of adaptability, easily absorbing the gods and the wisdom of every country it touched.

By 400 CE, China had more than 1,700 Buddhist monasteries and about 80,000 monks and nuns. By contrast, in 600 CE (after two centuries of monastic growth), Gaul and Italy—the two richest regions of western Europe—had, altogether, only 320 monasteries, many with fewer than 30 monks. Yet, in the two ends of Afro-Eurasia, the principal bearers of the new religions were monks. Set apart from "worldly" affairs in their refuges, they enjoyed the pious support of royal courts and warriors whose lifestyles differed sharply from their own. Through their devoted faith in the divine and the support of secular rulers, these two universalizing religions—Buddhism and Christianity—would continue to grow, flourish, and revitalize themselves.

Faith and Cultures in the Worlds Apart

In most areas of sub-Saharan Africa and Mesoamerica, it was not easy for ideas, institutions, peoples, and commodities to circulate broadly. Thus, we do not see the development of universalizing faiths like those in Eurasia. Rather, belief systems and their associated deities remained local. Nonetheless, sub-Saharan Africans and peoples living in Mesoamerica revered prophetic figures who, they believed, communicated with deities and brought to humankind divinely prescribed rules of behavior. Peoples in both regions honored beliefs and rules that were passed down orally across generations. These unifying spiritual traditions guided behavior and established social customs.

BANTUS OF SUB-SAHARAN AFRICA

Today, most of Africa south of the equator is home to peoples who speak some variant of more than 400 Bantu languages. Although scholars using oral traditions and linguistic evidence can trace a clear narrative of the Bantu people no farther back than 1000 CE, it appears that the first Bantu speakers lived in the southeastern part of modern Nigeria, where about 4,000 or 5,000 years ago they likely shifted from hunting, gathering, and fishing to practicing settled agriculture. Preparing just 1 acre of tropical rain forest for farming required removing 600 tons of moist vegetation. To accomplish this arduous task, Bantus used mainly machetes, billhooks, and controlled burning. Bantus cultivated woodland plants such as yams and mushrooms, as well as palm oils and kernels. Yet the difficulties in preparing the land for settled agriculture did not keep the Bantus from being the most expansionist of African peoples. (See Map 8.6.)

Bantu Migrations Following riverbeds and elephant trails, Bantu migrants traveled out of West Africa in two great waves. One wave moved across the Congo forest region to East Africa. Their knowledge of iron smelting enabled them to deploy iron tools for agriculture. Because their new habitats supported a mixed economy of animal husbandry and sedentary agriculture, this group became relatively prosperous. A second wave of migrants moved southward through the rain forests in present-day Congo, eventually reaching the Kalahari Desert. The tsetse fly–infested environment did not permit them to rear livestock, so they were limited to subsistence farming. These Bantus learned to use iron later than those who had moved to the Congo region in the east.

Precisely when these **Bantu migrations** began is unclear, but once underway, the travelers moved rapidly. Genetic and linguistic evidence reveals that they absorbed most of the hunting and gathering populations who originally inhabited these areas. What enabled the Bantus to prevail and prosper was their skill as settled agriculturalists. They adapted their farming techniques and crops to widely different environments, including the tropical rain forests of the Congo River basin, the savanna lands of central Africa, the high grasslands around Lake Nyanza (formerly Lake Victoria), and the highlands of Kenya.

For the Bantu of the rain forests of central Africa (the western Bantu), the introduction of the banana plant from tropical South and Southeast Asia was decisive. Linguistic evidence suggests that it first arrived in the Upper Nile region and then traveled into the rest of Africa with small groups migrating from one favorable location to another; the earliest proof of its presence is a record from the East African coast dating to 525 CE. The banana adapted well to the equatorial rain forests, withstanding the heavy rainfalls, requiring less clearing of rain forests, reducing the presence of the malaria-carrying *Anopheles* mosquito, and providing more nutrients than the indigenous yam crop. Exploiting banana cultivation, the western Bantu filled the equatorial rain forests of central Africa between 500 and 1000 CE.

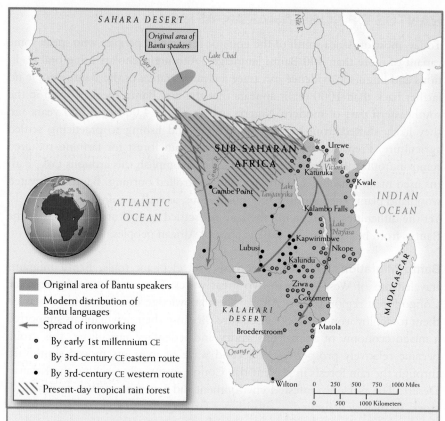

Map 8.6 Bantu Migrations in Africa

The migration of Bantu speakers throughout much of sub-Saharan Africa in the first millennium CE dramatically altered the cultural landscape.

- According to the map, where did the Bantu speakers originate? Into which areas did the Bantu speakers migrate? Why might they have migrated in that direction?
- Trace the spread of ironworking with the Bantu speakers. How might ironworking have enabled Bantu speakers to dominate the peoples already living in the regions to which they migrated?
- What range of topography and ecological zones did the Bantu speakers encounter as they moved southward and eastward? How might that have influenced their spread into new regions?

Bantu Cultures, East and West The widely different ecological zones into which the Bantu-speaking peoples spread made it difficult to establish the same political, social, and cultural institutions. In the Great Lakes area of the East African savanna lands and the savanna lands of central Africa, where communication was relatively easy, the eastern Bantu speakers developed centralized polities whose kings ruled by divine right. They moved into heavily forested areas similar to those they had left in southeastern Nigeria. These locations supported a way of life that remained fundamentally unaltered until European colonialism in the twentieth century.

The western Bantu-speaking communities of the lower Congo River rain forests formed small-scale societies based on family and clan connections. They organized themselves socially and politically into age groups, the most important of which were the ruling elders. Within these age-based networks, individuals who demonstrated talent in warfare, commerce, and politics provided leadership. Certain rights and duties were imposed on different social groups based mainly on their age. Males moved from child to warrior to ruling elder, and females transitioned from child to married child-bearer. Bonds among age groups were powerful, and movement from one to the next was marked by meaningful and well-remembered rituals. So-called big men, supported by followers attracted by their valor and wisdom as opposed to inheritance, promoted territorial expansion. Individuals who could attract a large community of followers, marry many women, and sire many children could lead their bands into new locations and establish dominant communities.

These rain forest communities held a common belief that the natural world was inhabited by spirits, many of whom were their own heroic ancestors. These spiritual beings intervened in mortals' lives and required constant appeasement. Diviners helped men and women understand the spirits' ways, and charms warded off the misfortune that aggrieved spirits might wish to inflict. Diviners and charms also protected against the injuries that living beings—witches and sorcerers—could inflict. In fact, much of the misfortune that occurred in the Bantu world was attributed to these malevolent forces. The Bantu migrations ultimately filled up more than half the African landmass. The Bantus spread a political and social order based on family and clan structures that rewarded individual achievement—and maintained an intense relationship to the world of nature that they believed was imbued with supernatural forces.

MESOAMERICANS

As in sub-Saharan Africa, the process of settlement and expansion in Mesoamerica differed from that in the large empires of Afro-Eurasia. Mesoamerica had no integrating artery of a giant river and its floodplain, and so it lacked the extensive resources that a state could harness for monumental ambitions. Nonetheless, some remarkable polities developed in the region, ranging from the city-state of Teotihuacán to the more widespread influence of the Maya. (See Map 8.7.)

Teotihuacán Around 300 BCE, people in the central plateau and the southeastern districts of Mesoamerica where the dispersed villages of Olmec culture had risen and fallen (see Chapter 5) began to gather in larger settlements. Soon, political and social integration led to city-states. Teotihuacán, in the heart of the fertile valley of central Mexico, became the largest center of the Americas before the Aztecs almost 1,500 years later.

Fertile land and ample water from the valley's marshes and lakes fostered high agricultural productivity despite the inhabitants' technologically rustic methods of cultivation. The local food supply sustained a metropolis of between 100,000 and 200,000 residents, living in more than 2,000 apartment compounds lining the city's streets. At one corner rose the massive pyramids of the sun and the moon— the focus of spiritual life for the city dwellers. Marking the city's center was the huge royal compound; the grandeur and refinement of its stepped stone temple, the Pyramid of the Feathered Serpent, were famous throughout Mesoamerica.

The feathered serpent was central to the spiritual lives of Teotihuacán's people. It was a symbol of fertility that governed reproduction and life. The feathered serpent's temple was the core of a much larger structure. From it radiated the awesome promenade known as the Street of the Dead, which culminated in the hulking Pyramid of the Moon, where foreign warriors and dignitaries were mutilated, sacrificed, and often buried alive to consecrate the holy structure.

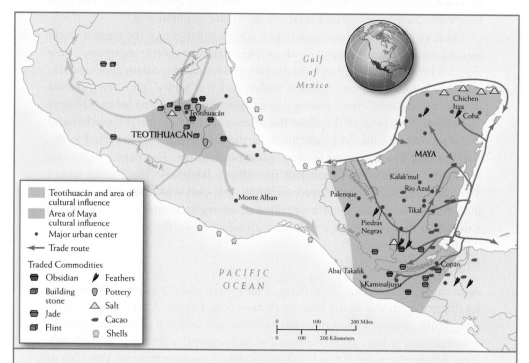

Map 8.7 Mesoamerican Worlds, 200–700 CE

At this time, two groups dominated Mesoamerica: one was located at the city of Teotihuacán, in the center, and the other, the Maya, was in the south.

- Locate the traded commodities on the map. What do you note about the distribution of these commodities?
- Where are the trade routes located? What might have fostered interaction between Teotihuacán and the Maya?

Teotihuacán The ruins of Teotihuacán convey the importance of monumental architecture to its culture. Looking down from the Pyramid of the Moon, in the foreground is the Plaza of the Moon leading to the Street of the Dead. The Pyramid of the Sun stands in the distance and beyond it, out of sight, are the remains of the Pyramid of the Feathered Serpent. These massive structures were meant to confirm the importance of spiritual affairs in urban life.

Teotihuacán was a powerful city-state that flexed its military muscle to overtake its rivals. By 300 CE, Teotihuacán controlled the entire basin of the Valley of Mexico. It dominated its neighbors and demanded gifts, tribute, and humans for ritual sacrifice. Its massive public architecture displayed art that commemorated decisive battles, defeated neighbors, and captured fighters.

While the city's political influence beyond the basin was limited, its cultural and economic diffusion were significant. Making use of porters, Teotihuacán's merchants traded their ceramics, ornaments of marine shells, and all sorts of decorative and valued objects (especially of green obsidian) far and wide. At the same time, Teotihuacán imported pottery, feathers, and other goods from distant lowlands.

This kind of expansion left much of the political and cultural independence of neighbors intact, with only the threat of force keeping them in check. In the fifth century CE, however, invaders burned Teotihuacán and smashed the carved figurines of the central temples and palaces, targeting Teotihuacán's institutional and spiritual core.

The Maya In the Caribbean region of Yucatán and its interior, the Maya people flourished from about 250 CE to their zenith in the eighth century. The Maya lived in an inhospitable region—hot, infertile, lacking navigable river systems, and vulnerable to hurricanes. Yet the Maya established hundreds, possibly thousands, of agrarian villages scattered across the diverse ecological zones of present-day southern Mexico to western El Salvador. Villages were linked by their shared Mayan language and through tribute payments, chiefly from lesser settlements to sacred towns. Until recently, scholars believed that at their peak the Maya may have numbered as many as 10 million. Today, as scholars reevaluate their assumptions based on new LIDAR (light detection and ranging) imaging, many conclude that population estimates may have been too low. LIDAR mapping tools are revealing Maya settlements that are much more elaborate than those that were previously excavated in the jungles of Guatemala, Belize, Honduras, and El Salvador; as a result, population estimates may need to increase many times over.

Maya Political and Social Structure The Maya established a variety of kingdoms around major ritual centers—such as Palenque, Copán, and Piedras Negras—and their hinterlands. Such hubs were politically independent but culturally and economically interconnected through commerce. Some larger settlements, such as Tikal and Kalak'mul, became sprawling centers with dependent provinces. In 2018, scientists using jungle-penetrating laser scanning determined that many of the Maya centers were much larger and more densely settled than had been previously thought and that they had defensive walls, had extensive irrigation systems, and were connected by roads.

Maya culture encompassed about a dozen kingdoms that shared many features. Ambitious rulers in these larger states frequently engaged in hostilities with one another. Highly stratified, with an elaborate class structure, each kingdom was topped by a shamanistic king who legitimated his position via his lineage, reaching back to a founding father and, ultimately, the gods. The vast pantheon of gods included patrons of each subregion, as well as a creator god and deities for rain, maize, war, and the sun. Gods were neither especially cruel nor benevolent; rather, they focused on the dance that sustained the axis connecting the underworld and the skies. What humans had to worry about was making sure that the gods got the attention and reverence they needed.

This was the job of Maya rulers. Kings sponsored elaborate public rituals to reinforce their divine heritages, including ornate processions down their cities' main boulevards to honor gods and their descendants, the rulers. Lords and their wives performed ritual blood sacrifice to feed their ancestors. A powerful priestly elite, scribes, legal experts, military advisers, and skilled artisans were vital to the hierarchy.

Most of the Maya people remained tied to the land, which could sustain a high population only through dispersed settlements. Poor soil quality and limited water supply prevented large-scale agriculture. Through terraces, the draining of fields, and slash-and-burn agriculture, the Maya managed a subsistence economy of diversified agrarian production. Villagers cultivated maize, beans, and squash, rotating them to prevent the depletion of soil nutrients. Farmers supplemented these staples with root crops such as sweet potato and cassava. Cotton—the basic fiber used for clothing—frequently grew amid rows of other crops as part of a diversified mix.

Maya Writing, Mathematics, and Architecture A common set of beliefs, codes, and values connected the dispersed Maya villages. Sharing a similar language, the Maya developed writing and an important class of scribes, who were vital to the society's integration. Rulers rewarded scribes for writing grand epics about dynasties and their founders, major battles, marriages, deaths, and

Palenque Deep in the Lacandon jungle lies the ruin of the Maya city of Palenque. Its pyramid, on the left, overlooks the site; on the right, the Tower of the Palace shadows a magnificent courtyard where religious figures and nobles gathered. There is no mistaking how a city like Palenque could command its hinterland with religious authority.

sacrifices. Such writings offered to Maya shared common histories, beliefs, and gods—always associated with the narratives of ruling families.

The best-known surviving Maya text is the *Popol Vuh*, a "Book of Community." It narrates one community's creation myth, extolling its founders (twin heroes) and the experiences—wars, natural disasters, human ingenuity—that enabled a royal line to rule the Quiché kingdom. The text begins with the gods' creation of the earth and ends with the rituals the kingdom's tribes must follow to avoid a descent into social and political anarchy, which had occurred several times throughout their history.

The Maya also had skilled mathematicians, who devised a calendar and studied astronomy. They accurately charted regular celestial movements and marked the passage of time by precise lunar and solar cycles. The Maya kept sacred calendars, by which they rigorously observed their rituals at the proper times. Each change in the cycle had particular rituals, dances, performances, and offerings to honor the gods with life's sustenance.

Cities reflected a ruler's ability to summon his subjects to contribute to the kingdom's greatness. Plazas, ball courts, terraces, and palaces sprawled out from neighborhoods. Activity revolved around grand royal palaces and massive ball courts, where competing teams treated enthusiastic audiences to contests that were more religious ritual than game. The Maya also excelled at building monumental structures. In Tikal, for instance, surviving buildings include six massive, steep funerary pyramids featuring elaborately carved and painted masonry walls, vaulted ceilings, and royal burial chambers; the tallest temple soars more than 220 feet high (40 feet higher than Justinian's Hagia Sophia).

Maya Bloodletting and Warfare

Maya elites were obsessed with spilling blood as a way to honor rulers and ancestors as well as gods. This gory rite led to frequent warfare, especially among rival dynasties, the goal of which was to capture victims for these rituals. Rulers would also shed their own blood at intervals set by the calendar. Royal wives drew blood from their tongues and men had their penises perforated. Such bloodletting by means of elaborately adorned and sanctified instruments was reserved for those of noble descent. Carvings and paintings portray blood cascading from rulers' mutilated bodies.

Wood Tablet This detail of a wood-carved tablet from a temple in the city of Tikal (c. 741 CE) is a fine example of the ornate form of scribal activity, which combined images and portraits with glyphs that tell a narrative.

Internal warfare eventually doomed the Maya, especially after devastating confrontations between Tikal and Kalak'mul during the fourth through seventh centuries CE. With each outbreak, rulers drafted larger armies and sacrificed greater numbers of captives. Crops perished. People fled. After centuries of misery, it must have seemed as if the gods themselves were abandoning the Maya people. The cycle of violence destroyed the cultural underpinnings of elite rule that had held the Maya world together. There was no single catastrophic event, no great defeat by a rival power. The Maya people simply abandoned their spiritual centers, and cities became ghost towns. As populations declined, jungles overtook temples. Eventually, the hallmark of Maya unity—the ability to read a shared script—vanished. While vibrant religious traditions thrived in sub-Saharan Africa and in Mesoamerica, they served more to reinforce the political and social situations from which they came rather than to spread a universalizing message far beyond their original context.

Conclusion

The breakdown of two imperial systems—Rome around the Mediterranean, and Han China in East Asia—introduced an era in which religion and shared culture rather than military conquest and political institutions linked large areas of Afro-Eurasia.

The Roman Empire gave way to a new religious unity, first represented by Christian dissenters and then co-opted by the emperor Constantine. In western

Europe, the sense of unity unlimited by imperial frontiers gave rise to a universal, or "Catholic," church—the "true" Christian religion that believers felt all peoples should share. In the eastern Mediterranean, where the Roman Empire survived, Christianity and empire coalesced to reinforce one another. Christians here held that beliefs about God and Jesus found their most correct expression within the Eastern Roman Empire and in its capital, Constantinople.

Similarly, in East Asia, the weakening of the Han dynasty enabled Buddhism to dominate Chinese culture. Without a unified state in China, Confucian officials lost their influence, while Buddhist priests and monks enjoyed patronage from regional rulers, local warriors, and commoners. In India, Brahman elites exploited population movements beyond the reach of traditional rulers as they established ritual forms for daily life on every level of society, while melding aspects of their own Vedic faith with those of Buddhism to create a new Hindu synthesis.

Not all regions felt the spread of universalizing religions, however. In most of sub-Saharan Africa, belief systems were much more localized. Similarly, in Mesoamerica, where long-distance transportation was harder and political authority more diffuse, religion was a unifying force but nothing like the widespread universalizing religions of Afro-Eurasia. Nevertheless, spiritual life was no less profound. Here, a strong sense of a shared worldview, a shared sense of purpose, and a shared sense of faith enabled common cultures to develop. Indeed, the Bantus and the Maya became large-scale common cultures—but ruled at the local level.

Thus, the period 300–600 CE saw the emergence of three great cultural units in Afro-Eurasia, each defined in religious terms: Christianity in the Mediterranean and parts of Southwest Asia, Hinduism in South Asia, and Buddhism in East Asia. They illustrate the ways in which peoples were converging under larger religious tents, while also becoming more distinct. Universalizing religions, whether Christian or Buddhist, and codes of behavior, such as the Brahmanic Code of Manu, gave people a new way to define themselves and their loyalties.

Maya Court Procession Brilliantly painted scenes from the late eighth-century CE Temple of the Murals in Bonampak, Mexico, include images of tribute processions, brutal conflicts, and bloody rituals associated with the installation of a ruler. In Room 1, pictured here, the upper panel shows Maya dignitaries, while the lower panel features singers and musicians playing rattles and drums.

 **Focus On**

The Rise of Christianity, the Spread of Buddhism, and the Beginnings of Common Cultures

Europe and Southwest Asia

- Christianity moves from a minority, persecuted faith to a state religion in the Roman Empire.

- The Sasanian state in Iran provides fertile ground for a tolerant mixture of Zoroastrianism, Nestorian Christianity, Judaism, Buddhism, and Brahmanic religion.

South Asia and East Asia

- Brahmanism, or Hinduism, becomes the dominant religion among the Vedic peoples of South Asia.

- Buddhism spreads out of South Asia along the Silk Roads through central Asia and into East Asia (now fractured politically, but with the Buddhist-leaning Northern Wei having a dominant influence).

Sub-Saharan Africa and Mesoamerica

- Large parts of sub-Saharan Africa are influenced by the spread of Bantu-speaking, ironworking migrants who adapt to a range of ecological zones.

- In Mesoamerica, urban kingdoms thrive in Teotihuacán (central Mexico) and among the Maya (of Yucatán).

Key Terms

Bantu migrations p. 307	creed p. 288	martyr p. 283	universalizing religions p. 281
Byzantium p. 292	Hinayana Buddhism p. 301	Sanskrit cosmopolis p. 301	
Code of Manu p. 301	Hinduism p. 299		

CHRONOLOGY

	1 CE	100 CE	200 CE	300 CE	400 CE
The Mediterranean and Southwest Asia			Emperor Constantine legalizes Christianity in Roman Empire 313 CE		
Central Asia					
South Asia			Transformation of Brahmanism into Hinduism begins first or second century C		
East Asia		Six Dynasties period 220–589 CE			
Sub-Saharan Africa					
Mesoamerica					

- **Thinking about Crossing Borders and Universalizing Religions** Why did borders seem to infuse vitality into Christianity and Buddhism in the fourth through sixth centuries CE? Which religions in this period did not seem to cross borders and why? What effect did this have on those religions?

- **Thinking about Changing Power Relationships and Universalizing Religions** Universalizing religions, like Christianity and Buddhism, were successful in part because of their diverse personalized appeal to men and women, rich and poor, and the upper and lower classes. How might this diverse appeal enable a universalizing religion like Christianity to undermine and alter traditional power relationships? In what ways did Buddhism do the same?

- **Thinking about Worlds Together, Worlds Apart and Universalizing Religions** Why did universalizing religions like Christianity and Buddhism develop in some parts of the world but not in others in the period 300 to 600 CE? How did these universalizing religions allow for continuity in Eurasia, even as empires fell away? In the "worlds apart," how might the lack of universalizing religion have influenced continuity, as political entities rose and fell over time?

 Go to **INQUIZITIVE** to see what you've learned—and learn what you've missed—with personalized feedback along the way.

500 CE	600 CE	700 CE	800 CE	900 CE	1000 CE

Sasanian Empire flourishes in Iran and Mesopotamia third–sixth centuries CE

"Barbarian" invasions of Roman Empire fourth–fifth centuries CE

Byzantine Empire flourishes in eastern Mediterranean fifth–seventh centuries CE

Byzantine and Sasanian wars sixth–seventh centuries CE

Buddhism spreads through central Asia fourth–sixth centuries CE

Sogdian merchant communities dominate Silk Road trade through central Asia fourth–sixth centuries CE

Gupta Empire 320–550 CE

Buddhism gains in popularity fourth–sixth centuries CE

Bantu migrations from western Africa to south, central, and east 1 CE–1000 CE

Maya culture dominates Yucatán Peninsula and surrounding area third–ninth centuries CE

City of Teotihuacán dominates Valley of Mexico fourth–fifth centuries CE

9

New Empires and Common Cultures

600–1000 CE

Core Objectives

- **DESCRIBE** and **EXPLAIN** the spread of Islam, Buddhism, and Christianity from 600 to 1000 CE.

- **COMPARE** the organizational structures of the Abbasids, Tang China, and Christendom.

- **COMPARE** the internal divisions within the Islamic, Tang, and Christian worlds.

- **EVALUATE** the relationships between religion, empire, and commercial exchange across Afro-Eurasia during this period.

In 754 CE al-Mansur, ruler of the new Muslim Abbasid dynasty, decided to relocate his capital city from Damascus (the capital of Islam's first dynasty) closer to the Abbasids' home region on the Iranian plateau. Islam was barely a century old, yet it flourished under this second dynasty. The caliph al-Mansur chose, for both practical and symbolic reasons, to build his capital near an unimposing village called Baghdad. Not only did the site lie between Mesopotamia's two great rivers, at the juncture of the canals that linked them, but it was also close to the ancient capital of the earlier Sasanian Empire and the site of ancient Sumerian and Babylonian power. By building at Baghdad, al-Mansur could reaffirm Mesopotamia's centrality in the world and promote the universalizing ambitions of Islam.

Al-Mansur's choice had enduring effects. Baghdad became a vital crossroads for commerce. Overnight, the city exploded into a bustling world entrepôt.

Chinese goods arrived by land and sea; commodities from Inner Eurasia flowed in over the Silk Roads; and cargo-laden camel caravans wound across Baghdad's western desert, linking the capital with Syria, Egypt, North Africa, and southern Spain. The unity that the Abbasids imposed from Baghdad intensified the movement of peoples, ideas, innovations, and commodities.

While Islam was gaining ground in central Afro-Eurasia, Chinese might was surging in East Asia under the Tang dynasty. Yet Islam and Tang China were clearly different worlds. The Islamic state had a universalizing religious mission: to bring humankind under the authority of the religion espoused by the Prophet Muhammad. In contrast, the Tang state had no such grandiose religious goals; the ruling elites supported religious variety within China, and they did not use Buddhism to expand their control into areas outside China. Instead, the Tang rulers expected that their neighbors would copy Chinese institutions and pay tribute as symbols of respect to the greatness of the Tang Empire. Though not as expansive as Islam and the Tang Empire, Christianity also strived in this period to extend its domain and add to its converts. With Islam's warriors, traders, and scholars crossing into Europe, Chinese influences taking deeper root in East Asia, and Christendom extending itself across Europe, religion and empire once again intertwined to serve as the social foundation across much of Afro-Eurasia.

Global Storyline

Religion and Empires: Islam, the Tang Dynasty, Christendom, and Common Cultures

- The universalizing religion of Islam, based on the message of the Prophet Muhammad, originates on the Arabian Peninsula and spreads rapidly across Afro-Eurasia.

- The expanding Tang dynasty in East Asia consolidates its bureaucracy, struggles with religious pluralism, and extends its influence into central and East Asia.

- Christianity splits over religious and political differences, leading to a divide between Roman Catholicism in the west and Greek Orthodoxy in the east.

The Origins and Spread of Islam

Islam began on the Arabian Peninsula. Despite its remoteness and sparse population, by the sixth century CE Arabia was brushing up against exciting outside currents: long-distance trade, religious debate, and imperial politics. The Hijaz—the western region of Arabia bordering the Red Sea—knew the outside world through trading routes reaching up the coast to the Mediterranean. Mecca, located in the Hijaz, was an unimposing village of simple mud huts. Mecca's inhabitants included both merchants and the caretakers of a revered sanctuary called the Kaaba, a dwelling place of deities. In this remote region, one of the world's major prophets emerged, and the universalizing faith he founded soon spread from Arabia through the trade routes stretching across Southwest Asia and North Africa.

A VISION, A TEXT, A NEW COMMUNITY

Born in Mecca around 570 CE into a well-respected tribal family, Muhammad enjoyed only limited financial success as a trader. Then came a revelation that would convert this merchant into a proselytizer of a new faith. In 610 CE, while the forty-year-old Muhammad was on a month-long spiritual retreat in a cave near Mecca, he believed that God came to him in a vision and commanded him to recite a series of revelations.

The early revelations were short and powerful, emphasizing a single, all-powerful God (Allah) and providing instructions for Muhammad's fellow Meccans to carry this message to nonbelievers. Muhammad's early preaching had a clear message. He urged his small band of followers to act righteously, to set aside false deities, to submit themselves to the one and only true God, and to care for the less fortunate—for the Day of Judgment was imminent. Muhammad's most insistent message was the oneness of God, a belief that has remained central to the Islamic faith ever since.

These teachings, compiled into an authoritative version after the Prophet's death, constituted the foundational text of Islam: the Quran. Accepted as the word of God, the Quran's verses were understood to have flowed flawlessly through God's perfect instrument, the Prophet Muhammad. Muhammad believed that he was a prophet in the tradition of Moses, other Hebrew prophets, and Jesus and that he communicated with the same God that they did. The Quran and Muhammad proclaimed the tenets of a new faith intended to unite a people and to expand the faith's spiritual frontiers. Islam's message already had universalizing elements, though how far it was to be extended, whether to the tribesmen living in the Arabian Peninsula or well beyond, was not at all clear at first.

In 622 CE, Muhammad and a small group of followers, opposed by Mecca's leaders because of their radical religious beliefs and their challenge to the ruling

Mecca At the great mosque at Mecca, which many consider the most sacred site in Islam, hundreds of thousands of worshippers gather for Friday prayers. Many are performing their religious duty to go on a pilgrimage to the holy places in the Arabian Peninsula.

elite's authority, escaped to Yathrib (later named Medina). The perilous 200-mile journey, known as *the hijra* ("breaking off of relations" or "departure"), yielded a new form of communal unity: the *umma* ("band of the faithful"). So significant was this moment that Muslims date the beginning of the Muslim era from this year.

Medina became the birthplace of a new faith called Islam ("submission"—in this case, to the will of God) and a new community called Muslims ("those who submit"). The city of Medina had been facing tribal and religious tensions, and by inviting Muhammad and his followers to take up residence there, its elders hoped that his leadership and charisma would bring peace and unity to their city. Early in his stay Muhammad drew on the pragmatic business mindset he no doubt had acquired from years of working as a merchant to put forth the Constitution of Medina. This document laid down rules intended to promote harmony among the different groups in the city (including its Muslim and Jewish inhabitants), in part by requiring the community's people to refer all unresolvable disputes to God and Muhammad. Now the residents were expected to replace traditional family, clan, tribal, and religious affiliations with loyalty to Muhammad as the one and true Prophet of God.

Over time, the core practices and beliefs of every Muslim would crystallize as the **five pillars of Islam**. Muslims were expected to (1) *proclaim* the phrase "there is no God but God and Muhammad is His Prophet"; (2) *pray* five times daily facing Mecca; (3) *fast* from sunup until sundown during the month of Ramadan; (4) *travel on a pilgrimage* (or *hajj*) to Mecca at least once in a lifetime if their personal resources permitted; and (5) *pay alms* in the form of taxation that would alleviate the hardships of the poor. These clear-cut expectations gave the imperial system that soon developed a doctrinal and legal structure and a broad appeal to diverse populations.

MUHAMMAD'S SUCCESSORS AND THE EXPANDING *DAR AL-ISLAM*

In 632 CE, in his early sixties, the Prophet passed away; but Islam remained vibrant thanks to the energy of its early followers—especially Muhammad's first four successors, the "rightly guided caliphs" (the Arabic word *khalīfa* means "successor"). These caliphs ruled over Muslim peoples and the expanding state. They institutionalized the new faith. They set the new religion on the pathway to imperial greatness by linking religious uprightness with territorial expansion, empire building, and an appeal to all peoples.

Driven by religious fervor and a desire to acquire the wealth of conquered territories, Muslim soldiers embarked on military conquests and sought to found a far-reaching territorial empire. This expansion of the Islamic state was one aspect of the struggle that they called *jihad*, between the *dar al-Islam* ("the world of Islam") and the *dar al-harb* ("the world of warfare"). Within fifteen years, their skill in desert warfare and their inspired military leadership enabled Muslim soldiers to expand the *dar al-Islam* into Syria, Egypt, and Iraq—centerpieces of the former Byzantine and Sasanian Empires. The Byzantines saved the core of their empire by pulling back to the highlands of Anatolia, where they could defend their frontiers. In contrast, the Sasanians hurled their remaining military resources against the Muslim armies, only to be annihilated.

A political vacuum opened in the new and growing Islamic empire with the assassination of Ali, the last of the "rightly guided caliphs." Ali was arguably the first male convert to Islam and had proved a fierce leader in the early battles for expansion. The Umayyads, a branch of one of the Meccan clans, laid claim to Ali's legacy. Having been governors of the province of Syria under Ali, the Umayyads relocated the capital to the Syrian city of Damascus and introduced a hereditary monarchy, the Umayyad caliphate, in 661 CE to resolve leadership disputes. Although tolerant of conquered populations, Umayyad dynasts did not permit non-Arabic-speaking converts to hold high political offices, an exclusive policy that contributed to their ultimate demise.

DIFFICULTIES IN DOCUMENTATION

Little can be gleaned about Muhammad himself and the evolution of Islam from Arabic-Muslim sources known to have been written in the seventh century CE. Non-Muslim sources, especially Christian and Jewish texts, which are often unsympathetic to Muhammad and early Islam, are more abundant and contain useful data on the Prophet and the early messages of Islam. These non-Muslim sources raise questions about Muhammad's birthplace, his relationship to the most powerful of the clans during his stay in Mecca, and even the date of his death. Many of these sources, as well as the Quran itself, stress the end-times content of Muhammad's preachings and the actions of his followers. The conclusion that scholars derive from these sources is that it was only during the eighth century CE, in the middle of the Umayyad period, that Islam lost its end-of-the-world emphasis and settled into a long-term religious and political system.

The only Muslim source that we have on Muhammad and early Islam is the Quran itself, which, according to Muslim tradition, was compiled during the caliphate of Uthman (r. 644–656 CE). Recent scholarship has questioned this claim, suggesting a later date, sometime in the early eighth century CE, for the standardization of the Quran. Some scholars even contend that the text by then had additions to, and redactions of, Muhammad's message. The Quran, in fact, is quiet on some of the most important events of Muhammad's life. It mentions the name of Muhammad only four times. For more information, scholars have depended on biographies of Muhammad, one of the first of which was compiled by Ibn Ishaq (704–767 CE); this work is not available to present scholars, but it was used by later Muslim authorities, notably Ibn Hisham (d. 833 CE), who wrote *The Life of Muhammad*, and Islam's most illustrious historian, Muhammad Ibn al-Jarir al-Tabari (838–923 CE). Although the works of these later writers come from the ninth and tenth centuries CE, Muslim tradition ever since has held these sources to be reliable on Muhammad's life and the evolution of Islam after the death of the Prophet.

THE ABBASID REVOLUTION

As the Umayyads spread Islam beyond Arabia, some peoples resisted what they experienced as Arab Umayyad religious impurity and repression. In particular, these peoples believed that the continuing discrimination against them despite their conversion to Islam was humiliating and unfair. The Arab Umayyad conquerors enslaved large numbers of non-Arabs. These enslaved people could leave their servile status only through manumission. Even so, the non-Arab freed peoples who converted found that they, too, were still regarded as lesser persons, although they lived in Arab households and had become Muslims. This situation existed even though the Arabs totaled about 250,000 to 300,000 during the Umayyad era, while non-Arab populations were 100 times as populous, totaling between 25 and 30 million. The area where protest against Arab domination reached a crescendo was in the east, notably in Khurasan, which included portions of modern-day Turkmenistan, Uzbekistan, Tajikistan, and Afghanistan. In Khurasan, most of the Arab conquerors did not live separately from the local populations but instead lived in close contact with them and intermarried local, ethnically different women. Ultimately, a new coalition emerged under the Abbasi family, which claimed descent from the Prophet.

Disgruntled provincial authorities and their military allies, as well as non-Arab converts, joined the movement.

After amassing a sizable military force, the Abbasid coalition trounced the Umayyad ruler in 750 CE and began its caliphate, which would last 500 years. The center of the Muslim state then shifted to Baghdad in Iraq (as we saw at the start of this chapter), signifying the eastward sprawl of the faith and its empire. This shift represented a success for non-Arab groups within Islam without eliminating Arab influence at the dynasty's center—the capital, Baghdad, in Arabic-speaking Iraq.

Islam's appeal to converts during the Abbasid period was diverse. Some turned to it for practical reasons, seeking reduced taxes or enhanced power. Others, particularly those living in ethnically and religiously diverse regions, welcomed the message of a single all-powerful God and a single community united by a clear code of laws. Islam, drawing its original impetus from the teachings and actions of a prophetic figure, followed the trajectory of Christianity and Buddhism and became a faith with a universalizing message and appeal. It owed much of its success to its ability to merge the contributions of vastly different geographic, economic, and intellectual territories into a rich yet unified culture. (See Map 9.1.)

The Caliphate An early challenge for the Abbasid rulers was to determine how traditional, or "Arab," they could be and still rule so vast an empire. They chose to keep the bedrock political institution of the early Islamic state—the **caliphate** (the line of political rulers reaching back to Muhammad). Although the caliphs exercised political authority over the Muslim community, they were not understood to have inherited Muhammad's prophetic powers or any authority in religious doctrine. That power was reserved for religious scholars, called *ulama*.

Abbasid rule borrowed practices from successful predecessors in its mixture of Persian absolute authority and the royal seclusion of the Byzantine emperors who lived in palaces far removed from their subjects. This blend of absolute authority and decentralized power involved a delicate and ultimately unsustainable balancing act. As the empire expanded, it became increasingly decentralized politically, enabling wily regional governors and competing caliphates in Spain and Egypt to grab power. Even as Islam's political center diffused, though, its spiritual center remained fixed in Mecca, where many of the faithful gathered to fulfill their pilgrimage obligation.

The Army The Abbasids, like all rulers, relied on force to integrate their empire. Yet they struggled with what the nature of that military force should be: a citizen-conscript, all-Arab force or a professional, even non-Arab, army. In the early stages, leaders conscripted military forces from local Arab populations, creating citizen armies. Ultimately, however, the Abbasids recruited professional soldiers from Turkish-speaking communities in central Asia and from the non-Arab, Berber-speaking peoples of North and West Africa. Their reliance on foreign—that is, non-Arab—military personnel represented a major shift in the Islamic world. Not only did the change infuse the empire with dynamic new populations, but soon these groups gained political authority. Having begun as an Arab state and then incorporated strong Persian influence, the Islamic empire now embraced Turkish elements from the pastoral belts of central Asia.

Islamic Law (the *Sharia*) and Theology Islamic law, or the ***sharia***, began to take shape in the Abbasid period. The work of generations of religious scholars, the *sharia* covers all aspects of practical and spiritual life, providing legal principles for marriage contracts, trade regulations, and religious prescriptions such as prayer, pilgrimage rites, and ritual fasting. The most influential early scholar of the *sharia* was an eighth-century CE Palestinian-born Arab, al-Shafi'i, who insisted that Muhammad's laws as laid out in the Quran, in addition to his sayings and actions as written in later reports (*hadith*), provided all the legal guidance that Islamic judges needed. This shift gave *ulama* (Muslim scholars) a central place in Islam since only their spiritual authority, and not the political authority of the caliphs, was qualified to define religious law. The *ulama*'s ascendance opened a sharp division within Islam: between the secular realm of the caliphs and the religious sphere of religious judges, experts on Islamic law, teachers, and holy men.

Gender in Early Islam Pre-Islamic Arabia was one of the last regions in Southwest Asia where patriarchy had not triumphed. Instead, men still married into women's families and moved to those families' locations, as was common in tribal communities. Some women engaged in a variety of occupations and, if they became wealthy, even married more than one husband. But contact with the rest of Southwest Asia, where men's power over women prevailed, was already altering women's status in the Arabian Peninsula before the birth of Muhammad.

Muhammad's relations with women reflected these changes. As a young man, he married a woman fifteen years his senior—Khadija, an independent trader—and took no other wives before she died. It was Khadija to whom he went in fear following his first revelations. She wrapped him in a blanket and assured him of his sanity. She was also his first convert. Later in life, however, he took younger wives, some of whom were widows of his companions, and insisted on their veiling (partly as a sign of their modesty and privacy). He married his favorite wife, Aisha, when she was only nine or ten years old. As a major source for collecting Muhammad's sayings, Aisha became an important figure in early Islam.

By the time Islam reached Southwest Asia and North Africa, where strict gender rules and women's subordinate status were entrenched, the new faith was adopting a patriarchal outlook. Muslim men could divorce freely; women

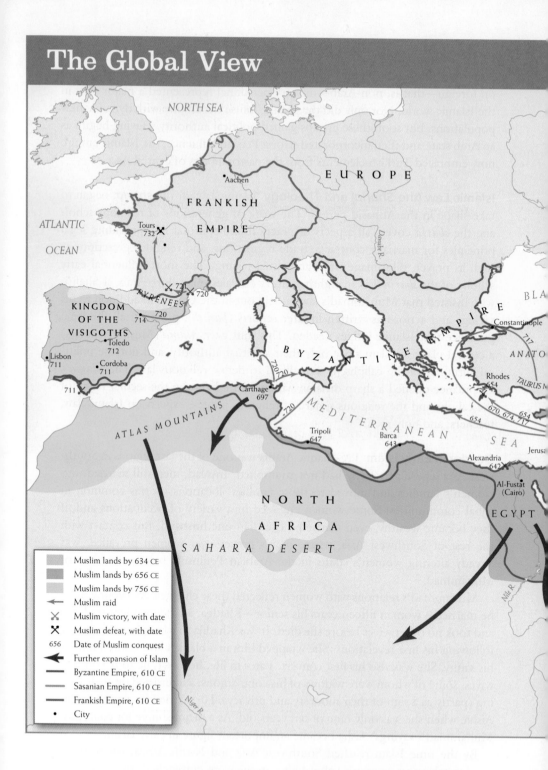

The Global View

NORTH SEA

EUROPE

ATLANTIC
OCEAN

•Aachen

FRANKISH

EMPIRE

Tours
732 ✗

BYZANTINE EMPIRE

Constantinople

717

ANATO

Danube R.

✗ 721
✗ 720

720

PYRENEES

KINGDOM
OF THE
VISIGOTHS

714   720

•Toledo
712

•Lisbon
711

•Cordoba
711

711

BYZANTINE

720 720

720

Carthage
697

Rhodes
654

TAURUS M

MEDITERRANEAN   SEA   654

670 674 717

654

Tripoli
647

Barca
643•

Alexandria
642✗

ATLAS MOUNTAINS

NORTH

AFRICA

SAHARA DESERT

Jerusa

Al-Fustat
(Cairo)

EGYPT

Nile R.

	Muslim lands by 634 CE
	Muslim lands by 656 CE
	Muslim lands by 756 CE
←	Muslim raid
✗	Muslim victory, with date
✗	Muslim defeat, with date
656	Date of Muslim conquest
←	Further expansion of Islam
—	Byzantine Empire, 610 CE
—	Sasanian Empire, 610 CE
—	Frankish Empire, 610 CE
•	City

Niger R.

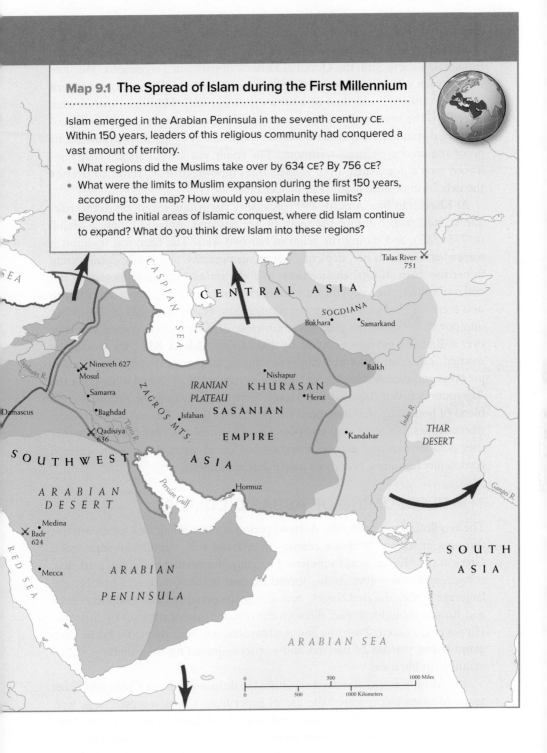

Map 9.1 The Spread of Islam during the First Millennium

Islam emerged in the Arabian Peninsula in the seventh century CE. Within 150 years, leaders of this religious community had conquered a vast amount of territory.

- What regions did the Muslims take over by 634 CE? By 756 CE?
- What were the limits to Muslim expansion during the first 150 years, according to the map? How would you explain these limits?
- Beyond the initial areas of Islamic conquest, where did Islam continue to expand? What do you think drew Islam into these regions?

Talas River ✖
751

CENTRAL ASIA

CASPIAN SEA

SOGDIANA
Bukhara•   •Samarkand

SEA

✖ Nineveh 627
Mosul   •Nishapur   •Balkh

•Samarra   IRANIAN   KHURASAN
                PLATEAU   •Herat
Damascus   •Baghdad   Isfahan•   SASANIAN
         ✖ Qadisiya
           636   EMPIRE   •Kandahar   THAR
                                                        DESERT

ZAGROS MTS.

Tigris R.

Euphrates R.

Indus R.

SOUTHWEST   ASIA

ARABIAN
DESERT

Persian Gulf

•Hormuz

Ganges R.

•Medina
✖ Badr
  624   SOUTH
                                                        ASIA
•Mecca
         ARABIAN

         PENINSULA

RED SEA

ARABIAN SEA

0		500		1000 Miles
0	500		1000 Kilometers	

could not. A man could take four wives and numerous concubines; a woman could have only one husband. Well-to-do women, always veiled, lived secluded from male society. Still, the Quran did offer women some protections. Men had to treat each wife with respect if they took more than one. Women could inherit property (although only half of what a man inherited). Marriage dowries went directly to the bride rather than to her guardian, indicating women's independent legal standing; and while a woman's adultery drew harsh punishment, its proof required eyewitness testimony. The result was a legal system that reinforced men's dominance over women but empowered magistrates to oversee the definition of male honor and proper behavior.

Al-Khayzurān Bint Atta (d. 789) provides a fascinating exception to this rule. She exerted power during the reign of her husband, Abbasid caliph al-Mahdi (r. 775–785), and during the reign of her two sons. The historical tradition is somewhat hostile to her, depicting her as manipulative and overly domineering in her rise from an total enslavement, to *umm walad* (unsellable mother of her enslaver's child), to wife, and then to mother of caliphs. Her reported ruthlessness even included maneuvering her younger son, Harun al-Rashid (r. 786–809), into power by having her elder son murdered. Al-Khayzurān's reputed influence over al-Rashid is perhaps matched by that of Zubaidah (d. 831), the woman he married. Zubaidah was a well-educated woman, who went on pilgrimage multiple times and even donated money for the construction of several wells along the *hajj* route between Baghdad and Mecca. Either al-Khayzurān or Zubaidah, or a blend of both, may well have been the inspiration for the learned Scheherazade, whose stories to a jilted king compose *One Thousand and One Nights*. Together they demonstrate how extraordinary women could assert power even within a community becoming ever more patriarchal in outlook.

THE BLOSSOMING OF ABBASID CULTURE

The arts flourished during the Abbasid period, a blossoming that left its imprint throughout society. Within a century of Abbasid rule, Arabic had superseded Greek as the Muslim world's preferred language for poetry, literature, medicine, science, and philosophy. Arabic spread beyond native speakers to become the language of the educated classes. Arabic scholars preserved and extended Greek and Roman thought, in part through the transmission of treatises by Aristotle, Hippocrates, Galen, Ptolemy, and Archimedes, among others. To house such manuscripts, patrons of the arts and sciences—including the caliphs—opened magnificent libraries.

The Muslim world absorbed scientific breakthroughs from China and other areas: Muslims incorporated the use of paper from China, adopted siege warfare from China and Byzantium, and assimilated knowledge of plants from the ancient Greeks. From Indian sources, scholars borrowed a numbering system based on the concept of zero and units of ten—what we today call Arabic numerals. Arab mathematicians were pioneers in arithmetic, geometry, algebra, and trigonometry. Since much of Greek science had been lost in the west and later was reintroduced via the Muslim world, the Islamic contribution to the west was of immense significance. Thus, this intense borrowing, translating, storing, and diffusing of ideas brought worlds together.

ISLAM IN A WIDER WORLD

As Islam spread and decentralized, it generated dazzling and often competitive dynasties in Spain, North Africa, and points farther east. Each dynastic state revealed the Muslim talent for achieving high levels of artistry far from its heartland. But growing diversity led to a problem: Islam fragmented politically. No single political regime could hold its widely dispersed believers together. (See Map 9.2.)

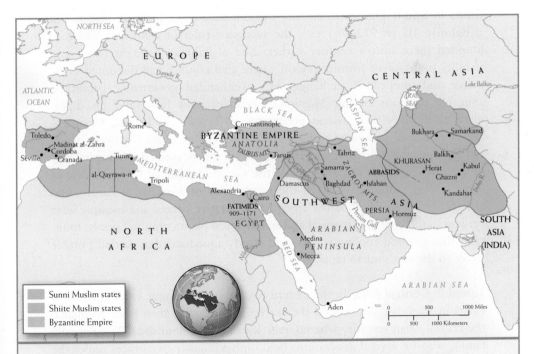

Map 9.2 Political Fragmentation in the Islamic World, 750–1000 CE

By 1000 CE, the Islamic world was politically fractured and decentralized. The Abbasid caliphs still reigned in Baghdad, but they wielded very limited political authority.

- What are the regions where major Islamic powers emerged?
- What areas were Sunni? Which were Shiite?
- Looking back to empires in the Mediterranean and Southwest Asia in earlier periods, how would you compare the area controlled by Islam with the extent of the Roman Empire (Chapter 7), Hellenistic kingdoms (Chapter 6), and the Persian Empire (Chapter 4)? What do you think accounts for the differences?

The Great Mosque of Cordoba The great mosque of Cordoba was built in the eighth century CE by the Umayyad ruler Abd al-Rahman I and added to by other Muslim rulers, including al-Hakim II (who succeeded Abd al-Rahman III), considered by many historians to have been the most powerful and effective of the Spanish Umayyad caliphs.

Cities in Spain One extraordinary Muslim state arose in Spain under Abd al-Rahman III (r. 912–961 CE), the successor ruler of a Muslim kingdom founded there over a century earlier. Abd al-Rahman brought peace and stability to a violent frontier region where civil conflict had disrupted commerce and intellectual exchange. His evenhanded governance promoted amicable relations among Muslims, Christians, and Jews, and his diplomatic relations with Christian potentates as far away as France, Germany, and Scandinavia generated impressive commercial exchanges between western Europe and North Africa. He expanded and beautified the capital city of Cordoba, and his successor made the Great Mosque of Cordoba one of Spain's most stunning sites. In the nearby city of Madinat al-Zahra, Abd al-Rahman III surrounded the city's administrative offices and mosque with verdant gardens of lush tropical and semitropical plants, tranquil pools, fountains that spouted cooling waters, and sturdy aqueducts that carried potable water to the city's inhabitants.

Talent in Central Asia In the eastern regions of the Islamic empire, Abbasid rulers in Baghdad surrounded themselves with learned men from Sogdiana, the central Asian territory where Greek learning had flourished. The Barmaki family, who for several generations held high administrative offices under the Abbasids, came from the central Asian city of Balkh. Loyal servants of the caliph, the Barmakis made sure that wealth and talent from the crossroads of Asia were funneled into Baghdad. Devoted patrons of the arts, the Barmakis promoted and collected Arabic translations of Persian, Greek, and Sanskrit manuscripts. They also encouraged central Asian scholars to enhance their learning by moving to Baghdad. These scholars included the Islamic cleric al-Bukhari (d. 870 CE), who was a renowned collector of *hadith*; the mathematician al-Khwarizmi (c. 780–850 CE), who modified Indian digits into Arabic numerals and wrote the first book on algebra; and the philosopher al-Farabi (d. 950 CE), from a Turkish military family, who also made his way to Baghdad, where he studied eastern Christian teachings and promoted the Platonic ideal of a philosopher-king. Even when the Abbasid caliphate began to decline, intellectual vitality continued under the patronage of local rulers. The best example of this is, perhaps, the polymath Ibn Sina (known in the west as Avicenna; 980–1037 CE), whose *Canon of Medicine* stood as the standard medical text in both Southwest Asia and Europe for centuries.

Trade in Sub-Saharan Africa Carried by traders and scholars, Islam also crossed the Sahara Desert and penetrated well into Africa, where merchants exchanged weapons and textiles for gold, salt, and enslaved people. (See Map 9.3.) Trade did more than join West Africa to North Africa. It generated prodigious wealth, which allowed centralized political kingdoms to develop. The most celebrated was Ghana, which lay at the terminus of North Africa's major trading routes and was often hailed in Arab sources for its gold, as well as its pomp and power. Seafaring Muslim traders carried Islam into East Africa via the Indian Ocean. As early as the eighth century CE, coastal trading communities in East Africa were exporting ivory and possibly exporting enslaved people. By the tenth century, the East African coast featured a mixed African-Arab culture. The region's evolving Bantu language absorbed Arabic words and before long gained a new name, Swahili (derived from the Arabic plural of the word meaning "coast").

Green Revolution in the Islamic World New crops, especially food crops, leaped across political and cultural borders during this period, offering expanding populations more diverse and nutritious diets and the ability to feed increased numbers. Most of these crops originated in Southeast Asia, made their way to India, and dispersed throughout the Muslim world and into China. They included new strains of rice, taro, sour oranges, lemons, limes, and most likely coconut palm trees, sugarcane, bananas, plantains, and mangoes. Sorghum and possibly cotton and watermelons arrived from Africa.

Once Muslims conquered the Sindh in northern India in 711 CE, the crop innovations pioneered in Southeast Asia made their way to the west. Soon a "green revolution" in crops and diet swept through the Muslim world. Sorghum supplanted millet and the other grains of antiquity because it was hardier, had higher yields, and required a shorter growing season. Citrus trees added flavor to the diet and provided refreshing drinks during the summer heat. Increased cotton cultivation led to a greater demand for textiles.

For over 300 years, farmers from northwest India to Spain, Morocco, and West Africa made impressive use of the new crops. They increased agricultural output, slashed fallow periods, and grew as many as three crops on lands that formerly had yielded one. (See Map 9.4.) As a result, farmers could feed larger communities; even as cities grew, the countryside became more densely populated and even more productive.

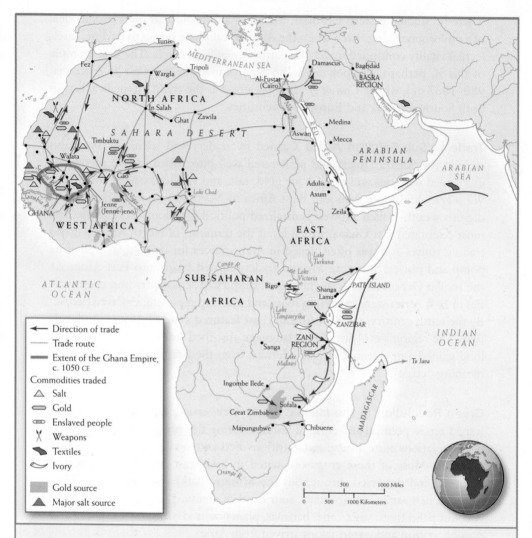

Map 9.3 Islam and Trade in Sub-Saharan Africa, 700–1000 CE

Islamic merchants and scholars, not Islamic armies, carried Islam into sub-Saharan Africa. Trace the trade routes in Africa, making sure to follow the correct direction of trade.

- According to the map key and icons, what commodities were Islamic merchants seeking below the Sahara?
- What were the major trade routes and the direction of trade in Africa?
- How did trade and commerce shape the geographic expansion of the Islamic faith?

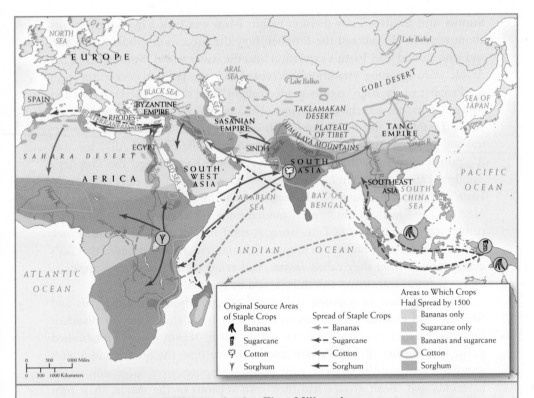

Map 9.4 Agricultural Diffusion in the First Millennium

The second half of the first millennium saw a revolution in agriculture throughout Afro-Eurasia. Agriculturalists across the landmass increasingly cultivated similar crops.

- Where did the staple crops originate? In what direction and where did most of them flow?
- What role did the spread of Islam and the growth of Islamic empires (see Map 9.1) play in the process?
- What role did Southeast Asia and the Tang dynasty play in the spread of these crops?

OPPOSITION WITHIN ISLAM: SHIISM AND THE FATIMIDS

Islam's whirlwind rise generated internal tensions from the start. It is hardly surprising that a religion that extolled territorial conquests and created a large empire in its first decades would also spawn dissident religious movements that challenged the existing imperial structures. Muslims shared a reverence for a basic text and a single God but often had little else in common. Religious and political divisions only grew deeper as Islam spread into new corners of Afro-Eurasia.

Sunnis and Shiites Early division within Islam was fueled by disagreements about who should succeed the Prophet, how the succession should take place, and who should lead Islam's expansion into the wider world. **Sunnis** (from the Arabic word meaning "tradition") accepted that the political succession from the Prophet to the four "rightly guided caliphs" and then to the Umayyad and Abbasid dynasties was the correct one. The vast majority of Muslims today are Sunni. Dissidents, like the Shiites, contested the Sunni understanding of political and spiritual authority. **Shiites** ("members of the party of Ali") felt that the proper successors should have been Ali, who had married the Prophet's daughter Fatima, and then his descendants. Ali was one of the early converts to Islam and one of the band of Meccans who had migrated with the Prophet to Medina. The fourth of the "rightly guided caliphs," he ruled over the Muslim community from 656 to 661 CE, dying at the hands of an assassin who struck him down as he was praying in a mosque in Kufa, Iraq. Shiites believed that Ali's descendants, whom they called *imams*, had religious and prophetic power as well as political authority—and thus should be spiritual leaders.

Shiism appealed to regional and ethnic groups whom the Umayyads and Abbasids had excluded from power; it became Islam's most potent dissident force and created a permanent divide within Islam. Shiism was well established in the first century of Islam's existence, and over time the Sunnis and Shiites diverged even more than these early political disputes over succession might have indicated. Both groups had their own versions of the *sharia*, their own collections of *hadith*, and their own theological tenets.

The Fatimids Repressed in what is present-day Iraq and Iran, Shiite activists made their way to North Africa, where they joined with dissident Berber groups to topple several rulers. In 909 CE, a Shiite religious and military leader, Abu Abdallah, overthrew the Sunni ruler there. Thus began the Fatimid regime.

After conquering Egypt in 969 CE, the Fatimids set themselves against the Abbasid caliphs of Baghdad, refusing to acknowledge their legitimacy and claiming to speak for the whole Islamic world. The Fatimid rulers established their capital at al-Qahira (or Cairo). Early on they founded al-Azhar Mosque, which attracted scholars from all over Afro-Eurasia and spread Islamic learning outward. They also built other elegant mosques and centers of learning. The Fatimid regime lasted until the late twelfth century, though its rulers made little headway in persuading the Egyptian population, most of whom remained Sunnis, to embrace their Shiite beliefs.

By 1000 CE Islam, which had originated as a radical religious revolt in a small corner of the Arabian Peninsula, had grown into a vast political and religious empire. It had become the dominant force in the middle regions of Afro-Eurasia. Like its rival in this part of the world, Christianity, it aspired to universality. But unlike Christianity, it was linked from its outset to political power. Muhammad and his early followers created an empire to facilitate the expansion of their

The Jenne Mosque and al-Azhar Mosque The Jenne Mosque (*left*) arose in the kingdom of Mali when that kingdom was at the height of its power. The mosque speaks to the depth and importance of Islam's roots in the Malian kingdom. The mosque of al-Azhar (*right*) is Cairo's most important ancient mosque. Built in the tenth century CE by the Fatimid conquerors and rulers of Egypt, it quickly became a leading center for worship and learning, frequented by Muslim clerics and admired in Europe.

faith, while their Christian counterparts inherited an empire when Constantine embraced the new faith. A vision of a world under the jurisdiction of Muslim caliphs, adhering to the dictates of the *sharia*, drove Muslim armies, merchants, and scholars to territories thousands of miles away from Mecca and Medina. Yet as Islam's reach stretched thin, political fragmentation within the Muslim world meant that Islam could not extend to much of western Europe and China.

The Tang State

The rise of the powerful Tang Empire (618–907 CE) in China paralleled Islam's explosion out of Arabia and its impact throughout Afro-Eurasia. Once again the landmass had two centers of power, as Islam replaced the Roman Empire in counterbalancing the power and wealth of China. Like the Umayyads and the Abbasids, the Tang dynasty promoted a cosmopolitan culture. Under Tang rule Buddhism, medicine, and mathematics from India gave China's chief cities an international flavor. China became a hub for East Asian integration and spread its influence to Korea and Japan.

TERRITORIAL EXPANSION UNDER THE TANG DYNASTY

The Tang dynasty expanded the boundaries of the Chinese state and reestablished its dominance in East and central Asia. After the fall of the Han, China had faced a long period of political fragmentation (see Chapter 8). As had happened several times before, yet another sudden change in the course of the Yellow River caused extensive flooding on the North China plain and set the stage for the emergence of the Tang dynasty. Revolts ensued as the population faced starvation. Li Yuan, the governor of a province under the short-lived Sui dynasty (589–618 CE), marched on Chang'an and took the throne in 618 CE. He promptly established the Tang dynasty and began building a strong central government by increasing the number of provinces and doubling the number of government offices. By 624 CE, the initial steps of establishing the Tang dynasty were complete, but Li Yuan's ambitious son, Li Shimin, forced his father to abdicate and took the throne in 627 CE.

An expanding Tang state required a large and professionally trained army, capable of defending far-flung frontiers and squelching rebellious populations. Toward these efforts the Tang built a military organization of aristocratic cavalry and peasant soldiers. The cavalry regularly clashed on the northern steppes with encroaching nomadic peoples, who also fought on horseback; at its height the Tang military had 700,000 horses. At the same time, between 1 and 2 million peasant soldiers garrisoned the south and toiled on public works projects.

Much like the Islamic forces, the Tang's frontier armies increasingly relied on pastoral nomadic soldiers from the Inner Eurasian steppe. Notable were the Uighurs, Turkish-speaking peoples who had moved into western China and by 750 CE constituted the empire's most potent military force. These warriors mobilized fearsome cavalries, fired longbows at distant range, and wielded steel swords and knives in hand-to-hand combat. The Tang military also pushed the state into Tibet, the Red River valley in northern Vietnam, Manchuria, and Bohai (near the Korean Peninsula).

At the empire's height, Tang armies controlled more than 4 million square miles of territory—an area as large as the entire Islamic world in the ninth and tenth centuries CE. (See Map 9.5.) Once the Tang administrators brought South China's rich farmlands under cultivation (by draining swamps, building an intricate network of canals and channels, and connecting lakes and rivers to the rice lands), the state was able to collect taxes from roughly 10 million families, representing 57 million individuals. Most of these taxes took the form of agricultural labor, which propelled the expansion of cultivated frontiers throughout the south.

ORGANIZING THE TANG EMPIRE

The Tang Empire emulated the Han in many ways, but its rulers also introduced new institutions. The heart of the agrarian-based Tang state was the magnificent capital city of Chang'an, whose population reached 1 million, half of whom lived within its impressive city walls. The outer walls enclosed a 30-square-mile area. Internal security arrangements made it one of the safest urban locales for its age. Its more than 100 quarters were separated from each other by interior walls with gates that were closed at night, after which no one was permitted on the streets. Horsemen patrolled the streets until the gates reopened in the morning. Chang'an had a large foreign population, estimated at one-third of its total, and a diverse religious life. Zoroastrian fires burned as worshippers

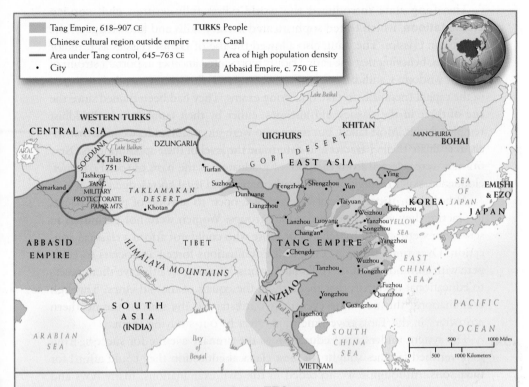

Map 9.5 The Tang State in East Asia, 750 CE

The Tang dynasty, at its territorial peak in 750 CE, controlled a state that extended from central Asia to the East China Sea.

- Which parts of the Tang dynasty benefited from the canal system that had been enhanced by its short-lived predecessor, the Sui?

- How did the area under Tang control change over time? Based on your reading of the chapter and the information on the map, what factors shaped the area controlled by the Tang?

- What foreign areas were under Tang control? What areas were heavily influenced by Tang government and culture?

sacrificed animals and chanted temple hymns. Nestorian Christians from Syria found a welcoming community, and Buddhists could boast ninety-one of their own temples in Chang'an in 722 CE.

Confucian Administrators Despite the Tang's reliance on the fruits of agriculture and a military force, the day-to-day control of the empire required an efficient and loyal civil service. Entry into the Tang ruling group required knowledge of Confucian ideas and all the commentaries on the Confucian classics. It also required skill in the intricate classical Chinese language, in which this literature was written.

The Tang state introduced the world's first fully written **civil service examinations**, which tested sophisticated literary skills and knowledge of the Confucian classics. The Tang also allowed the use of Daoist classics as texts for the exams, believing that the early Daoists represented another important stream of ancient wisdom. Candidates for office, whom local elites recommended, gathered in the capital triennially to take qualifying exams. They had been trained since the age of three in the classics and histories, either by their families or in Buddhist temple schools. Most failed, but those who were successful underwent further trials to evaluate their character and determine the level of their appointments. New officials were selected from the pool of graduates on the basis of social conduct, eloquence, skill in calligraphy and mathematics, and legal knowledge.

Although in theory official careers were open to anyone of proven talent, in practice they were closed to certain groups. Women were not permitted to serve, nor were sons of merchants or those who could not afford a classical education. Over time, though, Tang civil examinations forced aristocrats to compete with commoner southern families, whose growing wealth gave them access to educational resources that made them the equals of the old elites. Through examinations, this new elite eventually outdistanced the sons of the northern aristocracy in the Tang government, in effect by out-studying them.

The system underscored education as the primary avenue for success. Even impoverished families sought the best classical education they could afford for their sons. Although few succeeded in the civil examinations, many boys and even some girls learned the fundamentals of reading and writing. The Buddhists played a crucial role in extending education across society: as part of their charitable mission, their temple schools introduced many children to primers based on classical texts. Many Buddhist monks, in fact, entered the clergy only after not qualifying for or failing the civil examinations.

China's Female Emperor Not all Tang power brokers were men. The wives and mothers of emperors wielded influence in the court—usually behind the scenes, but sometimes publicly. The most striking example is Empress Wu.

Born into a noble family, Wu Zhao played music and mastered the Chinese classics as a young girl. Because she was witty, intelligent, and beautiful, Wu was recruited before age thirteen to Li Shimin's court and became his favorite concubine. When Li Shimin died, his son assumed power and became Emperor Gaozong. Wu became the new emperor's favorite concubine and gave birth to the sons he required to succeed him. As the mother of the future emperor, Wu enjoyed heightened political power. Subsequently, she took the place of Gaozong's empress, Wang, by accusing her of killing Wu's newborn daughter. Emperor Gaozong believed his favorite concubine, Wu, and married her. Following Gaozong's death, Wu Zhao made herself Empress Wu (r. 684–705 CE). She expanded the military and recruited her administrators from the civil examination candidates to oppose her enemies at court.

Christianity in China Nestorian Christianity made a lasting impression on the Tang Empire. *Left:* This mural created in Xinjiang, China, by a Tang artist records a procession on Palm Sunday (the Sunday before Easter, when Christians remember Jesus's triumphal entry into Jerusalem prior to his trial and crucifixion). *Right:* The 9-foot-tall Nestorian Stele, also called the Xi'an Stele, records details about the Nestorian community in China in the seventh and eighth centuries CE, including theological doctrine and missionary visits as well as church leadership and interactions between Nestorians and Tang emperors.

Wu ordered scholars to write biographies of famous women, and she empowered her mother's clan by assigning high political posts to her relatives. Later, she moved her court from Chang'an to Luoyang, where she tried to establish a new "Zhou dynasty," seeking to imitate the widely admired era of Confucius. Empress Wu elevated Buddhism over Daoism as the favored state religion, invited the most gifted Buddhist scholars to her capital at Luoyang, built Buddhist temples, and subsidized spectacular cave sculptures. In fact, Chinese Buddhism achieved its highest officially sponsored development in this period.

Eunuchs Tang rulers protected themselves, their possessions, and especially their women with loyal and well-compensated **eunuchs** (men surgically castrated as youths and thus sexually impotent). By the late eighth century CE, more than 4,500 eunuchs were fully entrenched in the Tang Empire's institutions, wielding significant power not only within the imperial household but at the court and beyond. For instance, the Chief Eunuch controlled the military. Through him, the military power of court eunuchs extended to every province and garrison station in the empire, forming an all-encompassing network. This eunuch bureaucracy mediated between the emperor and the provincial governments.

Under Emperor Xianzong (r. 805–820 CE), eunuchs acted as a third pillar of the government, working alongside the official bureaucracy and the imperial

The Tang Court *Left:* This tenth-century CE painting of elegant ladies of the Tang imperial court enjoying a feast and music tells us a great deal about the aesthetic tastes of elite women in this era. It also shows the secluded "inner quarters," where court ladies passed their daily lives far from the hurly-burly of imperial politics. *Right:* Castrated males, known as eunuchs, guarded the women and protected the royal family of Tang emperors. By the late eighth century CE, eunuchs were fully integrated into the government and wielded a great deal of military and political power.

court. Yet by 838 CE, the delicate balance of power among throne, eunuchs, and civil officials had evaporated. Eunuchs became an unruly political force in late Tang politics, and their competition for influence produced political instability.

AN ECONOMIC REVOLUTION

At its height, Tang China's economic achievements included agricultural production based on an egalitarian land allotment system, an increasingly fine handicrafts industry, a diverse commodity market, and a dynamic urban life. The earlier short-lived Sui dynasty had started this economic progress by reunifying China and building canals, especially the Grand Canal linking the north and south. The Tang continued by centering their efforts on the Grand Canal and the Yangzi River, which flows from west to east. These waterways aided communication and transport throughout the empire. The south grew richer, largely through the backbreaking labor of immigrants from the north. Fertile land along the Yangzi became China's new granary, and areas south of the Yangzi became its demographic center.

Green Revolution in Tang China The same agricultural revolution that was sweeping through South Asia and the Muslim world also took East Asia by storm. China received the same crops that Muslim cultivators were carrying westward. Rice was critical. New varieties entered from the south, and groups migrating from the north (after the collapse of the Han Empire) eagerly took them up. Soon Chinese farmers became the world's most intensive wet-field rice cultivators. Early- and late-ripening seeds supported two or three plantings a year. Champa rice, introduced from central Vietnam, was especially popular for its drought resistance and rapid ripening.

Because rice needs ample water, Chinese hydraulic engineers went into the fields to design water-lifting devices, which peasant farmers used to construct hillside rice paddies. This new rice cultivation was also the partial impetus for the canal building already mentioned. Engineers dug canals linking rivers and lakes, and they even drained swamps, alleviating the malaria that had long troubled the region. Their efforts yielded a booming and constantly moving rice frontier.

Trade in Luxuries Chinese merchants took full advantage of the Silk Roads to trade with India and the Islamic world; when rebellions in northwest China and the rise of Islam in central Asia jeopardized the land route, the "silk road by the sea" became the avenue of choice. From all over Asia and Africa, merchant ships arrived in South China ports bearing spices, medicines, and jewelry in exchange for Chinese silks and porcelains. In the large cities of the Yangzi delta, workshops produced rich brocades (silk fabrics), fine paper, intricate wood-block prints, unique iron casts, and exquisite porcelains. Art collectors all across Afro-Eurasia especially valued Tang "tricolor pottery," decorated with brilliant hues. Chinese artisans transformed locally grown cotton into highest-quality clothing. Painting and dyeing technology improved, and the resulting superb silk products generated significant tax revenue. These Chinese luxuries dominated the trading networks that reached Southwest Asia, Europe, and Africa via the Silk Roads and the Indian Ocean.

ACCOMMODATING WORLD RELIGIONS

The early Tang emperors tolerated remarkable religious diversity. Nestorian Christianity, Zoroastrianism, and Manichaeanism (a radical Christian sect) had entered China from Persia during the time of the Sasanian Empire. Islam came later. These spiritual impulses—together with Buddhism and the indigenous teachings of Daoism and Confucianism—spread throughout the Tang Empire and at first were widely used to enhance state power.

The Growth of Buddhism Buddhism, in particular, thrived under Tang rule. Initially, Emperor Li Shimin distrusted Buddhist monks because they avoided serving the government and paying taxes. Yet after Buddhism gained acceptance as one of the "three ways" of learning—joining Daoism and Confucianism—Li endowed huge monasteries, sent emissaries to India to collect texts and relics, and commissioned Buddhist paintings and statuary. Caves along the Silk Roads, such as those at Dunhuang, provided ideal venues for monks to paint the inside walls where religious rites and meditation took place.

Anti-Buddhist Campaigns By the mid-ninth century CE, however, the growing influence of China's hundreds of thousands of Buddhist monks and nuns threatened Confucian and Daoist leaders, who responded by arguing that Buddhism's values conflicted with native traditions. One Confucian-trained scholar-official, Han Yu, even attacked Buddhism as a foreign doctrine of barbarian peoples who were different in language, culture, and knowledge. Although Han Yu was exiled for his objections, two decades later the state began suppressing Buddhist monasteries and confiscating their wealth, fearing that religious loyalties would undermine political ones. Increasingly intolerant Confucian scholar-administrators argued that the Buddhist monastic establishment threatened the imperial order.

By the mid-ninth century CE, the Tang state openly persecuted Buddhism. Emperor Wuzong (814–846 CE), for instance, closed more than 4,600 monasteries and destroyed 40,000 temples and shrines. More than 260,000 Buddhist monks and nuns endured a forced return to secular life, after which the state parceled out monastery lands to taxpaying landlords and peasant farmers. To expunge the cultural impact of Buddhism, classically trained literati revived ancient prose styles and the teachings of Confucius and his followers. Their efforts reversed some of the early Buddhist successes in China.

Although Buddhism remained important, the Tang era represented the triumph of homegrown ideologies (Confucianism and Daoism) over a foreign universalizing religion (Buddhism). In addition, by permanently dismantling huge monastic land holdings, the Tang ensured that no religion would rival its power. Successor dynasties continued to keep religious establishments weak and fragmented, although Confucianism maintained a more prominent role within

society as the basis of the ruling classes' ideology and as a quasi-religious belief system for a wider portion of the population. The result was persistent religious diversity within China.

TANG INTERACTIONS WITH KOREA AND JAPAN

While China was opening up to the cultures of its western regions, its own culture was reaching out to the east—to Korea and, eventually, to Japan. (See Map 9.6.) Chinese influence, both indirect and direct, had reached into Korea for more than a millennium, and later into Japan, but not without local resistance and the flourishing of entirely indigenous and independent political and religious developments.

Early Korea Interactions with China played a fundamental role in the history of the Korean Peninsula. Unification in 668 CE under the Silla—one of three rival states in Korea—enabled Koreans to establish an autonomous government, but their opposition to the Chinese did not deter them from modeling their government on the Tang imperial state. The Silla rulers dispatched annual emissaries bearing tribute payments to the Chinese capital and regularly sent students and monks. As a result, literary Chinese—not their own dialect—became the written language of Korean elites. Chinese influence extended to the way in which the Silla state organized its court and bureaucracy and to the construction of the Silla capital city of Kumsong, which imitated the Tang capital of Chang'an. Silla's fortunes became entwined with the Tang's to such an extent, however, that once the Tang declined, Silla also began to fragment and ultimately surrendered to the Koryo kingdom in 935 CE.

Early Japan Like Korea, Japan also felt influences emanating from China, and it responded by thwarting and accommodating them at the same time. But Japan enjoyed added autonomy: it was an archipelago of islands, separated from the mainland although internally fragmented. In the mid-third century CE, a warlike group had arrived by sea from Korea and imposed military and social control over southern Japan. These conquerors—known as the "Tomb Culture" because of their elevated burial sites—unified Japan by extolling their imperial ancestors and maintaining their social hierarchy. In time, the complex aristocratic society that had developed within the Tomb Culture gave rise to a Japanese state on the Yamato plain in the region now known as Nara. In becoming the ruling faction in this area, the Yamato clan incorporated native Japanese as well as Korean migrants.

After 587 CE, the Soga kinship group—originally from Korea but by 500 CE a minor branch of the Yamato imperial family—became Japan's leading family and

◀ **One of the Four Sacred Mountains** This monastery on Mount Song is famous because in 527 CE an Indian priest named Bodhidharma arrived there to initiate the Zen school of Buddhism in China.

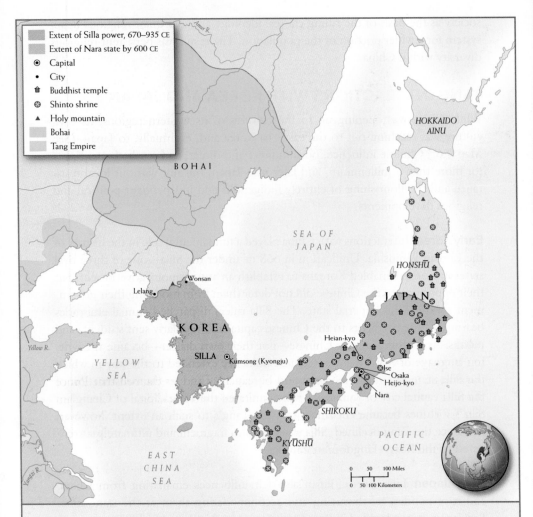

Extent of Silla power, 670–935 CE
Extent of Nara state by 600 CE
⊙ Capital
• City
🏯 Buddhist temple
⊛ Shinto shrine
▲ Holy mountain
Bohai
Tang Empire

BOHAI

HOKKAIDO
AINU

SEA OF
JAPAN

HONSHŪ

Wonsan

Lelang

JAPAN

Yellow R.

KOREA

Heian-kyo

YELLOW
SEA

SILLA Kumsong (Kyongju)

Ise
Osaka
Heijo-kyo

Nara

SHIKOKU

PACIFIC
OCEAN

KYŪSHŪ

EAST
CHINA
SEA

0   50   100 Miles

0   50 100 Kilometers

Map 9.6 Tang Borderlands: Korea and Japan, 600–1000 CE

The Tang dynasty held great power over emerging Korean and Japanese states, although it never directly ruled either region.

- Based on the map, what connections do you see between Korea and Japan and the Tang Empire?
- What, if any, relationship do you see between the proliferation of Buddhist temples and Shinto shrines?

Horyuji Temple The main hall of the Horyuji Temple in Nara, Japan (*left*), was built in the seventh century CE. Several murals from the seventh and eighth centuries CE cover the walls inside the temple. In this fresco (*right*), the Yakushi (or medicine/healing) Buddha sits with bodhisattvas and other attendants, while winged celestial beings, called *apsaras* (or *tennin*, in Japanese Buddhism), fly above. Some scholars have argued that the artists who created the frescoes in the Horyuji Temple based the images on drawings made of the Buddha in Tang China.

controlled the Japanese court through intermarriage. Soon they were attributing their cultural innovations to their own Prince Shotoku (574–622 CE), of Soga and Yamato descent. Contemporary Japanese scribes claimed that Prince Shotoku, rather than Korean immigrants, introduced Buddhism to Japan and that his illustrious reign sparked Japan's rise as an exceptional island kingdom. Shotoku promoted both Buddhism and Confucianism, thus enabling Japan, like its neighbor China, to accommodate numerous religions.

Indeed, religious influences flowed into Japan, contributing to spiritual diversity while bolstering the Yamato rulers. Although Prince Shotoku and later Japanese emperors turned to Confucian models for government, they also dabbled in occult arts and Daoist purification rituals. In addition, governmental edicts promoted Buddhism as the state religion of Japan. Association with Buddhism gave the Japanese state extra status by lending it the prestige of a universalizing religion whose appeal stretched to Korea, China, and India. State-sponsored spiritual diversity led native Shinto cults—which believed that after death a person's soul (or spirit) became a Shinto *kami*, or local deity, provided that it was nourished and purified through proper rituals and festivals—to formalize a creed of their own. The introduction of Confucianism and Buddhism motivated Shinto adherents to assemble their diverse religious practices into a well-organized belief system. Shinto priests now collected ancient liturgies, and Shinto rituals (such as purification rites to ward off demons and impurities) gained recognition in the state's official Department of Religion.

Political integration under Prince Shotoku did not mean political stability, however. In 645 CE, the Nakatomi kinship group seized the throne and eliminated the Soga and their allies. Via intermarriage with the imperial clan, the

Nakatomi became the new spokesmen for the Yamato tradition. Thereafter, Nakatomi no Kamatari (614–669 CE) enacted a series of reforms that reflected Confucian principles of government allegedly enunciated by Shotoku. These reforms enhanced the power of the ruler, no longer portrayed simply as an ancestral kinship group leader but now depicted as an exalted "emperor" (*tenno*) who ruled by the mandate of heaven, as in China, and exercised absolute authority.

THE FALL OF TANG CHINA

Hence, at the eastern end of Afro-Eurasia, the Tang, as well as the Silla of Korea and the Yamato state of Japan, interacted with one another and blended both religious and political authority to maintain stability. The peak of Chinese power in East Asia occurred just as the Abbasids were expanding into Tang portions of central Asia. Yet, despite the Abbasid Empire's spread, China in 750 CE was still the most powerful and best-administered empire in the world. When Muslim forces drove the Tang from Turkistan in 751 CE at the Battle of Talas River, however, their success emboldened groups such as the Sogdians and Tibetans to challenge the Tang and even take their capital. As a result, the Tang gradually retreated into the old heartlands along the Yellow and Yangzi Rivers. Thereafter, misrule, court intrigues, economic exploitation, and popular rebellions weakened the empire, but the dynasty held on for over a century more until northern invaders toppled it in 907 CE.

The Emergence of European Christendom

European historians debate whether or not to label this period in Europe "the Dark Ages." Scholars who have spurned the term "Dark Ages," in favor of the term "Late Antiquity," emphasize the political and cultural continuities between Rome and its successor states, especially in the eastern Mediterranean, and the new dynamic institutions that arose in Rome's wake. Scholars who favor the term "Dark Ages" stress what they see as a sharp cultural, political, and economic decline accompanying the Roman Empire's fall, especially in the western Mediterranean. "The Dark Ages," as a label for this period, has been resurrected by environmental historians, who argue that the period was indeed dark, as a result of a colder and drier climate. Agricultural production declined, famines occurred year after year, and infectious diseases spread across Afro-Eurasia (for example, the plague during the reign of Justinian; see Chapter 8). This harsher climate and the diseases that accompanied it between 400 and 900 CE caused dying and mortality on a large scale. The drought that was wreaking havoc in Europe is the same one that helped spur Arab tribal peoples, carrying the banner of Islam, to pour out of their severely affected lands in the Arabian Peninsula in search of better lands and a better life, as other nomadic groups had done.

Although western Europe lacked a highly developed political empire like that of the Abbasids or the Tang dynasty, Christianity increasingly unified the peoples of Europe. In fifth-century CE western Europe, the mighty Roman military machine gave way to a multitude of warrior leaders whose principal allegiances were local. The political ideal of the Roman Empire certainly influenced western Europeans, but the true inheritor of Rome in the west was the Roman Catholic Church, with its priests, missionaries, and monks. In northern Europe, a frontier mentality and the Viking threat shaped Christianity. In eastern Europe and Byzantium, a form of Christianity known as Greek Orthodoxy had become dominant by 1000 CE. Together, these two major strands of the faith—the western Roman Catholic Church and eastern Greek Orthodoxy—constituted the realm of Christendom, the entire portion of the world in which Christianity prevailed as a unifying institution. (See Map 9.7.)

CHARLEMAGNE'S FLEDGLING EMPIRE

Far removed from the old centers of high culture, Charlemagne (r. 768–814 CE), ruler of the Franks, expanded his western European kingdom through constant warfare and plunder. In 802 CE, Harun al-Rashid, the Abbasid ruler of Baghdad, sent the gift of an elephant to Charlemagne, already the king of the Franks for three decades and recently crowned by the pope in Rome as "Holy Roman Emperor" (on Christmas Day in 800 CE). While the Franks interpreted the caliph's gift as an acknowledgment of Charlemagne's power, al-Rashid more likely sent the rare beast as a gracious reminder of his own formidable sway. In al-Rashid's eyes, Charlemagne's "empire" was a minor principality. Although Charlemagne claimed the lofty title of emperor and ultimately controlled much of western Europe, compared with the Islamic world's rulers and vast domain, he was a political lightweight.

Charlemagne's empire had a population of less than 15 million; he rarely commanded armies larger than 5,000; and his tax system was rudimentary. At a time when the caliph's palace at Baghdad covered nearly 250 acres, Charlemagne's palace at Aachen was merely 330 by 655 feet. Baghdad itself was almost 40 square miles in area, whereas there was no "town" outside the palace at Aachen. The palace was essentially a large country house set in open countryside, where Charlemagne and his Franks hunted wild boar from horseback.

Charlemagne and his men were representatives of the warrior class that dominated post-Roman western Europe. After Roman control faded away, war became once again the duty and joy of the aristocrats. Although the Franks vigorously engaged in trade, even that trade was based on war. Europe's principal export at this time was Europeans, and the massive sale of prisoners of war, in markets at Alexandria, Tunis, and southern Spain, financed the Frankish Empire. The main victims of this trade were Slavic-speaking peoples,

Map 9.7 Christendom, 600–1000 CE

The end of the first millennium saw much of Europe divided between two versions of Christianity, each with different traditions. On the map, locate Rome and Constantinople, the two seats of power in Christianity.

- According to the map, what were the two major regions where Christianity held sway? In what directions did Roman Catholic Christianity and Greek Orthodox Christianity spread?
- Where were important churches and monasteries heavily concentrated? Why do you think they were focused in those regions?
- The map suggests that missionaries played important roles in spreading Roman Catholicism and Greek Orthodoxy. Why do you think this was the case?

tribal hunters and cultivators from eastern Europe. This trade in Slavs gives us the modern—and troubled—term *slave*.

Yet Charlemagne's seemingly uncivilized and inhospitable empire offered fertile ground for Christianity to sink down roots. As Christianity grew in western and northern Europe, the rough frontier mentality fueled its expansionist ambitions.

CHRISTIANITY IN WESTERN EUROPE

Christians of the west, including those in northern Europe, felt that theirs was the one truly universal religion. Their goal was to bring rival groups into a single Roman "catholic" (from the Greek for "universal") church that was replacing a political unity lost in western Europe when the Roman Empire fell. Drawing on Augustine of Hippo's centuries-old ideas (c. 410 CE), the western Christians believed that the "city of God" would take earthly shape in the form of a catholic church, and that this catholic church was not just for Romans—it was for all times and for all peoples.

The arrival of Christianity in northern Europe provoked a cultural revolution. Preliterate societies now encountered a sacred text—the Bible—in a language that seemed utterly strange. Latin had become a sacred language, and books themselves were vehicles of the holy. The bound codex, which had replaced the clumsy scroll, was still messy: it had no divisions between words, no punctuation, no paragraphs, no chapter headings. Readers who knew Latin as a spoken language could understand the script. But Irishmen, Saxons, and Franks could not, for they had never spoken Latin. Consequently, manuscript copyists in the newly Christian north lavished great care on the few parchment texts—like the Gospels in

Scenes from the Life of Charlemagne A thirteenth-century stained glass window from Chartres Cathedral in France depicts several scenes from the life of Charlemagne. This portion of the massive window captures several scenes of the Frankish king in action: in the center, from top to bottom, are Charlemagne commissioning the construction of a church, going on a trip to Spain, and offering relics to the church at Aachen. On the left are scenes of Charlemagne at prayer and gazing to the heavens, and on the right are images of him besieging a city and being visited by a saint in his dreams.

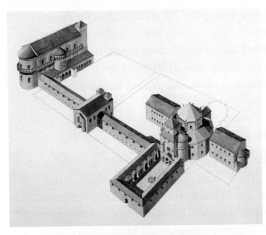

Charlemagne's Palace and Chapel Though not large by Byzantine or Islamic standards, Charlemagne's palace and chapel were heavy with symbolic meaning. A royal hall for banqueting in Frankish, "barbarian" style was linked by a covered walkway to the imperial domed chapel, which was meant to look like a miniature version of Hagia Sophia in Constantinople. Outside the chapel was a courtyard, like the one outside the shrine of Saint Peter in Rome.

the Book of Kells (c. 800 CE)—that were prepared with words separated, sentences correctly punctuated and introduced by uppercase letters, and chapter heading marked.

Those producing these stunning Bibles were starkly different from ordinary men and women. They were monks and nuns. Christian **monasticism** had originated in Egypt, but it suited well the missionary tendencies of Christianity in northern Europe. The root of "monastic" and "monk" is the Greek *monos*, "alone": a monastic was a man or a woman who chose to live alone, without the support of marriage or family. In Muslim (and Jewish) communities, religious leaders emphasized what they had in common with those around them. Accordingly, many Islamic scholars, theologians, and mystics were married men, even merchants and courtiers. In the Christian west, the opposite was true: warrior societies honored small groups of monks and nuns who were utterly unlike themselves: unmarried, unfit for warfare, and intensely literate in an incomprehensible tongue.

Monasticism appealed to a deep sense that the very men and women who had little in common with ordinary people were best suited to mediate between believers and God. Laypersons (common believers, not clergy) gave gifts to the monasteries and offered them protection. In return, they gained the prayers of monks and nuns and the reassurance that although they themselves were warriors and men of blood, the monks' and nuns' interventions on their behalf would keep them from going to hell. Payment for human sin, the atoning power of Jesus's crucifixion, and the efficacy of monastic prayers were significant theological emphases for western Roman Catholics.

The Catholic Church of northern Europe was a religion of monks, whose communities represented an otherworldly alternative to the warrior societies of the time. By 800 CE, most regions of northern Europe held great monasteries, many of which were far larger than the local villages. Supported by thousands of serfs donated by kings and local warlords, the monasteries became powerhouses of prayer that kept the regions safe.

Northern Christianity also gained new ties to an old center: the city of Rome. The Christian bishop of Rome had always enjoyed much prestige but often took second place to other bishops in Carthage, Alexandria, Antioch, and Constantinople. Though people spoke of him with respect as *papa* ("the grand old man"), many others shared that title.

By the ninth century CE, this picture had changed. Believers from the distant north saw only one *papa* left in western Europe: Rome's pope. New Christians in northern borderlands wanted to find a religious leader for their hopes, and the Catholic Church of western Europe united behind the symbolic center of Rome and its popes. Charlemagne fed this desire when, in 800 CE, he went out of his way to celebrate Christmas Day by visiting the shrine of Saint Peter in Rome. There, Pope Leo III acclaimed him as the new "emperor" of the west. A "modern" Rome—inhabited by popes, famous for shrines of the martyrs, and protected by a "modern" Christian monarch from the north—was what Charlemagne's subjects wanted.

VIKINGS AND CHRISTENDOM

Vikings from Scandinavia exposed the weakness of Charlemagne's Christian empire. When al-Rashid's elephant died in 813 CE, the Franks viewed it as an omen of coming disasters. The great beast keeled over when his handlers marched him out to confront a Viking army from Denmark. Charlemagne died the next year. In the next half century, Charlemagne's empire of borderland peoples met its match on the wide border between the European landmass and the Atlantic. (See Map 9.8.)

The **Vikings**' motives were announced in their name, which derives from the Old Norse *vik*, "to be on the warpath." The Vikings sought to loot the now-wealthy Franks and replace them as the dominant warrior class of northern

Monasticism *Left:* The great monasteries of the age of Charlemagne, such as the Saint Gallen Monastery, were like Roman legionary settlements. Placed on the frontiers of Germany, they were vast stone buildings, around which entire towns would gather. Their libraries, the largest in Europe, were filled with parchment volumes, carefully written out and often lavishly decorated in a "northern," Celtic style. *Right:* Monasticism was also about the lonely search for God at the very end of the world, which took place in these Irish monasteries on the Atlantic coast. The cells, made of loose stones piled in round domes, are called "beehives."

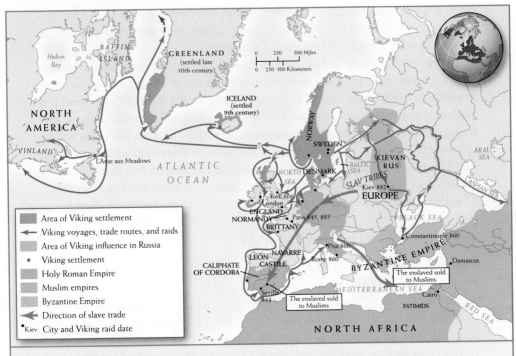

Map 9.8 The Age of Vikings and the Slave Trade, 800–1000 CE

Vikings from Scandinavia dramatically altered the history of Christendom.

- In what directions did the Vikings carry out their voyages, trade routes, and raids?
- What were the geographical limits of the Viking explorations in each direction?
- In what direction did the slave trade move, and what role did the Vikings and the Holy Roman Emperors play in expanding it?

Europe. They succeeded in their plundering and enslaving because of a deadly technological advantage: ships of unparalleled sophistication. Light and agile, Viking ships traveled far up the rivers of northern Europe and could even be carried overland from one river system to another. Under sail, the same boats could tackle open water and cross the North Atlantic. In the ninth century CE, the Vikings set their ships on both courses. They sacked the great monasteries along the coasts of Ireland and Britain and overlooking the Rhine and Seine Rivers. At the same time, Norwegian adventurers colonized the uninhabited island of Iceland, and then Greenland. By 982 CE, they had even reached continental North America and established a settlement at L'Anse aux Meadows on the Labrador coast.

More long-lasting than their settlements in North America was the Viking incursion into eastern Europe. The Vikings sailed east along the Baltic and then turned south, edging up the rivers that crossed the watershed of central Russia.

Here the Dnieper, the Don, and the Volga Rivers flow south into the Black Sea and the Caspian. Consequently, the Vikings created an avenue of commerce that linked Scandinavia and the Baltic directly to Constantinople and Baghdad. Muslim geographers bluntly called this route "the Highway of the Slaves" because so much of the trade was in human cargo.

In 860 CE, more than 200 Viking longships gathered ominously beneath the walls of Constantinople in the straits of the Bosporus. What they found was not poorly defended monasteries or Charlemagne's rustic Aachen, but a city with a population exceeding 100,000 protected by well-engineered late Roman walls. For nearly two centuries, Constantinople had resisted almost yearly campaigns launched by the successive Islamic empires of Damascus and later Baghdad. These campaigns were deflected by Constantinople's highly professional generals, a line of skillfully constructed fortresses that controlled the roads across Anatolia, and a deadly technological advantage in naval warfare: Greek fire. This combination of petroleum and potassium, when sprayed from siphons, would explode in a great sheet of flame on the water. The experience and weaponry of Byzantium were too much for the Vikings, and their raid of the most significant city in eastern Christendom was a spectacular failure. Despite their inability to take Byzantium, the Vikings asserted an enduring influence through their forays across the North Atlantic, their brutal interactions with Christian communities in northern Europe, and their expansion into eastern Europe, especially the slave trade they facilitated there.

GREEK ORTHODOX CHRISTIANITY

Outlasting so many military emergencies bolstered the morale of the eastern Christians and led to a flowering of Christianity in this region. Not just Constantinople but Justinian's Hagia Sophia—its heart—had survived significant threats. That great building and the solemn Greek divine liturgy that reverberated within its domed spaces symbolized the branch of Christian belief that dominated in the east: **Greek Orthodoxy**. Greek Orthodox theology held that Jesus became human less to atone for humanity's sins (as emphasized in Roman Catholicism) and more to facilitate *theosis* (a transformation of humans into divine beings). This was a truly distinct message from that which prevailed in the Roman Catholicism of the west.

Oseberg Ship The Viking ship was a triumph of design. It could be rowed up the great rivers of Europe, or its sails could take it across the Atlantic. The Oseberg ship pictured here contained the early ninth-century CE burial of a high-status Viking woman.

In the tenth century CE, as Charlemagne's empire collapsed in western Europe, large areas of eastern Europe became Greek Orthodox, not Roman Catholic. In addition, Greek Christianity gained a spiritual empire in Southwest Asia. The conversion of Russian peoples, Balkan Slavs, and Arab peoples to Greek Orthodox Christianity was a complex process. It reflected a deep admiration for Constantinople on the part of Russians, Bulgarians, Arabs, and Slav princes. It was an admiration as intense as that of any western Catholic for the Roman popes. This admiration amounted to awe, as shown by the famous story of the conversion to Greek Christianity of the rulers of Kiev (descendants of Vikings). Unimpressed by the religious practice and structures of Catholic Franks, these Russian Christians were overwhelmed by what to their eyes was the almost heavenly splendor of the churches they encountered in Greece and Constantinople.

By the year 1000 CE, then, there were two Christianities: the new and confident "borderland" **Roman Catholicism** of western Europe and an ancient Greek Orthodoxy. Western Roman Catholics believed that their church was destined to expand everywhere. Greek Orthodox Christians were less euphoric but believed that their church would forever survive the regular ravages of invasion. This was a significant difference in attitude; Greek Orthodox Christians considered the Franks barbarous and grasping, and western Roman Catholics contemptuously called the eastern Christians "Greeks" and condemned them for "Byzantine" cunning.

Thus, like Islam, the Christian world was divided, with differences in heritage, theology, customs, and levels of urbanization. At that time, the Orthodox world was considerably more ancient and more cultured than the world of the Catholic west. And each dealt with Islam differently. In Constantinople, eastern Christianity held off Muslim forces that constantly threatened the great city and its Christian hinterlands. In the west, by contrast, Muslim expansionism reached all the way to the Iberian Peninsula. Western Christendom, led by the Roman papacy, set about spreading Christianity to pagan tribes in

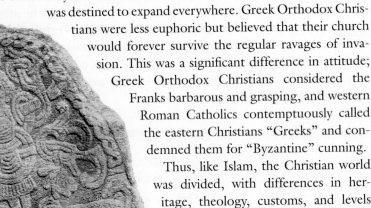

Jelling Stone Carved on the side of this great stone, Christ appears to be almost swallowed up in an intricate pattern of lines. For the Vikings, complicated interweaving like serpents or twisted gold jewelry was a sign of majesty: hence, in this, the first Christian monument in Denmark, Christ is part of an ancient pattern of carving, which brought good luck and victory to the king.

the north, and it began to contemplate retaking lands from the Muslims. Yet in spite of their deep political, ethnic, and theological differences, the two regions of Christianity conducted a brisk trade in commodities and ideas.

Conclusion

Despite the intermixing of peoples, ideas, and goods across Afro-Eurasia, new political and cultural boundaries were developing that would split this landmass in ways previously unimaginable. The most important dividing force was religion, as Islam challenged and slowed the spread of Christianity and as Buddhism challenged the ruling elite of Tang China. As a consequence, Afro-Eurasia's major cultural zones began to compete in terms of religious and cultural doctrines. The Islamic Abbasid Empire pushed back the borders of the Tang Empire. But the conflict grew particularly intense between the Islamic and Christian worlds, where the clash involved faith as well as frontiers.

The Tang Empire revived Confucianism, insisting on its political and moral primacy as the foundation of a new imperial order, and it embraced the classical written language as another unifying element. By doing so, the Tang counteracted universalizing foreign religions—notably Buddhism but also Islam—spreading into the Chinese state. The same adaptive strategies influenced new systems on the Korean Peninsula and in Japan.

In some circumstances, faith followed empire and relied on rulers' support or tolerance to spread the word. This was the case especially in East Asia. At the opposite extreme, empire followed faith—as in the case of Islam, whose believers endeavored to spread their empire in every direction. The Islamic empire and its successors represented a new force: expanding political power backed by one God whose instructions were to spread his message. In the worlds of Christianity, a common faith absorbed elements of a common culture (shared books, a language for the learned classes). But in the west, political rulers never overcame inhabitants' intense allegiance to local authority.

While universalizing religions expanded and common cultures grew, debate raged within each religion over foundational principles. In spite of the diffusion of basic texts in "official" languages, regional variations of Christianity, Islam, and Buddhism proliferated as each belief system spread. The period from 600 to 1000 CE demonstrated that religion, reinforced by prosperity and imperial resources, could bring peoples together in unprecedented ways. But it could also, as the next chapter will illustrate, drive them apart in bloody confrontations.

Focus On
Religion and Empires: Islam, the Tang Dynasty, Christendom, and Common Cultures

The Islamic Empire

- Warriors from the Arabian Peninsula defeat Byzantine and Sasanian armies and establish an Islamic empire stretching from Morocco to South Asia.

- The Abbasid state takes over from the Umayyads, crystallizes the main Islamic institutions of the caliphate and Islamic law, and promotes cultural achievements in religion, philosophy, and science.

- Disputes over Muhammad's succession lead to a deep and enduring split between Sunnis and Shiites.

Tang China

- The Tang dynasty dominates East Asia and exerts a strong influence on Korea and Japan.

- Tang rulers balance Confucian and Daoist ideals with Buddhist thought and practice.

- A common written language and shared philosophy, rather than a single universalizing religion, integrate the Chinese state.

Christian Europe

- Charlemagne establishes an empire in part of western Europe, while the Vikings raid and trade from their homeland in Scandinavia westward to North America, southward to the Mediterranean, and eastward to the Caspian Sea.

- Monks, nuns, and Rome-based popes spread Christianity throughout western Europe.

- Constantinople-based Greek Orthodoxy survives the spread of Islam.

Key Terms

caliphate p. 324	five pillars of Islam p. 321	*sharia* p. 325
civil service examinations p. 338	Greek Orthodoxy p. 353	Shiites p. 334
eunuchs p. 339	monasticism p. 350	Sunnis p. 334
	Roman Catholicism p. 354	Vikings p. 351

CHRONOLOGY

600 CE   700 CE

The Islamic World

Life of Muhammad 570–632 CE

Umayyad caliphate 661–750 CE

East Asia

Prince Shotoku initiates reforms in Japan 574–622 CE

Europe

Arab armies conquer much of Byzantine Empire but the empire survives 632–661 CE

THINKING ABOUT GLOBAL CONNECTIONS

- **Thinking about Crossing Borders and Faith & Empire** As Islam spread outside its initial Arabian context, the faith underwent a range of developments. As Christianity and Buddhism continued to spread, these traditions underwent changes as well. Compare the shifts that took place within Islam as it expanded (600–1000 CE) with those within Buddhism and Christianity, not only in their earlier periods (see Chapter 8) but also during the period from 600 to 1000 CE.

- **Thinking about Changing Power Relationships and Faith & Empire** As each of the empires discussed in this chapter matured, divisions developed within the faiths that initially had helped to bring unity to their respective regions. In the Abbasid world, a split developed between Sunni and Shiite Muslims. In Tang China, Buddhism and Confucianism vied for political influence. Christendom divided into the Roman Catholic west and the Greek Orthodox east. What was the exact nature of each religious disagreement? How do these divisions compare in terms of the root of the internal rifts and their impact in the political realm?

- **Thinking about Worlds Together, Worlds Apart** The empires described in this chapter reached across wide swaths of territory and interacted with vibrant societies on their margins. The peoples of Europe struggled with the onslaught of the fierce Vikings. The peoples of Tang China interacted with neighboring Korea and Japan. How does the interaction of Europe and the Vikings compare with the relations of the Tang and the external influences that they experienced? To what extent did the Abbasids contend with similar exchanges?

 Go to INQUIZITIVE to see what you've learned—and learn what you've missed—with personalized feedback along the way.

800 CE	900 CE	1000 CE

Abbasid caliphate 750–1258 CE

Fatimid Shiite regime founded in Egypt 969 CE ●

Tang dynasty in China 618–907 CE

Silla unify Korean state 668–935 CE

Catholic Church based in Rome begins converting much of northern Europe into Christian communities eighth century CE

Charlemagne unites much of western Europe into a short-lived Christian kingdom 768–814 CE

Vikings raid much of Europe and establish strong commercial links across eastern Europe ninth and tenth centuries CE

10

Becoming "The World"

1000–1300 CE

Core Objectives

- **IDENTIFY** technological advances of this period, especially in ship design and navigation, and **EXPLAIN** how they facilitated the expansion of Afro-Eurasian trade.

- **DESCRIBE** the varied social and political forces that shaped the Islamic world, India, China, and Europe, and **EVALUATE** the degree to which these forces integrated cultures and geographic areas.

- **COMPARE** the internal integration and external interactions of sub-Saharan Africa with those of the Americas, and with the connected Eurasian world.

- **ASSESS** the impacts that the Mongol Empire had on Afro-Eurasian peoples and places.

In the late 1270s two Nestorian Christian monks, Bar Sāwmā and Markōs, voyaged from the court of the Mongol leader Kublai Khan in what is now Beijing into the heart of the Islamic world and beyond. They were not Europeans. They were Uighurs, a Turkish people of central Asia, many of whom had converted to Christianity centuries earlier. The monks hoped to make a pilgrimage to Jerusalem in order to visit the tombs of the martyrs enshrined there and along the way.

On their journey westward, Bar Sāwmā and Markōs traveled a world bound together by economic and cultural exchange. The two monks lingered at the magnificent trading hub of Kashgar in what is now western China, where caravan routes converged in a market for jade, exotic spices, and precious silks. Unable to continue on to Jerusalem due to the route's dangers (including murderous robbers), the monks parted ways at Baghdad. Later, in 1287, Bar Sāwmā was appointed an ambassador by the Buddhist Mongol il-Khan of Persia, Arghūn, to drum up support among European leaders for an attack on Jerusalem to wrest it from Muslim control. He visited Constantinople (where the Byzantine emperor gave him gold and silver), Rome (where he met with the pope at the shrine of Saint Peter), Paris (where he saw that city's vibrant university), and Bordeaux (where he was welcomed by the English king, Edward I). In the end, neither monk ever reached Jerusalem or returned to China. Bar Sāwmā ended his days in Baghdad, and Markōs became patriarch of the Nestorian branch of Christianity, centered in modern-day Iran. Yet their voyages exemplified the crisscrossing of people, money, goods, and ideas along the trade routes and sea-lanes that connected the world's regions.

Three related themes dominate the period from 1000 to 1300 CE, at the end of which a monk like Bar Sāwmā could make such a journey. First, trade along sea-based routes increased and coastal trading cities began to expand dramatically. Second, greater trade and religious integration generated the world's four major cultural "spheres," whose inhabitants were linked by shared institutions and beliefs: the Islamic world, India, China, and Europe. Sub-Saharan Africa and the Americas also thrived during this period; however, they remained more fragmented, experiencing more limited political and economic integration. Third, the Mongol Empire, stretching from China to Persia and as far as eastern Europe, ruled over huge swaths of land in many of the world's major cultural spheres. Each of these three themes contributes to an understanding of how Afro-Eurasia became a "world" unified through trade, migration, and even religious conflict.

Global Storyline

The Emergence of the World We Know Today

- Advances in maritime technology lead to increased sea trade, transforming coastal cities into global trading hubs and elevating Afro-Eurasian trade to unprecedented levels.

- Intensified trade and religious integration shape four major cultural "spheres": the Islamic world, India, China, and Europe.

- Sub-Saharan Africa is drawn into Eurasian exchange, resulting in a true Afro-Eurasia–wide network, while the Americas experience more limited political, economic, and cultural integration.

- The Mongol Empire integrates many of the world's major cultural spheres.

Development of Maritime Trade

By the tenth century CE, sea routes were becoming more important than land networks for long-distance trade. Improved navigational aids, better mapmaking, refinements in shipbuilding, and new political support for shipping made seaborne trade easier and slashed its cost. These developments also fostered the growth of maritime commercial hubs (called anchorages), which further facilitated the expansion of maritime trade.

A new navigational instrument spurred this boom: the magnetic needle compass. This Chinese invention initially identified promising locations for houses and tombs, but eleventh-century sailors from Guangzhou (Canton) used it to find their way on the high seas. The use of this device eventually spread among navigators. The compass not only allowed sailing under cloudy skies but also improved mapmaking.

An array of new ship types—dhows, junks, and cogs—allowed for more impressive mastery of the seas. Dhows, ships with triangular sails called lateens, maximized the power of the monsoon trade winds on the Arabian Sea and the wider Indian Ocean. Sailing the South China Sea were junks, large, flat-bottomed ships with internal sealed bulkheads, stern-mounted rudders, as many as four decks, six masts with a dozen sails, and the space to carry as many as 500 men. And, in the Atlantic, cogs, with their single mast and square sail, linked Genoa to

Belitung Dhow This museum display in Singapore cleverly depicts a reconstruction of the Belitung dhow (albeit without the signature triangular sail) rising on a wave of Changsha bowls excavated from the actual wreck on the floor of the Java Sea.

locations as distant as the Azores and Iceland. The numbers testify to the power of the maritime revolution: while a porter could carry about 10 pounds over long distances, and animal-drawn wagons could move 100 pounds of goods over small distances, the Arab dhows could transport up to 5 tons of cargo, Atlantic cogs as much as 200 tons, and Chinese junks more than 500 tons. One particularly fascinating recent archaeological discovery that demonstrates the connectivity brought by these ships is the Belitung dhow. Shipwrecked in the Java Sea off the coast of the Indonesian island of Belitung in the early ninth century CE, this 50-foot ship likely hailed from the southern coast of the Arabian Peninsula (modern-day Oman or Yemen), based on analysis of the wood from which it was constructed. But the sunk ship was filled with more than 60,000 artifacts from Tang dynasty China. The artifacts offer evidence for the kind of direct, long-distance maritime trade between China and the Abbasid world that was bringing the world closer together by 1000 CE.

Although it may seem ironic to assert after invoking a shipwreck as evidence, the business of shipping, on the whole, became less dangerous in the period from 1000 to 1300 CE thanks not only to these innovations in shipbuilding but also to local political support. Maritime traders enjoyed the protection of political authorities such as the Song rulers in China, who maintained a standing navy that protected traders and lighthouses that guided trading fleets in and out of harbors. The Fatimid caliphate in Egypt profited from maritime trade and defended merchant fleets from pirates, using armed convoys of ships to escort commercial fleets and regulate the ocean traffic. This system of protection soon spread to North Africa and southern Spain.

Long-distance trade spawned the growth of commercial cities. These cosmopolitan **entrepôts** served as transshipment centers, located on land between borders or in ports where ships could drop anchor. In these cities, traders exchanged commodities and replenished supplies. Beginning in the late tenth century CE, several regional centers became major anchorages of the maritime trade: in the west, the Egyptian port city of Alexandria on the Mediterranean (and Cairo, just up the Nile); near the tip of the Indian subcontinent, the port of Quilon (now Kollam); in the Malaysian Archipelago, the city of Melaka; and in the east, the Chinese city of Quanzhou. (See Map 10.1.) These hubs thrived under the political stability of powerful rulers who recognized that trade would generate wealth for their regimes.

Cairo and Alexandria were the Mediterranean's main maritime commercial centers. Cairo was home to numerous Muslim and Jewish trading firms, and Alexandria was their lookout post on the Mediterranean. The Islamic legal system prevalent in Egypt promoted a favorable business environment. With the clerics' blessing, Muslim traders formed partnerships between those who had capital to lend and those who needed money to expand their businesses: owners of capital entrusted their money or commodities to agents who, after completing their work, returned the investment and a share of the profits to

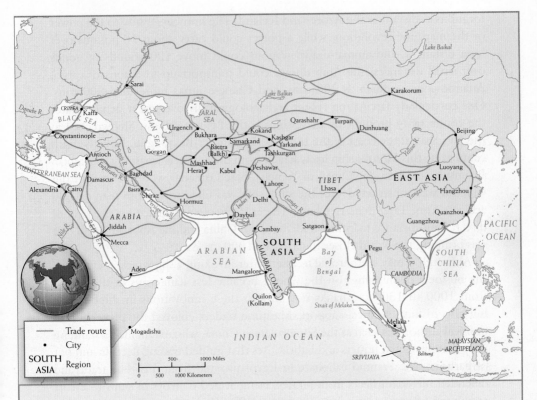

Map 10.1 Afro-Eurasian Trade, 1000–1300 CE

....

During the early second millennium, Afro-Eurasian merchants increasingly turned to the Indian Ocean to transport their goods. Locate the global hubs of Quilon, Alexandria, Cairo, Melaka, and Quanzhou on this map.

- What regions do each of these global hubs represent?
- Based on the map, why would sea travel have been preferable to overland travel?
- According to the text, what revolutions in maritime travel facilitated this development?

the owners—and kept the rest as their reward. The English word *risk* derives from the Arabic *rizq*, the extra allowance paid to merchants in lieu of interest. Through Alexandria, Europeans acquired silks from China, especially the coveted *zaytuni* (satin) fabric from Quanzhou. But many more goods passed through the Egyptian anchorage: from the Mediterranean, olive oil, glassware, flax, corals, and metals; from India, gemstones and aromatic perfumes; and from elsewhere, minerals and chemicals for dyeing or tanning, and raw materials such as timber and bamboo. Paper and books (including hand-copied Bibles, Talmuds, and Qurans) traveled along this network as well.

In South India during the tenth century CE, the Chola dynasty supported the port of Quilon, which was the nerve center of maritime trade between China and the Red Sea and the Mediterranean. Trade through Quilon continued to flourish long after the Chola golden age passed away. Personal relationships were key to trade at this anchorage, as elsewhere; for instance, when striking a deal with a local merchant, a Chinese trader might mention his Indian neighbor in Quanzhou and that family's residence in Quilon. Dhows arrived in Quilon laden not only with goods from the Red Sea and Africa, but also with traders, sojourners, and fugitives. Chinese junks unloaded silks and porcelain, and picked up passengers and commodities for East Asian markets. Muslims, the largest foreign community in Quilon, lived in their own neighborhoods and shipped horses from Arab countries to India and its southeastern islands, where kings viewed them as symbols of royalty. There was even trade through Quilon in elephants and cattle from tropical countries, though the most common goods were spices, perfumes, and textiles.

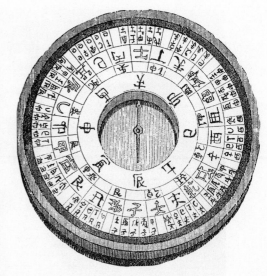

Antique Chinese Compass Chinese sailors from Guangzhou (Canton) started to use magnetic needle compasses in the eleventh century. By the thirteenth century, magnetic needle compasses were widely used on ships in the Indian Ocean and were starting to appear in the Mediterranean.

East of Quilon, across the Bay of Bengal, Melaka became a key cosmopolitan entrepôt because of its strategic location and proximity to Malayan tropical produce. Indian, Javanese, and Chinese merchants and sailors spent months in such ports selling their goods, purchasing return cargo, and waiting for the winds to change direction so they could reach their next destination. During peak season, Southeast Asian ports were crowded with colorfully dressed foreign sailors, local Javanese artisans who produced finely textured batik handicrafts, and traders eager for profit. The traders converged from all over Asia to flood the markets with their merchandise and to search for pungent herbs, aromatic spices, and agrarian staples such as quick-ripening strains of rice to ship out.

In China, the Song government set up offices of seafaring affairs in its three major ports: Quanzhou, Guangzhou (Canton), and a third near present-day Shanghai. In return for a portion of the taxes on the goods passing through these entrepôts, these offices registered cargoes, sailors, and traders, while guards kept a keen eye on the traffic. All foreign traders in Song China were guests of the governor, who doubled as the chief of seafaring affairs. Every year,

Mazu As much as sailors used compasses, they could still appeal for divine help at shrines devoted to Mazu, the goddess of seafarers. While many Mazu temples of varying size dotted the shorelines of the East and South China Seas, the shrine at Guangzhou now includes a 48-foot-tall statue of Mazu gazing out into the harbor. Mazu's origin-story is rooted in the life of a young girl named Lin Mo (living in the late 900s CE) who miraculously saved her family from stormy seas.

the governor conducted a wind-calling ritual. Traders of every origin—Arabs, Persians, Jews, Indians, and Chinese—witnessed the ceremony, then joined together for a sumptuous banquet. Although most foreign merchants did not reside apart from the rest of the city, they did maintain buildings for religious worship according to their faiths. A mosque from this period still stands on a busy street in Quanzhou. Hindu traders living in Quanzhou worshipped in a Buddhist shrine where statues of Hindu deities stood alongside those of Buddhist gods. Each of these bustling ports teemed with a cosmopolitan mix of peoples, goods, and ideas that flowed through growing maritime networks thanks to improved ships and better navigational tools.

The Islamic World in a Time of Political Fragmentation

While the number of Muslim traders began to increase in commercial hubs from the Mediterranean to the South China Sea, it was not until the ninth and tenth centuries CE that Muslims became a majority within their own Abbasid Empire (see Chapter 9), and even then rulers struggled to unite the diverse Islamic world. From the outset, Muslim rulers and clerics dealt with large non-Muslim populations, even as these groups were converting to Islam. Rulers accorded non-Muslims religious toleration as long as the non-Muslims accepted Islam's political dominion. Jewish, Christian, and Zoroastrian communities within Muslim lands were free to choose their own religious leaders and to settle internal disputes in their own religious courts. They did, however, have to pay a special tax, the *jizya*, and defer to their Muslim rulers. While tolerant, Islam was an expansionist, universalizing faith. Intense proselytizing—especially by Sufi missionaries (whose ideas are discussed later in this chapter)—carried the sacred word to new frontiers and, in the process, reinforced the spread of Islamic institutions that supported commercial exchange.

ENVIRONMENTAL CHALLENGES AND POLITICAL DIVISIONS

Severe climate conditions—freezing temperatures and lack of rainfall—afflicted the Eastern Mediterranean and the Islamic lands of Mesopotamia, the Iranian plateau, and the steppe region of central Asia in the late eleventh and early twelfth centuries. The Nile's low water levels devastated Egypt, the breadbasket for much of the area. At least one-quarter of the summer floods that normally brought sediment-enriching deposits to Egypt's soils and guaranteed abundant harvests failed in this period. Driven in part by drought, Turkish nomadic pastoralists poured out of the steppe lands of central Asia in search of better lands, wreaking political and economic havoc everywhere they invaded.

At the same time these climate-driven Turkish pastoralists were migrating and the Islamic faith was increasing its reach across Afro-Eurasia, the political institutions of Islam were fragmenting. (See Map 10.2.) From 950 to 1050 CE, it appeared that Shiism would be the vehicle for uniting the Islamic world. The Fatimid Shiites had established their authority over Egypt and much of North Africa (see Chapter 9), and the Abbasid state in Baghdad was controlled by a Shiite family, the Buyids. Each group created universities, in Cairo and Baghdad respectively, ensuring that leading centers of higher learning were Shiite. But divisions also sapped Shiism, and Sunni Muslims began to challenge Shiite power and establish their own strongholds. In Baghdad, the Shiite Buyid family surrendered to the invading Seljuk Turks, a Sunni group, in 1055. A century later, the last of the Shiite Fatimid rulers gave way to a new Sunni regime in Egypt.

The Seljuk Turks who took Baghdad had been migrating into the Islamic heartland from the Asian steppes as early as the eighth century CE, bringing superior military skills and an intense devotion to Sunni Islam. When they flooded into the Iranian plateau in 1029, they contributed to the end of the magnificent cultural flourishing of the early eleventh century. When Seljuk

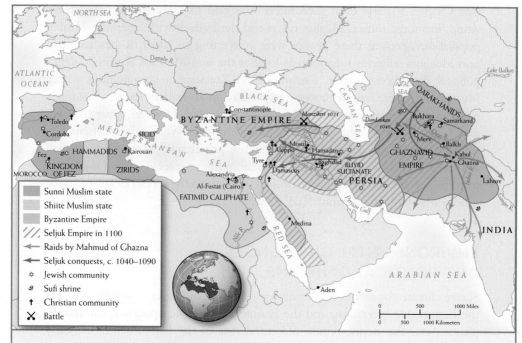

Map 10.2 The Islamic World, 900–1200 CE

The Islamic world experienced political disintegration in the first centuries of the second millennium.

- According to the map key, what were the two major types of Islamic states in this period? What were some of the major political entities?
- What were the sources of instability in this period, according to the map?
- What do you note about the locations of Jewish and Christian communities, as well as Sufi shrines, across the Islamic world?

warriors ultimately took Baghdad in 1055, they established a nomadic state in Mesopotamia in place of the once powerful Abbasid state that now lacked the resources to defend its lands and its peoples, weakened by famines and pestilence. The Seljuk invaders destroyed institutions of learning and public libraries and looted the region's antiquities. Once established in Baghdad, they founded outposts in Syria and Palestine, then moved into Anatolia after defeating Byzantine forces in 1071.

By the thirteenth century the Islamic heartland had fractured into three regions. In the east (central Asia, Iran, and eastern Iraq), the remnants of the old Abbasid state persevered, with a succession of caliphs claiming to speak for all of Islam yet deferring to their Turkish military commanders. In the core of the Islamic world—Egypt, Syria, and the Arabian Peninsula—where Arabic was the primary language, military men of non-Arab origin held the reins of power.

Farther west in North Africa, Arab rulers prevailed, but the influence of Berbers, some from the northern Sahara, was extensive. Islam was a vibrant faith, but its polities were splintered.

THE SPREAD OF SUFISM

Even in the face of this political splintering, Islam's spread was facilitated by a popular, highly mystical, and communal form of the religion, called **Sufism**. The term *Sufi* comes from the Arabic word for wool (*suf*), which many of the early mystics wrapped themselves in to mark their penitence. Seeking closer union with God, Sufis performed ecstatic rituals such as repeating over and over again the name of God. In time, groups of devotees gathered to read aloud the Quran and other religious tracts. Sufi mystics' desire to experience God's love found ready expression in poetry. Most admired of Islam's mystical love poets was Jalal al-Din Rumi (1207–1273), spiritual founder of the Mevlevi Sufi order, which became famous for the ceremonial dancing of its whirling devotees, known as dervishes.

Although many *ulama* (scholars) despised the Sufis and loathed their seeming lack of theological rigor, the movement spread with astonishing speed and offered a unifying force within Islam. Sufism's emotional content and strong social bonds, sustained in Sufi religious orders, or brotherhoods, added to its appeal for many. Sufi missionaries from these brotherhoods carried the universalizing faith to India, to Southeast Asia, across the Sahara Desert, and to many other distant locations. It was through these brotherhoods that Islam became truly a religion for the people. As trade increased and more converts appeared in the Islamic lands, urban and peasant populations came to understand the faith practiced by the political, commercial, and scholarly upper classes even while they remained attached

Dervishes The dance of Sufi mystics was an important means of reaching union with God. This illustration from a fifteenth-century publication of Firdawsi's *Shah Namah* depicts whirling dervishes with one hand stretching toward heaven and the other reaching toward the earth. Their richly colored robes and long streaming hair differ from the white garb and tall hats of modern dervishes.

to their Sufi brotherhood ways. Over time, Islam became even more accommodating, embracing Persian literature, Turkish ruling skills, and Arabic-language contributions in law, religion, literature, and science.

WHAT WAS ISLAM?

Buoyed by Arab dhows on the high seas and carried on the backs of camels following commercial routes, Islam had been transformed from Muhammad's original vision of a religion for Arab peoples (see Chapter 9). By 1300, its influence spanned Afro-Eurasia and reached multitudes of non-Arab converts. While Arabic remained the primary language of religious devotion, Persian became the language of Islamic philosophy and art and Turkish the language of Islamic law and administration. Islam attracted city dwellers and rural peasants alike, as well as its original audience of desert nomads. Muslim scholars formed universities, such as al-Qarawiyyin in Fez, Morocco (859 CE), and al-Azhar in Cairo, Egypt (970 CE). Islam's extraordinary universal appeal generated an intense cultural flowering around 1000 CE.

That cultural blossoming in all fields of high learning was marked by diversity in both language and ideas. Representing the new Persian ethnic pride was Abu al-Qasim Firdawsi (920–1020 CE), a devout Muslim who believed in the importance of pre-Islamic Sasanian traditions. In the epic poem *Shah Namah* (Book of Kings), he celebrated the origins of Persian culture and narrated the history of the Iranian highland peoples from the dawn of time to the Muslim conquest. Indicative of the enduring prominence of the Islamic faith and the Arabic language in thought was the legendary Ibn Rushd (1126–1198), known as Averroës in the western world. Steeped in the writings of Aristotle, Ibn Rushd's belief that faith and reason were compatible even influenced the thinking of the Christian world's leading philosopher and theologian, Thomas Aquinas (1225–1274).

The Islamic world's achievements in science were truly remarkable. Its scholars were at the pinnacle of scientific knowledge throughout the world in this era. Ibn al-Shatir (1304–1375), working on his own in Damascus, produced non-Ptolemaic models of the universe that later researchers noted were mathematically equivalent to those of Copernicus. Even earlier, the Maragha school of astronomers (1259 and later) in western Iran had produced a non-Ptolemaic model of the planets. Some historians of science believe that Copernicus must have seen an Arabic manuscript written by a thirteenth-century Persian astronomer that contained a table of the movements of the planets. In addition, scholars in the Islamic world produced works in medicine, optics, and mathematics as well as astronomy that were in advance of the achievements of Greek and Roman scholars.

During this period, the Islamic world became one of the four cultural spheres that would play a major role in world history, laying the foundation for what would become known as the Middle East up through the middle of the twentieth century. Islam became the majority religion of the inhabitants of Southwest Asia and North Africa, Arabic language use became widespread, and the Turks began to establish themselves as a dominant force, ultimately creating the Ottoman Empire, which would last into the twentieth century. The Islamic world became integral in transregional trade and in the creation and transmission of knowledge.

India as a Cultural Mosaic

With its pivotal location along land- and sea-based trade routes, India became an intersection for the trade, migration, and culture of Afro-Eurasian peoples. With 80 million inhabitants in 1000 CE, it had the second-largest population in the region, not far behind China's 120 million. Turks ultimately spilled into India as they had into the Islamic heartlands, bringing their newfound Islamic beliefs. But the Turkish newcomers encountered an ethnic and religious mix of which they were just one part. (See Map 10.3.)

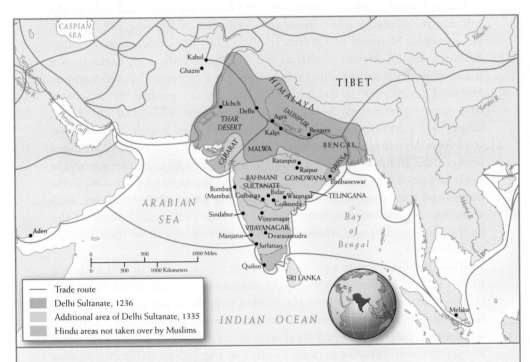

Map 10.3 South Asia in 1300

As the fourteenth century began, India was a blend of many cultures. Politically, the Turkish Muslim regime of the Delhi Sultanate dominated the region.

- What region was controlled by the Delhi Sultanate in 1236? How did the area controlled by the Delhi Sultanate change in just 100 years?
- How does the map suggest that trade routes helped spread the Muslims' influence in India?
- Where on the map do Hindu areas resist Muslim political control? Based on your reading, what factors may have accounted for Hinduism's continued appeal despite the Muslims' political power?

SHIFTING POLITICAL STRUCTURES

Before the Turks arrived, India was splintered among rival chiefs called *rajas*. These leaders gained support from Brahmans by doling out land grants to them. Since much of the land was uncultivated, the Brahmans first built temples, then converted the indigenous hunting and gathering peoples to the Hindu traditions, and finally taught the converts how to cultivate the land. In this way, Brahmans simultaneously spread their faith and expanded the agrarian tax base for themselves and the *rajas*. They also repaid the *rajas'* support by compiling elaborate genealogies for them, endowing them with lengthy and legitimizing ancestries. In return, the *rajas* demonstrated that they, too, were well versed in Sanskrit culture, including equestrian skills and courtly etiquette, and were prepared to patronize artists and poets.

When Turkish warlords began entering India, the *rajas* had neither the will nor resources to resist them after centuries of fighting off invaders. For example, Mahmud of Ghazna (r. 998–1030 CE) launched many expeditions from the Afghan heartland into northern India and, eager to win status within Islam, made his capital, Ghazna, a center of Islamic learning. Mahmud's expansion in the early eleventh century marked the height of what came to be known as the Ghaznavid Empire (977–1186 CE). Later, in the 1180s, Muhammad Ghuri led another wave of Islamic Turkish invasions from Afghanistan across the Delhi region in northern India. Wars raged between the Indus and Ganges Rivers until, one by one, all the way to the lower Ganges Valley, the fractured kingdoms of the *rajas* toppled. The Turks introduced their own customs while accepting local social structures, such as the hierarchical *varna* system. The Turks constructed grand mosques and built impressive libraries where scholars could toil and share their wisdom with the court.

While the Ghaznavids were impressive, the most powerful and enduring of the Turkish Muslim regimes of northern India was the **Delhi Sultanate** (1206–1526), whose rulers brought political integration but also strengthened the cultural diversity and tolerance that were already a hallmark of the Indian social order. Sultans recruited local artisans for numerous building projects, and palaces and mosques became displays of the Indian architectural tastes adopted by Turkish newcomers. But Islam never fully dominated South Asia because the sultans did not force their subjects to convert. Nor did they display much interest in the flourishing commercial life along the Indian coast. The sultans permitted these areas to develop on their own: Persian Zoroastrian traders settled on the coast around modern-day Mumbai, while farther south, Arab traders controlled the Malabar coast. The Delhi Sultanate was a rich and powerful regime that brought political integration but did not enforce cultural homogeneity.

WHAT WAS INDIA?

During the eleventh, twelfth, and thirteenth centuries, India became the most diverse and, in some respects, the most tolerant region in Afro-Eurasia. India in this era arose as an impressive but fragile mosaic of cultures, religions, and ethnicities. When the Turks arrived, the local Hindu population, having had much experience with foreign invaders and immigrants, assimilated these intruders as they had done earlier peoples. Before long, the newcomers thought of themselves as Indians who, however, retained their Islamic beliefs and steppe ways. They continued to wear their distinctive trousers and robes and flaunted their horse-riding skills. At the same time, the local population embraced some of their conquerors' ways, donning the tunics and trousers that characterized central Asian peoples.

Diversity and cultural mixing became most visible in the multiple languages that flourished in India. Although the sultans spoke Turkish languages, they regarded Persian literature as a high cultural achievement and made Persian their courtly and administrative language. Meanwhile, most of their Hindu subjects spoke local languages, adhered to the regulations of the *varna* system of hierarchies, and practiced diverse forms of Hindu worship. The rulers in India did

Hindu Temple When Buddhism started to decline in India, Hinduism was on the rise. Numerous Hindu temples were built, many of them adorned with ornate carvings like this small tenth-century CE temple in Bhubaneshwar in East India.

what Muslim rulers in Southwest Asia and the Mediterranean did with Christian and Jewish communities living in their midst: they collected the *jizya* tax and permitted communities to worship as they saw fit and to administer their own communal law. Ultimately, Islam proved in India that it did not have to be an intolerant conquering religion to prosper.

Although Buddhism had been in decline in India for centuries, it, too, became part of the cultural intermixing of this period. As Vedic Brahmanism evolved into Hinduism (see Chapter 8), it absorbed many Buddhist doctrines and practices, such as nonviolence (*ahimsa*) and vegetarianism. The two religions became so similar in India that Hindus simply considered the Buddha to be one of their deities—an incarnation of the great god Vishnu. Many Buddhist moral teachings mixed with and became Hindu stories. Artistic motifs reflected a similar process of adoption and adaptation. Goddesses, some beautiful and others fierce, appeared alongside Buddhas, Vishnus, and Shivas as their consorts. The Turkish invaders' destruction of major monasteries in the thirteenth century deprived Buddhism of local spiritual leaders. Lacking dynastic support, Buddhists in India were more easily assimilated into the Hindu population or converted to Islam.

Once the initial disruptive effects of the Turkish invasions were absorbed, India remained a highly diverse and tolerant region during this period. Most important, India also emerged as one of the four major cultural spheres, enjoying a tremendous level of integration as Turkish-Muslim rulers and their traditions and practices were successfully intermixed with the native Hindu society, leading to a more integrated and peaceful India.

Song China: Insiders versus Outsiders

The preeminent world power in 1000 CE was still China, despite its recent turmoil. In 907 CE the Tang dynasty splintered into regional kingdoms, mostly led by military generals. In 960 CE one of these generals, Zhao Kuangyin, ended the fragmentation, reunified China, and assumed the mandate of heaven for the Song dynasty (960–1279 CE). The following three centuries witnessed many economic and political successes, but northern nomadic tribes kept the Song dynasty from completely securing its reign. (See Map 10.4 and Map 10.5.) Ultimately, one of those nomadic groups, the Mongols, would bring the Song dynasty to an end, but not before Song influence had fanned out into Southeast Asia, helping to create new identities in the polities that developed there.

ECONOMIC AND POLITICAL DEVELOPMENTS

Chinese merchants, like those from India and the Islamic world, participated in Afro-Eurasia's powerful long-distance trade. Yet China's commercial successes could not have occurred without the country's strong agrarian base—especially

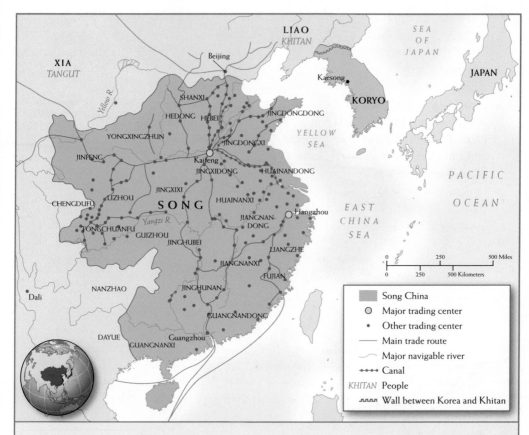

Map 10.4 East Asia in 1000 CE

Several states emerged in East Asia between 1000 and 1300 CE, but none were as strong as the Song dynasty in China. Using the key to the map, try to identify the factors that contributed to the Song state's economic dynamism.

- What do you note about the location of the major trading centers?
- What do you note about the distribution of the other trading centers?
- According to the map, what external factors kept the Song dynasty from completely securing its reign?

its vast wheat, millet, and rice fields, which fed a population that reached 120 million. Crop cultivation benefited from breakthroughs in metalworking that produced stronger iron plows, which Song farmers harnessed to sturdy water buffalo to extend the agricultural frontier.

Manufacturing also flourished. With the use of piston-driven bellows to force air into furnaces, Song iron production in the eleventh century equaled that of Europe in the early eighteenth century. In the early tenth century CE, Chinese alchemists mixed saltpeter with sulfur and charcoal to produce a product that

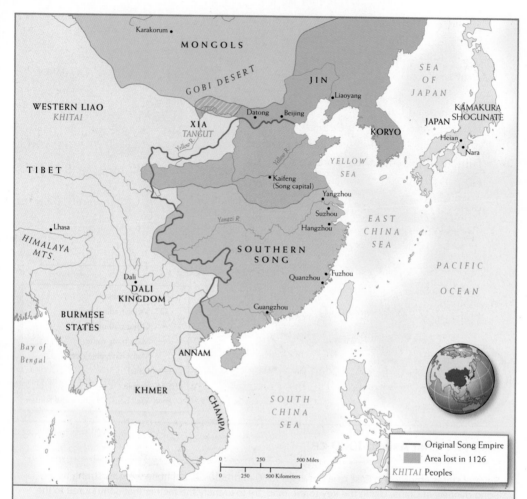

Map 10.5 East Asia in 1200

The Song dynasty regularly dealt with "barbarian" neighbors with a balance of military response and outright bribery.

- What were the major "barbarian" tribes on the borders of Song China during this period?
- Approximately what percentage of Song China was lost to the Jin in 1126?
- Apart from so-called barbarians, what other polities existed on the borders of Song China?

would burn and could be deployed on the battlefield: gunpowder. Song entrepreneurs were soon inventing a remarkable array of incendiary devices that flowed from their mastery of techniques for controlling explosions and high heat. At the same time, artisans were producing increasingly light, durable, and exquisitely beautiful porcelains. Before long, their porcelain was the envy of all Afro-Eurasia (hence the modern term *china* for fine dishes). Also flowing from the artisans' skillful hands were vast amounts of clothing and handicrafts, made from the fibers grown by Song farmers. In effect, the Song Chinese oversaw the world's first manufacturing revolution, producing finished goods on a large scale for consumption far and wide.

Expanding commerce transformed the role of money and its wide circulation. By now the Song government was annually minting nearly 2 million strings of currency, each containing 1,000 copper coins. As the economy grew, the supply of metal currency could not match the demand, which fueled East Asia's desire for gold from East Africa. At the same time, merchant guilds in northwestern Shanxi developed the first letters of exchange, or paper money, which they called **flying cash**. These letters linked northern traders with their colleagues in the south. Before long, printed money became more common than minted coins

Flying Cash Among the many innovations fueling the economic boom of the Song dynasty was paper money, called flying cash. Produced with woodblock printing technology that was relatively new at the time, the images printed on this example include, from top to bottom, coins, an inscription, and laborers at a warehouse. The inscription describes how much the bill was worth and in what regions it could be used as payment.

for trading purposes. Eventually, the Song dynasty began to issue more notes to pay its bills—a practice that ultimately contributed to runaway inflation.

Song emperors built on Tang political institutions by expanding a central bureaucracy of scholar-officials chosen even more extensively through competitive civil service examinations. Zhao Kuangyin, or Emperor Taizu (r. 960–976 CE), himself administered the final test for all who had passed the highest-level palace examination. In subsequent dynasties, the emperor was the nation's premier examiner, symbolically demanding oaths of allegiance from successful candidates. By 1100 these ranks of learned men had accumulated sufficient power to become China's new ruling elite. This expansion of the civil service examination system was crucial to a shift in power from the still significant hereditary aristocracy to a less wealthy but more highly schooled class of scholar-officials.

CHINA'S NEIGHBORS: NOMADS, JAPAN, AND SOUTHEAST ASIA

China's prosperity influenced its neighbors and its interactions with them. As Song China flourished, nomads on the outskirts eyed the Chinese successes closely. To the north, nomadic societies formed their own dynasties and adopted Chinese institutions. These non-Chinese nomads sought both to conquer and to copy China proper. Despite its sophisticated weapons, the Song army could not match its enemies on the steppe when the nomads united against it. Steel tips improved the arrows that Song soldiers shot from their crossbows, and flamethrowers and "crouching tiger" catapults sent incendiary bombs streaking into their enemies' ranks. But none of these breakthroughs was secret. Warrior neighbors on the steppe mastered the new arts of war more fully than did the Song military. Consequently, China drew on its economic success (and the innovation of paper money) to "buy off" the borderlanders. This short-term

Angkor Wat Mistaken by later European explorers for a remnant of Alexander the Great's conquests, the enormous temple complexes built by the Khmer people in Angkor borrowed their intricate layout and stupa (a moundlike structure containing religious relics) architecture from the Brahmanic Indian temples of the time. As their capital, Angkor was a microcosm of the world for the Khmer, who aspired to represent the macrocosm of the universe in the magnificence of Angkor's buildings and their geometric layout.

solution, however, led to economic instability (particularly inflation) and military weakness, especially as the Song forces were cut off, via the steppe nomads, from their supply of horses for warfare purposes.

Feeling the pull of China's economic and political gravity, cultures around China consolidated their own internal political authority and defined their own identities in order to keep from being swallowed up by China. At the same time, they increased their commercial transactions with China. In Japan, for instance, leaders distanced themselves from Chinese

Chinese and Barbarian After losing the north, the Chinese grew resentful of outsiders. They drew a dividing line between their own agrarian society and the nomadic warriors, calling them "barbarians." Such identities were not fixed, however. Chinese and so-called barbarians were mutually dependent.

influences, but they also developed a strong sense of their islands' distinctive identity. Even so, the long-standing dominance of Chinese ways remained apparent at virtually every level of Japanese society, and was most pronounced at the imperial court in the capital city of Heian (present-day Kyoto), which was modeled after the Chinese capital city of Chang'an. Outside Kyoto, however, a less China-centered way of life existed and began to impose itself on the center. Here, local notables, mainly military leaders and large landowners, began to challenge the imperial court for dominance. This challenge was accompanied by the arrival of an important new social group in Japanese society—samurai warriors. By the beginning of the fourteenth century, Japan had multiple sources of political and cultural power: an imperial family with prestige but little authority; an endangered and declining aristocracy; powerful landowning notables based in the provinces; and a rising and increasingly ambitious class of samurai.

During the Song period, Southeast Asia became a crossroads of Afro-Eurasian influences. The Malay Peninsula became home to many entrepôts for traders shuttling between India and China, because it connected the Bay of Bengal and the Indian Ocean with the South China Sea. (See Map 10.6.) Consequently, Southeast Asia was characterized by a fusion of religions and cultural influences: Vedic Brahmanism in Bali and other islands, Islam in Java and Sumatra, and Mahayana Buddhism in Vietnam and other parts of mainland Southeast Asia. Important Vedic and Buddhist kingdoms emerged in Southeast Asia. The most powerful and wealthy of these kingdoms was the Khmer Empire (889–1431 CE), with its capital at Angkor, in present-day Cambodia. Public works and magnificent temples dedicated to the revived

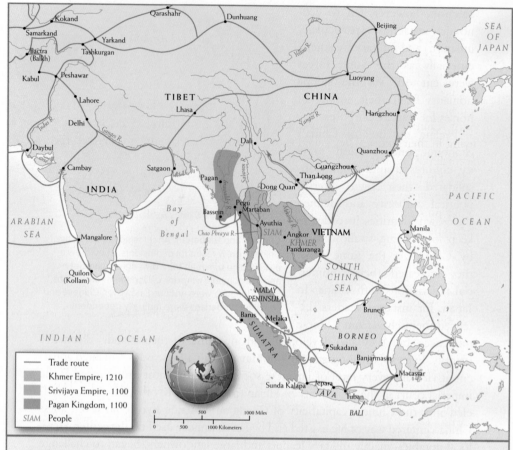

Map 10.6 Southeast Asia, 1000–1300 CE

Cross-cultural influences affected Southeast Asian societies during this period.

- What geographic features (rivers, mountains, islands, straits, etc.) shape Southeast Asia?
- What makes Southeast Asia unique geographically compared to other regions of the world?
- Based on the map, why were the kingdoms of Southeast Asia exposed to so many cross-cultural influences?

Vedic gods from India went hand in hand with the earlier influence of Indian Buddhism. One of the greatest temple complexes in Angkor—Angkor Wat— exemplified the Khmers' heavy borrowing from Vedic Indian architecture and the revival of the Hindu pantheon within the Khmer royal state. Kingdoms like the Khmer Empire functioned as political buffers between the strong states of China and India and brought stability and further commercial prosperity to the region.

WHAT WAS CHINA?

Paradoxically, the increasing exchange between outsiders and insiders within China hardened the lines that divided them and gave residents of China's interior a highly developed sense of themselves as a distinct people possessing a superior culture. Exchanges with outsiders nurtured a "Chinese" identity among those who considered themselves true insiders and referred to themselves as "Han." Song Chinese grew increasingly suspicious and resentful toward the outsiders living in their midst. They called these outsiders "barbarians" and treated them accordingly.

Print culture crystallized the distinct Chinese identity. Of all Afro-Eurasian societies in 1300, the Chinese were the most advanced in their use of printing, book publishing, and circulation, in part due to the invention of a movable type printing press by the artisan Bi Sheng around 1040. Song dynasty printed books established classical Chinese as the common language of educated classes in East Asia. The Song government used its plentiful supply of paper to print books, especially medical texts, and to distribute calendars. The private publishing industry expanded, and printing houses throughout the country produced Confucian classics, works on history, philosophical treatises, and literature—all of which figured in the civil service examinations. Buddhist publications, too, were available everywhere.

China's huge population base, coupled with a strong agrarian base and manufacturing innovations, made it the wealthiest of the four major cultural spheres, and its common language and Confucian civil service system, which enabled a transfer of power from hereditary aristocrats to Confucian scholars, made it the most unified. China's influence on the surrounding region was tremendous.

Christian Europe

Europe, from 1000 to 1300 CE, was a region of strong contrasts. Intensely localized power was balanced by a shared sense of Europe's place in the world, especially with respect to Christian identity. Some inhabitants even began to believe in the existence of something called "Europe" and increasingly referred to themselves as "Europeans" (see Map 10.7), especially in contrast to the world of Islam to the east and south.

LOCALIZATION OF POWER

The collapse of Charlemagne's empire had exposed much of northern Europe to invasion, principally from the Vikings, and left the peasantry there with no central authority to protect them from local warlords. Armed with deadly weapons, these strongmen collected taxes, imposed forced labor, and became the unchallenged rulers of society. Peasants toiled under the authority of these

Map 10.7 Western Christendom in 1300

....

Catholic Europe expanded geographically and integrated culturally during this era.

- According to this map, into what areas did western Christendom successfully expand?
- What were the different means by which western Christianity expanded?
- Which are the earliest universities on the map? What might account for the flourishing of universities where they were located?

landholding lords, who controlled every detail of their subjects' lives. The Franks (in northern France) were the trendsetters for this development in eleventh- and twelfth-century Europe.

The peasantry's subjugation to this knightly class was at the heart of a system scholars have called feudalism (emphasizing the power of the local lords over the peasantry), but a more accurate term for the system is **manorialism**, which emphasizes instead the manor's role as the basic unit of economic power. The manor comprised the lord's fortified home (or castle), the surrounding fields controlled by the lord but worked by peasants (as free tenants or as serfs tied to the land), and the village in which those peasants lived. Although manorialism was driven by agriculture, limited manufacturing and trade augmented the manor economy. This system harnessed agrarian energy and helped western Europe shed its identity as a somewhat "barbarian" appendage of the Mediterranean.

Between 1100 and 1200, as many as 200,000 pioneering peasants emigrated from present-day Belgium, Holland, and northern Germany to the frontiers of Europe (now Poland, the Czech Republic, Hungary, and the Baltic states). Despite its harsh climate and landscape, the area offered the promise of freedom from feudal lords' arbitrary justice and the imposition of forced labor that the peasants had experienced in western Europe. In a fragile balance between the native elites and liberty-seeking newcomers, castles and villages echoing the landscape of manorial France now replaced local economies that had been based on gathering honey, hunting, and the slave trade. For a thousand miles along the Baltic Sea, forest clearings dotted with new farmsteads and small towns edged inward from the coast up the river valleys.

Russian lands modeled themselves after Byzantium, not Rome or western Europe. Set in a giant borderland between the steppes of Inner Eurasia and the booming centers of Europe, Russia's cities lay at the crossroads of overland trade and migration. These cities were not agrarian centers, but hubs of expanding long-distance trade. Kiev became one of the region's greatest urban centers, a small-scale Constantinople with its own miniature Hagia Sophia (see Chapter 8). Russian Christians looked not to the Roman Catholic faith associated with the

The Bayeux Tapestry This tapestry was allegedly prepared by Queen Matilda, wife of William the Conqueror, and her ladies to celebrate the successful invasion of England in 1066. These embroidering women captured the intense brutality of the invasion not only in the central narrative thread showing spears flying, long shields studded with arrows, and cavalry galloping in on great horses, but also in the margins where chain mail is being ripped off corpses.

popes in Rome, but rather to Byzantium's Hagia Sophia and the Orthodoxy of the east as the source of religious authority. Russian Christianity remained that of a borderland—vivid oases of high culture set against the backdrop of vast forests and widely scattered settlements. Like the agricultural manors of western Europe, these Russian cities demonstrate the highly localized nature of power in Europe in this period.

WHAT WAS CHRISTIAN EUROPE?

Christianity in this era—primarily the Roman Catholicism of the west, but also the Orthodoxy of the east—became a universalizing faith that transformed the region becoming known as "Europe." The Christianity of post-Roman Europe had been a religion of monks, and its most dynamic centers were great monasteries. Members of the laity were expected to revere and support their monks, nuns, and clergy, but not to imitate them. By 1200, all this had changed. The internal colonization of western Europe—the clearing of woods and founding of villages—ensured that parish churches arose in all but the wildest landscapes. Now the clergy reached more deeply into the private lives of the laity. Marriage and divorce, previously considered family matters, became the domain of the church.

New understandings of religious devotion and innovative institutions for learning developed in the west. For instance, the followers of Francis of Assisi (1182–1226) emerged as an order of preachers who brought a message of repentance. Franciscans encouraged the laity—from the poorest to the elite—to feel remorse for their wrongdoings, to confess their sins to local priests, and to strive to be better Christians. At nearly the same time, intellectuals were beginning to gather in Paris to

Crusader Kneeling, this Crusader promises to serve God (as he would serve a feudal lord) by going to fight on a Crusade (as he would fight for any lord to whom he had sworn loyalty). The two kinds of loyalty—to God and to one's lord—were deliberately intertwined in promoting the Crusades. Both were about war. But fighting for God was unambiguously good, while fighting for a lord was not always so clear-cut.

form one of the first European universities, a sort of trade guild of scholars. These professional thinkers endeavored to prove that Christianity was the only religion that fully addressed the concerns of all rational human beings. Such was the message of Thomas Aquinas, who wrote *Summa contra Gentiles* (Summary of Christian Belief against Non-Christians) in 1264. The growing number of churches, new religious orders, and universities began to change what it meant to live in a "Christian Europe."

RELATIONS WITH THE ISLAMIC WORLD

In the late eleventh century, western Europeans launched the Crusades, a wave of attacks against the Muslim world. The First Crusade began in 1095, when Pope Urban II appealed to the warrior nobility of France to put their violence to good use: they should combine their role as pilgrims to Jerusalem with that of soldiers in order to free the Christian "holy land" from Muslim rule. Such a just war, the clergy proposed, was a means for absolution, not a source of sin.

Starting in 1097, an armed host of around 60,000 men set out from north-western Europe to seize Jerusalem. The crusading forces included knights in heavy armor as well as people drawn from Europe's impoverished masses, who joined the movement to help besiege cities and construct a network of castles as the Christian knights drove their frontier forward. The fleets of Venice, Genoa, and Pisa helped transport later Crusaders and supplied the kingdoms they created as they moved eastward. Later Crusaders, especially those from the upper class, brought their wives, who found a degree of autonomy away from their homeland. Eleanor of Aquitaine, for example, led her own army. Melisende (r. 1131–1152), born Armenian royalty in the Crusader state of Edessa, ruled as queen of Jerusalem after her father's death, despite occasional attempts by her husband and later her son to challenge her authority. Regarded as wise and experienced in affairs of the state, she was popular with local Christians. As a result, the society of the Crusader states remained more open to women and the lower classes than in Europe. There are even accounts of a children's crusade (1212), inspired by the visions of a boy. Over time, the Crusades drew together a range of peoples from varied walks of life in common purpose.

No fewer than nine Crusades were fought over the two centuries that followed Urban II's call; but none of the coalitions, in the end, created lasting Christian kingdoms in the lands the Crusaders "reconquered." Most knights returned home, their epic pilgrimages completed. The remaining fragile network of Crusader lordships barely threatened the Islamic heartland. The real prosperity and the capital cities of Muslim kingdoms lay inland, away from the coast—at Cairo, Damascus, and Baghdad. The assaults' long-term effect was to harden Muslim feelings against the Franks and the millions of nonwestern Christians who had previously lived peacefully in Egypt and Syria.

Even so, a range of sources offer Muslim and Christian perspectives that show tolerance of, and curiosity about, each other. For example, Usāmah

Ibn Munqidh (1095–1188), a learned Syrian leader, describes his shock at the Frankish Crusaders' backward medical practices and the freedom they offered their wives, in addition to well-meaning exchanges such as a particular Frank's confusion about the direction in which Muslims pray. Similarly, Jean de Joinville (1224–1317), a French chronicler of Louis X of France who led the Seventh Crusade, marveled at the order within the sultan's camp and the role of musicians in calling the Muslim forces to hear the sultan's orders.

Other campaigns of Christian expansion, like the Iberian efforts to drive out the Muslims, were more successful. Beginning with the capture of Toledo in 1061, the Christian kings of northern Spain slowly pushed back the Muslims. Eventually they reached the heart of Andalusia in southern Iberia and conquered Seville, adding more than 100,000 square miles of territory to Christian Europe. Another force, from northern France, crossed Italy to conquer Muslim-held Sicily, ensuring Christian rule in that strategically located mid-Mediterranean island. Unlike the Crusaders' fragile foothold at the edge of the Middle East, these two conquests were a turning point in relations between Christian and Muslim power in the Mediterranean. Christianity—and in particular the rise of the Roman Catholic Church, the spread of universities, and the fight against the Muslims in their native and spiritual homelands—was a force that helped create a cultural sphere known as Europe, whose peoples would become known as European, at the western end of the Afro-Eurasian landmass during this period.

Worlds Coming Together: Sub-Saharan Africa and the Americas

From 1000 to 1300 CE, sub-Saharan Africa and the Americas became far more internally integrated—culturally, economically, and politically—than before. Islam's spread and the growing trade in gold, enslaved people, and other commodities brought sub-Saharan Africa more fully into the exchange networks of the Eastern Hemisphere, but the Americas remained isolated from Afro-Eurasian networks for several more centuries.

SUB-SAHARAN AFRICA COMES TOGETHER

During this period, sub-Saharan Africa's relationship to the rest of the world changed dramatically. While sub-Saharan Africa had never been a world entirely apart before 1000 CE, its integration with Eurasia now became much stronger. Increasingly, its hinterlands found themselves touched by the commercial and migratory impulses emanating from the Indian Ocean and Arabian Sea transformations. (See Map 10.8.)

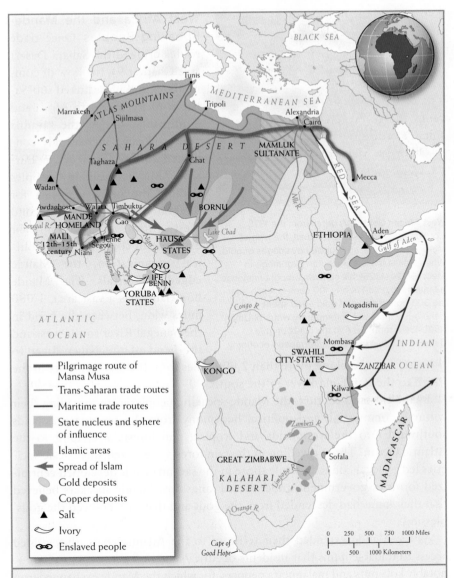

Map 10.8 Sub-Saharan Africa, 1300

Increased commercial contacts influenced the religious and political dimensions of sub-Saharan Africa at this time. Compare this map with Map 9.3.

- Where had strong Islamic communities emerged by 1300? By what routes might Islam have spread to those areas?

- According to this map, what types of activity were taking place in sub-Saharan West Africa?

- What goods were traded in sub-Saharan Africa, and along what routes did those exchanges take place?

West Africa and the Mande-Speaking Peoples Once trade routes bridged the Sahara Desert (see Chapter 9), the flow of commodities and ideas linked sub-Saharan Africa to North Africa and Southwest Asia. As the savanna region became increasingly connected to developments in Eurasia, Mande-speaking peoples became the primary agents for integration within and beyond West Africa. Exploiting their expertise in commerce and political organization, the Mande edged out rivals. The Mande homeland was a vast area, 1,000 miles wide, between the bend in the Senegal River to the west and the bend of the Niger River to the east, and stretching more than 2,000 miles from the Senegal River in the north to the Bandama River in the south.

West African Gold This detail from the 1375 *Catalan Atlas* shows Mansa Musa, the king of Mali, on his throne, surrounded by images of gold. When Mansa Musa traveled on pilgrimage to Mecca (1324–1325), his caravan brought immense quantities of gold—nearly 100 camels, each bearing 300-pound sacks of gold—and spent it so generously that the contemporary writer al-Umari (1301–1349) reported that the influx of gold deflated its value in the Mediterranean economy.

By the eleventh century, the Mande-speaking peoples were spreading their cultural, commercial, and political hegemony from the savanna grasslands southward into the woodlands and tropical rain forests stretching to the Atlantic Ocean. Those dwelling in the rain forests organized small-scale societies led by local councils, while those in the savanna lands developed centralized forms of government under sacred kingships. Mande speakers believed that their kings had descended from the gods and that they enjoyed the gods' blessing.

As the Mande extended their territory to the Atlantic coast, they gained access to tradable items that residents of Africa's interior were eager to have—notably kola nuts and malaguetta peppers, for which the Mande exchanged iron products and manufactured textiles. Mande-speaking peoples, with their far-flung commercial networks and highly dispersed populations, dominated trans-Saharan trade in salt from the northern Sahel, gold from the Mande homeland, and enslaved people. By 1300, Mande-speaking merchants had followed the Senegal River to its outlet on the Atlantic coast and then pushed their commercial frontiers farther inland and down the coast. Thus, even before European explorers and traders arrived in the mid-fifteenth century, West African peoples had created dynamic networks linking the hinterlands with coastal trading hubs.

The Mali Empire In the early thirteenth century, the **Mali Empire** became the Mande successor state to the kingdom of Ghana (see Chapter 9). The origins of the Mali Empire and its legendary founder are enshrined in *The Epic of Sundiata*. Sundiata's triumph, which occurred in the first half of the thirteenth century, marked the victory of new cavalry forces over traditional foot soldiers. Horses now became prestige objects for the savanna peoples, symbols of state power.

Under the Mali Empire, commerce was in full swing. With Mande trade routes extending to the Atlantic Ocean and spanning the Sahara Desert, West Africa was no longer an isolated periphery of the central Muslim lands. Mansa Musa (r. 1312–1332), perhaps Mali's most famous sovereign, made a celebrated *hajj*, or pilgrimage to Mecca, in 1324–1325. He traveled through Cairo and impressed crowds with the size of his retinue—including soldiers, wives, consorts, and as many as 12,000 enslaved people—and his displays of wealth, especially many dazzling items made of gold. Mansa Musa's lengthy three-month stopover in Cairo, one of Islam's primary cities, astonished the Egyptian elite and awakened much of the world to the fact that Islam had spread far below the Sahara and that a sub-Saharan state could mount such an impressive display of power and wealth.

The Mali Empire boasted two of West Africa's largest cities. Jenne, an entrepôt dating back to 200 BCE, was a vital assembly point for caravans laden with salt, gold,

and enslaved people preparing for journeys west to the Atlantic coast and north over the Sahara. More spectacular was the city of Timbuktu; founded around 1100 as a seasonal camp for nomads, it grew in size and importance under the patronage of various Mali kings. By the fourteenth century, it was a thriving commercial, intellectual, and religious center famed for its three large mosques, which are still standing.

Great Zimbabwe Massive stone walls, at points as high as 36 feet, surrounded the "Great Enclosure" that makes up part of the ruins of Great Zimbabwe. The city, covering almost 3 square miles, was a center of the gold trade between the East African coastal peoples and traders sailing on the Indian Ocean. Great Zimbabwe flourished during the thirteenth, fourteenth, and fifteenth centuries.

Trade between East Africa and the Indian Ocean Africa's eastern and southern regions were also integrated into long-distance trading systems. Because of the monsoon winds, East Africa was a logical end point for much of the Indian Ocean trade. Swahili peoples living along that coast became brokers for trade from the Arabian Peninsula, the Persian Gulf territories, and the western coast of India. Merchants in the city of Kilwa on the coast of present-day Tanzania brought ivory, gold, enslaved people, and other items from the interior and shipped them to destinations around the Indian Ocean.`

Enslaved, Bought, and Sold Enslaved men and women were a common commodity in the marketplaces of the Islamic world. Turkish conquests during the years from 1000 to 1300 CE put many prisoners on the slave market.

Shona-speaking peoples grew rich by mining the gold ore in the highlands between the Limpopo and Zambezi Rivers. By 1000 CE, the Shona had founded up to fifty small religious and political centers, each one erected from stone to display its power over the peasant villages surrounding it. Around 1100, one of these centers, Great Zimbabwe, stood supreme among the Shona. Built on the fortunes made from gold, its most impressive landmark was a massive elliptical building made of stones fitted so expertly that they needed no grouting.

Enslaved African people were as valuable as African gold in shipments to Indian Ocean as well as Mediterranean markets. After Islam spread into Africa and sailing techniques improved, the slave trade across the Sahara Desert and Indian Ocean boomed. Although the Quran mitigated the severity of slavery by requiring Muslim enslavers to treat their workers kindly and praising those who freed the enslaved, the African slave trade flourished under Islam. Africans became enslaved either by being taken as prisoners of war or by being sold into slavery as punishment for committing a crime. Enslaved people might work as soldiers, seafarers on dhows, domestic servants, or plantation workers. Conditions for plantation laborers on the agricultural estates of lower Iraq were so oppressive that they led, in the ninth century CE, to one of the most significant slave wars documented in world history (the Zanj rebellion). Yet in this era, plantation slave labor, like that which later became prominent in the Americas in the nineteenth century, was the exception, not the rule.

THE AMERICAS

During this period, the Americas were untouched by the connections reverberating across Afro-Eurasia. Apart from limited Viking contacts in North America (see Chapter 9), navigators still did not cross the large oceans that separated the Americas from other lands. Yet, here, too, commercial and expansionist impulses fostered closer contact among peoples who lived there.

Andean States of South America Growth and prosperity in the Andean region gave rise to South America's first empire. The **Chimú Empire** developed early in the second millennium in the fertile Moche Valley bordering the Pacific Ocean. (See Map 10.9.) Ultimately, the Moche people expanded their influence across numerous valleys and ecological zones, from pastoral highlands to rich valley floodplains to the fecund fishing grounds of the Pacific coast. As their geographic reach grew, so did their wealth.

The Chimú economy was successful because it was highly commercialized. Agriculture was its base, and complex irrigation systems turned the arid coast into a string of fertile oases capable of feeding an increasingly dispersed population. Cotton became a lucrative export to distant markets along the Andes. Parades of llamas and porters lugged these commodities up and down the steep mountain chains that form the spine of South America. A well-trained bureaucracy oversaw the construction and maintenance of canals, and a hierarchy of provincial administrators watched over commercial hinterlands.

Chan Chan The image shows some of the remains of Chan Chan. The city covered 15 square miles and was divided into neighborhoods for nobles, artisans, and commoners, with the elites living closest to the hub of governmental and spiritual power.

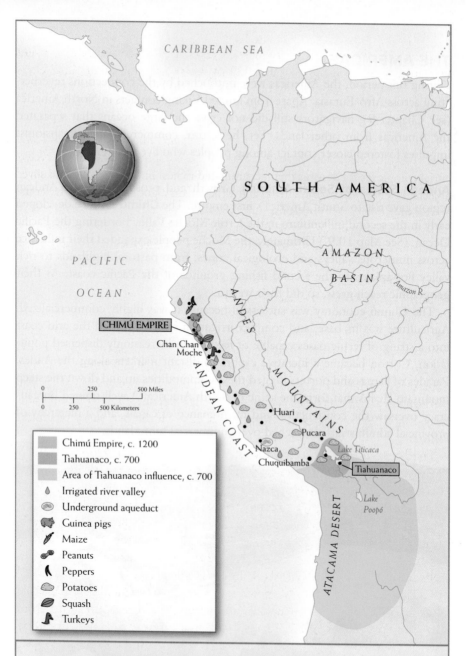

CARIBBEAN SEA

SOUTH AMERICA

PACIFIC

OCEAN

AMAZON

BASIN

Amazon R.

ANDES

CHIMÚ EMPIRE

Chan Chan
Moche

ANDEAN COAST

MOUNTAINS

| 0 | 250 | 500 Miles |
| 0 | 250 | 500 Kilometers |

Huari

Pucara

Nazca

Lake Titicaca

Chuquibamba

Tiahuanaco

Chimú Empire, c. 1200

Tiahuanaco, c. 700

Area of Tiahuanaco influence, c. 700

Irrigated river valley

Underground aqueduct

Guinea pigs

Maize

Peanuts

Peppers

Potatoes

Squash

Turkeys

Lake
Poopó

ATACAMA DESERT

Map 10.9 Andean States, c. 700–1400 CE

Although the Andes region of South America was isolated from Afro-Eurasian developments before 1500, it was not stagnant. Indeed, political and cultural integration brought the peoples of this region closer together.

- Where are the areas of Chimú Empire and Tiahuanaco influence on the map?
- What was the ecology and geography of each region, and how might that have shaped each region's development?
- What crops and animals did the Chimú and Tiahuanaco benefit from?

The Chimú Empire's biggest city was Chan Chan, which had been growing ever larger since its founding around 900 CE. By the time the Chimú Empire was thriving, Chan Chan held a core population of 30,000 inhabitants. A sprawling walled metropolis covering nearly 10 square miles, with extensive roads circulating through its neighborhoods, Chan Chan boasted ten huge palaces at its center. Protected by thick walls 30 feet high, these opulent residence halls symbolized the rulers' power. Within the compound, emperors erected burial complexes for storing their accumulated riches: fine cloth, gold and silver objects, splendid *Spondylus* shells, and other luxury goods. Around the compound spread neighborhoods for nobles and artisans; farther out stood rows of commoners' houses. The Chimú regime, centered at Chan Chan, lasted until Inca armies invaded in the 1460s and incorporated the Pacific state into their own immense empire.

Toltecs in Mesoamerica Additional hubs of regional trade developed farther north. By 1000 CE, Mesoamerica had seen the rise and fall of several complex societies, including Teotihuacán and the Maya (see Chapter 8). Caravans of porters bound the region together, working the intricate roads that connected the coast of the Gulf of Mexico to the Pacific and the southern lowlands of Central America to the arid regions of modern Texas. (See Map 10.10.) The **Toltecs** filled the political vacuum left by the decline of Teotihuacán and tapped into the commercial network radiating from the rich valley of central Mexico.

The Toltecs grew to dominate the valley of Mexico between 900 and 1100 CE. They were a combination of migrant groups, farmers from the north and refugees from the south fleeing the strife that followed Teotihuacán's demise. These migrants settled northwest of Teotihuacán as the city waned, making their capital at Tula. They relied on a maize-based economy supplemented by beans, squash, and dog, deer, and rabbit meat. Their rulers made sure that enterprising merchants provided them with status goods such as ornamental pottery, rare shells and stones, and precious skins and feathers.

Tula was a commercial hub, a political capital, and a ceremonial center. While its layout differed from Teotihuacán's, many features revealed borrowings from other Mesoamerican peoples. Temples consisted of giant pyramids topped by colossal stone soldiers, and ball courts where subjects and conquered peoples alike played their ritual sport were found everywhere. The architecture and monumental art reflected the mixed and migratory origins of the Toltecs in a combination of Maya and Teotihuacáno influences. At its height, the Toltec capital teemed with 60,000 people, a huge metropolis by contemporary European standards (if small by Song Chinese and Abbasid standards).

Cahokians in North America As in South America and Mesoamerica, cities took shape at the hubs of trading networks across North America. The largest was

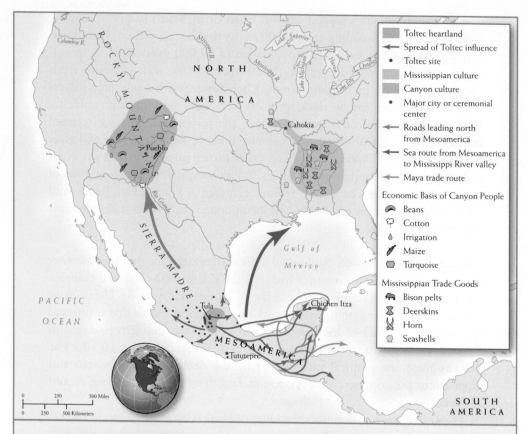

Map 10.10 Commercial Hubs in Mesoamerica and North America, 1000 CE

Both Cahokia and Tula were commercial hubs of vibrant regional trade networks.
- What routes linked Tula and the Toltecs with other regions?
- What goods circulated in the regions of Pueblo and Cahokia?
- Based on the map, what appear to be some of the differences between Canyon culture, Mississippian culture, and the Toltecs?

Cahokia, along the Mississippi River near modern-day East St. Louis, Illinois. A city of about 15,000, it approximated the size of London at the time. Farmers and hunters had settled in the region around 600 CE, attracted by its rich soil, its woodlands that provided fuel and game, and its access to trade via the Mississippi. Eventually, fields of maize and other crops fanned out toward the horizon. The hoe replaced the trusty digging stick, and satellite towns erected granaries to hold the growing harvests.

By 1000 CE, Cahokia was an established commercial center for regional and long-distance trade. The hinterlands produced staples for Cahokia's urban consumers, and in return its crafts rode inland on the backs of porters and to distant markets in canoes. Woven fabrics and ceramics from Cahokia were exchanged for mica from the Appalachian Mountains, seashells and sharks' teeth from the Gulf of Mexico, and copper from the upper Great Lakes. Cahokia became more than an importer and exporter: it was the exchange hub for an entire regional network trading in salt, tools, pottery, woven stuffs, jewelry, and ceremonial goods.

Toltec Temple Tula, the capital of the Toltec Empire, carried on the Mesoamerican tradition of locating ceremonial architecture at the center of the city. The Pyramid of the Morning Star cast its shadow over all other buildings. And above them stood columns of the Atlantes, carved Toltec god-warriors, the figurative pillars of the empire itself. The walls of this pyramid were likely embellished with images of snakes and skulls. The north face of the pyramid has the image of a snake devouring a human.

Dominating Cahokia's urban landscape were enormous earthen mounds of sand and clay (thus the Cahokians' nickname of "mound people"). It was from these artificial hills that the people honored spiritual forces. Building these types of structures without draft animals, hydraulic tools, or even wheels was labor-intensive, so the Cahokians recruited neighboring people to help. A palisade around the city protected the metropolis from marauders.

Ultimately, Cahokia's success bred its downfall. As woodlands fell to the axe and the soil lost its nutrients, timber and food became scarce. In contrast to the sturdy dhows of the Arabian Sea and the bulky junks of the China seas, Cahokia's river canoes could carry only limited cargoes. Cahokia's commercial networks met their limits. When the creeks that fed its water system could not keep up with demand, engineers changed their course, but to no avail. By 1350 the city was practically empty. But Cahokia represented the growing networks of trade and migration in North America and the ability of North Americans to organize vibrant commercial societies.

Two forces contributed to greater integration in sub-Saharan Africa and the Americas from 1000 to 1300 CE: commercial exchange (of salt, gold, ivory, and enslaved people in sub-Saharan Africa and shells, pottery, textiles, and metals in the Americas) and urbanization (at Jenne, Timbuktu, and Great Zimbabwe in sub-Saharan Africa and at Chan Chan, Tula, and Cahokia in the Americas). By 1300, trans-Saharan and Indian Ocean exchange had brought Africa into full-fledged Afro-Eurasian networks of exchange and, as we will see in Chapter 12, transatlantic exchange would soon bring the Americas into a global network.

The Mongol Transformation of Afro-Eurasia

Commercial networks were clearly one way to integrate the world. But just as long-distance trade could connect people, so could conquerors. The Inner Eurasian steppes had already unleashed horse-riding warriors such as the Kushans and Xiongnu (see Chapters 6 and 7). Now, the Mongols created an empire that straddled east and west, expanding their reach not only through brutal conquest but also through intensified trade and cultural exchange. (See Map 10.11.)

WHO WERE THE MONGOLS?

The Mongols were a combination of forest and steppe peoples. Residing in circular, felt-covered tents, which they shared with some of their animals, they lived by hunting and livestock herding. They changed campgrounds with the seasons. Life on the steppes was such a constant struggle that only the strong survived. Their food, primarily animal products, provided high levels of protein, which built up their muscle mass and their strength. Always on the march, their society resembled a perpetual standing army with bands of well-disciplined military units led by commanders chosen for their skill.

Wielding heavy compound bows made of sinew, wood, and horn, Mongol archers were deadly accurate at over 200 yards—even at full gallop. Their small but sturdy horses, capable of withstanding extreme cold, bore saddles with high supports in front and back, enabling the warriors to maneuver at high speeds. With their feet secure in iron stirrups, the archers could rise in their saddles to aim their arrows without stopping. These expert horsemen often remained in the saddle all day and night, even sleeping while their horses continued on. Each warrior kept many horses, replacing tired mounts with fresh ones so that the armies could cover up to 70 miles per day.

Mongol tribes solidified their conquests by extending kinship networks, building an empire out of an expanding confederation of familial tribes. The tents, or households, were interrelated mostly by marriage: they were alliances sealed by the exchange of daughters. Conquering men married conquered women, and conquered men were selected to marry the conquerors' women. Chinggis Khan (the founder of the Mongol dynasty) may have had more than 500 wives, most of them daughters of tribes that he conquered or that allied with him.

Elite women could play important political roles. Chinggis Khan's mother, Hoelun, and his first wife, Börte, were instrumental in his rise to power, but even before playing the role of khan maker, women had figured large in Mongol tribal politics. In the generation after Chinggis, Sorghaghtani Beki, a Nestorian Christian and the mother of Kublai Khan (the first official Mongol ruler of China), helped engineer her sons' rule. Illiterate herself, she made sure that each son acquired a second language to aid in administering conquered lands. Despite her own Christian faith, Sorghaghtani gathered Confucian scholars to prepare Kublai Khan to rule China. Chabi, Kublai's senior wife, offered patronage to Tibetan monks who set about converting the Mongol elite in China to Tibetan Buddhism. While some elite Mongol women played a role in fostering religious diversity, others took part in battles. Khutulun, a niece of Kublai Khan, became famous for besting men in wrestling matches and claiming their horses as spoils.

Yet the political influence wielded by these later *khātūns* (Mongol queens) and other elite women of the Mongol ruling class is only one part of the story. Women in Mongol society were responsible for bearing and rearing children, shearing and milking livestock, and processing animal pelts for clothing. They organized camp logistics in times of peace and war. Although women were often bought and sold, Mongol wives had the right to own property and to divorce. More recent studies of Mongol women have emphasized the economic influence they wielded as they acquired this wealth and property of their own. Central to making sense of Mongol women is recognizing that theirs was a changing story. Mongol family dynamics and gender roles changed due not only to the dramatic and relatively swift transformation of the Mongols from a pastoral steppe society to a settled empire, but also to the regional differences in ideas about women's roles in the varied regions into which the Mongols spread.

CONQUEST AND EMPIRE

The Mongols' need for grazing lands contributed to their desire to conquer distant fertile belts and rich cities. The Mongols depended on settled peoples for grain and manufactured goods, including iron for tools, wagons, weapons, bridles, and stirrups. Their first expansionist forays followed caravan routes.

The Mongol expansion began in 1206 under a united cluster of tribes. These tribes were unified by a gathering of clan heads who chose one of those present, Temüjin (c. 1162–1227), as khan, or supreme ruler. Taking the name Chinggis (Genghis) Khan, he launched a series of conquests southward across the Great Wall of China and westward to Afghanistan and Persia. The Mongols even invaded Korea in 1231. The armies of Chinggis's sons reached both the Pacific Ocean and the Adriatic Sea. Chinggis's grandsons founded dynasties in Persia, in China, and on the southern Eurasian steppes. Thus, a realm took shape that touched all four of Afro-Eurasia's cultural spheres.

Mongols in Abbasid Baghdad In the thirteenth century, Mongol tribes were streaming out of the steppes, crossing the whole of Asia and entering the eastern parts of Europe. Mongke Khan, a grandson of Chinggis, made clear the Mongol aspiration to world domination: he commanded his brother, Hulagu, to conquer

Map labels:
BALTIC SEA
POLAND
Moscow
RUSSIAN PRINCIPALITIES
KHANATE OF THE GOLDEN HO
Liegnitz 1240
Kiev
UKRAINE
Buda Pest
New Sarai
Old Sarai
Lake Bal
URAL MOUNTAINS
ARAL SEA
BLACK SEA
CAUCASUS MTS.
CASPIAN SEA
Constantinople
BYZANTINE EMPIRE
Tabriz
Aleppo
Samarkand
KHANATE C
Balkh
HINDU KUSH MTS.
MEDITERRANEAN SEA
Damascus
1258
Herat
HIM
Jerusalem
Baghdad
IL-KHANATE
RED SEA
ARABIA
SUL
OF

Map 10.11 Mongol Conquests and Campaigns, 1200–1300

Mongol campaigns and conquests brought Afro-Eurasian worlds together as never before. Trace the outline of the entire area of Mongol influence shaded on this map.

- What regions and cultural groups did the Mongol armies conquer, partially conquer, or invade? Which did the Mongols not invade?
- How many different khanates did the Mongols establish across Eurasia, and what were they? In what ways do these khanates essentially rewrite the political map of Eurasia?
- What role did geography play in shaping the spread of their influence?

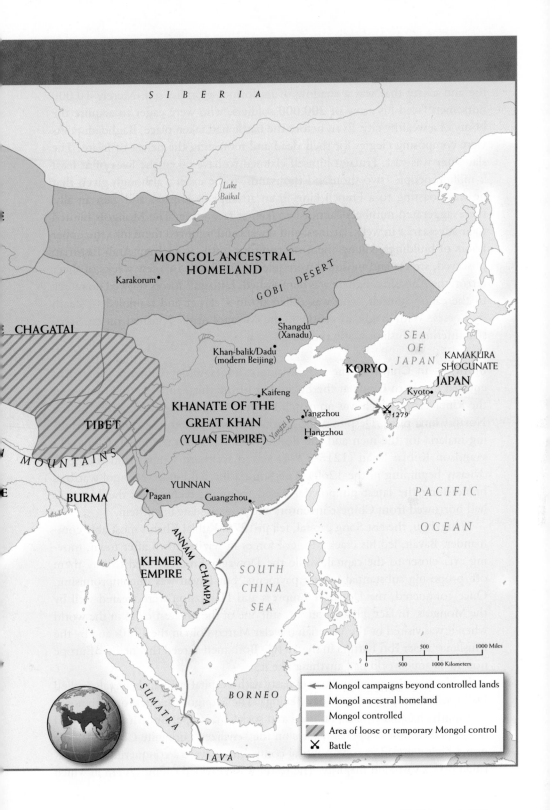

SIBERIA

Lake Baikal

MONGOL ANCESTRAL HOMELAND

Karakorum

GOBI DESERT

CHAGATAI

Shangdu (Xanadu)

Khan-balik/Dadu (modern Beijing)

SEA OF JAPAN

KAMAKURA SHOGUNATE

KORYO

JAPAN

Kyoto

Kaifeng

KHANATE OF THE GREAT KHAN (YUAN EMPIRE)

TIBET

Yangzhou

1279

Yangzi R.

Hangzhou

MOUNTAINS

YUNNAN

PACIFIC

Pagan

Guangzhou

BURMA

OCEAN

KHMER EMPIRE

ANNAM

CHAMPA

SOUTH CHINA SEA

BORNEO

SUMATRA

JAVA

	0	500	1000 Miles
0	500	1000 Kilometers	

→ Mongol campaigns beyond controlled lands

Mongol ancestral homeland

Mongol controlled

Area of loose or temporary Mongol control

✕ Battle

Iran, Syria, Egypt, Byzantium, and Armenia, and he appointed another brother, Kublai, to rule over China, Tibet, and the northern parts of India.

When Hulagu reached Abbasid Baghdad in 1258, he encountered a feeble foe and a city that was a shadow of its former glorious self. Merely 10,000 horsemen faced his army of 200,000 soldiers, who were eager to acquire the booty of a wealthy city. Even before the battle had taken place, Baghdadi poets were composing elegies for their dead and mourning the defeat of Islam. The slaughter was vast. Hulagu himself claimed to have taken the lives of at least 2 million people (two thousand thousands, to be exact), although given that he was boasting to a French king in an attempt to impress and gain an ally, the exaggerated numbers cannot be taken at face value. The Mongols hunted their adversaries in wells, latrines, and sewers and followed them into the upper floors of buildings, killing them on rooftops until, as an Iraqi Arab historian observed, streets and mosques were filled with blood. In a few weeks of sheer terror, the Abbasid caliphate was demolished. Hulagu's forces showed no mercy to the caliph himself, who was rolled up in a carpet and trampled to death by horses. With Baghdad crushed, the Mongol armies pushed on to Syria, slaughtering Muslims along the way.

Mongols in China In the east, Mongol forces under Chinggis Khan had entered northern China at the beginning of the thirteenth century, defeating the Khitai army, which was no match for the Mongols' superior cavalry on the North China plain. Despite some serious setbacks due to the climate (including malaria for the men and the deaths of horses from the heat), Chinggis's grandson Kublai Khan (1215–1294) seized southern China from the Song dynasty beginning in the 1260s. The Song army fell before Mongol warriors brandishing the latest gunpowder-based weapons, technology the Mongols had borrowed from Chinese inventors and now used against them.

Hangzhou, the last Song capital, fell in 1276. Kublai Khan's most able commander, Bayan, led his crack Mongol forces in seizing town after town, moving ever closer to the capital, while the Dowager Empress tried to buy them off, proposing substantial tribute payments, but Bayan was uncompromising. Once conquered, the Dowager Empress and Hangzhou were treated well by the Mongols. In fact, Hangzhou was still one of the greatest cities in the world when it was visited by the Venetian traveler Marco Polo in the 1280s and by the Muslim traveler Ibn Battuta in the 1340s. Both men agreed that neither Europe nor the Islamic world had anything like it.

Kublai Khan founded his Yuan dynasty with a capital at Khan-balik (also called Dadu, which became present-day Beijing). The Mongol conquest of both north and south changed China's political and social landscape. But Mongol rule did not impose rough steppe-land ways on the "civilized" urbanite Chinese. While non-Chinese outsiders took political control, they were a conquering elite that ruled over a vast Han majority. The result was a divided ruling system in which

Mongol Warriors This miniature painting is one of the illustrations for *History* by Rashid al-Din, the most outstanding scholar under the Mongol regimes. Note the relatively small horses and strong bows used by the Mongol soldiers.

incumbent Chinese elites governed locally, while the newcomers managed the unifying central dynasty and collected taxes for the Mongols.

Southeast Asia also felt the whiplash of Kublai Khan's conquest. Circling Song defenses in southern China, the Mongols galloped southwest and conquered states in Yunnan and in Burma. From there, in the 1270s, the armies headed directly back east into the soft underbelly of the Song state. In this sweep, portions of mainland Southeast Asia became annexed to China for the first time. Kublai Khan used the conquered Chinese fleets to push his expansionism onto the high seas—meeting with failure during his unsuccessful 1274 and 1281 invasions of Japan from Korea. An ill-fated Javanese expedition to extend Mongol reach beyond the South China Sea in 1293 was Kublai Khan's last.

In the end, the Mongol Empire reached its outer limits. In the west, the Egyptian Mamluks stemmed the advancing Mongol armies and prevented Egypt from falling into their hands. In the east, the waters of the South China Sea and the Sea of Japan foiled Mongol expansion into Java and Japan. Better at conquering than governing, the Mongols struggled to rule their vast possessions in makeshift states. Bit by bit, they yielded control to local administrators and rulers who governed as their surrogates. There was also frequent feuding among the Mongol rulers themselves. In China and in Persia, Mongol rule collapsed in the fourteenth century. Ultimately, the Mongols would meet a deadly adversary even more brutal than they were: the plague of the fourteenth century (see Chapter 11).

Mongol conquest reshaped Afro-Eurasia's social landscape. Islam would never again have a unifying authority like the caliphate or a powerful center like Baghdad. China, too, was divided and changed by the Mongols' introduction of Persian, Islamic, and Byzantine influences into China's architecture, art, science, and medicine. The Yuan policy of benign tolerance brought elements from Christianity, Judaism, Zoroastrianism, and Islam into the Chinese mix. The Mongol thrust also facilitated the flow of fine goods, traders, and technology from China to the rest of the world. Finally, the Mongol conquests encouraged an unprecedented Afro-Eurasian interconnectedness, surpassing even the Hellenistic connections that Alexander's conquests had brought in the late fourth century BCE (see Chapter 6). Out of Mongol conquest and warfare would come centuries of trade, migration, and increasing contacts among Africa, Europe, and Asia.

Conclusion

Between 1000 and 1300 CE, Afro-Eurasia was forming large cultural spheres. As trade and migration spanned longer distances, these spheres prospered and became more integrated. In central Afro-Eurasia, Islam was firmly established, its merchants, scholars, and travelers acting as commercial and cultural intermediaries as they spread their universalizing faith. As seaborne trade expanded, India, too, became a commercial crossroads. Merchants in its port cities welcomed traders arriving from Arab lands to the west, from China, and from Southeast Asia. China also boomed, pouring its manufactures into trading networks that reached throughout Eurasia and even into Africa. Christian Europe had two centers—at Rome and at Constantinople—both of which were at war with Islam.

Neither sub-Saharan Africa nor the Americas saw the same degree of integration, but trade and migration in these areas had profound effects. Certain African cultures flourished as they encountered the commercial energy of trade on the Indian Ocean. Africans' trade with one another linked coastal and interior regions in an ever more integrated world. American peoples also built cities that dominated cultural areas and thrived through trade. American cultures shared significant features: reliance on trade, maize, and the exchange of goods such as shells and precious feathers. And larger areas honored the same spiritual centers.

By 1300, trade, migration, and conflict were connecting Afro-Eurasian worlds in unprecedented ways. When Mongol armies swept into China, into Southeast Asia, and into the heart of Islam, they applied a thin coating of political integration to these widespread regions and built on existing trade links. At the same time, most people's lives remained quite localized, driven by the need for subsistence and governed by spiritual and governmental representatives acting at the behest of distant authorities.

Still, locals noticed the evidence of cross-cultural exchanges everywhere—in the clothing styles of provincial elites, such as Chinese silks in Paris or quetzal plumes in northern Mexico; in enticements to move (and forced removals) to new frontiers; in the news of faraway conquests or advancing armies. Worlds were coming together within themselves and across territorial boundaries, while remaining apart as they sought to maintain their own identities and traditions. In Afro-Eurasia especially, as the movement of goods and peoples shifted from ancient land routes to sea-lanes, these contacts were more frequent and far-reaching. Never before had the world seen so much activity connecting its parts, nor had there ever been so much cultural similarity within those parts. By the time the Mongol Empire arose, the regions composing the globe were those that we now recognize as the cultural spheres of today's world.

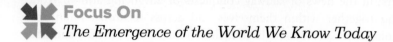

Focus On
The Emergence of the World We Know Today

The Islamic World

- The Islamic world undergoes a burst of expansion, prosperity, and cultural diversification but remains politically fractured.

- Arab merchants and Sufi mystics spread Islam over great distances and make it more appealing to other cultures, helping to transform Islam into a distinct cultural sphere.

- Islam travels across the Sahara Desert; the powerful gold- and enslaved people-supplying empire of Mali arises in West Africa.

China

- The Song dynasty reunites China after three centuries of fragmented rulership, reaching into the past to reestablish a sense of a "true" Chinese identity as the Han through a widespread print culture and denigration of outsiders.

- Agrarian success and advances in manufacturing—including the production of both iron and porcelain—fuel an expanding economy, complete with paper money.

India

- India remains a mosaic under the canopy of Hinduism despite cultural interconnections and increasing prosperity.

- The invasion of Turkish Muslims leads to the Delhi Sultanate, which rules over India for three centuries, strengthening cultural diversity and tolerance.

Christian Europe

- Roman Catholicism becomes a "mass" faith and helps create a common European cultural identity.

- Feudalism organizes the relationship between elites and peasants, while manorialism forms the basis of the economy.

- Europe's growing confidence is manifest in its efforts, including the Crusades and the reconquering of Iberia, to drive Islam out of "Christian" lands.

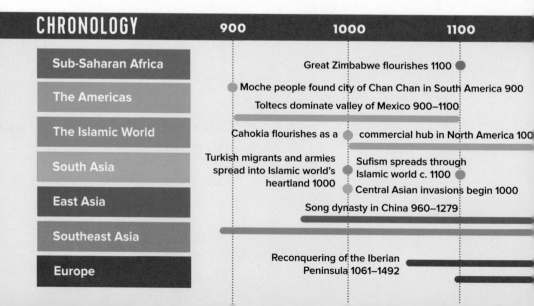

CHRONOLOGY

	900	1000	1100
Sub-Saharan Africa			Great Zimbabwe flourishes 1100
The Americas	Moche people found city of Chan Chan in South America 900 Toltecs dominate valley of Mexico 900–1100		
The Islamic World	Cahokia flourishes as a	commercial hub in North America 100	
South Asia	Turkish migrants and armies spread into Islamic world's heartland 1000	Sufism spreads through Islamic world c. 1100 Central Asian invasions begin 1000	
East Asia		Song dynasty in China 960–1279	
Southeast Asia			
Europe		Reconquering of the Iberian Peninsula 1061–1492	

THINKING ABOUT GLOBAL CONNECTIONS

- **Thinking about Worlds Together, Worlds Apart** From 1000 to 1300 CE, a range of social and political developments contributed to the consolidation of four cultural spheres that still exist today: Europe, the Islamic world, India, and China. In what ways did these spheres interact with one another? In what ways was each sphere genuinely distinct from the others? To what extent were sub-Saharan Africa and the Americas folded into these spheres and with what result?

- **Thinking about Transformation & Conflict and Becoming the World** As the four cultural spheres of Afro-Eurasia consolidated, shocking examples of conflict between them began to take place. Whether from Pope Urban II's call in 1095 to reclaim the "holy land" from Muslims or the Mongol Hulagu's brutal sack of Baghdad

in 1258, this period was marked by large-scale warfare between rival cultural spheres. To what extent was such conflict inevitable? In what ways did conflict transform the groups involved?

- **Thinking about Crossing Borders and Becoming the World** Major innovations facilitated economic exchange in the Indian Ocean and in Song China. The magnetic needle compass, better ships, and improved maps shrank the Indian Ocean to the benefit of traders. Similarly, paper money in Song China changed the nature of commerce. How did these developments shift the axis of Afro-Eurasian exchange? What evidence suggests that bodies of water and the routes across them became more significant than overland exchange routes in binding together Afro-Eurasia? What might be the longer-term implications of these developments?

Key Terms

Cahokia p. 392
Chimú Empire p. 389
Delhi Sultanate p. 370

entrepôts p. 361
flying cash p. 375
jizya p. 365

Mali Empire p. 387
manorialism p. 380

Sufism p. 367
Toltecs p. 391

 Go to **INQUIZITIVE** to see what you've learned—and learn what you've missed—with personalized feedback along the way.

	1200	1300	1400

Kingdom of Mali emerges 1230–1670

King Mansa Musa 1312–1332

Chimú Empire in South America 1000–1470

Mongol forces sack Baghdad and end Abbasid caliphate 1258

Delhi Sultanate 1206–1526

Mongol Yuan dynasty 1279–1368

Khmer Empire 889–1431

Crusades 1095–1291

11

Crises and Recovery in Afro-Eurasia

1300–1500

Core Objectives

- **DESCRIBE** the nature and origins of the crises spanning Afro-Eurasia during the fourteenth century.

- **ASSESS** the impact of the Black Death on China, the Islamic world, and Europe.

- **COMPARE** the ways in which regional rulers in post-plague Afro-Eurasia attempted to construct unified states, and **ANALYZE** the extent and nature of their successes.

- **EXPLAIN** the role that religious belief systems played in rebuilding the Islamic world, Europe, and Ming China in the fourteenth and fifteenth centuries.

- **EXAMINE** the way art and architecture reflected the political realities of the Islamic world, Europe, and Ming China after the Black Death.

- **COMPARE** how Ottoman, Iberian, and Ming rulers extended their territories and regional influence.

When Mongol armies besieged the Genoese trading outpost of Caffa on the Black Sea in 1346, they not only damaged trading links between East Asia and the Mediterranean but also unleashed a devastating disease: the bubonic plague. Defeated Genoese merchants and soldiers withdrew, unknowingly taking the germs with them aboard their ships. By the time they arrived in Messina, Sicily, half the passengers were dead. The rest were dying. People waiting on shore for the ships' cargoes were horrified at the sight and turned the ships away. Desperately, the captains went to the next port, only to face the same fate. Despite these efforts at isolation, Europeans could not keep the plague (later called the Black Death) from reaching their shores. As it spread from port to port, it eventually contaminated all of Europe, killing nearly two-thirds of the population.

This story illustrates the magnitude and complexity of the Mongol invasions. They devastated polities, ravaged trade routes, and unwittingly unleashed the bubonic plague. The invasions left behind a series of khanates ruled by local warlords, rather than a centralized state. But Mongol invasions also intensified cultural and political contacts. The channels of exchange—the land trails and sea-lanes of human voyagers—became accidental conduits for deadly microbes. Indeed, these germs devastated societies far more decisively than did Mongol warfare. They were the real "murderous hordes" of world history. So staggering was the Black Death's toll that population densities did not recover for 200 years. Most severely affected were regions that the Mongols had brought together: settlements and commercial hubs along the old Silk Roads and around the Mediterranean and South China Seas. While segments of the Indian Ocean trading world experienced death and disruption, South Asian societies, which had escaped the Mongol conquest, also escaped the great loss of life and political disruptions associated with the Black Death.

Out of the rubble of Mongol conquest and disease emerged the green shoots of a new world. This chapter explores the ways in which Afro-Eurasian peoples restored what they thought was valuable from old traditions after these crises, while discarding what they thought had failed them in favor of radically new institutions and ideas. Much of the recovery had striking similarities across Afro-Eurasia, as societies reaffirmed their most deeply held and long-standing beliefs. Chinese rulers looked to Confucian thought and well-known dynastic institutions to provide guidance going forward. In the Muslim heartland, a small band of Turkish-speaking warriors—the Ottomans—channeled the energies of a revived Islam to expand their own territory and the Muslim world. Europeans also invoked their traditions. In the Iberian Peninsula, political elites used a resurgent Catholicism to spread their political power and drive Muslim communities out of Europe. Europeans also created new dynastic monarchies and looked to their distant past in Greek and Roman culture for inspiration.

Collapse and Consolidation

Although the Mongol invasions overturned political systems, the plague devastated society itself. The pandemic killed millions, disrupted economies, and threw communities into chaos. Rulers could explain to their people the assaults of "barbarians," but it was much harder to make sense of an invisible enemy. Nonetheless, in response to the upheaval, new ruling groups moved to reorganize their states. By making strategic marriages and building powerful armies, these rulers enlarged their territories, formed alliances, and built dynasties.

SPREAD OF THE BLACK DEATH

The spread of the Black Death was the fourteenth century's most significant historical development. (See Map 11.1.) Originating in Inner Asia, the disease afflicted peoples from China to Europe and killed 25 to 65 percent of infected populations.

How did the **Black Death** move so far and so fast? One explanation may lie in climate changes. The cooler climate of this period—scholars refer to a "Little Ice Age"—may have weakened populations and left them vulnerable to disease. In Europe, for instance, beginning around 1310, harsh winters and rainy summers shortened growing seasons and ruined harvests. Exhausted soils no longer supplied the resources required by growing urban and rural populations, while nobles squeezed the peasantry in an effort to maintain their luxurious lifestyle. The ensuing famine lasted from 1315 to 1322, during which time millions of Europeans died of starvation or of diseases against which the malnourished population had little resistance. Climate change and famine crippled populations on the eve of the Black Death. Climate change also spread drought across central Asia, where bubonic plague had lurked for centuries. So when steppe peoples migrated in search of new pastures and herds, they carried the germs with them and into contact with more densely populated agricultural communities. Rats also joined the exodus from the arid lands and transmitted fleas to other rodents, which then skipped to humans.

The resulting epidemic was terrifying, for its causes were unknown at the time. Infected victims died quickly—sometimes overnight—and in agony, coughing up blood and oozing pus and blood from black sores the size of eggs.

But it was the trading network that spread the germs across Afro-Eurasia into famine-struck western Europe. This wider Afro-Eurasian population was vulnerable because its members had no immunity to the disease. The first outbreak in a heavily populated region occurred in the 1320s in southwestern China. From there, the disease spread through China and then continued its death march along the major trade routes westward. Many of these routes terminated at the Italian port cities, where ships with dead and dying people aboard arrived in 1347. From there, what Europeans called the Pestilence or the Great Mortality engulfed the western end of the landmass. Societies in China, the Muslim world, and Europe suffered the disastrous effects of the Black Death.

Plague in China China was ripe for the plague pandemic. Its population had increased under the Song dynasty (960–1279) and subsequent Mongol rule. But by 1300, hunger and scarcity spread as resources were stretched thin. The weakened population was especially vulnerable. For seventy years, the Black Death ravaged China, reduced the size of the already small Mongol population, and shattered the Mongols' claim to a mandate from heaven. In 1331, plague may have killed 90 percent of the population in Bei Zhili (modern Hebei) Province. From there it spread throughout other provinces, reaching Fujian and the coast at Shandong. By the 1350s, most of China's large cities had suffered severe outbreaks.

Even as the Black Death was engulfing China, bandit groups and dissident religious sects were undercutting the power of the last Mongol Yuan rulers.

Popular religious movements warned of impending doom. Most prominent was the Red Turban movement, which blended China's diverse cultural and religious traditions, including Buddhism, Daoism, and other faiths. Its leaders emphasized strict dietary restrictions, penance, and ceremonial rituals and made proclamations that the world was drawing to an end.

Plague in the Islamic World

The plague devastated parts of the Muslim world as well. The Black Death reached Baghdad by 1347. By the next year, the plague overtook Egypt, Syria, and Cyprus, causing as many as 1,000 deaths a day according to a Tunisian report. Animals, too, were afflicted. One Egyptian writer commented: "The country

Plague Victim The plague was highly contagious and quickly led to death. Here a physician and his helper cover their noses to avoid the unbearable stench emanating from the patient.

was not far from being ruined. . . . One found in the desert the bodies of savage animals with the bubos under their arms. It was the same with horses, camels, asses, and all the beasts in general, including birds, even the ostriches." In the eastern Mediterranean, plague left much of the Islamic world in a state of near political and economic collapse. The great Arab historian Ibn Khaldûn (1332–1406), who lost his mother and father and a number of his teachers to the Black Death in Tunis, underscored the desolation. "Cities and buildings were laid waste, roads and way signs were obliterated, settlements and mansions became empty, dynasties and tribes grew weak," he wrote. "The entire world changed."

Plague in Europe In Europe, the Black Death made landfall on the Italian Peninsula; then it seized France, the Netherlands, Belgium, Luxembourg, Germany, and England in its deathly grip. Overcrowded and unsanitary cities were particularly vulnerable. All levels of society—the poor, craftspeople, aristocrats—were at risk, although flight to the countryside offered some protection from infection. Nearly 50 million of Europe's 80 million people perished between 1347 and 1351. After 1353, the epidemic waned, but the plague returned every seven years or so for the rest of the century and sporadically through the fifteenth century. Consequently, the European population continued to decline, until by 1450 many areas had only one-quarter the number of a century earlier.

In the face of the Black Death, some Europeans turned to debauchery, determined to enjoy themselves before they died. Others, especially in urban settings in Flanders, the Netherlands, and parts of Germany, claimed to find God's grace outside what they saw as a corrupt Catholic Church. Semimonastic orders like the Beghards and Beguines, which had begun in the century or so before the plague, expanded in its wake. These laypeople (unordained men and women) argued that people should trust their own "interior instinct" more than the Gospel as then preached. By contrast, the Flagellants were so convinced that man had incurred God's wrath that they whipped themselves to atone for human sin.

For many who survived the plague, disappointment with the clergy smoldered. Famished peasants resented priests and monks for living lives of luxury. In addition, they despaired at the absence of clergy when they were so greatly needed. While many clerics had perished attending to their parishioners during the Black Death, others had fled to rural retreats far from the ravages of the plague, leaving their followers to fend for themselves.

The Black Death wrought devastation throughout Afro-Eurasia. The Chinese population plunged from around 115 million in 1200 to 75 million or less in 1400, as the result of the Mongol invasions of the thirteenth century and the disease and disorder of the fourteenth century. Over the course of the fourteenth century, Europe's population shrank by more than 50 percent. In the most densely settled Islamic territory—Egypt—a population that had totaled around 6 million in 1400 was cut in half. When farmers fell ill with the plague, food production collapsed. Famine followed and killed off the survivors. Worst afflicted were the crowded cities, especially coastal ports. Some cities lost up to two-thirds of their population. Refugees from urban areas fled their homes, seeking security and food in the countryside. The shortage of food and other necessities led to rapidly rising prices, work stoppages, and unrest. Political leaders added to their unpopularity by repressing the unrest. Everywhere, regimes trembled and collapsed. The Mongol Empire, which had held so much of Eurasia together commercially and politically, disintegrated. Thus, the way was prepared for experiments in state building, religious beliefs, and cultural achievements.

REBUILDING STATES

Starting in the late fourteenth century, Afro-Eurasians began the task of reconstructing both their political order and their trading networks. By then the plague had died down, though it continued to afflict peoples for

The Global View

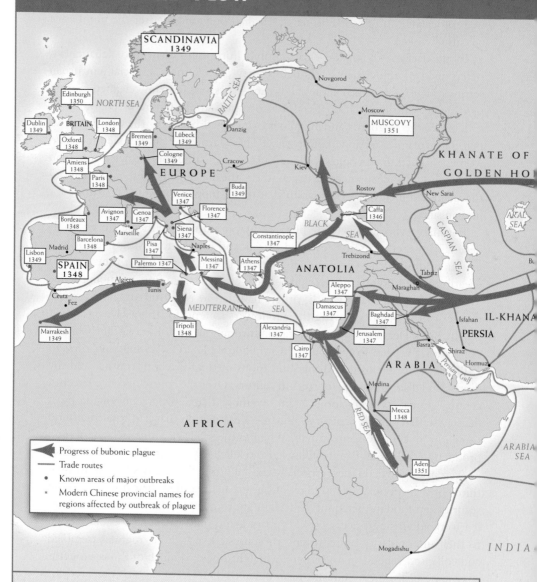

Map 11.1 The Spread of the Black Death, 1320–1354

The Black Death was an Afro-Eurasian pandemic of the fourteenth century.

- What was the origin point of the Black Death? How far did it travel?
- Which trade routes did the Black Death follow? Which trade routes did the Black Death appear not to have followed? What do you think accounts for the difference?
- Where was the earliest instance of the Black Death? Where did it occur latest? What hypotheses can you assert about the Black Death based on the dates on the map?

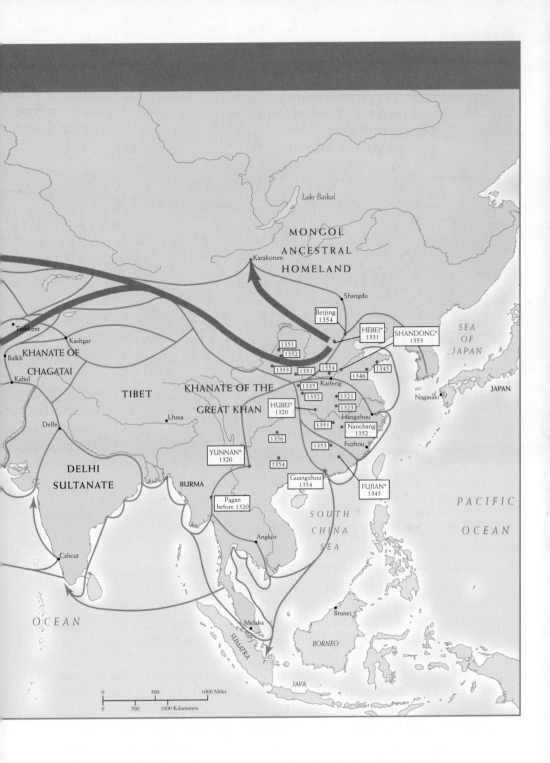

Lake Baikal

MONGOL
ANCESTRAL
HOMELAND

Karakorum

Shangdu

Beijing
1354

HEBEI*
1331

SHANDONG*
1353

SEA
OF
JAPAN

Tashkent

Kashgar

KHANATE OF
CHAGATAI

Balkh

Kabul

1351

1352

1353   1351   1354

1345

1346

JAPAN

TIBET

KHANATE OF THE

GREAT KHAN

1335   Kaifeng

1332

1321

1323

Nagasaki

Delhi

Lhasa

HUBEI*
1320

1351

1351

Nanchang
1352

Hangzhou

DELHI

SULTANATE

BURMA

YUNNAN*
1320

1356

1353   Fuzhou

1354

Guangzhou
1354

FUJIAN*
1345

PACIFIC

OCEAN

Pagan
before 1320

Calicut

Angkor

SOUTH
CHINA
SEA

OCEAN

Melaka

Brunei

BORNEO

SUMATRA

JAVA

0   500   1000 Miles

0   500   1000 Kilometers

The text in the image (medieval French manuscript):

E nfuere alerent chafcu lor
ad efter lor en ext a besoing
ad out lor coment agerre loing.
L i filz le roi furent ploze
L uoz qil furent enterre

S arqeus ozent trop
S iles mistret euz a
d eleg leur frere b.
E nterre furent n

r lpuis furent z euiseloz
Bien diun an eoit lautoz

A la plus belle rei
S ouz ael ni cuei
n ela plus belle
L er bimtez ne la

The Plague Pandemic's Destruction Bubonic plague tore through the countries of western Christendom. Italy, depicted in this detail from a fourteenth-century Italian illuminated manuscript page, was among the regions most devastated by the Black Death. Neighbors buried neighbors, parents buried children, and the rich and poor suffered alike.

centuries. However, the rebuilding of military and civil administrations—no easy task—also required political legitimacy. With their people deeply shaken by the extraordinary loss of life, rulers needed to revive confidence in themselves and their regimes, which they did by fostering beliefs and rituals that confirmed their legitimacy and by increasing their control over subjects.

The basis for power was a political institution well known to Afro-Eurasians for centuries, the **dynasty**—the hereditary ruling family that passed control from one generation to the next. Like those of the past, the new dynasties sought to establish their legitimacy in three ways. First, ruling families insisted that their power derived from a divine calling: Ming emperors in China claimed for themselves what previous dynastic rulers had asserted—the "mandate of heaven"—while European monarchs claimed to rule by "divine right." From their base in Anatolia, Ottoman warrior-princes asserted that they now carried the banner of Islam. In these ways, ruling households affirmed that God or the heavens intended for them to hold power. Second, leaders attempted to prevent squabbling among potential heirs by establishing clear rules about succession to the throne. Many European states tried to standardize succession by passing titles to the eldest male heir, thus ensuring political stability at a potential time of crisis, but in practice there were countless complications and quarrels. In the Islamic world, successors could be designated by the current ruler or elected by the community; here, too, struggles over succession were frequent. Third, ruling families elevated their power through conquest or alliance—by ordering armies to forcibly extend their domains or by marrying their royal offspring to rulers of other states or members of other elite households, a technique widely practiced in Europe. Once it established legitimacy, the typical royal family would consolidate power by enacting coercive laws and punishments and sending emissaries to govern distant territories. A ruling family would also establish standing armies and new administrative structures to collect taxes and to oversee building projects that proclaimed royal power.

As we will see in the next three sections of this chapter, the innovative state building that followed the plague's devastating wake would not have been as successful had it not drawn on older traditions. The peoples of the Islamic world held fiercely to their religion as successor states, notably the Ottoman Empire, absorbed numerous Turkish-speaking groups. In Europe, a cultural flourishing based largely on ancient Greek and Roman models gave rise to thinkers who proposed new views of governance. The Ming renounced the Mongol expansionist legacy and emphasized a return to Han rulership, consolidating control of Chinese lands and concentrating on internal markets rather than overseas trade. Many of these regimes lasted for centuries, long enough to set deep roots for political institutions and cultural values that molded societies long after the Black Death.

The Islamic Heartland

The devastation of the Black Death followed hard on the heels of the Mongol destruction of Islam's most important city, Baghdad, and Islam's old political order. The double shock of conquest and disease shattered whatever was left of Islamic unity and cleared the way for new Islamic states to emerge. The old, Arabic-speaking Islamic world remained vital in Islam's geographic heartland, but it now had to yield authority to new rulers and religious men. This new Islamic world included large Turkish- and Persian-speaking populations as well. The implosion of the Abbasid caliphate in Baghdad made way for powerful, more militarized, expansionist successors capable of extending

Islam's reach into Christian heartlands in the west and the Delhi Sultanate in the east.

The recovery from conquest and disease was slow. Eventually, the Ottomans, the Safavids, and the Mughals emerged as the dominant states in the Islamic world in the early sixteenth century. They exploited the rich agrarian resources of the Indian Ocean regions and the Mediterranean basin, and they benefited from a brisk seaborne and overland trade. By the mid-sixteenth century the Mughals controlled the northern Indus River valley; the Safavids occupied Persia; and the Ottomans ruled Anatolia, the Arab world, and much of southern and eastern Europe. Here we will explore in depth the Ottoman Empire, which emerged first and endured the longest of the three. (See Chapter 12 for a fuller discussion of the Mughals and Chapter 14 for more on the Safavids.)

THE OTTOMAN EMPIRE

The rise of the **Ottoman Empire** owed as much to innovative administrative techniques and religious tolerance as to military strength. Although the Mongols considered Anatolia to be a borderland region of little economic importance, their military forays in the late thirteenth century opened up the region to new political forces. The ultimate victors here were the Ottoman Turks. They transformed themselves from warrior bands roaming the borderlands between the Islamic and Christian worlds into rulers of a settled state and, finally, into sovereigns of a far-flung, highly bureaucratic empire. (See Map 11.2.)

Under their chief, Osman (r. 1299–1326), the Turkish Ottomans formalized a stern and disciplined warrior ethos. In addition to deploying their fierce warriors, knowns as *ghazis*, Osman and his son Orhan (r. 1326–1362), both Sunni Muslims, proved skilled at working with those who held different religious beliefs, including Byzantine Christians, Sufi dervishes, and Shiites. Osman and Orhan offered genuine opportunities for others to exercise power and gain wealth. While other Turkish warrior bands fought for booty under charismatic military leaders, they failed because, unlike the Ottomans, they did not integrate these religious groups and the range of artisans, merchants, bureaucrats, and clerics whose support was essential in the Ottoman rise to power. The Ottomans triumphed over their rivals by adapting techniques of administration from neighboring groups and by attracting those groups to their rule. In time, not only did the Ottoman state win the favor of Islamic clerics, but it also became the champion of Sunni Islam throughout the Islamic world.

By the mid-fourteenth century, the Ottomans had expanded into the Balkans, becoming the most powerful force in the eastern Mediterranean and western Asia. By the early sixteenth century, the Ottoman state controlled a vast territory, stretching in the west to the Moroccan border, in the north to Hungary and Moldavia, in the south through the Arabian Peninsula, and in the east to the Persian border. What was impressive and new within the Islamic world was the Ottomans' elaborate administrative hierarchy, atop which stood the sultan. Below him was a military and civilian bureaucracy whose task was to demand obedience and revenue from subjects. The bureaucracy's discipline enabled the sultan to expand his realm, which in turn forced him to invest in an even larger bureaucracy.

The empire's spectacular expansion was primarily a military affair. To recruit followers, the Ottomans promised wealth and glory to new subjects. This was an expensive undertaking, but territorial expansion generated vast financial and administrative rewards. Moreover, by spreading the spoils of conquest and lucrative administrative positions, rulers bought off potentially unhappy subordinates. Still, without military might, the Ottomans would not have enjoyed the successes associated with the brilliant reigns of Murad II (r. 1421–1451) and his appropriately

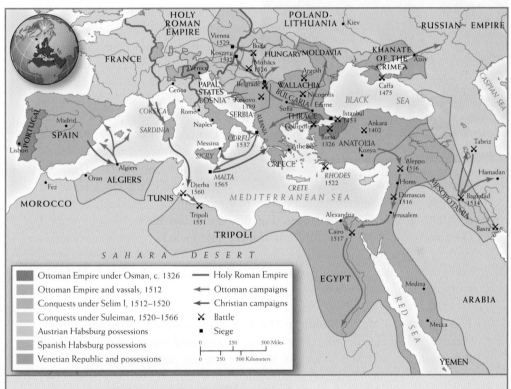

Map 11.2 The Ottoman Empire, 1300–1566

This map charts the expansion of the Ottoman state from the time of its founder, Osman, through the reign of Suleiman, the empire's most illustrious ruler.

- Where did the Ottoman Empire originate under Osman? Into what regions did the Ottomans expand between the years 1326 and 1566?
- What were the geographic limits of the Ottoman Empire?
- What governments were able to resist Ottoman expansion?

The Siege of Constantinople A depiction of the Turkish siege of Constantinople from Burgundian spy Bertrandon de la Broquière's 1453 book of travels, *Voyage d'Outre-Mer*. The use of heavy artillery in the fifty-three-day siege of Constantinople was instrumental to the Ottoman victory.

named successor, Mehmed the Conqueror (r. 1451–1481).

Mehmed's most spectacular triumph was the conquest of Constantinople, an ambition for Muslim rulers ever since the birth of Islam. Mehmed left no doubt that this was his primary goal: shortly after his coronation, he vowed to capture Constantinople, the ancient Roman and Christian capital of the Byzantine Empire, and a city of immense strategic and commercial importance, which had withstood Muslim efforts at conquest for centuries. First, Mehmed built a fortress of his own to prevent European vessels from reaching the capital. Then, by promising his soldiers free access to booty and portraying the city's conquest as a holy cause, he amassed a huge army that outnumbered the defending force of 7,000 by more than ten times. For fifty-three days his troops bombarded Constantinople's massive walls with artillery that included enormous cannons built by Hungarian and Italian engineers. On May 29, 1453, Ottoman troops overwhelmed the surviving defenders and took Constantinople—which Mehmed promptly renamed Istanbul.

The Tools of Empire Building The Ottomans adopted Byzantine administrative practices to unify their enlarged state and incorporated many of Byzantium's powerful families into it. Their dynastic power, however, was not only military; it also rested on a firm religious foundation. At the center of this empire was the sultan, who combined a warrior ethos with an unwavering devotion to Islam. Describing himself as the "shadow of God" on earth, the sultan claimed the role of caretaker for the Islamic faith. Throughout the empire, he devoted substantial resources to the construction of elaborate mosques and to the support of Islamic schools. As self-appointed defender of the faith, the sultan assumed the role of protector of the holy cities on the Arabian Peninsula and of Jerusalem, while working to unite the realm's diverse lands and peoples and constantly striving to extend the borders of Islam. During the reign of

Suleiman (r. 1520–1566), the Ottomans reached the height of their territorial expansion. Under his administration, the Ottoman state ruled 20 to 30 million people. By the time Suleiman died, the Ottoman Empire bridged Europe and the Arab world.

Istanbul's **Topkapi Palace** exhibited the Ottomans' view of governance, the sultans' emphasis on religion, and the continuing influence of Ottoman familial traditions. Laid out by Mehmed II, the palace complex projected a vision of Istanbul as the center of the world. As a way to promote the sultan's magnificent power, architects designed the complex so that the buildings containing the imperial household were nestled behind layers of outer courtyards, in a mosaic of mosques, courts, and special dwellings for the sultan's harem. The harem had its own hierarchy of thousands of women, from the sultan's mother and consorts to the enslaved women who waited on them, and it became a formidable political force at the heart of Ottoman power.

The growing importance of Topkapi Palace as the command post of empire represented a crucial transition in the history of Ottoman rulers. Not only was the palace the place where future bureaucrats received their training; it was also the place where the chief bureaucrat, the grand vizier, carried out the day-to-day running of the empire. Whereas the early sultans had led their soldiers into battle personally and had met face-to-face with their kinsmen, the later rulers withdrew into the sacredness of the palace, venturing out

The Süleymaniye Mosque Built by Sultan Suleiman to crown his achievements, the Süleymaniye Mosque was designed by the architect Sinan to dominate the city. Four tall minarets called the faithful to prayer. Location mattered to Suleiman. The Bosporus Strait, the vital route connecting the Mediterranean with the Black Sea, is visible beyond the mosque, and Justinian's Hagia Sophia (not visible here) is located just across a park from the mosque.

only occasionally for grand ceremonies. Still, every Friday, subjects lined up outside the palace to introduce their petitions, ask for favors, and seek justice. If they were lucky, the sultans would be there to greet them—but they did so behind grated glass, issuing their decisions by tapping on the window. The palace thus projected a sense of majestic, distant wonder, a home fit for semi-divine rulers.

Diversity and Control The Ottoman Empire's endurance into the twentieth century owed much to the ruling elite's ability to gain the support and employ the talents of exceedingly diverse populations. After all, neither conquest nor conversion eliminated cultural differences among the empire's distant provinces. Thus, for example, the Ottomans' language policy was one of flexibility and tolerance. Although Ottoman Turkish was the official language of administration, Arabic was the primary language of the Arab provinces, the common tongue of street life. Within the empire's European lands, many people spoke their own languages. From the fifteenth century onward, the Ottoman Empire was perhaps more multilingual than any of its rivals.

In politics, as in language, the Ottomans showed flexibility and tolerance. The imperial bureaucracy permitted extensive regional autonomy. In fact, Ottoman military cadres perfected a technique for absorbing newly conquered territories into the empire by parceling them out as revenue-producing units among loyal followers and kin. Regional appointees could collect local taxes, part of which they earmarked for Istanbul and part of which they pocketed for themselves. This approach was a common administrative device for many world dynastic empires ruling extensive domains.

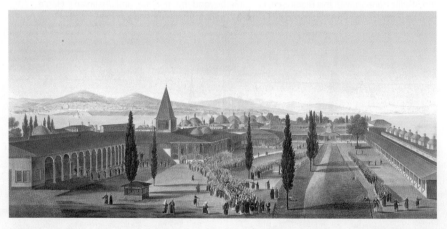

The Topkapi Palace A view of the inner courtyard of the Topkapi Palace complex. Note the grand construction with entrances leading to the Council Hall, the Treasury, and the Tower of Justice. This courtyard was the site of important Ottoman ceremonies, such as the accession of sultans, the distribution of janissaries' salaries, and the reception of foreign emissaries.

Like other empires, the Ottoman state was always in danger of losing control over its provincial rulers. Local potentates—the group that the imperial center allowed to rule in their distant regions—found that great distances enabled them to operate independently from central authority. These rulers kept larger amounts of tax revenues than Istanbul deemed proper. So, to limit their autonomy, the Ottomans established the janissaries, a corps of infantry soldiers and bureaucrats who owed direct allegiance to the sultan. The system at its high point involved conscription of Christian youths from the empire's European lands. This conscription, called the *devshirme*, required each village to hand over a certain number of males between the ages of eight and eighteen. Uprooted from their families and villages, these young men—selected for their fine physiques and good looks—were converted to Islam and sent to farms to build up their bodies and learn Turkish. A select few were moved on to Topkapi Palace to learn Ottoman military, religious, and administrative techniques. Some of these men—such as the architect Sinan, who designed the Süleymaniye Mosque—later enjoyed exceptional careers in the arts and sciences. Recipients of the best education available in the Islamic world, trained in Ottoman ways, instructed in the use of modern weaponry, and deprived of family connections, the *devshirme* recruits were prepared to serve the sultan (and the empire as a whole) rather than the interests of any particular locality or ethnic group.

Thus, the Ottomans established their legitimacy via military skill, religious backing, and a loyal bureaucracy. They artfully balanced the decentralizing tendencies of the outlying regions with the centralizing forces of the imperial capital. Relying on a careful mixture of religious faith, imperial patronage, and cultural tolerance, the sultans curried loyalty and secured political stability. Indeed, the Ottoman Empire was so strong and stable that it dominated the coveted and highly contested trading crossroads between Europe and Asia for many centuries. Thus, its consolidation had powerful consequences for Europeans' efforts to rebuild their societies after the plague; above all, it closed off their traditional overland trade routes to India and China.

Western Christendom

No region suffered more from the Black Death than western Christendom, and arguably no region made a more spectacular comeback. From 1100 to 1300, Europe had enjoyed a surge in population, rapid economic growth, and significant technological and intellectual innovations, only to see these achievements halted in the fourteenth century by famine and the Black Death. Europeans responded by creating new political and cultural forms. New dynastic states arose, competing with one another, and a movement called the Renaissance revived Europe's connections with its Greek and Roman past and produced masterpieces of art, architecture, and other forms of thought.

THE CATHOLIC CHURCH, STATE BUILDING, AND ECONOMIC RECOVERY

In the aftermath of famine and plague, the peoples of western Christendom, like those in the Muslim world, looked to their religious beliefs and institutions as foundations for recovery. The faith of many had been severely tested, and religious authorities had to struggle to reclaim their power. To begin with, the late medieval western church found itself divided at the top (at one point during this period there were three popes) and challenged from below, both by individuals pursuing alternative kinds of spirituality and by increasing demands on the clergy and church administration. Disappointment with the clergy smoldered. The peasantry despaired at the absence of clergy when they were so greatly needed during the famines and Black Death. With groups like the Beghards and Beguines challenging the clergy's right to define religious doctrine and practices, the church fought back, identifying all that was suspect and demanding strict obedience to the true faith. This response included the persecution of Jews, Muslims in the Iberian Peninsula, gays, sex workers, "witches," and others considered by the church to be heretical. During this period the church also expanded its charitable and bureaucratic functions, providing alms to the urban poor and registering births, deaths, and economic transactions. Crucially, when faced with challenges to its authority, the church associated itself with secular rulers, lending moral authority to kings who claimed to rule "by divine right."

At the same time, the high death toll of the fourteenth and fifteenth centuries emboldened those who survived to seek higher wages or reductions in their feudal obligations. When landlords resisted or kings tried to impose new taxes, there were uprisings, including a 1358 peasant revolt in France that was dubbed the Jacquerie (the term derived from "Jacques Bonhomme," a name that contemptuous "masters" used for all peasants). Armed with only knives and staves, the peasantry went on a rampage, killing hated nobles and clergy and burning and looting all the property they could get their hands on. At issue was the peasants' insistence that they should no longer be tied to their land or have to pay for the tools they used in farming.

A better-organized uprising took place in England in 1381. Although the English Peasants' Revolt began as a protest against a tax levied to raise money for a war on France, it was also fueled by postplague labor shortages: serfs demanded the freedom to move about, and free farmworkers called for higher wages and lower rents. When landlords balked at these demands, aggrieved peasants assembled at the gates of London. The protesters demanded abolition of the feudal order, but the king ruthlessly suppressed them. Nonetheless, in both France and England a free peasantry gradually emerged as labor shortages made it impossible to keep peasants bound to the soil.

Europe's political rulers aligned themselves with church leaders to rebuild their states and consolidate their power. One royal family, the Habsburgs, drew on their Catholic religious traditions and established a powerful, long-lasting

The Imperial Crown Creating new emblems of authority and a culture of grandeur was important to rising monarchies of Afro-Eurasia. In an effort to distance themselves from their time-worn, conquering reputations, they invested heavily in palaces and elaborate courtly cultures. Above all, the crown and the throne became the symbols of imperial regality, as wearing the crown or sitting on the throne conferred supremacy. It was important, therefore, for these emblems to exude wealth and ostentation. This is the crown of the Holy Roman Emperor. Studded with pearls and large sapphires, emeralds, and amethysts, it combined piety (note the cross and the inlaid plaques of biblical scenes) with authority.

dynasty that would rule large parts of central Europe for centuries to follow. This family provided continuous emperors from 1445 to 1806 for the federation of states known as the Holy Roman Empire, and for a time they ruled Spain and its New World colonies. Yet even at the height of its power in the early sixteenth century, the Habsburg monarchy never succeeded in restoring an integrated empire to western Europe.

In 1450, western Christendom had no central government, no official tongue, and only a few successful commercial centers, mostly in the Mediterranean basin. (See Map 11.3.) The feudal system of a lord's control over the peasantry (see Chapter 10), which was now in decline, left a legacy of political fragmentation and enduring elite privileges, which made the consolidation of a unified Christian Europe even more difficult to achieve. Europe's linguistic diversity reflected its political fragmentation. No single ruler or language united peoples, even when they shared a religion. Europe saw Latin lose ground as rulers chose various regional dialects (such as French, Spanish, or English) to be their official state languages, in contrast with China, whose written literary Chinese script remained a key administrative tool for the new dynasts, and the Islamic world, where Arabic was the common language of faith and Turkish the language of administration.

Those who sought to rule the emerging states faced numerous obstacles. For example, rival claimants to the throne financed threatening private armies. Also, the clergy demanded and received privileges in the form of access to land and relief from taxation; they often meddled in politics, and the church became a formidable economic powerhouse. And once the printing press became more widely available in Europe in the 1460s, printers circulated anonymous pamphlets criticizing the court and the clergy. Some states had consultative political bodies—such as the Estates-General in France, the Cortes in Spain, and Parliament in England—in which princes formally asked representatives of their people for advice and, in the case of the English Parliament, for consent to new forms of taxation. Such political bodies gave no voice to common men and no representation to women. But they did allow the collective expression of grievances against overbearing policies.

Out of the chaos of famine, disease, and warfare, the diverse peoples of Europe found a political way forward. This path involved the formation of centralized dynastic monarchies. While not new to this period, the political institution of **monarchy** was particularly instrumental to western Christendom in the fifteenth century. Often in competition with the new monarchies, a handful of European city-states, in which a narrow group of wealthy and influential voters selected their leaders, survived right up to the nineteenth century and in some cases into the twentieth. Consolidation of these states occurred sometimes through strategic marriages but more often through warfare, both between princely families and with local aristocratic allies and foreign mercenaries.

One striking example of this political turmoil was the Hundred Years' War (1337–1453), in which the French sought to throw off English domination. The Black Death raged in the early years of this intermittent conflict. A central figure toward the end of the war was the peasant girl Joan of Arc, whose visions of various saints inspired her to support the French monarch Charles VII and see him crowned at Reims Cathedral. While Joan was a charismatic leader of troops, commanding as many as 8,000 at the decisive battle at Orléans, eventually the French nobility turned on her, and she was captured by the English. Joan was tried for heresy and burned at the stake in Rouen in 1431. Joan's brief, but remarkable, part in the Hundred Years' War illustrates the role an exceptional woman, even a peasant girl, could play on the predominantly male, elite political stage.

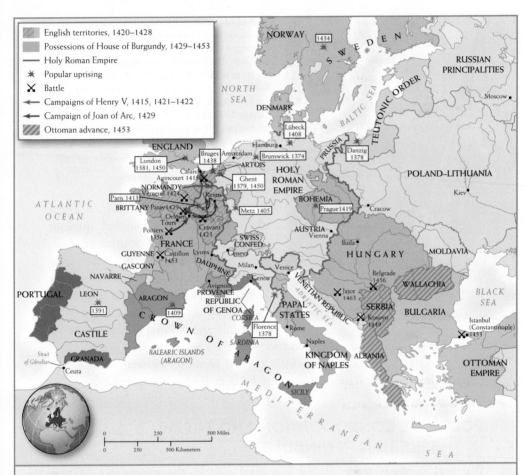

Legend:
- English territories, 1420–1428
- Possessions of House of Burgundy, 1429–1453
- Holy Roman Empire
- ✳ Popular uprising
- ✗ Battle
- ← Campaigns of Henry V, 1415, 1421–1422
- ← Campaign of Joan of Arc, 1429
- Ottoman advance, 1453

Map labels:

NORWAY 1434

SWEDEN

RUSSIAN PRINCIPALITIES

NORTH SEA

BALTIC SEA

TEUTONIC ORDER

DENMARK

Moscow

PRUSSIA

Lübeck 1408

Hamburg

Danzig 1378

ENGLAND

Bruges 1438 • Amsterdam

Brunswick 1374

London 1381, 1450

Calais

Agincourt 1415

ARTOIS

HOLY ROMAN EMPIRE

POLAND–LITHUANIA

Ghent 1379, 1450

NORMANDY

Verneuil 1424

Reims

Kiev

ATLANTIC OCEAN

Paris 1413

BRITTANY Patay 1429

Metz 1405

BOHEMIA

Orléans

Prague 1419

Cracow

Tours

Poitiers 1356

Cravant 1423

AUSTRIA

Vienna

Buda

FRANCE

SWISS CONFED.

Geneva

HUNGARY

MOLDAVIA

GUYENNE ✗ Castillon 1453

Lyons

Milan

Venice

Belgrade 1456

WALLACHIA

GASCONY

DAUPHINÉ

Genoa

VENETIAN REPUBLIC

Jajce 1463

BLACK SEA

NAVARRE

Avignon

PROVENCE

ADRIATIC SEA

SERBIA

BULGARIA

PORTUGAL

LEON

ARAGON

1391

REPUBLIC OF GENOA

1409

CORSICA

PAPAL STATES

Rome

Kosovo 1449

Istanbul (Constantinople) 1453

CASTILE

CROWN OF ARAGON

Florence 1378

Naples

SARDINIA

KINGDOM OF NAPLES

ALBANIA

OTTOMAN EMPIRE

Strait of Gibraltar

GRANADA

Ceuta

BALEARIC ISLANDS (ARAGON)

SICILY

MEDITERRANEAN SEA

0 — 250 — 500 Miles
0 — 250 — 500 Kilometers

Map 11.3 Western Christendom, 1400–1500

Europe was a region divided by dynastic rivalries during the fifteenth century. Locate the most powerful regional dynasties on the map: Portugal, Castile, Aragon, France, Burgundy, England, and the Holy Roman Empire.

- Using the scale, contrast the sizes of political units in this map with those in Maps 11.2 (Ottoman Empire) and 11.4 (Ming China). Explain the significance of the differences.
- Where did popular uprisings take place? Based on your reading, why did those regions experience popular unrest?
- Based on the map, why might the Venetian Republic have been particularly engaged, both in trade and intermittent warfare, with the Ottomans?

Joan of Arc Joan of Arc became an icon of French identity. Inspired by divine visions of the archangel Michael as well as Saint Margaret and Saint Catharine, she was famous for leading troops to battle in the drive to repel English forces during the Hundred Years' War. But for many French nobles, she was a troublemaker; they captured her and gave her to the English, who burned her at the stake in 1431. She was nineteen years old. It was only later, as the French monarchy consolidated itself and cast about for popular symbols, that she was rebranded from popular rebel to martyr for the nation.

Elsewhere, in southern Europe, where economies rebounded through seaborne trade with Southwest Asia, political stabilization was swifter. The stabilization of Italian city-states such as Venice and Florence, and of monarchical rule in Portugal and Spain, led to an economic and cultural flowering known as the Renaissance. In northern and western Europe, the process took longer. In England and France, in particular, internal feuding, regional warfare, and religious fragmentation delayed recovery for decades (see Chapter 12).

POLITICAL CONSOLIDATION AND TRADE IN THE IBERIAN PENINSULA

War and overseas trade played a central role in the emergence of new dynasties in Portugal and Spain. Through the fourteenth century, Portuguese Christians devoted themselves to fighting the Moors, who were Muslim occupants of North Africa, the western Sahara, and the Iberian Peninsula. After the Portuguese crossed the Strait of Gibraltar and seized the Moorish fortresses at Ceuta, in Morocco, their ships could sail between the Mediterranean and the Atlantic without Muslim interference. With that threat diminished, the Portuguese perceived their neighbor Castile (a region in what is now Spain) as their chief foe. Under João I (r. 1385–1433), Portugal defeated the Castilians, becoming the dominant power on the Iberian Peninsula. No longer preoccupied with Castilian competition, the Portuguese sought new territories and trading opportunities in the North Atlantic and along the West African coast. João's son Prince Henrique, known later as Henry the Navigator, further expanded the royal family's domain by supporting expeditions down the coast of Africa and offshore to the Atlantic islands of Madeira and the Azores. The west and central coasts of Africa and the islands of the North and South Atlantic, including the

Cape Verde Islands, São Tomé, Principe, and Fernando Po, soon became Portuguese ports of call.

Portuguese monarchs granted the Atlantic islands to nobles as hereditary possessions on condition that the grantees colonize them, and soon the colonizers were establishing lucrative sugar plantations. In gratitude, noble families and merchants threw their political weight behind the king. Subsequent monarchs continued to cultivate local aristocrats' support for monarchical authority, thus ensuring smooth succession to the crown for members of the royal family.

In Spain, a new dynasty also emerged, though the road was difficult. Medieval Spain comprised rival kingdoms that quarreled ceaselessly. Within those kingdoms, several religions coexisted: Muslims, Jews, and Christians lived side by side in relative harmony, and Muslim armies still occupied strategic posts in the south. Over time, marriages and the formation of kinship ties among nobles and between royal lineages yielded a new political order. One by one, the major houses of the Spanish kingdoms intermarried, culminating in the wedding of Isabella of Castile and Ferdinand of Aragon in 1469. This marriage linked Castile, wealthy and populous, to Aragon, which enjoyed an extended trading network in the Mediterranean. Together, the monarchs brought unruly nobles and distant towns under their control. They topped off their achievements by marrying their children into other European royal families—especially the Habsburgs, central Europe's most powerful dynasty. Thus, Spain's two most important provinces were joined, and Spain later became a state to be reckoned with.

The new Spanish rulers sent Christian armies south to push Muslim forces out of the Iberian Peninsula. By the mid-fifteenth century, only Granada, a strategic linchpin overlooking the straits between the Mediterranean and the Atlantic, remained in Muslim hands. After a long and costly siege, Christian forces captured the fortress there in 1492. This was a victory of enormous symbolic importance, as joyous as the fall of Constantinople to Mehmed and the Ottomans in 1453 was depressing (for Christians).

The Inquisition and Westward Exploration Isabella and Ferdinand sought to drive all non-Catholics out of Spain. Terrified by Ottoman incursions into Europe, they launched the **Inquisition** in 1481, taking aim especially against *conversos*—converted Jews and Muslims, whom they suspected were Christians only in name. When Granada fell, the crown ordered the expulsion of all Jews from Spain. After 1499, a more tolerant attempt to convert the Moors (Muslims) by persuasion gave way to forced conversion—or emigration. All told, almost half a million people were forced to flee the Spanish kingdoms. This lack of tolerance meant that Spain, like other European states in this era, became increasingly homogeneous. With fewer groups vying for influence within their territories, rulers' attention turned outward, fueling rivalries between the various European states.

So strong was the tide of Spanish fervor by late 1491 that the monarchs listened now to a Genoese navigator whose pleas for patronage they had previously rejected. Christopher Columbus promised them unimaginable riches that could finance their military campaigns and bankroll a crusade to liberate Jerusalem from Muslim hands. Off he sailed with a royal patent that guaranteed the monarchs a share of all he discovered. Soon the Spanish economy was reorienting itself toward the Atlantic, and Spain's merchants, missionaries, and soldiers were preparing for conquest and profiteering in what the Spanish had perceived, just a few years before, as a blank space on the map.

Ferdinand and Isabella Entering Granada This altar relief, sculpted by Felipe Vigarny in the early sixteenth century, depicts the triumphant entrance of King Ferdinand and Queen Isabella into the city of Granada after their conquest of this last Muslim stronghold in Spain.

THE RENAISSANCE

Just as the Ming invoked Han Chinese traditions and the Ottomans looked to Sunni Islam to point the way forward, European elites drew on their own traditions for guidance as they rebuilt after the devastation of the plague. They found inspiration in ancient Greek and Roman institutions and ideas. Europe's extraordinary political and economic revival also involved a powerful outpouring of cultural achievements, led by Italian scholars and artists and financed by bankers, churchmen, and nobles. Much later, scholars coined the word **Renaissance** ("rebirth") to characterize the cultural flourishing of the Italian city-states, France, the Netherlands, England, and the Holy Roman Empire in the period 1430–1550. What was being "reborn" was ancient Greek and Roman art and learning—knowledge that could help people understand an expanding world and support the rights of secular individuals to exert power in it.

Although Christians generally portrayed the "fall" of Constantinople as a calamity, in fact the Muslim conquest brought benefits to western Europe. Many Christian survivors fled to ports in the west, bringing with them classical and Arabic manuscripts previously unknown in Europe. The well-educated, Greek-speaking émigrés generally became teachers and translators, thereby helping to revive Europeans' interest in classical antiquity and spreading knowledge of ancient Greek (which had virtually died out in medieval times). These manuscripts and teachers would play a vital role in Europe's Renaissance.

Although the Renaissance was largely funded by popes, Christian kings, and powerful wealthy merchants, it challenged the authority of traditional religious elites, breaking the medieval church's monopoly on answers to the big questions. Religious topics and themes, such as David and Goliath, Judith and Holofernes, and various scenes from Jesus's story (the annunciation of his birth to Mary, Jesus's adoration by the magi, and his baptism and crucifixion), dominated much of Renaissance art, but these themes took on new meaning as warnings to overbearing rulers and reminders to the obscenely wealthy, who sponsored many of these works, of their place in the cosmos and the civic responsibility that stemmed from their wealth. These religious themes were also joined by classical topics, such as scenes from mythology and the ancient past. The movement valued secular forms of learning, rather than just Christian doctrine, and a more human-centered understanding of the cosmos.

The Renaissance was all about new exposure to the old—to classical texts and ancient art and architectural forms. Although some Greek and Roman texts were known in Europe and the Islamic world, the use of the printing press made others accessible to western scholars for the first time. Scholars now realized that the pre-Christian Greeks and Romans had developed powerful means of representing and caring for the human body. Having studied the world directly, without the need to square their observations with biblical information, the ancients had much to teach about geography, astronomy, and architecture and about how to govern states and armies. For Renaissance scholars it was no longer enough to understand Christian doctrine and to concern themselves with the next world. One had to go back to the original, classical sources in order to understand the human condition. This in turn required the learning of languages and history. Scholarship that attempted to return to Greek and Roman sources became known as **humanism**.

Because political and religious powers were not united in Europe (as they were in China and the Islamic world), scholars and artists seeking sponsors for their work could play one side against the other or, alternatively, could suffer both clerical and political persecution. Michelangelo, a leading painter, sculptor, architect, and engineer of the age, completed commissions for the famous Florentine bankers and political leaders of the Medici family, for the Florentine Wool Guild, and for Pope Julius II. Peter Paul Rubens painted for the courts of France, Spain, England, and the Netherlands, as well as selling paintings on the open market. These two painters, renowned for showing a great deal of flesh, frequently offended conservative church officials. Even so, most support for the arts came either from the church or from individual clergymen, and virtually all secular donors were devout believers who commissioned works with religious themes. The Dutch scholar Desiderius Erasmus ridiculed corrupt popes and the clergy under the patronage of English, Dutch, and French supporters while remaining a Catholic, an ordained cleric, and an opponent of Reformation doctrines. Conflicts within the Catholic Church,

Renaissance Masterpieces *Left:* Leonardo da Vinci's *The Last Supper* depicts Christ's disciples reacting to his announcement that one of them will betray him. *Right:* Michelangelo's *David* stands over 13 feet high and was conceived as an expression of Florentine civic ideals.

between the church and secular leaders, and among secular leaders and wealthy private citizens enabled artists to present challenging images and ideas with an unusual independence.

Gradually, a network of educated men and women took shape that was not wholly dependent on the church, the state, or a single princely patron. Classical knowledge gave individuals the means to challenge political, clerical, and aesthetic authority. Moreover, rivalries between Europe's relatively small states and city-states allowed many of these scholars to dodge the authorities by fleeing to neighboring communities. Of course, they could also use their learning to defend the older elites: for example, numerous lawyers and scholars continued to work for the popes in defending the papacy. At the same time, men like Erasmus and later Martin Luther (the leading figure of the Reformation in the sixteenth century) looked to secular princes to support their critical scholarship. In Florence, Niccolò Machiavelli wrote the most famous treatise on authoritarian power, *The Prince* (1513). Machiavelli argued that political leadership required mastering the rules of modern statecraft, even if in some cases this meant disregarding moral imperatives. Holding and exercising power were vital ends in themselves, he claimed; traditional ideas of civic virtue should not deter rulers, like those of the Medici family, from maintaining control over society.

The Printing Press Over time one major technological advance, the invention of the **printing press**, would serve to increase the spread of knowledge more than any other phenomenon. The earliest advances in printing were made in China, where wood block printing first appeared around 220 CE, followed by movable type around 1040, and then the first metal movable type was used in Korea around 1300. In the 1450s, Johannes Gutenberg, the son of a German goldsmith, applied a technology to printing that was similar to the technology used to stamp metal coins. The first printed newspapers, leaflets, pamphlets, and books were printed on large wood frame presses that used rows of movable type to stamp the ink on the printed pages. Now hundreds of copies could be made in a few hours, hundreds of hours faster than handwritten and hand-bound copies of books could be produced. A second key factor that made this communication revolution possible was readily available cheap paper, made from old rags turned into pulp at local mills. Rising literacy rates, which increased the demand for books, were a third factor.

Artistic and intellectual experiments, specifications for innovative weapons, and humanist writings were rapidly exported from Renaissance Italy to other parts of Europe. Major news like Columbus's first voyage and the resulting encounters and conquests spread rapidly around Europe, as did major criticisms of this new form of European imperialism. Rulers also used this revolution in communication to expand and centralize their own power through widely distributed printed propaganda and the creation of standardized national languages. The powerful impact of printing was immediate, and its role in communication would continue to grow and evolve for the centuries ahead both in Europe and globally.

With Renaissance ideas challenging traditional authority and rulers facing a range of internal and external obstacles, the new monarchies of Europe were not all immediately successful in consolidating power and unifying peoples. In France and England, for example, the great age of monarchy had

Invention of the Printing Press Around 1450, the German goldsmith Johannes Gutenberg invented the printing press. It was not a complex or elaborate device. Consider the simplicity of this mechanical device, with few moving parts and the use of a modest screw to push plates together. Nonetheless, its ability to reproduce thousands of pages per day—as opposed to only dozens at the hands of scribes—slashed the cost of printing and made information cheap. Just as important, the device itself was inexpensive and easy to build. Within a few decades, printing presses were in operation throughout western Europe, reading books became commonplace, and religious and secular authorities lost what control was left to them over the creation and flow of information.

yet to dawn. Even when stable states did arise in Europe, they were fairly small compared with the Ottoman and Ming Empires. In the mid-sixteenth century, Portugal and Spain, Europe's two most expansionist states, had populations of 1 million and 9 million, respectively. England, excluding Wales, had a mere 3 million in 1550. Only France, with 17 million, had a population close to the Ottoman Empire's 25 million. And these numbers paled in comparison with Ming China's population of nearly 200 million in 1550 and Mughal India's 110 million in 1600. But in Europe, small could be advantageous. Portugal's relatively small population meant that the crown had fewer groups to control. In the world of finance, the most successful merchants were those inhabiting the smaller Italian city-states and, a bit later, the cities of the northern Netherlands. The Florentines developed sophisticated banking techniques, created extensive networks of agents throughout Europe and the Mediterranean, and served as bankers to the popes. At the same time, the Renaissance—which flourished in the city-states and newly stabilized monarchies—made elite European culture more cosmopolitan and independent from government authority, even if it could not unify the states and peoples who cultivated it.

Ming China

Like the Europeans, the Chinese saw their stable worldview and political order crumble under the catastrophes of human and microbial invasions. Moreover, like the Europeans, people in China had long regarded outsiders as "barbarians" and balked at being ruled by them. Together, the Mongols and the Black Death upended the political and intellectual foundations of what had appeared to be the world's most integrated society. The Mongols brought the Yuan dynasty to power; then the plague devastated China and prepared the way for the emergence of a new dynasty. The **Ming dynasty**, ruled by ethnically Han Chinese, defined itself against its foreign predecessors. Ming emperors sought to reinforce everything Chinese. In particular, they supported China's vast internal agricultural markets in an attempt to minimize dependence on merchants and foreign trade.

RESTORING ORDER

In the chaotic fourteenth century, as plague and famine ravaged China and the Mongol Yuan dynasty collapsed, only a strong military movement capable of overpowering other groups could restore order. That intervention began at the hands of a poor young man who had trained in the **Red Turban movement**: Zhu Yuanzhang, a successful warlord who had led a rebellion against the waning power of the Mongols and any others who would assert control in their wake.

It soon became clear that Zhu had a much grander design for China than the ambitions of most warlords. When he took Nanjing in 1356, he renamed it Yingtian ("in response to heaven"). Buoyed by subsequent successful military campaigns, Zhu (r. 1368–1398) took the imperial title of Hongwu ("expansive and martial") Emperor and proclaimed the founding of the Ming ("brilliant") dynasty in 1368. Soon thereafter, his troops met little resistance when they seized the Yuan capital of Khan-balik (soon renamed Beijing), causing the Mongol emperor to flee to his homeland in the steppe. It would, however, take the Hongwu Emperor almost another twenty years to reunify the entire country.

CENTRALIZATION UNDER THE MING

The Hongwu Emperor and successive Ming emperors had to rebuild a devastated society from the ground up. Although in the past China had experienced natural catastrophes, wars, and social dislocation, the plague's legacy was devastation on an unprecedented scale. It left the new rulers with the formidable challenge of rebuilding the great cities, restoring respect for ruling elites, and reconstructing the bureaucracy.

Imperial Grandeur and Kinship The rebuilding began with the Hongwu Emperor, whose capital at Nanjing reflected imperial grandeur. When the dynasty's third emperor, the Yongle ("perpetual happiness") Emperor, relocated the capital to Beijing, he flaunted an even more grandiose style, employing around 100,000 artisans and 1 million laborers to build this new capital. The city had three separate walled enclosures. Inside the outer city walls sprawled the imperial city; within its walls lay the palace compound, the Forbidden City. Traffic within the walled sections navigated through broad boulevards leading to the different gates, above which imposing towers soared. The palace compound, where the imperial family resided, had more than 9,000 rooms. Anyone standing in the front courts, which measured more than 400 yards on a side and boasted marble terraces and carved railings, would gasp at the awe-inspiring projection of power. That was precisely the effect the Ming emperors wanted (just as the Ottoman sultans did in building Topkapi Palace).

Marriage and kinship buttressed the power of the Ming imperial household, much as dynastic strategies did in Europe. The Ming dynasty's founder married the adopted daughter of a leading Red Turban rebel (her father, according to legend, was a convicted murderer), thereby consolidating his power and eliminating a threat. Empress Ma, as she was known, became the Hongwu Emperor's principal wife and was praised for her compassion. Emerging as the kinder face of the regime, she tempered the harsh and sometimes cruel disposition of her spouse. He had numerous other consorts as well, including Korean and Mongol women, who bore him twenty-six sons and sixteen daughters. (His household was similar to, although on a smaller scale than, the Ottoman sultan's harem at Topkapi Palace.)

Building a Bureaucracy Faced with the challenge of reestablishing order out of turmoil, the Hongwu Emperor initially sought to rule through his kinsmen—by giving imperial princes generous stipends, command of large garrisons, and significant autonomy in running their domains. However, when the princes' power began to threaten the court, the Hongwu Emperor slashed their stipends, reduced their privileges, and took control of their garrisons. No longer dependent on these men, he established an imperial bureaucracy beholden only to him and to his successors. Its officials won appointments through their outstanding performance on a reinstated civil service examination.

In addition, the Hongwu Emperor took other steps to install a centralized system of rule. He assigned bureaucrats to oversee the manufacture of porcelain, cotton, and silk products as well as tax collection. He reestablished the Confucian school system as a means of selecting a cadre of loyal officials (not unlike the Ottoman janissaries and administrators). He also set up local networks of villages to rebuild irrigation systems and to supervise reforestation projects to prevent flooding—with the astonishing result that the amount of land reclaimed nearly tripled within eight years. For water supply and flood

The Forbidden City The Yongle Emperor relocated the capital to Beijing, where he began the construction of the Forbidden City, or imperial palace. The palace was designed to inspire awe in all who saw it.

control, over 40,000 reservoirs underwent repairs or new construction. Historians estimate that the Hongwu Emperor's reign oversaw the planting around Nanjing of about 1 billion trees, which were later used in building a maritime expedition fleet in the early fifteenth century.

The imperial palace not only projected the image of a power center; it *was* the center of power. Every official received his appointment by the emperor through the Ministry of Personnel. The Hongwu Emperor also eliminated the post of prime minister (he executed the man who held the post) and ruled directly. Ming bureaucrats had to kneel before the emperor. The drawback of this centralized control, of course, was that the Ming emperor had to keep tabs on this immense system. The Hongwu Emperor constantly moved his bureaucrats around, sometimes fortifying the administration, sometimes undermining it lest it become too autonomous. Over time, the Hongwu Emperor nurtured a bureaucracy far more extensive than that of the Ottomans. The Ming thus established the most highly centralized system of government of all the monarchies of this period.

RELIGION UNDER THE MING

Just as the Ottoman sultans projected themselves as Muslim rulers, calling themselves the shadow of God, and European monarchs claimed to rule by divine right, the Ming emperors enhanced their legitimacy by drawing on ancient Chinese religious traditions. Citing the mandate of heaven, the emperor revised and strengthened the elaborate rites and ceremonies that had supported dynastic power for centuries. Official rituals, such as those related to the gods of soil and grain, reinforced political and social classes, portraying the rulers as the moral and spiritual benefactors of their subjects. In lavish ceremonies, the emperor engaged in sacrificial rites, cultivating his image as mediator between the human and the spiritual worlds. The message was clear: the gods were on the side of the Ming household.

MING RULERSHIP

Conquest and defense helped establish the Ming empire, and bureaucracy kept it functioning. The empire's scale required complex administration. (See Map 11.4.) To many outsiders (especially Europeans, whose region was in a state of constant war), Ming stability and centralization appeared to be political wizardry.

Ming rulers worried in particular about maintaining the support of ordinary people in the countryside. The emperor wished to be seen as the special guardian of his subjects. He wanted their allegiance as well as their taxes and labor. But during hard times, poor farmers were reluctant to provide resources—taxes or services—to distant officials. A popular Chinese proverb was "The mountain is high and the

Ming Deities A pantheon of deities were worshipped during the Ming dynasty, demonstrating the rich religious culture of the period and the elaborate way in which faith reinforced hierarchy.

emperor is far away." For these reasons, and because he distrusted state bureaucrats, the Hongwu Emperor preferred to entrust the management of rural communities to local leaders, whom he appointed as village chiefs, village elders, or tax captains. Within these communities, the dynasty created a social hierarchy based on age, sex, and kinship. While women's labor remained critical for the village economy, the government reinforced a gender hierarchy by promoting women's chastity and constructing commemorative arches for widows who honored their husbands by refraining from remarrying.

Like the European and Islamic states, the Ming Empire faced periodic unrest and rebellion. Rebels often proclaimed their own brand of religious beliefs and local elites resented central control. Outright terror helped stymie these threats to central authority. In a massive wave of carnage, the Hongwu Emperor slaughtered anyone who posed a threat to his authority, from the highest of ministers to the lowliest of scribes. From 1376 to 1393, four of his purges condemned close to 100,000 subjects to execution.

Yet, despite the emperor's immense power, the Ming Empire remained undergoverned. Indeed, as the population multiplied, there were too few loyal officials to handle local affairs. By the sixteenth and early seventeenth centuries, for example, some 10,000 to 15,000 officials shouldered the responsibility of managing a population exceeding 200 million people. Nonetheless, the Hongwu Emperor bequeathed to his descendants a set of tools for ruling that drew on subjects' direct loyalty to the emperor and on the intricate workings of an extensive bureaucracy. His legacy enabled his successors to balance local sources of power with the needs of dynastic rulership.

TRADE AND EXPLORATION UNDER THE MING

Gradually, the political stability brought by the Ming dynasty allowed trade to revive. Now the new dynasty's merchants reestablished China's preeminence in long-distance commercial exchange. Chinese silk and cotton

Map 11.4 Ming China, 1500–1600

The Ming state was one of the largest empires at this time—and the most populous. Using the scale, determine the length of its coastline and its internal borders.

- What were the two Ming capitals and the three main seaport trading cities? How far are they from one another?
- According to the map, where did the Ming rulers expect the greatest threat to their security?
- How many provinces are outlined on the map? How far is Beijing from some of the more distant provinces? What sorts of challenges did that create for the centralized style of Ming rule, and how does the chapter suggest those challenges were resolved?

textiles, as well as fine porcelains, ranked among the world's most coveted luxuries. When a Chinese merchant ship sailed into a port, trading partners and onlookers crowded the docks to watch the unloading of precious cargoes. Although Ming rulers' support for overseas ventures wavered and eventually declined, this period saw important developments in Chinese trade and exploration.

Overseas Trade: Success and Suspicion During the Ming period, Chinese traders based in the three main ports—Hangzhou, Quanzhou, and Guangzhou (Canton)—were as energetic as their Muslim counterparts in the Indian Ocean. These and other ports were home to prosperous merchants and the point of convergence for vast sea-lanes. Leaving the mainland ports, Chinese vessels carried precious wares to offshore islands, the Pescadores, and Taiwan. From there, they sailed on to the ports of Southeast Asia. As entrepôts for global goods, East Asian ports flourished. Former fishing villages developed into major urban centers.

The Ming dynasty viewed overseas expansion with suspicion, however. The Hongwu Emperor feared that too much contact with the outside world would cause instability and undermine his rule. In fact, he banned private maritime commerce in 1371. But enforcement was lax, and by the late fifteenth century maritime trade had once again surged. Because much of the thriving business took place in defiance of official edicts, constant friction occurred between government officials and maritime traders. Although the Ming government ultimately agreed to issue licenses for overseas trade in the mid-sixteenth century, its policies continued to vacillate. To Ming officials, unlike their counterparts in Portugal and Spain, the sea represented problems of order and control rather than opportunities.

The Expeditions of Zheng He One spectacular exception to the early Ming attitude toward maritime trade was a series of officially sponsored expeditions in the early fifteenth century. It was the ambitious third Ming emperor, the Yongle Emperor, who took this initiative. One of his loyal followers was a Muslim whom the Ming army had captured as a boy. The youth was castrated and sent to serve at the court (as a eunuch, he could not continue his family line and so theoretically owed allegiance solely to the emperor). Given the name **Zheng He** (1371–1433), he grew up to be an important military leader. The emperor entrusted him with venturing out to trade, collect tribute, and display China's power to the world.

From 1405 to 1433, Zheng He commanded the world's greatest armada and led seven naval expeditions. His larger ships stretched 400 feet in length (Columbus's *Santa Maria* was 85 feet), carried hundreds of sailors on four tiers of decks, and maneuvered with sophisticated rudders, nine masts, and

Zheng He's Ships and Exotic Cargo The largest ship in Zheng He's armada had nine staggered masts and twelve silk sails. This graphic demonstrates just how large and complex Zheng He's ships were, compared with Christopher Columbus's *Santa Maria*. With ships so large, Zheng He's fleet could return to China with magnificent and exotic cargo, like the giraffes brought as tribute from Bengal in 1414 and Malindi in 1415. These tribute giraffes were recorded in several paintings, some inscribed with a poem attributed to his contemporary Shen Du that described the giraffes as *qilin*, mythical creatures that appear during the rule of a great leader.

watertight compartments. The first expedition set sail with 28,000 men aboard a flotilla of sixty-two large ships and over 200 lesser ones. Zheng He and his entourage aimed to establish tributary relations with far-flung territories—from Southeast Asia to the Indian Ocean ports, to the Persian Gulf, and to the east coast of Africa. (See Map 11.5.) These expeditions sought not territorial expansion but rather control of trade and tribute. When the Yongle Emperor died in 1424, the expeditions lost their most enthusiastic patron. Moreover, by the mid-fifteenth century, there was a revival of military threats from the north. Recalling how the maritime-oriented Song dynasty had been overrun by invaders from the north (see Chapter 10), Ming officials withdrew imperial support for seagoing ventures and instead devoted their energies to overland ventures and defense.

Even though maritime commerce continued without official patronage, the Ming decision to forgo overseas ventures was momentous. Although China remained the wealthiest, most densely settled region of the world, with fully developed state structures and thriving markets, the empire's wariness of overseas projects deprived merchants and would-be explorers of vital support in an age when others were beginning to look outward and overseas.

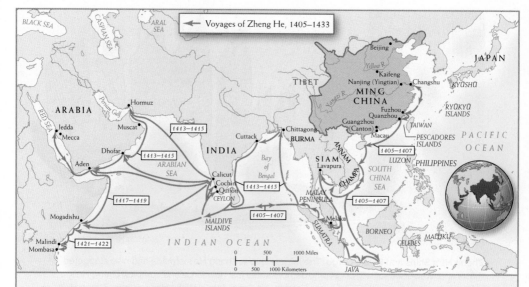

Map 11.5 Voyages of Zheng He, 1405–1433

Zheng He's voyages are some of the most famous in world history. Many have speculated about how history might have been different if the Chinese emperors had allowed the voyages to continue.

- What routes did Zheng He's armada follow?
- Referring to other maps in this chapter and earlier chapters, with what peoples did Zheng He's armada come into contact?
- Using the scale on the map, estimate how far Zheng He's armada sailed. How does this distance compare with the distances covered by other world travelers you've encountered in this text?

Conclusion

The dying and devastation that came with the Black Death caused many transformations, but certain underlying ideals and institutions endured. What changed were mainly the political regimes; they took the blame for the catastrophes. The Yuan dynasty collapsed, and regimes in the Muslim world and western Christendom were replaced by new political forms. And yet, universal religions and wide-ranging cultural systems endured. A fervent form of Sunni Islam found its champion in the Ottoman Empire. In Europe, centralizing monarchies appeared in Spain, Portugal, France, and England. The Ming dynasts in China set the stage for a long tenure by claiming the mandate of heaven and stressing China's place at the center of their universe.

The new states and empires had notable differences. These differences were evident in the ambition of a Ming warlord who established a new dynasty, the military expansionism of Turkish warrior bands bordering the Byzantine

Empire, and the desire of various European rulers to consolidate power. But interactions among peoples also mattered; this era saw an eagerness to reestablish and expand trade networks and a desire to convert unbelievers to "the true faith"—be it a form of Islam or an exclusive Christianity.

All the dynasties surveyed in this chapter faced similar problems. They had to establish legitimacy, ensure smooth succession, deal with religious movements, and forge working relationships with nobles, townspeople, merchants, and peasants. Yet each state developed a distinctive identity. They all combined political innovation, traditional ways of ruling, and ideas borrowed from neighbors. European monarchies achieved significant internal unity, often through warfare with competing states. Ottoman rulers perfected techniques for ruling an ethnically and religiously diverse empire: they moved military forces swiftly, allowed local communities a degree of autonomy, and trained a bureaucracy dedicated to the Ottoman and Sunni Islamic way of life. The Ming fashioned an imperial system based on a Confucian bureaucracy and intense subordination to the emperor so that they could manage a mammoth population. The rising monarchies of Europe and the Ottoman state all blazed with religious fervor and sought to eradicate or subordinate the beliefs of other groups.

The new states displayed unprecedented political and economic powers. All demonstrated military prowess, a desire for stable political and social hierarchies and secure borders, and a drive to expand. Each legitimized its rule via dynastic marriage and succession, state-sanctioned religion, and administrative bureaucracies. Each supported vigorous commercial activity. The Islamic regimes, especially, engaged in long-distance commerce and, by conquest and conversion, extended their holdings.

For western Christendom, the Ottoman conquests were decisive. They provoked Europeans to establish commercial connections to the east, south, and west. The consequences of their new toeholds would be momentous—just as the Chinese decision to turn away from overseas exploration and commerce meant that China's contact with the outside world would be overland and more limited. As we shall see in Chapter 12, both decisions were instrumental in determining which worlds would come together and which would remain apart.

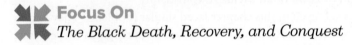

Focus On
The Black Death, Recovery, and Conquest

Collapse and Consolidation

- Bubonic plague originates in Inner Asia and afflicts people from China to Europe.

- Climate change and famine leave people vulnerable to infection, while commerce facilitates the spread of disease.

- The plague kills 25 to 65 percent of infected populations and leaves societies in turmoil.

The Islamic Heartland

- Ottomans overrun Constantinople and become the primary Sunni regime in the Islamic world.

- The Ottomans establish their legitimacy with military prowess, religious backing, and a loyal bureaucracy.

- Sultans manage the decentralizing tendencies of outlying provinces with flexibility and tolerance, relying on religious faith, patronage, and bureaucracy.

Western Christendom

- New dynastic monarchies that claim to rule by divine right appear in Portugal, Spain, France, and England.

- The Inquisition takes aim against *conversos*—converted Jews and Muslims.

- A rebirth of classical learning, known as the Renaissance, originates in Italian city-states and spreads throughout western Europe.

Ming China

- The Ming dynasty replaces the Mongol Yuan dynasty and rebuilds a strong state from the ground up, claiming a mandate from heaven.

- An elaborate, centralized bureaucracy oversees the revival of infrastructure and long-distance trade.

- The emperor and bureaucracy concentrate on developing internal markets and overland trade at the expense of overseas commerce.

CHRONOLOGY

	1200	1300

The Islamic World

Osman founds Ottoman Empire 1299 ●

Black Death arrives in Baghdad 1347 ●

Western Christendom

Black Death reaches Italian port cities 1347 ●

East Asia

Black Death begins in China 1320 ●

The Hongwu Emperor founds Ming dynasty 1368

THINKING ABOUT GLOBAL CONNECTIONS

- **Thinking about Exchange Networks** By the fourteenth century, most of the Afro-Eurasian landmass was bound together by multiple exchange networks that functioned on many levels—political, cultural, and commercial. How did these exchange networks facilitate the spread of the plague? In what ways did the spread of the Black Death correspond with and diverge from existing political, cultural, and commercial networks?

- **Thinking about Changing Power Relationships** Fourteenth-century famine and plague, and the accompanying political, economic, and natural crises, together triggered powerful,

often differing, responses in western Europe, the Ottoman lands, and Ming China. How did men and women at different levels of society respond to the fourteenth-century crises? How did their responses reshape their societies? Pay special attention to the relationships among ordinary men and women, elites, and imperial bureaucracies in all three regions.

- **Thinking about Environmental Impacts** Climate change laid the groundwork for the devastation of the Black Death. What environmental developments in Europe, central Asia, and China set the stage for the Black Death?

Key Terms

Black Death p. 407
devshirme p. 419
dynasty p. 412
humanism p. 427

Inquisition p. 425
Ming dynasty p. 430
monarchy p. 422

Ottoman Empire p. 414
printing press p. 428
Red Turban movement p. 430

Renaissance p. 426
Topkapi Palace p. 417
Zheng He p. 436

 Go to **INQUIZITIVE** to see what you've learned—and learn what you've missed—with personalized feedback along the way.

1400	1500	1600

- Ottoman armies conquer Constantinople 1453

Suleiman expands and consolidates Ottoman Empire 1520–1566

The printing press is invented by Johannes Gutenberg and enters commercial use 1450

Castile and Aragon unite to form Spain 1469

The Inquisition 1481–1826

Spain conquers Granada 1492

Zheng He's voyages 1405–1433

12

Contact, Commerce, and Colonization

1450-1600

Core Objectives

- **DESCRIBE** the broad patterns of world trade after 1450, and **COMPARE** major features of world trade in Asia, the Americas, Africa, and Europe.

- **ANALYZE** the factors that enabled Europeans to increase their trade relationships with Asian empires in the fifteenth and sixteenth centuries, and **ASSESS** their significance.

- **COMPARE** the practices and the impact of European explorers in Asia and the Americas.

- **ANALYZE** the social and political relationships, and **EXPLAIN** the sources of conflict within the Afro-Eurasian polities.

- **ASSESS** how European colonization of the Americas affected African and Amerindian peoples, and **DESCRIBE** their responses.

At the time of Christopher Columbus's birth in 1451, the great world power on the rise was neither Spain nor Portugal, but the Ottoman Empire. For the Ottomans, unlike the other major Asian empires, the fifteenth and sixteenth centuries marked a period of frenzied territorial expansion in the Mediterranean as well as the Indian Ocean. The Ottomans sought to fulfill what they considered to be Islam's primary mission: world dominion. Sultans Bayezid II (r. 1481–1512), Selim I (r. 1512–1520), and Suleiman the Magnificent (r. 1520–1566) continued the conquests of Mehmed the Conqueror and led the thrust into Arab lands and the Indian Ocean even while pressing ahead in Europe. Indeed, Selim I boasted that "he was the ruler of the east and the west."

As the Ottomans turned their attention to conquest of the Red Sea, the Arabian Peninsula, and North Africa, reestablishing under their own control trade routes disrupted by the Mongols and the Black Death, they forced others seeking shares in South and East Asian luxuries to seek new sea passages. European states gave the Ottomans no cause for alarm when they began to make inroads in South Asia in the mid-sixteenth century. After all, it was not Ottoman territory they were contesting, and the Ottomans, looking westward, had bigger fish to fry. No one could have predicted that European conquests of a few South Asian trading cities were particularly significant, compared with the Ottomans' relentless annexations of large territories, including great stretches of southeastern Europe.

Even more unpredictable, though hugely consequential, was the accidental discovery made by Christopher Columbus. Seeking to circumvent Ottoman power in the eastern Mediterranean, Columbus opened up a "New World" about which Afro-Eurasians had no previous knowledge. Although Columbus did not intend to "discover" America when he went looking for Asia, his voyages convinced Europeans that there were still new territories to exploit and peoples to convert to Christianity. For the first time since the Ice Age migrations, large numbers of people moved from Afro-Eurasian landmasses to the Americas. Two different **biomes** (distinct biological systems, including humans, that have formed in response to shared physical conditions) came into contact and converged, including plants, commercial products, and—most momentous—deadly germs. The encounter of the New and Old Worlds was as if two separate planets that had not known of each other suddenly merged into one. Europeans now began building empires different in kind from the land empires of Africa and Asia: overseas empires. While the new colonies generated vast riches, they also brought unsettling changes to the rulers and the ruled.

Despite the significance of Europeans' activity in the Americas, most Africans and Asians were barely aware of the Americas. Asian empires continued to flourish after recovering from the Black Death. Nor was Europe's attention exclusively on the Americas, for its royal houses competed with one another for power and territory at home. Religious revolt in the form of the Protestant Reformation intensified these rivalries. In the wake of Columbus, the drive to build and protect empires across oceans began a very long process that would profoundly change the terms on which people around the globe interacted with one another.

Ottoman Expansion and World Trade

Ottoman expansion overland pushed Europeans to probe westwards overseas. Both Ottoman and European expansion caused important global shifts in the organization of polities as well as in patterns of trade. The two were interconnected, as increasing Ottoman control in the eastern Mediterranean motivated Portuguese and Spanish explorers to turn toward the Atlantic in hopes of reaching the rich trading posts of China and the Indian Ocean by another route. Ottoman expansion was made possible by the Ottomans' domination of Afro-Eurasian trade routes as they recovered in the wake of the Black Death, and it was marked by the sultanate's co-optation of local elites and a relatively tolerant attitude toward other peoples and religions.

For the Europeans, in contrast, expansion overseas was quite new and experimental. Mariners and traders, searching for new routes to South and East Asia, began exploring the Atlantic coast of Africa. Lured by the prospect of spices, silks, and the enslaved, and aided by new maritime technology, Portuguese expeditions made their way around Africa and onward to India. Although Europeans still had little to offer would-be trading partners in Asia, their developing capability in overseas trade laid the foundations for a new kind of global commerce.

Both the new and the old expansionism knitted worlds together that had previously been apart or only loosely interconnected. Together they laid the foundations for a new chapter in world history. But we must not forget that even in the midst of this global transformation, the peoples of each continent continued to focus on local, and often religious, struggles closer to their everyday lives.

THE REVIVAL OF ASIAN ECONOMIES

Trade all across Afro-Eurasia benefited enormously from China's economic dynamism, which was driven primarily by China's vast internal economy. Chinese demand for silver fueled a revival of trade across the Indian Ocean and traditional overland routes. After the Ming dynasty relocated its capital from Nanjing in the prosperous south to the northern city of Beijing, Chinese merchants, artisans, and farmers exploited the surging domestic market. Reconstruction of the Grand Canal now opened a major artery that allowed food and riches from the economically vibrant lower Yangzi area to reach the capital region of Beijing. Urban centers, such as Nanjing with a population approaching a million and Beijing at half a million, became massive and lucrative markets. Despite official restrictions on trade, merchants thrived and coastal cities remained active harbors. (See Map 12.5.)

What did foreign buyers have to trade with the Chinese? The answer was silver, which became essential to the Ming monetary system. Whereas their predecessors had used paper money, Ming consumers and traders mistrusted anything other than silver or gold for commercial dealings. Once the rulers adopted silver as a means of tax payment in the 1430s, it became the predominant medium for larger transactions. China, however, did not produce sufficient silver for its booming economy. Indeed, silver and other precious metals were about the only commodities for which the Chinese would trade their precious manufactures. Through most of the sixteenth century, China's main source of silver was Japan, which one Florentine merchant called the "silver islands." After the 1570s, however, the Philippines, now under the control of the Spanish, became a gateway for silver coming from the New World. One-third of all silver mined in the Americas during the sixteenth and seventeenth centuries wound up in Chinese hands.

China's economic expansion contributed to the revival of Indian Ocean trade. Long-distance merchants developed a brisk commerce that tied the whole of the Indian Ocean together. Ports as far off as East Africa and the Red Sea enjoyed links with coastal cities of India, South Asia, and the Malay Peninsula. Muslims dominated this trade. India was the geographic and economic center of numerous trade routes. With a population expanding as rapidly as China's, its large cities (such as Agra, Delhi, and Lahore) each boasted nearly half a million residents. India's manufacturing center, Bengal, exported silk and cotton textiles and rice throughout South and Southeast Asia. Like China, India exported more than it imported, selling textiles and pepper in exchange for silver.

Overland commerce also thrived anew. One well-trafficked route linked the Baltic Sea, Muscovy, the Caspian Sea, the central Asian oases, and China. Other land routes carried goods to the ports of China and the Indian Ocean; from there, they crossed to the Ottoman Empire's heartland and went by land farther into Europe. Ottoman authorities took a keen interest in the caravan trade, since the state gained considerable tax revenue from it. To facilitate the caravans' movement, the government maintained refreshment and military stations along the route. The largest had individual rooms to accommodate the chief merchants and could provide lodging for up to 800 travelers, as well as care for all their animals. But gathering so many traders, animals, and cargoes could also attract marauders, especially desert tribesmen. To stop the raids, authorities and merchants offered cash payments to tribal chieftains as "protection money." This was a small price to pay in order to protect the caravan trade, whose revenues ultimately supported imperial expansion.

OTTOMAN EXPANSION

Having built the period's most powerful military forces and armed themselves with the latest maps and scientific instruments, the Ottomans began the sixteenth century in possession of Constantinople and great swaths of southeastern Europe and Anatolia. During the sultanate of Suleiman the Magnificent (r. 1520–1566), Ottoman forces carried the empire southward into Egypt, eastward to the Iranian borderlands, and westward into Europe. By 1550, the Ottoman Empire stretched from Hungary and the Crimea in the north to the Arabian Peninsula in the south, from Morocco in the west to the contested border with Safavid Iran in the east. (See Map 12.1 and Chapter 13.)

The Ottomans had become a world power, and their armada dwarfed that of all others at the time. It consisted of seventy-four ships, including twenty-seven large and small galleys and munitions ships, mounted with cannons. Piri Reis—an Ottoman admiral and cartographer—conducted research in the Indian Ocean, an area previously unknown to the Ottomans. Not only did he produce a map of the world, but in 1526 he presented to Sultan Suleiman a masterpiece of geography and cartography known as *The Book of the Sea*. The book drew on Arab sources as well as Indian maps obtained from the Portuguese and offered full information on the geography of the world. In no small part thanks to Piri, the Ottomans made important gains in the Red Sea and ventured into the Indian Ocean as rivals to the Portuguese. But their main energies were devoted to the lands around the eastern Mediterranean, the Black Sea, and the Arabian Peninsula.

The conquest of Syria and Egypt in 1516–1517 was decisive in allowing Ottoman leaders to regard their Sunni state as the preeminent Muslim empire from that moment forward, even enabling some sultans to call themselves caliphs. Egypt became the Ottomans' most lucrative and important acquisition, the breadbasket of the empire and the province that provided Istanbul with the largest revenue stream. But the conquest was no easy matter. The Mamluk rulers resisted mightily, losing a bloody battle in 1516 at Marj Dabiq, north of Aleppo, after which, according to Ibn Iyas, the Arab chronicler of the age, "the battlefield was strewn with corpses and headless bodies and faces covered with

Overland Caravans and Caravanserais Muslim governments and merchants' associations constructed inns, or caravanserais, along the major trading routes. These areas were capable of accommodating a large number of traders and their animals in great comfort. This illustration of a caravanserai comes from the 1581 travel journal of Venetian envoy Jacopo Soranzo.

dust and grown hideous." Nor did the conquest of Egypt prove any easier, for the Mamluks were determined to hold on to their most precious possession. The conquest of Constantinople and the Arab lands transformed the Ottoman Empire, creating a Muslim majority in an empire once mainly populated by conquered Christians and enabling Ottoman sultans to see themselves as heirs of a long line of empires that had ruled over these regions.

Yet on the eastern front, in conflicts with the Safavid Empire, the Ottomans encountered their earliest military failures and their most determined foe, an enemy state that plagued the Ottoman Empire until its collapse early in the eighteenth century (see Chapters 11 and 13). Blocked from eastward expansion, the Ottomans moved westward into Europe, which terrified Europeans. Having taken Constantinople in 1453, Sultan Mehmed II took Athens in 1458. The Ottomans also took large swaths of Balkan territory before turning to North Africa and Egypt and exerted more control than ever over commerce in the Mediterranean.

Ottoman conquests in southeastern and central Europe resulted in the subordination of Christians and Jews to Muslim rule. Centuries of Ottoman rule left a multiethnic legacy in places like Bosnia, including large populations of Muslims in areas later taken by the Habsburg Empire. Thus, the Ottomans, too,

The Global View

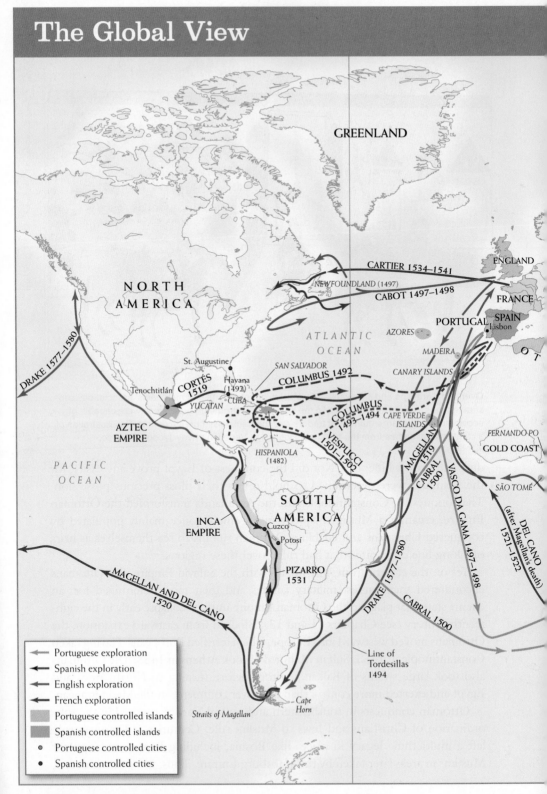

GREENLAND

NORTH AMERICA

CARTIER 1534–1541

NEWFOUNDLAND (1497)

CABOT 1497–1498

ENGLAND

FRANCE

SPAIN

PORTUGAL · Lisbon

ATLANTIC OCEAN

AZORES

MADEIRA

CANARY ISLANDS

DRAKE 1577–1580

St. Augustine

SAN SALVADOR

COLUMBUS 1492

CORTÉS 1519

Havana (1492)

Tenochtitlán

YUCATAN

CUBA

COLUMBUS 1493–1494

CAPE VERDE ISLANDS

VESPUCCI 1501–1502

MAGELLAN 1519

CABRAL 1500

VASCO DA GAMA 1497–1498

FERNANDO PO

GOLD COAST

SÃO TOMÉ

DEL CANO (after Magellan's death) 1521–1522

AZTEC EMPIRE

PACIFIC OCEAN

HISPANIOLA (1482)

SOUTH AMERICA

INCA EMPIRE

Cuzco

· Potosí

PIZARRO 1531

MAGELLAN AND DEL CANO 1520

DRAKE 1577–1580

CABRAL 1500

Line of Tordesillas 1494

Cape Horn

Straits of Magellan

- → Portuguese exploration
- → Spanish exploration
- → English exploration
- → French exploration
-   Portuguese controlled islands
-   Spanish controlled islands
- • Portuguese controlled cities
- • Spanish controlled cities

Map 12.1 European Exploration, 1420–1580

In the fifteenth and sixteenth centuries, sailors from Portugal, Spain, England, and France explored and mapped the coastline of most of the world. Their activities took place in the shadow of the leading empires of the day, with the Ottomans, Safavids, Mughals, and Ming largely unconcerned and unthreatened by them. They established contacts and made connections that, over time, became increasingly important.

- Explain why Europeans would have chosen sea routes to reach Asia rather than land routes.
- Trace the voyages that started from Portugal, and then the voyages that started from Spain. Explain why Portuguese explorers concentrated on Africa and the Indian Ocean, whereas their Spanish counterparts focused on the Americas.
- Contrast the different patterns of exploration in the New World with those in the Indian Ocean and the South China Sea.

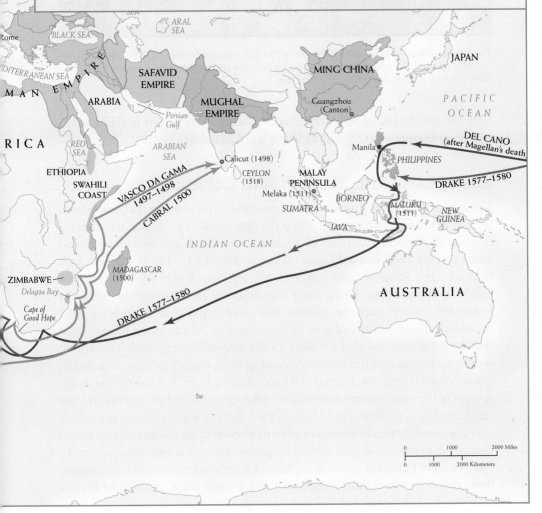

The Catalan Atlas This 1375 map shows the world as it was then known. Not only does it depict the location of continents and islands, but it also includes information on ancient and medieval tales, regional politics, astronomy, and astrology.

from the eastern end of the Mediterranean, became key players in the transformation of Europe in the age of da Gama and Columbus.

EUROPEAN EXPLORATION AND EXPANSION

The emergence of the Ottoman Empire prompted Europeans to find new links to the east in the sixteenth century. When the Ottomans took control of traditional overland trade routes from Europe to Asia, Europeans began to look south and west—and ventured across the seas. (See again Map 12.1.) The Portuguese took the lead. Their search for new routes to Asia led them first to Africa. Europeans had long believed that Africa was a storehouse of precious metals. In fact, a fourteenth-century map, the Catalan Atlas, had depicted a single black ruler controlling a vast quantity of gold in the interior of Africa. As the price of gold skyrocketed during and after the Black Death, ambitious men decided to venture southward in search of this commodity and its twin, silver. While precious metals initially drove Portuguese interest in Africa's Atlantic coast, it would be the development of the sugar plantations on the islands they controlled off the African coast (the Canaries, Cape Verde, and Madeira, then São Tomé and Principe in the Gulf of Guinea) and the need for enslaved labor to work on those plantations that would come to dominate trade with African kingdoms during the sixteenth century. In order to trade European goods in exchange for enslaved humans, the Portuguese built trading forts along major regions of Africa's west coast, establishing trading

Caravel Caravels became the classic vessel for European exploration. They had many decks and plenty of portholes for cannons, could house a large crew, and had lots of storage for provisions, cargo, and booty.

relationships with prominent African kingdoms and rulers extending southward from Senegambia in the north through Sierra Leone, the Gold Coast, the Kongo kingdom, and Angola. This initial version of the African slave trade would expand dramatically in later centuries to fuel the development of the European colonies in the New World. Once European merchants had found sea routes around Africa and established a flourishing trade with the Atlantic kingdoms, they sought to reap the riches abounding in Asian ports, especially when Asian states were firmly established across the Indian Ocean in the seventeenth century.

Innovations in maritime technology and information from other mariners helped Portuguese sailors navigate the treacherous waters along the African coast. New vessels included the carrack, a three- or four-masted ship, developed by the Portuguese to deal with rough waters like the Atlantic Ocean and the Mediterranean. The caravel, with specially designed triangular sails, enabled European sailors to nose in and out of estuaries and navigate unpredictable currents and winds. By using highly maneuverable caravels and perfecting the technique of tacking (sailing into the wind rather than before it), the Portuguese advanced far along the West African coast. In addition, newfound expertise with the compass and the astrolabe helped navigators determine latitude.

Portuguese seafarers ventured from the coasts of Africa into the Indian Ocean and inserted themselves into its thriving commerce. In Asia, Portugal did not attempt to rule directly or to establish colonies. Rather, it aimed to exploit Asian commercial networks and trading systems. To do so, the Portuguese took advantage of a technology developed centuries earlier in China: gunpowder. Mounting small cannons on their warships, they bombarded ports and rival navies or merchant vessels.

The first Portuguese mariner to reach the Indian Ocean was Vasco da Gama (1469–1524). Like Columbus, da Gama was relatively unknown before his extraordinary voyage commanding four ships around the Cape of Good Hope. He found a network of commercial ties spanning the Indian Ocean, as well as skilled Muslim mariners who knew the currents, winds, and ports of call. Once established in the key ports, the Portuguese attempted to take over the trade or, failing this, to tax local merchants. From Sofala, Kilwa, and other important ports on the East African coast, from Goa and Calicut in India, and from Macau in southern China, the Portuguese soon dominated the most active sea-lanes of the Indian Ocean. The Portuguese did not interrupt the flow of luxuries among Asian and African elites; rather, their naval captains simply kept a portion of the profits for themselves, content to benefit from Asian prosperity without imposing Portuguese rule. Only with the discovery of the Americas and the conquest of Brazil did Portugal become an empire with large overseas colonies. For this to transpire, mariners would have to traverse the Atlantic Ocean itself.

The Atlantic World

By opening new sea-lanes in the Atlantic, European explorers set the stage for a major transformation in world history: the establishment of overseas colonies. After the discovery of the Americas, Europeans conquered the native peoples and created colonies for the purpose of enriching themselves and their monarchs.

Crossing the Atlantic changed the course of world history. It did not occur, however, with an aim to discover new lands. Columbus set out to open a more direct—and more lucrative—route to Japan and China. As we saw in Chapter 11, Ferdinand and Isabella hoped Columbus would bring them riches that would finance a crusade to liberate Jerusalem. Neither they nor Columbus expected he would find a "New World."

Europeans arrived in the Americas with cannons, steel weapons and body armor, horses, and, above all, deadly diseases that caused a catastrophic decline of Amerindian populations. Europeans arrived at a time of political upheaval and took advantage of divisions among the indigenous peoples. The combination of material advantages and local allies enabled Europeans to conquer and colonize the Americas, as they could not do in Asia or Africa, where long-standing patterns of trade had resulted in the development of shared immunities and stable states resisted outside incursions.

The devastation of the Amerindian population also resulted in severe labor shortages. Thus began the large-scale introduction of enslaved laborers imported from Africa, which led to the "Atlantic system" that connected Europe, the Americas, and Africa. The precious metals of the New World now gave Europeans something to offer their trading partners in Asia and enabled them to grow rich. In the process, they brought together peoples and ecosystems that had developed separately for thousands of years.

FIRST ENCOUNTERS

Christopher Columbus set sail from Spain in early 1492, stopped in the Canary Islands for supplies and repairs, and cast off into the unknown. It is important to see Columbus as a man of his time. He had no vision for a "new world," no plan for the Atlantic system that would ultimately enrich Europeans. He sought instead to break into older, established trade routes to raise money for the conquest of Muslim-ruled Granada and the reconquest of the Holy Land. Yet his accidental discoveries did usher in a new era in world history.

When Columbus made landfall in the Caribbean Sea, he unfurled the royal standard of Ferdinand and Isabella and claimed the "many islands filled with people innumerable" for Spain. It is fitting that the first encounter with Caribbean inhabitants, in this case the Tainos, drew blood. Columbus noted, "I showed them swords and they took them by the edge and through ignorance cut themselves." The Tainos had their own weapons but did not forge steel—and thus had no knowledge of such sharp edges.

For Columbus, the Tainos' naïveté in grabbing his sword symbolized the childlike primitivism of these people, whom he would mislabel "Indians" because he thought he had arrived off the coast of Asia. In Columbus's view the Tainos had no religion, but they did have at least some gold (found initially hanging as pendants from their noses). Likewise, Pedro Álvares Cabral, a Portuguese mariner whose trip down the coast of Africa in 1500 was blown off course across the Atlantic, wrote that the people of Brazil had all "the innocence of Adam." He also noted that they were ripe for conversion and that the soils "if rightly cultivated would yield everything." But, as with Africans and Asians, Europeans also developed a contradictory view of

Columbus As Columbus made landfall and encountered Indians, he planted a cross to indicate the spiritual purpose of the voyage and read aloud a document proclaiming the sovereign authority of the king and queen of Spain. Quickly, he learned that the Spanish could barter for precious stones and metals.

the peoples of the Americas. From the Tainos, Columbus learned of another people, the Caribs, who (according to his informants) were savage, warlike cannibals. For centuries, these contrasting images—innocents and savages—shaped European (mis)understandings of the native peoples of the Americas.

We know less about what the Indians thought of Columbus or other Europeans on their first encounters. Certainly they were impressed with the Europeans' appearance and their military prowess. The Tainos fled into the forest at the approach of European ships, which they thought were giant monsters; others thought they were floating islands. European metal goods, in particular weaponry, struck them as otherworldly. The Amerindians found the newcomers different not for their skin color (only Europeans drew the distinction based on skin pigmentation) but for their hairiness. Indeed, the Europeans' beards, breath, and bad manners repulsed their Indian hosts. The newcomers' inability to live off the land also stood out. In due course, the Indians realized not just that the strange, hairy people bearing metal weapons were odd trading partners, but that they meant to stay and to force the local population to labor for them. The explorers had become **conquistadors** (conquerors).

FIRST CONQUESTS

First contacts between peoples gave way to dramatic conquests in the Americas; then conquests paved the way to mass exploitation of native peoples. After the first voyage, Columbus claimed that on Hispaniola (present-day Haiti and the Dominican Republic) "he had found what he was looking for"—gold. That was sufficient to persuade the Spanish crown to invest in larger expeditions. Whereas Columbus first sailed with three small ships and 87 men, ten years later the Spanish outfitted an expedition with 2,500 men.

Between 1492 and 1519, the Spanish experimented with institutions of colonial rule over local populations on the Caribbean island that they renamed Hispaniola. Ultimately they created a model that the rest of the New World colonies would adapt. But the Spaniards faced problems that would recur. The first was Indian resistance. As early as 1494, starving Spaniards raided and pillaged Indian villages. When the Indians revolted, Spanish soldiers replied with punitive expeditions and began enslaving them to work in mines extracting gold. As the crown rewarded conquistadors with grants (*encomiendas*) giving them control over Indian labor, a rich class of **encomenderos** arose who enjoyed the fruits of the system. Although the surface gold mines soon ran dry, the model of granting favored settlers the right to coerce Indian labor endured. In return, those who received the labor rights paid special taxes on the precious metals that were extracted. Thus, both the crown and the *encomenderos* benefited. The same cannot be said of the Amerindians, who perished in great numbers from disease, malnutrition, and overwork.

As Spanish colonists saw the bounty of Hispaniola dry up, they set out to discover and conquer new territories. Finding their way to the mainlands of the American landmasses, they encountered larger, more complex, and more militarized societies than those they had overrun in the Caribbean. Great civilizations had arisen there centuries before, boasting large cities, monumental buildings, and riches based on wealthy agrarian societies. In both Mesoamerica, starting with the Olmecs (see Chapter 5), and the Andes, with the Chimú (see Chapter 10), large states had laid the foundations for the subsequent Aztec Empire and **Inca Empire**. These empires were powerful. But they had evolved untouched by Afro-Eurasian developments; as worlds apart, they were unprepared for the kind of assaults that European invaders had honed. In pre-Columbian Mesoamerica and then the Andes, warfare was more ceremonial, less inclined to wipe out enemies than to make them pay tribute. As a result, the wealth and vulnerability of these empires made them irresistible to outside conquerors.

Aztec Society In Mesoamerica, the Mexica had created an empire known to us as "Aztec." Around Lake Texcoco, Mexica cities grew and in 1430 formed a three-city league, which then expanded through the Central Valley of Mexico to incorporate neighboring peoples. Gradually the **Aztec Empire** united numerous small, independent states under a single monarch who ruled with the help of counselors, military leaders, and priests. By the late fifteenth century, the Aztec realm may have embraced 25 million people. Tenochtitlán, situated on an immense island in Lake Texcoco, ranked among the world's largest cities.

Tenochtitlán spread in concentric circles, with the main religious and political buildings in the center and residences radiating outward. The city's outskirts

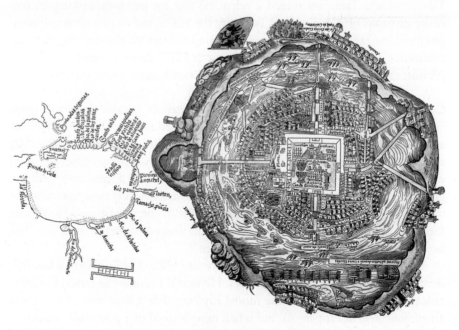

Tenochtitlán At its height, the Aztec capital, Tenochtitlán, was as populous as Europe's largest city. As can be seen from this map, it spread in concentric circles, with the main religious and political buildings in the center and residences radiating outward.

connected a mosaic of floating gardens producing food for urban markets. Canals irrigated the land, waste served as fertilizer, and high-yielding produce found easy transport to markets. Entire households worked: men, women, and children all had roles in Aztec agriculture.

Extended kinship provided the scaffolding for Aztec statehood. Marriage of men and women from different villages solidified alliances and created clan-like networks. In Tenochtitlán, powerful families married their children to each other or found nuptial partners among the prominent families of other important cities. Soon a lineage emerged to create a corps of "natural" rulers. Priests legitimized new emperors in rituals to convey the image of a ruler close to the gods and to distinguish the elite from the lower orders.

Ultimately Aztec power spread through much of Mesoamerica, but the empire's constant wars and conquests deprived it of stability. In military campaigns, the Aztecs defeated their neighbors, forcing the conquered peoples to pay tribute of crops, gold, silver, textiles, and other goods that financed Aztec grandeur. Such conquests also provided a constant supply of humans for sacrifice, because the Aztecs believed that the great god of the sun required human hearts to keep on burning and blood to replace that given by the gods to moisten the earth through rain. Priests escorted captured warriors up the temple steps and tore out their hearts, offering their lives and blood as a sacrifice to the sun god.

Those whom the Aztecs sought to dominate did not submit peacefully. From 1440, the empire faced constant turmoil as subject populations rebelled. Tlaxcalans and Tarascans waged a relentless war for freedom, holding at bay entire divisions of Aztec armies. To pacify the realm, the empire diverted more and more men and money into a mushrooming military. By the time the electoral committee chose Moctezuma II as emperor in 1502, divisions among elites and pressures from the periphery had placed the Aztec Empire under extreme stress.

Cortés and Conquest Not long after Moctezuma became emperor, news arrived from the coast of ships bearing pale, bearded men and monsters (horses and dogs). Here distinguishing fact from fiction is difficult. Some accounts left after the conquest by indigenous witnesses reported that Moctezuma consulted with his ministers and priests, and the observers wondered if these men were the god Quetzalcoatl and his entourage. Most historians dismiss the importance of these omens, describing them as the efforts of rival elites to blame Moctezuma for their own inaction. In any case, Moctezuma sent emissaries bearing gifts, but he did not prepare for a military engagement.

Aboard one of the ships was Hernán Cortés (1485–1547), a former law student from one of the Spanish provinces. He would become the model conquistador, just as Columbus was the model explorer. For a brief time, Cortés was an *encomendero* in Hispaniola, but when news arrived of a potentially wealthier land to the west, he set sail with over 500 men, eleven ships, sixteen horses, and artillery. When the expedition arrived near present-day Veracruz, Cortés acquired two translators, including the daughter of a local Indian noble family, who became known as Doña Marina, also known as La Malinche. With the assistance of Doña Marina and other native allies, Cortés marched his troops to Tenochtitlán. Upon entering, he gasped in wonder, "This city is so big and so remarkable [that it is] almost unbelievable." One of his soldiers wrote, "It was all so wonderful that I do not know how to describe this first glimpse of things never heard of, seen or dreamed of before."

How did this tiny force overcome an empire of many millions with an elaborate warring tradition? Crucial to Spanish conquest was their alliance, negotiated through translators, with Moctezuma's enemies—especially the Tlaxcalans. After decades of yearning for release from the Aztec yoke, the Tlaxcalans and other Mesoamerican peoples embraced Cortés's promise of help. The Spaniards' second advantage was their method of warfare. The Aztecs were seasoned fighters, but they fought to capture, not to kill. Nor were they familiar with gunpowder or sharp steel swords. Although outnumbered, the Spaniards killed their foes with abandon, using superior weaponry, horses, and war dogs. When Cortés arrived at Tenochtitlán, the Aztecs were still unsure who these strange men were and allowed Cortés to enter their city. With the aid of the Tlaxcalans and a handful of his own men, in 1519 Cortés captured Moctezuma, who became a puppet of the Spanish conqueror.

Cortés Meets Mesoamerican Rulers *Left:* This colonial image depicts the meeting of Cortés (second from right) and Moctezuma (seated on the left), with Doña Marina serving as an interpreter and informer for the Spanish conquistador. Notice at the bottom what are likely Aztec offerings for the newcomer. *Right:* This detail from a twentieth-century Mexican mural depicts the meeting of Cortés and the king of Tlaxcala (an enemy of the Aztecs). As Mexicans began to celebrate their mixed-blood heritage, Doña Marina (in the middle) became the symbolic mother of the first mestizos. But she remains controversial and has also been viewed in Mexico as a traitor for the help she provided to the Spanish.

The Aztecs quickly changed their approach to fighting. When Spanish troops massacred an unarmed crowd in Tenochtitlán's central square while Cortés was away, they provoked a massive uprising. The Spaniards led Moctezuma to one of the palace walls to plead with his people for a truce, but the Aztecs kept up their barrage of stones, spears, and arrows—striking and killing Moctezuma. Cortés returned to reassert control, but realizing this was impossible, he gathered his loot and escaped. He left behind hundreds of Spaniards, many of whom were dragged up the temple steps and sacrificed by Aztec priests.

With the Tlaxcalans' help, Cortés regrouped. This time he bombarded Tenochtitlán with artillery, determined to defeat the Aztecs completely. Even more devastating was the spread of smallpox, brought by the Spanish, which ran through the Aztec soldiers and commoners like wildfire. In the end, starvation, disease, lack of artillery, and Cortés's ability to rally Amerindian allies to his side vanquished the Aztec forces in 1521. More died from disease than from fighting—the total number of Aztec casualties may have reached 240,000. As Spanish troops retook the capital, now in ruins, the Spaniards and their allies had to engage in house-to-house combat to secure control over Tenochtitlán. The Aztecs lamented their defeat in verse: "We have pounded our hands in despair against the adobe walls, for our inheritance, our city, is lost and dead." Cortés became governor of the new Spanish colony, renamed "New Spain." He promptly allocated *encomiendas* to his loyal followers and dispatched expeditions to conquer the more distant Mesoamerican provinces.

The Mexica experience taught the Spanish an important lesson: an effective conquest had to be swift—and it had to remove completely the symbols of legitimate authority. Their winning advantage, however, was disease. The Spaniards unintentionally introduced germs that made their subsequent efforts at military conquest much easier.

The Incas The other great Spanish conquest occurred in the Andes, where Quechua-speaking rulers, called Incas, had established an impressive state. Sometime around 1200, a band of Andean villagers settled into the valleys near what is now Cuzco, in Peru, which soon became the hub of South America's greatest empire. A combination of raiding neighbors and intermarrying into elite families raised the Incas to regional supremacy. Their power radiated along the valley routes that carved up the chain of great mountains until they finally ran up against the mighty warrior confederacy of the Chanca. After defeating the Chanca rivals around 1438, the Inca warrior Yupanqui renamed himself Pachacuti and began the royal line of Inca emperors. They eventually ruled a vast domain from what is now Chile to southern Colombia. At its center was the capital, Cuzco, with the magnificent fortress of Sacsayhuamán as its head. Built of huge boulders, the citadel was the nerve center of a complex network of strongholds that held the empire together.

As in most empires of the day, political power depended on a combination of tribute and commercial exchange to finance an extensive communication and military network. The empire developed an elaborate system of sending messages by runners who relayed up and down a system of stone highways carrying instructions to allies and roving armed divisions. None of this would have been possible without a wealthy agrarian base. Peasants paid tribute to village elders in the form of labor services to maintain public works, complex terraces, granaries, and food storage systems in case of drought or famine. In return, Inca rulers were obliged to shelter their people and allies in case of hardship. They oversaw rituals, festivals, and ceremonies to give spiritual legitimacy to their power. At their peak, the Incas may have governed a population of up to 6 million people. But as the empire stretched into distant provinces, especially into northern frontiers, ruling Incas lost touch with their base in Cuzco. Fissures began to open in the Andean empire as European germs and conquistadors appeared on South American shores.

When the Spaniards arrived in 1532, they found a fractured empire, a situation they quickly learned to exploit. Francisco Pizarro, who led the Spanish campaign, had been inspired by Cortés's victory and yearned for his own glory. Commanding a force of about 600 men, he invited Atahualpa, the Inca ruler, to meet at the town of Cajamarca. There he laid a trap, intending to overpower the Incas and capture their ruler. As columns of Inca warriors and servants covered with colorful plumage and plates of silver and gold entered the main square, the Spanish soldiers were awed. One recalled, "Many of us urinated without noticing it, out of sheer terror." But Pizarro's plan worked. His guns and horses shocked the Inca forces. Atahualpa himself fell into Spanish hands, later to be decapitated. Pizarro's conquistadors overran Cuzco in 1533 and then vanquished the rest of the Inca forces, a process that took decades in some areas.

The defeat of the New World's two great empires had enormous repercussions for world history. First, it set the Europeans on the road to controlling the human and material wealth of the Americas and opened a new frontier that the Europeans could colonize. Second, it gave Europeans a market for their own products—goods that found little favor in Afro-Eurasia. Now, following the Portuguese push into Africa and Asia (as well as a Russian push into northern Asia; see Chapter 13), the New World conquests introduced Europeans to a new scale of imperial expansion.

The Columbian Exchange Spanish conquests led to the merger of two separate biomes, leading to an exchange of previously unknown plants, people, and products—and pathogens. Regions that had evolved independently for 10,000 years merged, often violently, into one. The Spanish came to the Americas for gold and silver, but in the course of conquest and settlement they also learned about crops such as potatoes and corn. They brought with them pigs, horses, wheat, grapevines, and sugarcane, as well as devastating diseases. Historians call this transfer of previously unknown plants, animals, people, diseases, and products in the wake of Columbus's voyages the **Columbian exchange**. Over time, this exchange transformed environments, economies, and diets in both the new and the old worlds.

The first and most profound effect of the Columbian exchange was a destructive one: the decimation of the Amerindian population by European diseases. For millennia, the isolated populations of the Americas had been cut off from Afro-Eurasian microbe migrations. Africans, Europeans, and Asians had long interacted, sharing disease pools and gaining immunities; in this sense, in contrast, the Amerindians were indeed worlds apart. Sickness spread from almost the moment the Spaniards arrived. One Spanish soldier noted, upon entering the conquered Aztec capital, "The streets were so filled with dead and sick people that our men walked over nothing but bodies." As each wave of disease retreated, it left a population weaker than before, even less prepared for the next wave. The scale of death was unprecedented: imported pathogens wiped out up to 90 percent of the Indian population. A century after smallpox arrived on Hispaniola in 1519, no more than 5 to 10 percent of the island's population was alive. Diminished and weakened by disease, Amerindians could not resist European settlement and colonization of the Americas. Thus were Europeans the unintended beneficiaries of a horrifying catastrophe.

As time passed, all sides adopted new forms of agriculture from one another. After Amerindians taught Europeans how to grow potatoes and corn, the crops became staples all across Afro-Eurasia. The Chinese found that they could grow corn in areas too dry for rice and too wet for wheat, and in Africa corn gradually replaced sorghum, millet, and rice to become the continent's principal food crop by the twentieth century. Europeans also took away tomatoes, beans, cacao, peanuts, tobacco, and squash, while importing livestock such as cattle, swine, and horses to the New World. The environmental effects of the introduction of livestock to the Americas were significant. For example, in regions of central Mexico where Native Americans had once cultivated maize and squash, Spanish settlers introduced large herds of sheep and cattle. Without natural predators, these animals reproduced with lightning speed, destroying entire landscapes with their hooves and their foraging.

As Europeans cleared trees and other vegetation for ranches, mines, or plantations, they undermined the habitats of many indigenous mammals and birds. On the islands of the West Indies, described by Columbus as "roses of the sea," the Spanish chopped down lush tropical and semitropical forests to make way for sugar plantations. Before long, nearly all of the islands' tall trees as well as many shrubs and ground plants were gone, and residents lamented the absence of birdsong.

Over ensuing centuries, the plants and animals of the Americas took on an increasingly European appearance, a process that the historian Alfred Crosby has called ecological imperialism. At the same time, the interactions between Europeans and Native Americans would continue to shape societies on both sides of the Atlantic.

THE IBERIAN EMPIRES IN THE AMERICAS

The European presence in the New World went beyond the control of commercial outposts. Unlike in the Indian Ocean—where they had to contend with stable, powerful states—European colonizers in the Americas encountered less densely settled, less centralized indigenous societies. (See Map 12.2.) They harnessed those Native Americans who survived the original encounters as a means to siphon tribute payments to their imperial coffers. We should be careful, however, not to mistake the expansive claims made by European empires in the Americas. Through the fifteenth and sixteenth centuries—and as we will see in Chapter 13, through the seventeenth and eighteenth—Amerindians still maintained their dominion over much of the Americas, even as disease continued to diminish their numbers.

By fusing traditional tribute taking with their own innovations, Spanish masters made villagers across their new American empire deliver goods and services. But because the Spanish authorities also bestowed *encomiendas*, those favored individuals could demand labor from their lands' Indian inhabitants—for mines, estates, and public works. Whereas Aztec and Inca rulers had used conscripted labor to build up their public wealth, the Spaniards did so for private gain.

Most Spanish migrants were men; very few were women. One, Inés Suárez, reached the Indies only to find her husband, who had arrived earlier, dead. She then became mistress of the conquistador Pedro de Valdivia, and the pair worked as a conquering team. Initially, she joined an expedition to conquer Chile as Valdivia's domestic servant, but she soon became much more—nurse, caretaker, adviser, and guard, having uncovered several plots to assassinate her lover. Suárez even served as a diplomat between warring Indians and Spaniards in an effort to secure the conquest. Later, she helped rule Chile as the wife of Rodrigo de Quiroga, governor of the province. Admittedly, hers was an exceptional story. More typical were women who foraged for food, tended wounded soldiers, and set up European-style settlements.

Spanish migrants and their descendants preferred towns to the countryside. With the exception of ports, the major cities of Spanish America were the former centers of Indian empires. Mexico City took shape on the ruins of Tenochtitlán; Cuzco arose from the razed Inca capital. In their architecture, economy, and family life, the Spanish colonies adopted as much as they transformed the worlds they encountered.

The next European power to seize land in the Americas, the Portuguese, were no less interested in immediate riches than the Spanish were. Disappointed by the absence of tributary systems and precious metals in the area they controlled, Brazil, they found instead abundant, fertile land, which they doled out with massive royal grants. These estate owners governed their plantations like feudal lords (see Chapter 10). Failing to find established cities, the Portuguese created enclaves along the coast and lived in more dispersed settlements than

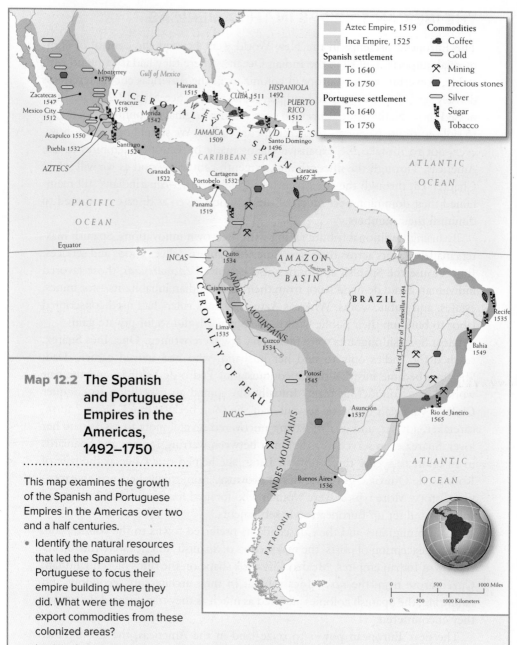

Map 12.2 legend:

- Aztec Empire, 1519
- Inca Empire, 1525

Spanish settlement
- To 1640
- To 1750

Portuguese settlement
- To 1640
- To 1750

Commodities
- Coffee
- Gold
- Mining
- Precious stones
- Silver
- Sugar
- Tobacco

Map labels: Monterrey 1579, Gulf of Mexico, Zacatecas 1547, Veracruz 1519, Havana 1515, CUBA 1511, HISPANIOLA 1492, PUERTO RICO 1512, Mexico City 1512, Merida 1542, VICEROYALTY OF NEW SPAIN, WEST INDIES, Acapulco 1550, Puebla 1532, Santiago 1524, JAMAICA 1509, Santo Domingo 1496, AZTECS, CARIBBEAN SEA, Granada 1522, Cartagena 1532, Portobelo, Caracas 1567, Panama 1519, PACIFIC OCEAN, ATLANTIC OCEAN, Equator, INCAS, Quito 1534, AMAZON BASIN, Amazon R., BRAZIL, VICEROYALTY OF PERU, Cajamarca, ANDES MOUNTAINS, Recife 1535, Lima 1535, Cuzco 1534, Line of Treaty of Tordesillas 1494, Bahia 1549, Potosí 1545, INCAS, Asunción 1537, Rio de Janeiro 1565, ANDES MOUNTAINS, Buenos Aires 1536, ATLANTIC OCEAN, PATAGONIA

0 500 1000 Miles / 0 500 1000 Kilometers

Map 12.2 The Spanish and Portuguese Empires in the Americas, 1492–1750

This map examines the growth of the Spanish and Portuguese Empires in the Americas over two and a half centuries.

- Identify the natural resources that led the Spaniards and Portuguese to focus their empire building where they did. What were the major export commodities from these colonized areas?

- Looking back to Map 12.1, explain why Spanish settlement covered so much more area than Portuguese settlement.

- According to your reading, describe how the production and export of silver and sugar shaped the labor systems that evolved in both empires.

the Spanish settlers did. Unlike the Spanish, they rarely intermarried with Amerindians, most of whom had fled or had died from imported diseases. By the late seventeenth century, Brazil's white population was 300,000.

The problem was where to find labor to work the rich lands of Brazil. Because there was no centralized government to deal with the labor shortage, Portuguese settlers initially tried to enlist the dispersed native population. But when recruitment became increasingly coercive, Indians turned on the settlers. Some Indians fought; others fled to the vast interior. Reluctant to pursue the Indians inland, the Portuguese continued to hug their beachheads, extracting brazilwood (the source of a beautiful red dye) and sugar from their coastal enclaves. Enslaved Africans became the solution to this labor problem. What had worked for the Portuguese on sugarcane plantations in the Azores and other Atlantic islands now found application on their Brazilian plantations.

Silver, Sugar, and Slavery The Iberian empires in the Americas concentrated on three commodities that would transform Europe's relationship to the rest of the world: silver, sugar—and enslaved human beings. Silver enabled Spain and Portugal to enter established trade networks in Asia. The slave trade was a big business in itself: it subsidized shipbuilding and new insurance schemes. Above all, the use of enslaved labor made sugar cultivation

Silver Silver was an important discovery for Spanish conquerors in Mesoamerica and the Andes. Conquerors expanded the customs of Inca and Aztec labor drafts to force Amerindians to work in mines, often in brutal conditions.

fantastically profitable, fueling economic growth and political instability around the world.

The first Europeans in the Americas hoarded vast quantities of gold and silver for themselves and their monarchs. But they also introduced precious metals into the world's commercial systems, which electrified them. In the twenty years after the fall of Tenochtitlán, conquistadors took more gold and silver from Mexico and the Andes than all the gold accumulated by Europeans over the previous centuries.

Having looted Indian coffers, the Spanish entered the business of mining directly, opening the Andean Potosí mines in 1545. Between 1560 and 1685, Spanish America sent 25,000 to 35,000 tons of silver annually to Spain. From 1685 to 1810, this sum doubled. The two mother lodes were Potosí in present-day Bolivia and Zacatecas in northern Mexico. Silver brought bounty not only to the crown but also to a privileged group of families based in Spain's colonial capitals; thus, private wealth funded the formation of local aristocracies.

Colonial mines epitomized the Atlantic world's new extractive economy. They relied on an extensive network of Amerindian labor, at first enslaved, subsequently drafted. Here again, the Spanish adopted Inca and Aztec practices of requiring labor from subjugated villages. Each year, under the *mita*, the local system for recruiting labor, village elders selected a stipulated number of men to toil in the shafts, refineries, and smelters. Under the Spanish, the digging, hauling, and smelting taxed human limits to their capacity—and beyond. Mortality rates were appalling. The system pumped so much silver into European commercial networks that it transformed Europe's relationship to all its trading partners, especially those in China and India. It also shook up trade and politics within Europe itself.

Along with silver, sugar emerged as the most valuable export from the Americas. It also was decisive in rearranging relations between peoples around the Atlantic. Cultivation of sugarcane had originated in India, spread to the Mediterranean region, and then reached the coastal islands of West Africa. The Portuguese, the Spanish, and other European settlers transported the West African model to the Americas, first in the sixteenth century in Brazil, and then in the Caribbean. By the early seventeenth century, sugar had become a major export from the New World. Because Amerindians resisted recruitment and their numbers were greatly reduced by disease, European plantation owners began importing enslaved Africans. By the eighteenth century, sugar production required continuous and enormous transfers of labor from Africa, and its value surpassed that of silver as an export from the Americas to Europe.

At first, most sugar plantations were fairly small, employing between 60 and 100 enslaved people. But they were efficient enough to create an alternative model of empire, one that resulted in more complete and dislocating control of the existing population. The enslaved lived in wretched conditions: their barracks were miserable, and their diets were insufficient to keep them alive under backbreaking work routines. Moreover, they were disproportionately men. As they rapidly died off, the only way to ensure replenishment was to import more Africans. This model of settlement relied on the transatlantic flow of enslaved human beings.

As European demand for sugar increased, the slave trade expanded. Although enslaved Africans were imported into the Americas starting in the fifteenth century, the first direct voyage carrying them from Africa to the Americas occurred in 1525. From the time of Columbus until 1820, five times as many Africans as Europeans moved to the Americas: approximately 2 million Europeans (voluntarily) and 10 million Africans (involuntarily) crossed the Atlantic.

Well before European merchants arrived off its western coast, Africa had known long-distance slave trading. In fact, the overall number of Africans sold into captivity in the Muslim world exceeded that of the Atlantic slave trade. Moreover, Africans kept a population of enslaved people locally. African slavery, like its American counterpart, was a response to labor scarcities. In many parts of Africa, however, enslaved people did not face permanent servitude. Instead, they were assimilated into families, gradually losing their servile status.

With the additional European demand for enslaved individuals to work New World plantations alongside the ongoing Muslim slave trade, pressure on their supply intensified. Only a narrow band stretching down the spine of the African landmass, from present-day Uganda and the highlands of Kenya to Zambia and Zimbabwe, escaped the impact of African rulers engaged in the slave trade and Asian and European slave traders.

By the late sixteenth century, important pieces had fallen into place to create a new Atlantic world, one that could not have been imagined a century earlier. This was the three-cornered **Atlantic system**, with Africa supplying labor, the Americas land and minerals, and Europe the technology and military power to hold the system together. In time, the wealth flows to Europe and the slavery-based development of the Americas would alter the world balance of power.

The Transformation of Europe

Despite the flow of American silver into Spanish coffers, most European rulers and their subjects were focused on Europe, not the New World, in the sixteenth century. The period's frequent warfare centered on purely European concerns, above all on a religious split within the Roman Catholic Church, known as the Reformation. This conflict led to profound religious rifts among states and brought additional political rivalries to the continent.

THE REFORMATION

Like the Renaissance, the **Protestant Reformation** in Europe began as a movement devoted to returning to ancient sources—in this case, to biblical scriptures. Yet returning to the sources and interpreting Christian doctrine for oneself was dangerous in the fourteenth and fifteenth centuries, for the church feared that challenges to its authority would arise if laypersons were allowed to read the scriptures as they pleased. The church was right: when Luther and his followers seized the right to read and interpret the Bible in a new way, they paved the way for a "Protestant" Reformation that split Christendom for good.

The opening challenge to the authority of the Catholic Church originated in Germany. Here a monk and a professor of theology, **Martin Luther** (1483–1546), used his knowledge of the Bible to criticize the church's ideas and practices. For Luther, God's gift of forgiveness did not depend on taking sacraments or performing good deeds. This faith was something Christians could obtain from reading the Bible—rather than by having a priest tell them what to believe. Finally, Luther concluded that Christians did not need specially appointed mediators to speak to God for them; all believers were equally bound by God's laws and obliged to minister to one another's spiritual needs.

These became the three main principles that launched Luther's reforming efforts: (1) belief that faith alone saves, (2) belief that the scriptures alone hold the key to Christian truth, and (3) belief in the priesthood of all believers. Luther also reacted against corrupt practices in the church, such as the keeping of mistresses by monks, priests, and even popes; and the selling of indulgences, certificates that would supposedly shorten the buyer's time in purgatory. In the 1510s, clerics were hawking indulgences across Europe in an effort to raise money for the sumptuous new Saint Peter's Basilica in Rome. In 1517, Luther formulated ninety-five statements, or theses, and posted them on the doors to the Wittenberg cathedral, hoping to stir up his colleagues in debate.

In response, Pope Leo X and the Habsburg emperor, Charles V, demanded that Luther take back his criticisms and theological claims. When he refused, he was declared a heretic and narrowly avoided being burned at the stake. Luther wrote many more pamphlets attacking the church and the pope, whom he now described as the anti-Christ. Luther also translated the New Testament from Latin into German so that laypersons could have direct access, without the clergy, to the word of God. This act spurred many other reformers across Europe to undertake translations of their own, and it encouraged the Protestant clergy to teach children (and adults) to read their local languages.

Spread by printed books and ardent preachers in all the common languages of Europe, Luther's doctrines and those put forward by other reformers won widespread support in some regions, particularly among urban populations. In France and Switzerland, the reformer **Jean Calvin** (1509–1564) emphasized moral regeneration through church teachings and laid out a doctrine of predestination—the notion that each person is "predestined for damnation or salvation even before birth." Those who followed the new faith of Luther and Calvin identified themselves as "Protestants." They promised that their reformed version of Christianity provided both an answer to individual spiritual needs and a new moral foundation for community life. The renewed Christian creed appealed to commoners as well as elites, especially in communities that resented rule by Catholic "outsiders." For example, Protestantism was popular among the Dutch, who resented being ruled by Philip II, an Austrian Catholic who lived in Spain. Although Protestants were rarely a majority before the seventeenth century, the new ideas gained a wide following in the German states, France, Switzerland, the Low Countries, England, and Scotland. (See Map 12.3.) Later, following the sociologist Max Weber (1864–1920), many European historians and economists, in their efforts to explain the origins of capitalism, would look back to these ideas—especially the emphasis on discipline, industriousness, and the individual's relation to God—as distinguishing Europeans from other peoples.

Counter-Reformation The Catholic Church responded to Luther and Calvin by embarking on its own renovation, which became known as the **Counter-Reformation**. At the Council of Trent, whose twenty-five sessions stretched from 1545 to 1563, Catholic leaders reaffirmed the church's doctrines. But the council also enacted reforms to answer the Protestants' assaults on clerical corruption. Like the Protestants, the reformed Catholics carried their message overseas—especially through an order established by a Spaniard, Ignatius Loyola (1491–1556). Loyola founded a brotherhood of priests, the Society of Jesus, or **Jesuits**, dedicated to the revival of the Catholic Church. From bases in Lisbon, Rome, Paris, and elsewhere in Europe, the Jesuits opened missions as far as South and North America, India, Japan, and China.

Yet the Vatican continued to use repression and persecution to combat what it regarded as heretical beliefs. Priests in Augsburg performed public exorcisms, seeking to free Protestant parishioners from possession by "demons." The Index of Prohibited Books (a list of books and theological treatises banned by the Catholic Church) and the medieval Inquisition (which began around 1184 CE) were weapons against those deemed the church's enemies. But the proliferation of printing presses and the spread of Protestantism made it impossible for the Catholic Counter-Reformation to turn back the tide leading toward increased autonomy from the papacy.

In Lima, Peru, the Inquisition reached a fever pitch in the 1630s. Almost 100 people were arrested for committing treason and practicing heresy in a "Great Jewish Conspiracy." The inquisitors held trials for two men and one woman accused of practicing Judaism. Doña Mencia de Luna, Manuel Hernández, and Manuel Bautista Pérez were charged as Judaizers and infidels, which led to a wave of unrests and mass torture. The convicted faced a dramatic public judgment and acts of ritual penance. Inquisitors ordered Manuel Bautista Pérez and ten others lashed to the stake and burned alive. Fifty-two others were publicly whipped, then exiled. Doña Mencia de Luna, Manuel Hernández, and the remaining conspirators wallowed in prison for decades while the inquisitors gathered evidence.

Both Catholics and Protestants persecuted witches. Between about 1500 and 1700, up to 100,000 people, mostly women, were accused of being

Map 12.3 Religious Divisions in Europe after the Reformation, 1590

. . . .

The Protestant Reformation divided Europe religiously and politically.

- Within the formerly all-Catholic Holy Roman Empire, list the Protestant groups that took hold.
- Looking at the map, what geographic patterns can you identify in the distribution of Protestant communities?
- List the regions in which you would expect Protestant-Catholic tensions to be the most intense, and explain why.

Inquisition in Lima The Catholic drive to be rid of heresy spread throughout the Spanish and Portuguese empires, which were at their zenith. Campaigns to rid the colonies of idols and pre-Columbian symbols were ferocious. Since many Jews and Muslims took flight to the colonies, there was also perpetual fear of infidels. In Lima, Peru, the Inquisition staged a spectacular public ceremony to display the power of church authority in the 1630s.

witches. Many were tried, tortured, burned at the stake, or hanged. Older women, widows, and nurses were vulnerable to charges of cursing or poisoning babies. Other charges included killing livestock, causing hailstorms, and tampering with marriage arrangements. People also believed that weak and susceptible women might have sex with the devil or be tempted to do his bidding. Clearly, neither the Reformation—nor the Catholic response to it—made Europe a more tolerant society. Indeed, the Reformation split European society deeply as both Catholics and Protestants promoted their faiths.

RELIGIOUS WARFARE IN EUROPE

The religious revival led Europe into another round of ferocious wars. Their ultimate effect was to weaken the **Holy Roman Empire**—a loose confederation of principalities that were clustered mainly in central Europe and presided over in this period by the Habsburgs (see Chapter 11)—and strengthen the English, French, and Dutch. Already in the 1520s, the circulation of books presenting Luther's ideas sparked peasant revolts across central Europe. Some peasants, hoping that Luther's assault on the church's authority would help liberate them, rose up against repressive feudal landlords. In contrast to earlier wars in which one noble's retinue fought a rival's, the defense of the Catholic mass and the Protestant Bible brought crowds of simple folk to arms. Now wars between and within central European states raged for nearly forty years.

Religious conflicts weakened European dynasties. Spain, with its massive empire and its silver mines in the New World, spent much of its new fortune waging war in Europe. Most debilitating was its costly effort to subdue recently acquired Dutch territories. After a series of wars spanning nearly a hundred years, Catholic Spain finally conceded the Protestant Netherlands its independence. Wars took their toll on the Spanish Empire, which was soon wallowing in debts; not even the riches of its American silver mines could bail out the court. In the late 1550s, Philip II could not meet his obligations to creditors, and, within two decades, Spain was declared bankrupt three times. Its decline opened the way for the Dutch and the English to extend their trading networks into Asia and the New World, and the center of power within Europe shifted to the north.

Religious conflicts also sparked civil wars. In France, the divide between Catholics and Protestants exploded in the St. Bartholomew's Day Massacre of 1572. Catholic crowds rampaged through the streets of Paris murdering Huguenot (Protestant) men, women, and children and dumping their bodies into the Seine River. The number of dead reached 3,000 in Paris and 10,000 in provincial towns. Slaughter on this scale did not break the Huguenots' spirit, but it did bring more disrepute to the monarchy for failing to ensure peace. Another round of warfare exhausted the French and brought Henry of Navarre, a Protestant prince, to the throne. To become king, Henry IV converted to Catholicism. Shortly thereafter, he issued the Edict of Nantes, a proclamation that declared France a Catholic country but also tolerated some Protestant worship.

As princes sought to resolve religious questions within their domains, states increasingly became identified with one or another form of Christian faith—and, for Protestants, with a local language. (Protestants translated the Bible from Latin so that more people could read it.) In this way, religious strife propelled forward the process of state building and the forming of national identities. At the same time, religious conflict fueled rivalries for wealth and territory overseas. Thus, Europe entered its age of overseas exploration as a collection of increasingly powerful yet irreconcilably competitive rival states, whose differences stemmed not just from language but from the ways they worshipped the Christian God.

Wealth from Asian trade, the African slave trade, and American colonization and silver fueled Europe's religious civil war and splintered its state system. This would mean that European powers paled in comparison with the cohesive dynasties of Asia, at least for the moment.

Prosperity in Asia

While Europe was experiencing religious warfare, Asian empires were expanding and consolidating their power, and trade was flourishing. If anything, the arrival of European sailors and traders in the Indian Ocean strengthened trading ties across the region and enhanced the political power and expansionist interests of Asia's imperial regimes. The Mughal ruler of India, Akbar, and the Ottoman sultan, Suleiman the Magnificent (see Chapter 11), were effective and esteemed rulers. The Ming dynasty's elegant manufactures enjoyed worldwide renown, and its ability to govern vast numbers of highly diverse peoples led outsiders to consider China the model imperial state.

MUGHAL INDIA AND COMMERCE

The **Mughal Empire** became one of the world's wealthiest empires just when Europeans were establishing sustained connections with India. These connections, however, only touched the outer layer of Mughal India, one of Islam's greatest regimes. Established in 1526, it was a vigorous, centralized state whose political authority encompassed most of modern-day India. During the sixteenth century, it had a population of between 100 and 150 million.

The Mughals' strength rested on their military power. The dynasty's founder, Babur, had introduced horsemanship, artillery, and field cannons from central Asia, and gunpowder had secured his swift military victories over northern India. Under his grandson, Akbar (r. 1556–1605), the empire enjoyed expansion and consolidation that continued (under his own grandson, Aurangzeb) until it covered almost all of India. (See Map 12.4.) Known as the "Great Mughal," Akbar was skilled not only in military tactics but also in the art of alliance making. Deals with Hindu chieftains through favors and intermarriage also undergirded his empire.

Mughal rulers were flexible toward their realm's diverse peoples, especially in spiritual affairs. Though its primary commitment to Islam stood firm, the imperial court also patronized other beliefs, displaying a tolerance that earned it widespread legitimacy. The contrast with Europe, where religious differences drove deep fractures within and between states, was stark. Unlike European monarchs, who tried to enforce religious uniformity, Akbar studied comparative religion and hosted regular debates among Hindu, Muslim, Jain, Parsi, and Christian theologians. His tolerance kept a multifaceted spiritual kingdom under one political roof.

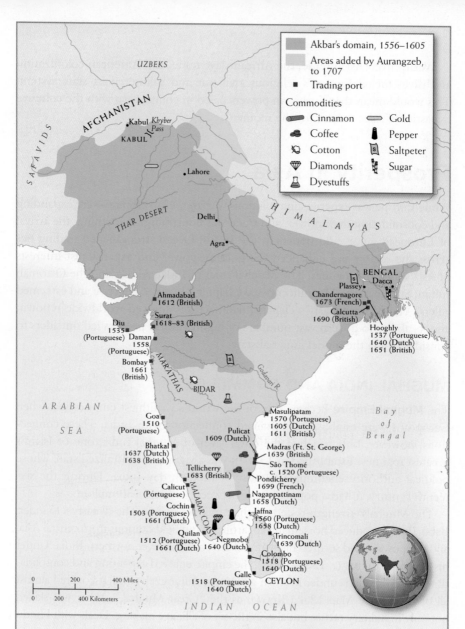

Map 12.4 Expansion of the Mughal Empire, 1556–1707

....

Under Akbar and Aurangzeb, the Mughal Empire expanded and dominated much of
South Asia. Yet, by looking at the trading ports along the Indian coast, one can see
the growing influence of Portuguese, Dutch, French, and English interests.

- Look at the dates for each port, and identify which traders came first and which
  came last.

- Compare this map with Map 12.1 (showing a period that begins earlier, 1420–1580).
  To what extent do the trading posts shown here reflect increased European
  influence in the region?

- According to your reading, explain how these European outposts affected
  Mughal policies.

During the sixteenth century, expanded trade with Europe brought more wealth to the Mughal polity, while the empire's strength limited European incursions. Although the Portuguese occupied Goa and Bombay on the Indian coast, they had little presence elsewhere and dared not antagonize the Mughal emperor. In 1578, Akbar recognized the credentials of a Portuguese ambassador and allowed a Jesuit missionary to enter his court. Thereafter, commercial ties between Mughals and Portuguese intensified, but the merchants were still restricted to a handful of ports. In the 1580s and 1590s, the Mughals ended the Portuguese monopoly on trade with Europe by allowing Dutch and English merchantmen to dock in Indian ports.

Centered in northern India, the Mughal Empire used surrounding regions' wealth and resources—military, architectural, and artistic—to glorify the court. Over time, the enhanced wealth caused friction between wealthy and poorer Indian regions, and even between merchants and rulers. Yet as long as merchants relied on rulers for their commercial gains, and as long as rulers balanced local and imperial interests, the realm maintained a formal unity and kept Europeans on its margins.

PROSPERITY IN MING CHINA

China also prospered from increased commerce in the late sixteenth century. Like the Mughals, the Ming seemed unconcerned with the increasing appearance of foreigners, including Europeans bearing silver. As in India, the Ming confined European traders to port cities. Silver from the Americas did, however, circulate widely in China. It allowed employers to pay their workers with money rather than with produce or goods, which in turn motivated those workers to produce more. China also experienced soaring production in agriculture and handicrafts. A cotton boom, for example, made spinning and weaving China's largest industry.

One measure of greater prosperity under the Ming was its population surge. By the mid-seventeenth century, China's population probably accounted for more than one-third of the total world population. Although 90 percent of Chinese people lived in the countryside, large numbers

Chinese Porcelain Box There were two distinct markets for Chinese porcelains in this period, one external and one internal, for consumption within China itself. Although it ultimately ended up in a French museum, this box was produced for the vibrant internal Chinese market, for Persian eunuchs serving the Ming court. The inscription on top, in Arabic script, says, "Strive for excellence in penmanship, for it is one of the keys of livelihood"; the inscription on the sides, in Persian, says, "Ignorance is an irremediable evil, [but] knowledge is a priceless elixir." Neither comes from the Quran, but they both express Islamic sentiments in favor of calligraphy and intellectualism glorying God and testify to extensive commercial activity in China.

filled the cities. Beijing, the Ming capital, grew to over 1 million; Nanjing, the secondary capital, nearly matched that number. Cities offered diversions ranging from literary and theatrical societies to schools of learning, religious societies, urban associations, and manufactures from all over the empire. The elegance and material prosperity of Chinese cities dazzled European visitors. One Jesuit missionary described Nanjing as surpassing all other cities "in beauty and grandeur. . . . It is literally filled with palaces and temples and towers and bridges. . . . There is a gaiety of spirit among the people who are well mannered and nicely spoken."

Urban prosperity fostered entertainment districts where people could indulge themselves anonymously and in relative freedom. Some Ming women found a place here as refined entertainers and courtesans, others as midwives, poets, sorcerers, and matchmakers. Female painters, mostly from scholar-official families, emulated males who used the home and garden for creative pursuits. The expanding book trade also accommodated women, who were writers as well as readers, not to mention literary characters and archetypes (especially of Confucian virtues). But Chinese women made their greatest fortunes inside the emperor's Forbidden City as healers, consorts, and power brokers. The vitality that commerce brought to Ming society continued even after the dynasty's fall in 1644, laying the foundation for further population growth and territorial expansion.

ASIAN RELATIONS WITH EUROPE

As actors in the world of Asian commerce, Europeans were the newest, and weakest, kids on the block. Europeans' overseas expansion had originally looked toward Asia in hopes of acquiring greater access to luxury goods such as silk and spices. It took some time for them to acquire access to these markets. But silver, followed by maritime and military advances and state-backed trading companies, offered Europeans the opportunity to gradually insert themselves into the Eurasian luxury trade. They did not conquer it; before the advent of the industrial revolution, Europeans grafted onto Asian commercial networks and their powerful actors.

The Portuguese blazed the way as collectors of customs duties from Asian traders and, after 1557, as trans-shippers of Chinese porcelains and silks from the coastal enclave of Macau. (See Map 12.5.) The Portuguese also dominated the silver trade from Japan. Envying Portuguese profits, the Spanish, English, and Dutch also ventured into Asian waters.

The real breakthrough came when the American silver supply got hitched directly to Asian silver demand—and Europeans could play the intermediaries. With its monopoly on American silver, Spain enjoyed a competitive advantage. In 1565, the first Spanish trading galleon reached the mouth of the Pasig River on one of the islands in the current-day Philippines. The town of Maynila was a vibrant marketplace in 1570. Merchants from China and Borneo did a swift business there, trading in gold, beeswax, porcelains, and forest products. Maynila was a strategic spot on the sea routes that connected China, Japan,

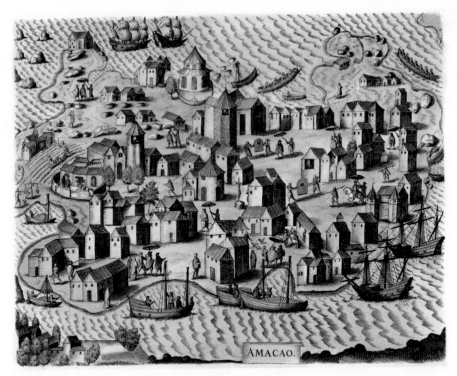

Macau This color engraving depicts the Portuguese enclave of Macau, on the southern border of China, in 1598.

and the Spice Islands—the exclusive source of prized nutmeg and cloves. The Spanish eyed the town not from Europe, but from the other side of the Pacific, in Mexico. Officials and adventurers mortgaged their fortunes in Mexico to fund an expedition to Maynila, taking control of the chieftainship after a series of skirmishes. Thus, in 1571, was born Manila, an administrative dependency of distant Mexico and eventually the capital of the Philippines, the Spanish colony named after the king, Philip II.

Taking Manila opened up a direct portal to China. Each year, ships from Peru and Mexico crossed the Pacific to Manila bearing cargoes of silver. They returned with a ballast of porcelains and silks. Merchants in Manila also procured silks, tapestries, and feathers from the China seas for shipment to the Americas, where the mining elite eagerly awaited these imports.

Cultural sharing and influences were not limited to just trade. Mexican theater groups represented the work of the great writer Sor Juana Inés de la Cruz on a Manila stage. Africans and Filipinos joined the same religious brotherhoods in Mexico and Manila. Filipino migrants taught Mexican Indians how to produce wine from palm trees. Even Chinese migrants and traders joined the flow from Manila to Mexico. In 1635, Spanish barbers in the Viceroyalty complained that a glut of cheap Chinese hair and beard trimmers was driving them out

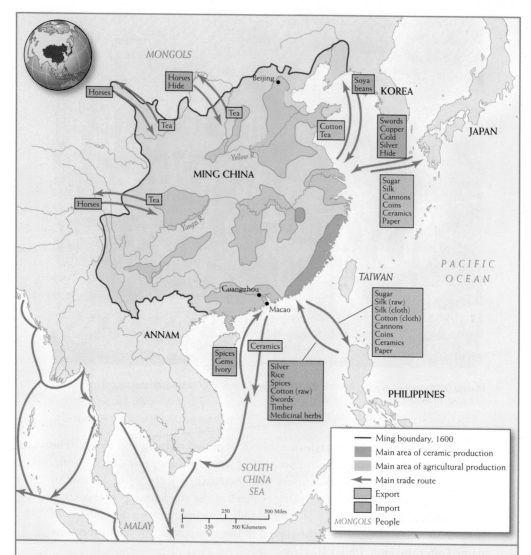

Map 12.5 Trade and Production in Ming China

The Ming Empire in the early seventeenth century was the world's most populous state and arguably its wealthiest.

- According to this map, list the main items involved in China's export-import trade, and identify some of the regions that purchased its exports.
- Evaluate the relative importance of China's internal and overland trade, and contrast it with overseas commerce.
- Evaluate the balance between raw materials, agricultural products, and manufactured goods.

of business. Not only did the Chinese barbers' stalls around the Plaza Mayor offer discounts, but they also provided acupuncture, bloodletting, and coveted Chinese herbal medicines. Missions as far away as California boasted lavish silk vestments brought back on the galleons from Manila. Spain's conquests of Manila and Mexico created a booming Pacific world system.

The year 1571 was decisive in the history of the modern world, for in that year Spain inaugurated a trade circuit that made good on Ferdinand Magellan's earlier achievement of circumnavigating the globe. As Spanish ships circled the globe from the New World to China and from China back to Europe, the world became commercially interconnected. Silver solidified the linkage, as it was the only foreign commodity for which the Chinese had an insatiable demand. From the mother lodes of the Andes and Mesoamerica, silver made the commerce of the world go round. Between 1500 and 1800, the Spanish colonies pumped out 150,000 tons of silver, dwarfing all other supplies combined; much of it sailed east, directly to Asia to monetize and fuel its commercial boom. The silver also coursed through European trading systems and financiers' accounts, growing Europe's economy—despite the political and religious mayhem. Though the Dutch were caught in an endless war with Spanish and Portuguese forces, business was lucrative enough that blue and white Chinese porcelain became commonplace on dinner tables in Amsterdam. Soon, there were imitation items made in Europe, later called "chinoiserie." Whether imported or imitation, Chinese styles became all the rage among prosperous European urbanites. Well-to-do aristocratic women had to be seen in the finest—and latest—of Chinese silks.

By creating an interconnected trading system and finding the means for Europeans to trade with Asian suppliers of precious commodities, the Spanish and the Portuguese created the first world market. It was increasingly integrated. But it also set off a scramble and ramped up competition from envious latecomers. Bristling with their Protestant faiths and determined to muscle in on the Iberian empires' terrain and traffic, the English and the Dutch reached the

Manila Galleon For centuries after 1571, there was continual direct trade between the New World and China. The most famous example was the regular "Manila Galleon," which carried precious metals and enslaved human beings from Mexico to the Philippines. From there, the silver was transported to China in return for silks, porcelains, and other fine goods to be shipped back to Mexico, creating a vibrant transpacific trading system.

South China Sea late in the sixteenth century. Captain James Lancaster made the first English voyage to the East Indies between 1591 and 1594. Five years later, 101 English subscribers pooled their funds and formed a joint-stock company (an association in which each member owns shares of capital). This English East India Company soon won a royal charter granting it exclusive rights to import East Indian goods. Soon the company displaced the Portuguese in the Arabian Sea and the Persian Gulf. Doing a brisk trade in indigo, saltpeter, pepper, and cotton textiles, the English East India Company eventually acquired control of ports on both coasts of India—Fort St. George (Madras; 1639), Bombay (1661), and Calcutta (1690).

Though they fought among themselves for toeholds and trade, Europeans trading in Asia remained dependent on local power brokers and commercial traders. The number of European settlers was miniscule, their cultural inroads few. Trade in Asia continued, largely in Asian hands, and focused on older routes. Although Europeans came to control some small coastal enclaves, they did not have large colonial lands to rule. In Asia, Europeans were, for all intents and purposes, consigned to the role of intermediaries or predators. This contrasted with the Atlantic world, where Europeans created trading and colonizing systems that placed them increasingly at the center—and buoyed their fledgling empires.

Conclusion

In the multicentered world of the fifteenth century, Europe was a poor cousin. However, a new spirit of adventure and achievement animated its peoples, stirred up by the rediscovery of antiquity (the Renaissance), the ambitions of merchants and other elites, and the spiritual fervor of the Reformation and Counter-Reformation. Desiring Asian luxury goods, European merchants and mariners were eager to exploit trade routes leading eastward, and new navigational techniques enabled them to sail into dangerous waters. More important, Europe's location promoted expansion across the largely unknown Atlantic Ocean. With the Ottomans controlling Constantinople and the eastern Mediterranean, Atlantic sea-lanes offered an alternative route to Asia. As Europeans searched for routes around Islamic territory, they first sailed down the coast of Africa and then across the Atlantic.

Encountering the "New World" was an accident of monumental significance. In the Americas, Europeans found riches. Mountains of silver and rivers of gold gave them the currency they needed for dealing with Asian traders. Europeans also found opportunities for exchange, conquest, and colonization. Yet establishing these transatlantic empires heightened tensions within Europe, as rivals fought over the spoils and a religious schism turned into a divisive political and spiritual struggle.

Thus, two conquests characterize this age of increasing world interconnections. The Islamic conquest of Constantinople drove Europeans to find new links to Asia. In turn, the Spanish conquest of the Aztecs and the Incas gave Europeans access to silver, which bought them an increased presence in Asian trading networks.

Amerindians also played an important role, as Europeans sought to conquer their lands, exploit their labor, and confiscate their gold and silver. Sometimes Amerindians worked with Europeans, sometimes under Europeans, sometimes against Europeans—and sometimes none were left to work at all. Then Europeans brought in African laborers, compounding the calamity of the encounter with the tragedy of slavery. Out of the catastrophe of contact, a new oceanic system arose to link Africa, America, and Europe. This was the Atlantic system. Unlike the Indian Ocean and China seas, which supported a system of tributary and trading orders, the Atlantic Ocean supported a system of formal imperial control and settlement of distant colonies. These would become more important to how worlds connected and collided in the following centuries.

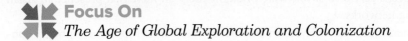

Focus On
The Age of Global Exploration and Colonization

Europe

- Portugal creates a trading empire in the Indian Ocean and the South China Sea.

- Spain and Portugal establish colonies in the Americas, discover silver, and establish export-oriented plantation economies.

- The Protestant Reformation breaks out in northern and western Europe, splitting the Catholic Church.

The Americas

- Millions of Amerindians, lacking immunity to European diseases, perish in every region of the New World.

- Spanish conquest and disease destroy the two great Native American empires in Mexico (the Aztecs) and Peru (the Incas).

Africa

- Trade in enslaved African peoples fuels the Atlantic slave trade, which furnishes labor for European plantations in the Americas.

Asia

- Asian empires—the Mughals in India, the Ming in China, and the Ottomans in western Asia and the eastern Mediterranean—barely notice the Americas but profit economically from enhanced global trade.

Key Terms

Atlantic system p. 465
Aztec Empire p. 455
biomes p. 443
Jean Calvin p. 466
Columbian exchange p. 460

conquistadors p. 454
Counter-Reformation p. 467
encomenderos p. 454
Holy Roman Empire p. 469

Inca Empire p. 455
Jesuits p. 467
Martin Luther p. 466
Mughal Empire p. 471
Protestant Reformation p. 465

CHRONOLOGY   1500

Europe	Luther begins Protestant Reformation 1517 ●
The Americas	Columbus discovers the "New World" 1492 ●
	Cortés conquers Aztec Empire 1521
South Asia	Da Gama sails to India 1498 ●
	Portuguese establish bases around Indian Ocean 1508–1511 ●
East Asia	

THINKING ABOUT GLOBAL CONNECTIONS

- **Thinking about Exchange Networks and the Age of Exploration** In the fifteenth and sixteenth centuries, the densest trade networks and most powerful states remained centered in Asia. How did Columbus's "discovery" of the New World alter the terms on which peoples across Afro-Eurasia interacted with one another? What commodities and trade networks brought peoples together, and on what terms? What new inequalities did those contacts create around the world?

- **Thinking about Changing Power Relationships and the Age of Exploration** The effort to expand empires and trading networks differed substantially across Afro-Eurasia and the Americas in the fifteenth and sixteenth centuries. How did men and women at all levels of society contribute to this expansion? How did that participation shape or reshape their societies? Pay particular attention to the relationship between lower classes and elites.

- **Thinking about Environmental Impacts and the Age of Exploration** The Columbian exchange led to demographic catastrophe and environmental transformation in the New World. Why did the indigenous populations of the Americas get sick so much more often than Europeans did? Why did the plants and animals of the New World increasingly come to resemble those of Afro-Eurasia?

 Go to INQUIZITIVE to see what you've learned—and learn what you've missed—with personalized feedback along the way.

1600

Religious and dynastic wars 1520s–1570s

Pizarro conquers Inca Empire 1533

Expansion and consolidation of Mughal Empire 1556–1605

Portuguese establish trading port in Macau 1557

Spanish make Manila their major port in the Pacific Ocean 1571

13

Worlds Entangled

1600–1750

Core Objectives

- **DESCRIBE** and **EXPLAIN** the impact of climate change on societies and economies across the globe.

- **IDENTIFY** and **EXPLAIN** the major steps in the integration of global trade networks in the seventeenth and eighteenth centuries, and **ANALYZE** examples of resistance to this integration.

- **ANALYZE** the consequences of the Atlantic slave trade across the Atlantic world.

- **EXPLAIN** the effects of New World silver and increased trade on the Asian empires, and their response to them.

- **COMPARE** the impact of trade and religion on state power in various regions.

- **EXPLAIN** the significance of European consumption of goods (like tobacco, textiles, and sugar) for the global economy.

The leading Ottoman intellectual of the sixteenth century, Mustafa Ali, was a gloomy man, convinced that the Ottoman Empire had slipped into an irreversible decline. When he published his magnum opus, *The Essence of History* (1591), the empire's fortunes looked grim. The first half of the century had witnessed the conquest of Egypt and the reign of Suleiman the Magnificent and the Lawgiver, arguably the most successful of sultans. But by century's end, the Ottomans had lost territory to their main European adversaries; military rioting had occurred in protest against payments in debased silver coinage; and uprisings against the empire were widespread in eastern Anatolia. In addition, Ottoman rulers had to grapple with the integration of Old and New World biomes and a series of environmental shocks to their agrarian systems. Getting entangled brought bounty and opportunity, but also competition and disruption. How different parts of the world responded to the upheavals of the global conjuncture of "the long seventeenth century" (the period running from the 1590s to the early 1700s) would have deep, long-term consequences.

We are now becoming aware of how decisive climate change can be on human evolution, because many of the problems of this period stemmed from a severe cold and arid spell that swept the entire world. The seventeenth century is now known as the Little Ice Age. A plunge in global temperatures lasted from 1620 to 1680 (and in some regions dragged into the next centuries), bringing in its wake a decline in precipitation; it laid waste to agricultural and pastoral lands and spread hunger and famines worldwide.

The result was a global, double-edged crisis. Just as world empires ramped up their competition and warfare, they squeezed their peasants for resources to pay for the fighting. At the same time, global cooling meant that peasants produced less food and fewer surpluses and could ill afford the exactions of their rulers. Across much of Afro-Eurasia, the result was mass suffering and a wave of peasant unrest and political upheaval.

Mustafa Ali captured the sentiments of this age well: "Prosperity had turned to famine, the government careers had become confused, venality was rampant, and the military class was being overrun by re'aya [tax-paying subjects]." Even more apocalyptic were his poems. He wrote that "in the social sphere the world is upside down; the ulama are no longer learned or pious; the pillars of the state are fiends and lions; the truly learned are disdained and dismissed and government service now brings pain and poverty rather than pride and wealth. The plague destroying the world is moral as well as physical, for bribery and corruption are the order of the day."

In spite of the turmoil, the period 1600–1750 saw the world's oceans give way to booming sea-lanes for global trading networks. Sugar flowed from Brazil and the Caribbean, spices from Southeast Asia, cotton textiles from India, silks from China, and silver from Mesoamerica and the Andes. New World silver was crucial to these networks: it gave Europeans a commodity to exchange with Asians, and it tilted the balance of wealth and power in a westerly direction across Afro-Eurasia.

Europeans conquered and colonized more of the Americas, the demand for enslaved Africans to work New World plantations leaped upward, and global trade intensified, fueled by New World silver. In the Americas, Spain and Portugal faced new competitors—primarily England and France. With religious tensions added to the mix, the stage was set for decades of bloody warfare in Europe and the Americas. At the same time, in the East, rulers in India, China, and Japan enlarged their empires, while Russia's tsars incorporated Siberian territories into their domain. Meanwhile, the Ottoman, Safavid, and Mughal dynasties, though resisting most European intrusions, found their stability profoundly shaken by climate change and global commerce.

Global Storyline

The Emergence of Global Trade

- Transoceanic trade networks (on an unprecedented scale) create vast wealth and new kinds of inequality.

- Silver gives Europeans a commodity to exchange with Asians and begins to tilt the balance of wealth and power from Asia toward Europe.

- New World sugar also accelerates the shift of power in the Atlantic world from the Spanish and Portuguese to the British and French.

- European merchants and African leaders radically increase the volume and violence of the slave trade, destabilizing African societies.

- Asian rulers in India, China, and Japan and Russian tsars enlarge their empires.

- The Ottoman, Safavid, and Mughal dynasties all struggle to resist European assaults.

Global Commerce and Climate Change

In spite of the worldwide trauma brought on by the plunge in temperatures, global trade flourished during this period. Increasing economic ties brought new places and products into world markets. Closer economic contact enhanced the power of certain states and destabilized others. It bolstered the legitimacy of England and France, and it prompted strong local support of new rulers in Japan and parts of sub-Saharan Africa. But elsewhere, linkages led to civil wars and social unrest. In the Ottoman state, outlying provinces slipped from central control; the Safavid regime foundered and then collapsed; the Ming dynasty imploded and gave way to the Qing. In India, rivalries among princes and merchants eroded the Mughals' authority, compounding the instability caused by peasant uprisings.

The plunge in temperatures also forced people from marginal agricultural lands into the cities. The world had never experienced such massive urbanization: 2.5 million Japanese lived in cities, roughly 10 percent of the population, and in Holland over 200,000 lived in ten cities close to Amsterdam. But city officials were ill equipped to deal with the influx. Disease swept through overcrowded houses, and fire ravaged whole districts. London had an excess of 228,000 deaths over births, yet continued to grow through in-migration. Hardly an escape from rural poverty, cities had inordinately high mortality rates.

EXTRACTING WEALTH: MERCANTILISM

Transformations in global relations began in the Atlantic, where the extraction and shipment of gold and silver siphoned wealth from the New World (the Americas) to the Old World (Afro-Eurasia). (See Map 13.1.) Mined mainly by coerced Amerindians and delivered into the hands of merchants and monarchs, silver from the Andes and Mesoamerica boosted the world's supply of money and spurred trade. During the boom years of the sixteenth century, the increased supply of silver inflated prices. But there could also be sharp contractions, especially after 1620, which deflated prices and led to shortages. Then, a new boom began after 1690. New silver veins opened in Mexico and a gold rush made Brazil the world's largest producer of that gilded ore. For societies that depended on precious metals for their money supply, the ups and downs of mining output could be severely disruptive.

Overall, a rising money supply and new institutions like stock markets and lending houses spurred global trade. American exports were so lucrative for Spain and Portugal that other European powers wanted a share of the bounty, so they too launched colonizing ventures in the New World. Although these latecomers found few precious metals, they devised other ways to extract wealth, for the Americas had fertile lands on which to cultivate sugarcane, cotton, tobacco, indigo, and rice.

The Global View

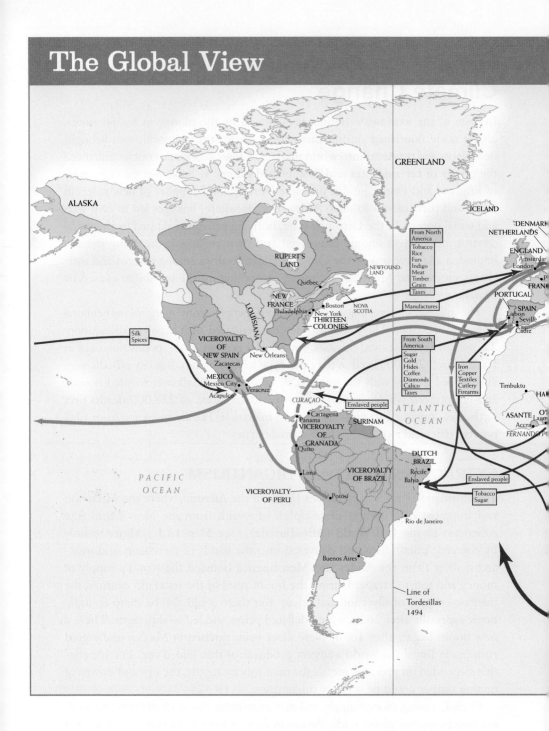

From North America
Tobacco
Rice
Furs
Indigo
Meat
Timber
Grain
Taxes

Manufactures

From South America
Sugar
Gold
Hides
Coffee
Diamonds
Calico
Taxes

Iron
Copper
Textiles
Cutlery
Firearms

Silk
Spices

Enslaved people

Enslaved people

Tobacco
Sugar

GREENLAND

ICELAND

DENMARK
NETHERLANDS
ENGLAND
Amsterdam
London
FRAN
PORTUGAL
SPAIN
Lisbon
Seville
Cadiz

Timbuktu
HA

ASANTE
Accra
FERNANDO P

ALASKA

RUPERT'S
LAND

NEWFOUND-
LAND

Québec

NEW
FRANCE
Philadelphia
New York
THIRTEEN
COLONIES
Boston
NOVA
SCOTIA

LOUISIANA

VICEROYALTY
OF
NEW SPAIN
Zacatecas
New Orleans

MEXICO
Mexico City
Acapulco
Veracruz

CURAÇAO

Cartagena
Panama
VICEROYALTY
OF
GRANADA
Quito

Lima

SURINAM

DUTCH
BRAZIL
Recife
Bahia

VICEROYALTY
OF BRAZIL

VICEROYALTY
OF PERU
Potosí

Rio de Janeiro

Buenos Aires

ATLANTIC
OCEAN

PACIFIC
OCEAN

Line of
Tordesillas
1494

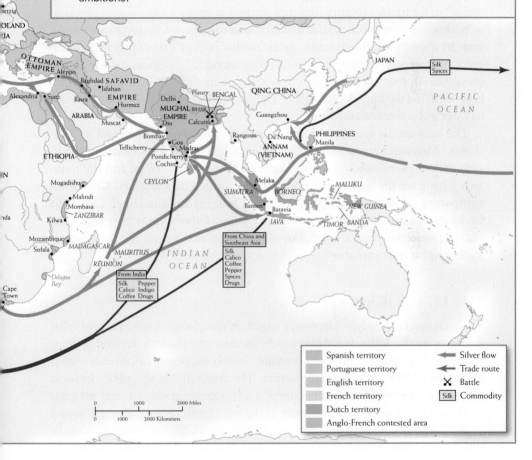

Map 13.1 Trade in Silver and Other Commodities, 1650–1750

The seventeenth and eighteenth centuries were the first centuries of true global commerce. Silver was the one item that was traded all over the world.

- Trace the flows of silver from the Americas around the globe (by following the thick orange arrows), and identify the commodities that silver was exchanged for in different parts of the world.
- Explain the relationship between the trade of manufactures and natural resources.
- According to this map, how did increased trade shape European states' territorial ambitions?

(Map labels:) ARCTIC O; St.; anzig; ĐEN; POLAND; IA; OTTOMAN EMPIRE; Aleppo; Alexandria; Suez; Basra; Baghdad; Isfahan; SAFAVID EMPIRE; Hormuz; ARABIA; Muscat; ETHIOPIA; IN; Mogadishu; Malindi; Mombasa; ZANZIBAR; Kilwa; nda; Mozambique; Sofala; MADAGASCAR; MAURITIUS; RÉUNION; Delagoa Bay; Cape Town; Delhi; MUGHAL EMPIRE; BIHAR; Plassey; BENGAL; Diu; Calcutta; Bombay; Goa; Madras; Tellicherry; Pondicherry; Cochin; CEYLON; Rangoon; Da Nang; ANNAM (VIETNAM); Guangzhou; QING CHINA; JAPAN; Silk Spices; PACIFIC OCEAN; PHILIPPINES; Manila; Melaka; SUMATRA; BORNEO; MALUKU; Banten; Batavia; JAVA; TIMOR; BANDA; NEW GUINEA; INDIAN OCEAN

From China and Southeast Asia
Silk
Calico
Coffee
Pepper
Spices
Drugs

From India
Silk   Pepper
Calico   Indigo
Coffee   Drugs

0   1000   2000 Miles
0   1000   2000 Kilometers

Legend:
- Spanish territory
- Portuguese territory
- English territory
- French territory
- Dutch territory
- Anglo-French contested area
- Silver flow
- Trade route
- ✕ Battle
- Silk Commodity

If silver quickened the pace of global trade, sugar transformed the European diet. First domesticated in Polynesia, sugar rarely appeared in European diets before the New World plantations started exporting it. Previously, Europeans had used honey as a sweetener, but they soon became insatiable consumers of sugar. Between 1690 and 1790, Europe imported 12 million tons of sugar—approximately 1 ton for every African enslaved in the Americas.

No matter what products they supplied, colonies were supposed to provide wealth for their "mother countries"—according to the economic theory of mercantilism, which drove European empire builders. The term **mercantilism** describes a system that saw the world's wealth as fixed, meaning that any one country's wealth came at the expense of other countries. Mercantilism further assumed that overseas possessions existed solely to enrich European motherlands. Thus, colonies should ship more "value" to the mother country than they received in return. Colonies were supposed to be closed to competitors, so that foreign traders would not drain precious resources from an empire's exclusive domain. As the mother country's monopoly over its colonies' trade generated precious metals for royal treasuries, European states grew rich enough to wage almost unceasing wars against one another. Ultimately, mercantilists believed, as did the English philosopher Thomas Hobbes (1588–1679), that "wealth is power and power is wealth."

The mercantilist system required an alliance between the state and its merchants. Mercantilists understood economics and politics as interdependent, with the merchant needing the monarch to protect his interests and the monarch relying on the merchant's trade to enrich the state's treasury. **Chartered companies**, such as the (English) Virginia Company and the Dutch East India Company were the most visible examples of the collaboration between the state and the merchant classes. European monarchs awarded these firms monopoly trading rights over vast areas.

THE LITTLE ICE AGE

While commerce brought the world together, the global climate entered what is known as the **Little Ice Age**, which shocked the planet's survival systems with plunging temperatures and drought. It also happened to coincide with a downturn in New World mining output. The combination was toxic. In some places, the effect of falling temperatures, shorter growing seasons, and irregular precipitation patterns was felt as early as the fourteenth century. But the impact of the Little Ice Age reached farther and deeper in the seventeenth century. What caused this climate change is a matter of debate. But scholars agree that a combination of low sunspot activity, changing ocean currents, and volcanic eruptions that choked the atmosphere ravaged an integrated world. What's more, new research has revealed that the great dying of Amerindians in the sixteenth and seventeenth centuries, as described in the previous chapter, was a major factor producing the Little Ice Age. The decimation of millions of people cleared the way for a return of trees and bushes to what was once densely tilled land. With time, reforestation absorbed vast quantities of carbon dioxide; this in turn intensified cooling and drying all across planet earth. In a sense, this was the reverse of the trend we see today, in which deforestation is reducing the planet's capacity to absorb carbon dioxide, leading to warming. While the seventeenth century was especially severe, the cold lasted well into the next century and in parts of North America into the nineteenth. Climate change brought mass suffering because harvests failed. Famine spread across Afro-Eurasia. In West Africa, colder and drier conditions saw an advance of the Sahara Desert, leading to repeated famines in the Senegambia region. Timbuktu and the region around the Niger bend suffered their greatest famines in the seventeenth century. It was still so cold in the early nineteenth century that the English novelist Mary Shelley and her husband spent their summer vacation indoors in Switzerland telling each other horror stories, which inspired Shelley to write *Frankenstein*.

There were also political consequences. As droughts, freezing, and famine spread across Afro-Eurasia, herding societies invaded settled societies. Starving peasants lashed out against their lords and rulers. Political divides opened up. In Europe, the Thirty Years' War raged out of control, stoked by farmers' anger (see later in this chapter). Although religious and political strife fueled the violence, it owed much to the decline of food production. In the Americas, centuries of plagues had already ripped through indigenous populations. The long cold snap brought even more suffering. Bitter cold and drought afflicted the Rio Grande basin in northern Mexico, culminating in a deep freeze in 1680. The Pueblo Indians rose up en masse against Spanish rulers in a desperate bid for survival. Tensions between Iroquois and Huron rose in the Great Lakes region of North America. Civil war between Portugal and Spain in Europe wreaked havoc in Iberian colonies and led to invasion and panic. The Ottomans faced a crippling revolt, while in China the powerful Ming regime could not deal with the climate shock. It was invaded, as was so often the case when pastures turned to dust, by Manchurian peoples from beyond the Great Wall. They installed a new regime, the Qing dynasty. The English philosopher Thomas Hobbes famously wrote in *Leviathan* (1651) that "man's natural state . . . was war; and not simply war, but the war of every man against every other man." "The life of man," he continued, is "solitary, poor, nasty, brutish, and short."

The Little Ice Age had a devastating impact on populations. It is hard, however, to separate the victims of starvation from the victims of war, since warfare aggravated starvation and famine contributed to war. But in continental Europe, the Thirty Years' War carried off an estimated two-thirds of the total population, on a par with the impact of the Black Death (see Chapter 11). Elsewhere, estimates were closer to one-third. Not until the twentieth century did the world again witness such extensive warfare.

Winter Landscapes *Top:* Hendrick Avercamp was one of the most prolific Dutch painters of the seventeenth century. He often painted skaters on frozen ponds, lakes, and canals. This painting is from around 1608, when the Little Ice Age was at its most intense, and shows skaters on one of the large frozen-over canals in Amsterdam. *Bottom:* Francisco de Goya's *The Snowstorm or Winter* (1786) is set later in the chronology of the Little Ice Age. The painting's subjects huddle against the wind and cold. The peasants are returning home from a futile effort to buy a pig. Behind them are servants from a rich manor house with a recently slaughtered swine.

Exchanges and Expansions
in the Americas

As rulers in England, France, and Holland granted monopolies to merchant companies, those countries began to dominate the settlement and trade of new colonies in the Americas and compete with the established colonies of Spain and Portugal. (See Map 13.2.) Although the search for precious metals or water routes to Asia had initially spurred British, French, and Dutch efforts to establish New World colonies, colonizers soon learned that only by exploiting other resources could they generate profits.

EXPANDING MAINLAND COLONIES

The Little Ice Age hit mainland North America hard. The first English, French, and Spanish settlers faced daunting challenges in freezing woodlands or in areas where native peoples were already scrambling for survival. Early settlements ended badly: the Spanish in Florida, the French in the mouth of the St. Lawrence River, and then the English in Jamestown in 1607 on the northern bank of the James River in what would become Virginia. The English arrived in the midst of a severe drought that lasted from 1606 to 1612; 80 percent of the settlers died of starvation and disease. The survivors were desperate to return to England. It was not until June 10, 1610, when a relief fleet arrived, that the struggling base avoided calamity. The first English settlement in North America could sink its roots.

How the interlopers grappled with the challenges and opportunities laid the foundations for different models of North American colonialism. The important determinants were the resources they found and the relations between newcomers and natives. While the Dutch relied primarily on commerce, the British and the French exploited natural resources in their North American colonies: the British established farms in a number of ecological zones, while the French relied primarily on the fur trade, especially in the interior.

In their colonies along the Atlantic seaboard, the English established one model for new colonies in the Americas. Although these territories failed to yield precious metals or a waterway across the continent, they did boast land suitable for growing a variety of crops. Different climates and soils made for very different agricultural possibilities: wheat, rye, barley, and oats in the Middle Colonies; tobacco in Virginia and North Carolina; and rice and indigo farther south. In all of England's North American colonies, population growth fed greater hunger for farmlands, which put pressure on Indian holdings. The result: a souring of relations between Native Americans and colonists, often ferocious wars between natives and newcomers, and, over the course of the seventeenth and eighteenth centuries, the dispossession of Indians from lands between the Atlantic Ocean and the Appalachian Mountains.

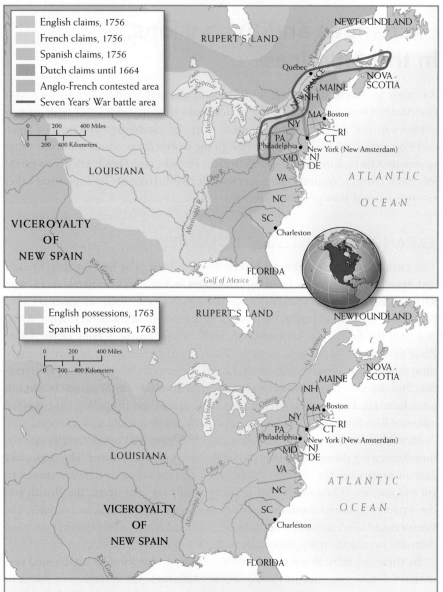

Map 13.2 Empires in North America, 1607–1763

France, England, and Spain laid claim to much of North America at this time.

- Where was each of these colonial powers strongest before the outbreak of the Seven Years' War in 1756? (See p. 525 for a discussion of the Seven Years' War.)

- Which empire gained the most North American territory, and which lost the most at the end of the war in 1763?

- How do you think Native American peoples reacted to the territorial arrangements agreed to by Spain, France, and England at the Peace of Paris, which ended the war?

By contrast, Dutch and French colonies rested not on the expulsion of natives but on dependence on them. Holland's North American venture, however, proved short-lived, as the English took over New Netherland and renamed it New York in 1664. French claims were more enduring and extended across a vast swath of the continent, encompassing eastern Canada, the Great Lakes, and the Mississippi Valley. Crucial to the trade between Europeans and Native Americans in the northern parts of North America was the beaver, an animal for which Native Americans previously had little use.

The distinctive aspect of the fur trade was the Europeans' utter dependence on Native American know-how. After all, trapping required familiarity with the beavers' habits and habitats, which Europeans lacked. This reliance forced the French to adapt to Native American ways, which is evident in their pattern of exchange. Responding to Native American desires to use trade as an instrument to cement familial bonds, the French gave gifts, participated in Native American diplomatic rituals, and even married into Native American families. Women and girls were crucial mediators and brokers in the relationships between newcomers and natives. French–Native American offspring, *métis,* inherited the mantle in New France as interpreters, traders, and guides. Thus, the French colonization of the Americas—owing to French reliance on Native Americans as trading partners, military allies, and mates—rested more on cooperation than conquest, especially compared with the empires built by their Spanish and English rivals. Intermarriage and the creation of mixed-race peoples became commonplace across the rest of the Americas as well, with the notable exception of the English colonies.

As French (and English) traders introduced guns into the exchange networks, however, they initiated an arms race among Native Americans. To get more guns, Native Americans had to collect more skins, which resulted in the depletion of the beaver population in heavily trapped areas. That, in turn, pushed Native Americans to expand their hunting/trapping zones, which heightened conflicts between groups now increasingly competing for hunting territories. Alcohol, too, became a potent weapon for Europeans. It gave them a commodity that Native Americans wanted badly enough to undermine long-standing understandings of the relationship between humans and animals and to overwhelm strictures against overhunting.

NEW NATIVE AMERICAN EMPIRES

Through the seventeenth century and into the middle of the eighteenth century, the majority of lands in the interior of the North American continent remained firmly in Amerindian hands, despite the European empires' expanding claims. On the Great Plains in the center of North America, some Indian peoples lost ground to newcomers, but here the winners were other Indian groups. On the northern plains, the Lakotas, who had migrated westward onto the grasslands, emerged as the most successful expansionists. Migrating eastward, the Comanches reigned across a vast swath of the southern plains. These and other invaders displaced existing indigenous societies from some lands, added to their ranks by capturing and often enslaving large numbers of people (especially women), and enriched themselves by their raiding and through their control over trading. The control that the Comanches asserted extended not only over other Amerindians whom they captured and whose horses they plundered, but also over would-be European colonizers. From the eastern Plains almost to the Pacific Ocean, with the exception of a few enclaves of European settlement, it was Amerindians who largely determined where Europeans could go, stay, and trade. Thus, while early eighteenth-century maps drawn by European empire makers divvied up North America principally among British, French, and Spanish realms, the reality on the ground mocked these imperial pretentions.

There was considerable irony in the fact that Spanish colonizers had empowered the Plains Amerindians. The Spanish, after all, had brought horses to the Americas, and it was the acquisition of these animals that revolutionized Amerindian life and enabled the expansions occurring on the Great Plains. Recognizing the role that horses played in their conquests, the Spanish had tried to keep them out of Indian hands. They failed. Raiders targeted horses. Once introduced into Amerindian circuits, the animals dispersed and flourished on the grasses of the Plains. So did the Indians who had greatest access to horses and who most decisively adapted to equestrianism. On horseback, Amerindians could kill bison much more effectively, which encouraged some groups to forsake farming for hunting and other groups, like the Lakotas and Comanches, to move

NORTH AMERICAN TRADERS AND INDIANS.
Ganthier and Faden's Map of Canada, 1777.

The Fur Trade *Left:* For Europeans in northern North America, no commodity was as important as beaver skins. For the French especially, the fur trade determined the character of their colonial regime in North America. For Indians, it offered access to European goods, but overhunting depleted resources and provoked intertribal conflicts. *Right:* A hand-colored woodcut of the seal of New Netherland depicts a beaver surrounded by wampum, a string of beads used by Indians in religious ceremonies and as currency.

onto the Plains in pursuit of buffalo. Astride horses, Amerindians also gained military superiority over more sedentary peoples, whose villages and cornfields were vulnerable to mobile forces.

Not all Native Americans prospered, however, and certainly not all equally. The gains of nomadic equestrians often came at the expense of those who remained wedded to a mixture of horticulture and hunting. Within horse cultures, new inequalities materialized. More successful raiders and hunters not only earned greater honor but also acquired more horses. One effect was to create new divides within Indian households between women who remained closer to the villages and worked on their sustenance and men who became more ambulatory and devoted to hunting. For victorious men, capturing more horses usually brought higher status and more wives. At the same time, the status of women generally declined in the transition from horticultural to hunting societies. Their burdens, however, did not, as there were now more buffalo waiting to be turned by women into the products that sustained Plains Amerindian life.

The Plantation Complex in the Caribbean

The initial agricultural endeavors in the New World were modest. They relied on crops like tobacco that required relatively modest capital investments and could be profitably farmed on a small scale, with few workers. Sugar, by contrast, required major investments. It had to be processed near the cane fields, which meant mills had to be built, and it required massive amounts of labor. Produced on a large scale with enslaved labor, sugar was enormously profitable. From the middle of the seventeenth century, the British and French devoted their energies to replicating the Portuguese sugar plantations of Brazil on the islands they controlled in the Caribbean. All was not sweet there, however.

Large European plantations in the Caribbean relied on enslaved labor to produce sugar for export. Sugar was a killing crop. So deadly was the hot, humid environment in which sugarcane flourished (as fertile for disease as for sugarcane) that many sugar barons spent little time on their plantations. Management fell to overseers, who worked the people they enslaved to death. Despite having immunities to yellow fever and malaria from their homelands' similar environment, the enslaved Africans who worked on the plantations could not withstand the regimen. Inadequate food, atrocious living conditions, and a lack of sanitation added to their miseries. Moreover, plantation managers on large sugar plantations treated those they enslaved as nonhuman— and as subhuman: one English gentleman commented that enslaved people were like cows, "as near as beasts may be, setting their souls aside."

Slavery and Sugarcane Sugar was the preeminent agricultural export from the New World for centuries. Owners of sugarcane plantations relied almost exclusively on enslaved Africans to produce the sweetener. This 1640 drawing by Frans Post shows enslaved Africans working in a sugar mill in Brazil.

More than disease and inadequate rations, the work itself decimated the enslaved. Average life expectancy was three years. Six days a week enslaved laborers rose before dawn, labored until noon, ate a short lunch, and then worked until dusk. At harvest time, sixteen-hour days saw hundreds of men, women, and children doubled over to cut the sugarcane and transport it to refineries, sometimes seven days per week. Entire households labored in the fields, erasing distinctions of age and gender. Under this brutal schedule, people occasionally dropped dead from exhaustion.

Amid disease and toil, the enslaved resisted as they could. The most dramatic expression of resistance was violent revolt. A more common form of resistance was flight. Seeking refuge from overseers, thousands of resisters took to the hills—for example, to the remote mountains of Caribbean islands or to Brazil's vast interior. Those who remained on the plantations resisted via foot-dragging, pilfering, and sabotage.

Caribbean settlements and slaveholdings were not restricted to any single European power. But it was the latecomers—especially the English and the French—who concentrated on the islands of the Caribbean. (See Map 13.3.) The English took Jamaica from the Spanish and made it the premier site of Caribbean sugar by the 1740s. When the French seized half of Santo Domingo in the 1660s (renaming it Saint-Domingue, which is present-day Haiti), they created one of the wealthiest societies based on slavery of all time. This French colony's exports eclipsed those of all the Spanish and English islands combined. By 1789, French

Saint-Domingue produced nearly half of the world's supply of sugar and coffee. Its principal port city, Cap-Français, was among the richest in the Atlantic world. The colony's merchants and planters built immense mansions worthy of the highest European nobles. Thus, the Atlantic system benefited elite Europeans, who amassed new fortunes by exploiting the colonies' rich soil (which they eroded) and tropical climate and the labor of the African people that they enslaved.

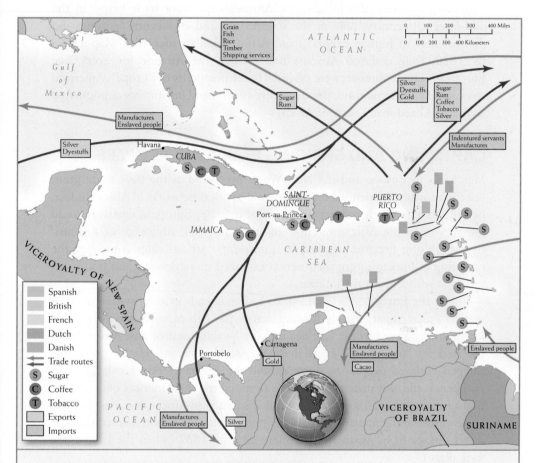

Map 13.3 Caribbean Colonies, 1625–1763

The Caribbean was a region of expanding trade in the seventeenth and eighteenth centuries.

- What were its major exports and imports?
- Who were its main colonizers and trading partners?
- According to your reading, how did the transformation of this region shape other societies in the Atlantic world?

The Slave Trade and Africa

Wiping out native populations, pushing them farther afield, cleared the way for European occupation in the Americas. But there was a problem: Who was going to work the land? Where indigenous labor could not be recruited or forced, Europeans turned to indentured workers and increasingly to importing enslaved African laborers. Although the slave trade began in the mid-fifteenth century, only in the seventeenth and eighteenth centuries did the numbers of human exports from Africa begin to soar. (See Map 13.4.) By 1820, four enslaved Africans had crossed the Atlantic for every free European. Those numbers were essential to the prosperity of Europe's American colonies. At the same time, the departure of so many inhabitants depopulated and destabilized many parts of Africa.

CAPTURING AND SHIPPING ENSLAVED PEOPLES

Merchants in Europe and the New World prospered as the slave trade grew, but their fortunes depended on trading and political networks in Africa. In fact, before the nineteenth-century discovery of quinine, European enslavers could not survive in the African interior. Instead they took advantage of Africans' rivalries. Using firearms supplied by Europeans, African elites controlled the capturing of human cargo; their networks linked moneylenders and traders on the coast with allies in the interior.

Before the Europeans' arrival, Africa had an already existing system of commercial enslavement, mainly flowing across the Sahara to North Africa and Egypt and eastward to the Red Sea and the Swahili coast of East Africa. From the Red Sea and Swahili coast destinations, Muslim and Hindu merchants shipped enslaved peoples to ports around the Indian Ocean. However, their numbers could not match the volume destined for the Americas once plantation agriculture began to spread. Indeed, 12.5 million Africans survived forcible enslavement and shipment to Atlantic ports from 1525 (the date of the first direct voyage from Africa to the Americas) until 1867 (when the last voyage took place).

Now the ports along the African coast became gruesome holding pens. Many of the enslaved who perished did so before losing sight of Africa. Stuck in vast camps where disease and hunger were rampant, the enslaved were then forced aboard vessels in cramped and wretched conditions. These ships waited for weeks to fill their holds while their human cargoes wasted away below deck. Crew members tossed dead Africans overboard as they loaded on other Africans from the shore. When the "cargo" was complete, the ships set sail. In their wake, crews continued to dump bodies. Most died of dehydration brought on by gastrointestinal diseases and a lack of fresh water. Smallpox and dysentery were also scourges. Either way, death was slow and agonizing.

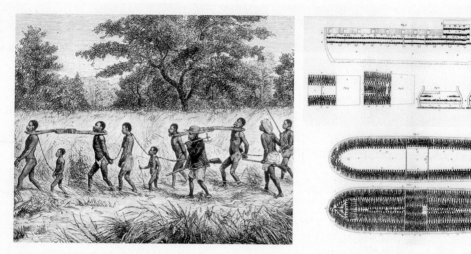

The Slave Trade *Left*: Africans were captured in the interior and then bound and marched to the coast. *Right*: After reaching the coast, the captured Africans would be crammed into the holds of enslaving vessels, where they suffered grievously from overcrowding and unsanitary conditions. Long voyages were especially deadly. If the winds failed or ships had to travel longer distances than usual, many of the men, women, and children held captive would die en route to the slave markets across the ocean.

SLAVERY'S GENDER IMBALANCE

In moving so many people from Africa to the Americas, the slave trade played havoc with the ratios of men to women in both places because most of the people shipped to the Americas were adult men. Although the numbers indicated Europeans' preferences for male laborers, they also reflected African enslavers' desire to keep enslaved women, primarily for household work. The gender imbalance made it difficult for enslaved men and women to have children in the Americas. So planters and enslavers had to return to Africa to procure more human beings to force into bondage—especially for the Caribbean islands, where death rates were so high.

Enslaved men outnumbered women in the New World, but in the enslaving supplier regions of Africa women outnumbered men. Enslaved women were especially prized in Africa because of their traditional role in the production of grains, leathers, and cotton. Moreover, the slave trade reinforced the traditional practice of polygamy—allowing relatively scarce men to take several wives, which helped minimize the loss of population.

AFRICA'S NEW ENSLAVING SUPPLIER STATES

Africans did not passively let captives fall into the arms of European buyers; instead, local political leaders and merchants were active suppliers. This activity promoted the growth of centralized political structures, particularly in West

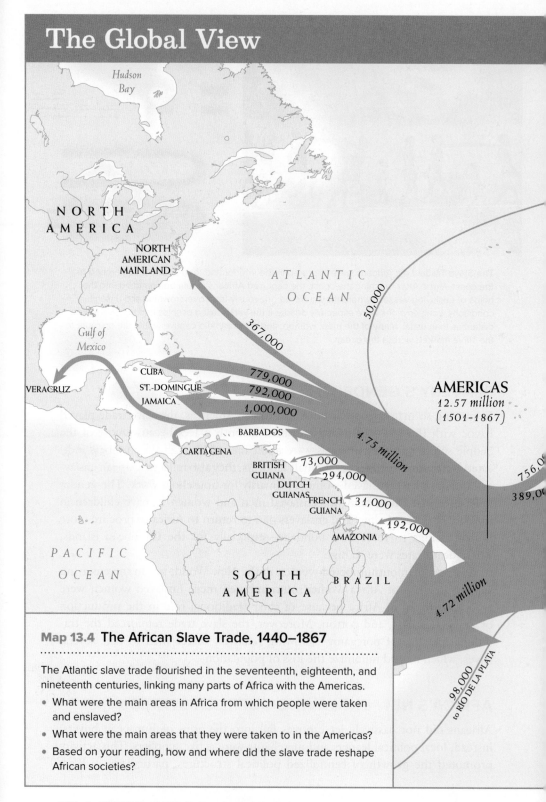

The Global View

Hudson Bay

NORTH AMERICA

NORTH AMERICAN MAINLAND

ATLANTIC OCEAN

50,000

367,000

Gulf of Mexico

VERACRUZ

CUBA

ST.-DOMINGUE

JAMAICA

779,000

792,000

1,000,000

BARBADOS

CARTAGENA

BRITISH GUIANA   73,000

DUTCH GUIANAS   294,000

FRENCH GUIANA   31,000

AMAZONIA   192,000

PACIFIC OCEAN

SOUTH AMERICA   BRAZIL

AMERICAS
12.57 million
(1501–1867)

4.75 million

756,0

389,00

4.72 million

98,000 to RIO DE LA PLATA

Map 13.4 The African Slave Trade, 1440–1867

The Atlantic slave trade flourished in the seventeenth, eighteenth, and nineteenth centuries, linking many parts of Africa with the Americas.

- What were the main areas in Africa from which people were taken and enslaved?
- What were the main areas that they were taken to in the Americas?
- Based on your reading, how and where did the slave trade reshape African societies?

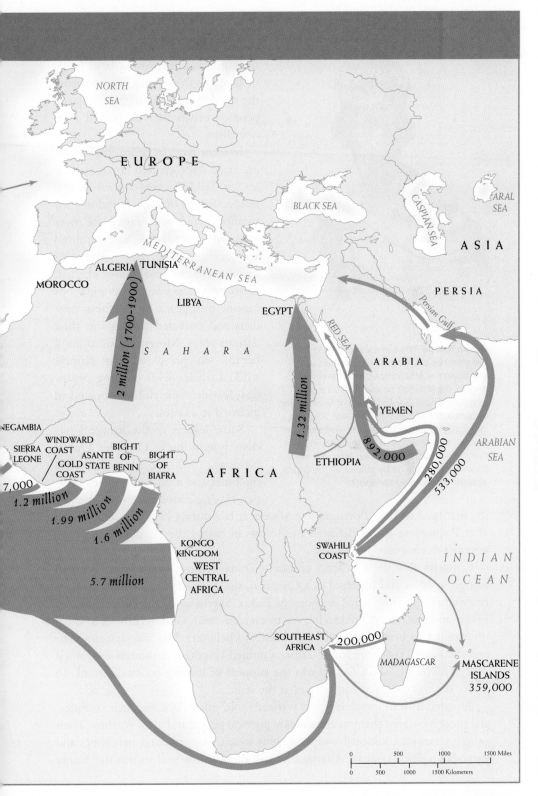

NORTH
SEA

EUROPE

BLACK SEA

CASPIAN SEA

ARAL
SEA

ASIA

MEDITERRANEAN SEA

MOROCCO

ALGERIA TUNISIA

LIBYA

EGYPT

PERSIA

Persian Gulf

RED SEA

ARABIA

2 million (1700–1900)

S A H A R A

4.32 million

YEMEN

ARABIAN
SEA

280,000

533,000

NEGAMBIA

SIERRA
LEONE

WINDWARD
COAST
GOLD
COAST

ASANTE
STATE

BIGHT
OF
BENIN

BIGHT
OF
BIAFRA

A F R I C A

ETHIOPIA

8.92,000

7,000

1.2 million

1.99 million

1.6 million

5.7 million

KONGO
KINGDOM
WEST
CENTRAL
AFRICA

SWAHILI
COAST

I N D I A N

O C E A N

SOUTHEAST
AFRICA

200,000

MADAGASCAR

MASCARENE
ISLANDS
359,000

0   500   1000   1500 Miles

0   500   1000   1500 Kilometers

Queen Nzinga The slave trade shifted political alliances and created new politics up and down the African coast. In what is now Angola, the Mbundu people formed a great kingdom. Under Queen Nzinga of Ndongo and Matamba, they flourished. She was adept at managing Portuguese relations, and after her brother died she rose to the throne to rule for thirty-seven years. Under her reign, her state flourished and she deftly played off the Dutch against Portuguese interlopers.

African rain forest areas. The trade also shifted control of wealth away from households owning large herds or lands to those who profited from the capture and exchange of enslaved people—urban merchants and warrior elites.

In some parts of Africa, the booming slave trade created chaos as local leaders feuded over control of the traffic. In the Kongo kingdom, for example, civil wars raged for over a century after 1665, and captured warriors were sold into slavery. As members of the royal family clashed, entire provinces saw their populations vanish. Europeans fueled these conflicts and provided weapons to their African allies. Moreover, kidnapping became so prevalent that farmers worked their fields bearing weapons, leaving their children behind in guarded stockades.

Some leaders of the Kongo kingdom fought back. Consider Queen Nzinga (1583–1663), a masterful diplomat and a shrewd military planner. Having converted to Christianity, she managed to keep Portuguese enslavers at bay during her long reign. Even after Portuguese forces defeated her troops in battle, she conducted effective guerrilla warfare into her sixties.

Consider also the Christian visionary Dona Beatriz Kimpa Vita. Born in Kongo in 1684 and baptized as a Christian, she claimed at age twenty to have received visions from Saint Anthony of Padua. She believed that she died every Friday and was transported to heaven to converse with God, returning to earth on Monday to broadcast God's commands to believers. Her message aimed to end the Kongo civil wars and re-create a unified kingdom. Although she gained a large following, she failed to win the support of leading political figures. In 1706, she was captured and burned at the stake.

As some African merchants and warlords sold other Africans, their commercial success enabled them to consolidate political power and grow wealthy. Their wealth financed additional weapons, with which they subdued neighbors and extended political control. Among the most durable new polities was the Asante state, which arose in the West African tropical rain forest in 1701 and expanded through 1750. This state benefited from its access to gold, which it used to acquire firearms (from European traders) to raid nearby communities for captives to be sold into slavery in the Americas. From its capital city at Kumasi, the state eventually encompassed almost all of present-day Ghana. Main roads spread out from the capital like spokes of a wheel, each approximately twenty days' travel from the center. Through the Asante trading networks African traders bought, bartered, and sold captives, who wound up in the hands of European merchants waiting in ports with vessels carrying manufactures and weaponry.

Slavery and the emergence of new states enriched and empowered some Africans, but they cost Africa dearly. For the princes, warriors, and merchants who organized the slave trade, their business enabled them to obtain European goods—especially alcohol, tobacco, textiles, and guns. The Atlantic system also tilted wealth away from rural dwellers and village elders and increasingly toward port cities. Across the landmass, the slave trade thinned the population. True, Africa was spared a demographic catastrophe equal to the devastation of American Indians. The introduction of American food crops—notably maize and cassava, producing many more calories per acre than the old staples of millet and sorghum—blunted the trade's depopulating aspects. Yet some areas suffered grievously from three centuries of heavy involvement in the slave trade. The Atlantic trade enhanced the warrior class, who carried out raids for captives;

The Port of Loango Partly as a result of the profits of the slave trade, African rulers and merchants were able to create large and prosperous port cities such as Loango (pictured), which was on the west coast of south-central Africa.

the dislocations, internal power struggles, and economic hardships that followed precipitated the rise and fall of West African kingdoms.

Asia in the Seventeenth and Eighteenth Centuries

Global trading networks grew as vigorously in Asia as they did in the Americas. In Asia, however, the Europeans were less dominant. Although they could gain access to Asian markets with American silver, they could not conquer Asian empires or colonize vast portions of the region. Nor were they able to enslave Asian peoples as they had Africans. The Mughal Empire continued to grow, and the Qing dynasty, which had wrested control from the Ming, significantly expanded China's borders. China remained the richest state in the world, but in some places the balance of power was tilting in Europe's direction. Not only did the Ottomans' borders contract, but by the late eighteenth century Europeans had established economic and military dominance in parts of India and much of Southeast Asia.

THE DUTCH IN SOUTHEAST ASIA

In Southeast Asia, the Dutch already enjoyed considerable influence by the seventeenth century. Although the Portuguese had seized the vibrant port city of Melaka in 1511 and the Spaniards had taken Manila in 1571, neither was able to monopolize the lucrative spice trade. To challenge them, the Dutch government persuaded its merchants to charter the Dutch East India Company (abbreviated as VOC) in 1602. Benefiting from Amsterdam's position as the most efficient money market with the lowest interest rates in the world, the VOC raised ten times the capital of its English counterpart—the royal chartered English East India Company. The advantages of chartered companies were evident in the VOC's scale of operation: at its peak the company had 257 ships and employed 12,000 persons. Throughout two centuries it sent ships manned by a total of 1 million men to Asia.

The VOC's main impact was in Southeast Asia, where spices, coffee, tea, and teak wood were key exports. (See again Map 13.1.) The company's objective was to secure a trade monopoly wherever it could, fix prices, and replace the local population with Dutch planters. Under the leadership of Jan Pieterszoon Coen (who once said that trade could not be conducted without war and war could not be conducted without trade), the Dutch swept into the Javanese port of Jakarta in 1619 and took over the nearby Banda Islands two years later. In Banda, the traditional chiefs and almost the entire population were killed outright, left to starve, or taken into slavery. Dutch enslavers and the people they held in bondage replaced the decimated local population and sent their produce to the VOC. The motive for such rapacious action was the huge profit to be made by buying nutmeg at a low price in the Banda Islands and selling it at many times that price in Europe. The islands, once rich with dense forests and ecologically complex, became monocrop (single-crop) plantations. Although this aggressive expansion met widespread resistance from the local population and other merchants involved in the region's trade, by 1670 the Dutch had also taken Melaka from the Portuguese and controlled all of the lucrative spice trade from the Maluku islands. Next, the VOC set its sights on pepper. However, the Dutch had to share this commerce with Chinese and English competitors. Moreover, since there was no demand for European products in Asia, the Dutch had to participate more in inter-Asian trade as a way to reduce their need to make payments in precious metals.

TRANSFORMATIONS IN THE ISLAMIC HEARTLAND

Compared with Southeast Asia, the major Islamic empires did not feel such direct effects of European intrusion. They did, however, face internal difficulties, which were exacerbated by trade networks that eluded state control and, in some important instances, by climate change. From its inception, the Safavid Empire had always required a powerful, religiously inspired ruler to enforce Shiite religious orthodoxy and to hold together the realm's tribal, pastoral, mercantile, and agricultural factions. With a succession of weak rulers and declining tax revenues—aggravated by a series of droughts and epidemics—the state foundered, and ultimately collapsed in 1722 (see Chapter 14). The Ottoman and Mughal Empires, in contrast, remained more resilient.

The Ottoman Empire Climate change hit the eastern Mediterranean earlier than other regions. Fierce cold and endless drought brought famine and high mortality. In 1620, the Bosporus froze over, enabling people to walk from the European side of Istanbul to the Asian side. In lands dependent on floodwaters for their well-being, such as Egypt and Iraq, food was in short supply and death rates skyrocketed. In addition, the import of New World silver led to high levels of inflation and a destabilized economy.

Having attained a high point under Suleiman (see Chapter 11), the Ottoman Empire ceased expanding. After Suleiman's reign, Ottoman armies and navies tried unsuccessfully to expand the empire's borders—losing, for example, on the western flank to the European Habsburgs. As military campaigns and a growing population strained the realm's limited resources, Ottoman intellectuals worried that the empire's glory was ebbing. A series of administrative reforms in the seventeenth century reinvigorated the state, but it never recaptured the vast power it enjoyed at its height.

Even as the empire's strength waned, by the seventeenth century its sultans faced a commercially more connected world. The introduction of New World silver into Ottoman networks of commerce and moneylending eventually destabilized the empire. Although early Ottoman rulers had avoided trade with the outside world, the lure of silver broke through state regulations. Now Ottoman merchants established black markets for commodities that eager European buyers paid for in silver—especially wheat, copper, and wool. Because these exports were illegal, their sale did not generate tax revenues to support the state's civilian and military administration. So Ottoman rulers had to rely on loans of silver from the merchants. Some European royal houses, notably the Dutch and English, would grant those who bankrolled them a say in government, which vastly increased the crown's credit and ultimately its power. Ottoman sultans, by contrast, feuded with their financiers, which undermined the sultans' authority.

More silver and budget deficits were a recipe for inflation. Prices tripled between 1550 and 1650. Runaway inflation caused hard-hit peasants in Anatolia, suffering from bad harvests and increasing taxes (used to pay off dynastic debts), to join together in uprisings that threatened the state's stability. A revolt, begun in central Anatolia in the early sixteenth century, continued in fits and starts throughout the century, reaching a crescendo in the early seventeenth century. Known as the Celali revolts, after Shaykh Celali, who had led one of the initial uprisings, the rebellion challenged the sultan's authority with an army of 30,000 and turned much of Anatolia into a danger zone. Disorder at the center of the empire was accompanied by difficulties in the provinces, where breakaway regimes appeared.

The most threatening of the breakaway pressures occurred in Egypt beginning in the seventeenth century. In 1517, Egypt had become the Ottoman Empire's greatest conquest. As the wealthiest Ottoman territory, it was an important source of revenue, and its people shouldered heavy tax burdens. The group that asserted Egypt's political and commercial autonomy consisted of military men, known as **Mamluks** (Arabic for "owned" or "possessed"), who had ruled Egypt as an independent regime until the Ottoman conquest. Although the Ottoman army had routed Mamluk forces on the battlefield, Ottoman governors in Egypt allowed the Mamluks to remain in place, in a subordinate position. But by the seventeenth century, these military men were nearly as powerful as their ancestors had been in the fifteenth century when they ruled Egypt independently. Mamluk leaders enhanced their power by aligning with Egyptian merchants and catering to the religious elites of Egypt, the *ulama*. Turning the Ottoman administrator of Egypt into a mere figurehead, this new provincial elite kept much of the area's fiscal resources for themselves at the expense not only of the imperial coffers but also of the local peasantry.

Amid new economic pressures and challenges from outlying territories, the Ottoman system also had elements of resilience—especially at the center, where decaying leadership provoked demands for reform from administrative elites. Known as the Köprülü reforms (1656–1683), a combination of financial reform and anticorruption measures gave the state a new burst of energy and enabled the military to reacquire some of its lost possessions. Revenues again increased, and inflation decreased. Fired by revived expansionist ambitions, Istanbul decided to renew its assault on Christianity—beginning with rekindled plans to seize Vienna. Although the Ottomans gathered an enormous force outside the Habsburg capital in 1683, both sides suffered heavy losses and the Ottoman forces ultimately retreated. Under the treaty that ended the Austro-Ottoman war, the Ottomans lost major European territorial possessions, including Hungary.

Thus, the Ottoman Empire began the eighteenth century dealing with serious economic and environmental challenges. Whereas in the sixteenth century rulers of the Ottoman Empire had wanted to create a self-contained and self-sufficient imperial economy, silver undermined this vision as it had elsewhere in the global economy. Indeed, the influx of silver opened Ottoman-controlled lands to trade with the rest of the world, producing breakaway regimes, widespread inflation, social discontent, and conflict between the state and its financiers. The crop shortages and population crises of the Little Ice Age made all of those problems more difficult to manage.

The Mughal Empire In contrast to the Ottomans' military reversals, the Mughal Empire reached its height in the seventeenth century. The period saw

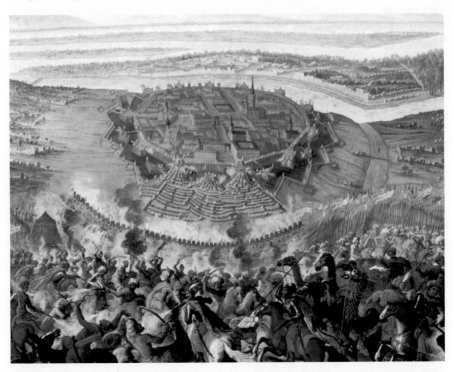

Siege of Vienna This seventeenth-century painting depicts the Ottoman siege of Vienna, which began on July 14, 1683, and ended on September 12. The city might have fallen if the Polish king, John III, had not answered the pope's plea to defend Christendom and sent an army to assist German and Austrian troops in defeating the Ottomans.

Mughal rulers extend their domain over almost all of India and enjoy increased domestic and international trade. But they, too, eventually had problems governing dispersed and resistant provinces, where many villages retained traditional religions and cultures and suffered from the effects of the Little Ice Age on their land's productivity.

Before the Mughals, India had never had a single political authority. Akbar and his successors had conquered territory in the north (see Chapter 12, Map 12.4), so now the Mughals turned to the south and gained control over most of that region by 1689. As the new provinces provided an additional source of resources, local lords, and warriors, the Mughal bureaucracy grew better at extracting services and taxes.

Imperial stability and prosperity did not depend entirely on the Indian Ocean trading system. Indeed, although the Mughals profited from seaborne trade, they never undertook overseas expansion. The main source of their wealth was land rents, which increased via incentives to bring new land into cultivation. But the imperial economy also benefited from Europeans' increased demand for Indian goods, including a sixfold rise in the English East India Company's textile purchases.

Eventually, the Mughals were victims of their own success. More than a century of imperial expansion, commercial prosperity, and agricultural development placed substantial resources in the hands of local and regional authorities. As a result, local warrior elites became more autonomous. By the late seventeenth century, many regional leaders were well positioned to resist Mughal authority. As in the Ottoman Empire, distant provinces began to challenge central rulers. Now the Indian peasants (like their counterparts in Ming China, Safavid Persia, and the Ottoman Empire) capitalized on weakening central authority. Many rose in rebellions, especially when drought and famine hit; others took up banditry.

At this point, the Mughal emperors had to accept diminished power over a loose unity of provincial states. Most of these areas accepted Mughal control in name only, administering their own affairs with local resources. Yet India still flourished, and landed elites brought new territories into agrarian production. Cotton, for instance, supported a thriving textile industry as peasant households focused on weaving and cloth production. Much of their production was destined for export as the region deepened its integration into world trading systems.

The Mughals themselves paid scant attention to commercial matters, but local rulers welcomed Europeans into Indian ports. As more European ships arrived, these authorities struck deals with merchants from Portugal and, increasingly, from England and Holland. Some Indian merchants formed trading companies of their own to control the sale of regional produce to competing Europeans; others established intricate trading networks that reached as far north as Russia. Mercantile houses grew richer and gained greater political influence over

Indian Cotton European traders were drawn to India by its famed cotton textiles. This image from around 1800 shows a woman separating the cotton from the seeds; it captures the preindustrial technology of cotton production in India.

financially strapped emperors. Thus, even as global commercial entanglements enriched some in India, the effects undercut the Mughal dynasty.

FROM MING TO QING IN CHINA

Like India, China prospered in the seventeenth and eighteenth centuries; but here, too, growing wealth and climate change undermined central control and, in this case, contributed to the fall of a long-lasting dynasty. As in Mughal India, local power holders in China increasingly defied the Ming government. Moreover, because Ming sovereigns discouraged overseas commerce and forbade travel abroad, they did not reap the rewards of long-distance exchange. Rather, such profits went to traders and adventurers who evaded imperial edicts. Together, the persistence of local autonomy and the accelerating economic and social changes brought unprecedented challenges until finally, in 1644, the Ming dynasty collapsed.

Administrative and Economic Problems How did a dynasty that in the early seventeenth century governed the world's most economically advanced society (and perhaps a third of the world's population) fall from power? As in the Ottoman Empire, responsibility often lay with the rulers and their inadequate response to economic and environmental change. Zhu Yijun, the Wanli Emperor (r. 1572–1620), was secluded despite being surrounded by a staff of 20,000 eunuchs and 3,000 women. The "Son of Heaven" rarely ventured outside the palace compound, and when he moved within it a large retinue accompanied him, led by eunuchs clearing his path with whips. Ming emperors like Wanli quickly discovered that despite the elaborate arrangements and ritual performances affirming their position as the Son of Heaven, they had little control over the vast bureaucracy. An emperor frustrated with his officials could do little more than punish them or refuse to cooperate.

The timing of administrative breakdown in the Ming government was unfortunate, because expanding opportunities for trade led many individuals to circumvent official rules. From the mid-sixteenth century, bands of supposedly Japanese pirates ravaged the Chinese coast. Indeed, the Ming government had difficulties regulating trade with Japan and labeled all pirates as Japanese, but many of the marauders were in fact Chinese who flouted imperial authority. In tough times, the roving gangs terrorized sea-lanes and harbors. In better times, some functioned like mercantile groups: their leaders mingled with elites, foreign trade representatives, and imperial officials. What made these predators so resilient—and their business so lucrative—was their ability to move among the mosaic of East Asian cultures.

Just like in the Islamic empires, the influx of silver from the New World and Japan, while at first stimulating the Chinese economy, led to severe economic and, eventually, political problems. As we saw in Chapter 12, Europeans used New World silver to pay for their purchases of Chinese goods. As a result, by the early seventeenth century China imported more than twenty times more silver bullion (uncoined gold or silver) than it produced. Increasing monetization of the economy—which meant that silver currency became the primary medium of exchange—bolstered market activity and state revenues at the same time. Then, when silver shipments to China declined due to downturns in New World mining

Silver This seventeenth-century helmet from the Ming (1368–1644) or Qing (1644–1911) dynasty features steel, gold, silver, and textiles, all of which were vital to the Chinese economy during this century. Silver was especially important, for its large influx from Japan and the Americas led to severe economic problems, political unrest, and the overthrow of the Ming dynasty.

output and more precious metals were swallowed up in European wars, the supply of money contracted in China; inflation suddenly gave way to deflation and shortages.

Yet the use of silver pressured peasants, who now needed that metal to pay their taxes and purchase goods. When silver supplies were abundant, the peasants faced inflationary prices. When supplies were low, the peasants could not meet their obligations to state officials and merchants, and they took up arms in rebellion.

The Collapse of Ming Authority By the seventeenth century, the Ming's administrative and economic difficulties were affecting their subjects' daily lives. This was particularly evident when the regime failed to cope with devastation caused by natural disasters, as in the northwestern province of Shanxi after a drop in average temperatures shortened growing seasons and reduced harvests.

While the Little Ice Age was not wholly responsible for the fall of the Ming, it played a major role. As the price of grain soared there in 1627–1628, the poor and the hungry fanned out to find food by whatever means they could muster. To deal with the crisis, the government imposed heavier taxes and cut the military budget. Bands of dispossessed Chinese peasants and mutinous soldiers then vented their anger at local tax collectors and officials.

Now the cycle of rebellion and weakened central authority that played out in so many other places took its predictable toll. Outlaw armies grew large under charismatic leaders. The most famous rebel leader, the "dashing prince" Li Zicheng, arrived at the outskirts of Beijing in 1644. Only a few companies of soldiers and a few thousand eunuchs were there to defend the capital's 21 miles of walls, so Li Zicheng seized Beijing easily. Two days later, the emperor hanged himself. On the following day, the triumphant "dashing prince" rode into the capital and claimed the throne.

News of the fall of the Ming capital sent shock waves around the empire. One hundred and seventy miles to the northeast, where China meets Manchuria, the army's commander received the news within a matter of days. His task in the area was to defend the Ming against their menacing neighbor, a group that had begun to identify itself as Manchu. Immediately the commander's position became precarious. Caught between an advancing rebel army on one side and the Manchus on the other, he made a fateful decision: he appealed for the Manchus' cooperation to fight the "dashing prince," promising his new allies that "gold and treasure" awaited them in the capital. Thus, without shedding a drop of blood, the Manchus joined the Ming forces. After years of coveting the Ming Empire, the Manchus were finally on their way to Beijing. (See Map 13.5.)

The Qing Dynasty Asserts Control Despite their small numbers, the Manchus overcame early resistance to their rule and oversaw an impressive expansion of their realm. The **Manchus**—the name was first used in 1635—were descendants of a Turkic-speaking group known as the Jurchens. They emerged as a force early in the seventeenth century, when their leader claimed the title of khan after securing the allegiance of various Mongol groups in northeastern Asia, paving the way for their eventual conquest of China. By that time, a rising Manchu population, based in Inner China and unable to feed their people in Manchuria, was posed to breach the Great Wall in search of better lands. The Manchus found a Chinese government in disarray from warfare and fiscal crisis, with central authorities overwhelmed by roving bands of peasant rebels.

When the Manchus defeated Li Zicheng and seized power in Beijing, they numbered around 1 million. Assuming control of a domain that included perhaps 250 million people, they were keenly aware of their minority status. Taking power was one thing; keeping it was another. But keep it they did. In fact, during the eighteenth century the Manchu **Qing** ("pure") **dynasty** (1644–1911) incorporated new territories, experienced substantial population growth, and sustained significant economic growth.

The key to China's relatively stable economic and geographic expansion lay in its rulers' shrewd and flexible policies. The early Manchu emperors were able and diligent administrators. They also knew that to govern a diverse population, they had to adapt to local ways. At the same time, Qing rulers were determined to convey a clear sense of their own majesty and legitimacy. Rulers relentlessly promoted patriarchal values. Widows who remained "chaste" enjoyed public praise, and women in general were urged to lead a "virtuous" life serving male kin and family. To the majority Han population, the Manchu emperor represented himself as the worthy upholder of familial values and classical Chinese civilization. However, insinuating themselves into an existing order and appeasing subject peoples did not satisfy the yearning of the Manchus to leave their imprint. They also introduced measures that emphasized their authority, their distinctiveness, and the submission of their mostly Han Chinese subjects. For example, Qing officials composed or translated important documents into Manchu and banned intermarriage between Manchu and Han, although this proved difficult to enforce.

Manchu impositions fell mostly on the peasantry, for the Qing financed their administrative structure through taxes on peasant households. In response, the peasants sought new lands to cultivate in border areas, often planting New World crops that grew well in difficult soils. This move introduced an important change in Chinese diets: while rice remained the staple of the wealthy, peasants increasingly subsisted on corn and sweet potatoes.

While officials redoubled their reliance on an agrarian base, trade and commerce flourished. Chinese merchants continued to ply the waters stretching from Southeast Asia to Japan, exchanging textiles, ceramics, and medicine for spices and rice. Although the Qing state vacillated about permitting maritime

Map 13.5 From Ming to Qing China, 1644–1760

Qing China under the Manchus expanded its territory significantly during this period. Find the Manchu homeland and then the area of Manchu expansion after 1644, when the Manchus established the Qing dynasty.

- Where did the Qing dynasty expand? Explain what this tells us about the priorities of the ruling elite, in particular with respect to global commerce.
- Explain the significance of the chronology of Chinese expansion. Does this qualify your answer to the first question?
- What does the chronology of Chinese expansion tell us about the evolution of the ruling elite's priorities?
- Consider the scope of Chinese territorial expansion in this period, and, based on your reading, explain the challenges this posed for central authorities.

trade with foreigners in its early years, it sought to regulate external commerce more formally as it consolidated its rule. In 1720, in Canton, a group of merchants formed a monopolistic guild to trade with Europeans seeking coveted Chinese goods and peddling their own wares. Although the guild disbanded in the face of opposition from other merchants, it revived after the Qing restricted European trade to Canton. The **Canton system**, officially established by imperial decree in 1759, required European traders to have guild merchants act as guarantors for their good behavior and payment of fees.

Despite public disregard for certain imperial edicts, the Qing dynasty enjoyed a heyday during the eighteenth century. It forced Korea, Vietnam, Burma, and Nepal to pay tribute, and its territorial expansion reached far into central Asia, Tibet, and Mongolia. China, in sum, negotiated a century of political upheaval and climate change without dismantling established ways in politics and economics. The peasantry continued to practice popular faiths, cultivate crops, and stay close to fields and villages. Trade with the outside world was marginal to overall commercial life; like the Ming, the Qing cared more about the agrarian than the commercial health of the empire, believing the former to be the foundation of prosperity and tranquility. As long as China's peasantry could keep the dynasty's coffers full, the government was content to squeeze the merchants when it needed funds. Some historians view this practice as a failure to adapt to a changing world order, as it ultimately left China vulnerable to outsiders—especially Europeans. But this view projects later developments onto the past. By the mid-eighteenth century, Europe still needed China more than the other way around. For the majority of Chinese, no superior model of belief, politics,

Canton A painting by an unknown artist provides a view of the foreign factories in Canton. Not only were foreigners prohibited from trading with the Chinese outside of Canton, but they were also required to have Chinese guild members act as guarantors of their good behavior and payment of fees.

or economics was conceivable. Indeed, although the Qing had taken over a crumbling empire in 1644, a century later China was enjoying a new level of prosperity.

TOKUGAWA JAPAN

Integration with the Asian trading system exposed Japan to new external pressures, even as the islands grappled with internal turmoil. But the Japanese dealt with these pressures more successfully than the mainland Asian empires (Ottoman, Safavid, Mughal, and Ming), which saw political fragmentation and even the overthrow of ruling dynasties. In Japan, a single ruling family emerged. This dynastic state, the **Tokugawa shogunate**, accomplished something that most of the world's other regimes did not: it regulated foreign intrusion. While Japan played a modest role in the expanding global trade, it remained free of outside exploitation.

Unification of Japan During the sixteenth century, Japan had suffered from political instability as banditry and civil strife disrupted the countryside. Regional ruling families, called *daimyos*, had commanded private armies of warriors known as samurai. The daimyos sometimes brought order to their domains, but no one family could establish preeminence over others. Although Japan had an emperor, his authority did not extend beyond the court in Kyoto.

Following an effort by military leaders to unify Japan, one of the daimyos, Tokugawa Ieyasu, seized power. This was a decisive moment. In 1603, Ieyasu assumed the title of shogun (military ruler), retaining the emperor in name only while taking the reins of power himself. He also solved the problem of succession, declaring that rulership would be hereditary and that his family would be the ruling household. Administrative authority shifted from Kyoto to the site of Ieyasu's domain headquarters: the castle town called Edo (later renamed Tokyo). (See Map 13.6.) By the time Ieyasu died, Edo had become a major urban center with a population of 150,000. This hereditary Tokugawa shogunate lasted until 1867.

The Tokugawa shoguns ensured a flow of resources from the working population to the rulers and from the provinces to the capital. Villages paid taxes to the daimyos, who transferred resources to the seat of shogunate authority. No longer engaged in constant warfare, the samurai became administrators. Peace brought prosperity. Agriculture thrived. Improved farming techniques and land reclamation projects enabled the country's population to grow from 10 million in 1550 to 16 million in 1600 and 30 million in 1700.

Foreign Affairs and Foreigners Internal peace and prosperity did not insulate Japan from external challenges. When Japanese rulers tackled foreign

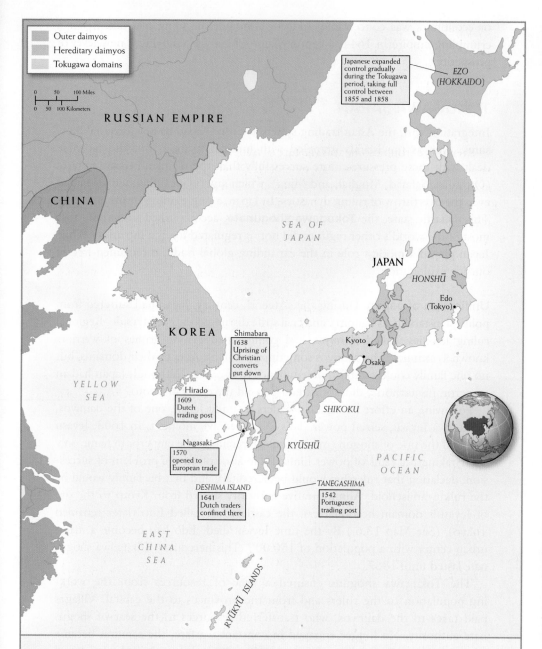

Legend (map):
- Outer daimyos
- Hereditary daimyos
- Tokugawa domains

0   50   100 Miles
0   50   100 Kilometers

RUSSIAN EMPIRE

CHINA

Japanese expanded control gradually during the Tokugawa period, taking full control between 1855 and 1858

EZO (HOKKAIDO)

SEA OF JAPAN

JAPAN

HONSHŪ

Edo (Tokyo)

KOREA

Shimabara
1638
Uprising of Christian converts put down

Kyoto

Osaka

YELLOW SEA

Hirado
1609
Dutch trading post

Nagasaki
1570
opened to European trade

SHIKOKU

KYŪSHŪ

PACIFIC OCEAN

DESHIMA ISLAND
1641
Dutch traders confined there

TANEGASHIMA
1542
Portuguese trading post

EAST CHINA SEA

RYŪKYŪ ISLANDS

Map 13.6 Tokugawa Japan, 1603–1867

....

The Tokugawa shoguns created a strong central state in Japan at this time.

- According to this map, how extensive was their control?
- Based on your reading, what foreign states were interested in trade with Japan?
- How, according to the chapter, did Tokugawa leaders attempt to control relations with foreign states and other entities?

affairs, their most pressing concern was the intrusion of Christian missionaries and European traders. Initially, Japanese officials welcomed these foreigners out of an eagerness to acquire muskets, gunpowder, and other new technology. But once the ranks of Christian converts swelled, Japanese authorities realized that Christians were intolerant of other faiths, believed Christ to be superior to any authority, and fought among themselves. The government thus suppressed Christianity and drove European missionaries from the country.

Even more troublesome was the lure of trade with Europeans. The Tokugawa knew that trading at various Japanese ports would pull the commercial regions in various directions, away from the capital. When it became clear that European traders preferred the ports of Kyūshū (the southernmost island), the shogunate restricted Europeans to trading only in ports under Edo's direct rule in Honshū. Then, Japanese authorities expelled all European competitors. Only the Protestant (and nonproselytizing) Dutch won permission to remain in Japan, confined to an island near Nagasaki. The Dutch were allowed to unload just one ship each year, under strict supervision by Japanese authorities.

These measures did not close Tokugawa Japan to the outside world, however. Trade with China and Korea flourished, and the shogun received missions from Korea and the Ryūkyū Islands. Edo also gathered information about the outside world from the resident Dutch and Chinese (who included monks, physicians, and painters). A few Japanese were permitted to learn Dutch and to study European technology, shipbuilding, and medicine (see Chapter 14).

Edo in the Rain This facsimile of an *ukiyo-e* ("floating world") print by Hiroshige (1797–1858) depicts one of several bridges in the bustling city of Edo (later Tokyo), with Mount Fuji in the background.

By limiting such encounters, the authorities ensured that foreigners would not threaten Japan's security.

The arrival of New World silver provided at least an initial boost to the major Asian economies. The Mughal Empire achieved its greatest influence in the seventeenth century. Despite a change in the ruling dynasty, China remained the world's center of wealth and power, although there, as elsewhere in Asia, silver caused inflation and altered relations between center and periphery. Ottoman domains shrank, and Europeans achieved important commercial footholds in parts of India and Southeast Asia.

Transformations in Europe

Between 1600 and 1750, religious conflict and the consolidation of dynastic power, spurred on by long-distance trade and climate change, transformed Europe. Commercial centers shifted northward, and Spain and Portugal lost ground to England and France. To the east, the state of Muscovy expanded dramatically to become the sprawling Russian Empire.

EXPANSION AND DYNASTIC CHANGE IN RUSSIA

During this period the Russian Empire expanded to become one of the world's largest-ever states. It gained positions on the Baltic Sea and the Pacific Ocean, and it established political borders with both the Qing Empire and Japan. These momentous shifts involved the elimination of steppe nomads as an independent force. Culturally, Europeans as well as Russians debated whether Russia belonged more to Europe or to Asia. The answer was both.

Muscovy Becomes the Russian Empire The principality of Moscow, or Muscovy, like Japan and China, used territorial expansion and commercial networks to consolidate a powerful state. This was the Russian Empire, the name given to Muscovy by Tsar Peter the Great around 1700. (*Tsar* was a Russian word derived from the Latin *Caesar* to refer to the Russian ruler.) Originally a mixture of Slavs, Finnish tribes, Turkic speakers, and many others, **Muscovy** spanned parts of Europe, much of northern Asia, numerous North Pacific islands, and even—for a time—a corner of North America (Alaska).

Like Japan, Russia emerged out of turmoil. Security concerns inspired the Muscovite regime to seize territory in the fifteenth and sixteenth centuries. Because the steppe, which stretches deep into Asia, remained a highway for nomadic peoples (especially descendants of the powerful Mongols), Muscovy sought to dominate the areas south and east of Moscow. Beginning in the 1590s, Russian authorities built forts and trading posts along Siberian rivers, and by 1639 the state's borders reached the Pacific. Thus, in just over a century

Muscovy had claimed an empire straddling Eurasia and incorporating peoples of many languages and religions. (See Map 13.7.)

Much of this expansion occurred despite the dynastic chaos that followed the death of Tsar Ivan IV in 1584. Ultimately, a group of prominent families reestablished central authority and threw their weight behind a new family of rulers. These were the Romanovs, court barons who set about reviving the Kremlin's fortunes. (The Kremlin was a medieval walled fortress where the Muscovite grand princes—later, tsars—resided.) Like the Ottoman and Qing dynasts, Romanov tsars and their aristocratic supporters would retain power into the twentieth century.

Map 13.7 Russian Expansion, 1462–1795

The state of Muscovy incorporated vast territories through overland expansion as it grew and became the Russian Empire.

- Using the map key, identify the different expansions the Russian Empire underwent between 1462 and 1795 and the directions it generally expanded in.
- With what countries and cultures did the Russian Empire come into contact?
- According to the text, what drove such dramatic expansion?

Absolutist Government and Serfdom In the seventeenth and eighteenth centuries, the Romanovs created an absolutist system of government. Only the tsar had the right to make war, tax, judge, and coin money. The Romanovs also made the nobles serve as state officials. Now Russia became a despotic state that had no political assemblies for nobles or other groups, other than mere consultative bodies like the imperial senate. Indeed, away from Moscow, local aristocrats enjoyed nearly unlimited authority in exchange for loyalty and tribute to the tsar.

During this period, Russia's peasantry bore the burden of maintaining the wealth of the nobility and the monarchy. Most peasant families gathered into communes, isolated rural worlds where people helped one another deal with the harsh climate, severe landlords, and occasional poor harvests. Communes functioned like extended kin networks in which members supported one another. In 1649, peasants were legally bound as serfs to the nobles and the tsar, meaning that, in principle, they had to perform obligatory services and deliver part of their produce to their lords.

Imperial Expansion and Migration A series of military victories in the eighteenth century made it possible to consolidate the empire and sparked significant population movements. The conquest of Siberia brought vast territory and riches in furs. Victory in a prolonged war with Sweden and then the incorporation of the fertile southern steppes, known as Ukraine, proved decisive. Peter the Great (r. 1682–1725) accomplished the victory in Sweden, after which he founded a new capital at St. Petersburg. Under Peter's successors, including the brilliant and ruthless Catherine the Great, Russia, already a harsh and colossal space, added even more territory. By the late eighteenth century, Russia's grasp extended from the Baltic Sea, Ukraine, and Crimea on the Black Sea, and stretched eastward all the way to Siberia.

Many people migrated eastward to Siberia. Some were fleeing serfdom; others were being deported for rejecting religious reforms. Battling astoundingly harsh temperatures (falling to –40 degrees Celsius/Fahrenheit) and frigid Arctic winds, these individuals traveled on horseback and trudged on foot to resettle in the east. But the difficulties of clearing forested lands or planting crops in boggy Siberian soils, combined with extraordinarily harsh winters, meant that many settlers died or tried to return. Isolation was a problem, too. There was no established land route back to Moscow until the 1770s, when exiles completed the Great Siberian Post Road through the swamps and peat bogs of western Siberia. The writer Anton Chekhov later called it "the longest and ugliest road in the whole world."

ECONOMIC AND POLITICAL FLUCTUATIONS IN CENTRAL AND WESTERN EUROPE

During this period European economies became more commercialized, especially after the Thirty Years' War. As in Asia, developments in distant parts of the world shaped the region's economic upturns and downturns. Underlying the economic and political fluctuations taking place in Europe, especially the brutal warfare of the Thirty Years' War, was the powerful impact of the Little Ice Age. Freezing temperatures shortened agricultural growing seasons by one to two months. The result was escalating prices for essential grain products, now in short supply. Famines and death from diseases because of malnourishment followed. The cooling had a few benefits, however, including the magnificent violins, still prized today, crafted by Antonio Stradivari (1644–1737) from the denser wood that freezing temperatures produced.

The Thirty Years' War For a century after Martin Luther broke with the Catholic Church (see Chapter 12), religious warfare raged in Europe. So did contests over territory, power, and trade. The **Thirty Years' War** (1618–1648) was all three of these—a war between Protestant princes and the Catholic emperor for religious predominance in central Europe; a struggle for regional control among Catholic powers (the Spanish and Austrian Habsburgs and the French); and a bid for independence (from Spain) by the Dutch, who wanted to trade and worship as they liked.

The brutal conflict began as a struggle between Protestants and Catholics within the Habsburg Empire, but it soon became a war for preeminence in Europe. It took the lives of civilians as well as soldiers. In total, fighting, disease, and famine wiped out a third of the German states' urban population and two-fifths of their rural population. Ultimately the Treaty of Westphalia (1648) stated that as there was a rough balance of power between Protestant and Catholic states, they would simply have to put up with each other. The Dutch won their independence, but the war's enormous costs provoked severe discontent in Spain, France, and England. Central Europe was so devastated that it did not recover in economic or demographic terms for more than a century.

The Thirty Years' War The mercenary armies of the Thirty Years' War were renowned for pillaging and tormenting civilians. Here the artist Jacques Collot, from Nancy in eastern France, depicts the officially sanctioned punishment of renegade soldiers before an orderly group of townspeople. The caption that appeared with the image indicted the soldiers as "damned and infamous thieves, [hanging] like bad fruit, from this tree."

The Thirty Years' War transformed war making. Whereas most medieval struggles had been sieges between nobles leading small armies, centralized states fielding standing armies now waged decisive, grand-scale campaigns. The war also changed the ranks of soldiers: local enlisted men defending their king, country, and faith gave way to hired mercenaries or criminals doing forced service. Even officers, who previously obtained their stripes by purchase or royal decree, now had to earn them. Gunpowder, cannons, and muskets became standardized. By the eighteenth century, Europe's wars featured huge standing armies boasting a professional officer corps, deadly artillery, and long supply lines bringing food and ammunition to the front. The costs—material and human—of war began to soar.

Western European Economies In spite of the toll that warfare took on economic activity, the European states enjoyed significant commercial expansion in the seventeenth century. Northern Europe gained more than did the south, however. Spain, for example, started losing ground to its rivals as the costs of defending its empire soared and merchants from northern Europe cut in on its trading networks. The burden of its involvement in the Thirty Years' War dealt the Spanish economy a final, disastrous blow.

As European commercial dynamism shifted northward, the Dutch led the way with innovative commercial practices and a new mercantile elite. They specialized in shipping and in financing regional and long-distance trade. Their famous *fluitschips* carried heavy, bulky cargoes (like Baltic wood) with relatively small crews. Now shipping costs throughout the Atlantic world dropped as Dutch ships transported their own and other countries' goods. Amsterdam's merchants founded an exchange bank, established a rudimentary stock exchange, and pioneered systems of underwriting and insuring cargoes.

England and France also became commercial powerhouses, establishing aggressive policies to promote national business and drive out competitors. By stipulating that only English ships could carry goods between the mother country and its colonies, the English Navigation Act of 1651 protected English shippers and merchants—especially from the Dutch.

Economic development was not limited to port towns: the countryside, too, enjoyed breakthroughs in production. Most important was expansion in the production of food. In northwestern Europe, investments in water drainage, larger livestock herds, and improved cultivation practices generated much greater yields. Also, a four-field crop rotation involving wheat, clover, barley, and turnips kept nutrients in the soil and provided year-round fodder for livestock. As a result (and as we have seen many times before), increased agricultural output supported a growing urban population.

Production rose most where the organization of rural property changed. In England, in a movement known as **enclosure**, landowners took control of lands that traditionally had been common property serving local needs. Claiming exclusive rights to these lands, the landowners planted new crops or pastured sheep with the aim of selling the products in distant markets—especially cities. The largest landowners put their farms in the hands of tenants, who hired wage laborers to till, plant, and harvest. Thus, in England, peasant agriculture gave way to farms run by wealthy families who exploited the marketplace to buy what they needed (including labor) and to sell what they produced. In this regard, England led the way in a Europe-wide process of commercializing the countryside.

Dynastic Monarchies: France and England European monarchs had varying success with centralizing state power. In France, Louis XIII (r. 1610–1643) and especially his chief minister, Cardinal Richelieu, concentrated power in the hands of the king. Instead of sharing power with the aristocracy, much less commoners, the king and his counselors wanted him to rule free of external checks, to create an **absolute monarchy**. The ruler was not to be a tyrant, but his authority was to be complete and thorough, and his state free of bloody disorders. The king's rule would be lawful, but he, not his jurists, would dictate the last legal word. If the king made a mistake, only God could call him to account. Thus, the Europeans believed in the "divine right of kings," a political belief not greatly different from that of imperial China, where the emperor was thought to rule with the mandate of heaven.

In absolutist France, privileges and state offices flowed from the king's grace. All patronage networks ultimately linked to the king: these included financial supports the crown provided directly, as well as tax exemptions and a wide array of permissions—such as consent for a writer to publish a book or for people ranging from lawyers and professors to apothecaries, bookbinders, and butchers to work in a regulated trade. The great palace Louis XIV built at Versailles teemed with nobles from all over France seeking favor, dressing according to the king's expensive fashion code, and attending the latest tragedies, comedies, and concerts.

The French dynastic monarchy provided a model of absolute rule for other European dynasts, like the Habsburgs of the Holy Roman Empire, the Hohenzollerns of Prussia, and the Romanovs of Muscovy. The king and his ministers controlled all public power, while other social groups, from the nobility to the peasantry, had no formal body to represent their interests. Nonetheless, French absolutist government was not as absolute as the king would have wished. Pockets of stalwart Protestants practiced their religion secretly in the plateau villages of central France, despite Louis XIV's discriminatory measures against them. Peasant disturbances continued. Criticism of court life, wars, and religious policies filled anonymous pamphlets, jurists' notebooks, and courtiers' private journals. Members of the nobility also grumbled about their political misfortunes, but since the king had suppressed the traditional advisory bodies they had dominated, they had no formal way to express their concerns.

England might also have evolved into an absolutist regime, but there were important differences between England and France. Queen Elizabeth

(r. 1558–1603) and her successors used many policies similar to those of the French monarchy, such as control of patronage and elaborate court festivities. Above all, the English Parliament remained an important force. Whereas the French kings did not consult the Estates-General to enact taxes, the English monarchs had to convene Parliament to raise money.

Under Elizabeth's successors, fierce quarrels broke out over taxation, religion, and royal efforts to rule without parliamentary consent. Tensions ran high between Puritans (who preferred a simpler form of worship and more egalitarian church government) and Anglicans (who supported the state-sponsored, hierarchically organized Church of England headed by the king). Those tensions erupted in the 1640s into civil war that saw the victory of the largely Puritan parliamentary army and the beheading of the king, Charles I. Although the monarchy was restored a dozen years later, in 1660, the king's relation to Parliament and the relationship between the crown and religion remained undecided (in particular, the right of Protestants to assume the throne).

Subsequent monarchs who aspired to absolute rule came into conflict with Parliament, whose members insisted on shared sovereignty and the right of Protestant succession. This dispute culminated in the Glorious Revolution of 1688–1689. In a bloodless upheaval, King James II fled to France and Parliament offered the crown to William of Orange and his wife, Mary (both Protestants). The

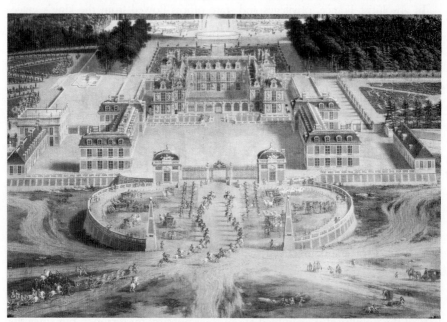

Versailles Louis XIV's Versailles, just southwest of Paris, was a hunting lodge that was converted at colossal cost in the 1670s–1680s into a grand royal chateau with expansive grounds. Much envied and imitated across Europe, the palace became the epicenter of a luxurious court life that included entertainments such as plays and musical offerings, state receptions, royal hunts, boating, and gambling. Thousands of nobles at Versailles vied with each other for closer proximity to the king in the performance of court rituals.

outcome of the conflict established the principle that English monarchs must rule in conjunction with Parliament. Although the Church of England was reaffirmed as the official state church, Presbyterians and Jews were allowed to practice their religions. Catholic worship, still officially forbidden, was tolerated as long as the Catholics kept quiet. By 1700, then, England's nobility and merchant classes had a guaranteed say in public affairs and assurance that state activity would privilege the propertied classes as well as the ruler. As a result, English rulers could borrow money much more effectively than their rivals could.

Mercantilist Wars The rise of new powers in Europe, especially France and England, intensified rivalries for control of Atlantic trade. As conflicts over colonies and sea-lanes replaced earlier religious and territorial struggles, commercial struggles became worldwide wars. Across the globe, European empires constantly skirmished over control of trade and territory. English and Dutch trading companies took aim at Portuguese outposts in Asia and the Americas, and then at each other. Ports in India suffered repeated assaults and counterassaults. In response, European powers built huge navies to protect their colonies and trade routes and to attack their rivals.

After 1715, a series of wars occurred mainly outside Europe, as empires feuded over colonial possessions. These conflicts were especially bitter in border areas, particularly in the Caribbean and North America. Each round of warfare ratcheted up the scale and cost of fighting.

The **Seven Years' War** (known as the French and Indian War in North America) marked the culmination of this rivalry among European empires around the globe. Fought from 1756 to 1763, it saw Native Americans, enslaved Africans, Bengali princes, Filipino militiamen, and European foot soldiers dragged into a contest over imperial possessions and control of the seas. The battles in Europe were relatively indecisive (despite being large), except in the hinterlands. After all, what sparked the war was a skirmish of British colonial troops (featuring a lieutenant colonel named George Washington) allied with Seneca warriors against French soldiers in the Ohio Valley. (See Map 13.2 for North American references.) In India, the war had a decisive outcome, for here the East India Company trader Robert Clive rallied 850 European officers and 2,100 Indian recruits to defeat the French (there were but 40 French artillerymen) and their 50,000 Maratha allies—men from an independent Indian empire in northern India—at Plassey. The British seized the upper hand, over everyone. Not only did the British drive off the French from the rich Bengali interior, but they also crippled Indian rulers' resistance against European intruders. (See Map 12.4 for India references.)

The Seven Years' War changed the balance of power around the world. Britain emerged as the foremost colonial empire. Its rivals, especially France and Spain, took a pounding; France lost its North American colonies, and Spain lost Florida (though it gained the Louisiana Territory west of the Mississippi in a secret deal with France). In India, as well, the French were losers and had to acknowledge British supremacy in the wealthy provinces of Bihar and Bengal. But overwhelmingly, the biggest losers were indigenous peoples everywhere. With the rise of one empire over all others, it was harder for Native Americans to play the Europeans off against each other. Maratha princes faced the same problem. Clearly, as worlds became more entangled, the gaps between winners and losers grew more pronounced.

Conclusion

A radical decline in temperatures worldwide made the seventeenth century a time of famine, dying, epidemic disease, and political turmoil that contributed to regime change in China, Persia, and England and threatened the rulers of the Ottoman and Mughal Empires. But by the 1750s, the world's regions were more economically connected than they had been a century and a half earlier. The process of integrating the resources of separated worlds, which had begun with Christopher Columbus's voyages, intensified during this period. Traders shipped a wider variety of commodities—from Baltic wood to Indian cotton, from New World silver and sugar to Chinese silks and porcelains—over longer distances. People increasingly wore clothes manufactured elsewhere, consumed beverages made from products cultivated in far-off locations, and used imported guns to settle local conflicts.

This integration and expansion of consumer opportunities came at a heavy price for some peoples. Nowhere was it more costly than in the Americas, where colonization and exploitation led to the expulsion of Native Americans from their lands and the decimation of their numbers. Nonetheless, in North America, Native Americans still held most of the land during a dynamic period of change that saw the emergence of the Lakota and Comanche Empires. The cost was also very high for the millions of Africans forced across the Atlantic to work New World plantations and for the millions more who did not survive the journey.

Silver was the product from the Americas that most transformed global trading networks and that showed how greater entanglements could both enrich and destabilize. Although Spanish colonizers mined New World silver and shipped it to western Europe and Asia, it was Spain's main competitors in Europe who gained the upper hand in the seventeenth and eighteenth centuries. Nearly one-third of the silver from the New World ended up in China as payment for products like porcelains and silks that consumers still regarded as the world's finest manufactures. But if China's economy remained vibrant, silver did play a part in the fall of one dynasty and the rise of another. For the Ottoman and Mughal Empires, the influx of silver created rampant inflation and undermined their previous economic autonomy.

Certain societies coped with increased commercial exchange, environmental change, and internal challenges more successfully than others did. The Safavid and Ming dynasties could not withstand the pressures; both collapsed. The Spanish, Ottoman, and Mughal dynasties managed to survive but faced increasing pressure from aggressive rivals. For newcomers to the integrating world, the opportunity to trade helped support new dynasties. Japan, Russia, and England emerged on the world stage. But even in these newer regimes, commerce and competition did not erase conflict. To the contrary, while the world was more fully integrated in economic terms than ever before, greater prosperity for some hardly translated into peace for most.

Focus On
The Emergence of Global Trade

The Americas
- England, France, and Holland join Spain and Portugal as colonial powers in the Americas.
- The English and French colonies in the Caribbean become the world's major exporters of sugar.

Africa
- The Atlantic slave trade increases to record proportions, creating gender imbalances, impoverishing some regions, and elevating the power of enslaving supplier states.

Southeast Asia
- The Dutch East India Company takes over the major islands of Southeast Asia.

The Islamic World
- World trade destabilizes the Safavid, Ottoman, and Mughal Empires.

East Asia
- The Ming dynasty in China loses the mandate of heaven and is replaced by the Qing.
- The Tokugawa shogunate unifies Japan and limits the influence of Europeans in the country.

Europe
- Tsarist Russia expands toward the Baltic Sea and the Pacific Ocean.
- Europe recovers from the Thirty Years' War (1618–1648), with Holland, England, and France emerging as economic powerhouses.

Key Terms

absolute monarchy p. 523
Canton system p. 514
chartered companies p. 488
enclosure p. 522
Little Ice Age p. 488

Mamluks p. 506
Manchus p. 512
mercantilism p. 488
Muscovy p. 518
Qing dynasty p. 512

Seven Years' War p. 525
Thirty Years' War p. 521
Tokugawa shogunate p. 515

CHRONOLOGY

1600

The Americas
Sugar complex emerges in the Caribbean region seventeenth century

French and Dutch merchants establish fur trade in North America seventeenth century

Africa
Massive expansion of Atlantic slave trade 1650–1800

South Asia

East Asia
Tokugawa shogunate formed in Japan 1603

Ming dynasty falls, Qing dynasty founded 1644

Europe
Thirty Years' War 1618–1648
England, France, Netherlands pursue mercantilist expansion abroad 1600–1800

The Islamic World
Köprülü reforms stabilize Ottoman Empire 1656–1683

Russia
Expansion into Siberia seventeenth century
Romanov dynasty founded 1613

THINKING ABOUT GLOBAL CONNECTIONS

- **Thinking about Exchange Networks and World Trade** How did silver, and then sugar, transform world trade? What political and cultural forces benefited from the development of long-distance trading networks? Which groups suffered and how? Contrast the effects of long-distance trade in major world regions.

- **Thinking about Changing Power Relationships and World Trade** The seventeenth and eighteenth centuries witnessed the rise of new powers in England, Japan, and Russia, as well as regional powers on the west coast of Africa. Several established empires continued to expand but confronted powerful new challenges to their authority. How did leaders of the Ottoman, Mughal, and Qing Empires respond to challenges to their authority? What major challenges did they face? How would you characterize the new powers that emerged around the world in this period?

- **Thinking about the Impact of World Trade on Gender Relations** The Atlantic slave trade wreaked havoc on sex ratios both in Africa and in the slavery-ridden societies of the New World because most people taken from Africa were men. How did this affect social life on New World plantations? What strategies did African communities utilize to mitigate the loss of so many men? Elsewhere around the world, increased trade challenged established social hierarchies. How did ruling elites mobilize gender to reinforce their authority?

 Go to **INQUIZITIVE** to see what you've learned—and learn what you've missed—with personalized feedback along the way.

1700	1750

British defeat French forces in North America during the Seven Years' War 1756–1763

Asante state founded 1701

Mughal dynasty reaches its high point 1658–1707

British assume control of French interests in South Asia during Seven Years' War 1756–1763

Seven Years' War 1756–1763

Safavid dynasty collapses 1722

Peter the Great reigns 1682–1725

14

Cultures of Splendor and Power

1500–1780

Core Objectives

- **EXPLAIN** the connections between cultural growth and the creation of a global market.

- **DESCRIBE** and **COMPARE** how each culture in this period reflected the ideas of the state in which it was produced.

- **ANALYZE** the different responses to foreign cultures across Afro-Eurasia in the period from 1500 to 1780.

- **DESCRIBE** how hybrid cultures emerged in the Americas, and **EXPLAIN** the connection between these cultures and Enlightenment ideology.

- **ANALYZE** the role that race and cultural difference played in the process of global integration.

In 1664, a sixteen-year-old girl from the provinces of New Spain asked her parents for permission to attend the university in the capital. Although she had mastered Greek logic, taught Latin, and become a proficient mathematician, she had two strikes against her: she was a woman, and her thinking ran against the grain of the Catholic Church. So keen was she to pursue her studies that she proposed to disguise herself as a man. But her parents denied her requests, and instead of attending the university she entered a convent in Mexico City, where she would spend the rest of her life. The convent turned out to be a sanctuary for her. There she studied science and mathematics and composed remarkable poetry. Sor (Sister) Juana Inés de la Cruz was her name, and she spoke for a new world where people mixed in faraway places, where new wealth created new customs, and where new ideas began to take hold.

Sor Juana's story attests to the conflicts between new ideas and old orders that occurred as commerce and the consolidation of empires intensified contact between diverse cultures. On the one hand, global commerce created riches that supported arts, architecture, and scientific ventures. On the other, experiments with new ways caused discomfort among defenders of the old order and provoked backlashes against innovation.

This chapter explores how global commerce enriched and reshaped cultures in the centuries after the Americas ceased to be worlds apart from Afro-Eurasia. As New World commodities invigorated global trade and states consolidated power, rulers and merchants on both sides of the Atlantic displayed their power by commissioning fabulous works of art and majestic

Sor Juana Inés de la Cruz In this portrait by Miguel Cabrera, Sor (Sister) Juana Inés de la Cruz (1651–1695) sits surrounded by scholarly artifacts, like her books, and symbols of piety. Sor Juana's writings exemplify how people around the world experimented with new cultural styles, often fusing disparate cultures. Frustrated by her exclusion from men's cultural circles, she also wrote in a personal, confessional style.

palaces and sprawling plazas. These cultural splendors were meant to impress, which they surely did. They also demonstrated the growing connections between distant societies, reflecting how foreign influences could blend with domestic traditions. Book production and consumption soared, with some publications finding their way around the world. Information from distant parts became valuable; books were the medium to buy and sell it. The circulation of books and ideas, alongside the movement of peoples and commodities, intensified cultural exchanges and led to experiments in religious tolerance. As a result, people became more aware of diversity as the world's parts were laced together.

For some, this was a threat. All over the world, many people doubled down on their traditions. For others, it was an opportunity for adventure, discovery—and exploitation. So with splendor and power came a mixture of innovation and resistance. It was in Europe, however, that new knowledge gave rise to efforts to organize and systematize the world into categories—and into Europeans' ideas of hierarchy and superiority.

The Creation of Global Cultures

- Growing global commerce enriches rulers and merchants, who express their power through patronage for the arts.

- Distinctive cultures flourish in the major regions of the world, blending new influences with local traditions to varying degrees.

- While the Islamic and Asian worlds confidently retain their own belief systems, the Americas and Oceania increasingly face European cultural pressures.

Trade and Culture

New wealth amassed by global commerce in the aftermath of Columbus's "discovery" created the conditions for cultural dynamism in the centuries after 1500. With newfound wealth, rulers promoted learning and the arts in order to legitimize their power and show their sophistication. In Europe, monarchs known as enlightened absolutists—divine-right rulers influenced by the Enlightenment—restricted the clergy and nobility and hired loyal bureaucrats who championed the knowledge of the new age. Mughal emperors, Safavid shahs, and Ottoman sultans glorified their regimes by bringing artists and artisans from all over the world to give an Islamic flavor to their major cities and buildings. Rulers in China and Japan also looked to artists to extol their achievements. In Africa, the wealth garnered from slave trading underwrote cultural productions of extraordinary merit.

Some rulers were more eager for change than others. Moreover, certain societies—in the Americas and the South Pacific, for example—found that contact, conquest, and commerce undermined indigenous cultural life. Although Europeans and native peoples often exchanged ideas and practices, these transfers were not equal. Native Americans, for example, adapted to European missionizing by creating mixed forms of religious worship—but only because they were under pressure to do so. And as the Europeans swallowed up new territories, it was *their* culture that spread and diversified. Indeed, the Europeans absorbed much from Native Americans and enslaved Africans but offered them little share of sovereignty or wealth in return.

Despite the unifying aspects of world trade, each society retained core aspects of its individuality. Ruling classes disseminated values based on cherished classical texts and long-established moral and religious principles. They used space in new ways to establish and project their power. They mapped their geographies and wrote their histories according to their traditional visions of the universe.

It is not surprising that in 1500 the world's most dynamic cultures remained in Asia, in areas profiting from the Indian Ocean and China Sea trades. It was in China and the Islamic world that the spice and luxury trades first flourished; here, too, rulers had successfully established political stability and centralized control of taxation, law making, and military force. Although older ways did not die out, both trade and empire building contributed to the spread of knowledge about distant people and foreign cultures.

Culture in the Islamic World

As the Ottoman, Safavid, and Mughal Empires gained greater expanses of territory in the sixteenth and seventeenth centuries, they acquired new resources to fund cultural development. Rulers supported new schools and building projects, and the elite produced books, artworks, and luxury goods. Cultural life was connected to the politics of empire building, as emperors and elites sought greater prestige by patronizing intellectuals and artists.

Forged under different empires, Islamic cultural and intellectual life now reflected three distinct worlds. In place of an earlier Islamic cosmopolitanism, unique cultural patterns prevailed within each empire. Although the Ottomans, the Safavids, and the Mughals shared a common faith, each developed a relatively autonomous form of Muslim culture.

THE OTTOMAN CULTURAL SYNTHESIS

By the sixteenth century, the Ottoman Empire enjoyed a remarkably rich culture that reflected a variety of mixing influences. As the Ottoman Empire absorbed more cultures and territories, its blend of ethnic, religious, and linguistic elements exceeded the diversity of previous Islamic empires. It also balanced the interests of military men and administrators with those of clerics. Finally, it allowed autonomy to the minority faiths of Christianity and Judaism. That ability to balance a wide array of local traditions and interests and yet maintain authority in the center, supported by new revenues drawn from global trade, constituted the Ottoman synthesis.

Religion and Education A sophisticated educational system was crucial for the empire's religious and intellectual integration and for its cultural achievements. Here, as in religious affairs, the Ottomans tolerated difference. They encouraged three educational systems that produced three streams of talent—civil and military bureaucrats, **ulama**, and **Sufi** religious masters. The administrative elite attended hierarchically organized schools that culminated in the palace schools at Topkapi (see Chapter 11). In the religious sphere, an equally elaborate system took students from elementary schools (where they learned reading, writing, and numbers) on to higher schools, or *madrasas* (where they learned

The Ottomans and the Tulip From the earliest times, the Ottomans admired the beauty of the tulip. *Left: Audience of an Ambassador with the Grand Vizier*, a painting by Jean Baptiste Vanmour (1671–1737), captures the power and influence of the Ottoman court, which drew envoys from around Europe and Asia, especially in what is called the Tulip Period. The sultan's affection for tulips was part of a wider spirit of reform, high consumption, and elite sociability. *Right:* The Ottomans used tulip motifs to decorate tiles in homes and mosques and to decorate pottery wares, as on the plate shown here.

law, religion, the Quran, and the natural sciences). These graduates became *ulama* who served as judges, experts in religious law, or teachers. Yet another set of schools, *tekkes*, taught the devotional strategies and religious knowledge for students to enter Sufi orders.

Science and the Arts During this period, the Ottomans integrated some foreign elements into their culture, especially in science and philosophy, while furthering their own traditions in architecture, literature, and music. Most of the foreign influences came from Europe, with which the Ottomans were in constant contact. The Ottomans' most impressive effort to spread European knowledge occurred when a Hungarian convert to Islam, Ibrahim Muteferrika, set up a printing press in Istanbul in 1729. Muteferrika published works on science, history, and geography. One included sections on geometry; others included the works of Copernicus, Galileo, and Descartes and a plea to the Ottoman elite to learn from Europe. When his patron was killed, however, the *ulama* promptly closed off this avenue of contact with western learning.

The Ottomans combined inherited traditions with new elements in art as well. For example, portraiture became popular after the Italian painter Gentile Bellini visited Istanbul and painted a portrait of Mehmed II. In other areas, though, the Ottomans kept their own styles. The magnificent architectural monuments built in the sixteenth through eighteenth centuries, including mosques, gardens, tombs, forts, and palaces, showed scant western influence. Nor were the Ottomans interested in western literature or music. For the most part, they believed that God had given the Islamic world a monopoly on truth and enlightenment and that their military successes proved his favor.

The Ottomans' capacity to celebrate their well-being and prosperity spread from elites to the broader public during the so-called Tulip Period, which occurred in the 1720s. The elite had long admired the tulip's bold colors and graceful blooms, and for centuries the flower served as the sultans' symbol. In fact, both Mehmed the Conqueror and Suleiman the Magnificent grew tulips in the most secluded and prestigious courtyards at Topkapi Palace in Istanbul. And many Ottoman warriors heading into battle wore undergarments embroidered with tulips to ensure victory. By the early eighteenth century, tulip designs appeared on tiles, fabrics, and public buildings, and authorities sponsored elaborate tulip festivals. Indeed, Ottoman enjoyment of luxury goods (including lemons, soap, pepper, metal tools, coffee, and wine) grew so extensive that a well-traveled diplomat looked askance at the supposed wealth of Europe. He wrote, "In most of the provinces [of Europe], poverty is widespread, as a punishment for being infidels. Anyone who travels in these areas must confess that goodness and abundance are reserved for the Ottoman realms." Thus, despite challenges from western Europe and fears that their best days were behind them, the Ottomans' cultural traditions flourished into the eighteenth century and beyond.

SAFAVID CULTURE, SHIITE STATE

If global trade ultimately strengthened Safavid rivals both within the empire and without (see Chapter 13), it also provided the wherewithal for a period of spectacular artistic and architectural creativity, especially at the height of Safavid power in the seventeenth century. The Safavid Empire in Persia (1501–1722) was not as long-lived as the Ottoman Empire, but it was significant for giving the Shiite branch of Islam a home base and a location for displaying Shiite culture. The brilliant culture that emerged during the Safavid period provided a unique blend of Shiism and Persia's distinctive historical identity.

The Safavids created a mixed political and religious system based on Shiism and loyalty to the royal family. The most effective architect of a cultural life based on Shiite religious principles and Persian royal absolutism was Shah Abbas I (r. 1587–1629). The location that he chose to display the wealth and royal power of his state, its Persian and Shiite heritages, and its artistic sensibility was Isfahan, the capital city from its creation in 1598 until the empire's end in 1722.

Architecture and the Arts The Safavid shahs were unique among Afro-Eurasian rulers of this era, for they sought to project both absolute authority and accessibility. Their dwellings were unlike those of other rulers—such as Topkapi Palace in Istanbul, the Citadel in Cairo, and the Red Forts of the Mughals. Those were enclosed and fortified buildings, designed to enhance rulers' power by concealing them from their subjects. In contrast, the buildings of Isfahan were open to the outside, demonstrating the Safavid rulers' desire to connect with their people. Isfahan's centerpiece was the great plaza next to the royal palace and the royal mosque at the heart of the capital.

Other aspects of intellectual life reflected the elites' aspirations, wealth, and commitment to Shiite principles. Safavid artists perfected the illustrated book, the outstanding example being *The King's Book of Kings*, which contained 250 miniature illustrations. Here, artists demonstrated their mastery of three-dimensional representation and their ability to harmonize different colors. Weavers produced ornate silks and carpets for trade throughout the world; artisans painted tiles in vibrant colors and created mosaics that adorned mosques and other buildings. Moreover, the Safavids developed an elaborate calligraphy that was the envy of artists throughout the Islamic world. All of these works celebrated Shiite visions of the sacred while at the same time reinforcing the authority and prestige of the empire's ruling elite.

POWER AND CULTURE UNDER THE MUGHALS

Like the Safavids and the Ottomans, the Mughals fostered a lavish high culture, supported primarily by taxes on agriculture but reliant on silver for its currency and, at its high point, open to global trade. Because the Mughals ruled over a large non-Muslim population, the culture they developed in South Asia was initially broad and open, welcoming non-Muslims into its circle. Thus, while Islamic traditions dominated the empire's political and judicial systems, Hindus shared with Muslims the flourishing of learning, music, painting, and architecture, especially from the middle of the sixteenth century to the middle of the seventeenth.

Religion, Architecture, and the Arts In the sixteenth and early seventeenth centuries, Mughal culture mixed diverse elements from within South Asia and

the broader Islamic world. The promise of an open Islamic high culture found its greatest fulfillment under the Mughal emperor Akbar (r. 1556–1605). This skillful military leader was also a popular ruler who allowed common people as well as nobles from all ethnic groups to converse with him at court. His quest for universal truths outside the strict *sharia* led him to develop a religion of his own known

Akbar Leading Religious Discussion This miniature painting from 1604 depicts Akbar's many different types of advisers, books, and elaborate accounts, fit for a powerful empire. The Jesuit priests (in black robes on the left) hold a page relating, in Persian, the birth of Christ, as they debate with Islamic authorities over whether the Bible or the Quran is the true word of God.

The Taj Mahal A symbol of Mughal splendor, the Taj Mahal was a mausoleum that was built of white marble. Often described as poetry in stone, it was constructed under Shah Jahan as an homage to his deceased wife, Mumtaz Mahal (*right*).

as "Divine Faith" (Dīn-i Ilāhī), which was a mix of Quranic, Hindu, Catholic, and other influences; it emphasized piety, prudence, gentleness, liberality, and a yearning for God.

A liberal religious attitude was not limited to Akbar's reign but remained an important feature of Mughal rule. Sufism was the most important expression of this attitude. Dara Shikoh, Emperor Shah Jahan's eldest son, for example, was an accomplished scholar of Sufism. He translated Sanskrit texts into Persian, including the Hindu Upanishads, which, in turn, was translated into French and circulated in Europe. Dara Shikoh declared there was no fundamental difference between Islam and Hinduism. His open religious attitude drew the ire of the orthodox *ulama*, who pressed for the supremacy of Islamic law and upheld religious purity.

A debate between conservative and liberal attitudes also characterized Hinduism. Orthodox writers reiterated Brahman privileges and opposed the entry of women and Shudras (members of the lower caste) into the spiritual sphere. But saints of the *bhakti* (devotional) sects offered a different vision. This movement, which had led to the establishment of Sikhism, swept through northern India between the fifteenth and seventeenth centuries. Devotion to the playful cowherd Krishna, rather than rituals officiated by Brahmans, gained popularity as the path to salvation. One famous *bhakti* saint was Mirabai (1498–1547), a woman who was compelled to marry a warrior's son but preferred the company of Krishna's devotees. She composed many poems mocking marriage and asceticism. If Mirabai challenged the prohibition of women in the spiritual sphere, another *bhakti* saint, Tukaram (1608–1649), asserted the fundamental equality of human beings and challenged caste inequality.

Shah Jahan In this 1629 painting, Emperor Shah Jahan is perched on the globe below angels bearing the insignia of sovereignty, as if the Mughal emperor mediated between the terrestrial and the divine with supreme authority and legitimacy. Shah Jahan took the Mughal Empire to its height, and he imagined his court—and himself—at the center of the world order.

While Persian and Sanskrit functioned as languages of the court and the elite, the *bhakti* movement addressed the common folk in regional languages. This promoted the development of Marathi, Hindi, Bengali, and other regional vernaculars. Religious life under the Mughals at both elite and popular levels presents a rich and diverse picture of dialogue and interaction between different religions,

In architecture, too, the Mughals produced masterpieces that blended styles. This was already evident as builders combined Persian, Indian, and Ottoman elements in tombs and mosques built by Akbar's predecessors. But Akbar enhanced this mixture in the elaborate city he built at Fatehpur Sikri, beginning in 1571. The buildings included residences for nobles (whose loyalty Akbar wanted), gardens, a drinking and gambling zone, and even an experimental school devoted to studying language acquisition in children.

Akbar's descendant Shah Jahan was also a lavish patron of architecture and the arts. In 1630, Shah Jahan ordered the building in Agra of a magnificent white marble tomb for his beloved wife, Mumtaz Mahal. Like many other women in the Mughal court, she had been an important political counselor. Designed by an Indian architect of Persian origin, this structure, the **Taj Mahal**, took twenty years and 20,000 workers to build. The 42-acre complex included a main gateway, a garden, minarets, and a mosque. The translucent marble mausoleum lay squarely in the middle of the structure, enclosed by four identical façades and crowned by a majestic central dome rising to 240 feet. The stone inlays of different types and hues, organized in geometrical and floral patterns and featuring Quranic verses inscribed in Arabic calligraphy, gave the surface an appearance of delicacy and lightness. Blending Persian and Islamic design with Indian materials and motifs, this poetry in stone represented the most splendid example of Mughal high culture and the combining of cultural traditions.

Foreign Influences versus Islamic Culture Although later emperors were less tolerant than Akbar, Mughal culture remained vibrant. Well into the eighteenth century, the Mughal nobility lived in unrivaled luxury. The presence of foreign scholars and artists enhanced the courtly culture, and the elite eagerly consumed exotic goods from China and Europe. Foreign trade also brought in more silver, advancing the money economy and supporting the nobles' sumptuous lifestyles. In addition, the Mughals assimilated European military technology: they hired Europeans as gunners and military engineers in their armies, employed them to forge guns, and bought guns and cannons from them.

Mughal appreciation for other European knowledge and technology was mixed. When a representative of the English East India Company presented an edition of Mercator's *Maps of the World* to the emperor Jahangir in 1617, the emperor returned it with the remark that no one could read or understand it. Others were more curious. Jahangir's successor, Shah Jahan, seized upon Europeans' introduction of terrestrial globes. He treated them as new ornaments that allowed him to imagine himself at the center of—if not the commander of—a wider world. Courtly portraits featured the emperor posed as a kind of world king or world conqueror, holding the orb in his magnanimous hands like a delicate object that he, and only he, could grasp.

For all their openness to outside influences, the Mughals, like the Ottomans, remained supremely confident of their own traditions. The centers of the Islamic world were still Istanbul, Cairo, and Delhi. Even while incorporating a few new European elements into their cultural mix, most Muslims regarded Europeans as rude barbarians. Elites in Persia, India, and the Ottoman Empire looked to China and the east, not to Europe and the west, for inspiration.

Culture and Politics in East Asia

In East Asia, prosperity, facilitated by China's vast importation of silver from Japan and the Americas, promoted cultural dynamism in the sixteenth through eighteenth centuries. Still, it was China's booming internal market, more than global trade, that fueled a Chinese culture inspired mainly by its own traditions. China had long been a renowned center of learning, with its emperors and elites supporting artists, poets, musicians, scientists, and teachers. But in late Ming and early Qing China, a growing population and extensive commercial networks propelled the circulation of ideas as well as goods.

In Japan, too, economic growth supported elite and popular culture. Because of its giant neighbor across the sea, the Japanese people had always been aware of outside influences. Like the Chinese government, the Tokugawa shogunate tried to promote Confucian notions of a social hierarchy organized on the basis of social position, age, gender, and kin. It also tried to shield the country from egalitarian ideas that would threaten the strict social hierarchy. But the forces that undermined governmental control of knowledge in China proved even stronger in Japan.

CHINA: THE CHALLENGE OF EXPANSION AND DIVERSITY

While China had become increasingly connected with the outside world in the sixteenth and seventeenth centuries, the sources for its cultural flourishing during the period came primarily from within. The circulation of books spread ideas among the literate, and religious rituals instilled cultural values among the broader population. Advances in cartography reflected the distinctive worldview of Chinese elites.

Publishing and the Transmission of Ideas The decentralization of book production and the domestic market helped circulate ideas within China. Woodblock and movable type printing had been present in China for centuries. Although initially the state had spurred book production by printing Confucian texts, before long the economy's increasing commercialization weakened government controls over what got printed. Even as officials clamped down on unorthodox texts, there was no centralized system of censorship, and unauthorized opinions circulated freely.

By the late Ming era, a burgeoning publishing sector catered to the diverse social, cultural, and religious needs of educated elites and urban populations. European visitors admired the vast collections of printed materials housed in Chinese libraries, describing them as "magnificently built" and "finely adorn'd." Perhaps more important, books and other luxury goods were now more affordable. Increasingly, publishers offered a mix of wares: guidebooks for patrons of the arts, travelers, or merchants; handbooks for performing rituals, choosing dates for ceremonies, or writing proper letters; almanacs and encyclopedias; morality books; medical manuals; and, above all, study guides.

Study aids for the civil service examination dominated the literary marketplace. In 1595, Beijing reeled with scandal over news that the second-place graduate had reproduced verbatim several model essays published by commercial printers. Ironically, then, the increased circulation of knowledge led critics to bemoan a decline in real learning; instead of mastering the classics, they charged, examination candidates were simply memorizing the work of others.

Elite women also joined China's literary culture. Women's poetry was especially popular, not only in anthologies published for the general market but in volumes produced for limited circulation to celebrate the refinement of the writer's family. Men of letters soon recognized the market potential of women's writings; some also saw women's less regularized style (usually acquired through family channels rather than state-sponsored schools) as a means to challenge stifling stylistic conformity. On rare occasions, women even served as publishers themselves.

Although elite women enjoyed success in the world of culture, the period brought increasing restrictions on their lives. The practice of footbinding (which elite women first adopted at least as far back as the twelfth century) continued to spread among common people, as small, delicate feet came to signify femininity and respectability. The thriving publishing sector indirectly promoted stricter morality by printing plays and novels that echoed the government's conservative attitudes.

Popular Culture and Religion Important as the book trade was, it had only an indirect impact on most men and women in late Ming China. Those who could not read well or at all absorbed cultural values through oral communication, ritual performance, and daily practices.

Villagers participated in various religious and cultural practices, such as honoring local guardian spirits, patronizing Buddhist and Daoist temples, or watching performances by touring theater groups. At the grassroots level, there was little distinction among Buddhist, Daoist, and local cults. The Chinese believed in cosmic unity, and although they celebrated spiritual forces, they did not consider any of them to be a Supreme Being who favored one sect over another. They believed it was the emperor, rather than any religious group, who held the mandate of heaven. Unless sects posed an obvious threat, the emperor had no

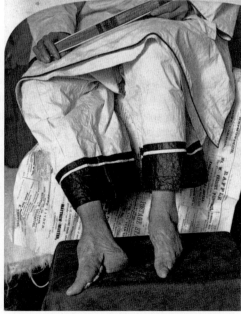

Footbinding Two images of bound feet: (*left*) as an emblem of feminine respectability when wrapped and concealed, as on this well-to-do Chinese woman; and (*right*) as an object of curiosity and condemnation when exposed for the world to see.

reason to regulate their spiritual practices. This situation promoted religious tolerance and avoided the sectarian warfare that plagued post-Reformation Europe.

Technology and Cartography Belief in cosmic unity did not prevent the Chinese from devising technologies to master nature's operations in this world. For example, the magnetic compass, gunpowder, and the printing press were all Chinese inventions. Chinese astronomers also compiled accurate records of eclipses, comets, novae, and meteors. In part, the emperor's needs drove their interest in astronomy and calendrical science. It was the emperor's job as the Son of Heaven, and thus mediator between heaven and earth, to determine the best dates for planting, holding festivities, scheduling mourning periods, and convening judicial court sessions.

Convinced that their sciences were superior, Christian missionaries in China tried to promote their own knowledge in areas such as astronomy and cartography (mapmaking). In 1583, the Jesuit missionary Matteo Ricci brought European maps to China, hoping to impress the elite with European learning. Challenging their belief that the world was flat, his maps demonstrated that the earth was spherical—and that China was just one country among many others. Chinese critics complained that Ricci treated the Ming Empire as "a small unimportant country." As a concession, he placed China closer to the center of the maps and provided additional textual information. Still, his maps had a negligible impact, as neither the earth's shape nor precise scale was particularly important to most Chinese geographers.

Before the nineteenth century, the Chinese had fairly incomplete knowledge about foreign lands despite a long history of contact. Chinese writers, for example, often identified groups of other people through distinctive and, to them, odd physical features. A Ming geographical publication portrayed the Portuguese as "seven feet tall, having eyes like a cat, a mouth like an oriole, an ash-white face, thick and curly beards like black gauze, and almost red hair." Chinese elites glorified their "white" complexions as compared to the dark skin of the peasants, the "black," skin of the wavy-haired "devils" of Southeast Asia, and the "ash-white" pallor of the Europeans. Qing authors in the eighteenth century confused France with the Portugal known during Ming times, and they characterized England and Sweden as dependencies of Holland. During this period of cultural flourishing, in short, most Chinese did not feel compelled to revise their view of the world.

CULTURAL IDENTITY AND TOKUGAWA JAPAN

The culture that developed in Japan in this period drew on local traditions and, increasingly, foreign influences from China and Europe. Chinese cultural influence had long crossed the Sea of Japan, but under the Tokugawa shogunate there was also interest in European culture. This interest grew via the Dutch presence in Japan and limited contacts with Russians. At the same time, there was a surge in the study of Japanese traditions and culture. Thus, Tokugawa Japan engaged in a three-cornered conversation among time-honored Chinese ways, European teachings, and distinctly Japanese traditions.

Native Arts and Popular Culture Elite and popular culture featured elements that were distinctly Japanese. Until the seventeenth century, the main patrons of Japanese culture were the imperial court in Kyoto, the hereditary shogunate, religious institutions, and a small upper class. These groups developed an elite culture of theater and stylized painting. Samurai (former warriors turned bureaucrats) and daimyos (regional lords) favored a masked theater, called Noh, and an elegant ritual for making tea and engaging in contemplation.

Alongside the elite culture arose a rougher urban one that artisans and merchants patronized. Urban dwellers could purchase works of fiction and colorful prints made from carved wood blocks, and they could enjoy the company of female entertainers known as geisha. These women were skilled (*gei*) in playing the three-stringed instrument (*shamisen*), storytelling, and performing; some were also prostitutes. Geisha worked in the cities' pleasure quarters, which were famous for their geisha houses, public baths, brothels, and theaters. Kabuki—a type of theater that combined song, dance, and skillful staging to dramatize conflicts between duty and passion—became wildly popular. This art form featured dazzling acting, brilliant makeup, and sumptuous costumes.

Much popular entertainment chronicled the world of the common people rather than politics or high society. The urbanites' pleasure-oriented culture was known as "the floating world" (*ukiyo*), and the woodblock prints depicting it were called *ukiyo-e* (*e* meaning "picture"). Here, the social order was temporarily turned upside down. Those who were usually considered inferior—actors, musicians, courtesans, and others seen as possessing low morals—became idols.

Literacy in Japan now surged, especially among men. The most popular novels sold 10,000 to 12,000 copies. In the late eighteenth century, Edo had some sixty booksellers and hundreds of book lenders. In fact, the presence of so many lenders allowed books to spread to a wider public that previously could not afford to buy them. By the late eighteenth century, as more books circulated and some of them criticized the government, officials tried to censor certain publications. The government's response testified to the uncommon power wielded by people of modest means and the relative significance of popular culture in Japan.

Religion and Chinese Influence In the realm of higher culture and religion, China loomed large in the Tokugawa world. Japanese scholars wrote imperial histories of Japan in the Chinese style, and Chinese law codes and other books attracted a significant readership. Some Japanese traveled south to Nagasaki to meet Zen Buddhist masters and Chinese residents there. Buddhism originally came

Artist and Geisha at Tea The erotic, luxuriant atmosphere of Japan's urban pleasure quarters was captured in a new art form, the *ukiyo*-e, or "pictures from a floating world." In this image set in Tokyo's celebrated Yoshiwara district, several geisha flutter about a male artist.

to Japan from China and remained associated with Chinese monks. A few of those monks even won permission to found monasteries outside Nagasaki and to give lectures and construct temples in Kyoto and Edo.

Although Buddhist temples grew in number, they did not displace the native Japanese practice of venerating ancestors and worshipping gods in nature. Later called Shintō ("the way of the gods"), this practice boasted a network of shrines throughout the country. Shintō developed from time-honored beliefs in spirits, or *kami*, who were associated with places (mountains, rivers, waterfalls, rocks, the moon) and activities (harvest, fertility). Seeking healing or other assistance, adherents appealed to these spirits in nature and daily life through incantations and offerings. Some women under Shintō served as *mikos*, a kind of shaman with special divinatory powers.

Reacting to the influence of Chinese Buddhism and desiring to honor their own country's greatness, some thinkers promoted intellectual traditions from Japan's past. These efforts stressed "native learning," Japanese texts, and Japanese uniqueness. In so doing, they formalized a Japanese religious and cultural tradition, and they denounced Buddhism as a foreign contaminant.

European Influences Not only did Chinese intellectual influences compete with revived native learning, but by the late seventeenth century Japan was also tapping other sources of knowledge. By 1670, a guild of Japanese interpreters in Nagasaki who could speak and read Dutch accompanied Dutch merchants on trips to Edo. As European knowledge spread to high circles in Edo, in 1720 the shogunate lifted its ban on foreign books. Thereafter European ideas, called "Dutch learning," circulated more openly. Scientific, geographical, and medical texts appeared in Japanese translations and in some cases displaced Chinese texts. A Japanese-Dutch dictionary appeared in 1745, and the first official school of Dutch learning followed. Students of Dutch and other European teachings remained a limited segment of Japanese society, but the demand for translations intensified.

Japan's internal debates about what to borrow from the Europeans and the Chinese illustrate the changes that the world had undergone in recent centuries. A few hundred years earlier, products and ideas generally did not travel beyond coastal regions and had only a limited effect (especially inland) on local cultural practices. By the eighteenth century, though, expanded networks of exchange and new prosperity made the integration of foreign ideas feasible and, sometimes, desirable. The Japanese did not consider the embrace of outside influences as a mark of inferiority or subordination, particularly when they could put those influences to good use. This was not the case for the cultures that thrived within the great Asian land-based empires, which were eager lenders but hesitant borrowers.

African Cultural Flourishing

The wealth that spurred artistic achievement and displays of power in Asia and the Islamic world did not bypass African states. Proceeds from the slave trade enabled African upper classes to fund cultural activities and invigorate strong artisanal and artistic traditions that dated back many centuries. African artisans, like those in East Asia, maintained local forms of cultural production, such as wood carving, weaving, and metalworking.

Cultural traditions in Africa varied from kingdom to kingdom, but there were patterns among them. For example, all West African elites encouraged craftsmen to produce carvings, statues, masks, and other objects that would glorify the power and achievements of rulers. (Royal patrons in Europe, Asia, and the Islamic world did the same with architecture and painting.) There was also a widespread belief that rulers and their families had the blessing of the gods. Arts and crafts not only celebrated royal power but also captured the energy of a universe that people believed was suffused with spiritual beings. Starting in the sixteenth century and continuing through the eighteenth century when the slave trade reached its peak, African rulers who benefited from that trade had even more reason—and means—to support cultural pursuits.

THE ASANTE, OYO, AND BENIN CULTURAL TRADITIONS

The kingdom of Asante led the way in cultural attainments, and the Oyo Empire and Benin also promoted rich artistic traditions.

The Asante kingdom's access to gold and the revenues that it derived from selling captives made it the richest state in West Africa, perhaps even in the whole of sub-Saharan Africa. The citizens of Asante accorded the highest respect to entrepreneurs who made money and were able to surround themselves with retainers and enslaved people. The adages of the age were inevitably

Kente Cloth Kente cloth originated among the Asante people and spread to other parts of West Africa. Threads of silk and cotton were interwoven to produce patterns with dazzling colors and geometric shapes. The colors represented different meanings important to the Asante peoples. Gray stood for healing and gold for royalty. Red was said to engender spiritual moods.

about becoming rich: "money is king" or "nothing is as important as money" or "money is what it is all about."

Asante's artisans celebrated these traditions through the crafting of magnificent seats or stools coated with gold as symbols of authority; the most ornate were reserved for the head of the Asante federation, the Asantehene, who ruled this far-flung empire from the capital city of Kumasi. By the eighteenth century, these monarchs ventured out from the secluded royal palace only on ceremonial and feast days, when they wore sumptuous silk garments featuring many dazzling colors and geometric patterns all joined together in interwoven strips. Known as Kente cloth, this fabric could be worn only by the rulers. Kings also had a golden elephant tail, which was carried in front of them. It symbolized the highest level of wealth and power. Also held aloft on these celebratory occasions were maces, spears, staffs, and other symbols of power fashioned from the kingdom's abundant gold supplies. These reminded the common people of the Asantehene's connection to the gods.

Equally resplendent were rulers of the Oyo Empire and Benin, located in the territory that now constitutes Nigeria. Elegant, refined metalwork in the form of West African bronzes reflects these rulers' power and their peoples' high esteem. In the Oyo Empire, the Yoruba people drew on craft and artistic traditions dating back to the first millennium CE. The bronze heads of Ife, capital city of the Yoruba Oyo Empire, are among the world's most sophisticated pieces of art. According to one commentator, "Little that Italy or Greece or Egypt ever produced could be finer, and the appeal of their beauty is immediate and universal." Artisans fashioned the best known of these works in the thirteenth century (before the slave trade era), but the tradition continued and became more elaborate in the seventeenth and eighteenth centuries.

Stunning bronzes were produced in Benin as well. Although historical records have portrayed Benin as one of Africa's most brutal slave-trading regimes, it produced art of the highest order. Whether Benin's reputation for brutality was deserved or simply part of Europeans' desire to label African rulers as "savage" in order to justify their intervention in African affairs, it cannot detract from the splendor of its artisans' creations.

Brass Oba Head The brass head of an Oba, or king, of Benin. The kingdom's brass and bronze work was among the finest in all of Africa.

Although supported by funds from the Atlantic slave trade, the cultural traditions of western Africa remained little influenced by intellectual and artistic influences from the wider world. African culture during this period was relatively autonomous, even as Africa became increasingly entangled in the global webs of economic exchange and political domination.

The Enlightenment in Europe

An extraordinary cultural flowering also occurred in Europe during the seventeenth and eighteenth centuries. Ironically, its origins lay in the period of the Little Ice Age, a time of devastating religious and civil wars, events that provoked many European thinkers to turn their backs on religious strife and to develop useful ways for understanding and improving *this* world. But it was also an era of intensifying commercial exchange. Europe's empires drew in commodities and observations from all corners of the planet, adding to the pool of learning that set the stage for Europe's scientific revolution. Historians call it

Europe's creation, but the change relied on global encounters, discoveries, and importation of knowledge from elsewhere. It was the product of exchange.

THE NEW SCIENCE

The search for new, testable knowledge began centuries before the **Enlightenment**, in the efforts of Nicolaus Copernicus (1473–1543) and Galileo Galilei (1564–1642) to understand the behavior of the heavens. These men were both astronomers and mathematicians. Making their own mathematical calculations and observations of the stars and planets, they came to conclusions that contradicted age-old assumptions. This entailed considerable risk: when Galileo confirmed Copernicus's claims that the earth revolved around the sun, he was tried for heresy.

In the seventeenth century, a small but influential group of scholars committed themselves, similarly, to experimentation, calculation, and observation. They adopted a method for "scientific" inquiry laid out by the philosopher Sir Francis Bacon (1561–1626), who claimed that real science entailed the formulation of hypotheses that could be tested in carefully controlled experiments. Bacon was chiefly wary of classical and medieval authorities, but his principle also applied to traditional knowledge that European scientists were encountering in the rest of the world. Confident of their calculations performed according to the new **scientific method**, scientists like Isaac Newton (1642–1727) sought universal laws that applied to all matter and motion; they criticized older conceptions of nature (from Aristotelian ideas to folkloric and foreign ones) as absurd and obsolete. Thus, in his *Principia Mathematica* (1687) Newton set forth the laws of motion—including the famous law of gravitation, which simultaneously explained falling bodies on earth and planetary motion.

Observations from around the world stoked a hunger for uncovering new information and borrowing knowledge from others. Consider the example of botany and **bioprospecting**, the taking of botanical information from one place and using it in another—and thereby adding value to it. Merchants from China, India, and the Arabian Peninsula had been transporting plants and minerals, like opium, pepper, and frankincense, as they traveled in caravans and ships to distant lands around the Indian Ocean and South China Sea. European naturalists and explorers acquired knowledge of plants from local herbalists and apothecaries who studied them for their healing powers. They then returned to Europe to publish their findings and gave botany added commercial value.

It was not just the pursuit of commerce that drove Europeans to develop novel ways of thinking. Competition between rival states for markets and prestige fueled these activities. By the late seventeenth century, many rulers saw that getting an edge in the knowledge business could give them strategic advantages. They established royal academies of science to encourage local endeavors. By incorporating the British Royal Society in 1662, for example, Charles II hoped to show not only that the crown backed scientific progress but also that

England's great minds backed the crown against critics and rivals. Similar reasoning lay behind Louis XIV's founding of the French Academy of Science. The result was an escalation of the drive to learn.

Proponents of the new science agreed that useful knowledge came from collecting data and organizing them into universally valid systems, rather than from studying revered classical texts. The new math was useful for the science of ballistics and the new astronomy for building better clocks and navigational devices, such as the chronometer. More technical sophistication necessitated, in turn, the establishment of military schools, which increasingly stressed engineering methods, made advances in surveying and mapping, and introduced a culture of meritocracy into the previously noble-dominated armies. In rural areas, landowners began to read books about crop rotation and formed societies to discuss the latest methods of animal breeding. In Italy, numerous female natural philosophers emerged, and the genre of scientific literature for "ladies" took hold. By about 1750, even artisans and journalists were applying Newtonian mechanics to their practical problems and inventions.

ENLIGHTENMENT THINKERS

Enlightenment thinkers, called **philosophes** in France, applied scientific reasoning to human interaction and society as opposed to nature. The English scientist and political writer John Locke (1632–1704), the French writers Voltaire (1694–1778) and Denis Diderot (1713–1784), and the Scottish economist Adam Smith (1723–1790) believed in the power of human reason to criticize and improve existing institutions and practices. They claimed that oppressive governments, religious superstition, and irrational social inequalities were not ills people simply had to accept.

In general, Enlightenment thinkers distrusted institutions and conventions and argued that societies should be governed by applying reason and natural laws rather than by following traditions. The application of reason to history, Locke claimed, showed that divine-right monarchies were a myth. Early peoples had voluntarily *made* their political institutions, binding themselves to their rulers according to a "social contract." When a government became tyrannical, it violated that contract, and the people had the right to rebel and create a new contract. All men were born equal in God's eyes, Locke argued, and were equally endowed by nature with the facility to flourish; hence, they must be equal under human law. Jean-Jacques Rousseau (1712–1778) reversed the pessimistic principle that humankind was inherently sinful and in need of a master. "Man is born good," he countered. "It is society that corrupts him." Other Enlightenment thinkers, similarly, believed that the only true inequalities among men were those produced by natural talents and education, and they criticized the European social order in which status was based on birth rather than on merit. Voltaire ridiculed the nobility and clergy for their stupidity, greed, and injustice. In *The Wealth of Nations*, Smith remarked that there was little difference (other than education) between a philosopher and a street porter: both were born, he claimed, with the ability to reason, and both were (or should be) free to rise in society according to their talents. Yet Locke, Rousseau, and Voltaire did not believe that women could act as independent, rational individuals in the same way that all men, presumably, could. Although educated women like Mary Wollstonecraft and Olympe de Gouges took up the pen to protest these inequities (see Chapter 15 for further discussion), the Enlightenment did little to change women's subordinate status in European society.

The Enlightenment touched all of Europe, but to varying extents. In the Netherlands, France, and Britain, where population density and urbanization were greatest, enlightened learning spread widely; in Spain, Poland, and Russia, enlightened circles were small and barely influenced the general population. Enlightened thought flourished in commercial centers such as Amsterdam and Edinburgh and in colonial ports such as Philadelphia and Boston. As education and literacy levels rose in these cities, book sales and newspaper circulation surged.

The expanding reading public grew increasingly omnivorous and increasingly difficult to police. In England, the Netherlands, and Switzerland, authorities essentially gave up censoring, and radical books and pamphlets printed there were smuggled into other markets, where they found readers of many sorts. Some of the most popular works were not from high intellectuals but from more sensationalist essayists. Pamphlets charging widespread corruption, fraudulent stock speculation, and insider trading circulated widely. Sex, too, sold well. Works like *Venus in the Cloister or the Nun in a Nightgown* racked up as many sales as the now-classic works of the Enlightenment. Bawdy and irreligious, these vulgar best-sellers exploited consumer demand—but they also seized the opportunity to mock authority figures, such as nuns and priests. Some even dared to go after the royal family, portraying Marie Antoinette as having sex with her court confessor. In these cases, pornography—some of it even philosophical—spilled into the literary marketplace for political satire. Such works displayed the seamier side of the Enlightenment, but they also revealed a willingness (on the part of high and low intellectuals alike) to challenge established beliefs and institutions and to undermine royal and clerical authority.

New readerships generated new cultural institutions and practices. In Britain and Germany, book clubs and coffeehouses sprang up to cater to sober men of business and learning; here, aristocrats and well-to-do commoners could read news sheets or discuss stock prices, political affairs, and technological novelties. Similar noncourtly socializing occurred in Parisian salons, where aristocratic women presided. The number of female readers and writers soared, and the relatively new genre of the novel, as well as specialized women's journals, appealed especially to them.

Inspired by the new science, many thinkers sought to discover the "laws" of human behavior. Explaining the laws of economic relations was chiefly the

Salon of Madame Geoffrin Much of the important work—and wit—of the Enlightenment was the product of private gatherings known as salons. Often hosted, like the one depicted here, by aristocratic women, these salons also welcomed down-at-the-heels writers and artists, offering everyone, at least in theory, the opportunity to discuss the sciences, the arts, politics, and the idiocies of their fellow humans on an equal basis.

work of Adam Smith, whose book *The Wealth of Nations* (1776) described universal economic principles. According to Smith, all people have what he called the propensity to truck, barter, and exchange—an innate desire to trade with one another. He complained that mercantilist controls and guild restrictions stifled economic growth and argued instead that a division of labor, spurred on by free and fair competition in a laissez-faire economy, provided the best conditions for producing wealth, though he did not advocate completely free, unregulated markets. (Laissez-faire expresses the concept that the economy works best when it is left alone—that is, when the state does not regulate or interfere with the workings of the market.) Assuming that all people, everywhere, shared Protestant notions of thrift and discipline, Smith claimed that by pursuing their own rational self-interest, virtuous individuals would advance the common good without meaning to do so—as if, as he put it in *The Theory of Moral Sentiments* (1759), by an "invisible hand." Smith was conscious of growing economic gaps between "civilized and thriving" nations and "savage" ones. He believed that until the poorer nations behaved virtuously and learned to abide by what he regarded as nature's laws, they could not expect a happy fate.

The Enlightenment produced numerous works that attempted to encompass universal knowledge. Most important was the French *Encyclopédie*, which ultimately comprised twenty-eight volumes containing essays by more than 130 intellectuals. It was popular among the elite despite its political, religious, and intellectual radicalism. Its purpose was "to collect all the knowledge scattered over the face of the earth" and to make it useful to men and women in the present and future. Indeed, the *Encyclopédie* offered a wealth of information about the rest of the world, including more than 2,300 articles on Islam. Here, the authors typically praised Arab culture for preserving and extending Greek and Roman science—and in doing so, preparing the way for scientific advances in Europe. But at the same time, the authors portrayed Islam with the same ill will that they applied to other organized religions, condemning Muhammad for promoting a bloodthirsty religion and Muslim culture in general for not rejecting superstition.

CONSEQUENCES OF THE ENLIGHTENMENT

The Enlightenment—or, more properly, Enlightenments, as there was much variation across Europe—was a movement with numerous consequences, both for religious and political institutions and for Europe's relationship with the rest of the world.

Although few Enlightenment thinkers were atheists, most criticized what they perceived to be the irrational rituals, superstitions, persecutions, and expenditures defended by clergy. The Scottish philosopher and historian David Hume (1711–1776) attacked biblical miracles, and Voltaire underscored the bloodiness of the Crusades. They insisted that the use of reason, rather than force or rote repetition of formulas, was the best way to create a community of believers and morally good people. Some governments bowed to clerical pressure and censored the most radical books or exiled writers, but many absolutist monarchs saw an advantage in reducing the church's power and introducing at least some measure of tolerance of religious minorities into their realms.

Tolerance did not mean full civil rights—for Catholics in England, for example, or for Jews anywhere in Europe. Tolerance simply meant a loosening of religious uniformity, and the population as a whole often resented even this. Few Europeans entirely lost their faith as a result of the spread of enlightened ideas and critiques. But it is unquestionably the case that the Enlightenment succeeded in spreading the suspicion of religious authorities and the distaste for religious persecution, and it did create new forms of religious belief and practice.

The application of enlightened ideas to non-European religions had conflicting effects. On the one hand, enlightened thinkers sought information about other religions and wrote books discussing similarities between Christian and non-Christian practices and beliefs. On the other hand, their imposition of enlightened categories and principles often resulted in severe misunderstandings, as differences were increasingly explained as others' "backward" refusal to evolve along European lines.

The *Encyclopédie* Originally published in 1751, the *Encyclopédie* was the most comprehensive work of learning of the French Enlightenment. *Left:* The title page features an image of light and reason being dispersed throughout the land. The title itself identifies the work as a dictionary, based on reason, that deals not just with the sciences but also with the arts and occupations. It identifies two of the leading literati (*gens de lettres*), Denis Diderot and Jean le Rond d'Alembert, as the primary authors of the work. Contributors to the *Encyclopédie* included craftsmen as well as intellectuals. *Below:* The detailed illustrations of a pin factory and the processes and machinery employed in pin making are from a plate in the fourth volume of the *Encyclopédie* and demonstrate its emphasis on practical information.

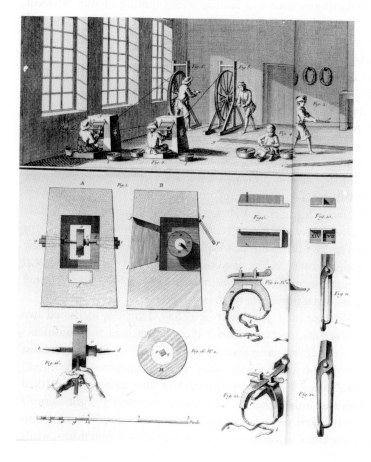

Absolutist governments did not entirely reject enlightened ideas, which included ideas that were in most cases reformist or critical of religious authorities rather than directly political. Rulers, like astronomers, recognized the virtues of universality (as in a universally applicable system of taxation) and precision (as in a well-drilled army). Also, social mobility allowed more skilled bureaucrats to rise through the ranks, while commerce provided the state with new riches. The idea of collecting knowledge, too, appealed to states that wanted to have greater control over their subjects and to extend their reach overseas. Consider Louis XIV, who was persuaded to establish a census (though he never carried it out) so that he could "know with certitude in what consists his grandeur, his wealth, and his strength." Many enlightened princes supported innovations in the arts and agriculture or sent scientific missions out to explore the world and plant their flags. Like the philosophes, they were convinced that the improvement of trade, agriculture, and national productivity was the right way forward, even though some were also beholden to the older values of the nobility and clergy. Merit and religious tolerance could also be useful in attempts to make states more profitable and armies more efficient. In this way, cultural efflorescence and secular state building in Europe went hand in hand.

The Enlightenment introduced new ways of thinking about human difference. Scientists sought objective, rational ways to classify peoples and cultures in the same way that botanists classified plants—indeed, many leaders in this field were botanists. To do so, they relied on new concepts of race.

Before the eighteenth century, the word *race* referred to a swift current in a stream or a test of speed; sometimes it meant a family lineage (mainly that of a royal or noble family). The Frenchman François Bernier (1620–1688), who had traveled in Asia, may have been the first European to attempt to classify the peoples of the world. He used a variety of criteria, including those that were to become standard from the late eighteenth century down to the present, such as skin color, facial features, and hair texture. Bernier published these views in his *New Division of the Earth by the Different Groups or Races Who Inhabit It* (1684). The Swedish naturalist Carolus Linnaeus (1707–1778); the French scholar Georges-Louis Leclerc, the comte de Buffon (1707–1788); and the German anatomist Johann Friedrich Blumenbach (1752–1840) also were among the first to use racial principles to classify humankind.

In his *Systema Naturae* (first published in 1735), Linnaeus identified five subspecies of *Homo sapiens*, or "wise man." He gave each of the continents a subspecies: there were *Homo europaeus*, *Homo americanus*, *Homo afar*, and *Homo asiaticus*, to which he added a fifth category, *Homo monstrosus*, for "wild" men and "monstrous" types. He believed that each of these groups was marked by distinctive social and intellectual characteristics, contrasting light-skinned Europeans, who he believed were governed by laws, to "sooty" Asians, who were governed by opinion. Custom governed copper-skinned Americans, while

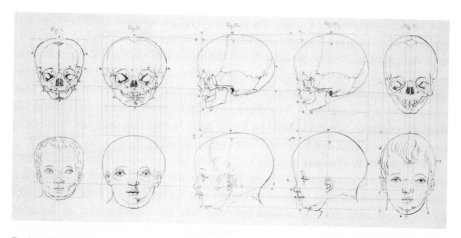

Racial "Classification" The Dutch anatomist Petrus Camper (1722–1789) advocated a theory of facial angles to create new, scientifically classified ranks of species and humans. In this drawing, Camper sought to illustrate the differences and commonalities among primates, including humans, and to devise a stratified classification system. In his system, which is broadly understood today as "scientific" racism, some humans resembled apes more than other humans did.

only personal whim ruled Africans, whom he consigned to the lowest rung of the human ladder.

Linnaeus thought these categories were malleable, both under environmental pressure and through mixing to create new species. He did not suggest that skin color, facial features, and hair type directly and permanently correlated to intelligence or morality—his system was far removed from the racial thought that emerged a century later. But the idea that human beings could be classified in a few large groups proved enormously influential.

Enlightened Europeans were not the first to remark on other peoples' distinctive—and to them, unpleasing—physical features and to see themselves as superior. Amerindians, for example, commented critically on the hairiness of European invaders. What the Enlightenment added was the drive to classify all of humankind and impose a hierarchy, one that put White Europeans on top.

THE EUROPEAN ENLIGHTENMENT IN GLOBAL PERSPECTIVE

Europe's new science and enlightened thought arose in reaction both to Europe's expanding interaction with the rest of the world and to the period's environmental, religious, and political chaos. But why Europe? What of China, India, and the Muslim world, where scientific work had been well in advance of Europe before the sixteenth century? Between 800 and 1450 CE, the Muslim world possessed the most important centers for this study. Throughout Islam, the mathematical sciences of arithmetic, geometry, and trigonometry flourished and broke open fields of astronomy, astrology, geography, cartography, and optics. The Maragha Observatory (1259 and later) in Persia produced the first non-Ptolemaic planetary models; Nasir al-Din al-Tusi (1201–1271), a Persian astronomer and mathematician who was the director of the Maragha Observatory, created a diagram of the movements of the planets, written in Arabic, that some historians claim must have been seen by Copernicus and influenced his thinking of the universe. Finally, Ibn Sina's great work of medicine, *Canon*, held sway in Europe until the sixteenth century.

While many Europeans resisted the advent of new ways of knowing, opposition was often stronger elsewhere. In the Islamic world, novelty produced a defense of tradition. The rise of Sufi orders and Sufi mysticism posed challenges to the dominance that the *ulama* believed they should have over all fields of thought and principles of belief. The *ulama* responded to this threat in conservative, even fundamentalist ways, reiterating the importance of the religious sciences, which included studies of the Quran, the sayings of the Prophet (*hadith*), the *sharia* (religious law), theology, poetry, and the Arabic language. They questioned the value of the foreign sciences and the study of the natural world. Occasionally scholars were able to challenge the *ulama*'s monopoly on learning and to look outward for inspiration, but such efforts relied on reformist patrons, who were not in great abundance. While in Europe a diverse set of quarreling and competing churches and patrons made possible the articulation of new and more secular sciences, in Ottoman lands the established authorities and ideas could not so easily be dislodged.

What of China? The English philosopher Francis Bacon credited the Chinese with three of the most influential inventions in the world at that time, namely the magnetic compass, gunpowder, and printing. Chinese science, however, suffered a fundamental disadvantage compared with that of Europe. Although both European and Chinese scientists focused on practical applications, the European scientists were more open to theoretical applications—which enabled breakthroughs to have wider effects. Chinese thinkers were less inclined than their European counterparts to mathematize the study of the natural world.

Chinese elites welcomed European learning, but they did so on their own terms. The two first Jesuit missionaries to reach China, Michele Ruggieri (1543–1607) and the aforementioned Matteo Ricci (1552–1610), arrived in China in 1582 and 1583, respectively. As was the case with many Jesuits at this time, both were brilliantly educated not just in religious and theological matters but in Europe's evolving new science. At the time of their arrival, China was in the midst of debates over its solar calendar, which now was out of sync with the seasons and causing difficulties coordinating ceremonial rites and rituals. Thus, Chinese officials were eager to employ Jesuit knowledge of mathematics and astronomy—based on Copernicus and Galileo's heliocentrism—to assist them in bringing ceremonial dates and political and economic activities into a better relationship with the seasons.

For their part, the Jesuits participated in Confucian ceremonies, hoping to win favor with the emperor and arguing that the rites were compatible with Catholicism. But, to the Jesuits' great disappointment, the Chinese did not accept their religious and theological tenets, and the men made only a very small number of converts. When Pope Clement XI issued a papal bull condemning the missionaries' participation in the rites, the project of cultural exchange broke down. Offended, the Kangxi Emperor, who had once been sympathetic to the missionaries, banned Christian missionaries from practicing in China. His successor went even further, ordering the closing of all churches and the expulsion of Jesuits from China. Thus, starting in the mid-eighteenth century, the European window on China and the Chinese window on Europe were closed. China turned away from European contact, most notably Europe's new science that had once intrigued the Chinese ruling classes.

Matteo Ricci Adapts to Chinese Culture This image depicts Jesuit father Matteo Ricci with one of his most high-profile converts to Christianity, the scholar and official Xu Guangqi. Behind them stands a painting of the Madonna and baby Jesus with a text in literary Chinese, demonstrating Ricci's commitment to adapting Christianity and European culture to the text-oriented Chinese cultural world.

In the contest between innovators and traditionalists worldwide, two factors made Europe the hub of new knowledge. First, Europeans feuded with one another for regional mastery by scrambling overseas. This made them more open to learning from and appropriating from local sources in a way that Chinese and Islamic scientists, who started out ahead, were not. Second, Europe had internal diffusion mechanisms for practical and theoretical discoveries. Printing presses and the circulation of scientists allowed European competitors to share the pool of breakthroughs.

Once Europeans seized their advantage and found ways to commercialize new knowledge, they reversed the knowledge gap that separated Asian scientists from Europeans. But the more they learned in their interactions with others and the more they succeeded in secularizing and spreading their ideas at home, the more European intellectuals became convinced not only that their culture was superior—after all, such ethnocentricity was hardly rare—but that they had discovered a set of universal laws that applied to everyone, everywhere around the globe.

Creating Hybrid Cultures in the Americas

As European empires expanded in the Americas, mingling between colonizers and native peoples, as well as enslaved Africans, produced hybrid cultures. But the mixing of cultures grew increasingly unbalanced as Europeans
imposed authority over more of the Americas. In addition to guns and germs,
many European colonizers brought Bibles, prayer books, and crucifixes. With
these, they set out to Christianize and "civilize" Amerindian and African
populations in the Americas. Yet missionary efforts produced uneven and
often unpredictable outcomes. Even as Amerindians and enslaved Africans
adopted Christian beliefs and practices, they often retained older religious
practices too.

European colonists likewise borrowed from the peoples they subjugated and
enslaved. This was especially true in the sixteenth and seventeenth centuries,
when the colonists' survival in the New World often depended on adapting.
New sorts of hierarchies emerged, and elites in Latin America and North
America increasingly followed the tastes and fashions of European aristocrats.
Yet, even as they imitated Old World ways, these colonials forged identities that
separated them from Europe.

SPIRITUAL ENCOUNTERS

Although the Jesuits had little impact in China and the Islamic world, Christian
missionaries in the Americas had armies and officials to back up their insistence
that Native Americans and enslaved Africans abandon their own deities and
spirits for Christ. Nonetheless, their attempts to force conversions were rarely a
complete success, and some European settlers became interested in Amerindian
culture.

European missionaries, especially Catholics, used numerous techniques
to bring Amerindians within the Christian fold. They smashed idols, razed
temples, and whipped backsliders. Catholic orders (principally Dominicans,
Jesuits, and Franciscans) also learned what they could about Indian beliefs and
rituals—and then exploited that knowledge to make converts to Christianity.
For example, many missionaries found it useful to demonize local gods, subvert
indigenous spiritual leaders, and transform Indian iconography into Christian
symbols.

Neither gentle persuasion nor violent coercion produced the results that
missionaries desired. When conversions did occur, the Christian practices that
resulted were usually syncretic: mixed forms in which indigenous deities and
rituals merged with Christian ones. Those who did convert saw Christian spiritual power as an addition to, not a replacement for, their own religions.

Europeans also attempted to Christianize enslaved people from Africa, though many enslavers doubted the wisdom of converting persons they regarded as mere property. Sent forth with the pope's blessing, Catholic priests targeted enslaved populations in the American colonies of Portugal, Spain, and France. Applying many of the same techniques that missionaries used with Indian "heathens," these priests produced similarly mixed results.

More distressing to missionaries than the blending of beliefs or outright defiance were the Amerindians' successes in assimilating captured colonists. It deeply troubled the missionaries that quite a few captured colonists adjusted to their situation, accepted adoptions into local societies, and refused to return to colonial society when given the chance. Moreover, some Europeans voluntarily chose to live among the Amerindians. Comparing the records of cultural conversion, one eighteenth-century colonist suggested that "thousands of Europeans are Indians," yet "we have no examples of even one of those Aborigines having from choice become European." (Aborigines, or aboriginals, are original, native inhabitants of a region, as opposed to invaders, colonizers, or later peoples of mixed ancestry.) While this calculation was no doubt exaggerated, it shows that despite the missionaries' intentions, cultural exchange went in more than one direction.

INTERMARRIAGE AND CULTURAL MIXING

In the early stages of colonization, Europeans mixed with Amerindians in part because there were many more men than women among the colonists. Almost all the early European traders, missionaries, and settlers were men. The British North American settlements saw more women arrive relatively early on, and, as a result, English settlers were the least inclined to forge voluntary liaisons with native peoples. In some parts of the Andes and in Central America, where European settlement was scarcer, natives and newcomers mingled less. But in many parts of New France, New Spain, and Brazil, for instance, mixing was a norm. In response to the scarcity of women and as a way to help Amerindians accept the newcomers' culture, the Portuguese crown authorized intermarriage between Portuguese men and local women. These relations often amounted to little more than rape, but longer-lasting relationships developed in places where Amerindians kept their independence—as among French fur traders and Amerindian women in Canada, the Great Lakes region, and the Mississippi Valley. Whether by coercion or consent, sexual relations between European men and Amerindian women resulted in offspring of mixed ancestry. In fact, the Mestizos of Spanish colonies and the *Métis* of French outposts soon outnumbered settlers of wholly European descent.

The increasing numbers of enslaved Africans in the Americas complicated the mix of New World cultures even further. Unlike marriages between fur traders and Indian women, in which the women held considerable power because

Racial Mixing *Left*: This *casta* painting shows racial mixing in colonial Mexico—the father is a Spaniard, the mother Amerindian, and the child Mestizo. (Like the word *caste*, *casta* refers to a group within a social hierarchy, in this case defined by race and racial mixing.) The image indicates that Indians who married Whites achieved elevated status. *Right*: Here, too, we see a racially mixed family. The father is a Spaniard, the mother is African, and the child is what was then called "Mulatto" (a term for a person of mixed White and Black ancestry that is considered offensive today). Observe, however, the less aristocratic and markedly less peaceful portrayal of this family.

of their connections to Indian trading partners, sexual intercourse between European men and enslaved African women was almost always forced. Children born from such unions swelled the ranks of mixed-ancestry people in the colonial population, contributing to the new cultural mix that was emerging.

FORMING AMERICAN IDENTITIES

Over time, as European colonies in the Americas became more securely established, the colonists developed a sense of their own distinctive "American" identities. The colonization of the Americas brought Europeans, Africans, and Indians into sustained contact, though the nature of the colonies and the character of the contact varied considerably. Where European dominance was most secure, colonists imposed their ways on subjugated populations and imported what they took to be the chief cultural and institutional attributes of the countries they had left behind. Yet Europeans were not immune to cultural influences from the groups they dispossessed and enslaved.

Creole Identities In Spanish America, ethnic and cultural mixing produced a powerful new class, the **Creoles**—people born in the Americas. By the late eighteenth century, Creoles increasingly resented the control that ***Peninsulares***—men and women born in Spain or Portugal but living in the Americas—had over colonial society. Creoles especially resented the exclusive privileges given to peninsular rulers, like those that forbade Creoles from trading with other colonial ports. Also, they disliked the fact that royal ministers gave most official posts to *Peninsulares*.

In many cities of the Spanish and Portuguese Empires, reading clubs and salons hosted energetic discussions of fresh Enlightenment ideas and contributed to the growing Creole identity. The Spanish crown, recognizing the role of printing presses in spreading troublesome ideas, strictly controlled the number and location of printers in the colonies. In Brazil, royal authorities banned them altogether. Nonetheless, books, pamphlets, and simple gossip allowed new notions of science, history, and politics to circulate among literate Creoles.

The global Enlightenment also inspired a quest for modern science as a basis for Creole reform. The Spanish government sent Royal Botanical Expeditions composed of scientists and artists to Chile and Peru (1777–1788), New Granada (1783–1816), and New Spain (1787–1803). These campaigns collected and classified an astonishing array of flora; they also produced beautifully illustrated publications that launched an American style of natural painting, and several new and marketable commodities.

Perhaps the most significant of these commodities was the cinchona plant, popularized by the Spanish-born physician José Celestino Mutis, who moved to New Granada as a young man. He oversaw the making of thousands of botanical illustrations of New World plants and was especially interested in the medical properties of the cinchona plant; its bark had been used by Amerindians and Jesuit missionaries for centuries to cure malaria. Mutis recognized that cinchona, or quinine, if scientifically cultivated, could enable more Europeans to settle in the tropics. This botanical conquest of the New World added to the global warehouse of what Europeans and Creoles knew about natural diversity, improved global health, *and* yielded riches for the Spanish colonies. It also situated Spanish American Creoles as part of the "century of light."

Anglicization In one important sense, wealthy colonists in British America were similar to the Creole elites in Spanish and Portuguese America: they, too, copied European ways. For example, they constructed "big houses" (in Virginia and elsewhere—especially the Caribbean) modeled on the country estates of English gentlemen and imported opulent furnishings and fashions from the finest British stores. Imitating the British also involved tightening patriarchal authority. In seventeenth-century Virginia, men had vastly outnumbered women, which gave women some power (widows, in particular, gained greater control over property and more choices when they remarried). During the eighteenth century, however, sex ratios became more equal, and women's property rights diminished as British customs took precedence.

Intellectually, too, British Americans were linked to Europe. Importing enormous numbers of books and journals, these Americans played a significant role in the Enlightenment as producers and consumers of political pamphlets,

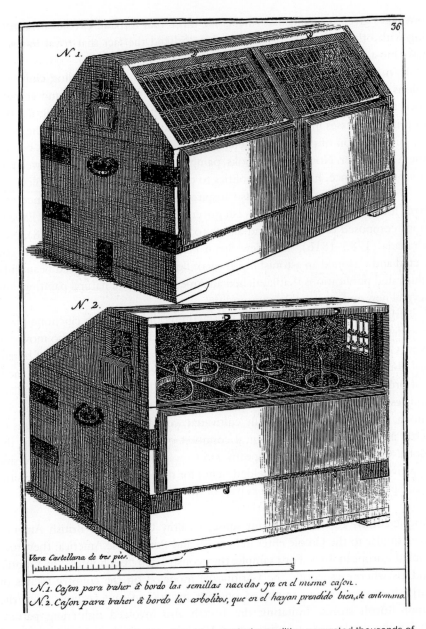

N.1. *Cafon para traher à bordo las femillas nacidas ya en el mismo cafon.*
N.2. *Cafon para traher à bordo los arbolitos, que en el hayan prendido bien, de antemano.*

The Cinchona Plant The Creole New Granada botanical expedition generated thousands of scientific illustrations of previously unknown tropical plants. One of the enlightened leaders of this expedition, José Celestino Mutis, recommended the intensive cultivation of the cinchona plant, whose bark could be used to make the most effective antimalarial medicine of the day, quinine. This image is of maritime crates used to transport live plants and saplings from the tropics to botanical gardens or from experimental stations in Spain to the colonies.

scientific treatises, and social critiques. Indeed, drawing on the words of numerous Enlightenment thinkers, American intellectuals created the most famous of enlightened documents: the Declaration of Independence. It announced that all men were endowed with equal rights and were created to pursue worldly happiness. In this way, Anglicized Americans showed themselves, like the Creole elites of Latin America, to be products of both European and New World cultures.

The Influence of European Culture in Oceania

In the South Pacific, as in the Americas, European influence had powerful consequences in the eighteenth century. Although in centuries past Hindu, Buddhist, and Islamic missionaries and Chinese traders had traveled to Malaysia and nearby islands, they had not ventured beyond Timor. (See Map 14.1.) Europeans began to do so in the years after 1770, turning their sights on **Oceania** (Australia, New Zealand, and the islands of the southwest Pacific). Using their new wealth to fund voyages with scientific and political objectives, Europeans invaded these remaining unexplored areas. The results were mixed: while some islands maintained their autonomy, the biggest prize, Australia, underwent thorough Anglicization.

Until Europeans colonized it in the late eighteenth century, Australia was, like the Americas before Columbus, truly a world apart. Separated by water and sheer distance from other regions, Australia featured harsh natural conditions and a sparse population. At the time of the European colonization, the island was home to around 300,000 people, mostly hunters and gatherers. Now the intrusion into Oceania presented Europeans with a previously unknown region that could serve as a laboratory for studying other peoples and geographical settings.

THE SCIENTIFIC VOYAGES OF CAPTAIN COOK

In Oceania and across the South Pacific, Europeans experimented with a scientific form of imperialism. The story of the region's most famous explorer, Captain James Cook (1728–1779), shows how closely related science and imperialist ventures could be. Cook's voyages and his encounter with the South Sea Islanders opened up the Pacific, particularly Australia, to European colonizers.

Captain Cook has become a legendary figure in European cultural history, portrayed as one of the saintly scientists of enlightened progress. His first voyage had two objectives. The Royal Society charged him with the scholarly task of observing the movement of the planet Venus from the Southern Hemisphere, and the British government assigned him the secret mission of finding and claiming "the southern continent" for Britain. Cook set sail in 1768, and his

The Global View

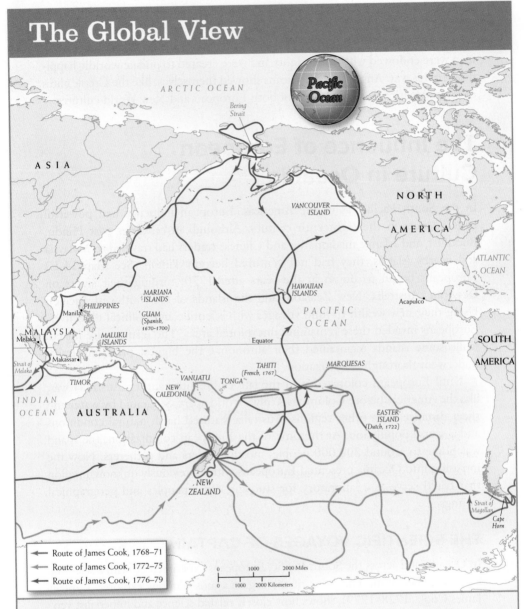

ARCTIC OCEAN

Bering Strait

ASIA

NORTH AMERICA

VANCOUVER ISLAND

ATLANTIC OCEAN

MARIANA ISLANDS

PHILIPPINES

Manila

GUAM (Spanish, 1670–1700)

HAWAIIAN ISLANDS

Acapulco

PACIFIC OCEAN

MALAYSIA

Melaka

MALUKU ISLANDS

Makassar

Equator

SOUTH AMERICA

Strait of Melaka

TIMOR

TAHITI (French, 1767)

MARQUESAS

INDIAN OCEAN

AUSTRALIA

VANUATU

TONGA

NEW CALEDONIA

EASTER ISLAND (Dutch, 1722)

NEW ZEALAND

Strait of Magellan

Cape Horn

← Route of James Cook, 1768–71
← Route of James Cook, 1772–75
← Route of James Cook, 1776–79

0   1000   2000 Miles
0 1000   2000 Kilometers

Map 14.1 Cook's Global Voyages

Captain Cook's voyages throughout the Pacific Ocean symbolized a new era in European exploration of other societies.

- Where did Cook explore, and what peoples did he encounter?
- Contrast the routes Cook selected for his three voyages. How do they differ? What does that tell us about his project?
- According to your reading, how did Cook's endeavors symbolize "scientific" imperialism?

The Voyages of Captain James Cook *Left:* During his celebrated voyages to the South Pacific, Cook kept meticulous maps and diaries. Although he had little formal education, he became one of the great exemplars of enlightened learning through experience and experiment. *Right:* Kangaroos were unknown in the western world until Cook and his colleagues encountered (and ate) them on their first visit to Australia. This engraving of the animal (which, unlike most animals, plants, and geographical features, actually kept the name the Aboriginals had given it) from Cook's 1773 travelogue, *A Voyage Round the World in the Years 1768–1771*, lovingly depicts the kangaroo's environs and even emotions.

voyage was so fruitful that he subsequently undertook two more scientific-imperial adventures.

Cook was chosen to head the first expedition because of his scientific interests and skills. Besides Cook, the Royal Society sent along one of its members who was a botanist; a doctor and student of the renowned Swedish naturalist Carolus Linnaeus; and numerous artists and other scientists. The crew also carried sophisticated instruments and had instructions to keep detailed diaries. This was to be a grand data-collecting journey. Cook's voyages surpassed even the Royal Society's hopes. The scientists made approximately 3,000 drawings of Pacific plants, birds, landscapes, and peoples never seen in Europe.

ECOLOGICAL AND CULTURAL EFFECTS

More than science was at stake, however, for Australia was intended to supply Britain with raw materials. As in the Americas, extracting those materials required a labor force, and the Aboriginals of Australia, like the Indians of the Americas, perished in great numbers from imported diseases. Those who survived generally fled to escape control by British masters. Thus, to secure a labor force, plans arose for grand-scale conquest and resettlement by British colonists. On his third voyage, Cook took along a wide array of animals and plants with which to turn the South Pacific into a European-style garden, with massive ecological consequences. His lieutenant later brought apples, quinces, strawberries, and rosemary to Australia; the seventy sheep imported in 1788 laid the foundations for the region's wool-growing economy. In fact, the domestication of Australia arose from the Europeans' certainty about their superior know-how and a desire to make the entire landmass serve British interests.

In 1788, a British military expedition took official possession of the eastern half of Australia. The intent was, in part, to establish a prison colony far from home. This plan belonged as well to the realm of "enlightened" dreams: removing people from an environment that did not suit them and sending them to new climes where they could be reformed, or, if they couldn't be, at least be prevented from causing problems back home. The intent was also to exploit Australia for its timber and flax and to use it as a strategic base against Dutch and French expansion. By 1860, immigration—free and forced—had increased the Anglo-Australian population from an original 1,000 to about 1.2 million. Importing their customs and their capital, British settlers turned Australia into a frontier version of home, just as they had done in British America. Yet such large-scale immigration had disastrous consequences for the surviving Aboriginals. Like the Native Americans, the original inhabitants of Australia were decimated by diseases and increasingly forced westward by European settlement. As in the Americas, European ideas and institutions proved to be far more influential and disruptive in Oceania than they were in the major land empires of Afro-Eurasia.

Conclusion

New wealth produced by commerce and state building created the conditions for a global cultural renaissance in the sixteenth, seventeenth, and eighteenth centuries. It began in the Chinese and Islamic empires and then stretched into Europe, Africa, and previous worlds apart in the Americas and Oceania. Experiments in religious toleration encouraged cultural exchange; book production and consumption soared; grand new monuments took shape; luxury goods became available for wider enjoyment.

Although the Islamic and Chinese worlds confidently retained their own systems of knowing, believing, and representing, the Americas and Oceania increasingly faced European cultural pressures. Here, while hybrid practices became widespread by the late eighteenth century, European beliefs and habits took over as the standards for judging degrees of "civilization." African cultures largely escaped this influence, though their homelands felt the impact of European expansionism because of the slave trade.

From a commercial standpoint, the world was more integrated than ever before. But the exposure and cultural borrowing that global trade promoted did not obliterate established cultural traditions. The Chinese, for instance, still believed in the superiority of their traditional knowledge and customs. Muslim rulers, confident of the primacy of Islam, allowed others to form subordinate cultural communities within their realm and adopted the Europeans' knowledge only when it served their own imperial purposes.

Only the Europeans were constructing knowledge that they believed was both universal and objective, enabling mortals to master the world of nature and all its inhabitants. This view would prove consequential, as well as controversial, in the centuries to come.

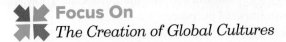

Focus On
The Creation of Global Cultures

The Islamic World

- The Ottomans' unique cultural synthesis accommodates not only mystical Sufis and ultraorthodox *ulama* but also military men, administrators, and clerics.

- The Safavid state proclaims the triumph of Shiism and Persian influences in the sumptuous new capital, Isfahan.

- Mughal courtly culture values art and learning and, at its high point, welcomes non-Muslim contributions.

East Asia

- China's cultural flourishing, coming from within, is evident in the broad circulation of traditional ideas, publishing, and mapmaking.

- Japan's imperial court at Kyoto develops an elite culture of theater, stylized painting, tea ceremonies, and flower arranging.

Europe

- Cultural flourishing known as the Enlightenment yields a faith in reason and a belief in humans' ability to fathom the laws of nature and human behavior.

- European thinkers articulate a belief in unending human progress.

- Europeans expand into Australia and the South Pacific.

Africa

- Slave-trading states such as Asante, Oyo, and Benin celebrate royal power and wealth through art.

The Americas

- Even as Euro-Americans participate in the Enlightenment, their culture reflects Native American and African influences.

CHRONOLOGY

	1500	1550	1600
The Islamic World		Shah Abbas I builds Isfahan 1598–1629	
Africa			
Europe			
East Asia			
The Americas			

- **Thinking about Exchange Networks and Cultural Change** How did increased exchanges of goods and ideas change established traditions? What institutions and ideas proved most hospitable to foreign influence, even in established cultures, and why? Which fields proved more resistant to outside ideas? Why were some regions more receptive to foreign influences than others were? Consider religion, natural science, and art.

- **Thinking about Changing Power Relationships and Cultural Change** How did established cultures respond to the inclusion of the Americas in an increasingly integrated world? Which cultures flourished, and why? What relationship(s) can you see between new wealth and cultural change?

- **Thinking about Environmental Impacts and Cultural Change** The isolation of the Americas and Oceania paved the way for ecological catastrophe when Europeans arrived. How, in turn, did ecological catastrophes leave indigenous cultures vulnerable? Consider the nature of religious change in the Americas and the Afro-Eurasian core regions and population movements in Australia.

Key Terms

bioprospecting p. 548
Creoles p. 560
Enlightenment p. 548
Oceania p. 563

Peninsulares p. 560
Philosophes p. 549

scientific method p. 548
Sufis p. 533

ulama p. 533
Taj Mahal p. 538

 Go to INQUIZITIVE to see what you've learned—and learn what you've missed—with personalized feedback along the way.

1650	1700	1750	1800

Taj Mahal built in Mughal dynasty 1630–1650

Tulip Period in Ottoman Empire 1720s

Oyo and Asante kingdoms produce vibrant artistic works seventeenth century

Isaac Newton publishes *Principia Mathematica* 1687

Enlightenment philosophy spreads among educated elites eighteenth century

Carolus Linnaeus publishes *Systema Naturae* 1735

Adam Smith publishes *The Wealth of Nations* 1776

Voyages of Captain Cook 1768–1779

Growing circulation of books and ideas in China seventeenth century

Study aids for the civil service examination are especially popular seventeenth century

Anthologies of women's poetry circulate widely seventeenth century

"Floating worlds" appear in Japanese cities seventeenth century

Hybrid cultures appear seventeenth century

Enlightenment philosophy spreads among colonial elites eighteenth century

15

Reordering the World

1750–1850

Core Objectives

- **DESCRIBE** the new ideas of freedom, and **EXPLAIN** how they differed from earlier understandings of this term.

- **COMPARE** political and economic developments in the Atlantic world with those of regions elsewhere around the globe during the period 1750–1850.

- **IDENTIFY** and **EXPLAIN** the key developments that constituted the industrial revolution.

- **EXPLAIN** patterns of global trade and economic growth, and **CONNECT** them to political changes during the period 1750–1850.

- **COMPARE** the groups of people who held power in each of the regions in 1750 and then in 1850, and **EXPLAIN** the changes that took place during this period in these societies.

In 1798, the French commander Napoleon Bonaparte invaded Egypt. At the time, Europeans regarded this territory as the cradle of a once-great culture, a land bridge to the Red Sea and trade with Asia, and an outpost of the Ottoman Empire. Occupying the country would allow Napoleon to introduce some of the principles of the French Revolution and to seize control of trade routes to Asia. Napoleon also hoped that by defeating the Ottomans, who controlled Egypt, he would augment his and France's historic greatness. Although Napoleon's adventure backfired, it challenged Ottoman rule and threatened the balance of power in Europe. Indeed, Napoleon's actions in Africa, the Americas, and Europe, combined with the principles of the American and French Revolutions, laid the foundations for a new era—one based on a radically new understanding of freedom as the absence of constraint, the opposite of privileges handed down by a lord or master.

That new idea of freedom first rang out across western Europe and the Americas and reverberated around the world. It destroyed the American colonial domains of Spain, Portugal, Britain, and France; brought new nations to the stage; and challenged established elites everywhere, leading in some cases to the expansion of colonial rule. The impulse for change was a belief that governments should enact laws that apply to all people, though in practice there were significant exceptions (enslaved peoples, women, and colonized subjects). Free speech, free markets, free labor, and governments freely chosen by freeborn men, it was thought, would benefit everyone. In Europe and the Americas, though not elsewhere, the era also witnessed the emergence of the nation-state. This new form of political organization derived legitimacy from its inhabitants, often referred to as citizens, who, in theory, if not always in practice, shared a common culture, ethnicity, and language.

Underlying many of these political and social upheavals were major changes in the world economy. Countries began to produce goods less for their own population and more for people living in other places around the globe. This specialization for export markets further integrated the world. But results were paradoxical. While the world became more integrated and economic growth took off, social disparities grew wider—both within and across countries. What is called "the industrial revolution" set in motion great divides between Europe and North America and the rest of the world and even within industrializing societies.

Freedom in some corners of the globe set the stage for depriving people of freedom elsewhere and led inexorably to changes in the worldwide balance of power. Even as western European countries lost their New World colonies, they gained economic and military strength, which further challenged Asian and African governments.

Global Storyline

The Global Impact of the Atlantic and Industrial Revolutions

- A new era based on radically new ideas of freedom and the nation-state emerges in the Atlantic world.
- The industrial revolution transforms communities and the global economy.
- The worldwide balance of power shifts decisively toward northwestern Europe.

Revolutionary Transformations and New Languages of Freedom

In the eighteenth century, the circulation of goods, people, and ideas created pressures for reform around the Atlantic world. As economies expanded, many people felt that the restrictive mercantilist system prevented them from sharing in the new wealth and power. Similarly, an increasingly literate public called for their states to adopt just practices, including the abolition of torture and the accountability of rulers. In several places, power holders could not stamp out these demands before they became full-scale revolutions.

Reformers wanted to expand the franchise, to enable property holders to vote. Claims of **popular sovereignty**, the idea that political power depends on "the people," became rooted in the idea of the nation: people who shared a common language, common culture, and common history. This in turn gave rise to the nation-state as a form of political organization. Over the course of the nineteenth century, political movements began to emphasize nationalism, the idea that a fully fledged nation should have a state of its own, and democracy, the idea that the people, the *demos*, should choose their own representatives and be governed by them (see Chapter 16). In this chapter, we concentrate on the first expressions of this new thinking in four empires—the British, French, Spanish, and Portuguese—where new ideas of freedom broke old loyalties.

This chapter also concentrates on far-reaching economic developments that came in tandem with revolutionary political change. Economic reformers argued that unregulated economies would produce faster economic growth. Going well beyond the work of Adam Smith, they called for **free trade** (or **laissez-faire**), unencumbered by tariffs, quotas, and fees; free markets, which would be unregulated; and free labor, which meant using the labor of paid, rather than enslaved, workers. They insisted that these economic freedoms would yield more just and more efficient societies, ultimately benefiting everyone, everywhere in the world.

Ideas and practices spread on the backs of a transformation in communications after 1750. First, changes in the media disseminated new ideas about political and economic freedom. The idea of a "people" could be shared only if there were shared stories and information. Second, faster, cheaper, and easier access to valuable information helped mobilize resources and intensify pressures to open markets around the world. As a result, newspapers, news agencies, and global reporting helped promote national identities within societies while also creating more interlinked and interdependent markets across societies.

There was a quiet revolution in how information was organized and exchanged. Technologies changed. Iron frames replaced wood hand printing presses; then cylinders allowed continuous sheets to be printed, and steam could power bigger cylinders. The circulation of information became a more complex business and eventually involved sprawling multinationals with agents operating around the world. Printers became bigger businesses with elaborate divisions of labor. The most prized jobs, like typesetting, went to men. Women, too, performed printing jobs, but they were assigned the hardest ones. They worked as sheet feeders, which was not just back-breaking and mind-numbing, but also risky: a tired or distracted woman could lose a hand or fingers as the presses clamped down. Eventually, as cylinders and steam replaced flatbed stamp presses, those dangerous jobs were replaced. The creation of guilds and unions of more skilled workers ultimately drove women from the industry.

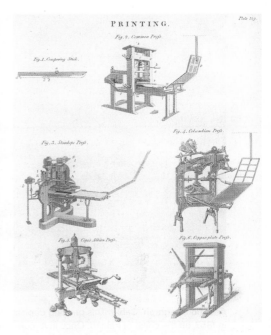

The Printing Press The printing press underwent important transformations after 1750. This illustration shows how the original wood presses gave way to iron presses, which were more durable, printed larger sheets, and could hold movable type more easily. Eventually, cylinders could roll long sheets through the presses for a continuous flow. Hand stamping and rolling eventually ceded to steam-driven machinery.

The cost of printing declined sharply, making newspapers, magazines, pamphlets, and broadsheets more accessible. These would become the mechanisms for spreading seditious ideas, which often spurred authorities to clamp down on their sales, often with mixed results. Booklets like *Common Sense* (1776) by the rebel Thomas Paine or *What Is the Third Estate?* (1789) by Abbé Sieyès explained what was at stake and why common people deserved more rights than the powerful gave them. As the Spanish Empire went into convulsions along with the French and British Empires, the printing press became a weapon of war there, too. When the Venezuelan patriot Francisco de Miranda set out to liberate the colony from Spanish rule in 1804, he brought with him a printing press, which the colony did not yet have, to spread his revolutionary message.

Many women also seized the opportunities afforded by cheap printing to claim their rights. The idea of giving them the vote might have been unthinkable, but it was hard to deny them a voice. One of the most prominent was Mary Wollstonecraft, whose *Vindication of the Rights of Woman* (1792) echoed men's demands for rights but criticized revolutionary men for their convenient hypocrisy—for claiming that women were unequal while denying them educational opportunities to be equal. It was published on both sides of the Atlantic and immediately translated into French.

Atlantic Telegraph Cable This painting depicts the laying of the first Atlantic telegraph cable in 1857, off the coast of Ireland. Once inventors figured out how to protect underwater cables, there was a scramble to tether the continents together after the 1851 connection from England to France. Within a few years, companies were dreaming bigger. They were also able to use other new technologies, like the steam-powered vessel especially designed to lay cable that is shown here. The breakthroughs were also labor-intensive, as this image also illustrates.

Technological developments enabled information in one part of the world to reach others more easily and more cheaply. In the 1820s, the news from London could still take two to three months to reach Buenos Aires or Cape Town, and over four months to reach India and then New South Wales. When innovators figured out how to transmit messages by cable, the cost of information plunged. New coatings made of colonial Malaysian latex and Bengali hemp allowed cables to be laid under water. A cable linking Dover to Calais was laid in 1851; after that, lines stretched all over the planet to link commercial and political entrepôts. The number of days it took to dispatch news from London went from one month to two days for New York, from 145 days to 3 days for Bombay, and from 97 days to 3 days for Buenos Aires.

Political Reorderings

Empires became more connected with each other through the cross-border flow of commodities and information. But the expansion of world markets also led to a scramble to control these markets. Global rivalries between empires plunged them all into a crisis, and escalating mercantilist wars mired them deeper and deeper into debt. Debt meant more borrowing and thus inflation, and more taxes and thus resistance. A global arms race ignited basic questions about the legitimacy of governments and the rights of people to defend themselves from what they saw as predatory policies.

Late in the eighteenth century, revolutionary ideas spread across the Atlantic world (see Map 15.1), following the trail of Enlightenment ideas about freedom and reason. As more newspapers, pamphlets, and books circulated in European countries and American colonies, readers began to discuss their societies' problems and to believe they had the right to participate in governance.

The slogans of independence, freedom, liberty, and equality seemed to promise an end to oppression, hardship, and inequities. In the North American colonies and in France, revolutions ultimately brought down monarchies and blossomed into republics. The examples of the United States and France soon encouraged other people in the Caribbean and Central and South America to reject the rule of monarchs. In these revolutionary environments, new institutions—such as written constitutions and permanent parliaments—claimed to represent the people.

THE NORTH AMERICAN WAR OF INDEPENDENCE, 1776–1783

The American Revolution was the beginning of the end of British rule in North America. It was the first of a series of revolutions to shake the Atlantic world, inspired by new ideas of freedom.

By the mid-eighteenth century, Britain's colonies in North America swelled with people and prosperity. Bustling port cities like Charleston, Philadelphia, New York, and Boston saw inflows of enslaved Africans, European migrants, and manufactured goods, while agricultural staples flowed out. A "genteel" class of merchants and landowning planters dominated colonial affairs.

Land was a constant source of dispute. Planters struggled with independent farmers (yeomen). Sons and daughters of farmers, often unable to inherit or acquire land near their parents, moved westward, where they came into conflict with Amerindian peoples. To defend their lands, many Amerindians allied with Britain's rival, France. After losing the Seven Years' War (see Chapter 13), however, France ceded its Canadian colony to Britain to secure the return of its much more lucrative Caribbean colonies, especially Saint-Domingue. This forced many Native Americans to turn to the British government for help in fending off land-hungry colonists. British officials did make some concessions to Native American interests, but they did not have the troops or financial strength to enforce them.

Asserting Independence from Britain Despite these tensions, Britain stood supreme in the Atlantic world in the mid-1760s, with its greatest foes defeated and its empire expanding. Political revolution in North America seemed unimaginable. And yet, a decade later, that is what occurred.

The Global View

RUSSIA

BRITISH NORTH AMERICA

Hudson Bay

OREGON
(Claimed by Spain, Russia, and Britain)

LOUISIANA
(Louisiana was a Spanish possession from 1762 to 1801, then French, then sold to the United States.)

Québec

Boston
New York

UNITED STATES
✳1776
(independence recognized by Great Britain 1783)

Philadelphia
Washington, D.C.
Charleston

A T L A N T I C

O C E A N

Santa Fe

MEXICO
✳1821

FLORIDA

Gulf of Mexico

Mexico City

CUBA

PUERTO RICO

GUADELOUPE (Fr.)
MARTINIQUE (Fr.)

BELIZE JAMAICA REPUBLIC OF HAITI
✳1804

UNITED PROVINCES OF CENTRAL AMERICA
✳1823 Cartagena

Caracas

TRINIDAD (Br.)

P A C I F I C

O C E A N

REPUBLIC OF COLOMBIA
✳1819

GUIANA

Quito

PERU
✳1821
Lima

B R A Z I L
✳1822

BOLIVIA
✳1825

Rio de Janeiro

PARAGUAY
✳1811

CHILE
✳1818

PROVINCES OF LA PLATA
✳1816

URUGUAY
✳1828

Buenos Aires Montevideo

British possessions
Spanish possessions
French possessions
Portuguese possessions
Dutch possessions
Ottoman possessions
Russian Empire
✳1776 Date of political independence from European (or Ottoman) colonial rule

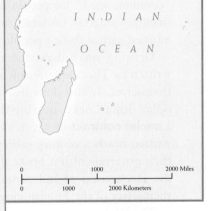

SWEDEN-
NORWAY

St. Petersburg

DENMARK
NETHERLANDS
GREAT BRITAIN
London
BELGIUM
Paris
FRANCE

Berlin
GERMAN
STATES AUSTRIAN
Vienna EMPIRE

Moscow

R U S S I A N   E M P I R E

PORTUGAL

ITALIAN

Madrid
Lisbon SPAIN

Rome
STATES
GREECE Athens
※1829 O T T O M A N

M E D I T E R R A N E A N   S E A

E M P I R E
Cairo
E G Y P T
(occupied by
French troops
1798–1801)

A F R I C A

I N D I A N

O C E A N

Map 15.1 Revolutions and Empires in the Atlantic World, 1776–1829

....

Influenced by Enlightenment thinkers and the
French Revolution, colonies gained independence
from European powers (and in the case of Greece,
from the Ottoman Empire) in the late eighteenth
and early nineteenth centuries.

- Which European powers granted
  independence to their colonial possessions in
  the Americas during this period?

- What were the first two colonial territories to
  become independent in the Americas?

- Based on the chronology presented in this
  map and on your reading, consider the
  relative importance of European influence
  and local developments in the Americas in
  accounting for the timing of independence
  in different countries. Why, in particular, did
  colonies in Spanish and Portuguese America
  obtain political independence decades after
  the United States won its independence?

0   1000   2000 Miles

0   1000   2000 Kilometers

The Boston Massacre Paul Revere's idealized view of the Boston Massacre of March 5, 1770. In the years after the Seven Years' War, Bostonians grew increasingly disenchanted with British efforts to enforce imperial regulations. When British troops fired on and killed several members of an angry mob in what came to be called the "Boston Massacre," the resulting frenzy stirred revolutionary sentiments among the populace.

The spark came from the government of King George III, which insisted that colonists contribute to the crown that protected them, notably in the Seven Years' War (known in North America as the French and Indian War). The king's officials imposed taxes on a variety of commodities and tried to put an end to smuggling by colonists who sought to evade mercantilist restrictions on trade. To the king's surprise and dismay, colonists objected to the new measures and protested having to pay taxes when they lacked political representation in the British Parliament.

In 1775, resistance in the form of petitions and boycotts turned into open warfare between a colonial militia and British troops in Massachusetts. Once blood was spilled, more radical voices came to the fore. Previously, leaders of the protest had claimed to revere the British Empire. Now calls for severing the ties to Britain became more prominent. Thomas Paine, a recent immigrant from England, captured the new mood in a pamphlet he published in 1776, arguing that it was "common sense" for people to govern themselves. Later that year, the Continental Congress (in which representatives from thirteen colonies gathered) adapted part of Paine's popular pamphlet for the Declaration of Independence.

Drawing on Enlightenment themes (see Chapter 14), the declaration written by Thomas Jefferson affirmed the people's "natural right" to govern themselves. It also drew inspiration from the writings of the British philosopher John Locke, notably the idea that governments should be based on a **social contract** in which the law binds both ruler and people. Locke had written nearly a century earlier that the people had the right to rebel against their government if it broke the contract and infringed on their rights. With the Declaration of Independence, the rebels announced their right to rid themselves of the English king and form their own government.

The Declaration's assertion that "all men are created equal" overturned former social hierarchies in the thirteen colonies (now calling themselves states). Thus, common men no longer automatically deferred to gentlemen of higher rank. Many women claimed that their contributions to the revolution's cause (by managing farms and shops in their husbands' absence) earned them greater equality in marriage, including property rights. However, the political arrangements Americans designed during their War of Independence gave voting rights only to White, male property owners—not women, not the enslaved, not Amerindians, not poor White men without property. Indeed, many enslaved people sided against the revolution, for it was the British who offered them freedom most directly, in exchange for military service. Backed by France and Spain, the Continental Army under the command of General George Washington finally broke the British back. With the Treaty of Paris (1783), the United States gained its independence.

Building a Republican Government With independence, the former colonists had to build a new government. They generally agreed that theirs was not to be a monarchy. But what it *was* to be remained through the 1780s a source of heated words and sometimes heated action. As a loose confederation of relatively autonomous states, the new national state struggled to deal with local rebellions, foreign relations, and crushing levels of debt. To save the young nation from falling into "anarchy," propertied men convened the Constitutional Convention in Philadelphia in 1787.

This gathering aimed to forge a document that would create a more powerful national government and a more unified nation. After fierce debate, the convention drafted a charter for a republican government in which power would rest with representatives of the people—not with a king. When it went before the states for approval, the Constitution was controversial. Critics known as Anti-Federalists feared the growth of a potentially tyrannical national government and insisted on including a Bill of Rights to protect individual liberties from abusive government intrusions. Ultimately the Constitution was ratified by the states and then amended by the Bill of Rights.

This did not end arguments about the scope and power of the national government of the United States. Some Americans called for the national government to abolish slavery. However, many others—especially leaders in the south, where slavery was a mainstay of the economy—argued that the national government did not have the power to do so. In an uneasy truce, political leaders agreed not to let the debate over whether to abolish slavery escalate into a cause for disunion. As the frontier pushed westward, however, the question of which new states would or would not allow slavery again posed a vexing challenge. Initially the existence of ample land postponed a confrontation. In 1800, Thomas Jefferson's election as the third president of the United States marked the triumph of a model of sending pioneers out to new lands in order to reduce conflict on old lands. In the same year, however, an enslaved Virginian named Gabriel Prosser raised an army of fellow enslaved Virginians to seize the state capital at Richmond and won support from White artisans and laborers for a more inclusive republic. His dream of an egalitarian revolution fell victim to White terror and Black betrayal, though: twenty-seven freedom fighters, including Prosser, went to the gallows. With them, for the moment, died the dream of a multiracial republic in which all men were truly created equal.

In the larger context of the Atlantic world, the successful defiance of Europe's most powerful empire and the establishment of a nonmonarchical, republican form of government sent shock waves through the Americas and Europe and into Asia and Africa. It also helped pave the way for other revolts over the next several decades.

THE FRENCH REVOLUTION, 1789–1799

Partly inspired by reports from the American Revolution, French men and women soon began to call for liberty too—and the result profoundly shook Europe's dynasties and social hierarchies. Its impact, though, reached well beyond Europe, for the French Revolution, even more than the American, inspired rebels and terrified rulers around the globe.

Origins and Outbreak The French king himself opened the door to revolution. Eager to weaken his rival, England, Louis XVI spent huge sums in support of the American rebels—and thereby overloaded the state with debt. To restore his credit, Louis needed to raise taxes on the privileged classes; to do so, he was forced to convene the Estates-General, a medieval advisory body that had not met for 175 years. Like the American colonists, French nobles argued that taxation gave them the right of representation.

When the delegates assembled in 1789, however, a procedural dispute spun out of control. The delegates of the clergy (the First Estate) and the aristocracy (the Second Estate) hoped to vote by estate and overrule the delegates representing everyone else (the Third Estate). But the Third Estate, which had more representatives than the first two estates combined, refused to be outvoted. It demanded that all delegates sit together in one chamber and vote as individuals. Soon delegates of the Third Estate declared themselves to be the "National Assembly," the body that should determine France's future.

Afraid that the king would crush the reform movement, a Parisian crowd attacked a medieval armory in search of weapons on July 14, 1789. Not only did this armory—the Bastille—hold gunpowder, but it was also an infamous jail for political prisoners. The crowd stormed the prison and murdered the commanding officer, then cut off his head and paraded it through the streets of Paris. On this day (Bastille Day), the king made the fateful decision not to call out the army, and the capital city belonged to the crowd. As news spread to the countryside, peasants torched manor houses and destroyed municipal archives containing records of feudal dues, payments they owed to landlords of specially designated properties. Barely three weeks later, the French National Assembly abolished the privileges of the nobility and the clergy. It declared a new era of liberty, equality,

The "Tennis Court Oath" Locked out of the chambers of the Estates-General, the deputies of the Third Estate reconvened at a nearby indoor tennis court in June 1789; there they swore an oath not to disband until the king recognized the sovereignty of a national assembly.

and fraternity. Liberty, like freedom, now meant the absence of constraint rather than a special privilege granted by the king.

Revolutionary Transformations The French Revolution connected the concept of a people more closely with a nation. The Declaration of the Rights of Man and of the Citizen (1789) echoed the Americans' Declaration of Independence, but in more radical terms. It guaranteed all citizens of the French nation inviolable liberties and gave all men equality under the law. It also proclaimed that "the principle of all sovereignty rests essentially in the nation." Both the rhetorical and the real war against old-regime privileges threatened to end dynastic and aristocratic rule in Europe.

Social relations changed too, as women felt that the new principles of citizenship should include women's rights. In 1791, a group of women demanded the right to bear arms to defend the revolution, but they stopped short of claiming equal rights for both sexes. In their view, women would become citizens by being good revolutionary wives and mothers, not because of any natural rights. In the same year, Olympe de Gouges composed the Declaration of the Rights of Woman and the Female Citizen, proposing rights to divorce, hold property in marriage, be educated, and have public careers. The all-male assembly did not take up these issues, believing that a "fraternity" of free *men* composed the nation.

As the revolution gained momentum, deep divisions emerged. In 1790, all clergy had to take an oath of loyalty to the new state—an action that bitterly divided the country. The most divisive, destructive turn in the revolution came

Women March on Versailles On October 5, 1789, a group of market women, many of them fishwives (traditionally regarded as leaders of the poor), marched on the Paris city hall to demand bread. Quickly, their numbers grew, and they redirected their march to Versailles, some 12 miles away and the symbol of the entire political order. In response to the women, the king finally appeared on the balcony and agreed to sign the revolutionary decree and return with the women to Paris.

in 1792, when the French declared a preemptive war against Austria, and then Prussia, Britain, and Russia. They soon had foreign armies on their soil and a civil war to contend with, when peasants outraged by the loyalty oath and city dwellers in major provincial cities rose up against the revolutionary government and its wartime demands.

The Terror In response to this self-induced crisis, elite reformers made common cause with urban radicals in Paris, who demanded price controls, direct democracy, and the violent suppression of dissent. Together, they launched the Terror. The Committee of Public Safety, including the lawyer Maximilien Robespierre, oversaw the execution of as many as 40,000 so-called enemies of the people—mostly peasants and laborers who had taken up arms against them—justified in terms of defending the Republic. Although most victims were of modest means, the term *aristocrat* was often equated with treason. Even before terror was declared as government policy, Louis XVI and his wife, Marie Antoinette, had lost their heads to the guillotine (itself a novel and supposedly rational, enlightened way to execute prisoners painlessly).

By 1794 France's army numbered some 800,000 soldiers, making it the world's largest. Most French officers now came from the middle classes, some even from the lower class. Foot soldiers identified with the French fatherland. Having vowed to wage a defensive war, they now pushed foreign armies off French soil and waged a war to "liberate" the disenfranchised from their rulers across Europe.

Battle of the Pyramids The French army invaded Egypt with grand ambitions and high hopes. Napoleon brought a large cadre of scholars along with his 36,000-man army, intending to win Egyptians to the cause of the French Revolution and to establish a French imperial presence on the banks of the Nile. This idealized portrait of the famous Battle of the Pyramids, fought on July 21, 1798, shows Napoleon and his forces crushing the Mamluk military forces.

When the military emergency ended, Robespierre's measures lost popular support, and Robespierre himself went to the guillotine on 9 Thermidor (according to the new, revolutionary calendar, or July 28, 1794). His execution marked the end of the Terror but did not restore order. Several years later, following yet more political turmoil, a coup d'état brought to power a thirty-year-old general from the recently annexed Mediterranean island of Corsica.

The general, **Napoleon Bonaparte** (1769–1821), put security and order ahead of social reform. His regime retained significant revolutionary changes, especially those associated with more efficient state government. He eased religious tensions by working out an accord with the Vatican. However, Napoleon was determined not only to reform France but also to prevail over its enemies, and he retreated from republican principles. Taking the title Emperor of the French, he centralized government administration and established a system of rational tax collection. Most important, he created a civil legal code—the Napoleonic Code—that applied throughout all of France (and the French colonies).

THE NAPOLEONIC ERA, 1799–1815

Determined to extend the reach of French influence, Napoleon launched a series of military campaigns in an effort to build a vast empire. He had his armies trumpet the principles of liberty, equality, and fraternity wherever they went. Many local populations initially embraced the French, regarding them as liberators from the old order. Although Napoleon thought the entire world would take up his cause, this was not always the case.

In Portugal, Spain, and Russia, French troops faced fierce popular resistance. Portuguese and Spanish soldiers and peasants formed bands of resisters called guerrillas, and British troops joined them to fight the French in the Peninsular War (1808–1813). In Germany and Italy, as local inhabitants grew tired of paying tribute, many looked to their past for inspiration to oppose the French. Now they discovered something they had barely recognized before: *national* traditions and borders. One of the ironies of Napoleon's attempt to bring all of Europe under French rule was that it laid the foundations for nationalist strife.

In Europe, Napoleon extended his empire from the Iberian Peninsula to the Austrian and Prussian borders. (See Map 15.2.) By 1812, when he invaded Russia, however, his forces were too overstretched and undersupplied to survive the harsh winter. After his failed attack on Russia, all the major European powers united against him. At the Battle of Waterloo in Belgium in 1815, armies from Prussia, Austria, Russia, and Britain crushed his troops as they made their last stand. The stage was now set for a century-long struggle on the continent between those who wanted to restore society as it had been before the French Revolution and those who wanted to guarantee a more liberal order based on individual rights, limited government, and free trade.

Revolution in Saint-Domingue In 1791, enslaved Black freedom fighters and free people of color rose up against White planters. This engraving was based on a German report on the uprising and depicts White fears of rebellion as much as the actual events themselves.

REVOLUTION IN SAINT-DOMINGUE (HAITI)

France also saw colonies break away in this age of new freedoms, notably Saint-Domingue. Unlike most of British North America, revolution here came from the bottom rungs of the social ladder: enslaved people. In this Caribbean colony, freedom therefore meant not just liberation from Europe but emancipation from White planters. It posed a powerful question: How universal were these new rights?

At the outset of the French Revolution the island's enslaved Black population numbered 500,000, compared with 40,000 White French settlers and about 30,000 free "people of color" (individuals of mixed Black and White ancestry, as well as formerly enslaved

Map 15.2 Napoleon's Empire, 1812

Early in the first decade of the nineteenth century, Napoleon controlled almost all of Europe.

- What major states were under French control? What countries were allied with France?
- Compare this map with the European part of Map 15.1, and explain how Napoleon redrew the map of Europe. What major country was not under French control?
- According to your reading, how was Napoleon able to control and build alliances with so many states and kingdoms?

Blacks). Almost two-thirds of the enslaved were relatively recent arrivals from Africa, with fresh memories of freedom; they had been brought to the colony to toil on its renowned sugar plantations, which were exceptional in their brutality. The enslaved population was an angry majority without local ties, producing wealth for rich absentee landlords of a different race.

The breakdown of authority in France unleashed conflict in Saint-Domingue, where local tensions were already high. White settlers sought self-government; they wanted to break free of the exclusive trade arrangement with France and to control the island themselves. Free Blacks wanted to end racial discrimination among property holders without, initially, calling slavery into question. Enslaved people, by contrast, invoked revolutionary language to denounce their enslavers and air long-standing grievances. As civil war erupted, the enslaved fought French forces that had arrived to restore order. In 1793, the National Convention in France abolished slavery. In part, the motive was to declare the universality of liberty, equality, and fraternity within the French nation, which included colonies. In part, it was to restore order to the colony. Once liberated, the newly freed men and women took control of the island. But their struggles were not over. They had to fight off British and Spanish forces. Then, after Napoleon took power in France, bringing with him a strong commitment to order and France's imperial ambitions, they had to slay their own emperor's armies. Toussaint L'Ouverture, who was formerly enslaved, became the leader of the slave revolution—fighting not just for the abolition of slavery but for freedom from France. Soon, a combination of guerrilla fighters and yellow fever decimated the French army. In 1804, General Jean-Jacques Dessalines declared the island, newly named Haiti, independent.

The specter of a free country ruled by emancipated Black people sent shudders across the Atlantic world, and above all in Britain and Spain, which had neighboring colonies. A version of martial law was declared in Venezuela. Thomas Jefferson, author of the Declaration of Independence and U.S. president at the time, refused to recognize Haiti. Like other American enslavers, he worried that the example of a successful uprising of the enslaved might inspire similar revolts in the United States and elsewhere in the Americas. One by one, European and American governments began to question the wisdom of importing more enslaved Africans lest they lose control of their colonies.

REVOLUTIONS IN SPANISH AND PORTUGUESE AMERICA

Revolutionary enthusiasm also spread through Spanish and Portuguese America. As in Haiti, subordinated people of color took advantage of the period's political instability; they mobilized European ideas against European colonizers and challenged the established order. (See Map 15.3.)

Even before the French Revolution, Andean Indians rebelled against Spanish colonial authority. In a major uprising in the 1780s, of which Túpac Amaru II was an early leader, they demanded freedom from forced labor and compulsory consumption of Spanish wares. After an army of 40,000 to 60,000 Andean Indians besieged the ancient capital of Cuzco and nearly vanquished Spanish armies, it took Spanish forces many years to eliminate the insurgents.

After this uprising, Iberian American elites who feared their Indian or enslaved Black majorities renewed their loyalty to the Spanish or Portuguese crown.

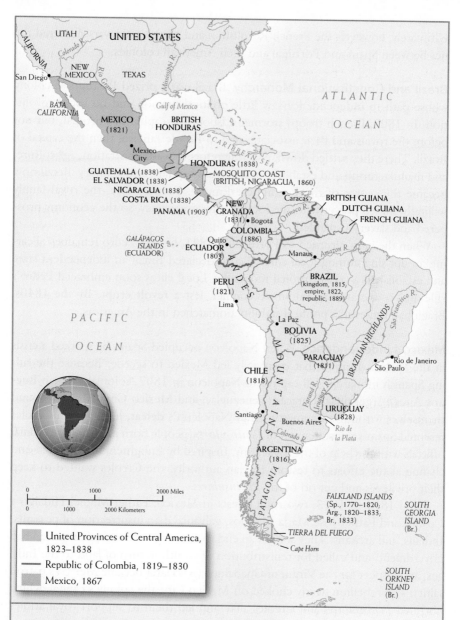

United Provinces of Central America, 1823–1838

— Republic of Colombia, 1819–1830

Mexico, 1867

Map 15.3 Latin American Nation Building

Creating strong, unified nation-states proved difficult in Latin America. The map shows where boundaries were drawn in Mexico, the United Provinces of Central America, and the Republic of Colombia. In each case, the governments' territorial and nation-building ambitions failed to some degree.

- During what period did a majority of the colonies in Latin America gain independence?
- Which European countries lost the most in Latin America during this period?
- Why did all these colonies gain their independence during this time?

Ultimately, however, the French Revolution and Napoleonic wars shattered the ties between Spain and Portugal and their American colonies.

Brazil and Constitutional Monarchy Brazil was a prized Portuguese colony whose path to independence saw little political turmoil and no social revolution. In 1807, French troops stormed Lisbon, the capital of Portugal, but not before the royals and their associates fled to Rio de Janeiro, then the capital of Brazil. There they settled down, enacting reforms in administration, agriculture, and manufacturing and establishing schools, hospitals, and a library. Brazil now became the center of the Portuguese Empire. Furthermore, the royal family willingly shared power with the local planter aristocracy, so the economy prospered and slavery expanded.

When the king returned to Portugal in 1821, his son Pedro remained. Fearing an uprising among local elites, Pedro declared Brazil an independent state and established a constitutional monarchy. Local elites soon embraced Pedro's rule and cooperated to minimize conflict, lest a revolt erupt. By the 1840s, Brazil had achieved a political stability unmatched in the Americas.

Mexico's Independence When Napoleon occupied Spain, he sparked a crisis in the Spanish Empire that eventually led Mexico to secede. Because the ruling Spanish monarchy fell captive to Napoleon in 1807, colonial elites in Buenos Aires (Argentina), Caracas (Venezuela), and Mexico City (Mexico) found themselves without an emperor. After Napoleon's defeat, locally born Creoles resented Spain's reinstatement of *Peninsulares* (people born in Spain) as colonial officials with the help of the royal army. Inspired by Enlightenment thinkers and chafing at the efforts to restore Iberian authority, the Creoles wanted to keep their privileges and get rid of the *Peninsulares*.

From 1810 to 1813, two rural priests in Mexico, Father Miguel Hidalgo y Costilla and Father José María Morelos, galvanized an insurrection of peasants, Indians, and artisans. They sought an end to abuses by the elite, denounced bad government, and called for redistribution of wealth, return of land to the Indians, and respect for the Virgin of Guadalupe (who later became Mexico's patron saint). The rebellion nearly choked off Mexico City, the colony's capital, which horrified *Peninsulares* and Creoles alike and led them to support royal armies that eventually crushed the uprising.

Despite the military victory, Spain's hold on its colony weakened. Mexico's Creoles identified themselves more as Mexicans than as Spanish Americans, and as the Spanish king appeared less and less able to govern effectively, Mexican generals (with support of the Creoles) proclaimed Mexican independence in 1821. Unlike in Brazil, Mexican secession did not lead to stability.

Other South American Revolutions The loosening of Spain's grip on its colonies was more prolonged and militarized than Britain's separation from its American colonies. Venezuela's Simón Bolívar (1783–1830), the son of a merchant-planter family who was educated on Enlightenment texts, dreamed of a land governed by reason. He revered Napoleonic France as a model state built on military heroism and constitutional proclamations. So did the Argentine leader General José de San Martín (1778–1850). Men like Bolívar, San Martín, and their many generals waged extended wars of independence against Spanish armies and their allies between 1810 and 1824.

What started in South America as a political revolution against Spanish colonial authority escalated into a social struggle among Indians, mestizos, enslaved Black people, and Whites. The armed populace threatened the planters and merchants; rural folk battled against aristocratic Creoles; Andean Indians fled the mines and occupied great estates. Popular armies, having defeated Spanish forces by the 1820s, fought civil wars over the new postcolonial order.

New states and collective identities of nationhood now emerged. A narrow elite led these political communities, and their guiding principles were often contradictory. Bolívar, for instance, encouraged his followers to become "American," to overcome their local identities. He wanted the liberated countries to form a Latin American confederation, urging Peru and Bolivia to join Venezuela, Ecuador, and Colombia in the "Gran Colombia." But local identities prevailed, giving way to unstable national republics. Bolívar died surrounded by opponents; San Martín died in exile. The real heirs to independence were local military chieftains, who often forged alliances with landowners, which perpetuated the power of local patriarchs. In the face of so much uncertainty, for many, the prior obligation was to family and kin rather than state and public interests. Though many women yearned for more room to become educated and to choose their spouses, political instability tended to favor traditional private norms. Thus, the legacy of the Spanish American revolutions was contradictory. All the mainland colonies broke free of Spain. Wealthy elites survived under a banner of liberty, at the continued expense of poorer, non-White, and mixed populations.

Change and Trade in Africa

Africa also was swept up in revolutionary tides, as increased domestic and world trade—including the selling of enslaved Africans—shifted the terms of state building across the continent. The main catalyst for Africa's political shake-up was the rapid growth and then the demise of the Atlantic slave trade. The abolition of the Atlantic slave trade, which European reformers believed would lead to economic prosperity based on "legitimate trade," had the perverse effect of intensifying domestic slavery. As Africa became an exporter of raw materials rather than human beings, the hard work done on African farms and plantations—producing palm, palm kernels, peanuts, and gum for export—was done by enslaved people.

ABOLITION OF THE SLAVE TRADE

Even as it enriched and empowered some Africans and many Europeans, the slave trade became a subject of fierce debate in the late eighteenth century. Some European and American revolutionaries argued that enslaved labor was inherently less productive than free wage labor and ought to be abolished. At the same time, another group favoring abolition of the slave trade insisted that traffic in the enslaved was immoral. In London abolitionists created committees, often led by Quakers, to lobby Parliament for an end to the slave trade. Quakers in Philadelphia did likewise. Pamphlets, reports, and personal narratives denounced the traffic in people.

In response to abolitionist efforts, North Atlantic powers moved to prohibit the slave trade. Denmark acted first in its Caribbean colonies in 1803, Great Britain followed in 1807, and the United States joined the campaign in 1808. Over time, the British persuaded the French and other European governments to do likewise. To enforce the ban, Britain posted a naval squadron off the coast of West Africa to prevent any slave trade above the equator and compelled Brazil's emperor to end imports of enslaved people. After 1850, Atlantic slave shipping dropped sharply, though slavery did not end for several decades due to the continued profitability of cotton in the southern United States, sugar in the Caribbean, and coffee in Brazil. The last known Atlantic slave ship discharged its cargo in Cuba in 1867.

Chasing Enslaver Dhows Transformed from a major proponent of the Atlantic slave trade to its chief opponent, the British used their naval forces to suppress European and African slave traders who attempted to subvert the injunction against slave trading. Here a British vessel chases an East African dhow trying to run enslaved Africans from the island of Zanzibar.

NEW TRADE WITH AFRICA

Even as the Atlantic slave trade died down, Europeans promoted commerce with Africa. Now they wanted Africans to export raw materials and to purchase European manufactured goods. What Europeans liked to call "legitimate" trade aimed to raise the Africans' standards of living by substituting trade in produce for trade in enslaved people. West Africans responded by exporting palm kernels and peanuts. The real bonanza was in vegetable oils to lubricate machinery and make candles and in palm oil to produce soap. European merchants argued that by becoming vibrant export societies, Africans would earn the wealth to profitably import European wares.

The new trade gave rise to a generation of successful West African merchants. There were many rags-to-riches stories, like that of King Jaja of Opobo (1821–1891). Kidnapped and sold into slavery as a youngster, he started out paddling canoes carrying palm oil to coastal ports. Ultimately becoming the head of a coastal canoe house, he founded the port of Opobo and could summon a flotilla of war canoes on command. Another freed man, a Yoruba, William Lewis, made his way back to Africa and in 1828 settled in Sierra Leone (a British colony for freed people, notably Blacks from the United States who were loyal to Great Britain). Starting with a few utensils and a small plot of land, he became a successful merchant and sent his son Samuel to England for his education. Samuel eventually became an important political leader in Sierra Leone.

However, the rise of free labor in the Atlantic world and the dwindling foreign slave trade had an unanticipated effect: it strengthened slavery within Africa. In some areas, by the mid-nineteenth century enslaved people accounted for more than half the population. No longer did they comfortably serve in domestic employment; instead, they toiled on palm oil plantations or, in East Africa, on clove plantations. They also served in the military forces, bore palm oil and ivory to markets as porters, or paddled cargo-carrying canoes along rivers leading to the coast. In 1850, northern Nigeria's ruling class had more enslaved men, women, and children than independent Brazil and almost as many as the United States. As Africa ceased to be the world's supplier of enslaved people, it became in time the world's largest enslaving region.

Economic Reorderings

Behind the political and social upheavals, profound changes were occurring in the world economy. Until the middle of the eighteenth century, global trade touched only the edges of most societies, which produced for their own subsistence. Surpluses of special goods, from porcelains to silks, entered trade arteries but did not change the cultures that produced them. By the middle of the nineteenth century global trade began to boom. Basic staples, food, fibers, and fuel became more and more important in the basket of world trade, while precious commodities and metals declined as a share of overall trade. What started with sugar, tea, and coffee spread to other basics like clothing, wheat, and meat. Likewise, what started as elite consumption percolated down to become mass consumption. This shift evinced a dramatic change in the global division of labor, with entire societies gearing more and more of their economic activity to the production of long-distance goods.

Many factors contributed to this reorganization of world trade: state policies changed; elites promoted free trade in parts of Europe and Latin America, and new technologies like steam allowed commerce to reach deeper inland and slashed the cost of transportation and information. In addition, financiers pooled their money to invest in government bonds as well as private stocks. But one of the most important forces in this new trading system was the industrial revolution, which slashed the prices of manufactured goods and required new staple inputs, many of which had to be imported.

One effect of this global reordering was to open a gap between the haves and the have-nots across countries. Societies that industrialized tended to see their incomes grow, sometimes substantially. In contrast, societies that remained basically agrarian tended to fall behind. The new international division of labor produced wealth and inequality at the same time. Global reintegration and a commercial bonanza created a new global economic divide.

MERGING SPHERES OF TRADE

Access to new and cheaper commodities yielded a consumer revolution and reconfigured Europe's place in the world. The lure of products that had once been available as luxuries only to the wealthy classes fueled regional and global trade. More food, including new food items, and better clothes, made of cotton instead of heavy, scratchy wool, trickled down the social ladder. By the eighteenth century, other staples joined the long-distance trading business. Tea, for instance, became a beverage of world trade. Its leaves came from China, the sugar to cut its bitterness from the Caribbean, the enslaved people to harvest the sweetener from Africa, and the ceramics from which to drink a proper cup from the English Midlands.

Shopping became a verb. It denoted going out with a specific purpose: to buy. The act of shopping itself became a status symbol for people who had climbed out of the working classes; by shopping, they demonstrated that they had time for public leisure and the means to spend money on luxuries. In addition, shops increasingly marketed products not only to men but to wives and daughters of the new leisured classes, who created a customer base for another new sector: fashion. Paying attention to one's looks was no longer just for aristocrats but now also for the new rich (and even the professional middling sectors), and was for women and men alike. In women's fashion, it became increasingly in vogue to reveal the actual curvature of the body, freeing it from layers upon layers of heavy fabric and the steel hoops that were needed to keep the mountain of garb up. Men, meanwhile, gave up long coats and knee breeches, suiting themselves with trousers and waistcoats. Practicality became "cool," as did hygiene: it became increasingly important to wear clothes that were lighter and more easily washed. Not to mention underwear, knitted from cotton.

By 1850, there was a booming advertising business, which in turn fueled the expansion of the press. The press, for its part, drew more and more revenue not from the sales of papers and magazines but from ads, many pitched at women. As a result, the consumer and communications revolutions became mutually reinforcing.

This consumer revolution was not just about Europeans importing from the rest of the world. The rest of the world also imported from Europe. Alcohol was a major export to Native Americans as payment for furs and to African slave traders in return for captives. Another European export was guns. The city of Birmingham became the world firearms capital,

The Rise of Fashion Fashion became a business just as business became a fashion. The rise of new commercial and industrial classes living in cities created a market for high-end clothing made of new fabrics, especially cotton. These were assimilated into the taste for older fabrics like silk and—as the top hat of this model German gentleman around 1800 indicates—felted beaver fur. This image provides a fine display of how new urban fashion appealed to women and men alike.

based on gradual technological adaptations that were typical of the hardware trades (as we will see, software trades, like textiles, were a different story). By tinkering with high-precision tools and machines—for example, by boring metal, refining files, and becoming more adept at ironwork to weld barrels (without an accurate barrel, muskets and later rifles were useless)—the general machine tool industry created the right conditions for other production breakthroughs. But despite these developments, the boom in gunmaking would have been impossible without global trade. Why? The never-ending appetite for weapons to duel with world rivals made empires into military-industrial complexes. In this way, European imperial wars globalized an arms race.

Empires were also export systems selling large-scale munitions on a global scale. On the North American frontier, the bow and arrow had long been eclipsed by muskets. Birmingham gunsmiths made fortunes by supplying muskets, pistols, locks, and ordnance to the East India Company, which equipped armies of sepoys (Indian soldiers serving in the company ranks) with small arms and sold stockpiles to Indian allies (called nabobs) in the struggle to subdue Bengal after driving out the French in 1757 (the Battle of Plassey). One Scottish businessman, Lawrence Dundas, made so much money supplying British troops during the Seven Years' War that people called him "the Nabob of the North." Gunmakers also turned to the African market. By 1800, 150,000 to 200,000 guns were shipped to Africa per year.

Britain's edge in the arms race was a critical factor in boosting its global ascent in the nineteenth century. Once the Napoleonic wars ended in 1815 and gunmakers faced the prospect of a sharp contraction in demand for their commodities, they appealed to the government to promote military exports to clients in warring Latin America, the Middle East, and the expanding frontiers in the United States. Competition among gunmakers produced a scramble to lower production costs and prices to gun consumers by using interchangeable parts, which put small firearms into the hands of consumers worldwide.

The combination of war-making capacities and a consumer revolution transformed the world division of labor. The expansion of European exports and imports boosted European standards of living; spurred institutions and industries connected to global trade, such as shipping and shipbuilding; and fueled financial institutions, such as insurance companies, stock exchanges, and banks. These latter institutions were to serve the Europeans, especially the British, well during the industrial revolution. They became the instruments to channel more and more money into manufacturing enterprises.

But the rise of European manufactured exports led to the world's first deindustrialization, in Asia. Access to cheap raw materials, finance, and support from the state and war making gave Europeans an edge over native industries in India and China. European—and especially British—producers began to undercut Indians in their home market for exquisite artisanal textiles. In China, cheaper delftware from the Netherlands and stoneware from England cut deeply into the market for Chinese porcelain.

The state played an important role in nurturing European industries. States began to see the benefits of a strong merchant and manufacturing class: not only did manufacturing increase the wealth of nations, as Adam Smith had argued, but it created pools of money that the state could borrow in times of need. States also enacted new laws to defend the rights of private property owners and inventors, so they could reap rewards from patents and be encouraged to innovate further. If the state encouraged the making of money, it also agreed to protect those who loaned money. Capitalists could rely on the government to force debtors to honor their obligations, thus protecting lenders from risk. These measures formed a pact between merchants and the state that would make some parts of Europe and some colonies of Europe distinctive.

Nowhere was this new alliance clearer than in England. Critical for the take-off of the English cotton manufacturing industry were tariffs against Indian textile imports. Here, the pressure came from the woolen and linen industries, which wanted to shut out their Indian competitors. The chief beneficiaries, however, would be cotton entrepreneurs. In 1701, the English Parliament passed a law against the importation of dyed or printed calicoes coming from China, India, and Persia. The state followed this act of Parliament by passing a law that fined anyone wearing printed or dyed calicoes, though Indian muslins were exempted.

SOCIAL AND POLITICAL CONSEQUENCES OF GLOBAL TRADE

The expansion of global trade had important social and political consequences. Global trading now trickled its way down from elites to ordinary folk, especially in western Europe. Even ordinary people could purchase imported goods with their earnings. Thus, the poor began to enjoy—some would say became addicted to—coffee, tea, and sugar and eventually felt the need to use soap. European artisans and farmers purchased tools, furnishings, and home decorations. Colonial laborers also used their meager earnings to buy imported cotton cloth made in Europe from the raw cotton they themselves had picked several seasons earlier.

As new goods flowed from ever more distant corners of the globe, immense fortunes grew. To support their enterprise, traders needed new services, in insurance, bookkeeping, and the recording of legal documents. Trade helped nurture the emergence of new classes of professionals—accountants and lawyers. The new cities of the commercial revolution, hubs like Bristol, Bombay, and Buenos Aires, provided the homes and flourishing neighborhoods for a class of men and women known as the **bourgeoisie**: urban businessmen, financiers, and other property owners without aristocratic origins.

As Europe moved to the center of this new global economic order, one class in particular moved to the top of the social ladder: the trader-financiers. Like the merchandiser, the financier did not have to emerge from the high and mighty of Eurasia's dynasties. Consider Mayer Amschel Rothschild (1744–1812): born the son of a money changer in the Jewish ghetto of Frankfurt, Rothschild progressed from coin dealing to money changing, then from trading textiles to lending funds to kings and governments. By the time of his death, he owned the world's biggest banking operation and his five sons were running powerful branches in London, Paris, Vienna, Naples, and Frankfurt.

By extending credit, families like the Rothschilds also enabled traders to ship goods across long distances without having to worry about immediate payment.

All these financial changes implied world integration through the flow of goods as well as the flow of money. In the 1820s, sizable funds amassed in London flowed to Egypt, Mexico, and New York to support trade, public investment, and, of course, speculation.

THE INDUSTRIAL REVOLUTION

Trade and finance repositioned western Europe's relationship with the rest of the world. So did the emergence of manufacturing. Like agricultural production, output of cheap industrial commodities surged. The heart of this process was a gradual accumulation and diffusion of technical knowledge. Lots of little inventions, their applications, and their spread across the Atlantic world gradually built up a stock of technical knowledge and practice. Historians have traditionally called these changes the **industrial revolution**.

Nowhere was this industrial revolution more evident than in Britain. Britain had access to waterways, constructed a network of canals, and had large supplies of coal and iron—key materials used in manufactured products. It also had a political and social environment that allowed merchants and industrialists to invest heavily while also expanding their internal and international markets. Among their investments was the application of steam power to textile production, which enabled Britain's manufacturers to produce cheaper goods in larger quantities. Finally, Britain had access to New World lands as sources of financial investment, raw materials, and markets for manufactured goods. These factors' convergence promoted self-sustaining economic growth.

Consider the relationship between inventor and investor in the advent of the steam engine. Such engines burned coal to boil water, and the resulting steam drove mechanized devices. There were several tinkerers working on such an engine over a long period of time. But the most famous was James Watt (1736–1819) of Scotland, who managed to separate steam condensers from piston cylinders so that pistons could stay hot and run constantly; he joined forces with the industrialist Matthew Boulton, who marketed the steam engine and set up a laboratory where Watt could refine his device. Invented in 1769, the steam engine catalyzed a revolution in transportation. Steam-powered engines also improved sugar refining, pottery making, and other industrial processes, generating more products at lower cost than when workers had made them by hand.

Textile production was critical. Most raw cotton for the British cloth industry had come from colonial India until 1793, when the American inventor Eli Whitney (1765–1825) patented a "cotton gin" that separated cotton seeds from fiber. After that, cotton farming spread so quickly in the southern United States that by the 1850s it was producing more than 80 percent of the world's cotton supply. In turn, every enslaved Black man and woman in the Americas and many Indians in British India were consumers of cheap, British-produced

A Cotton Textile Mill in the 1830s The region of Lancashire became one of the major industrial hubs for textile production in the world. By the 1830s, mills had made the shift from artisanal work to highly mechanical mass production. Among the great breakthroughs was the discovery that cloth could be printed with designs, such as paisley or calico (as in this image), and marketed to middle-class consumers.

cotton shirts. The price of cotton cloth declined by nearly 50 percent between 1780 and 1850, as textiles became the world's most dynamic industry. England became the world's largest cloth producer, driving most of the other centers of textile production, notably those in the Indian subcontinent, out of business.

What, in sum, was the industrial revolution? First, it should be clear that it did not always mean the creation of large-scale factories. In fact, the large factory was rare in manufacturing. Moreover, the largest production units at the time were sugar plantations in the Americas. Small-scale production remained the norm, mass production the exception. Gunmakers in Birmingham and Harpers Ferry, Virginia, and the pioneering ballistic manufacturer Honoré Blanc in France, whose interchangeable and uniform parts for artillery dazzled buyers around the world, shipped their weapons from small plants. The silks of Lyon, cutlery of Solingen, calicoes of Alsace, and cottons of Pawtucket, Rhode Island, were all products of small firms in heavily industrialized belts.

The industrial revolution combined three decisive forces: the application of energy sources like coal that allowed production in more efficient locations, the use of machinery to augment the productivity of specialized labor, and the deployment of interchangeable parts that made machinery more effective and cheaper to use. Knowledge and science could be harnessed to the pooling of investments to launch manufacturers into a new age, an age capable of seizing the opportunity afforded by wars and empires to create demand for new products and new markets—and to crush rivals in old Asian markets.

WORKING AND LIVING

The industrial revolution brought more demanding work routines—not only in the manufacturing economies of western Europe and North America but also on the farms and plantations of Asia and Africa.

Urban Life and Work Routines Increasingly, Europe's workers made their livings in cities. London, Europe's largest city in 1700, saw its population nearly double over the next century to almost 1 million. By the 1820s, population growth was even greater in the industrial hubs of Leeds, Glasgow, Birmingham, Liverpool, and Manchester. (See Map 15.4.)

For most urban dwellers, cities were not healthy places. Water that powered the mills, along with chemicals used in dyeing, went directly back into waterways that provided drinking water. Overcrowded tenements shared just a few outhouses. Most European cities as late as 1850 had no running water, no garbage pickup, and no underground sewer system. The result was widespread disease. (In fact, no European city at this time had as clean a water supply as the largest towns of the ancient Roman Empire once had.)

Changes in work affected the understanding of time. Whereas most farmers' workloads had followed seasonal rhythms, after 1800 industrial settings imposed a rigid concept of work discipline. To keep the machinery operating, factory and mill owners installed huge clocks and used bells or horns to signify the workday's beginning and end. Employers also measured output per hour and compared workers' performance.

Industrialization imposed numbing work routines and paltry wages. Worse, however, was having no work at all. As families abandoned their farmland and depended on wages, being idle meant having no income. Periodic downturns in the economy put wage workers at risk, and many responded by organizing protests.

Social Protest and Emigration While entrepreneurs accumulated private wealth, the effects of the industrial revolution on working-class families raised widespread concern, sometimes leading to protests or emigration. In the 1810s in England, groups of jobless craftsmen, called Luddites, smashed the machines that had left them unemployed. Social advocates sought protective legislation for workers, including curbing child labor, limiting the workday, and, in some countries, legalizing prostitution for the sake of monitoring the prostitutes' health.

Some people, however, could not wait for legislative reform. The period saw unprecedented emigration, as unemployed workers or peasants abandoned their homes to seek their fortunes in America, Canada, and Australia. During the Irish Potato Famine of 1845–1849, at least 1 million Irish citizens left their country (and a further million or so died) when fungi attacked their subsistence crop. Desperate to escape starvation, they booked cheap passage to North America on ships so notorious for disease and malnutrition that they earned the name "coffin ships."

Map 15.4 Industrial Europe around 1850

By 1850, much of western Europe was industrial and urban, with major cities linked to one another through a network of railroads.

- According to this map, what natural resources contributed to the growth of the industrial revolution? What effects did it have on urban population densities?
- Compare the courses of major rivers with those of the railways.
- Why did the United Kingdom have such a large concentration of cities with more than 100,000 inhabitants? How was the United Kingdom able to support such large population centers?

The industrial revolution produced wealth on an unprecedented scale, but that wealth was distributed unevenly. Enormous inequalities resulted, both within societies and between them. Free trade resulted, in the long run, not in the proliferation of ever-more-productive small workshops but in massive industrial concentration, a concentration that would prove dynamic, creative, and unstable.

Persistence and Change in Afro-Eurasia

As western Europe pulled ahead of the rest of the world economically and technologically, it became a threat to the remaining Afro-Eurasian empires. Western European merchants and industrialists sought closer economic and (in some cases) political ties once they commanded an advantage. They did so in the name of gaining "free" access to Asian markets and products, putting regional competitors in tough spots. Rulers in Russia, the Ottoman Empire, India, and China all sought to borrow from the ideas and institutions emerging from western Europe, but they did so on their own terms, intent on defending the core of their social and political traditions.

REVAMPING THE RUSSIAN MONARCHY

Russian rulers responded to the new western European commercial and industrial powerhouses by strengthening their traditional authority through modest reforms and the suppression of domestic opposition. Tsar Alexander I (r. 1801–1825) was fortunate that Napoleon committed several blunders and lost his formidable army in the Russian snows. Yet the French Revolution and its massive armies struck at the heart of Russian political institutions, which rested upon a huge peasant population laboring as serfs. The tsars could no longer justify their absolutism by claiming that enlightened despotism was the most advanced form of government, since a new model, rooted in popular sovereignty and the concept of the nation, had arisen.

In December 1825, when Alexander died unexpectedly and childless, there was a question over succession. Some Russian officers launched a patriotic revolt. The Decembrists, as they were called, came primarily from elite families and were familiar with western European life and institutions. Some called for a constitutional monarchy to replace Russia's despotism; others favored a tsar-less republic and the abolition of serfdom. Their conspiracy failed to win over conservatives or the peasantry, who still believed in the tsar's divine right to rule. Nicholas (r. 1825–1855) became tsar and brutally suppressed the insurrectionists.

Still, Alexander's successors faced a world in which powerful European states had constitutions and national armies of citizens, not subjects. In trying to maintain absolutist rule, Russian tsars portrayed the monarch's family as the ideal historical embodiment of the nation with direct ties to the people. Nicholas himself prevented rebellion by expanding the secret police, enforcing censorship, conducting impressive military exercises, and maintaining serfdom. And in the 1830s he introduced a conservative ideology that stressed religious faith, hierarchy, and obedience. For the time being, the influence of the French Revolution was quashed in Russia.

REFORMING EGYPT AND THE OTTOMAN EMPIRE

Unlike Russia, where Napoleon's army had reached Moscow, the Ottoman capital in Istanbul never faced a threat from French troops. Still, Napoleon's invasion of Egypt shook the Ottoman Empire. Even before this trauma, Ottoman authorities faced the challenge posed by increased trade with Europe—and the greater presence of European merchants and missionaries. In addition, many non-Muslim religious communities in the sultan's empire wanted the European powers to advance their interests. In the wake of Napoleon, who had promised to remake Egyptian society, reformist energies swept from Egypt to the center of the Ottoman domain.

Reforms in Egypt In Egypt, far-reaching changes came with the rule of **Muhammad Ali**. After the French withdrawal in 1801, Muhammad Ali (r. 1805–1848) won a chaotic struggle for supreme power in Egypt and aligned himself with influential Egyptian families. Yet he looked to revolutionary France for a model of modern state building. As with Napoleon (and with Simón Bolívar in Latin America), the key to his hold on power was the army.

Muhammad Ali also made reforms in education and agriculture. He established a school of engineering and opened the first modern medical school in Cairo under the supervision of a French military doctor. And his efforts in the countryside made Egypt one of the world's leading cotton exporters. A summer crop, cotton required steady watering when the Nile's irrigation waters were in short supply. So Muhammad Ali's Public Works Department, advised by European engineers, deepened the irrigation canals and constructed a series of dams across the Nile. These efforts transformed Egypt, making it the most powerful state in the eastern Mediterranean and alarming the Ottoman state (which still controlled Egypt) and the great powers in Europe. At the same time, European merchants pressed for free access to Egyptian markets, just as they did in Latin America and Africa.

Ottoman Reforms Under political and economic pressures like those facing Muhammad Ali in Egypt, Ottoman rulers also made reforms. Indeed, military defeats and humiliating treaties with Europe were painful reminders of the sultans' vulnerability. In 1805, Sultan Selim III tried to create a new infantry, trained by western European officers. But before he could bring this force up to fighting strength, the janissaries stormed the palace, killed its officers, and deposed Selim in 1807. Over the next few decades, janissary military men and clerical scholars (*ulama*) cobbled together an alliance that thwarted reformers.

Why did reform falter in the Ottoman state before it could be implemented? Reform was possible only if the forces opposed to reform—especially in the military—were weak and the reformers strong. In the Ottoman Empire, the janissary class had grown powerful, providing the main resistance to change. Ottoman authority depended on clerical support, and the Muslim clergy also resisted change. Blocked at the top, Ottoman rulers hesitated to appeal for popular support. Such an appeal, in the new age of popular sovereignty and national feeling, would be dangerous for an unelected dynasty in a multiethnic and multireligious realm.

Mahmud II (r. 1808–1839) broke the political deadlock, shrewdly manipulating his conservative opponents. Like Muhammad Ali in Egypt, Mahmud brought in European officers to advise his forces. Here, too, military reform spilled over into nonmilitary areas. The Ottoman modernizers created a medical college, then a school of military sciences. To understand Europe better and to create a first-rate diplomatic corps, the Ottomans schooled their officials in European languages and had European classics translated into Turkish. As Mahmud's successors extended reforms into civilian life, this era—known as the Tanzimat, or reorganization period (1826–1839)—saw legislation that guaranteed equality for all Ottoman subjects, regardless of religion.

The reforms, however, stopped well short of revolutionary change. Reform relied too much on the personal whim of rulers, and the bureaucratic and religious infrastructure remained committed to old ways. Any effort to reform the rural sector met resistance by the landed interests. Finally, the merchant classes profited from business with a debt-ridden sultan. By preventing the empire's fiscal collapse through financial support to the state, bankers lessened the pressure for reform and removed the spark that had fired revolutions in Europe.

COLONIAL REORDERING IN INDIA

Europe's most important colonial possession in Asia between 1750 and 1850 was British India. Unlike in North America, the changes that the British fostered in Asia did not lead to political independence. Instead, India was increasingly dominated by the **East India Company**, which the crown had chartered in 1600. The company's control over India's imports and exports in the eighteenth and nineteenth centuries, however, contradicted British claims about their allegiance to a world economic system based on "free trade."

The East India Company's Monopoly In enforcing the East India Company's monopoly on trade, the British soon took control of much of the region. Initially, the British tried to control India's commerce by establishing trading posts along the coast without taking complete political control. After conquering the state of Bengal in 1757, the company began to fill its coffers and its officials began to amass personal fortunes. In spite of violent opposition, the British secured the right for the East India Company to collect tax revenues in Bengal, Bihar, and Orissa and to trade free of duties throughout Mughal territory. In return, the Mughal emperor would receive a hefty annual pension. The company went on to annex other territories, bringing much of South Asia under its rule by the early nineteenth century. (See Map 15.5.)

To rule with minimal interference required knowing the conquered society. This led to Orientalist scholarship: British scholar-officials wrote the first modern histories of South Asia, translated Sanskrit and Persian texts, identified philosophical writings, and compiled Hindu and Muslim law books. Through their efforts, the company-state presented itself as a force for revitalizing authentic Hinduism and recovering India's literary and cultural treasures. However, although the Orientalist scholars admired Sanskrit language and literature, they still supported British colonial rule and did not necessarily agree with local beliefs.

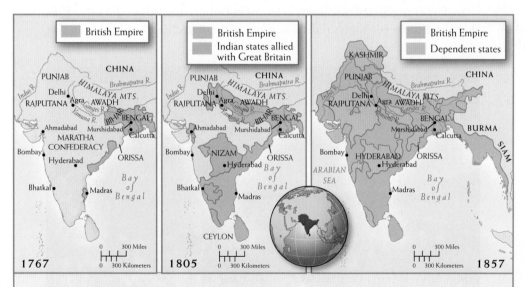

Map 15.5 The British in India, 1767–1857

Starting from locations in eastern and northeastern India, the British East India Company extended its authority over much of South Asia prior to the outbreak of the Indian Rebellion of 1857.

- What type of locations did the British first acquire in India?
- According to your reading, how did the British East India Company expand into the interior of India and administer these possessions?
- Why did the company choose a strategy of direct rule over some areas and indirect rule over other areas in India?

Effects in India Company rule and booming trade altered India's urban geography. By the early nineteenth century, colonial cities like Calcutta, Madras, and Bombay became the new centers at the expense of older Mughal cities like Agra, Delhi, Murshidabad, and Hyderabad. As the colonial cities attracted British merchants and Indian clerks, artisans, and laborers, their populations surged. Calcutta's reached 350,000 in 1820; Bombay's jumped to 200,000 by 1825. In these cities, Europeans lived close to the company's fort and trading stations, while migrants from the countryside clustered in crowded quarters called "black towns."

India now became an importer of British textiles and an exporter of raw cotton—a reversal of its traditional pattern of trade. In the past, India had been an important textile manufacturer, exporting fine cotton goods throughout the Indian Ocean and to Europe. But its elites could not resist the appeal of cheap British textiles. As a result, India's industrial sector declined. In addition, the import of British manufactures caused unfavorable trade balances that changed India from a net importer of gold and silver to an exporter of these precious metals.

Led by evangelical Christians and liberal reformers, the British did more than alter the Indian economy; they also advocated far-reaching changes in Indian

Indian Resistance to Company Rule Tipu Sultan, the Mysore ruler, put up a determined resistance against the British. This painting by Robert Home shows Charles Cornwallis, the East India Company's governor, receiving Tipu's two sons as hostages after defeating him in the 1792 war. The boys remained in British custody for two years. Tipu returned to fighting the British and was killed in the war of 1799.

culture. For example, they sought to stop the practice of *sati*, by which women burned to death on the funeral pyres of their dead husbands. Now the mood swung away from the Orientalists' respect for India's classical languages, philosophies, cultures, and texts. In 1835, when the British poet, historian, and liberal politician Lord Macaulay was making recommendations on educational policies, he urged that English replace Persian as the language of administration and that European education replace Oriental learning. The result, reformers hoped, would be a class that was Indian in blood and color but English in tastes and culture.

This was a new colonial order, but it was not stable. Most wealthy landowners resented the loss of their land and authority. Peasants, thrown to the mercy of the market, moneylenders, and landlords and subject to high taxation, were in turmoil. The non-Hindu forest dwellers and roaming cultivators, faced with the hated combination of a colonial state and moneylenders, revolted. Dispossessed artisans stirred up towns and cities. And merchants and industrialists chafed under the British-dominated economy. As freedom expanded in Europe, exploitation expanded in India.

PERSISTENCE OF THE QING EMPIRE

The Chinese empire was largely unaffected by the upheavals in Europe and America until the Opium Wars (1839–1842, 1856–1860) forced the Chinese to acknowledge their military weaknesses. The Qing dynasty, which had taken power in 1644, was still enjoying prosperity and territorial expansion as the nineteenth century dawned. Their sense of imperial splendor continued to rest on the political structure and social order inherited from the Ming (see Chapter 11). However, they could not resist European demands for access to their resources and markets.

The Qing had a talent for extending the empire's boundaries and settling frontier lands. Before 1750, they conquered Taiwan (the stronghold of remaining Ming forces), pushed westward into central Asia, and annexed Tibet. To secure these territorial gains, the Qing encouraged settlement of frontier lands like Xinjiang. New crops from the Americas aided this process—especially corn and sweet potatoes, which grow well in less fertile soils.

Like their European counterparts, Chinese peasants were on the move. But migration occurred in Qing China for different reasons. The state-sponsored westward movement into Xinjiang, for example, aimed to secure a recently pacified frontier region through military colonization, after which civilians would follow. So peasants received promises of land, tools, seed, and the loan of silver and a horse—all with the dual objectives of producing enough food to supply the troops and relieving pressure on the poor and arid northwestern part of the country. These efforts brought so much land under cultivation by 1840 that the region's ecological and social landscape completely changed.

Despite their success in expanding the empire, the Qing faced nagging problems. As a ruling minority, they looked warily at innovation, and only late in the eighteenth century did they deal with their rapidly expanding population. On the one hand, the tripling of China's population since 1300 demonstrated the realm's prosperity; on the other, a population of over 300 million severely strained resources—especially soil for growing crops and wood for fuel. In the late eighteenth and early nineteenth centuries, uprisings inspired by mystical beliefs in folk Buddhism, and at times by the idea of restoring the Ming, engulfed northern China.

By the mid-nineteenth century, extraordinary changes had made western European powers stronger than ever before, and the Qing could no longer dismiss their demands. The first clear evidence of an altered global balance of power was not the rise of Napoleon but a British-Chinese war over a narcotic. Indeed, the **Opium Wars** exposed China's vulnerability in a new era of European ascendancy.

The Opium Wars and the "Opening" of China Europeans had been selling staples and intoxicants in China for a long time, and by the late eighteenth century opium, which had previously been used as a medicine or an aphrodisiac, was being smoked in long-stemmed pipes at every level of Chinese society. Sensing opium's economic potential, the East India Company established a monopoly over the export of opium from India in 1773 to help pay for a rapid growth in the company's purchase of tea from China. Because the Chinese showed little taste for British goods, the British had been financing their tea imports with exports of silver to China. But by the late eighteenth century, the company's tea purchases had become too large to finance with silver. Fortunately for the company, the Chinese were eager for Indian cotton and opium, and then mostly just opium. In the early nineteenth century the company's revenues from the sale of opium in China exceeded all its revenues from India, and by the 1830s opium had become one of the most lucrative commodities in world trade.

Opium's impact on China's balance of trade was devastating. In a reversal from earlier trends, silver began to flow out of instead of into China. Once silver shortages occurred, the peasants' tax burden grew heavier. Consequently, long-simmering unrest in the countryside gained momentum. At the Qing court, some officials wanted to legalize the opium trade so as to eliminate corruption and boost revenues. (After all, as long as opium was an illegal substance, the government could not tax its traffic.) In 1838, the emperor sent a special commissioner to Canton, the main center of the trade, to eradicate the influx of opium.

When British merchants in Canton resisted, war broke out. In June 1840, British warships bombarded coastal regions near Canton and sailed upriver for a short way. On land, Qing soldiers used spears, clubs, and a few imported matchlock muskets against the modern artillery of British troops, many of whom were Indians supplied with percussion cap rifles. Along the Yangzi River, outgunned

Opium Having established a monopoly in the 1770s over opium cultivation in India, the British greatly expanded their manufacture and export of opium to China to balance their rapidly growing import of Chinese tea and silk. This picture from the 1880s shows an opium warehouse in India where the commodity was stored before being transported to China.

Qing forces fought fiercely, as soldiers killed their own wives and children before committing suicide themselves. But they were no match for British military technology.

The Qing ruling elite capitulated to European pressure, and through the 1842 Treaty of Nanjing, the British acquired the island of Hong Kong and the right to trade directly with the Chinese in five treaty ports and to reside there. (See Map 15.6.) They also forced the Chinese to repay the costs that the British had incurred in the war.

Subsequent treaties guaranteed that the British and other foreign nationals would be tried in their own courts for crimes, rather than in Chinese courts, and would be exempt from Chinese law. Moreover, the British insisted that any privileges granted through treaties with other parties would also apply to them. Other western nations followed the British example in demanding the same right, and the arrangement thus guaranteed all Europeans and North Americans a privileged position in China.

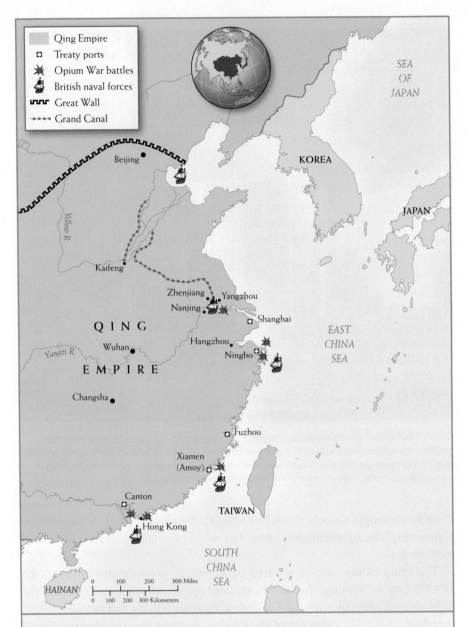

Map 15.6 The Qing Empire and the Opium Wars

The Opium Wars demonstrated the superiority of British military technology. Their victory granted the British control of Hong Kong and established a series of treaty ports, which gave Europeans access to Chinese trade and were subject to the laws of designated European countries.

- How many treaty ports were there after the Opium Wars? What was their significance?
- How were the treaty ports distributed along China's coastline?
- According to the text, how did the Opium Wars change relations between China and the western powers?

Still, China did not become a formal colony. To the contrary, in the mid-nineteenth century Europeans and North Americans were trading only on its outskirts. Most Chinese did not encounter Europeans. Daily life for most people went on as it had before the Opium Wars. Only the political leaders and urban dwellers were beginning to feel the foreign presence and wondering what steps China might take to acquire European technologies, goods, and learning.

Conclusion

During the period 1750–1850, changes in politics, commerce, industry, and technology reverberated throughout the Atlantic world and, to varying degrees, elsewhere around the globe. By 1850, the world was more integrated economically, with Europe increasingly at the center.

In the Americas, colonial ties broke apart. In France, the people toppled the monarchy. Dissidents threatened the same in Russia. Such upheavals introduced a new public vocabulary—the language of the nation—and made the idea of revolution empowering. In the Americas and parts of Europe, nation-states took shape around redefined hierarchies of class, gender, and color. Britain and France emerged from the political crises of the late eighteenth century determined to expand their borders. Their drive forced older empires such as Russia and the Ottoman state to make reforms.

As commerce and industrialization transformed economic and political power, European governments compelled others (including Egypt, India, and China) to expand their trade with European merchants. Ultimately, such countries had to participate in a European-centered economy as exporters of raw materials and importers of European manufactures. By the 1850s, many of the world's peoples became more industrious, producing less for themselves and more for distant markets. Through changes in manufacturing, some areas of the world also made more goods than ever before. With its emphasis on free trade, Europe began to force open new markets—even to the point of colonizing them. Gold and silver now flowed out of China and India to pay for European products like opium and textiles.

However, global reordering did not mean that Europe's rulers had uncontested control over other people or that the institutions and cultures of Asia and Africa ceased to be dynamic. Some countries became dependent on Europe commercially; others became colonies. China escaped colonial rule but was forced into unfavorable trade relations with the Europeans. In sum, dramatic changes combined to unsettle systems of rulership and to alter the economic and military balance between western Europe and the rest of the world.

Focus On
The Global Impact of the Atlantic and Industrial Revolutions

The Atlantic World

- North American colonists revolt against British rule and establish a nonmonarchical, republican form of government.

- In the wake of the American Revolution, the French citizenry proclaims a new era of liberty, equality, and fraternity and executes opponents of the revolution, notably the king and queen of France.

- Napoleon's French Empire extends many principles of the French Revolution throughout Europe.

- In the midst of the French Revolution, enslaved Haitians throw off French rule, abolish slavery, and create an independent state.

- Napoleon's invasion of Iberia frees Portuguese and Spanish America from colonial rule.

- The British lead a successful campaign to abolish the Atlantic slave trade and promote new sources of trade with Africa.

- An industrial revolution spreads outward from Britain to a few other parts of the Atlantic world.

Africa, India, and Asia

- In Egypt, a military leader, Muhammad Ali, modernizes the country and threatens the political integrity of the Ottoman Empire.

- The British East India Company increasingly dominates the Indian subcontinent.

- The Qing Empire persists despite major European encroachments on its sovereignty.

Key Terms

Muhammad Ali p. 601
Napoleon Bonaparte
  p. 583
bourgeoisie p. 595

East India Company p. 602
free trade (laissez-faire)
  p. 572
industrial revolution p. 596

Opium Wars p. 606
popular sovereignty
  p. 572
social contract p. 578

CHRONOLOGY

	1700	1750
The Americas		
Europe		James Watt invents the steam engine 1769
Africa		
Ottoman Empire		
South Asia		
East Asia		

- **Thinking about Exchange Networks and Sociopolitical Change** How did established dynasties respond to pressures created by increased exchanges of goods, ideas, and peoples? To what degree did established elites respond by forging a partnership with "the people"? Who defined "the people," and on what terms?

- **Thinking about Changing Power Relationships and Sociopolitical Change** What new kinds of political organizations emerged in this period? Where did new political systems take root, and where did established elites resist most successfully?

- **Thinking about Environmental Impacts and Sociopolitical Change** Although new technologies only gradually transformed agriculture—by far the most common economic activity in the world—the spread of more intensive cultivation demanded considerable capital investment. How did the relationship between town and countryside change as a result? How did living conditions change in cities as their populations swelled?

Go to INQUIZITIVE to see what you've learned—and learn what you've missed—with personalized feedback along the way.

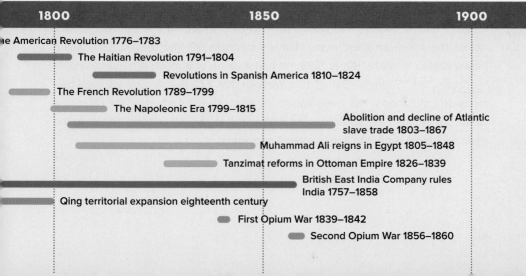

1800	1850	1900

ne American Revolution 1776–1783

The Haitian Revolution 1791–1804

Revolutions in Spanish America 1810–1824

The French Revolution 1789–1799

The Napoleonic Era 1799–1815

Abolition and decline of Atlantic slave trade 1803–1867

Muhammad Ali reigns in Egypt 1805–1848

Tanzimat reforms in Ottoman Empire 1826–1839

British East India Company rules India 1757–1858

Qing territorial expansion eighteenth century

First Opium War 1839–1842

Second Opium War 1856–1860

16

Alternative Visions of the Nineteenth Century

Core Objectives

- **DESCRIBE** the challenges to the ideals of industrial capitalism, colonialism, and nation-states in this period.

- **COMPARE** the utopian goals, immediate outcomes, and longterm influence of rebel movements around the world.

- **ANALYZE** the connections between nineteenth-century protest movements and organized religion.

- **ASSESS** the role religion played in these alternative social visions.

By the late nineteenth century, territorial expansion in the United States confined almost all Native Americans to reservations. The buffalo that once supported many tribes disappeared: White settlers built towns, farms, and railroads throughout the buffalo's natural habitat, and Native Americans overhunted the shrinking herds. Across the American West, many Native Americans fell into despair. One was a Paiute named Wovoka. But in 1889, he had a vision of a much brighter future. In his dream, the "Supreme Being" told Wovoka that if Native Americans lived harmoniously, shunned White ways (especially alcohol), and performed the cleansing Ghost Dance, then the buffalo would return, and Native Americans, including the dead, would be reborn to live in eternal happiness.

As word spread of Wovoka's vision, Native Americans from hundreds of miles around made pilgrimages to the lodge of this new prophet. Many proclaimed him the Native Americans' messiah or the "Red Man's Christ," an impression fostered by scars on his hands. Soon, increasing numbers joined in the ritual Ghost Dance, hoping it would restore the good life that European colonialism in the Americas had extinguished. Among the hopefuls was Sitting Bull, a revered Sioux chief who was himself famous for his visions. Yet, less than two years after Wovoka's vision, Sitting Bull died at the hands of police forces on a Sioux reservation. A few days later, on December 29, 1890, the U.S. Seventh Cavalry Regiment massacred Sioux Ghost Dancers at a South Dakota creek called Wounded Knee.

Though it failed, this movement was one of many prophetic crusades that challenged an emerging nineteenth-century order. The ideals of the French and American Revolutions in politics—equality before the law, and government for and by property-holding citizens in a world of nation-states—now provided the dominant answers to age-old questions of who should govern and how. Emerging from the industrial revolution, the ideas of free market (laissez-faire) capitalism, in which private owners competed against one another to maximize profits using new technologies and industrial organizations, provided the dominant answers to questions about how productive activity should be organized. But these political and economic answers were not powerful enough to entirely stamp out other views. A diverse assortment of political radicals, charismatic prophets, peasant rebels, and anticolonial insurgents put forward striking counterproposals to those that capitalists, colonial modernizers, and nation-state builders had developed. The people making these counterproposals were motivated by the impending loss of their existing worlds and were energized by visions of ideal, utopian futures.

This chapter presents the voices and visions of those who opposed a nineteenth-century world in which capitalism, colonialism, and nation-states held sway. It puts the spotlight on challengers who shared a dislike of global capitalism and European (and North American) colonialism. Beyond that similarity, these challengers differed in significant ways, for the alternatives they proposed reflected the local circumstances in which each of them developed. Although many of these challengers suffered devastating defeats, like the Ghost Dancers at Wounded Knee, the dreams that aroused their fervor did not always die with them. Some of these alternative visions of the nineteenth century endured to propel the great transformations of the twentieth.

Reactions to Social and Political Change

The transformations of the late eighteenth and early nineteenth centuries had upset polities and economies around the globe. In Europe, the tide of political and economic revolutions either swept aside or severely battered the old order. In North America, the newly independent United States began an expansion westward. Territorial growth led to the dispossession of hundreds of Indian tribes and the acquisition of nearly half of Mexico by conquest. In Latin America, fledgling nation-states that now replaced the Spanish Empire struggled to control their subject populations. And in Asia and Africa, rulers and common people alike confronted the growing might of western military and industrial power. At stake were issues of how to define and rule territories and what social and cultural visions they would embody.

The alternatives to the emerging order of the nineteenth century varied considerably. Some rebels and dissidents called for the revitalization of traditional religions; others wanted to strengthen village and communal bonds; still others imagined a society where there was no private property and where people shared goods equally. The actions of these dissenters depended on their local traditions and the degree of contact they had with the effects of industrial capitalism, European colonialism, and centralizing nation-states.

This era of rapid social change, when differing visions of power and justice vied with one another, offers unique opportunities to hear the voices of the lower orders—the peasants and workers, whose perspectives the elites often ignored or suppressed. While there are few written records that capture the views of the illiterate and the marginalized, we do have traditions of folklore, dreams, rumors, and prophecies. Handed down orally from generation to generation, these resources illuminate the visions of common people.

Prophecy and Revitalization in the Islamic World and Africa

In regions that experienced European and North American influence but not direct colonial rule, alternative perspectives were strongest far from the main trade and cultural routes. People outside the emerging capitalist world order led these movements. In the Islamic world and Africa, leaders on the margins were especially important in articulating alternative views.

Even though much of the Islamic world and non-Islamic Africa had not been colonized and was only partially involved with European-dominated trading networks, these regions had reached turning points. By the late eighteenth century, the era of Islamic expansion and cultural flowering under the Ottomans, Safavids, and Mughals was over. Their empires had extended Muslim trading orbits, facilitated cross-cultural communication, and promoted common knowledge over vast territories. Their political and military decline, however, brought new challenges to the faithful. The sense of alarm intensified as Christian Europe's power spread from the edges of the Islamic world to its centers. While this perception of danger motivated military men in Egypt and the Ottoman sultans to modernize their states (see Chapter 15), it also bred religious revitalization movements that sought to recapture the glories of past traditions. Led by prophets who feared that the Islamic faith was in trouble, these movements spoke the language of revival and restoration as they sought to establish new religiously based governments across lands in which Muslims ruled and Islamic law prevailed.

Prophecy also exerted a strong influence in non-Islamic Africa, where long-distance trade and population growth were upending the social order. Just as Muslim clerics and political leaders sought solutions to unsettling changes by rereading Islamic classics, African communities looked to charismatic leaders who drew strength from their peoples' spiritual and magical traditions. Often uniting disparate groups behind their dynamic visions, prophetic leaders and other "big men" gained power because they were able to resolve local crises—mostly caused by drought, a shortage of arable land, or some other issue related to the harsh environment.

ISLAMIC REVITALIZATION

Movements to revitalize Islam took place on the peripheries—at a certain remove from trade networks and the changes wrought by global capitalism. (See Map 16.1.) Here, religious leaders rejected the westernizing influences they felt encroaching on their authority and way of life. Revitalization movements looked back to Islamic traditions and modeled their revolts on the life of Muhammad. But even as they looked to the past, they attempted to establish something new: full-scale theocracies. These reformers conceived of the state as the primary instrument of God's will and as the vehicle for purifying Islamic culture.

Wahhabism One of the most powerful reformist movements arose on the Arabian Peninsula, the birthplace of the Muslim faith. In the Najd region, an area surrounded by mountains and deserts, a religious cleric named Muhammad Ibn Abd al-Wahhab (1703–1792) galvanized the population by attacking what he regarded as lax religious practices. His message found a ready response among local inhabitants, who felt threatened by the new commercial activities and fresh intellectual currents swirling around them. Abd al-Wahhab demanded a return to the pure Islam of Muhammad and the early caliphs.

Although Najd was far removed from the centers of the expanding world economy, Abd al-Wahhab himself was not. Having been educated in Iraq, Iran, and the Hijaz (a region on the western end of modern Saudi Arabia, on the Red Sea), he believed that Islam had fallen into a degraded state, particularly in its birthplace. He railed against the polytheistic beliefs that had taken hold of the people, complaining that in defiance of Muhammad's tenets men and women were worshipping trees, stones, and tombs and making sacrifices to false images. Abd al-Wahhab's movement stressed the absolute oneness of Allah and severely criticized Sufi sects for extolling the lives of saints over the worship of God.

As **Wahhabism** swept across the Arabian Peninsula, the movement threatened the Ottomans' hold on the region. Wahhabism gained a powerful political ally in the Najdian House of Saud, a leading family whose followers, inspired by the Wahhabis' religious zeal, undertook a militant religious campaign in the final years of the eighteenth century. Frightened by the Wahhabi challenge, the Ottoman sultan persuaded the provincial ruler of Egypt to send troops to the Arabian Peninsula to suppress the movement. The Egyptians defeated the Saudis in 1818, but Wahhabism and the House of Saud continued to represent a pure Islamic faith that attracted clerics and ordinary people throughout the Muslim world.

Usman dan Fodio and the Fulani In West Africa, Muslim revolts erupted from Senegal to Nigeria in the early nineteenth century, partly in response to increased trade with the outside world and the circulation of religious ideas from across the Sahara Desert. In this region, the Fulani people were decisive in religious uprisings that sought, like the Wahhabi movement, to re-create a

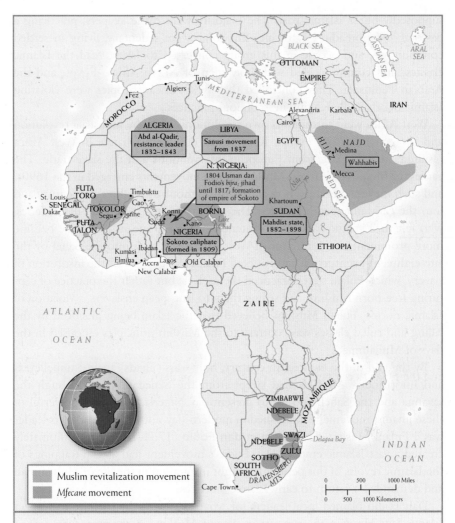

Map 16.1 Muslim Revitalization Movements in the Middle East and Africa and the *Mfecane* Movement in Southern Africa

During the nineteenth century, a series of Muslim revitalization movements took place throughout the Middle East and North Africa.

• According to this map, in how many different areas did the revitalization movements occur?

• Based on their geographic location within their larger regions, did these movements occur in central or peripheral areas?

• According to your reading, were any of the same factors that led to Islamic revitalization involved in the *Mfecane* developments in southern Africa?

supposedly purer Islamic past. The majority were cattle keepers, practicing a pastoral and nomadic way of life. But some were sedentary, living in settled communities, and people in this group converted to Islam, read the Islamic classics, and communicated with holy men of North Africa, Egypt, and the Arabian Peninsula. They concluded that West African peoples were violating Islamic beliefs and engaging in irreligious practices.

West Africa went through its own revolutions while the industrial revolution and the American and French Revolutions unfolded. Change in West Africa resulted, in large part, from European interventions and the slave trade. The earliest of these West African Muslim reform movements emerged in the 1690s, and such movements steadily occurred throughout the eighteenth century and into the early nineteenth century. The primary agents were the Fulani clerics, who felt their religious beliefs threatened as the European slave trade became more prominent in the interior of West Africa, reaching into the Sahel by the late eighteenth century. What troubled Fulani clerics was not the institution of slavery, which Fulani states practiced themselves, but rather the practice of capturing free-born Muslims and selling them to European enslavers, a violation of Islamic norms. Fulani Muslims believed that the Islam being practiced by the ruling and ruled classes was contrary to the Muslim principles espoused in the days of Muhammad.

By the end of the eighteenth century, holy wars (jihads) against unbelievers and unorthodox Muslims had swept from the Senegal Valley, through the savanna and the Sahel, and up to present-day Nigeria. The most powerful of these jihadist movements flourished in modern-day northern Nigeria. Its leader was a Fulani Muslim cleric, **Usman dan Fodio** (1754–1817), who ultimately created a vast Islamic empire. Dan Fodio's movement had all the trappings of the Islamic revolts of this period. It sought inspiration in the life of Muhammad and demanded a return to early Islamic practices.

Dan Fodio blamed local leaders for what he saw as their failure to respect Islamic law. He won the support of devout Muslims in the area, who agreed that the people were not properly practicing Islam. He also gained the backing of his Fulani tribes and many Hausa-speaking peasants, who had suffered under the rule of the Hausa landlord class. The revolt, initiated in 1804, resulted in the overthrow of the Hausa rulers and the creation of a confederation of Islamic emirates, almost all of which were in the hands of the Fulani allies of dan Fodio.

Fulani women of northern Nigeria made critical contributions to the success of the religious revolt. Although dan Fodio and other male leaders of the purification movement expected women to obey the *sharia* (Islamic law), being modest in their dress and their association with men outside the family, they also expected women to support the community's military and religious endeavors. In this effort, they cited women's important role in the first days of Islam. The best known of the Muslim women leaders was Nana Asma'u (1793–1864), daughter of dan Fodio. Fulani women of the upper ranks acquired an Islamic education, and Asma'u was as astute a reader of Islamic texts as any of the learned men in her society. Like other Muslim Fulani devotees, she accompanied the warriors on their campaigns, encamped with them, prepared food for them, bound up their wounds, and provided daily encouragement. According to many accounts, Asma'u inspired the warriors at their most crucial battle, hurling a burning spear into the midst of the enemy army. Her poem "Song of the Circular Journey" celebrates the triumphs of military forces that trekked thousands of miles to bring a reformed Islam to the area.

Usman dan Fodio considered himself a cleric first and a political and military man second. Although his political leadership was decisive in the revolt's success, thereafter he retired to a life of scholarship and writing. He delegated the political and administrative functions of the new empire to his brother and his son. An enduring decentralized state structure, which became known as the Sokoto caliphate in 1809, developed into a stable empire that helped spread Islam through the region. In 1800, on the eve of dan Fodio's revolt, Islam was the faith of a small minority of people living in northern Nigeria; a century later, it had become the religion of the vast majority, thanks to dan Fodio's military prowess and success in creating a stable political structure, and the increasing Fulani contacts with the broader Islamic world.

CHARISMATIC MILITARY LEADERS IN NON-ISLAMIC AFRICA

Non-Islamic Africa saw revolts, new states, and prophetic movements arise from the same combination of factors that influenced the rest of the world—particularly long-distance trade and population increase. Local communities here also looked to religious traditions and, as was so often the case in African history, expected charismatic clan leaders, known as "big men," to provide political leadership.

In southern Africa, early in the nineteenth century, a group of political revolts reordered the political map. Collectively known as the **Mfecane** ("the crushing" in Zulu) **movement**, its epicenter was a large tract of land lying east of the Drakensberg Mountains, an area where growing populations and land resources existed in a precarious balance. (See again Map 16.1.) Many branches of Bantu-speaking peoples had inhabited the southern part of the African landmass for centuries. At the end of the eighteenth century, however, their political organizations still operated on a small scale. These tiny polities could not cope with the competition for land that now dominated southern Africa. That competition intensified with the arrival of British colonizers, who fought both with Dutch settlers and indigenous African communities over natural resources. The import of European goods that flowed into southern Africa from Delagoa Bay also was a destabilizing factor. A branch of the Nguni, the Zulus, produced a fierce war leader, Shaka (1787–1828), who created a ruthless warrior state.

BAKA KING OF THE ZOOLUS.

London, Published by E.Churton, 26 Holles St.

Shaka and His Zulu Regiments *Left:* Though he is renowned for his reforms and infamous for his brutality, the only existing image of Shaka is this engraving by English trader Henry Francis Fynn, the first White settler in Natal, a British colony near the Zulu kingdom. Nonetheless, Shaka's awesome presence and strength is as obvious to modern viewers as it would have been to his young warriors, who were deeply loyal to him and superbly trained. *Right:* In the image shown here, a Zulu regiment dances, arrayed in concentric circles.

His state drove other populations out of the region and forced a shift from small clan communities to large, centralized monarchies throughout southern and central Africa.

The son of a minor chief, Shaka emerged victorious in a struggle for cattle-grazing and farming lands that arose during a severe drought. A physically imposing figure, Shaka used terror to intimidate his subjects and to overawe his adversaries. His enemies knew that the price of opposition would be a massacre, even of women and children. Nor was he kinder to his own people. Following the death of his beloved mother, he executed those who were not properly contrite and did not weep profusely. Reportedly, it took 7,000 lives to assuage his grief.

Shaka built a new Zulu state in southern Africa from 1818 to 1828 around his military and organizational skills and the fear that his personal ferocity produced. He drilled his men relentlessly in the use of short stabbing spears and in discipline under pressure. Like the Mongols, he had a remarkable ability to incorporate defeated communities into the state and to absorb young men into his military. His army of 40,000 men comprised regiments that lived, studied, and fought together. Forbidden from marrying until they were discharged from the army, Shaka's warriors developed an intense esprit de corps and regarded no sacrifice as too great in the service of the state. So overpowering were these forces that other peoples of the region fled from their home areas, and Shaka claimed their estates for himself and his followers. Peoples in nearby areas who weren't absorbed into the Zulu state adopted many of Shaka's military and political innovations, at first to defend themselves and then to take over new land as they fled their old areas. The new states of the Ndebele in present-day Zimbabwe and the Sotho of southern Africa came into existence in this way in the mid-nineteenth century.

In turning southern Africa from a region of smaller polities into an area with larger and more powerful states, Shaka seemed very much a man of the modern, nineteenth-century world. Yet he was, in his own unique way, a familiar kind of African leader. He shared a charismatic and prophetic style with others who emerged during periods of acute social change. His new state built an enduring Zulu community and established its traditions against encroachments by outside, European forces.

Prophecy and Rebellion in China

In the mid-nineteenth century, China experienced an explosive popular rebellion that incorporated Christian beliefs into its long tradition of peasant revolts. Whereas movements promoting alternative visions in the Islamic world and Africa appeared in areas distant from western influences and drew substantially on their own traditions, China was no longer isolated. In fact, it had been conducting a brisk trade in opium with Europe. Until 1842, the Chinese had confined trade with Europeans to the port city of Canton. After the Opium Wars, however, westerners forced Qing rulers to open up a number of other ports to trade.

The Port of Canton Before the Opium Wars, Canton (now Guangzhou) was the only Chinese port open to western traders. This nineteenth-century painting depicts the "factories" or trading stations operated by a number of different countries (note the flags), including Denmark, Great Britain, Sweden, the United States, and the Netherlands.

As in the Islamic world and other parts of sub-Saharan Africa, population increases in China—from 250 million in 1644 to around 450 million by the 1850s—were putting considerable pressure on land and other resources. Moreover, the rising consumption of opium, grown in India and brought to China by British traders, produced further social instability and financial crisis. As banditry and rebellions spread, the Qing rulers turned to the landed elites, the gentry, to maintain order in the countryside. But as the gentry raised its militia to suppress these troublemakers, it whittled away at the authority of the Qing Manchu rulers. Faced with these changes, the Qing dynasty struggled to maintain control.

Searching for an alternative present and future, hundreds of thousands of disillusioned peasants joined what became known as the Taiping Rebellion. If one regards the Taiping uprising as a civil war rather than a rebellion, as many scholars now do, it was probably the most lethal civil war of all time, with a death toll thirty times that of the American civil war. Beginning in 1850, the uprising drew on China's long history of peasant revolts. Traditionally, these rebellions ignited within popular religious sects whose visions were egalitarian or **millenarian** (convinced of the imminent coming of a just and ideal society). Moreover, in contrast to orthodox institutions, here women played important roles. Inspired by Daoists, who revered a past golden age before the world was corrupted by human conventions, or by Buddhist sources, these sects threatened the established order.

THE DREAM OF HONG XIUQUAN

The story of the rebellion begins with a complex dream that inspired its founding prophet, Hong Xiuquan (1814–1864). A native of Guangdong Province in the southernmost part of the country (see Map 16.2), Hong first encountered Christian missionaries in the 1830s. He was then trying, unsuccessfully, to pass the civil service examination. After failing the exam for the third time, Hong suffered a strange "illness" in which he had visions of combating demons; these dreams included a mysterious "Old Father" and an "Elder Brother." He also began proclaiming himself the Heavenly King. Relatives and neighbors thought he might have gone mad, but Hong gradually returned to his normal state.

In 1843, after failing the exam for the fourth time, Hong immersed himself in a Christian tract titled *Good Words for Exhorting the Age*. Reportedly, reading this tract enabled Hong to realize the full significance of his earlier visions. All the pieces suddenly fell into place, and he began to grasp their meaning. The "Old Father," he concluded, was the Lord Ye-huo-hua (a Chinese rendering of "Jehovah"), the creator of heaven and earth. His visions of cleansing rituals in heaven foretold Hong's baptism. The "Elder Brother" was Jesus the Savior, the son of God. He, Hong Xiuquan, was the younger brother of Jesus—God's other son. Just as God had previously sent Jesus to save mankind, Hong thought, God was now sending *him* to rid the world of evil. What was once a series of dreams now became a prophetic vision.

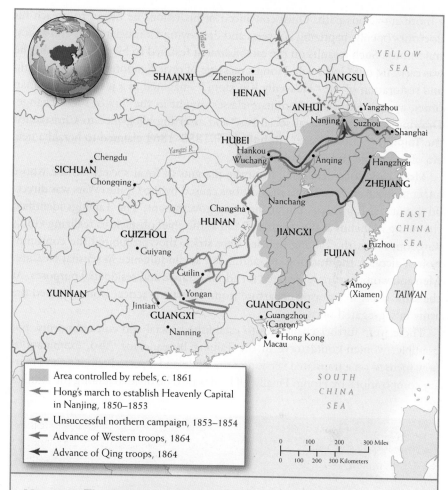

Map 16.2 The Taiping Rebellion in China, 1850–1864

The Taiping Rebellion started in the southwestern part of the country. The rebels, however, went on to control much of the lower Yangzi region and part of the coastal area.

- What cities did the rebels' march start and end in?
- Why do you think the Taiping rebels were so successful in southern China and not in northern regions?
- How did western powers react to the Taiping Rebellion? Would they have been as concerned if the rebellion took place farther to the north or west?

THE REBELLION

Hong's prophecy tapped into a millenarian tradition, inspiring a movement that spread rapidly from southern China. Unlike earlier sectarian leaders whose plots for rebellion were secret before exploding onto the public arena, Hong chose a more audacious path. Once convinced of his vision, he began to preach his doctrines openly, baptizing converts and destroying Confucian idols and ancestral shrines. Such assaults on the establishment testified to his conviction that he was carrying out God's will. Hong's message of revitalization of a troubled land and restoration of the "Heavenly Kingdom," imagined as a just and egalitarian order, appealed to the subordinate classes caught in the flux of social change. Drawing on a largely rural social base and asserting allegiance to Christianity, the **Taiping** ("Great Peace") **Rebellion** of 1850–1864 claimed to herald a new era of economic and social justice.

Many early followers came from the margins of local society—those whose anger at social and economic dislocations caused by the Opium Wars was directed not at the Europeans but at the Qing government. The Taipings identified the ruling Manchus as the "demons" and as the chief obstacle to realizing God's kingdom on earth. Taiping policies were strict: they prohibited the consumption of alcohol, the smoking of opium, and any indulgence in sensual pleasure. Men and women were segregated for administrative and residential purposes. At the same time, in a drastic departure from dynastic practice, women joined the army in segregated units.

There were further challenges to established social and cultural norms. For example, women could serve in the Taiping bureaucracy. Also, examinations now focused on a translated version of the Bible and assorted religious and literary compositions by Hong. Finally, all land was to be divided among the families

Taiping Rebellion The tens of thousands who had joined the "Heavenly King" became such a formidable force that they swiftly conquered and settled in many of the cities they encountered. Depicted in this mid-nineteenth-century painting are imperial Chinese troops driving the Taiping rebels from their stronghold in Tientsin.

according to family size, with men and women receiving equal shares. Once each family met its own needs for sustenance, the communities would share the remaining surplus. These were all radical departures from Chinese traditions. But the Taiping opposition to the Manchus did not involve the formation of a modern nation-state. The rebellion remained caught between the modern and the traditional.

By 1850, Hong's movement had amassed a following of over 20,000, giving Qing rulers cause for concern. When they sent troops to arrest Hong and other rebel leaders, Taiping forces repelled them and then took their turmoil beyond the southwestern part of the country. In January 1851, Hong declared himself Heavenly King of the "Taiping Heavenly Kingdom" (or "Heavenly Kingdom of Great Peace"). By 1853, the rebels had captured major cities. Upon capturing Nanjing, the Taipings cleansed the city of "demons" by systematically killing all the Manchus they could find—men, women, and children. Then they established their own "heavenly" capital in the city.

Although many missionaries considered the Taiping leader, Hong Xiuquan, to be mad, they and many other Europeans in China had a better opinion of his cousin Hong Rengan: he was the second-in-command of the Taiping movement, held the Taiping title of Shield King, and was in charge of the civil service in Nanking, the Taiping capital. They believed Hong Rengan would bring about the westernization and Christianization of China and fully open it to European influences. Hong Rengan had a strikingly different background from Hong Xiuquan. He had spent his early years in Hong Kong, absorbing the teachings of Protestant missionaries. Furthermore, he articulated his vision for China's modernization in a document titled "A New Work for the Aid of Government," expressing his belief that China was no longer the center of the universe and that the British now held that place. He also wrote of his desire for the Chinese to stop calling outsiders "barbarians," believing that China could and must benefit from the achievements of the west. In the end, however, the rebellion collapsed.

Several factors contributed to the fall of the Heavenly Kingdom: struggles within the leadership, an excessively rigid code of conduct, and the rallying of Manchu and Han elites around the embattled dynasty. Disturbed by the Taiping rejection of Confucianism and wanting to protect their property, landowning gentry led militias against the Taipings. Moreover, western governments also eventually opposed the rebellion, claiming that its doctrines represented a perversion of Christianity. Thus, a mercenary army led by foreign officers took part in suppressing the rebellion. Hong Xiuquan himself perished as his heavenly capital fell in 1864. All told, at least 20 million people died in the Taiping Rebellion.

Like their counterparts in the Islamic world and Africa, the Taiping rebels promised to restore lost harmony. Despite all their differences in cultural and historical background, what Muhammad Ibn Abd al-Wahhab, Usman dan Fodio, Shaka, and Hong Xiuquan had in common was the perception that the present world was unjust. Thus, they sought to reorganize their communities—an endeavor that involved confronting established authorities. In this regard, the language of revitalization used by prophets in Islamic areas and China was crucial, for it provided an alternative vocabulary of political and spiritual legitimacy. By mobilizing masses eager to return to an imagined golden age, these prophets and charismatic leaders gave voice to those dispossessed by global change, while producing new, alternative ways of organizing society and politics.

Socialists and Radicals in Europe

Europe and North America were the core areas of economic growth, based on the industrial revolution and free trade, nation-state building, and colonial expansion. But there, too, the main currents of thought and activity encountered challenges. Prophets of all stripes—political, social, cultural, and religious—voiced antiestablishment values and dreamed of alternative arrangements. Radicals, liberals, utopian socialists, nationalists, abolitionists, and religious mavericks made plans for better worlds to come.

RESTORATION AND RESISTANCE

The social and political ferment of the efforts to restore the old order, known as the Restoration period (1815–1848), owed a great deal to the ambiguous legacies of the French Revolution and the Napoleonic wars. (See Map 16.3.) Kings had been toppled and replaced by republics, and then by Napoleon and his relatives; these experiments gave Restoration-era states and radicals many political options from which to choose in the years between Napoleon's downfall in 1815 and the revolutions of 1848.

This period has often been called the Age of Ideology because revolutionary upheavals forced everyone, even those in power, to justify their vision of the social order. Appeals to tradition no longer sufficed. Those called reactionaries or conservatives wanted a return to the world that existed before the French Revolution; they rejected change. Liberals, by contrast, accepted the French Revolution's overthrow of aristocratic privilege. They wanted to hold on to the principles of 1789—above all free trade and equality before the law—without accepting the price controls and political violence of the Terror. Free markets rather than government controls, they believed, would make the most sensible decisions. These proponents of **liberalism** insisted on the individual's right to think, speak, act, and vote as he or she pleased without government interference, so long as no harm came to people or property. Both reactionaries and liberals could find elements to their taste in all the states of the post-Napoleonic world. Much more threatening to the ruling elite were the radicals who believed that the French Revolution had not gone far enough. They longed for a grander revolution that would sweep away the Restoration's political *and* economic order.

Map key:

— German Confederation
✳ Revolutionary activity

Foreign intervention to put down revolutions
◀— Austrian   ◀— French
◀— British   ◀-- Russian
◀— Egyptian

Map 16.3 Civil Unrest and Revolutions in Europe, 1819–1848

Civil unrest and revolutions swept Europe after the Congress of Vienna established a peace settlement at the end of the French Revolution and Napoleon's conquests. Conservative governments had to fight off liberal rebellions and demands for change.

- How many sites of revolutionary activity can you locate on this map?
- What parts of Europe appear to have been politically stable, and what parts rebellious? Based on your reading and the map, can you explain the stability of some parts of Europe and the instability of others?

RADICAL VISIONS

Reactionaries and liberals did not form the only alternative groups of importance at this time. Most discontented of all—and most determined to effect grand-scale change—were the radicals.

The term *radicals* refers to those who favored the total reconfiguration of the old regime's state system: going to the root of the problem and continuing the revolution, not reversing it or stopping reform. In general, radicals shared a bitter hatred for the status quo and an insistence on popular sovereignty, but beyond this consensus much disagreement remained. If some radicals demanded the equalization or abolition of private property, others—like Serbian, Greek, Polish, and Italian nationalists—were primarily interested in throwing off the oppressive overlordship of the Ottoman and Austrian Empires and creating their own nation-states. It was the radicals' threat of a return to revolutions that ultimately reconciled both liberals and reactionaries to preserving the status quo.

Nationalists In the period before the revolutions of 1848, nationalism was a cause dear to both liberals and radicals, and it threatened conservative rulers who claimed to rule by divine right. The idea of popular sovereignty spread, especially during and after Napoleon's occupation of the continent, but who exactly were "the people"? The "people," or the nation, were generally considered to be those who shared a common language, culture, and history, but nationalists fought bitterly over which people counted and who decided. All nationalists believed that governments should represent the "people" and that each people—or, at least, their people—should have a state of their own.

Each fledgling nationalist movement—whether Polish, Czech, Greek, Italian, or German—had different contours, but they all drew backers from the liberal aristocracy and the well-educated, commercially active middle classes. Most nationalist movements were, at first, weak and easily crushed, such as attempted Polish uprisings inside tsarist Russia in 1830–31 and 1863–64. Unable to win political power, the movements' leaders instead pursued educational and cultural programs to arouse and unite their nation for eventual statehood. By contrast, the Greeks, inspired by religious revivalism and enlightened ideas, managed to wrest independence from the Ottoman Turks after a years-long series of skirmishes, in 1832.

Other nationalist movements were suppressed or at least slowed down with little bloodshed. In places like the German principalities, the Italian states, and the Hungarian parts of the Habsburg Empire, secret societies of young men—students and intellectuals—gathered to plan bright, republican futures. Regrettably for these patriots, however, organizations like Young Italy, founded in 1832 to promote national unification and renewal, had little popular or foreign support. Censorship and a few strategic executions suppressed them. Yet many of these movements ultimately succeeded in the century's second half, when conservatives and liberals alike in western Europe employed nationalist fervor to advance their own ambitions. Kings, aristocrats, and bourgeois businessmen realized that they could mobilize popular support in their capacity as Germans, Frenchmen, or Italians, even as they limited poor people's political rights. However, in central Europe, nationalism pitted many claimants for the same territories against one another, like the Czechs, Serbs, Slovaks, Poles, and Ruthenians (Ukrainians). They did not understand why they could not have a nation-state too. Indeed, the idea of a "nation," like that of a "people," was so abstract and vague that it unleashed a series of competing claims that were incompatible with one another and would prove enormously destructive in the twentieth century.

Socialists and Communists Early socialists and communists (the terms were more or less interchangeable in the nineteenth century) insisted that political reforms offered no effective answer to the more pressing "social question": What was to be done about the inequalities so powerfully magnified by industrial capitalism? The socialists worried in particular about two things. One was the growing gap between impoverished workers and newly wealthy employers. The other concern was that the division of labor—that is, the dividing up and simplifying of tasks so that each worker performs most efficiently—might make people into soulless, brainless machines. Socialists believed that the whole free market economy, not just the state, had to be transformed to save the human race from self-destruction. Liberty and equality, they insisted, could not be separated; liberal capitalism and free markets belonged on history's ash heap, in their view, along with aristocratic privilege.

No more than a handful of radical prophets hatched revolutionary plans in the years after 1815, but they were not the only participants in strikes, riots, peasant uprisings, and protest meetings. Indeed, ordinary workers, artisans, domestic servants, and women employed in textile manufacturing all joined in attempts to answer the "social question" to their satisfaction. A few socialists and feminists—like the English thinker John Stuart Mill and his wife, Harriet— campaigned for social and political equality of the sexes. In Britain in 1819, Manchester workers at St. Peter's Field demonstrated peacefully for increased representation in Parliament, but panicking guardsmen fired on the crowd, leaving 11 dead and 460 injured in an incident later dubbed the Peterloo Massacre. In 1839 and 1842, nearly half the adult population of Britain signed the People's Charter, which called for universal suffrage for all adult males, the secret ballot, equal electoral districts, and annual parliamentary elections. Like most such endeavors, this mass movement, known as Chartism, ended in defeat. Parliament rejected the charter in 1839, 1842, and 1848.

Fourier and Utopian Socialism Despite their many defeats, the radicals kept trying. Charles Fourier's **utopian socialism** was perhaps the most visionary and influential of all Restoration-era alternative movements.

Fired by the egalitarian hopes and the cataclysmic failings of the French Revolution, Fourier (1772–1837) believed himself to be the scientific prophet of the new world to come. He was an imaginative, self-taught man who earned his keep in the cloth trade, an occupation that gave him an intense hatred for merchants and middlemen. Convinced that the division of labor and repressive moral conventions were destroying mankind's natural talents and passions, Fourier concluded that a revolution grander than that of 1789 was needed. But this utopian transformation of economic, social, and political conditions, he thought, could occur through organization, not through bloodshed. Indeed, by 1808 Fourier believed that the thoroughly corrupt world was on the brink of giving way to a new and harmonious age, of which he was the oracle.

First formulated in 1808, his "system" envisioned the reorganization of human communities into what he called phalanxes. In these harmonious collectives of 1,500 to 1,600 people, diversity would be preserved but efficiency maintained; best of all, work would become enjoyable. All members of the phalanx, rich and poor, would work, though not necessarily at the same tasks. All would work in short spurts of no more than 2 hours, so as to make labor more interesting and sleep, idleness, and overindulgence less attractive. Truly undesirable jobs, like sweeping out stables or cleaning latrines, would fall to young adolescents, who, Fourier argued, actually liked mucking about in filth.

Fourier's writings gained popularity in the 1830s, appealing to radicals who supported a variety of causes. In France, women were particularly active in spreading his ideas, notably founders of the feminist press in France, including Désirée Gay and Jeanne Deroin. Longing for social and moral reforms that would address problems such as prostitution, poverty, illegitimacy, and the exploitation of workers (including women and children), some women saw in Fourier's ideas a higher form of Christian communalism. By reshaping the phalanx to accommodate monogamous families and Christian values, women helped make his work more respectable to middle-class readers. In Russia, Fourier's works inspired the imaginations of the young writer Fyodor Dostoyevsky. He and fourteen others in the radical circle to which he belonged

The Phalanx The phalanx, as one of Fourier's German followers envisioned it. In this rendering, the idealized home for the residents of the cooperative social system is represented as a building architecturally similar to the home of the French kings, the Louvre.

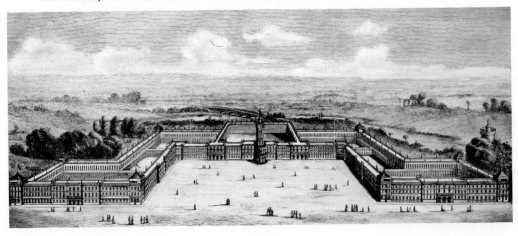

were sentenced to death for their views (though their executions were called off at the last minute). The German thinker Karl Marx read Fourier with great care, and there are many remnants of utopian thought in his work. In *The German Ideology*, Marx describes life in an ideal communist society; in a post-revolutionary world, he predicts, people would no longer have to commit to a single profession or sphere of activity. Everyone could develop their talents in a range of areas. A well-ordered society would make it possible, as he put it in a famous phrase, "for me to do one thing today and another tomorrow, to hunt in the morning, fish in the afternoon, rear cattle in the evening, [and] criticize after dinner."

Marxism University-educated and philosophically radical, Karl Marx (1818–1883) produced the most influential critique of capitalism on record. After being expelled from the university for his radical views, Marx took up a career in journalism. In that capacity, he covered legislative debates over property rights and taxation and developed an interest in economics. His understanding of *capitalism*, a term he was instrumental in popularizing, deepened through his collaboration with Friedrich Engels (1820–1895). Engels was a German-born radical who, after observing conditions in the factories owned by his wealthy father in Manchester, England, published a devastating indictment of industrial wage labor titled *The Condition of the Working Class in England*.

Together, Marx and Engels developed what they called "scientific social-ism," which they contrasted with the "utopian socialism" of others like Fourier. Scientific socialism was rooted, they argued, in a materialist theory of history: what mattered in history was the production of material goods and the ways in which society was organized into classes of producers and exploiters. History, they claimed, consisted of successive forms of exploitative production and rebellions against them. Capitalist exploitation of the wage worker was only the latest, and worst, version of class conflict, Marx and Engels contended. In industrialized societies, capitalists owned the means of production (the factories and machinery) and exploited wage workers. Marx and Engels were confident that the clashes between industrial wage workers with nothing to sell but their labor—or **proletarians**—and capitalists would end in a colossal transformation of human society and would usher in a new world of true liberty, equality, and fraternity. These beliefs constituted the fundamentals of **Marxism**. For Marx and Engels, history moved through stages: from feudalism to capitalism, and then, finally, to socialism (or communism).

From these fundamentals, Marx and Engels issued a comprehensive cri-tique of post-1815 Europe. They identified a whole class of the exploited—the working class. They believed that more and more people would fall into this class as industrialization proceeded and that the masses would not share in the rising prosperity that capitalists monopolized. Marx and Engels predicted that there would be overproduction, and underconsumption of goods would lead to lower profits for capitalists and, consequently, to lower wages or unemployment for workers—which would ultimately spark a proletarian revolution. This revolution would result in a "dictatorship of the proletariat" and the end of private property. With the destruction of capitalism, the men claimed, exploitation would cease and the state would wither away.

After a decade of hardship across Europe known as the hungry forties, revolutions erupted in 1848 in France, Austria, Russia, Italy, Hungary, and the German states. After hearing that revolution had broken out in France, Marx and Engels published *The Communist Manifesto*, calling on the workers of all nations to unite in overthrowing capitalism. These were not proletarian revolutions. By midcentury, modern industry had not developed beyond a few key locations, mostly in northern and western Europe. Instead the revolutions were cross-class affairs, lead by an uneasy coalition of liberal doctors, lawyers, and university professors; often-radical students and urban artisans; and a mass of poor peasants. As a group, they shared little more than a frustration with old elites and a desire for independent nations. Marx and Engels were sorely disappointed (not to mention exiled) by the reactionary crackdowns that quickly crushed the 1848 revolutions. The failure of those revolutions, however, did not doom their prophecy itself or diminish commitment to alternative social landscapes.

Insurgencies against Colonizing and Centralizing States

Outside Europe, for Native Americans and for Britain's colonial subjects in India, the greatest threat to traditional worlds was colonialism. While European radicals looked back to revolutionary legacies in imagining a transformed society, Native American insurgents and rebels in British India drew on their traditional cultural and political resources to imagine local alternatives to foreign impositions. Like the peoples of China, Africa, and the Middle East, native groups in the Americas and India met the period's challenges with prophecy, charismatic leadership, and rebellion. The insurgents all sought to defend their cultures and looked to an idealized past free from outside influences, but the new worlds they envisioned bore unmistakable marks of the present as well.

NATIVE AMERICAN PROPHETS

Like other native peoples threatened by imperial expansion, the Native Americans of North America dreamed of a world in which intrusive colonizers disappeared. Taking such dreams as prophecies, many Native Americans in the Ohio Valley flocked in 1805 to hear the revelations of a Shawnee named Tenskwatawa. Facing a dark present and a darker future, they enthusiastically embraced the

Shawnee Prophet's visions, which (like those of the Paiute prophet Wovoka nearly a century later) foretold how invaders would vanish if Native Americans returned to their customary ways and traditional rites.

Early Calls for Resistance and a Return to Tradition Tenskwatawa's visions—and the anticolonial uprising they inspired—drew on a long tradition of visionary leaders. Often these prophets inspired their followers not only to engage in cleansing ceremonies but also to cooperate in violent anticolonial uprisings. In the 1760s, for example, the preachings of the Delaware shaman Neolin encouraged Native Americans of the Ohio Valley and Great Lakes to take up arms against the British, leading to the capture of several British military posts. Although the British put down the uprising, imperial officials learned a lesson from the conflict: they assumed a less arrogant posture toward Ohio Valley and Great Lakes Native Americans, and they forbade colonists from trespassing on lands west of the Appalachian Mountains. The British, however, were incapable of restraining the flow of settlers across the mountains, and the problem became much worse for the Native Americans once the American Revolution ended. With the Ohio Valley transferred to the new United States, American settlers crossed the Appalachians and flooded into Kentucky and Tennessee.

Despite the settlers' considerable migration, much of the territory between the Appalachian Mountains and the Mississippi River, which Americans referred to as the "western country," remained a Native American country. North and south of Kentucky and Tennessee, Native American warriors more than held their own against American forces. But in 1794 Native American warriors failed to repel invading American armies, and their leaders had to surrender lands in what is now the state of Ohio to the United States. (See Map 16.4.)

Tenskwatawa: The Shawnee Prophet The Shawnees, who lost most of their land, were among the most bitter—and bitterly divided—of Native American peoples living in the Ohio Valley. Some Shawnee leaders concluded that their people's survival now required that they cooperate with American officials and Christian missionaries. This strategy, they realized, entailed wrenching changes in Shawnee culture. European reformers, after all, insisted that Native American men give up hunting and take up farming, an occupation that the Shawnees and their neighbors had always considered "women's work." Moreover, the Shawnees were pushed to abandon communal traditions in favor of private property rights.

Among the demoralized Shawnees was **Tenskwatawa** (1775–1836), whose story of overcoming personal failures through religious visions and embracing a strict moral code has parallels with that of Hong Xiuquan, the Taiping leader. In his first thirty years, Tenskwatawa could claim few accomplishments. He had failed as a hunter and as a medicine man, had blinded himself in one eye, and had earned a reputation as an obnoxious braggart. All this changed

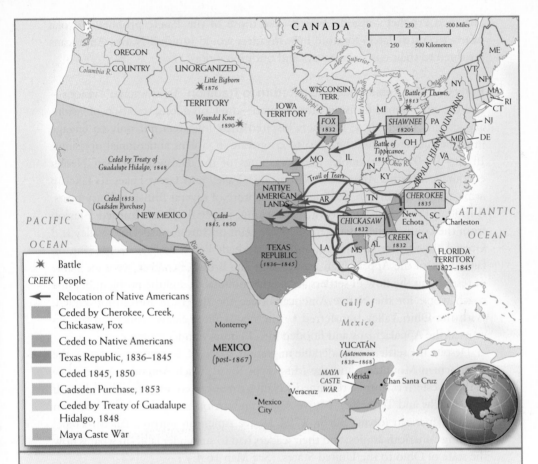

Map 16.4 Native American Revolts in the United States and Mexico

The new world order of expanding nation-states and industrial markets strongly affected indigenous peoples in North America.

- According to this map, where did the fiercest resistance to centralizing states and global market pressures occur?
- What regions of the United States were Native Americans forced to leave?
- According to your reading, to what extent, if any, did the natives' alternative visions create or preserve an alternative to the new emerging order?

in the spring of 1805, however, after he fell into a trance and experienced a vision. In this dream, Tenskwatawa encountered a heaven where the virtuous enjoyed the traditional Shawnee way of life and a hell where evildoers suffered punishments. Additional revelations followed, and Tenskwatawa soon stitched these together into a new social gospel that urged disciples to abstain from alcohol and return to traditional customs.

Like other prophets, Tenskwatawa exhorted Native Americans to avoid contact with outside influences, to reduce their dependence on European trade goods, and to sever their connections to Christian missionaries. If Native Americans obeyed these dictates, Tenskwatawa promised, the deer, which "were half a tree's length under the ground," would come back in abundant numbers to the earth's surface. Likewise, he claimed, Native Americans killed in conflict with colonial intruders would be resurrected, while evil Americans would depart from the country west of the Appalachians.

Like the Qing who responded to Hong Xiuquan's visions, American officials grew concerned as the Shawnee Prophet gathered followers. The spread of Tenskwatawa's message raised fears of a pan–Native American confederacy. Hoping to undermine the Shawnee Prophet's claims to supernatural power, territorial governor William Henry Harrison challenged Tenskwatawa to make the sun stand still. But Tenskwatawa one-upped Harrison. Having learned of an impending eclipse from White astronomers, Tenskwatawa assembled his followers on June 16, 1806. Right on schedule, and as if on command, the sky darkened. Claiming credit for the eclipse, Tenskwatawa saw his standing soar, as did the ranks of his disciples.

At the same time, however, Tenskwatawa had made plenty of enemies among his fellow Native Americans. His visions consigned drinkers to hell and singled out those who cooperated with colonial authorities for punishment in this

Visions of American Indian Unification *Left:* A portrait of Tenskwatawa, the "Shawnee Prophet," whose visions stirred thousands of Indians in the Ohio Valley and Great Lakes to renounce dependence on colonial imports and resist the expansion of the United States. *Right:* A portrait of his brother, Tecumseh, who succeeded in building a significant pan-Indian confederation, although it unraveled following his death at the Battle of Thames in 1813.

world and the next. Indeed, Tenskwatawa condemned as witches those Native Americans who rejected his preaching in favor of the teachings of Christian missionaries and American authorities. (To be sure, Tenskwatawa's damnation of Christianized Native Americans was somewhat paradoxical, for missionary doctrines obviously influenced his vision of a burning hell for sinners and his crusade against alcohol.)

Tecumseh and the Wish for Native American Unity Although Tenskwatawa's accusations alienated some Native Americans, his prophecies gave heart to many more. This was particularly the case once his brother, Tecumseh (1768–1813), helped circulate the message of Native American renaissance among Native American villages from the Great Lakes to the Gulf Coast. On his journeys after 1805, Tecumseh did more than spread his brother's visions; he also wedded them to the idea of an enlarged Native American confederation. Moving around the Great Lakes and traveling across the southern half of the western country, Tecumseh preached the need for Native American unity. Always, he insisted that Native Americans resist any American attempts to get them to sell more land. In response, thousands of followers renounced their ties to colonial ways and prepared to combat the expansion of the United States.

By 1810, Tecumseh had emerged, at least in the eyes of American officials, as even more dangerous than his brother. Impressed by Tecumseh's charismatic organizational talents, Harrison warned that this new "Indian menace" was forming "an Empire that would rival in glory" that of the Aztecs and the Incas. In 1811, while Tecumseh was traveling among southern tribes, Harrison had his troops attack Tenskwatawa's village, Prophet's Town, on the Tippecanoe River in what is now the state of Indiana. The resulting battle was evenly fought, but the Native Americans eventually gave ground and American forces burned Prophet's Town. That defeat discredited Tenskwatawa, who had promised his followers protection from destruction at American hands. Spurned by his former disciples, including his brother, Tenskwatawa fled to Canada. Tecumseh soldiered on, supporting the British in the War of 1812 in the hope that a British victory would check American expansionism. But in 1813, with the war's outcome still in doubt and the pan–Native American confederacy still fragile, he perished at the Battle of the Thames, north of Lake Erie.

Native American Removals The discrediting of Tenskwatawa and the death of Tecumseh damaged the cause of Native American unity; then British betrayal dealt it a fatal blow. Following the war's end in 1814, the British withdrew their support and left the Native Americans south of the Great Lakes to fend for themselves against land-hungry American settlers and the armies of the United States. By 1815, American citizens outnumbered Native Americans in the western country by a seven-to-one margin, and this gap dramatically widened in the next few years. Recognizing the hopelessness of military resistance, Native

Indian Removals after 1815 After the failure of efforts to forge Native American solidarity, the American government forced Native Americans to relocate west of the Mississippi. Often these measures were extremely violent, as in the case of the removal of the Cherokee Nation from its southern lands to present-day Oklahoma, an event so traumatic for the Cherokee as to be known afterwards as "the Trail of Tears."

Americans south of the Great Lakes resigned themselves to relocation. During the 1820s, most of the peoples north of the Ohio River were removed to lands west of the Mississippi River. During the 1830s, the southern tribes were cleared out, completing what amounted to an ethnic cleansing of Native American peoples from the region between the Appalachians and the Mississippi.

In the midst of these final removals, Tenskwatawa died, though his dream of an alternative to American expansion had faded for his people years earlier. Through the rest of the nineteenth century, however, other Native American prophets emerged, and their visions continued to inspire followers with the hope of an alternative to life under the colonial rule of the United States. But like the efforts of Wovoka and the Ghost Dancers in 1890, these dreams failed to halt the expansion of the United States and the contraction of Native American lands.

THE CASTE WAR OF YUCATÁN

As in North America, the creation of expansionist nation-states in Latin America sparked widespread revolts by indigenous peoples. The difference was that after the secession from Spain and Portugal, Latin America went through decades of political instability. Across the region, rural people seized the opportunity to resist encroachers. The Maya revolt in the Yucatán Peninsula was the most protracted. It started in 1847, and its flames were doused only with the full occupation of Yucatán by Mexican national troops in 1901.

The strength and endurance of the Maya revolt stemmed in large measure from the unusual features of the Spanish conquest in southern Mesoamerica. Because this area lacked precious metals and fertile lands, Spain and its rivals focused elsewhere—on central and northern Mexico and the Caribbean islands. As a result, the Maya Indians escaped forced recruitment for silver mines or sugar plantations. This does not mean that global processes sidestepped the Maya Indians. In fact, the production of dyes and foodstuffs for shipment to other regions drew Yucatán into long-distance trading networks. Nonetheless, cultivation and commerce were much less disruptive to indigenous lives in Yucatán than elsewhere in the New World.

After Mexico gained independence, it plunged into a series of civil wars, which culminated in the loss of its northern provinces, first Texas and then almost half of the rest of its territory from California to New Mexico. For the Maya, this was largely a relief; they could survive without much intrusion from the federal government and its troops. Their villages still constituted the chief political domain, ruled by elders; breaking away from Spain meant that old colonial institutions, notably the Catholic Church, weakened, while new republican ideas could be adapted to village self-government. Ownership of land remained collective, the property of families and not individuals. Even food retained its communal and spiritual significance. Corn, a mere staple to White consumers, continued to enjoy sacred status in Maya culture.

Growing Pressures from the Sugar Trade Local developments, however, encroached on the Maya world in the nineteenth century. First, regional elites—mainly White, but often with the support of mixed-race (Mestizo) populations—bickered for supremacy so long as the central authority of Mexico City remained weak. Weaponry flowed freely through the peninsula, and some rivals even appealed for Maya support. Second, regional and international trade spurred the spread of sugar estates and commercial farming, which threatened traditional corn cultivation in Yucatán. Over the decades, plantations slowly encroached on Maya properties. Planters used several devices to lure independent Maya to work, especially in the harvest. The most important device, debt peonage, involved giving small cash advances to Indian families, which obligated fathers and sons to work for meager wages to pay off the debts. Back in the village, it fell to women and daughters to till the land and defend collective property. The real threat came from tax collectors. Mexico's costly wars, culminating in a showdown with the United States in 1846, drove tax collectors and army recruiters into villages in search of revenues and soldiers. There they confronted subsistence farmers, many of them women, struggling to hang on.

This was the pressure cooker when General Zachary Taylor invaded Mexico and American warships blockaded Mexican ports. Suddenly, all the internal tensions in Yucatán blew open. Rival political elites took up arms and appealed to the peasantry for support. Peasants, in turn, mobilized into militia, starting as foot soldiers of urban clans—but soon became independent rebel fighting forces that took a half century to subdue. The rebels were primarily free Maya who had not yet been absorbed into the sugar economy. They wanted to dismantle old definitions of Indians as a caste—a status that deprived the Indians of legal and political equality with Whites and that also subjected the Indians to special taxes. Thus, local Maya leaders, like Jacinto Pat and Cecilio Chi, upheld a republican model of formal equality of all political subjects and devotion to a spiritual order that did not distinguish between Christians and non-Christians. "If the Indians revolt," one Maya rebel explained, "it is because the whites gave them reason; because the whites say they do not believe in Jesus Christ, because they have burned the cornfield."

The Caste War Horrified, the local White elites reacted to the uprising with vicious repression and dubbed the ensuing bloody conflict a caste war. In their view, the **Caste War of Yucatán** was a struggle between forward-looking liberals and backward-looking Indians. This narrative helped frighten Whites into

Caste War of Yucatán The conflict in the Yucatán Peninsula came to be called the "Caste War" and came to symbolize indigenous resistance in Mexico. For twentieth-century muralists like Fernando Castro Pacheco, it became the subject for a public memorial for native resistance against Mexican elites. This mural, like so many of its kind in Mexico, hangs in the government palace in Mérida, the capital city of the region that was nearly overrun by Maya insurgents in the late 1840s. Note the use of peasant tools, like the machete, as weapons; the angry, muscular faces and fiery coloration of the insurgents; and the huddling, naked innocents behind the protective arm of the rebel.

a common cause. The irony is that the classification of the Maya as a "caste" was the effect, not the cause, of the war—and the narrative helped justify the repression that ensued. At first, Whites and Mestizos were no match for the determined peasants, whose forces seized town after town. They especially targeted symbols of White power. With relish they demolished the whipping posts where Indians had endured public humiliation and punishment.

In the end, luck helped save Yucatán's Whites. Settlement of the war with the United States in 1848 enabled Mexico City to rescue local elites in Yucatán. With the help of a $15 million payment from Washington for giving up its northern provinces, Mexico could spend freely to build up its southern armies. The Mexican government soon fielded a force of 17,000 soldiers and waged a scorched-earth campaign to drive back the depleted Maya forces. By 1849, the confrontation had entered a new phase in which Mexican troops engaged in mass repression of the Maya. Mexican armies set Indian fields and villages ablaze. Between 30 and 40 percent of the Maya population perished in the war and its repressive aftermath.

Reclaiming a Maya Identity Warfare prompted a spiritual transformation that reinforced the value of a purely Maya identity to counter the Mexican invaders' efforts to create a strong, centralized state. Thus, a struggle that began with demands for legal equality and relative cultural autonomy became a crusade for spiritual salvation and the complete cultural separation of the Maya Indians. A particularly influential group under José María Barrera retreated to a hamlet called Chan Santa Cruz. There, at the site where he found a cross shape carved into a mahogany tree, Barrera had a vision of a divine encounter. Thereafter, people in a swath of Yucatán villages around Chan Santa Cruz refashioned themselves as moral communities. Leaders created a polity, with soldiers, priests, and tax collectors pledging loyalty to the Speaking Cross. Like the followers of Hong Xiuquan in China's Taiping Rebellion, Indian rebels forged an alternative religion: it blended Christian rituals, faiths, and icons with Maya legends and beliefs. At the center was a stone temple, Balam Na ("House of God"), 100 feet long and 60 feet wide. Through pilgrimages to Balam Na and the secular justice of Indian judges, many Maya soon governed their domain in Yucatán autonomously, almost completely cut off from the rest of Mexico.

Among the fugitives were women. The old Catholic Church had confined them to duties as tenders of altars and protectors of private domesticity. Disenchantment with colonial spiritual authority presented opportunities for women to press for access to schools as a condition to fulfill sacred duties, new and old. One woman teacher in the town of Dzemul, Josefa Ortega, argued that educating "the fairer sex" was key to preserving "civil order."

The Mexican government threw its weight behind the strong-arm ruler General Porfirio Díaz (r. 1876–1911). The general sent one of his veteran commanders, Ignacio Bravo, to do what no other Mexican could accomplish: vanquish Chan Santa Cruz. When General Bravo finally entered the town, he found the once-imposing temple Balam Na covered in vegetation. Nature was reclaiming the territories of the Speaking Cross. Hunger and Bravo's soldiers finally drove the Maya to work on Mexican plantations; the alternative vision was vanquished. A combination of declining economic conditions and the soldiers under Ignacio Bravo brought an end to the Maya revolt.

THE REBELLION OF 1857 IN INDIA

Like Native Americans, the peoples of nineteenth-century India had a long history of opposition to colonial domination. Armed revolts had occurred since the onset of rule by the British East India Company (see Chapter 15). Nonetheless, the uprising of 1857 was unprecedented in its scale, and it posed a greater threat than had any previous rebellion.

India under Company Rule During the first half of the nineteenth century, the British rulers of India had dismantled most of the traditional powers of the nobility and the rights of peasants. Believing that the princely powers and landed aristocracies were out-of-date, the East India Company instituted far-reaching changes in administration. The Charter Act of 1833 wound up almost all of the East India Company's trading activities. It gave absolute power to the governor-general of India, enabling him to make laws that all the courts had to administer. In addition, it required the East India Company to recruit its officials by merit on the basis of competitive exams. In short, the Charter Act made clear that the East India Company was no longer a commercial enterprise but a governing body. The government dispatched the noted Whig historian and political figure Thomas Macaulay to India. During his three-year stint in the country, he noted that he was expected "to legislate for a conquered race, to whom the blessings of our constitution cannot as yet be extended." Macaulay produced a comprehensive code of laws that bore no relationship to traditional Indian laws or any legislation that the company had introduced.

These changes infuriated local peoples and laid the foundations for one of the world's most violent and concerted movements of protest against colonial authority. Lord Dalhousie, upon his appointment as governor-general in 1848, immediately began annexing what had been independent princely domains and stripping native aristocrats of their privileges. Swallowing one princely state after another, the British removed their former allies. The government also decided to collect taxes directly from peasants, displacing the landed nobles as intermediaries. In disarming the landed nobility, the British threw the retainers and militia of the notables into unemployment, and by demanding high taxes from peasants, the British forced them to rely on moneylenders, who could take ownership of land when peasant proprietors failed to pay. Meanwhile, the company transferred judicial authority to an administration that was insulated from the Indian social hierarchy.

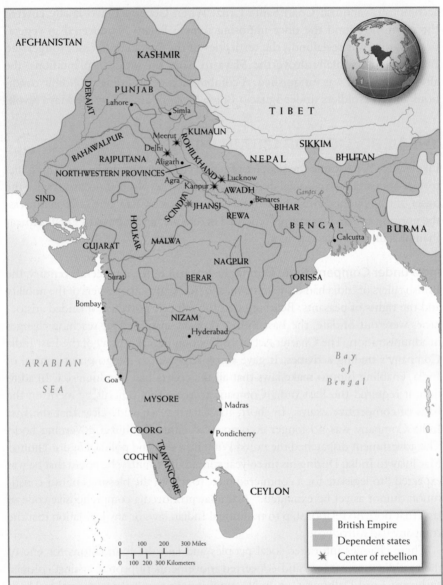

Map 16.5 Indian Rebellion of 1857

The Indian Rebellion of 1857 broke out first among the Indian soldiers of the British army. Other groups soon joined the struggle.

- According to this map, how many centers of rebellion were located in British territory and how many in dependent states?
- Why do you think the rebellion occurred in the interior of the subcontinent rather than along the coasts?
- In what way was the East India Company's expansion into formerly autonomous areas during the first half of the nineteenth century a factor in the rebellion?

The Indian Sepoys Pictured here are Indian soldiers, or sepoys, who were armed, drilled, and commanded by British officers. The sepoys were drawn from indigenous groups that the British considered "martial races." This photograph shows the Sikhs, designated as one such "race."

The most prized object for annexation was the kingdom of Awadh in northern India. (See Map 16.5.) Founded in 1722 by an Iranian adventurer, it was one of the first successor states to have gained a measure of independence from the Mughal ruler in Delhi. With access to the fertile resources of the Ganges plain, its opulent court in Lucknow was one place where Mughal splendor still survived. In 1765, the company imposed a treaty on Awadh under which the ruler paid an annual tribute for British troops stationed in his territory to "protect" his kingdom from internal and external enemies.

Treaty Violations and Annexation In 1856, citing misgovernment and deterioration in law and order, the East India Company violated its treaty obligations and sent its troops to Lucknow to take control of the province. Nawab Wajid Ali Shah, the poet-king of Awadh, whom the British saw as weak and immoral, refused to sign the treaty ceding control to the British.

The annexation of princely domains and the abolition of feudal privileges formed part of the developing practices of European imperialism. To the policy of annexation, Dalhousie added an ambitious program of building railroads, telegraph lines, and a postal network to unify the disjointed territory into a single "network of iron sinew" under British control. Dalhousie saw these infrastructures as key to developing India into a productive colony—a supplier of raw materials for British industry and a market for its manufactures.

A year after Dalhousie's departure in 1856, India went up in flames. The spark that ignited the simmering discontent into a furious rebellion—the Great Rebellion of 1857—was the "greased cartridge" controversy. At the end of 1856, the British army, which consisted of many Hindu and Muslim recruits (sepoys) commanded by British officers, introduced the new Enfield rifle to replace the old-style musket. To load the rifle, soldiers had to bite the cartridge open. Although manufacturing instructions stated that linseed oil and beeswax be used to grease the cartridge, a rumor circulated that cow and pig fat had been used. Biting into cartridges greased with animal fat meant violating the Hindu and Muslim sepoys' religious traditions. The sepoys became convinced that there was a plot afoot to defile them and to compel their conversion to Christianity. So a wave of rebellion spread among the 270,000 Indian soldiers, who greatly outnumbered the 40,000 British soldiers employed to rule over 200 million Indians.

Rebellion Breaks Out The mutiny broke out on May 10, 1857, at the military barracks in Meerut. The revolt soon turned from a limited military mutiny into a widespread civil rebellion that involved peasants, artisans, day laborers, and religious leaders. While the insurgents did not eliminate the power of the East India Company, which managed to retain the loyalty of princes and landed aristocrats in some places, they did throw the company into a crisis. Before long, the mutineers in Delhi issued a proclamation declaring that because the British were determined to destroy the religion of both Hindus and Muslims, it was the duty of the wealthy and the privileged to support the rebellion. To promote Hindu-Muslim unity, rebel leaders asked Muslims to refrain from killing cows in deference to Hindu sentiments.

Although the dispossessed aristocracy and petty landholders led the rebellion, leaders also appeared from the lower classes. Bakht Khan, who had been a junior noncommissioned officer in the British army, became commander in chief of the rebel forces in Delhi, replacing one of the Mughal emperor's sons. And Devi Singh, a wealthy peasant, set himself up as a peasant king. Dressed in yellow, the insignia of Hindu royalty, he constituted a government of his own, modeling it on the British administration. While his imitation of company rule showed his respect for the British bureaucracy, he defied British authority by leading an armed peasantry against the hated local moneylenders.

The call to popular forces also marked the rebel career of Maulavi Ahmadullah Shah, a Muslim theologian. He stood at the head of the rebel forces in Lucknow, leading an army composed primarily of ordinary soldiers and people from the lower orders. Claiming to be an "Incarnation of the Deity" and thus inspired by divine will, he emerged as a prophetic leader of the common people. He voiced his undying hatred of the British in religious terms, calling on Hindus and Muslims to destroy British rule and warning his followers against betrayal by landed authorities.

Participation by the Peasantry The presence of popular leadership points to the important role of the lower classes. Although feudal chieftains often brought them into the rebellion, the peasantry made it their own. The organizing principle of their uprising was the common experience of oppression. Thus, they destroyed anything that represented the authority of the company: prisons, factories, police posts, railway stations, European bungalows, and law courts. Equally significant, the peasantry attacked native moneylenders and local power holders who were seen as benefiting from company rule.

Vigorous and militant as the popular rebellion was, it was limited in its territorial and ideological horizons. To begin with, the uprisings were local in scale and vision. Peasant rebels attacked the closest seats of administration and sought to settle scores with their most immediate and visible oppressors. They generally did not carry their action beyond the village or collection of villages. Their loyalties remained intensely local, based on village attachments and religious, caste, and clan ties. Nor did popular militants seek to undo traditional hierarchies of caste and religion.

British Response Convinced that the rebellion was the result of plotting by a few troublemakers, the British reacted with brutal vengeance. Villages were torched, and rebels were tied to cannons and blown to bits to teach Indians a lesson in power. Delhi fell in September 1857, Lucknow in March 1858. The British exiled the unfortunate Mughal emperor to Burma, where he died, and murdered his sons. Most of the other rebel leaders were either killed in battle or captured and executed. When, at the same time, the British also moved to annex the state of Jhansi in northern India, its female leader, Lakshmi Bai, mounted a counterattack. After a two-week siege, Jhansi fell to the British; Lakshmi Bai escaped on horseback, only to die in the fighting for control of a nearby fortress. Her intelligence, bravery, and youth (she was twenty-eight) made her the subject of many popular Indian ballads in the decades to follow.

By July 1858, the vicious campaign to restore British control had achieved its goal. Yet, in August, the British Parliament abolished company rule and the company itself and transferred responsibility for the governing of India to the crown. In November, Queen Victoria issued a proclamation guaranteeing religious toleration, promising improvements, and allowing Indians to serve in the government. She promised to honor the treaties and agreements with princes and chiefs and to refrain from interfering in religious matters. The insurgents had risen up not as a nation but as a multitude of communities acting independently; their determination to find a new order shocked the British and threw them into a panic. Having crushed the uprising, the British resumed the work of transforming India into a modern colonial state and economy. But the desire for radical alternatives and traditions of popular insurgency, though vanquished, did not vanish.

The East India Company provoked the rebellion with desperate attempts to hold on to power. Unsure of its ability to bring westernization and modernity to India,

The Rani of Jhansi The Rani of Jhansi, who was deposed by the British, rose up during the revolt of 1857. In subsequent nationalist iconography, as this twentieth-century watercolor illustrates, she is remembered as a heroic rebel, all the more so because of her gender.

Secundra Bagh Palace Courtyard The Great Rebellion's aftermath was captured by Italian photographer Felice Beato, who covered conflicts across Asia and is regarded as the first global wartime photographer. Beato arrived in Lucknow in 1858 to record the wreckage after most of the fighting in the rebellion was quashed. For this photo, he relied on local witnesses to move bones and skulls around in the foreground to dramatize the violence.

the company became increasingly authoritarian, which transformed discontent into an insurgency. This was why the violence was most acute in northern India, where the opposition to company rule ran deep, where the company had only recently imposed itself, and where it wielded only limited military capacity. It was there that the rebels posed the greatest threat to British rule and thus had to be quashed mercilessly.

Conclusion

The nineteenth century was a time of turmoil and transformation. Powerful forces reconfigured the world as a place for capitalism, colonialism, and nation-states, while prophets, charismatic leaders, radicals, peasant rebels, and anticolonial insurgents arose to offer alternatives. Reflecting local circumstances and traditions, the struggles of these men and women for a different future opened up spaces for the ideas and activities of subordinate classes.

Conventional historical accounts either neglect these struggles or fail to view them as a whole. These individuals were not just romantic, last-ditch resisters, as some scholars have argued. Even after defeat, their messages remained alive within their communities. Nor were their actions isolated and atypical events, for when viewed on a global scale they bring to light a world that looks very different from the one that became dominant. To see the Wahhabi movement in the Arabian Peninsula together with the Shawnee Prophet in North America, the utopians and radicals in Europe with the peasant insurgents in British India, and the Taiping rebels with the Maya in Yucatán is to glimpse a world of marginalized regions and groups. It was a world that more powerful groups endeavored to suppress but could not erase.

In this world, prophets and rebel leaders usually cultivated power and prestige locally; the emergence of an alternative political or social movement in one region did not impinge on communities and political organizations in others. As much as these individuals had in common, they envisioned widely different kinds of futures. Even Karl Marx, who exhorted the workers of the world to unite, was acutely aware that the call for a proletarian revolution applied only to the industrialized countries of Europe. Other dissenters had even more localized horizons. A world fashioned by movements for alternatives meant a world with multiple centers and different historical timelines.

What gave force to a different mapping of the world was the fact that common people were at the center of these alternative visions, and their voices, however muted, gained a place on the historical stage. The quest for various forms of equality defined efforts to reconstitute alternative worlds. In Islamic regions, the emphasis on equality in revitalization movements was evident in their mobilization of all Muslims, not just the elites. Likewise, charismatic military leaders in Africa, for all their use of raw power, used the framework of community to build new polities. The Taiping Rebellion distinguished itself by seeking to establish an equal society of men and women in service of the Heavenly Kingdom. Operating under very different conditions, European radicals imagined a society free from aristocratic privileges and bourgeois property. Anticolonial rebels and insurgents depended on local solidarities and proposed alternative moral communities. In so doing, these movements compelled ruling elites to adjust the way they governed. The next chapter explores this challenge.

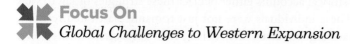

Focus On
Global Challenges to Western Expansion

Europe

- European socialists and radicals envision a world free of exploitation and inequalities, while nationalists work to create new independent nation-states.

The Americas

- Native American prophets in the United States imagine a world restored to its customary ways and traditional rites.

- The Maya defy the central Mexican government in a rebellion known as the Caste War of Yucatán.

The Islamic World and Africa

- Revivalist movements in the Arabian Peninsula and West Africa demand a return to traditional Islam.

- A charismatic warrior, Shaka, creates a powerful state in southern Africa.

Semicolonial China

- An inspired prophetic figure, Hong Xiuquan, leads the Taiping Rebellion against the Qing dynasty and European encroachment on China.

Colonial India

- Indian troops mutiny against the British and attempt to restore Mughal rule.

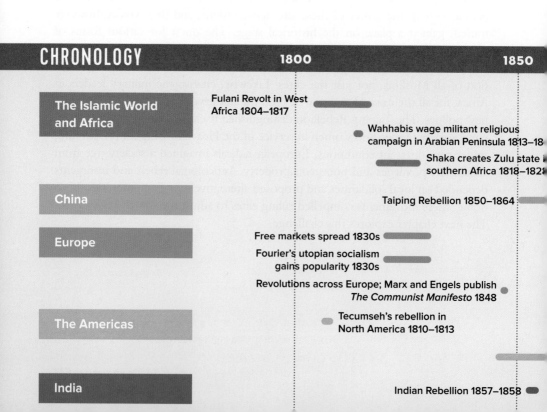

CHRONOLOGY 1800 1850

The Islamic World and Africa

Fulani Revolt in West Africa 1804–1817

Wahhabis wage militant religious campaign in Arabian Peninsula 1813–18

Shaka creates Zulu state southern Africa 1818–1828

China

Taiping Rebellion 1850–1864

Europe

Free markets spread 1830s

Fourier's utopian socialism gains popularity 1830s

Revolutions across Europe; Marx and Engels publish *The Communist Manifesto* 1848

The Americas

Tecumseh's rebellion in North America 1810–1813

India

Indian Rebellion 1857–1858

THINKING ABOUT GLOBAL CONNECTIONS

Key Terms

- **Thinking about Exchange Networks and Alternative Visions** How did people around the world respond to the major changes of the French, American, and industrial revolutions? What difference did proximity to the European and American "core" make?

- **Thinking about Changing Power Relationships and Alternative Visions** What kind of challenges did the new order provoke? What kinds of traditions did those challenges draw on, and what kind of success did they have?

- **Thinking about Gender and Alternative Visions** Describe the role women played in millenarian protest movements during the nineteenth century, and explain the significance of gender to those movements.

Key Terms

Caste War of Yucatán p. 639

Usman dan Fodio p. 618

liberalism p. 626

Marxism p. 631

Mfecane movement p. 619

millenarian p. 622

proletarians p. 631

Taiping Rebellion p. 624

Tenskwatawa p. 633

utopian socialism p. 629

Wahhabism p. 616

Go to INQUIZITIVE to see what you've learned—and learn what you've missed—with personalized feedback along the way.

	1900		1950

Ghost Dance movement in North America 1889–1890

Caste War in Yucatán, Mexico 1847–1901

17

Nations and Empires

1850–1914

Core Objectives

- **IDENTIFY** the institutions that enabled elites in western Europe, the Americas, and Japan to consolidate nation-states, and **ANALYZE** the degree to which they succeeded during this period.

- **EXPLAIN** the roles that industrialization, science, and technology played in the expansion of powerful states into the rest of the world.

- **COMPARE** the reactions to imperialism in Africa and Asia, and **EVALUATE** how effective these responses were.

- **ANALYZE** the extent to which colonies contributed to the wealth and political strength of the nation-states that controlled them.

In 1895, the Cuban patriot José Martí launched a rebellion against the last Spanish holdings in the Americas. The anti-Spanish struggle continued until 1898, when Spain withdrew from Cuba and Puerto Rico. Martí hoped to bring freedom to a new Cuban nation and equality to all Cubans. But even as he helped secure freedom from the declining Spanish Empire, he could not prevent military occupation and political domination of Cuba by the world's newest imperial power, the United States. Martí's hopes and frustrations found parallels around the world.

After 1850, the building of nation-states in Europe, the Americas, and Oceania and the expansion of their empires changed the map of the world, exhilarating some peoples and frustrating others. Those who benefited most were Europeans and peoples of European descent. During these decades the nation-states of Europe, now locked in intense political and economic rivalry, projected their power across the entire world. Much of the rivalry among European states intensified through disruptions in the European balance of power, caused by the unification of two new states (Italy and Germany). Across the Atlantic, the United States abandoned its anticolonial origins and annexed overseas possessions. Yet imperial expansion did not go unchallenged. It encountered resistance from communities being incorporated into the new empires. In Asia and Africa resisters struggled to repel their invaders, often demanding the right to govern themselves.

The second half of the nineteenth century witnessed the simultaneous—and entwined—advance of nationalism and imperialism. These decades also saw the further expansion of industrialization. Taken together, the era's political and economic developments allowed western Europe and the United States to attain primacy in world affairs. But tensions inside these states and their empires, as well as within other states, made the new world order anything but stable.

Global Storyline

How Nation-States Became Global Empires

- Nation-state building and imperial expansion change the map of the world.

- Industrialization, science, and technology enable states in North America and western Europe—and, to a lesser extent, Japan—to overpower other regions politically, militarily, and economically.

- European, American, and Japanese imperialists encounter significant opposition in Africa and Asia.

Consolidating Nations and Constructing Empires

During the second half of the nineteenth century, the idea of building nation-states engulfed the globe, and nationalism became closely linked to imperialism. Enlightenment thinkers had emphasized the importance of nations, defined as peoples who shared a common past, territory, and culture. To many people it seemed natural that once absolutist rulers had fallen, governments should draw their power and legitimacy from those who lived within their borders and that the body of institutions governing each territory should be uniquely concerned with promoting the welfare of that particular people. This seemed such a natural process that little thought was given to the relationship between "nation" and "state," between the people and their government; national states were simply supposed to well up from the people's longing for liberty and togetherness.

BUILDING NATIONALISM

More often than not, however, local elites created nations. They did so by compelling diverse groups of people and regions to accept a unified network of laws, a central administration, time zones, national markets, and a single regional dialect as the "national" language. To overcome strong regional identities, state administrators broadened public education in the national language and imposed universal military service to build a national army. In this way, dominant elites spread their values and institutions outward to regions throughout each nation and beyond their borders. While a handful of nation-states were already well established in the mid-nineteenth century (Japan, Great Britain, France, Spain, Portugal, and the United States), two of the most important—Italy and Germany—were newly created in this period, forged through strategic military contests.

EXPANDING THE EMPIRES

The processes of nation building also required the acquisition of new territories, often overseas, a development that was called **imperialism**. Rulers measured national strength not only by their people's unity but also by their economic power and the conquest of new territories. Thus, Germany, France, the United States, Russia, and Japan challenged Britain's leadership in overseas trade by developing their industries and seizing new territories. By the century's end, gaining new territory had become so important that these states scrambled to colonize peoples from Africa to the Amazon, from California to Korea.

Imperial rule facilitated a widespread movement of labor, capital, commodities, and information. As scholars studied previously unknown tribes and races, new schools taught colonized peoples the languages, religions, scientific practices, and cultural traditions of their colonizers. Publications and products from the "mother country" circulated widely among indigenous elites. Yet empire builders did not extend to non-White inhabitants of their colonies the same rights that they gave to inhabitants of their own nations; here, nation and empire were incompatible. Not only were colonial subjects largely prohibited from participating in their own governments, but they were, with extremely modest exceptions, also not considered members of the nation at all. As a result, imperialism produced diametrically opposed reactions: exultation among the colonizers and bitterness among the colonized.

Expansion and Nation Building in the Americas

Once freed from European control, the elites of the Americas set about creating political communities of their own. By the 1850s, they shared a desire both to create widespread loyalty to their political institutions and to expand territorial domains. This required refining the tools of government to include national laws and court systems, standardized money, and national political parties. This also meant finding ways to settle hinterlands that previously belonged to indigenous populations.

Although nation-states took shape throughout the world, the Americas saw the most complete assimilation of new possessions. Instead of treating outlying areas as colonial outposts, American nation-state builders turned them into new provinces. With the help of rifles, railroads, schools, and land surveys, frontiers became staging areas for the expanding populations of North and South American societies. For indigenous peoples, however, such national expansion meant the loss of traditional lands on a vast scale, and many lost lives. Not all national consolidations in the Americas were the same. The United States, Canada, and Brazil, for example, experienced different processes of nation building, territorial expansion, and economic development.

THE UNITED STATES

Military might, diplomacy, and the power of numbers enabled the United States to claim territory that spanned the North American continent. (See Map 17.1.) At its independence, the new country established a barely united confederation of states. Native American resistance and Spanish and British rivalry hemmed in the Americans of European descent. At the same time, the disunited states threatened to break apart between "North" and "South," as questions of states' rights and of slavery versus free labor intruded into national politics. Yet, rallying to the rhetoric of **Manifest Destiny**, the idea that it was God's will for the United States to "overspread" North America, American Whites pushed their territorial claims and boundaries westward. They acquired territories via purchase agreements and treaties

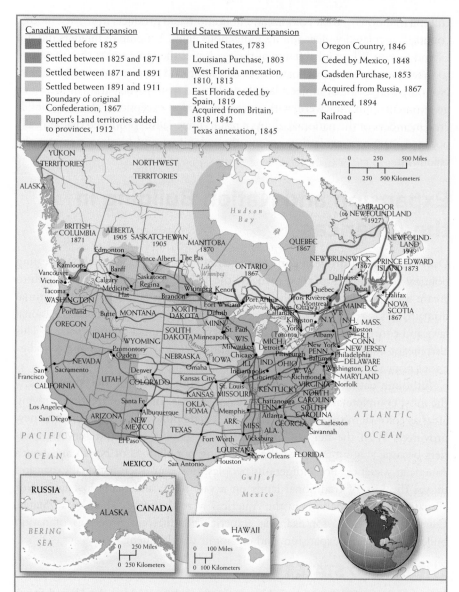

Canadian Westward Expansion

■ Settled before 1825

■ Settled between 1825 and 1871

■ Settled between 1871 and 1891

■ Settled between 1891 and 1911

— Boundary of original Confederation, 1867

■ Rupert's Land territories added to provinces, 1912

United States Westward Expansion

■ United States, 1783

■ Louisiana Purchase, 1803

■ West Florida annexation, 1810, 1813

■ East Florida ceded by Spain, 1819

■ Acquired from Britain, 1818, 1842

■ Texas annexation, 1845

■ Oregon Country, 1846

■ Ceded by Mexico, 1848

■ Gadsden Purchase, 1853

■ Acquired from Russia, 1867

■ Annexed, 1894

— Railroad

Map 17.1 U.S. and Canadian Westward Expansion, 1803–1912

Americans and Canadians expanded westward in the second half of the nineteenth century, aided greatly by railways.

- How do you account for the differences between the transcontinental railroads in the United States and Canada?

- When did Canada and the United States complete their respective territorial expansions? Why were these expansions not continuous, moving from east to west?

with France, Spain, and Britain and via warfare and treaties with diverse Native American nations and Mexico.

As part of the territories taken from Mexico after the Mexican-American War (1846–1848), the United States gained California, where the discovery of gold brought migration on an unprecedented scale. As news of the find spread, hopeful prospectors raced to stake their claims. In the next few years, over 100,000 Americans took to the overland trails and to the seas in quest of California's riches, transforming it almost overnight into the most cosmopolitan place on earth, where worlds truly came together.

Civil War and Citizenship Rights Westward expansion proved the undoing of the American nation. The question was whether newly acquired lands would be open to slavery or restricted to free labor. Following the 1860 election of President Abraham Lincoln, who pledged to halt the expansion of slavery, the United States divided between North and South and plunged into a gruesome Civil War (1861–1865).

The bloody conflict led to the abolition of slavery, and the struggle to extend voting and citizenship rights to formerly enslaved men qualified the Civil War as a second American Revolution. Abraham Lincoln had promised a new model of freedom for a state reborn out of bloodshed. Its cornerstone would be the incorporation of freed people as citizens of the United States. Yet experiments in biracial democracy during the Reconstruction period (1867–1877) were short-lived. In the decades after the Civil War, counterrevolutionary pressure led to the denial of voting rights to African Americans and the restoration of (White, patriarchal) planter rule in the Southern states. This pressure was spearheaded by the terrorism of former Confederate supporters and secret society groups like the Ku Klux Klan, who used a combination of legalized and criminal tactics like making people take literacy tests to vote, creating new forms of coerced labor like chain gangs, willfully destroying people's property, and employing vigilante justice through widespread public lynchings.

Nonetheless, the war brought enduring changes across the United States. The defeat of the South established the preeminence of the national government. After the Civil War, Americans learned to speak of their nation in the singular ("the United States is" in contrast to "the United States are"). With an invigorated nationalism came a stronger national government.

Economic and Industrial Development Even more dizzying were social and economic changes that followed the Civil War. Within ten years of the war's end, the industrial output of the United States had climbed by 75 percent. Americans made such impressive industrial gains that the United States soon joined Britain and Germany atop the list of economic giants.

A potent instrument of capital accumulation appeared at this time—the **limited-liability joint-stock company**. Firms such as Standard Oil and U.S.

African American Gains and Losses *Left:* In the immediate aftermath of the American Civil War, "Radical Republicans" asserted political control by passing laws and constitutional amendments ending slavery, guaranteeing equal rights, and enfranchising freedmen. One result was the election of African Americans to the U.S. Congress. During the 1870s, however, White leaders retreated from the commitment to Black rights, allowing ex-Confederates to reassert control over Southern politics. *Right:* The Ku Klux Klan terrorized African Americans in the post–Civil War South. Klan violence reversed many of the legal and political gains made by freedmen and helped restore planters to power in the South.

Steel attracted money from well-to-do investors via a stock market. These investors, called shareholders, in theory owned the company; nonetheless, they left the running of these enterprises to paid managers. Intermediaries, like J. Pierpont Morgan, the New York financial giant who became the world's wealthiest man, loaned money and brokered big deals on the New York Stock Exchange. So great were the fortunes amassed by leading financiers and industrialists that by 1890 the richest 1 percent of Americans owned nearly 90 percent of the nation's wealth.

The expansion of railroad lines symbolized American economic and territorial growth. In 1865, the United States boasted 35,000 miles of track. By 1900, nearly 200,000 miles of track connected the Atlantic to the Pacific and crisscrossed the American territory in between. Americans continued their migrations west. Joined by throngs of immigrants from Europe, they were attracted by homestead acts promising nearly free acreage to settlers and by promoters from the railroads. The migrations sparked another round of wars with Amerindians, which resulted in their dispossession and concentration on reservations.

By now the United States had become a major world power. It boasted an economy that, despite troubles in the 1890s, had expanded rapidly over the last decades of the nineteenth century. It also was a more integrated nation after the Civil War, with an amended constitution that claimed to uphold the equality of all members of the American nation, even those men who were not White. But there was disagreement on what that equality should involve (for example, should it include women as voters?) and how the country would adjust to a new century in which the nation's "destiny" had already been fulfilled.

CANADA

Canadians also built a new nation, enjoyed economic success, and followed an expansionist course. Like the United States, Canada had access to vast western lands for growing agricultural exports. And as in the United States, these lands became the homes and farms of more European immigrants. However, whereas the United States had waged a war to gain independence, Canada's separation from Britain was peaceful. From the 1830s to the 1860s, Britain gradually passed authority to the colonies, leaving Canadians to grapple with the task of creating a shared community.

Building a Nation Sharp internal divisions made that task especially difficult. For one thing, there was a well-established French population. Wanting to keep their villages, their culture, their religion, and their language intact, these French Canadians did not feel integrated into the emerging Canadian national community. Nor were they eager to join the English-speaking population in settling new areas, lest such migration dilute their French-Canadian presence.

The English speakers were equally unenthusiastic about creating an independent Canadian state. Fear of being absorbed into the American republic reinforced these Canadians' loyalty to the British crown and made them content with colonial status. Indeed, when Canada finally began to take its own steps away from colonial status in 1867, it was by an Act of Parliament in London and not by revolution.

Territorial Expansion Lacking cultural and linguistic unity, Canadians used territorial expansion to build an integrated state. In response to the U.S. purchase of Alaska from Russia in 1867 and the movement of settlers onto the American plains, Canadian leaders realized that they had to incorporate their own western territories, lest these, too, fall into American hands.

Pioneers seemed unwilling to venture to these western lands—it was far, it was cold, and the growing season was cruelly short. So the state lured emigrant farmers from Europe and the United States with subsidized railway rates and the promise of fortunes to be made. It also offered attractive terms to railway companies to connect agrarian hinterlands with Montreal and Toronto (see again Map 17.1) and *not* with commercial cities in the United States.

The Canadian state also faced friction with indigenous peoples. Warfare in the western lands threatened to drive away investors and settlers, who could always find property south of the border instead. To prevent the kind of bloodletting that characterized the United States' westward expansion, the Canadian government signed treaties with indigenous peoples to ensure strict separation between natives and newcomers.

The Canadian government acquired significant powers to intervene in, regulate, and mediate social conflict between Anglo and French residents, and among both groups and the Native American population. These powers, in fact, were fuller than those of the U.S. government. But even though the state was relatively strong, the sense of a national identity was comparatively weak. Expansionism helped Canada remain an autonomous state, but it did not solve the question of what it meant to belong to a Canadian nation.

LATIN AMERICA

Latin American elites also engaged in nation-state building and expanded their territorial borders. But unlike in the United States and Canada, expansion did not always create homesteader frontiers that could help expand democracy and forge national identities. Instead, civil conflict fractured certain countries in the region and rural elites hung on to their private properties and political privileges (see Chapters 15 and 16).

Far more than in North America, the richest lands in Latin America went to large estate holders producing exports such as sugar, coffee, or beef. The result: while Latin America shared in the world's frontier expansion and general economic growth, elites hoarded opportunities at the expense of the poor, the indigenous people, and people of color.

Amerindian and peasant uprisings were a major worry in new Latin American republics. Fearing insurrections, elites devised governing systems that protected private property while limiting the political rights of the poor. Likewise, the specter of revolts by enslaved resisters, driven home not just by earlier, brutal events in Haiti (see Chapter 15) but also by daily rumors of rebellions, kept elites in a state of alarm. Creating strong states, it seemed to many Latin American elites, required excluding large groups of people from power.

Brazil's "Exclusive" Nation-State Brazil illustrates the process by which Latin American rulers built nation-states that excluded much of the population from both the "nation" and the "state." Through the nineteenth century, rulers in Rio de Janeiro defused political conflict by allowing planters to retain the reins of power.

The official prohibition of the importation of enslaved people in 1830, coupled with freedom seekers' resistance, began to choke the planters' system by driving up the price of enslaved labor within the region. Thereafter, Brazilian elites retained some formerly enslaved people as gang-workers or sharecroppers (who received tools and seeds in return for a share of the crop), and they also imported new workers— especially from Italy, Spain, and Portugal—as seasonal migrant workers or indentured tenant farmers. Indeed, European and even Japanese migration to Brazil helped planters preserve their holdings in the post-slavery era. In all, 2 million Europeans and some 70,000 Japanese moved to Brazil.

The Brazilian state was exclusive by design. As in the United States, elites imposed severe restrictions on suffrage and set rules that reduced political competition. However, given the greater share of the Black population in Brazil, restrictions there excluded a larger share of the potential electorate than in the United States.

Abolition in Brazil The abolition of slavery in Brazil was by far the most popular act of the country's monarchy, though it immediately alienated the planter class and led to the bloodless downfall of the royal family. *Left:* A large crowd is gathered before the Imperial Palace in Rio de Janeiro to applaud Princess Isabel in particular. Observe the number of umbrellas used to protect against the sun. *Right:* Although the abolition of slavery had widespread support, it was immediately turned into a political symbol. In *Libertação dos Escravos* (1889), the painter, Pedro di Figueredo Americo, idealizes the act as a republican gesture of salvation for pleading freedom seekers who are surrounded by ennobled Whites (represented as women) showering their praise on Princess Isabel. Note how the artist relegates the monarch to the background, in contrast to the immense support she receives in the photo. Note also the racial stratification suggested by the depiction of enlightened Whites and prostrate, bawling Blacks. Such racist imagery makes for a sharp contrast with the uniform, unified scene in the black-and-white photograph.

Brazilian Expansion and Economic Development

Like Canada and the United States, the Brazilian state extended its reach to distant areas and incorporated them as provinces. The biggest land grab occurred in the Amazon River basin, the world's largest drainage watershed and tropical forest. It had built up over millennia around the meandering tributaries that convey runoffs from the eastern slopes of the Andes all the way to the Atlantic Ocean. It was a massive yet delicate habitat of balanced biomass suspended by towering trees with a canopy of leaves and vines that kept the basin ecologically diverse. Here, the Brazilian state gave giant concessions to local capitalists to extract rubber latex. When combined with sulfur, rubber was a key raw material for tire manufacturing in European and North American bicycle and automobile industries.

For a time, Brazil became the world's exclusive exporter of rubber; as a result, its planters, merchants, and workers prospered. Rich merchants became lenders and financiers, not only to workers but also to landowners. The mercantile elites of Manaus, the capital of the Amazon region, designed and decorated their city to reflect their new fortunes. Although the streets were still paved with mud, the town's elites built a replica of the Paris Opera House, and Manaus became a regular stopover for European opera singers on the circuit between Buenos Aires and New York. Rubber workers also benefited from the boom. Men migrated from farms and villages around the Amazon and from the impoverished northeast. Mostly either Amerindians or mixed-blood people, they saved meager sums to take home to their kin. Meanwhile, women and girls

Opera House in Manaus The turn-of-the-century rubber boom brought immense wealth to the Amazon jungle. As in many boom-and-bust cycles in Latin America, the proceeds flowed to a small elite and diminished when the rubber supply outstripped the demand. But the wealth produced was sufficient to prompt the local elite to build temples of modernity in the midst of the jungle. Pictured here is the Opera House in the rubber capital of Manaus. Like other works built by Latin American elites of the period, this one emulated the original in Paris.

took care of subsistence plots or worked as domestics. In this fashion, the benefits of the commodity boom in the Amazon trickled down to the poor. But economic growth came with substantial environmental costs. Such a diversified biomass could not tolerate a regimented form of production. Cultivating rubber trees at the expense of other vegetation made the forest vulnerable to non-human predators. Leaf blights and ferocious ants destroyed all experiments at creating more sustainable rubber plantations.

The Brazilian rubber boom, moreover, soon went bust. Brazilian rubber faced severe competition after a British scientist smuggled rubber plant seeds out of Brazil in 1876. Following years of experimentation, British patrons transplanted a blight-resistant hybrid to the British colony of Ceylon (present-day Sri Lanka). As competition led to increased supplies and reduced prices, Brazilian producers went bankrupt. Merchants called in their loans, landowners forfeited their titles, and rubber workers returned to their small subsistence farms. Tropical vines crept over the Manaus Opera House, and it gradually fell into disrepair.

Throughout the Americas, nineteenth-century elites, working with outdated ideas of who should wield power, nonetheless attempted to satisfy popular demands for inclusion. While the ideal was to construct nation-states that could reconcile differences among their citizens and pave the way for economic prosperity, political autonomy did not bring prosperity, or even the right to vote, to all. As each nation-state expanded its territorial boundaries, many inhabitants were left out of the political realm.

Consolidation of Nation-States in Europe

In Europe, no "frontier" existed into which new states could expand. Instead, nation-states took shape out of older monarchies and empires, and their borders were determined by diplomats or by battles. In the wake of the French Revolution, the idea caught on that "the people" should form the basis for the nation and that nations should share a common culture—but no one could agree on who "the people" should be. Yet, over the course of the nineteenth century, as literacy, cities, industrial production, and the number and prosperity of property owners expanded, ruling elites had no choice but to share power with a wider group of citizens. These citizens, in turn, increasingly defined themselves as, say, French or German, rather than as residents of Marseilles or subjects of the king of Bavaria.

DEFINING "THE NATION"

For a very long time, in most places, "the nation" was understood to comprise kings, clergymen, nobles—and occasionally rich merchants or lawyers—and no one else. Although some peoples, such as the English and the Spanish, were already self-conscious about their unique histories, only in the late eighteenth century were the crucial building blocks of European nationalism put in place.

Cultural changes laid the foundations of the nation. Increasingly literate urban populations met in coffeehouses and other public places to discuss the issues of the day. Their collective debates—public opinion—weighed for the first time on the decisions of kings and statesmen. During the nineteenth century, a huge expansion of the periodical press made it possible for people all across Europe to read books and newspapers in their own languages. The emerging industrial economy made merchants anxious to standardize laws, taxation policies, and weights and measures. States invested huge sums in building roads and then railroads—and these linked provincial towns and bigger cities, laying the foundations for a closer political integration.

But who were the people, and what constituted a viable nation-state? For some, the nation was a collection of all those who spoke one language; for others, it was all those who lived in a certain territory and who shared a common religious heritage. This was a particularly acute problem in multiethnic central and southeastern Europe, where many people were multilingual, rich and poor alike. But some who shared the same language objected to being lumped into one nation-state. The Irish, for example, spoke English but were predominantly Catholics and wanted to be free from Anglican rule.

UNIFICATION IN GERMANY AND ITALY

Two of Europe's fledgling nation-states came into being when the dynastic states of Prussia and Piedmont-Sardinia incorporated their smaller, linguistically related neighbors, creating the German and Italian nation-states. (See Map 17.2.) In both regions, conservative prime ministers—Count Otto von Bismarck of Prussia and Count Camillo di Cavour of Piedmont—exploited liberal, nationalist sentiment to rearrange the map of Europe.

Building Unified States The unifications of Germany and Italy, both completed in 1871, posed all the familiar problems of who should be included in

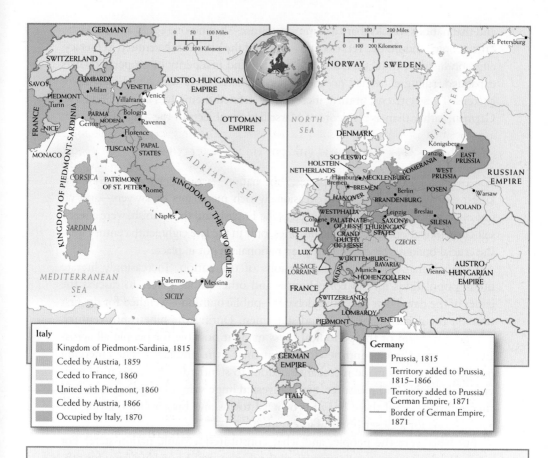

Map 17.2 Italian Unification and German Unification, 1815–1871

Italian unification and German unification altered the political map of Europe.

- What were the names of the two original states that grew to become Italy and Germany?
- Who were the big losers in these territorial transfers?
- According to your reading, what problems did the new Italian and German states face in creating strong national communities?

the new nation-states. To begin with, German speakers were spread all across central and eastern Europe; for centuries they had lived in many different states. Similarly, Italians had lived separately in city-states and small kingdoms on the Italian Peninsula and spoke a range of dialects. The historical experiences and economic developments had made Bavarian Germans (Catholic) quite different from Prussian Germans (Protestant); likewise, the Milanese (who lived in a wealthy urban industrial center) shared little, language included, with the typical Sardinian peasant. But liberal nationalists had made the case that their high culture—especially their literary, musical, and theatrical traditions—overrode these differences, and emotional appeals by poets, composers, and orators convinced many people that this was indeed the case. Bismarck and Cavour merged this nationalist rhetoric with clever diplomacy—and the use of military force in a series of small conflicts—to forge united German and Italian nation-states.

These "unified" states rejected democracy. In the new Italy, which was a constitutional monarchy, less than 5 percent of the 25 million people could vote. The new German Empire (the Second Reich) had an assembly elected by all adult males (the Reichstag), but it had little power. The country was ruled by a combination of aristocrats and bureaucrats under a monarch. Liberals dominated in many localities, but only the emperor (the kaiser) could depose the prime minister. In fact, Bismarck continued to dominate Prussian politics for twenty-eight years, until fired in 1890 by Kaiser Wilhelm II. By that time, unification had yielded brisk economic growth both in Italy and, especially, Germany, but conflict between regions and political groups continued.

NATION BUILDING AND ETHNIC CONFLICT IN THE AUSTRO-HUNGARIAN EMPIRE

Bismarck's unification of Germany came at the expense of Habsburg supremacy in central Europe and (as we will see in the next section) of French territory and influence in the west. After Germany won a victory over the Austrian army in 1866, the Hungarian nobles who controlled the eastern Habsburg Empire forced the weakened dynasts to grant them home rule. In the Compromise of 1867, the Habsburgs agreed that their state would officially be known as the Austro-Hungarian Empire. But this move did not solve Austria-Hungary's nationality problems. In both the Hungarian and the Austrian halves of the dual state, Czechs, Poles, and other Slavs now began to clamor for their own power-sharing "compromise" or autonomous national homelands. They would, however, have to wait until the end of World War I.

DOMESTIC DISCONTENTS IN FRANCE AND BRITAIN

Although already unified as nation-states, Britain and France faced major difficulties. For the French, dealing with defeat at the hands of the Germans was the primary national concern in the decades leading up to World War I. For the British, issues of Irish separatism, the rise of the working class, and feminists' demands troubled the political arena.

Destabilization in France The Franco-Prussian War of 1870–1871 completed the unification of Germany. Germany took the French provinces of Alsace and Lorraine, and its victory destabilized France. The German siege of Paris, which lasted for more than three months, devastated the capital. Unprepared, Parisians had no food stocks and were compelled to eat all sorts of things, including two zoo elephants. Under terrible conditions and without effective leadership, the French capital resisted until January 1871, when the government signed a humiliating peace treaty. The Germans left in place a weak provisional French government. Refusing the negotiated peace, furious Parisians vented their rage and established their own government, proclaiming the city a utopia for workers. The leftist commune they established lasted until the provisional national government's army stormed Paris a few months later. At least 25,000 Parisians died in the bloody mop-up that followed. A "Third Republic" took the place of Napoleon III's empire, but it struggled to achieve stability. In the years following the Franco-Prussian War, France saw increasing conflict between classes and the rise of anti-German nationalism.

Irish Nationalism in Great Britain Although the English had long thought of themselves as a nation, the idea that all British people belonged in the same state was much more problematic. The kingdom of England—which was originally composed of England, clearly the dominant state, and Wales—became the kingdom of Great Britain when it united with Scotland in 1707 and Ireland in 1801. It was home to peoples whose historical experiences, religious backgrounds, and economic opportunities were very different. In the nineteenth century, British leaders wrestled in particular with demands for independence from Irish nationalists and lower-class agitation, especially in England. Beginning in 1832, England responded to class conflict at home by extending political rights to most men but not women. England finally established universal suffrage for all adult males after World War I, in 1918; roughly one-quarter of British women gained the right to vote at that time, and the rest did so a decade later.

Yet Ireland remained Britain's Achilles' heel. The British government was widely condemned for its failure to relieve Irish suffering during the potato famine of 1845–1849. Over the course of the early nineteenth century, Irish peasants had planted energy-rich and easy-to-cultivate potatoes on their remaining rocky and sandy land. A relatively healthy diet of potatoes and milk had fueled population growth and put more pressure on the land. When a continent-wide potato blight ravaged the island's crops in 1845, this monoculture turned into a recipe for widespread famine. Although the blight continued to decimate harvests for the next four years, the English stuck to their laissez-faire principles and were slow to send grain to relieve Irish suffering, resulting in the death of as many as a million and the emigration of about the same number. Many of these Irish emigrants made their way to England, seeking either passage to North America or work in the English mill towns. Like their Scottish brethren, they did not assimilate easily and often got the lowliest jobs. All of this, on top of 300 years of repressive English domination, spawned a mass movement for Irish home rule that continued into the twentieth century.

Born in opposition to the old monarchical regimes, European nationalism by the end of the nineteenth century had become a means used by liberal and conservative leaders alike to unite the people behind them. But just what they meant by "the people" remained bitterly contested. Continental powers increasingly resorted to an aggressive foreign policy and imperial expansion to maintain

The Irish Potato Famine Many families in Ireland were left desperate and starving in the aftermath of the potato crop failure and were forced to find sustenance wherever they could. In this engraving from the late nineteenth century, a group of people by the coast collect limpets and seaweed to eat.

popular support without granting political power to ordinary people. France alone, of the European great powers, had a parliamentary democracy elected by universal manhood suffrage.

Industry, Science, and Technology

A powerful combination of industry, science, and technology shaped the emerging nation-states in North America and western Europe. It also reordered the relationships among different parts of the world. One critical factor was that after 1850 western Europe and North America experienced a new phase of industrial development—essentially a second industrial revolution. Japan, too, joined the ranks of industrializing nations as its state-led program of industrial development started to pay dividends. These changes transformed the global economy and intensified rivalries among industrial societies.

NEW TECHNOLOGIES, MATERIALS, AND BUSINESS PRACTICES

New technologies and materials drove economic development in the late nineteenth century and led to new business practices. This period witnessed major technological changes with the arrival of new organic sources of power (like oil) and new ways to get old organic sources (like coal) to processing plants. These changes freed manufacturers from having to locate their plants close to their fuel sources. Not only did the most important new source of energy—electricity—permit factories to arise in areas with plenty of skilled workers, but it also slashed production costs. **Steel**, now cheaply produced because of technical innovations, became essential for shipbuilding and railways. Electricity and steel were part of a bundle of innovations that included chemicals and pharmaceuticals, which together transformed northwestern Europe, the United States, and Japan. Scientific research, too, boosted industrial development. German companies led the way in creating laboratories where university-trained chemists and physicists conducted research to serve industrial production. The United States likewise wedded scientific research with capitalist enterprise: universities and corporate laboratories produced swelling ranks of engineers and scientists, as well as patents.

The breakthroughs of the second industrial revolution ushered in new business practices, especially mass production and the giant integrated firm. No longer would modest investments suffice, as they had in Britain a century earlier. Now large banks were the major providers of funds. In Europe, limited-liability joint-stock companies were as wildly successful in raising capital on stock markets as they were in the United States. Companies like Standard Oil, U.S. Steel, and Siemens mobilized investments from large numbers of shareholders. The scale of these firms was awesome. U.S. Steel alone produced over half of the world's steel ingots, castings, rails, and heavy structural shapes—and nearly half of all its steel plates and sheets, which were vital in the construction of buildings, railroads, ships, and the like.

INTEGRATION OF THE WORLD ECONOMY

Not only did industrial change concentrate power in North Atlantic societies, but it also reinforced their power on the world economic stage and created a more integrated global economy. Europe and the United States increased their exports of new products; they also grew eager to control the importation of tropical commodities such as cocoa and coffee. While the North Atlantic societies were still largely self-sufficient in coal, iron, cotton, wool, and wheat (the major commodities of the first industrial revolution), the second industrial revolution bred a need for rubber, copper, oil, and bauxite (an ore used to make aluminum), which were not available domestically. Equally important, large pools of money became available for investing overseas. London may have lost its industrial leadership, but it retained dominance over the world's financial operations.

Movements of Labor and Technology Vast movements of workers took place to satisfy the labor demands of an increasingly integrated world economy. Indians moved thousands of miles from Asia to work on sugar plantations in the

Caribbean, Mauritius, and Fiji; to labor in South African mines; and to build railroads in East Africa. Chinese workers constructed railroads in the western United States and toiled on sugar plantations in Cuba. The Irish, Poles, Jews, Italians, and Greeks flocked to North America to fill its burgeoning factories. Italians also moved to Argentina to harvest wheat and corn.

With steam-powered gunboats and breech-loading rifles, Europeans opened new territories for trade and conquest. At home and in their colonial possessions, imperial powers constructed networks of railroads that carried people and goods from hinterlands to the coasts. From there, steamships bore them across the seas. Completion of the Suez Canal in 1869 shortened ship voyages between Europe and Asia and lowered the costs of interregional trade. Information moved even faster than cargoes, thanks to the laying of telegraph cables under the oceans, supplemented by overland telegraph lines.

Charles Darwin and Natural Selection Although machines were the most visible evidence that humans could master the universe, perhaps the most momentous shift in the conception of nature derived from the travels of one British scientist: **Charles Darwin** (1809–1882). Longing to see exotic fauna, he signed on for a four-year voyage in 1831 on a surveying vessel bound for Latin America and the South Seas. As the ship's naturalist, Darwin collected large quantities of specimens and recorded observations daily. After returning to England, he became convinced that the species of organic life had evolved under the uniform pressure of natural laws, not by means of a special, one-time creation as described in the Bible.

Darwin's theory, articulated in his *On the Origin of Species* (1859), laid out the principles of **natural selection**. Inevitably, he claimed, populations grew faster than the food supply; this condition created a "struggle for existence" among species. In later work he showed how the passing on of individual traits was also determined by what he called sexual selection—according to which the "best" mates are chosen for their strength, beauty, or talents and the less fit fail to reproduce at comparable rates. The outcome: the "fittest" survive to reproduce, while the less adaptable do not. Although Darwin's book dealt exclusively with animals (and mostly with birds), his readers immediately wondered what his theory implied for humans.

A passionate debate began among scientists and laymen, clerics and anthropologists. Some read Darwin's doctrine of natural selection to mean that it was natural for the strong nations to dominate the weak, or justifiable to allow disabled persons to die—something Darwin explicitly rejected. As more groups (mis)interpreted Darwin's theory to suit their own objectives, a set of beliefs known as social Darwinism legitimated the suffering of the underclasses in industrial society. In subsequent years Europeans would repeatedly suggest that they had evolved more than Africans and Asians. Extending Darwinian ideas far beyond the scientist's intent, some Europeans came to believe that nature itself gave them the right to rule others.

Imperialism and the Origins of Anticolonial Nationalism

Increasing rivalries among nations and social tensions within them produced an expansionist wave late in the nineteenth century. Although Africa became the primary focus of interest, a frenzy of territorial conquest overtook Asia as well. In China's territories, competition by foreign powers to establish spheres of influence heated up in the 1890s. And in India, imperial ambitions provoked the British to conquer Burma (present-day Myanmar). Moreover, Britain and Russia competed for preeminence from their respective outposts in Afghanistan and central Asia. In the Americas, new territories were usually incorporated as provinces of the expansionist state, making them integral parts of the nation.

In Asia and Africa, however, European and American imperialism turned far-flung territories into colonial possessions. The inhabitants of these colonial possessions were generally designated as subjects of the empire without the rights and privileges of citizens. Britain's imperial regime in India provided lessons to a generation of European colonial officials in Africa and other parts of Asia. Yet, even as Europe's colonial administrators looked to earlier imperial practices in India and the Caribbean for use in Africa, they also regarded African communities as less economically and culturally developed than Asian communities. Hence, they believed that Africans would require an extended period of colonial tutelage.

The proponents of European and North American colonization argued that colonial rule produced benefits for both the colonial peoples and the colonizers. Economically, colonies would be drawn into and profit from an emerging world economy. They would export primary products in high demand in the industrialized parts of the global economy—most notably cocoa, tea, coffee, diamonds, gold, and copper from Africa; rubber from the Dutch East Indies; huge quantities of cotton from India and Egypt; and beginning mainly after World War I, oil from the Middle East to fuel industrial economies. In return, colonial peoples would import much-needed manufactured commodities—clothing made from their raw cotton; processed foods made from coffee, cocoa, and tea; railway engines; and oceangoing vessels. But were the benefits evenly distributed, as some imperialist proponents claimed? A balance sheet of imperialism is difficult to construct, but the biggest beneficiaries were clearly not African and Asian peasant cultivators, as apologists asserted, or even the workers in western factories, whose wages, while rising, still remained low. Profits flowed mainly to European-run export-import firms, large global banks, and wealthy industrialists.

Not surprisingly, colonized peoples resisted the imposition of economic systems that destroyed older trading and agricultural systems and benefited only the colonial extractors. Resistance took different forms, including the demand for national self-determination. In many parts of colonial Asia, early forms of resistance, usually put down with savage reprisals, were followed by organized political protest and the formation of nationalist political parties. The African continent, the last to be colonized, at first went through an early phase of armed resistance to colonial rule, which was repressed with considerable bloodshed. After World War I, colonial critics followed in the footsteps of the Asian anticolonial nationalists. They, too, created anticolonial, mainly nonviolent, political organizations, seeking at first the redress of colonial grievances, such as lost lands. Many of these nations would have to wait until the post–World War II period to achieve full independence.

INDIA AND THE IMPERIAL MODEL

Britain's rule in India provided a model for other imperialist governments by developing the colony's infrastructure in order to maximize British profits from trade. Having suppressed the Indian Rebellion of 1857 (see Chapter 16), authorities revamped the colonial administration. From the British point of view, Indians were not to be appeased—and certainly not to be brought into British public life. But they did have to be governed, and the economy had to be revived. So, after replacing the East India Company's rule with crown government in 1858, the British set out to make India into a more secure and productive colony. This period of British sovereignty was known as the **Raj** ("rule").

Sinews of the Raj The British allowed several native princes to remain in power as long as they accepted imperial paramountcy. This photograph shows a roadbuilding project in one such princely state. Officials of the Muslim princely ruler and British advisers supervise the workers.

The most urgent tasks facing the British in India were modernizing its transportation and communication systems and transforming the territory into an integrated colonial state. These changes had begun under the governor-general of the East India Company, Lord Dalhousie, who oversaw the development of India's modern infrastructure. After the British suppressed the revolt, they took up the construction of public works with renewed vigor. Railways were a key element both in the pacification (they shuttled troops to danger zones) and in the later reform project. The first railway line opened in 1853, and by 1910 India had 30,627 miles of track in operation—making it the fourth-largest railway system in the world.

Construction of other public works followed. Engineers built dams across rivers to tame their force and to irrigate lands; workers installed a grid of telegraph lines that opened communication between distant parts of the region. These public works served imperial and economic purposes: India was to become a consumer of British manufactures and a supplier of primary staples such as cotton, tea, and wheat. On the hillsides of the island of Ceylon (now Sri Lanka) and the northeastern plains of India, the British established vast plantations to grow tea—which was then marketed in England as a healthier alternative to Chinese green tea. India also became an important consumer of British manufactures, especially textiles, in an ironic turnabout of its centuries-old tradition of exporting its own cotton and silk textiles.

The reform efforts of the Raj made India into a unified territory and enabled its inhabitants to begin to regard themselves as "Indians." These were the first steps to becoming a "nation" like Italy and the United States, but there were profound differences. Above all, as colonial subjects Indians did not enjoy basic

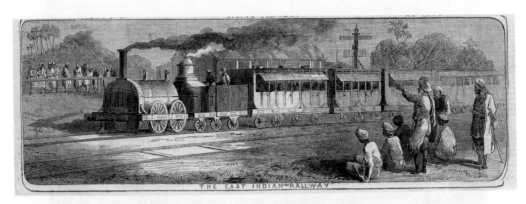

Railways in India Following the uprising of 1857, India came under the rule of the British crown and government through the newly established Department of India and was no longer a concession of the East India Company. The British then built an extensive system of railroads to develop India as a profitable colony and to maintain military security. Railways and telegraphs, which connected the interior of the country to the cities and ports of the coast, were more instrumental than anything else in integrating the colony—and eventually the nation. This engraving shows the East India Railway around 1863. The train and the telegraph post overshadow the lush vegetation in the background and the cheering Indians who watch in idealized marvel.

civic and human rights, and even elites lacked the vote. Other European powers followed the British example in trying to modernize and integrate their colonies economically without welcoming colonial peoples into the life of the nation.

DUTCH COLONIAL RULE IN INDONESIA

Decades before the British government took control of India away from the East India Company, Holland had terminated the rule of the Dutch East India Company over Indonesia. Beginning in the 1830s, the Dutch government took administrative responsibility over Indonesian affairs. Holland's new colonial officials envisioned a more regulated colonial economy than that of their British counterparts in India. For example, they ordered Indonesian villagers to allocate one-third of their land for cultivating coffee beans, an important export. In return, the colonial government paid a set price (well below world market prices) and placed a ceiling on rents owed to landowners.

These policies had dreadful local consequences. For example, increased production of the export crops of coffee beans, sugar, and tobacco meant reduced food production for the local population. By the 1840s and 1850s, famine spread across Java; over 300,000 Indonesians perished from starvation. Surviving villagers voiced growing discontent, prompting harsh crackdowns by colonial forces. Back in Holland, the embarrassing spectacle of colonial oppression prompted calls for reform. Thus, in the 1860s the Dutch government introduced what it called an ethical policy for governing Asian colonies: it reduced governmental exploitation and encouraged Dutch settlement of the islands and more private enterprise. For Indonesians, however, the replacement of government agents with private merchants made little difference. In some areas, islanders put up fierce resistance. On the sprawling island of Sumatra, for instance, armed villagers fought off Dutch invaders. After decades of warfare, Sumatra was finally subdued in 1904. The shipping of Indonesian staples continued to enrich the Dutch.

COLONIZING AFRICA

No region felt the impact of European colonialism more powerfully than Africa. In 1880, the only two large European colonial possessions there were French Algeria and two British-ruled South African states, the Cape Colony and Natal. But within a mere thirty years, seven European states had carved almost all of Africa into colonial possessions.

Partitioning the African Landmass In the context of heightened international rivalries, Portugal called for an international conference to discuss claims to Africa. Meeting in Berlin between 1884 and 1885, delegates from Europe, the United States, and the Ottoman Empire agreed to carve up Africa and to recognize the claims of the first European power that claimed control of a given territory. Colonizers rushed to plant their flags as widely as possible, lest they be outmaneuvered by their rivals.

The consequences for Africa were devastating. Nearly 70 percent of the newly drawn borders failed to correspond to older demarcations of ethnicity, language, culture, and commerce—for Europeans knew little of the landmass beyond its coast and rivers. They based their new colonial boundaries on European trading centers rather than on the location of African population groups. (See Map 17.3.) In West Africa, for example, the Yoruba were split between the French in Dahomey and the British in southwestern Nigeria, and a segment of the very large and dynamic Mandara peoples came under British-ruled Nigeria.

Several motives led the European powers into their frenzied partition of Africa. Although European businesses were primarily interested in Egypt and southern Africa, where their investments were lucrative, small-scale traders and investors harbored fantasies of great treasures locked in the vast uncharted interior. Politicians, publicists, and the reading public also took an interest. The writings of explorers like David Livingstone (1813–1873), a Scottish doctor and missionary, and Henry Morton Stanley (1841–1904), an adventurer in the pay of the *New York Herald*, excited readers with accounts of Africa as a continent of unlimited economic potential.

The most determined of the African empire builders was Leopold II (r. 1865–1909), king of the Belgians. In southern Africa, the British champion of imperialism Cecil Rhodes (1853–1902) brought the Rhodesias, Nyasaland, Bechuanaland, the Transvaal, and the Orange Free State into the British Empire as part of a design to have British territories stretching all the way from the Cape of Good Hope in South Africa to Cairo in Egypt.

Other Europeans saw Africa as a grand opportunity for converting souls to Christianity. In fact, Europe's civilizing mission was an important motive in the scramble for African territory. In Uganda, northern Nigeria, and central and western Africa, missionaries went ahead of European armies, begging the European statesmen to follow their lead.

African Resistance Africans faced two unappealing options: they could capitulate to the Europeans and negotiate to limit the loss of their autonomy, or they could fight to preserve their sovereignty. Only a few chose to negotiate. Lat Dior, a Muslim warlord in Senegal, refused to let the French build a railway through his kingdom. "As long as I live, be well assured," he wrote the French commandant, "I shall oppose with all my might the construction of this railway. I will always answer no, no, and I will never make you any other reply. Even were I to go to rest, my horse, *Malay*, would give you the same answer." Conflict was inevitable, and Lat Dior lost his life in a battle with the French in 1886. Most Africans who resisted were unaware of the Europeans' superior military technology, and even those who adapted their tactics to meet the challenge were unable to keep the Europeans out indefinitely.

Only Menelik II of Ethiopia successfully repulsed the Europeans, for he knew how to play rivals off one another. By doing so, he procured weapons from the

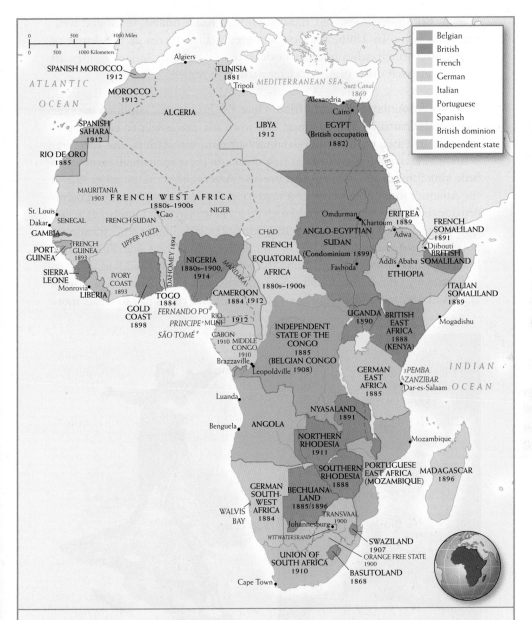

Legend:
- Belgian
- British
- French
- German
- Italian
- Portuguese
- Spanish
- British dominion
- Independent state

Map 17.3 Partition of Africa, 1880–1914

....

The partition of Africa took place between the early 1880s and the outbreak of World War I.

- Which two European powers gained the most territory in Africa?
- Which two African states managed to remain independent? What kind of economic and political gain did European powers realize through the colonization of Africa? Did any of the European states realize their ambitions in Africa?

French, British, Russians, and Italians. He also had a united, loyal, and well-equipped army. In 1896, his troops routed Italian forces at the Battle of Adwa, after which Adwa became a celebrated moment in African history. Its memory inspired many of Africa's later nationalist leaders.

Colonial Administrations in Africa Once the Europeans' euphoria over the gains of the partition and conquest had worn off, the power to rule the colonies fell to "men on the spot"—military adventurers, settlers, and entrepreneurs whose main goal was to get rich quick. As these individuals established little kingdoms in some areas, Africans (like Amerindians on the other side of the Atlantic) found themselves confined to territories where they could barely provide for themselves. To uphold such an invasive system at minimal expense, Europeans created permanent standing armies by equipping their African supporters, whom they either bribed or compelled to join their side. Such armies bullied local communities into doing the colonial authorities' bidding.

Eventually, these rough-and-ready systems led to violent revolts from aggrieved Africans, and in their aftermath the colonial rulers had to create more

Europeans in Africa *Left:* Henry Morton Stanley was one of the most famous of the nineteenth-century explorers in Africa. He first made his reputation when he located the British missionary-explorer David Livingstone, feared dead, in the interior of Africa, uttering the famous words, "Dr. Livingstone, I presume." Stanley worked on behalf of King Leopold, establishing the Belgian king's claims to territories in the Congo and often using superior weaponry to cow African opponents. *Right:* The zealous British imperialist Cecil Rhodes endeavored to bring as much of Africa as he could under British colonial rule. He had an ambition to create a swath of British-controlled territory that would stretch from the Cape in South Africa to Cairo in Egypt, as this cartoon shows.

efficient administrations, dedicated to providing health care and education for the colonized. As in India, colonial powers in Africa laid the foundations for future nation-state organizations. Once information trickling out of Africa revealed that the imperial governments were not realizing their goal of bringing "civilization" to the "uncivilized" and creating easy profits, each European power implemented a new form of colonial rule, stripping the strongman conquerors of their absolute powers, monitoring them more closely, and assuming greater responsibility for the conquered peoples.

Europeans brought their extreme racial attitudes toward peoples of color into Africa. They discovered similar views toward Whiteness and Blackness within African societies and were quick to take advantage of this overlap. In West Africa, the British, French, and Germans lacked a large administrative staff and were wholly dependent on noncommissioned African soldiers and police forces to maintain their authority. They quickly gravitated to those ethnic groups who regarded themselves as superior, at least those willing to make themselves available as collaborators with their conquerors. The Tuareg peoples, the Arabs, or Fulani, and the notables among the Songhai peoples looked down on others, many of whom were their vassals or were actually enslaved to them. They used the Arabic words for the colors white (*bidan*) and black (*sudan*) as markers of their superiority and the inferiority of others. In particular, the Tuareg and Fulani ruling elites accepted European rule in hopes that the colonial period would be a short one, from which they would emerge with powers intact. In response, the Europeans delegated much local authority to these former rulers.

Over time, stabilized colonies began to deliver on their economic promise. Whereas early imperialism in Africa had relied on the export of ivory and wild rubber, after these resources became depleted, the colonies pursued other exports. From the rain forests came cocoa, coffee, palm oil, and palm kernels. From the highlands of East Africa came tea, coffee, sisal (used in cord and twine), and pyrethrum (a flower used to make insecticide). Another important commodity was long-staple, high-quality cotton, grown in Egypt and the Anglo-Egyptian Sudan. Indeed, tropical commodities from all across Africa (as from India and Latin America) flowed to industrializing societies.

Battle of Adwa Portrait of King Menelik, who defeated the Italian forces at the Battle of Adwa in 1896, thus saving his country from European colonization.

The boom in late nineteenth-century colonial trade had far-reaching effects. It enabled western corporations to grab land in southeast Asia and especially Africa. It also made it possible for the industrialized nations of western Europe and North America to gain access to valuable natural resources beyond their borders. To take one notable example, between 1800 and 1914, world production of cotton rose by a factor of twenty-five. By the century's end, cotton cultivation covered an area the size of the United Kingdom, and some 1.5 percent of the world's population was involved in growing and shipping the crop and turning it into textiles.

European colonizers thought Africans would benefit from their role in global trade, but, in truth, Africans gained little, while the price they paid was substantial. Mining was particularly destructive. The discovery of diamonds and gold in the late nineteenth century in South Africa not only created unheard-of fortunes for ardent imperialists like Cecil Rhodes but threatened family life and traditional agriculture all over the region. Mining required an immense labor supply, often recruited by force. While European-run companies made huge profits, the absence of adult African males meant that the task of maintaining small subsistence farms fell to those who remained behind—older men and women, wives of mine workers, and children.

To observers, the European empires in Africa seemed solid and durable, but in fact European colonial rule there was fragile. For all of British Africa, the only all-British force was 5,000 men garrisoned in Egypt. Elsewhere, European officers depended on African military and police forces. And prior to 1914, the number of British administrative officers available for the whole of northern Nigeria was less than 500. These were hardly strong foundations for colonial rule. It would not take much to destabilize the European order in Africa.

Tuareg Resistance Tuareg warriors put up stiff resistance against European intruders. The Tuareg people ran the caravan routes across the Sahara from North to West Africa and became powerful and wealthy thanks to expanding trade. Since they were also nomadic, they had large herds of camels, which they deployed in battle with peerless skill. Trade also gave them access to weapons and they played European rivals against one another. The Sahara, therefore, was a perennial source of resistance to colonization. This image depicts Tuareg warriors wiping out a French patrol in the early twentieth century at a time when publics in Europe were starting to question the legitimacy of empire.

THE AMERICAN EMPIRE

The United States, like Europe, was drawn into the mania of overseas expansion and empire building. Echoing the earlier rhetoric of Manifest Destiny, the expansionists of the 1890s claimed that Americans still had a divine mission to spread their superior civilization and their Christian faith around the globe. However, America's new imperialists followed the European model of colonialism from Asia and Africa: colonies were to provide harbors for American vessels, supply raw materials to American industries, and purchase the surplus production of American farms and factories. These new territorial acquisitions were not intended for American settlement or statehood. Nor were their inhabitants to become American citizens, for non-White foreigners were considered unfit for incorporation into the American nation.

The pressure to expand came to a head in the late 1890s, when the United States declared war on Spain and invaded the Philippines, Puerto Rico, and Cuba. The United States annexed Puerto Rico after minimal protest, but Cubans and Filipinos resisted becoming colonial subjects. Bitterness ran particularly high among Filipinos, to whom American leaders had promised independence if they joined in the war against Spain. Betrayed, Filipino rebels launched a war for independence in the name of a Filipino nation. In two years of fighting, over 5,000 Americans and perhaps 200,000 Filipinos perished. The outcome: the Philippines became a colony of the United States.

Colonies in the Philippines and Puerto Rico laid the foundations for a revised model of U.S. expansionism. The earlier pattern had been to turn Native American lands into privately owned farmsteads and to extend the Atlantic market across the continent. But now, in this new era, the nation's largest corporations (with government support) aggressively intervened in the affairs of neighbors near and far. Following the Spanish-American War (1898), the United States repeatedly sent troops to many Caribbean and Central American countries. The Americans preferred to turn these regimes into dependent territories, rather than making them part of the United States itself (as with Alaska and Hawaii) or converting them into formal colonies (as the Europeans had done in Africa and Asia).

IMPERIALISM AND CULTURE

Europeans and Americans set out to bring "civilization" to the peoples of their colonies. At least since the Crusades, Europeans had regularly written and thought about others. These images and ideas had grown more numerous and varied as commerce and colonialism in Asia and the Atlantic world increased; they served various purposes, including those of informing, entertaining, and flattering Europeans as well as criticizing their own culture. As Europeans and Americans grew more and more confident in their achievements, they became convinced that their arts and sciences were superior—and curiosity often turned to disdain. In time Europeans presumed that the only true modern civilization was their own; other peoples might have reigned over great empires in antiquity but had since fallen into decadence and decline. Artists and writers portrayed nonwestern peoples as exotic, sensuous, and economically backward in a genre scholars have come to call Orientalism.

Although Darwin remained ambivalent about the nature of race, his followers embraced the idea of stable racial differences that evolved only on the longest of time horizons, at a glacial pace, over thousands of years rather than decades or centuries. They ratified a view of "lower" and "higher" races, the former stuck in the past and the latter anointed by God (or, in the case of social Darwinists, by nature itself) to define and dictate civilization's future. Europeans' relationship to others might now be one of condescending sympathy or of ruthless exploitation, but the result was that it was up to White Europeans and Americans to create modern culture. The darker people, social Darwinists argued, were not nearly as fully "evolved" as the Europeans and could not hope to catch up. At best they could be taught European languages, sciences, and religions, and perhaps be made to evolve more quickly. It is telling

The Women of Algiers in Their Apartment An oil painting by Eugène Delacroix (1798–1863) of Algerian women being attended by a Black servant. European painters in the nineteenth century often used images of women to portray Arab Muslim society.

that French colonial subjects who did well at French schools were known as *evolués*, "the evolved ones."

Celebrating Imperialism Especially in middle- and upper-class circles, Europeans celebrated their imperial triumphs. After the invention of photographic film and the Eastman Kodak camera in 1888, imperial images surfaced in popular forms such as postcards and advertisements. Imperial themes also decorated packaging materials; tins of coffee, tea, tobacco, and chocolates featured pictures highlighting the commodities' colonial origins. Cigarettes often had names like "Admiral," "Royal Navy," "Fighter," and "Grand Fleet." Some of this served as propaganda, produced by investors in imperial commodities or by colonial pressure groups.

Propaganda promoted imperialism abroad but also inspired changes at home. For example, champions of empire argued that if the British population did not grow fast enough to fill the world's sparsely settled regions, then the population of other nations would. Population was power, and the number of healthy children provided an accurate measure of global influence. "Empire cannot be built on rickety and flat-chested citizens," warned a British member of Parliament in 1905. Empire and imperialism carried European, American, and, to a lesser extent, Japanese power and culture throughout the world. In terms of the size of the populations they ruled, this era was the high point of European and Euro-American predominance.

Pressures of Expansion in Japan, Russia, and China

The challenge of integrating political communities and extending territorial borders was a problem not just for western Europe and the United States. Other societies also aimed to overcome domestic dissent and establish larger domains. Japan, Russia, and China provide three contrasting models; their differing forms of expansion eventually led them to fight over possessions in East Asia.

JAPAN'S TRANSFORMATION AND EXPANSION

Starting in the 1860s, Japanese rulers tried to recast their country less as an old dynasty and more as a modern nation-state. Since the early seventeenth century, the Tokugawa shogunate had kept outsiders within strict limits and thwarted internal unrest. But after an American naval officer, Commodore Matthew Perry, entered Edo Bay in 1853 with a fleet of steam-powered ships, other Americans, Russians, Dutch, and British followed in his wake. These

Perry Arrives in Japan A Japanese woodblock print portraying the uninvited arrival in Edo (Tokyo) Bay on August 7, 1853, of a tall American ship, which was commanded by Matthew Perry. This arrival marked the end of Japan's ability to fully control the terms of its interactions with foreigners.

outsiders forced the Tokugawa rulers to sign humiliating treaties that opened Japanese ports, slapped limits on Japanese tariffs, and exempted foreigners from Japanese laws. Younger Japanese, especially among the military (samurai) elites, felt that Japan should respond by adapting, not rejecting, western practices.

In 1868, a group of reformers toppled the Tokugawa shogunate and promised to return Japan to its mythic greatness by creating a modern empire, as in Britain, Russia, and France. Emperor Mutsuhito—the Meiji ("Enlightened Rule") Emperor—became the symbol of a new Japan; he ruled over a professionalized military that sidelined the old samurai class while the aristocratic daimyos gave way to a parliament. Women emerged from private seclusion. Schools for women, like the "Tokyo Women's School," popped up around the country. Furthermore, the cult of "a good wife and a wise mother" authorized women to take a more important role in promoting national welfare.

Mutsuhito's reign (1868–1912) was called the **Meiji Restoration**. By founding schools, initiating a propaganda campaign, and revamping the army to create a single "national" fighting force, the Meiji government promoted a political community that stressed linguistic and ethnic homogeneity, as well as superiority compared to others. In this way the Meiji leaders overcame age-old regional

Economic Transformation of Japan During the Meiji period, the government transformed the economy by building railroads, laying telegraph lines, founding a postal system, and encouraging the formation of giant firms known as *zaibatsu*, which were family organizations consisting of factories, import-export businesses, and banks. Here we see a raw-silk-reeling factory that was run by one of the *zaibatsu*.

divisions, subdued local political authorities, and mobilized the country to face rivals for Pacific supremacy.

Economic Development One of the Meiji period's remarkable achievements was the nation's economic transformation. After 1871, when the government banned the feudal system and allowed peasants to become small landowners, farmers improved their agrarian techniques and saw their standard of living rise. The energetic new government unified the currency around the yen, created a postal system, introduced tax reforms, and established an advanced civil service system. In 1889, the Meiji government introduced a constitution (based largely on the German model). The following year, 450,000 people— about 1 percent of the population—elected Japan's first parliament, the Imperial Diet.

As the government sold valuable enterprises to the people who had provided strong support, it created private economic dynasties. The new large companies (such as Sumitomo, Yasuda, Mitsubishi, and Mitsui) were trusted family organizations. Fathers, sons, cousins, and uncles ran different parts of large integrated corporations—some in charge of banks, some running the trade wing, some overseeing factories. Women played a crucial role, not just as custodians of the home but also as cultivators of important family alliances, especially among potential marriage partners. In contrast to American limited-liability firms, which issued shares on stock markets to anonymous buyers, Japan's version of large-scale managerial capitalism was a personal affair.

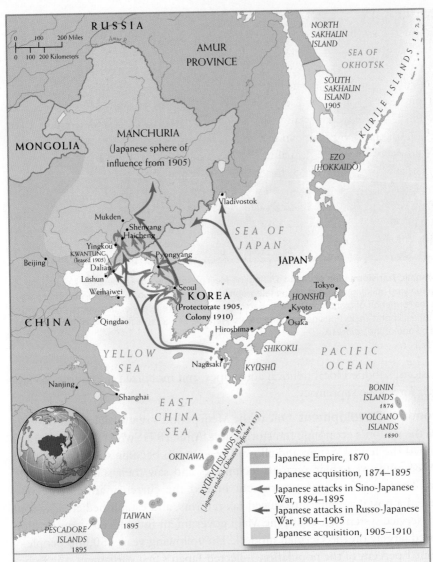

Map within image contains the following labels:

RUSSIA

AMUR PROVINCE

Amur R.

0 100 200 Miles
0 100 200 Kilometers

NORTH SAKHALIN ISLAND

SEA OF OKHOTSK

SOUTH SAKHALIN ISLAND 1905

KURILE ISLANDS 1875

MONGOLIA

MANCHURIA
(Japanese sphere of influence from 1905)

EZO (HOKKAIDŌ)

Mukden

Shenyang
Haicheng

Yingkou

KWANTUNG (leased 1905)

Beijing

Dalian

Lüshun

Weihaiwei

Pyongyang

Vladivostok

SEA OF JAPAN

JAPAN

Tokyo

HONSHŪ

Kyoto

Osaka

Seoul

KOREA
(Protectorate 1905, Colony 1910)

CHINA

Qingdao

Hiroshima

SHIKOKU

PACIFIC OCEAN

YELLOW SEA

Nagasaki

KYŪSHŪ

Nanjing

Shanghai

EAST CHINA SEA

BONIN ISLANDS 1876

VOLCANO ISLANDS 1890

OKINAWA

RYŪKYŪ ISLANDS 1874
(Japanese establish Okinawa Prefecture 1879)

Japanese Empire, 1870

Japanese acquisition, 1874–1895

Japanese attacks in Sino-Japanese War, 1894–1895

Japanese attacks in Russo-Japanese War, 1904–1905

Japanese acquisition, 1905–1910

TAIWAN 1895

PESCADORE ISLANDS 1895

Map 17.4 Japanese Expansion, 1870–1910

Under the Meiji Restoration, the Japanese state built a strong national identity and competed with foreign powers for imperial advantage in East Asia.

- According to the map, what were the first areas that the Japanese Empire acquired as it started to expand?

- What two empires' spheres of influence were affected by Japan's aggressive attempts at expansion?

- According to your reading, what were the new Japanese state's objectives? How were they similar to or different from those of expansionist European states in the same period?

Expansionism and Conflict with Neighbors As in many other emerging nation-states, expansion was a tempting prospect to the Japanese. It offered the promise of more markets for selling goods and obtaining staples, and it was a way to burnish the image of national superiority and greatness. The Meiji moved first to take over the kingdom of the Ryūkyūs, southwest of Japan. (See Map 17.4.) A small show of force, only 160 Japanese soldiers, was enough to establish the new Okinawa Prefecture there in 1879. The Japanese regarded the people of the Ryūkyūs as an ethnic minority and refused to incorporate them into the nation-state on equal terms. In contrast with the British in India or the Americans in Puerto Rico, the Japanese conquerors refused to train a native Ryūkyūan governing class. Meiji intellectuals insisted that the "backward" Okinawans were unfit for local self-rule and representation.

The Japanese fixed upon Korea, which put their plans on a collision course with China's. In a formal treaty, the Japanese recognized Korea as an independent state (expected to be no longer dominated by China), opened Korea to trade, and won the right to apply Japanese law in Korea. As a result, the Chinese worried that soon the Japanese would try to take over Korea. These fears were well founded, for Japanese designs on Korea eventually sparked the Sino-Japanese War of 1894–1895, in which the upstart Japan delivered a humiliating defeat to the Chinese military.

The Sino-Japanese War accelerated Japan's rapid transformation into a nation-state and a colonial power with no peer in Asia. Having lost the war, China ceded the province of Taiwan to the Japanese. Japan also annexed Korea in 1910 and converted Taiwan and Korea into the twin jewels of its young empire. Like the British in India, the Japanese regarded their colonial subjects as racially inferior and unworthy of the privileges of citizenship. And like other imperial powers, the Japanese expected their possessions to serve the metropolitan center.

RUSSIAN TRANSFORMATION AND EXPANSION

Russia expanded out of a sense of a civilizing mission and a need to defend against other countries expanding along its immense borders. Facing an emerging Germany, a British presence in the Middle East and Persia, a consolidating China, and an increasingly powerful Japan, Russia knew it would have to extend its already large territorial domain. So it established a number of expansionist fronts simultaneously: southwest to the Black Sea, south into the Caucasus and Turkestan, and east into Manchuria. (See Map 17.5.) Success depended on annexing territories and establishing protectorates over conquered peoples.

Looking west and south, Russia invaded the Ottoman territories of Moldavia (present-day Moldova) and Walachia (present-day Romania) in 1853. The invasion provoked opposition from Britain and France, which joined with the Ottomans to defeat Russia in the Crimean War (1853–1856). By exposing

Russia's lack of modern weapons and its problems in supplying troops without a railway system, the defeat spurred a course of aggressive modernization and expansion.

Modernization and Internal Reform In the 1860s, Tsar Alexander II launched a wave of "Great Reforms" to make Russia more modern and to preserve its status as a great power. In 1861, for example, a decree emancipated peasants from serfdom. Other changes included a sharp reduction in the duration of military service, a program of education for the conscripts, and the beginnings of a mass school system to teach children reading, writing, and Russian culture. Starting in the 1890s, state-sponsored industrialization led to the building of railroads and factories and stimulated the expansion of the steel, coal, and petroleum industries. But while the reforms strengthened the state, they did not enhance

Map 17.5 Russian Expansion, 1801–1914

....

The Russian state continued to expand in the nineteenth century.

• According to this map, what lands did Russia acquire during the period 1796–1855? What lands did it acquire next?

• Compare this map of Russian expansion with Map 13.7. How did the direction of Russia's expansion change in the nineteenth century?

• Which states did the expanding Russian Empire more resemble in this era, western European states (such as Great Britain) or American states (such as the United States)?

The Trans-Siberian Railroad Russia's decision to build a railway across Siberia to the Pacific Ocean derived from a desire to expand the empire's power in East Asia and to forestall British advances in Asia. The colossal undertaking, which claimed the lives of thousands of workers, reached completion just as Russia clashed militarily with Japan. The new railroad ferried Russian troops over long distances to battles, such as the one at Mukden, in Manchuria, which was then the largest land battle in the history of warfare.

the lives of common people. Workers in Russia were brutally exploited, even by the standards of the industrial revolution. Also, large landowners had kept most of the empire's fertile land, and the peasants had to pay substantial redemption fees for the poorer-quality plots they received.

The reforms revealed a fundamental problem: the rulers were eager to reform society, but not the basis of government (autocracy). This caused liberals, conservatives, and malcontents alike to question the state-led modernizing mission. Before long, in the press, courtrooms, and streets, men and women denounced the regime. Revolutionaries engaged in terror and assassination. In 1881, a terrorist bomb killed the tsar. In the 1890s, following a period of famine, the radical doctrines of Marxism (see Chapter 16) gained popularity in Russia. Even aristocratic intellectuals, such as the author of *War and Peace*, Count Leo Tolstoy, lamented their despotic government.

Territorial Expansion Yet the critics of internal reform did not hold back the Russian expansionists, who believed they had to take over certain lands to keep them out of rivals' hands. So they conquered the highland people of the Caucasus Mountains to prevent Ottomans and Persians from encroaching on Russia's southern flank. And they battled the British over areas between Turkestan and British India, such as Persia (Iran) and Afghanistan. Although some Russians moved to these lands, they never became a majority there. The new provinces were multiethnic, multireligious communities that were only partially integrated into the Russian nation.

Perhaps the most impressive Russian expansion occurred in East Asia, where the Amur River basin offered rich lands, mineral deposits, and access to the Pacific Ocean. The Chinese also wanted to colonize this area, which lay just north of Manchuria. After twenty years of struggle, Russia claimed the land north and south of the Amur River and in 1860 founded Vladivostok, a port on the Pacific Ocean whose name signified "Rule the East." Deciding to focus on these areas in Asia, the Russian government sold its one territory in North America (Alaska) to the United States. Then, to link central Russia and the western part of the country to its East Asian spoils, the government began construction of the Trans-Siberian Railroad in the 1890s. When it was fully completed in 1916, the new railroad bridged the east and the west.

Governing a Diverse Empire Russia was a huge empire whose rulers were only partially effective at integrating its diverse regions into a political community. Unlike the United States, which displaced or slaughtered native populations during its expansion across an entire continent, Russia tolerated and taxed many of the new peoples. The state's approach ranged from outright repression (of Poles and Jews) to favoritism (toward Baltic Germans and Finns), although the beneficiaries of favoritism often later lost favor if they became too strong. Further, unlike the United States, which managed to pacify borders with its weaker neighbors, Russia faced the constant suspicions of Persians and Ottomans and the menace of British troops in Afghanistan. In East Asia, a clash with expansionist Japan loomed on the horizon.

CHINA UNDER PRESSURE

While the Russians and Japanese scrambled to copy European models of industrialism and imperialism, the Qing were slower to mobilize against threats from the west. Even as the European powers were dividing up China into spheres of influence, Qing officials were much more worried about internal revolts and threats from their northern borders than European incursions.

Adopting Western Learning and Skills A growing number of Chinese officials recognized the superior armaments and technology of rival powers and were deeply troubled by the threat posed by European military might. Starting in the 1860s, reformist bureaucrats sought to adopt elements of western learning and technological skills—but with the intention of keeping the core Chinese culture intact.

This so-called **Self-Strengthening movement** included a variety of new ventures: arsenals, shipyards, coal mines, a steamship company to contest the foreign domination of coastal shipping, and schools for learning foreign ways and languages. Most interesting was the dispatch abroad of about 120 schoolboys under the charge of Yung Wing. The first Chinese graduate of an American college (Yale University, 1854), Yung believed that western education would greatly benefit Chinese students, so he took his charges to Connecticut in the 1870s to attend school and live with American families. Conservatives at the Qing court were soon dismayed by reports of the students' interest in Christianity and aptitude for baseball. In 1881, after the U.S. government refused to admit the boys into military academies, the court summoned the students home.

Yung Wing's abortive educational mission was not the only setback for the Self-Strengthening movement, for skepticism about western technology was rife among conservative officials. Some insisted that the introduction of machinery would lead to unemployment; others worried that railways would facilitate western military maneuvers and lead to an invasion; still others complained that the crisscrossing tracks disturbed the harmony between humans and nature. The first short railway track ever laid in China was torn up in 1877 shortly after being built, and the country had only 179 miles of track prior to 1895.

Although they did not acknowledge the railroad's usefulness, the Chinese did adopt other new technologies to access a wider range of information. For example, by the early 1890s there were about a dozen Chinese-language newspapers (as distinct from the foreign-language press) published in major cities, with the largest ones having a circulation of 10,000 to 15,000. To avoid government intervention, these papers sidestepped political controversy; instead, they featured commercial news and literary contributions. In 1882, the newspaper *Shenbao* made use of a new telegraph line to publish dispatches within China.

Internal Reform Efforts China's defeat by Japan in the Sino-Japanese War (1894–1895), sparked by quarrels over Korea, prompted a more serious attempt at reform by the Qing. Known as the Hundred Days' Reform, the episode lasted only from June to September 1898. The force behind it was a thirty-seven-year-old scholar named Kang Youwei and his twenty-two-year-old student Liang Qichao. Citing rulers such as Peter the Great of Russia and the Meiji Emperor of Japan as their inspiration, the reformers urged Chinese leaders to develop a railway network, a state banking system, a modern postal service, and institutions to foster the development of agriculture, industry, and commerce. The reform failed when a group of conservative leaders placed the Dowager Cixi on the throne, rescinded the reformist laws, and executed six of the reform movement's major leaders. They did not, however, capture Kang Youwei, who fled to Japan.

But, in truth, the reforms of the Self-Strengthening movement were ineffectual: they were too modest and poorly implemented. Very few Chinese acquired new skills. Despite talk of modernizing, the civil service examination remained based on Confucian classics and still opened the only doors to government service. Governing elites were not yet ready to reinvent the principles of their political community, and they adhered instead to the traditional dynastic structure.

By the late nineteenth century, the success of the Qing regime in expanding its territories a century earlier seemed like a distant memory, as various powers repeatedly forced it to make economic and territorial concessions. Unlike Japan or Russia, however, the Qing government resisted comprehensive social reforms (until after the turn of the twentieth century), and its policies left the country vulnerable to both external aggression and internal instability.

Conclusion

Between 1850 and 1914, most of the world's people lived not in nation-states but in land empires or in the overseas colonies of nation-states. But leaders in colonial territories, often responding to popular upheavals and destabilizing economic changes, began to see independent nation-states as the most desirable form of governance for their regions.

Although the ideal of "a people" united by territory, history, and culture grew increasingly popular worldwide, it was not easy to make it a reality. Official histories, national heroes, novels, poetry, and music helped, but central to the process of nation formation were the actions of bureaucrats. Asserting sovereignty over what it claimed as national territory, the state "nationalized" diverse populations by creating a unified system of law, education, military service, and government.

Colonization beyond borders was another part of nation building in many societies. In these efforts, territorial conquests took place under the banner of nationalist endeavors. In Europe, the Americas, Japan, and to some extent Russia, the intertwined processes of nation building and territorial expansion were most effective. Expansion abroad consolidated national identities at home.

However, the integrating impulses of imperialist nation-states did not wipe out local differences, mute class antagonisms, or eliminate gender inequalities. Even as Europeans and Americans came to see themselves as chosen—by God or by natural selection—to rule the rest, they suffered deep divisions. Not everyone identified with the nation-state or the empire, or agreed on what it meant to belong or to conquer. But by the century's end, racist advocates and colonial lobbyists seem to have convinced many that their interests and destinies were bound up with their countries' unity, prosperity, and global clout.

Ironically, imperial expansion had an unintended consequence, for self-determination could also apply to racial or ethnic minorities at home and in the colonies. Armed with the rhetoric of progress and uplift, colonial authorities tried to subjugate distant people, but colonial subjects themselves often asserted the language of "nation" and accused imperial overlords of betraying their own lofty principles. As the twentieth century opened, Filipino and Cuban rebels used Thomas Jefferson's Declaration of Independence to oppose American invaders, Koreans defined themselves as a nation crushed under Japanese heels, and Indian nationalists made colonial governors feel shame for violating British standards of "fair play."

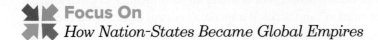

Focus On
How Nation-States Became Global Empires

The Americas and Europe: Consolidating Nations

- Residents of the United States claim territory across the North American continent after fighting a bloody civil war to preserve the union and abolish slavery.

- Canadians build a new nation and expand across the continent.

- Brazilians create a prosperous nation-state that excludes much of the population from the privileges of belonging to the "nation" and the "state."

- The dynastic states of Prussia and Piedmont-Sardinia create German and Italian nation-states at the expense of France and the Austrian Empire.

Industry, Science, and Technology on a Global Scale

- Continued industrialization transforms the global economy.

- New technologies of warfare, transportation, and communication lead to greater global economic integration.

- Charles Darwin's *On the Origin of Species* overturns previous conceptions of nature, arguing that present-day life-forms evolved from simpler ones over long periods.

Empires

- After suppressing the Indian Rebellion of 1857, the British reorganize their rule in India, providing a model for other imperialist powers.

- European powers partition the entire African continent (except for Ethiopia and Liberia) despite intense African resistance.

- Americans win the Spanish-American War, annex Puerto Rico, and establish colonial rule over the Philippines.

- The expansionist aims of Japan, Russia, and China lead to clashes

CHRONOLOGY   1800   1850

The Americas	
	U.S. Civil War 1861–1865
	Canada gains self-rule 1867

Europe	
	On the Origin of Species published 1859
	Unifications of Germany and Italy 1870–1871

East Asia and Southeast Asia	
	Commodore Perry "opens" Japan 1853

Africa and the Middle East

South Asia

Russia	
	Crimean War 1853–1856
	Great Reforms to modernize Russia 1860s

THINKING ABOUT GLOBAL CONNECTIONS

over possessions in East Asia, with Russia gaining much territory and Japan defeating the Chinese.

- Colonial rule spurs nationalist sentiments among the colonized.

- **Thinking about Worlds Together, Worlds Apart and Nations & Empires** Compare the eighteenth-century empires of Spain, Portugal, and Britain with the new empires arising in Africa at the end of the nineteenth century. What were the sources of their wealth and power? How and to what degree were colonial territories and economies integrated with their imperialist states?

- **Thinking about Changing Power Relationships and Nations & Empires** How did the growth of western influence and Japanese power lay the basis for opposition movements in Africa and Asia? How did people respond to imperialism? Where was resistance most effective?

- **Thinking about Environmental Impacts and Nations & Empires** Describe the second industrial revolution and explain how it differed from the first industrial revolution. Pay special attention to the new technologies used in the late nineteenth century, especially the sources of power and new materials that were used.

Key Terms

Charles Darwin p. 667

imperialism p. 652

limited-liability joint-stock company p. 655

Manifest Destiny p. 653

Meiji Restoration p. 680

natural selection p. 667

Raj p. 669

Self-Strengthening movement p. 686

steel p. 666

 Go to **INQUIZITIVE** to see what you've learned—and learn what you've missed—with personalized feedback along the way.

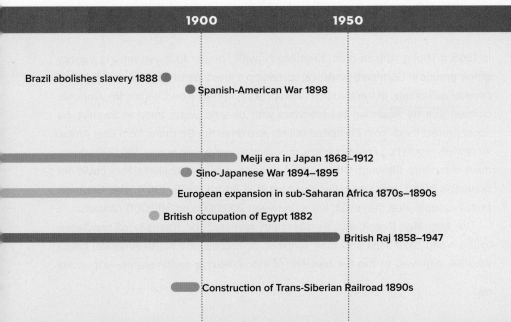

1900

1950

Brazil abolishes slavery 1888

Spanish-American War 1898

Meiji era in Japan 1868–1912

Sino-Japanese War 1894–1895

European expansion in sub-Saharan Africa 1870s–1890s

British occupation of Egypt 1882

British Raj 1858–1947

Construction of Trans-Siberian Railroad 1890s

18

An Unsettled World

1890–1914

Core Objectives

- **EXPLAIN** the connections between migration and the development of nationalism in this period.

- **COMPARE** Chinese responses to imperialism with responses to imperialism in Africa.

- **IDENTIFY** and **DESCRIBE** political, economic, and social crises that swept through the world in this period, and **ANALYZE** the impact they had on different regions of the world.

- **EXPLAIN** the ways in which new cultural forms at the turn of the century reflected challenges to the world order as it then existed.

- **EVALUATE** the ways in which race, nation, and religion unified populations but also made societies more difficult to govern and economies more difficult to manage.

In 1905 a young African man, Kinjikitile Ngwale, began to move among various ethnic groups in German East Africa, spreading a message of opposition to German colonial authorities. In the tradition of visionary prophets (see Chapter 16), Kinjikitile claimed that by anointing his followers with blessed water (*maji* in Swahili), he could protect them from European bullets and drive the Germans from East Africa. Kinjikitile's reputation spread rapidly, drawing followers from across 100,000 square miles of territory. Although German officials soon executed Kinjikitile, they could not prevent a broad uprising, called the Maji Maji Revolt (1905–1907). The Germans brutally suppressed the revolt, killing between 200,000 and 300,000 Africans.

The Maji Maji Revolt and its aftermath revealed the intensity of resistance to the world of nations and their empires. In Europe and North America, critics who felt deprived of the full benefits of industrializing nation-states—especially women, workers, and frustrated nationalists—demanded far-reaching reforms. In Asia, Africa, and Latin America, anticolonial critics and exploited classes protested European domination. In the face of so much unrest from within their nations and from their colonies, Europeans' faith in the idea of progress and the superiority of their "civilization" was shaken. Ironically, this occurred at the very moment when Europeans and people of European descent seemed to have established preeminence in world affairs.

This chapter tackles the anxieties and insecurities that unsettled the world around the turn of the twentieth century. It ties them in particular to three key factors: (1) the uprooting of millions of people from countryside to city and from one continent to another, (2) discontent with the poverty that many suffered even as economic production increased, and (3) resentment of and resistance to European domination. Around the globe, this tumult caused a questioning of established ideas that led to a flowering of new thinking and fresh artistic expression under the label of "modernism." This unsettling movement was a defining feature of the era.

Global Storyline

The Global Impact of Modernity

- Numerous factors lead to global instability: vast population movements, worldwide financial crises, class conflict, the rise of women's consciousness, and hatred of colonial domination.

- Class conflict, economic instability, and great power rivalry within Europe combine with growing protest from overseas to undermine Europe's dominant position in world affairs.

- New forms of scientific thinking and artistic expression, known as cultural modernism, challenge the dominant western view of progress and open Europe and North America to the cultural achievements of nonwestern societies.

Progress, Upheaval, and Movement

Rapid economic progress in the decades leading up to 1914 brought challenges to the established order and the people in power. In Europe, the United States, and Latin America, radicals and middle-class reformers agitated for political and social change, the former stressing land reform and economic rights and the latter giving priority to the interests of property owners. In areas colonized by European countries and the United States, resentment focused on either colonial rulers or indigenous elites. Even in nations such as China, which had not been formally colonized but which faced repeated intrusions, popular discontent targeted domination by Europeans. At the same time, millions of people migrated to cities and different countries in search of a better life.

In the late nineteenth century, whole new industries fueled economic growth, especially in the industrial countries and in territories that exported vital raw materials to Europe and the United States. But advanced capitalism also spurred inequalities within industrial countries and, especially, between the world's industrial and nonindustrial regions. It also brought unwelcome changes in how and where people worked and lived. Rural folk flocked into the cities, hoping to escape the poverty that encumbered most people in the countryside. In the cities, even though public building projects produced sewer systems, museums, parks, and libraries, the poor had little access to them. Periodic economic downturns left thousands out of work. This led, in some cases, to organized opposition to authoritarian regimes or to the free market system; it also provoked new critiques of the industrial order and the values that supported it.

In Europe and North America, a generation of young artists, writers, and scientists broke with older conventions and sought new ways of seeing and describing the world. In Asia, Africa, and Latin America as well, many of these innovators were energized by the idea of moving beyond traditional forms of art, literature, music, and science. But this generation's exuberance worried those who were not ready to give up their cultural traditions and institutions.

PEOPLES IN MOTION

If the world was being *unsettled* by political, economic, and cultural changes, it was also being *resettled* by mass emigration. (See Map 18.1.) The emigration of throngs of Europeans to temperate zones in the Americas and Oceania began after the Napoleonic wars and gathered momentum in the 1840s, when the Irish fled their starving communities to seek better lives in places like Ontario (Canada), New York (United States), and Patagonia (Argentina); the Irish exodus and the end of the slave trade meant that, for the first time, European migration eclipsed that of African captives. The United States was the favored destination. The high point occurred between 1901 and 1910, when over 6 million Europeans entered the United States. This was nothing less than a demographic revolution.

Emigration, Immigration, Internal Migration Europeans were not the only peoples on the move. Between the 1840s and the 1940s, 29 million South Asians migrated into the Malay Peninsula and Burma (British colonies), the Dutch Indies (Indonesia), East Africa, and the Caribbean. Most were recruited to labor on plantations, railways, and mines in British-controlled territories. Meanwhile, the Chinese, too, emigrated in massive numbers. Between 1845 and 1900, population pressure, a shortage of cultivable land, and social turmoil drove 800,000 Chinese to seek new homes in North and South America, New Zealand, Hawaii, and the West Indies. Nearly four times as many settled in Southeast Asia. Moreover, industrial changes caused millions to migrate *within* their own countries or to neighboring ones, seeking employment in the burgeoning cities or other opportunities in frontier regions. In North America, hundreds of thousands headed west, while millions relocated from the countryside to the cities. In Asia, about 10 million Russians went east to Siberia and central Asia, and 2 million Koreans moved northwest to Manchuria. In Africa, small numbers of South Africans moved north into Northern and Southern Rhodesia in search of arable land and precious metals. Across the world, gold rushes, silver rushes, copper rushes, and a diamond rush took people across landmasses and across oceans. Mostly men, these emigrants were hell-bent on profit and were often willing to destroy the land in order to extract precious commodities as quickly as possible.

Until 1914, governments imposed almost no controls on immigration or emigration. In China, the Qing government failed in its effort to restrict emigration into the dominant Manchus' northeastern homelands. The United States allowed entry to anyone who was not a prostitute, a convict, or a "lunatic," but in 1882 racist reactions spurred legislation that barred entry to almost all Chinese. Travel within Europe required no passports or work permits; foreign-born criminals were subject to deportation, but that was the extent of immigration policy.

Urban Life Cities boomed, with both positive and negative effects. Tokyo's population climbed from 500,000 in 1863 to 2 million in 1905. The population of Buenos Aires rose from 180,000 in 1869 to 1.58 million in 1914, and London's increased from 3.2 million in 1861 to 6.5 million in 1901. Major cities faced housing shortages, despite governments' massive rebuilding and beautification projects. This was the era when city planning came into its own—to widen and regularize thoroughfares for train and streetcar traffic, and to make crowded city life attractive to new inhabitants. City governments in New York, Cairo, Buenos Aires, Bombay, and Brussels spent lavishly on opera houses, libraries, sewers, public transportation, wide open avenues, and parks, hoping to ward off disease and crime and to impress others with their modernity. And yet, for all those efforts, cholera and tuberculosis remained major killers, and suicide and alcoholism became growing problems.

The Global View

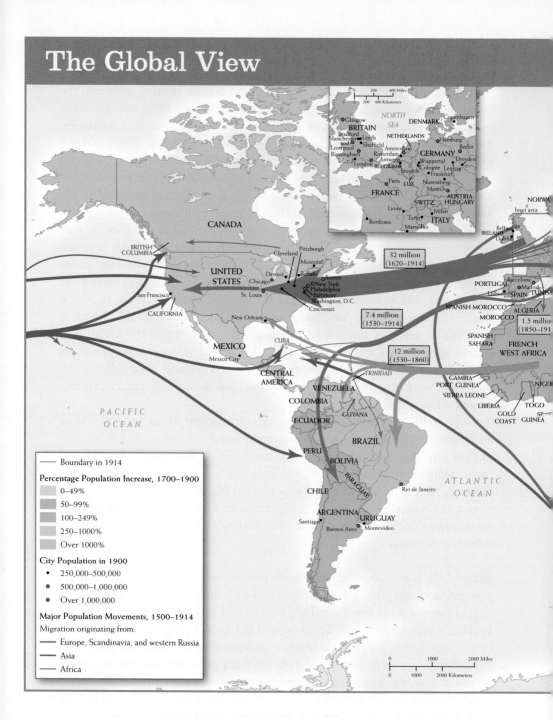

Boundary in 1914

Percentage Population Increase, 1700–1900
- 0–49%
- 50–99%
- 100–249%
- 250–1000%
- Over 1000%

City Population in 1900
- • 250,000–500,000
- ⦿ 500,000–1,000,000
- ⦿ Over 1,000,000

Major Population Movements, 1500–1914
Migration originating from:
- —— Europe, Scandinavia, and western Russia
- —— Asia
- —— Africa

32 million
(1620–1914)

7.4 million
(1530–1914)

12 million
(1530–1860)

1.5 million
(1850–191[?])

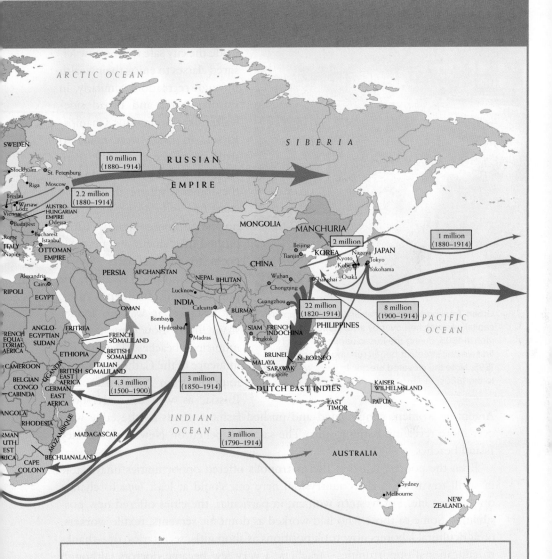

Map 18.1 Nineteenth-Century Migration

The nineteenth century witnessed a demographic revolution in terms of migration, urbanization patterns, and population growth. The world's population also rose from roughly 625 million in 1700 to 1.65 billion in 1900 (a two-and-a-half-fold increase).

- To what areas did most of the migrants from Europe go? What about the migrants from China, India, and Africa?

- What four areas saw the greatest population increase by 1900?

- How were migration flows and urbanization connected? What factors most accounted for these global population changes? Was internal growth more important than external migration in the case of the world's population growth? In what countries was population growth most affected by external or internal migration?

Urban Transportation Streetcars in Tokyo, Japan's capital, are watched over by sword-bearing patrolmen in 1905, during the Russo-Japanese War. The first electric streetcar began running in Japan in 1895. Note the elevated electricity lines, which date to the 1880s.

Tokyo, like so many other booming metropolitan areas, had made the city safe for the new leisured classes to enjoy their wealth through recreation. Similarly, in Europe, parks and broad sidewalks, like the famous Champs-Élysées in Paris, were made to stroll in, to see and to be seen. Women, no longer cooped up in the domestic sphere, donned the latest furs and dresses; men were no less fashion conscious. Cities pushed their smelly and pestilent ports to the outskirts. Shores were ideal, in good weather, for public bathing. In Buenos Aires, for instance, it was no longer shameful to show some flesh on municipal beaches. Despite the influence of the Catholic Church, migrants from Italy, Spain, and Russia, as well as native-born Argentine women, congregated and pushed fashion trends to the edge with ever more revealing bathing suits. The same happened on New York's Coney Island beaches.

Even the poorest felt that the metropolis offered opportunities unavailable in small towns or in the countryside; here one could at least *hope* to change one's lot in life. For western women, in particular, the cities offered new possibilities. Some of those who had worked as domestic servants, textile workers, or agricultural laborers now took positions as shop girls, secretaries, or—thanks to educational opportunities—teachers; a very few became doctors, although their practices were largely limited to treating other women. Increasing female literacy and the falling price of books and magazines gave western women access to new models of acceptable behavior. In cities it became respectable, even fashionable, for women to be seen on the boulevards. The availability in some places of ready-made clothes and packaged goods changed the way wealthier women shopped and cooked. Yet, for most women, leisure time, professional work, and luxury consumption remained dreams rather than realities.

Increased population density made possible more collective action—and collective amusement—but did not necessarily lead to greater social harmony. The turn of the century was marked by the construction of new parks, soccer and baseball stadia, theaters, and pubs, but also by an increasing number of conflicts between workers and business owners or police. Social clubs, political

Coney Island in 1905 As societies grew richer and more consumer oriented, cities cleared space for promenades, parks, and beaches for leisure time. Coney Island in New York became a model for local escapes from the work week and the bustle of the metropolis. Sites like this were designed to be spectacular and to provide images for even distant consumers to gawk at. Visiting Coney Island meant leaving with memorabilia to show off—like the postcard pictured here.

organizations, and charitable associations met more and more frequently—but often battled with one another for members or influence. As cities grew, they often developed ethnically homogenous neighborhoods—"Little Italies" or "Chinatowns" in the United States, Basque *barrios* in Buenos Aires, and Jewish or Irish neighborhoods in England—where inhabitants kept to themselves and were sometimes feared and hated by their neighbors. Seeking to unify nations internally, many writers, artists, and political leaders created mythic histories that aimed to give diverse groups a common story of nationhood. Such inventions were crucial in nation building, but they also fueled conflict among nations that in 1914 erupted in the Great War, an event that would generate another huge wave of emigration and urban expansion—and hostility to "foreigners." Population movement and the growth of cities were distinct features of the later nineteenth century all over the world, opening up new opportunities to become rich or to sink into poverty.

Discontent with Imperialism

In the decades before the Great War, as World War I was known before there was a World War II, opposition to European domination in Asia and Africa gathered strength. During the nineteenth century, as Europeans touted imperialism as a "civilizing mission," local prophets had voiced alternative visions contesting European supremacy (see Chapter 16). While imperialists consolidated their hold, suppression of unrest in the colonies required ever more force and bloodshed. As the cycle of resistance and repression escalated, many Europeans back home, mainly on the left and out of power, questioned the harsh means of controlling their colonies. By 1914, these questions were intensifying as colonial subjects across Asia and Africa challenged imperial domination.

UNREST IN AFRICA

Africa witnessed many anticolonial uprisings in the first decades of colonial rule. (See Map 18.2.) Violent conflicts embroiled not only the Belgians and the Germans, who paid little attention to African political traditions, but also the British, whose colonial system left traditional African rulers in place. These uprisings made Europeans uneasy. Why, they wondered, were Africans resisting regimes that had huge advantages in firepower and transport and that were bringing medical skills, literacy, and other fruits of European civilization? Some Europeans concluded that Africans were too stubborn or unsophisticated to appreciate Europe's generosity. Others, shocked by colonial cruelty, called for reform. A few radicals even demanded an end to imperialism.

The Anglo-Boer War Africa witnessed many anticolonial uprisings in the first decades of colonial rule, especially in areas where colonial rulers imposed forced labor, increased taxes, and appropriated land. The continent's most devastating anticolonial uprising occurred in South Africa. This unique struggle pitted two White communities against each other: the British in the Cape Colony and Natal against the Afrikaners, descendants of original Dutch settlers who lived in the Transvaal and the Orange Free State. (See Map 18.2 inset.) Although two White regimes were the main adversaries, the **Anglo-Boer War** (1899–1902) involved the area's 4 million Black inhabitants as fully as its 1 million Whites.

The war's origins lay in the discovery of gold in the Transvaal in the mid-1880s. As the area rapidly became Africa's richest state, the prospect that Afrikaner republics might become the powerhouse in southern Africa was more than British imperialists could accept. They also fretted over rumors of German influence on Afrikaners. Fearing that war was inevitable, the president of the Transvaal launched a preemptive strike against the British. In late 1899, Afrikaner forces crossed into South Africa. Fighting a relentless guerrilla campaign, Afrikaners waged a war that would last three years and cost Britain 20,000 soldiers and £200 million.

In a frustrated effort to respond to Afrikaner hit-and-run tactics, British commanders also borrowed a Spanish innovation from the counterinsurgency in Cuba: the concentration camp. At one moment in the war, giant prison camps surrounded by barbed wire held over 155,000 people, many of them women

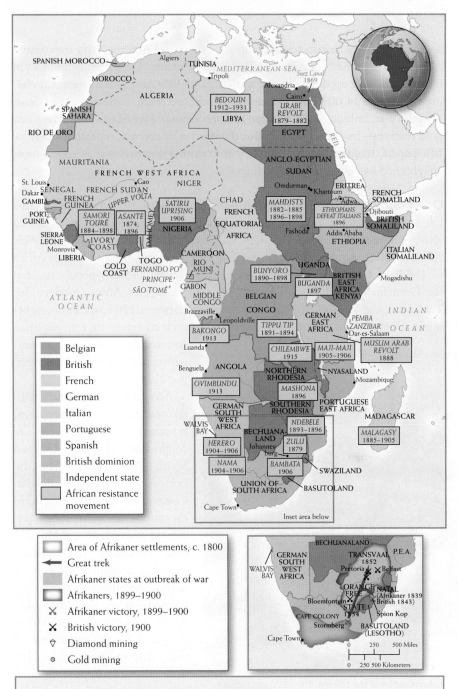

Map key:

- Belgian
- British
- French
- German
- Italian
- Portuguese
- Spanish
- British dominion
- Independent state
- African resistance movement

Inset key:

- Area of Afrikaner settlements, c. 1800
- → Great trek
- Afrikaner states at outbreak of war
- Afrikaners, 1899–1900
- ✕ Afrikaner victory, 1899–1900
- ✕ British victory, 1900
- � Diamond mining
- ⊙ Gold mining

Map 18.2 Uprisings and Wars in Africa

....

The European partition and conquest of Africa were violent affairs.

- How many separate African resistance movements can you count on this map?
- Where was resistance the most prolonged?
- According to your reading, why were Ethiopians (see Chapter 17), who sustained their autonomy, able to do what other African opponents of European armies were not?

and children. The British rounded up Afrikaners and Africans, who they feared would side with the "anticolonial" Dutch descendants. The suffering and loss in these camps were appalling; by the war's end, 28,000 Afrikaner women and children, as well as 14,000 Black Africans, had perished there. Ultimately, the British won the war, bringing the Transvaal and the Orange Free State—with their vast gold reserves—into their empire. But the horrors of the war, reported widely by newspapers, traumatized the British, who regarded themselves as Europe's most enlightened and efficient colonial rulers.

Other Struggles in Colonized Africa The disgust that some Europeans felt toward imperial violence deepened after Germany's activities in Africa also went brutally wrong. Germany had established colonies in South West Africa (present-day Namibia), Cameroon, and Togo in 1884 and in East Africa in 1885. In German South West Africa, the Herero and San people resisted the Germans in the Herero Revolt, and in German East Africa (modern-day Tanzania), the Muslim Arab peoples rebelled. Between 1904 and 1906, fighting in German South West Africa escalated to such an extent that the German commander issued an extermination order against the Herero population.

According to those who favored European imperialism, however, the atrocities of the Anglo-Boer War and German South West Africa, like the horrors of Leopold's Belgian Congo (see Chapter 17), were exceptions to what they considered Europeans' enlightened rule. Europeans saw Africans either as accepting subjects or as childlike primitives when they resisted—as in the Maji Maji Revolt in German East Africa, described at the beginning of this chapter—and redoubled their efforts to impose colonial order. The problem, in their view, was that they had not tried hard enough to bring civilization. In many cases, the number of officials stationed in the colonies increased.

Extermination of the Herero This 1906 photograph shows a soldier guarding Herero women and children in a prison camp on the coast of German South West Africa (present-day Namibia). The Germans carried out a campaign of near-extermination against the Herero population in German South West Africa in 1904–1906. Nearly 90 percent of the Herero were killed.

THE BOXER UPRISING IN CHINA

Although not formally colonized, China too struggled against European intrusions. As the population swelled to over half a billion and outstripped the country's resources, problems of landlessness, poverty, and peasant discontent (long-standing concerns in China's modern history) left the established order vulnerable to internal revolts and foreign intervention.

The breakdown of Qing dynastic authority originated largely with foreign pressure. For one thing, China's defeat in the Sino-Japanese War of 1894–1895 (see Chapter 17) was deeply humiliating. Japan acquired Taiwan as its first major colony, and European powers demanded that the weakened Qing government grant them specific areas within China as their respective "spheres of influence." (See Map 18.3.) The United States argued instead for maintaining an "open door" policy in China that would keep access available to all traders, while supporting missionary efforts to spread Christianity.

The most explosive reaction to these pressures, the **Boxer Uprising**, started within the peasantry in 1899. Like colonized peoples in Africa, the Boxers violently resisted European meddling. And as in the Taiping Rebellion decades earlier (see Chapter 16), the story of the Boxers was tied to missionary activities. Whereas in earlier centuries Jesuit missionaries had sought to convert the court and the elites, by the mid-nineteenth century the missionary goal was to convert commoners. After the Taiping Rebellion, Christian missionaries had streamed into China, impatient to make new converts in the hinterlands and confident of their governments' backing.

In early 1899, several martial arts groups united under the name Boxers United in Righteousness and adopted the slogan "Support the Qing, destroy the foreign." Like the African followers of Kinjikitile, the Boxers believed that divine protection made them immune to all earthly weapons. As one fighter noted, "We requested the gods to attach themselves to our bodies. When they had done so, we became Spirit Boxers, after which we were invulnerable to swords and spears, our courage was enhanced, and in fighting we were unafraid to die and dared to charge straight ahead." Especially in regions suffering from natural disasters and economic hardship, activists provided assistance to the dispossessed. Idle, restless, and often hungry, many peasants, boatmen, and peddlers turned to the Boxers for support. They also liked the Boxers' message that the gods were angry over the foreign presence in general and Christian activities in particular.

Women played a prominent role in the uprising. The so-called Red Lanterns were mostly teenage girls and unmarried women who announced their loyalty by wearing red garments. Although segregated from the male Boxers—Red Lanterns worshipped at their own altars and practiced martial arts at separate boxing grounds—they were important to the movement in counteracting the influence of Christian women. Indeed, one of the Boxers' greatest fears was that cunning Christian women would use their guile to weaken the Boxers' spirits. They claimed that the "purity" of the Red Lanterns could counter this threat.

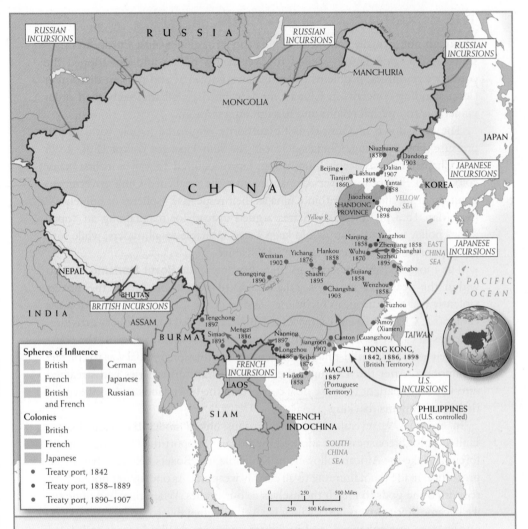

Map 18.3 Foreign Spheres of Influence in China, 1842–1907

....

While technically independent, the Qing dynasty could not prevent foreign penetration and domination of its economy during the nineteenth century.

- Which five powers established spheres of influence in China?
- At what time was the greatest number of treaty ports established?
- According to your reading, what did the foreign powers hope to achieve within their spheres of influence? What kinds of local opposition did the foreign influence inspire?

The Red Lanterns were supposedly capable of incredible feats: they could walk on water or fly through the air. Belief in their magical powers provided critical assistance for the uprising.

As the movement gained momentum, the Qing vacillated between viewing the Boxers as a threat to order and embracing them as a force to check foreign intrusion. Early in 1900, Qing troops clashed with the Boxers in an escalating cycle of violence. By spring, however, the Qing could no longer control the tens of thousands of Boxers roaming the vicinities of Beijing and Tianjin. Embracing the Boxers' cause, the empress dowager, who had gained power when the Qing emperor was placed under house arrest by his opponents for implementing reforms, declared war against the foreign powers in June 1900.

Acting without any discernible plan or leadership, the Boxers attacked Christian and foreign symbols and persons. They harassed and sometimes killed Chinese Christians in parts of northern China, destroyed railroad tracks and telegraph lines, and attacked owners of foreign objects such as lamps and clocks. In Beijing, the Boxers besieged foreign embassy compounds, where diplomats and their families cowered in fear.

The Boxer Uprising in China The Boxer Uprising was eventually suppressed by a foreign army made up of Japanese, European, and American troops that arrived in Beijing in August 1900. The picture here shows fighting between the foreign troops and the combined forces of Qing soldiers and the Boxers. After a period of vacillation, the Qing court, against the advice of some of its officials, finally threw its support behind the quixotic struggle of the Boxers against the foreign presence, laying the ground for the military intervention of the imperialist powers.

Foreign Involvement and Aftermath In August 1900, a foreign army of 20,000 troops crushed the Boxers. About half came from Japan; the rest came primarily from Russia, Britain, Germany, France, and the United States. Thereafter, the victors forced the Chinese to sign the punitive Boxer Protocol. It required the regime to pay an exorbitant compensation in gold (about twice the empire's annual income) for damages to foreign life and property. The protocol also authorized western powers to station troops in Beijing.

Even in defeat, the Boxers' anti-western uprising showed how much had changed in China since the Taiping Rebellion. Although the Boxers were primarily peasants, even they had felt the unsettledness generated by European inroads into China. Indeed, the Europeans' commercial and spiritual reach, once confined to elites and port cities, had extended across much of China. Whereas the Taiping Rebellion had mobilized millions against the Qing, the Boxers remained loyal to the dynasty and focused their wrath on foreigners and Chinese Christians. The Boxer Uprising, like the Maji Maji Revolt in East Africa, revealed the widespread political opposition to westernization and the willingness of disaffected populations to resist western programs.

Worldwide Insecurities

While news of unrest in the distant colonies and in China generally did not lead Europeans to seriously question their ways, it did reinforce public belief in the supposed inferiority of other cultures. Conflicts closer to home tore the most at European confidence in this era. The rise of a European-centered world deepened rivalries within Europe. Numerous factors fostered conflict, including France's smoldering resentment at its defeat in the Franco-Prussian War (see Chapter 17), and led to a buildup of military forces, especially in Britain, Germany, and France. Tensions also increased as the European states competed for raw materials and colonial footholds. Not everyone, however, supported vast expenditures on the military. Many Europeans disapproved of spending on massive steam-powered warships. Others warned that the arms race would end in a devastating war. At the same time, the booms and busts of expanding industrial economies, challenges about the proper roles of women, and problems of uncontrolled urbanization shook the established order and had an impact across the globe. (See again Map 18.1.) These changes and insecurities transformed Europe and swept through the world.

FINANCIAL, INDUSTRIAL, AND TECHNOLOGICAL CHANGE

Economic development helped make powers "great," but it could also unsettle societies. Indeed, pride about wealth and growth coincided with laments about changes in national and international economies. To begin with, Americans and

Europeans recognized that the small-scale, laissez-faire capitalism championed by Adam Smith (see Chapter 14) was giving way to an economic order dominated by huge, heavily capitalized firms. Gone, it seemed, was Smith's vision of many small producers in vigorous competition with one another, all benefiting from efficient—but not exploitative—divisions of labor.

Instead of progressing smoothly, the economy of Europe and North America in the nineteenth century bounced between booms and busts: long-term business cycles of rapid growth followed by countercycles of stagnation. Late in the century, the pace of economic change accelerated. Large-scale steel production, railroad building, and textile manufacturing expanded at breakneck speed, while waves of bank closures, bankruptcies, and agricultural crises ruined many small property owners, including farmers. By the century's end, a few large-scale firms, such as John D. Rockefeller's Standard Oil and the large banking institutions, dominated in France, Britain, Germany, and the United States. The same was true in Japan, where *zaibatsu*—large companies with banking subsidiaries for finance and industrial wings dominating different sectors of the market—like Sumitomo, Mitsui, and Mitsubishi were the engine of Japan's extraordinary economic growth.

Financial Integration and Crises These were years of heady international financial integration. More and more countries joined the world system of borrowing and lending; more and more countries were linked financially through global loans and the fact that all the major national currencies in the world, such as the American dollar, the British pound, and the French franc, were exchanged at reliable rates. At the hub of this world system were the banks of London, which since the Napoleonic wars had been a major source of capital for international borrowers.

The rise of giant banks and huge industrial corporations caused alarm, for it seemed to signal an end to free markets and competitive capitalism. In the United States, an entire generation of journalists cut their teeth exposing the skullduggery (shady dealings) of financial and industrial giants. Ida Tarbell grew up in company towns in Pennsylvania and watched as bigger oil firms drove out little ones until they fall under one mantle: the Standard Oil Company of John D. Rockefeller. As one of the investigative "muckraker" journalists, Tarbell published a celebrated book about Standard Oil in 1904, a work that heavily influenced the drafting of new regulatory policies. Rather than longing for the return of truly free markets, many critics sought reforms that would protect people from economic instability. The solution, many economists and politicians thought, was for the state to manage the national economies.

Banking especially seemed in need of closer government supervision. Many industrial societies already had central banks (banks that issued national currencies, fixed underlying interest rates, and in general controlled monetary policy); London's Bank of England had long overseen local and international money

Ida Tarbell Ida Minerva Tarbell (1857–1944) grew up near oilfields in Pennsylvania, where her father was an oilman. Her family was rocked by the boom and bust of American finance when their savings were wiped out in the Panic of 1857, only to recover with the oil boom in 1859. Tarbell attended college and began her career as a teacher, eventually becoming an intrepid investigative reporter. She parlayed her research into the abuses of oil magnates into a series of articles in *McClure's* magazine exposing the ruthless practices of Standard Oil. Such "muckraking" became a new model for investigative journalism directed against the high and the mighty.

markets. But governments did not have the resources to protect all—or even most—investments during times of crisis. Between 1890 and 1893, 550 American banks collapsed, and only the intervention of J. P. Morgan, a banker who dominated corporate finance, prevented the depletion of the nation's reserves of gold that stood behind the dollar.

In 1907, a more serious crisis threatened. A panic on Wall Street led to a run on the banks. Once again, J. P. Morgan rescued the American economy from financial panic. Morgan himself lost $21 million and emerged from the bank panic convinced that some sort of public oversight was needed. In 1913, the U.S. Congress ratified the Federal Reserve Act, creating boards to monitor the supply and demand of the nation's money. The crisis of 1907 also showed how national financial matters could quickly become international affairs as panicked American investors withdrew their funds from other countries, many of which relied on American capital.

Industrialization and the Modern Economy Backed by big banks, industrialists extended their enterprises to new places. For example, with loans from European investors, Russia built railways, telegraph lines, and factories. By 1900, Russia was producing half of the world's oil and a considerable amount of steel. Yet industrial development remained uneven: southern Europe and the American South continued to lag behind northern regions. The gap was even more pronounced in colonial territories, which contained few industrial enterprises aside from railroad building and mining.

By 1914, the factory and the railroad had become global symbols of the modern economy—and of its positive and negative effects. Everywhere, the coming of the railroad to one's town or village was a big event: for some, it represented an exhilarating leap into the modern world; for others, a terrifying abandonment of the past. Ocean liners, automobiles, and airplanes likewise could be both dazzling and disorienting.

For ordinary people, the new economy brought benefits and drawbacks. Factories produced cheaper goods, but they belched clouds of black smoke.

Railways offered faster transport, but they ruined small towns unlucky enough to be left off the branch line. Machines (when operating properly) were more efficient than human and animal labor, but workers who used them felt reduced to machines themselves. Indeed, the American Frederick Winslow Taylor proposed a system of "scientific management" to make human bodies perform more like machines, maximizing the efficiency of workers' movements. But workers did not want to be managed or to cede control of the pace of production to employers. "Taylorization" provoked massive resistance and numerous strikes. For strikers, as for those left out of the new economy, progress had taken an unsettling turn.

THE "WOMAN QUESTION"

Complicating the situation was turmoil about the "woman question." In the west, female activists demanded that women be given more rights as citizens; more radical voices called for fundamental changes to the family and the larger society. At the same time, imperialists claimed that colonial rule was bringing great improvements to women in Asia and Africa. But the "woman question" was no more easily settled there than elsewhere.

Women's Issues in the West In western countries, for most of the nineteenth century, a belief in "separate spheres" had supposedly confined women to domestic matters, while leaving men in charge of public life and economic undertakings. (In practice, only women from middle- and upper-class families avoided working outside the home for wages.) However, as economic developments created new jobs for women and greater access to education, women increasingly found work as teachers, secretaries, typists, department store clerks, social workers, and telephone operators. These jobs offered greater economic and social independence. Some educated women spearheaded efforts to improve conditions for the urban poor and to expand the government's role in regulating economic affairs. Nonetheless, much of the population continued to think that higher education and public activism were not suitable for women.

In one important change, many women began to assert control over reproduction. Although in numerous countries the use of contraceptive devices was illegal, women still found a variety of ways to limit the number of children they bore. In addition to marrying late and sleeping apart, some used spermicidal herbs, which sometimes worked but sometimes killed the woman; others relied on a variety of sponges and other barriers, had their partners use condoms, or insisted on the practice of *coitus interruptus* (withdrawal). When contraception failed, many women turned to abortion, even though it was illegal. Successful contraception, by whatever means, depended on cooperation and communication and tended to be more effective as educational levels increased.

Early in the twentieth century, the birthrate in America was half of what it had been a century before. By having fewer children, families could devote more income to education, food, housing, and leisure activities. Declining birthrates, along with improved medicine, also meant that fewer women died in childbirth; more would see their children reach adulthood.

Still, changes in women's social status did not translate into full political rights at the national level, such as the vote. By the mid-nineteenth century, women's suffrage movements had appeared in several countries, but these campaigns bore little immediate fruit. In 1868, women received the right to vote in local elections in Britain. Within a few years, Finland, Sweden, and some American states allowed single, property-owning women the right to cast ballots—again, only in local elections. Women obtained the right to vote in national elections in New Zealand in 1893, in Australia in 1902, in Finland in 1906, and in Norway in 1913.

As in the labor and socialist movements, feminists also formed cross-border alliances and, thanks to the media, followed each other's news. When the English suffragette Emily Davison dashed into the lanes at the aristocratic Epsom Derby horse race and got trampled to death by the king's horse, the news made headlines around the world. The clamor for women's rights was a truly global one. Komako Kimura, trained in Japanese dance and theater and raised to be a "proper wife," was also an avid reader of western literature and developed a reputation as a rebel for her daring performances. She soon became one of Japan's early suffragettes and cofounded the True New Woman's Association and labored to send her magazine to Europe and North America. She finally traveled to the United States in 1917 to study how American activists had succeeded in winning the vote there. She was among the celebrities who marched through New York demanding women's emancipation worldwide.

Despite these gains, male alarmists portrayed women's suffrage and women's rights as the beginning of civilization's end. Among women, views on feminism varied. Most

Komako Kimura Komako Kimura (1887–1980) was a pioneering Japanese feminist. She traveled widely and drew inspiration from suffragist movements in Europe and North America to campaign in Japan. But she also became a global celebrity, making the case for women's suffrage in an international crusade. Conscious that mass politics was becoming a media phenomenon, she used her training in dance and theater to cultivate her public persona. She also got in trouble. The Japanese government censored her magazine, *The True Woman*, for advocating women's right to choose their husbands and practice birth control. In this photo, she poses during a massive suffragist march in New York.

middle-class women in Europe and the Americas were not seeking to make women equal to men. Indeed, many bourgeois women recoiled from the close relationships between socialism and feminism. In Latin America, for example, anarchists championed a version of feminism arguing that the abolition of private property would liberate women from their misery and that the traditional family was a bourgeois convention. Other women feared becoming too "mannish," and a few worried that equality would destroy female sensuality. Most, probably, looked to reform less in terms of voting rights and more in terms of better treatment within families and local communities.

Women's Status in Colonies In the colonial world, the woman question was also a contentious issue—but it was mainly argued among men. European authorities liked to boast that colonial rule improved women's status. Citing examples of traditional societies' treatment of women, they criticized the veiling of women in Islamic societies, the binding of women's feet in China, widow burning (*sati*) in India, and female genital mutilation in Africa. Europeans believed that prohibiting such acts was a justification for colonial intervention.

And yet, colonialism only added to women's burdens. As male workers headed into the export economy, formerly shared agricultural work fell exclusively on women's shoulders. In Africa, for example, the opening of vast gold and diamond mines drew thousands of men away to work in the mines, leaving women to tend to the farmstead and to do colonial tasks that men once did. Similarly, the rise of European-owned agricultural estates in Kenya and Southern Rhodesia depleted surrounding villages of male family members, who went to work on the estates. In these circumstances, women kept the local, food-producing economy afloat.

Nor did colonial "civilizing" rhetoric improve women's political or cultural circumstances. In fact, European missionaries preached a message of domesticity to Asian and African families, emphasizing that women's place was in the home raising children and that women's education should be different from men's. Thus, males overwhelmingly dominated the new schools that Europeans built. Moreover, the chiefs who collaborated with colonial officials consistently favored men. As a result, African women often lost landholding and other rights that they had enjoyed before the Europeans' arrival.

CLASS CONFLICT

As capitalism's volatility shook confidence in free market economies and sharpened conflicts between classes, the tone of political debate was transformed as new voices called for radical change. Although living conditions for European and North American workers improved over time, widening inequalities in income and the slow pace of reform bred frustration. Most workers remained committed to peaceful agitation, but some radicals favored violence against the state and its agents.

Strikes and Revolts In the Americas and in Europe, radicals adopted numerous tactics for asserting the interests of the working class. In Europe, the franchise was gradually expanded in hopes that the lower classes would prefer voting to revolution—and indeed, most of the new political parties that catered to workers had no desire to overthrow the state. But conservatives feared them anyway, especially as they gained electoral clout. The Labour Party, founded in Britain in 1900, quickly boasted a large share of the vote. By 1912, the German Social Democratic Party was the largest party in the Reichstag, though it lacked power since the Reichstag was only an advisory body. But it was not the legally sanctioned parties that sparked violent street protests and strikes in the century's last decades. A whole array of **syndicalists** (labor activists), **anarchists** (those who opposed government altogether), royalists, and socialists sprang up in this period, making work stoppages everyday affairs.

Although the United States did not have similarly radical factions or successful labor parties, American workers were also organizing. The labor movement's power burst forth dramatically in 1894. Spawned by wage cuts and firings following an economic downturn, the Pullman Strike (directed against the maker of railway sleeping cars, George Pullman) involved approximately 3 million workers. The strike's conclusion, however, revealed the enduring power of the status quo. After hiring replacement workers to break the strike, Pullman requested federal troops to protect his operation. After its leaders were jailed, the strike collapsed. Although strikes and protests in the United States and Europe often failed to achieve their immediate goals, they worried those in power and ultimately led to important changes.

Revolution in Mexico Perhaps the most successful turn-of-the-century revolution occurred in Mexico. This peasant uprising thoroughly transformed the country. Fueled by the unequal distribution of land and by disgruntled workers, the **Mexican Revolution** erupted in 1910 when political elites split over the succession of General Porfirio Díaz after decades of his strong-arm rule. Dissidents balked when Díaz refused to step down, and peasants and workers rallied to the call to arms.

From the north (led by the charismatic Pancho Villa) to the south (under the legendary Emiliano Zapata), peasants, farmers, and other rural workers helped topple the Díaz regime. In the name of providing land for farmers and ending oligarchic rule, peasant armies defeated Díaz's troops and proceeded to destroy many large estates. The fighting lasted for ten brutal years, during which almost 10 percent of the country's population perished.

Thereafter, political leaders had to accept popular demands for democracy, respect for the sovereignty of peasant communities, and land reform. The revolution's most lasting legacy was perhaps the creation of rural communes for Mexico's peasantry. These communal village holdings, called *ejidos*, looked back to a precolonial heritage. The revolution spawned a set of new national myths based on the heroism of rural peoples, Mexican nationalism, and a celebration of the Aztec past.

Preserving Established Orders

Although the Mexican Revolution succeeded in toppling the old elite, elsewhere in Latin America the ruling establishment remained united against assaults from below. Already, in 1897, the Brazilian army had mercilessly suppressed a peasant movement in the northeastern part of the country. Moreover, in Cuba, the Spanish and then the American armies crushed tenant farmers' efforts to reclaim land from sugar estates. In Guatemala, Maya Indians lost land to coffee barons.

In Europe and the United States, the preservation of established orders did not rest on repression alone.

The Mexican Revolution By the 1920s, Mexican artists and writers were putting recent events into images and words. Pictured here is a detail from a mural by Diego Rivera. Notice the nationalist interpretation: Porfirio Díaz's troops defend foreign oil companies and White aristocrats against middle-class and peasant (and darker-skinned) reformers who call for a "social revolution." Observe also the absence of women in this epic mural.

Here, elites also grudgingly agreed to gradual change. Indeed, by the century's end, left-wing agitators, muckraking reporters, and middle-class reformers began to win meaningful social improvements. Unable to suppress the socialist movement, Otto von Bismarck, the German chancellor, defused the appeal of socialism by enacting social welfare measures in 1883–1884, insuring workers against illness, accidents, and old age and establishing maximum working hours. In the United States, it took lurid journalistic accounts of unsanitary practices in Chicago slaughterhouses (including tales of workers falling into lard vats and being rendered into cooking fat) to spur the federal government into action. In 1906, President Theodore Roosevelt signed a Meat Inspection Act that provided for government supervision of meatpacking operations. In other cases (banking, steel production, railroads), the federal government's enhanced supervisory authority served corporate interests as well.

These consumer and family protection measures reflected a broader reform movement, one dedicated to creating a more efficient society and correcting the undesirable consequences of urbanization and industrialization. At local and state levels, these **progressive reformers** attacked corrupt city governments that had allegedly fallen into the hands of immigrant-dominated "political machines." The progressives also attacked other vices, such as gambling, drinking, and prostitution—all associated with industrialized, urban settings. The creation of city parks preoccupied urban planners, who hoped parks' green spaces would serve as the city's "lungs" and offer healthier forms of entertainment than houses of prostitution, gambling dens, and bars. From Scandinavia to California, the proponents of old-age pensions and public ownership of utilities put pressure on lawmakers. Thousands of associations took shape against capitalism's harsher effects, and they occasionally succeeded in changing state policies. Indeed, the period leading up to World War I was one of rapid change, in which financial crises reverberated across the globe, European and American women pressed for their rights and also agitated for the rights of Asian and African women, and elites were forced to make reforms, though they tended to be limited, in the colonial and colonializers' worlds.

Cultural Modernism

As revolutionaries and reformers wrestled with the problems of progress, intellectuals, artists, and scientists struggled to make sense of change in their own societies and beyond. What we call **modernism**—the sense of having broken with tradition—came to prominence in many fields, from physics to architecture, from painting to the social sciences.

Modernist movements were notably international. Egyptian social scientists read the works of European thinkers, while French and German painters flocked to museums to inspect artifacts from Egypt and artworks from other parts of Africa, Asia, and Oceania. As education spread and political reforms enfranchised more Americans and Europeans, changes in the meaning of culture occurred, causing it to be less elitist and more popular. Yet European elites did not give up their opera houses and paintings in favor of arts and entertainments that were appealing to urban workers or colonized peoples. Instead, the arts became more abstract: musicians abandoned the comfort of harmonic and diatonic sound (the eight-tone scale standard in classical western music at the time); writers and visual artists left realistic representation behind.

Above all, modernism in arts and sciences replaced the certainties of the Enlightenment with the unsettledness of the new age. Modernists challenged claims to provide complete, coherent explanations and representations of all kinds. With growing doubts about civilizing missions or urban and industrial "progress," artists and scientists struggled to understand a world in which human reason seemed inadequate.

POPULAR CULTURE COMES OF AGE

From the late eighteenth to the late nineteenth century, production and consumption of the arts, books, music, and sports changed dramatically. The change derived mainly from new urban settings, technological innovations, mass education, and increased leisure time. Middle-class art lovers eagerly purchased mass-produced engravings; millions attended dance halls and vaudeville shows (entertainment by singers, dancers, and comedians). For the first time, sports attracted mass followings. Soccer in Europe, baseball in the United States, and cricket in India had wildly devoted middle- and working-class fans. Thus did a truly **popular culture** emerge, delivering affordable and accessible forms of art and entertainment to the masses.

By the nineteenth century's close, the press stood as a major form of popular entertainment and information. This was partly because publishers were offering different wares to different classes of readers and partly because many more people could read, especially in Europe and the Americas. By that time, the English *Daily Mail* and the French *Petit Parisien* boasted circulations of over 1 million. In the United States, urban dwellers, many of them immigrants, avidly read newspapers— some in English, others in their native languages. Banner headlines, sensational stories, and simple language drew in readers with little education or poor English skills.

Pablo Picasso The Franco-Spanish artist Pablo Picasso was one of the first to incorporate "primitive" artistic forms into his work, as displayed in his breakthrough canvas *Les Demoiselles d'Avignon* (The Courtesans of Avignon; 1907), which was inspired by the artist's study of African sculpture and masks.

By now the kind of culture one consumed had become a reflection of one's real (or desired) status in society. For many Latin American workers, for example, reading one's own newspaper or comic strip was part of being a worker. Argentina's socialist newspaper, *La Vanguardia*, was one of Buenos Aires's most prominent periodicals, read and debated at work and in the cafés of working-class neighborhoods. Anyone seen reading the bourgeois paper, *La Prensa*, faced heckling and ridicule by fellow workers. As the community of cultural consumers broadened and as ideas from across the globe flooded in, writers, artists, and scholars struggled to adapt.

MODERNISM IN EUROPEAN CULTURE

In intellectual and artistic terms, Europe at the turn of the twentieth century experienced perhaps its richest age since the Renaissance. Artists' work reflected their doubts about the modern world, as represented by the railroad, the big city, and the factory. While the artists and writers of the mid-nineteenth century had largely celebrated progress, the painters and novelists of the century's end took a darker view. They turned away from reason, which the Enlightenment had championed, and descriptive prose as they searched for meanings that came

Impressionism Emerging in Paris in the last third of the nineteenth century, impressionism was an artistic movement that was radical in its day. Its members broke away from the conventional art community and its official, academic salons. With small, visible brushstrokes, the impressionists stressed the changing qualities of light, the passage of time, and movement. Rather than compete with photography and present a facsimile of a stable, static, coherent external reality, they sought to capture perceptions of a world in rapid flux. These two paintings, Claude Monet's *The Gare Saint-Lazare* (*left*) and Camille Pissarro's *Sunset over the Boieldieu Bridge at Rouen* (*right*), exemplify the impressionists' ambivalent view of nineteenth-century progress.

from instinct and emotion. The primitive came to symbolize both Europe's lost innocence and the forces that reason could not control, such as sexual drives, religious fervor, or brute strength.

Europeans began to see the world in a fundamentally different way, aided by the experience of nonwestern visual arts. The painter who led the way in incorporating nonwestern themes into modern art was Pablo Picasso (1881–1973), who found in African art forms a radically new way of expressing human sentiments that was shocking to most European and American observers. Other artists were inspired by the sleekness and syncopation of machines or by the irrational content of dreams. And painting was not the only art form that displayed a modern style. Arnold Schoenberg (1874–1951) led the movement to reject western tonality in music. World-famous dancers like Isadora Duncan (1877–1927) pioneered the expressive, free-form movements that laid the foundations for modern dance.

However, the arts alone did not undermine older views of the world. Even science, in which the Enlightenment had placed so much faith, challenged the idea that the world functioned according to easily understood natural laws. After 1900, pioneering physicists and mathematicians like Albert Einstein (1879–1955) challenged the idea that a single scientific theory, like Newton's, could explain everything. They took apart the Enlightenment's conviction that man could achieve full knowledge of, and control over, nature. In a series of papers published between 1905 and 1915, Einstein worked out the special and general theories of relativity, which demonstrated that measurements of speed and gravitational pull were not purely objective but always conditioned by the relative position and conditions of the observer. Although most scientists continued to collect data, feeling certain that they could plumb nature's depths, some of their colleagues began to question the arrogance of this view.

From the time of the Enlightenment, Europeans had prided themselves on their "reason." To be rational was to be civilized and to master irrational urges; respectable, middle-class nineteenth-century men were thought to embody these virtues. But in the late nineteenth century, faith in rationality began to falter. Perhaps reason was *not* man's highest attainment, said some; perhaps reason was impossible for man to sustain, said others. Friedrich Nietzsche (1844–1900) claimed that conventional European attempts to assert The Truth—including science and Judeo-Christian moral codes—were nothing more than life-destroying quests for power. Sigmund Freud (1856–1939) began to excavate layers of the human subconscious, where irrational desires and fears lay buried. For Freud, human nature was not as simple as it had seemed to Enlightenment thinkers. Instead, he asserted, humans were driven by sexual longings and childhood traumas. Neither Nietzsche nor Freud was well loved among nineteenth-century liberal elites. But in the new century, Nietzsche would become the prophet for many antiliberal causes, from nudism to Nazism, and Freud's dark vision would become central to the twentieth century's understanding of the self.

CULTURAL MODERNISM IN CHINA

What it meant to be modern sparked debate beyond western Europe. Europeans provided one set of answers; thinkers elsewhere offered quite different answers. Chinese artists and scientists at the turn of the century selectively engaged western ideas and transformed them. Indeed, some scholars have described the late Qing period as a time of competing cultural *modernities*, in contrast to the post-Qing era, which pursued a single, western-oriented *modernity*. These forms of modernity involved critical reflection on Chinese traditions and mixed reactions to western culture.

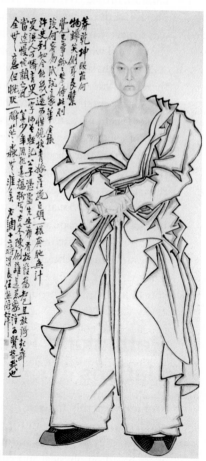

Ren Xiong, *Self-Portrait* This famous self-portrait of Ren Xiong was most likely produced in the 1850s. Ren Xiong was probably familiar with the new practice of portrait photography in the treaty ports. Although his self-portrait reproduced some old conventions of Chinese scholarly art, such as the unity of the visual image with a lengthy self-composed inscription, it is also clear that through its rather unconventional pose and image, it reflects the trend of cultural modernism in China during this period.

As in the west, Chinese writers now had a wider readership. By the late nineteenth century, more than 170 presses in China were serving a potential readership of 2 to 4 million, concentrated mostly in the urban areas. These cities were more economically and culturally vibrant than the hinterlands. Not only was there an expanding body of readers, but newly rich beneficiaries of the treaty-port economy now patronized the arts.

Painters from the Lower Yangzi region, collectively known as the **Shanghai School**, adopted elements from both indigenous and foreign sources. Although classically trained, they appropriated new western techniques into their art.

Similarly, fantasy novels drew on both western science and indigenous supernatural beliefs. Some experimental writers explicitly addressed Chinese–western relations. Depicting China at war with western powers, the novel *New Era* (1908) by Bigehuan Zhuren celebrated conventional military themes but also introduced actual western inventions such as electricity-repellent clothing and bulletproof satin. More visionary still was *The Stone of Goddess Nüwa* (1905), whose male author, Haitian Duxiaozi, imagined a technologically advanced feminist utopia. Its female residents studied subjects ranging from the arts to physics, drove electric cars, and ate purified liquid food extracts. Their mission was to save China by eliminating corrupt male officials. Such works, combining the fanciful with the critical, offered a new and provocative vision of China.

Although steamships, telegraphs, and railroads captured public attention, there was little interest in changing fundamental Chinese beliefs. Indeed, even as Chinese intellectuals recognized new modes of knowledge, many of the elite insisted that Chinese learning remain the principal source of all knowledge. What kind of balance should exist between western thought and Chinese learning, or even whether the ancient classics should keep their fundamental role, was an issue that would haunt generations to come. In this respect, the Chinese dilemma reflected a worldwide challenge to accepting the impulses of modernism.

Modernism arose at a time when intellectuals began to question the values that had sustained Europe and North America throughout most of the nineteenth century. It reflected discontent with industrialization, income inequality, and colonial repression. Even though modernism had its origins and most profound impact in Europe, in many ways, especially in art, it drew upon nonwestern traditions and spread its influence throughout Asia and Africa among the educated classes.

Rethinking Race and Reimagining Nations

Ironically, at this time of huge population transfers and shared technological modernization, many European and American elites embraced the idea that the identities of peoples and nations were deeply rooted and unchangeable and were based on physical and cultural characteristics. By the century's close, racial roots had become a crucial part of identity. People wanted to know who they (and their neighbors) were—especially in terms of *biological* ancestry. Now the idea of inheritance took on new weight, in both cultural and biological forms. Nationalists spoke of the uniqueness of the Slavic soul, the German mind, Hindu spirituality, and the Hispanic race.

Nationalist and racial ideas were different in different parts of the world. In Europe and America, debates about race and national purity reflected several concerns—above all, fear of being overrun by the brown, black, and yellow peoples beyond the borders of "civilization." By contrast, in India these ideas were part of the anticolonial debate, and they helped mobilize people politically. This was also the case in China, Latin America, and the Islamic world, where discussions of identity went hand in hand with opposition to western domination and corrupt indigenous elites.

As we will see, these new impulses produced a variety of national movements, from China's anti-Qing campaign to India's Swadeshi movement. At the same time, panethnic movements looked beyond the nation-state, envisioning communities based on ethnicity. Behind these movements was the notion that political communities should be built on racial purity.

NATION AND RACE IN NORTH AMERICA AND EUROPE

Americans and Europeans greeted the end of the century with a combination of pride and pessimism, and this mood influenced attitudes about national identity, race, and religion. In the early 1890s, for example, Americans flocked to extravagant commemorations of the 400th anniversary of Christopher Columbus's discovery. Yet, at the same time, Americans—like many Europeans—feared for their future.

Regulating the Environment and Immigration Americans especially worried that the United States had exhausted its supposedly infinite supply of new land and resources—as evidenced by the disappearance of the buffalo, the erosion of soils, and the depletion of timber stands by aggressive logging companies. Conservationists' alarm grew more intense with the Census Bureau's 1890 announcement that the American frontier had "closed." When Theodore Roosevelt became president of the United States in 1901, he translated concerns about conserving natural resources into government policy. The market, insisted Roosevelt and like-minded conservationists, could not be trusted to protect "nature." Instead, federal regulation was necessary. This led in 1902 to the passage of the National Reclamation Act, which provided funding for large-scale dams and irrigation projects. Three years later, the Roosevelt administration orchestrated the establishment of the National Forest Service to manage the development of millions of acres of permanent public lands.

Another issue troubled the Americans: the need to maintain the dominance of persons of European descent. As a result, the government initiated new forms of racial discrimination where old forms (like slavery) had broken down. In the

American West, animosity toward Chinese workers led to the 1882 Exclusion Act, which prohibited almost all immigration from China. In the American South, where most of the nation's 7 million African Americans resided, a system of "Jim Crow" laws—enacted after Reconstruction, especially in the 1890s and later, and in force until the 1960s—upheld racial segregation and inequality.

Americans from western Europe grew even more anxious as throngs of "swarthy" immigrants entered the United States from southern and eastern Europe. Even more threatening were darker peoples who were colonial subjects in the Philippines, Puerto Rico, and Cuba. Talk of the end of "White America" fueled support for more restrictive immigration policies.

Across the North Atlantic, European elites engaged in similar discussions about immigration and the environment. For them, the final divvying up of Africa was in many respects equivalent to the closing of the American frontier. The Germans and Italians, in particular, complained about the lack of new territories on which to plant their flags. The French and British, by contrast, worried about how to preserve their overseas empires in a period of intense international competition; both experienced widespread nativist campaigns on their respective mainlands, and England all but closed its borders with the Aliens Act of 1905.

New Social Issues in Europe Darwinist theory provoked new anxieties about inherited diseases, racial mixing, and the dying out of White "civilizers." Sexual relations between European colonizers and indigenous women—and their mixed offspring—had always been a part of European expansionism, but as racial identities hardened, many saw racial mixing as harmful to the supposedly superior White races. In addition, medical attention focused on homosexuality, regarding it as a disease and a threat to civilization.

Some people debated whether Jews—defined by religious practice or, increasingly, by ethnicity—could be fully assimilated into European society. Even though Jews had gained rights as citizens in most European countries by the late nineteenth century, powerful prejudices persisted. In the 1880s and 1890s, violent attacks known as pogroms, often involving police complicity, targeted the large Jewish populations in the Russian Empire's western territories and pushed the persecuted farther westward. These emigrants' presence, in turn, stirred up fear and resentment, especially in Austria, Germany, and France. Rumors circulated about Jewish bankers' conspiratorial powers, and anxieties over the "pollution" of the European races became widespread.

RACE-MIXING AND THE PROBLEM OF NATIONHOOD IN LATIN AMERICA

In Latin America, debates about identity chiefly addressed ethnic intermixing and the legacy of a system of government that, unlike in much of the North Atlantic world, excluded rather than included most people. Social hierarchies reaching back to the sixteenth century ranked Whites born in Spain and Portugal at the top, creole elites in the middle, and indigenous and African populations at the bottom. Thus, the higher they were on the social ladder, the more likely people were to be White.

Contested Mixtures and Invented Traditions "Mixing" did not lead to a shared heritage. Nor did it necessarily lead to homogeneity. In fact, the "racial" order did not stick, since some Iberians occupied the lower ranks, while a few people of color managed to ascend the social ladder. Moreover, starting in the 1880s, the racial hierarchy saw further disruption by the deluge of poor European immigrants; they flooded into prospering Latin American countrysides or into booming cities like Buenos Aires in Argentina and São Paulo in Brazil. Latin American societies, then, did not easily become homogeneous "nations."

Latin American leaders began to exalt bygone glories as a way to promote national identity and foster unity. Inventing successful myths could make a government seem more legitimate—as the heir to a rightful struggle of the past. In Mexico, many parades celebrated Aztec grandeur, thereby creating a mythic arc from the greatness of the Aztec past to the triumphal story of Mexican independence. As the government glorified the Aztecs with pageants, statues, and pavilions, however, it continued to ignore modern Aztec descendants, who lived in squalor. Thus, race in Latin America was a more fluid category than it was in North America and Europe.

Diego Rivera's *History of Mexico* This is one of the most famous works of Mexican art, a portrait of the history of Mexico by the radical nationalist painter Diego Rivera. Earlier in this chapter, we showed a detail from this mural. In stepping back to view the whole work, which is in the National Palace in Mexico City, we can see how Rivera envisioned the history of his people generally. Completed in 1935, this work seeks to show a people fighting constantly against outside aggressors; it winds like a grand epic from their glorious preconquest days (lower center) to the conquest, the colonial exploitation, the revolution for independence, nineteenth-century invasions from France and the United States, and the popular 1910 Mexican Revolution. It culminates in an image of Karl Marx, framed by a "scientific sun" (not shown here)—pointing to a future of progress and prosperity for all, as if restoring a modern Tenochtitlán of the Aztecs. This work captured many Mexicans' efforts to return to the indigenous roots of the nation and to fuse them with modern scientific ideas.

SUN YAT-SEN AND THE MAKING OF A CHINESE NATION

Just as Latin Americans celebrated their past, Chinese writers emphasized the power and depth of Chinese culture—in contrast to the Qing Empire's failing political and social strength. Here, writers used race to emphasize the superiority of the Han Chinese. Here, too, the pace of change generated a desire to trace one's roots back to secure foundations. Moreover, traditions were reinvented in the hope of saving a Chinese culture threatened by modernity.

Among those who thought most intensely about the future of China was **Sun Yat-sen** (1866–1925), whose life story symbolized the challenge of nation building. Sun was part of an emerging generation of critics of the old regime. Like his European counterparts, Sun dreamed of a political community reshaped along national lines. Born into a modest rural household in southern China, he studied medicine in the British colony of Hong Kong and then turned to politics during the Sino-Japanese War. When the Qing government rejected his offer of service to the Chinese cause, he became convinced that China's rulers were out of touch with the times. Subsequently he established an organization based in Hawaii to advocate the Qing downfall and the cause of republicanism. The cornerstone of his message was Chinese nationalism—specifically, Han (the majority of the population) nationalism. Sun blasted the feeble rule by the non-Han "outsiders," the Manchus, and trumpeted a sovereign political community of "true" Chinese.

Replacing the Qing and Reconstituting a Nation Realizing that reforms were necessary, the Manchu court began overhauling the administrative system and the military in the aftermath of the Boxer Uprising. Yet these changes came too late. The old elites grumbled, and the new class of urban merchants, entrepreneurs, and professionals (who often benefited from business with westerners) regarded the government as outmoded. Peasants and laborers resented the high cost of the reforms, which seemed to help only the rulers.

A mutiny, sparked in part by the government's nationalization of railroads and its low compensation to native Chinese investors, broke out in the city of Wuchang in central China in 1911. As it spread to other parts of the country, Sun Yat-sen hurried home from traveling in the United States. Few people rallied to the emperor's cause, and the Qing dynasty collapsed and was replaced by the Republic of China, bringing an abrupt end to a dynastic tradition of more than 2,000 years.

China was soon reconstituted, and Sun's ideas, especially those regarding race, played a central role. The original flag of the republic, for example, consisted of five colors representing the citizenry's major racial groups: red for the Han, yellow for the Manchus, blue for the Mongols, white for the Tibetans, and black for the Muslims. But Sun had reservations about this multiracial flag, believing there should be only one Chinese race. The

Sun Yat-sen These two images of Sun Yat-sen (1866–1925), the man generally known as the "father of the Chinese nation," capture the evolution of China's cultural identity during this period. *Left:* In early 1912, Sun and the officials of the new republic appeared in public in full western-style jackets and ties. *Right:* Sun is pictured here shortly before his death. Chiang Kai-shek (1887–1975), standing behind him, had just been appointed commandant of the Wham-poa Military Academy. By the time this photo was taken, China was sliding into civil war, and Sun was relying increasingly on the army. He feared that sovereignty could be assured only through a strong military.

existence of different groups in China, he argued, was the result of incomplete assimilation—a problem that the modern nation now had to confront.

NATIONALISM AND INVENTED TRADITIONS IN INDIA

British imperial rule persisted in India, but the turn of the century saw cracks in its stranglehold. Four strands had woven the territory together: the consolidation of colonial administration, the establishment of railways and telegraphs, the growth of western education and ideas, and the development of colonial capitalism. Now it was possible to speak of India as a single unit. It was also possible for anticolonial thinkers to imagine seizing and ruling India by themselves. Thus a new form of resistance emerged, different from peasant rebellions of the past. Now, dissenters talked of Indians as "a people" who had both a national past and national traditions.

A Modernizing Elite Leaders of the nationalist opposition were western-educated intellectuals from colonial cities and towns. Although a tiny minority of the Indian population, they gained influence through their access to the official world and their familiarity with European knowledge and history. This elite group used their knowledge to develop modern cultural forms. For example, they turned colloquial languages (such as Hindi, Urdu, Bengali, Tamil, and

Malayalam) into standardized, literary forms for writing novels and dramas. Now the publication of journals, magazines, newspapers, pamphlets, novels, and dramas surged, facilitating communication throughout British India.

Along with print culture came a growing public sphere where intellectuals debated social and political matters. By 1885, voluntary associations in big cities had united to establish a political party, the **Indian National Congress**. Lawyers, prominent merchants, and local notables dominated its early leadership. The congress demanded greater representation of Indians in administrative and legislative bodies, criticized the government's economic policies, and encouraged India's industrialization.

Underlying this political nationalism, embodied by the Indian National Congress, was cultural nationalism. The nationalists claimed that Indians might not be a single race but were at least a unified people, because of their unique culture and common colonial history.

Rewriting Traditions The recovery of traditions became a way to establish a modern Indian identity without acknowledging the recent subjugation by British colonizers. So Indian intellectuals (like those in Latin America) turned to the past and rewrote the histories of ancient empires and kingdoms. In this way, Indian intellectuals promoted the idea of India as a nation-state.

To portray Indians as a people with a unifying religious creed, intellectuals reconfigured Hinduism so that it resembled western religion. This was no easy task, for traditional Hinduism did not have a supreme textual authority (like the Bible or the Quran), a monotheistic God, an organized church, or an established creed. Nonetheless, nationalist Hindu intellectuals combined various philosophical texts, cultural beliefs, social practices, and Hindu traditions into a mix that they labeled the authentic Hindu religion. While fashioning hybrid forms, revivalists also narrowed the definition of Indian traditions. As Hindu intellectuals looked back, they identified Hindu traditions and the pre-Islamic past as the only sources of India's culture. Other contributors to the region's mosaic past were forgotten; the Muslim past, in particular, had no prominent role.

Hindu Revivalism Hindu revivalism became a powerful political force in the late nineteenth century, when the nationalist challenge to the colonial regime took a militant turn. New leaders rejected constitutionalism and called for militant agitation. The British decision to partition Bengal in 1905 into two provinces—one predominantly Muslim, the other Hindu—drew militants into the streets to urge the boycott of British goods. Rabindranath Tagore, a famous Bengali poet and future Nobel laureate, composed stirring nationalist poetry. Activists formed voluntary organizations, called Swadeshi ("one's own country") Samitis ("societies"), that championed indigenous enterprises for manufacturing soap, cloth, medicine, iron, and paper, as well as schools for imparting nationalist education. Although few of these ventures succeeded, the efforts reflected the nationalist desire to assert Indians' autonomy as a people.

Rabindranath Tagore The Bengali writer, philosopher, and teacher Rabindranath Tagore became the poet laureate of the Swadeshi movement in Bengal in 1903–1908. The first Asian Nobel laureate, he became disenchanted with nationalism, viewing it as narrow and not universalistic. The photo shows Tagore reading to a group of his students in 1929.

Unlike the insurgents of 1857, nationalist leaders in India at the turn of the twentieth century imagined a modern national community. Invoking religious and ethnic symbols, they formed modern political associations to operate in a national public arena. They did not seek a radical alternative to the colonial order; instead, they fought for the political rights of Indians as a secular, national community. In these new nationalists, British rulers discovered an enemy not so different from themselves.

THE PAN MOVEMENTS

India and China were not the only places where activists dreamed of founding new states. Across the globe, groups had begun to imagine new communities based on ethnicity or, in some cases, religion. **Pan movements** (from the Greek *pan*, "all") sought to link people across state boundaries. The grand aspiration of all these movements—which included pan-Asianism, pan-Islamism, pan-Africanism, pan-Slavism, pan-Turkism, pan-Arabism, pan-Germanism, and Zionism—was the rearrangement of borders in order to unite dispersed communities. But such remappings posed a threat to rulers of the Russian, Austrian, and Ottoman Empires, as well as to overseers of the British and the French colonial empires.

Pan-Islamism Within the Muslim world, intellectuals and political leaders begged their fellow Muslims to put aside their differences and unite under the banner of Islam in opposition to European incursions. The leading spokesman for pan-Islamism was the well-traveled Jamal al-Din al-Afghani (1838–1897). Born in Iran and given a Shiite upbringing, he nonetheless called on Muslims worldwide to overcome their Sunni and Shiite differences so that they could work together against the west. Afghani called for unity and action, for an end to corruption and stagnation, and for acceptance of the true principles of Islam.

The pan-Islamic message only added to Muslims' confusion as they confronted the west. Indeed, Arab Muslims living as Ottoman subjects had many calls on their loyalties. Should they support the Ottoman Empire to resist European encroachments? Or should they embrace the Islamism of Afghani? Most decided to work within the fledgling nation-states of the Islamic world, looking to a Syrian or Lebanese identity, for example, as the way to deal with the west and

Sultan Abdul Hamid II Agrees to a Constitution
In 1876, the new Ottoman sultan, Abdul Hamid II, agreed to reign as a constitutional monarch. Thanks in part to a war with Russia, which commenced the next year, and in part to the sultan's own dictatorial instincts, within two years' time the Ottoman Empire had reverted to absolute monarchy, and the sultan had begun to promote himself as a Muslim leader.

gain autonomy. But Afghani and his disciples had struck a chord in Muslim culture, and their Islamic message has long retained a powerful appeal.

Pan-Germanism and Pan-Slavism

Pan-Germanism found followers across central Europe, where it often competed with a pan-Slavic movement that sought to unite all Slavs against their Austrian, German, and Ottoman overlords. This area had traditionally been ruled by German-speaking elites, who owned the land farmed by Slavic peasants. German elites began to feel increasingly uneasy as Slavic nationalisms (spurred by the midcentury revivals of traditional Czech, Polish, Serbian, and Ukrainian languages and cultures) became more popular. Even more threatening was the fact that the Slavic populations were growing faster than the German population. As pogroms in the Russian Empire's borderlands in the 1880s, as well as economic opportunities, drove crowds of eastern European Jews westward, German resentment toward these newcomers also increased.

The rhetoric of pan-Germanism inspired mass, grassroots political activism. It motivated central Europeans to think of themselves as members of a German *race*, their identities determined by blood rather than defined by state boundaries. This, too, was the lesson of pan-Slavism. Both movements led extremists to take actions that were dangerous to existing states. The organization of networks of radical southern Slavs, for example, unsettled Bosnia and Herzegovina (annexed by the Austrians in 1908). Indeed, it was a Serbian proponent of plans to carve an independent Slav state out of Austrian territory in the Balkans who assassinated the heir to the Habsburg throne in June 1914. By August, the whole of Europe had descended into mass warfare, bringing much of the rest of the world directly or indirectly into the conflict as well. Eventually, the war would fulfill the pan-Slav, pan-German, and anti-Ottoman Muslim nationalist longing to tear down the Ottoman and Habsburg Empires. Intellectuals articulated the pan movements, but aspiring political leaders and secret societies took up their ideologies, leaving Europe and much of Asia at the end of the nineteenth century boiling with ideas of how to change the borders of states and the dominance of France and Britain.

Conclusion

Ever since the Enlightenment, Europeans had put their faith in "progress." Through the nineteenth century, educated, secular elites took pride in booming industries, bustling cities, and burgeoning colonial empires. Yet by the century's end, urbanization and industrialization seemed more disrupting than uplifting, more disorienting than reassuring. Moreover, colonized people's resistance to the "civilizing mission" fueled doubts about the course of progress.

The realization that "the people" were developing ways to unseat them terrified ruling elites. In colonial settings, nationalists learned how to mobilize large populations. In Europe, socialist and right-wing leaders likewise challenged liberals by appealing to the idea of popular sovereignty. A politics that relied on closed-door negotiations between "rational" gentlemen was unprepared to deal with modern ideas and identities.

Nor were elites able to control the scope of change, for the expansion of empires had drawn ever more people into an unbalanced global economy. Everywhere, disparities in wealth appeared. Moreover, the size and power of industrial operations threatened small firms and made individuals seem insignificant. Even some cities seemed too big and too dangerous. All these social and economic challenges stretched the capacities of gentlemanly politics.

They also stimulated creative energy. Western artists borrowed nonwestern images and vocabularies; nonwestern intellectuals looked to the west for inspiration, even as they formulated anti-western ideas. The upheavals of modern experience propelled scholars to study the past and to fabricate utopian visions of the future.

Even as these changes unsettled the European-centered world, they intensified rivalries among Europe's powers themselves. Although the world had become a smaller place and travel was easier and quicker, at least for those who had wealth and came from powerful societies, this increasing global integration had its limitations and contradictions. At its center—Europe—the global order was unstable. And in the massive conflict that destroyed this era's faith in progress, Europe would ravage itself. The Great War (described in Chapter 19) would yield an age of even more rapid change—with even more violent consequences.

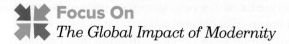

Focus On
The Global Impact of Modernity

Global Trends
- Mass migrations and unprecedented urban expansion challenge national identities.

Africa and China: Anticolonialism
- The Anglo-Boer War and violent uprisings against colonial rule in Africa call Europe's imperializing mission into question.
- The Chinese rebel against European encroachments in the Boxer Uprising.

Europe and North America: Mounting Tensions
- Intense political rivalries, financial insecurities and crises, rapid industrialization, feminism, and class conflict roil Europe and spread to the rest of the world.

Mexico: Resentment toward Elites
- The most widespread revolution from below takes place in Mexico.

Cultural Modernism
- Increased earning power gives workers in wealthy nations the leisure to enjoy music, vaudeville shows, sports, and other forms of popular culture and to read mass-circulation newspapers.
- Elite culture explores new forms in painting, architecture, music, literature, and science in order to break with the past and differentiate itself more dramatically from popular culture.
- New ideas of race emerge, as does a renewed emphasis on the nation-state and nationalism.

CHRONOLOGY	1870	1880	1890
Africa			
The Americas		Jim Crow laws in the United States 1890s	
Europe			
South Asia			
		Indian National Congress founded 1885 ●	
East Asia			

THINKING ABOUT GLOBAL CONNECTIONS

- **Thinking about Crossing Borders and an Unsettled World** How did mobility of different kinds unsettle established certainties in this period? Think in particular of the massive flight of farmers toward cities and the erosion of traditional social hierarchies; the prevalence of steamships and rail travel, which made long-distance journeys easier than ever before; and the emergence of the telephone and telegraph, which revolutionized communications.

- **Thinking about Changing Power Relationships and an Unsettled World** To what extent were challenges to western influence internal to the western tradition—the product of growing doubts and contradictions within the Enlightenment project—articulated by Europeans like Nietzsche and Freud? To what degree were they external to that tradition—a reaction against the massive concentration of wealth and power centered in the west and the values that supported western dominance?

- **Thinking about Women and Gender in an Unsettled World** To what degree did the economic and technological breakthroughs of the nineteenth century improve women's lives? To what extent were women able to make claims on governments in different parts of the world? How did ordinary women take control of their bodies and their lives, and how did feminists challenge patriarchal cultures?

 Go to **INQUIZITIVE** to see what you've learned—and learn what you've missed—with personalized feedback along the way.

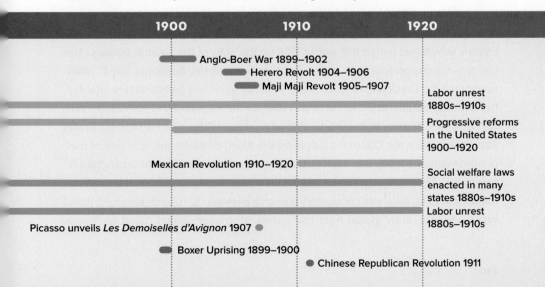

1900	1910	1920

Anglo-Boer War 1899–1902
Herero Revolt 1904–1906
Maji Maji Revolt 1905–1907

Labor unrest 1880s–1910s

Progressive reforms in the United States 1900–1920

Mexican Revolution 1910–1920

Social welfare laws enacted in many states 1880s–1910s

Labor unrest 1880s–1910s

Picasso unveils *Les Demoiselles d'Avignon* 1907

Boxer Uprising 1899–1900

Chinese Republican Revolution 1911

19

Global Crisis

1910–1939

Core Objectives

- **IDENTIFY** the causes of World War I, and **ANALYZE** the effects of the war on regions both within and outside Europe.

- **EXPLAIN** how the development of modern, mass societies both caused and was affected by the Great Depression.

- **COMPARE** the ideologies of liberal democracy, authoritarianism, and anticolonialism, and **EVALUATE** the success of each in this period.

- **EXPLAIN** how access to consumer goods and other aspects of mass society influenced political conflict in Asia, Africa, and Latin America.

In early 1916, the British First Lord of the Admiralty, Sir Winston Churchill, prevailed upon his colleagues and allies to undertake an unconventional effort to knock Germany and the Central Powers out of the Great War, as World War I was known before 1939. Instead of attacking Germany or Austria directly, a British-led Allied coalition would hit the Central Powers from the south, invading the Ottoman Empire, which had joined the war in 1914 on the side of the Central Powers. The Gallipoli Campaign took aim at the Dardanelles and the Bosporus Strait, which connected the Black and Aegean Seas, in order to clear a path to attack Istanbul, the Ottoman capital, and then provide relief for the Russian army (an Allied force) via sea-lanes. Thanks to the leadership of a young officer named Mustafa Kemal Ataturk, however, the Ottomans surprised the Allied coalition and won one of their greatest victories in the war. That victory prolonged the conflict, which dragged on for another two years, and expanded the war dramatically, spreading it throughout the Middle East. As a war conducted primarily between European empires, World War I was inherently global from the outset. Moreover, Britain relied on troops and resources from its empire and commonwealth—from Australia, New Zealand, and above all, India (which contributed over a million men)—to wear down the Ottomans in battles from Iraq to Palestine (present-day Israel and Palestinian territories). The result was that the war drew in belligerents from around the globe on an unprecedented scale. Furthermore, the power vacuum left after the Ottoman Empire collapsed in 1922 would give rise to political conflicts in the Middle East, the longest-lasting, most intractable conflicts to emerge from the war.

This chapter deals with the Great War and its global impact. First, because the war was fought among European powers with sprawling empires, resources from all over the world were brought to bear. The war prompted production and consumption on a mass scale. Wartime leaders also used new media such as radio and film to promote national loyalties and to discredit enemies—and thereby helped spread mass culture. Second, the incomplete nature of the peace settlement contributed to the outbreak of the Great Depression. Third, political turmoil surrounding the war inflamed disputes over how to manage mass societies and build a better world. To this end, three distinct visions arose: liberal democracy, authoritarianism, and anticolonialism. These ideologies competed for preeminence in the decades leading up to World War II.

Global Storyline

World War I and the Growth of Mass Societies

- The Great War (World War I) engulfs the globe, exhausts Europe, and promotes production and consumption on a mass scale.

- The victors' peace imposed on Germany produces resentment and economic instability, while Woodrow Wilson's League of Nations struggles to keep the peace.

- European countries' efforts to rebuild their economies after the Great War by cutting expenses and returning to the gold standard cause the Great Depression, whose severe repercussions reverberate globally.

- Three strikingly different visions for building a better world compete: liberal democracy, authoritarianism, and anticolonialism.

The Great War

Few events were more decisive in drawing men and women worldwide into national and international politics than the **Great War (World War I)**. For over four years, millions of soldiers from Europe, its dominions, and its colonies killed and mutilated one another. Such carnage damaged European claims to civilized superiority and encouraged colonial subjects to break from imperial masters. Among Europeans, too, the war's effects shook the hierarchies of prewar society. Above all, the war made clear how much the power of the state now depended on the support of the people, not just the elites, and showed how powerful those states could be.

The war's causes were complex. Underlying European tensions were great-power rivalries, which pitted a rising Germany and a conflict-ridden Austria-Hungary against Britain, France, and Russia. Through most of the nineteenth century, Britain had been the preeminent power. By century's end, however, Germany's industrial output had surpassed Britain's, and Germany had begun building a navy. For the British, who controlled the world's seas, the German navy was an affront; for the French, still seething from their defeat in the Franco-Prussian War of 1870–1871 (see Chapter 17), German military buildup seemed a mortal threat; for the Germans, it was a logical step in their expanding ambitions. British hawks, wielding their might in the international financial system, wanted to destroy German power. German hawks felt surrounded—by the French to the west, the Russians to the east—and argued for launching war before Russia grew too strong militarily. Germany joined Austria-Hungary to form the **Central Powers** (later adding the Ottoman Empire), and Britain affiliated itself with France and Russia in the Triple Entente (called the **Allied Powers** later, after Italy joined).

Well armed and secretly pledged to defend their partners, the rivals were provided with a spark in June 1914, when the heir to the Habsburg throne was assassinated in Sarajevo, the capital of Austrian-annexed Bosnia. The assassin, a teenage Bosnian Serb named Gavrilo Princip, hoped to trigger an independence movement that would unite South Slav territories in the Austro-Hungarian Empire (see Chapter 18) with independent Serbia. The Austro-Hungarian emperor decided to take a firm stand, and the German kaiser backed him; the Russians declared support for the Serbs in an effort to uphold state prestige and stifle domestic political opposition. The British and French were determined to prevent Germany and Austria from taking advantage of a possible Ottoman collapse and were keen to realize their own ambitions at German expense in the colonial world. Unable to diffuse mounting tensions diplomatically, contestants braced for war.

BATTLE FRONTS, STALEMATE, AND CARNAGE

At the outset, the belligerents expected the war to end quickly. But it soon became infamous for its duration and horrors. As casualties mounted, the war became more intractable, each side determined to slug it out for a final victory that never came. It began on July 29 with a massive Austrian bombardment of Serbian Belgrade, followed by the invasion of Austro-Hungarian troops who committed atrocities against civilians. The German offensive, a thrust through neutral Belgium into France, ran into French and Belgian resistance. German troops came close to Paris at the First Battle of the Marne in September 1914. (See Map 19.1.) A stalemate ensued. Instead of a quick war, vast land armies dug trenches along the Western Front—from the English Channel through Belgium and France to the Alps—installing barbed wire and setting up machine-gun posts.

It would be hard to exaggerate the terror and futility. Lord Kitchener—who had conquered Sudan in part by unleashing the machine gun on Sudanese warriors—had predicted to the British cabinet that the war in Europe "will not end until we have plumbed our manpower to the last military man." The fear of having to "go over the top" and into the withering fire and gas of "no man's land" to attack the enemy's entrenched position created severe mental health issues for many soldiers, including what was then called "shell shock" and is known today as post-traumatic stress disorder. Between panic attacks and bombardment, soldierly life in the trenches combined boredom, dampness, vermin, disease, depression, and terror.

The war quickly ground to a gruesome standstill. Although neither the Allies nor the Central Powers could substantially advance, they refused to negotiate peace. At Ypres in 1915, the Germans tried to break the stalemate by introducing poison gas, but a countermove of equipping soldiers with gas masks nullified that advantage. In July 1916, the British launched an offensive along the Somme River in northeastern France. By November, when the futile attack halted, approximately 600,000 British and French and 500,000 Germans had perished. When the smoke lifted, the battle lines had hardly budged.

On the other side of Europe, Russian troops advanced into German East Prussia and Austria-Hungary along the Eastern Front. Although they defeated Austro-Hungarian troops in Galicia (between present-day Poland and Ukraine) and scored initial victories in eastern Germany, they suffered devastating reversals once the Germans threw in well-trained divisions that were better armed and better provisioned than the Russian troops.

Strategically, World War I (like World War II, later) pitted the Germans' need to overwhelm opponents quickly against the Allies' ability to maintain cohesion. Germany had the most powerful military and the most productive industries in Europe, but it was surrounded by enemies, lacked basic resources, and was badly outnumbered. Germany consistently tried to escalate and expand the conflict to relieve pressure on its primary, European fronts. Berlin convinced the Ottomans to join its alliance and urged the sultan to proclaim a jihad against the British, French, and Russians so the Muslims inside those empires would rise up. In the end, the scheme failed, as did German efforts to lure the Allies into conflict in places like the Falkland Islands, Nigeria, and East Africa.

Map 19.1 World War I: The European and Middle Eastern Theaters

Most of the fighting in World War I occurred in Europe, and most of it was concentrated across a few agonizingly static fronts. Millions of soldiers perished over relatively thin belts of land, which became pulverized lunar landscapes.

- Which countries had to fight a two-front war?
- Did the armies of the Central Powers or the Allies gain the most territory?
- According to your reading, how did those territorial gains affect the war's outcome?

Armenian Genocide Armenian civilians being escorted by Ottoman troops to a mass prison in Mezireh in April 1915. As the war ground to a stalemate, Talaat Pasha, the minister of the navy, became the dictator of Syria and suspected Christians of colluding with Ottoman enemies. He became known as "the Blood Shedder" for his cruelty to unarmed civilians.

Attempts to win by opening other fronts only added to the carnage. The sprawling Ottoman Empire battled British- and Russian-led forces in Egypt, Iraq, Anatolia, and the Caucasus. In 1915–1916, after initially conscripting many Armenian soldiers into coerced forms of labor to support the war effort, Ottoman forces turned violent. They massacred or deported 1.5 million Armenians, whom they accused en masse of collaborating with the Russians. Some analysts regard these attacks as the world's first genocide, the intentional elimination of a whole people.

The fighting between European imperial colonies in Africa pitted German colonial armies against neighboring Allied colonial armies, with the heaviest fighting in central and East Africa. The results were twofold. Over 100,000 African soldiers died in the fighting, and over 300,000 civilians died from war-related famine and disease. The fighting also generated dozens of localized rebellions against imperial rulers.

A war of this scale, toll, and duration forced governments to call up more men than ever before. More than 70 million men worldwide fought in the war, including almost all of Europe's young adult males. From 1914 to 1918, 13 million served in the German army. In Russia some 15 million took up arms. In France around 8 million served, roughly 80 percent of men aged fifteen to forty-nine, a greater proportion than in any other major power. The British Empire mobilized nearly 9 million soldiers, and the 5.25 million troops of the

United Kingdom (England, Scotland, Wales, and Ireland) constituted almost half the prewar population of men aged fifteen to forty-nine. Over half of all the men mobilized for World War I were killed, injured, taken prisoner, or unaccounted for. Mass mobilization also undermined traditional gender boundaries. Tens of thousands of women served at or near the front as doctors, nurses, and technicians. Even more women mobilized on the "home front," taking on previously male occupations—especially in munitions plants. But women could also turn against the state. Particularly in central Europe and Russia, the war's demands for soldiers and supplies left farms untended and caused food shortages. Bread riots and peaceful protests by women, traumatized by loss and desperate to feed their children, put states on notice that their citizens expected compensation for their sacrifices. Indeed, civilian pressure forced many states to make promises they would have to fulfill after the war, in the form of welfare provisions, expanded suffrage, and pensions for widows and the wounded.

Military demobilization, meanwhile, hit societies hard, especially working women; when soldiers hobbled home, women faced layoffs from their wartime jobs. Still, their wartime roles helped women win the vote in Denmark (1915), the former Russian Empire (1917), Britain (1918), Germany (1918), and the United States (1920). (France held out until 1944.) Young, unmarried

Trenches in World War I The anticipated war of mobility turned out to be an illusion; instead, armies dug trenches and filled them with foot soldiers and machine guns. To advance entailed walking into a hail of machine-gun fire. Life in the trenches meant cold, dampness, rats, disease, and boredom.

Women's War Effort, 1915 With armies drafting nearly every able-bodied man, women filled their places in factories, especially in those that manufactured war materials.

women went out in public unescorted, dressed as they saw fit, and maintained their own apartments, to the shock of cultural conservatives.

Empire and War The war's horrors reached around the globe. (See Map 19.2.) To increase their forces, the British and the French conscripted colonial subjects: India provided 1 million soldiers, who fought exclusively in the Middle Eastern theater; over 1 million Africans fought in Africa and Europe for their colonial masters, and another 3 million transported war supplies. Even the sparsely populated British dominions of Australia, New Zealand, and Canada dispatched over 1 million young men to fight for the empire. Colonial recruits were also put to work in factories. In France, the international labor force numbered over 250,000, including workers from China, Vietnam, Egypt, India, the West Indies, and South Africa.

The Russian Revolution The war ravaged all empires; some it destroyed. The first to go was Romanov Russia. In February 1917, Tsar Nicholas II stepped down under pressure from his generals. They wanted to quash the mass unrest in the capital, St. Petersburg, which, they believed, threatened the war effort along the Eastern Front. Some members of the Russian parliament formed a Provisional Government; at the same time, grassroots councils (soviets) sprang up in factories, garrisons, and towns. With the tsar removed, millions of peasants seized land, soldiers and sailors abandoned the front, and borderland non-Russian groups split from the crumbling Russian Empire.

In October 1917, left-wing socialists calling themselves **Bolsheviks** seized power. A minority political group in February, the Bolsheviks gained enormous influence over the spring and summer by promising to pull Russia out of the war, controlling the price of bread for urban workers, and recognizing peasant land seizures. Led by Vladimir Lenin and Leon Trotsky, the Bolsheviks drew support among radicalized soldiers, sailors, and factory workers organized in the soviets. Arresting Provisional Government members, they claimed power in the name of the soviets. Several months later, Soviet Russia signed the Treaty of Brest-Litovsk, acknowledging German victory on the Eastern Front as the Russian army collapsed. For protection, the Bolshevik leadership relocated the capital to Moscow and set up a dictatorship. Lenin insisted on accepting the peace treaty and the loss of vast territories to safeguard the socialist revolution.

The Global View

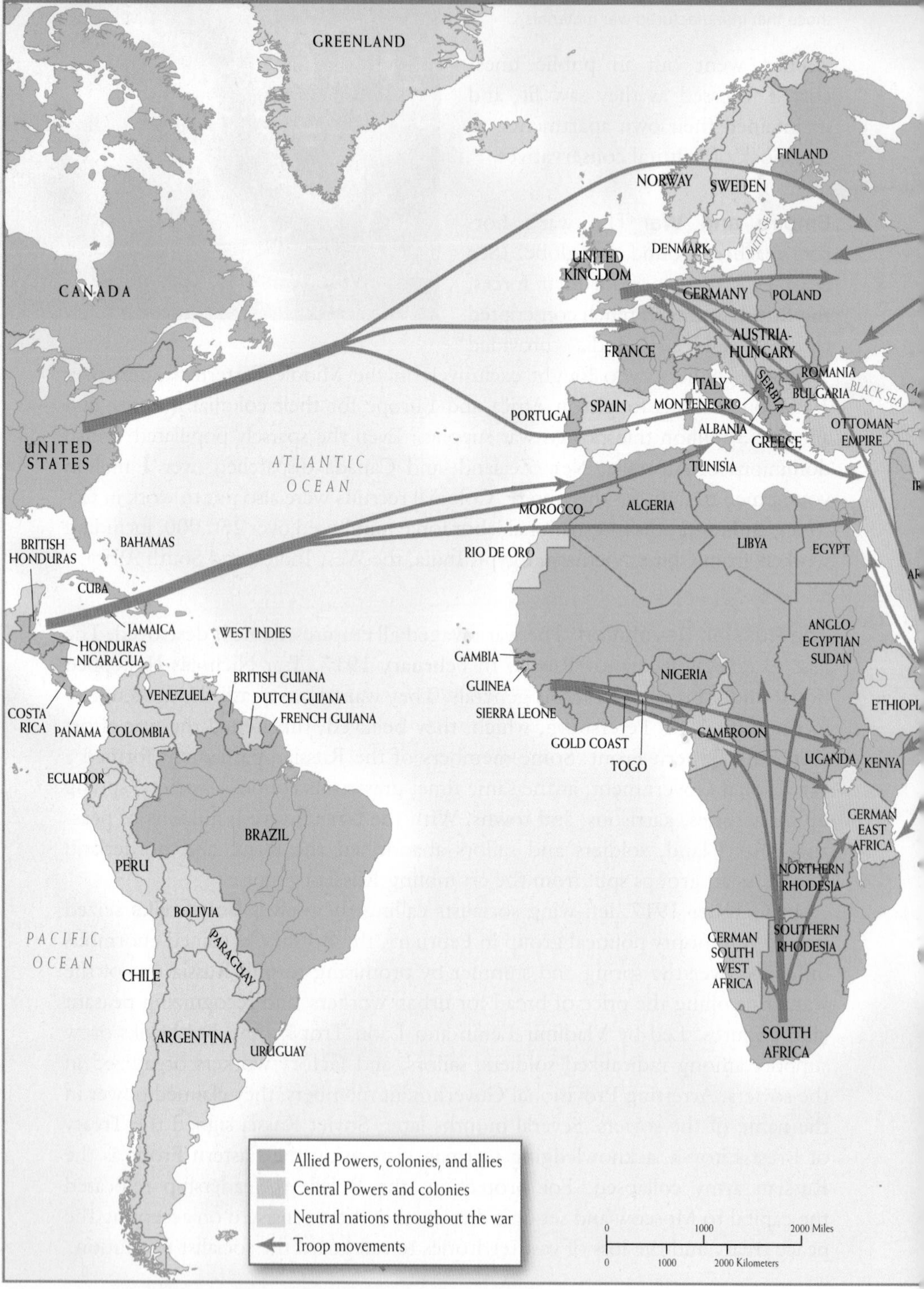

GREENLAND

FINLAND

NORWAY SWEDEN

DENMARK

UNITED
KINGDOM

GERMANY POLAND

CANADA

FRANCE

AUSTRIA-
HUNGARY

ROMANIA

ITALY

SERBIA BULGARIA BLACK SEA

PORTUGAL SPAIN

MONTENEGRO

ALBANIA GREECE

OTTOMAN
EMPIRE

UNITED
STATES

ATLANTIC
OCEAN

TUNISIA

MOROCCO ALGERIA

LIBYA EGYPT

BRITISH
HONDURAS

BAHAMAS

RIO DE ORO

ANGLO-
EGYPTIAN
SUDAN

CUBA

JAMAICA WEST INDIES

GAMBIA

NIGERIA

HONDURAS
NICARAGUA

GUINEA

ETHIOPIA

VENEZUELA

BRITISH GUIANA

SIERRA LEONE

COSTA
RICA PANAMA COLOMBIA

DUTCH GUIANA
FRENCH GUIANA

GOLD COAST

CAMEROON

UGANDA KENYA

ECUADOR

TOGO

BRAZIL

GERMAN
EAST
AFRICA

PERU

NORTHERN
RHODESIA

BOLIVIA

PACIFIC
OCEAN

PARAGUAY

GERMAN
SOUTH
WEST
AFRICA

SOUTHERN
RHODESIA

CHILE

ARGENTINA URUGUAY

SOUTH
AFRICA

Allied Powers, colonies, and allies

Central Powers and colonies

Neutral nations throughout the war

Troop movements

0   1000   2000 Miles

0   1000   2000 Kilometers

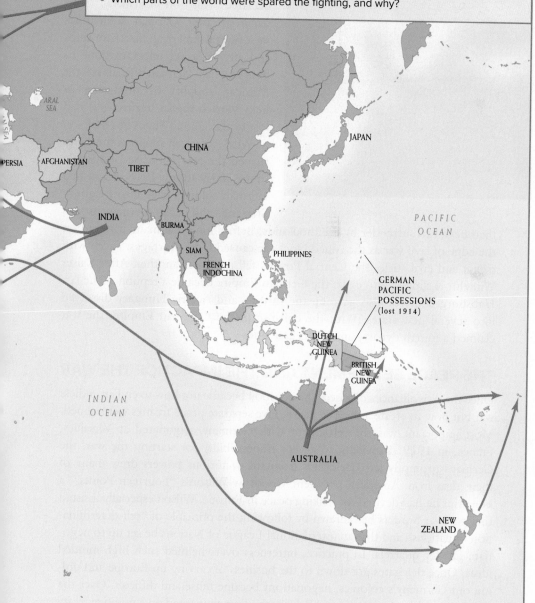

Map 19.2 World War I: The Global Theater

This map illustrates the ways in which World War I was a truly global conflict.

- Which states outside Europe became involved?
- Other than Europe, which continent experienced the most warfare?
- Which parts of the world were spared the fighting, and why?

The Russian Revolution Vladimir Lenin died just six years and three months after the October 1917 revolution, but he lived on in his writings and in images, such as this painting by Alexander Gerasimov called *Lenin on the Stand*. Artists and propagandists helped make Lenin an icon of the new Soviet order.

The Fall of the Central Powers

On April 2, 1917, the United States declared war on Germany. This occurred after German submarines sank several American merchant ships and after a secret telegram came to light in which German officials sought Mexican support by promising to help Mexico regain territories it had lost to the United States in 1848.

With American support, the Allies turned the tide at the Second Battle of the Marne in July 1918 and pushed German soldiers back into Belgium. Starving and sick, German troops then began to surrender by the thousands. Before long, Germany tottered on the edge of civil war as the Allied blockade caused food shortages. Faced with defeat and civil strife, the Central Powers fell one after another. After Kaiser Wilhelm II slipped into exile, the German Empire became a republic. The last Habsburg emperor also gave up the throne, and Austria-Hungary dissolved into several new states. With the collapse of the Ottoman Empire, the war claimed a fourth dynasty among its casualties.

THE PEACE SETTLEMENT AND THE IMPACT OF THE WAR

Once the Axis alliance collapsed, the question became not how to end an endless war but how to create a durable peace. Five separate peace treaties were signed. Most important was the settlement with Germany, negotiated at Versailles, France, in 1919. Unwilling to accept responsibility for starting the war, the Germans promptly left. Delegates from the victorious powers drew many of their ideas from American president Woodrow Wilson's "Fourteen Points," a blueprint he had devised for making peace in Europe. Wilson especially insisted that postwar borders be redrawn by following the principle of "self-determination of nations" and that an international League of Nations be set up to negotiate further quarrels. In practice, bitterness overwhelmed such high-minded ideas. Once delegates got down to the business of carving up Europe and doling out Germany's colonies, negotiations became tense and difficult. Over the objections of the Americans and British, the French insisted on a punitive treaty that assigned Germany sole blame for the war and forced it to pay reparations. When a League of Nations was created in 1920, the United States Congress refused to join.

BROKEN PROMISES AND POLITICAL TURMOIL

Violence became an enduring part of politics. Home fronts suffered grim impoverishment as states failed the challenges of the total war their rulers had launched. Left-wing elements grew stronger even as they divided between moderate socialists and communists; the right underwent a radical and dangerous mutation toward fascism and other forms of hypernationalism; and the center tried to accommodate itself to mass democracy. The polarization also unfolded on racial lines. Anti-Semitism spread everywhere. And African American soldiers who returned from service in Europe walked into a storm of racial hatred and lynching.

The American goal of making the world safe for democracy proved illusory. The idea of self-determination created intractable problems. Although President Wilson had intended self-determination to apply principally to the ethnic minorities within the Russian and Austro-Hungarian Empires and to European peoples still under Ottoman rule, other groups expected the term to apply to themselves as well. In Europe, making ethnic and political boundaries coincide proved impossible. Suddenly, 60 million people in central and eastern Europe emerged as inhabitants of new nation-states. (See Map 19.3.) Many were unhappy, as perhaps 25 million now lived in states where they were ethnic minorities and thus vulnerable to persecution in the tumultuous years after the armistice.

Beyond Europe, colonial peoples also seized upon the rhetoric of self-determination. But France's and Britain's imperial ambitions dashed these sentiments. The issue came up immediately at the Versailles peace negotiations. A photographer's assistant living in Paris named Nguyen Ai Quoc, the future Ho Chi Minh, famously challenged the American secretary of state, Robert Lansing, to take his own country's principles seriously and support the Vietnamese people's liberation from French rule, to no avail. Beyond Versailles, the British suppressed a 1919 rebellion in Egypt, albeit only after promising Egyptian nationalists a limited form of autonomy. The Syrians, too, did not understand why they were less deserving of self-rule than the Czechs or Yugoslavs, but the French put down a Syrian nationalist revolt. In India, similarly inspired by Wilsonian ideals, peaceful protesters gathered in a garden in the city of Amritsar in the Punjab. The British army mowed down 370 men and women and wounded 2,000 (although Indian eyewitnesses claimed that the dead totaled more than 1,000). In China, students, offended by the minor status accorded to their country at Versailles, launched a widespread protest in the name of Wilsonianism that solidified nationalist sentiment for this generation of students and later ones.

The bloodiest of all conflicts occurred in Iraq, where nearly 600,000 people— more than 20 percent of the population—rose up against British military efforts to force them into a colonial state. The rebellion's first stages were so successful that the Iraqis established an independent state in the middle Euphrates region, one that brought together Sunni and Shiite leaders and Arab officers and soldiers who had formerly served with the Ottoman army but desired an independent Iraqi state. Ultimately, British forces totaling 73,000, of whom 63,000 were Indian soldiers, were needed to crush the rebellion. Having broken their

Map 19.3 Outcomes of World War I in Europe, North Africa, and Some of the Middle East

The political map of Europe and the Middle East changed greatly after the peace treaty of 1919.

- Comparing this map with Map 19.1, which shows the European and Middle Eastern theaters of war, identify the European countries that came into existence after the war.
- What happened to the Ottoman Empire, and what powers gained control over many territories of the Ottoman state?
- What states emerged from the Austro-Hungarian Empire?

wartime promise to support an independent Arab empire from Palestine to the Fertile Crescent with both the Sykes-Picot Agreement (1916) and the Balfour Declaration (1917), the British installed Emir Faisal, a major leader in the Arab nationalism movement, as king of Iraq, where he ruled under the British mandate of the League of Nations from 1921 to 1933. (See Map 19.4.)

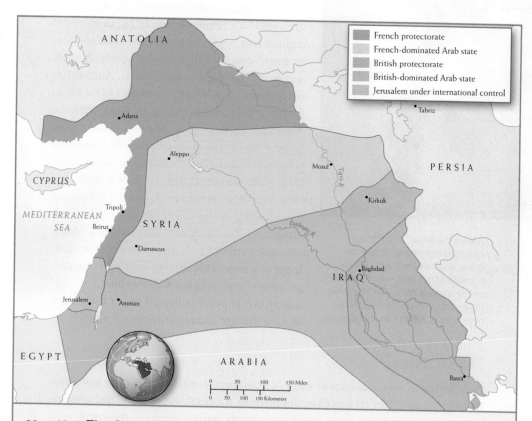

Map 19.4 The Sykes-Picot Agreement

The Sykes-Picot Agreement was a secret pact negotiated between British diplomat Mark Sykes and French diplomat François Georges-Picot in 1916. While the agreement reserved protectorates for the French in Syria and the British in Iraq, it also supported the creation of a politically independent Arab state or confederation of Arab states under an Arab chief.

- Why did the British and French governments want to divide up the Arab provinces of the Ottoman Empire?
- Compare the areas that were to be the Arab confederation, though dominated by the French and the British, with the map of ISIS (the Islamic State) that appears in Chapter 22 (Map 22.3). How similar are the territories in both maps?
- Why do you think that Arabs in particular and Muslims in general believed that this agreement was antithetical to their wishes and was an inadequate recompense for their contributions to the war effort? Why do you think that it continues to this day to fuel powerful grievances against the west?

Mass Society: Culture, Production, and Consumption

The war dramatically extended the making of mass societies. Even before 1914, democratic regimes had begun to extend the right to vote, in many cases making non–property holders and women eligible to cast ballots. Authoritarian regimes, meanwhile, had begun to mobilize the people via rallies and mass organizations. And new technologies, such as radio, were helping to create mass cultures that spanned geographic and class divides. The radio, coupled with mass-circulation tabloids featuring vivid snapshot photography, created the means to turn wider circles of listeners and readers into integrated communities—like nations. Mass consumer culture only compounded the challenge of a peace that needed nations to cooperate rather than compete with one another. Ultimately, world peace collapsed under the weight of mass-culture-induced national rivalries.

Josephine Baker The African American entertainer Josephine Baker, unable to perform in America because of her race, was a sensation on the stage in Paris after World War I. Many of her shows exoticized or even caricatured her African descent.

MASS CULTURE

New forms of communication and entertainment contributed to the new mass culture. In an effort to mobilize populations for total war, leaders had disseminated propaganda as never before—through public lectures, theatrical productions, musical compositions, and (censored) newspapers. Indeed, the war's impact had politicized cultural activities while broadening the audience for nationally oriented information and entertainment.

Postwar mass culture was distinctive. It differed from elite culture (opera, classical music, paintings, literature) because it reflected the tastes of the working and the middle classes, who now had more time and money to spend on entertainment. Moreover, mass culture relied on new technologies, like the cheap penny press (tabloid-style newspapers), photography, and, especially, film and radio, which could reach an entire nation's population and consolidate its sense of being a single nation-state.

Radio Radio entered its golden age after World War I. Invented in the 1890s, it made little impact until the 1920s, when powerful transmitters permitted stations to reach much larger audiences—often with nationally syndicated programs. Radio "broadcasts" gave listeners a sense of intimacy with newscasters and stars, addressing consumers as personal friends and drawing them in to the lives of serial heroes.

Radio also was a way to mobilize the masses, especially in authoritarian regimes. The Italian dictator Benito Mussolini pioneered the radio address to the nation; later, Soviet and Nazi propagandists used it to great effect, as did the right-wing Japanese government. But even dictatorships could not exert total control over mass culture. For example, although the Nazis regarded African American jazz as the music of an inferior race and the Soviets regarded it as "bourgeois," neither could prevent young or old from tuning in to foreign radio broadcasts, smuggling gramophone records over the borders, or creating their own jazz bands.

Film and Advertising Film, too, had profound effects. For traditionalists, Hollywood by the 1920s signified vulgarity and decadence because the silver screen prominently displayed modern sexual habits. Like radio, film served political purposes. Here, again, antiliberal governments took the lead. German filmmaker Leni Riefenstahl's movie of the Nazi Nuremberg rally of 1934, *Triumph of the Will*, is a key example of propagandistic cinema. Nazi-era films were comedies, musicals, melodramas, detective films, and adventure epics—sometimes framed by racial stereotypes and political goals. Soviet film studios also produced Hollywood-style musicals alongside didactic pictures about socialist triumphs.

In market economies, radio and film grew into big businesses, and with expanded product advertising they promoted other enterprises as well. Especially in the United

Mass Cultural Propaganda *Above:* The movie poster for the Soviet propaganda film *Jolly Fellows* by Grigori Aleksandrov. *Right:* The shooting of *Triumph of the Will*, directed by Leni Riefenstahl, who made a series of films for the annual Nazi Party rallies in Nuremberg. This one, perhaps the greatest propaganda film ever, won gold medals in Venice in 1935 and at the World's Fair in 1937.

States, advertising became a major industry, with radio commercials shaping national consumer tastes. Increasingly, too, American-produced entertainment, radio programs, and cinematic epics reached an international audience. Thanks to new media, America and the world began to share mass-produced images and fantasies.

MASS PRODUCTION AND MASS CONSUMPTION

The same factors that promoted mass culture also enhanced production and consumption on a mass scale. In fact, World War I had relied on industrial might, for machine technologies produced war materials with abundant and devastating effect.

Never before had armies had so much firepower at their disposal. Whereas in 1809 Napoleon's artillery had discharged 90,000 shells over two days during the largest battle waged in Europe to that point, by 1916 German guns were firing 100,000 rounds of shells per hour for 12 hours at a time in the Battle of Verdun. To sustain military production, millions of men and women worked in factories at home and in the colonies. Producing huge quantities of identical guns, gas masks, bandage rolls, and boots, these factories reflected the modern world's demands for greater volume, faster speed, reduced cost, and standardized output—key characteristics of mass production.

The war reshuffled the world's economic balance of power, boosting the United States as an economic powerhouse. As the United States' share of world industrial production climbed above one-third in 1929 (roughly equal to that of Britain, Germany, and Russia combined), people around the globe regarded it as a "working vision of modernity" in which not only production but also consumption boomed.

The Automobile Assembly Line The most outstanding example of the relationship between mass production and consumption in the United States was the motor car. Before World War I, the automobile had been a toy of the rich. Then came Henry Ford, who founded the Ford Motor Company in 1903. Seeking to make more cars more efficiently and sell them at prices affordable to workers, Ford used mechanized conveyors to send the auto frame along a track, or assembly line, where each worker performed one simplified task. By standardizing the manufacturing process and substituting machinery for manual labor, Ford's assembly line brought a new efficiency to the mass production of automobiles.

By the 1920s, a finished car rolled off Ford's assembly line in Detroit every 10 seconds. Although workers complained about becoming "cogs" in a depersonalized labor process, the system boosted output and reduced costs. Altogether, nearly 4 million jobs related directly or indirectly to the automobile—an impressive total in a labor force of 45 million workers.

After World War I, automobile ownership became more common among Americans. Ford further expanded the market for cars by paying his own workers $5 per day—approximately twice the average manufacturing wage in the United

States. He understood that without mass consumption, increased purchasing power in the middle classes, and the public's appetite for goods, there could be no mass production. Whereas in 1920 Americans owned 8 million motor cars, a decade later they owned 23 million. The automobile's rapid spread seemed to demonstrate that mass production worked.

The Great Depression Not all was easy listening and smooth motoring in countries where mass societies were taking root. The advent of mass societies and mass markets heightened the sense of instability and turmoil. Many worried that democracies were vulnerable to the whims of public opinion. Furthermore, economists worried about underlying market problems. Just as the peace treaties did not put an end to war, they could not wind the economic clock back to the prewar global prosperity. Instead, the world economy went through seismic ups and downs—and finally crashed dramatically in 1929, bringing a decade of misery, political polarization, and eventually nationalist-fueled war.

World War I had several lingering effects on the world economy. Primary producers of foodstuffs and fibers struggled to adjust to the new industrial age. In frontier areas like the North American West or in colonial plantation regions of West Africa, farmers began to overproduce their wheat and palm oil, driving down their prices by the late 1920s. These edges of the world market turned into weak links.

The war also led to runaway inflation. Conservative governments, desperate to restore stability, turned to austerity measures to place their countries back on a creaky gold standard. Some societies never fully recovered from the economic trauma of the first wave of mass unemployment caused by government policy.

Finally, the war left all belligerents burdened with massive public debts. France and Britain, once big lenders, became net borrowers; they owed creditors a whopping $8.5 billion in 1918. Germany, the crippled powerhouse at the center of Europe's economy, was stuck not only with its war debts but with the burden of indemnities. The Treaty of Versailles imposed reparations on Germany that totaled $33 billion, of which it ultimately paid $21 billion. The whole financial

German Reparations The Versailles peace treaty imposed heavy burdens on the German people. Stripped of colonial possessions, coal from the Saar region, and industries in other provinces, Germany still shouldered heavy "reparations" payments. When Germany fell into arrears, Belgian and French forces began to invade industrial pockets. This 1923 photo captures French troops moving into the manufacturing heartland of the Ruhr. In response, German coal and rail workers refused to work. The country plunged off a hyperinflationary cliff, stabilizing only after French withdrawal and a financial bailout. The economic cost and the memory of hurt pride led to lasting German grievances.

system became dependent on loans from the United States. Through the 1920s, American lenders recycled old loans while European debtors struggled to pay them off. This meant that if there was ever a crisis in the nerve center of New York, it would send riptides around the world.

The world market had no coordinating authorities to deal with a crisis. This made it fragile. Sure enough, when American bankers who worried about overheated markets at home called in their loans, their debtors were pushed into insolvency. Western farmers could not pay; banks started to go belly up. Then New York financiers started to call in their loans abroad.

This set off a spiral into the **Great Depression**. Bankers panicked, stock prices plunged, debtors walked away from their loans, banks failed, and as big lending from New York slammed shut, countries went off the gold standard one by one, letting their currencies fall.

Financial turmoil produced a major reduction in world trade. Striving to protect workers and investors from the influx of cheap foreign goods, governments raised tariffs against imports. After the United States enacted protective tariffs, other governments abandoned free trade in favor of protectionism. Manufacturers cut back production, laid off millions of workers, and often went out of business. By 1935, world trade had shrunk to one-third of its 1929 level. The producers of raw materials, mainly found in the less developed economies, felt the harshest effects, for their international markets shut down almost completely. For example, world prices for Argentine beef, Chilean nitrates, and Indonesian sugar all dropped sharply.

The Great Depression forced people to rethink the core of laissez-faire liberalism (see Chapter 15), the idea that free markets regulate themselves and free trade leads to economic progress. By the late 1930s, the exuberant embrace of private mass production had ceded to a new conviction: state intervention to regulate the economy was critical to prevent disaster. In 1936, the British economist John Maynard Keynes published a landmark treatise, *The General Theory of Employment, Interest, and Money*. He argued that the market could not always adjust to its own failures and that sometimes the state had to stimulate it by increasing the money supply and creating jobs. Although the "Keynesian Revolution" took years to transform economic policy, many governments had doubts about whether capitalism could be saved. The Great Depression did more than any other event to challenge the belief that liberal democracy and capitalism were the best way to achieve political stability and economic progress.

Mass Politics: Competing Visions for Building Modern States

In the aftermath of World War I, societies grappled with the question of how to build modern, prosperous states. The war upset class, gender, and colonial relations, which were already unsettled in the prewar period. On battlefronts and home fronts, countless workers, peasants, women, and colonial subjects had sacrificed and now expected to share in the fruits of peace. Even in victorious nations, many lost confidence in traditional authorities who had caused the human wastage. Amid widespread political turmoil, the states that retained some form of democracy revised the liberal vision, while authoritarianism gained in popularity and anticolonial movements gathered steam.

LIBERAL DEMOCRACY UNDER PRESSURE

The demands of fighting a total war had a profound effect on all the European states. All of them, including the democracies in Britain and France, seized the opportunity to experiment with illiberal policies. Indeed, the war brought both the suspension of many democratic rights and an effort by governments to manage industry and distribution. States on both sides of the conflict jailed many individuals who opposed the war. Governments regulated both production and, through rationing, consumption. Above all, the war and the economic crises that followed revolutionized the size and scope of the state.

British and French Responses to Economic Crises Britain and France retained their democracies, but even here, old-fashioned liberal democracy was on the run. Strife rippled across the British Empire, and in the home isles Britain gave independence to what became the Republic of Ireland in 1922. Britain's working-class Labour Party came to power twice between 1923 and 1931, but whether alone or in coalition with Liberals and Conservatives, Labour could not lift the country out of its economic crisis.

Disorder was even more pronounced in France, which had lost 10 percent of its young men and had seen the destruction of vast territory. In 1932–1933, six government coalitions came and went over the course of just nineteen months. Against the threat of a rightist coup, a coalition of the moderate and radical left, including the French Communist Party, formed the Popular Front government (1936–1939). It introduced the right of collective bargaining, a 40-hour workweek, two-week paid vacations, and minimum wages.

The American New Deal In the United States, too, markets and liberalism faced challenges. When the Great Depression shattered the nation's fortunes, pressure intensified to create a more secure political and economic system.

By the end of 1930, more than 4 million American workers had lost their jobs. As President Herbert Hoover, a Republican, insisted that citizens' thrift and self-reliance, not government handouts, would restore prosperity, the economic situation worsened. By 1933, industrial production had dropped by a staggering 50 percent since 1929. The hard times were even worse in the countryside, where farm income plummeted by two-thirds between 1929 and 1932.

In the 1932 presidential election, a Democrat, Franklin Delano Roosevelt, won in a landslide. He promptly launched what came to be called the New Deal, a set of programs and regulations that dramatically expanded the scope of the American national government and its role in the nation's economic life. In his first 100 days in office, Roosevelt obtained legislation to provide relief for the jobless and to rebuild the shattered economy. Among his administration's experiments were the Federal Deposit Insurance Corporation to guarantee bank deposits up to $5,000, the Securities and Exchange Commission to monitor the stock market, and the Federal Emergency Relief Administration to help states and local governments assist the needy. Subsequently, in 1935, the Works Progress Administration (WPA) put nearly 3 million people to work building roads, bridges, airports, and post offices. In addition, the Social Security Act inaugurated old-age pensions supported by the federal government.

Never before had the U.S. federal government expended so much on social welfare programs or intervened so directly in the national economy. Nonetheless, Roosevelt refrained from substantially redistributing national income. Privately owned enterprises continued to dominate American society. Roosevelt's aim was not to destroy capitalism but to save it. In this regard the New Deal succeeded, for it staved off authoritarian solutions to modern problems.

During the interwar years, liberal democratic regimes respected elections and defended private property against challenges from labor movements. But they intervened in markets and regulated people's lives in ways their prewar counterparts never would have contemplated.

"Jim Crow" "Jim Crow" laws mandated the segregation of races in the American South, with African Americans forced to use separate, and usually unequal, facilities, including schools, hotels, and theaters, such as this one in Mississippi.

AUTHORITARIANISM AND MASS MOBILIZATION

Like the liberal systems they challenged, authoritarian regimes came in various stripes. Right-wing dictatorships arose in Italy, Germany, and Japan. Although differing in important respects, they all disliked the left-wing dictatorship of the Soviet Union. The Soviets, in turn, hated the fascists. Yet all the postwar dictatorships shared a visceral dislike of liberal democracy as weak and corrupt, unsuited to muscular nations. These regimes touted their success in mobilizing the masses to create dynamic yet orderly societies. They also had charismatic leaders who personified the power and unity of the societies over which they ruled.

Although rejecting liberal democracy, post–World War I dictators insisted that they had their people's support. True, they treated their people as a mass conscript army that needed firm leadership to build new societies and guarantee well-being. But their demands, the leaders maintained, would yield robust economies, restore order, and renew pride. In addition, dictators gained support by embracing public welfare programs. They also vowed to deliver prosperity, national pride, and technology without having to endure the class divisions, unemployment, urban-industrial squalor, or moral decay of liberal societies. For a time, many believed them.

The Soviet Union and Socialism The most dramatic blow to liberal capitalism occurred in Russia, where the Bolshevik Party established a socialist regime. Fearing the spread of revolutions, Britain, France, Japan, and the United States sent armies to Russia to contain Bolshevism. But after executing Tsar Nicholas II and his family, the Bolsheviks rallied support by defending the homeland against its invaders. They also mobilized people to fight (and win) a horrific civil war (1918–1921) in the name of defending the revolution.

To revive a ravaged economy after losing 7 to 10 million people to a famine between 1921 and 1923, the Bolsheviks grudgingly legalized private trade and private property. In 1924, with the country still recovering from civil war, the undisputed leader of the revolution, Lenin, died. Lenin had done more than anyone to shape the institutions of the revolutionary regime, including creating expectations for a single ruler. After eliminating his rivals, **Joseph Stalin** (1878–1953) emerged as the new leader of the Communist Party and the country, which had become the Union of Soviet Socialist Republics (USSR), or Soviet Union.

Since socialism as a fully developed social and political order did not exist anywhere in the 1920s, no one was sure how it would actually work. Stalin resolved this dilemma by defining Soviet or revolutionary socialism in opposition to capitalism. Since capitalism had "bourgeois" parliaments serving the interests of the rich, socialism, as elaborated by Stalinist leaders, would have soviets (councils) of worker and peasant deputies. Since capitalism had unregulated and unruly markets, socialism would have economic planning and full employment. And since capitalism relied on the "exploitation" of private ownership, socialism would outlaw private trade and private property. In short, socialism would eradicate

УДАРНУЮ УБОРКУ—

БОЛЬШЕВИСТСКОМУ УРОЖАЮ

Collectivized Agriculture Soviet plans for the socialist village envisioned the formation of large collectives supplied with advanced machinery, thereby transforming peasant labor into an industrial process. The realities behind the images of smiling farmers—such as in this poster, exhorting "Give first priority to gathering the Soviet harvest!"—were low productivity, enormous waste, and often broken-down machinery.

capitalism and then invent social-ist forms in housing, culture, values, dress, and even modes of reasoning.

The efforts to build a noncapitalist society required class war, and these efforts began in the heavily populated countryside. As Stalin solidified his control over the Soviet Union in the late 1920s, he sought to combine indi-vidual farms into larger units owned and worked collectively and run by regime loyalists. Tens of thousands of urban activists and Red Army soldiers led the forced drive to establish these collective farms and to compel farmers to sell all their grain and livestock at state-run collection points at depressed state prices. In protest, many peas-ants burned their crops, slaughtered their livestock, and destroyed their farm machinery. The government responded by deporting the protest-ers, along with many bystanders, to remote areas. Meanwhile, harvests again declined, and famine claimed between 5 and 7 millions more lives.

When it came to industry, the regime rolled out Five-Year Plans to "catch and overtake" the lead-ing capitalist countries. Millions of enthusiasts (as well as deported peas-ants) set about building a socialist urban utopia founded on advanced tech-nology, almost all of it purchased from the Depression-mired capitalist coun-tries. Tens of millions of people built thousands of factories, hospitals, and schools. Huge hydroelectric dams, automobile and tractor factories, and heavy-machine-building plants symbolized the promise of Soviet-style modernity, which wiped out unemployment during the capitalist Great Depression. Soviet authorities also started building socialism in the borderlands, and the USSR soon included several new republics (see Map 19.5), all of which acquired their own institutions—but under central rule from Moscow.

Mass Terror and Stalin's Dictatorship The Soviet political system became more ruthless as the state expanded. Police power grew the most, partly from forcing peasants into collectives and organizing mass deportations. As the party's ranks swelled, ongoing loyalty tests also led to the removal of party members, even when they professed absolute loyalty. From 1936 to 1938, trials of supposedly treasonous "enemies of the people" resulted in the execution of around 750,000 people and the arrest or deportation of more than 2 million more. They were sent to forced-labor camps, collectively known as the Gulag. Such purges decimated the loyal Soviet elite—party officials, state officials, intelligentsia, army officers, and even members of the police who had enforced the terror. Lenin and Stalin secured a communist regime based in Russia but did so through highly coercive and deeply resented methods. Nonetheless, Stalin's efforts at heavy industrialization were to pay off when Nazi Germany invaded the Soviet Union in World War II (see Chapter 20).

Map 19.5 The Soviet Union

The Union of Soviet Socialist Republics (USSR) came into being after World War I.

- How did its boundaries compare with those of the older Russian Empire, as shown in Map 17.5?
- Identify the Soviet republics other than Russia.
- What does the large number of Soviet republics suggest about the ethnic diversity within the Soviet Union?

Mussolini Benito Mussolini, known as Il Duce, liked to puff out his chest, particularly when appearing in public. He pioneered radio addresses to the people and encouraged fascist versions of the mass spectacles that also became common in Soviet Russia.

Italian Fascism Disillusionment with the costs of the Great War and fear of a communist takeover like that in Russia inspired violent political movements in many European countries, above all in Italy and Germany. In Italy, mass strikes, occupations of factories, and peasant land seizures swept the country in 1919 and 1920. Amid this disorder, authoritarian nationalists seized power. Their leader was **Benito Mussolini** (1883–1945), a former socialist journalist, who coined the term **fascism**. In the wake of the Russian Revolution of 1917, fascism represented a counterrevolution. It combined mass movements, which had emerged on the political left, with an aggressive, authoritarian nationalism and antisocialist and antiliberal values.

In 1919, Mussolini sought to organize alienated veterans into a mass political movement. In the early years, black-shirted vigilante squads received money from landowners and industrial magnates to beat up socialist leaders. Still, the fascists presented themselves as champions of the little guy—of peasants and (nonsocialist) workers—as well as of war veterans, students, and white-collar professionals.

In 1922, Mussolini announced a march on Rome. The march was a bluff, since Mussolini had no military support, yet it intimidated the king, who disliked fascist ruffians but feared bloodshed more. So the king withheld use of the army against the lightly armed marchers. When the Italian government resigned in protest, the monarch invited Mussolini to become prime minister, even though fascists had won only a small minority of seats in the 1921 elections. Soon a series of decrees transformed Italy from a constitutional monarchy into a dictatorship. Within a few years, all parties except that of the fascists had been dissolved. The regime used parades, films, radio, and visions of recapturing Roman imperial grandeur to boost support during the troubled times of the Depression. Mussolini used his personal charisma to promote the idea that as Il Duce ("the leader"), he personified the power and unity of Italy.

Mussolini's dictatorship made deals with big business and the church. He left traditional elites in place and preserved their powerful institutions; thus, his regime fell short of a total social revolution. By the mid-1930s, Italian fascism had settled into a traditional form of conservatism. Nonetheless, as the first antiliberal, antisocialist alternative, the early phase of Italian fascism served as a model for other countries.

German Nazism In Germany, too, fear of Bolshevism and anger over the war propelled a violent, authoritarian party to power. Here, the dictator was **Adolf Hitler** (1889–1945), backed by the nationalist workers' movement, whose name he changed to the National Socialist German Workers' Party (*National-Sozialistische Arbeits-Partei*, or **Nazis**).

Unlike Mussolini, the young Hitler was never a socialist, but the Nazis' Twenty-Five Points (1920) combined nationalism with a heavy dose of anticapitalism. The party platform called for the renunciation of the Treaty of Versailles, for a defense of workers against war profiteers, and for discrimination against Jews. It was an assertion of Germany's grievances against the world and of the small man's grievances against those whom the Nazis perceived as the rich. At first, Hitler and the Nazis were unsuccessful, and Hitler himself was arrested. He was sentenced to five years in prison for treason but served less than a year. While in prison he wrote an autobiographical and fanatically anti-Semitic treatise called *Mein Kampf* (My Struggle, 1925), which subsequently became wildly popular among Nazis.

As the Great Depression eroded popular support for the Weimar Republic (the democratic regime that came into existence after the Treaty of Versailles), conservative leaders sought to profit from Hitler's popularity. Germany's president appointed Hitler chancellor (prime minister) in 1933, even as the Nazi movement was declining as an electoral force. Like Mussolini, Hitler came to power legally, with the help of traditional elites. Yet neither leader won an electoral majority.

Hitler's first step as chancellor was to heighten fears of communist conspiracy. The burning of the Reichstag (parliament) building in Berlin gave the Nazis an opportunity to blame the fire on the communists. They immediately suspended civil liberties, including free speech and freedom of association, and attacked and imprisoned their opponents, especially communists. By July 1933, the Nazis were the only legal party and Hitler was dictator of Germany. Like Mussolini, Hitler relied on choreographed mass rallies and new media like film and radio, as well as his own personal charisma, to mobilize a mass following.

Hitler also unleashed a campaign of persecution against Jews. Like many other right-wing Germans, he believed that a Jewish-socialist conspiracy had stabbed the German army in the back, causing its surrender in World War I, and that intermarriage with Jews was destroying the supposed purity of the

Aryan race (which included northern, White Europeans). Hitler and the Nazis did not believe that religious practice defined Jewishness; instead, they held, it was transmitted biologically from parents to children. Hitler encouraged the use of terror against Jews, destroying their businesses, homes, and marriages with non-Jews and ultimately eliminating all traces of Jewish life and culture in Nazi-dominated central Europe (see Chapter 20).

The Nazis won popular support by restoring order and reviving the economy, although the economic gains had more to do with timing than Nazi policy. In any case, Germany reemerged as a great power with expansionist aspirations. Just as Mussolini reached back to ancient Rome to connect fascism to the Italian past, Hitler, too, invoked history. He called his state the Third Reich—he considered the Holy Roman Empire (or Reich) the first and the Reich created by Bismarck in 1871 the second—to bolster its legitimacy.

Dictatorships in Spain and Portugal As authoritarian regimes spread across Europe, the military instituted dictatorships in Spain and Portugal. Their effort to seize power in Spain provoked a brutal civil war from 1936 to 1939, which left 250,000 dead.

The Spanish civil war was, from the start, an international war. When the Spanish republican government introduced reforms to break the hold of the church and landlords on the state, the military launched a coup and received weapons, advisers, and other backing from fascist Italy and Nazi Germany. The Soviet Union supported the republic with weapons and advisers, and many volunteers fought in international brigades. Britain and France dithered, leading Stalin and many others to conclude that the democratic powers would not stand up to fascism. The leader of the military coup, Generalissimo Francisco Franco (who had risen to prominence as an army officer in the campaign to establish a Spanish protectorate over what became Spanish Morocco), gained the upper hand in the civil war thanks to foreign support, his brutal tactics, and his forging of a broad political coalition of the traditional and radical right.

Militarist Japan Unlike authoritarian regimes in Europe, the right-wing movement that emerged in Japan did not spring from wounded power and pride during World War I. In fact, because wartime disruptions reduced European and American competition, Japanese products found new markets in Asia. Although the government expanded the electorate and seemed headed toward liberal democracy in the early 1920s, Japan veered to the political right in 1926 when Emperor Hirohito came to power.

Here, as in Germany, the Great Depression spurred the eventual shift to dictatorship. Japan's trade with the outside world had more than tripled between 1913 and 1929, but after 1929 China and the United States imposed barriers on Japanese exports in preference for domestic products. These measures contributed to a 50 percent decline in Japanese exports, and unemployment surged.

Such turmoil invited calls for stronger leadership, which military commanders were eager to provide. As in Germany and Italy, Japanese rulers dreamed of empire to defend the homeland against rivals.

Adding Manchuria to its Korean and Taiwanese colonies in 1932 (see Map 19.6), Japan established the puppet state of Manchukuo. Meanwhile, at home, "patriots" carried out a campaign of terror against uncooperative businessmen and critics of the military. By 1940, Hirohito and his closest advisers had merged all political parties into the Imperial Rule Assistance Association, ending even the semblance of democracy, and they advocated a radical form of racial purity. The Imperial Army divided the peoples of Asia into "master races," "friendly races," and "guest races," reserving a dominant position for the Japanese "Yamato Race."

Common Features of Authoritarian Regimes All the major authoritarian regimes of this period claimed that modern economies required state direction. In Japan, the government fostered huge business conglomerates (*zaibatsu*); in Italy, it encouraged big business to form cartels. The German state also regarded the private sector as the vehicle of economic growth, but it expected entrepreneurs to support the Nazis' racial, antidemocratic, and expansionist aims. The most thorough form of economic coordination occurred in the Soviet Union, which adopted American-style mass production while eliminating private enterprise. Instead, the Soviet state owned and managed all the country's industry.

All these states relied heavily on mass organizations. The Soviet Union, Italy, and Germany had single mass parties; Japan had various rightist groups until the 1940 merger. All promoted dynamic youth movements, such as the Hitler Youth and the Union of German Girls, the Soviet Communist Youth League, and the Italian squads marching to the anthem "Giovinezza" (Youth).

All these regimes, except the Soviet Union, were ambivalent about women in public roles. Even the Soviets, who claimed to support gender equality, eventually restricted abortion and rewarded mothers who had many children. Officials were eager to honor new mothers as a way to repair the loss of so many young men during the Great War. Yet many more women were also entering professional careers, and some were becoming their families' primary wage earners.

Finally, all the dictatorships used violence and terror as tools for remaking the sociopolitical order. The Italians and the Japanese were not shy about arresting political opponents, particularly in their colonies. However, it was the Nazis and especially the Soviets who filled concentration and labor camps with alleged enemies of the state, whether Jews or supposed counterrevolutionaries.

THE HYBRID REGIMES IN LATIN AMERICA

Latin American countries felt the same pressures that produced liberal democratic and authoritarian responses in Europe, Russia, and Japan. However, the Latin American leaders devised solutions that combined democratic and authoritarian elements.

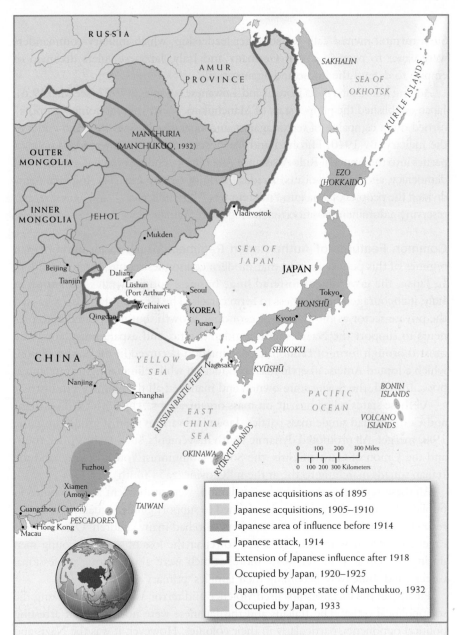

Map 19.6 The Japanese Empire in Asia, 1933

Hoping to become a great imperial power like the European states, Japan established numerous colonies and spheres of influence early in the twentieth century.

- What were the main territorial components of the Japanese Empire?
- How far did the Japanese succeed in extending their political influence throughout East Asia?
- According to your reading, what problems did the desire to extend Japanese influence in China present to Japanese leaders?

Economic Turmoil Latin American states had stayed out of the fighting in World War I, but their export economies had suffered. As trade plummeted, popular confidence in oligarchic regimes fell, and radical agitation surged.

As in Europe, Latin American governments stepped in to manage volatile economic markets. More than in any other region, the Depression battered Latin America's trading and financial systems, as well as the standards of living of laborers, because all were so dependent on exports. Exporters of basic staples, from sugar to wheat, faced stiff competition from other exporters and evaporating demand for their commodities. The region, in fact, suffered doubly because it had borrowed so much money to invest in infrastructure and expansion. When the world's major banks failed, creditors called in their loans from Latin America. This move drove borrowers to default. In an effort to improve their economic prospects, Latin American governments—with enthusiastic backing from the middle classes, nationalist intellectuals, and urban workers—turned to their domestic rather than foreign markets as the main engine of growth. Here, too, the state took a much more interventionist role in market activity than it was expected to do under the model of classical liberalism.

After the war, Latin American elites confronted the age of mass politics by establishing mass parties and encouraging interest groups to associate with them. Collective bodies such as chambers of commerce, trade unions, peasant associations, and organizations for minorities like Blacks and Indians all operated with state sponsorship. This form of modern politics, often labeled corporatist, used social groups to bridge the gap between ruling elites and the general population.

Corporatist Politics in Brazil Corporatist politics took hold especially in Brazil, where the old republic collapsed in 1930. In its place, a coalition led by the skilled politician Getúlio Vargas (1883–1954) cultivated a strong following by enacting socially popular reforms.

Dubbing himself the "father of the poor," Vargas encouraged workers to organize, erected monuments to national heroes, and supported the building of schools and the paving of roads. He made special efforts to appeal to Black Brazilians, who had been excluded from public life since the abolition of slavery. Thus, he legalized many previously forbidden Afro-Brazilian practices, such as the ritual *candomblé* dance, whose African and martial overtones seemed threatening to White elites. Vargas also supported samba schools, organizations that not only taught popular dances but also raised funds for public works. Moreover, Vargas addressed maternity and housing policies and enfranchised women (although they had to be able to read, as did male voters). Although he condemned the old elites for betraying the country to serve the interests of foreign consumers and investors, he also arranged foreign funding and technical transfers to build steel mills and factories. However, he took this step to create domestic industry so that Brazil would not be so dependent on imports.

Samba Dancers The dance started in the shanty towns of Rio de Janeiro and eventually became popular throughout the world, thanks to films, photographs, and long-playing records that featured samba music.

In these and other ways, Brazil and other Latin American governments combined democratic and authoritarian institutions and methods as a response to the economic downturn of the depression.

ANTICOLONIAL VISIONS OF MODERN LIFE

Debates over liberal democratic versus authoritarian models engaged the world's colonial and semicolonial regions as well. But in Asia and Africa there was a larger concern: What should be done about colonial authority? Throughout Asia, most educated people wanted to roll back the European and American imperial presence. Some Asians even accepted Japanese imperialism as an antidote, under the slogan "Asia for the Asians." In Africa, however, where the European colonial presence was more recent, intellectuals still questioned the real meaning of colonial rule: Were the British and the French sincerely committed to African improvement, or were they obstacles to African peoples' well-being?

In Africa as well as Asia, anticolonialism was the preeminent vision. To overcome the contradictions of the democratic liberalism Europeans practiced at home and the authoritarianism they exercised in colonial areas, educated Asians and Africans proposed various forms of nationalism.

Behind the Asian and African nationalist movements were profound disagreements about how best to govern nations once they gained independence and how to define citizenship. The democratic ethos of the imperial powers appealed to many intellectuals. Others liked the radical authoritarianism of fascism and communism, with their promises of rapid change. Whatever their political preferences, most literate colonial subjects also regarded their own religious and cultural traditions as sources for political mobilization. Thus Muslim, Hindu, Chinese, and African nationalist leaders used traditional values to gain the support of the rank and file. The colonial figures involved in political and intellectual movements insisted that the societies they sought to establish were going to be modern *and* at the same time retain their indigenous characteristics.

Sub-Saharan African Stirrings Africa contained the most recent territories to come under the Europeans' control, so anticolonial nationalist movements there were quite young. The region's fate remained very much in the hands of Europeans. After 1918, however, African peoples probed more deeply for the meaning of Europe's imperial presence.

There was some room (but not much) for voicing African interests under colonialism. The French had long held to a vision of assimilating their colonial peoples into French culture. In France's primary West African colony, Senegal, four coastal cities had traditionally elected one delegate (of mixed African and European ancestry) to the French National Assembly. This practice, limiting African representation to men of mixed ancestry, lasted until 1914, when Blaise Diagne (1872–1934), an African candidate, ran for office and won the seat in the French National Assembly, invoking his African origins and garnering the African vote. While the British allowed Africans to elect delegates to municipal bodies, they refused to permit colonial representatives to sit in Parliament.

Opposition was still not widespread in Africa, for protests ran up against not only colonial administrators but also western-educated African elites. Yet even this privileged group began to reconsider its relationship to colonial authorities. In Kenya, immediately after World War I, a small contingent of mission-educated Africans called on the British to provide more and better schools and to return lands they claimed European settlers had stolen. Although defeated in this instance, the young nationalists drew important lessons from their confrontation with the authorities. Their new spokesperson, Jomo Kenyatta (1898–1978), invoked their precolonial Kikuyu traditions as a basis for resisting colonialism. These early anticolonial movements prepared the foundations for more widespread resistance to colonial rule after World War II.

Imagining an Indian Nation As Africans explored the use of modern politics against Europeans, the war and its aftermath brought full-blown challenges to British rule in India. Indeed, the Indian nationalist challenge provided inspiration for other anticolonial movements.

For over a century, Indians had heard British authorities extol the virtues of liberal democracy, yet they were excluded from participation. In 1919, the British did slightly enlarge the franchise in India and allowed more local self-government, but these moves did not satisfy Indians' nationalist longings. During the 1920s and 1930s, the nationalists, led by **Mohandas Karamchand (Mahatma) Gandhi** (1869–1948), laid the foundations for an alternative, anticolonial movement.

Gandhi and Nonviolent Resistance When Gandhi returned to India in 1915, after studying law in England and gaining a reputation for working on behalf of Indian immigrants in South Africa, he immediately became the focus of the Indian nationalist movement. He spelled out the moral and political philosophy of *satyagraha*, or **nonviolent resistance**, which he had developed while in South Africa. His message to Indians was simple: develop your own resources and inner strength and control the instincts and activities that encourage participation in colonial economy and government, and you shall achieve *swaraj* ("self-rule"). Faced with Indian self-reliance and self-control pursued nonviolently, Gandhi claimed, the British eventually would have to leave.

Indian nationalists urged people to oppose cooperation with government officials, to boycott goods made in Britain, to refuse to send their children to British schools, and to withhold taxes. Gandhi added his voice, calling for an all-India *satyagraha*. He also formed an alliance with Muslim leaders and began transforming the Indian National Congress from an elite organization of lawyers and merchants into a mass organization open to anyone who paid dues, even the illiterate and poor.

When the Depression struck India in 1930, Gandhi singled out salt as a testing ground for his ideas on civil disobedience. Every Indian used salt, whose producer was a heavily taxed government monopoly. Thus, salt symbolized the Indians' subjugation to an alien government. To break the colonial government's monopoly, Gandhi began a 240-mile march from western India to the coast to gather sea salt for free. Accompanying him were seventy-one followers representing different regions and religions of India. News wire services and mass-circulation newspapers worldwide reported on the drama of the sixty-one-year-old Gandhi, wooden staff in hand, dressed in coarse homespun garments, leading the march. Thousands of people gathering en route were moved by the sight of the frail apostle of nonviolence encouraging them to embrace independence from colonial rule. By insisting that Indians follow their conscience (always through nonviolent protest), by exciting the masses through his defiance of colonial power, and by using symbols like homespun cloth to counter foreign, machine-spun textiles, Gandhi instilled in the people a sense of pride, resourcefulness, and Indian national awareness.

A Divided Anticolonial Movement in India Although Gandhi gained a mass following, his program met opposition from within, for many in the Indian National Congress Party did not share his vision of community as the source of public life. Cambridge-educated Jawaharlal Nehru (1889–1964), for example, believed that only by embracing science and technology could India develop as a modern nation.

Even less enamored were radical activists who wanted a revolution, not peaceful protest. In the countryside, these radicals sought to organize peasants to overthrow colonial domination. Other activists galvanized the growing industrial proletariat by organizing trade unions. Their stress on class conflict ran against Gandhi's ideals of national unity.

Religion, too, threatened to fracture Gandhi's hope for anticolonial unity. The Hindu-Muslim alliance crafted by nationalists in the early 1920s splintered over who represented them and how to ensure their political rights. The Muslim community found an impressive leader in Muhammad Ali Jinnah, who set about making the Muslim League the sole representative organization of the Muslim

Gandhi and the Road to Independence *Left:* Gandhi launched a civil disobedience movement in 1930 by defying the British government's tax on salt. Calling it "the most inhuman poll tax the ingenuity of man can devise," Gandhi, accompanied by his followers, set out on a monthlong march on foot covering 240 miles to Dandi, on the Gujarat coast. The picture shows Gandhi arriving at the sea, where he and his followers broke the law by scooping up handfuls of salt. *Right:* Gandhi believed that India had been colonized by becoming enslaved to modern industrial civilization. Indians would achieve independence, he argued, when they became self-reliant. Thus, he made the spinning wheel a symbol of *swaraj* and handspun cloth the virtual uniform of the nation.

community. In 1940, the Muslim League passed a resolution demanding independent Muslim states in provinces where Muslims constituted a majority, on the grounds that they were not a religious minority of the Indian nation but a nation themselves.

In 1937, the British belatedly granted India provincial assemblies, a national legislature with two chambers, and an executive. By then, however, India's people were deeply politicized. The Indian Congress Party, which inspired the masses to overthrow British rule, struggled to contain the different ideologies and new political institutions, such as labor unions, peasant associations, religious parties, and communal organizations. Seeking a path to economic modernization, Gandhi, on one side, envisioned independent India as an updated collection of village republics organized around the benevolent authority of male-dominated households. Nehru, on another side, hoped for a socioeconomic transformation powered by science and state-sponsored economic planning. Both believed that India's traditions of collective welfare and humane religious and philosophical practices set it apart from the modern west. By the outbreak of World War II, India was well on its way toward political independence, but British policies and India's divisions foretold a violent end to imperial rule (see Chapter 20).

Chinese Nationalism Unlike India and Africa, China was never formally colonized. But foreign powers' "concession areas" on Chinese soil compromised its sovereignty. Indeed, foreign nationals living in China enjoyed many privileges, including immunity from Chinese law. Furthermore, unequal treaties imposed on the Qing government had robbed China of its customs and tariff autonomy. Thus,

Chiang Kai-shek Riding the current of anti-imperialism, Chiang Kai-shek, shown here in 1924 in military dress, led the Guomindang on a military campaign in 1926–1928 and seized power, establishing a new national government based in Nanjing.

the Chinese nationalists' vision of a modern alternative echoed that of the Indian nationalists: ridding the nation of foreign domination was the initial condition of national fulfillment. For many, the 1911 Revolution (as the fall of the Qing dynasty came to be known; see Chapter 18) symbolized the first step toward transforming a crumbling agrarian empire into a modern nation.

Despite high hopes, the new republic could not establish legitimacy. For one thing, factional and regional conflicts made the government little more than a loose alliance of rural elites, merchants, and military leaders. Its intellectual inspiration came from the ideas of Sun Yat-sen, founder of the nationalist political party, the Guomindang. Under the banner of anti-imperialism, the party sponsored large-scale organizations of workers' unions, peasant leagues, and women's associations that looked to students and workers as well as the Russian Revolution for inspiration.

In 1926, amid a renewed tide of anti-foreign agitation, **Chiang Kai-shek** (1887–1975) seized control of the party following Sun's death. Chiang launched a partially successful military campaign to reunify the country and established a new national government in 1928 with its capital in Nanjing.

Peasant Populism in China: White Wolf For many Guomindang leaders, the peasant population represented a backward class. Thus, the leadership failed to tap into the revolutionary potential of the countryside, which was alive with grassroots movements such as that of White Wolf.

From late 1913 to 1914, Chinese newspapers circulated reports about a roving band of armed men led by a mysterious figure known as White Wolf. This figure terrified members of the elite. It is unlikely that the band, rumored to have close to a million followers, had more than 20,000 members even at its height. But the mythology surrounding White Wolf was so widespread that the movement's impact reverberated well beyond its physical presence.

Popular myth depicted White Wolf as a Chinese Robin Hood with the mission to restore order. The band's objective was to rid the country of government injustices. Raiding major trade routes and market towns, White Wolf's followers gained a reputation for robbing the rich and aiding the poor. Stories of helping the poor won the White Wolf army many followers in rural China, where local peasants joined temporarily as fighters and then returned home when the band moved on. Although the White Wolf army lacked the power to restore order in the countryside, its presence reflected the changes that had to come in China.

A Postimperial Turkish Nation Of all the postwar anticolonial movements, none was more successful or more committed to European models than that of **Mustafa Kemal Ataturk** (1881–1938), who helped forge the modern Turkish nation-state. Until 1914, the Ottoman Empire was a colonial power in its own right. But having fought on the losing German side, it saw its realm shrink to a part of Anatolia under the Treaty of Sèvres, which ended the war between the Allies and the Ottoman Empire.

In 1920, an Ottoman army officer and military hero named Mustafa Kemal harnessed an outpouring of Turkish nationalism into opposition to Greek troops that had been sent to enforce the peace treaty. Rallying his own troops to defend the fledgling Turkish nation, Kemal reconquered most of Anatolia and the area around Istanbul and secured international recognition for the new state in 1923 in the Treaty of Lausanne. Thereafter, a vast, forcible exchange of populations occurred. Approximately 1.2 million Greek Christians left Turkey to settle in Greece, and 400,000 Muslims relocated from Greece to Turkey.

Ataturk In the 1920s, Mustafa Kemal, known as Ataturk, introduced the Latin alphabet for the Turkish language as part of his campaign to modernize and secularize Turkey. He underscored his commitment to change by having a photographer record his demonstration of the new alphabet.

With the Ottoman Empire gone, Kemal and his followers moved to build a state based on Turkish national identity. First they deposed the sultan. Then they abolished the Ottoman caliphate and proclaimed Turkey a republic, whose supreme authority would be an elected House of Assembly. Later, after Kemal insisted that the people adopt European-style surnames, the assembly conferred on Kemal the mythic name Ataturk, "father of the Turks."

In forging a Turkish nation, Kemal looked to construct a European-style secular state and to eliminate Islam's hold over civil and political affairs. The Turkish elites replaced Muslim religious law with the Swiss civil code, instituted the western (Christian) calendar, and abolished the once-powerful dervish religious orders. They also sought to eliminate Arabic and Persian words from Turkish, substituted Roman script for Arabic letters, forbade polygamy, made wearing the fez (a brimless cap associated in Kemal's mind with old-fashioned ways) a crime, and instructed Turks to wear European-style hats. The veil, though not outlawed, was denounced as a relic. In 1934, the government enfranchised Turkish women, granted them property rights in marriage and inheritance, and allowed them to enter the professions. Schools were taken out of the hands of Muslim clerics, placed under state control, and, along with military service, became the chief instrument for making the masses conscious of belonging to a Turkish nation. Yet many villagers did not accept Ataturk's non-Islamic nationalism, remaining devoted to Islam and resentful of the prohibitions against dervish dancing.

In imitating Europe, Kemal also borrowed many of its antidemocratic models. Inspired by the Soviets, he inaugurated a five-year plan for the economy emphasizing centralized coordination by the government. During the 1930s, Turkish nationalists also drew on Nazi examples by advocating racial theories that celebrated central Asian Turks as the founders of all civilization. In another authoritarian move, Kemal occasionally rigged parliamentary elections, while using the police and judiciary to silence his critics. The Kemalist revolution in Turkey was the most far-reaching and enduring transformation that had occurred outside Europe and the Americas up to that point. It offered an important model for the founding of secular, authoritarian states in the Islamic world.

Nationalism and the Rise of the Muslim Brotherhood in Egypt Elsewhere in the Middle East, where France and Britain had expanded their holdings at the Ottomans' expense, anticolonial movements borrowed from European models while putting their own stamp on nation-making and modernization campaigns. In Egypt, the British occupation predated the fall of the Ottoman Empire, but here, too, World War I energized the forces of anticolonial nationalism.

When the war ended, Sa'd Zaghlul (1857–1927), an educated Egyptian patriot, pressed for an Egyptian delegation to be invited to the peace conference at Versailles. He hoped to present Egypt's case for national independence. Instead, British officials arrested and exiled him and his most vocal supporters. When news of this action came out, Egypt burst into revolt. Rural rebels broke away from the central government, proclaiming local republics. Villagers tore up railway lines and telegraph wires, the symbols of British authority.

After defusing the conflict, British authorities tried to appease the Egyptian desire to control their own destiny. In 1922, Britain proclaimed Egypt independent, although it retained the right to station British troops on Egyptian soil. Ostensibly, this provision was intended to protect traffic through the Suez Canal and foreign populations residing in Egypt, but it also enabled the British to continue to influence Egyptian politics. Two years later, elections placed Zaghlul's nationalist party, the Wafd, in office. But the British prevented the Wafd from exercising real power.

This subversion of independence and democracy provided an opening for antiliberal versions of anticolonialism in Egypt. During the Depression years, a fascist group, Young Egypt, garnered wide appeal. Much more influential and destined to have an enduring influence throughout the Arab world was an Islamic group founded in 1928, the Muslim Brotherhood, which attacked liberal democracy as a façade for middle-class, business, and landowning interests. The Muslim Brotherhood was anticolonial and anti-British, but its members considered mere political independence insufficient. Egyptians, they argued, must also renounce the lure of the west (whether liberal capitalism or godless communism) and return to a purified form of Islam. For the Muslim Brotherhood, Islam offered a complete way of life. A "return to Islam" through the nation-state created yet another model of modernity for colonial and semicolonial peoples.

Conclusion

The Great War and its aftermath accelerated the trend toward mass participation in a broad range of activities and the debate over how to define progress and organize the people. Because mass society meant production and consumption on a staggering scale, satisfying the populace became a pressing concern for rulers worldwide. Competing programs vied for influence in the new, broader, public domain.

Most programs fell into one of three categories: liberal democratic, authoritarian, or anticolonial. Liberal democracy defined the political and economic systems in most of western Europe and the Americas in the decade following World War I. Resting on faith in free enterprise and representative democracy (with a restricted franchise), liberal regimes had already been unsettled before the Great War. Turn-of-the-century reforms broadened electorates and brought government oversight and regulation into private economic activity. But during the Great Depression, dissatisfaction again deepened. Only far-reaching reforms, introducing greater regulation and more aggressive government intervention to provide for the citizenry's welfare, saved capitalist economies and democratic political systems in Britain, France, and North America from collapse.

Through the 1930s, liberal democracy was in retreat. Authoritarianism seemed better positioned to satisfy the masses while representing the dynamism of modernity. While authoritarians differed about the faults of capitalism, they joined in the condemnation of electoral democracy. Authoritarians mobilized the masses to put the interests of the nation above the individual. That mobilization often involved brutal repression, yet it seemed also to restore pride and purpose to a great number of people.

Meanwhile, the colonial and semicolonial world searched for ways to escape from European domination. In Asia and Africa, anticolonial leaders sought to eliminate foreign rule while turning colonies into nations and subjects into citizens. Some looked to the liberal democratic west for models of nation building, but others rejected liberalism because it was associated with colonial rule. Instead, socialism, communism, fascism, and a return to religious traditions offered more promising paths.

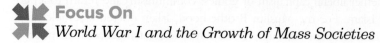

Focus On
World War I and the Growth of Mass Societies

The Great War

- The war destroys empires, starting with the Bolshevik Revolution against the tsarist regime in Russia, followed by the defeat and dissolution of the German, Austro-Hungarian, and Ottoman Empires.

- Mass mobilization sees almost 70 million men join the fighting, undermines traditional gender boundaries, and forces states to recognize their peoples' demands for compensation afterward.

- Popular culture spreads as leaders use the new media of radio and film to promote national loyalties and discredit enemies.

The Aftermath

- Liberal democracies in France, Britain, and the United States survive the Great Depression by enacting far-reaching changes in their political systems and free market economies.

- Authoritarian (communist and fascist) dictatorships with many political similarities emerge in the Soviet Union, Italy, Germany, Spain, and Portugal.

- Latin American leaders devise hybrid solutions that combine democratic and authoritarian elements.

- Peoples living under colonial rule in Asia and Africa mobilize traditional values to oppose imperial rulers.

- Key individuals emerge in the struggle to define newly independent nations: Kenyatta, Gandhi, Chiang Kai-shek, and Ataturk.

Key Terms

Allied Powers p. 732
Mustafa Kemal Ataturk p. 765
Bolsheviks p. 737
Central Powers p. 732

Chiang Kai-shek p. 764
fascism p. 754
Mohandas Karamchand (Mahatma) Gandhi p. 761

Great Depression p. 748
Great War (World War I) p. 732
Adolf Hitler p. 755
Benito Mussolini p. 754

Nazis p. 755
nonviolent resistance p. 761
Joseph Stalin p. 751

CHRONOLOGY

	1900	1910	1920
The Americas		United States enters World War I 1917	
Europe		World War I 1914–1918	Mussolini takes over Italy 1922
Soviet Union		Bolshevik Revolution 1917 / Russian civil war 1918–1921	
East Asia			
South Asia		Sykes-Picot Agreement 1916 / Balfour Declaration 1917	
Middle East		Mustafa Kemal creates modern Turkish nation-state 1923	

THINKING ABOUT GLOBAL CONNECTIONS

- **Thinking about Transformation & Conflict and Visions of the Modern** What was the relationship between war and progress in the early twentieth century? What new political, social, and cultural movements grew out of the Great War? Think in particular of the role of former soldiers in politics; the adaptation in peacetime of production practices developed for the war effort; and governments' willingness and ability to regulate the economy and people's everyday lives.

- **Thinking about Changing Power Relationships and Visions of the Modern** What, if anything, was left in this period of the tradition of classical liberalism, which trusted markets to regulate themselves and believed progress would result when individuals pursued their own self-interest? What

role did government intervention—in the economy and society—play for the three major traditions discussed in this chapter: liberal democratic, authoritarian, and anticolonial? How central was state intervention to their respective views of progress and modernity?

- **Thinking about Gender and Visions of the Modern** What role did women play in the social transformations of the early twentieth century, both as participants and as symbols? Pay special attention to the role of women workers in war production and, increasingly, in professional careers thereafter; to women consumers in an era of mass production; and to governments' commitment to the ideal of gender equality and their (faltering) willingness to abide by that ideal.

 Go to **INQUIZITIVE** to see what you've learned—and learn what you've missed—with personalized feedback along the way.

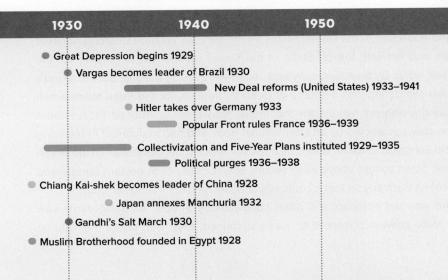

1930	1940	1950

- Great Depression begins 1929
- Vargas becomes leader of Brazil 1930
- New Deal reforms (United States) 1933–1941
- Hitler takes over Germany 1933
- Popular Front rules France 1936–1939
- Collectivization and Five-Year Plans instituted 1929–1935
- Political purges 1936–1938
- Chiang Kai-shek becomes leader of China 1928
- Japan annexes Manchuria 1932
- Gandhi's Salt March 1930
- Muslim Brotherhood founded in Egypt 1928

20

The Three-World Order

1940–1975

Core Objectives

- **EXPLAIN** the relationship between World War II and the three-world order.

- **ANALYZE** the extent to which World War II was a global war.

- **ANALYZE** the roles that the United States and the Soviet Union played in the Cold War.

- **IDENTIFY** the goals of Third World states in this period, and **EVALUATE** the degree to which these goals were achieved.

- **COMPARE** the civil rights issues in the First, Second, and Third Worlds, and **ASSESS** the ways each "world" addressed these and other basic rights.

In February 1945, the three leaders of the World War II Allies—President Franklin Delano Roosevelt of the United States, Prime Minister Winston Churchill of Great Britain, and Premier Joseph Stalin of the Soviet Union—met to prepare for the postwar world. By then, Germany and Japan were losing the war. But the world's postwar reordering was a source of deep contention, for the three leaders had profoundly different visions for the future. Roosevelt envisioned independent nation-states protected by an international body and had no interest in restoring the old European empires. Churchill, however, resisted decolonization of the British Empire. Stalin sought above all to secure Soviet influence in eastern Europe and to weaken Germany so that it could never again menace the Soviet Union.

The war had complex and often contradictory effects. All belligerents saw their state powers bolstered to wage sustained, total war. When the fighting stopped, the European-centered order, shocked by World War I, had been shattered by World War II. Empires either lay in ruins or faced an upsurge of independence movements. The nation-state had emerged as the prevailing global political organization.

With the weakening of western Europe, a new three-world order emerged. Heading the "First World," the United States championed capitalism and democracy as the best way to bring unprecedented prosperity in the decades after 1945. The Soviet Union, despite having been the United States' crucial ally during World War II, became its chief adversary in the decades that followed. As leader of the communist "Second World," the Soviet Union contested capitalist societies' claims and trumpeted socialism's accomplishments. As their spheres of influence expanded, the Americans and the Soviets (and their respective allies) engaged in a bitter ideological rivalry, known as the **Cold War** because no direct military conflict occurred between these two superpowers. Caught in between were formerly colonized and semicolonized peoples. Lumped together as the "Third World" by western intellectuals and by Asian, Latin American, and African leaders who embraced the idea of an alternative to the two dominant blocs, these nations emerged from the war eager to seek their own ways forward.

Global Storyline

World War II and the Emergence of the First, Second, and Third Worlds during the Cold War

- World War II shatters the European-centered global order, weakening Europe and Japan and unsettling empires.

- The United States and its liberal democratic allies (the First World) engage in a cold war with the Soviet Union and its communist allies (the Second World).

- Decolonized states in Asia, Africa, and Latin America (the Third World) struggle to find a "third way" but find themselves caught between the rival superpowers.

World War II and Its Aftermath

World War II was truly a global conflict, a devastatingly total one. It grew out of unresolved problems connected to the Great War. World War I had not been, as many had prophesied, "the war to end all wars." Especially influential were the resentments bred by the harsh provisions and controversial state boundaries set out in the treaties signed at the war's end. World War II also resulted from the aggressive ambitions and racial theories of Germany and Japan. By the late 1930s, German and Japanese ambitions to become imperial powers brought these dictatorships (which, along with Italy, constituted the Axis Powers) into conflict with France, Britain, the Soviet Union, and eventually the United States (the Allied Powers).

Compared to the First World War, the Second World War was more global, stretching across Europe, Africa, and Asia; the Atlantic and the Pacific Oceans; and the Northern and Southern Hemispheres. Belligerents mobilized entire societies, including the colonized, into armed forces and placed enormous demands on civilians. Civilians in places such as India and Greece, Yugoslavia and Korea, Poland and the Philippines suffered terrible hardships, including famines, reprisal killings, and deportations in the course of this war without mercy. Moreover, as aerial bombardment of cities caused colossal civilian casualties, the total war erased the old distinction between soldiers and civilians. Women—as victims and as collaborators, as volunteers and as forced laborers, as workers behind the scenes and as witnesses to the conflict—were involved as never before. They, together with children, the infirm, and the elderly, also swelled the enormous population of refugees seeking safety in the midst of worldwide chaos.

World War II also completed the decline of European world dominance that World War I had set in motion. The unspeakable acts of barbarism perpetrated during the Second World War, including the Nazi genocides directed against Jews and others, robbed Europe of its lingering claims of superiority. In the war's wake, anticolonial movements demanded national self-determination from battered and morally bankrupted European powers.

THE WAR IN EUROPE

World War II began in September 1939 with Germany's invasion of Poland and Britain's and France's decision to oppose it. Before it was all over in 1945, much of Europe, including Germany, had been leveled.

Blitzkrieg and Resistance Germany's early success was staggering. Nazi troops overran western Poland, France, Norway, Denmark, Luxembourg, Belgium, and the Netherlands. Within less than two years, the Germans controlled virtually all of Europe from the English Channel to the Soviet border. (See Map 20.1.) Only Britain among major countries escaped Axis control, although Nazi

Map 20.1 World War II: The European Theater

The Axis armies achieved great success during the early stages of World War II.

- Which parts of the European theater did the Allies control? The Axis? Which countries were neutral in 1941?
- Where did the major Allied and Axis campaigns take place?
- What was Germany's greatest geographic obstacle during World War II?

Map labels:

ICELAND

NORTH SEA

NORWAY

SWEDEN

FINLAND

SOVIET UNION

Leningrad besieged Sept. 1941–Jan. 1944

ESTONIA

LATVIA

•Moscow

IRELAND

GREAT BRITAIN

DENMARK

LITHUANIA

Gdańsk

EAST PRUSSIA (Ger.)

Stalingrad Aug. 21, 1942– Jan. 31, 1943

ATLANTIC OCEAN

NETHERLANDS

Battle of Britain Aug. 1–Oct. 12, 1940

•London

GERMANY Berlin•

Germany invades Soviet Union June 1941

POLAND

•Kiev

D-Day June 6, 1944

BEL.
LUX.

Battle of the Bulge Dec. 16, 1944– Jan. 31, 1945

UKRAINE

Paris liberated Aug. 25, 1944

FRANCE

SLOVAKIA

VICHY FRANCE (occupied Nov. 1942)

SWITZ.

HUNGARY

ROMANIA

PORTUGAL

SPAIN

ITALY

YUGOSLAVIA

BLACK SEA

CORSICA (Fr.)

BULGARIA

SARDINIA (It.)

Rome liberated June 4, 1944

ALBANIA (It.)

TURKEY

SPANISH MOROCCO

GREECE

•Athens

SICILY

DODECANESE IS. (It.)

CYPRUS (Br.)

SYRIA (Fr.)

MOROCCO (Fr.)

ALGERIA (Fr.)

TUNISIA (Fr.)

MALTA (Br.)

CRETE

LEBANON

Axis Powers, August 1939

MEDITERRANEAN SEA

PALESTINE (Br.)

TRANS-JORDAN

Extent of Axis control, May 1941

Allies

Neutral nations

Axis offenses

Allied offenses

Major battles

LIBYA (It.)

El Alamein June–Nov. 1942

EGYPT

SAUDI ARABIA

RED SEA

0   250   500 Miles

0   250   500 Kilometers

bombers pulverized British cities. In 1939 Germany signed a nonaggression pact with the Soviets, but in 1941 the German army broke the pact and invaded the Soviet Union with 170 divisions, 3,000 tanks, and 3.2 million men—an invasion force of a size unmatched before or since. Here, as elsewhere, the Germans fought a *blitzkrieg* (lightning war) of tank-led assaults followed by motorized infantrymen and then foot soldiers. By October 1941, the Germans had reached the outskirts of Moscow. The Soviet Union seemed on the verge of a monumental defeat.

The Nazi war was not just a grab for land and raw materials; it was also a crusade for a new order based on race. Throughout Europe, Hitler established puppet governments that complied with deportation orders against Jews and dissidents. His new order made Europe a giant police state. It gave rise to collaborators, who worked with the Germans; resistance fighters, who opposed the German occupiers for varying reasons; and a wide range of options in between, as people struggled to make their way and take care of their families as best they could.

In the east, the tide turned against the Germans and their collaborators after the ferocious battles of Stalingrad in 1942–1943 and Kursk in 1943. The Battle of Stalingrad raged for six months in bitterly cold temperatures—below –30°C/–22°F—and blinding snowstorms, a fight to the death over a city that had been obliterated. It ended with the Soviet encirclement and destruction of an entire German field army, the worst defeat in German military history up to that time. A German infantryman wrote in his last diary entry: "The horses

The Devastation of War In November 1942, Nazi troops entered Stalingrad, some 2,000 miles from Berlin. Hitler wanted to capture the city not only to exploit the surrounding wheat fields and the oil of the Caucasus, but also for its very name. With handheld flamethrowers and sometimes just their fists, Soviet troops drove out the Germans in February 1943.

have already been eaten. I would eat a cat. They say its meat is also tasty. The soldiers look like corpses or lunatics. . . . They no longer take cover from Russian shells." The battle and subsequent imprisonment claimed 295,000 German lives (190,000 on the battlefield; 105,000 in captivity). Conservative estimates place the number of Soviet soldiers dead at 479,000, with estimates ranging as high as 1 million. Only six months later, at the Battle of Kursk, the largest tank conflict in world history, the Germans, boasting a tank force of more than 2,000, lost to a Soviet tank force twice its size. Once the Soviet army had blunted the initial German assault, it launched a massive counteroffensive. This move initiated the defeat of the German war effort on the Eastern Front, but full retreat took another two years as the Soviets drove Hitler's army slowly westward. Before 1944, the Soviets bore the brunt of the fighting but in turn caused more than 85 percent of all German casualties. The spectacular D-Day landing of western Allied forces in Normandy on June 6, 1944 (when the Germans had a mere 15 divisions in France, as compared with more than 300 on the Eastern Front), initiated Germany's defeat in the west. On April 30, 1945, as Soviet and Anglo-American forces converged on Berlin, Hitler committed suicide. Days later, Germany surrendered unconditionally.

The Bitter Costs of War The war in Europe had devastating human and material costs. This was particularly true in eastern Europe, where German forces leveled more than 70,000 Soviet villages, obliterated one-third of the Soviet Union's wealth, and inflicted 7 million Soviet military deaths (by contrast, the Germans lost 3.5 million soldiers) and at least 20 million civilian deaths. German bombing of British cities, such as London, took a heavy toll on civilians and buildings, as did Allied bombing of Axis war plants and cities like Dresden and Tokyo. Tens of millions were left homeless. Urban casualties were perhaps greatest in Leningrad, a city that was surrounded and besieged for 900 days; 900,000 people lost their lives during this struggle. By the war's end, Poland had lost 6 million people and Great Britain had lost 400,000.

Europe's Jews paid an especially high price. Hitler had long talked of "freeing" Europe of all Jews. At the war's outset, the Nazis herded Jews into ghettos and labor camps, then seized their property. As the German army moved eastward, more and more Jews came under their control.

At first the Nazi bureaucrats considered deportation of Jews, but they then ruled out transporting "subhumans" as too costly and began instead to starve them and crowd them together in unsanitary ghettos. By summer 1941 special troops operating behind the army on the Eastern Front had begun mass shootings of communists and Jewish civilians, and by fall 1941 Hitler and the S.S.—the *Schutzstaffel*, or special security forces—were building a series of killing centers in the east. At a conference in Wannsee, just outside Berlin, in late January 1942, German decision makers finalized plans to kill all the Jews of Europe. This murderous departure from the work camps and ghettos meant

The Ovens at Auschwitz (Reconstruction) One of the most horrifying aspects of Nazi behavior during World War II was the attempt to make mass killing efficient, scientific, and hygienic. At Auschwitz, the deadliest of the extermination camps, more than 1 million Jews and other racial and political "enemies" of the regime were murdered according to carefully designed plans. Many of the bodies were then burned in specially built ovens like these so the Nazis could avoid digging potentially unhygienic mass graves and could hide the evidence that genocide was being committed. Still, prisoners and guards at the camp reported enduring the terrible smell of burning flesh and the falling of ash containing fragments of human bones.

a systematic eradication of Jews to clear the way for Nazi settlement in the east and racial purification across Europe. When the German invasion of Russia stalled in the winter of 1941, the German leaders abandoned their plans to ship Jews to locations beyond the Ural Mountains. Cattle cars shipped Jews from all over Europe to these extermination sites, where Nazis used the latest technology, including the arsenic-based poison gas Zyklon B, to kill men, women, and children. The largest facility, Auschwitz, combined an extermination center and work camp in a single complex.

The deliberate extermination of the Jews, known as the **Holocaust**, claimed around 6 million lives. About half of this number died in the gas chambers of death camps; the others were shot, gassed in mobile vans, or succumbed to starvation or disease. The shift to a policy of extermination was both unimaginably brutal and rapid. At its core, the Holocaust was brief, intense mass murder. In mid-March 1942, roughly three-quarters of all victims of the Holocaust were still alive and one-quarter had been killed; within a year—by March 1943—the proportions were reversed, with three-quarters of the victims dead. The Nazis also turned their mass killing apparatus against Sinta and

Roma, gay people, communists, and Slavs, with deportations to the death camps continuing to the very end of the war.

These Nazi genocides stood as a powerful challenge to European claims that science, technology, and an efficient bureaucracy would make life better for everyone. Lamenting connections between European culture and the Holocaust, German philosopher Theodor Adorno wrote in 1949, "To write poetry after Auschwitz is barbaric." Nazi crimes, he suggested, defied human understanding.

THE WAR IN THE PACIFIC

Like the war in Europe, the conflict in the Pacific transformed the military and political landscape. (See Map 20.2.) The war broke out when Japan's ambitions to dominate Asia targeted American interests and military might.

Japan's Efforts to Expand Japanese efforts to expand in Asia were already underway in the 1930s, but the outbreak of war in Europe opened opportunities for further expansion. Having fought with the Allies in World War I, Japan was granted control of the South Pacific Mandate (1919–1947) by the League of Nations. Japan's military forces invaded and occupied Manchuria in 1931—creating a puppet state called Manchukuo (1937–1945)—and then launched an offensive against the rest of China in 1937. Although the Japanese did not gain China's complete submission, the invaders exacted a terrible toll on the population. Most infamous was the ravaging of Nanjing, in which Japanese aggressors slaughtered at least 100,000 civilians and raped thousands of women in the Chinese city between December 1937 and February 1938.

Meanwhile, Germany's swift occupation of western Europe left the defeated nations' Asian colonies at the mercy of Japanese forces. After concluding a pact with Germany in 1940, the Japanese seized French Indochina (Vietnam) in 1941 and squeezed the Dutch East Indies for oil and rubber. The chief remaining obstacle to their further expansion in the Pacific was the United States, which already had imperial interests in China and the Philippines as well as other Pacific islands. Hoping to strike the United States before it was prepared for war, the Japanese launched a surprise air attack on the American naval base at Pearl Harbor in Hawaii on December 7, 1941.

Now Japan's expansion shifted into high gear. With French Indochina already under their control, the Japanese turned against the American colony of the Philippines and against the Dutch East Indies, both of which fell in 1942. By coordinating their army, navy, and air force units and using tactical surprise, the Japanese seized a huge swath of territory that included British-ruled Hong Kong, Singapore, Malaya, and Burma while threatening the British Empire's hold on India as well.

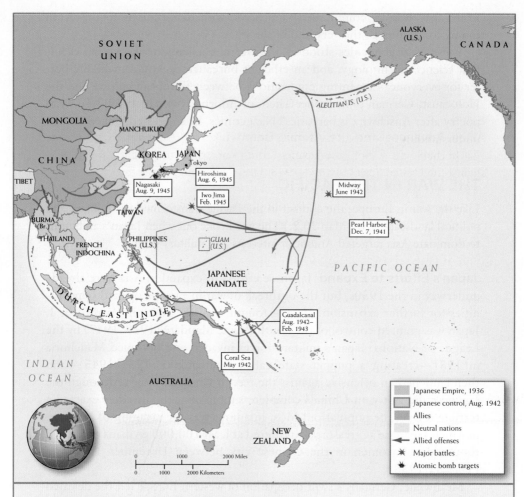

Map 20.2 World War II: The Pacific Theater

Like Germany and Italy, Japan experienced stunning military successes in the war's early years.

- In August 1942, which areas in the Pacific theater were under the control of the Japanese, and which were under Allied control?
- What does tracing the routes of the Allied offense tell you about the Allies' main strategy?
- What geographic factors influenced the American decision to drop atomic bombs on Hiroshima and Nagasaki to end the war, instead of invading Japan?

Japan justified its aggression on the grounds that it was anticolonial and pan-Asian: Japan promised to drive out the European imperialists and to build a new order reflecting "Asia for Asians." In practice, however, the Japanese made oppressive demands on fellow Asians for resources, developed myths of Japanese racial purity and supremacy, and treated Chinese and Koreans with brutality. During the war, Japan put up to 4 million Koreans to work for its empire, forcibly imported another 700,000 Korean men as laborers, and pressed up to 200,000 young women into service as prostitutes for Japanese soldiers. (In a similar move, the Nazi war effort in Europe involved forcing 12 million foreign laborers—including 2 million prisoners of war—to settle and work in Germany.)

Allied Advances and the Atomic Bomb Like the Germans in their war against the Soviet Union, the Japanese could not sustain their military successes against the United States. By mid-1943, U.S. forces had put the Japanese on the defensive. Fighting their way from island to island, American troops recaptured the Philippines, and a combined force of British, American, and Chinese troops returned Burma to Britain. The Allies then moved toward the Japanese mainland. By summer 1945, American bombers had all but devastated the major cities of Japan. Yet Japan did not surrender.

Japanese Aggression The brutal Battle of Shanghai (August–November 1937) marked the beginning of what turned out to be World War II in Asia. Claiming to be "protecting" China from European imperialists and expecting a relatively easy victory, the Japanese instead met with stiff resistance from the Chinese troops under Chiang Kai-shek. Here we see Japanese marines parading through the streets of the city after they finally broke through Chinese defenses. About a quarter of a million Chinese soldiers, close to 60 percent of Chiang's best troops, were killed or wounded in the campaign, a blow from which Chiang's regime never recovered. The Japanese sustained more than 40,000 casualties.

Anticipating that an invasion of Japan would cost hundreds of thousands of American lives, U.S. president Harry Truman unleashed the Americans' secret weapon. It was the work of a team of scientists who were predominantly European refugees. On August 6, 1945, an American plane dropped an atomic bomb on the city of Hiroshima, killing or maiming over 100,000 people and poisoning the air, soil, and groundwater for decades to come. Three days later, the Americans dropped a second atomic bomb on Nagasaki. Within days, Emperor Hirohito announced Japan's surrender, bringing the war to an official end. After the six years of World War II, much of East Asia and Europe lay in ruins; millions had died, and millions more were wounded, displaced, widowed, and orphaned. What the postwar world would look like, however, remained unclear.

The Beginning of the Cold War

The destruction of Europe and the defeat of Japan left a power vacuum, which the United States and the Soviet Union rushed to fill. Avoiding direct warfare, the Americans and Soviets vied for influence in postwar Europe and around the globe in a series of smaller, indirect conflicts.

REBUILDING EUROPE

Communism and liberal democracy offered competing approaches to rebuilding states and societies in Europe after World War II. The task of political rebuilding was daunting, for the old order had been discredited. Liberal democrats had to distance themselves from their prewar predecessors. Communism, by contrast, gained new appeal. Many eastern Europeans, reacting to the horrors of fascism and not knowing the extent of Stalin's crimes, looked to the Soviets for answers.

Europe's leftward tilt alarmed U.S. policymakers. They feared that the Soviets would use their ideological influence and the territory taken from the Nazis by the Red Army to spread communism. They also worried that Stalin might seize Europe's overseas possessions and create communist regimes outside Europe. But no one wished to fight another "hot" war. As President Truman began advocating a policy of containment to prevent the further advance of communism, an American journalist popularized the term *cold war* in 1946 to describe a new form of struggle in which both sides endeavored to avoid direct warfare.

Truman's containment policy was tested when the Soviets attempted to seize control of Berlin. Like the rest of Germany, Berlin had been partitioned into British, French, American, and Soviet zones of occupation, but the city itself was an island lying within the Soviet zone. In 1948, the Soviets attempted to cut the city off from western access by blocking routes between the western zones of Germany and the western zones of Berlin. The United States and its western allies responded with the Berlin Airlift, transporting supplies in planes to West Berlin in hope of keeping the population from capitulating to the Soviets. This crisis lasted for almost a year, until Stalin lifted the blockade in May 1949.

In that same year, occupied Germany was split into two hostile states: the democratic Federal Republic of Germany (West Germany) in the west, and the communist German Democratic Republic (East Germany) in the east. In 1961, leaders in the German Democratic Republic built a wall around West Berlin to insulate the east from what they considered capitalist propaganda and to halt a flood of émigrés fleeing communism. The Berlin Wall became the great symbol of a divided Europe and of the Cold War.

U.S. policymakers wanted to shore up democratic governments in Europe, so Truman promised American military and economic aid. Containing the spread of communism meant securing a capitalist future for Europe, a job that fell to Truman's secretary of state, General George C. Marshall. He launched the Marshall Plan, an ambitious program that provided over $13 billion in grants and credits to reconstruct Europe and facilitate an economic revival. U.S. policymakers hoped the aid would dim communism's appeal by fostering economic prosperity, muting class tensions, and integrating western European nations into an alliance of capitalist democracies.

The Berlin Airlift In summer 1948, a new currency was issued for the united occupation zones of West Germany. It began to circulate in Berlin at more favorable exchange rates than the eastern zone's currency, and Berlin seemed poised to become an outpost of the west inside the Soviet occupation zone. The Soviets responded by blocking western traffic into Berlin; the west countered with an airlift, forcing the Soviets to back down in May 1949 but hastening the division of Germany into two countries.

Soviet troops had occupied eastern European nations at the war's end, and both communist and leftist members of other parties formed Soviet-backed coalition governments there. By tricking their moderate leftist allies and repressing their critics and opponents, the communists established dictatorships in Bulgaria, Romania, Hungary, and Czechoslovakia in 1948. Stalin saw the Marshall Plan as a threat to the Soviet Union and rejected the offer of support. He felt the same way about the formation in 1949 of the **North Atlantic Treaty Organization (NATO)**, a military alliance between countries in western Europe and North America. He believed that the Soviet Union, having sacrificed millions of people to the war against fascism, deserved to be dominant in eastern Europe. Soviet troops had occupied eastern European nations at the war's end, and in those nations, communists and leftist members of other parties formed Soviet-backed coalition governments. In 1955, the Soviets formally allied themselves with these communist nations in the **Warsaw Pact**, a military alliance of their own. (See Map 20.3.) The tense confrontations between NATO and the Warsaw Pact countries in Europe and in other parts of the world in the 1950s and 1960s brought the world to the brink of an atomic World War III.

WAR IN THE NUCLEAR AGE: THE KOREAN WAR

The dropping of the atomic bombs on Japan in 1945 changed military affairs forever. Spurred by the onset of the Cold War, the Soviets worked hard to catch up to the Americans and in 1949 tested their first nuclear bomb. Thereafter, each side rushed to stockpile nuclear weapons and update its military technologies. By 1960, the explosive power of these weapons had increased so greatly that nuclear war had the potential to destroy the world without a soldier firing a single shot. This sobering realization changed the rules of the game. Each side now possessed the power to inflict total destruction on the other, a circumstance that inhibited direct confrontations but sparked smaller conflicts in parts of Asia such as Korea, where Japan's defeat resulted in an uneasy standoff between the communist north, backed by the Soviet Union, and the south, backed by the United States.

In 1950, North Korean troops invaded South Korea, setting off the Korean War. (See Map 20.4.) President Truman ordered American troops to drive back the North Koreans. The Security Council of the United Nations—an international body established in 1945 to help prevent another world war—also sent troops from fifteen nations to restore peace. Within a year, the invaders had been routed and were near collapse. When U.N. troops advanced north to the Chinese border, however, Stalin maneuvered his communist Chinese allies into rescuing the communist regime in North Korea and driving the South Korean and U.N. forces back to the old boundary in the middle of the Korean peninsula. The fighting continued until 1953, when an armistice divided the country at roughly the same spot as at the start of the war.

Map 20.3 NATO and Warsaw Pact Countries

....

The Cold War divided Europe into two competing blocs: those allied with the
United States in the North Atlantic Treaty Organization (NATO) and those linked to
the Soviet Union under the Warsaw Pact.

- Which nations had borders with nations belonging to the opposite bloc?
- Comparing this map with Map 20.1, explain how combat patterns in World War II
  shaped the dividing line between the two blocs.
- According to the map, where would you expect Cold War tensions to be the
  most intense?

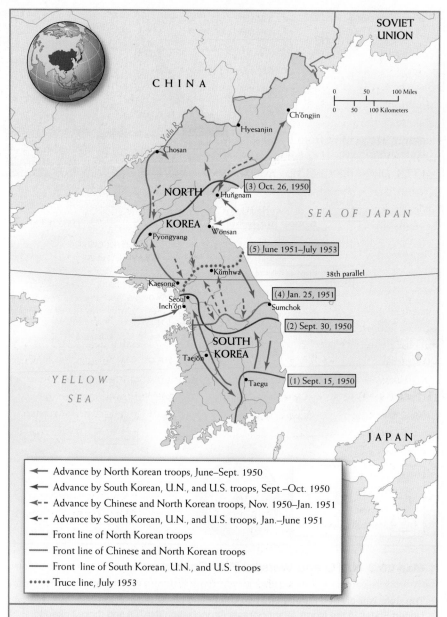

Map 20.4 The Korean War

The Korean War was an early confrontation between the capitalist and communist blocs during the Cold War era.

- What were the dates of each side's farthest advance into the other side's territory?
- Why was the Korean Peninsula strategically important?
- According to your reading, how did the outcome of the war shape political affairs in East Asia for the next several decades?

The Korean War energized America's anticommunist commitments and spurred a rapid increase in NATO forces. The United States now saw Japan as a bulwark against communism and resolved to rebuild Japanese economic power. Like West Germany, Japan went from being the enemy in World War II to being a valued U.S. ally as the Cold War rivalry between the United States and the Soviet Union propelled both sides to shore up alliances around the globe.

Atom Bomb Anxiety Schoolchildren take shelter under their desks during an A-bomb drill in Brooklyn, New York, in 1951. The Soviets had exploded their first test bomb in 1949. Underground bomb shelters were built in many American urban areas as places in which to survive a doomsday attack.

Decolonization

The unsettling of empires, including those established by Japan before and during World War II and the longer-standing colonies held by European states, inspired colonial peoples to reconsider their political futures. The resulting process of **decolonization** and nation building, creating national identities to replace previous colonial and precolonial loyalties, followed four general patterns: civil wars, negotiated independence, wars of independence, and incomplete decolonization.

THE CHINESE REVOLUTION

In China, the ousting of the Japanese occupiers intensified a civil war that eventually brought the Chinese Communist Party to power. The communist movement in China had its origins in the struggle since the early twentieth century to free the country from western domination. In that period, the communists had vowed to free China from colonialism, but had been outgunned by Chiang Kai-shek's Nationalist regime and driven from China's cities; they retreated into the interior, where they founded base camps. In 1934, under attack by Chiang's forces, the communists, led by **Mao Zedong** (1893–1976), abandoned their bases and undertook an arduous 6,000-mile journey through the rugged terrain of northwestern China. (See Map 20.5.) In the course of this great escape, glorified in communist lore as the Long March, fewer than 10,000 of the approximately 80,000 people who started the journey reached their destination. Fortunately for the communists, the Japanese invasion in 1937 diverted Nationalist troops and offered Mao and the survivors a chance to regroup.

Mao's followers cultivated popular support by advocating the lowering of taxes, cooperative farming, and policies aimed at women's emancipation, such

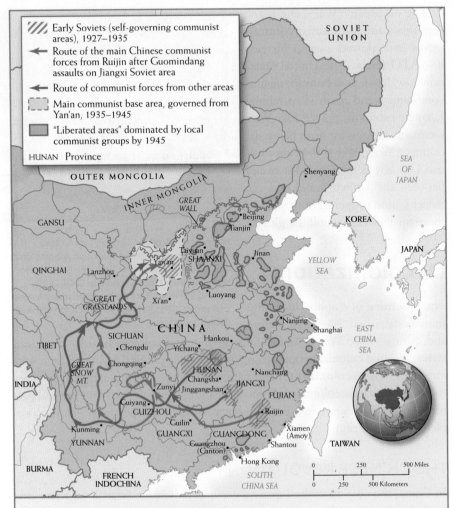

Legend:
- Early Soviets (self-governing communist areas), 1927–1935
- Route of the main Chinese communist forces from Ruijin after Guomindang assaults on Jiangxi Soviet area
- Route of communist forces from other areas
- Main communist base area, governed from Yan'an, 1935–1945
- "Liberated areas" dominated by local communist groups by 1945
- HUNAN Province

Map 20.5 The Long March, 1934–1935

During the Long March, which took place during the struggle for power between the Nationalists and the communists within China, communist forces traveled over 6,000 miles to save their lives and their movement.

- What route did the communist forces take?
- Why did the communists take this particular route?
- How did this movement affect the outcome of this internal struggle in the long run?

as the outlawing of arranged marriages and the legalization of divorce. Like many anticolonial reformers, Mao regarded women's emancipation as a key component in building a new nation, since he considered their oppression to be both unjust and an obstacle to progress.

Communist expansion in rural areas during World War II swelled the membership of the Communist Party from 40,000 in 1937 to over a million in 1945. After Japan's surrender, China's civil war between Nationalists and communists resumed. But the communist forces now had the numbers, the guns (mostly supplied by the Soviet Union), and the popular support to assault Nationalist strongholds and seize power. By contrast, although the Nationalist government had weapons and financing from the United States, as well as control of the cities, it had not recovered from its defeat at the hands of the Japanese. No match for the invigorated communists, the Nationalists fled to the island of Taiwan, where they established a rival Chinese state. The communists established the People's Republic of China in 1949. Mao proclaimed that China had "stood up" to the world and had experienced a "great people's revolution." Subsequently, many of his ventures proved disastrous failures (see later in this chapter), but China's model of an ongoing people's revolution provided much hope in the Third World.

NEGOTIATED INDEPENDENCE IN INDIA AND AFRICA

In India and most of colonial Africa, gaining independence involved little bloodshed, although the aftermath was often extremely violent. The British, realizing that they could no longer rule India without coercion, bowed to the inevitable and withdrew. The same happened in many African colonies, where nationalists also succeeded in negotiating independence from European empires, although, as we shall see, there were notable exceptions.

India Unlike China, India achieved political independence without an insurrection. But it did veer dangerously close to civil war. The leadership of the Indian National Congress Party retained tight control over the mass movement that it had mobilized in the 1920s and 1930s (see Chapter 19). Even Gandhi hesitated to leave the initiative to the common people, believing that they had not yet assimilated the doctrine of nonviolence. Gandhi and the party leadership worked hard to convince the British that they, the middle-class leaders, spoke for the nation. At the same time, the threat of a mass peasant uprising with radical aims (like the communist revolution in China) encouraged the British to transfer power quickly.

As negotiations moved forward, Hindu-Muslim relations deteriorated. Whose culture would define the new nation? The Indian nationalism that had existed in the late nineteenth century reflected the culture of the Hindu majority. Yet this movement masked the multiplicity of regional, linguistic, caste, and class differences *within* the Hindu community, just as Muslim movements that arose in reaction to Hindu-dominated Indian nationalism overlooked divisions within their own ranks. Now the prospect of defining "India" created a grand contest between newly self-conscious communities. Riots broke out between Hindus and Muslims in 1946, which increased the mutual distrust between the Congress Party and Muslim League leaders. The specter of civil war haunted the proceedings as outgoing colonial rulers decided to divide the subcontinent into two states: India and Pakistan.

On August 14, 1947, Pakistan gained independence from Britain; a day later, India did the same. The euphoria of decolonization, however, was drowned in a frenzy of brutality. Shortly after independence, as many as 1 million Hindus and Muslims killed one another. Fearing further violence, 12 million Hindus and Muslims left their homes to relocate in the new countries where they would be in the majority. Although the British departed peacefully from India, the peoples inhabiting the subcontinent engaged in open warfare over differences that haunt the relationship between India and Pakistan to this day.

Africa for Africans Shortly after Indian independence, most African states also gained their sovereignty. Except in southern Africa, where minority White rule persisted, the old colonial states gave way to indigenous rulers.

The postwar years saw Africans move to cities in search of a better life. As expanding educational systems produced a wave of primary and secondary school graduates, these educated young people and other new urban dwellers became disgruntled when attractive employment opportunities were not forthcoming. Three groups—former servicemen, the urban unemployed or underemployed, and the educated—led the nationalist agitation that began in the late 1940s and early 1950s. (See Map 20.6.)

Faced with rising nationalist demands, and too much in debt to invest more in pacifying the discontented colonies, European powers agreed to decolonize. The Soviet Union and the United States also favored decolonization. Thus, decolonization in most of Africa was a rapid and relatively sedate affair. In 1957, the Gold Coast (renamed Ghana), under Prime Minister Kwame Nkrumah, became tropical Africa's first independent state. Other British colonial territories followed in rapid succession, so that by 1963 all of British-ruled Africa, except for Southern Rhodesia, was independent.

Decolonization in much of French-ruled Africa followed a similarly smooth path, although the French were initially resistant. Instead of negotiating independence, they tried first to accord fuller voting rights to their colonial subjects, even allowing Africans and Asians to send delegates to the French National Assembly. In the end, however, the French electorate had no desire to share the privileges of French citizenship with African and Asian populations. Thus, France dissolved its political ties with French West Africa and French Equatorial Africa in 1960, having given protectorates in Morocco and Tunisia their independence in 1956. Algeria, considered an integral part of France, was a different matter. France's desperate efforts to hold onto Algeria (see below) facilitated independence movements elsewhere in Africa.

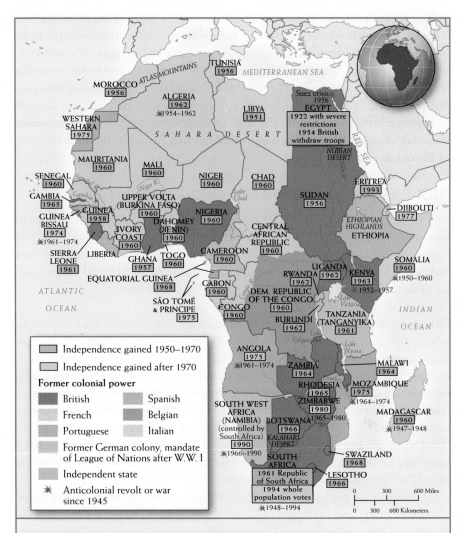

Independence gained 1950–1970
Independence gained after 1970

Former colonial power
- British
- French
- Portuguese
- Spanish
- Belgian
- Italian
- Former German colony, mandate of League of Nations after W.W. I
- Independent state
- ✳ Anticolonial revolt or war since 1945

Map 20.6 Decolonization in Africa

African decolonization occurred after World War II, largely in the 1950s, 1960s, and 1970s.

- Find at least four areas that won independence in the 1950s, and identify which former colonial power had ruled each area.
- What areas took longer to gain independence?
- According to your reading, what problems and tensions contributed to this uneven process across Africa?

The leaders of African independence movements believed that Africa's pre-colonial traditions would enable the region to move from colonialism right into a special African form of socialism, escaping the ravages of capitalism. Without rejecting western culture completely, they praised the so-called African personality, exemplified by the idea of "Negritude" developed by Senegal's first president, Léopold Sédar Senghor. Negritude, they claimed, was steeped in common African traditions and able to embrace social justice and equality while rejecting the unrestrained individualism that Africans felt lay at the core of European culture.

VIOLENT AND INCOMPLETE DECOLONIZATIONS

In Palestine, Algeria, Kenya, and southern Africa, the presence of European immigrant groups created violent conflicts that aborted any peaceful transfer of power—or left the process incomplete. In Vietnam, the process was also violent and delayed, partly because of France's desire to reimpose colonial control and partly because of the power politics of Cold War competition.

Palestine, Israel, and Egypt In Palestine, Arabs and Jews had been on a collision course since the end of World War I. Before that war, a group of European Jews, known as Zionists, had argued that only a large-scale migration from existing states to their place of origin in Palestine could lead to Jewish self-determination. Zionism combined a yearning to return to the holy lands with a fear of anti-Semitism and anguish over increasing Jewish assimilation. Zionists wanted to create a Jewish state, and they won a crucial victory during World War I when the British government, under the Balfour Declaration, promised a homeland for the Jews in Palestine. But when the British took control of Palestine after 1918, they also guaranteed the rights of Palestinian Arabs.

As more Jews settled in Palestine, tensions arose between Zionists and Palestinian Arabs, and both grew dissatisfied with British rule. Arabs resented the presence of Jews, who displaced farmers who had lived on the land for generations and who openly sought their own independent state. Zionists became especially enraged when British authorities wavered in supporting their demands for more immigration. After World War II, the pressure to allow more immigration increased as hundreds of thousands of concentration camp survivors clamored for entry into Palestine, and Zionist militants began using force to attempt to gain control of the state.

In 1947, the British could no longer control the festering region and announced that they would leave negotiations over the area's fate to the United Nations; in May 1948, the British planned to transfer the mandate to the U.N. That body then voted to partition Palestine into Arab and Jewish territories. The Arab states rejected the partition, and the Jewish Agency, a nongovernmental organization that supported the immigration of Jews to Israel, only reluctantly accepted it. Although the Jews were delighted to have an independent state, they were unhappy about its small size, its indefensible borders, and the fact that it did not include all the lands that had belonged to ancient Israel. For their part, the Palestinians were shocked at the partition, and they looked to their better-armed Arab neighbors to regain the territories set aside for the new state of Israel.

The ensuing Arab-Israeli War of 1948–1949 shattered the legitimacy of Arab ruling elites. Arab states entered the war poorly prepared to take on the well-run and enthusiastically supported Israeli Defense Force. By the time the United Nations finally negotiated a truce, Israel had declared its independence (May 14, 1948) and extended its boundaries; more than 1 million Palestinians had become refugees in surrounding Arab countries.

Embittered by this defeat, a group of young army officers in Egypt plotted to overthrow the Egyptian regime, which they felt was corrupt and still under European influence. One of the officers, Gamal Abdel Nasser, became the head of a secret organization of junior military officers called the Free Officers movement. These men had ties with communists and other dissident groups, including the Muslim Brotherhood, which favored a return to Islamic rule. They launched a successful coup in 1952, forcing the king to abdicate and leave the country. The new regime dissolved the parliament, banned political parties (including the communists and the Muslim Brotherhood), and stripped the old elite of its wealth.

In 1956, Nasser moved to nationalize the Suez Canal Company (an Egyptian company, mainly run by French businessmen and experts), inciting the Israelis, the British, and the French to invade Egypt and seize territory along the Suez

The Creation of the State of Israel Standing beneath a portrait of Theodor Herzl, the founder of the Zionist movement, David Ben-Gurion, the first Israeli prime minister, proclaimed independence for the state of Israel in May 1948.

Canal. Opposition by the United States and the Soviet Union forced the invading countries to withdraw, providing Nasser with a spectacular diplomatic triumph. As Egyptian forces reclaimed the canal, Nasser's reputation as leader of the Arab world soared. He became the chief symbol of a pan-Arab nationalism that swept across the Middle East and North Africa and especially through the camps of Palestinian refugees.

The Algerian War of Independence The appeal of Arab nationalism was particularly strong in Algeria, where a population of 1 million European settlers (the *colons*) stood in the way of decolonization. Indeed, French leaders claimed that Algeria was an integral part of France. Although the *colons* were a minority in Algeria, they held the best land and generally lived in the major cities near the coast. They controlled Algeria's finances and all its major public institutions.

Anticolonial nationalism in Algeria gathered force after World War II. The Front de Libération Nationale (FLN) emerged as the leading nationalist party in the 1950s, using violence to provoke its opponents and to make the local population choose between supporting the nationalist cause or the *colons*. The full-fledged revolt that erupted in 1954 pitted FLN troops and guerrillas against hundreds of thousands of French troops and indigenous allies. Atrocities and terrorist acts occurred on both sides.

The war dragged on for eight years, at a cost of perhaps 300,000 lives. On the French mainland, the war came as a terrible shock, for many, though not all, French citizens had accepted the idea that Algeria was not a colonial territory but part of France itself—the three northern administrative *départements* had been incorporated into the French mainland since 1848. The *colons* insisted that they had emigrated to Algeria in response to their government's promises and that yielding power to the nationalists would be a betrayal. After an insurrection led by *colons* and army officers brought down the French government in 1958, the new French president, Charles de Gaulle, negotiated a peace accord. Shortly after the handover of power to FLN leaders, 800,000 *colons* left Algeria. By late 1962, over nine-tenths of its European and indigenous Jewish population had departed. While struggling for independence, the FLN and its Armée de Libération Nationale (ALN) became a symbol for decolonizing movements worldwide.

Eastern and Southern Africa The bloody conflict in Algeria highlights a harsh reality of African decolonization: the presence of European settlers prevented the smooth transfer of power. Even in British-ruled Kenya, where the European settler population had never been large, a violent war of independence broke out between European settlers and African nationalists. Employing secrecy and intimidation, the Kikuyu peoples, Kenya's largest ethnic group, organized a revolt. This uprising, which began in 1952, forced the British to fly in troops to suppress it, but ultimately the British government conceded independence to Kenya in 1963. Decolonization proved even more difficult in the southern third of the continent, where Portuguese Angola, Portuguese Mozambique, and British Southern Rhodesia (present-day Zimbabwe) did not gain independence until 1980.

South Africa, which held the continent's largest and wealthiest settler population (a mixture of Afrikaans- and English-speaking peoples of European descent), defied Black majority rule longer than other African states. After winning the elections of 1948, the White Afrikaner–dominated National Party enacted an extreme form of racial segregation known as apartheid. Under apartheid, laws stripped Africans, Indians, and "colored" persons (those of mixed descent) of their few political rights. Racial mixing of any kind was forbidden, and schools were strictly segregated.

The ruling party tolerated no protest. Nelson Mandela, one of the leaders of the African National Congress (ANC), a group that campaigned for an end to discriminatory legislation, was repeatedly harassed, detained, and tried by the government, even though he had at first urged peaceful resistance. After the Sharpeville massacre in 1960, in which police killed demonstrators who were peacefully protesting the oppressive laws, Mandela and the ANC decided to oppose the apartheid regime with violence. A South African court sentenced Mandela to life imprisonment, and the government banned the ANC.

Women helped keep resistance flames burning. The most dynamic of these individuals was Winnie Mandela, wife of the imprisoned Nelson Mandela. Unlike many of the ANC leaders, who opposed the regime from exile, she remained in South Africa and openly and courageously spoke out against the apartheid government. Nonetheless, Whites retained external support. Through the 1950s and 1960s, western powers (especially the United States) saw South Africa as a bulwark against the spread of communism in Africa.

Vietnam The same desire to contain communism also drew the United States into support for a conservative and pro-western regime in South Vietnam. Vietnam had come under

Apartheid Protest In Johannesburg, South Africans march in the street to protest the new restrictions on African citizens, soon to be known worldwide as apartheid, implemented by the White minority government of Daniel Malan. During the Malan administration (1948–1954), informal discrimination was systematically made law, and all electoral, housing, civil, and employment rights of African citizens were dismantled.

French rule in the 1880s, and by the 1920s approximately 40,000 Europeans were living among and ruling over roughly 19 million Vietnamese. To promote an export economy of rice, mining, and rubber, the colonial rulers granted vast land concessions to French companies and local collaborators while leaving large numbers of peasants landless.

The colonial system also generated a new intelligentsia. Primarily schooled in French and Franco-Vietnamese schools, educated Vietnamese worked as clerks, shopkeepers, teachers, and petty officials. Yet they had few opportunities for advancement. Discontented, they turned from the traditional ideology of Confucianism to modern nationalism. Vietnamese intellectuals overseas, notably Ho Chi Minh, one of the original founders of the French Communist Party, took the lead in imagining a new Vietnamese nation-state.

Ho had left Vietnam at an early age and found his way to London and Paris. During the interwar period he read the writings of Marx, Engels, and Lenin, and he discovered not only an ideology for opposing French exploitation but also a vision for transforming the common people into a political force. He was a founding member of the French Communist Party and subsequently founded the Indochinese Communist Party. After the Japanese occupied Indochina, he traveled to China, embraced the idea of an agrarian revolution, and established the Viet Minh (League for the Independence of Vietnam), a liberation force, in 1941. Back in Vietnam, the communist-led Viet Minh became a powerful nationalist organization as it mobilized the peasantry.

When the French tried to restore their rule in Vietnam after Japan's defeat in 1945, Ho led the resistance. War with France followed (1946–1954). The Viet Minh used guerrilla tactics to undermine French positions. They were most successful in the north, but even in the south their campaign bled the French. Finally, in 1954, the anticolonial forces won a decisive military victory. At a conference held in Geneva that year, Vietnam (like Korea) was divided into two zones. Ho controlled the north, while a government with French and American support took charge in the south.

During the early 1960s, U.S. involvement in Vietnam escalated as Ho's support for the Viet Cong (Vietnamese communist) guerrillas heightened American concerns about the spread of communism. In 1965, large numbers of American troops entered the country to fight on behalf of South Vietnam, while communist North Vietnam turned to the Soviet Union for supplies. Over the next several years, the United States sent some 500,000 soldiers to fight the Vietnam War, but peasant support enabled the Viet Cong to continue fierce guerrilla fighting. Even the bombing of villages and the deployment of counterinsurgency forces failed to prevent the spread of communism in Southeast Asia. In 1975, two years after the final withdrawal of American troops, the South Vietnamese government collapsed.

Thus, the process of decolonization varied across regions. Although most of the lands in Asia and Africa had gained independence by the mid-1960s, there were significant exceptions in Africa (South Africa, Southern Rhodesia, and the Portuguese colonies) and in Asia (notably Vietnam). Although the British and French realized that they no longer had the resources to stem the nationalist tide that was spreading through the Third World, they tried to use military might to support areas of European settlement, above all in Algeria.

Women, Nationalism, and Decolonization Decolonization mobilized women in struggles all over the world. Some of the most dramatic examples of their participation come from colonial Africa. In Kenya immediately after World War I, Kikuyu women assembled outside the prison where the colonial authorities were holding Harry Thuku, the leader of the first African political party in Kenya. The women indeed had much to protest. The British had expropriated substantial amounts of land for distribution to European settlers—land that the Kikuyu believed belonged to them. Land dispossession affected all segments of Kikuyu society, none more profoundly than women, who bore major responsibilities for feeding and looking after their families. Confined to reserves that they considered inadequate for feeding and supporting their families, particularly when the colonial authorities forcibly recruited many young adult males to work on settler estates, the women rallied to support Thuku and denounced colonial authorities for allowing their lands to be seized for settlers.

Much the same happened in 1929 in southeastern Nigeria, where Ibo women and women from other ethnic communities, believing that the colonial authorities planned to tax them as well as men, similarly feared that they

Agriculture and Decolonization Women pose with their farming implements before hoeing a field of maize in South Africa around 1923. Since men were often recruited for seasonal and mining work away from the village, women took charge of farms. When White settlers encroached on villages for their land, they often pushed women off their plots. Over the years, dispossessed women joined the vanguard of opposition to White and European rule.

would be unable to look after their families. Here, they turned against the British-appointed African warrant chiefs, who served as native-born officers of the empire. Surrounding the homes of these chiefs, the women insulted them and demeaned their manhood. This form of protest, called "sitting on a man," had traditionally been employed against men who had illegitimately wielded their powers over women, and was revived under British rule. The uprising was perhaps the biggest women's protest movement in colonial history at the time, covering an area of 6,000 square miles with an estimated population of 2 million. Fifty-five women lost their lives, and the British colonial administration, so deeply troubled by the women's uprising, abolished the system of warrant chiefs. They even appointed women to serve on African courts.

Three Worlds

World War II and postwar decolonization created a three-world order, in which the liberal democratic and capitalist First World and the communist Second World competed for global influence, notably among the newly decolonized Third World states. The war had made the Soviet Union and the United States into superpowers. Possessing nuclear weapons, superior armies, and industrial might, they vied for global influence. As decolonization spread, the two Cold War belligerents offered new leaders their models for modernization. The decolonized, however, had their own ideas. With the communist takeover in 1949, China had shrugged off semicolonial status, but Mao soon broke from Soviet direction. Other decolonized nations in Asia and Africa had underdeveloped economies and could not leap into either capitalist or communist industrial development. They drew some elements from communist and capitalist models, but politically tended to favor single-party states. Moreover, in some places colonial rule persisted, and civilians were not allowed even relative autonomy because the colonizers remained in place.

THE FIRST WORLD

As the Cold War spread in the early 1950s, western Europe and North America became known as the First World, or "the free world." Later on, Japan joined this group. First World states sought to organize the world on the basis of capitalism and democracy. Yet, in struggling against communism, the free world sometimes aligned with Third World dictators, thereby sacrificing its commitment to freedom and democracy for the sake of propping up pro-western regimes.

Western Europe The reconstruction of western Europe after World War II was a spectacular success. By the late 1950s, most nations' economies were thriving, thanks in part to massive American economic assistance. Improvements in agriculture were particularly impressive. With increased mechanization and the use of pesticides, fewer farmers were feeding more people. In 1950, for example, each French farmer had produced enough food for seven people; by 1962, one farmer could feed forty. As industrial production boomed and wages rose, goods that had been luxuries before the war—refrigerators, telephones, automobiles, indoor plumbing—became commonplace. Prosperity and the dismantling of national military establishments allowed governments to expand social welfare systems; by the late 1950s, education and health care were within the reach of virtually all citizens. Western Europe's economic recovery blunted the appeal of socialism and communism.

The United States While Europe lay in ruins in 1945, the United States boomed. The majority of Americans could afford more consumer goods than ever before—almost always U.S. manufactures. Home ownership became more common, especially in the burgeoning suburbs.

Yet anxieties about the future of the First World abounded. Following the Soviet Union's explosion of an atomic bomb, the communist revolution in China, and the outbreak of the Korean War, fear of the communist threat prompted increasingly harsh rhetoric. Anticommunist hysteria led a Republican senator from Wisconsin, Joseph McCarthy, to initiate a campaign to uncover closet communists in the State Department and in Hollywood in the 1950s. Televised congressional hearings broadcast his views to the entire nation, which pressured elected officials to support a strong anticommunist foreign policy and a large military budget.

Postwar American prosperity did not benefit all citizens equally. During the 1950s, nearly a quarter of the American population lived in poverty. But many African Americans, a group disproportionately trapped below the poverty line, participated in a powerful movement for equal rights and the end of racial segregation.

Civil Rights Movement The 1955 arrest of Rosa Parks, for refusing to give up her seat on a Montgomery, Alabama, bus to a White passenger, led to a boycott that brought Martin Luther King Jr. to prominence and galvanized the challenge to legal racial segregation in the American South.

The National Association for the Advancement of Colored People (NAACP) won court victories that mandated the desegregation of schools. Boycotts, too, became a weapon of the growing civil rights movement, with Martin Luther King Jr. (1929–1968) leading a successful strike against injustices in the bus system of Montgomery, Alabama. Here and in subsequent campaigns against White supremacy, King borrowed his most effective weapons—the commitment to nonviolent protest and the appeal to conscience—from Gandhi. As the civil rights movement spread, the federal government gradually supported programs promoting racial equality.

The Japanese "Miracle" Japan reemerged as an economic powerhouse in the postwar period. The war had ended with Japan's unconditional surrender in 1945, its dreams of dominating East Asia dashed and its homeland devastated. But after 1945, in an attempt to incorporate Japan into the First World, American military protection, investment, and transfers of technology helped rebuild Japanese society during the American postwar occupation. The Japanese government guided economic development through directed investment, partnerships with private firms, and protectionist trade policies. By the mid-1970s, Japan, formerly a dictatorship, was a politically stable civilian regime with a thriving economy, and the power of the emperor had been replaced with a parliamentary system.

THE SECOND WORLD

The Soviet Union, with its eastern and central European allies as well as Mongolia and North Korea, constituted the communist Second World. The scourge of World War II and the shadow of the Cold War fell heavily on the Soviets. Having suffered more deaths and more damage than any other industrialized nation, the Soviet Union was determined to insulate itself from future aggression from the west. That meant turning eastern Europe into a bloc of communist buffer states.

The Appeal of the Soviet Model The Soviet model's egalitarian ideology and success with rapid industrialization made it seem a worthy alternative to capitalism. Here, there was no private property and thus, in Marxist terms, no exploitation. Workers "owned" the factories and worked for themselves. The Soviet state promised full employment, boasting that a state-run economy would be immune from upturns and downturns in business cycles. Freedom from exploitation, combined with security, was contrasted with the capitalist model of owners hoarding profits and suddenly firing loyal workers when they were not needed.

The Soviet system touted protections for workers, inexpensive mass transit, paid maternity leave, free health care, and universally available education. Whereas under the Russian Empire less than one-third of the population had been literate, by the 1950s the literacy rate soared above 80 percent. True,

Soviet policies did not provide material abundance of the sort that First World nations were enjoying. But if consumer goods were often scarce, they were always cheap. Likewise, while it sometimes took ten years to obtain a small apartment through waiting lists at work, when one's turn finally came the apartment carried low annual rent and could be passed on to one's children.

Few Soviet citizens knew how people lived in the capitalist world, so it was easy to believe in the advantages of the Soviet system. Government censors skewed news about the First World and suppressed unfavorable information about the Soviet Union and the communist bloc. Critics did not typically seek to overthrow the system and restore capitalism. Rather, they wanted the Soviet regime to introduce reforms that would create "socialism with a human face."

Repression of Dissent Few people outside the Soviet sphere knew just how inhuman Soviet communism was, and few within knew the extent of its brutality. Under Stalin, anyone suspected of opposing the regime risked imprisonment, forced labor, and often torture or execution. By the time of Stalin's death in 1953, its vast Gulag (labor camp complex) confined several million people, who dug for gold and uranium and survived on hunks of bread and gruel.

Stalin's successors had to face hard questions, including what to do with so many prisoners, many of whom were incarcerated for fabricated political crimes. This problem became acute when mass strikes rocked the camps in 1953 and 1954, forcing the regime's hand. In 1956, the new party leader, Nikita Khrushchev, delivered a speech at a closed session of the Communist Party Congress in which he attempted to separate Stalin's crimes from true communism. The speech was never published in the Soviet Union, but party members distributed it to party organizations abroad. The crimes that Khrushchev revealed came as a terrible shock.

Repercussions were far-reaching. Eastern European leaders interpreted Khrushchev's speech as an endorsement for political liberation and economic experimentation. Right away, Polish intellectuals began a drive to break free from the communist ideological straitjacket. Hungarian intellectuals and students held demonstrations demanding an uncensored press, free elections with genuine alternative parties, and the withdrawal of Soviet troops. But the seeming liberalization promised by Khrushchev's speech proved short-lived.

Rather than let eastern Europeans stray, the Soviet leadership crushed dissent. In Poland, the security police massacred strikers. In Hungary, tanks from the Soviet Union and other Warsaw Pact members invaded, and the Soviet Union installed a new government that aimed to smash all "counterrevolutionary" activities. The Second World remained very much the dominion of the Soviet Union.

Despite its repressive policies, the Soviet Union's status surged after the launching of Sputnik, the first satellite, into space in 1957. Students from Third World countries flocked to the Soviets' excellent educational system for training as engineers, scientists, army commanders, and revolutionaries. The updated 1961 Communist Party program predicted euphorically that within twenty years the Soviet Union would surpass the United States and eclipse the First World, but reckless industrialization left terrible scars both on the population and on the landscape.

THE THIRD WORLD

In the 1950s, the French demographer Alfred Sauvy coined the term **Third World** (*tiers monde*) to describe those countries that, like the "Third Estate" in the 1789 French Revolution, represented the majority of the world's population but were oppressed. The term became a slogan of resistance and a declaration of independence from the other two blocs, the capitalist west and the communist east. The Third World's defenders believed capitalist countries were too materialistic and were ruled by oligarchic corporations, while they thought communist countries were soulless, godless, and tended toward dictatorship. Third Worlders aimed to defeat imperialism, which they regarded as a sinister force. They also challenged global inequality. By the early 1960s, most of the countries in Asia, Africa, and Latin America, having emerged from colonial domination, aimed to create more just societies than those of the First and Second Worlds. Their leaders believed that they could even build democratic societies and promote rapid economic development through economic planning.

The early 1960s were years of heady optimism in the Third World. Ghanaian prime minister Kwame Nkrumah trumpeted pan-Africanism as a way to increase the power of African nations in global politics. Egyptian president Gamal Abdel Nasser boasted that his democratic socialism was neither western nor Soviet and that Egypt would remain neutral in the Cold War struggle. Indian prime minister Jawaharlal Nehru blended democratic politics and vigorous state planning to promote India's quest for political independence and economic autonomy. Around Latin America, governments aggressively promoted industrialization and agrarian reform to break their dependence on exports and to break the grip of old elites.

Limits to Autonomy Charting a third way proved difficult. Both the Soviets and the Americans saw the Third World as "underdeveloped." The western powers looked to two new instruments of global capitalism, the **World Bank** and the **International Monetary Fund (IMF)**, to help them develop their economies. Both institutions raised capital from all participating nations—but the most from the United States—and provided economic guidance in the Third World. The World Bank funded loans for projects intended to lift societies out of poverty (such as providing electricity in India and building roads in Indonesia), while the IMF supported the new governments' monetary systems when they experienced economic woes (as in Ghana, Nigeria, and Egypt). Yet both institutions also intruded on these states' autonomy.

Another force that threatened Third World economic autonomy was the multinational corporation. In the rush to acquire advanced technology, Africans, Asians, and Latin Americans struck deals with multinational corporations to import their know-how. Owned primarily by American, European, and Japanese entrepreneurs, firms such as United Fruit, Firestone, and Volkswagen expanded cash-cropping and plantation activities and established manufacturing branches worldwide. But such corporations impeded the growth of indigenous firms. Although the world's nations were more economically interdependent, the west still made the decisions—and reaped most of the profits.

Whether dealing with the west or with the Soviet Union, Third World leaders had limited options because they faced pressure to choose one Cold War side or the other. In hope of adding subservient client states to its bloc, the Soviet Union backed communist insurgencies around the globe, while the United States supported almost all leaders who declared their anticommunism. Indeed, to contain communist expansion, the United States formed a number of military alliances. Following the 1949 creation of NATO, similar regional arrangements took shape in Southeast Asia (SEATO) and in the Middle East (the Baghdad Pact). These organizations brought many Third World nations into American-led alliances and allowed the United States to establish military bases in foreign territories. The Soviet Union countered by positioning its own forces in other Third World countries.

Nowhere was the militarization of Third World countries more threatening to economic development than in Africa. Whereas in the colonial era African states had spent little on military forces, this trend ended abruptly once the states became independent and were drawn into the Cold War. Civil wars, like the one that splintered Nigeria between 1967 and 1970, were opportunities for the superpowers to wield influence. When the west refused to sell weapons to the Nigerian government so it could suppress the breakaway eastern province of Biafra, the Soviets supplied MiG aircraft and other vital weapons, contributing to a destructive conflict and the ultimate triumph of the federal government of Nigeria. A similar situation occurred in Egypt, a strategic region to both superpowers. After the founding of Israel, Egypt's new military rulers insisted that their country never again be caught militarily unprepared. Aware of the west's support for Israel, the Egyptians turned to the Soviet bloc. The resulting arms race between Egypt and Israel left the region bristling with modern weaponry.

Thus, Third World nations now confronted a situation that has been called **neocolonialism**. How were they to apply liberal or socialist models to their own situations? How were they to deal with economic structures and institutions that seemed to reduce their autonomy and limit their development? And how might they escape being puppets of the west or the Soviet Union? No wonder Third World nations grew frustrated about prospects for an alternative way to modernity.

By the late 1960s, as the euphoria of decolonization evaporated and new states became mired in debt and dependency, many Third World nations fell into dictatorship and authoritarian rule. Although some dictators still spoke about forging a third way, they did so mainly to justify their own corrupt regimes. They had forgotten the democratic commitments that were made at independence. Most also had been drawn into the Cold War, the better to extract arms and assistance from one of the superpowers.

Revolutionaries and Radicals As postcolonial states increasingly found themselves mired in debt and dependency, dissatisfaction grew. While some radicals seized power in the 1950s and 1960s, revolutionary transformation of society proved elusive.

Third World revolutionaries drew on the pioneering writings of Frantz Fanon (1925–1961). While serving as a psychiatrist in French Algeria, Fanon (who was born in a French Caribbean colony) became aware of the psychological damage of European racism. He subsequently joined the FLN and became a radical theorist of liberation. His 1961 book *The Wretched of the Earth* urged Third World peoples to achieve personal and national independence through violence against their European oppressors.

The Maoist Model While Fanon moved people with his writings, others did so by building political organizations and undertaking revolutionary social experiments. In 1958, Mao Zedong introduced the Great Leap Forward. Mao's program organized China into 24,000 social and economic units, called communes. Peasants took up industrial production in their own backyards. The campaign aimed to catapult China past the developed countries, but the communes failed to feed the people and the industrial goods were inferior. As many as 45 million people may have perished from famine and malnutrition, forcing the government to abandon the experiment in 1961.

Fearing that China's revolution was losing spirit, Mao launched the Great Proletarian Cultural Revolution in 1966. This time Mao turned against his associates in the Communist Party and appealed to China's young people. They responded enthusiastically. Organized into "Red Guards," over 10 million of them journeyed to Beijing to participate in huge rallies. Chanting, crying, screaming, and waving the little red book of Mao's quotations, they pledged to cleanse the party of its corrupt elements and to thoroughly remake Chinese society.

With help from the army, the Red Guards set out to rid society of the "four olds"—old customs, old habits, old culture, and old ideas. They ransacked homes, libraries, museums, and temples. They destroyed classical texts, artworks, and monuments. With its rhetoric of struggle against American imperialism and Soviet revisionism, the Cultural Revolution also targeted anything foreign. Knowledge of a foreign language was enough to compromise a person's revolutionary

The Cultural Revolution in China Young women were an important part of the Red Guards during the Cultural Revolution. Here female Red Guards, armed with copies of the *Little Red Book*, march in the front row of a parade in the capital city of Beijing under a sign that reads "Rise."

credentials. The Red Guards attacked government officials, party cadres, or just plain strangers in an escalating cycle of violence. Even family members and friends were pressured to denounce one another; all had to prove themselves faithful followers of Chairman Mao.

Given the costs of the Great Leap Forward and the Cultural Revolution, many of Mao's revolutionary policies were hard to admire. But in spite of the upheaval inside China, the Maoist model had great appeal outside China for people seeking radical alternatives to the three-world order. For example, a young philosopher from Ayacucho in Peru, Abimael Guzmán, traveled to Beijing in 1965 to learn about the miracles of Maoism and to meet the legendary chairman. Like thousands of other activists, he came away dazed. "It was one of the most transcendental and unforgettable experiences of my life," he reported. When Guzmán returned to Peru, he vowed to lead a peasant revolution in the Andes; disseminated translations of Mao's *Little Red Book*; converted teachers, especially women; and organized guerrilla militias. Peruvians woke up to graffiti all over prominent walls announcing, "Viva Beijing!" Guzmán renamed himself "Chairman Gonzalo" in honor of Chairman Mao and formed an insurgency movement that plunged Peru into a spiral of violence in the 1980s that left tens of thousands dead.

Latin American Revolution Most Third World radicals did not go as far as Mao, but they still dreamed of overturning the social order. In Latin America, such dreams excited those who wished to throw off the influence of U.S.-owned multinational corporations and local elites.

Reform programs in Latin America addressed numerous concerns. Economic nationalists urged greater protection for domestic industries and sought to curb the multinationals. Liberal reformers wanted to democratize political systems and redistribute land, lest discontent erupt into full-blown revolutions like China's. But when liberals and nationalists joined forces, as in Guatemala in the 1950s, their reforms met resistance from local conservatives and from the United States.

In Cuba, the failure of the government to address political, social, and economic concerns spurred a revolution. Since gaining its independence in the

Spanish-American War of 1898, Cuba had been ruled by governments better known for their compliance with U.S. interests than with popular sentiment. In the 1930s, sugar planters, casino operators, and North American investors prospered, but middle- and working-class Cubans did not. In 1953, a group composed heavily of university students launched a botched assault on a military garrison. One of the leaders, a law student named **Fidel Castro** (1926–2016), gave a stirring speech at the rebels' trial, which made him a national hero. After his release from prison in 1955, he fled to Mexico. Several years later, he returned and started organizing guerrilla raids that brought him to power in 1959.

Castro then elbowed aside rivals and wrested control of the economy from the wealthy elite, who fled to exile. As his policies grew increasingly radical, American leaders began to plot his demise. Then, in 1961, the CIA mounted an invasion by Cuban exiles, landing at the Bay of Pigs. The invasion not only failed to overthrow Castro but further radicalized his ambitions for Cuba. He now declared himself a socialist and aligned himself with the Soviet Union. It was over Cuba and its radicalizing revolution that the world came closest to nuclear Armageddon in the Cuban Missile Crisis of 1962. To deter U.S. attacks, Castro appealed to the Soviet Union to install nuclear weapons in Cuba—a mere ninety miles off the coast of Florida. When U.S. intelligence detected the weapons, President John F. Kennedy ordered a blockade of Cuba, just as weapons-bearing Soviet ships were heading toward Havana. For several weeks, the world was paralyzed with anxiety as Kennedy, Khrushchev, and Castro matched threats.

Latin American Human Rights By the early 1980s, human rights movements were gaining strength all over Latin America, even in Chile under the repressive General Pinochet. Here, a crowd of 400,000 demonstrates against his rule in November 1983.

In the end, Kennedy succeeded in getting the Soviets to withdraw their nuclear missiles from Cuba.

By rejecting the power of capitalist industrial societies, Castro and his followers promoted revolution, not reform, as a way to achieve Third World liberation. The symbol of this new spirit was Castro's closest lieutenant, Ernesto "Che" Guevara (1928–1967). Shortly after receiving his medical degree in 1953, Guevara arrived in Guatemala in time to witness the CIA-backed overthrow of the progressive Jacobo Arbenz government. Thereafter, he became increasingly bitter about U.S. influences in Latin America. He joined Castro's forces and helped topple the pro-American regime in Cuba in 1958. After 1959, he held several posts in the Cuban government, but grew restive for more action. Latin America, he believed, should challenge the global power of the United States. Soon his casual military uniform, his patchy beard, his cigar, and his moral energy became legendary symbols of revolt.

To combat the germ of revolution, the Kennedy administration sent U.S. advisers throughout Latin America to dole out aid, explain how to reform local land systems, and demonstrate the benefits of liberal capitalism. Working with American advisers, Latin American militaries were trained to root out radicalism. Even Salvador Allende's democratically elected socialist government in Chile was not spared; the CIA and U.S. policymakers aided General Augusto Pinochet's military coup against the regime in 1973 and looked the other way while political opponents were butchered. By 1975, protesters had been liquidated in Argentina, Uruguay, Brazil, Mexico, Bolivia, and Venezuela.

Tensions within the Three Worlds

Each of the three "worlds" was beset by vulnerabilities and divisions. The United States experienced social unrest in this period on a scale not seen since the Great Depression, and other First World countries also experienced major protest movements. In the Second World, too, dissent challenged the Soviet Union's hold on world communism. In the Third World, the optimism generated at independence gave way quickly to discouragement and eventually despair. Finally, in the 1970s, the rising fortunes of oil-producing nations and of Japan introduced new problems in the relations within and among worlds.

TENSIONS WITHIN THE FIRST WORLD

Although the First World enjoyed great prosperity in the decades after World War II, a variety of issues created friction within these societies and between allies.

Women's Issues, Civil Rights, and Environmental Concerns In the First World, groups that believed that they had been left behind in the surge of economic growth expressed deep unhappiness. One issue was women's economic and political opportunities. Women in Italy, France, and Belgium did not obtain the right to vote until the end of World War II. Although women made gains in employment outside the home, they still awaited a decrease in domestic responsibilities.

A second source of concern, articulated most forcefully by students in Europe, was the deployment of nuclear weapons in their countries, as well as the rigid social and educational institutions that preserved power and high culture for the elite few. Protests reached their apex in Paris in 1968, when workers joined students in a general strike and clashed violently with police.

In the United States, a crescendo of protests against racial discrimination propelled the U.S. federal government to enact civil rights legislation and to promote programs designed to end poverty. The Civil Rights Act of 1964 banned segregation in public facilities and outlawed racial discrimination in employment, and the Voting Rights Act of 1965 gave millions of previously disenfranchised African Americans an opportunity to exercise equal political rights. The Lyndon Baines Johnson administration also supported programs providing social security, health, and education. Aided by impressive economic growth, these War on Poverty programs nearly halved the U.S. poverty rate.

But legacies of racism and inequality were not easy to overcome, and protest movements proliferated. In spite of Supreme Court decisions, most schools remained racially homogeneous not only in the South but across the United States, as "White flight" to the suburbs left inner-city neighborhoods and schools to minorities. Militant voices, like those of Malcolm X and the Black Panthers, became prominent. Instead of integration, these radicals advocated Black separatism; instead of Americanism, they espoused embracing their African origins.

African American struggles inspired Native Americans, Mexican Americans, gay people, and women to initiate their own campaigns for equality and empowerment. Women now questioned a life built around taking care of home and family. In fact, the introduction of the birth control pill in 1960 and the publication of Betty Friedan's *The Feminine Mystique* in 1963 stand as watershed moments in American women's history. Because oral contraception allowed women to limit childbearing and to have sex with less fear of pregnancy, the resulting freedom helped unleash a sexual revolution. Moreover, Friedan blasted the myth of middle-class domestic contentment, describing the idealized 1950s suburban home as a "comfortable concentration camp" from which women must escape. Despite rising numbers of married women and college-educated women in the workforce, their compensation and opportunities for advancement lagged far behind those of men.

A year before Friedan authored her challenge to the subordination of women, Rachel Carson published *Silent Spring*, a book that was equally revolutionary in its attack against long-standing practices. In particular, Carson's book took on

Women Protest Sexism Insisting that "the private is public," many women in the 1960s and 1970s argued that the problem of sexism went beyond equal rights and income equality: women's oppression began in the home, where they were treated merely as homemakers or as sex objects. At this 1971 rally in London, protesters suggested that women were being "crucified" by their association with these everyday objects: an apron, a net shopping bag, silk stockings, and an item of washing.

the use of synthetic pesticides such as dichlorodiphenyltrichloroethane (DDT), which she said caused cancer, devastated wildlife, and destroyed natural ecosystems. Although chemical manufacturers responded that pesticides had vastly multiplied agricultural yields, *Silent Spring* stirred opposition that ultimately led to the banning of DDT in the United States in 1972. More broadly, Carson's book spurred the development of an environmental movement that questioned many of the ideas about economic progress and material prosperity upon which the "American Dream" had rested.

The escalation of the Vietnam War prompted many White American college students to question the ideals of American society. As the United States increased troop levels there in the 1960s, it conscripted more and more men. After President Richard Nixon sent American troops into Cambodia in 1970 to root out North Vietnamese soldiers, students at over 500 campuses occupied buildings and closed down universities. At Kent State University in Ohio, National Guardsmen attempting to stop the protests killed four students. The United States withdrew from Vietnam in 1973, but not before the divisions created by the war had strained the country almost to the breaking point.

TENSIONS WITHIN WORLD COMMUNISM

The unity of the communist world also came under increasing pressure. As early as 1948, Yugoslavia had broken free of the Soviet yoke and embarked on its own road to building socialism. Other satellite states within the Soviet bloc had more trouble freeing themselves. In 1956, Poland and Hungary were forced back into line. Twelve years later, Czechoslovakia experienced the Prague Spring, in which communist authorities experimented with creating a democratic and pluralist socialist world. Workers and students rallied behind the reformist government of Alexander Dubček, calling for more freedom of expression, more autonomy for workers and consumers, and more debate within the ruling party. Once again, the Soviets crushed what they branded a "counterrevolutionary" movement. As their tanks rolled into Prague, the Czech capital, one desperate student doused himself with gasoline and lit a match—his public suicide a gesture of defiance against communist rule.

Thereafter, the Prague Spring served as a symbol for dissenters, who were divided between those who still wanted to reform socialism and those who wanted to overturn it. Underground reading groups proliferated throughout eastern Europe, and many Russians renewed their faith in Orthodox Christianity, their prerevolutionary religion. Many dissidents were exiled from the Soviet Union. Most famous by the early 1970s was the Russian novelist Aleksandr Solzhenitsyn. His masterwork, *The Gulag Archipelago,* rejected the notion that socialism could be reformed simply by a turn away from Stalin's policies. Yet very few people in the Soviet Union could obtain copies of Solzhenitsyn's

Prague Spring In the spring of 1968, a movement demanding economic self-determination and freedom of speech took hold in Czechoslovakia, especially among students in its capital city, Prague. The Soviets allowed the movement to unfold for several months, but in late August they organized an invasion with troops and tanks from the USSR and several other Warsaw Pact countries. Although Czech students rallied to oppose the invaders—shouting "Ivan, go home!"—the Soviets suppressed the movement, afterward purging intellectuals from all leadership positions.

exposé, which had been published abroad and was a best-seller in the west. In 1974, the author himself was expelled from the USSR.

Still, there were important changes within the Second World. During the 1950s and 1960s, "national communism" became the rule throughout eastern Europe, even in countries that experienced Soviet invasions. National variations also arose within the Soviet Union, where Moscow conceded some autonomy to the Communist Party machines of its fifteen republics—in exchange for their fundamental loyalty. Dissidents were still persecuted, but by the 1970s many fewer were murdered outright, and the population of the gulags declined.

A shared dislike of the United States created a Sino-Soviet alliance in the years just after the Chinese Revolution of 1949. By the late 1950s, the Soviet Union had contributed massive military and economic aid to China. But the Chinese increasingly sought to define their own brand of Marxism and criticized Khrushchev's efforts to reduce tensions with the United States and the west. The divide raised China's profile throughout Asia and even in eastern Europe. Indeed, Romania achieved a measure of autonomy in foreign policy by playing off China and the Soviet Union. Albania declared its allegiance to China. African nations seeking Soviet aid increased their demands with subtle hints that they might consider deepening ties with China instead. Clearly, the Second World was no monolith.

TENSIONS WITHIN THE THIRD WORLD

In contrast to the First and Second Worlds, the Third World was never unified by economic, military, or political alliances. The Cold War pushed Third World states to choose between alignment with the First World or the Second. Nonetheless, radicalism nourished new hopes for unifying and empowering the Third World.

One effort at collaboration was the formation in 1960 of an alliance of oil exporters. The Organization of the Petroleum Exporting Countries (OPEC)—which included Algeria, Ecuador, Gabon, Indonesia, Iran, Iraq, Kuwait, Libya, Nigeria, Qatar, Saudi Arabia, the United Arab Emirates, and Venezuela—had little success in raising oil revenues through the 1960s, even though several members nationalized their oil fields. But after the fourth major Arab-Israeli war broke out in 1973, OPEC's Arab members decided to pressure Israel's First World allies by halting oil exports to them. Overnight, the embargo raised oil prices more than threefold, a bonanza that enriched all oil producers and led to an oil crisis in the west. To many, the bulging treasuries of OPEC nations seemed like the Third World's revenge. Here were Saudi Arabian princes, Venezuelan magnates, and Indonesian ministers dictating world prices to industrial consumers.

But the realignment was incomplete. Third World producers of raw materials such as coffee and rubber tried unsuccessfully to duplicate OPEC's model, and OPEC itself had trouble controlling the world's oil market. During the 1970s, oil discoveries in the North Sea, Mexico, and Canada reduced pressures on the large oil-consuming states to be more fuel efficient. With supply up, prices fell. To compensate for lost revenue, various OPEC states raised their own production, putting further downward pressure on prices.

Nor did oil revenues help overcome poverty and dependency in the Third World as a whole. To the contrary, most revenue surpluses from OPEC simply flowed back to First World banks or were invested in real-estate holdings in Europe and the United States. Some of these funds, in turn, were reloaned to the world's poorest countries in Africa, Asia, and Latin America, at high interest rates, to pay for more expensive imports—including oil! The biggest bonanza went to multinational petroleum firms, whose control over production, refining, and distribution yielded enormous profits.

For all the talk in the mid-1970s of changing the balance of international economic relations between the world's rich and poor countries, fundamental inequalities persisted. Those few Third World nations that appeared to break out of the cycle of poverty, like South Korea and Taiwan, did not achieve success through free trade and private-sector development. Rather, these nations regulated domestic markets, nurtured new industries, educated the populace, and required multinationals to work with local firms.

Conclusion

The three-world order arose on the ruins of European empires and their Japanese counterpart. First, the Soviet Union and the United States became superpowers. Second, World War II affirmed the nation-state rather than the empire as the primary form for organizing communities. Third, in spite of the rhetoric of individualism and the free market, the war and postwar reconstruction enhanced the reach and functions of the modern state. In the Third World, too, leaders of new nations saw the state as the primary instrument for promoting economic development.

The organization of the world into three blocs lasted into the mid-1970s. This arrangement fostered the economic recovery of western Europe and Japan from the wounds inflicted by war. These nations' recovery grew out of a Cold War alliance with the United States, where anticommunist hysteria accompanied an economic boom. The Cold War also cast a shadow over the citizens of the Soviet Union and eastern Europe. Gulags and political surveillance became widespread, while the Soviets and their satellite regimes mobilized resources for military purposes. The Third World, squeezed by its inability to reduce poverty on the one hand and by superpower rivalry on the other, struggled to pursue a "third way." While some states maintained democratic institutions and promoted economic development, many tumbled into dictatorships and authoritarian regimes, marked by high levels of corruption. In addition, they often suffered irreparable environmental damage.

In this context, Third World revolutionaries sought radical social and political transformation, seeking paths different from both western capitalism and Soviet communism. Though not successful, they energized considerable tensions in the three-world order. These tensions intensified in the late 1960s and early 1970s as Vietnamese communists defeated the United States, an oil crisis struck the west, and protests escalated in the First and Second Worlds. Thirty years after the end of World War II, the world order forged after 1945 was beginning to give way.

 **Focus On**

World War II and the Emergence of the First, Second, and Third Worlds during the Cold War

World War II

- World War II grows out of unresolved problems connected to World War I, especially the aggressive plans of Germany and Japan to expand their political and economic influence.

- The war brings huge human and material costs and ushers in an age of nuclear weapons.

- At the war's end, the United States, fearing the spread of communism and Soviet influence, helps rebuild war-torn Europe and Japan and creates military and political alliances to contain Soviet expansionist ambitions.

A New Global Order

- The Soviet Union and the United States become superpowers.

- Japan emerges as an economic powerhouse and a U.S. ally.

- A weakened Europe cannot resist demands for independence from Asian and African nationalists.

- Chinese communists engineer a revolution, while Indian nationalists and many African leaders achieve independence through negotiations.

- Elsewhere, especially in territories with large settler populations, decolonization is violent (Palestine, Algeria) or incomplete (eastern and southern Africa).

- Actions by Latin American reformers and revolutionary insurgents spark counterinsurgency efforts by the United States and its regional allies.

- An insecure three-world order emerges after most Asian and African states achieve independence.

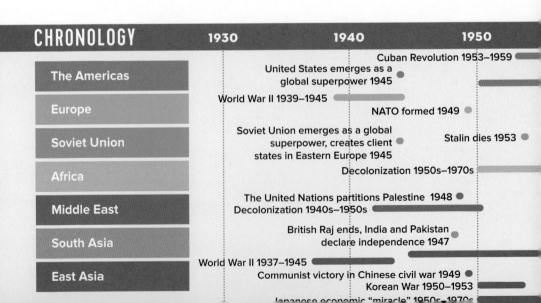

CHRONOLOGY

	1930	1940	1950
The Americas		United States emerges as a global superpower 1945	Cuban Revolution 1953–1959
Europe	World War II 1939–1945		NATO formed 1949
Soviet Union		Soviet Union emerges as a global superpower, creates client states in Eastern Europe 1945	Stalin dies 1953
Africa			Decolonization 1950s–1970s
Middle East		The United Nations partitions Palestine 1948 / Decolonization 1940s–1950s	
South Asia		British Raj ends, India and Pakistan declare independence 1947	
East Asia	World War II 1937–1945	Communist victory in Chinese civil war 1949 / Korean War 1950–1953	
		Japanese economic "miracle" 1950s–1970s	

THINKING ABOUT GLOBAL CONNECTIONS

- **Thinking about Worlds Together, Worlds Apart and the Three-World Order** Explain how the collapse of a Europe-centered world changed how states interacted with one another. In what ways did the division of the globe into three rival worlds differ from the dominance of the European "great powers" that preceded it? Which world order do you think was more stable, the Europe-centered world or the three-world order that followed it? Do you think one system was more equitable than the other?

- **Thinking about Changing Power Relationships and the Three-World Order** Analyze Third World revolutionaries' ability to alter the dynamic of the Cold War. Where do you think power was located in this period? To what degree did Washington and Moscow determine the course of world affairs, and to what degree were politicians in places like Cuba, Vietnam, and Algeria able to play the superpowers off against each other? How and to what degree were revolutionaries able to make claims on the First and Second Worlds for economic, political, or military assistance?

- **Thinking about Environmental Impacts and the Three-World Order** In this period, for the first time, organized groups set out to defend the environment. What sparked their protests? Where were those organizations most fully developed? Where was ecological devastation most extreme? What force or forces opposed environmentalists?

Key Terms

Fidel Castro p. 804

Cold War p. 771

decolonization p. 785

Holocaust p. 776

International Monetary Fund (IMF) p. 800

Mao Zedong p. 785

neocolonialism p. 801

North Atlantic Treaty Organization (NATO) p. 782

Third World p. 800

Warsaw Pact p. 782

World Bank p. 800

 Go to **INQUIZITIVE** to see what you've learned—and learn what you've missed—with personalized feedback along the way.

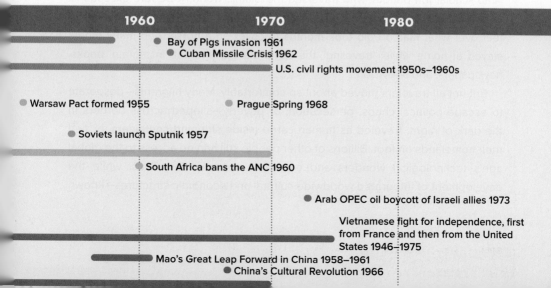

1960	1970	1980

Bay of Pigs invasion 1961

Cuban Missile Crisis 1962

U.S. civil rights movement 1950s–1960s

Warsaw Pact formed 1955

Prague Spring 1968

Soviets launch Sputnik 1957

South Africa bans the ANC 1960

Arab OPEC oil boycott of Israeli allies 1973

Vietnamese fight for independence, first from France and then from the United States 1946–1975

Mao's Great Leap Forward in China 1958–1961

China's Cultural Revolution 1966

21

Globalization

1970-2000

Core Objectives

- **DESCRIBE** the relationship between global migration, new technologies, and the spread of cultural influences during and after the Cold War.

- **EVALUATE** the degree to which globalization after the end of the Cold War changed societies, and **COMPARE** that globalization with earlier forms of globalization.

- **DESCRIBE** how globalization and population changes affected the environment, and vice versa.

- **IDENTIFY** the transnational forces that eroded the power of the nation-state in the last third of the twentieth century, and **EXPLAIN** how they did so.

In the thirteenth century, few people could imagine moving beyond their local regions. The Venetian explorer Marco Polo, who traveled through China, and the Arab scholar Ibn Battuta, who traversed the Islamic world, were rare exceptions. In contrast, by the end of the twentieth century, many slept while flying at 30,000 feet over what Marco Polo took months to cover on a horse. And many others stayed at home while "traveling" the world via the Internet, Instagram, books, newspapers, and television.

But not all travelers moved about so comfortably. Many migrants—desperate to escape political chaos, persecution, or poverty—slipped across borders in the dark of night, traveled as human cargo inside shipping containers, or fled their homelands on foot. Billions of other people still had no access to the global age's technological wonders and economic opportunities. Thus, while the development of integrated worldwide cultural and economic structures—known as **globalization**—created new possibilities for some, it also caused deeper inequalities.

The forces driving global integration—and inequality—were no longer the empires of old. For centuries, these empires had been the engines of convergence and conflict. By the mid-twentieth century, however, they were in retreat. The Cold War and decolonization movements produced the three-world order. But within three decades, the three-world order was also in retreat. Power structures in the First World, under stress in the 1970s, did not crack, but those in the Second World did. The Cold War ended with the implosion of the Soviet bloc. The Third World also splintered, with some areas becoming highly advanced and others falling into deep poverty; the term **developing world** obscured these differences. Now a new architecture of power organized the world into a unified marketplace with unhindered flows of capital, commerce, culture, and labor. By 2000, most societies had endorsed electoral systems and adopted some form of market economy.

Because the United States promoted these changes, globalization has looked to some like Americanization. The United States unquestionably stood as the world's most influential society, with its music, food, principles of representative government, and free markets spreading worldwide. Yet the process did not run one way. The world also came to America and shaped its society: people living in the United States—along with their inventions, sports stars, and musical inspirations—increasingly came from somewhere else.

Nor was the United States immune from transnational forces challenging the power of the nation-state itself. In the United States, as elsewhere, globalization functioned through networks of investment, trade, and migration that operated relatively independently of nation-states. In the process, globalization shook entrenched forms of political and social identification, including religious and military authority. Members of societies now often identified more with local, sub-national, or international movements or cultures than with nation-states. To be sure, nation-states remained essential for establishing democratic institutions and protecting human rights, but supranational organizations—institutions that transcended nation-state borders, like the European Union and the International Monetary Fund (IMF)—often impinged on their autonomy. A new global order emerged with a unified marketplace and unhindered flows of capital, commerce, culture, and labor.

Removing Obstacles to Globalization

The collapse of the Soviet Union brought the Cold War to an end. At the same time, the capitalist First World gave up its last colonial possessions and the remnants of White settler supremacy disintegrated. But as this occurred, the formerly colonized Third World's dream of a "third way" also vanished. As empires withdrew, they revealed a world integrated by markets for capital and labor, culture, and technology, rather than by forced loyalties to imperial masters or rival superpowers.

ENDING THE COLD WAR

A world split between hostile factions limited the prospects for a global exchange of peoples, ideas, and resources. There was widespread exchange within each of the rival blocs, but for other countries the pressure from the Soviet Union and the United States to align with one of the two existing superpowers imposed limits to their interactions, even with neighboring states. Tiny Nicaragua received support from the eastern bloc but was isolated in Central America. Egypt, on the other hand, had enough clout to leave the Soviet orbit and changed the political geography of the Arab world. At the same time, the rivalry between blocs posed rising tolls. The cost was highest in contested hot spots of the Third World, but even the superpowers paid a price. Eventually economic pressures, technological changes, and political crumbling brought down the walls that defined the three-world order and widened the scope for an explosion of trade, migration, and cultural exchange across borders.

Mounting Costs Other pressures within and outside the United States and the Soviet Union also strained the Cold War order. Vietnam became a battleground for Russian, Chinese, and American ambitions. This war spilled over into Laos and Cambodia, dragging them to ruin along with Vietnam. In Central America, U.S. president Ronald Reagan and his advisers opposed the victory of the left-leaning Nicaraguan Sandinista coalition in 1979. During the 1980s the U.S. government pumped millions of dollars to the Contras (right-wing opponents of the left-wing Sandinistas) and lent military and monetary assistance to other Central American anticommunist forces.

Rivalry was enormously costly to the superpowers. The 1970s and 1980s saw the largest peacetime accumulation of arms in history. Despite myriad treaties and summits, the United States and the Soviet Union stockpiled nuclear and conventional weaponry. Furthermore, in 1983 U.S. president Ronald Reagan unveiled the Strategic Defense Initiative (nicknamed "Star Wars"), an elaborate and expensive plan to use satellites and space missiles to insulate the United States from incoming nuclear bombs. For both sides, these military spending sprees brought economic troubles.

Cracks on either side of the conflict appeared in the 1970s. The intelligence organizations of both the Soviet Union and the United States produced secret memos questioning whether the Soviet bloc could sustain its global position. The Soviet Union sent troops to prop up a puppet regime in Afghanistan, only to fall into a bloody war against insurgents financed and armed by the United States. The resulting stalemate undermined the image of the mighty Soviet armed forces, and mothers of Soviet soldiers protested their government's involvements abroad. In Europe and North America, the antinuclear movement rallied millions to the streets, while western industrialists worried about competition from Japan, which had been plowing money into rapid industrialization rather than arms. Political leaders also grappled with distressingly high unemployment rates.

The Soviet Bloc Collapses In the end, the Soviet bloc collapsed. (See Map 21.1.) Even though planned economies employed the entire Soviet population, they failed to fill stores with sufficient consumer goods. Socialist health care and benefits generally lagged behind those provided in wealthy, capitalist countries—though there were notable exceptions, like Cuba. Authoritarian political structures in the Soviet bloc relied on deception and coercion rather than elections and civic activism. Although communists had promised to beat capitalism by building socialism on the way to achieving full communism, the communist paradise was nowhere on the horizon.

Events in Poland were one catalyst in socialism's undoing. In 1978, the Catholic Church appointed a new pope, John Paul II, who came from Poland—the first non-Italian pope in over 450 years. The pope supported mass strikes at the Lenin Shipyard in Gdańsk, which led to the formation of the Soviet bloc's

1989: Mass demonstrations, fall of the Berlin Wall
1990: Reunited with West Germany

1980 onward: Solidarity leads opposition
1981: Crackdown against Solidarity, driving it underground
1989: Solidarity wins 99 of the 100 seats in parliament that it is permitted to contest

1989: Mass demonstrations
1990: Multiparty elections
1993: Czechoslovakia splits into Czech Republic and Slovakia

1989: Removal of barbed wire on border with Austria allows East German tourists to cross westward
1990: Multiparty elections

1989: National uprising against Ceausescu
1992: First multiparty general election
1996: First noncommunist government

1990: Multiparty elections

1990: Multiparty elections
1991–1992: War between Croats and Serbs

1992: Fighting begins between Serbs and Bosnian Muslims
1995: Divided in two

1990: Multiparty elections
1991: Dissolved into warring states

1989: Loses autonomy from Serbia
1998–1999: Fighting between Serbs and ethnic Albanians
2000: First free elections

1989: Demonstrations
1990: Multiparty elections

1990: Multiparty elections
2001: Fighting erupts between Macedonians and ethnic Albanians

1990: Demonstrations, civil war
1991: Multiparty elections

Civil unrest

DENMARK
BALTIC SEA
NETHERLANDS
EAST GERMANY
Berlin
Leipzig
BELGIUM
LUX.
WEST GERMANY
Prague
CZECH REPUBLIC
CZECHOSLOVAKIA
SLOVAKIA
Bratislava
FRANCE
SWITZERLAND
AUSTRIA
HUNGARY
Budapest
SLOVENIA
CROATIA
BOSNIA-HERZOGOVINA
Belgrade
YUGOSLAVIA
SERBIA
ITALY
MONTE-NEGRO
KOSOVO
MACEDONIA
Tirana
ALBANIA
Gdańsk
POLAND
Warsaw
SOVIET UNION
ROMANIA
Timisoara
Bucharest
Danube R.
BLACK SEA
BULGARIA
Sofia
GREECE
TURKEY
MEDITERRANEAN SEA

0 100 200 300 Miles
0 100 200 300 Kilometers

Map 21.1 Collapse of the Communist Bloc in Europe

The Soviet Union's domination of eastern Europe ended precipitously in 1989. The political map of eastern and central Europe took on a different shape under European integration.

- What significant event in many communist countries signaled the collapse of communism?
- In what part of eastern and central Europe did the most political instability and conflict occur?
- According to your reading, why did the end of communist rule cause the reshuffling of political boundaries in the region?

first independent trade union, Solidarity. As Communist Party members in Poland defected to its side, the union became a society-wide movement; it aimed not to reform socialism (as in Czechoslovakia in 1968; see Chapter 20) but to overcome it. A crackdown by the Polish military and police put most of Solidarity's leadership in prison and drove the movement underground, but Soviet intelligence officials secretly worried that Solidarity could not be easily eradicated.

Lech Wałęsa A Polish electrician from the Lenin Shipyard in the Baltic port city of Gdańsk, Wałęsa spearheaded the formation of Solidarity, a mass independent trade union of workers who battled the communist regime that ruled in their name. He later was elected president of post-communist Poland.

The most consequential factor in the collapse of the Soviet superpower was the reform effort launched by Mikhail Gorbachev, who became general secretary of the Soviet Communist Party in 1985. Under this effort (known as *perestroika*, meaning "reconstruction"), Gorbachev permitted competitive elections for Communist Party posts, relaxed censorship, allowed civic associations, legalized small nonstate businesses, granted autonomy to state firms, and encouraged the Soviet republics to be responsible for their own affairs within the Soviet Union. His foreign policy also upended decades of Soviet central control. He sought arms control to lessen the burden on the Soviet Union. He pulled troops from Afghanistan and informed eastern European leaders that they could not count on Moscow's armed intervention to prop up their regimes.

Having wanted to rescue socialism, Gorbachev instead destabilized it. His political changes allowed civic groups to call not for the system's reform but for its liquidation. Eastern Europe bolted from the Soviet orbit, and some of the Soviet republics began to push for independence. In response, disgruntled factions within the Communist Party and the Soviet military tried to preserve the destabilized old order by staging a coup in 1991. It was a fiasco. The former Communist Party boss of Moscow and elected president of the Russian republic, Boris Yeltsin, rallied the opposition and faced down the hard-liners. Discontented Soviet elites saw an opportunity. They abandoned the socialist cause and divided up state property among themselves—and became the so-called oligarchs of the post-Soviet order. Thus, the Soviet Union broke apart into independent states. (See Map 21.2.)

Map 21.2 The Breakup of the Soviet Union

The Soviet Union broke apart in 1991. Compare this map with Map 17.5, which illustrates Russian expansion in the nineteenth century.

- Which parts of the old Russian Empire remained under Russian rule, and which of its territories established their own states?
- In what areas did large migrations accompany the breakup, and for what reasons?
- According to your reading, how did the breakup of the Soviet Union change Russia's status in Europe and Asia?

The fall of the Berlin Wall and the collapse of the Soviet Union allowed eastern European states to resume their cultural, political, and economic ties with western Europe and the United States, ties previously severed by the 1945 partition of Europe. No sooner had the Berlin Wall come down than new countries lined up to join the European Union. With the Cold War over, traditionally neutral countries like Austria and Sweden applied for admission. Then came a flood of eastern European, Balkan, and Baltic applicants. By 2004, the European Union had grown from 322 million people to 495 million. European integration and the turn west went beyond economic matters. Many of the countries that joined the European Union also entered the North Atlantic Treaty Organization (NATO) alliance, much to the distaste of Russia.

By historical standards the Cold War had been relatively brief, spanning four decades. But communism had played a major role in the military conflicts and the headlong modernization of Russia and China, and it exercised important influence on India and elsewhere in the Third World, where proxy wars were devastating. Communism, however, faced a trilemma: it could not keep up the Cold War *and* deliver the good life to its adherents *and* survive in a more competitive world economy. But ultimately, it was the inability to keep up with the consumption and technology race more than the inability to keep up with the arms race that doomed the USSR and unleashed in the early 1990s economic and cultural energies that would buoy global integration.

AFRICA AND THE END OF WHITE RULE

Although the aftermath of World War II saw the dismantling of most of Europe's empires, remnants of colonial rule remained in southern Africa. (See Chapter 20, Map 20.6.) Here, Whites clung to centuries-old notions of their racial superiority over non-Europeans. Final decolonization meant that self-rule would return to all of Africa. The end of colonialism also set the stage for former colonies to find new trading and investment partners and to become more integrated with the wider world.

The Last Holdouts The last African territories under direct European control were the Portuguese colonies of southern and western Africa. However, by the mid-1970s, efforts to suppress African nationalist movements in those colonies had exhausted Portugal's resources. As African nationalist demands led to a hurried Portuguese withdrawal from Guinea-Bissau, Angola, and Mozambique, formal European colonialism in Africa came to an end.

But White rule still prevailed elsewhere in Africa. In Rhodesia, a White minority resisted international pressure to allow Black rule. In the end, independent African states helped support a liberation guerrilla movement under Robert Mugabe. Surrounded, Rhodesian Whites finally lost control in 1979. The new constitutional government renamed the country Zimbabwe, erasing the name of the long-deceased British expansionist Cecil Rhodes (see Chapter 17).

South Africa and Nelson Mandela The final outpost of White rule was South Africa, where the European minority was larger, richer, and more entrenched than elsewhere in the region. Although powerful international firms operated there, they were reluctant to risk their investments by boycotting the racist regime. In addition, the U.S. government regarded South Africa's large army as a useful tool to fight Soviet allies elsewhere in southern Africa. Yet in the countryside and cities, defiance of White rule was growing. Black South Africans lobbed rocks and crude bombs at tanks and organized mass strikes against the multinational-owned mines.

At the same time, pressures from abroad to end the racist apartheid system were mounting. The International Olympic Committee banned South African athletes starting in 1970. American students insisted that their universities divest themselves from companies with investments in South Africa. As international pressures grew, foreign governments—even that of the United States, once South Africa's staunchest ally—applied economic sanctions against South Africa. A swelling worldwide chorus demanded that **Nelson Mandela** (1918–2013), the imprisoned leader of the African National Congress (ANC), be freed. The White political elite eventually realized that it was better to negotiate new arrangements than to endure international condemnation and years of internal warfare against a majority population. In 1990, President F. W. de Klerk (of the National Party) released Mandela from prison and legalized the ANC and the Communist Party of South Africa. Ensuing negotiations produced South Africa's first free, mass elections in 1994. These elections brought an overwhelming victory to the ANC and to Nelson Mandela, who was elected president. Majority rule had finally come to South Africa, and for the first time in centuries, Africans ruled over all of Africa.

In Nelson Mandela, South Africa's White rulers found a man of exceptional integrity and political savvy. He had spent more than two decades in prison, much of it at hard labor. But he looked beyond past injustices to ease the transition to full democracy. Besides, he was aware that with the country

The End of Apartheid Nelson Mandela, running for president in 1994 as the candidate of the African National Congress, here casts a ballot in the first all-races election in South Africa. This election ended apartheid and saw the African National Congress win a sweeping victory.

veering toward civil war, only a negotiated change would preserve South Africa's industries, wealth, and educational system.

Still, African leaders faced immense problems in building stable political communities. Although they set out to destroy the vestiges of colonial political structures and build African-based public institutions, those leaders struggled to find a third way between capitalism and communism. Ethnic and religious rivalries, held in check during the colonial period, now blazed forth. Civil wars erupted in many countries—most violently in Nigeria, Sudan, and Zaire (later called the Democratic Republic of the Congo)—and military leaders were drawn into politics. By the 1990s, the continent was aflame with civil strife. Armed conflicts that started with the Cold War endured well after it ended, even though White rule had finally come to an end throughout the entire continent.

Unleashing Globalization

As obstacles to international integration began to dissolve, capital, commodities, people, and culture crossed borders with ever-greater freedom. Even though trade, foreign investment, migration, and cultural borrowing had long been hallmarks of modern history, the global age changed their scale. At the same time, never had there been such unequal access to the fruits of globalization. Several factors contributed to increasing integration and to new power arrangements: international banking, expanded international trade, population migrations, and technical breakthroughs in communications that facilitated the worldwide spread of cultural influences.

FINANCE AND TRADE

The increase in the international flow of goods and capital was well underway in the 1970s, but the end of the Cold War removed many impediments to globalization. During the 1990s, even the strongest nation-states felt the effects of economic globalization.

Global Finance and Deregulated Markets Major transformations in the world's financial system occurred in the 1970s. America's budget and trade deficits prompted President Richard Nixon to take the dollar off the gold standard, an action that enabled the yen, the lira, the pound, the franc, and other national currencies to cut their ties to the American dollar. Now international financiers enjoyed greater freedom from national regulators and found fresh business opportunities.

The primary agents of the heightened global financial activity were banks. Based mainly in London, New York, and Tokyo, big banks attracted large amounts of capital for lucrative ventures around the world. Revenues from oil producers provided a large infusion of cash into the global economy in the 1970s. At the same time, banks joined forces to issue mammoth loans to developing countries.

No international financial organization was more influential than the International Monetary Fund (IMF). Created after World War II at the Bretton Woods Conference by an international community led by the United States and Great Britain, the IMF raised capital from all participating states to lend funds to states in need. During the 1980s, it emerged as a central player, especially in response to the debt crises that surfaced in poor countries as the prospect of finding a third way between the superpower blocs began to fade. Throughout the 1970s, European, Japanese, and North American banks had loaned money on very easy terms to cash-strapped Third World and eastern-bloc borrowers. But what was once good business soon turned sour. In 1982, a wave of defaults, in which governments and other borrowers found themselves unable to repay their loans, threatened to overrun Latin America in particular. Throughout the 1980s, international banks and the IMF kept heavily indebted customers solvent. The IMF offered short-term loans to governments on condition that recipients produce balanced budgets, compel civilian populations to give up subsidies on essential products, and cease to import far more than they exported. Latin Americans led the way in reorganizing their finances and thus pioneered the process of expanding domestic production while at the same time engaging in robust international trade. All across the world, tariffs and other barriers to foreign trade crumbled, state enterprises became private firms, and foreign banks and multinational companies took a great interest in investing in these newly reformed economies.

Effects of Integrated Networks New technologies and institutions enabled many more financial investors and traders to participate in the integrated networks of world finance. The Internet and online trading accelerated the movement of capital across borders. Rapid changes in financial and currency markets soon created problems, however. When the Mexican economy went into paralysis in 1994, the crisis was so extreme that not even the IMF could bail it out; the U.S. Treasury issued the largest international loan in history to pull Mexico out of its economic tailspin. Despite its role as the lender in that instance, the United States emerged in the new financial order as the world's largest borrower because it imported far more than it exported. Early in the new millennium, its net foreign debt soared past $2 trillion—a 700 percent increase since the early 1990s. Much of this debt was owed to China, which had a huge trade surplus with the United States.

Globalization increased commercial, as well as financial, interdependence. The total value of goods and services exchanged through world trade increased nearly tenfold between 1973 and 1998, and trade in Asia grew even faster. Whereas an American would once have worn American-made clothes (Levi's), driven an American car (a Ford), and watched an American television (made by Zenith), such was rarely the case by the century's end. Increasingly, American consumers bought foreign goods and services and sold a greater share of their own output abroad. This pattern had always been true of smaller regions like Central America and southern Africa. But in the 1980s, it intensified as countries with cheap and skilled labor, like China, India, and Brazil, were able to undersell their competitors in world markets.

Globalization East Asian countries, starting with Japan and South Korea in the 1970s and including China more recently, became major exporters of manufactured goods while North America and Europe began their long deindustrialization. Shipping containers (like those pictured here) were crucial to this new global division of labor. Invented to haul expensive military hardware for the U.S. war in Vietnam, they proved instrumental in lowering shipping costs. They allowed ever-more-fragile goods, like electronics, to be transported safely and did away with labor-intensive systems of loading and unloading massive transport vessels. The results were massive layoffs from manufacturing and transportation jobs in some parts of the world and rapid industrialization in emerging economies.

International trade also shifted the international division of labor. After World War II, Europeans and North Americans dominated manufacturing, while Third World countries supplied raw materials. But by the 1990s, this was no longer the case. Brazil became a major airplane maker, South Korea exported millions of automobiles, and China emerged as the world's largest source of textiles, footwear, and electronics.

The most remarkable global shift involved East Asian industry and commerce. Manufactured goods, including high-technology products, now came from the eastern fringe of Afro-Eurasia as often as from its western fringe. Japan blazed the Asian trail: between 1965 and 1990, its share of world trade doubled to almost 10 percent. China, too, flexed its economic muscle, especially after Deng Xiaoping took power in 1978. It's hard to imagine now, but at the time China was very poor. Even as late as 1990, China's per capita income was 30 percent lower than that of the countries of sub-Saharan Africa. Moreover, China barely registered on the global economic scale, commanding a mere 1.6 percent of global GDP. To improve China's economy, Deng threw open the country's doors to foreign trade and investment. In addition, study missions abroad brought back ideas and encouragement. By globalizing China, Deng turned it into an economic powerhouse. By 2010, China had become the world's second-largest economy, producing 8.6 percent of global GDP. It muscled past Germany, the United States, and Japan to become the largest exporter of goods in the world. China's per capita income was now three times that of sub-Saharan Africa. For the three decades from 1990 to 2019, China chalked up astounding 10 percent annual growth rates, even maintaining 6 percent GDP growth during the global recession of 2008 to 2009 (see Chapter 22).

For East Asia as a whole, the share of exports doubled in the same period. Smaller states whose governments subsidized economic development, like Singapore, Taiwan, South Korea, and Hong Kong, became mini-powerhouses. By the early 1990s, these countries and Japan were also major investors abroad. As East Asia's share of world production quickly increased, the U.S. and European shares decreased.

Regional Trade Blocs and Growing Inequalities The industrialization of poor countries, combined with lower trade barriers, increased the pressures of world competition on national economies. Some areas responded by establishing regional trade blocs to create larger markets for themselves and stay competitive in an ever more integrated world economy.

The most complete regional integration occurred in Europe, where states slashed trade barriers and harmonized their commercial policies toward the rest of the world. In 1993, the Maastricht Treaty established the **European Union (EU)** under its current name, and what had been conceived as a trading and financial bloc began to evolve into a political union as well, a supranational organization with legislative and judicial powers. EU members agreed to eliminate border controls and visas and created a vast, open migrant zone across the old Cold War divide, which sparked substantial movement from east to west. By 2000, the European Union had fifteen member states. In 2002, a number of those states deepened their economic interdependence by adopting a single currency, the euro. A few of them—most notably the United Kingdom—did not want to give up control of their own national currency. (The United Kingdom would later withdraw from the EU—the so-called Brexit—in 2020).

"Great. You move to Mexico, and we all end up working at McDonald's."

CartoonCollections.com

Trade Blocs and Outsourcing The creation of regional trade agreements led to more trade and migration within blocs, such as within Europe and North America. But as manufacturers sought out new locations for their factories to take advantage of cheaper labor elsewhere, they generated backlash from workers. Many had to seek out new jobs in the service sectors as assembly lines closed. This cartoon captures the resentments directed against business elites.

European countries may have gone the farthest in dismantling national borders and sovereignties. But they were not alone. The Unites States, Mexico, and Canada agreed in 1994 to create a common trade bloc. In South America, Brazil and Argentina formed the backbone of a regional fusion. Since 2000, Asian countries have formed what is often called a "noodle bowl" of trade agreements to create regional partnerships and multilateral agreements to liberalize trade among countries of the Asian Pacific.

Although international trade increased during this period, it also became increasingly unequal. High-technology and high-value goods now occupied an ever-greater share of the manufacturing and exports of the world's richest countries. For rich countries as a whole, about half of total GDP reflected the production and distribution of goods such as computers, software, and pharmaceuticals and services such as insurance and banking, which, collectively, gave those countries a competitive advantage. Poor nations, by contrast, generally remained locked in the production of low-tech goods and the export of raw materials. Increasingly, technology and knowledge divided the world into affluent, technically sophisticated countries and poor, technically underdeveloped regions.

MIGRATION

Migration, a constant feature of world history, became more pronounced in the twentieth century. (See Map 21.3.) After 1970 fewer Europeans were on the move, despite the opening up of borders within Europe and movement from the poorer south and east to the wealthier north and west. But many more Asians, Africans, and Latin Americans were chasing jobs in the richer countries. By 2000, there were 120 million migrants scattered across 152 countries, up from 75 million in 1965.

Patterns of Migration Migratory flows often followed the contours of past colonial and political ties. Where North America and Europe had had colonies or dependencies, their political withdrawal left tracks for migrants to follow. Indians and Pakistanis moved to Britain; so did Jamaicans. Dominicans, Haitians, and Mexicans went to the United States. Algerians and Vietnamese moved to France. Where emerging rich societies cultivated close diplomatic ties, these relations opened migratory gates. This was true of Germany's relationship with Turkey, of Japan's with South Korea, and of Canada's with Hong Kong.

International migration was often an extension of regional and national migration from poorer rural areas to urban centers. In Nigeria, for example, rural-urban migration intensified after 1970. In 1900, Nigeria's capital at the time, Lagos, had a population of 41,847. At the century's end, Lagos had more than 10 million people, with this number predicted to double by 2025. The key to Lagos's boom in the 1970s was the existence of large oil reserves in the country and the high prices that oil fetched in international markets. When the Organization of the Petroleum Exporting Countries (OPEC) sent oil prices

East Europeans 1918–1919

East Europeans 1918–1919

Russian Jews to USA 1980s and 1990s

European Jews to USA 1930s

Jamaicans, Haitians, and Dominicans to USA 1990–

West Indians to Britain

Spaniards to Mexico 1936

Algerian colons to France 1962

CANADA

UNITED STATES

MEXICO

BELIZE

GUATEMALA

NICARAGUA

CUBA

HAITI

COLOMBIA

BRAZIL

ARGENTINA

GREAT BRITAIN

SWITZ. FRANCE

SPAIN

MOROCCO

TUNISIA

ALGERIA

NIGER

IVORY COAST

NIGERIA

ATLANTIC OCEAN

PACIFIC OCEAN

1950–

1960–

1960–1980

1950–

1970–

1980

Foreign-born people as percentage of total population (latest available year)

- Less than 1.5%
- 1.5%–2.9%
- 3.0%–7.5%
- More than 7.5%
- Data not available
- ← Migration

0   1000   2000 Miles

0   1000   2000 Kilometers

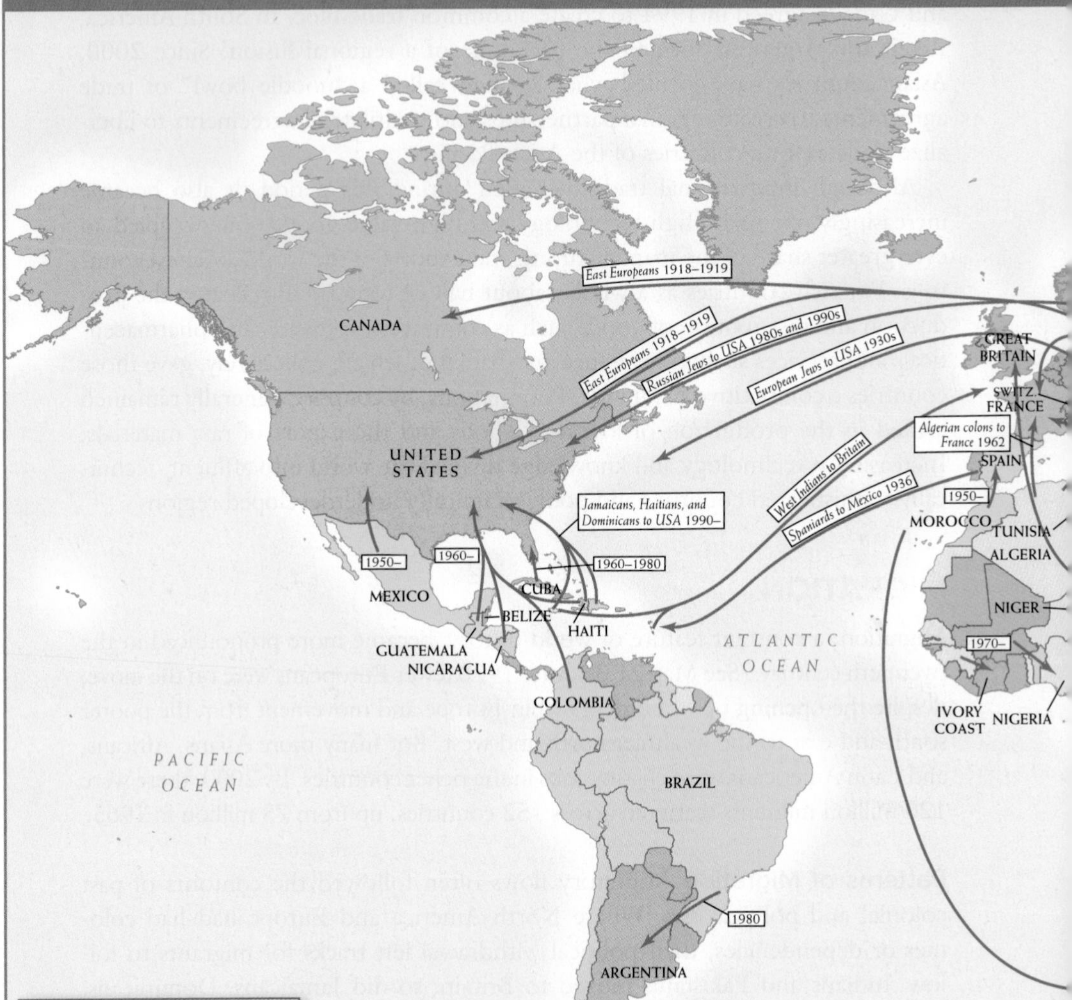

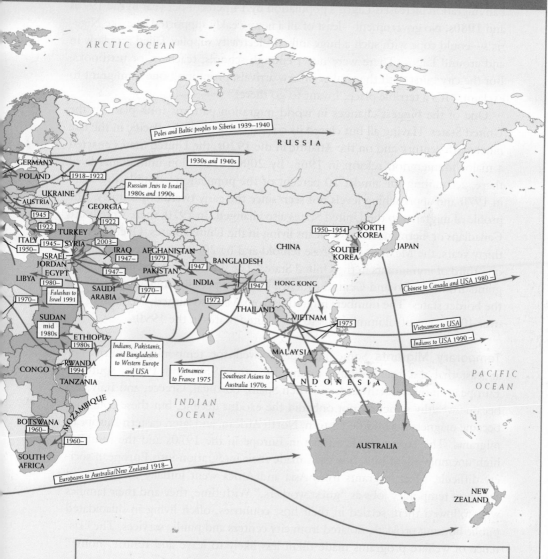

ARCTIC OCEAN

Poles and Baltic peoples to Siberia 1939–1940

RUSSIA

1930s and 1940s

GERMANY

POLAND 1918–1922

Russian Jews to Israel 1980s and 1990s

UKRAINE

AUSTRIA

1945

GEORGIA

1922

1922

TURKEY

ITALY 1945 **SYRIA** 2003–

1950– **IRAQ** **AFGHANISTAN**

ISRAEL 1947– 1979

JORDAN

EGYPT 1947–

LIBYA **PAKISTAN**

1980– **SAUDI** **INDIA**

Falashas to **ARABIA** 1970–

1970– Israel 1991 1972

SUDAN **THAILAND**

mid 1980s

ETHIOPIA

1980s Indians, Pakistanis, and Bangladeshis to Western Europe and USA

CONGO **RWANDA** 1994 Vietnamese to France 1975

TANZANIA Southeast Asians to Australia 1970s

1950–1954 **NORTH KOREA**

CHINA **SOUTH** **JAPAN**

KOREA

Chinese to Canada and USA 1980–

BANGLADESH

1947

HONG KONG

1947

VIETNAM 1975 Vietnamese to USA

Indians to USA 1990–

MALAYSIA

INDONESIA **PACIFIC OCEAN**

INDIAN OCEAN

BOTSWANA

1960–

1960–

SOUTH AFRICA

Europeans to Australia/New Zealand 1918–

AUSTRALIA

NEW ZEALAND

MOZAMBIQUE

Map 21.3 World Migration, 1918–1998

....

The world's population continued to grow and move around in the twentieth century.

- Looking at this map, identify the countries that had the greatest increase in foreign-born people as a percentage of total population.

- Compare the areas of most rapid population growth during the nineteenth century with the parts of the world that, according to this map, had the highest percentage of foreign-born people in the twentieth century. What are the similarities and differences?

- During the twentieth century, which parts of the world were the sending areas, and which were the receiving territories? See also Map 18.1.

soaring, money poured into Nigeria. The government kept most of that money in its largest city. That, in turn, spurred people to move to Lagos. This rural-urban migration increased Lagos's population by 14 percent per year in the 1970s and 1980s. No government—least of all a new, weakly supported one like Nigeria's—could cope with such a huge influx. Electricity supplies failed regularly in and around Lagos. There were never enough schools, teachers, or textbooks. But the city burst with the vitality of new arrivals, prompting one immigrant to exclaim, "It's a terrible place; I want to go there!"

One of the biggest changes in world migration patterns took place in the United States. Having all but closed its coastal borders on the Pacific in the late nineteenth century and on the Atlantic in the 1920s, the United States enacted a major immigration reform in 1965. By 2000, 27 million immigrants lived there, accounting for almost 10 percent of the population—double the share in 1970 and approaching levels not seen since the early twentieth century. The profile of migrants to the United States also changed. In 1970, there were more Canadians or Germans than Mexicans living in the United States. Over the next thirty years, the Mexican influx rose tenfold and by 2000 accounted for almost one-third of immigrants in the United States. The flow of legal and illegal immigrants from Mexico and Central America had an especially dramatic impact on the border states. The numbers migrating from Asia also surged, accounting for over 40 percent of all immigrants to the United States in the 1990s.

Temporary Migrants Some migrants moved for temporary sojourns—or at least that was their original intent. Into the 1950s and 1960s, southern Europeans moved northward; yet when Spain, Portugal, Greece, and Italy also became wealthy societies, not only did the exodus decline, but these countries became magnets for Middle Eastern, North African, and later, eastern European migrants. The economic downturn in Europe in the 1970s and the resulting high unemployment rate, however, made their integration into European society difficult. Most migrants from Asia and Africa went initially to Europe in search of temporary jobs as "guest workers." With time, they and their families who followed them settled in their host countries, often living in dilapidated public housing projects, isolated from city centers and public services. The existence of welfare programs made them less likely to leave and return "home" than were earlier generations of labor migrants.

In Japan, too, immigrants were not easily incorporated. Tokyo's immigration policy in the 1970s resembled a guest-worker program. Discouraging permanent settlement and immigration, Japan encouraged itinerant workers to move to the country temporarily, yet its expanding economy required increasing numbers of these temporary migrants. Indeed, Japan's deep reluctance to recruit large numbers of foreign workers, for fear of their settling down, led to dire labor shortages. After Japan, the economic tigers of Hong Kong, Taiwan, and Malaysia all became hosts for temporary migrants. Millions of guest workers moved there, and ultimately those migrants sank deeper roots, especially once their children entered school.

Resident Noncitizens and Refugees Arguments in Los Angeles over schools and health care for resident noncitizens became part of a global debate over the rights and protections afforded to migrants in the late twentieth century. In Argentina, up to 500,000 undocumented Peruvians, Bolivians, and Paraguayans lived without the approval of host countries or basic rights as citizens. Even more staggering were the numbers of migrants—between 3 and 8 million—who moved from Mozambique, Zimbabwe, and Botswana to South Africa with the election of the ANC and an end to apartheid. In some Middle Eastern countries, like Saudi Arabia and Kuwait, foreign-born workers constituted over 70 percent of the workforce. In general, migrants were only partially accommodated by their host societies, while many were fully excluded. Thus, even though population movements flowed across political, kinship, and market networks, this demographic reshuffling heightened national concerns about the ethnic makeup of political communities.

Forced migrations remained a major problem. In contrast to earlier centuries' forced migration of enslaved people from Africa, this period's involuntary flows involved refugees fleeing civil war and torture. Many suffered for weeks, months, or years in refugee camps on the periphery of violence. The greatest concentration of refugees occurred in the world's poorest region—Africa. Many Africans were caught up in ethnic and religious conflicts that generated vast refugee camps, where their survival depended on the generosity of host governments and international contributions.

Whether migrants traveled in search of work or fled persecution, they posed a series of challenges for host countries. If migrants crossed borders easily, they

Sudanese Refugees During the late twentieth century, Africa became a continent of displaced persons and refugee camps. Pictured here is a camp in Chad for Sudanese driven out of the Darfur region by government-sponsored raids.

often struggled to receive basic rights. Especially during economic downturns, discrimination often led to violent conflicts among recent immigrants, long-time residents (often themselves of immigrant origin), and the host country's security forces. Conflicts erupted over religion and culture, notably in French efforts to prevent women from wearing Muslim headscarves in public and the English-only movement in the United States. Governments in immigrant-receiving countries everywhere grappled with the challenge of extending citizenship to newcomers and then respecting their desires to dress, worship, and celebrate traditions as they did in their families' homelands.

GLOBAL CULTURE

Migrations and new technologies helped create a more global entertainment culture. In this domain, globalization was often equated with Americanization. Yet American entertainments themselves reflected artistic practices from across the globe as one mass culture met another. On the global scale, there was less cultural diversity in 2000 than in 1300, but in terms of individuals' everyday lives, the potential for experiencing cultural diversity, if one could afford the technology to do so, increased.

New Media Technology was key in spreading entertainment. In the 1970s, for example, cassette tapes became the dominant medium for popular music, sidelining the long-playing record and the short-lived eight-track tape. Television was another globalizing force, as American producers bundled old dramas and situation comedies for stations worldwide. Brazilian soap operas began to appear in Spanish-language TV markets throughout the Americas in the 1980s, often inducing Mexican viewers to rush home from work to catch the latest episode. Latin American television shows and music were distributed in the United States in areas with large Spanish-speaking populations. Bombay (now called Mumbai) also produced its fair share of programs for viewers of British television and today produces more than three times as many films per year as Hollywood. In terms of box-office revenues, Hollywood remained the leading producer of films in the world before 2000 but has been eclipsed since then by dynamic industries in India (Bollywood, named for Bombay), Nigeria (Nollywood), and, more recently, China.

Television's globalizing effects were especially evident in sports. Soccer (known as football outside the United States) became an international passion, with devoted national followings for national teams. Indeed, by the 1980s, soccer was *the* world sport, with television ratings increasingly determining its schedule. Organizers of the 1986 World Cup in Mexico insisted that big soccer matches take place at midday so that the games could be televised live at prime time in Europe, even though teams had to play under the scorching sun. In many parts of the globe, major American sports also made particularly deep inroads as more people participated in them and as television broadcast American games in other countries. The National

Basketball Association (along with the athletic footwear firm Nike) was particularly successful in international marketing; in the process, it made Michael Jordan the world's best-known athlete in the late twentieth century.

Cultural Exchanges Technology was not the only driving force of world cultures; migration and exchange were also important. For example, as people moved around, they brought their own musical tastes with them and borrowed others. Reggae, born in the 1960s among Jamaica's Rastafarians, became a sensation in London

Bob Marley In the 1970s, young Europeans and North Americans began to listen to music from the Third World. Among the most popular was Jamaican-based reggae, and its most renowned artist was Bob Marley. Marley's music combined rock and roll with African rhythms and lyrics about freedom and redemption for the downtrodden of the world.

and Toronto, where large West Indian communities had migrated. Reggae's lyrics and realist imagery invoked a Black countercultural spirit and a call for a return to African roots. Soon, Bob Marley and the Wailers, reggae's flagship band, played to audiences worldwide. In northeastern Brazil, where African culture was emerging from decades of disdain, Bob Marley became a folk hero. In Soweto, South Africa, populated by Black workers, he was a symbol of resistance.

Reggae propelled a shift in Black American music. In broadcasting reggae, DJs often merged sounds and chanted lyrics over a beat, a "talkover" form that soon characterized rap music as well. This was a disruptive concept in the late 1970s, but within ten years rap had become mainstream. Rap lyrics emulated reggae's realism by focusing on Black problems, but they also opened a new domain of controversies by reflecting gang worldviews. On the world stage, Latino rappers stressed multicultural themes, often in "Spanglish." Asian rap stressed the genre as a vehicle for cross-cultural sharing and epitomized the ability of new cultural forms to bring peoples together.

The effects of migration on global music were also evident in Latin American transformations of North American genres. Latin music came into its own thanks to Latin American migrants to the United States. In New York and New Jersey, Puerto Ricans and Dominicans popularized boogaloo, salsa, and merengue. In Los Angeles, Mexican *corridos* (ballads) became pop hits.

What reinforced cross-cultural borrowing was not just the medium of production and distribution of entertainment across borders, but also the message. Increasingly, world popular culture was youth culture—especially its message of generational opposition. Consider Egypt's popular TV serial *The School of Troublemakers*, which carried a resolutely antiestablishment message: it showed schoolboys challenging their teachers' authority and then reveling in the chaos that resulted. In Argentina, rock and roll was crucial to the counterculture during the military dictatorship of the 1970s and 1980s. Charlie García urged Buenos Aires audiences to defy authorities by daring to dream of a different order. Indeed, in countries where repressive regimes quashed public cultures, pop culture was usually counterculture.

The same globalizing effects influenced sports. Consider the staple of American identity, baseball, whose major league teams took on a more global cast. Beginning in the 1960s, the number of Latin Americans playing in North American professional leagues grew steadily. Notable in the 1980s was the Mexican pitcher Fernando Valenzuela, whose exploits as a member of the Los Angeles Dodgers made him a hero to that city's Mexican population and in his native land as well. The Dodgers also took the lead in reaching for Asian talent. In the 1990s, as Los Angeles experienced a growing Asian immigrant population, the Dodgers signed the Japanese pitcher Hideo Nomo. Meanwhile, in the Dominican Republic, baseball fans were riveted by their favorite players in the big leagues: slugger Sammy Sosa and ace pitcher Pedro Martínez. The emergence of so many Latin American and Asian baseball players epitomized the ability of what were once purely American cultural forms to spread their influences and to bring peoples all over the world together.

Local Culture World cultures may have become more integrated and homogeneous, but they did not completely replace national and local cultures. Indeed, technology and migration often reinforced the appeal of "national" cultural icons as national celebrities gained popularity among emigrant groups abroad. Inexpensive new technology introduced these stars to more and more people. In Egypt, the most popular singer of the Nasser years was Umm Kulthum, who became the favorite of Arab middle classes via radio. In 1975, she was given a state funeral, the likes of which had rarely been seen.

Fairuz Street art depicting the singer Fairuz. Born in Lebanon in 1934, Fairuz is an icon in the Arab world. Her record sales top 150 million worldwide. Although she was raised in a conservative Christian household, her voice and lyrics crossed religious and sectarian divides. Even through the horrors of the Lebanese civil wars of the 1970s and 1980s, she appealed to all sides and refused to abandon her country. Occasionally, however, her crossovers upset her fans. For instance, in 2008, when Syrian dictator Bashar al-Assad's troops occupied part of Lebanon, Fairuz performed in Syria, claiming that culture should not be politicized. Some accused her of turning a blind eye.

Nonetheless, as the market for world cultures grew increasingly competitive, performers increasingly employed a wider array of styles and also challenged biases and conventions. Among the breakthroughs that have occurred since the 1970s are the triumphs of Black performers (Bob Marley, Whitney Houston, Michael Jackson), Black athletes (Pelé, Michael Jordan, Carl Lewis), and Black writers (Toni Morrison, Chinua Achebe). Competition also shattered some biases of gender and sexuality. Women performers such as Madonna became popular icons. So did gay performers, starting with the Village People, whose campy multicultural anthem "YMCA" created a place for a new generation of gay, lesbian, and bisexual artists. In American television, the comedian and talk show host Ellen DeGeneres broke barriers as a popular lesbian performer who could elicit peals of laughter from gay and straight audiences alike. Of course, beyond Europe and North America, challenging sexual conventions had its limits. In the Middle East, female video artists continued to wear headscarves—but now they swung their hips. Relatively homogeneous national cultures, often dominated by men representing the ethnic majority, gave way to a wider variety of entertainers and artists who broke loose from confining local cultures.

COMMUNICATIONS

Computer technology drove a revolution in global communications networks. In the late 1980s, while working in Switzerland, the British physicist Tim Berners-Lee devised a way to pool data stored on various computers. Whereas previous electronic links had existed only between major universities and research stations, Berners-Lee made data more accessible by creating the World Wide Web. With each use, each connection, and each datum entered, however, the Web grew unmanageably crowded and difficult to navigate. The early 1990s saw the first commercial browsers used in navigating the Web. Suddenly people were communicating across global networks more easily than with neighbors and more inexpensively than with local phone calls.

These changes created a new generation of wealth. CEOs of top companies like General Motors, Royal Dutch Shell, and Merck now had less net worth than Michael Dell (computer hardware maker), Bill Gates (software maker), and Jeff Bezos (creator of online retailer Amazon). Shares of Internet firms, known as dot-coms, swept the world's stock markets. Money from these companies flowed globally as they established offices worldwide. Software and Internet technology firms developed enormous economies of scale and thus became prone to monopolization as they took over smaller companies.

Hardware, software, and the Internet were not purely American innovations. Within a few years of their invention, personal computers were being made in Mexico and computer chips were being mass-produced in Taiwan. The brains behind the Internet were likely to be students from Indian institutes of technology. Originally engineering schools, these institutes trained a whole generation of pioneering computing engineers, many of whom resettled in California's Silicon Valley. By 1996, Indians held half of the 55,000 temporary work visas issued by the U.S. government for high-tech employees. Roughly half of Silicon Valley start-up companies in the late 1990s were the brainchildren of Indian entrepreneurs. Google, the biggest of them all, was founded by a couple of graduate students at Stanford. One of them, Sergey Brin, was a Jewish Russian fugitive. The current CEO of the giant firm is Sundar Pichai, who grew up in Chennai, India, before moving to the United States for graduate studies.

While the Internet revolution provided new means to share and sell information, it also reinforced hierarchies between haves and have-nots. Great swaths of the world's population living outside big cities, especially in low-income countries, had no access to the Internet. The have-nots were poor not just from lack of capital, but from lack of access to knowledge and new media.

Characteristics of the New Global Order

While providing access to an unimaginable array of goods and services, globalization also deepened world inequalities. Family structures changed, and life spans increased. Education and good health determined one's status in society as never before. Populations expanded dramatically, requiring greater industrial and agricultural output from all parts of the world. While many parts of the world consumed more than ever before, others struggled with famine and the consequences of **global climate change**.

THE DEMOGRAPHY OF GLOBALIZATION

It took 160 years (1800–1960) for the world's population to increase from 1 billion to 3 billion; over the next 40 years (1960–2000), it jumped from 3 billion to over 6 billion. Behind this steepening curve were two important developments: a decline in mortality, especially among children, and a rise in life expectancy.

Population growth was hardly equal worldwide. (See Map 21.4.) In Europe, population peaked around 1900, in terms of both its rate of increase and its share of global population in absolute terms. It increased only gradually, from 400 million to 730 million, during the twentieth century, with little growth after the 1970s, while populations elsewhere grew faster. North America's population quadrupled over the same period, mainly because of immigration. The other population booms in the twentieth century occurred in Asia (whose population grew by 400 percent), Africa (550 percent), and Latin America (700 percent). China and India each passed the billion-person mark. Population increases were greatest in cities. By the 1980s, the world's largest cities were Asian, African, and Latin American. Greater Tokyo-Yokohama had 30 million inhabitants, while Mexico City had 20 million, São Paulo 17 million, Cairo 16 million, Calcutta 15 million, and Jakarta 12 million.

Population growth slowed most dramatically in richer societies. For some, like Italy, the growth rate declined to zero, as the number of births no longer exceeded the number of deaths. More recently enriched societies like South Korea, Taiwan, and Hong Kong also had fewer births. Societies that did not see their birthrates decline by the same rate (much of Africa, southern Asia, and impoverished parts of Latin America) had difficulty raising income levels. But even among poor nations, birthrates declined after the 1970s.

The most remarkable turnaround occurred in China, where the government instituted a "one-child family" policy in 1979 with rewards for compliance and penalties for transgression. The bias in favor of sons (long a feature of China's patrilineal system, which emphasized descent through the male line), together with the availability of ultrasound scanners, promoted the widespread—albeit illegal—practice of prenatal sex selection.

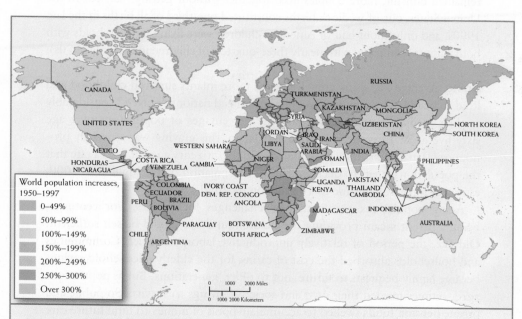

Map 21.4 World Population Increases, 1950–1997

The world's population more than doubled between 1950 and 1997, rising from approximately 2.5 billion to nearly 6 billion.

- Which countries had the largest population increases over these five decades? Why do you suppose these countries experienced such high population increases?

- According to your reading, why did western Europe and Russia have the lowest population increases?

In general, however, declining family size resulted from choice. In rich countries, more women deferred having children as education, career prospects, and birth-control devices provided incentives and methods to postpone starting a family. In addition, love became a precondition to marriage and family formation in societies that had previously emphasized arranged marriages.

Families In many countries, the legal definition of families became more fluid in this period. Here again, the changes reflected women's choices and the relationship between love and marriage. First, couples chose to end their marriages at unprecedented rates. In Belgium and Britain late in the twentieth century, fewer than half of all marriages survived. China's divorce rate soared too. In Beijing, by century's end, it approached 25 percent—double the 1990 rate. As of 2000, women initiated more than 70 percent of divorces.

As marriages became shorter-lived, new forms of child-rearing proliferated. Europeans, including the supposedly more traditional Italians and Greeks, abandoned nuclear family conventions. In those European countries where divorce remained difficult, more couples lived together without getting married. In the United States, out-of-wedlock births constituted one-third of all births in the late 1990s, and only about half of American children were living in households with both parents (compared with nearly three-quarters of children in the early 1970s).

Aging Average life spans grew longer as more infants survived childhood and lived to be old. The populations of industrialized nations "grayed" considerably as their median ages increased and the percentages of populations over age sixty-five grew. In western Europe and Japan, this graying was especially pronounced. Japan's birthrate plummeted, and the citizenry aged at such a rate that the population began to decrease. From a population of 127 million in 2000, estimates forecast a decline to 105 million by 2050.

Aging populations presented new challenges for families. For centuries, being a parent meant providing for children until they could be self-sufficient. Old age, the period of relatively unproductive labor, was brief. Communities and households absorbed the cost of caring for the elderly. Household savings became family bequests to future, not to older, generations. But as populations aged, retirees needed their own and society's savings to survive. So public and private pension funds swelled to accumulate pools of money to fund future care for the aged. In Germany, over 30 percent of the government's social policy spending went into the state pension fund.

In Africa, where publicly supported pension funds were rare, the aged faced bleaker futures. Whereas in earlier times the elderly were respected founts of wisdom, colonial rule and the postcolonial world elevated the status of the young—especially those with western educations and lifestyles. Then, in the 1970s, as birthrates soared, the demand on family resources for infant and child care rose at the very moment when societies' resource bases began to shrink.

The elderly could no longer work, but neither could they rely on the household's support.

INEQUALITY AND ENVIRONMENTAL DEGRADATION

Health The spread of contagious diseases also reflected inequities in the globalized world. Although microbes have no respect for borders, the effects of public health regulations, antibiotics, and vaccination campaigns reduced the spread of contagions in some countries. By the late twentieth century, not only did nutrition and healthy habits determine social status (as they always had), but access to medicines did too.

What used to be universal afflictions in previous centuries now affected only certain peoples. Water treatment and proper sewerage, for example, had banished cholera from most urban centers by the mid-twentieth century. More recently, however, its deadly grip again reached across Asia and into the eastern Mediterranean, parts of Latin America and the Caribbean, and much of sub-Saharan Africa. Thus, diseases proliferated where urban squalor was most acute—in cities with the greatest post-1970s population growth.

In the 1970s, entirely new diseases began to devastate the world's population. Consider **HIV/AIDS**, an epidemic that, in its first two decades, killed 12 million people. Acquired immunodeficiency syndrome (AIDS) is caused by the human immunodeficiency virus (HIV), which spreads through blood and other body fluids. The virus may remain dormant in the bodies of infected people for some time, but eventually attacks the immune system, leaving them unable to fight off even the most common microbes. First detected in 1981, HIV/AIDS was initially stigmatized as a "gay cancer" (as it then appeared primarily in gay men) and received little attention. Gay activists in San Francisco, New York, Toronto, and Rio de Janeiro mobilized and pressured public authorities to be more responsive; at first, they were greeted with derision. But as it spread to heterosexuals and public awareness about it increased, new campaigns urged the practice of safe sex, control of blood supplies, and restrictions on sharing hypodermic needles.

In Europe and North America, where the campaigns intensified and new drugs were eventually developed to keep the virus inactive, HIV/AIDS rates stabilized. The new drugs were very expensive, however, leaving the poor and disadvantaged still vulnerable to developing AIDS. By 2000, 33 million people had AIDS (the vast majority in poor countries) and even more were infected with HIV. (See Map 21.5.) At least two-thirds of those with AIDS lived in sub-Saharan Africa. In India, 7 million carried HIV; in China, the figure topped 1 million.

Education Access to education increasingly separated the haves from the have-nots. Moreover, because educational opportunities usually favored men, schooling shaped economic opportunities available to men and women. In sub-Saharan Africa and in India, for example, literacy rates as of 2000 were, respectively, 63 and 64 percent for men and only 39 and 40 percent for women. In the Arab world, the literacy gap between men and women had decreased somewhat by the end of the twentieth century. Yet low levels of literacy overall and the depressed levels for women continued to impede each region's efforts to combat poverty.

Gender bias also remained in rich societies. For decades, however, women and girls pressed for equal access to education, with some astounding results. In the United States, by the late 1980s, more than half of all college degrees went to women. Chinese women made even greater strides, although roadblocks persisted. Ironically, with China's market reforms (described later in this chapter), women's access to basic education regressed as families, particularly in rural areas, reverted to spending their limited resources on educating sons. Thus, in 2000, up to 70 percent of China's 140 million illiterate people were women.

Women and Work Although more women held jobs outside the home, they lacked full equality at work. Limited by job discrimination and the burdens

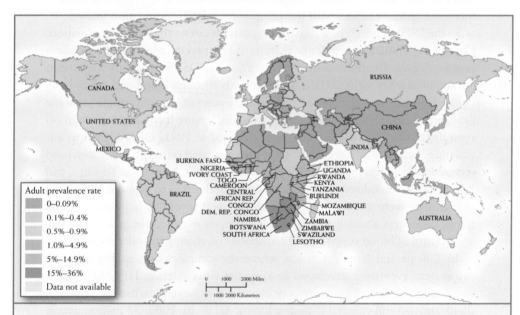

Map 21.5 HIV Infection across the World, 1999

HIV, which leads to AIDS, spread across the whole world within two decades, providing further evidence of global interconnectedness. The outbreak began in Africa.

- Where in Africa have the highest rates of HIV infection occurred?
- Which countries *outside* the African continent have had the highest rates of infection, and why is this so?
- Which countries have the lowest rates of HIV infection, and why is this so?

of child-rearing, women's participation in the workforce reached a fairly stable level by the 1980s. The percentage of women at the top of the corporate pyramid was considerably lower than their proportion in the labor force or their college graduation rates. Women worldwide had difficulties breaking through the "glass ceiling"—the seemingly invisible barrier that kept them from advancing to these high-level positions. Consequently, while the difference between men's and women's incomes narrowed, a significant gap persisted.

African Women and Education Though women's education lagged behind that of men in Africa, a number of women, like Stella Kenyi, pictured here (left), graduated from African high schools and attended universities at home or abroad. Kenyi taught business skills to men and women in Sudan after completing an undergraduate degree at Davidson College in North Carolina.

Working outside the home led to a problem inside the home: Who would take care of the children? Changing gender norms in rich countries sparked major migration streams. Jamaican and Filipino women, for example, migrated by the thousands in the 1970s and 1980s to Canada and Australia to work as nannies to raise money to send back home, where they had often left their own children. In South Africa and Brazil, local women worked as domestic servants and nannies. They were doing the jobs that once belonged to middle- and upper-class homemakers, women who now wanted the same rights as men: to parent *and* to work.

The deeply ingrained inequality between men and women prompted calls for change. Feminist movements arose mainly in Europe and North America in the 1960s, then became global in the 1970s. In 1975, the first truly international women's forum took place in Mexico City. But becoming global did not necessarily imply overturning local customs. What feminists called for was not the abolition of gender differences but equal treatment—equal pay and equal opportunities for jobs and advancement.

Women took increasingly active stances against discrimination in government and in the workplace. Indeed, as economic integration intensified as a result of regional trade pacts (usually negotiated by men in the interest of male-owned and male-run firms), women struggled to ensure that globalization did not cut them out of new opportunities. For instance, after Argentina, Uruguay, Paraguay, and Brazil negotiated the Mercosur free trade pact, member governments built new highways and bridges, and traffic across South American borders soared. But as government efforts to foster approved trade grew, so did efforts to monitor illegal commerce. Women were responsible for one kind of illicit commerce: for generations, they had transported goods across the river separating Argentina and Paraguay. When customs officers tried to stop this practice in the mid-1990s, Argentine and Paraguayan women locked arms to occupy the new bridge that male truckers were using to ship Mercosur products, protesting the restrictions on their age-old enterprise.

The rising tide of global feminism culminated in the Fourth World Conference on Women, held in Beijing in 1995. Delegates from more than 180 governments attended the conference to produce "a platform for action" regarding women's rights in politics, business, education, and health. Alongside the official conference was the NGO Forum, a parallel conference for nearly 30,000 grassroots activists, who represented 2,000 nongovernmental organizations from every corner of the globe. Representatives planned strategies and coordinated programs for improving women's living and working conditions. What emerged from the conference were associations and groups that pledged to lobby for the rights of women and girls worldwide. One effect was to spotlight the ongoing shortage of opportunities for the advancement of women leaders.

Agricultural Production The most immediate challenge facing many societies was how to feed their increasing populations. Yet changing agrarian practices resulted in a huge increase in food production. Starting in the 1950s, the "green revolution," which relied on chemical fertilizers, herbicides, and pesticides, produced dramatically larger harvests. Then, in the 1970s, biologists began developing genetically engineered crops, which multiplied yields at an even faster rate.

But these breakthroughs were not evenly distributed. American farmers, the biggest innovators, were also the greatest beneficiaries. For example, by century's end, they produced approximately one-ninth of the world's wheat and two-fifths of its corn. American exports accounted for about one-third of the world's international wheat trade and four-fifths of all corn exports. At the heart of the innovation was political power, for farmers had the clout to force officials to maintain roads, subsidize credit and prices, and mop up surplus supply. But Asian rice farmers made impressive innovations, too. In Taiwan and Korea, chemical and biological breakthroughs allowed rice yields to jump by 53 and 132 percent, respectively, between 1965 and 1985. And as Indian wheat farmers deployed chemical fertilizers, new seed varieties, and irrigation systems to double their output, the Ganges River basin supported an ever-larger urban population. The most dramatic transformation of agriculture, however, occurred in China. Beginning in the late 1970s, the Chinese government broke up some of the old collective farms and restored the individual household as the basic economic unit in rural areas. Thereafter, agricultural output surged by roughly 9 percent per year and nearly doubled between 1978 and 1986.

Other agricultural producers also replied to world demand, but sometimes their added production was disruptive. While biology and chemistry allowed farmers in some countries to get more out of their land, others simply opened up new lands to cultivation. Lacking access to credit, seed, and good land, small farmers had to go where land was cheap. In Java, farmers cleared sloping woodland to make way for coffee plantings. In southern Colombia, peasants moved into semitropical woodlands to cultivate coca bushes (the source of cocaine) at profits that other cultivators could never realize.

The most notorious frontier expansion occurred in the Amazon River basin. Migrants flocked to the Amazon frontier, largely from impoverished areas in northeastern Brazil. They cleared (by fire) cheap land, staked their claims, and, like nineteenth-century American homesteaders, tried to get ahead by cultivating crops and raising livestock. But the promise of bounty failed: the soils were poor and easily eroded, and land titles provided little security, especially once large speculators moved into the area. So the frontiersmen moved farther inland to repeat the cycle. By the 1980s, migrants to the Amazon River basin had burned away much of the rain forest, contaminated the environment, reduced the stock of diverse plant and animal life, and fostered social conflict in the Brazilian hinterland.

Not even "breadbasket" areas were always able to feed exploding populations. This was especially true in Africa from the 1970s onward, when domestic food production could not keep pace with population growth. (See Map 21.6.) Food shortages increased in frequency and duration, wiping out large numbers of people in sub-Saharan Africa.

What explained Africa's famines? As the Indian economist and Nobel laureate Amartya Sen observed, famines—and their increasing frequency—are not natural disasters; they are human-made. Food shortages in Africa stemmed largely from governments that ignored the rural sector and its politically unorganized farmers. Unable to persuade their governments to raise prices for their crops, the farmers lacked incentives to expand production. Food shortages were also by-products of global inequalities. At the urging of the IMF, African countries devoted hefty chunks of their economies to crops that could be exported to repay debts incurred in the 1970s. This focus left them without enough foodstuffs domestically, and thus they actually became food importers.

Natural Resources and the Environment While American farmers now produced a large share of the world's food, Americans also consumed a high proportion of its natural resources. Energy consumption presented a similar story, although America's enormous appetite for fossil fuels generated a domestic debate about reliance on foreign sources and pollution of the environment. In the 1970s, OPEC raised the price of crude oil (see Chapter 20). The cartel weakened in the 1980s, partly because new oil fields opened elsewhere in the world and partly because internal struggles divided the exporters.

The harshest conflict over oil occurred in the mid-1980s between Iran and Iraq, followed by the 1990 Iraqi invasion of Kuwait. Iraq was poised to become

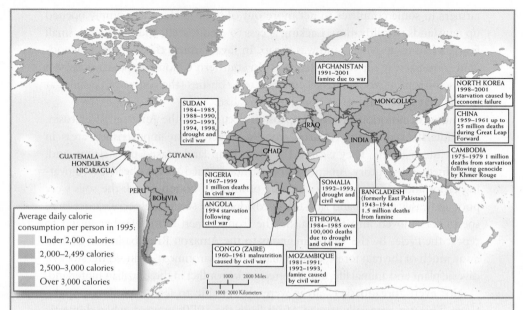

Map 21.6 Food Consumption and Famine since the 1940s

··

There is perhaps no better indicator of the division of the world into rich and poor, haves and have-nots, than average food consumption and famine.

- Which parts of the world have had the most difficulty in feeding their populations?
- What have been some of the causes of famine and malnourishment in these regions?
- How much have famine and malnourishment been due to human actions, and how much to climate and other matters over which human beings have little control?

dominant in the area and thus to control oil policies. The conquest of Kuwait would have given Iraq control over about 7 percent of the world's oil supplies and nearly 20 percent of the world's known reserves. Only Iraq's neighbors, Saudi Arabia and Iran, would have been larger oil exporters, and Iraq would have been in a position to menace both. As the situation threatened to unsettle the regional balance of power, the U.S. government moved to restore it. Rallying a coalition of other nations, the Americans and their allies turned to the United Nations to gain approval for a military invasion called Operation Desert Storm. The ensuing Gulf War, which ended with Iraq's expulsion from Kuwait, restored an order in which the global distribution of power favored oil consumers over producers and preserved a regional balance of power.

The consumption of water, oil, and other natural resources became matters of international concern late in the twentieth century. So did pollution control and the disposal of waste products. Part of this internationalization reflected the recognition that individual nations could not solve environmental issues on their own. Air and water, after all, do not stop flowing at political boundaries.

Americans consumed a disproportionate share of the world's natural resources. By 2000, they were using water at a per capita rate three times the world's average. Indeed, extensive irrigation was crucial to California's agricultural sector, the most productive and profitable in the world. And piping water to desert cities like Los Angeles allowed them to grow. The North American Free Trade Agreement, approved in 1992, encouraged urban development in the southwestern United States and agricultural development in northern Mexico, both of which put further strains on water supplies.

In the United States and Canada, attempts to curb energy consumption saw little success, and the United States grew more dependent on imported oil. In the late 1990s, North American demand for fuel-guzzling sport utility vehicles intensified the demand for oil imports. Dependence on foreign sources locked oil importers into recurring clashes with oil exporters.

As Canadians saw their northern lakes fill up with acid rain (precipitation laced with sulfur, mainly from coal-fired power plants), they urged their southern neighbor to curb emissions. Reciprocal agreements between Canada and the United States to cut sulfur emissions took shape in the 1980s. Europeans, also beset by acid rain, likewise negotiated regional environmental treaties. But some polluting industries simply moved overseas to poorer and less powerful nations. As the west cleaned up its environment, the rest of the world paid the price.

Other problems crossed human-made borders as well, especially the growing problem of global climate change. The world was now confronted with the greenhouse effect and **global warming** (worldwide rising temperatures caused in large part by the release into the air of human-made carbons), ocean pollution, and declining biological diversity. An increase in vehicles, factories, and air-conditioned homes—the general betterment of middle-class living—meant more combustion of coal, gas, and oil. Moreover, liberalizing world trade and industrializing Asia released 4 billion metric tons of carbon into the atmosphere in 1970; the figure by 2009 was 10 billion. Fully half of the fossil fuel–induced carbon dioxide emissions worldwide since 1750 took place after 1985.

People around the planet were emitting more carbon and at the same time were increasingly aware of the catastrophic risks. On June 26, 1974, *Time* magazine announced provocatively to the world that our "prolonged streak of exceptionally good climate has probably come to an end." But it took years to turn words and science into action plans. In 1992, Rio de Janeiro hosted a massive Earth Summit of state and NGO leaders, as well as scientists from around the world, that spotlighted the global threat of climate change. The follow-up in Kyoto, Japan, did lead to a major treaty that pledged countries to curb carbon emissions. But when President George W. Bush entered the White House in early 2001, he scrapped the Kyoto Protocol—to the dismay of many scientists, activists, and partner governments.

The response to these environmental crises has been uneven at best. Carbon emissions continued to grow with the rise in automobile traffic in cities like

Saving the Amazon The rise of an international environmental movement in the 1970s led to alliances with local indigenous and environmental leaders, especially in the Amazon. One of the most prominent advocates of the rights of indigenous people and the need to protect imperiled jungles was the British musician Sting. Here he is pictured alongside one of the Amazon's foremost Indian leaders, Bep Koroti Paiakan.

Tokyo, Mexico City, and Los Angeles. Where environmentalists acquired political power, they forced regulators to curb carbon emissions. But controls on emissions depended on power and wealth, for it was hard to impose restrictions in societies where high energy use seemed a necessity of economic life. Even the Japanese, pioneers of clean fuel as early as the 1960s, were polluters in other spheres long thereafter. For example, with increasing controls at home, Japanese industrialists went abroad to unload hazardous waste. U.S. industrialists did the same, sending hazardous waste to Mexico. Argentina and Canada sent their nuclear waste not abroad but to poor provinces desperate for jobs.

Environmental problems gained new urgency after the meltdown of a Soviet nuclear reactor in Chernobyl in 1986. Initially, communist authorities tried to cover up the disaster, but when the fallout reached Sweden, they had to accept responsibility. The delayed response was disastrous for Ukraine and Belorussia (present-day Belarus). Being relatively powerless under a centralized authoritarian regime, they had no political voice to cry out for help in addressing the contamination. As Chernobyl and global warming demonstrated, environmental concerns do not observe boundary lines. Yet at the end of the twentieth century, global guidelines for regulating the impact of human activities on the environment had eluded the world's leaders.

Citizenship in the Global World

Globalization distributed its benefits unequally. In general, people with access to better education and more opportunities profited from the border-crossing freedoms that the new order permitted. For most of the world's population, however, the new power structure was not so kind. Finding little opportunity in the globalized world, disadvantaged groups often invoked older religious and nationalist ideals. As globalization fostered human rights, environmental and labor standards, and women's rights worldwide, critics claimed that the language of international rights and standards was promoting neocolonial power in the form of a new "civilizing mission."

In particular, globalization posed massive problems for the nation-state. Since the nineteenth century, nation-states were supposed to be key in defining the rights of citizens. But now the rapid movement of ideas, goods, capital, and people across national boundaries undercut the authority of even the most powerful nations. Accordingly, other political spheres emerged to define and defend citizens. After the 1970s, people realized that international and supranational organizations often had more influence over their lives than did their own national governments. These organizations became increasingly important in shaping the meaning of citizenship. This was true especially in the Third World, where nation-states struggled hardest to accommodate globalization.

SUPRANATIONAL ORGANIZATIONS

New organizations with goals and responsibilities that transcended national boundaries and governments took shape after World War II for the purpose of facilitating global activities. These **supranational organizations**, which were intended to facilitate globalization and manage crisis situations, impinged on the autonomy of all but the most powerful states.

Among the most prominent supranational organizations were the World Bank and the International Monetary Fund, which provided vital economic assistance to poorer nations. The World Bank, originally named the International Bank for Reconstruction and Development, was designed primarily to provide financial assistance for big development projects. In contrast, the IMF provided funds and technical assistance to countries whose economies were in trouble. A good example of the World Bank's agenda was the financial support that it gave to the government of Ghana in the 1960s for the Volta River project, which was intended to create an electrical grid for that country. Nonetheless, both the World Bank and the IMF required that recipient governments implement far-reaching economic reforms, such as devaluation of the currency and the privatization of public-sector companies; these reforms were often deeply unpopular and led to charges that these international groups were agents of a new kind of imperialism.

Another set of supranational bodies, international nongovernmental organizations (NGOs), also stepped forward late in the twentieth century. Many championed human rights or highlighted environmental problems. Others, like the International Committee of the Red Cross, once dedicated to war relief, became more active in peacetime, sheltering survivors of natural disasters or providing food for famine victims. What united NGOs was not so much their goals but the way they pursued them: autonomously, rather than through state power.

International NGOs reached a new level of influence in the 1970s because most nation-states at that time were still not democracies. Of the 121 countries in the world in 1980, only 37 were democracies, accounting for only 35 percent of the globe's population. People found it difficult to rely on authoritarians to uphold their rights as citizens. Indeed, despite adopting a Universal Declaration of Human Rights in 1948, the United Nations (another international organization created after World War II and intended to provide a forum for settling international problems) was a latecomer to enforcing human rights provisions, largely because its own members were the selfsame authoritarians.

NGOs, then, took the lead in trying to make the language of human rights stick. The brutality of military regimes in Latin America inspired the emerging network of international human rights organizations to take action. After the overthrow of Chile's Salvador Allende in 1973, political groups created by the Catholic Church protested the military junta's harsh repression. When the Argentine military began killing tens of thousands of innocent civilians in 1976 and news of their torture techniques leaked out, human rights organizations again took action. Prominent among them was Amnesty International. Formed in 1961 to defend prisoners of conscience (detained for their beliefs, color, sex, ethnic origin, language, or religion), Amnesty International catalogued human rights violations worldwide. By 2000, an extensive network of NGOs was informing the public, lobbying governments, and pressuring U.N. member nations to live up to commitments to respect the rights of citizens.

VIOLENCE

Supranational organizations and NGOs could play only a limited role in preserving peace and strengthening human rights. The end of the Cold War left entire regions in such turmoil that even the most effective humanitarian agencies could not prevent mass killings.

Consider the Balkans in the 1990s. In the territorial remains of Yugoslavia, groups of Serbs, Croats, Bosnians, ethnic Albanians, and others fought for control. Former neighbors, fueled by opportunistic leaders' rhetoric, no longer saw themselves as citizens of diverse political communities. Instead, demagogues trumpeted the superiority of ethnically defined states. Ethnic Serbians took up arms against their Croat neighbors, and vice versa. When international agencies moved in to try to bolster public authority, they failed, and Yugoslavia's ethnic mosaic imploded into civil war and ethnic cleansing. The Dayton Accords of

1995 ended the bloodshed by partitioning Bosnia and assigning several international organizations to maintain peace. But in 1999, Serbian president Slobodan Milošević sent troops to suppress unrest in the province of Kosovo; only NATO air strikes on Serbia's capital, Belgrade, convinced Milošević to back down. Subsequently, Milošević was indicted by the International Criminal Tribunal on sixty-six counts of war crimes and crimes against humanity, but he died of a heart attack before he could be found guilty.

Some of the most gruesome scenes of political violence occurred in Africa, where many nation-states struggled to uphold the rule of law for all citizens. Here, tension often erupted into conflict between ethnic groups. The failure of African agriculture to sustain growing populations, as well as unequal access to resources like education, made ethnic rivalries worse. Droughts, famine, and corruption fanned the rivalries into riots and killings—even into bitter civil wars and the breakdown of centralized authority.

Events in Rwanda reflected Africa's horrifying experience with political violence. Friction grew between the majority Hutus (agrarian people, who were often very poor) and the minority Tutsis (herders, who were often better educated, were wealthier, and had been chosen by the Belgians to rule over the Hutus) after the two peoples had intermarried and lived side by side for many generations. Some resentful Hutus blamed the Tutsis for all their woes. As tensions mounted, the United Nations dispatched peacekeeping troops. Moderate Hutus urged continued peaceful coexistence, only to be shouted down by government forces in command of radio stations and a mass propaganda machine. Although alerted to the impending problem, U.N. forces, fearing a clash and uncertain of their mandate, failed to prevent the violence.

The failure on the part of the international community, including the United States, which did not have troops on the ground and which had no clear policy toward Rwanda, gave the Hutu government a green light to wipe out its opponents. In 100 days of carnage in 1994, Hutu militias massacred as many as 800,000 Tutsis and moderate Hutus. This was not, as many proclaimed, the militarization of ancient ethnic rivalries, for many Hutus were butchered as they tried to defend Tutsi friends, relatives, and neighbors. Meanwhile, the ensuing refugee crisis destabilized neighboring countries. The Rwanda genocide sent riptides across eastern and central Africa, creating a whole new generation of conflicts. This catastrophe is the starkest example of the failure of supranational organizations to deal with a crisis before it mushroomed into a genocide. Elsewhere, in famine areas and big development projects, supranational relief agencies enjoyed more success.

Some societies tried to put political violence behind them. In Argentina, El Salvador, Guatemala, and South Africa, the transition to democracy compelled elected rulers to establish commissions to inquire into past rulers' human rights abuses. These **truth commissions** were vital for creating a new aura of legitimacy for democracies and for promising to uphold the rights of individuals.

Rwandan Refugees Perhaps as many as 800,000 Tutsis and moderate Hutus were killed in 1994 as the Hutus turned against the local Tutsi population while Rwanda was being invaded by a Tutsi-led army from Uganda. Not surprisingly, the massacre led to an enormous refugee crisis.

In South Africa, many Blacks backed the new president, Nelson Mandela, but also demanded a reckoning with the punitive experience of the apartheid past. To avoid a backlash against the former White rulers, the South African leadership opted to record the past events rather than avenge them. Truth, the new leaders argued, would be powerful enough to heal old wounds. The Truth and Reconciliation Commission, chaired by Nobel Peace Prize winner and long-time opponent of apartheid Bishop Desmond Tutu, called on all who had been involved in political crimes, Whites as well as Blacks, to come before its tribunal and speak the truth. Although the truth alone did not fully settle old scores, a more open discussion of basic liberties fostered new bonds between public authorities and citizens.

RELIGIOUS FOUNDATIONS OF POLITICS

Secular concerns for human rights and international peace were not the only foundations for politics after the Cold War. In many regions, people wanted religion to define the moral fabric of political communities. Very often, religion provided a way to reimagine the nation-state just as globalization was undermining national autonomy.

Hindu Nationalism In India, Hindu nationalism offered a communal identity for a country being rapidly transformed by globalization. In the 1980s, India freed market forces, privatized state firms, and withdrew from its role as welfare provider. Economic reforms under the ruling Congress Party sparked economic growth, thereby creating one of Asia's largest, best-educated, and most affluent middle classes. But because these changes also widened the gap between rich and poor, lower classes and castes formed political parties to challenge the traditional elites. With established hierarchies and loyalties eroding, Hindu nationalists argued that religion could now fill the role once occupied by a secular state. Claiming that the ideology of *Hindutva* (Hinduness) would bring the help that secular nationalism had failed to give, Hindu militants trumpeted the idea of India as a nation of Hindus (the majority), with minorities relegated to a lesser status. The chief beneficiary of the politics established by economic liberalization was a Hindu nationalist party, the Bharatiya Janata Party (BJP), or Indian People's Party. It was the political arm of an alliance of Hindu organizations devoted to establishing India as a Hindu state. In 1998 a BJP coalition came to power and sought to transform the nation-state into a moral community, but without challenging the economic forces of globalization.

Islamic Conservatism In some cases, religion provided a way to resist seemingly American-dominated globalization. One of the most spirited challenges arose in the Islamic Middle East, where many people believed that modernizing and westernizing programs were leading their societies toward rampant materialism and unchecked individualism. Critics included both traditional clerics and young western-educated elites whose job prospects seemed bleak and who felt that the promise of modernization had failed. Having criticized modernizing processes since the nineteenth century, Islamic conservatives flourished once more in the 1970s as global markets and social tensions undermined secular leadership.

The most revolutionary Islamic movement arose in Iran, where clerics forced the shah, the country's ruler, from power in 1979. The revolt pitted a group of religious officials possessing only pamphlets, tracts, and tapes against the military arsenal and the vast intelligence apparatus of the Iranian state. Shah Mohammad Reza Pahlavi had enjoyed U.S. technical and military support since the Americans helped place him on the throne in 1953. His bloated army and police force, as well as his brutally effective intelligence service, had crushed all challenges to his authority. The shah had also benefited from oil revenues, which soared after 1973. Yet the uneven distribution of income, the oppressive police state, and the royal family's ostentatious lifestyle fueled widespread discontent.

The most powerful critique came from the mullahs (Muslim scholars or religious teachers), who found in the Ayatollah Ruhollah Khomeini a courageous leader. Khomeini used his traditional Islamic education and his training in Muslim ethics to accuse the shah's government of gross violations of Islamic norms. He also identified the shah's ally, America, as the Great Satan. With opposition to his rule mounting, the shah fled the country in 1979. In his wake, Khomeini established a theocratic state ruled by a council of Islamic clerics. Although some Iranians grumbled about aspects of this return to Islam, they prided themselves on having inspired a revolution based on principles other than those drawn from the west.

Religious Conservatism in the United States The search for religious foundations for politics in the global age reached into western societies. Indeed, in the United States, religion became a potent force after the 1970s as the membership and activism of conservative, fundamentalist Protestant churches eclipsed those of mainstream denominations. Insisting on a literal interpretation of the Bible, Protestant fundamentalists argued against secularizing trends in American society. This traditionalist crusade took up a broad range of cultural and political issues. Religious conservatives (predominantly evangelical Protestants, but also some Catholics and Orthodox Jews) attacked many of the social changes that had emerged from the liberation movements of the 1960s. Shifting sexual and familial relations were sore points, but the religious conservatives especially targeted public leaders who, they felt, had abandoned the moral purpose of authority by legalizing abortion and supporting secular values.

ACCEPTANCE OF AND RESISTANCE TO DEMOCRACY

New sources of power and new social movements drastically changed politics in the global age. Increasingly, supranational organizations were decisive in defining the conditions of democratic citizenship. Perhaps most remarkable was how much democracy spread toward the end of the twentieth century. In South Africa, Russia, and Guatemala, elections now decided politicians' fates. In this sense, the world's societies embraced the idea that people had a right to choose their own representatives. Nevertheless, democracy did not triumph everywhere.

An important holdout was China. Mao Zedong died in 1976, and within a few years his successor, Deng Xiaoping, opened the nation's economy to market forces. But Deng and other Chinese Communist Party leaders resisted multiparty competition. Instead of turning to capitalism and western-style democracy, they maintained that China should follow its own path to modernity. By the late 1980s, economic reforms had produced spectacular increases in production and rising standards of living for most of China's people. But the widening gap between rich and poor, together with increasing public awareness of corruption within the party and the government, triggered popular discontent. Worker strikes and slowdowns, peasant unrest, and student activism spread.

On April 22, 1989, some 100,000 people gathered in **Tiananmen Square** at the heart of Beijing in silent defiance of a government ban on assembling. The regime responded by declaring martial law. Two huge protest demonstrations followed, and residents erected barricades to defend the city against government troops. As the protest's momentum waned, a 28-foot icon, partly inspired by the Statue of Liberty, was unveiled at the square, capturing the imagination of the crowd and the attention of the cameras. But by then the government had assembled troops to crush the movement. In a night of terror that began at dusk on June 3, the People's Liberation Army turned its guns against the people. Estimates of the death toll range from 2,000 to 7,000.

In Mexico, democracy finally triumphed, as the single party that had dominated the country for seventy-one years fell after the election of Vicente Fox in 2000. Until that time, Mexican rulers had combined patronage and rigged elections to stay in office. By the 1980s, corruption and abuse permeated the system. The abuse of democratic rights fell hardest on poor communities, especially those with large numbers of indigenous people.

Consider the state of Chiapas. An impoverished area with many Maya descendants, Chiapas had trouble coping with social and economic change in the 1980s. The president stripped Indians of their right to communal land and let the ruling party run Chiapas like a fiefdom. By the early 1990s, the province was demanding material betterment, cultural recognition of Indian rights, and local democracy. When one group of rebels, the Zapatistas, rose up in Mexico City against the government in 1994, the government prepared to crush the insurgents. But no one anticipated how supranational forces

Tiananmen Square This white plaster and Styrofoam statue, inspired in part by the Statue of Liberty and dubbed the Goddess of Democracy, was created by students in Beijing in the spring of 1989. It was brought to Tiananmen Square and unveiled at the end of May in an attempt to reinvigorate the democracy movement and the spirits of the protesters. For five days it captured worldwide attention, until it was toppled by a tank on June 4 and crushed as the Chinese People's Liberation Army cleared the square of its democracy advocates.

would play a role in helping local democracy: Cable News Network (CNN) broadcast the clash worldwide, and the rebel leader created a website that drew thousands of hits. Thereafter, international news media flooded Chiapas, filming Indians waving flags and pronouncing victory. Leaders in Mexico City, deeply embarrassed, asked local church authorities to negotiate peace and spearhead a commission to hear the villagers' concerns. In 2000, national elections toppled the ruling party (including its representatives in Chiapas), and Mexico dismantled its one-party ruling system.

Mexico, South Africa, and China were powerful examples of how men and women in every corner of the earth yearned to choose their own leaders. In 1994, millions of previously disenfranchised South Africans lined up for hours to cast a vote for a new Black African president, Nelson Mandela. That same year, Zapatista rebels drew worldwide attention to the plight of poor indigenous

Protests in Mexico After generations of oppression and exclusion, the peasants of Chiapas, in southern Mexico, called for democracy and respect for their right to land. When Mexican authorities refused to bend, peasants took up arms. While they knew that they posed no military threat to the Mexican army, the Zapatista rebels used the world media and international organizations to embarrass the national political establishment into allowing reforms.

communities when militants occupied six towns in central and eastern Chiapas, Mexico, to protest the North American Free Trade Agreement. In China, the ruling Communist Party has repeatedly called on the army, police, and intelligence services to prevent regime change and democratic reforms.

Conclusion

In the thirteenth century (and long before), a few travelers like Ibn Battuta and Marco Polo ventured over long distances to trade, to explore, and to convert souls; yet communications technology was rudimentary, making long-distance mobility and exchange expensive, rare, and perilous. The world was more a series of communities set apart than a world bound together by culture, capital, and communications networks.

By the late twentieth century, that balance had changed. Food, entertainment, clothing, and even family life were becoming more similar worldwide. To be sure, some local differences remained. In 2000, local cultures lived on, and in some cases were revived, through challenges to the authority of nation-states.

No longer did the nation-state or any single level of community life define collective identities. At the same time, worldwide purveyors of cultural and commercial resources offered all local communities the same kinds of products, from aspirin to Nike shoes. Exchanges across local and national boundaries became easier. For the first time, many of the world's peoples felt they belonged to a global culture.

New technologies, new methods of production and investment, and the greater importance of personal health and education created new possibilities—and greater inequalities. Indeed, the gaps between haves and have-nots in 2000 were astonishing. For as humanity harnessed new technologies to accelerate exchanges across and within cultures, an ever-larger gulf separated those who participated in global networks from those on the margins. This inequality produced a range of different political and cultural forms after the collapse of the three-world order. Thus, as the world became more integrated, it also grew apart along ever-deeper lines.

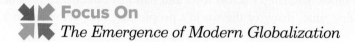

Focus On
The Emergence of Modern Globalization

Removing Obstacles to Globalization

- Communism's fall and the end of the Cold War improve prospects for global exchange of peoples, ideas, and resources.

- Final decolonization in Angola, Mozambique, and Guinea-Bissau and the end of apartheid in South Africa return self-rule throughout Africa.

Unleashing Globalization

- Financial deregulation and the end of gold and silver standards allow money to move freely across borders but lead to a Third World debt crisis.

- Widespread migrations occur as people in Africa, Asia, and Latin America move to Europe and America, following the tracks of their former colonizers.

- Revolutions in culture and communications make cultural diversity more possible for those who can afford it.

The New Global Order

- Globalization leads to dramatic population expansion, requiring greater agricultural and industrial output.

- Family structure changes, life spans increase, and more goods are available, yet inequalities deepen as education and good health determine social status as never before.

- As globalization erodes the power of the nation-state, greater violence occurs between and within states. Nongovernmental organizations (NGOs) and religion become resources for dealing with violence and inequality and for reimagining the nation-state.

CHRONOLOGY

	1970	1980
The Americas		United States announces Strategic Defense Initiative (SDI) 1983 ●
Europe		
Soviet Union		
Africa		
Middle East	Khomeini establishes theocratic state in Iran 1979 ●	
South Asia		
East Asia	Deng Xiaoping reforms China 1978–1992	

THINKING ABOUT GLOBAL CONNECTIONS

- **Thinking about Worlds Together, Worlds Apart and Globalization** How did globalization shape patterns of inequality? After the Cold War, trade, migration, and communications reshaped the terms on which peoples interacted with one another around the world. Industry, agriculture, culture, and the arts all linked peoples and regions together in different ways. Consider differences in all these domains. What kinds of inequalities were most significant?

- **Thinking about Changing Power Relationships and Globalization** What kind of resistance movements did globalization generate, both within the world's wealthiest societies and elsewhere? How did the feminist, labor, and environmental reform movements

resemble and differ from their predecessors? How did Hindu nationalism and religious conservatism differ from each other and from earlier nationalist and religious or pan movements?

- **Thinking about Environmental Impacts and Globalization** Explain the relationship between globalization, climate change, and the environment. The consumption of water, oil, and other natural resources became major national and international issues in this period. How did the organization of agricultural and industrial production change, and what influence did those changes have on global warming, acid rain, and pollution? Identify efforts to limit damage to the environment and evaluate their success.

Key Terms

developing world p. 815

European Union (EU) p. 826

global climate change p. 836

global warming p. 845

globalization p. 815

HIV/AIDS p. 839

Nelson Mandela p. 822

supranational organizations p. 847

Tiananmen Square p. 852

truth commissions p. 849

 Go to INQUIZITIVE to see what you've learned—and learn what you've missed—with personalized feedback along the way.

1990　　　　　　　　　**2000**

- North American Free Trade Agreement approved 1992
- Zapatista rebellion in Mexico 1994
- Eastern European communist regimes collapse 1989
- Yugoslavia dissolves, ethnic cleansing ensues 1989–1995
- European Union formed 1993
- Soviet-Afghan War 1979–1989
- Gorbachev assumes power 1985
- Chernobyl nuclear accident 1986
- Dissolution of the Soviet Union 1991
- Mandela released from prison 1990
- Free elections in South Africa 1994
- Genocide in Rwanda 1994

BJP heads up government in India 1998

Chinese state cracks down on Tiananmen Square protests 1989

22

Twenty-First-Century Global Challenges

2001–THE PRESENT

Core Objectives

- **DEFINE** modern globalization, and **COMPARE** it to earlier forms of global integration.

- **DESCRIBE** the global challenges we face in the twenty-first century.

- **IDENTIFY** the challenges posed by climate change around the world, and **EXPLAIN** what can be done to lessen or reverse the damage.

- **IDENTIFY** who modern globalization has benefited and how, as well as who it has not benefited and why.

- **EXPLAIN** how globalization has contributed to a resurgence in political populism, the growth of economic nationalism, the expansion of state violence, and the struggle for racial justice and LGBTQ rights.

The new millennium closed the chapter on the bloody wars and ideological rivalries of the twentieth century. Although the Cold War was over, and global integration seemed greater than ever before in human history, the twenty-first century brought new explosive hostilities and fresh economic and political challenges.

On September 11, 2001, nineteen hijackers commandeered four commercial airplanes. The hijackers slammed two of the planes into the World Trade Center in New York City and a third into the Pentagon, home of the U.S. Department of Defense, in Washington, D.C. The fourth plane was diverted from its intended target—the White House or the Capitol—and crashed in a field in southwestern Pennsylvania. A still rather unknown Muslim militant organization, al-Qaeda, headed by an equally little-known Saudi, Osama bin Laden, claimed responsibility for the attacks, which took the lives of more than 3,000 Americans. What followed was a predictable and determined American military response: the invasions of Iraq, incorrectly blamed for engineering the attacks, and Afghanistan, where a fundamentalist Islamic government provided a haven for bin Laden and his al-Qaeda affiliates.

Economic turmoil added to the turbulence of terrorism and wars. The global economy and new technologies had brought the world together as never before, but the benefits of integration were unequally distributed. Consequently, when an economic crisis broke out in 2008, its effects were felt globally but experienced unequally. An angry, populist politics of despair swept many parts of the world. In the United States, Brazil, India, Turkey, Britain, and parts of eastern Europe, ethnic and religious nationalists emerged, claiming to represent the "real," virtuous people in a face-off against out-of-touch elites. Many lashed out against the "globalists"—a term used to decry the champions of international cooperation—for betraying their nations economically and admitting too many foreigners.

Twenty-first-century **globalization** also promoted the rise of pandemics. The outbreaks of SARS, MERS, and Ebola foreshadowed the COVID-19 outbreak of 2020, which brought the world to a halt. Although flu pandemics hit periodically over the course of the twentieth century, none killed nearly as many as the so-called Spanish flu, which emerged in Haskell County, Kansas, in the United States in 1918, spread on troop transport and supply ships headed toward the battlefronts in Europe during World War I, and killed at least 50 million people worldwide, especially in a deadly second wave.

As the world became more fractured, many people became more and more aware of the common challenges they faced. Populists had gained the upper hand in many countries, notably the United States. But many citizens there and elsewhere worried about the future of the planet as climate change, looming economic and military tensions, and pandemics seemed to promise challenges that required governments to cooperate at the global level.

The Impact of Modern Globalization Today

- The "global war on terror" achieves successes and failures in its fight against fundamentalist terrorists.

- The benefits of a globally integrated economy are unequally distributed, creating substantial tensions within and across societies.

- Twenty-first-century globalization contributes to an increasing incidence and prevalence of pandemics.

- Economic development and human consumption cause climate change, with substantial negative effects on biodiversity, water quality, and food production.

- Mounting geopolitical and economic uncertainties lead to a rise in populist politics and economic nationalism, polarizing many countries politically and leading to state violence and struggles for racial justice and LGBTQ rights.

Global Challenges

WAR ON TERROR

The terrorist attack of 9/11 repulsed people around the world. Anger focused on Osama bin Laden and al-Qaeda, the loosely organized militant network of Islamist groups that had organized the attack. The militants claimed that it was a response to America's imperialist policies in the Middle East and retribution for American troops' presence in Saudi Arabia (during the first Iraq War). In the months and years that followed, countries grappled with a "war on terror," conflicts with militant Islamic groups, and a global economic crisis. George W. Bush, who had become president after a close and disputed election the year before the attack, gained broad public support for his tough talk about bringing terrorists to justice. Domestically, Bush pushed for security measures to curb future terrorist violence.

Internationally, President Bush declared a **"global war on terror."** With the backing of the majority of the American people, as well as strong support from many nations, Bush unsuccessfully sent American forces to Afghanistan in 2001 to hunt down bin Laden, destroy al-Qaeda training camps, and topple the Taliban government that had provided a haven for the terrorists. Expanding the battle-front of the war on terror, the Bush administration ordered an invasion of Iraq in 2003, falsely charging its dictator, Saddam Hussein, with abetting the terrorist assault of 9/11 and wielding weapons of mass destruction. As in Afghanistan, the initial offensive went well, but defeating the Iraqi army and finding Hussein proved easier than restoring order to the country or winning popular support.

In Afghanistan, U.S.-led coalition forces soon found themselves in a quagmire. Early successes collapsed as local warlords pursued their own goals and as the revitalized Taliban was able to regroup in neighboring Pakistan.

The faltering campaigns in Iraq and Afghanistan led to a growing chorus of disapproval at home. The American image had suffered internationally as news spread of programs of extensive surveillance (including that of U.S. citizens), "rendition" of suspected

9/11 With the North Tower already aflame, this photograph captures a second hijacked jet an instant before it crashed into the South Tower of New York's World Trade Center on September 11, 2001.

militants to sites where they could be tortured to extract information, the inhumane treatment of Iraqi prisoners at the Abu Ghraib prison, and the harsh and indefinite detention of suspected terrorists at Guantánamo. All of these factors helped Barack Obama secure the American presidency in 2008. President Obama then delivered on his campaign promises, announcing plans to end the Iraq War and refocus attention on Afghanistan. The Democratic president ended the Iraq occupation in 2011, and after promoting a surge of forces in Afghanistan, he reduced the number of American troops there. At the same time, however, while the campaigns in Iraq and Afghanistan faltered, the United States accelerated its efforts to hunt down terrorist leaders. Under President Obama, a daring operation in Pakistan ended with the death of Osama bin Laden in 2011. The prospect that the new century would be one of peace and prosperity under an American order seemed increasingly remote.

CRISIS AND ECONOMIC INEQUALITY IN THE GLOBAL ECONOMY

In 2008, the world economy fell into crisis. The problem began the previous year in the financial sector, the most globally interlinked sector of all. Seeking new sources of profits, investors from around the world had poured their money into riskier and riskier investments—many of which were so complex that not even the regulators in charge of monitoring the financial sector could understand them.

Risk and indebtedness were at record levels. Commercial and investments banks and insurance companies had tripled their indebtedness over the three decades leading up to 2008. Major banks, even the world's largest, began to fail, and governments largely watched from the sidelines. When Bear Stearns collapsed in March 2008, the U.S. Treasury Department finally intervened, providing a loan of nearly $30 billion to JPMorgan Chase to buy out Bear Stearns. But no support was forthcoming later that year when Lehman Brothers, a firm that had been in existence since 1850, filed for bankruptcy. Had the Treasury provided anywhere from $12 billion to $60 billion, the roiling financial crisis might have been averted. But it did not, and what had already been a dramatic economic and financial meltdown in the United States spread quickly to the United Kingdom, Ireland, Spain, and Iceland. As the shockwaves reverberated throughout Europe, Asia, Latin America, and parts of Africa, millions lost their livelihoods and houses, corporations failed, and trillions of dollars in financial wealth vaporized.

The **Great Recession** of 2008, as it soon came to be called, did not last as long as the Great Depression of 1929. The unemployment rate in the United States cratered at 10 percent, not 25 percent, and hundreds of banks, not thousands, failed. The fact that the financial downturn of 2008 was not as sharp or persistent as the 1929 depression was largely due to the innovative policies championed by Ben Bernanke at the Federal Reserve and officials at the U.S. Treasury. They thought it essential to shore up the U.S. financial system because it integrated so much of the world economy. This meant protecting the big banks, stimulating the economy with easy credit to keep consumers buying commodities, resisting protectionism, and promoting international cooperation. In keeping with these policies, the Treasury bailed out fourteen financial firms, including such heavy hitters as Goldman Sachs, Citigroup, and JPMorgan Chase, as well as two automobile manufacturers, General Motors and Chrysler. It did so by pressuring a rather unwilling Congress to set aside the stupendous sum of $700 billion in a program labeled TARP (Troubled Asset Relief Program). In the end, the U.S. Treasury disbursed only $430 billion of the allocated $700 billion. Supporters of the policy pointed out that it eventually turned a profit of $25 billion when the businesses repaid their debts. Critics noted that the stimulus was too small, given the scale of the crisis; moreover, the program did nothing to rein in the risk taking or punish those who brought the economy to its knees in the first place.

While the crisis started in the United States, it threatened the world economy. American authorities had less success getting European authorities to follow suit. Monetary authorities there were leery about bailing out troubled countries and were determined to keep the euro currency stable. But this meant that the European economy entered a prolonged slump and recovered very slowly. For the debtor countries in southern Europe, like Greece and Italy, and eastern Europe, notably Ukraine and Hungary, there was no help. Grievances soon piled up amid rising unemployment, especially for young people. Meanwhile, the Chinese government gave the green light to state firms to continue spending, and these firms embarked on a borrowing spree that was more monumental and more lasting than the American corporate bailouts. Together, U.S. and Chinese spending and lending were enough to keep the financial crash of 2008 from turning into a full-blown economic depression.

A major reason for the shock to the global economy was a belief in a **free market** ideology, based on the principle that free and unregulated markets will naturally make the most productive, rational use of resources. This view took over the economics profession globally after World War II, and at the same time, economists became increasingly influential in governments. The election of Ronald Reagan as president of the United States (1981–1989) and his appointment of Alan Greenspan as chairman of the Federal Reserve Board (1987–2006) brought free market ideology to the highest economic policy position of the country with the largest economy in the world.

Many benefits resulted from free market policies. Free global trade pulled millions of Chinese, Indian, and other economically developing peoples out of poverty. It made products available to consumers around the world at lower prices. Deregulation of businesses took place, and the worldwide privatization of state-run businesses promoted high economic growth rates, especially, but not only, in China, India, South Korea, Indonesia, and Brazil.

But there was a price to be paid: huge disparities in wealth emerged. Developing countries like China and India saw a rising middle class, but this was not the case in the United States, where the middle class shrank and a small number of individuals held the lion's share of the wealth. This situation was due in large part to the exportation of American manufacturing jobs to cheaper locations around the world and the decline in the power of labor unions, which had been critical in dramatically expanding the middle class in America after World War II.

The concentration of vast wealth in the hands of a few in the United States and other industrialized economies gave enormous political power to big corporations. A number of crucial U.S. Supreme Court decisions reinforced that power, notably the 2010 *Citizens United* ruling. In a 5–4 vote,

Occupy Wall Street Inspired by other stirrings around the world, this largely national movement was fueled by methods as novel as social media and as traditional as a sit-in. Here an Occupy Wall Street rally joins a labor union demonstration outside the New York County Courthouse in 2011.

the court ruled that in campaign financing the free speech of the First Amendment of the Constitution prohibited restricting the financial contributions of businesses as well as nonprofit corporations, trade unions, and other associations. Corporate wealth, power, and influence reached levels not seen for over a century.

Even as economies emerged from the Great Recession, **economic inequality** among individuals and between regions led to new challenges. This sparked protests, none more powerful and dramatic than those conducted by Occupy Wall Street (OWS), a movement that started in September 2011 in New York and was organized by a Canadian environmental activist group called Adbusters. The movement highlighted growing social and economic inequality and challenged the power of banks and corporations.

OWS was one among a wide range of emergent political upheavals around the world. Each one had a character specific to the region. Yet together they represented a new phenomenon. Almost all of them took shape outside conventional politics and ideological agendas. Expressing antiestablishment ideals and using social media to mobilize, the young took the lead in these new popular upsurges and became a permanent fixture on the political landscape worldwide. But instead of rallying to traditional parties, they preferred to take their activism to the streets and public squares.

While some groups and political factions protested over inequality, others pushed back to defend traditional definitions of citizenship and nationhood. In Europe, where, at last, economic and political integration within the European Union (EU) had seemed to promise an end to conflict between states, the crisis created new tensions. In Greece, radical new parties arose to protest austerity measures or to take out frustrations on immigrants, and many blamed the richer nations, especially Germany, for having profited from the creation of the EU at the expense of the poorer nations. For the first time in decades, vehement nationalist slogans came into wide circulation, and politicians of the left and right hostile to the European project were elected. Some commentators predicted that the common currency (the euro)—and perhaps even the European Union in its current form—would not last, as exemplified by Great Britain's decision to leave the European Union. In the Americas, Mexico elected a trade skeptic, Andrés Manuel López Obrador. In the United States, the Trump administration pulled out of the Trans-Pacific Partnership (TPP; a trade agreement with twelve nations), sought to renegotiate the North American Free Trade Agreement (NAFTA) with Mexico and Canada, and, in the name of national security, imposed restrictions on the importation of aluminum and steel.

CLIMATE CHANGE

Climate change has emerged as one of the most pressing issues for the new millennium. Scientists and activists had been ringing the alarm bells about rising atmospheric temperatures since the 1980s. By 2019, the evidence of systemic changes to the biosphere was undeniable. The Intergovernmental Science-Policy Platform on Biodiversity and Ecosystem Services (IPBES) published a definitive report in May 2019 concluding that climate change was responsible for significant and irreversible reductions in global biodiversity. A few months later, in August, the United Nations reported that **global climate change** was responsible for vast reductions in water supplies, especially in

The Amazon Ablaze Fire is a common method for clearing the Amazon forest. After Jair Bolsonaro was elected president of Brazil in 2018, loggers and land speculators began to torch thousands of acres of woodland. Satellites caught images of the alarming spread. This photo, taken in August 2019, is just one snapshot of the more than 900,000 hectares that were destroyed that year.

the tropics, and threatened food supplies, especially for large, precarious population belts. The threat of climate change mobilized global cooperation. The IPBES report, compiled by 145 environmental experts from 50 countries with inputs from another 310 contributors, and based on a review of 15,000 scientific and governmental sources, warned that 1 million of the 8 million plant and animal species in existence today would become extinct within the next two decades if the present trends in climate warming continue. This would be a rate of extinction hundreds of times higher than the averages of the last 10 million years. Moreover, innumerable climate reports made clear that humans were responsible for an impending disaster that threatens all regions of the world. More than a third of the world's land surface is now devoted to crop or livestock production. Tropical rain forests, essential for planetary control of global warming, have decreased by 50 percent since 1950 to make way for agriculture and livestock grazing. The oceans and rivers have been overfished. Since 1980 greenhouse gas emissions have doubled, raising global temperatures by at least 0.7°C. The reports called for transformative change in humanity's approach to the earth, stating that the various plans thus far accepted by the world's countries were inadequate. Much more needed to be done, and much more quickly, to make the planet carbon free and to reverse the decline of forests, the deterioration of the oceans and rivers, and the steady increase of lands devoted to agriculture and livestock.

Hurricane Katrina in 2005, for example, left much of New Orleans and the Mississippi Gulf Coast in ruins. Hurricane Sandy had similar catastrophic effects on the shorelines of New Jersey and New York in 2013; and in 2018, Hurricane Maria devastated Puerto Rico. Elsewhere, prolonged drought has led to agrarian crises and food shortages; this situation crept up on Syria over many years and led to an outburst of opposition to the despotic government of Bashar al-Assad and a bloody civil war. The resulting refugee crisis has spilled over into Turkey and Europe.

A major breakthrough occurred in Paris in 2015 when, under the sponsorship of the United Nations Framework Convention on Climate Change, most of the nations of the world gathered to hammer out an agreement that would limit the emission of greenhouse gases and hold down the increase in global temperature. The accord, scheduled to go into effect in 2020, aims to achieve a less than 1.5°C increase in global temperature. The two heaviest polluters, China and the United States, are crucial signatories. Yet the implementation of the agreement is left to the individual nations, each of which must file reports with the United Nations.

Donald Trump, the American president elected in 2016, repudiated American participation in the Paris Agreement and asserted that the entire science of climate change and global warming is a hoax. America was part of a wave of defections and noncompliance, though few nations had the temerity to leave the pact formally. Most, like Australia, Japan, and Canada, just ignored its provisions. Some, like Russia, Turkey, and Iran, never signed it. The new Brazilian president, Jair Bolsonaro, approved loggers' demands to clear the Amazon forest, the world's biggest carbon sink (a large and dense concentration of flora capable of transforming carbon dioxide into oxygen). But China and India, two countries that rely heavily on coal, have made great strides in meeting their carbon reduction targets. Tiny emitters, like Morocco and Gambia, have been standout examples in switching to renewable energy sources.

PANDEMICS

In late 2019, news started to leak out of the province of Hubei, China, of a new virus. As it ripped through the capital of Wuhan, Chinese authorities struggled to make sense of the threat—and to control the public relations fallout. At first, it looked unexceptional, as it is much less infectious than measles and less deadly than Ebola. But it soon became clear that this virus possessed a cunning balance of infectiousness and lethality—and the ability to spread undetected. Southern China was especially vulnerable to the transmission of viruses from other species. The numerous wet markets, where live animals were sold in unsanitary conditions, were one source. More dangerous were the massive chicken and pork farms in Hubei Province. As China lifted itself out of poverty and its cities boomed, these farms expanded—and they soon became disease incubators. Crowded, in such close proximity to dense cities, and neglected by inspectors, the meat production industry in China created the conditions for a perfect epidemic storm.

On December 31, 2019, China officially informed the World Health Organization (WHO) of the "unknown disease," and on January 9, 2020, Chinese researchers released the map of the virus's genetic makeup. When the first case

Wuhan Battles COVID-19 In late 2019, news reports began to circulate from China's Hubei Province of a new viral threat. Within months, the capital city of Wuhan was the epicenter of a pandemic. With the city shut down, Chinese doctors and hospital workers frantically sought to save lives while state officials struggled to contain the spread, often using strict, but effective, means.

appeared in Bangkok a few days later, the implications were clear. By then, reporters from around the world swarmed into Wuhan as the virus was flowing out. Faced with mounting evidence, the WHO announced on March 10 that this mysterious disease was now a **pandemic**, which meant that it no longer had one point of origin—it was thoroughly global.

This was not the first pandemic in history. But its global shock was unprecedented. While the Black Death ravaged an interconnected world in the fourteenth century, eruptive fevers devastated the native populations of the Americas after 1492, and the influenza of 1918–1919 killed millions of war-fatigued people, none of these slammed the breaks so violently on an interdependent world as did COVID-19. Country after country went into lockdown. Those that dithered after the first infections, like Italy, Great Britain, the United States, and Brazil, paid a heavy human toll. Those that acted quickly and deployed testing systems and contact tracing, like South Korea and Taiwan, suffered less. One source of their relative success was that they had learned from earlier pandemics and were more prepared. Societies with weak health care systems saw hospitals overwhelmed.

What started as a public health crisis exploded into an economic and social calamity. Airports worldwide emptied. Borders between trading nations were sealed. As interdependent economies seized up, the ranks of unemployed soared—within weeks, the U.S. jobless rate hit 15 percent. Middle-class people lined up at food banks. In the first two months of France's lockdown, its economy shrank by 20 percent. The most hard-hit economies were those most dependent on foreign trade. Oil exporters reeled as prices plunged; on April 20, 2020, the U.S. benchmark for crude oil dropped as low as *minus* $40 a barrel. Oil producers were paying people to buy their fuel. Across the board, global trade dropped in just a few weeks by more than it had dropped in the three years after the stock market crash of 1929. The collapse in world trade in turn crippled heavily indebted countries in the Global South. Argentina defaulted on a major interest payment to lenders and threatened to set off a cascade of defaults across Latin America and Africa.

The economic crisis sparked a social one. Despite the rhetoric about how viruses do not respect status or citizenship, this was a disease that afflicted the have-nots especially hard. No social group was punished more harshly than migrants and the households that depended on them. For millions of poor migrant workers, their remittances to families back home dried up. And as cities and countries went into lockdowns, many migrant workers faced an agonizing predicament: How could they get home if the transportation systems were paralyzed? Kenyan workers were forced to leave the Gulf States and returned empty-handed to a draconian curfew. In India, when Prime Minister Narendra Modi closed the economy down overnight, millions of migrant workers began to walk home, often hundreds of miles, with no wages for their families. Salvadoran migrants to the United States also stopped sending money home, thereby choking a fifth of El Salvador's GDP. Sub-Saharan Africa is full of millions of Somali migrant workers, and this diaspora normally sends modest sums back to poverty-stricken Somalia every day, accounting for almost one-third of the country's GDP. But when COVID-19 struck, these workers were unable to send remittances back to their families. Furthermore, women's savings clubs (known as *hagbad* in Somali), which are vital to family survival, had to close down for lack of funds.

Such peacetime suffering had few modern parallels. But it also spawned remarkable displays of solidarity. In northern Italy, people went out on their balconies in the evenings as hospital workers changed shifts to applaud their selflessness. China dispatched personal protective equipment to Europe and Africa. In Berlin, when Muslims entered their fasting month of Ramadan, one pastor, Monika Matthias, invited

Lockdown in India The worldwide spread of COVID-19 forced countries to lock down their economies. In India, this meant clearing the streets of vendors and paralyzing an important part of the national economy, the informal sector. This photo of the city of Kolkata in March 2020 shows a practically deserted streetscape, with empty stalls lining the sidewalks.

Muslims to hold their Friday prayers in her church—provided they observe social distancing norms. She said, "During prayer, I could only say yes, yes, yes, because we have the same concerns and we want to learn from you. And it is beautiful to feel that way about each other."

The United States, the European Union, and Japan

Although the global challenges of the twenty-first century have touched virtually every corner of the world, local contexts continue to weigh heavily. Countries and regions have experienced globalizing forces in very different ways.

THE UNITED STATES

In the United States, the Obama administration sought to cope with the economic crisis while introducing health care reform. It encountered a conservative backlash in 2009 in the shape of the Tea Party movement, which espoused the ideals of small government and market freedom and contributed to a stinging defeat of the Democrats in the 2010 congressional elections. From the opposite side of the ideological spectrum arose the aforementioned Occupy Wall Street movement in 2011. Claiming to speak on behalf of 99 percent of Americans against the wealthiest 1 percent, the Occupy activists, consisting largely of young people, railed against the banks and financial institutions that the federal government had rescued from bankruptcy. Although the movement ran out of steam by the end of the year, it succeeded in inserting the nation's growing inequality into political discussions.

The most stunning event in the second decade of the twenty-first century was the election of Donald Trump to the presidency. He repudiated globalization and championed what he called "America First" values. He also threatened the multilateral fabric of the post-1945 order. Trump, who had never held political office, inveighed against "inner-city" crime, immigrants, international trade, and long-standing American alliances and security arrangements. Although few pundits believed Trump had much of a chance against a field of well-established and well-financed Republican Party opponents, his platform resonated with primary voters and gained him the party's nomination. Facing Hillary Clinton in the general election, Trump once more defied pollsters by winning a majority in the Electoral College (though losing the popular vote by nearly 3 million). His coalition relied on swing votes in some key upper-midwestern states, as well as traditional conservatives motivated by economic and religious concerns. More modest and poor rural voters who had been left feeling hopeless also rallied to his angered rhetoric. This latter group was responding to a severe economic decline and an opioid drug crisis, which were ravaging their communities as America continued to move away from manufacturing and natural-resource-based industries and toward a service- and information-based economy. Coming on the heels of Brexit, Trump's victory reflected the rising populist and nationalist tide against globalization.

A CHANGING WESTERN EUROPE

The American invasion of Iraq in 2003 created fractures in the alliance between the United States and western Europe. Far more serious divisions, however, emerged over the fate of NATO and of the coherence of the European Union, whose membership peaked at twenty-eight countries, including ten that had formerly been part of the Soviet bloc. The sprawling EU incorporated debtor and creditor countries, low-productivity and high-productivity workers, frontline immigration societies and those that keep migrants out. After the shocks of the 2008 economic slump, the divisions came to the fore. In a 2016 referendum on EU membership in Britain, in which voters could choose "Leave" or "Remain," "Leave" secured a majority. The trend toward EU expansion, whereby member states relinquished a significant degree of sovereignty to redress the legacies of war, ethnic cleansing, and genocide, was reversed over the issues of free integration within the EU and the unlimited jurisdiction of the European Court of Justice.

In economic terms, the adoption of a single currency, the euro, by seventeen EU members had facilitated commerce, but it had also caused economic damage. The common currency meant that countries with different economies and needs, each making their own decisions about taxes and expenditures, could no longer adjust for imbalances and competitiveness by currency devaluations, typically among the most potent tools in a government's arsenal. Unemployment rose dramatically and remained high in Europe's southern tier, even as the northern tier did better, selling goods and services on credit to their southern neighbors. The calamity was most visible in Greece, where northern country debtors were protected at the expense of Greek jobs and the Greek standard of living, all in the name of preserving Greece's EU membership. The euro, which had promised prosperity, became a symbol of immiseration.

Resentment over unfettered immigration, mismanagement of the euro and the economy, and limitations on carbon emissions created fertile ground for self-styled populist politics. The EU's signature identity, democratic institutions, experienced significant erosion, beginning in Hungary and then Poland before spreading to much of the rest of the continent. In 2018, a wave of protest rocked France. When pro-EU President Emmanuel Macron increased the tax on petrol to protect the environment, working-class protesters from the provinces took to the streets. Ill served by public transport and dependent on their cars to work, they donned yellow vests to signal their outrage that they should be forced to pay. Europe's malaise put the long-term future of integration to the test.

DEMOGRAPHIC ISSUES IN WESTERN COUNTRIES

Two threats to future peace and prosperity in Europe—and in the United States and Japan as well—are the interlocking issues of aging and immigration. Women in the European Union would have to bear 2.1 children on average to maintain its population of 500 million, but women in the EU now average only 1.5 children. Adding to the problem is the graying of the European population. With the percentage of elderly Europeans rising rapidly, sustaining the present ratio of workers to retirees and paying for the region's burgeoning number of pensioners will require the EU to attract around 15 million immigrants annually.

Nonetheless, divisions have spilled into the open over how to respond to waves of migrants from Africa and the Middle East. In the summer of 2015, columns of refugees crossed into Europe through the Balkans. Many came by boat, setting sail from Turkey and Libya—and their crowded, rickety dinghies and rafts were sometimes no match for the waves. Thousands died, creating a massive humanitarian outcry. By year's end, Germany admitted an astonishing 1 million refugees. But many Europeans, especially in eastern Europe and in Italy, were less than welcoming.

Europe is not alone in confronting the problems of an aging population and the integration of immigrants. As its post–World War II baby boom generation ages, the United States faces a similar imbalance between retirees and workers that endangers its Social Security system. Likewise, the increase in immigration, particularly from Asia and Latin America, continues to shift the nation's ethnic composition. Donald Trump, who pledged to "build a wall" across the U.S.-Mexico border, made control of immigration central to his campaign for the presidency in 2016. Once he was in office, his efforts to "build a wall" became so divisive that they led to the longest shutdown of the federal government in American history in late 2018 and early 2019. (For a global look at population growth and life expectancies, see Maps 22.1 and 22.2.)

In many respects, the problem of an aging population presses hardest today on Japan. Like Europeans and North Americans, the Japanese are marrying later and having fewer children. Japan's female population now averages barely 1.37 children, compared with nearly 3.7 in 1950. At the same time, Japanese life expectancy has reached eighty-five, the highest in the world, which further tilts the nation's age pyramid. In 1970, the elderly (those over age sixty-five) represented around 7 percent of the population; in 2014, they made up more than 25 percent and are expected to hit 40 percent by 2050. Analysts surmise that Japan's population peaked at around 128 million and might decline to perhaps 120 million by 2050, with a substantial proportion over the working age. Such a downturn bodes ill for Japan's economy.

Like Europe and North America, Japan relies on immigrants to fill out its labor force. In the 1960s, the nation's booming economy led to labor shortages, but neither the government nor major corporations chose to invite foreign laborers. By the 1980s, however, deepening labor shortages and the yen's

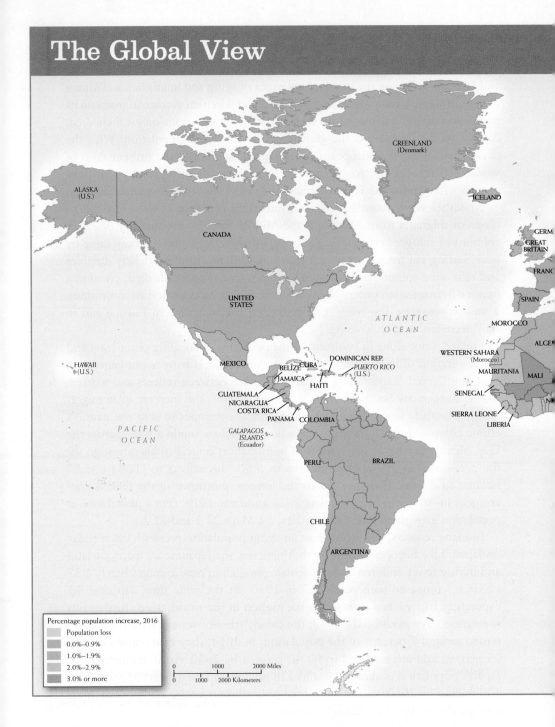

GREENLAND
(Denmark)

ICELAND

ALASKA
(U.S.)

CANADA

GERM

GREAT
BRITAIN

FRANC

UNITED
STATES

SPAIN

ATLANTIC
OCEAN

MOROCCO

ALGE

WESTERN SAHARA
(Morocco)

HAWAII
(U.S.)

MEXICO

BELIZE CUBA

DOMINICAN REP.

PUERTO RICO
(U.S.)

MAURITANIA

MALI

JAMAICA

HAITI

GUATEMALA

SENEGAL

NICARAGUA

COSTA RICA

PANAMA COLOMBIA

SIERRA LEONE

LIBERIA

N

PACIFIC
OCEAN

GALAPAGOS
ISLANDS
(Ecuador)

PERU

BRAZIL

CHILE

ARGENTINA

Percentage population increase, 2016

- Population loss
- 0.0%–0.9%
- 1.0%–1.9%
- 2.0%–2.9%
- 3.0% or more

0   1000   2000 Miles

0   1000   2000 Kilometers

Map 22.1 Population Growth, 2016

The demographic patterns observed early in the twenty-first century pose major problems for the industrialized societies of western Europe, North America, and Japan. As life expectancy increases and population growth slows, these regions' economies face labor shortages that have fueled immigration.

- According to this map and Map 22.2, which regions of the world are prime candidates for sending migrants to the industrialized world?
- What cultural and political dilemmas does this phenomenon create?
- Which states within the industrialized world do you think have created the best environment for immigrant residents?

The Global View

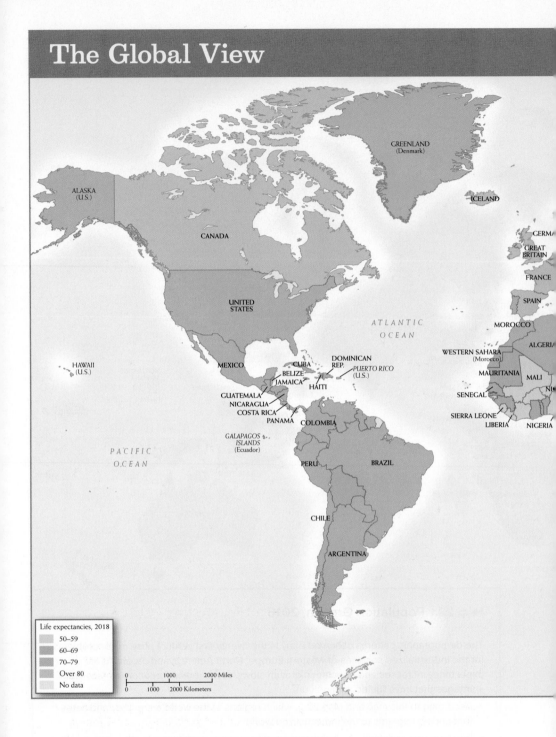

GREENLAND
(Denmark)

ICELAND

ALASKA
(U.S.)

CANADA

GERMA
GREAT
BRITAIN

FRANCE

SPAIN

UNITED
STATES

ATLANTIC
OCEAN

MOROCCO

HAWAII
(U.S.)

WESTERN SAHARA
(Morocco)

ALGERIA

MEXICO

CUBA

DOMINICAN
REP.

PUERTO RICO
(U.S.)

MAURITANIA

MALI

BELIZE

JAMAICA

HAITI

SENEGAL

NI

GUATEMALA
NICARAGUA
COSTA RICA
PANAMA

COLOMBIA

SIERRA LEONE

LIBERIA

NIGERIA

GALAPAGOS
ISLANDS
(Ecuador)

PERU

BRAZIL

PACIFIC
OCEAN

CHILE

ARGENTINA

Life expectancies, 2018
- 50–59
- 60–69
- 70–79
- Over 80
- No data

0   1000   2000 Miles

0 1000 2000 Kilometers

ARCTIC OCEAN

RUSSIA

KAZAKHSTAN

MONGOLIA

TURKEY
ALBANIA CYPRUS
LEBANON SYRIA
ISRAEL IRAQ
JORDAN
LIBYA EGYPT KUWAIT
SAUDI
ARABIA U.A.E.

AFGHANISTAN

IRAN

PAKISTAN

NEPAL

INDIA

PEOPLE'S REPUBLIC
OF
CHINA

NORTH
KOREA
SOUTH
KOREA

JAPAN

TAIWAN

HONG KONG

PACIFIC
OCEAN

CHAD
SUDAN

ERITREA OMAN
YEMEN
DJIBOUTI

ETHIOPIA
UGANDA
CONGO
DEMOCRATIC KENYA
REP. OF RWANDA
CONGO BURUNDI
TANZANIA

SOMALIA

SRI
LANKA

BANGLADESH
THAILAND
CAMBODIA

LAOS

VIETNAM

BRUNEI
MALAYSIA
SINGAPORE

PHILIPPINES

MARIANA
ISLANDS
(U.S.)
GUAM

MARSHALL
ISLANDS

ANGOLA

ZIMBABWE
BOTSWANA

SOUTH
AFRICA

MADAGASCAR

MOZAMBIQUE

INDIAN
OCEAN

INDONESIA

EAST TIMOR

AUSTRALIA

PAPUA
NEW GUINEA

SAMOA
FIJI

NEW
ZEALAND

Map 22.2 Life Expectancies in Global Perspective, 2018

....

Increased attention to public health, medicine, nutrition, and education since the early
nineteenth century has contributed to prolonging life expectancy around the world, as
have the many scientific breakthroughs and technological advancements of the twentieth
and twenty-first centuries.

- According to Map 22.1 and this map, which regions experienced population increases
  but low life expectancies? Population decreases and high life expectancies? Explain.

- Which countries do not match the life expectancy trends of their geographic regions? Why?

- Do you note any correlations between a region's life expectancy and its physical
  environment? Why or why not?

rising value led to an expanded dependence on immigrant workers. Recent estimates put the number of foreign nationals in Japan at nearly 2 million, or around 1.5 percent of the total population. Most of them hail from the Korean Peninsula, the Philippines, Southeast Asia, Brazil, and Iran.

ANTI-IMMIGRANT SENTIMENTS IN WESTERN COUNTRIES

In Europe, where unemployment rates have remained higher than in Japan or North America, the political reaction against immigration has been sharpest. Far-right groups have demanded that immigration be halted or "foreigners" expelled, and that stance has now been adopted by politicians across the far-right spectrum. Support for these views varies among countries, but across Europe the far right's electoral base appears to be around 15 percent; in some countries, it is above 25 percent. The Freedom Party in Austria regularly places cabinet representatives in coalition governments. Ultra-right forces such as France's National Front (renamed National Rally in 2018), Denmark's People's Party, and the League of Polish Families sometimes pressure governing coalitions to slow EU integration and immigration, especially from Muslim countries. The presence of Muslims in Europe's large cities seems threatening to those who still equate Europe with Christendom and challenges those who

"No Muslim Ban" Protesters against the U.S. Supreme Court's decision to uphold President Donald Trump's ban on travel from several mostly Muslim countries expressed their indignation on June 26, 2018, in New York.

believe that European integration requires complete cultural assimilation of all inhabitants. The issue of accepting Muslim refugees from war-torn Syria has galvanized supporters and opponents in the EU's most powerful country, Germany, and it played a key role in the Northern League's election as part of a populist coalition government in Italy.

The pushback against immigration has become intertwined with the issues of terrorism and assimilation of Muslims into European societies. In Holland, the precipitating event was the grisly murder of filmmaker Theo van Gogh by Mohammed Bouyeri in 2004. Bouyeri claimed he was fulfilling his duty as a Muslim by assassinating van Gogh, who had made a film about the abuse of Muslim women. Following the assassination, many in Holland questioned the nation's traditional tolerance of diversity and expressed concern that Muslims were too alien in their values to ever fit into Dutch society. Several terrorist attacks further inflamed the debate. In 2004, a series of bombings of commuter trains in Madrid killed 191 people and wounded more than 2,000; in 2005, terrorists struck London's subways, leaving 52 dead and 700 injured. In both cases, authorities pinned responsibility on al-Qaeda. But investigators also alleged that the operations were the work of Muslim residents of Spain or Britain. France confronted a similar debate after riots protesting police brutality and the country's failure to offer equal opportunity to all rocked a series of poor neighborhoods, notably in Paris, in 2005.

Although Europeans stepped up their security procedures and intensified intelligence gathering, violence continued. The French satirical weekly magazine *Charlie Hebdo* became the target of two terrorist attacks (in 2011 and 2015) after publishing deliberately irreverent depictions of the Prophet Muhammad. And on November 13, 2015, terrorists claiming allegiance to the Islamic State in Iraq and Syria (ISIS) carried out a series of coordinated attacks: while one group struck outside a Paris stadium where France was playing Germany in a football (soccer) match, others attacked restaurants, cafés, and a concert hall. In all, 130 people were killed and many more were injured. Just a few months later, a Tunisian, Anis Amri, also asserting allegiance to ISIS, struck in a market in Berlin, killing twelve.

In the United States, meanwhile, anti-immigrant sentiments also gathered popular support, fueled by candidate, and later president, Donald Trump's attacks on immigrants and restrictions on immigration from Muslim countries (the so-called Muslim ban). His administration expanded the policy that separated children from parents who crossed the U.S.-Mexico border without documentation and sought to end the Deferred Action for Childhood Arrivals (DACA) policy of his predecessor, Barack Obama. In the summer of 2020, the U.S. Supreme Court rejected the Trump administration's efforts to strip DACA students of their rights to remain and have access to education.

In just a few years, the mood of the world's most advanced industrial societies has shifted decisively. The triumphant atmosphere that ushered in the new millennium has given way to a pessimistic outlook. In the year 2000, talk of the blessings of global integration dominated the political and economic scene; two decades later, prognosticators warn about the dangers emanating from disaffected members of their societies and from radicals, especially Islamic radicals, willing and able to unleash terror anywhere in the world.

Russia, China, and India

Fueling the anti-immigrant fires in Europe, Japan, and North America is the increasing number of jobs being "outsourced" to China, India, and other countries. In the past, businesses had turned to immigrants to fill low-wage positions (and to keep all wages down). But by the end of the twentieth century, it had become more economical to relocate manufacturing to places where cheap labor was already available.

ECONOMIC GLOBALIZATION AND POLITICAL EFFECTS

In the twenty-first century, business mobility has not been limited to low-skill and low-wage jobs. Technological advances—particularly in computers and communication—have enabled all sorts of enterprises to operate from almost any point on the globe. No longer do educated workers have to leave India or China for employment in Europe or North America, because it is increasingly cost-effective for corporations to shift certain operations to those countries. The globalized market economy has leveled the playing field in the competition for jobs, although countries with vast labor reserves, such as Russia, China, and India, still have a long way to go to achieve the per capita income levels enjoyed in the older capitalist societies. Nonetheless, Russia, China, and India have had healthy economic growth in the first years of the new century. As the gap closed, China in particular moved from being a trading partner to a trade competitor. It once sent cheap commodities to Europe and North America in return for capital goods and advanced technology; now, it is selling 5G wireless technology and cornering the market on strategic technologies like solar panels.

RUSSIA: ECONOMIC EXPANSION AND AGGRESSIVE NATIONALISM

While Russia's economy was opening to the world, thanks to high oil prices, its political system seemed to be closing in on itself. President Vladimir Putin presided over a rebuilding of the central Russian state, which was widely welcomed in Russia. But the means used by Putin to reassert central state power led, once again, to personal rule. The president forcibly repossessed the two principal television stations from their billionaire owners and reassigned other valuable private properties, especially oil and gas companies, to the state, to be run by his former colleagues from the Soviet-era political police, the KGB. The Gorbachev-Yeltsin era's promise of a real legislature, an independent judiciary, and an end to arbitrary rule gave way, in the yearning for order and stability, to aggressive nationalism and an authoritarian executive, which have spurred Russia's annexation of Crimea in 2014 and its aggressive support of separatists in Ukraine.

Although Donald Trump and right-wing leaders in Europe have expressed admiration for Vladimir Putin and claimed to take Putin at his word that the Russian government did not interfere in the 2016 American elections and subsequent votes in Europe, American policies toward the Russians have been as hostile as they were during the Obama administration. Sanctions have been intensified, and the American military commitments to the eastern and central European member states of NATO have been strengthened.

CHINA: MARKET REFORMS AND SHIFTING FOREIGN POLICY

As in Russia, leaders in China have encouraged market reforms while quashing political liberalization. Their economic strategies seem to be successful. Over the last three decades, China's economy has maintained an average growth rate of over 9 percent annually, although it has recently shown signs of slowing down. Consumer goods made in China dominate so many markets that it is virtually impossible, as several newspaper reporters have found, to supply an American family's needs with a "China-free" shopping list. Indeed, the Chinese economy has been the second largest in the world since late 2010, and some projections suggest that it will be the largest by midcentury, even though China's per capita income will still lag behind that of the United States.

In many ways, China's fortunes illustrate both the promises and the pitfalls of the economic reforms undertaken by many developing countries in the era of globalization. On the one hand, China's entry into the World Trade Organization (WTO) in 2001 signified its full integration into the global capitalist economy. On the other hand, the reforms have caused political, social, and environmental problems that defy easy solutions. A 2016 report from Peking University found that 1 percent of Chinese households controlled a third of the country's assets, while the poorest 25 percent of households owned just 1 percent of the country's wealth.

There are concerns, both at home and abroad, about the environmental impact of China's economic development. China's homes and factories, for instance, use 40 percent more coal than those in the United States, and Chinese city dwellers suffer from some of the world's worst smog and poorest air quality. But as China's energy consumption and economy have soared, so has its global standing.

China's Trade War with America During his 2016 presidential campaign, Donald Trump excoriated American trade policies, claiming that they robbed Americans of jobs, created large trade deficits, and brought about large transfers of wealth to China and other countries. Upon coming to office, he immediately repudiated the Trans-Pacific Partnership (TPP) agreement, which had been signed on February 4, 2016, by countries with ports on the Pacific, though not the Chinese. During the campaign he also criticized the North American Free Trade Agreement (NAFTA), brought into effect on January 1, 1994, involving the United States, Canada, and Mexico. According to Trump, it was the worst American trade agreement ever negotiated, and he said that if he were elected president, he would either renounce it or renegotiate it. He did in fact renegotiate it in September 2018. But although the new treaty, known as the United States–Mexico–Canada Agreement (USMCA), included some beneficial updates to the now-twenty-five-year-old NAFTA, these improvements did not fundamentally change the original agreement.

In reality, Trump's chief economic target was China and the massive trade imbalance with the Chinese, brought about because of the American appetite for Chinese goods and the unwillingness or inability of the Chinese to purchase American exports. Claiming that trade wars were easily won, Trump began his conflict with China on March 22, 2018, by applying steep tariffs on

$50 billion to $60 billion worth of Chinese goods. China retaliated by placing tariffs on 128 U.S. imports to China, notably aluminum, airplanes, cars, and soybeans. The Americans and the Chinese, almost always with the Americans in the lead, continued to increase the rates and the products involved until July 2019, when Trump announced that the United States would impose a 10 percent tariff on an additional $300 billion worth of Chinese exports. He claimed that he was doing so because the Chinese had

An Economic Boom in China The opening of the Chinese economy in the 1980s made the country an export powerhouse. Today, computers, office machine parts, and electronics dominate China's export list. But at the outset, it was mainly textiles and low-tech assembly that powered the industrial boom. This photo was taken in 2007. Now female-dominated textile manufacturing has moved away from China to lower-wage producers, like Bangladesh.

not lived up to their agreement to buy agricultural products in larger quantities than before. The new tariff would be imposed on top of the 25 percent tariff already levied on $250 billion worth of Chinese imports, which would result in a tax on virtually all Chinese products entering the United States. The spat remained unresolved as negotiators wrangled.

Chinese Environmental Concerns Despite its prosperity, Hong Kong, like other major Chinese cities, suffers from severe air pollution, which threatens its future as a hub of international commerce. This picture shows part of the city's waterfront shrouded in smog.

Larry Kudlow, Trump's chief adviser, stated that the tariffs on Chinese imports would have little effect on the pocketbooks of American consumers. Most economists have disagreed, for that is not how tariffs usually work. The main groups to be hurt will be American businesses and consumers, who will have to pay more for valuable Chinese imports or go without them. Independent financial surveys estimated that the new tariffs will cost American households an average of $200 a year on top of the $831 imposed by the already existing tariffs. In addition, these tariffs will affect low-income families more directly than the earlier tariffs, which were mainly imposed on industrial products. The new tariffs target shoes, clothing, toys, and cell phones, and the increased costs to consumers will wipe out the gains middle-class households made from the Trump's 2017 tax cut.

Hong Kong Protests On July 1, 1997, the British ceded Hong Kong Island, Kowloon, and the New Territories to the Peoples Republic of China, effectively bringing an end to the British Empire. Hong Kong had been part of the British Empire for 156 years and had achieved a level of prosperity and personal freedom unknown on mainland China. The agreement between the British and Chinese governments, known as the "one country, two systems" accord, stipulated that the socialist system of the People's Republic would not be practiced in Hong Kong, where a capitalist way of life would be maintained for fifty years. Further, the agreement stated that the chief executive of Hong Kong as well as the legislature would be selected by a committee composed of professional and business leaders until 2017, when both the chief executive and members of the legislature would be chosen by all of Hong Kong's citizens. Alas, the People's Republic of China has chipped away at these arrangements, and ultimately Hong Kong's chief executive, Carrie Lam, elected in 2017, brought before the Hong Kong legislature an extradition law that would allow the government of Hong Kong to extradite Hong Kong citizens for trial on the mainland. Thousands of Hong Kongers, perhaps as many as 1 million out of a total of a little more than 6 million, turned out in protest on the grounds that the law violated the spirit of the original accord. Although the chief executive has withdrawn the law from the legislature, she has not repudiated the law, leading to further protests and clashes with the police. However, as the COVID-19 pandemic spread, forcing Hong Kong dissidents off the streets, Beijing seized the opportunity to extend new national security laws to the city, curbing its autonomy and slashing its cherished civil liberties.

INDIA: ECONOMIC AND SOCIAL LIBERALIZATION AND ITS EFFECTS

India has also registered impressive economic growth in the new millennium. Since the 1990s, the Indian economy has become increasingly open. The nation's information technology sector has boomed, and India has become a favorite destination for global corporations, attracted by its sizable English-speaking population. In some respects, India became a model of market-driven growth, an alternative to the state-dominated Chinese model. Its middle classes were booming and the wealthy lived more opulently than ever. But it was also unfair and fragile. When the COVID-19 pandemic hit, India's economy was sent reeling; many migrant workers and members of the middle class suddenly saw their precarious gains vanish.

India also experienced some social gains alongside economic ones. In 2005 Prince Manvendra Singh Gohil became the world's first openly gay royal, and in 2006 Nobel laureate Amartya Sen and other public figures urged the repeal of section 377 of the Indian penal code, due to its British-era provision that criminalized homosexuality. Another milestone arrived in 2008, when five Indian cities held LGBTQ pride parades for the first time. A decade later, in 2018, after many legal battles, India's Supreme Court decriminalized homosexuality in a victory for equality. Nonetheless, these gains need to be viewed side by side with rampant and violent homophobia, including numerous vigilante murders of gay, lesbian, and transgender people.

Unfortunately, the benefits of economic liberalization were experienced unequally. High inflation hit the income of the salaried class hard. Inequality and poverty remain acute problems. To boost the capitalist economy, the government declared an open season on land acquisition for real estate development, industrial parks, and mining, leading to the eviction of farmers and forest dwellers. The displaced people responded with armed insurgencies. Violence erupted in the state of Gujarat in February 2002 after sixty Hindu pilgrims perished in a fire that consumed a train compartment. Although the circumstances of the fire remain disputed, a rumor immediately spread that Muslims and a "foreign hand" were responsible. For the next few months, Hindu mobs went on a rampage, burning Muslim homes and hacking the residents to death. Over 2,000 Muslims lost their lives.

Right-Wing Hindu Nationalism Not long after Indian independence in 1947, Hindu nationalists began to organize against the idea of a secular, multicultural state. They recruited young men and women and trained them in the arts of street and paramilitary violence. The Bharatiya Janata Party (BJP), a coalition of right-wing Hindu nationalists, has been in power since 2014. Street violence and persecution of minorities and pro-democracy activists have been on the rise ever since. In this photo, members of the women's wing of a Hindu nationalist group perform a self-defense exercise.

Riding on the widespread revulsion against corruption, the populist Bharatiya Janata Party (BJP), under Narendra Modi, swept the national elections and came to power in 2014 and again in 2019. With opposition parties dispirited and weak, he skillfully used social media to portray himself as a leader working tirelessly to advance India's interests against its foreign and domestic enemies. Taking a cue from their leader's aggressive nationalism, BJP politicians and Hindu vigilante groups targeted minorities, particularly Muslims. Critics of the government's policies toward Muslims and Dalits were tarred as anti-national. In November 2016, Modi's government demonetized high-value currency notes, claiming the policy to be a measure directed against unaccounted wealth, the underground economy, and counterfeit money. This move shocked the financial system and caused grave distress to the significant section of the economy that is based on cash transactions. However, Modi successfully framed demonetization as a nationalist act; those opposed to it were labeled as anti-national and pro–"black money."

Hindu nationalists also took aim at Muslim-majority regions. Bolstered by his impressive win in the 2019 elections, Prime Minster Modi announced on August 8, 2019, that the part of Kashmir that was under Indian administration was being stripped of its autonomy. He claimed that his action would improve the lot of the poor and minorities and enhance the political and economic development of the region. But the action deprived 8 million Kashmiris of local self-rule, their own prime minister, and protections against non-Kashmiri Indians seeking to move to the province. Much of the authority of the Kashmiri administration had been lost over time. But making this situation formal was an affront to Muslims in India and India's Muslim neighbors. Modi's actions infuriated Pakistan and heightened tensions with Bangladesh, which was itself reeling from an influx of Muslim refugees coming from Myanmar, many of them spilling into India.

The ongoing tension with neighboring Pakistan poses further problems. Flexing its nationalist muscle, the Indian government exploded a nuclear device in 1998. Pakistan responded by exploding its own bombs, casting an ominous shadow over the two nations' unresolved conflict over Kashmir. In that contested province, terrorist violence repeatedly disturbed the peace and brought the nuclear-armed neighbors close to a potentially devastating war. The tension between the two countries escalated in 2008 when a small band of terrorists from Pakistan carried out raids in Mumbai, slaughtering many civilians and security personnel before being subdued.

The Middle East, Africa, and Latin America

THE MIDDLE EAST: RADICAL CHANGE OR CONTINUITY?

In the Middle East, radical changes have been brought about by the Arab Spring and the growth of Islamic militancy, while more than a few countries in Africa have begun to achieve economic progress and gained political stability through democratic elections.

The Arab Spring The trigger for what became known as the Arab Spring was a seemingly futile act of protest. On December 17, 2010, Mohamed Bouazizi, a twenty-six-year-old Tunisian vegetable vendor and father of eight, set himself on fire outside a provincial office to protest the constant police harassment he had undergone. This singular act aroused the entire population of Tunisia against the ruling elite. Not only had the police confiscated Bouazizi's vegetable stand (and not for the first time), but a policewoman had slapped him in the face. In explaining his decision to take his life, his sister exclaimed, "In Sidi Bouzidi [where he resided] those with no connections and no money for bribes are humiliated and insulted and not allowed to live." As the story circulated through the country, crowds poured into the streets, demanding an end to the long-term dictatorship of Zine al-Abidine Ben Ali, who had taken over from Habib Bourguiba, Tunisia's president from independence in 1956 until 1978. The catchword of the protesters was *dégage* ("get out"). With the army refusing to suppress the dissenters and the security police overwhelmed, Ben Ali took the only way open to him: he departed for Saudi Arabia on January 14, 2011.

Young Egyptian radicals watched events in Tunisia with growing interest. If the Tunisians could get rid of their dictator, why not the Egyptians? On January 25, 2011 (ironically, a holiday to honor Egypt's police forces, who were by then an object of people's hatred), Egyptians of all backgrounds and ages assembled in Cairo's major plaza, Tahrir ("Liberation") Square, to inform Egypt's president, Hosni Mubarak, that he was no longer wanted. On February 11, 2011, just three weeks after the first mass demonstration, Mubarak left office, turning the reins of power over to the Supreme Command of the Armed Forces.

The ouster of Ben Ali and Mubarak sent shock waves throughout the Arab world and sparked an outpouring of protest in all of its major cities. The protesters' demands were consistent: the end of repression, the establishment of democratic institutions, and the ousting of rulers who had stayed in power too long and who did not represent the will of the people. The results were astonishing. Monarchs in Jordan and Morocco promised new constitutions. Bahraini Shiites successfully demanded a new constitution from their Sunni king, and Ali Abdullah Saleh, ruler of Yemen since 1978, fled the country. Even Muammar al-Qaddafi, the Libyan strongman who had been in power since ousting King Idris in 1969, felt the sting of protest, though his ouster and eventual execution on October 20, 2011, owed as much to NATO air power as it did to the rebel army that rose up to unseat him.

Arab Spring The deaths of Egyptian Khaled Said (left on the poster) and Tunisian Mohamed Bouazizi (right) provided martyrs for an upheaval across the Arab world and toppled undemocratic regimes, like that of Hosni Mubarak in Egypt in 2011. In this photograph, one demonstrator holds the martyrs' images aloft to denounce the authoritarian rule around the region. Day and night, Cairo's Tahrir Square was thronged with Egyptians of all ages to protest the ongoing military rule after the ousting of Mubarak.

Where did the uprisings come from? In the first place, the Arab people, most of whom were young and had known only authoritarian rule, resented the fact that the wave of democratic reforms that had swept other regions had passed them by. They saw no reason why they, too, should not have leaders who represented their wishes, rather than rigged elections and fraudulent referendums that supported the wishes of the ruling elites. The young came to be known as the generation in waiting—waiting for jobs that never seemed to appear; waiting to have enough money to move out of their parents' homes; waiting to get married and start families. The fact that Hafez al-Assad of Syria had passed power to his son, Bashar al-Assad, and Hosni Mubarak of Egypt was grooming his son, Gamal, to succeed him, heightened their rage. Although the uprisings often took names that suggested peaceful protest—such as the Jasmine Revolution in Tunisia and the White Revolution in Egypt—in reality these outbursts reflected deep-seated and long-standing fury at rulers who were repressive, corrupt, and unresponsive to their people.

Dictatorships and monarchies lost control over the media. The Qatari television station and newspaper *Al Jazeera*, founded in 1995, became an open forum for all kinds of opinions. One of its most dramatic and widely quoted programs featured an intense discussion about whether the Arab people had the right, like those in the west, to criticize their leaders. In addition, mobile phones, Facebook, Twitter, and other social media helped dissenters communicate with one another and enabled groups to organize large assemblies outside the purview of the state.

The early results led euphoric protesters to believe that they could create new and more open societies. Dictators were ousted, free elections were held, and new constitutions were promised. But the progress was hard to sustain. In Tunisia, which thus far had accomplished more than the other states, a moderate Muslim Brotherhood party, al-Nahda, won control of the parliament. Egypt, too, held elections that were won by the Muslim Brotherhood party, Justice and Development, but nullified by the courts. It also elected a Muslim Brotherhood president, Mohamed Morsi. Yet President Morsi failed to establish an inclusive government and was ousted by Egypt's military leader, General Abdel Fattah al-Sisi. Rebels in Sinai and the western desert, drawing inspiration from the rise of ISIS (discussed shortly), have challenged Sisi's government. The liberals and secularists who initiated the revolt against Mubarak have seen their aspirations dashed. Once in power, Sisi dealt with the Muslim Brotherhood in a savage way, imprisoning at least 30,000 members, perhaps even 60,000, and massacring at least 1,000 Muslim Brother protesters in Cairo on August 14, 2013. In early 2014, Sisi resigned from the military and ran for the presidency against a single opponent. While he won 96 percent of the vote, many eligible voters boycotted the election as a protest against the new government. On June 4, 2014, Sisi was sworn in as Egypt's sixth president. On April 23, 2019, he carried out a referendum that would allow him to remain as president until 2030, by which time he would be seventy-five years old.

By far, the most lethal outcome of the Arab Spring has occurred in Syria. Beginning on March 15, 2011, protesters demanded the ouster of President Bashar al-Assad, formed the Free Syrian Army, gained international recognition for their movement from the United States and European states, and led protests that resulted in violent confrontation with Assad's forces, which resorted to the use of chemical weapons (sarin gas and chlorine bombs). In August 2012, U.S. president Obama declared that the use of chemical weapons would cross a "red line." A year later, on August 21, 2013, the Syrian military killed nearly 1,500 civilians in Damascus. Video footage showed people with their bodies twitching and their mouths foaming after exposure to sarin gas. Since 2013, thousands of Syrians have been injured and hundreds killed in chemical attacks. By the summer of 2014, when the United Nations stopped officially counting, more than 400,000 Syrians had lost their lives in the conflict and 12 million had been displaced, of whom 5 million sought refuge in Turkey, Lebanon, and Jordan. Another 1 million risked their lives on rickety boats bound for Europe. Even while the Americans and many others considered Assad's days to be numbered, the Syrian president defied the protesters and his western critics by gaining financial aid from Iran and crucial—indeed, regime-saving—military support from Hezbollah (a Shiite party established in Lebanon) and Russia. Assad's retaking of the rebel stronghold of Aleppo in January 2017 marked a significant military triumph for the Syrian president, driving the Free Syrian Army and its supporters into the governorates of Idlib and Hama in northwest Syria, near the border with Turkey, and calling into question whether the different groups battling the Assad regime could topple his government.

The turmoil of the Syrian civil war has produced catastrophic suffering. Eight years of war cost 500,000 lives, left over 1 million injured, displaced half the population, and reduced the economy to one-third the size it was at the outset of the conflict. In 2018, the United Nations High Commission for Refugees estimated that Syria had the largest number of the 70,800,000 worldwide refugees, returnees, internally displaced persons, and stateless persons. Indeed, more than half of the people in the refugee category came from Syria (5.5 million), Afghanistan (2.5 million), and South Sudan (2.3 million). Of these Syrian refugees, 600,000 found refuge in Germany. Assad won the war, but his country is in misery.

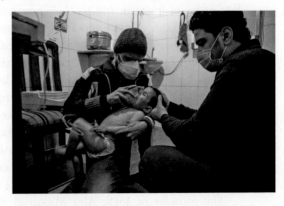

Syrian Chemical Weapons Use A child received treatment after an alleged gas attack on the Sakba and Hammuriye areas in Eastern Ghouta, Syria, on March 7, 2018.

Nor have events gone as the protesters wanted in Yemen and in other countries like Libya. In Yemen, the ousting of President Ali Abdullah Saleh created a political and leadership vacuum, which a marginalized Shiite Houthi community in north Yemen attempted to fill. Houthi forces invaded the southwest and established a new government, but the Saudi regime intervened militarily against the Houthis. The civil war in that country rages on and has pushed 10 million people to the brink of famine and nearly 250,000 to catastrophic levels of food security in a population of 29 million.

The Arab Spring began with such excitement and optimism, but nearly everywhere it has failed to deliver on its promises. The reasons for failure vary from country to country. In general, however, in Egypt, Syria, Saudi Arabia, and the other Arab countries, like Morocco and Jordan, that maintained their ruling elites, the regular militaries stayed in power and asserted their authority after the early protests. Nor did the original liberal leaders, almost all young people, create strong political parties or emerge as charismatic leaders. Sectarianism was also a factor, although it should not be overstated. In recent days, mainly young, liberal protesters in Iraq and Lebanon have demanded that the primarily Shiite government in Iraq and the multireligious elites step aside and allow less religious, more nationalist political elites to assume power.

Islamic Militancy As the old tyrants shook and states grew weak, Islamic movements grew stronger. The militant movement was dominated by al-Qaeda in the 1990s and the first decade of the twenty-first century, but changed significantly with the emergence of ISIS in the early 2000s. As the Americans clipped the power of al-Qaeda, killing many of its important leaders, ISIS rose to take its place, becoming an even more formidable opponent.

Al-Qaeda's agenda was based on the belief that the west, and especially the United States, was the main force standing in the way of Islam's rise. Thus, the first order of business was to challenge American power: hence the attack on the World Trade Center and the Pentagon. The leaders of al-Qaeda (notably the Saudi Osama bin Laden and the Egyptian Ayman al-Zawahiri) came from elite families and were gradualists in their vision of liberating the Muslim world from western influence, believing that an Islamic state could emerge only after American power had been eroded. They were also uncomfortable with the kinds of violence that more radical Islamists, like the founders of ISIS, urged upon their followers. U.S. Navy SEALs killed Osama bin Laden in 2011 when he was hiding out, though really in plain sight, in Abbottabad, Pakistan, but the United States has yet to find Zawahiri despite its offer of $25 million for information concerning his whereabouts.

The founder of ISIS, Abu Musab al-Zarqawi, was an unlikely leader. A heavy drinker, a brawler, and a high school dropout, he found religion—in his case, militant Islam—which became his salvation and the purpose of his life. Al-Zarqawi made his way to Afghanistan in the 1990s to meet Osama bin

ISIS Fighters ISIS assembled a powerful group of soldiers, many from foreign countries (including the United States and European nations), and created a territorial state in western Syria and northern Iraq.

Laden, whom he idolized. Those meetings did not generate much enthusiasm, probably because al-Qaeda's leadership considered him too violent and hotheaded. Nonetheless, some high-ranking members of al-Qaeda accepted him into their ranks. When the Americans chased al-Zarqawi out of Afghanistan, he made his way to Iraq, anticipating that the Americans would invade and that he could put his form of radical and militant Islam into action there.

As the American occupation of Iraq faltered, al-Zarqawi's vision of a violent jihadi world rose to prominence. Here, because of his willingness to employ extreme violence, such as beheading prisoners and burning them alive, he earned the nickname "the Sheikh of the Slaughterers." As much as al-Zarqawi hated Americans, his rage against Iraqi Shiites was even more intense. In a country where the Sunni minority had exercised power for centuries, the dominance of Shiites in the new American-supported government enraged al-Zarqawi and his Sunni followers.

Although American troops killed al-Zarqawi in June 2006, the movement he led resurrected itself and became known as ISIS. Its unlikely new leader, Abu Bakr al-Baghdadi, had neither military nor bureaucratic experience when he assumed leadership of ISIS in May 2010. He was an Islamic scholar who had trained in some of the minor Iraqi Muslim schools and had eventually gained his doctorate by writing an exegesis of the Quran. But he had something that the parent organization, al-Qaeda, lacked: a territorial state, based in northern and central Iraq, which became even more formidable following the departure of American forces from the country. After moving into war-torn Syria and conquering Mosul in northern Iraq in 2014, ISIS also took the name Islamic Caliphate, and al-Baghdadi announced to the world that he was the new state's first caliph.

At its height, after the conquest of Mosul in 2014, ISIS controlled territories in central Syria and northern Iraq equivalent in area to the United Kingdom. It also had a population of between 6 and 9 million; an army of 30,000; a capital city, Raqqa, in Syria; and large financial resources, amassed though oil revenues, looting, and taxes. (For a look at the territory held by the Islamic State and the population of Shiite Muslims in the Middle East, see Map 22.3 and Table 22.1.) By August 2016, ISIS was reported to operate in eighteen countries around the world, including Afghanistan and Pakistan.

By 2017, ISIS was losing its strongholds in Iraq and Syria. First to fall was the city of Mosul, the biggest and largest ISIS city in its caliphate. Compelled to retreat to its Syrian capital, Raqqa, it was finally dislodged there in 2019, overrun by anti-ISIS forces led by a well-disciplined and well-armed Kurdish force. On October 26–27, 2019, al-Baghdadi killed himself by detonating a suicide vest as he was about to be seized by an American military unit. Nonetheless, although ISIS is no longer a state, its appeal, like that of al-Qaeda, remains potent. Not only does it have deep roots in the writings of many earlier, and now modern, Muslim theoreticians, but it continues to appeal to marginalized Muslim groups around the world. It will be a force to be reckoned with for years.

Table 22.1 Population of Shiite Muslims, 2009

	Estimated 2009 Shiite Population	Approximate Percentage of Muslim Population That is Shiite
Iran	66–70 million	90–95
Iraq	19–22 million	65–70
Yemen	8–10 million	35–40
Azerbaijan	5–7 million	65–75
Syria	3–4 million	15–20
Lebanon	1–2 million	45–55
Kuwait	500,000–700,000	20–25
Bahrain	400,000–500,000	65–75
World total	154–200 million	10–13

Source: "Mapping the Global Muslim Population," Pew Research Center, October 7, 2009.

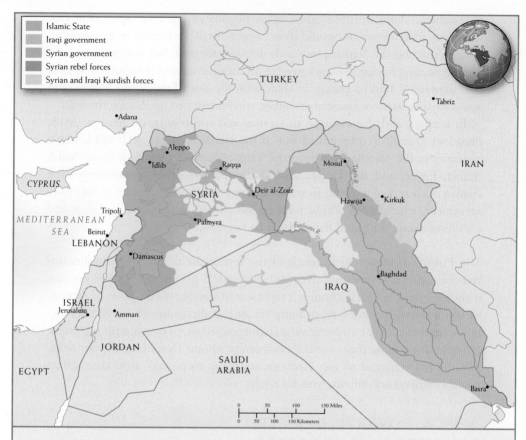

Map 22.3 Warring Factions in Iraq and Syria, March 27, 2017

This map shows the territories held by Kurdish fighters, ISIS, rebel Syrian fighters, and the Iraqi and Syrian governments.

- Compare the territories held by ISIS with the map of the boundaries set by the Sykes-Picot agreement (see Map 19.4). How similar are the territories that ISIS held in March 2017 to those that Sykes-Picot reserved for an Arab confederation?

- ISIS contends that the British-French agreements for the division of the Arab world after World War I need to be abolished. Why does ISIS hold these views?

- Why would the Turkish, Iraqi, and Syrian governments be dismayed that the Kurds have become the strongest militia fighting against ISIS?

The Iranian Nuclear Deal In mid-June 2015, Iran and the United States, Russia, China, Britain, France, Germany, and the European Union reached an agreement on an issue that had troubled Iran's relations with the outside world for more than a decade and that had resulted in the imposition of severe economic sanctions on Iran. The agreement dealt with Iran's nuclear program, which the Iranians claimed was entirely for civil use, but the United States and many other countries believed was to create nuclear weapon capability. The U.S.

government, along with five other states, negotiated a nuclear agreement that was to run for ten years and would allow inspections of the Iranian nuclear facilities while permitting the Iranians to enrich uranium for civil, but not military, uses. The negotiating foreign powers agreed to lift the financial and economic sanctions, thus permitting Iran to engage in trade with the rest of the world and to gain access to its substantial financial resources, which were tied up in western banks.

In keeping with his aversion to treaties and constraints, on May 6, 2018, President Donald Trump pulled out of the Iranian nuclear deal. While many countries in the Middle East endorsed Trump's action, including Israel, Saudi Arabia, Egypt, and the United Arab Emirates, the other signatories of the Iranian nuclear deal did not. In response, Iran breached significant parts of the agreement, exceeding a critical limit on how much fuel it could possess and enriching uranium beyond the purity it had agreed to.

The Future of Israel As in much of the rest of the world, where politicians favored national sovereignty over global laws and norms, a hard-line government took hold in Israel. Though it represented an unstable coalition of extremist and nationalist parties, its cunning leader and the country's longest-serving prime minister, Benjamin Netanyahu, has managed to survive and tilt the political spectrum ever further to anti-Palestinian positions. Despite corruption scandals, he has managed to win elections and cling to power—now through an unstable emergency alliance with his rivals.

AFRICA: POVERTY, DISEASE, GENOCIDE, AND PROGRESS

Globalization lifted many out of poverty, especially in China and elsewhere in East and Southeast Asia. But it also spread the benefits unfairly. So, while poverty decreased on the whole, inequality increased—and became more concentrated in specific regions. The result: in much of the developing world, poverty, disease, and violence persist. The new millennium did not begin auspiciously for the peoples of Africa. The region remained the poorest in the world and suffered the uncontrolled and uncontrollable spread of HIV/AIDS. (For a global look at hunger and disparities in income, see Maps 22.4 and 22.5.)

Of the thirty-eight sub-Saharan African countries surveyed in the *World Bank Development Report* for 2009, all but seven were low-income countries. The poorest of the poor (Burundi, the Republic of the Congo, and Liberia) reported per capita incomes of U.S. $150 or less. Botswana, which enjoyed Africa's second-highest per capita income at $6,120 (behind only mineral-rich Gabon), was so devastated by HIV/AIDS that its average life expectancy, once the highest in Africa at close to seventy years, had tumbled to fifty-one years by 2007 and was one of the lowest in the world. (For a global look at HIV/AIDS incidence, see Map 22.6.) As Asian economies have prospered, Africa's share of global poverty has increased. In 2013, more than half of the people living in extreme poverty lived in Africa.

There have, however, been signs of progress. Ghana embraced parliamentary and presidential elections. Civil strife ended in Mozambique and Angola. South Africa convened a Truth and Reconciliation Commission to put the trauma of apartheid behind it and to stay on the course of parliamentary democracy while addressing the gross income inequality between Whites and Blacks that was a legacy of the twentieth century.

But these countries have been exceptions to the rule in a region where political instability has wrought misery and devastation. Many of Africa's countries (Liberia, Sierra Leone, Mali, the Ivory Coast, and the Central African Republic) were torn asunder by ethnic and personal rivalries, and the resulting conflicts required foreign interventions. Nigeria finally rid itself of its unwanted military dictatorship and moved to a civil, parliamentary system. But Nigeria's democratically elected presidents have barely been able to hold the country together. The people of the Niger Delta in the south of the country continue to rebel and to demand a larger share of the oil wealth their region produces, while in the impoverished northeast a Muslim group calling itself Boko Haram (meaning "no western learning") has carried out acts of shocking violence.

In 2011, just when Africa's longest-running civil war, pitting the animists and Christians of southern Sudan against the Muslim peoples of the north, had seemingly been resolved through the creation of a new state for the southerners, known as South Sudan, an ongoing dispute in western Sudan kept the Sudanese government in civil strife. In the region of Darfur, the state allowed local horse-riding nomads to carry out ethnic-cleansing campaigns against settled agriculturalists. Thus, as in Rwanda in the 1990s (see Chapter 21), genocide has once more visited Africa. The conflict in Darfur has also led to one of Africa's worst cases of displacement: as of 2018, over 4 million refugees have fled government terror and civil war to huddle in vast, miserable camps. But there is some reason for hope. In the West African country of Liberia, after years of pitiless civil war, the belligerents agreed to put down their guns in 2004. In 2005, remarkable elections swept Africa's first woman president, Ellen Johnson Sirleaf, into office.

LATIN AMERICA: DEEPENING INEQUALITIES

Globalization has contributed to economic inequality in some of the poorest parts of the world. Compared with sub-Saharan Africa, Latin America's situation is not so bleak. But the divide between haves and have-nots has widened across the region, which has historically been the world's most unequal. The very rich in Buenos Aires live like the very rich in Paris; magnates in Mexico City drive the same cars, eat the same food, read the same books, and vacation

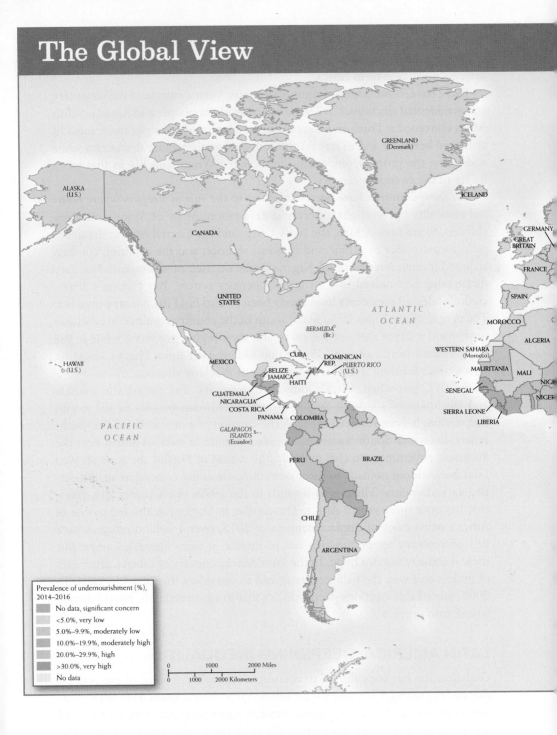

GREENLAND
(Denmark)

ICELAND

ALASKA
(U.S.)

CANADA

GERMANY

GREAT
BRITAIN

FRANCE

SPAIN

UNITED
STATES

ATLANTIC
OCEAN

BERMUDA
(Br.)

MOROCCO

ALGERIA

WESTERN SAHARA
(Morocco)

HAWAII
(U.S.)

MEXICO

CUBA

DOMINICAN
REP. PUERTO RICO
(U.S.)

BELIZE
JAMAICA
HAITI

MAURITANIA

MALI

NIG

GUATEMALA
NICARAGUA
COSTA RICA
PANAMA

SENEGAL

NIGER

COLOMBIA

SIERRA LEONE

LIBERIA

PACIFIC
OCEAN

GALAPAGOS
ISLANDS
(Ecuador)

PERU

BRAZIL

CHILE

ARGENTINA

Prevalence of undernourishment (%),
2014–2016

- No data, significant concern
- <5.0%, very low
- 5.0%–9.9%, moderately low
- 10.0%–19.9%, moderately high
- 20.0%–29.9%, high
- >30.0%, very high
- No data

0   1000   2000 Miles

0   1000   2000 Kilometers

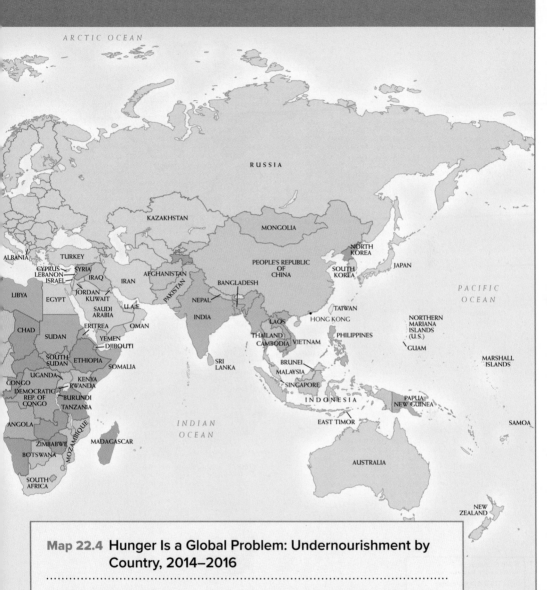

ARCTIC OCEAN

RUSSIA

KAZAKHSTAN

MONGOLIA

ALBANIA   TURKEY
CYPRUS   SYRIA
LEBANON   IRAQ
ISRAEL
JORDAN
EGYPT   KUWAIT
SAUDI   U.A.E.
ARABIA
ERITREA   OMAN
CHAD   SUDAN
YEMEN
DJIBOUTI
SOUTH
SUDAN   ETHIOPIA
SOMALIA
UGANDA
CONGO   KENYA
DEMOCRATIC   RWANDA
REP. OF   BURUNDI
CONGO   TANZANIA
ANGOLA

LIBYA

IRAN   AFGHANISTAN
PAKISTAN   BANGLADESH
NEPAL
INDIA

PEOPLE'S REPUBLIC
OF
CHINA

NORTH
KOREA
SOUTH
KOREA

JAPAN

PACIFIC
OCEAN

TAIWAN
HONG KONG

LAOS
THAILAND
CAMBODIA   VIETNAM

PHILIPPINES

NORTHERN
MARIANA
ISLANDS
(U.S.)
GUAM

MARSHALL
ISLANDS

SRI
LANKA

BRUNEI
MALAYSIA
SINGAPORE

INDONESIA

PAPUA
NEW GUINEA

SAMOA

ZIMBABWE   MADAGASCAR
BOTSWANA
MOZAMBIQUE

INDIAN
OCEAN

EAST TIMOR

AUSTRALIA

SOUTH
AFRICA

NEW
ZEALAND

Map 22.4 Hunger Is a Global Problem: Undernourishment by Country, 2014–2016

Despite much optimism on the part of world leaders, globalization has not yet met the basic human needs of the entire world population. In 2019, the proportion of undernourished people in the world declined to 8.9 percent. But a United Nations report predicted that the COVID-19 pandemic could push 130 million more people into chronic hunger by 2020's end.

- According to this map, in which regions is undernourishment very high?
- Comparing this map with Map 22.5, identify at least twelve countries where undernourishment is very high *and* per capita income is low. What other characteristics do these regions share?

The Global View

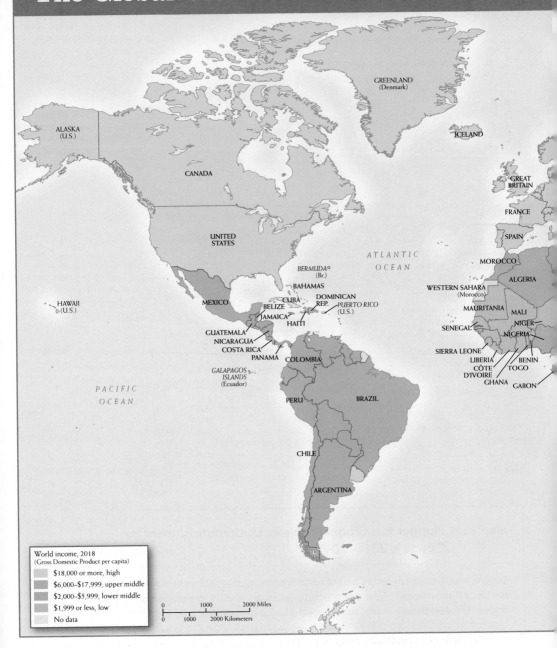

GREENLAND
(Denmark)

ALASKA
(U.S.)

ICELAND

CANADA

GREAT
BRITAIN

FRANCE

UNITED
STATES

SPAIN

ATLANTIC
OCEAN

MOROCCO

BERMUDA○
(Br.)

BAHAMAS

ALGERIA

WESTERN SAHARA
(Morocco)

HAWAII
○(U.S.)

MEXICO

CUBA

BELIZE

DOMINICAN
REP.

PUERTO RICO
(U.S.)

MAURITANIA

MALI

JAMAICA

NIGER

HAITI

SENEGAL

NIGERIA

GUATEMALA

NICARAGUA

COSTA RICA

SIERRA LEONE

LIBERIA

BENIN

PANAMA

COLOMBIA

CÔTE
D'IVOIRE

TOGO

GALAPAGOS
ISLANDS
(Ecuador)

GHANA

GABON

PACIFIC
OCEAN

PERU

BRAZIL

CHILE

ARGENTINA

World income, 2018
(Gross Domestic Product per capita)

$18,000 or more, high

$6,000–$17,999, upper middle

$2,000–$5,999, lower middle

$1,999 or less, low

No data

0   1000   2000 Miles

0   1000   2000 Kilometers

ARCTIC OCEAN

RUSSIA

GERMANY
UKRAINE
KAZAKHSTAN
MONGOLIA
ITALY
ALBANIA
TURKEY
CYPRUS SYRIA
LEBANON
ISRAEL
JORDAN
IRAQ
IRAN
AFGHANISTAN
PEOPLE'S REPUBLIC
OF
CHINA
NORTH
KOREA
SOUTH
KOREA
JAPAN
LIBYA
EGYPT
KUWAIT
SAUDI
ARABIA
U.A.E.
PAKISTAN
NEPAL
BHUTAN
INDIA
BANGLADESH
TAIWAN
HONG KONG
MACAU
PACIFIC
OCEAN
CHAD
SUDAN
ERITREA
YEMEN
DJIBOUTI
OMAN
LAOS
THAILAND
CAMBODIA VIETNAM
PHILIPPINES
MARIANA
ISLANDS
(U.S.)
GUAM
CAMEROON
C.A.R.
UGANDA
ETHIOPIA
SOMALIA
SRI
LANKA
BRUNEI
MALAYSIA
SINGAPORE
MARSHALL
ISLANDS
CONGO
DEMOCRATIC
REP. OF
CONGO
KENYA
RWANDA
BURUNDI
TANZANIA
INDONESIA
PAPUA
NEW GUINEA
SOLOMON
ISLANDS
ANGOLA
ZAMBIA
ZIMBABWE
NAMIBIA
BOTSWANA
MADAGASCAR
INDIAN
OCEAN
EAST TIMOR
VANUATU
FIJI
SAMOA
NEW CALEDONIA
(Fr.)
SOUTH
AFRICA
AUSTRALIA
NEW
ZEALAND

Map 22.5 Rich and Poor Countries: Per Capita Annual Income (U.S. $), 2018

Wealth and income derived from globalization have not been shared equally among the regions of the world.

- Using this map, identify the regions with the highest per capita income and those with the lowest. What factors do you think account for this disparity? What historical antecedents helped create this disparity?
- According to your reading, why have India and China, despite recent economic growth, failed to catch up with the United States, western European countries, and Japan in terms of per capita income?

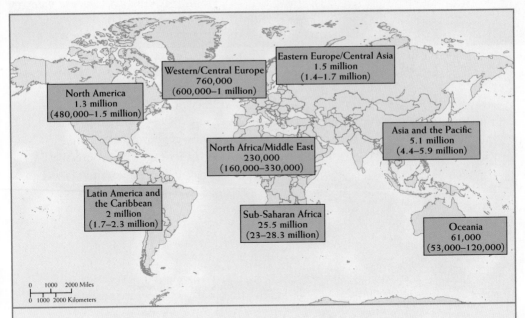

Map 22.6 Numbers of HIV-Positive People Worldwide, 2016

··

The spread of HIV/AIDS threatens the development of human capital in the twenty-first century.

- According to this map, which region has the highest rate of HIV infection?
- Using Maps 22.4 and 22.5 for reference, what connections do you see between poverty and HIV/AIDS prevalence?
- How does the spread of HIV/AIDS compromise economic development in poorer regions of the world?

in the same spots as their social cousins from New York. They send their children to private schools in the United States and the United Kingdom to join a cosmopolitan upper class. To Latin American elites, globalization has been a boon, as it has increased their wealth and has facilitated their integration into the international circulation of goods, ideas, and people. Many, in fact, identify less and less with a particular place in the world.

Some of the same features hold for the social bottom. Being disadvantaged and poor in southern Mexico looks a lot like being on the losing end in southern Africa: people cling to tiny parcels of land, migrate long distances for seasonal jobs, and fight against insensitive authorities for their basic needs. In many cases, the best solution to their problems is to leave—to move to cities or across borders in search of opportunities elsewhere.

Latin Americans have responded to these challenges in many ways. One sweeping trend is the election of left-wing governments. Most of these new leaders are not like the rebel firebrands of the 1960s. Instead, in Brazil, Chile,

Argentina, and Uruguay, left-wing governments have offered policies designed to soften the blows of globalization and meet basic needs for land, schools, and decent housing. However, the same pressures of globalization that contribute to leftist electoral triumphs limit what these fledgling governments can do. In Venezuela, Ecuador, and Bolivia, a more nationalist and populist brand of politics has emerged, one that rejects globalization altogether. Rather than softening the effects of globalization, the presidents of these countries promised to reverse them. Not all left-wing governments calling for greater equality have been repressive or even anti-American. The progressive president of Mexico, Andrés Manuel López Obrador (known commonly as AMLO) has been a shrewd pragmatist, deftly avoiding inflammatory relations with his mercurial neighbor Donald Trump.

But the left-wing turn boomeranged. Parts of Latin America followed the Indian, Russian, and American tilt to nativist, right-wing politics. This was most dramatic in Brazil, where the Workers' Party lost elections in 2018, bringing Jair Bolsonaro to power on a wave of racism and sexist sloganeering. Like other populists, he stoked resentments against minorities and women, and he blamed outside forces for the country's woes. Other left-wing regimes hung on, often with calamitous results for the country. In Venezuela, a once-wealthy country that is now wracked with a 44 percent unemployment rate, a "revolutionary" government has dragged the society into mass poverty and polarization. Up to 6 million people, 20 percent of the population, have fled, creating a refugee crisis in neighboring Colombia and Brazil.

The appeal of anti-globalist politics is not limited to Latin America, or even to the developing nations. In the most advanced industrial societies, as well as in rapidly rising nations like China and India, programs to check globalization or buffer people from its destabilizing effects have found receptive audiences. Still, opposition to deeper global integration continues to be greatest in the poorest parts of the world, where globalization's benefits are least apparent and its costs are often lethal.

State Violence and the Struggles for Racial Justice and LGBTQ Rights

If the shocks to globalization revealed underlying injustices and the unequal effects of climate change and public health threats, the spotlight also turned to the ways in which states openly discriminated and harassed some of their own citizens, while drawing ever-harder lines in excluding noncitizens. Consider the role of police violence. In France, Britain, Turkey, and the United States—not to mention countries with even more repressive regimes, like Syria and Hong Kong—policing became synonymous with a defense of privileged sectors and racial hierarchies.

Black Lives Matter in 2020 On May 25, 2020, a Black civilian named George Floyd was choked to death by a police officer in front of onlookers who pleaded to let Floyd live. Videos of the murder went viral. Across American cities and around the world, people demonstrated. Floyd, painted here in a mural in Nairobi, Kenya, became an emblem of defiance against police violence.

In the United States, the struggle over police violence and repression flared up in the wake of 2008. The struggle to reform policy became a social movement under the banner of **Black Lives Matter**. In 2013, a "neighborhood watchman" named George Zimmerman was acquitted of killing Trayvon Martin, a Black teenager who had been on the way to his father's house in Florida. A rash of news reports about brutal killings and torture hit the headlines. The deaths from excessive use of force by police of Eric Garner in New York, Michael Brown in Ferguson, Missouri, and others also prompted mass demonstrations. In 2015, twenty-eight-year-old Sandra Bland, who was arrested on a traffic stop and held for three days in a Texas jail, died in police custody. Black Lives Matter evolved quickly from a protest wave to a movement—one cofounded by three Black women, Alicia Garza, Patrisse Cullors, and Opal Tometi, two of whom identify with the LGBTQ community. They called for deep police and penal reform.

The drive to reform and to restore some sense of equal citizenship gained momentum in late spring 2020 in the United States, which had emerged as the symbolic epicenter of a global movement. On May 25, a Minneapolis police officer, Derek Chauvin, looked into cameras for 8 minutes and 47 seconds as his knee sank into the neck of a Black man named George Floyd. As onlookers called for help and warned Chauvin that George was choking, Floyd's eyes fluttered shut, he stopped breathing, and he died. The footage of the murder went viral. In the midst of a pandemic lockdown, the people of Minneapolis took to the streets to protest the long history of police abuse. Within days, small towns and cities across America became the stage for the largest single civilian mobilization since the protests against the Vietnam War in the 1960s. The protest also went global as citizens of other countries turned to their own police forces and called out local injustices. Thousands of protesters took to the streets in Japan, England, Denmark, Senegal, Spain, Turkey, Canada, Portugal, South Korea, Brazil, and France. This time, calls to defund or even abolish the police joined the calls for reform and the demands to hold individual officers accountable for their use of excessive force. Social media played a vital role as viral, smartphone-shot videos of police teargassing and shooting rubber bullets at unarmed protesters and members of the press—and of protesters wearing masks to reduce the risk of spreading COVID-19—lit up the Internet. The racial protests and cries for reform continued to erupt over the summer as more acts of excessive police force were caught on video in cities like Atlanta, Georgia, and Kenosha, Wisconsin.

The call for equal protection and rights for citizens also spurred mobilization for the rights of people who resist heterosexual norms and the binary gender labels of man or woman. The past decade has seen many global triumphs, as well as heightened visibility in the media and the public sphere, for **LGBTQ** people. The United Nations Human Rights Council (UNHRC) passed its first resolution affirming LGBTQ rights in 2011; actress and advocate Laverne Cox became the first transgender person on the cover of *Time* magazine in 2014; and *Moonlight* became the first LGBTQ-themed film to win the Best Picture award at the Oscars in 2017. In 2018, the Vatican used the acronym "LGBT" in an official document for the first time. And in 2019, Mattel released the world's first line of gender-neutral dolls, and Pete Buttigieg became the first openly gay Democratic presidential candidate in U.S. history—to name just a few milestones. As of August 2020, twenty-nine countries recognize marriage for same-sex couples, and only a single country,

Transgender Activism Laverne Cox, a prominent American actress and defender of the rights of LGBTQ people, became a standard-bearer for transgender activism. Here she serves as grand marshal of the New York City Pride March in 2014. Beside her is a framed picture of Islan Nettles, a young trans woman who was murdered in Harlem earlier that year, held by Nettles's mother. Since the election of Donald Trump, Cox has been working on lawsuits to defend against discrimination, and she appeared at rallies and demonstrations against police violence in the summer of 2020.

Iran, is still thought to enforce the death penalty for same-sex sexual intercourse. In an ever-swinging pendulum, even as some rights are gained, others are contested or taken away; in 2020, during a pandemic, the Trump administration rescinded Obama-era health care protections for transgender people.

The events of 2019 and 2020 have borne out the disproportionate impact of global challenges like climate change and pandemics on the members of marginalized groups. In Africa, at the border of Zimbabwe and Zambia, the Kariba Dam—which was installed by profiteering European colonial powers and the World Bank in the 1950s over the objections of local people—is on the brink of collapse due to climate change. A tsunami will rage through southern Africa when the dam falls. In the United States, enduring and systemic social inequities mean that Black people and indigenous people have a hospitalization rate from COVID-19 five times higher than that of (non-Hispanic) White people, and Hispanic or Latinx people are hospitalized at four times the rate of White people. Worldwide, in 2019 a total of 331 transgender and gender-diverse people were reported murdered, down from 369 in 2018; the majority of the homicides were catalogued in Brazil, and the vast majority of the victims were transgender women of color.

Conclusion: Globalization and Its Discontents

Globalization has had transforming effects, many of them decidedly good for large segments of the world's population, but some of them unsettling. Freer markets and international trade have created a global middle class, pulling nearly half a million Chinese out of poverty, as well as equally huge proportions of the poor in India, Southeast Asia, Egypt, Nigeria, South Africa, and many other communities around the world. Members of the new international middle class communicate with one another, read the same newspapers and journals, see the same films, wear the same clothes, and eat the same foods. Nor is everything made in America, as the Nobel Prize in Literature, the leading film actors of the world, and the major commentators on increasingly international television and radio networks demonstrate. The extremely high economic growth rates enjoyed by states once regarded as part of the developing world—countries like China, India, Brazil, Mexico, Indonesia, South Korea, Kenya, South Africa, and Mozambique, among others—could not have been achieved without international trade networks and significant free trade agreements.

Nonetheless, the negative effects of globalization have been much in evidence, especially since the financial crisis of 2008. While major banks and large multinational corporations were bailed out, the less well-off suffered grievously. In America, the hardest hit were White workers between the ages of forty-five and fifty-four who lacked a high school education. Their death rates became alarmingly high as the result of suicide, drug addiction and overdosing, and alcoholism, bringing about for the first time an overall decline in the average life span of White males. The marginalized no longer remained silent, however. They voted overwhelmingly for Brexit (Britain's departure from the European Union) and contributed to the rise of Islamic militancy, Hindu nationalism, Turkey's turn toward Islamism and authoritarianism, and the increasing popularity of right-wing, ethnic nationalist parties in Europe, many of which oppose immigrant communities and balk at allowing refugees into their countries. In the United States, they elected Donald Trump, thereby turning away from the economic and security agreements that were central to American leadership in the post–World War II period and the initial efforts to contain climate change. In short, globalization has drawn the world more closely together, opening doors for migrants and enhancing the life prospects for many. But trade competition and new technologies have threatened groups who, through a lack in education and skills, are ill equipped to take advantage of globalism's opportunities.

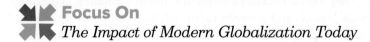

Focus On
The Impact of Modern Globalization Today

The United States, the European Union, and Japan

- Mounting geopolitical and economic uncertainties lead to a rise in populist politics and economic nationalism, expanding state violence, racial justice, and LGBTQ rights.

- The European Union begins to fracture over immigration, domestic terrorism, and support for debtor countries.

- An aging and declining population in Japan requires substantial immigration to fill jobs.

Russia, China, and India

- A return to authoritarianism in Russia and high oil prices increase personal income, state surpluses, and aggressive nationalism.

- China emerges as one of the largest trader and creditor nations, leading to trade frictions, internal inequalities, and authoritarianism.

- India experiences economic growth driven by foreign investment in the information technology sector. High inflation, political corruption, internal divisions (Hindu nationalism), and external divisions (conflicts in Kashmir and Pakistan) weaken economic gains.

The Middle East, Africa, and Latin America

- The Arab Spring generates revolutionary fever over inequality in many countries (Tunisia and Egypt) without creating change; others are torn apart by civil war (Syria) or by militant Islamic groups like ISIS (Iraq). Israeli and Palestinian relations deteriorate; American and Iranian relations worsen.

- While Africa benefits from globalization, many countries struggle with violence and unrest, HIV/AIDS, and other diseases.

- Globalization in Latin America deepens inequalities between wealthy urbanites while factory workers and farmers migrate in search of work elsewhere.

CHRONOLOGY

	2000	2005
Worldwide		The Great Recession 2008–2009
The Americas	9/11 terrorist attacks 2001	Barack Obama elected president of the United States 2008
Europe	Madrid terrorist bombings 2004	
Africa		
Middle East	Invasion of Afghanistan 2001 Invasion of Iraq 2003	
South Asia		
East Asia		

THINKING ABOUT GLOBAL CONNECTIONS

- **Thinking about Worlds Together, Worlds Apart and Twenty-First-Century Challenges** Identify the political, technological, and economic forces that brought into closer contact Europe, Asia, and the Americas, which came to resemble one another as never before, and the forces that excluded developing nations, especially in Africa and Latin America, from those networks of wealth, power, and influence.

- **Thinking about Environmental Impacts and Twenty-First-Century Challenges** Describe the key causal factors driving global climate change and pandemic disease. To what degree are climate change and pandemics connected, and to what degree are they distinct phenomena?

- **Thinking about Changing Power Relationships and Cultural Change and Twenty-First-Century Challenges** How has technological change, especially the emergence of computers and the Internet, changed the transmission of culture worldwide? Where are the leading centers of the film and music industries located today?

Key Terms

Go to INQUIZITIVE to see what you've learned—and learn what you've missed—with personalized feedback along the way.

Further Readings

Chapter 1: Becoming Human

Arsuaga, Juan Luis, *The Neanderthal's Necklace: In Search of the First Thinkers*, trans. Anthony Klatt (2002). A stimulating overview of prehistory that focuses on the Neanderthals and compares them with *Homo sapiens*.

Barham, Lawrence, and Peter Mitchell, *The First Africans: African Archaeology from the Earliest Toolmakers to Most Recent Foragers* (2008). New findings on the evolution of hominids and hominins in Africa.

Barker, Graeme, *Agricultural Revolution in Prehistory: Why Did Foragers Become Farmers?* (2006). The most recent truly global and up-to-date study of this momentous event in world history.

Bellwood, Peter, *First Farmers: The Origins of Agricultural Societies* (2005). A state-of-the-art global history of the origins of agriculture including recent archaeological, linguistic, and microbiological data.

Bender, Michael L., *Paleoclimate* (2013). A definitive overview of the world's climate over the entire life of our universe, written by a renowned geoclimatologist.

Bogucki, Peter, *The Origins of Human Society* (1999). An authoritative overview of prehistory.

Brooke, John L., *Climate Change and the Course of Global History: A Rough Journey* (2014). An excellent overview of the impact of climate on history; particularly useful for the hominin period and the emergence of *Homo sapiens*.

Callaway, Ewen, "Oldest *Homo sapiens* Fossil Claim Rewrites Our Species' History," *Nature News*, June 7, 2017, doi:10.1038/nature.2017.22114. Describes and contextualizes Hublin's (see below) early *Homo sapiens* finds at Jebel Irhoud in Morocco.

Cauvin, Jacques, *The Birth of the Gods and the Origins of Agriculture*, translated by Trevor Watkins from the original 1994 French publication (2000). An important work on the agricultural revolution of Southwest Asia and the evolution of symbolic thinking at this time.

Cavalli-Sforza, Luigi Luca, *Genes, Peoples, and Languages*, translated by Mark Seielstad from the original 1996 French publication (2000). An expert's introduction to the use of gene research for revealing new information about the evolution of human beings in the distant past.

Childe, V. Gordon, *What Happened in History* (1964). A classic work by one of the pioneers in studying the early history and evolution of human beings. Though superseded in many respects, it is still an important place to start one's reading and a work of great power and emotion.

Christian, David, *Maps of Time: An Introduction to Big History* (2004). Offers an outline of Big History from the formation of the universe and planets, to the beginnings of life on earth, to humans, to the modern era; emphasizes the value of examining both collective learning and human extensification/intensification of the earth's resources for making sense of human history at the grandest scale.

Clark, J. Desmond, and Steven A. Brandt (eds.), *From Hunters to Farmers: The Causes and Consequences of Food Production in Africa* (1984). Excellent essays on the agricultural revolution.

Cohen, Mark Nathan, *The Food Crisis in Prehistory: Overpopulation and the Origins of Agriculture* (1977). An older, but pioneering, work on the role of population growth in bringing about the domestication of plants and animals. Although disputed in recent studies, Cohen's work is an important starting point for studying this transformational development.

Coon, Carleton Stevens, *The Story of Man: From the First Human to Primitive Culture and Beyond*, 2nd ed. (1962). An important early work on the evolution of humans, emphasizing the distinctiveness of "races" around the world.

Cunliffe, Barry (ed.), *The Oxford Illustrated Prehistory of Europe* (1994). The definitive work on early European history.

Dalton, Rex, "Peking Man Older Than Thought," *Nature,* March 11, 2009, doi:10.1038/news.2009.149. Describes the use of aluminum-beryllium dating techniques to push back the date for *Homo erectus* (Peking Man) to 770,000 years ago and the implications of this revised date.

Ehrenberg, Margaret, *Women in Prehistory* (1989). What was the role of women in hunting and gathering societies, and how greatly were women affected by the agricultural revolution? The author offers a number of stimulating generalizations.

Ehret, Christopher, *The Civilizations of Africa: A History to 1800* (2002). Although this is a general history of Africa, the author, a linguist and an expert on early African history, offers new information and new overviews of African peoples in very ancient times.

Fagan, Brian, *People of the Earth: An Introduction to World Prehistory* (1989). An authoritative overview of early history, widely used in classrooms.

Fage, J. D., and Roland Oliver (eds.), *The Cambridge History of Africa,* 8 vols. (1975–1984). A pioneering work of synthesis by two of the first and foremost scholars of the history of Africa. Volume 1 deals with African prehistory.

Frison, George C., *Survival by Hunting: Prehistoric Human Predators and Animal Prey* (2004). An archaeologist applies his knowledge of animal habitats, behavior, and hunting strategies to an examination of prehistoric hunting practices in the North American Great Plains and Rocky Mountains.

Gebauer, Anne Birgitte, and T. Douglas Price (eds.), *Transition to Agriculture in Prehistory* (1992). Excellent essays on the agricultural revolution, especially those written by the two editors.

Gibbons, Ann, "World's Oldest *Homo sapiens* Fossils Found in Morocco," *Science,* June 7, 2017, doi:10.1126/science.aan6934. An accessible discussion of Jebel Irhoud fossils that explains how they "fit" the picture of other hominid finds.

Gokhman, David, et al., "Reconstructing Denisovan Anatomy Using DNA Methylation Maps," *Cell* 179 (2019): 180–92. Describes the process by which Gokhman and his team used aDNA to predict possible ways that genetic variations would manifest as physical differences between hypothetical Denisovan skeletons and those of *Homo sapiens* and Neanderthals.

Greshko, Michael, "Earliest Evidence for Humans on the 'Roof of the World' Found," *National Geographic,* November 29, 2018. Discusses evidence (including more than 3,600 stone artifacts) that humans occupied Nwya Devu, a site in the central Tibetan Plateau, 30,000 to 40,000 years ago.

Harari, Yuval Noah, *Sapiens: A Brief History of Humankind* (2015). A largely successful overview of human history from the hominins to the present.

Hershkovitz, Israel, et al., "The Earliest Modern Humans Outside Africa," *Science* 359 (January 26, 2018): 456–59. Reviews the scientific evidence for the *Homo sapiens* fossils found at Mount Carmel, pushing back the date of

Homo sapiens migration out of Africa closer to 180,000 years ago.

Hublin, Jean-Jacques, et al., "New Fossils from Jebel Irhoud, Morocco and the Pan-African Origin of *Homo sapiens*," *Nature* 546 (June 8, 2017): 289–92, doi:10.1038/nature22336. The report from Hublin's team that explains the significance of the Jebel Irhoud site and of the identification of the fossils found there as *Homo sapiens.*

"Inter-Group Violence among the Early Holocene Hunter-Gatherers of West Turkana, Kenya," *Nature* 529 (January 21, 2016): 394–98. Describes a spectacular discovery of the remains of hunters and gatherers who engaged in warfare.

Johanson, Donald, Lenora Johanson, and Blake Edgar, *Ancestors: In Search of Human Origins* (1999). A good overview of human evolution, with insightful essays on *Homo erectus* and *Homo sapiens.*

Johanson, Donald C., and Kate Wong, *Lucy's Legacy: The Quest for Human Origins* (2009). Describes Johanson's initial finding and classification of Lucy, and also reviews new discoveries in paleoanthropology since that important find.

Jones, Steve, Robert Martin, and David Pilbeam (eds.), *The Cambridge Encyclopedia of Human Evolution* (1992). A superb guide to a wide range of subjects, crammed with up-to-date information on the most controversial and obscure topics of human evolution and early history.

Ki-Zerbo, J. (ed.), *Methodology and African Prehistory*, vol. 1 of *General History of Africa* (1981). The first volume of UNESCO's general history of Africa, written for the most part by scholars of African heritage.

Klein, Richard G., and Blake Edgar, *The Dawn of Human Culture* (2002). A fine and reliable guide to the tangled history of human evolution.

Leakey, Richard, *The Origin of Humankind* (1994). A readable and exciting account of human evolution, written by the son of the pioneering archaeologists Louis and Mary Leakey, a scholar of equal stature to his parents.

Lewin, Roger, *The Origin of Modern Humans* (1993). Yet another good overview of human evolution, with useful chapters on early art and the use of symbols.

Lewis-Kraus, Gideon, "Is Ancient DNA Research Revealing New Truths—or Falling into Old Traps?" *New York Times Magazine,* January 17, 2019. Offers an accessible review of David Reich's groundbreaking paleogenetic claims, while leveling challenges against the findings and methods of David Reich and others who use aDNA to chart ancient genomes.

Loewe, Michael, and Edward Shaughnessy (eds.), *The Cambridge History of Ancient China: From the Origins of Civilization to 221 B.C.* (1999). A good review of the archaeology of ancient China.

Mathieson, Iain, et al., "Genome-Wide Patterns of Selection in 230 Ancient Eurasians," *Nature* 522 (November 23, 2015), published online. New DNA research on the skeletons of 230 West-Eurasians who lived between 6500 and 300 BCE shows the three waves of migrations into Europe in its distant past. These migrations came from Africa via Southwest Asia, Anatolia, and the Russian steppes.

Mellaart, James, *Çatal Höyük: A Neolithic Town in Anatolia* (1967). A detailed description of one of the first towns associated with the agricultural revolution in Southwest Asia.

Meredith, Martin, *Born in Africa: The Quest for Human Origins* (2011). A well-written and authoritative overview of the evolution of humankind from the earliest hominins to *Homo sapiens.*

Mithen, Steven, *The Prehistory of the Mind: The Cognitive Origins of Art and Science* (1996). A stimulating discussion of the impact of biological and cultural evolution on the cognitive structure of the human mind.

Olson, Steve, *Mapping Human History: Genes, Race, and Our Common Origins* (2003). Using the findings of genetics and attacking the racial thinking of an earlier generation of archaeologists, the author writes powerfully about the unity of all human beings.

Price, T. Douglas (ed.), *Europe's First Farmers* (2000). A discussion of the agricultural revolution in Europe.

Price, T. Douglas, and Anne Birgitte Gebauer (eds.), *Last Hunters—First Farmers: New Perspectives on the Prehistoric Transition to Agriculture* (1996). An exciting collection of essays by some of the leading scholars in the field studying the transition from hunting and gathering to settled agriculture.

Reich, David, *Who We Are and How We Got Here: Ancient DNA and the New Science of the Human Past* (2018). Offers an overview of the new findings of paleobiologists working with ancient DNA.

Richter, Daniel, et al., "The Age of the Hominin Fossils from Jebel Irhoud, Morocco, and the Origins of the Middle Stone Age," *Nature* 546 (June 8, 2017): 293–96, doi:10.1038/nature22335. Reviews the methods used by scientists to determine the date of the *Homo sapiens* fossils at Jebel Irhoud.

Sahlins, Marshall, "Notes on the Original Affluent Society," in *Man the Hunter,* edited by Richard B. Lee and Irven DeVore (1968), pp. 85–89. Sahlins coined the widely used and now famous expression "affluent society" for hunters and gatherers.

Scarre, Chris (ed.), *The Human Past: World Prehistory and the Development of Human Societies* (2005). An encyclopedia and an overview rolled up into one mammoth volume, written by leading figures in the field of early human history.

Shaw, Thurstan, et al. (eds.), *The Archaeology of Africa: Food, Metals, and Towns* (1993). Up-to-date research on the earliest history of human beings in Africa.

Shreeve, James, "Mystery Man," *National Geographic* 228 (October 2015): 30–57. An authoritative and up-to-date account of the extraordinary discovery of fossil remains of a hominid species, now named *Homo naledi.*

Smith, Bruce D., *The Emergence of Agriculture* (1995). How early humans domesticated wild animals and plants.

Stringer, Christopher, and Robin McKie, *African Exodus: The Origins of Modern Humanity* (1996). Detailed data on why Africa was the source of human origins and why *Homo sapiens* is a recent wanderer out of Africa.

Tattersall, Ian, *The Fossil Trail: How We Know What We Think We Know about Human Evolution* (1995). A passionately written book about early archaeological discoveries and the centrality of Africa in human evolution.

———, *Masters of the Planet: The Search for Our Human Origins* (2012). The most recent survey of human evolution.

———, *The World from Beginnings to 4000 BCE* (2008). A brief up-to-date overview of humanity's early history by a leading authority.

Van Oosterzee, Penny, *Dragon Bones: The Story of Peking Man* (2000). Describes how the late nineteenth-century unearthing of sites in China containing fossils of animals used for medicinal purposes led to the discovery of the fossils of Peking Man.

Wei-Haas, Maya, "DNA Reveals First Look at Enigmatic Human Relative," *National Geographic,* September 19, 2019. Reviews paleogeneticist David Gokhman's work in using ancient DNA to reconstruct the physical traits of Denisovans.

Weiss, Mark L., and Alan E. Mann, *Human Biology and Behavior: An Anthropological Perspective* (1996). The authors stress the contribution that biological research has made and continues to make to the unraveling of the mystery of human evolution.

Wrangham, Richard, *Catching Fire: How Cooking Made Us Human* (2009). The author shows how fire made it possible for humans to have a more varied and richer diet but also one that provided energy for the one organ—the brain—that consumes the most energy.

Chapter 2: Rivers, Cities, and First States, 3500–2000 BCE

Adams, Robert McCormick, *The Evolution of Urban Society* (1966). A classic study of the social, political, and economic processes that led to the development of the first urban civilizations.

Algaze, Guillermo, *Ancient Mesopotamia at the Dawn of Civilization* (2008). A compelling analysis of the complex environmental and social factors underlying the rise of the world's first urban culture in southern Mesopotamia.

———, *The Uruk World System: The Dynamics of Expansion of Early Mesopotamian Civilization* (1993). A compelling argument for the colonization of the Tigris-Euphrates basin by the proto-Sumerians at the end of the fourth millennium BCE.

Andrews, Carol, *Egyptian Mummies* (1998). An illustrated summary of Egyptian mummification and burial practices.

Bagley, Robert, *Ancient Sichuan: Treasures from a Lost Civilization* (2001). Describes the remarkable findings in southwestern China, particularly at Sanxingdui, that have challenged earlier accounts of the Shang dynasty's central role in the rise of early Chinese civilization.

Bar-Yosef, Ofar, and Anatoly Khazanov (eds.), *Pastoralism in the Levant: Archaeological Materials in Anthropological Perspectives* (1992). Classic study of the role of nomads in the development of societies in the Levant during the Neolithic period.

Bruhns, Karen Olsen, *Ancient South America* (1994). The best basic text on pre-Columbian South American cultures.

Butzer, Karl W., *Early Hydraulic Civilization in Egypt: A Study of Cultural Ecology* (1976). The best work on how the Egyptians dealt with the Nile floods and the influence that these arrangements had on the overall organization of society.

Cunliffe, Barry, *By Steppe, Desert, and Ocean: The Birth of Eurasia* (2015). A work that stresses the connections among the societies of China, India, Mesopotamia, Egypt, and Europe.

———, *Europe between the Oceans, 9000 BC–AD 1000* (2008). A very up-to-date and spectacularly illustrated account of early Europe.

Feng, Li, *Early China: A Social and Cultural History* (2013). An important new study on the origins of Chinese culture.

Fukuyama, Francis, *The Origins of Political Order: From Prehistoric Times to the French Revolution* (2011). A superb overview of the powerful political elements that were behind the great river-basin societies in ancient times.

Habu, Junko, *Ancient Jomon of Japan* (2004). Study of prehistoric Jomon hunters and gatherers on the Japanese archipelago that incorporates several different aspects of anthropological studies, including hunter and gatherer archaeology, settlement archaeology, and pottery analysis.

Horden, Peregrine, and Nicholas Purcell, *The Corrupting Sea: A Study of Mediterranean History* (2000). A global overview of the history of the Mediterranean over three millennia.

Jacobsen, Thorkild, *The Treasures of Darkness: A History of Mesopotamian Religion* (1976). Best introduction to the religious and philosophical thought of ancient Mesopotamia.

Kemp, Barry J., *Ancient Egypt: Anatomy of a Civilization* (1989). A synthetic overview of the culture of the pharaohs.

Kramer, Samuel Noah, *The Sumerians: Their History, Culture and Character* (1963). Classic study of the Sumerians and their culture by a pioneer in Sumerian studies.

Liverani, Mario, *The Ancient Near East: History, Society, and Economy* (2014). An important and recent history of Southwest Asia, incorporating the latest scholarship.

Manning, J. G., *The Open Sea: The Economic Life of the Ancient Mediterranean World from the Iron Age to the Rise of Rome* (2018). A survey of the main economic systems of the Mediterranean from the first millennium BCE to the rise of the Roman Empire.

Middleton, Guy D., *Understanding Collapse: Ancient History and Modern Myths* (2017). An important corrective to those who stress climate change as the primary factor undermining the societies in Mesopotamia, Egypt, and the Indus Valley.

Pollock, Susan, *Ancient Mesopotamia: The Eden That Never Was* (1999). An analysis of the social and economic development of Mesopotamia from the beginnings of settlement until the reign of Hammurabi.

Possehl, Gregory L., *Indus Age: The Beginnings* (1999). The second of four volumes analyzing the history of the Indus Valley civilization.

Postgate, J. N., *Early Mesopotamia: Society and Economy at the Dawn of History* (1992). A study of the economic and political development of the Sumerian civilization.

Preziosi, Donald, and L. A. Hitchcock, *Aegean Art and Architecture* (1999). One of the best general guides to the figurative and decorative art produced both by the Minoans and Mycenaeans and by related early societies in the region of the Aegean.

Ratnagar, Shereen, *Trading Encounters: From the Euphrates to the Indus in the Bronze Age,* 2nd ed. (2004). A comprehensive presentation of the evidence for the relationship between the Indus Valley and its western neighbors.

———, *Understanding Harappa: Civilization in the Greater Indus Valley* (2001). An overview, written by a leading Indian archaeologist, on the many features of Harappan civilization, including major settlements, trade, and writing.

Rice, Michael, *Egypt's Legacy: The Archetypes of Western Civilization, 3000–300 BC* (1997). The author argues for the decisive influence of Egyptian culture on the whole of the Mediterranean and its later historical development.

Roaf, Michael, *Cultural Atlas of Mesopotamia and the Ancient Near East* (1990). A comprehensive compendium of the historical and cultural development of the Mesopotamian civilization from the Neolithic background through the Persian Empire.

Scott, James C., *Against the Grain: A Deep History of the Earliest States* (2017). A work by a well-known and prolific sociologist who is intent on demonstrating that the rise of cities and territorial states imposed burdens of exploitation and suffering on most of humankind and destroyed the egalitarianism of pre-city-state life.

Shaw, Ian (ed.), *The Oxford History of Ancient Egypt* (2000). The most up-to-date and comprehensive account of the history of Egypt down to the Greek invasion.

Singh, Ajit, et al., "Counter-intuitive Influence of Himalayan River Morphodynamics on Indus Civilisation Urban Settlements," *Nature Communications* 8, article no. 1617 (2017), doi:10.1038/s41467-017-01643-9. Demonstrates how data from NASA's shuttle topography mission are being used to understand paleochannels of now-dried-up rivers and how those rivers influenced early Indus settlement patterns.

Tallet, Pierre, and Gregory Marouard, "The Harbor of Khufu on the Red Sea Coast at Wadi al-Jarf, Egypt," *Near Eastern Archaeology* 77, no. 1 (2014): 4–14. Accessible description of the archaeological work undertaken at an Egyptian site, arguably the world's oldest harbor. Includes excellent maps and photos of excavated materials, such as storage jars, ship debris, sandstone anchors, and the papyri that contain Merer's records.

Thorp, Robert, *The Chinese Neolithic: Trajectories to Early States* (2005). Uses the latest archaeological evidence to describe the development of early Bronze Age cultures in northern and northwestern China from about 2000 BCE.

Tignor, Robert L., *Egypt: A Short History* (2011). An overview of the history of Egypt from the rise of the pharaohs to the present.

Van de Mieroop, Marc, *A History of Ancient Egypt* (2011). A historian of ancient Southwest Asia undertakes to view Egypt through the lens of his interest in ancient cities and territorial states.

Wachsmann, Shelley, *Seagoing Ships and Seamanship in the Bronze Age Levant* (1998). Provides a compelling, in-depth, and well-documented review of the evidence for ships from several Bronze Age seafaring peoples (including Egyptians, Mycenaeans, and Sea Peoples) and also discusses activities such as shipbuilding, navigation, and piracy.

Wright, Rita P., *The Ancient Indus: Urbanism, Economy, and Society* (2010). A reconstruction of the Indus society with updated archaeological data.

Chapter 3: Nomads, Territorial States, and Microsocieties, 2000–1200 BCE

Allan, Sarah, *The Shape of the Turtle: Myth, Art, and Cosmos in Early China* (1991). Explains the roles of divination and sacrifice in artistic representations of the Shang cosmology.

Allen, James P., *Middle Egyptian: An Introduction to the Language and Culture of Hieroglyphs* (2000). An introduction to the system of writing and its use in ancient Egypt.

Anthony, David W., *The Horse, the Wheel, and Language: How Bronze-Age Riders from the Eurasian Steppes Shaped the Modern World* (2007). A superb analysis of the origins and spread of the Indo-European peoples.

Arnold, Dieter, *Building in Ancient Egypt: Pharaonic Stone Masonry* (1996). Details the complex construction of monumental stone architecture in ancient Egypt.

Baines, John, and Jaromir Málek, *Atlas of Ancient Egypt* (1980). Useful compilation of information on ancient Egyptian society, religion, history, and geography.

Beal, Richard H., *The Organization of the Hittite Military* (1992). A detailed study based on textual sources of the world's first chariot-based army.

Behringer, Wolfgang, *A Cultural History of Climate* (2010). A general history of the impact of climate on many different societies.

Bell, Barbara, "The Dark Ages in Ancient History. I. The First Dark Age in Egypt," *American Journal of Archaeology* 75 (January 1971): 1–26. An environmental analysis of the decline of the Old Kingdom and the emergence of the First Intermediate Period.

Bogucki, Peter, and Pam J. Crabtree (eds.), *Ancient Europe 8000 BC–AD 1000: Encyclopedia of the Barbarian World*, 2 vols. (2004). An indispensable handbook on the economic, social, artistic, and religious life in Europe during this period.

Breasted, James Henry (trans.), *Ancient Records of Egypt: Historical Documents from the Earliest Times to the Persian Conquest*, 5 vols. (1906). Breasted's five-volumes offer a collection of translated Egyptian inscriptions arranged by dynasty that give insight into a wide range of issues, including trade, military campaigns, royal edicts, biographical information of pharaohs, and religion.

Bruhns, Karen Olsen, *Ancient South America* (1994). The best basic text on pre-Columbian South American cultures.

Bryant, Edwin, *The Quest for the Origins of Vedic Culture: The Indo-Aryan Migration Debate* (2001). Insight into the highly charged debate on who the Indo-European speakers were, where they originated, and where they migrated to.

Castleden, Rodney, *The Mycenaeans* (2005). One of the best current surveys of all aspects of the Mycenaean Greeks.

Chadwick, John, *The Decipherment of Linear B*, 2nd ed. (1968). Not only a retelling of the story of the decipherment of the Linear B script, but also an introduction to the actual content and function of the tablets themselves.

Childs-Johnson, Elizabeth, "Fu Zi, the Shang Woman Warrior," in Lily Xiao Hong Lee, A. D. Stefanowska, and Sue Wiles (eds.), *Biographical Dictionary of Chinese Women, Antiquity through Sui, 1600 B.C.E.–618 C.E.* (2007), pp. 19–25. Offers a biography of Fu Hao (Fu Zi) that summarizes much Chinese-language scholarship as well as a thorough discussion of the items found in her tomb.

Cline, Eric H., *1177 B.C.: The Year Civilization Collapsed* (2014). An engaging account, drawing on a wide array of archaeological and literary evidence, that discusses the many factors—including internal political turmoil, invasions (like those of the Sea Peoples), and disruption of international trade—that contributed to a "systems collapse" at the end of the Mediterranean Bronze Age.

_____, *Sailing the Wine-Dark Sea: International Trade and the Late Bronze Age Aegean* (1994). An excellent account of the trade and contacts between the Aegean and other areas of the Mediterranean, Europe, and the Near East during the late Bronze Age.

Cunliffe, Barry, *Facing the Ocean: The Atlantic and Its Peoples, 8000 BC–AD 1500* (2001). An in-depth, highly useful treatment of western Europe during this period.

_____ (ed.), *Prehistoric Europe: An Illustrated History* (1997). A state-of-the-art treatment of first farmers, agricultural developments, and material culture in prehistoric Europe.

Curry, Andrew, "Slaughter at the Bridge," *Science* 351 (March 25, 2016): 1384–89. New information on a battle among hunting and gathering warriors in northern Europe in the thirteenth century BCE.

Davis, W. V., and L. Schofield, *Egypt, the Aegean and the Levant: Interconnections in the Second Millennium BC* (1995). A discussion of the complex interactions in the eastern Mediterranean during the "international age."

Doumas, Christos, *Thera: Pompeii of the Ancient Aegean* (1983). A study of the tremendous volcanic eruption and explosion that destroyed the Minoan settlement on the island of Thera.

Drews, Robert, *Coming of the Greeks: Indo-European Conquests in the Aegean and the Near East* (1988). A good survey of the evidence for the "invasions" or "movements of peoples" that reconfigured the world of the eastern Mediterranean and Near East.

Finley, M. I., *The World of Odysseus*, 2nd rev. ed. (1977; reprint, 2002). The classic work that describes what might be recovered about the social values and behaviors of men and women in the so-called Dark Ages of early Greek history.

Frankfort, Henri, *Ancient Egyptian Religion: An Interpretation* (1948; reprint, 2000). A classic study of Egyptian religion and culture during the pharaonic period.

Frayne, Douglas R., *The Royal Inscriptions of Mesopotamia, Early Periods*, vol. 4., *Old Babylonian Period, 2003–1595 BC.* (1990). A standard and still-useful study of this period in Babylonian history.

Keightley, David N., *The Ancestral Landscape: Time, Space, and Community in Late Shang China, ca. 1200–1045 BC* (2000). Provides insights into the nature of royal kinship that under-girded the Shang court and its regional domains.

Kemp, Barry J., *Ancient Egypt: Anatomy of a Civilization* (2006). A definitive presentation of the history, culture, and religion of ancient Egypt.

Klein, Jacob, "The Marriage of Martu: The Urbanization of 'Barbaric' Nomads," in Meir Malul (ed.), *Mutual Influences of Peoples and Cultures in the Ancient Near East* (1996). A crucial text in the corpus of scholarship on Sumerian literature.

Kristiansen, Kristian, *Europe before History* (1998). The finest recent survey of all the major developmental phases of European prehistory.

McIntosh, Jane, *Handbook to Life in Prehistoric Europe* (2006). Highlights the archaeological evidence that enables us to re-create the day-to-day life of different prehistoric communities in Europe.

Pines, Yuri, *The Everlasting Empire: The Political Culture of Ancient China and Its Imperial Legacy* (2012). How imperial unity became the norm in ancient China.

Preziosi, Donald, and L. A. Hitchcock, *Aegean Art and Architecture* (1999). One of the best general guides to the figurative and decorative art produced both by the Minoans and Mycenaeans and by related early societies in the region of the Aegean.

Quirke, Stephen, *Ancient Egyptian Religion* (1992). A highly readable presentation of ancient Egyptian religion that summarizes the roles and attributions of the many Egyptian gods.

The Rigveda, the Earliest Religious Poetry of India, trans. Stephanie W. Jamison and Joel P. Brereton (2014). A new translation of the earliest literature of South Asia, correcting errors made in earlier translations.

Robins, Gay, *The Art of Ancient Egypt* (1997). The most comprehensive survey to date of the art of pharaonic Egypt.

———, *Women in Ancient Egypt* (1993). An interesting survey of the place of women in ancient Egyptian society.

Romer, John, *Ancient Lives: Daily Life in Egypt of the Pharaohs* (1990). A discussion of the economic and social lives of everyday ancient Egyptians.

Roth, Martha T., *Law Collections from Mesopotamia and Asia Minor* (1995). An assemblage of law codes from Southwest Asia, including Hammurabi's famous legal edicts.

Sandars, N. K., *The Sea Peoples: Warriors of the Ancient Mediterranean* (1985). A readable discussion of a very complex period of Levantine history.

Simpson, William Kelly (ed.), *The Literature of Ancient Egypt: An Anthology of Stories, Instructions, and Poetry* (1972). A compilation of the most important works of literature from ancient Egypt.

Thapar, Romila, *The Past before Us: Historical Tradition of Early North India* (2013). A comprehensive evaluation of ancient Indian literature.

Thorp, Robert L., *China in the Early Bronze Age: Shang Civilization* (2005). Reviews the archaeological discoveries near Anyang, site of two capitals of the Shang kings.

Van De Mieroop, Marc, *King Hammurabi of Babylon: A Biography* (2004). A useful biography of an important Babylonian ruler and lawgiver.

Warren, Peter, *The Aegean Civilizations: From Ancient Crete to Mycenae*, 2nd ed. (1989). An excellent textual and pictorial guide to all the basic aspects of the Minoan and Mycenaean societies.

Wilson, John A., *The Culture of Ancient Egypt* (1951). A classic study of the history and culture of pharaonic Egypt.

Yadin, Yigael, *The Art of Warfare in Biblical Lands in the Light of Archaeological Discovery* (1963). A well-illustrated presentation of the machinery of war in the second and first millennia BCE.

Yoffee, Norman (ed.), *The Cambridge World History*, vol. 3, *Early Cities in Comparative Perspective* (2014). One of nine volumes that trace world history through individual articles written by experts.

Chapter 4: First Empires and Common Cultures in Afro-Eurasia, 1250–325 BCE

Ahlström, Gosta W., *The History of Ancient Palestine from the Paleolithic Period to Alexander's Conquests* (1993). An excellent survey of the history of the region by a renowned expert, with good attention to the recent archaeological evidence.

Assmann, Jan, *The Invention of Religion: Faith and Covenant in the Book of Exodus*, trans. Robert Savage (2018). An exposition by an expert on the evolution of early religions and a claim for the importance of the book of Exodus as the foundational work of monotheism.

Astour, Michael, "New Evidence on the Last Days of Ugarit," *American Journal of Archaeology* 69 (1965). An early and important article on the destruction of important cities in the Levant in the twelfth century BCE.

Aubet, Maria Eugenia, *The Phoenicians and the West*, 2nd ed. (2001). The basic survey of the Phoenician colonization of the western Mediterranean and Atlantic, with special attention to recent archaeological discoveries.

Behringer, Wolfgang, *A Cultural History of Climate*, trans. Patrick Camiller (2010). A summary view of the place of climate in historical change, written by an expert in historical climatology.

Benjamin, Craig (ed.), *The Cambridge World History*, vol. 4, *A World with States, Empires, and Networks, 1200 BCE–900 CE* (2015). An important overview of developments in the world, with individual chapters written by experts.

Briant, Pierre, *From Cyrus to Alexander: A History of the Persian Empire*, trans. Peter T. Daniels (2002). A complex and comprehensive history of the Persian Empire by its finest modern scholar.

Bright, John, *A History of Israel*, 4th ed. (2000). An updated version of a classic and still very useful overview of the whole history of the Israelite people down to the end of the period covered in this chapter.

Cook, J. M., *The Persian Empire* (1983). An older but still useful, and highly readable, standard history of the Persian Empire.

Fagan, Brian, *The Long Summer: How Climate Changed Civilization* (2004). An accessible overview of the role of climate in historical change, written by one of the leading historians of ancient history and an individual who has brought together considerable evidence about climate change and historical development.

Falkenhausen, Lothar von, *Chinese Society in the Age of Confucius (1000–250 BC): The Archaeological Evidence* (2006). A timely reassessment of early Chinese history that compares the literary texts on which it has traditionally been based with the new archaeological evidence.

Frahm, Eckart (ed.), *A Companion to Assyria* (2017). The work of expert Assyriologists and hence the most up-to-date study of these ancient states.

Frye, Richard N., *The Heritage of Persia* (1963). This classic study of ancient Iran gives the political and literary history of the Persians and their successors.

Fukuyama, Francis, *The Origins of Political Order: From Prehuman Times to the French Revolution* (2011). Argues that the first real kings in Chinese history and the first real states and dynasties did not appear until the Qin and Han.

Grayson, A. K., "Assyrian Civilization," in *Cambridge Ancient History*, vol. 3, pt. 2, pp. 194–228 (1992). The Neo-Assyrian and Neo-Babylonian

Empires and other states of the Near East, from the eighth to the sixth century BCE.

Hornung, Erik, *Akhenaten and the Religion of Light*, translated from the German by David Lorton (1999). An important, brief biography of Egypt's most controversial pharaoh.

———, *History of Ancient Egypt: An Introduction*, translated from the German by David Lorton (1999). An accessible overview of the history of ancient Egypt by a leading Egyptologist.

Isserlin, Benedikt J., *The Israelites* (1998). A very well-written and heavily illustrated history of all aspects of life in the regions of the Levant inhabited by the Israelites, equally good on the latest scholarship and the archaeological data.

Keay, John, *India: A History* (2010). A useful, readable overview of the sweep of Indian history.

Lancel, Serge, *Carthage: A History*, trans. Antonia Nevill (1997). By far the best single-volume history of the most important Phoenician colony in the Mediterranean (the first three chapters are especially relevant to materials covered in this chapter).

Lemche, Niels Peter, *Ancient Israel: A New History of Israelite Society* (1988). A quick, readable, and still up-to-date summary of the main phases and themes.

Lewis, Mark Edward, *Writing and Authority in Early China* (1999). A work that traces the changing uses of writing to command assent and obedience in early China.

Liu, Guozhong, *Introduction to the Tsinghua Bamboo-Strip Manuscripts*, trans. Christopher J. Foster and William N. French (2016). An important essay on the implications of these texts for our understanding of early Western Zhou history.

Liverani, Mario, *The Ancient Near East: History, Society and Economy* (2014). Parts 5 and 6 are especially relevant to the materials covered in this chapter.

Luckenbill, Daniel David, *Ancient Records of Assyria and Babylonia*, vol. 1, *Historical Records of Assyria from the Earliest Times to Sargon* (1926). Luckenbill's English translations of Neo-Assyrian documents (mostly inscriptions), arranged chronologically by king's reign, provide insight into Neo-Assyrian politics, religion, building programs, and much more. A short introduction accompanies each translation.

Markoe, Glenn E., *Phoenicians* (2000). A thorough survey of the Phoenicians and their society as it first developed in the Levant and then expanded over the Mediterranean, with excellent illustrations of the diverse archaeological sites.

Matthews, Victor H., and Don C. Benjamin, *Social World of Ancient Israel, 1350–587 BCE* (1993). A thematic overview of the main occupational groups and social roles that characterized ancient Israelite society.

Oates, Joan, and David Oates, *Nimrud: An Assyrian Imperial City Revealed* (2001). A fine and highly readable summary of the state of our knowledge of the Neo-Assyrian Empire from the perspective of the early capital of Ashurnasirpal II.

Oded, Bustenay, *Mass Deportations and Deportees in the Neo-Assyrian Empire* (1979). A detailed textual examination of the deportation strategy of the Neo-Assyrian kings. Good for in-depth research of the question.

Potts, D. T., *The Archaeology of Elam: Formation and Transformation of an Ancient Iranian State* (1999). The definitive study of the archaeology of western Iran from the Neolithic period through the Persian Empire.

Quinn, Josephine C., and Nicholas C. Vella (eds.), *The Punic Mediterranean* (2014). A valuable and readable collection of chapters on various aspects of how the Phoenician colonization of the Mediterranean led to the formation of new cultural identities.

Radner, Karen, *Ancient Assyria: A Very Short Introduction* (2015). A highly readable and up-to-date survey of all the important aspects of Neo-Assyrian government and society.

———, "The Neo-Assyrian Empire," in Michael Gehler and Robert Rollinger (eds.), *Imperien und Reiche in der Weltgeschichte* (2014), pp. 101–20. An outstanding overview by one of the most learned historians of ancient Assyria.

Shaughnessy, Edward L., *Sources of Western Zhou History: Inscribed Bronze Vessels* (1992). Detailed work on the historiography and interpretation of the thousands of ritual bronze vessels discovered by China's archaeologists.

Stein, Burton, *A History of India*, 2nd ed., edited by David Arnold (2010). One of the standard general histories of India, brought up to date by a leading historian of the subcontinent.

Tanner, Harold M., *China: A History* (2009). A readable and up-to-date overview of the sweep of Chinese history.

Thapar, Romila, *The Aryan: Recasting Constructs* (2011). On the rise of the theory of an Aryan race and the beginnings of Indian history.

———, *From Lineage to State* (1984). The only book on early India that uses religious literature historically and analyzes major lineages to reveal the transition from tribal society to state institutions.

Tignor, Robert L., *Egypt: A Short History* (2010). A succinct treatment of the entire history of Egypt from the pharaohs to the present, with three chapters on the ancient period.

Trautmann, Thomas, *India: Brief History of a Civilization* (2011). A highly readable survey of Indian history with emphasis on its early history.

Tubb, Jonathan N., *Canaanites* (1998). This well-illustrated book is the best recent survey of one of the main ethnic groups dominating the culture of the Levant.

Wunsch, Cornelia, "The Egibi Family," in Gwendolyn Leick (ed.), *The Babylonian World* (2007), pp. 232–42. An Assyriologist and expert on the Egibi family archive reviews the family connections and the wide-ranging business dealings reflected in this unique and valuable collection of Neo-Babylonian records.

Chapter 5: Worlds Turned Inside Out, 1000–350 BCE

Adams, William Y., *Nubia: Corridor to Africa* (1977). The authoritative historical overview of Nubia, the area of present-day Sudan just south of Egypt and a geographic connecting point between the Mediterranean and sub-Saharan Africa.

Allan, Sarah, *Buried Ideas: Legends of Abdication and Ideal Government in Early Chinese Bamboo-Slip Manuscripts* (2016). Four recently discovered Warring States texts challenge long-standing ideas about Chinese intellectual history.

Armstrong, Karen, *Buddha* (2001). A readable and impressive account of the life of the Buddha.

———, *The Great Transformation: The Beginning of Our Religious Traditions* (2006). A thorough investigation of a key moment in the evolution of religious thought, explaining the traditions that arose in the ninth century BCE in four regions of the civilized world as a response to the violence of the period.

Aubet, Maria Eugenia, *The Phoenicians and the West*, 2nd ed. (2001). The basic survey of the Phoenician colonization of the western Mediterranean and Atlantic, with special attention to recent archaeological discoveries.

Barker, Graeme, and Tom Rasmussen, *The Etruscans* (1998). The most up-to-date introduction to this important pre-Roman society in the Italian Peninsula, with strong emphasis on broad social and material patterns of development as indicated by the archaeological evidence.

Beckwith, Christopher I., *The Greek Buddha: Pyrrho's Encounter with Early Buddhism in Central Asia* (2015). A pioneering work on the introduction of Buddhist views into the Greek philosophical scene.

Bellah, Robert N., "What Is Axial about the Axial Age?" *European Journal of Sociology* 46, no. 1 (2005): 69–89. A useful categorical analysis of the four cases of axial "breakthrough"—ancient Israel, Greece, India, and China.

Benjamin, Craig (ed.), *The Cambridge World History*, vol. 4, *A World with States, Empires, and Networks, 1200 BCE–900 CE* (2015). Essays by experts on these centuries in world history. Especially important for thinking about the Axial Age is the chapter by Bjorn Wittrock, "The Axial Age in World History," pp. 101–19.

Bresson, Alain, *The Making of the Ancient Greek Economy: Institutions, Markets, and Growth in the City-States*, trans. Steven Rendall (2015). The most conceptually sophisticated and factually up-to-date account of the economic regimes of the Greek city-states.

Bruhns, Karen Olsen, *Ancient South America* (1994). A very useful overview of recent debates and conclusions about pre-Columbian archaeology in South America, including both the Andes and the lowland and coastal regions.

Burkert, Walter, *Greek Religion*, trans. John Raffan (1985). The best one-volume introduction to early Greek religion, placing the Greeks in their larger Mediterranean and Near Eastern contexts.

Cartledge, Paul (ed.), *The Cambridge Illustrated History of Ancient Greece* (2002). An excellent history of the Greek city-states down to the time of Alexander the Great.

Chakravarti, Uma, *The Social Dimensions of Early Buddhism* (1987). A description of the life of the Buddha drawn from early Buddhist texts.

Cho-yun, Hsu, *Ancient China in Transition* (1965). An account of the political, economic, social, and intellectual changes that occurred during the Warring States period.

Coarelli, Filippo (ed.), *Etruscan Cities* (1975). A brilliantly and lavishly illustrated guide to the material remains of the Etruscans: their cities, their magnificent tombs, and their architecture, painting, sculpture, and other art.

Coe, Michael, et al. (eds.), *The Olmec World: Ritual and Rulership* (1996). A collection of field-synthesizing articles with important illustrations, based on one of the most comprehensive exhibitions of Olmec art in the world.

Confucius, *The Analects (Lun Yü)*, trans. D. C. Lau (1979). An outstanding translation of the words of Confucius as recorded by his major disciples. Includes valuable historical material needed to provide the context for Confucius's teachings.

Eisenstadt, S. N. (ed.), *The Origins and Diversity of the Axial Age* (1986). An important, original analysis of the great ancient civilizations and a systematic exploration of the conditions under which they developed.

Elman, Benjamin A., and Martin Kern (eds.), *Statecraft and Classical Learning: The Rituals of Zhou in East Asian History* (2010). Traces the long-term political rise of classical learning and state rituals in East Asia from the decline of the Eastern Zhou kingdom to the rise of later imperial dynasties in China, Japan, and Korea.

Falkenhausen, Lothar von, *Chinese Society in the Age of Confucius (100–250 BC)* (2006). The larger Chinese society under the influence of Confucian thought.

Finley, M. I., and H. W. Pleket, *The Olympic Games: The First Thousand Years* (2005). A fine description of the most famous of the Greek games; it explains how they exemplify the competitive spirit that marked many aspects of the Greek city-states.

Garlan, Yvon, *Slavery in Ancient Greece*, trans. Janet Lloyd (1988). A treatment of the emergence, development, and institutionalization of "chattel slavery" in the Greek city-states.

———, *War in the Ancient World: A Social History*, trans. Janet Lloyd (1976). A discussion of the emergence of the forms of warfare, including male citizens fighting in hoplite phalanxes and the development of siege warfare, that were typical of the Greek city-states.

Iliffe, John, *Africans: The History of a Continent*, 2nd ed. (2007). A first-rate scholarly survey of Africa from its beginnings, with a strong emphasis on demography.

Jaspers, Karl, *The Origin and Goal of History*, trans. Michael Bullock (1953). A book that reckons with the philosophy of the history of humankind and heightens our awareness of the present by locating it within the framework of the obscurity of prehistory.

Kagan, Donald, *The Peloponnesian War* (2004). A vivid description of the war that pitted the major Greek city-states, including Athens and Sparta, against one another over the latter half of the fifth century BCE.

Lancel, Serge, *Carthage: A History*, trans. Antonia Nevill (1997). By far the best single-volume history of the most important Phoenician colony in the Mediterranean.

Lewis, Mark Edward, *Sanctioned Violence in Early China* (1990). An analysis of the use of sanctioned violence as an element of statecraft from the Warring States period to the formation of the Qin and Han Empires in the second half of the first millennium BCE.

———, *Writing and Authority in Early China* (1999). A revisionist account of the central role of writing and persuasion in models for the invention of a Chinese world empire.

Ling, Trevor, *The Buddha: Buddhist Civilization in India and Ceylon* (1972). An overview of Buddhism in India and Ceylon.

Lloyd, G. E. R., *Early Greek Science: Thales to Aristotle* (1970). An especially clear and concise introduction to the main developments and intellectuals that marked the emergence of critical secular thinking in the early Greek world.

Lloyd, G. E. R., and Nathan Sivin, *The Way and the Word: Science and Medicine in Early China and Greece* (2002). A comprehensive rethinking of the social and political settings in ancient China and city-state Greece that contributed to the different views of science and medicine that emerged in each place.

Morris, Ian, and Walter Scheidel (eds.), *The Dynamics of Ancient Empires: State Power from Assyria to Byzantium* (2010). A work by experts on ancient empires and city-states. The essay by Ian Morris on Athens is especially useful.

Mote, Frederick, *Intellectual Foundations of China* (1971). An early but still useful description of the seminal figures in China's early intellectual life.

Murray, Oswyn, *Early Greece*, 2nd ed. (1993). One of the best introductions to the emergence of the Greek city-states down to the end of the Archaic Age.

Ober, Josiah, *The Rise and Fall of Classical Greece* (2015). A compelling general interpretation of the rise of the Greek city-states in the sixth and fifth centuries BCE and their subsequent demise in the fourth century BCE.

Osborne, Robin, *Archaic and Classical Greek Art* (1998). An outstanding book that clearly explains the main innovations in Greek art, setting them in their historical context.

———, *Greece in the Making, 1200–479 BC* (1999). The standard history of the whole early period of the Greek city-states, characterized by an especially fine and judicious mix of archaeological data and literary sources.

Pallottino, Massimo, *The Etruscans*, rev. ed., trans. J. Cremona (1975). A fairly traditional but still classic survey of all aspects of Etruscan history and political and social institutions.

Pines, Yuri, Paul R. Goldin, and Martin Kern (eds.), *Ideology of Power and Power of Ideology in Early China* (2015). A new assessment of state ideology and political legitimation under the Eastern Zhou dynasty during the Warring States era.

Provan, Iain, *Convenient Myths: The Axial Age, Dark Green Religion, and the World That Never Was* (2013). An illumination of two deeply rooted myths—the first being Karl Jaspers's construct of world religions spontaneously emerging from a shared set of values, the second being David Suzuki's assertion that organized religion severed society's previous connection with nature—and their dangers.

Rayor, Diane J., and André Lardinois, *Sappho: A New Translation of the Complete Works* (2014). Offers commentary about the identification and reconstruction of the Sapphic fragments, as well as authentic and readable translations of the Greek.

Redford, Donald B., *From Slave to Pharaoh: The Black Experience of Ancient Egypt* (2004). A description of Egypt's twenty-fifth dynasty, which was made up of Sudanese conquerors.

The Sayings of Lao Tzu, trans. Lionel Giles (1904). A translated collection of Master Lao's sayings, which offer a third-century BCE expression of Daoist philosophy.

Schaberg, David, *A Patterned Past: Form and Thought in Early Chinese Historiography* (2002). A comprehensive study of the intellectual content of historical anecdotes by the followers of Confucius collected around the fourth century BCE.

Schaps, David, *The Invention of Coinage and the Monetization of Ancient Greece* (2004). A new analysis that offers a broad overview of the emergence of coined money in the Near East and the eastern Mediterranean and its effects on the spread of money-based markets.

Sharma, J. P., *Republics in Ancient India, c. 1500 B.C.–500 B.C.* (1968). Relying on information from early Buddhist texts, this book first revealed that South Asia had not only monarchies but also alternative polities.

Shaw, Thurston, *Nigeria: Its Archaeology and Early History* (1978). An important introduction to the early history of Nigeria by one of that country's leading archaeologists.

Shinnie, P. L., *Ancient Nubia* (1996). An excellent account of the history of the ancient Nubians, who, we are discovering, had great influence on Egypt and on the rest of tropical Africa.

Snodgrass, Anthony, *Archaic Greece: The Age of Experiment* (1981). A good introduction to the archaeological evidence of Archaic Greece.

Taylor, Christopher, Richard Hare, and Jonathan Barnes, *Greek Philosophers* (1999). A fine, succinct, one-volume introduction to the major aspects of the three big thinkers who dominated the high period of classical Greek philosophy: Socrates, Plato, and Aristotle.

Torok, Laszlo, *Meroe: Six Studies on the Cultural Identity of an Ancient African State* (1995). A good collection of essays on Meroe.

Welsby, Derek A., *The Kingdom of Kush: The Napatan and Meroitic Empires* (1996). A fine book on these two important Nubian kingdoms.

Chapter 6: Shrinking the Afro-Eurasian World, 350–100 BCE

al Quntar, Salam, and Brian A. Daniels, "Responses to the Destruction of Syrian Cultural Heritage: A Critical Review of Current Efforts," *International Journal of Islamic Architecture* 5, no. 2 (2016): 381–97. Describes the work of the Safeguarding the Heritage of Syria and Iraq (SHOSI) project to empower local "heritage activists" to document, protect, and raise awareness of the threats to Syrian cultural heritage

Bogdanos, Matthew, *Thieves of Baghdad: One Marine's Passion to Recover the World's Greatest Stolen Treasures* (2005). U.S. Marine Corps colonel, lawyer, and National Humanities Medal–winner Bogdanos offers a compelling first-person narrative of his team's work to track down thousands of antiquities looted from Baghdad's National Museum in the aftermath of the U.S. invasion in 2003.

Bradley, Keith, *Slavery and Rebellion in the Roman World, 140 B.C.–70 B.C.* (1989). A description of the rise of large-scale plantation slavery in Sicily and Italy, and a detailed account of the three great slave wars.

Bresson, Alain, *The Making of the Ancient Greek Economy: Markets and Growth in the City-States*, trans. Steven Rendall (2015). An up-to-date and theoretically well-informed analysis of the market economics of the Greek city-states in the Hellenistic era.

Briant, Pierre, *Alexander the Great and His Empire: A Short Introduction*, translated by Amélie Kuhrt from a work originally published in 1974 and revised in 2005 (2010). A classic account of Alexander the Great's life.

Browning, Iain, *Palmyra* (1979). A narrative of the history of the important desert city that linked eastern and western trade routes.

Carney, Elizabeth, *Olympias: Mother of Alexander the Great* (2006). Carney explores the hostile ancient sources that describe the role of Olympias in late fourth-century BCE political intrigue to peel back the gender-based critique and offer a more nuanced and sympathetic understanding of her actions and motivations.

Casson, Lionel, *The Periplus Maris Erythraei* (1989). An introduction to a typical ancient sailing manual, this one of the Red Sea and Indian Ocean.

————, *Ships and Seamanship in the Ancient World* (1995). The classic account of the ships and sailors that powered commerce and war on the high seas.

Colledge, Malcolm, *The Art of Palmyra* (1976). A well-illustrated introduction to the unusual art of Palmyra with its mixture of eastern and western elements.

Convention on the Means of Prohibiting and Preventing the Illicit Import, Export and Transfer of Ownership of Cultural Property 1970 (Paris, November 14, 1970), http://portal.unesco.org/en/ev.php-URL_ID=13039&URL_DO=DO_TOPIC&URL_SECTION=201.html. This document records the UNESCO agreement that limits illegal trade in cultural property, with the goals of both reducing the black market for art, artifacts, and manuscripts and returning improperly removed items to their rightful place of origin. It includes several post-2000 reports from member states.

Fowler, Barbara H., *The Hellenistic Aesthetic* (1989). How the artists in this new age saw and portrayed their world in new and different ways.

Green, Peter, *Alexander to Actium: The Historical Evolution of the Hellenistic Age* (1990). The best general guide to the whole period in all of its various aspects, and well illustrated.

Habicht, Christian, *Athens from Alexander to Antony,* trans. Deborah L. Schneider (1997). The authoritative account of what happened to the great city-state of Athens in this period.

Hansen, Valerie, *The Silk Road: A New History* (2012). A recent work on the Silk Roads; authoritative on the eastern terminus of this vital trade route.

Harmanşah, Ömür, "ISIS, Heritage, and the Spectacles of Destruction in the Global Media," *Near Eastern Archaeology* 78, no. 3 (September 2015): 170–77. Considers the voyeuristic element of the world's consumption of images of ISIS's destruction of cultural heritage, characterizing ISIS's behavior not as iconoclasm but rather as "iconoclash."

Herodotus, *The Histories,* 4 vols., trans. Tom Holland (2013). A basic work, which many scholars regard as the first world history.

Holt, Frank L., *Thundering Zeus: The Making of Hellenistic Bactria* (1999). A basic history of the most eastern of the kingdoms spawned by the conquests of Alexander the Great.

Hopkirk, Peter, *Foreign Devils on the Silk Road* (1984). A historiography of the explorations and researches on the central Asian Silk Roads in the nineteenth and early twentieth centuries.

Juliano, Annette L., and Judith A. Lerner (eds.), *Nomads, Traders and Holy Men along China's Silk Road* (2003). A description of the travelers along the Silk Roads in human terms, focusing on warfare, markets, and religion.

Kosmin, Paul J., *The Land of the Elephant Kings: Space, Territory, and Ideology in the Seleucid Empire* (2014). The best current analysis of the relationships of Seleucid kings, both with their own subjects and, especially, with the Mauryan kingdom of India and the nomadic peoples of central Asia.

Kuzima, E. E., *The Prehistory of the Silk Road* (2008). Valuable information on the early history of the Silk Roads.

Lane Fox, Robin, *Alexander the Great* (1973). Still the most readable and in many ways the sanest biography of the world conqueror.

Lewis, Naphtali, *Greeks in Ptolemaic Egypt* (1986). An account of the relationships between Greeks and Egyptians as seen through the lives of individual Greek settlers and colonists.

Liu, Xinru, *Ancient India and Ancient China* (1988). The first work to connect political and economic developments in India and China with the evolution and spread of Buddhism in the first half of the first millennium.

————, *The Silk Road in World History* (2010). A study of the history of the great trade and communications routes that connected the different regions of Afro-Eurasia between the third century BCE and the thirteenth century CE.

Long, Antony A., *Hellenistic Philosophy: Stoics, Epicureans, Sceptics*, 2nd ed. (1986). One of the clearest guides to the main new trends in Greek philosophical thinking in the period.

Manning, J. G., *The Last Pharaohs: Egypt under the Ptolemies, 305–30 BC* (2010). An important work on the way the Ptolemy dynasty merged Greek and Egyptian institutions.

Martin, Luther H., *Hellenistic Religions: An Introduction* (1987). An introduction to the principal new Hellenistic religions and cults that emerged in this period.

Mendels, Doron, *The Rise and Fall of Jewish Nationalism* (1992). A sophisticated account of the various phases of Jewish resistance in Judea to foreign domination.

Miller, James Innes, *The Spice Trade of the Roman Empire, 29 B.C. to A.D. 641* (1969). A first-rate study of the spice trade in the Roman Empire.

Penrose, Walter Duvall, Jr., *Postcolonial Amazons: Female Masculinity and Courage in Ancient Greek and Sanskrit Literature* (2016). A theoretically inflected exploration of Greek (Athenian and non-Athenian) ideas about female masculinity and a range of warrior women—from Artemisia of Caria (who fought on the side of the Persians against the Greeks), to Hellenistic warrior queens, to Persian and Indian female bodyguards—to historicize Greek legends of the Amazons.

Pomeroy, Sarah B., *Women in Hellenistic Egypt: From Alexander to Cleopatra* (1990). A highly readable investigation of women and family in the best-documented region of the Hellenistic world.

Ray, Himanshu P., *The Wind of Change: Buddhism and the Maritime Links of Early South Asia* (1994). Ray's study of Buddhism and maritime trade stretches from the Arabian Sea to the navigations between South Asia and Southeast Asia.

Rosenfield, John, *The Dynastic Art of the Kushans* (1967). Instead of focusing on the Gandharan Buddhist art itself, Rosenfield selects sculptures of Kushan royals and those representing nomadic populations in religious shrines to display the central Asian aspect of artworks of the period.

Rostovtzeff, Michael Ivanovich, *Caravan Cities,* trans. D. and T. Talbot Rice (1932). Though published more than seven decades ago, this small volume contains accurate descriptions of the ruins of many caravan cities in modern Jordan and Syria.

———, *The Social and Economic History of the Hellenistic World* (1941). A monumental achievement; one of the great works of history written in the twentieth century. An unsurpassed overview of all aspects of the politics and social and economic movements of the period. Despite its age, there is still nothing like it.

Schoff, Wilfred H. (ed. and trans.), *The Periplus of the Erythraean Sea* (1912). An invaluable tool for mapping names and places from the Red Sea to Indian coastal areas during this period.

Shipley, Graham, *The Greek World after Alexander, 323–30 BC* (2000). A more up-to-date survey than Peter Green's work (above), with more emphasis on the historical detail in each period.

Tarn, W. W., *Greeks in Bactria and India* (1984). The most comprehensive coverage of Greek sources on Hellenistic states in Afghanistan and northwest India.

Thapar, Romila, *Ashoka and the Decline of the Mauryas* (1973). Using all available primary sources, including the edicts of Aśoka and Greek authors' accounts, Thapar gives the most authoritative analysis of the first and the most important empire in Indian history.

Vainker, Shelagh, *Chinese Silk: A Cultural History* (2004). A work that traces the cultural history of silk in China from its early origins to the twentieth century and considers its relationship to the other decorative arts. The author draws on the most recent archaeological evidence to emphasize the role of silk in Chinese history, trade, religion, and literature.

Wood, Frances, *The Silk Road: Two Thousand Years in the Heart of Asia* (2004). Illustrated with drawings, manuscripts, paintings, and artifacts to trace the Silk Roads to their origins as far back as Alexander the Great, with an emphasis on their importance to cultural and religious movements.

Young, Gary K., *Rome's Eastern Trade: International Commerce and Imperial Policy, 31 BC–AD 305* (2001). This study examines the taxation and profits of eastern trade from the perspective of the Roman government.

Chapter 7: Han Dynasty China and Imperial Rome, 300 BCE–300 CE

Barbieri-Low, Anthony J., and Robin D. S. Yates, *Law, State, and Society in Early Imperial China: A Study with Critical Edition and Translation of the Legal Texts from Zhangjiashan Tomb No. 247,* 2 vols. (2015). A new account of changes in Western (Former) Han dynasty law in terms of its moralization via instituting Confucianism.

Bodde, Derk, *China's First Unifier: A Study of the Ch'in Dynasty as Seen in the Life of Li Ssu (280?–208 B.C.)* (1938). A classic account of the key Legalist adviser, Li Si, who formulated the Qin policy to enhance its autocratic power.

Bowman, Alan K., *Life and Letters on the Roman Frontier: Vindolanda and Its Peoples* (1994). An introduction to the exciting discovery of writing tablets at a Roman army base in northern Britain.

Bradley, Keith, *Slavery and Society at Rome* (1994). The best single overview of the major aspects of the slave system in the Roman Empire.

Chevallier, Raymond, *Roman Roads,* trans. N. H. Field (1976). A guide to the fundamentals of the construction, maintenance, administration, and mapping of Roman roads.

Coarelli, Fillipo (ed.), *Pompeii,* trans. Patricia Cockram (2006). A lavishly illustrated large volume that allows the reader to sense some of the wondrous wealth of the buried city of Pompeii.

Colledge, Malcolm A. R., *The Parthians* (1967). A bit dated but still a fundamental introduction to the Parthians, the major power on the eastern frontier of the Roman Empire.

Cornell, Tim, *The Beginnings of Rome: Italy and Rome from the Bronze Age to the Punic Wars, c. 2000 to 264 B.C.* (1995). The single best one-volume history of Rome through its early history to the first war with Carthage.

Cornell, Tim, and John Matthews, *Atlas of the Roman World* (1982). A history of the Roman world; much more than simply an atlas. It is provided not only with good maps and a gazetteer, but also with marvelous color illustrations and a text that guides the reader through the basics of Roman history.

Csikszentmihalyi, Mark, *Readings in Han Chinese Thought* (2006). A volume presenting a representative selection of primary sources to illustrate the growth of ideas in early imperial times; a useful introduction to the key strains of thought during this crucial period.

Di Cosmo, Nicola, and Michael Maas (eds.), *Empires and Exchanges in Eurasia in Late Antiquity* (2018). Expert historians examine commercial and other connections between the west and the east during the Late Antique period.

Dien, Albert E., "The Qin Army and Its Antecedents," in Liu Yang (ed.), *China's Terracotta Warriors: The First Emperor's Legacy* (2013). An account of the Qin army in light of its Warring States precedents.

Dixon, Suzanne, *The Roman Family* (1992). The best one-volume guide to the nature of the Roman family and family relations.

Garnsey, Peter, and Richard Saller, *The Roman Empire: Economy, Society, and Culture,* 2nd ed. (2014). A perceptive and critical introduction to three basic aspects of social life in the empire.

Giardina, Andrea (ed.), *The Romans,* trans. Lydia Cochrane (1993). Individual studies of important typical figures in Roman society, from the peasant and the bandit to the merchant and the soldier.

Goldsworthy, Adrian, *The Roman Army at War: 100 B.C.–A.D. 200* (1996). A summary history and analysis of the Roman army in action during the late Republic and early Empire.

Goodman, Martin, *The Roman World: 44 B.C.–A.D. 180* (1997). A newer basic history text covering the high Roman Empire.

Graf, David F., "The Silk Road between Syria and China," in Andrew Wilson and Alan Bowman (eds.), *Trade, Commerce, and the State in the Roman World* (2018), pp. 443–529. An exhaustive overview of relations between the Roman Empire and Han China, based on the most recent research of historians.

Hansen, Valerie, *The Silk Road: A New History* (2012). An important study of the Silk Roads, based on much original research.

Harper, Kyle, *The Fate of Rome: Climate, Disease, and the End of an Empire* (2017). A vigorous and persuasive argument that climate played a significant role in the decline of the Roman Empire.

Harris, William, *Ancient Literacy* (1989). A basic survey of what is known about communication in the form of writing and books in the Roman Empire.

Hopkins, Keith, *Death and Renewal: Sociological Studies in Roman History,* vol. 2 (1983). Innovative studies in Roman history, including one of the best on gladiators and another on death and funerals.

————, *A World Full of Gods: Pagans, Jews and Christians in the Roman Empire* (1999). A somewhat unusual but interesting and provocative look at the world of religions in the Roman Empire.

Hughes, J. Donald, *Environmental Problems of the Greeks and Romans: Ecology in the Ancient Mediterranean*, 2nd ed. (2014). A much improved and expanded edition of a classic work on the environment in Greek and Roman antiquity and a state-of-the-art summary of our current knowledge.

Juliano, Annette L., and Judith A. Lerner (eds.), *Nomads, Traders and Holy Men along China's Silk Road* (2003). A description of the travelers along the Silk Roads in human terms, focusing on warfare, markets, and religion.

Kern, Martin, and Michael Hunter (eds.), *The Analects: A Western Han Text?* (2013). Challenges the assumption that the Confucian *Analects* was compiled before the Han Dynasty.

Knapp, Robert C., *Invisible Romans* (2011). A highly readable introduction to the lower orders of Roman imperial society: the poor, the enslaved, freedmen, prostitutes, gladiators, bandits, and pirates (among others).

Kraus, Theodore, and Leonard von Matt, *Pompeii and Herculaneum: The Living Cities of the Dead*, trans. Robert E. Wolf (1975). A huge, lavishly illustrated compendium of all aspects of life in the buried cities of Pompeii and Herculaneum as preserved in the archaeological record.

Liang, Cai, *Witchcraft and the Rise of the First Confucian Empire* (2014). A new account of the rise of the Confucians at the Western (Former) Han court during the famous witchcraft trials circa 91–87 BCE.

Liu, Xinru, *The Silk Road in World History* (2010). A short overview of the Silk Roads, written by a scholar whose specialty is India, and of the manifold connections involving East Asia, South Asia, Southwest Asia, North Africa, and Europe.

Loewe, Michael, *The Government of the Qin and Han Empires: 221 BCE–220 CE* (2006). A useful overview of the government of the early empires of China. Topics include the structure of central government, provincial and local government, the armed forces, officials, government communications, the laws of the empire, and control of the people and the land.

Millar, Fergus, *The Crowd in the Late Republic* (1998). An innovative study of the democratic power of the citizens in the city of Rome itself.

————, *The Emperor in the Roman World, 31 B.C.–A.D. 337* (1992). Everything you might want to know about the Roman emperor, with special emphasis on his civil role as the administrator of an empire.

Potter, David S., *The Roman Empire at Bay, A.D. 180–395*, 2nd ed. (2014). A new basic text covering the later Roman Empire, including the critical transition to a Christian state.

Potter, David S., and David J. Mattingly (eds.), *Life, Death, and Entertainment in the Roman Empire* (1999). A good introduction to basic aspects of Roman life in the empire, including the family, feeding the cities, religion, and popular entertainment.

Qian, Sima, *Records of the Grand Historian: Qin Dynasty*, trans. Burton Watson, 3rd ed. (1995). The classic work of Chinese history in a readable translation. The Han dynasty's Grand Historian describes the slow rise and meteoric fall of the Qin dynasty from the point of view of the succeeding dynasty, which Sima Qian witnessed or heard of during his lifetime.

Scheidel, Walter (ed.), *Rome and China: Comparative Perspectives on Ancient World Empires* (2009). Historians of the Roman and Han Empires offer a series of essays that compare these two empires.

———— (ed.), *The Science of Roman History: Biology, Climate, and the Future of the Past* (2018). Experts apply biology, climatology, and other scientific subjects to the study of the Roman Empire.

Southern, Pat, *The Roman Army: A Social and Institutional History* (2006). A fundamental guide to all aspects of the Roman army.

Todd, Malcolm, *The Early Germans,* rev. ed. (2004). A basic survey of the peoples in central and western Europe at the time of the Roman Empire.

Vainker, Shelagh, *Chinese Silk: A Cultural History* (2004). A work that traces the cultural history of silk in China from its early origins to the twentieth century and considers its relationship to the other decorative arts. The author draws on the most recent archaeological evidence to emphasize the role of silk in Chinese history, trade, religion, and literature.

Wells, Peter S., *The Barbarians Speak: How the Conquered Peoples Shaped Roman Europe* (1999). The cultures of the peoples of central and northern Europe at the time of the Roman Empire and their impact on Roman culture.

Wood, Frances, *The Silk Road: Two Thousand Years in the Heart of Asia* (2004). A work illustrated with drawings, manuscripts, paintings, and artifacts to trace the Silk Roads to their origins as far back as Alexander the Great. The author stresses the importance of the Silk Roads to cultural and religious movements.

Woolf, Greg (ed.), *The Cambridge Illustrated History of the Roman World* (2005). A good guide to various aspects of Roman history, culture, and provincial life.

————, *Rome: An Empire's Story* (2012). An up-to-date narrative of the Roman Empire told according to major themes that are particularly relevant to world history.

Chapter 8: The Rise of Universalizing Religions, 300–600 CE

Bowersock, Glen W., *Empires in Collision in Late Antiquity* (2013). Brilliant, short studies of the relations between Ethiopia, Arabia, and Byzantium as a background to the origins of Islam.

Bowersock, Glen W., Peter Brown, and Oleg Grabar (eds.), *Late Antiquity: A Guide to the Postclassical World* (1999). Essays and items for the entire period 150–750 CE. The volume covers the Roman, East Roman, Sasanian, and early Islamic worlds.

Brown, Peter, *The Rise of Western Christendom: Triumph and Diversity, A.D. 200–1000,* 2nd ed. (2003). The rise and spread of Christianity in Europe and Asia, with up-to-date bibliographies on all topics, maps, and time charts.

————, "The Silk Road in Late Antiquity," in V. H. Maier and J. Hickman (eds.), *Reconfiguring the Silk Road* (2014). The Silk Roads from the perspective of their western outlets and influences.

————, *Through the Eye of a Needle: Wealth, the Fall of Rome, and the Making of Christianity in the West, 350–550* (2012). Christianity and Roman society before and after the end of the empire.

————, *Treasure in Heaven: The Holy Poor in Early Christianity* (2016). On the social role of early Christian monasticism in Syria and Egypt.

————, *The World of Late Antiquity: From Marcus Aurelius to Muhammad, AD 150–750* (1989). A social, religious, and cultural history of the late Roman and Sasanian empires, with illustrations and a time chart.

Bühler, G. (trans.), *The Laws of Manu* (1886). The classic translation of one of India's most important historical, legal, and religious texts.

Canepa, Matthew P., *The Two Eyes of the Earth: Art and Ritual of Kingship between Rome and Sasanian Iran* (2009). An interesting look at how two great global powers, Rome and Iran, shared images of rulership.

Clynes, Tom, "Laser Scans Reveal Maya 'Megalopolis' below Guatemalan Jungle," *National Geographic*

News, February 1, 2018, https://news. nationalgeographic.com/2018/02/ maya-laser-lidar-guatemala-pacunam/. Highlights the use of LIDAR laser technology to uncover extensive Maya ruins, including additional pyramids, intercity road systems, defensive walls, irrigation systems, quarries, and other structures.

Coe, Michael D., *The Maya,* 6th ed. (1999). A work by the world's most famous Mayanologist, with recent evidence, analyses, and illustrations.

Cowgill, George L., "The Central Mexican Highlands and the Rise of Teotihuacan to the Decline of Tula," in Richard Adams and Murdo Macleod (eds.), *The Cambridge History of the Native Peoples of the Americas,* vol. 2, *Mesoamerica,* pt. 1 (2000). A thorough review of findings about urban states in central Mexico.

Fash, William L., *Scribes, Warriors and Kings: The City of Copan and the Ancient Maya* (2001). A fascinating and comprehensive study of one of the most elaborate of the Maya city-kingdoms.

Fisher, Greg (ed.), *Arabs and Empires before Islam* (2015). A collection of up-to-date studies on the relationships of various Arab groups with imperial powers, especially Rome and Persia.

―――. *Between Empires: Arabs, Romans, and Sasanians in Late Antiquity* (2011). Arab, Roman, and Sasanian empires compared.

Fowden, Elizabeth Key, *The Barbarian Plain: Saint Sergius between Rome and Iran* (1999). The study of a major Christian shrine and its relations to Romans, Persians, and Arabs.

Fowden, Garth, *Empire to Commonwealth: The Consequences of Monotheism in Late Antiquity* (1993). A study of the relationship between empire and world religions in western Asia.

Fried, Johannes, *The Middle Ages,* trans. Peter Lewis (2015). An impressive overview of the Late Antique period and the Early Middle Ages.

Gombrich, Richard F., and Sheldon Pollack (eds.), *Clay Sanskrit Library* (2005–2006). All major works from the Gupta and post-Gupta periods, in both Sanskrit and English versions. During the Gupta period, classical Sanskrit literature reached its apex, with abundant drama, poetry, and folk stories.

Gordon, Charles, *The Age of Attila* (1960). The last century of the Roman Empire in western Europe, vividly illustrated from contemporary sources.

Haldon, John, *The Empire That Would Not Die: The Paradox of Eastern Rome's Survival* (2010). Incorporates much new climatological evidence.

Hansen, Valerie, *The Silk Road: A New History* (2012). A detailed history of the Silk Roads, based largely on Chinese sources.

Harper, Prudence, *The Royal Hunter: The Art of the Sasanian Empire* (1978). The ideology of the Sasanian Empire as shown through excavated hoards of precious silverware.

Heather, Peter, *The Fall of the Roman Empire: A New History of Rome and the Barbarians* (2006). A military and political narrative based on up-to-date archaeological material.

Herrmann, Georgina, *Iranian Revival* (1977). The structure and horizons of the Sasanian Empire as revealed in its monuments.

Hillgarth, Jocelyn (ed.), *Christianity and Paganism, 350–750: The Conversion of Western Europe,* rev. ed. (1986). A collection of contemporary sources.

Holcombe, Charles, *In the Shadow of the Han: Literati Thought and Society at the Beginning of the Southern Dynasties* (1994). A clear and concise account of the evolution of thought in China after the fall of the Han dynasty in 220 CE. The book presents the rise of Buddhism and Daoism as popular religions as well as elite interests in classical learning in a time of political division and barbarian conquest in North and South China.

La Vaissière, Étienne de, *Sogdian Traders: A History*, trans. James Ward (2005). A summary of historical facts about the most important trading community and its commercial networks on the Silk Roads, from the early centuries CE to its demise in the ninth century CE.

Little, Lester (ed.), *Plague and the End of Antiquity: The Pandemic of 541–750* (2008). A series of debates over the nature and impact of the first great pandemic attested in global history.

Liu, Xinru, and Lynda Norene Shaffer, *Connections across Eurasia: Transportation, Communication, and Cultural Exchanges on the Silk Roads* (2007). A survey of trade and religious activities on the Silk Roads.

Lopez, Ariel G., *Shenoute of Atripe and the Uses of Poverty: Rural Patronage, Religious Conflict, and Monasticism in Late Antique Egypt* (2013). Places a leading Egyptian abbot in his full social context.

Maas, Michael, *The Age of Attila: The Cambridge Companion to the Age of Attila* (2013). Essays on this important age in the Late Antique period.

——— (ed.), *The Cambridge Companion to the Age of Justinian* (2005). A survey of all aspects of the eastern Roman Empire in the sixth century CE.

———, *Readings in Late Antiquity: A Source Book* (1999). Well-chosen extracts that illustrate the interrelation of Romans and non-Romans, and of Christians, Jews, and pagans.

Moffett, Samuel, *A History of Christianity in Asia*, vol. 1 (1993). Particularly valuable on Christians in China and India.

Munro-Hay, Stuart, *Aksum: An African Civilization of Late Antiquity* (1991). The origins of the Christian kingdom of Ethiopia.

Murdock, George P., *Africa: Its Peoples and Their History* (1959). A vital introduction to the peoples of Africa and their history.

Oliver, Roland, *The African Experience: From Olduvai Gorge to the Twenty-First Century* (1999). An important overview, written by one of the pioneering scholars of African history and one of the leading authorities on the Bantu migrations.

Payne, Richard. *A State of Mixture: Christians, Zoroastrians, and Iranian Political Culture in Late Antiquity* (2015). A new view of Christianity in Sasanian Iran.

Pines, Yuri, *Envisioning Eternal Empire: Chinese Political Thought of the Warring States Era* (2009). A critical comparative work that focuses on the Warring States period and discusses how the rise of an imperial ideology was formative in the Chinese commitment to imperial rule.

———, *The Everlasting Empire: The Political Culture of Ancient China and Its Imperial Legacy* (2012). Stresses the critical role that the Warring States period played in the formulation of an enduring imperial ideology.

Pourshariati, Parvaneh, *The Decline and Fall of the Sasanian Empire: The Sasanian-Parthian Confederacy and the Arab Conquest of Iran* (2008). An innovative perspective on the demise of the Sasanians and the relevance of their decline for the Arab conquest of Iran.

Pregadio, Fabrizio, *Great Clarity: Daoism and Alchemy in Early Medieval China* (2006). An examination of the religious aspects of Daoism. The book focuses on the relation of alchemy to the Daoist traditions of the third to sixth centuries CE and shows how alchemy was integrated into the elaborate body of doctrines and practices of Daoists at that time.

Rea, Jennifer A., and Liz Clarke, *Perpetua's Journey: Faith, Gender, and Power in the Roman Empire* (2018). An innovative graphic history that includes a new translation of the martyrdom text and scholarly essays on Perpetua's historical context.

Rosenthal, Jean-Laurent, and R. Bin Wong, *Before and Beyond Divergence: The Politics of Economic Change in China and Europe* (2011). A spirited attempt to understand why Europe outperformed China in the period leading up to the twenty-first century.

Scheidel, Walter (ed.), *Rome and China: Comparative Perspectives on Ancient World Empires* (2009). The essays by Walter Scheidel and Nathan Rosenstein expertly compare the Roman and Han Empires.

Tannous, Jack, *The Making of the Medieval Middle East: Religion, Society, and Simple Believers* (2018). An essential study of how Southwest Asia, Egypt, and North Africa, the birthplace of Judaism and Christianity, became an Islamic area.

Tempels, Placide, *Bantu Philosophy* (1959). A highly influential effort to argue for the underlying cultural unity of all the Bantu peoples.

Vansina, Jan, *Paths in the Rainforests: Toward a History of Political Tradition in Equatorial Africa* (1990). The best work on Bantu history.

Walker, Joel, *The Legend of Mar Kardagh: Narrative and Christian Heroism in Late Antique Iraq* (2006). Christians and Zoroastrians in northern Iraq and in Iran.

Yarshater, Ehsan, *Encyclopedia Iranica* (1982–). A guide to all aspects of the Sasanian Empire and to religion and culture in the regions between Mesopotamia and central Asia.

Zürcher, E., *The Buddhist Conquest of China: The Spread and Adaptation of Buddhism in Early Medieval China,* 3rd ed. (2007). A reissue of the classic account of the assimilation of Buddhism in China during the medieval period, with particular focus on the religious and philosophical success of Buddhism among Chinese elites in South China.

Chapter 9: New Empires and Common Cultures, 600–1000 CE

Ahmed, Leila, *Women and Gender in Islam* (1992). A superb overview of the relations between men and women throughout the history of Islam.

al-Azmeh, Aziz, *The Emergence of Islam in Late Antiquity: Allah and His People* (2014). A detailed and comprehensive treatment of the origins of Islam, written by a scholar aware of all historical sources of this period.

Aneirin, *Y Gododdin: Britain's Oldest Heroic Poem,* ed. and trans. A. O. H. Jarman (1988). A sixth-century CE Welsh text that describes the battle of the last Britons against the invading Anglo-Saxons.

Arberry, Arthur J., introduction to *The Koran Interpreted: A Translation,* trans. Arthur J. Arberry (1986). One of the most eloquent appreciations of this classical work of religion.

Augustine, *The City of God,* trans. H. Bettenson (1976). An excellent translation of Augustine's monumental work of history, philosophy, and religion.

Berkey, Jonathan P., *The Formation of Islam: Religion and Society in the Near East, 600–1800* (2005). A recent overview of the history of Islam before the modern era. It is particularly sensitive to the influence of external elements on the history of the Muslim peoples.

Bol, Peter, *This Culture of Ours: Intellectual Transitions in T'ang and Sung China* (1994). A study tracing the transformation of the shared culture of the Chinese learned elite from the seventh to the twelfth centuries.

Bowersock, G. W., *The Crucible of Islam* (2017). A classicist treatment of the origins of Islam.

———, *The Throne of Adulis: Red Sea Wars on the Eve of Islam* (2013). A vital study of the kingdom of Himyar, in present-day Yemen, a center of Judaism and Christianity before the rise of Islam in the Arabian Peninsula.

Brooke, John L., *Climate Change and the Course of Global History: A Rough Journey* (2014). An overview of a changing climate and its impact on historical developments.

Brown, Peter, *The Rise of Western Christendom: Triumph and Diversity,*

AD 200–1000, 2nd ed. (2003). A description of the changes in Christianity in northern Europe and the emergence of the new cultures and political structures that coincided with this development.

Bulliet, Richard W., *Conversion to Islam in the Medieval Period: An Essay in Quantitative History* (1979). A study of the rate at which the populations overrun by Arab conquerors in the seventh century CE embraced the religion of their rulers.

———, *Cotton, Climate, and Camels in the Early Islamic State* (2009). A fascinating account of economic development on the Iranian plateau, with an emphasis on climate.

Cook, Michael, *The Koran: A Very Short Introduction* (2000). A useful overview of Islam's holy book.

———, *Muhammad* (1983). A brief but careful life of the Prophet that takes full account of the prolific and often controversial preexisting scholarship.

Creswell, K. A. C., *A Short Account of Early Muslim Architecture, revised and supplemented by James W. Allan* (1992). The definitive treatment of the subject, brought up to date.

Crone, Patricia, *The Nativist Prophets of Early Islam: Rural Revolt and Local Zoroastrianism* (2012). The rise of protest movements in Islam that led to the Abbasid takeover from the Umayyads.

Cross, S. H., and O. P. Sherbowitz-Westor (trans.), *The Russian Primary Chronicle* (1953). A vivid record of the Viking settlement of Kiev, of the conversion of Kiev, and of the princes of Kiev in the tenth and eleventh centuries.

Donner, Fred M., *The Early Islamic Conquests* (1981). The best account of the Arab conquests in the Persian and Byzantine Empires in the seventh century CE.

———, *Muhammad and the Believers at the Origins of Islam* (2010). An Islamicist reexamines early historical sources on the origins of Islam and contends that the early Muslim believers did not separate from Christianity and Judaism until more than a half century had elapsed from Muhammad's first proclamations.

Duncan, John, *The Origins of the Chosŏn Dynasty* (2000). A historical account of the early Korean dynasties from 900 to 1400 CE.

Elman, Benjamin, *Precocious China: Civil Examinations, 1400–1900* (2013). Summary of civil exams in China from medieval times.

Fage, J. D., *Ghana: A Historical Introduction* (1966). A brief but authoritative history of Ghana from earliest times to the twentieth century.

Fisher, Humphrey J., *Slavery in the History of Muslim Black Africa* (2001). A general history of the relations between North Africa and black Africa, focusing on one of the most important aspects of contact—the slave trade.

Fowden, Garth, *Before and after Muhammad: The First Millennium Refocused* (2014). The author sets Islam in its larger Greek and Christian context; part of the work of the Late Antique scholarly community.

Grabar, Oleg, *The Shape of the Holy: Early Islamic Jerusalem* (1996). The best account of the architecture of early Islam, including the building and the purposes of the Dome of the Rock, one of Islam's early and iconic places of worship.

Graham-Campbell, James, *Cultural Atlas of the Viking World* (1994). A positioning of the Vikings against their wider background in both western and eastern Europe.

Haider, Najam, *The Origins of the Shi'a: Identity, Ritual, and Sacred Space in Eighth-Century Kufah* (2011). A definitive study on the origin of Shiism.

Hawting, G. R., *The First Dynasty of Islam: The Umayyad Caliphate, A.D. 661–750* (2000). The essential scholarly treatment of Islam's first dynasty.

Herrmann, Georgina, *Iranian Revival* (1977). The structure and horizons of the Sasanian Empire as revealed in its monuments.

Hillgarth, J. N. (ed.), *Christianity and Paganism, 350–750: The Conversion of Western Europe,* rev. ed. (1986). A collection of contemporary sources.

Hodges, Richard, and David Whitehouse, *Mohammed, Charlemagne, and the Origins of Europe* (1983). A spirited comparison of Islam and the rise of Europe.

Hodgson, Marshall G. S., *The Venture of Islam: Conscience and History in a World Civilization*, 3 vols. (1977). A magnificent history of the Islamic peoples. Its first volume, *The Classical Age of Islam*, is basic reading for anyone interested in the history of the Muslim world.

Holdsworth, May, *Women of the Tang Dynasty* (1999). An account of women's lives during the Tang dynasty.

Hourani, Albert, *History of the Arab Peoples* (2002). The best overview of Arab history.

Hoyland, Robert G., *In God's Path: The Arab Conquests and the Creation of an Islamic Empire* (2015). An overview of new findings about the origins of Islam.

Jones, Gwynn, *The Norse Atlantic Saga* (1986). The Viking discovery of America.

Kennedy, Hugh, *The Prophet and the Age of the Caliphate: The Islamic Near East from the Sixth to the Eleventh Century* (2004). A very good synthesis of the rise and spread of Islam.

Lee, Peter, et al. (eds.), *Sources of Korean Tradition*, vol. 1 (1996). A unique view of Korean history through the eyes and words of the participants or witnesses themselves, as provided in translations of official documents, letters, and policies.

Levtzion, Nehemia, *Ancient Ghana and Mali* (1980). The best introduction to the kingdoms of West Africa.

Levtzion, Nehemia, and Jay Spaulding, *Medieval West Africa: Views from Arab Scholars and Merchants* (2003). An indispensable source book on early West African history.

Levy-Rubin, Milka, *Non-Muslims in the Early Islamic Empire: From Surrender to Co-existence* (2011). The exploitation of non-Muslims in early Islam and their later conversion and rise to prominence.

Lewis, Bernard (trans.), *Islam from the Prophet Muhammad to the Capture of Constantinople*, vol. 2, *Religion and Society* (1974). A fine collection of original sources that portray various aspects of classical Islamic society.

———, *The Middle East: Two Thousand Years of History from the Rise of Christianity to the Present Day* (1995). A stimulating introduction to an area that has seen the emergence of three of the great world religions.

Lewis, David Levering, *God's Crucible: Islam and the Making of Europe, 570–1215* (2008). An exciting and well-written overview of the high period of Islamic power and cultural attainments.

Middleton, John, *The Swahili: The Social Landscape of a Mercantile Community* (2000). An exciting synthesis of the Swahili culture of East Africa.

Miyazaki, Ichisada, *China's Examination Hell* (1981). A study of China's examination system.

Nurse, Derek, and Thomas Spear, *The Swahili: Reconstructing the History and Language of an African Society, 800–1500* (1984). A work that explores the history of the Muslim peoples who lived along the coast of East Africa.

Peters, F. E., *Muhammad and the Origins of Islam* (1994). A work that explores the early history of Islam and highlights the critical role that Muhammad played in promoting a new religion and a powerful Arab identity.

Pourshariati, Parveneh, *Decline and Fall of the Sasanian Empire* (2008). Fundamental analysis of the end of the Sasanian Empire and the reasons for the success of the Arab/Muslim invasions.

Robinson, Chase F., *'Abd al-Malik* (2005). A short biography of the powerful Umayyad ruler who played a critical role in distinguishing Islam from the other monotheisms in the region, namely, Christianity, Judaism, and Zoroastrianism.

————, *The Formation of the Islamic World, Sixth to Eleventh Centuries*, vol. 1 of *The New Cambridge History of Islam* (2010). The first volume of an authoritative and up-to-date six-volume overview of the history of Islam from the sixth century CE to the present.

Schirokauer, Conrad, David Lurie, and Suzanne Gay, *A Brief History of Japanese Civilization*, 2nd ed. (2005). A balanced account; chapters focus on developments in art, religion, literature, and thought as well as on Japan's economic, political, and social history in medieval times.

Shoemaker, Stephen J., *The Death of a Prophet: The End of Muhammad's Life and the Beginnings of Islam* (2012). A careful revision of the standard biographies of Muhammad, based on non-Muslim sources.

Smith, Julia, *Europe after Rome: A New Cultural History, 500–1000* (2005). A vivid analysis of society and culture in so-called Dark Age Europe.

Totman, Conrad, *History of Japan* (2004). A recent and readable summary of Japanese history from ancient to modern times.

Twitchett, Denis, *The Birth of the Chinese Meritocracy: Bureaucrats and Examinations in T'ang China* (1976). A description of the role of the written civil examinations that began during the Tang dynasty.

————, *Financial Administration under the T'ang Dynasty* (1970). A pioneering account—based on rare Dunhuang documents that survived from medieval times in Buddhist grottoes in central Asia—of the political and economic system undergirding the Chinese imperial state.

Whittow, Mark, *The Making of Byzantium, 600–1025* (1996). A study on the survival and revival of the eastern Roman Empire as a major power in eastern Europe and Southwest Asia.

Wood, Ian, *The Missionary Life: Saints and the Evangelization of Europe, 400–1050* (2001). The horizons of Christians on the frontiers of Europe.

Chapter 10: Becoming "The World," 1000–1300 CE

Allsen, Thomas, *Commodity and Exchange in the Mongol Empire: A Cultural History of Islamic Textiles* (1997). A study that uses golden brocade, the textile most treasured by Mongol rulers, as a lens through which to analyze the vast commercial networks facilitated by the Mongol conquests and control.

————, *Culture and Conquest in Mongol Eurasia* (2001). A work that emphasizes the cultural and scientific exchanges that took place across Afro-Eurasia as a result of the Mongol conquest.

Bagge, Svere, Michael Gelting, and Thomas Lundkvist (eds.), *Feudalism: New Landscapes of Debate* (2011). A collection of essays on interpretations of feudalism by experts on the topic.

Bartlett, Robert, *The Making of Europe: Conquest, Colonization and Cultural Change, 950–1350* (1993). The modes of cultural, political, and demographic expansion of feudal Europe along its frontiers, especially in eastern Europe.

Bay, Edna G., *Wives of the Leopards: Gender, Politics, and Culture in the Kingdom of Dahomey* (1998). A work that stresses the role of women in an important West African society and dips into the early history of this area.

Beach, D. N., *Shona and Zimbabwe, 900–1850: An Outline of Shona History* (1980). A good place to start for exploring the history of Great Zimbabwe.

Broadbridge, Anne F., *Women and the Making of the Mongol Empire* (2018). By examining the lives of women in Chinggis Khan's orbit, this study uncovers not only details about the lives of well-known elite Mongol women but also a larger picture of the roles of women in kinship strategies binding Mongol tribes, the economy fueling nomadic life, and the political machinations driving conquest.

Brooks, George E., *Landlords and Strangers: Ecology, Society, and Trade in Western Africa, 1000–1630* (1993). A survey assembled from primary sources of early West African history that stresses transregional connections.

Bulliet, Richard W., *Cotton, Climate, and Camels in Early Islamic Iran* (2009). An analysis of the upswing of the Iranian plateau economy after the Muslim conquest and its subsequent decline as a result of climate change.

Buzurg ibn Shahriyar of Ramhormuz, *The Book of the Wonders of India: Mainland, Sea and Islands,* ed. and trans. G. S. P. Freeman-Greenville (1981). A collection of stories told by sailors, both true and fantastic; they help us imagine the lives of sailors of the era.

Chappell, Sally A. Kitt, *Cahokia: Mirror of the Cosmos* (2002). A thorough and vivid account of the "mound people"; it explores not just what we know of Cahokia but how we know it.

Christian, David, *A Short History of Russia, Central Asia, and Mongolia,* vol. 1, *Inner Eurasia from Prehistory to the Mongol Empire* (1998). Essential reading for students interested in interconnections across the Afro-Eurasian landmass.

Curtin, Philip, *Cross-Cultural Trade in World History* (1984). A groundbreaking book on intercultural trade with a primary focus on Africa, especially the cross-Saharan trade and Swahili coastal trade.

Dawson, Christopher, *Mission to Asia* (1980). Accounts of China and the Mongol Empire brought back by Catholic missionaries and diplomats after 1240.

De Nicola, Bruno, *Women in Mongol Iran: The Khātūns, 1206–1335* (2017). Drawing on a wide range of source material, De Nicola explores the political, economic, and religious influence of women in Mongol society from the pre-imperial steppe nomadic context to the settled empire, in particular the Il-Khanate of Persia.

Di Cosmo, Nicola, Allen J. Frank, and Peter Golden (eds.), *The Cambridge History of Inner Asia: The Chinggisid Age* (2009). A definitive study of the Mongol period, written by the leading scholars of this period.

Ellenblum, Ronnie, *The Collapse of the Eastern Mediterranean: Climate Change and the Decline of the East, 950–1072* (2012). An analysis of the impact of freezing temperatures and drought on the societies of the eastern Mediterranean.

Flecker, Michael, "A 9th-Century Arab or Indian Shipwreck in Indonesian Waters," *International Journal of Nautical Archaeology* 29, no. 2 (2000): 199–217. Offers an early detailed description of the Belitung dhow's excavation, likely place of origin, construction, and cargo.

———, "A 9th-Century Arab or Indian Shipwreck in Indonesian Waters: Addendum," *International Journal of Nautical Archaeology* 37, no. 2 (2008): 384–86. An update on the origin of the Belitung dhow that, based on a comparative analysis of wood fibers, argues that the ship's timbers suggest it was built in Oman or Yemen (on the southern coast of the Arabian Peninsula), not India as was earlier considered to be a possibility.

———, "A 9th-Century Arab Shipwreck in Indonesia," in Regina Krahl et al. (eds.), *Shipwrecked: Tang Treasures and Monsoon Winds* (2010), pp. 100–119. Flecker's most recent consideration of the Belitung dhow, published in a collection of essays to accompany an exhibition focused on the important shipwreck.

Foltz, Richard C., *Religions of the Silk Road: Overland Trade and Cultural Exchange from Antiquity to the Fifteenth Century* (1999). A study of the populations and the cities of the Silk Roads as transmitters of culture across long distances.

Franklin, Simon, and Jonathan Shepherd, *The Emergence of Rus: 750–1200* (1996). The formation of medieval Russia between the Baltic and Black Seas.

Gibb, Hamilton A. R., *Saladin: Studies in Islamic History,* ed. Yusuf Ibish (1974). A sympathetic portrait of one of Islam's leading political and military figures.

Glahn, Richard von, "Re-examining the Authenticity of Song Paper Money Specimens," *Journal of Song-Yuan Studies* 36 (2006): 79–106. Provides a close examination, including descriptions, images, and translations, of many examples of paper money from the Song and Yuan dynasties. The article offers a detailed discussion (on pp. 93–94) of the flying cash example reproduced in Chapter 10.

Goitein, S. D., *Letters of Medieval Jewish Traders* (1973). The classic study of medieval Jewish trading communities based on the commercial papers deposited in the Cairo Geniza (a synagogue storeroom) during the tenth and eleventh centuries CE; it explores not only commercial activities but also the personal lives of the traders around the Indian Ocean basin.

———, *A Mediterranean Society: An Abridgment in One Volume,* rev. and ed. Jacob Lassner (1999). A portrait of the Jewish merchant community with ties across the Afro-Eurasian landmass, based largely on the documents from the Cairo Geniza (of which Goitein was the primary researcher and interpreter).

———, "New Light on the Beginnings of the Karim Merchant," *Journal of Social and Economic History of the Orient* 1 (1958). Goitein's description of Egyptian trade.

Goitein, S. D., and Mordechai A. Friedman, *India Traders of the Middle Ages: Documents from the Cairo Geniza* (2008). Collection of documents (translated into English) and authoritative essays that explore the eleventh- and twelfth-century trade conducted by several prominent Jewish families along the Mediterranean and Indian Ocean routes.

Harris, Joseph E., *The African Presence in Asia: Consequences of the East African Slave Trade* (1971). One of the few books that looks broadly at the impact of Africans and African slavery on the societies of Asia.

Hartwell, Robert, "Demographic, Political, and Social Transformations of China, 750–1550," *Harvard Journal of Asiatic Studies* 42 (1982): 365–442. A pioneering study of the demographic changes that overtook China during the Tang and Song dynasties, which are described in light of political reform movements and social changes in this crucial era.

Historical Relations across the Indian Ocean: Report and Papers of the Meeting of Experts Organized by UNESCO at Port Louis, Mauritius, from 15 to 19 July, 1974 (1980). Excellent essays on the connections of Africa with Asia across the Indian Ocean.

Hitti, Philip, *An Arab-Syrian Gentleman and Warrior in the Period of the Crusades: Memoirs of Usāmah ibn-Munqidh* (1929). The Crusaders seen through Muslim eyes.

Hodgson, Natasha, *Women, Crusading, and the Holy Land in Historical Narrative* (2007). A book dealing with the Crusades and focusing on the place of women in them.

Holt, P. M., *The Age of the Crusades: The Near East from the Eleventh Century to 1517* (1984). The Crusades period as seen from the eastern Mediterranean and through the lens of a leading British scholar of the area.

Huff, Toby E., *The Rise of Early Modern Science* (2009). A bold attempt to look at the rise of scientific work in the Islamic world, premodern China, and Europe, seeking to explain why the scientific revolution occurred in Europe rather than the Islamic world or China.

Hymes, Robert, and Conrad Schirokauer (eds.), *Ordering the World: Approaches to State and Society in Sung Dynasty China* (1993). A collection of essays that traces the intellectual, social, and political movements that shaped the Song state and its elites.

Ibn Battuta, *The Travels of Ibn Battuta*, trans. H. A. R. Gibb (2002). A readable translation of the classic book, originally published in 1929.

Ibn Fadlan, Ahmad, *Ibn Fadlan's Journey to Russia: A Tenth Century Traveler from Baghdad to the Volga River,* translated with commentary by Richard Frye (2005). A coherent summary of the observations of an envoy who traveled from Baghdad to Russia.

Irwin, Robert, *The Middle East in the Middle Ages: The Early Mamluk Sultanate, 1250–1582* (1986). Egypt under Mamluk rule.

Jeppie, Shamil, and Souleymane Bachir Diagne (eds.), *The Meanings of Timbuktu* (2008). New materials on the ancient Muslim city of Timbuktu by scholars who have been preserving its manuscripts and writing about its historical importance.

Khazanov, Anatoly M., *Nomads and the Outside World*, 2nd ed., trans. Julia Crookurden, with a foreword by Ernest Gellner (1994). A classic overview of nomadism, based on years of research, covering all the nomadic communities of Afro-Eurasia.

Lambourn, Elizabeth A., *Abraham's Luggage: A Social Life of Things in the Medieval Indian Ocean World* (2018). Uses Abraham Ben Yiju's 173-item luggage list to unpack a fascinating social and economic history of a North African Jewish trader living in southern India.

Lancaster, Lewis, Kikun Suh, and Chai-shin Yu (eds.), *Buddhism in Koryo: A Royal Religion* (1996). A description of Buddhism at its height in the Koryo period, when the religion made significant contributions to the development of Korean culture.

Levtzion, Nehemia, and Randall L. Pouwels (eds.), *The History of Islam in Africa* (2000). A useful general survey of the place of Islam in African history.

Lewis, Bernard (trans.), *Islam: From the Prophet Muhammad to the Capture of Constantinople,* vol. 2, *Religion and Society* (1974). A fine collection of original sources that portray various aspects of classical Islamic society.

Lopez, Robert S., *The Commercial Revolution of the Middle Ages, 950–1350* (1976). An account focusing on the development around the Mediterranean of commercial practices such as the use of currency, accounting, and credit.

Lyons, Malcolm C., and D. E. P. Jackson, *Saladin: The Politics of the Holy War* (1984; reprint, 2001). The fundamental revisionist work on one of the more important historical figures of the time.

Maalouf, Amin, *The Crusades through Muslim Eyes*, trans. Jon Rothschild (1984). The European Crusaders as seen by the Muslim world.

Marcus, Harold G., *A History of Ethiopia* (2002). An authoritative overview of the history of this great culture.

Mass, Jeffrey, *Yoritomo and the Founding of the First Bakufu: The Origins of Dual Government in Japan* (1999). A revisionist account of how the Kamakura military leader Minamoto Yoritomo established the "dual polity" of court and warrior government in Japan.

McDermott, Joseph, *A Social History of the Chinese Book: Books and Literati Culture in Late Imperial China* (2006). The history of the book in China since the Song dynasty, with comparisons to the book's role in other civilizations, particularly the European.

McEvitt, Christopher, *The Crusaders and the Christian World of the East: Rough Tolerance* (2008). Excellent work on the relations of religious groups in the Crusader kingdoms.

McIntosh, Roderik, *The Peoples of the Middle Niger: The Island of Gold* (1988). A historical survey of an area often omitted from other textbooks.

Moore, Jerry D., *Cultural Landscapes in the Ancient Andes: Archaeologies of Place* (2005). The most recent and up-to-date analysis of findings based on recent archaeological evidence, emphasizing the importance of local cultures and diversity in the Andes.

Mote, Frederick W., *Imperial China, 900–1800* (1999). Still the best work on this period, written by an expert on the full scope of Chinese history. The chapter on the Mongols is superb.

Niane, D. T. (ed.), *Africa from the Twelfth to the Sixteenth Century,* vol. 4 of *General History of Africa* (1984). The fourth volume of UNESCO's history of Africa covers four centuries of African history. This work features the scholarship of Africans.

Oliver, Roland (ed.), *From c. 1050 to c. 1600,* vol. 3 of *The Cambridge History of Africa,* ed. J. D. Fage and Roland Oliver (1977). Another general survey of African history. This volume draws heavily on the work of British scholars.

Peters, Edward, *The First Crusade* (1971). The Crusaders as seen through their own eyes.

Petry, Carl F. (ed.), *Islamic Egypt, 640–1517,* vol. 1 of *The Cambridge History of Egypt* (1998). A solid overview of the history of Islamic Egypt up to the Ottoman conquest.

Polo, Marco, *The Travels of Marco Polo,* ed. Manuel Komroff (1926). A solid translation of Marco Polo's famous account.

Popovic, Alexandre, *The Revolt of African Slaves in Iraq in the 3rd/9th Century,* trans. Leon King (1999). The account of a massive revolt against their enslavers by enslaved Africans taken to labor in Iraq's mines and fields.

Rossabi, Morris, *A History of China* (2014). Part of the Blackwell History of the World series and an excellent overview of Chinese history.

———, *Voyager from Xanadu: Rabban Sauma and the First Journey from China to the West* (2010). Rossabi's exploration in this second/revised edition uses additional historical sources and speculation to imaginatively expand on E. A. Wallis Budge's 1920s translation of Bar Sāwmā's late thirteenth-century account of his westward travels from Mongol territories to European cities like Rome and Paris.

Scott, Robert, *Gothic Enterprise: A Guide to Understanding the Medieval Cathedral* (2003). The meaning and social function of religious building in medieval cities in northern Europe.

Shaffer, Lynda Norene, *Maritime Southeast Asia to 1500* (1996). A history of the peoples of the southeast fringe of the Eastern Hemisphere, up to the time that they became connected to the global commercial networks of the world.

Shimada, Izumi, "Evolution of Andean Diversity: Regional Formations (500 BCE–CE 600)," in Frank Salomon and Stuart Schwartz (eds.), *South America,* vol. 3 of *The Cambridge History of the Native Peoples of the Americas* (1999), pt. 1, pp. 350–517. A splendid overview that contrasts the varieties of lowland and highland cultures.

Steinberg, David Joel, et al., *In Search of Southeast Asia: A Modern History,* rev. ed. (1987). An account of the emergence of the modern Southeast Asian polities of Cambodia, Burma, Thailand, and Indonesia.

Tanner, Harold M., *China: A History* (2009). Along with Rossabi (2014), an excellent overview of the full history of China.

Tyerman, Christopher, *God's War: A New History of the Crusades* (2006). The balance of religious and nonreligious motivations in the Crusades.

Waley, Daniel, *The Italian City-Republics*, 3rd ed. (1988). The structures and culture of the new cities of medieval Italy.

Watson, Andrew, *Agricultural Innovation in the Early Islamic World: The Diffusion of Crops and Farming Techniques, 700–1100* (1983). An impressive study of the spread of new crops throughout the Muslim world.

West, Charles, *Reframing the Feudal Revolution: Political and Social Transformation between Marne and Moselle, c. 800–c. 1100* (2013). Big change seen through an intensely studied region.

Wickham, Chris, *Sleepwalking into a New World: The Emergence of Italian City Communes in the Twelfth Century* (2015). Origins of the city democracies of medieval Italy.

Chapter 11: Crises and Recovery in Afro-Eurasia, 1300–1500

Barkey, Karen, *Empire of Difference: The Ottomans in Comparative Perspective* (2008). A revisionist view of the rise and flourishing of the Ottoman Empire.

Bois, Guy, *The Crisis of Feudalism: Economy and Society in Eastern Normandy, c. 1300–1550* (1984). A good case study of a French region that illustrates the turmoil in fourteenth-century Europe.

Brook, Timothy, *Praying for Power: Buddhism and the Formation of Gentry Society in Late Ming China* (1994). An analysis of the role of a significant religious force in the political and social developments of the Ming.

Clunas, Craig, and Jessica Harrison-Hall (eds.), *Ming: 50 Years That Changed China* (2014). Developed to accompany an exhibition at the British Museum, this catalog includes richly illustrated scholarly essays that explore clothing, jewelry, courtly objects, and commerce during the Ming dynasty.

Dardess, John, *A Ming Society: T'ai-ho County, Kiangsi, Fourteenth to Seventeenth Centuries* (1996). A work that covers the different changes and developments of a single locality in China through the centuries.

Dols, Michael Walter, *The Black Death in the Middle East* (1977). One of the few scholarly works to examine the Black Death outside Europe.

Dreyer, Edward, *Early Ming China: A Political History, 1355–1435* (1982). A useful account of the early years of the Ming dynasty.

Faroqhi, Suraiya N., and Kate Fleet (eds.), *The Cambridge History of Turkey*, vol. 2, *The Ottoman Empire as a World Power, 1453–1603* (2013). An overview of this crucial period in Ottoman history, written by experts in the field.

Finkel, Caroline, *Osman's Dream: The Story of the Ottoman Empire, 1300–1923* (2005). The most authoritative overview of Ottoman history.

Finnane, Antonia, *Changing Clothes in China: Fashion, History, Nation* (2008). An exploration of changing Chinese identities from the perspective of clothing.

Hale, John, *The Civilization of Europe in the Renaissance* (1994). A beautifully crafted account of the politics, economics, and culture of the Renaissance period in western Europe.

He, Yuming, *Home and the World: Editing the "Glorious Ming" in Woodblock-Printed Books of the Sixteenth and Seventeenth Centuries* (2013). An insightful exploration of Ming society through a close look at its vibrant print culture and market for books.

Hodgson, Marshall, *The Venture of Islam: Conscience and History in a World Civilization*, vol. 3 (1974). A good volume on the workings of the Ottoman state.

Hoffman, Philip T., *Why Did Europe Conquer the World?* (2015). Makes an interesting case for the importance of Europe's use of gunpowder technologies.

Itzkowitz, Norman, *Ottoman Empire and Islamic Tradition* (1972). Another good book on the Ottoman state.

Jackson, Peter, *The Delhi Sultanate* (1999). A meticulous, highly specialized political and military history.

Jackson, Peter, and Lawrence Lockhart (eds.), *The Cambridge History of Iran*, vol. 6 (1986). A volume that deals with the Timurid and Safavid periods in Iran.

Jones, E. L., *The European Miracle* (1981). A provocative work on the economic and social recovery from the Black Death.

Kafadar, Cemal, *Between Two Worlds: The Construction of the Ottoman State* (1995). A thorough reconsideration of the origins of one of the world's great land empires.

Karamustafa, Ahmed, *God's Unruly Friends: Dervish Groups in the Islamic Later Middle Period, 1200–1550* (1994). A book that describes the unorthodox Islamic activities that were occurring in the Islamic world prior to and alongside the establishment of the Ottoman and Safavid Empires.

Levathes, Louise, *When China Ruled the Seas: The Treasure Fleet of the Dragon Throne, 1405–33* (1994). A book that provides a lively account of the Zheng He expeditions.

Lowry, Heath W., *The Nature of the Early Ottoman State* (2003). New perspectives on the rise of the Ottomans to prominence.

McNeill, William, *Plagues and Peoples* (1976). A pathbreaking work with a highly useful chapter on the spread of the Black Death throughout the Afro-Eurasian landmass.

Morgan, David, *Medieval Persia, 1040–1797* (1988). Contains an informative discussion of the Safavid state.

Peirce, Leslie, *The Imperial Harem: Women and Sovereignty in the Ottoman Empire* (1993). A work that describes the powerful place that imperial women had in political affairs.

Pirenne, Henri, *Economic and Social History of Medieval Europe* (1937). A classic study of the economic and social recovery from the Black Death.

Reid, James J., *Tribalism and Society in Islamic Iran, 1500–1629* (1983). A useful account of how the Mongols and other nomadic steppe peoples influenced Iran in the era when the Safavids were establishing their authority.

Savory, Roger. *Iran under the Safavids* (1980). A standard and still-useful work on Safavid history.

Schäfer, Dagmar, *The Crafting of the 10,000 Things: Knowledge and Technology in Seventeenth-Century China* (2011). An innovative study of the philosophy of technology and crafts in the late Ming period with important implications for the global history of science.

Singman, Jeffrey L. (ed.), *Daily Life in Medieval Europe* (1999). An introductory description of the social and material world experienced by Europeans of different walks of life.

Tuchman, Barbara W., *A Distant Mirror: The Calamitous Fourteenth Century* (1978). A book that shows, in a vigorous way, how war, famine, and pestilence devastated Europeans in the fourteenth century.

Wittek, Paul, *The Rise of the Ottoman Empire* (1958). A work that contains vital insights on the emergence of the Ottoman state amid the political chaos in Anatolia.

Chapter 12: Contact, Commerce, and Colonization, 1450–1600

Axtell, James, *Beyond 1492: Encounters in Colonial North America* (1992). A wonderfully informed speculation about Indian reactions to Europeans.

Brady, Thomas A., Heiko A. Oberman, and James D. Tracy (eds.), *Handbook of European History 1400–1600: Late Middle Ages, Renaissance, and Reformation*, vol. 1, *Structures and*

Assertions (1996). A good synthetic survey of recent literature and historiographical debates.

Brook, Timothy, *Vermeer's Hat: The Seventeenth Century and the Dawn of the Global World* (2008). An interesting look at the connections forged across the globe through the works of a well-known European artist.

Casale, Giancarlo, *The Ottoman Age of Exploration* (2010). The author places Ottoman exploration in a comparative context alongside European overseas expansion.

Cass, Victoria, *Dangerous Women: Warriors, Grannies, and Geishas of the Ming* (1999). An original study of Chinese female archetypes in memoirs, miscellanies, short stories, and novels.

Chaudhuri, K. N., *Trade and Civilisation in the Indian Ocean: An Economic History from the Rise of Islam to 1750* (1985). An excellent, comprehensive work that deals with the Indian Ocean economy and the appearance of European merchants there from the sixteenth century onward.

Clendinnen, Inga, *Aztecs: An Interpretation* (1991). Brilliantly reconstructs the culture of Tenochtitlán in the years before its conquest.

Crosby, Alfred W., *The Columbian Exchange: Biological and Cultural Consequences of 1492* (1972). A provocative discussion of the ecological consequences that followed the European "discovery" of the Americas.

———, *Ecological Imperialism: The Biological Expansion of Europe, 900–1900* (1986). Another important work on the ecological consequences of European expansion.

Curtin, Philip, *Cross-Cultural Trade in World History* (1984). A work stressing the role of trade and commerce in establishing cross-cultural contacts.

Faroqhi, Suraiya N. (ed.), *The Cambridge History of Turkey*, vol. 3, *The Later Ottoman Empire, 1603–1839* (2008). Definitive articles on this important period in Ottoman history.

Faroqhi, Suraiya N., and Kate Fleet (eds.), *The Cambridge History of Turkey*, vol. 2, *The Ottoman Empire as a World Power, 1453–1603* (2013). A collection of articles written by leading scholars of this crucial period in Ottoman history.

Febvre, Lucien, *The Problem of Unbelief in the Sixteenth Century: The Religion of Rabelais* (1982). A tour de force of intellectual history by the man who moved the study of the Reformation away from great men to the broader question of religious revival and mentalities.

Flynn, Dennis, and Arturo Giráldez (eds.), *Metals and Monies in an Emerging Global Economy* (1997). Contains several articles relating to silver and the Asian trade.

Frank, Andre Gunder, *ReOrient: Global Economy in the Asian Age* (1998). A reassessment of the role of Asia in the economic development of the world from around 1400 onward.

Giraldez, Arturo, *The Age of Trade: The Manila Galleons and the Dawn of the Global Economy* (2015). The best analysis of the origins and effects of the Spanish colonization of the Philippines and the making of the Pacific Ocean world.

Glahn, Richard von, *The Economic History of China: From Antiquity to the Nineteenth Century* (2016). A masterful new survey of Chinese economic history.

———, *Fountain of Fortune: Money and Monetary Policy in China, 1000–1700* (1996). Includes an excellent analysis of the history of silver in Ming China.

Gruzinski, Serge, *The Conquest of Mexico* (1993). An important work on the conquest of Mexico.

Habib, Irfan, *The Agrarian System of Mughal India* (1963). One of the best studies on the subject.

Hall, Richard Seymour, *Empires of the Monsoon: A History of the Indian Ocean and Its Invaders* (1996). A very engaging journalistic account with fabulous details.

Hodgson, Marshall, *The Venture of Islam,* vols. 2 and 3 (1974). A magisterial work that includes the Indian subcontinent in its careful study of the political and cultural history of the whole Islamic world.

Hulme, Peter, *Colonial Encounters: Europe and the Native Caribbean, 1492–1797* (1986). Presents an interesting interpretation of the encounters of Europeans and Native Americans.

Lach, Donald F., *Asia in the Making of Europe,* 5 books in 3 vols. (1965–). Perhaps the single most comprehensive and innovative guide to the European voyages of discovery.

Lockhart, James, and Stuart Schwartz, *Early Latin America* (1983). One of the finest studies of European expansion in the late fifteenth century.

McCann, James, *Maize and Grace: Africa's Encounter with a New World Crop, 1500–2000* (2005). A significant study of how maize, a New World crop, became Africa's most widely grown grain.

Melville, Elinor G. K., *A Plague of Sheep: Environmental Consequences of the Conquest of Mexico* (1994). A history of the transformation of a valley in Mexico from the Aztec period to the era of Spanish rule.

Mignolo, Walter D., *The Darker Side of the Renaissance: Literacy, Territoriality, and Colonization* (1995). Uses literary theory and literary images to present provocative interpretations of the encounter of Europeans and Native Americans.

Ozbaran, Salih, *Ottoman Expansion toward the Indian Ocean in the 16th Century* (2009). An important treatment of the Ottoman entry into the Indian Ocean at a time when the Portuguese were also expanding there.

Pagden, Anthony, *European Encounters with the New World* (1993). A complex look at the deep and lasting imprint of the New World on its conquerors.

Parker, Geoffrey, *The Military Revolution: Military Innovation and the Rise of the West, 1500–1800* (1996). Traces the changes in technology and tactics in the early modern period and discusses the political significance of this "revolution."

Pelikan, Jaroslav, *Reformation of Church and Dogma (1300–1700)* (1988). An important overview of major religious controversies.

Phillips, William D., and Carla Rahn Phillips, *The World of Christopher Columbus* (1992). One of the finest studies of European expansion in the late fifteenth century.

Remensnyder, Amy G., *La Conquistadora: The Virgin Mary at War and Peace in the Old and New Worlds* (2014). The author illuminates the continuities of the spiritual reconquest of Iberia and the conquest of the Americas and the symbolic importance of the Virgin as the mother of conversion in a man's world.

Roper, Lyndal, *Martin Luther: Renegade and Prophet* (2016). A magisterial biography that demonstrates the ways in which Luther was a rebel but also a man of his time.

Russell-Wood, A. J. R., *The Portuguese Empire, 1415–1808* (1992). An important survey of early Portuguese exploration.

Chapter 13: Worlds Entangled, 1600–1750

Alam, Muzaffar, *The Crisis of Empire in Mughal North India* (1993). Represents the best of the new scholarly interpretations of the subject.

Bay, Edna, *Wives of the Leopard: Gender, Politics, and Culture in the Kingdom of Dahomey* (1998). A useful treatment of gender issues in Dahomey.

Blackburn, Robin, *The Making of New World Slavery: From the Baroque to the Modern, 1492–1800* (1997). A good place to begin when studying African slavery and the Atlantic slave trade, this book compares the early expansion of the plantation systems across the Atlantic and throughout the Americas.

Bushkovitch, Paul, *Peter the Great* (2016). An updated version of a standard work, offering a concise overview of one of Russia's most celebrated and energetic rulers.

Calloway, Colin G., *One Vast Winter Count: The Native American West before Lewis and Clark* (2003). A sweeping survey of North American Indian histories prior to the nineteenth century.

Crossley, Pamela, *A Translucent Mirror: History and Identity in Qing Imperial Ideology* (1999). The author deals with the formation of identities such as "Manchu" and "Chinese" during the Qing period.

Dale, Stephen F., *The Muslim Empires of the Ottomans, Safavids, and Mughals* (2010). A comparative overview of Islam's three most powerful empires of the sixteenth and seventeenth centuries.

Eltis, David, and David Richardson, *Atlas of the Transatlantic Slave Trade* (2010). This work contains the most up-to-date data on the Atlantic slave trade, including the numbers transported, where the captives came from, and where they landed.

Flynn, Dennis O., and Arturo Giráldez (eds.), *Metals and Money in an Emerging World Economy* (1997). A collection of articles about the place of silver in the world economy.

Forsyth, James, *A History of the Peoples of Siberia: Russia's North Asian Colony 1581–1990* (1992). A narrative overview of a violent history reminiscent of the western expansion of the United States.

Glahn, Richard von, *Fountains of Fortune: Money and Monetary Policy in China, 1000–1700* (1996). A discussion of the place of silver in the Chinese economy.

Halperin, Charles J., *Russia and the Golden Horde: The Mongol Impact on Medieval Russian History* (1985). A book on the rise of Muscovy, forebear of the Russian Empire, from within the Mongol realm.

Hämäläinen, Pekka, *The Comanche Empire* (2008). A book that inverts the conventional history of empires in North America by arguing that the Comanches were the most successful expansionist power in the middle of the continent during the eighteenth century.

Hartley, Janet, *Siberia: A History of the People* (2014). A vivid portrait of the diverse conquerors—fur traders, Cossack adventurers, political criminals—of a region larger than almost all continents.

Hattox, Ralph S., *Coffee and Coffeehouses: The Origins of a Social Beverage in the Medieval Near East* (1985). This work shows how widespread and popular coffee consumption and coffeehouses were around the world.

Herzog, Tamar, *Frontiers of Possession: Spain and Portugal in Europe and the Americas* (2015). An exploration of how Spanish and Portuguese rulers carved up the New World, less by military action and diplomatic treaties than by quarrels over land settlement and rights to trade and travel.

Heywood, Linda M., and John K. Thornton, *Central Africans, Atlantic Creoles, and the Foundation of the Americas, 1585–1660* (2007). Examines how Africans repopulated the Americas and created hybrid cultures.

Huang, Ray, *1587, A Year of No Significance: The Ming Dynasty in Decline* (1981). An insightful analysis of the problems confronting the late Ming.

Koch, Alexander, et al., "Earth System Impacts of the European Arrival and Great Dying in the Americas after 1492," *Quarternary Science Review* 207 (March 2019): 13–39. The findings of a group of climatologists at the University of London on the impact of the morbidity of Native American populations on the climate.

Lensen, George, *The Russian Push toward Japan: Russo-Japanese Relations 1697–1875* (1959). A discussion of why and how Japan established its first border with another state and how Russia pursued its ambitions in the Pacific.

Lockhart, James, *The Nahuas after the Conquest* (1992). A landmark study of the social reorganization of Meso-american societies under Spanish rule.

Lovejoy, Paul, *Transformations in Slavery: A History of Slavery in Africa* (1983). An excellent discussion of African slavery.

Mathee, Rudi, *Persia in Crisis, Safavid Decline, and the Fall of Isfahan* (2012). A study of the disintegration of the Safavid state.

Mikhail, Alan, *Nature and Empire in Ottoman Egypt: An Environmental History* (2011). An important study of the impact of the environment on Egypt in the eighteenth century.

Monahan, Erika, *The Merchants of Siberia: Trade in Early Modern Eurasia* (2016). A stirring account of entrepreneurs battling the harshest imaginable conditions to establish trading networks connecting the far-flung territories north of the ancient Silk Road.

Moon, David, *The Plough That Broke the Steppes: Agriculture and Environment in Russia's Grasslands, 1700–1913* (2013). A bold incorporation of environmental aspects to retell the epic story of Russia's most numerous social group.

Nakane, Chie, and Shinzaburo Oishi (eds.), *Tokugawa Japan: The Social and Economic Antecedents of Modern Japan* (1990). First-rate essays on Japanese village society, urban life, literacy, and culture.

Nwokeji, G. Uko, *The Slave Trade and Culture in the Bight of Biafra: An African Society in the Atlantic World* (2010). A study of the Aro peoples of southeastern Nigeria and their use of their commercial powers to promote a vigorous trade with European enslavers on the coast.

Pamuk, Sevket, *A Monetary History of the Ottoman Empire* (2000). A discussion of the place of silver in the Ottoman Empire.

Parker, Geoffrey, *Global Crisis: War, Climate Change, and Catastrophe in the Seventeenth Century* (2013). A comprehensive and exhaustively researched study of the effects of the Little Ice Age on the governments and societies of the entire world in the seventeenth century.

———— (ed.), *The Thirty Years' War* (1997). The standard account of the conflict and its outcomes.

Pendergrast, Mark, *Uncommon Grounds: The History of Coffee and How It Transformed Our World* (2010). A narrative of coffee's history and attendant culture, from its Abyssinian origins to the present day.

Perdue, Peter C., *China Marches West: The Qing Conquest of Central Asia* (2005). This volume chronicles the expansion of the Qing Empire to its northwest, drawing comparisons to other colonial empires and their legacies.

Platonov, S. F., *Ivan the Terrible* (1986). Covers the controversies over Russia's infamous tsar.

Rawski, Evelyn, *The Last Emperors: A Social History of Qing Imperial Institutions* (1998). This volume explores the mechanisms and processes through which the Qing court negotiated its Manchu identity.

Reid, Anthony, *Charting the Shape of Early Modern Southeast Asia* (1999). A collection of articles by a leading historian of Southeast Asia.

Reséndez, Andrés, *The Other Slavery: The Uncovered Story of Indian Enslavement in America* (2016). The most comprehensive treatment of how Europeans tried to enslave indigenous people of the Americas.

Spence, Jonathan, and John Wills (eds.), *From Ming to Ch'ing: Conquest, Region, and Continuity in Seventeenth-Century China* (1979). Covers the various aspects of a tumultuous period of dynastic transition.

Subramanyam, Sanjay, *From the Tigris to the Ganges: Explorations in Connected History* (2012). A study that demonstrates that Afro-Eurasia in the seventeenth and eighteenth centuries contained a porous network of empires, cultures, and economies.

Subramanyam, Sanjay, and Muzaffar Alam, *Indo-Persian Travels in the Age of Discoveries, 1400–1800* (2012). A lively portrait of cultural exchanges between Persia, central Asia, and India as seen in travel literature.

Taylor, Alan, *American Colonies: The Settling of North America* (2001). Brings together British, French, and Spanish colonial histories and shows how the fortunes of each were entangled with one another and with those of diverse Native American peoples.

Thornton, John K., *Africa and Africans in the Making of the Atlantic World, 1400–1800* (1998). A wonderful discussion of the large role enslaved Africans played in the formation of the Atlantic world.

———, *The Kongolese Saint Anthony: Dona Beatriz Kimpa Vita and the Antonian Movement, 1684–1706* (1998). An excellent monograph on religious movements in Kongo.

Toby, Ronald P., *State and Diplomacy in Early Modern Japan: Asia in the Development of the Tokugawa Bakufu* (1984). The author shows that the Japanese, far from being isolated from the outside world, engaged in vigorous and successful diplomacy.

Van Dusen, Nancy E., *Global Indios: The Indigenous Struggle for Justice in Sixteenth-Century Spain* (2015). A remarkable study of the ways that Spanish rulers enslaved Amerindians in the Americas and even exported them back to Europe.

Vilar, Pierre, *A History of Gold and Money* (1991). An excellent study of the development of the early silver and gold economies.

White, Sam, *A Cold Welcome: The Little Ice Age and Europe's Encounter with North America* (2017). A discussion of the problems encountered by the first European settlers in mainland North America.

Chapter 14: Cultures of Splendor and Power, 1500–1780

Axtell, James, *The Invasion of America: The Contest of Cultures in Colonial North America* (1985). Discusses the strategies of Christian missionaries in converting the Indians, as well as the success of Indians in converting Europeans.

Babaie, Sussan, *Isfahan and Its Palaces: Statecraft, Shi'ism and the Architecture of Conviviality in Early Modern Iran* (2008). An overview of the city of Isfahan as the capital of the Safavid state.

Barmé, Geremie R., *The Forbidden City* (2008). A concise introduction to the history of one of the most important physical emblems of Chinese imperial power.

Berlin, Ira, *Many Thousands Gone: The First Two Centuries of Slavery in North America* (1998). Surveys the development of African American culture in colonial North America.

Bleichmar, Daniela, *Visible Empire: Botanical Expeditions and Visual Culture in the Hispanic Enlightenment* (2012). A fascinating and beautifully illustrated history of creole botanical expeditions in the eighteenth century.

Brook, Timothy, *The Confusions of Pleasure: Commerce and Culture in Ming China* (1999). An insightful survey of Ming society.

Clunas, Craig, *Superfluous Things: Material Culture and Social Status in Early Modern China* (1991). A good account of the late Ming elite's growing passion for material things.

Collcutt, Martin, Marius Jansen, and Isao Kumakura, *A Cultural Atlas of Japan* (1988). A sweeping look at the many different forms of Japanese cultural expression over the centuries, including the flourishing urban culture of Edo.

Crèvecoeur, Hector St. John de, *Letters from an American Farmer*, reprinted from the original edition, with a prefatory note by W. P. Trent and an introduction by Ludwig Lewisohn (1904). Powerful and informative letters of a French settler in the Americas in the eighteenth century.

Darnton, Robert, *The Business of the Enlightenment: A Publishing History of the Encyclopédie, 1775–1800* (1979). The classic study of Europe's first great compendium of knowledge.

Dash, Mike, *Tulipomania: The Story of the World's Most Coveted Flower and the Extraordinary Passions It Aroused* (1999). A global perspective on and lively account of the spread of the tulip around the world as a flower signifying both beauty and status.

Dikötter, Frank, *The Discourse of Race in Modern China* (1992). A good survey of Chinese discussions of race in the modern era.

Doniger, Wendy, *The Hindus: An Alternative History* (2009). A deeply scholarly yet accessibly written history of Hinduism that takes into account both texts and popular practices and contains a lively account of dissenting traditions.

Elman, Benjamin A., *On Their Own Terms: Science in China, 1550–1900* (2005). A study of the development of "native" Chinese science and how the process interacted with the introduction of western science to China over the course of three and a half centuries.

Eze, Emmanuel Chukwudi (ed.), *Race and the Enlightenment: A Reader* (1997). Readings examining the idea of race in the context of the Enlightenment.

Fleischer, Cornell, *Bureaucrat and Intellectual in the Ottoman Empire: The Historian Mustafa Ali (1540–1600)* (1986). Offers good insight into the world of culture and intellectual vitality in the Ottoman Empire.

Gómez, Nicolás Wey, *The Tropics of Empire: Why Columbus Sailed South to the Indies* (2008). Argues that early scientific efforts to study hotter tropical latitudes were the origins of Europe's new science.

Grafton, Anthony, April Shelford, and Nancy Siraisi, *New Worlds, Ancient Texts: The Power of Tradition and the Shock of Discovery* (1995). A concise discussion of the impact of the New World on European thought.

Gutiérrez, Ramón, *When Jesus Came, the Corn Mothers Went Away: Marriage, Sexuality, and Power in New Mexico, 1500–1846* (1991). A provocative dissection of the spiritual dimensions of European colonialism in the Americas.

Harley, J. B., and David Woodward (eds.), *The History of Cartography*, vol. 2, book 2, *Cartography in the Traditional East and Southeast Asian Societies* (1994). An authoritative treatment of the subject.

Hart, Roger, *Imagined Civilizations: China, the West, and Their First Encounter* (2013). A treatment of the Jesuit mission to China as the first contact between Chinese and European cultures.

Horton, Robin, *Patterns of Thought in Africa and the West: Essays on Magic, Religion, and Science* (1993). Reflections on African patterns of thought and attitudes toward nature, which can help us understand African American religious beliefs and resistance movements.

Huff, Toby, *Intellectual Curiosity and the Scientific Revolution: A Comparative Perspective* (2011). This book deals with Europe's scientific revolution comparatively, asking why it occurred in Europe and not in China or the Islamic world.

Kai, Ho Yi (ed.), *Science in China, 1600–1900: Essays by Benjamin Elman* (2015). Elman, an expert on Chinese science, offers his latest word on

China's scientific achievements in a context of Europe's transmission of science through the Jesuit mission.

Keene, Donald, *The Japanese Discovery of Europe: Honda Toshiaki and Other Discoverers, 1720–1798* (1952). A study of the ways Japan managed to incorporate knowledge from the outside world with the development of national traditions.

Ko, Dorothy, *Teachers of the Inner Chambers: Women and Culture in Seventeenth-Century China* (1994). Explores the lives of elite women in late Ming and early Qing China.

Lewis, Bernard, *Race and Color in Islam* (1979). Examines the Islamic attitude toward race and color.

Mazower, Mark, *Salonica, City of Ghosts: Christians, Muslims and Jews, 1430–1900* (2006). An overview of one of the most important cities of the Ottoman Empire.

Mokyr, Joel, *A Culture of Growth: The Origins of the Modern Economy* (2016). Traces how the search for new knowledge yielded practical and valuable applications and set the stage for Europe's economic breakthrough.

Morgan, Philip D., *Slave Counterpoint: Black Culture in the Eighteenth-Century Chesapeake and Lowcountry* (1998). Describes the development of African American culture in colonial North America.

Munck, Thomas, *The Enlightenment: A Comparative Social History, 1721–1794* (2000). A wonderful survey, with unusual examples from the periphery, especially from Scandinavia and the Habsburg Empire.

Necipoğlu, Gülru, *Architecture, Ceremonial, and Power: The Topkapi Palace in the Fifteenth and Sixteenth Centuries* (1991). A magnificently illustrated book that shows the enormous artistic talent that the Ottoman rulers poured into their imperial structure.

Parker, Kenneth, *Early Modern Tales of the Orient: A Critical Anthology* (1999). A collection of travelers' accounts of the Near East.

"Publishing and the Print Culture in Late Imperial China," special issue, *Late Imperial China* 17, no. 1 (June 1996). Contains a collection of important articles with a foreword by the French cultural historian Roger Chartier.

Qaisar, Ahsan Jan, *The Indian Response to European Technology, AD 1498–1707* (1998). A meticulous, scholarly work on this little-studied subject.

Ramaswamy, Sumathi, "Conceit of the Globe in Mughal Visual Practice," *Comparative Studies in Society and History* 49, no. 4 (2007): 751–82. An excellent article that shows how Mughal rulers were aware of the world and adapted its discoveries to their Indo-centric visions.

Rizvi, Athar Abbas, *The Wonder That Was India*, vol. 2, *A Survey of the History and Culture of the Indian Subcontinent from the Coming of the Muslims to the British Conquest, 1200–1700* (1987). A deeply learned work in intellectual history.

Safier, Neil, *Measuring the New World: Enlightenment Science and South America* (2008). Examines the ways in which European, and especially Parisian, surveyors set about gauging the curvature of the earth, starting in Quito, Ecuador. Along the way, they learned much more about local natural history, which flowed back to Paris to inform the Enlightenment.

Smith, Bernard, *European Vision and the South Pacific* (1985). An excellent cultural history of Cook's voyages.

Smith, Richard J., *Chinese Maps: Images of "All under Heaven"* (1996). Provides a good introduction to the history of cartography in China.

Sorkin, David, *The Religious Enlightenment: Protestants, Jews, and Catholics from London to Vienna* (2008). Discusses a wide range of thinkers who were able to reconcile Enlightenment thought with religious belief.

Subrahmanyam, Sanjay, *Courtly Encounters: Translating Courtliness and Violence in Early Modern Eurasia* (2012). Explores the place of South Asia as a point of convergence for artists and scientists and the role of the Mughal court as a hub for global exchange.

Tignor, Robert L., "W. R. Bascom and the Ife Bronzes," *Africa: Journal of the International African Institute* 60, no. 3 (1990): 425–34. Explores controversies over issues of where antiquities of great artistic value like the Ife bronzes should reside.

Welch, Anthony, *Shah Abbas and the Arts of Isfahan* (1973). Describes the astonishing architectural and artistic renaissance of the city of Isfahan under the Safavid ruler Shah Abbas.

Whitfield, Peter, *The Image of the World: Twenty Centuries of World Maps* (1994). A good introduction to the history of cartography in different parts of the world.

Wilks, Ivor, *Forests of Gold: Essays on the Akan and the Kingdom of Asante* (1993). A study that focuses on the Asantes' drive for wealth.

Zilfi, Madeline C., *The Politics of Piety: The Ottoman Ulema in the Post-Classical Age (1600–1800)* (1988). Explores the cultural flourishing that took place within the Islamic world in this period.

Chapter 15: Reordering the World, 1750–1850

Allen, Robert C., *The British Industrial Revolution in Global Perspective* (2009). An authoritative study of the industrial revolution in Britain and its implications around the world.

———, *Global Economic History: A Very Short Introduction* (2011). A more globally oriented overview of industrialization than Robert Allen's book on British industrialization from a comparative perspective (above).

Anderson, Fred, *Crucible of War: The Seven Years' War and the Fate of Empire in British North America,* 1754–1766 (2000). The best synthesis of the "great war for empire" that set the stage for the American Revolution.

Bayly, C. A., *Indian Society and the Making of the British Empire* (1998). A useful work on the early history of the British conquest of India.

Blackburn, Robin, *The Overthrow of Colonial Slavery, 1776–1848* (1988). Places the abolition of the Atlantic slave trade and colonial slavery in a large historical context.

Cassel, Par Kristoffer, *Grounds of Judgement: Extraterritoriality and Imperial Powers in Nineteenth-Century China and Japan* (2012). A study of the idea and practice of extraterritoriality within the context of the triangular relationship between China, Japan, and the west.

Chaudhuri, K. N., *The Trading World of Asia and the East India Company, 1660–1760* (1978). An authoritative economic history of the East India Company's operations.

Crafts, N. F. R., *British Economic Growth during the Industrial Revolution* (1985). A pioneering study that emphasizes a long-term, more gradual process of adaptation to new institutional and social circumstances.

Daly, M. W. (ed.), *Cambridge History of Egypt*, vol. 2, *Modern Egypt, from 1517 to the End of the Twentieth Century* (1998). Contains authoritative essays on all aspects of modern Egyptian history, including the impact of the French invasion and the rule of Muhammad Ali.

de Vries, Jan, *Industrious Revolution: Consumer Behavior and the Household Economy, 1650 to the Present* (2008). A book on the lead-up to the industrial revolution, written by the leading economic historian who coined the term "industrious revolution."

Diamond, Jared, and James A. Robinson (eds.), *Natural Experiments of History* (2010). This book consists of eight comparative studies drawn from history, archaeology, economics, economic history, geography, and political science, covering a spectrum of approaches, ranging from a nonquantitative narrative style to quantitative statistical analyses.

Drescher, Seymour, *Abolition: A History of Slavery and Anti-Slavery* (2009). An authoritative overview of slavery and its opponents.

Dubois, Laurent, *Avengers of the New World: The Story of the Haitian Revolution* (2004). An authoritative synthesis on the Haitian Revolution.

Eacott, Jonathan, *Selling Empire: India in the Making of Britain and America, 1600–1830* (2016). Argues that the conquest of India and the resources extracted from India were vital to attitudes toward expansion in the Americas and the financing of Britain's American empire.

Elvin, Mark, *The Retreat of the Elephants: An Environmental History of China* (2004). A study of the different ways in which China's natural environment was shaped.

Findley, Carter, *Bureaucratic Reform in the Ottoman Empire: The Sublime Porte, 1789–1922* (1980). A useful guide to Ottoman reform efforts in the nineteenth century.

Geggus, David (ed.), *The Impact of the Haitian Revolution in the Atlantic World* (2001). A lively effort to disentangle the effects of the Haitian Revolution from those of the French Revolution.

Hevia, James, *Cherishing Men from Afar: Qing Guest Ritual and the Macartney Embassy of 1793* (1995). Offers a definitive interpretation of the nature of Sino-British conflict in the Qing period.

Hobsbawm, Eric, *Nations and Nationalism since 1780* (1990). An important overview of the rise of the nation-state and nationalism around the world.

Howe, Daniel Walker, *What Hath God Wrought: The Transformation of America, 1815–1848* (2007). A Pulitzer Prize–winning interpretation of how new technologies and new ideas reshaped the economy, society, culture, and politics of the United States in the first half of the nineteenth century.

Hunt, Lynn, *Politics, Culture and Class in the French Revolution* (1984). Examines the influence of sociocultural shifts as causes and consequences of the French Revolution, emphasizing the symbols and practice of politics invented during the revolution.

Inikori, Joseph, *Africans and the Industrial Revolution in England* (2002). Demonstrates the important role that Africa and Africans played in facilitating the industrial revolution.

Isset, Christopher Mills, *State, Peasant, and Merchant in Qing Manchuria, 1644–1862* (2007). A study of the relationships between sociopolitical structures and peasant lives in a key region during the Qing.

James, C. L. R., *The Black Jacobins: Toussaint L'Ouverture and the San Domingo Revolution* (1938). This classic chronicle of the only successful revolt of the enslaved in history provides a critical portrait of its leader, Toussaint L'Ouverture.

Jones, E. L., *Growth Recurring* (1988). Discusses the controversy over why the industrial revolution took place in Europe, stressing the unique ecological setting that encouraged long-term investment.

Kinsbruner, Jay, *Independence in Spanish America* (1994). A fine study of the Latin American revolutions that argues that the struggle was as much a civil war as a fight for national independence.

Landers, Jane, *Atlantic Creoles in the Age of Revolutions* (2011). A collection of fascinating and unique portraits of Atlantic world creoles who managed to move freely and purposefully through French, Spanish, and English colonies, and through Indian territory, in the unstable century between 1750 and 1850.

Lieven, Dominic, *Russia against Napoleon* (2010). Explains how outnumbered Russian forces were able to defeat the massive army that Napoleon assembled for his conquest of Russia.

Mokyr, Joel, *Enlightened Economy: An Economic History of Britain, 1700–1850* (2009). Perspectives on the evolution of the British economy in the era that produced the industrial revolution.

————, *The Lever of Riches* (1990). An important study of the causes of the industrial revolution that emphasizes the role of small technological and organizational breakthroughs.

Naquin, Susan, and Evelyn Rawski, *Chinese Society in the Eighteenth Century* (1987). A survey of mid-Qing society.

Neal, Larry, *The Rise of Financial Capitalism* (1990). An important study of the making of financial markets.

Nikitenko, Aleksandr, *Up from Serfdom: My Childhood and Youth in Russia, 1804–1824* (2001). One of the very few recorded life stories of a Russian serf.

Parthasarathi, Prasannan, *Why Europe Grew Rich and Asia Did Not: Global Economic Divergence, 1600–1800* (2011). A work that places the British industrial revolution in a global context, with much emphasis on India's textile industry before it was superseded by British manufacturers.

Platt, Stephen R., *Imperial Twilight: The Opium War and the End of China's Last Golden Age* (2018). A major work on the lead-up to and the long-term impact of the Opium Wars.

Pomeranz, Kenneth, *The Great Divergence: Europe, China, and the Making of the Modern World Economy* (2000). Offers explanations of why Europe and not some other place in the world, like parts of China or India, forged ahead economically in the nineteenth century.

Popkin, Jeremy D., *You Are All Free: The Haitian Revolution and the Abolition of Slavery* (2010). A revisionist account that calls attention to the role of local factors in the emancipation of enslaved Haitians.

Tackett, Timothy, *The Coming of the Terror in the French Revolution* (2017). An authoritative account of the most controversial phase of the French Revolution.

Taylor, Alan, *American Revolutions: A Continental History, 1750–1804* (2016). A sweeping interpretation of the founding of the United States that places the War of Independence in a North American perspective, bringing together the diverse revolutions that transformed societies and borders across the continent.

Wakeman, Frederic, Jr., "The Canton Trade and the Opium War," in John K. Fairbank (ed.), *The Cambridge History of China*, vol. 10 (1978), pp. 163–212. The standard account of the episode.

Wong, R. Bin, *China Transformed: Historical Change and the Limits of European Experience* (2000). Draws attention to the relative autonomy of merchant capitalists in relation to dynastic states in Europe as compared with China.

Wood, Gordon S., *Empire of Liberty: A History of the Early Republic, 1789–1815* (2009). An excellent synthesis of the history of the United States in the tumultuous years between the ratification of the Constitution and the War of 1812.

Wortman, Richard, *Scenarios of Power: Myth and Ceremony in Russian Monarchy*, 2 vols. (1995–2000). Examines how dynastic Russia confronted the challenges of the revolutionary epoch.

Chapter 16: Alternative Visions of the Nineteenth Century

Anderson, David M., *Revealing Prophets: Prophets in Eastern African History* (1995). Good discussion of the prophets in eastern Africa.

Beecher, Jonathan, *The Utopian Vision of Charles Fourier* (1983). A fine biography of this important thinker.

Boyd, Jean, *The Caliph's Sister: Nana Asma'u, 1793–1865, Teacher, Poet, and Islamic Leader* (1988). A study of the most powerful female Muslim leader in the Fulani religious revolt.

Brower, Benjamin Claude, *A Desert Named Peace: The Violence of France's Empire in the Algerian Sahara, 1844–1902* (2009). Examines colonial violence across a few fields of research and through multiple stories to reveal some unexpected causes—for instance, France's difficult revolutionary past and its sway on the military's institutional culture.

Caplan, Karen D., *Indigenous Citizens: Local Liberalism in Early National Oaxaca and Yucatán* (2009). Shows the ways in which indigenous people adapted liberalism for their own political imaginations and practices.

Clancy-Smith, Julia, *Rebel and Saint: Muslim Notables, Populist Protest, Colonial Encounter (Algeria and Tunisia, 1800–1904)* (1994). Examines Islamic protest movements against western encroachments in North Africa.

Clogg, Richard, *A Concise History of Greece* (1997). A good introduction to the history of Greece in its European context.

Dalrymple, William, *The Last Mughal: The Fall of a Dynasty: Delhi, 1857* (2007). A deeply researched and riveting account of Delhi during the 1857 revolt.

Danziger, Raphael, *Abd al-Qadir: Resistance to the French and Internal Consolidation* (1977). Still the indispensable work on this important Algerian Muslim leader.

Dowd, Gregory E., *A Spirited Resistance: The North American Indian Struggle for Unity, 1745–1815* (1992). Emphasizes the importance of prophets like Tenskwatawa in the building of pan-Indian confederations in the era between the Seven Years' War and the War of 1812.

Guardino, Peter, *The Dead March: A History of the Mexican-American War* (2017). A definitive account of the war from the Mexican side of the struggle.

Guha, Ranajit, *Elementary Aspects of Peasant Insurgency in Colonial India* (1983). Not specifically on the Indian Rebellion of 1857, but includes it in its pioneering "subalternist" interpretation of South Asian history.

Hamilton, Carolyn (ed.), *The Mfecane Aftermath: Reconstructive Debates in Southern African History* (1995). Debates on Shaka's *Mfecane* movement and its impact on southern Africa.

Hiskett, Mervyn, *The Sword of Truth: The Life and Times of the Shehu Usman dan Fodio* (1994). An authoritative study of the Fulani revolt in northern Nigeria.

Johnson, Douglas H., *Nuer Prophets: A History of Prophecy from the Upper Nile in the Nineteenth and Twentieth Centuries* (1994). Deals with African prophetic and charismatic movements in eastern Africa.

Keddie, Nikki, *An Islamic Response to Imperialism: Political and Religious Writings of Sayyid Jamal ad-Din "al-Afghani"* (1968). Definitive information on the Afghani's life and influence, coupled with a translation of one of his most important essays.

Lovejoy, Paul E., *Jihād in West Africa during the Age of Revolutions* (2016). This book should be read alongside the one by Lamin Sanneh (below), since these two scholars look at the revolutionary movements taking place in West Africa from differing perspectives. Lovejoy stresses jihads, while Sanneh emphasizes the peaceful uses of Islam.

Michael, Franz, and Chung-li Chang, *The Taiping Rebellion: History and Documents*, 3 vols. (1966–1971). The basic source for the history of the Taipings.

Mukherjee, Rudrangshu, *Awadh in Revolt, 1857–58* (1984). A careful case study of the Indian Rebellion.

Omer-Cooper, J. D., *The Zulu Aftermath: A Nineteenth-Century Revolution in Bantu Africa* (1966). A good place to start in studying Shaka's *Mfecane* movement, which greatly rearranged the political and ethnic makeup of southern Africa.

Ostler, Jeffrey, *The Plains Sioux and U.S. Colonialism from Lewis and Clark to Wounded Knee* (2004). Uses the lens of colonial theory to track relations between the Sioux and the United States, offering fresh insights about the Ghost Dance movement.

Peires, J. B. (ed.), *Before and After Shaka* (1981). Discusses elements in the debate over Shaka's *Mfecane* movement.

Pilbeam, Pamela, *French Socialists before Marx: Workers, Women and the Social Question in France* (2001). Describes the development of a variety of socialist ideas in early nineteenth-century France.

Platt, Stephen R., *Autumn in the Heavenly Kingdom: China, the West, and the Epic Story of the Taiping Civil War* (2012). A study of the Taiping Rebellion from a global perspective.

———, *Provincial Patriots: The Hunanese and Modern China* (2007). A well-argued essay on the important role that leaders born in Hunan have played in modern Chinese history. The book includes information on the role of Hunanese leaders in suppressing the Taiping uprising and on Mao Zedong, whose home province was Hunan.

Reed, Nelson, *The Caste War of Yucatan* (1964). A classic narrative of the Caste War of Yucatán.

Restall, Matthew, *The Maya World* (1997). Describes in economic and social terms the origins of the Yucatán upheaval in southern Mexico.

Robinson, David, *Muslim Societies in African History* (2004). A valuable overview of Muslim Africa, written by an expert on African Islam.

Rugeley, Terry, *Rebellion Now and Forever: Mayans, Hispanics, and Caste War Violence in Yucatán, 1800–1880* (2009). Explains the combination of economic and cultural pressures that drove the Maya in Yucatán to revolt in the Caste War.

———, *Yucatán's Maya Peasantry and the Origins of the Caste War* (1996). Examines the ways in which agrarian pressures, new taxes, and military recruitment put increasing strain on Maya farmers.

Sanneh, Lamin, *Beyond Jihad: The Pacifist Tradition in West African Islam* (2016). A powerful and often persuasive argument that the Muslim clerics in West Africa preferred peaceful means rather than violence to spread the tenets of Islam.

Spence, Jonathan, *God's Chinese Son: The Taiping Heavenly Kingdom of Hong Xiuquan* (1996). A fascinating portrayal of the Taipings through the prism of its founder.

Sperber, Jonathan, *Karl Marx: A Nineteenth-Century Life* (2013). An engaging and authoritative biography of Marx that emphasizes his role as a radical journalist.

Stedman Jones, Gareth, *Karl Marx: Greatness and Illusion* (2016). Now the authoritative biography of the founder of communism, showing Marx's own ambivalence about what he had created.

Wagner, Rudolf, *Reenacting the Heavenly Vision: The Role of Religion in the Taiping Rebellion* (1982). A brief but insightful analysis of the religious elements in the Taipings' doctrines.

Ware, Rudolph T., III, *The Walking Qur'an: Islamic Education, Embodied Knowledge, and History in West Africa* (2014). An overview of the Muslim clerics in Senegambia from the origins of Islam in the region up to the present.

White, Richard, *The Middle Ground: Indians, Empires, and Republics in the Great Lakes Region, 1650–1815* (1991). A pathbreaking exploration of intercultural relations in North America that offers a provocative interpretation of the visions of Tenskwatawa and the efforts of Tecumseh to resist the expansion of the United States.

Wilson, Jon, *The Chaos of Empire: The British Raj and the Conquest of India* (2018). This book challenges the image of an efficient British regime bringing order to decaying Indian kingdoms. It reveals just how brutal and improvised the conquest of India was.

Chapter 17: Nations and Empires, 1850–1914

Berry, Sara, *Cocoa, Custom and Socio-Economic Change in Western Nigeria* (1975). Innovative study based on interviews with local farmers that suggests that farmer enterprise and microeconomic theory better explain the spectacular growth in cocoa production than grand economic theory.

Cain, P. A., and A. G. Hopkins, *British Imperialism: Innovation and Expansion, 1688–1914* (1993). An excellent discussion of British imperialism, especially British expansion into Africa.

Clark, Christopher, *Iron Kingdom: The Rise and Downfall of Prussia, 1600–1947* (2009). Includes an excellent discussion of the rise of German nationalism and Prussian power.

Cooper, Frederick, *Colonialism in Question: Theory, Knowledge, History* (2005). A collection of essays by one of the leading scholars of colonial studies.

Cronon, William, *Nature's Metropolis: Chicago and the Great West* (1991). Makes connections among territorial expansion, industrialization, and urban development.

Davis, John, *Conflict and Control: Law and Order in Nineteenth-Century Italy* (1988). A superb study of the north-south and other rifts after Italian political unification.

Frankel, S. Herbert, *Capital Investment in Africa: Its Course and Effects* (1938). A careful study based on a mass of detailed figures and statistics on the general economic development of states in sub-Saharan Africa.

Friesen, Gerald, *The Canadian Prairies* (1984). The most comprehensive account of Canadian westward expansion.

Gluck, Carol, *Japan's Modern Myths: Ideology in the Late Meiji Period* (1985). A study of how states fashion useful historical traditions to consolidate and legitimize their rule.

Hall, Bruce S., *A History of Race in Muslim West Africa, 1600–1960* (2011). A study of racial consciousness in precolonial Africa and the uses made of it by the colonial conquerors of West Africa.

Harms, Robert, *Land of Tears: The Exploration and Exploitation of Equatorial Africa* (2019). A thorough and gripping account of the role scientists and surveyors played in the penetration of the interior of Africa and the pursuit of ivory and rubber.

Headrick, Daniel R., *The Tools of Empire: Technology and European Imperialism in the Nineteenth Century* (1981). A useful general study of the relationship between imperialism and technology.

Herbst, Jeffrey, *States and Power in Africa: Comparative Lessons in Authority and Control* (2000). An overview of the impact of colonial rule on contemporary African states.

Hill, Polly, *The Gold Coast Cocoa Farmer: A Preliminary Survey* (1965). A socioeconomic report detailing three issues facing the cocoa farmer: labor; indebtedness and pledging; and income and expenditure.

Hine, Robert V., and John Mack Faragher, *The American West: A New Interpretive History* (2000). Presents an excellent synthesis of the conquests by which the United States expanded from the Atlantic to the Pacific.

Hobsbawm, Eric J., *Nations and Nationalism since 1780: Programme, Myth, Reality* (1993). An insightful survey of the origins and development of nationalist thought throughout Europe.

Hochschild, Adam, *King Leopold's Ghost* (1998). A full-scale, eminently readable study of Europe's most egregiously destructive colonial regime in Africa.

Judson, Peter, *The Habsburg Empire: A New History* (2016). An innovative history of the relationship between "the people" and the state in a multiethnic empire.

Lee, Leo Ou-fan, and Andrew Nathan, "The Beginnings of Mass Culture: Journalism and Fiction in the Late Ch'ing and Beyond," in David Johnson, Andrew Nathan, and Evelyn Rawski (eds.), *Popular Culture in Late Imperial China* (1985), pp. 360–95. An important article on the emergence of a mass-media market in late nineteenth- and early twentieth-century China.

Lieven, Dominic, *Empire: The Russian Empire and Its Rivals* (2000). A comparison of the British, Ottoman, Habsburg, and Russian Empires.

Mackenzie, John M., *Propaganda and Empire* (1984). Contains a series of useful chapters showing the importance of the empire to Britain.

Mamdani, Mahmood, *Citizen and State: Contemporary Africa and the Legacy of Late Colonialism* (1996). A survey of the impact of European colonial powers on African political systems.

McClintock, Anne, *Imperial Leather: Race, Gender and Sexuality in the Colonial Contest* (1995). A study of the imperial relationship between Victorian Britain and South Africa from the point of view of cultural studies.

McNeil, William, *Europe's Steppe Frontier: 1500–1800* (1964). An excellent study of the definitive victory of Russia's agricultural empire over grazing nomads and independent frontier people.

Mitchell, B. R., *International Historical Statistics: Africa, Asia, and Oceania, 1750–2005* (2007). This comparative volume provides data from over two centuries for all principal areas of economic and social activity in both eastern and western Europe.

Montgomery, David, *The Fall of the House of Labor: The Workplace, the State, and American Labor Activism, 1865–1925* (1987). An excellent discussion of changes in work in the late nineteenth century.

Myers, Ramon, and Mark Peattie (eds.), *The Japanese Colonial Empire, 1895–1945* (1984). A collection of essays exploring different aspects of Japanese colonialism.

Needell, Jeffrey, *A Tropical Belle Epoque: Elite Culture and Society in Turn-of-the-Century Rio de Janeiro* (1987). Shows the strength of the Brazilian elites at the turn of the century.

Pan, Lynn (ed.), *The Encyclopedia of Chinese Overseas* (1999). A comprehensive coverage of the history of the Chinese diaspora.

Porter, Bernard, *The Absent-Minded Imperialists: What the British Really Thought about Empire* (2004). A careful dissection of the ways in which empire changed the British—and did not.

Prasad, Ritika, *Tracks of Change: Railways and Everyday Life in Colonial India* (2016). A detailed analysis of how railways transformed the everyday experience of Indians under colonial rule.

Rosenthal, Jean-Laurent, and R. Bin Wong, *Before and Beyond Divergence: The Politics of Economic Change in China and Europe* (2011). The authors challenge Kenneth Pomeranz's claims that China and Europe were roughly at the same level economically at the beginning of the eighteenth century and that Europe's industrial revolution, led by Great Britain, did not happen in China because of unique factors in Britain and the rest of Europe.

Ross, Corey, *Ecology and Power in the Age of Empire: Europe and the Transformation of the Tropical World* (2017). Marshals evidence that western corporations used empire to gain access to tropical raw materials, thus changing the relationship between the west and the rest of the world and altering work routines around the world.

Stengers, Jean, *Combien le Congo a-t-il coûté à la Belgique* (1957). A detailed financial accounting of how much Leopold put into the Congo and how much he took out, underscoring just how ruthlessly he exploited this possession.

Topik, Steven, *The Political Economy of the Brazilian State, 1889–1930* (1987). An excellent discussion of the Brazilian state, and especially of its elites.

Walker, Mack, *German Home Towns: Community, State, and the General State, 1648–1871* (1971; reprint, 1998). A brilliant, street-level analysis of the Holy Roman Empire (the First Reich) and the run-up to the German unification of 1871 (the Second Reich).

Wasserman, Mark, *Everyday Life and Politics in Nineteenth-Century Mexico* (2000). Wonderfully captures the way in which people coped with social and economic dislocation in late nineteenth-century Mexico.

Weeks, Theodore R., *Nation and State in Late Imperial Russia: Nationalism and Russification on the Western Frontier, 1863–1914* (1996). A good discussion of the Russian Empire's responses to the concept of the nation-state.

White, Richard, *Railroaded: The Transcontinentals and the Making of Modern America* (2011). A searing exposé of the corruptions and a startling critique of the economic and environmental costs associated with the expansion of railroad lines across Canada, the United States, and Mexico.

Wilson, Jon, *India Conquered: Britain's Raj and the Chaos of Empire* (2016). Stresses the violence and chaos involved in the British conquest and administration of Indian societies.

Yung, Wing, *My Life in China and America* (1909). The autobiography of the first Chinese graduate of an American university.

Zarrow, Peter, *After Empire: The Conceptual Transformation of the Chinese State, 1885–1924* (2012). A history of the changing ideas regarding the Chinese state that eventually led to the abandonment of monarchical rule by the Chinese people.

Chapter 18: An Unsettled World, 1890–1914

Aydin, Cemil, *The Idea of the Muslim World: A Global Intellectual History* (2017). Explores the creation of pan-Islamism in the nineteenth century and its complex relations with pan-Arabism, with a particular focus on the intellectual currents from Egypt to Indonesia.

Bayly, C. A., *The Birth of the Modern World, 1780–1914: Global Connections and Comparisons* (2004). A general study of the key political, economic, social, and cultural features of the modern era in world history.

Bergère, Marie-Claire, *Sun Yat-sen* (1998). Originally published in French in 1994, this is a judicious biography of the man generally known as the father of the modern Chinese nation.

Brinkley, Douglas, *Wilderness Warrior: Theodore Roosevelt and the Crusade to Save America* (2010). An important account of Roosevelt's environmental policies, based on new research.

Chatterjee, Partha, *The Nation and Its Fragments* (1993). One of the most important works on Indian nationalism by a leading scholar of "subaltern studies."

Conrad, Joseph, *Heart of Darkness* (1899). First published in a magazine in 1899, this novella contained a searing critique of King Leopold's oppressive and exploitative policies in the Congo and was part of a growing concern for the effects that European empires were having around the world, especially in Africa.

Esherick, Joseph, "How the Qing Became China," in Joseph W. Esherick,

Hasan Kayali, and Eric Van Young (eds.), *Empire to Nation: Historical Perspectives on the Making of the Modern World* (2006). A study of the processes through which the Qing Empire became the nation-state of China.

_____, *The Origins of the Boxer Uprising* (1987). The definitive account of the episode.

Everdell, William R., *The First Moderns: Profiles in the Origins of Twentieth-Century Thought* (1997). A rich account of the many faces of modernism, focusing particularly on science and art.

Finnane, Antonia, *Changing Clothes in China: Fashion, History, Nation* (2008). An exploration of changing Chinese identities from the perspective of clothing.

Gay, Peter, *The Cultivation of Hatred* (1994). A provocative discussion of the violent passions of the immediate pre–Great War era.

Gilmartin, Christina, et al. (eds.), *Engendering China: Women, Culture, and the State* (1994). Analyzes politics and society in modern China from the perspective of gender.

Hochschild, Adam, *King Leopold's Ghost: A Story of Greed, Terror, and Heroism in Colonial Africa* (1998). A well-written account of the violent colonial history of the Belgian Congo under King Leopold in the late nineteenth century.

Judge, Joan, *The Precious Raft of History: The Past, the West, and the Woman Question in China* (2008). An insightful exploration of the "woman question" in China at the turn of the twentieth century.

Katz, Friedrich, *The Life and Times of Pancho Villa* (1998). An exploration of the Mexican Revolution that shows how Villa's armies destroyed the forces of Díaz and his followers.

Keddie, Nikki, *An Islamic Response to Imperialism: Political and Religious Writings of Sayyid Jamal ad-Din "al-Afghani"* (1968). Definitive information on Afghani's life and influence, coupled with a translation of one of his most important essays.

Kern, Stephen, *The Culture of Time and Space 1880–1918* (1986). A useful study of the enormous changes in the experience of time and space in the age of late industrialism in Europe and America.

Kuhn, Philip, *Chinese among Others: Emigration in Modern Times* (2008). An overview of the history of Chinese migration.

McKeown, Adam, *Melancholy Order: Asian Migration and the Globalization of Borders* (2008). An examination of global migration patterns since the mid-nineteenth century and how regulations designed to restrict Asian migration to other parts of the world led to the modern regime of migration control.

Meade, Teresa, *"Civilizing" Rio: Reform and Resistance in a Brazilian City, 1889–1930* (1997). A wonderful study of cultural and class conflict in Brazil.

Mishra, Pankaj, *From the Ruins of Empire: The Intellectuals Who Remade Asia* (2012). Argues that an Asian tradition of thinking came into being in the late nineteenth century as a result of rising European empires and the emergence of Japan as an alternative model of modernization.

Moon, David, *The Plough That Broke the Steppes: Agriculture and Environment on Russia's Grasslands, 1700–1914* (2013). A pathbreaking study of Russian environmental history before the twentieth century.

Morris, Edmund, *Theodore Rex* (2002). A thorough biography of Theodore Roosevelt.

Nightingale, Carl H., *Segregation: A Global History of Divided Cities* (2012). Shows how, in the late nineteenth century, migration, investment, and booming exports coincided with increasing social partition within global cities.

Pick, Daniel, *Faces of Degeneration: A European Disorder, c. 1848–c. 1918* (1993). A study of Europe's fear of social and biological decline, particularly focusing on France and Italy.

Pretorius, Fransjohn (ed.), *Scorched Earth* (2001). A study of the Anglo-Boer War in terms of its environmental impacts.

Saler, Michael (ed.), *The Fin de Siècle World* (2014). A comprehensive anthology of essays on turn-of-the-century politics and culture across the world.

Sarkar, Sumit, *The Swadeshi Movement in Bengal* (1973). A comprehensive study of an early militant movement against British rule.

Schorske, Carl E., *Fin-de-Siècle Vienna: Politics and Culture* (1980). The classic treatment of the birth of modern ideas and political movements in turn-of-the-century Austria.

Trachtenberg, Alan, *The Incorporation of America: Culture and Society in the Gilded Age* (1982). A provocative synthesis of changes in the American economy, society, and culture in the last decades of the nineteenth century.

Wang, David Der-wei, *Fin-de-Siècle Splendor: Repressed Modernities of Late Qing Fiction, 1849–1911* (1997). A fine work that attempts to locate the "modern" within the writings of the late Qing period.

Warren, Louis, *Buffalo Bill's America: William Cody and the Wild West Show* (2005). A superb portrait of William F. Cody, the person; of Buffalo Bill, the persona Cody (and others) created; and of the popular culture his Wild West shows brought to audiences in Europe and North America.

Warwick, Peter, *Black People and the South African War, 1899–1902* (1983). An important study that reminds readers of the crucial involvement of Black South Africans in this bloody conflict.

Womack, John, Jr., *Zapata and the Mexican Revolution* (1968). A major work on the Mexican Revolution that discusses peasant struggles in the state of Morelos in great detail.

Chapter 19: Global Crisis, 1910–1939

Akcam, Taner, *The Young Turks' Crime against Humanity: The Armenian Genocide and Ethnic Cleansing in the Ottoman Empire* (2012). An exhaustive examination of the factors that impelled the Turkish authorities to carry out ethnic cleansing against the Armenians during World War I.

Akin, Yiğit, *When the War Came Home: The Ottomans' Great War and the Devastation of an Empire* (2018). A social history of the reactions of Ottoman citizenry to conscription and the efforts of the state to fight a modern war with modern means.

Aksakal, Mustafa, *The Ottoman Road to War in 1914: The Ottoman Empire and the First World War* (2008). A detailed treatment of the Ottomans' decision to align with Germany rather than with Britain, France, and Russia, and to not remain neutral throughout the conflict.

Anderson, Scott, *Lawrence in Arabia: War, Deceit, Imperial Folly, and the Making of the Middle East* (2013). A new and authoritative biography of T. E. Lawrence, with significant new material on British policies in the Middle East as seen through the eyes of a strong pro-Arab figure.

Bloxham, Donald, *The Great Game of Genocide: Imperialism, Nationalism, and the Destruction of the Ottoman Armenians* (2005). The definitive work on the Armenian genocide, set in a wide historical context.

Boyce, Robert, *The Great Interwar Crisis and the Collapse of Globalization* (2009). How the collapse of the world trading system and the failure of national leaders to resolve the effects of World War I led to the Great Depression.

Brown, Judith, *Gandhi: Prisoner of Hope* (1990). A biography of Gandhi as a political activist.

Clark, Christopher, *The Sleepwalkers: How Europe Went to War in 1914*

(2013). A rigorous examination of how interlaced European elites went to war with one another.

De Grazia, Victoria, and Ellen Furlough (eds.), *The Sex of Things: Gender and Consumption in Historical Perspective* (1996). Pathbreaking essays on how gender affects consumption.

Dumenil, Lynn, *The Modern Temper: America in the 1920s* (1995). A general discussion of American culture in the decade after World War I.

Eichengreen, Barry, *Gold Fetters: The Gold Standard and the Great Depression, 1919–1939* (1992). The definitive work on the Great Depression as a global crisis.

Fainsod, Merle, *Smolensk under Soviet Rule* (1989). The most accessible and sophisticated interpretation of the Stalin revolution in the village.

Friedman, Edward, *Backward toward Revolution: The Chinese Revolutionary Party* (1974). An insightful look at the failure of liberalism in early republican China through the prism of the short-lived Chinese Revolutionary Party.

Gelvin, James, *Divided Loyalties: Nationalism and Mass Politics in Syria at the Close of Empire* (1998). Offers important insights into the development of nationalism in the Arab world.

Gingeras, Ryan, *Fall of the Sultanate: The Great War and the End of the Ottoman Empire, 1908–1922* (2016). An essay on why the Ottomans entered the war and the consequences thereof.

Horne, John (ed.), *A Companion to World War I* (2010). A collection of articles written by leading scholars of World War I; the most comprehensive and up-to-date work on this war.

————, *State, Society, and Mobilization during the First World War* (1997). Essays on what it took to wage total war among all the belligerents.

Johnson, G. Wesley, *The Emergence of Black Politics in Senegal* (1971). A useful examination of the stirrings of African nationalism in Senegal.

Kennedy, David M., *Freedom from Fear: The American People in Depression and War, 1929–1945* (1999). A wonderful narrative of turbulent years.

Kershaw, Ian, *Hitler*, 2 vols. (1998–2000). A masterpiece combining biography and context.

Kieser, Hans-Lukas, *Talaat Pasha: Father of Modern Turkey, Architect of Genocide* (2018). An important biography of one of the most important Ottoman statesmen, who took Turkey into the war and carried out the Armenian genocide.

Kimble, David, *A Political History of Ghana* (1963). An excellent discussion of the beginnings of African nationalism in Ghana.

Kotkin, Stephen, *Magnetic Mountain: Stalinism as a Civilization* (1995). Recaptures the atmosphere of a time when everything seemed possible, even creating a new world.

————, *Stalin*, vol. 1, *Paradoxes of Power* (2014). A sweeping history of the tsarist regime, world war, Russian Revolution, civil war, and rise of Stalin.

Lambert, Nicholas A., *Planning Armageddon: British Economic Warfare and the First World War* (2012). Mines new archives to show that the British had an aggressive plan before the war to destroy Germany financially, which the British government approved and began to enact until the United States forced it to back off.

LeMahieu, D. L., *A Culture for Democracy: Mass Communication and the Cultivated Mind in Britain between the Wars* (1988). One of the great works on mass culture.

Leonhard, Jörn, *Pandora's Box: A History of the First World War* (2018). A masterful account of how a war predicted to produce a swift victory became so unwinnable for all sides.

Lyttelton, Adrian, *The Seizure of Power: Fascism in Italy, 1919–1929* (1961). Still the classic account.

Marchand, Roland, *Advertising the American Dream: Making Way for*

Modernity, 1920–1945 (1985). An excellent discussion of the force of mass production and mass consumption.

Mazower, Mark, *Dark Continent: Europe's Twentieth Century* (1999). A wide-ranging overview of Europe's tempestuous twentieth century.

McGirr, Lisa, *The War on Alcohol: Prohibition and the Rise of the American State* (2016). Emphasizes the power of cultural reaction against modernity that brought about Prohibition and the irony that its enforcement helped expand the power of the modern state.

McKeown, Adam, *Melancholy Order: Asian Migration and the Globalization of Border* (2008). A major study of the vast movement of peoples around the globe between the middle of the nineteenth and the twentieth centuries.

Morrow, John H., Jr., *The Great War: An Imperial History* (2004). Places World War I in the context of European imperialism.

Musgrove, Charles D., *China's Contested Capital: Architecture, Ritual, and Response in Nanjing* (2013). An exploration of how the Chinese Nationalist capital of Nanjing served as a focal point for the making of a nation and a new form of mass politics.

Nottingham, John, and Carl Rosberg, *The Myth of "Mau Mau": Nationalism in Kenya* (1966). Dispels the myths in describing the roots of nationalism in Kenya.

Patel, Kiran Klaus, *The New Deal: A Global History* (2016). A view that places Franklin Delano Roosevelt's New Deal in a global perspective, pointing out the ways in which other powers, mainly European, responded to the Great Depression, the gold standard, and Keynesianism.

Pedersen, Susan, *The Guardians: The League of Nations and the Crisis of Empire* (2015). Skillfully reexamines the neglected effort to regulate the colonial world under a so-called mandate system.

Rogan, Eugene, *The Fall of the Ottomans: The Great War in the Middle East* (2015). Emphasizes how international the war became when the Ottomans decided to join with the Central Powers.

Rosenberg, Clifford, *Policing Paris: The Origins of Modern Immigration Control between the Wars* (2006). Explores the first systematic efforts to enforce distinctions of nationality and citizenship status in a major urban setting.

Rutledge, Ian, *Enemy on the Euphrates: The British Occupation of Iraq and the Great Arab Revolt, 1914–1921* (2014). An impassioned investigation of Britain's effort to take control of the oil-rich territory of Iraq and the determined resistance of the Iraqi peoples.

Smith, S. A., *Russia in Revolution: An Empire in Crisis, 1890–1928* (2018). A masterpiece that shows how the Russian Empire went to war, how war created a civil war, and how out of civil war revolutionaries triumphed.

Strand, David, *An Unfinished Republic: Leading by Word and Deed in Modern China* (2011). A study of how the need for popular support led to a new political culture characterized by public speaking and performance in early twentieth-century China.

Suny, Ronald Gregor, *"They Can Live in the Desert but Nowhere Else": A History of the Armenian Genocide* (2015). A careful, document-based analysis of the Armenian genocide.

Taylor, Jay, *The Generalissimo: Chiang Kai-shek and the Struggle for Modern China* (2009). The first serious biographical study of Chiang Kai-shek in English, although its reliance on Chiang's own diary as a source does raise some questions of historical interpretation.

Thorp, Rosemary (ed.), *Latin America in the 1930s* (1984). An important collection of essays on Latin America's response to the shakeup of the interwar years.

Tsin, Michael, *Nation, Governance, and Modernity in China: Canton,*

1900–1927 (1999). An analysis of the vision and social dynamics behind the Guomindang-led revolution of the 1920s.

Vianna, Hermano, *The Mystery of Samba* (1999). Discusses the history of samba, emphasizing its African heritage as well as its persistent popular content.

Wakeman, Frederic, Jr., *Policing Shanghai, 1927–1937* (1995). An excellent account of Guomindang rule in China's largest city during the Nanjing decade.

Wilder, Gary, *Freedom Time: Negritude, Decolonization, and the Future of the World* (2015). Illustrates how anticolonialism grew into a global movement committed to a new idea of racial freedom and equality.

Winter, J. M., *The Experience of World War* (1988). A comprehensive presentation of the many sides of the twentieth century.

Young, Louise, *Japan's Total Empire: Manchuria and the Culture of Wartime Imperialism* (1998). An innovative case study of Japanese imperialism and mass culture with broad implications.

Chapter 20: The Three-World Order, 1940–1975

Aburish, Said K., *Nasser: The Last Arab* (2004). An impressive look at Egypt's most powerful political leader in the 1950s and 1960s.

Anderson, Jon Lee, *Che Guevara: A Revolutionary Life* (1997). A sweeping study of the radicalization of Latin American nationalism.

Bayly, Christopher, and Tim Harper, *Forgotten Armies: Britain's Asian Empire and the War with Japan* (2004). A brilliant social and military history of the Second World War as fought and lived in South and Southeast Asia.

Bruce-Lockhart, Katherine, "'Unsound Minds' and Broken Bodies: The Detention of 'Hardcore' Mau Mau Women at Kamiti and Gitamayu Detention Camps in Kenya, 1954–1960," *Journal of Eastern African Studies* 8, no. 4 (2014): 590–608. Examines a newly discovered British archive on the Mau Mau Uprising that reveals that the British opened a second detention camp for hardcore Mau Mau women at Gitamayu and sheds light on the treatment doled out by the British to women detained in both detention camps.

Byrne, Jeffrey James, *Mecca of Revolution: Algeria, Decolonization, and the Third World Order* (2016). Stresses the widespread influence of the Algerian revolution on other struggles for independence from imperial powers.

Chatterjee, Partha, *Nationalist Thought and the Colonial World: A Derivative Discourse* (1986). An influential interpretation of the ideological and political nature of Indian nationalism and the struggle for a postcolonial nation-state.

Cook, Alexander C. (ed.), *Mao's Little Red Book: A Global History* (2014). A look at the global impact of the Chinese Cultural Revolution through the lens of the iconic "little red book" of quotations from Mao.

Crampton, R. J., *Eastern Europe in the Twentieth Century and After*, 2nd ed. (1997). Comprehensive overview covering all Soviet-bloc countries.

Dikötter, Frank, *Mao's Great Famine: The History of China's Most Devastating Catastrophe, 1958–1962* (2010). A recent detailed account of one of the greatest man-made disasters in twentieth-century history.

Dower, John W., *Embracing Defeat: Japan in the Wake of World War II* (1999). A prize-winning study of the transformation of one of the war's vanquished.

Elkins, Caroline, *Imperial Reckoning: The Untold Story of Britain's Gulag in Kenya* (2005). Pulitzer Prize–winning study of the brutal war to suppress the nationalist uprising in Kenya in the

1950s that ultimately led to independence for that country.

Evans, Martin, *Algeria: France's Undeclared War* (2011). Gives the history of the Algerian nationalist movements and provides an overview of the Algerian war for independence.

Feshbach, Murray, and Alfred Friendly, Jr., *Ecocide in the USSR: Health and Nation under Siege* (1992). A crucial study of ecological disasters in the Soviet Union.

Gao, Yuan, *Born Red: A Chronicle of the Cultural Revolution* (1987). A gripping personal account of the Cultural Revolution by a former Red Guard.

Gerard, Emmanuel, and Bruce Kuklick, *Death in the Congo: Murdering Patrice Lumumba* (2015). The most recent study of the Congo independence movement and the execution of its major nationalist.

Getachew, Adom, *Worldmaking after Empire: The Rise and Fall of Self-Determination* (2019). An excellent study of how decolonization spread the national form of sovereignty while economic integration then weakened the idea of political self-determination.

Gordon, Andrew (ed.), *Postwar Japan as History* (1993). Essays covering a wide range of topics on postwar Japan.

Hargreaves, John D., *Decolonization in Africa* (1996). A good place to start when exploring the history of African decolonization.

Hasan, Mushirul (ed.), *India's Partition: Process, Strategy and Mobilization* (1993). A useful anthology of scholarly articles, short stories, and primary documents on the partition of India.

Iriye, Akira, *Power and Culture: The Japanese-American War, 1941–1945* (1981). A discussion that goes beyond the military confrontation in Asia.

Jackson, Kenneth T., *Crabgrass Frontier: The Suburbanization of the United States* (1985). An insightful and influential consideration of the movement of the American population from cities to suburbs.

Jalal, Ayesha, *The Sole Spokesman: Jinnah, the Muslim League and the Demand for Pakistan* (1985). A study of the high politics leading to the violent partition of British India.

Keep, John L. H., *Last of the Empires: A History of the Soviet Union, 1945–1991* (1995). A detailed overview of the core of the "Second World."

Lovell, Julia, Maoism: *A Global History* (2019). Traces the myth of Mao's revolution and its dissemination across the global south as well as Europe and North America.

Mba, Nina Emma, *Nigerian Women Mobilized: Women's Political Activity in Southern Nigeria, 1900–1965* (1982). An overview of women's political protests against the British in southern Nigeria.

Micklin, Philip, N.V. Aladin, and Igor Plotnikov (eds.), *The Aral Sea: The Devastation and Partial Rehabilitation of a Great Lake* (2014). Catalogues how Soviet irrigation plans drained a giant lake and destroyed the habitat of locals who depended on it for survival.

Morris, Benny, *Righteous Victims: A History of the Zionist-Arab Conflict, 1881–1999* (2000). A book on the Arab-Israeli War of 1948.

Pantsov, Alexander V., *Mao: The Real Story*, trans. Steven I. Levine (2012). A well-researched biography of Mao Zedong.

Patterson, James T., *Grand Expectations: The United States, 1945–1974* (1996). Synthesizes the American experience in the postwar decades.

Patterson, Thomas, *Contesting Castro* (1994). The best study of the tension between the United States and Cuba. Culminating in the Cuban Revolution, it explores the deep American misunderstanding of Cuban national aspirations.

Presley, Cora Ann, *Kikuyu Women, the Mau Mau Rebellion, and Social Change in Kenya* (1992). An overview of the impact of British policies on the most colonized group of African women.

Roberts, Geoffrey, *Stalin's Wars: From World War to Cold War, 1939–1953* (2007). A reassessment of Stalin's wartime leadership that conveys the vast scale of what took place.

Saich, Tony, and Hans van de Ven (eds.), *New Perspectives on the Chinese Communist Revolution* (1995). A collection of essays reexamining different aspects of the Chinese communist movement.

Schram, Stuart, *The Thought of Mao Tse-tung* (1989). Standard work on the subject.

Tignor, Robert L., *W. Arthur Lewis and the Birth of Development Economics* (2006). An intellectual biography of the Nobel Prize–winning, West Indian–born economist, who proposed formulas to promote the economic development of less developed societies and then sought to implement them in Africa and the West Indies.

Turshen, Meredeth, "Algerian Women in the Liberation Struggle and the Civil War: From Active Participants to Passive Victims?" *Social Research: An International Quarterly* 69, no. 3 (Fall 2002): 889–911. How women participated in Algeria's war of independence from France, and the benefits this brought women afterwards.

Van Allen, Judith, "'Sitting on a Man': Colonialism and the Lost Political Institutions of Igbo Women," *Canadian Journal of African Studies* 6, no. 2 (1972): 165–81. A crucial and early article on the women's uprising against the warrant chiefs in southeastern Nigeria.

Weiner, Douglas R., *A Little Corner of Freedom: Russian Nature Protection from Stalin to Gorbachev* (1999). A groundbreaking book about Russian environmentalism.

Weiss, Herbert, "The Congo's Independence Struggle Viewed Fifty Years Later," *African Studies Review* 55,

no. 1 (April 2012): 109–15. A statement by an American scholar who was in the Congo at the time of its independence.

Zubkova, Elena, *Russia after the War: Hopes, Illusions, and Disappointments, 1945–1957* (1998). Uses formerly secret archives to catalogue the devastation and difficult reconstruction of one of the war's victors.

Chapter 21: Globalization, 1970–2000

Anand, Nikhil, *Hydraulic City: Water and the Infrastructures of Citizenship in Mumbai* (2017). Illustrates how huge cities rely on basic infrastructures, like water circulation and treatment, and shows how the uneven distribution of water is a major cause of poverty and inequality. In the case of Mumbai, access to water maps onto access to power.

Collier, Paul, *The Bottom Billion: Why the Poorest Countries Fail and What Can Be Done about It* (2007). Shows that despite the world's advancing prosperity, more than a billion people have been left behind in abject poverty.

Connelly, Mathew, *Fatal Misconception: The Struggle to Control World Population* (2008). A savage attack on mainly American and United Nations population specialists, who supported China's autocratic one-child policy and other efforts to reduce fertility rates largely in Third World countries.

Davis, Deborah (ed.), *The Consumer Revolution in Urban China* (2000). A look at the different aspects of the recent, profound social transformation of urban China.

Davis, Mike, *City of Quartz: Excavating the Future in Los Angeles* (1990). Offers provocative reflections on the recent history, current condition, and possible future of Los Angeles.

Dutton, Michael, *Streetlife China* (1999). A fascinating portrayal of the survival tactics of those inhabiting the margins of society in modern China.

Eichengreen, Barry, *Globalizing Capital: A History of the International Monetary System* (1996). An insightful analysis of how international capital markets changed in the period from 1945 to 1980.

Ferguson, Niall, and Moritz Schularick, "'Chimerica' and the Global Asset Market Boom," *International Finance* 10, no. 3 (Winter 2007): 215–39. Coined the term "Chimerica" to designate a single, intertwined economic entity made up of a productive partner, China, and a consuming partner, the United States.

Gourevitch, Philip, *We Wish to Inform You That Tomorrow We Will Be Killed with Our Families: Stories from Rwanda* (1999). A volume that reveals the hatreds that culminated in the Rwanda genocide.

Guillermoprieto, Alma, *Looking for History: Dispatches from Latin America* (2001). A collection of articles by the most important journalist reporting on Latin American affairs.

Han Minzhu (ed.), *Cries for Democracy: Writings and Speeches from the 1989 Chinese Democracy Movement* (1990). A collection of documents from the events leading up to the incident in Tiananmen Square on June 4, 1989.

Herbst, Jeffrey, *States and Power in Africa: Comparative Lessons in Authority and Control* (2000). Explores the political dilemmas facing modern African polities.

Honig, Emily, and Gail Hershatter, *Personal Voices: Chinese Women in the 1980's* (1988). A record of Chinese women during a period of rapid social change.

Huang, Yasheng, *Capitalism with Chinese Characteristics: Entrepreneurship and the State* (2008). A sharp, unsentimental inside look at China's market economy and its future prospects.

Jacques, Martin, *When China Rules the World: The End of the Western World and the Birth of a New Global Order* (2009). A provocative essay on the rise of China as a world power and the overthrow of western cultural, political, and economic dominance.

Kavoori, Anandam P., and Aswin Punathambekar (eds.), *Global Bollywood* (2008). A collection of essays by leading scholars of Indian cinema on different aspects of the processes by which the Hindi film industry became Bollywood.

Kershaw, Ian, *The Global Age: Europe, 1950–2017* (2018). An overview of European developments from the end of World War II to the present.

Klitgaard, Robert, *Tropical Gangsters* (1990). On the intimate connections between corrupt native elites and international aid agencies.

Kotkin, Stephen, *Armageddon Averted: The Soviet Collapse, 1970–2000* (2001). Places the surprise fall of the Soviet Union in the context of the great shifts in the post–World War II order.

Lin, Justin Yifu, "China and the Global Economy," *China Economic Journal* 4, no. 1 (2011): 1–14. Originally presented as a luncheon address to businesspeople, this article provides useful statistics on China's economic and financial development from 1990 to 2010.

Macekura, Stephen, *Of Limits and Growth: The Rise of Global Sustainable Development in the Twentieth Century* (2016). Explores the rise of global environmental politics in the 1970s and 1980s and the debate about resources and climate change.

Maddison, Angus, *Chinese Economic Performance in the Long Run*, 2nd ed., revised and updated, 960–2030 AD (2007). Full of useful financial and economic statistics, this report is the best resource on China's economic miracle.

Mamdani, Mahmood, *When Victims Become Killers: Colonialism, Nativism, and the Genocide in Rwanda* (2001). Discusses the genocide in Rwanda in light of the legacy of colonialism.

Mehta, Suketu, *Maximum City: Bombay Lost and Found* (2005). Examines one of the great, and contradictory, cities in the era of globalization.

Miller, Chris, *The Struggle to Save the Soviet Economy: Mikhail Gorbachev and the Collapse of the USSR* (2016). An insightful analysis of internal debates in Moscow over rival directions for the Soviet economy and the response to Chinese reforms after 1978.

Mottahedeh, Roy, *The Mantle of the Prophet: Religion and Politics in Iran,* 2nd ed. (2008). Perhaps the best book on the 1979 Iranian Revolution and its aftermath.

Nathan, Andrew, and Perry Link, *The Tiananmen Papers* (2002). An inside look at the divisions within the Chinese elite in connection with the 1989 crackdown.

Portes, Alejandro, and Rubén G. Rumbaut, *Immigrant America,* 2nd ed. (1996). A good comparative study of how immigration has transformed the United States.

Prakash, Gyan, *Mumbai Fables* (2010). A spirited account of the rise of India's most modern city, a center of intellectual, commercial, and political vitality.

Prunier, Gerald, *Africa's World War: Congo, the Rwandan Genocide, and the Making of a Continental Catastrophe* (2009). A chilling discussion of the spillover effects of the Rwandan genocide on central, eastern, and southern Africa.

Punathambekar, Aswin, *From Bombay to Bollywood: The Making of a Global Media Industry* (2013). A study of the transformation of the Indian film industry that globalizes its content and reach.

Rao, D. S. Prasada, and Bart van Ark, *World Economic Performance: Past, Present and Future* (2013). Essays in honor of economist Angus Maddison, including an essay by Maddison on China's long-term economic performance.

Reinhart, Carmen, and Kenneth Rogoff, *This Time Is Different: Eight Centuries of Financial Folly* (2009). Explains the latest financial crash using historical perspective.

Ruggie, John Gerard, *Just Business: Multinational Corporations and Human Rights* (2013). Shows how even big businesses became involved in human rights advocacy.

Sen, Amartya, *Poverty and Famines: An Essay on Entitlement and Deprivation* (1982). A major study that reoriented the study of famines from a narrow concentration on food supply to broader questions of ownership, exchange, and democracy.

Sikkink, Kathryn, *The Justice Cascade: How Human Rights Prosecutions Are Changing World Politics* (2011). Shows how new forms of global organizing and new social norms are changing the political rules across borders.

Stein, Judith, *Pivotal Decade: How the United States Traded Factories for Finance in the Seventies* (2010). A comprehensive study of the rise of American banking and the decline of heartland industries.

Ther, Philipp, *Europe since 1989: A History* (2016). A concise account of European integration and neoliberalism since the fall of the Berlin Wall.

Van Der Wee, Hermann, *Prosperity and Upheaval: The World Economy, 1945–1980* (1986). Describes very well the transformation and problems of the world economy, particularly from the 1960s onward.

Vogel, Ezra F., *Deng Xiaoping and the Transformation of China* (2011). The definitive biography of China's leading reformer, based on exhaustive interviews and full source material.

Westad, Odd Arne, *The Global Cold War: Third World Interventions and the Making of Our Times* (2007). A genuinely global perspective on the Cold War and its consequences.

Winn, Peter, *Americas: The Changing Face of Latin America and the Caribbean* (1992). A useful portrayal of Latin America since the 1970s.

Chapter 22: Twenty-First-Century Global Challenges, 2001–the Present

Achcar, Gilbert, *Morbid Symptoms: Relapse in the Arab Uprising* (2016). An up-to-date overview of the difficulties that the proponents of the Arab Spring encountered, with long and detailed treatments of Syria and Egypt.

Blinder, Alan S., *After the Music Stopped: The Financial Crisis, the Response, and the Work Ahead* (2013). A definitive and detailed treatment of the Great Recession.

Chamie, Joseph, "Replacement Fertility Declines Worldwide," YaleGlobal Online, July 22, 2018, https://yaleglobal.yale.edu/content/replacement-fertility-declines-worldwide. A useful article on worldwide fertility rates.

Christensen, Thomas J., *The China Challenges: Shaping the Choices of a Rising Power* (2015). A survey of China's rise and the challenges and choices the country faces in the contemporary world.

Cleveland, William L., and Martin Bunton, *A History of the Modern Middle East*, 6th ed. (2016). The sixth edition of an important textbook that covers the whole of the Middle East from 1800 to the present.

Cooper, Frederick, *Africa in the World: Capitalism, Empire, Nation-State* (2014). An overview of Africa's place in global history, based on the most recent scholarship.

Crutzen, Paul J., and Eugene F. Stoermer, "The 'Anthropocene,'" IGBP Newsletter, no. 41 (May 2000): 17–18. The first coining of the term *Anthropocene* and the argument for a new geologic epoch.

Darwall, Rupert, *The Age of Global Warming: A History* (2013). An accessible narrative describing how scientists became increasingly aware of the threat of climate change and the multinational effort to reduce carbon emissions.

Deaton, Angus, *The Great Escape: Health, Wealth, and the Origins of Inequality* (2013). An examination of rising inequality by a Nobel Prize–winning authority who emphasizes that contemporary well-to-do individuals have largely failed to help those not so fortunate to achieve their potential.

Eichengreen, Barry J., *Hall of Mirrors: The Great Depression and the Great Recession, and the Uses—and Misuses—of History* (2015). The expert on the Great Depression now writes about the Great Recession.

Esposito, John L., Tamara Sonn, and John O. Voll, *Islam and Democracy after the Arab Spring* (2016). An analysis of the prospects of democracy in Muslim countries, with case studies of Tunisia, Egypt, and Turkey, among others.

Ferguson, James, *Give a Man a Fish: Reflections on the New Politics of Distribution* (2015). An analysis of social welfare programs in southern Africa, which involve cash payments to the poorest members of societies, and their implications for neoliberal capitalism.

Franco, Jean, *Cruel Modernity* (2013). An examination of the cultural dimensions of Latin America's experience with recent neoliberal policies and the tensions and violence of relatively stateless societies.

Friedman, Milton, and Anne Jacobson Schwartz, *A Monetary History of the United States, 1867–1960* (1963). A classic account of monetary policy. Still essential reading even though it leaves off in 1960.

Gallagher, James, "Remarkable Decline in Fertility Rates," BBC News, November 9, 2018, https://www.bbc.com/news/health-46118103. Written by the health and science correspondent for BBC News, this article provides the best overview of Christopher Murray et al's definitive article on fertility (see below), which is packed with statistics and details.

Gerges, Fawaz A., *ISIS: A History* (2016). One of a series of books that explores the rise of ISIS and stresses the place of violence in building a new Islamic state.

Guillen, Mauro F., *The Architecture of Collapse: The Global System in the 21st Century* (2015). A work that stresses the interconnectedness and complexity of the global capitalist system and argues that global financial systems have an "intrinsic propensity to instability, disruption, and crisis."

Jaffrelot, Christophe, *Saffron Modernity in India: Narendra Modi and His Experiment with Gujarat* (2014). A political history of how Narendra Modi emerged dominant in Gujarat using anti-Muslim nationalist ideology, captured the leadership of the BJP, and built a personality cult that catapulted him to national leadership.

Judis, John, *The Populist Explosion: How the Great Recession Transformed American and European Politics* (2016). A book by a journalist and political analyst that argues that the contemporary populist upsurges on both the right and the left are responses to neoliberal globalization.

Kindleberger, Charles P., and Robert Aliber, *Manias, Panics, and Crashes: A History of Financial Crises*, 5th edition (2005). A brilliant overview of the financial crises that have beset the global economy prior to the Great Recession of 2008.

Lepore, Jill, *The Whites of Their Eyes: The Tea Party's Revolution and the Battle over American History* (2011). A history of the American far right and the Tea Party and their imagination of a nostalgic American past.

Lynch, Marc, *The New Arab Wars: Uprisings and Anarchy in the Middle East* (2016). Brings the narrative of the Arab Spring and the ambitions of its diverse proponents up to the present.

McCants, William, *The ISIS Apocalypse: The History, Strategy, and Doomsday Vision of the Islamic State* (2015). An important study of ISIS based on a wide reading of its own publications.

McNeill, J. R., *Something New under the Sun: An Environmental History of the Twentieth Century* (2000). An important overview of the environmental history of the twentieth century, with considerable statistical data that underscore the impact of humans on the environment and the atmosphere.

McNeill, J. R., and Peter Engelke, "Into the Anthropocene: People and Their Planet," in Akira Iriye (ed.), *Global Interdependence: The World after 1945* (2014), pp. 365–533. Two environmental historians embrace the concept of the Anthropocene Epoch.

Milankovic, Brian, *Global Inequality: A New Approach for the Age of Globalization* (2016). Using the most up-to-date data on worldwide incomes, the author shows how the last quarter century has yielded a convergence in global income distribution across societies and the widening of a gap within societies.

Moubayed, Sami, *Under the Black Flag: At the Frontier of the New Jihad* (2015). A study of the rise of jihadism within the Arab world, with a concentration on Syria.

Muller, Jan-Werner, *What Is Populism?* (2016). The sharpest analysis yet of the nature and prospects of populism, especially its relations to political establishments, which it condemns but on which it depends.

Murray, Christopher, et al., "Population and Fertility by Age and Sex for 195 Countries and Territories, 1950–2017: A Systemic Analysis for the Global Burden of Disease Study, 2017," *Lancet* 392, no. 10159 (November 10–16, 2018): 1995–2051. The definitive article on total fertility worldwide.

Owen, Roger, *The Rise and Fall of Arab Presidents for Life, with a New Afterword* (2014). A study that examines the emergence of Arab leaders who endeavored to hold on to power for as long as they lived, with insights into the actions of those who brought many of those leaders down during the Arab Spring.

Pietz, David A., *The Yellow River: The Problem of Water in Modern China* (2015). A critical look at health and environmental issues in China today, from a historical perspective through the lens of one of its major rivers.

Population Reference Bureau, *2018 World Population Data Sheet*, 2018, https://www.prb.org/wp-content/uploads/2018/08/2018_WPDS.pdf, and *2019 World Population Data Sheet*, 2019, https://www.prb.org/2019-world-population-data-sheet/. Useful statistics on world population.

Radelet, Steven, *Emerging Africa: How Seventeen Countries Are Leading the Way* (2010). An Afro-optimist sees many African countries enjoying economic growth and political stability, proving that Africa can join much of the rest of the world in achieving economic and political progress.

———, *The Great Surge: The Ascent of the Developing World* (2015). An overview of the extraordinary progress that many of the countries in what once was called the Third World have achieved in the economic and political realms.

Reid, Michael, *Forgotten Continent: The Battle for Latin America's Soul* (2009). A journalistic account of how Latin America grappled with market openings, new democratic forces, and the search for policies to close the gap between the haves and have-nots.

Shambaugh, David, *China Goes Global: The Partial Power* (2013). An analysis of China's role in the global arena and its impact, from economics to culture.

Trenin, Dmitri, *Should We Fear Russia?* (2016). A clear-eyed view of what contemporary Russia is and is not.

Warwick, John, *Black Flags Flying: The Rise of ISIS* (2015). A detailed account of the leadership groups within ISIS and its relationship to al-Qaeda.

Weiss, Michael, and Hassan Hassan, *ISIS: Inside the Army of Terror* (2015). An account based on interviews and wide reading of western and Arabic sources on the rise of ISIS.

Wright, Lawrence, *The Looming Tower: Al-Qaeda and the Road to 9/11* (2006). A Pulitzer Prize–winning study of the origins and evolution of al-Qaeda.

———, *The Terror Years: From al-Qaeda to ISIS* (2016). Primarily a study of the decline of the power of al-Qaeda, which created an opening for the more territorially based ISIS.

Glossary

Abd al-Rahman III Islamic ruler in Spain who held a countercaliphate and reigned from 912 to 961 CE.

aboriginals Original, native inhabitants of a region, as opposed to invaders, colonizers, or later peoples of mixed ancestry.

absolute monarchy Form of government in which one body, usually the monarch, controls the right to tax, judge, make war, and coin money. The term *enlightened absolutist* was often used to refer to state monarchies in seventeenth- and eighteenth-century Europe.

acid rain Precipitation containing large amounts of sulfur, which comes mainly from coal-fired power plants.

adaptation Ability to alter behavior and to innovate, finding new ways of doing things.

African National Congress (ANC) Multiracial organization founded in 1912 in an effort to end racial discrimination in South Africa.

Afrikaners Descendants of the original Dutch settlers of South Africa; formerly referred to as Boers.

Agones Athletic contests in ancient Greece.

Ahmosis Egyptian ruler in the southern part of the country who ruled from 1550 to 1525 BCE; Ahmosis used Hyksos weaponry—chariots in particular—to defeat the Hyksos themselves.

Ahura Mazda Supreme God of the Persians, believed to have created the world and all that is good and to have appointed earthly kings.

AIDS *See* HIV/AIDS.

Akbarnamah Mughal intellectual Abul-fazl's *Book of Akbar*, which attempted to reconcile the traditional Sufi interest in the inner life within the worldly context of a great empire.

Alaric II Visigothic king who issued a simplified code of innovative imperial law.

Alexander the Great (356–323 BCE) Leader who used novel tactics and new kinds of armed forces to conquer the Persian Empire, which extended from Egypt and the Mediterranean Sea to the interior of what is now Afghanistan and as far as the Indus River valley. Alexander's conquests broke down barriers between the Mediterranean world and Southwest Asia and transferred massive amounts of wealth and power to the Mediterranean, transforming it into a more unified world of economic and cultural exchange.

Alexandria Port city in Egypt named after Alexander the Great. Alexandria was a model city in the Hellenistic world. It was built up by a multiethnic population from around the Mediterranean world.

al-Khwarizmi Scientist and mathematician who lived from 780 to 850 CE and is known for having modified Indian digits into Arabic numerals.

Allied Powers Name given to the alliance between Britain, France, Russia, and Italy, all of which fought against Germany and Austria-Hungary (the Central Powers) in World War I. In World War II, the name was used for the alliance between Britain, France, and the United States, all of which fought against the Axis powers (Germany, Italy, and Japan).

allomothering System in which mothers relied on other women, including their own mothers, daughters, sisters, and friends, to help in the nurturing and protecting of their children.

alluvium Area of land created by river deposits.

alphabet A mid-second-millennium BCE Phoenician system of writing based on relatively few letters (twenty-two) that combined to make sounds and words. Adaptable to many languages, the alphabet was simpler and more flexible than writing based on symbols for syllables and ideas.

American Railway Union Workers' union that initiated the Pullman strike of 1894, which led to violence and ended in the leaders' arrest.

Amnesty International Nongovernmental organization formed to defend "prisoners of conscience"—those detained for their beliefs, race, sex, ethnic origin, language, or religion.

Amorites Name, which means "westerners," used by Mesopotamian urbanites to describe the transhumant herders who began to migrate into their cities in the late third millennium BCE.

Amun Once-insignificant Egyptian god elevated to higher status by Amenemhet I (1985–1955 BCE). *Amun* means "hidden" in Ancient Egyptian; the name was meant to convey the god's omnipresence.

Analects, The Texts that included the teachings and cultural ideals of Confucius.

anarchists Advocates of anarchism, the belief that society should be a free association of its members, not subject to government, laws, or police.

Anatolia The area now mainly known as modern Turkey. In the sixth millennium BCE, people from Anatolia, Greece, and the Levant took to boats and populated the Aegean. Their small villages endured almost unchanged for two millennia.

Angkor Wat Magnificent temple complex that crowned the royal palace of the Khmer Empire in Angkor, adorned with statues representing the Hindu pantheon of gods.

Anglo-Boer War (1899–1902) Anticolonial struggle in South Africa between the British and the Afrikaners over the gold-rich Transvaal. In response to the Afrikaners' guerrilla tactics and in order to contain the local population, the British instituted the first concentration camps. Ultimately, Britain won the conflict.

animal domestication Gradual process that occurred simultaneously with or just before the domestication of plants, depending on the region.

annals Historical records. Notable annals are the cuneiform inscriptions that record successful Neo-Assyrian military campaigns.

Anti-Federalists Critics of the U.S. Constitution who sought to defend the people against the power of the federal government and insisted on a Bill of Rights to protect individual liberties from government intrusion.

apartheid Racial segregation policy of the Afrikaner-dominated South African government. Legislated in 1948 by the Afrikaner National Party, it had existed in South Africa for many years.

Arab-Israeli War of 1948–1949 Conflict between Israeli and Arab armies that arose in the wake of a U.N. vote to partition Palestine into Arab and Jewish territories. The war shattered the legitimacy of Arab ruling elites.

Aramaic Dialect of a Semitic language spoken in Southwest Asia; it became the lingua franca of the Persian Empire.

Aristotle (384–322 BCE) Philosopher who studied under Plato but came to different conclusions about nature and politics. Aristotle believed in collecting observations about nature and discerning patterns to ascertain how things worked.

Aryans Nomadic charioteers who spoke Indo-European languages and entered South Asia in 1500 BCE. The early Aryan settlers were herders.

Asante state State located in present-day Ghana, founded by the Asantes at the end of the seventeenth century. It grew in power in the next century because of its access to gold and its involvement in the slave trade.

ascetic One who rejects material possessions and physical pleasures.

Asiatic Society Cultural organization founded by British Orientalists who supported native culture but still believed in colonial rule.

Aśoka Emperor of the Mauryan dynasty from 268 to 231 BCE; he was a great conqueror and unifier of India. He is said to have embraced Buddhism toward the end of his life.

Assur One of two cities on the upper reaches of the Tigris River that were the heart of Assyria proper (the other was Nineveh).

Aśvaghosa First known Sanskrit writer. It is believed that he lived from 80 to 150 CE and composed a biography of the Buddha.

Ataturk, Mustafa Kemal (1881–1938) Ottoman army officer and military hero who helped forge the modern Turkish nation-state. He and his followers deposed the sultan, declared Turkey a republic, and constructed a European-like secular state, eliminating Islam's hold over civil and political affairs.

Atlantic system New system of trade and expansion that linked Europe, Africa, and the Americas. It emerged in the wake of European voyages across the Atlantic Ocean.

atma Vedic term signifying the eternal self, represented by the trinity of deities.

atman In the Upanishads, an eternal being who exists everywhere. The atman never perishes, but is reborn or transmigrates into another life.

Attila Sole ruler of all Hunnish tribes from 434 to 453 CE. Harsh and much feared, he formed the first empire to oppose Rome in northern Europe.

Augustus Latin term meaning "the Revered One"; title granted by the Senate to the Roman ruler Octavian in 27 BCE to signify his unique political position. Along with his adopted family name, *Caesar*, the military honorific *imperator*, and the senatorial term *princeps*, *Augustus* became a generic term for a leader of the Roman Empire.

australopithecines Hominin species, including *anamensis*, *afarensis* (Lucy), and *africanus*, that appeared in Africa beginning around 4 million years ago and, unlike other animals, sometimes walked on two legs. Their brain capacity was a little less than one-third of a modern human's. Although not humans, they carried the genetic and biological material out of which modern humans would later emerge.

Austro-Hungarian Empire Dual monarchy established by the Habsburg family in 1867; it collapsed at the end of World War I.

authoritarianism Centralized and dictatorial form of government, proclaimed by its adherents to be superior to parliamentary democracy and especially effective at mobilizing the masses. This idea was widely accepted in parts of the world during the 1930s.

Avesta Compilation of Zoroastrian holy works transmitted orally by priests for millennia and eventually recorded in the sixth century BCE.

Awadh Kingdom in northern India; one of the first successor states to have gained a measure of independence from the Mughal ruler in Delhi, and the most prized object for annexation by the East India Company.

Axial Age Pivotal period in the mid-first millennium BCE when radical thinkers, such as Zoroaster in Persia, Confucius and Master Lao in East Asia,

Siddhartha Gautama (the Buddha) in South Asia, and Socrates in the Mediterranean, offered dramatically new ideas that challenged their times.

Axis Powers The three aggressor states in World War II: Germany, Japan, and Italy.

Aztec Empire Mesoamerican empire that originated with a league of three Mexica cities in 1430 and gradually expanded through the Central Valley of Mexico, uniting numerous small, independent states under a single monarch who ruled with the help of counselors, military leaders, and priests. By the late fifteenth century, the Aztec realm may have embraced 25 million people. In 1521, the Aztecs were defeated by the conquistador Hernán Cortés.

baby boom Post–World War II upswing in U.S. birthrates, which reversed a century of decline.

Bactria (c. 250–50 BCE) Hellenistic kingdom in Gandhara region (modern Pakistan) that became an independent state around 200 BCE, with a major city at Aï Khanoum. Its people and culture are sometimes called "Indo-Greek" because of the blending of Indian and Greek populations and ideas.

Bactrian camel Two-humped animal domesticated in central Asia around 2500 BCE. The Bactrian camel was heartier than the one-humped dromedary and became the animal of choice for the harsh and varied climates typical of Silk Road trade.

Baghdad Capital of the Islamic empire under the Abbasid dynasty, founded in 762 CE (located in modern-day Iraq). In the medieval period, it was a center of administration, scholarship, and cultural growth for what came to be known as the Golden Age of Islamic science.

Baghdad Pact (1955) Middle Eastern military alliance between countries friendly with America that were also willing to align themselves with the western countries against the Soviet Union.

Balam Na Stone temple and place of pilgrimage for the Maya people of Mexico's Yucatán Peninsula.

Balfour Declaration Letter (November 2, 1917) written by Lord Arthur J. Balfour, British foreign secretary, that promised a homeland for the Jews in Palestine.

Bamboo Annals Shang stories and foundation myths that were written on bamboo strips and later collected.

Bantu Language first spoken by people who lived in the southeastern region of modern Nigeria around 1000 CE.

Bantu migrations Waves of population movement from West Africa into eastern and southern Africa during the first millennium CE, bringing new agricultural practices to these regions and absorbing much of the hunting and gathering population.

barbarian Derogatory term used to describe pastoral nomads, painting them as enemies of civilization; the term *barbarian* used to have a more neutral meaning than it does today.

barbarian invasions Violent migration of people in the late fourth and fifth centuries CE from the frontiers of the Roman Empire into its western provinces. These migrants had long been used as non-Roman soldiers.

basilicas Early Christian churches modeled on Roman law-court buildings that could accommodate over a thousand worshippers.

Battle of Adwa (1896) Battle in which the Ethiopians defeated Italian colonial forces; it inspired many of Africa's later national leaders.

Battle of Wounded Knee (1890) Bloody massacre of Sioux Ghost Dancers by U.S. armed forces.

Bay of Pigs (1961) Unsuccessful invasion of Cuba by Cuban exiles supported by the U.S. government. The invaders intended to incite an insurrection in Cuba and overthrow the communist regime of Fidel Castro.

Bedouins Nomadic pastoralists in the deserts of Southwest Asia.

Beer Hall Putsch (1923) Nazi intrusion into a meeting of Bavarian leaders in a Munich beer hall in an attempt to force support for their cause; Adolf Hitler was imprisoned for a year after the incident.

Beghards Eccentric sixteenth-century European group whose members claimed to be in a state of grace that allowed them to do what they pleased—ranging from adultery, free love, and nudity to murder; also called Brethren of Free Speech.

bell beaker Ancient drinking vessel, an artifact from Europe, so named because its shape resembles an inverted bell.

Berenice of Egypt Egyptian queen who helped rule over the kingdom of the Nile from around 320 to 280 BCE.

Beringia Prehistoric thousand-mile-long land bridge that linked Siberia and North America (which had not been populated by hominins). About 30,000 years ago, *Homo sapiens* edged into this landmass.

Berlin Airlift (1948) Supply of vital necessities to West Berlin by air transport, primarily under U.S. auspices, initiated in response to a land and water blockade of the city instituted by the Soviet Union in the hope that the Allies would be forced to abandon West Berlin.

Berlin Wall Wall dividing the city of Berlin, built in 1961 by communist East Germany to prevent its citizens from fleeing to West Germany; torn down in 1989.

bhakti Religious practice that grew out of Hinduism and emphasizes personal devotion to gods.

big men Leaders of the extended household communities that formed village settlements in African rain forests.

big whites Literal translation of *grands blancs;* French plantation owners in Saint-Domingue (present-day Haiti) who created one of the wealthiest enslaver societies.

Bilad al-Sudan Arabic for "the land of the Blacks"; it consisted of the land lying south of the Sahara.

bilharzia Debilitating waterborne illness that was widespread in Egypt, where it infected peasants who worked in the irrigation canals.

Bill of Rights First ten amendments to the U.S. Constitution; ratified in 1791.

biomes Distinct biological systems, including humans, that have formed in response to shared physical conditions.

bioprospecting Transferring knowledge about biological, chemical, and botanical resources from one location on the planet to another with commercial aims, especially in agriculture and pharmaceuticals. Often, this involves the exploitation of indigenous forms of knowledge. In the modern age, it frequently leads to patents, which reward the owner of the patent and not necessarily the discoverer of the knowledge.

bipedalism Walking on two legs, thereby freeing hands and arms to carry objects such as weapons and tools; one of several traits that distinguished hominins.

Black Death Plague pandemic that ravaged Europe, East Asia, and North Africa in the fourteenth century, killing large numbers of people, including perhaps as much as one-third of the European population.

Black Jacobins Nickname for the rebels in Saint-Domingue, including Toussaint L'Ouverture, a formerly enslaved man who led the enslaved people of this French colony in the world's largest and most successful insurrection of its kind.

Black Lives Matter A decentralized and eventually global movement founded in 2013 that champions nonviolent civil disobedience in resistance to police brutality and violence against Black people.

Black Panthers Radical African American group in the 1960s and 1970s that advocated Black separatism and pan-Africanism.

black shirts Fascist troops of Mussolini's regime; these squads received money from Italian landowners to attack socialist leaders.

Black Tuesday (October 29, 1929) Historic day when the U.S. stock market crashed, plunging the United States and international trading systems into crisis and leading the world into the Great Depression.

blitzkrieg "Lightning war"; type of warfare waged by the Germans during World War II, using coordinated aerial bombing campaigns along with tanks and infantry in motorized vehicles.

bodhisattvas In Mahayana Buddhism, enlightened beings who have earned nirvana but remain in this world to help others reach it.

Bolívar, Simón (1783–1830) Venezuelan leader who urged his followers to overcome their local identities and become "American." He wanted the liberated South American countries to form a Latin American confederation, urging Peru and Bolivia to join Venezuela, Ecuador, and Colombia in the "Gran Colombia."

Bolsheviks Former members of the Russian Social Democratic Party who advocated the destruction of capitalist political and economic institutions and seized power in Russia in 1917 when the Russian Empire collapsed. In 1918, the Bolsheviks changed their name to the Russian Communist Party.

Book of the Dead Ancient Egyptian funerary text that contains drawings and paintings as well as spells describing how to prepare the jewelry and amulets that were buried with a person in preparation for the afterlife.

bourgeoisie A French term originally designating non-noble city dwellers (*Bürger* in German). They sought to be recognized not by birth or aristocratic title but by property and ability. In the nineteenth century, *bourgeois* came to refer to non-noble property owners, especially those who controlled modern industry. A bourgeois was an individual. We can refer to "bourgeois values." *Bourgeoisie* refers to the entire class, as in the French bourgeoisie as a whole.

Boxer Protocol Written agreement between the victors of the Boxer Uprising and the Qing Empire in 1901 that placed western troops in Beijing and required the regime to pay exorbitant damages for foreign life and property.

Boxer Uprising (1899–1900) Chinese peasant movement that opposed foreign influence, especially that of Christian missionaries; it was put down after the Boxers were defeated by an army composed mostly of Japanese, Russians, British, French, and Americans.

Brahma One of three major deities that form a trinity in Vedic religion. Brahma signifies birth. *See also* Vishnu *and* Shiva.

Brahmans Vedic priests who performed rituals and communicated with the gods. Brahmans provided guidance on how to live in balance with the forces of nature as represented by the various deities. Brahmanism was reborn as Hinduism sometime during the first half of the first millennium CE.

British Commonwealth of Nations Union formed in 1926 that conferred "dominion status" on Britain's White settler colonies in Canada, Australia, and New Zealand.

British East India Company *See* East India Company.

bronze Alloy of copper and tin brought into Europe from Anatolia; used to make hard-edged weapons.

brown shirts Troops of German men who advanced the Nazi cause by holding street marches, mass rallies, and confrontations and by beating Jews and anyone who opposed the Nazis.

Buddha "Enlightened One." The term was applied to Kshatriya-born Siddhartha Gautama (c. 563–483 BCE), whose ideas—about the relationship between desire and suffering and how to eliminate both through wisdom, ethical behavior, and mental discipline in order to achieve contentment (nirvana)—offered a radical challenge to Brahmanism.

Buddhism Major South Asian religion that aims to end human suffering through the renunciation of desire. Buddhists believe that removing the illusion of a separate identity would lead to a state of contentment (nirvana). These beliefs challenged the traditional Brahmanic teachings of the time and provided the peoples of South Asia with an alternative to established traditions.

bullion Uncoined gold or silver.

Byzantium Modern term for the Eastern Roman Empire (which would last until 1453), centered at its "New Rome," Constantinople, which was founded in 324 CE by Constantine on the site of the Greek city Byzantium.

Cahokia Commercial city on the Mississippi for regional and long-distance trade of commodities such as salt, shells, and skins and of manufactured goods such as pottery, textiles, and jewelry; marked by massive artificial hills, akin to earthen pyramids, used to honor spiritual forces.

calaveras Allegorical skeleton drawings by the Mexican printmaker and artist José Guadalupe Posada. The works drew on popular themes of betrayal, death, and festivity.

caliphate Islamic state, headed by a caliph—chosen either by election from the community (Sunni) or from the lineage of Muhammad (Shiite)—with political authority over the Muslim community.

Calvin, Jean (1509–1564) A French theologian during the Protestant Reformation. Calvin developed a Christianity that emphasized moral regeneration through church teachings and laid out a doctrine of predestination.

candomblé Yoruba-based religion in northern Brazil; it interwove African practices and beliefs with Christianity.

Canton system System officially established by imperial decree in 1759 that required European traders to have Chinese guild merchants act as guarantors for their good behavior and payment of fees.

caravan cities Cities (like Petra and Palmyra) that were located along land routes of the Silk Roads and served as hubs of commerce and cultural exchange between travelers and merchants participating in long-distance trade.

caravans Companies of men who transported and traded goods along overland routes in North Africa and central Asia; large caravans consisted of 600–1,000 camels and as many as 400 men.

caravanserais Inns along major trade routes that accommodated large numbers of traders, their animals, and their wares.

caravel Sailing vessel suited for nosing in and out of estuaries and navigating in waters with unpredictable currents and winds.

carrack Ship used on open bodies of water, such as the Mediterranean.

Carthage City in what is modern-day Tunisia; emblematic of the trading aspirations and activities of merchants in the Mediterranean. Pottery and other archaeological remains demonstrate that trading contacts with Carthage were as far-flung as Italy, Greece, France, Iberia, and West Africa.

cartography Mapmaking.

caste system Hierarchical system of organizing people and distributing labor.

Caste War of Yucatán (1847–1901) Conflict between Maya Indians and the Mexican state over Indian autonomy and legal equality, which resulted in the Mexican takeover of the Yucatán Peninsula.

Castro, Fidel (1926–2016) Cuban communist leader who seized power in January 1959. Castro became increasingly radical as he consolidated power, announcing a massive redistribution of land and the nationalization of foreign oil refineries; he declared himself a socialist and aligned himself with the Soviet Union in the wake of the 1961 CIA-backed Bay of Pigs invasion.

Çatal Hüyük Site in Anatolia discovered in 1958. It was a dense honeycomb of settlements filled with rooms whose walls were covered with paintings of wild bulls, hunters, and pregnant women. Çatal Hüyük symbolizes an early transition to urban dwelling and dates to the eighth millennium BCE.

cathedra Bishop's seat, or throne, in a church.

Catholic Church *See* Roman Catholicism.

Cato the Elder (234–149 BCE) Roman statesman, often seen as emblematic of the transition from a Greek to a Roman world. He wrote a manual for the new economy of plantation slavery in agriculture, invested in shipping and trading, learned Greek rhetoric, and added the genre of history to Latin literature.

caudillos South American local military chieftains.

cave drawings Images on cave walls. The subjects are most often large game, although a few are images of humans. Other elements are impressions made by hands dipped in paint and pressed on a wall as well as abstract symbols and shapes.

Celali revolts (1595–1610) Peasant and artisan uprisings against the Ottoman state.

Central Powers Alliance of Germany and Austria-Hungary in World War I.

Chan Chan City founded around 900 CE by the Moche people in what is now modern-day Peru. It became the largest city of the Chimú Empire with a core population of 30,000 inhabitants.

Chan Santa Cruz Separate Maya community formed as part of a crusade for spiritual salvation and the complete cultural separation of the Maya Indians; means "little holy cross."

Chandragupta Maurya (r. 321–297 BCE) Also called Chandragupta Mori (and mentioned, though not by name, in many contemporary Greek sources); founder of South Asia's first empire, as the Mauryan dynasty of India, in the power vacuum left by the withdrawal of Alexander of Macedon's Greek forces from the region.

Chandragupta I (r. c. 320–335 CE) Founder of the Gupta dynasty of India who took the title "King of Kings" and significantly expanded the territory of his empire to include all of the northern plain of India.

Chandragupta II (r. c. 380–415 CE) Grandson of Chandragupta I who further expanded Gupta territories and was a literary patron. During his reign the renowned Sanskrit author Kalidasa is thought to have flourished.

Chandravansha One of two main lineages (the lunar one) of Vedic society, each with its own creation myth, ancestors, language, and rituals. Each lineage included many clans. *See also* Suryavansha.

chapatis Flat, unleavened Indian bread.

chariot Horse-drawn vehicle with two spoked and metal-rimmed wheels. Made possible by the interaction of pastoralists and settled communities, the chariot revolutionized warfare in the second millennium BCE.

charismatic Person who uses personal strengths or virtues, often laced with a divine aura, to command followers.

Charlemagne Emperor of the west and heir to Rome from 768 to 814 CE.

chartered companies Firms that were awarded monopoly trading rights over vast areas by European monarchs (for example, the Virginia Company and the Dutch East India Company).

Chartism (1834–1848) Mass democratic movement to pass the Peoples' Charter in Britain, granting male suffrage, secret ballot, equal electoral districts, and annual parliaments and absolving the requirement of property ownership for members of the parliament.

chattel slavery Form of slavery in which people were sold as property, the rise of which coincided with the expansion of city-states. Chattel slavery was eschewed by the Spartans, who also rejected the innovation of coin money.

Chavín Agrarian people living from 1400 to 200 BCE in complex societies in what is now Peru. They manufactured goods (ceramics, textiles, and precious metals), conducted limited long-distance trade, and shared an artistic and religious tradition, most notably at Chavín de Huántar.

Chernobyl (1986) Site in the Soviet Union (in present-day Ukraine) of the meltdown of a nuclear reactor.

Chiang Kai-shek (1887–1975) Leader of the Guomindang following Sun Yat-sen's death who mobilized the Chinese masses through the New Life movement. In 1949, he lost the Chinese Revolution to the communists and moved his regime to Taiwan.

Chimú Empire South America's first empire, centered at Chan Chan, in the Moche Valley on the Pacific coast from 1000 through 1470 CE, whose development was fueled by agriculture and commercial exchange.

chinampas Floating gardens used by Aztecs in the 1300s and 1400s to grow crops.

China's Sorrow Name for the Yellow River, which, when it changed course or flooded, could cause mass death and waves of migration.

chinoiserie Chinese silks, teas, tableware, jewelry, and paper; popular among Europeans in the seventeenth and eighteenth centuries.

Christendom Entire portion of the world in which Christianity prevailed.

Christianity New religious movement originating in the Eastern Roman Empire in the first century CE, with roots in Judaism and resonance with various Greco-Roman religious traditions. The central figure, Jesus, was tried and executed by Roman authorities, and his followers believed he rose from the dead. The tradition was spread across the Mediterranean by his followers, and Christians were initially persecuted—to varying degrees—by Roman authorities. The religion was eventually legalized in 312 CE, and by the late fourth century CE it became the official state religion of the Roman Empire.

Church of England Established form of Christianity in England dating from the sixteenth century.

city Highly populated concentration of economic, religious, and political power. The first cities appeared in river basins, which could produce a surplus of agriculture. The abundance of food freed most city inhabitants from the need to produce their own food, which allowed them to work in specialized professions.

city-state Political organization based on the authority of a single, large city that controls outlying territories.

Civil Rights Act (1964) U.S. legislation that banned racial segregation in public facilities, outlawed racial discrimination in employment, and marked an important step in correcting legal inequality.

civil rights movement Powerful movement for equal rights and the end of racial segregation in the United States that began in the 1950s with court victories against school segregation and nonviolent boycotts.

civil service examinations Set of challenging exams instituted by the Tang to help assess potential bureaucrats' literary skill and knowledge of the Confucian classics.

Civil War, American (1861–1865) Conflict between the northern and southern states of America that led to the abolition of slavery in the United States.

clan A social group comprising many households, claiming descent from a common ancestor.

clandestine presses Small printing operations that published banned texts in the early modern era, especially in Switzerland and the Netherlands.

closing of the frontier In 1893, responding to the recent U.S. Census, the historian Frederick Jackson Turner popularized the idea that the western frontier—so long crucial to the making of American identity—had closed. His announcement spurred many to worry that having lost the manliness and self-reliance nurtured by the hard life on the frontier, Americans would grow soft and weak.

Clovis people Early humans in America who used basic chipped blades and pointed spears in pursuing prey. They extended the hunting traditions they had learned in Afro-Eurasia, such as establishing campsites and moving with the herds. They were known as "Clovis people" because the type of arrowhead point that they used was first found by archaeologists at a site near Clovis, New Mexico.

Code of Manu Brahmanic code of law that took shape in the third to fifth centuries CE and expressed ideas going back to Vedic times. Framed as a conversation between Manu (the first human and an ancient lawgiver) and a group of wise men, it articulated the rules of the hierarchical *varna* system.

codex Early form of book, with separate pages bound together; it replaced the scroll as the main medium for written texts. The codex emerged around 300 CE.

cognitive skills Skills such as thought, memory, problem solving, and—ultimately—language. Hominins were able to use these skills and their hands to create new adaptations, like tools, which helped them obtain food and avoid predators.

Cohong Chinese merchant guild that traded with Europeans under the Qing dynasty.

coins Form of money that replaced goods, which previously had been bartered for services and other products. Originally used mainly to hire mercenary soldiers, coins became the commonplace method of payment linking buyers and producers throughout the Mediterranean.

Cold War (1945–1990) Ideological rivalry in which the Soviet Union and eastern Europe opposed the United States and western Europe, but no direct military conflict occurred between the two rival blocs.

colonies Regions under the political control of another country.

colons French settlers in Algeria.

Colosseum Huge amphitheater in Rome completed by Titus and dedicated in 80 CE. Originally begun by Flavian, the structure is named after a colossal statue of Nero that formerly stood beside it.

Columbian exchange Movements between Afro-Eurasia and the Americas of previously unknown plants, animals, people, diseases, and products that followed in the wake of Columbus's voyages.

commanderies The thirty-six provinces (*jun*) into which Shi Huangdi divided territories. Each commandery had a civil governor, a military governor, and an imperial inspector.

Communist Manifesto, The Pamphlet published by Karl Marx and Friedrich Engels in 1848 at a time when political revolutions were sweeping Europe. It called on the workers of all nations to unite in overthrowing capitalism.

Compromise of 1867 Agreement between the Habsburg state and the peoples living in Hungarian parts of the empire that the state would be officially known as the Austro-Hungarian Empire.

concession areas Territories, usually ports, where Chinese emperors allowed European merchants to trade and European people to settle.

Confucian ideals The ideals of honoring tradition, emphasizing the responsibility of the emperor, and respecting the lessons of history, promoted by Confucius, which the Han dynasty made the official doctrine of the empire by 50 BCE.

Confucianism Ethics, beliefs, and practices stipulated by the Chinese philosopher Kong Qiu, or Confucius, which served as a guide for Chinese society up to modern times.

Confucius (551–479 BCE) Radical thinker whose ideas—especially about how ethical living that was centered on *ren* (benevolence), *li* (proper ritual), and *xiao* (filial piety toward ancestors living and dead) shaped the politically engaged superior gentleman—transformed society and government in East Asia.

cong tube Ritual object crafted by the Liangzhu, made of jade and used in divination practices.

Congo Free State Large colonial state in Africa created by Leopold II, king of Belgium, during the 1880s and ruled by him alone. After rumors of mass slaughter and enslavement, the Belgian parliament took possession of the colony.

Congress of Vienna (1814–1815) International conference to reorganize Europe after the downfall of Napoleon. European monarchies agreed to respect one another's borders and to cooperate in guarding against future revolutions and war.

conquistadors Spanish military leaders who led the conquest of the New World in the sixteenth century.

Constantine Roman emperor who converted to Christianity in 312 CE. In 313, he issued a proclamation that gave Christians new freedoms in the empire. He also founded Constantinople (at first called "New Rome").

Constantinople Capital city of Byzantium, which was founded as the New Rome by the emperor Constantine.

Constitutional Convention (1787) Meeting to formulate the Constitution of the United States of America.

Contra rebels Opponents of the Sandinistas in Nicaragua; they were armed and financed by the United States and other anticommunist countries (1980).

conversos Jewish and Muslim converts to Christianity in the Iberian Peninsula and the New World.

Coptic Form of Christianity practiced in Egypt. It was doctrinally different from Christianity elsewhere, and Coptic Christians had their own views of the nature of Christ.

Corn Laws Laws that imposed tariffs on grain imported to Great Britain, intended to protect British farming interests. The Corn Laws were abolished in 1846 as part of a British movement in favor of free trade.

cosmology Branch of metaphysics devoted to understanding the order of the universe.

cosmopolitans Meaning "citizens of the world," as opposed to a city-state, this term refers particularly to inhabitants of the large, multiethnic cities that were nodes of exchange in the Hellenistic world.

Council of Nicaea Church council convened in 325 CE by Constantine and presided over by him as well. At this council, a Christian creed was articulated and made into a formula that expressed the philosophical and technical elements of Christian belief.

Counter-Reformation Movement to counter the spread of the Reformation; initiated by the Catholic Church at the Council of Trent in 1545. The Catholic Church enacted reforms to attack clerical corruption and placed a greater emphasis on individual spirituality. During this time, the Jesuits were founded to help revive the Catholic Church.

coup d'état Overthrow of an established state by a group of conspirators, usually from the military.

creation narratives Narratives constructed by different cultures that draw on their belief systems and available evidence to explain the origins of the world and humanity.

creed From the Latin *credo*, meaning "I believe," an authoritative statement of belief. The Nicene Creed, formulated by Christian bishops at the Council of Nicaea in 325 CE, is an example of one such formal belief statement.

Creoles Persons of mixed European and African (or other) descent who were born in the Americas.

Crimean War (1853–1856) War waged by Russia against Great Britain and France. Spurred by Russia's encroachment on Ottoman territories, the conflict revealed Russia's military weakness when Russian forces fell to British and French troops.

crossbow Innovative weapon used at the end of China's Warring States period that allowed archers to shoot their enemies with accuracy, even from a distance.

Crusades Wave of attacks launched in the late eleventh century by western European Christians against Muslims. The First Crusade began in 1095, when Pope Urban II appealed to the warrior nobility of France to free Jerusalem from Muslim rule. Four subsequent Crusades were fought over the next two centuries.

Cuban Missile Crisis (1962) Diplomatic standoff between the United States and the Soviet Union that was provoked by the Soviet Union's attempt to base nuclear missiles in Cuba; it brought the world close to a nuclear war.

cult Religious movement, often based on the worship of a particular god or goddess.

cultigen Organism that has diverged from its ancestors through domestication or cultivation.

cuneiform Wedge-shaped form of writing. As people combined rebus symbols with other visual marks that contained meaning, they became able to record and transmit messages over long distances by using abstract symbols or signs to denote concepts; such signs later came to represent syllables, which could be joined into words. By impressing these signs into wet clay with the cut end of a reed, scribes engaged in cuneiform.

Cyrus the Great Founder of the Persian Empire. This sixth-century ruler (559–529 BCE) conquered the Medes and unified the Iranian kingdoms.

czar *See* tsar.

daimyo Ruling lord who commanded a private army in pre-Meiji Japan.

dan Fodio, Usman (1754–1817) Fulani Muslim cleric whose visions led him to challenge the Hausa ruling classes, who he believed were insufficiently faithful to Islamic beliefs and practices. His ideas gained support among those who had suffered under the Hausa landlords. In 1804, his supporters and allies overthrew the Hausa in what is today northern Nigeria.

Daoism East Asian philosophy of the Axial Age introduced by Master Lao and expanded by his student Zhuangzi. It was remarkable for its emphasis on following the *dao* (the natural way of the cosmos) and held that the best way to do that was through *wuwei* (doing nothing).

dar al-Islam Arabic for "the House of Islam"; describes a sense of common identity.

Darius I (r. 522–486 BCE) Leader who put the emerging unified Persian Empire onto solid footing after Cyrus the Great's death.

Darwin, Charles (1809–1882) British scientist who became convinced that the species of organic life had evolved under the uniform pressure of natural laws, not by means of a special, one-time creation as described in the Bible.

D-Day (June 6, 1944) Day of the Allied invasion of Normandy under General Dwight Eisenhower to liberate western Europe from German occupation.

Dear Boy Nickname of an early human skull discovered in 1931 by a team of archaeologists named the Leakeys. Other objects discovered with Dear Boy demonstrated that by his time, early humans had begun to fashion tools and to use them for butchering animals and possibly for hunting and killing smaller animals.

Decembrists Russian army officers who were influenced by events in revolutionary France and formed secret societies that espoused liberal governance. They launched a revolt that was put down by Nicholas I in December 1825.

Declaration of Independence U.S. document stating the theory of government on which America was founded.

Declaration of the Rights of Man and of the Citizen (1789) French charter of liberties formulated by the National Assembly that marked the end of dynastic and aristocratic rule. The seventeen articles later became the preamble to the new constitution, which the assembly finished in 1791.

decolonization End of empire and emergence of new independent nation-states in Asia and Africa as a result of the defeat of Japan in World War II and weakened European influence after the war.

degeneration In the later nineteenth century, many Europeans began to fear that Darwin had been wrong: urbanization, technology, racial hybridity, the emergence of the "modern" woman, and over-refinement were causing Europeans not to progress as a species but to degenerate. This fear was often combined with anxieties about colonialism, homosexuality, emigration, and/or the advancement of women.

Delhi Sultanate (1206–1526) A Turkish Muslim regime in northern India that, through its tolerance for cultural diversity, brought political integration without enforcing cultural homogeneity.

democracy The idea that people, through membership in a nation, should choose their own representatives and be governed by them.

Democritus Thinker in ancient Greece who lived from around 460 to 370 BCE; he deduced the existence of the atom and postulated that there was such a thing as an indivisible particle.

demotic writing The second of two basic forms of ancient Egyptian writing. Demotic was a cursive script written with ink on papyrus, on pottery, or on other absorbent objects. It was the most common and practical form of writing in Egypt and was used for administrative record keeping and in private or pseudo-private forms like letters and works of literature. *See also* hieroglyphs.

developing world Term applied to poor countries of the Third World and the former eastern communist bloc seeking to develop viable nation-states and prosperous economies. The term has come under sustained criticism for suggesting that there is a single path of economic growth that countries everywhere follow. It has been replaced by equally problematic terms like "advanced economy" and "emerging markets."

devshirme The Ottoman system of taking non-Muslim children in place of taxes in order to educate them in Muslim ways and prepare them for service in the sultan's bureaucracy.

dhamma Moral code espoused by Aśoka in the Kalinga edict, which was meant to apply to all—Buddhists, Brahmans, and Greeks alike.

dhimma system Ottoman law that permitted followers of religions other than Islam, such as Armenian Christians, Greek Orthodox Christians, and Jews, to choose their own religious leaders and to settle internal disputes within their religious communities as long as they accepted Islam's political dominion.

dhows Ships used by Arab seafarers whose large sails were rigged to maximize the capture of wind.

Dien Bien Phu (1954) Site of a defining battle in the war between French colonialists and the Viet Minh that secured North Vietnam for Ho Chi Minh and his army and left the south to form its own government with French and American support.

Diogenes Greek philosopher who lived from around 412 to 323 BCE and who espoused a doctrine of self-sufficiency and freedom from social laws and customs. He rejected cultural norms as out of tune with nature and therefore false.

Directory Temporary military committee in France that took over affairs of the state from the radicals in 1795 and held control until the coup of Napoleon Bonaparte.

divination Rituals used to communicate with gods or royal ancestors and to foretell future events. Divination was used to legitimize royal authority and demand tribute.

Djoser Ancient Egyptian king who reigned from 2630 to 2611 BCE. He was the second king of the Third Dynasty and celebrated the Sed festival in his tomb complex at Saqqara.

domestication Bringing a wild animal or plant under human control.

Dominion in the British Commonwealth Canadian promise to keep up the country's fealty to the British crown, even after its independence in 1867. Later applied to Australia and New Zealand.

Dong Zhongshu Emperor Wu's chief minister, who advocated a more powerful view of Confucius by promoting texts that focused on Confucius as a man who possessed aspects of divinity.

double-outrigger canoes Vessels used by early Austronesians to cross the Taiwan Straits and colonize islands in the Pacific. These sturdy canoes could cover over 120 miles per day.

Duma Russian parliament.

Dutch learning Broad term for European teachings that were strictly regulated by the shoguns inside Japan.

dynastic cycle Political narrative in which influential families vied for supremacy. Upon gaining power, they legitimated their authority by claiming to be the heirs of previous grand dynasts and by preserving or revitalizing the ancestors' virtuous governing ways. This continuity conferred divine support.

dynasty Hereditary ruling family that passed control from one generation to the next.

Earth Summit (1992) Meeting in Rio de Janeiro between many of the world's governments in an effort to address international environmental problems.

East India Company (1600–1858) British charter company created to outperform Portuguese and Spanish traders in Asia; in the eighteenth century the company became, in effect, the ruler of a large part of India.

Eastern Front Battlefront between Berlin and Moscow during World War I and World War II.

economic inequality Systematically uneven distribution of both income and opportunity among different groups of people or different nations.

economic nationalism An ideology that supports state interventionism over other means of regulating a nation's market, often involving restrictions on the movement of capital, labor, and goods.

Edict of Nantes (1598) Edict issued by Henry IV to end the French Wars of Religion. The edict declared France a Catholic country but tolerated some Protestant worship.

Eiffel Tower Steel monument completed in 1889 for the Paris Exposition. It was twice the height of any other building at the time.

eight-legged essay Highly structured essay form with eight parts, required on Chinese civil service examinations.

Ekklesia Church or early gathering committed to leaders chosen by God and fellow believers.

Ekpe Powerful slave trade institution that organized the supply and purchase of enslaved people inland from the Gulf of Guinea in West Africa.

Elamites A people with their capital in the upland valley of modern Fars who became a cohesive polity that incorporated transhumant people of the Zagros Mountains. A group of Elamites who migrated south and west into Mesopotamia helped conquer the Third Dynasty of Ur in 2400 BCE.

empire Group of states or ethnic groups governed by a single sovereign power with varying degrees of centralization using a range of methods, including common language, shared religious beliefs, trade, political systems, and military might.

Enabling Act (1933) Emergency act passed by the Reichstag (German parliament) that helped transform Hitler from Germany's chancellor, or prime minister, into a dictator following the suspicious burning of the Reichstag building and a suspension of civil liberties.

enclosure A movement in which landowners took control of lands that traditionally had been common property serving local needs.

encomenderos Commanders of the labor services of the colonized peoples in Spanish America.

encomiendas Grants from European Spanish governors to control the labor services of colonized peoples.

Endeavor Ship of Captain James Cook, whose celebrated voyages to the South Pacific in the late eighteenth century supplied Europe with information about the plants, birds, landscapes, and people of this uncharted territory.

Engels, Friedrich (1820–1895) German social and political philosopher who collaborated with Karl Marx on many publications, including *The Communist Manifesto*.

English Navigation Act of 1651 Act stipulating that only English ships could carry goods between the mother country and its colonies.

English Peasants' Revolt (1381) Uprising of serfs and free farm workers that began as a protest against a tax levied to raise money for a war on France. The revolt was suppressed, but led to the gradual emergence of a free peasantry as labor shortages made it impossible to keep peasants bound to the soil.

enlightened absolutists Seventeenth- and eighteenth-century monarchs who claimed to rule rationally and in the best interests of their subjects and who hired loyal bureaucrats to implement the knowledge of the new age.

Enlightenment Intellectual movement in eighteenth-century Europe, which extended the methods of the natural sciences, especially physics, to society, stressing natural laws and reason as the basis of authority.

entrepôts Multiethnic trading stations, often supported and protected by regional leaders, where traders exchanged commodities and replenished supplies in order to facilitate long-distance trade.

Epicurus Greek philosopher who espoused emphasis on the self. He lived from 341 to 279 BCE and founded a school in Athens called The Garden. He stressed the importance of sensation, teaching that pleasurable sensations were good and painful sensations bad. Members of his school sought to find peace and relaxation by avoiding unpleasantness or suffering.

Estates-General French quasi-parliamentary body called in 1789 to deal with the financial problems that afflicted France. It had not met since 1614.

Etruscans A dominant people on the Italian Peninsula until the fourth century BCE. The Etruscan states were part of the foundation of the Roman Empire.

eunuchs Surgically castrated men who rose to high levels of military, political, and personal power in several empires (for instance, the Tang and the Ming Empires in China; the Abbasid and Ottoman Empires; and the Byzantine Empire).

Eurasia The combined area of Europe and Asia.

European Union (EU) Supranational body organized in the 1950s as an attempt at reconciliation between Germany and the rest of Europe. It emerged from the European Coal and Steel Community and initially aimed to forge closer industrial cooperation. By 1993, through various treaties, many European states had relinquished important elements of their sovereignty, and the cooperation became a full-fledged union with a common parliament and a common currency. By 2020, all twenty-seven member states of the EU except Denmark had adopted, or pledged to adopt, the euro as their currency.

evolution Process by which species of plants and animals change over time, as a result of the favoring, through reproduction, of certain traits that are useful in that species' environment.

Exclusion Act of 1882 U.S. congressional act prohibiting nearly all immigration from China to the United States; fueled by animosity toward Chinese workers in the American West.

Ezo Present-day Hokkaido, Japan's fourth main island.

Farang Persian word meaning "Frank," which was used to describe Crusaders.

fascism Form of hypernationalism that emerged in Europe after the Great War (World War I), in which a charismatic leader was followed by a mass party and supported by established elites and churches and existing government institutions. Fascist movements were widespread but came to power only in Italy and Germany.

Fatehpur Sikri Mughal emperor Akbar's temporary capital near Agra.

Fatimids Shiite dynasty that ruled parts of the Islamic empire beginning in the tenth century CE. They were based in Egypt and founded the city of Cairo.

February Revolution (1917) The first of two uprisings of the Russian Revolution, which led to the end of the Romanov dynasty.

Federal Deposit Insurance Corporation (FDIC) Organization created in 1933 to guarantee all bank deposits up to $5,000 as part of the New Deal in the United States.

Federal Republic of Germany (1949–1990) Country formed from the areas of Germany occupied by the Allies after World War II. Also known as West Germany, this country experienced rapid demilitarization, democratization, and integration into the world economy.

Federal Reserve Act (1913) U.S. legislation that created a series of boards to monitor the supply and demand of the nation's money.

Federalists Supporters of the ratification of the U.S. Constitution, which was written to replace the Articles of Confederation.

feminist movements Movements that call for equal treatment for men and women—equal pay and equal opportunities for obtaining jobs and advancement. Feminism arose mainly in Europe and in North America in the 1960s and then became global in the 1970s.

Fertile Crescent An area in Southwest Asia, bounded by the Mediterranean Sea in the west and the Zagros Mountains in the east; site of the world's first agricultural revolution.

feudalism System instituted in medieval Europe after the collapse of the Carolingian Empire (814 CE) whereby each peasant was under the authority of a lord. *See also* manorialism.

fiefdoms Medieval economic and political units.

First World Term invented during the Cold War to refer to western Europe and North America (also known as the "free world" or the west); Japan later joined this group. Following the principles of liberal modernism, First World states sought to organize the world on the basis of capitalism and democracy.

five pillars of Islam Five practices that unite all Muslims: (1) proclaiming that "there is no God but God and Muhammad is His Prophet"; (2) praying five times a day; (3) fasting during the daylight hours of the holy month of Ramadan; (4) traveling on pilgrimage to Mecca; and (5) paying alms to support the poor.

Five-Year Plan Soviet effort launched under Stalin in 1928 to replace the market with a state-owned and state-managed economy in order to promote rapid economic development over a five-year period and thereby "catch and overtake" the leading capitalist countries. The First Five-Year Plan was followed by the Second Five-Year Plan (1933–1937), and so on, until the collapse of the Soviet Union in 1991.

Flagellants European social group that came into existence during the Black Death in the fourteenth century; they believed that the plague was the wrath of God.

floating population Poor migrant workers in China who supplied labor under Emperor Wu.

fluitschips Dutch shipping vessels that could carry heavy, bulky cargo with relatively small crews.

flying cash Letters of exchange—early predecessors of paper money—first developed by guilds in the northern Song province Shanxi that eclipsed coins by the thirteenth century.

fondûqs Complexes in caravan cities that included hostels, storage houses, offices, and temples; from the Arabic word for "hotel."

Forbidden City of Beijing Palace city of the Ming and Qing dynasties.

Force Publique Colonial army used to maintain order in the Belgian Congo; during the early stages of King Leopold's rule, it was responsible for bullying local communities.

Fourierism Form of utopian socialism based on the ideas of Charles Fourier (1772–1837), who envisioned communes where work was made enjoyable and systems of production and distribution were run without merchants. His ideas appealed to the middle class, especially women, as a higher form of Christian communalism.

free labor Wage-paying rather than enslaved labor.

free markets Unregulated markets.

Free Officers Movement Secret organization of Egyptian junior military officers who came to power in a coup d'état in 1952, forced King Faruq to abdicate, and consolidated their own control through dissolving the parliament, banning opposing parties, and rewriting the constitution.

free trade (laissez-faire) Domestic and international trade unencumbered by tariff barriers, quotas, and fees.

Front de Libération Nationale (FLN) Algerian anticolonial, nationalist party that waged an eight-year war against French troops, beginning in 1954, that forced nearly all of the 1 million European colonists to leave.

Fulani Muslim group in West Africa that carried out religious revolts at the end of the eighteenth and the beginning of the nineteenth centuries in an effort to return to the pure Islam of the past.

fur trade Trading of animal pelts (especially beaver skins) by Indians for European goods in North America.

Gandharan style Style of artwork, especially statuary, originating in the Gandharan region of modern Pakistan, that blends Hellenistic artistic influences with Buddhist stylistic features and subjects.

Gandhi, Mohandas Karamchand (Mahatma) (1869–1948) Indian leader who led a nonviolent struggle for India's independence from Britain.

garrison towns Stations for soldiers originally established in strategic locations to protect territorial acquisitions. Eventually, they became towns. Alexander the Great's garrison towns evolved into cities that served as centers from which Hellenistic culture was spread to his easternmost territories.

garrisons Military bases inside cities; often used for political purposes, such as protecting rulers, putting down domestic revolts, or enforcing colonial rule.

gauchos Argentine, Brazilian, and Uruguayan cowboys who wanted a decentralized federation, with autonomy for their provinces and respect for their way of life.

Gdańsk shipyard Site of mass strikes in Poland that led in 1980 to the formation of the first independent trade union, Solidarity, in the Soviet bloc.

gender relations A relatively recent development that implies roles emerged only with the appearance of modern humans and perhaps Neanderthals. When humans began to think imaginatively and in complex symbolic ways and give voice to their insights, perhaps around 150,000 years ago, gender categories began to crystallize.

genealogy History of the descent of a person or family from a distant ancestor.

Geneva Peace Conference (1954) International conference to restore peace in Korea and Indochina. The chief participants were the United States, the Soviet Union, Great Britain, France, the People's Republic of China, North Korea, South Korea, Vietnam, the Viet Minh party, Laos, and Cambodia. The conference resulted in the division of North and South Vietnam.

Genoa One of two Italian cities (the other was Venice) that linked Europe, Africa, and Asia as nodes of commerce in 1300. Genoese ships linked the Mediterranean to the coast of Flanders through consistent routes along the Atlantic coasts of Spain, Portugal, and France.

German Democratic Republic (1949–1990) Country formed from the areas of Germany occupied by the Soviet Union after World War II. Also known as East Germany.

German Social Democratic Party Founded in 1875, the most powerful socialist party in Europe before 1917.

Ghana The most celebrated medieval political kingdom in West Africa.

Ghost Dance American Indian ritual performed in the nineteenth century in the hope of restoring the world to precolonial conditions.

Gilgamesh, Epic of Heroic narrative written in the Babylonian dialect of Semitic Akkadian. This story and others like it were meant to circulate and unify the kingdom.

Girondins Liberal revolutionary group that supported the creation of a constitutional monarchy during the early stages of the French Revolution.

global climate change A wide range of phenomena caused by global warming. These changes encompass not only rising temperatures, but also changes in precipitation patterns; ice mass loss on mountain glaciers around the world; shifts in the life cycles and migration patterns of flora and fauna; extreme weather events; and sea level rise.

global war on terror Global crusade to root out anti-American, anti-western Islamist terrorist cells; launched by President George W. Bush as a response to the 9/11 attacks.

global warming Upward temperature trends worldwide due to the release of carbon into the air, mainly by the burning of fossil fuels and other human activities.

globalization Development of integrated worldwide cultural and economic structures.

globalizing empires Empires that cover immense territory; exert significant influence beyond their borders; include large, diverse populations; and work to integrate conquered peoples.

Gold Coast Name that European mariners and merchants gave to the part of West Africa from which gold was exported. This area was conquered by the British in the nineteenth century and became a British colony; upon independence, it became Ghana.

Goths One of the groups of "barbarian" migrants into Roman territory in the fourth century CE.

government schools Schools founded by the Han dynasty to provide an adequate number of officials to fill positions in the administrative bureaucracy. The Imperial University had 30,000 members by the second century BCE.

Gracchus brothers Two tribunes, the brothers Tiberius and Gaius Gracchus, who in 133 and 123–121 BCE attempted to institute land reforms that would guarantee all of Rome's poor citizens a basic amount of land that would qualify them for army service. Both men were assassinated.

Grand Canal A thousand-mile-long connector between the Yellow and Yangzi Rivers created in 486 BCE to link the north and south of China.

grand unity Guiding political idea embraced by Qin rulers and ministers with an eye toward joining the states of the Central Plains into one empire and centralizing administration.

"greased cartridge" controversy Controversy spawned by the rumor that cow and pig fat had been used to grease the shotguns of the sepoys in the British army in India. Believing that this was a British attempt to defile their religions and speed their conversion to Christianity, the sepoys mutinied against the British officers.

Great Depression Worldwide depression following the U.S. stock market crash on October 29, 1929.

great divide The division between economically developed nations and less developed nations.

Great East Asia Co-Prosperity Sphere Term used by the Japanese during the 1930s and 1940s to refer to Hong Kong, Singapore, Malaya, Burma, and other states that they seized during their attempt to dominate Asia.

Great Flood One of many traditional Mesopotamian stories that were transmitted orally from one generation to another before being recorded. The Sumerian King List refers to this crucial event in Sumerian memory and identity. The Great Flood narrative assigned responsibility for Uruk's demise to the gods.

Great Game Competition over areas such as Turkistan, Persia (present-day Iran), and Afghanistan. The British (in India) and the Russians believed that controlling these areas was crucial to preventing their enemies' expansion.

Great League of Peace and Power Iroquois Indian alliance that united previously warring communities.

Great Leap Forward (1958–1961) Plan devised by Mao Zedong to achieve rapid agricultural and industrial growth in China. The plan, which failed miserably, may have led to the deaths of as many as 45 million people from famine and malnutrition.

great plaza at Isfahan The center of Safavid power in the seventeenth century created by Shah Abbas (r. 1587–1629) to represent the unification of trade, government, and religion under one supreme political authority.

Great Proletarian Cultural Revolution (1966–1976) Mass mobilization of urban Chinese youth inaugurated by Mao Zedong in an attempt to reinvigorate the Chinese Revolution and to prevent the development of a bureaucratized Soviet style of communism; with this movement, Mao turned against his longtime associates in the Communist Party.

Great Recession The economic downturn, with global reverberations, provoked by the financial crash of 2008.

Great Trek Afrikaner migration to the interior of Africa after the British Empire abolished slavery in 1833.

Great War (World War I) (August 1914–November 1918) A total global war involving the armies of Britain, France, and Russia (the Allies) against those of Germany, Austria-Hungary, and the Ottoman Empire (the Central Powers). Italy joined the Allies in 1915, and the United States joined them in 1917, helping tip the balance in favor of the Allies, who also drew upon the populations and material of their colonial possessions.

Greek Orthodoxy Branch of eastern Christianity, originally centered in Constantinople, that emphasizes the role of Jesus in helping humans achieve union with God.

Greek philosophers "Wisdom lovers" of the ancient Greek city-states, including Socrates, Plato, Aristotle, and others, who pondered such issues as self-knowledge, political engagement and withdrawal, and evidence-based inquiry to understand the order of the cosmos.

Greenbacks An American political party of the late nineteenth century that worked to advance the interests of farmers by promoting cheap money.

griots Counselors and other officials serving the royal family in African kingships. They were also responsible for the preservation and transmission of oral histories and repositories of knowledge.

Group Areas Act (1950) Act that divided South Africa into separate racial and tribal areas and required Africans to live in their own separate communities, including the "homelands."

guerrillas Portuguese and Spanish peasant bands who resisted the revolutionary and expansionist efforts of Napoleon; after the French word *guerre*.

guest workers Migrants seeking temporary employment abroad.

Gulag Administrative name for the vast system of forced labor camps under the Soviet regime; it originated in a small monastery near the Arctic Circle and spread throughout the Soviet Union and to other Soviet-style socialist countries. Penal labor was required of both ordinary criminals (rapists, murderers, thieves) and those accused of political crimes (counterrevolution, anti-Soviet agitation).

Gulf War (1991) Armed conflict between Iraq and a coalition of thirty-two nations, including the United States, Britain, Egypt, France, and Saudi Arabia. It was started by Iraq's invasion of Kuwait, which it had long claimed, on August 2, 1990.

gunpowder Explosive powder. By 1040, the first gunpowder recipes were being written down. Over the next 200 years, Song entrepreneurs invented several incendiary devices and techniques for controlling explosions.

gunpowder empires Muslim empires of the Ottomans, Safavids, and Mughals that used cannonry and gunpowder to advance their military causes.

Guomindang Nationalist Party of China, founded just before World War I by Sun Yat-sen and later led by Chiang Kai-shek.

Habsburg Empire Ruling house of Austria, which once ruled both Spain and central Europe but came to settle in lands along the Danube River; it played a prominent role in European affairs for many centuries. In 1867, the Habsburg Empire was reorganized into the Austro-Hungarian Empire, and in 1918 it collapsed.

hadith Sayings, attributed to the Prophet Muhammad and his early converts, used to guide the behavior of Muslim peoples.

Hagia Sophia Enormous and impressive church sponsored by Justinian and built starting in 532 CE. At the time, it was the largest church in the world.

hajj Pilgrimage to Mecca; an obligation for Muslims.

Hammurabi's Code Legal code created by Hammurabi (r. 1792–1750 BCE). The code divided society into three classes—free, dependent, and enslaved—each with distinct rights and responsibilities.

Han agrarian ideal Guiding principle for the free peasantry that made up the base of Han society. In this system, peasants were honored for their labors, while merchants were subjected to a range of controls, including regulations on luxury consumption, and were belittled for not engaging in physical labor.

Han Chinese Inhabitants of China proper who considered others to be outsiders and felt that they were the only authentic Chinese.

Han Fei Chinese state minister who lived from 280 to 233 BCE; a proponent and follower of Xunzi.

Han military Like its Roman counterpart, a ruthless military machine that expanded the Han Empire and created stable conditions that permitted the safe transit of goods by caravans. Emperor Wu heavily influenced the transformation of the military forces and reinstituted a policy that made military service compulsory.

Hangzhou City and former provincial seaport that became the political center of the Chinese people in their ongoing struggles with northern steppe nomads. It was also one of China's gateways to the rest of the world by way of the South China Sea.

Hannibal Great general from Carthage whose campaigns in the third century BCE swept from Spain toward the Italian Peninsula. He crossed the Pyrenees and the Alps with war elephants. He was unable, however, to defeat the Romans in 217 BCE.

Harappa One of the two largest of the cities that, by 2500 BCE, began to take the place of villages throughout the Indus River valley (the other was Mohenjo Daro). Each covered an area of about 250 acres and probably housed 35,000 residents.

harem Secluded women's quarters in a Muslim household.

Harlem Renaissance Cultural movement in the 1920s that was based in Harlem, a part of New York City with a large African American population. The movement gave voice to Black novelists, poets, painters, and musicians, many of whom used their art to protest racism; also referred to as the "New Negro movement."

harnesses Tools made from wood, bone, bronze, and iron for steering and controlling chariot horses. Harnesses discovered by archaeologists reveal the evolution of headgear from simple mouth bits to full bridles with headpiece, mouthpiece, and reins.

Hatshepsut Leader known as ancient Egypt's most powerful woman ruler. Hatshepsut served as regent for her young son, Thutmosis III, whose reign began in 1479 BCE. She remained co-regent until her death.

Haussmannization Redevelopment and beautification of urban centers; named after the city planner who "modernized" mid-nineteenth century Paris.

Heian period Period from 794 to 1185 CE during which the pattern of regents ruling Japan in the name of the sacred emperor began.

Hellenism Process by which the individuality of the cultures of the earlier Greek city-states gave way to a uniform culture that stressed the common identity of all who embraced Greek ways. This culture emphasized the common denominators of language, style, and politics to which anyone, anywhere in the Afro-Eurasian world, could have access.

hieroglyphs One of two basic forms of Egyptian writing that were used in conjunction throughout antiquity. Hieroglyphs are pictorial symbols; the term derives from a Greek word meaning "sacred carving." They were employed exclusively in temple, royal, and divine contexts. *See also* demotic writing.

hijra Tradition of Islam whereby one withdraws from one's community to create another, holier, one. The practice is based on the Prophet Muhammad's withdrawal from the city of Mecca to Medina in 622 CE.

Hinayana Buddhism (termed "Lesser Vehicle" Buddhism by the Mahayana/"Greater Vehicle" school; also called Theraveda Buddhism) A more traditional, conservative branch of Buddhism that accepted the divinity of the Buddha but not of bodhisattvas.

Hindu revivalism Movement to reconfigure traditional Hinduism to be less diverse and more amenable to producing a narrowed version of Indian tradition.

Hinduism Ancient Brahmanic Vedic religion that emerged as the dominant faith in India in the third century CE. It reflected rural and agrarian values and focused on the trinity of Brahma (birth), Vishnu (existence), and Shiva (destruction).

Hiroshima Japanese port devastated by an atomic bomb on August 6, 1945.

Hitler, Adolf (1889–1945) German dictator and leader of the Nazi Party who seized power in Germany after its economic collapse in the Great Depression. Hitler and his Nazi regime started World War II in Europe and systematically murdered Jews and other non-Aryan groups in the name of racial purity.

Hittites An Anatolian chariot warrior group that spread east to northern Syria, though they eventually faced weaknesses in their own homeland. Rooted in their capital at Hattusa, they interacted with contemporary states both violently (as at the Battle of Qadesh against Egypt) and peacefully (as in the correspondence of the Amarna letters).

HIV/AIDS An epidemic of acquired immunodeficiency syndrome (AIDS) caused by the human immunodeficiency virus (HIV), which compromises the ability of the infected person's immune system to ward off other diseases. First detected in 1981, AIDS killed 12 million people in the two decades that followed.

Holocaust Deliberate racial extermination by the Nazis of Jews, along with some other groups the Nazis considered "inferior" (including Sinta and Roma [gypsies], Jehovah's Witnesses, homosexuals, and people with mental illness), which claimed the lives of around 6 million European Jews.

Holy Roman Empire Enormous realm that encompassed much of Europe and aspired to be the Christian successor state to the Roman Empire. In the time of the Habsburg dynasts, the empire was a loose confederation of principalities that obeyed an emperor elected by elite lower-level sovereigns. Despite its size, the empire never effectively centralized power; it was split into Austrian and Spanish factions when Charles V abdicated to his sons in 1556.

Holy Russia Name applied to Muscovy and then to the Russian Empire by Slavic Eastern Orthodox clerics who were appalled by the Muslim conquest in 1453 of Constantinople (the capital of Byzantium and of eastern Christianity) and who were hopeful that Russia would become the new protector of the faith.

home charges Fees India was forced to pay to Britain as its colonial master; these fees included interest on railroad loans, salaries to colonial officers, and the maintenance of imperial troops outside India.

hominids The family, in scientific classification, that includes gorillas, chimpanzees, and humans (that is, *Homo sapiens*, in addition to our now-extinct hominin ancestors such as the various australopithecines as well as *Homo habilis*, *Homo erectus*, and *Homo neanderthalensis*).

hominins A scientific classification for modern humans and our now-extinct ancestors, including australopithecines and others in the genus *Homo*, such as *Homo habilis* and *Homo erectus*. Researchers once used the term *hominid* to refer to *Homo sapiens* and extinct hominin species, but the meaning of *hominid* has been expanded to include great apes (humans, gorillas, chimpanzees, and orangutans).

Homo The genus, in scientific classification, that contains only "true human" species.

Homo caudatus "Tailed man," believed by some European Enlightenment thinkers to be an early human species.

Homo erectus Species that emerged about 1.8 million years ago, had a large brain, walked truly upright, migrated out of Africa, and likely mastered fire. *Homo erectus* means "standing human."

Homo habilis Species, confined to Africa, that emerged about 2.5 million years ago and whose toolmaking ability truly made it the forerunner, though a very distant one, of modern humans. *Homo habilis* means "skillful human."

Homo sapiens The first humans; emerged in Africa as early as 300,000 years ago and migrated out of Africa beginning about 180,000 years ago. They had bigger brains and greater dexterity than previous hominin species, whom they eventually eclipsed.

homogeneity Uniformity of the languages, customs, and religion of a particular people or place. It can also be demonstrated by a consistent calendar, set of laws, administrative practices, and rituals.

horses Animals used by full-scale nomadic communities to dominate the steppe lands in western Afro-Eurasia by the second millennium BCE. Horse-riding nomads moved their large herds across immense tracts of land within zones defined by rivers, mountains, and other natural geographic features. In the arid zones of central Eurasia, the nomadic economies made horses a crucial component of survival.

Huguenots French Protestants who endured severe persecution in the sixteenth and seventeenth centuries.

humanism The Renaissance aspiration to develop a greater understanding of the human experience than the Christian scriptures offered by reaching back into ancient Greek and Roman texts.

Hundred Days' Reform (1898)
Abortive modernizing reform program of the Qing government of China.

hunting and gathering Lifestyle in which food is acquired through hunting animals, fishing, and foraging for wild berries, nuts, fruit, and grains, rather than planting crops, vines, or trees. As late as 1500 CE, as much as 15 percent of the world's population still lived by this method.

Hyksos Chariot-driving, axe- and composite-bow-wielding, Semitic-speaking people (their name means "rulers of foreign lands") who invaded Egypt, overthrew the Thirteenth Dynasty, set up their own rule over Egypt, and were expelled by Ahmosis to begin the period known as New Kingdom Egypt.

Ibadat Khana "House of Worship" in which the Mughal emperor Akbar engaged in religious debate with Hindu, Muslim, Jain, Parsi, and Christian theologians.

Ibn Sina Philosopher and physician who lived from 980 to 1037 CE. He was also schooled in the Quran, geometry, literature, and Indian and Euclidian mathematics.

ideology Dominant set of ideas of a widespread culture or movement.

Il Duce (leader) Name used by the fascist Italian leader Benito Mussolini.

Iliad Epic Greek poem about the Trojan War, composed several centuries after the events it describes. It was based on oral tales passed down for generations.

Il-Khanate Mongol-founded dynasty in thirteenth-century Persia.

imam Muslim religious leader and politico-religious descendant of Ali; believed by some to have a special relationship with Allah.

Imperial University Institution founded in 136 BCE by Emperor Wu (Han Wudi) not only to train future bureaucrats in the Confucian classics but also to foster scientific advances in other fields.

imperialism Acquisition of new territories by a state and the incorporation of these territories into a political system as subordinate colonies.

Imperium Latin word used to express Romans' power and command over their subjects. It is the basis of the English words *empire* and *imperialism*.

Inca Empire Empire of Quechua-speaking rulers in the Andean valley of Cuzco that encompassed a population of 4 to 6 million. The Incas lacked a clear inheritance system, causing an internal split that Pizarro's forces exploited in 1533.

Indian Institutes of Technology (IIT) Institutions originally designed as engineering schools to expand knowledge and to modernize India, which produced a generation of pioneering computer engineers, many of whom moved to the United States.

Indian National Congress Formed in 1885, a political party deeply committed to constitutional methods, industrialization, and cultural nationalism.

Indian National Muslim League Founded in 1906, an organization dedicated to advancing the political interests of Muslims in India.

Indo-European migrations The migrations, tracked linguistically and culturally, of the peoples of a distinct language group (including Sanskrit, Persian, Greek, Latin, and German) from central Eurasian steppe lands into Europe, Southwest Asia, and South Asia.

Indo-Greek Of or relating to the fusion of Indian and Greek culture in the area under the control of the Bactrians, in the northwestern region of India, around 200 BCE.

Indu Name used for what we would today call India by Xuanzang, a Chinese Buddhist pilgrim who visited the area in the 630s and 640s CE.

indulgences Church-sponsored fund-raising mechanism that gave certification that one's sins had been forgiven in return for money.

industrial revolution Gradual accumulation and diffusion of old and new technical knowledge that led to major economic changes in Britain, northwestern Europe, and North America. It resulted in large-scale industry and the harnessing of fossil fuels, which allowed economic growth to outpace the rate of population increase.

innovation Creation of new methods that allowed humans to make better adaptations to their environment, such as the making of new tools.

Inquisition General term for a tribunal of the Roman Catholic Church that enforced religious orthodoxy. Several inquisitions took place over centuries, seeking to punish heretics, witches, Jews, and those whose conversion to Christianity was called into doubt.

internal and external alchemy In Daoist ritual, use of trance and meditation or chemicals and drugs, respectively, to cause transformations in the self.

International Monetary Fund (IMF) Agency founded in 1944 to help restore financial order in Europe and the rest of the world, to revive international trade, and to offer financial support to Third World governments.

invisible hand As described in Adam Smith's *The Wealth of Nations*, the idea that the operations of a free market produce economic efficiency and economic benefits for all.

iron Malleable metal found in combined forms almost everywhere in the world; it became the most important and widely used metal in world history after the Bronze Age.

Iron Curtain Term popularized by Winston Churchill after World War II to refer to a rift that divided western Europe, under American influence, from eastern Europe, under the domination of the Soviet Union.

irrigation Technological advance whereby water delivery systems and water sluices in floodplains or river-basin areas were channeled or redirected and used to nourish soil.

Islam A religion that dates to 610 CE, when the Prophet Muhammad believed God came to him in a vision. Islam (which means submission—in this case, to the will of God) requires its followers to act righteously, to submit themselves to the one and only true God, and to care for the less fortunate. Muhammad's most insistent message was the oneness of God, a belief that has remained central to the Islamic faith ever since.

Jacobins Radical French political group that came into existence during the French Revolution; executed the French king and sought to remake French culture.

Jacquerie (1358) French peasant revolt in defiance of feudal restrictions.

jade The most important precious substance in East Asia; associated with goodness, purity, luck, and virtue. Jade was carved into such items as ceremonial knives, blade handles, religious objects, and elaborate jewelry.

Jagat Seths Enormous trading and banking empire in eastern India during the first half of the eighteenth century.

Jainism System of thought, originating in the seventh century BCE, that challenged Brahmanism. Spread by Vardhamana Mahavira, Jainism encouraged purifying the soul through self-denial and nonviolence.

Jaja (1821–1891) A merchant prince who founded the Opobo city-state, in what is known in modern times as the Rivers state of Nigeria.

janissaries Corps of infantry soldiers conscripted as children under the *devshirme* system of the Ottoman Empire and brought up with intense loyalty to the Ottoman state and its sultan. The sultan used these forces to clip local autonomy and to serve as his personal bodyguards.

jatis Social groups as defined by Hinduism's *varna* (caste) system.

Jesuits Religious order founded by Ignatius Loyola to counter the inroads of the Protestant Reformation; the Jesuits, or the Society of Jesus, were active in politics, education, and missionary work.

jihad Literally, "striving" or "struggle." This word also connotes military efforts, or "striving in the way of God." In addition, it came to mean spiritual struggles against temptation or inner demons, especially in Sufi, or mystical, usage.

Jih-pen Chinese for "Japan."

Jim Crow laws Laws that codified racial segregation and inequality in the southern part of the United States after the Civil War.

jizya Special tax that non-Muslims were forced to pay to their Islamic rulers in return for which they were given security and property and granted cultural autonomy.

jongs Large oceangoing vessels built by Southeast Asians that plied the regional trade routes from the fifteenth century to the early sixteenth century.

Judah The southern kingdom of David, which had been a Neo-Assyrian vassal until 612 BCE, when it became a vassal of Neo-Assyria's successor, Babylon, against whom the people of Judah rebelled, resulting in the destruction of Jerusalem in the sixth century BCE.

Julius Caesar Formidable Roman general who lived from 100 to 44 BCE. He was also a man of letters, a great orator, and a ruthless military man who boasted that his campaigns had led to the deaths of over a million people.

junks Large seafaring vessels used in the South China Sea after 1000 CE, which helped make shipping by sea less dangerous.

Justinian Roman or Byzantine emperor who ascended to the throne in 527 CE.

In addition to his many building projects and military expeditions, he issued a new law code.

kabuki Theater performance that combined song, dance, and skillful staging to dramatize conflicts between duty and passion in Tokugawa Japan.

kamikaze Japanese for "divine winds," or typhoons; such a storm saved Japan from a Mongol attack.

kanun Highly detailed system of Ottoman administrative law that jurists developed to deal with matters not treated in the religious law of Islam.

karim Loose confederation of shippers banding together to protect convoys.

karma Literally, "fate" or "action"; in Confucian thought, a universal principle of cause and effect.

Kassites Nomads who entered Mesopotamia from the eastern Zagros Mountains and the Iranian plateau as early as 2000 BCE. They gradually integrated into Babylonian society by officiating at temples. By 1745 BCE, they had asserted order over the region, and they controlled southern Mesopotamia for the next 350 years, creating one of the territorial states.

Keynesian Revolution Post-Depression economic ideas developed by the British economist John Maynard Keynes, wherein the state took a greater role in managing the economy, stimulating it by increasing the money supply and creating jobs.

KGB Soviet political police and spy agency, formed as the Cheka not long after the Bolshevik coup in October 1917. Grew to more than 750,000 operatives with military rank by the 1980s.

khan Mongol ruler acclaimed at an assembly of elites, who was supposedly descended from Chinggis Khan on the male line; those not descended from Chinggis continually faced challenges to their legitimacy.

khanate Major political unit of the vast Mongol Empire. There were four khanates, including the Yuan Empire in China, forged by Chinggis Khan's grandson Kublai.

Kharijites Radical sect from the early days of Islam. The Kharijites seceded from the "party of Ali" (who themselves came to be known as the Shiites) because of disagreements over succession to the role of the caliph. They were known for their strict militant piety.

Khmer A people who created the most powerful empire in Southwest Asia between the tenth and thirteenth centuries in what is modern-day Cambodia.

Khomeini, Ayatollah Ruhollah (1902–1989) Iranian religious leader who used his traditional Islamic education and his training in Muslim ethics to accuse Shah Reza Pahlavi's government of gross violations of Islamic norms. He also identified the shah's ally, America, as the great Satan. The shah fled the country in 1979; in his wake, Khomeini established a theocratic state ruled by a council of Islamic clerics.

Khufu A pyramid, among those put up in the Fourth Dynasty in ancient Egypt (c. 2613–2494 BCE), which is the largest stone structure in the world. It is in an area called Giza, just outside modern-day Cairo.

Khusro I Anoshirwan Sasanian emperor who reigned from 531 to 579 CE. He was a model ruler and was seen as the personification of justice.

Kiev City that became one of the greatest cities of Europe after the eleventh century. It was built to be a small-scale Constantinople on the Dnieper.

Kikuyu Kenya's largest ethnic group; organizers of a revolt against the British in the 1950s.

King, Martin Luther, Jr. (1929–1968) Civil rights leader who borrowed his most effective weapon—the commitment to nonviolent protest and the appeal to conscience—from Gandhi.

Kingdom of Jerusalem What Crusaders set out to liberate from Muslim rule when they launched their attacks.

Kizilbash Mystical, Turkish-speaking tribesmen who facilitated the Safavid rise to power.

Knossos Area in Crete where, during the second millennium BCE, a primary palace town existed.

Koine **Greek** Simpler than regional versions of Greek such as Attic or Ionic, this "common Greek" dialect became an international language across the regions influenced by Hellenism and facilitated trade of goods and ideas.

Köprülü reforms Reforms named after two grand viziers who revitalized the Ottoman Empire in the seventeenth century through administrative and budget trimming as well as by rebuilding the military.

Korean War (1950–1953) Cold War conflict between Soviet-backed North Korea and U.S.- and U.N.-backed South Korea. The two sides seesawed back and forth over the same boundaries until 1953, when an armistice divided the country at roughly the same spot as at the start of the war. Casualties included 33,000 Americans, at least 250,000 Chinese, and up to 3 million Koreans.

Koryo dynasty Leading dynasty of the northern-based Koryo kingdom in Korea. It is from this dynasty that the name "Korea" derives.

Kremlin Moscow's walled city center, whose name was once synonymous with the Soviet government.

Kshatriyas Originally the warrior *varna* (caste) in Vedic society, the dominant clan members and ruling *varna* who controlled the land.

Ku Klux Klan Racist organization that first emerged in the U.S. South after the Civil War and then gained national strength as a radically traditionalist movement during the 1920s.

Kublai Khan (1215–1294) Mongol leader who seized southern China after 1260 and founded the Yuan dynasty.

kulak Originally a pejorative word used to designate better-off peasants, a term used in the late 1920s and early 1930s to refer to any peasant, rich or poor, perceived as an opponent of the Soviet regime. Russian for "fist."

Kumarajiva Renowned Buddhist scholar and missionary who lived from 344 to 413 CE. He was brought to China by Chinese regional forces from Kucha, modern-day Xinjiang.

Kushans Northern nomadic group that migrated into South Asia around 50 CE. They unified the tribes of the region and set up the Kushan Empire, which embraced a large and diverse territory and played a critical role in the formation of the Silk Roads.

Labour Party Political party founded in Britain in 1900 that represented workers and was based on socialist principles.

laissez-faire The concept that the economy works best when it is left alone—that is, when the state does not regulate or interfere with the workings of the market.

"Land under the Yoke of Ashur" Lands not in Neo-Assyria proper, but under its authority, which had to pay the Neo-Assyrian Empire exorbitant amounts of tribute.

language System of communication reflecting cognitive abilities. Natural language is generally defined as words arranged in particular sequences to convey meaning and is unique to modern humans.

language families Related tongues with a common ancestral origin; language families contain languages that diverged from one another but share grammatical features and root vocabularies. More than a hundred language families exist.

Laozi Also known as Master Lao; perhaps a contemporary of Confucius, and the person after whom Daoism is named. His thought was elaborated upon by generations of thinkers.

latifundia Broad estates that produced goods for big urban markets, including wheat, grapes, olives, cattle, and sheep.

League of Nations Organization founded after World War I to solve international disputes through arbitration; it was dissolved in 1946 and its assets were transferred to the United Nations.

Legalism Also called Statism, a system of thought about how to live an ordered life. Developed by Master Xun, or Xunzi (310–237 BCE), it is based on the principle that people, being inherently inclined toward evil, require authoritarian control to regulate their behavior.

Lenin, Vladimir (1870–1924) Leader of the Bolshevik Revolution in Russia and the first leader of the Soviet Union.

LGBTQ Acronym for people who identify as lesbian, gay, bisexual, transgender, or queer.

Liangzhu Culture spanning centuries from the fourth to the third millennium BCE that represented the last new Stone Age culture in the Yangzi River delta. One of the Ten Thousand States, it was highly stratified and is known for its jade objects.

liberalism Political and social theory that advocates representative government, free trade, and freedom of speech and religion.

limited-liability joint-stock company Company that mobilized capital from a large number of investors, called shareholders, who were not to be held personally liable for financial losses incurred by the company.

Linear A and B Two linear scripts first discovered on Crete in 1900. On the island of Crete and on the mainland areas of Greece, documents of the palace-centered societies were written on clay tablets in these two scripts. Linear A script, apparently written in Minoan, has not yet been deciphered. Linear B was first deciphered in the early 1950s.

"Little Europes" Urban landscapes between 1100 and 1200 composed of castles, churches, and towns in what are today Poland, the Czech Republic, Hungary, and the Baltic States.

Little Ice Age A period of global cooling—not a true ice age—that extended roughly from the sixteenth to the nineteenth century. The dates, especially for the start of the period, remain the subject of scientific controversy.

Liu Bang Chinese emperor from 206 to 195 BCE; after declaring himself the prince of his home area of Han, in 202 BCE, Liu declared himself the first Han emperor.

llamas Animals domesticated in the Americas that are similar in utility and function to camels in Afro-Eurasia. Llamas can carry heavy loads for long distances.

Long March (1934–1935) Trek of over 6,000 miles (or 10,000 kilometers) by Mao Zedong and his communist followers to establish a new base of operations in northwestern China.

Longshan peoples Peoples who lived in small agricultural and river-basin villages in East Asia during the third millennium BCE. They set the stage for the Shang dynasty in terms of a centralized state, urban life, and a cohesive culture.

lord Privileged landowner who exercised authority over the people who lived on his land.

lost generation The 17 million former members of the Red Guard and other Chinese youth who were denied education from the late 1960s to the mid-1970s as part of the Chinese government's attempt to prevent political disruptions.

Louisiana Purchase (1803) American purchase of French territory from Napoleon that included much of the present-day United States between the Mississippi River and the Rocky Mountains.

Lucy Relatively intact skeleton of a young adult female australopithecine unearthed in the valley of the Awash River in 1974 by an archaeological team working at a site in present-day Hadar, Ethiopia. The researchers nicknamed the skeleton Lucy. She stood just over 3 feet tall and walked upright at least some of the time. Her skull contained a brain within the ape size range, but her jaw and teeth were humanlike. Lucy's skeleton was relatively complete and at the time was the oldest hominin skeleton ever discovered.

Luftwaffe German air force.

Luther, Martin (1483–1546) A German monk and theologian who sought to reform the Catholic Church; he believed in salvation through faith alone, the importance of reading scripture, and the priesthood of all believers. His Ninety-Five Theses, which enumerated the abuses by the Catholic Church as well as his reforms, started the Protestant Reformation.

Maastricht Treaty (1993) Treaty that formed the European Union, a fully integrated trading and financial bloc with its own bureaucracy and elected representatives.

ma'at Term used in ancient Egypt to refer to stability or order, the achievement of which was the primary task of Egypt's ruling kings, the pharaohs.

Maccabees Leaders of a riot in Jerusalem in 167 BCE that was a response to a Seleucid edict outlawing the practice of Judaism. 1000 CE.

Madhyamika (Middle Way) Buddhism Chinese branch of Mahayana Buddhism established by Kumarajiva (344–413 CE) that used irony and paradox to show that reason is limited.

madrasas Higher schools of Muslim education that taught law, the Quran, religious sciences, and the regular sciences.

magnetic needle compass A navigational instrument invented by the Chinese that helped guide sailors on the high seas after.

Mahayana Buddhism "Great Vehicle" Buddhism; an accessible form of Buddhism that spread along the Silk Roads and included in its theology a divine Buddha as well as bodhisattvas.

Mahdi The "chosen one" in Islam whose appearance was believed to foretell the end of the world and the final day of reckoning for all people.

maize Grains, the crops that the settled agrarian communities across the Americas cultivated, along with legumes (beans) and tubers (potatoes).

Maji Maji Revolt (1905–1907) Swahili insurrection against German colonialists; inspired by the belief that those who were anointed with specially blessed water (*maji*) would be immune to bullets. It resulted in 200,000 to 300,000 African deaths.

Mali Empire West African empire, founded by the legendary king Sundiata in the early thirteenth century. It facilitated thriving commerce along routes linking the Atlantic Ocean, the Sahara, and beyond.

Mamluks (Arabic for "owned" or "possessed") Military men who ruled Egypt as an independent regime from 1250 until the Ottoman conquest in 1517.

Manaus Opera House Opera house built in the interior of Brazil in a lucrative rubber-growing area at the turn of the twentieth century.

Manchukuo Japanese puppet state in Manchuria in the 1930s.

Manchus Descendants of the Jurchens who helped the Ming army recapture Beijing in 1644 after its seizure by the outlaw Li Zicheng. The Manchus numbered around 1 million but controlled a domain that included perhaps 250 million people. Their rule lasted more than 250 years and became known as the Qing dynasty.

mandate of heaven Religious ideology established by Zhou leaders to communicate legitimate transfer and retention of royal power as the will of their supreme god. The mandate later became Chinese political doctrine.

Mande A people who lived in the area between the bend in the Senegal River to the west and the bend in the Niger River to the east and between the Senegal River to the north and the Bandama River to the south. Also known as the Mandinka. Their civilization emerged around 1100.

Mandela, Nelson (1918–2013) Leader of the African National Congress (ANC) who was imprisoned for more than two decades by the apartheid regime in South Africa for his political activities, until worldwide protests led to his release in 1990. In 1994, Mandela won the presidency in South Africa's first free mass elections.

Manifest Destiny Belief that it was God's will for the American people to expand their territory and political processes across the North American continent.

manorialism System in which the manor (a lord's home, its associated industry, and surrounding fields) served as the basic unit of economic power; an alternative to the concept of feudalism (the hierarchical relationships of king, lords, and peasantry) for thinking about the nature of power in western Europe from 1000 to 1300 CE.

Mao Zedong (1893–1976) Chinese communist leader who rose to power during the Long March (1934–1935). In 1949, Mao and his followers defeated the Nationalists and established a communist regime in China.

maroon community Sanctuary for formerly enslaved freedom seekers in the Americas.

Marshall Plan Economic aid package given by the United States to Europe after World War II in hopes of a rapid period of reconstruction and economic gain that would protect the countries that received the aid from a communist takeover.

martyr Literally meaning "witness," a person executed by Roman authorities for maintaining his or her Christian beliefs rather than worshipping the emperor.

Marx, Karl (1818–1883) German philosopher and economist who created Marxism and believed that a revolution of the working classes would overthrow the capitalist order and create a classless society.

Marxism A current of socialism created by Karl Marx and Friedrich Engels. It stressed the primacy of economics and technology—and, above all, class conflict—in shaping human history. Economic production provided the foundation, the "base" for society, which shaped politics, values, art, and culture (the superstructure). In the modern, industrial era, they believed class conflict boiled down to a two-way struggle between the bourgeoisie (who controlled the means of industrial production) and the proletariat (workers who had only their labor power to sell).

mass consumption Increased purchasing power and appetite for goods in the prosperous and mainly middle-class societies of the early twentieth century, stemming from mass production.

mass culture Distinctive form of popular culture that arose in the wake of World War I. It reflected the tastes of the working and middle classes, who now had more time and money to spend on entertainment, and relied on new technologies, especially film and radio, that could reach an entire nation's population and consolidate their sense of being a single state.

mass production System in which factories were set up to produce huge quantities of identical products, reflecting the early twentieth-century world's demands for greater volume, faster speed, reduced cost, and standardized output.

mastaba Word meaning "bench" in Arabic; it refers to a huge flat structure identical to earlier royal tombs of ancient Egypt.

Mau Mau Uprising (1952–1957) Uprising orchestrated by a Kenyan guerrilla movement; this conflict forced the British to grant independence to the Black majority in Kenya.

Mauryan Empire (321–184 BCE) The first large-scale empire in South Asia, stretching from the Indus in the west to the mouth of the Ganges in the east and nearly to the southern tip of the Indian subcontinent; begun by Chandragupta Maurya, in the aftermath of Alexander's time in India, and expanded to its greatest extent by his grandson Aśoka.

Mawali Non-Arab "clients" to Arab tribes in the early Islamic empire. Because tribal patronage was so much a part of the Arabian cultural system, non-Arabs who converted to Islam affiliated themselves with a tribe and became clients of that tribe.

Maxim gun European weapon that was capable of firing many bullets per second; it was used against Africans in the conquest of the continent.

Maya Civilization that ruled over large stretches of Mesoamerica; it was composed of a series of kingdoms, each built around ritual centers rather than cities. The Maya engaged neighboring peoples in warfare and trade and expanded borders through tributary relationships. They were not defined by a great ruler or one capital city, but by their shared religious beliefs.

McCarthyism Campaign by U.S. Republican senator Joseph McCarthy in the late 1940s and early 1950s to uncover closet communists, particularly in the State Department and in Hollywood.

Meat Inspection Act (1906) Legislation that provided for government supervision of meatpacking operations; it was part of a broader progressive reform movement dedicated to correcting the negative consequences of urbanization and industrialization in the United States.

Mecca Arabian city in which the Prophet Muhammad was born. Mecca was a trading center and pilgrimage destination in the pre-Islamic and Islamic periods. Exiled in 622 CE because of resistance to his message, Muhammad returned to Mecca in 630 CE and claimed the city for Islam.

Medes Rivals of the Neo-Assyrians and the Persians. The Medes inhabited the area from the Zagros Mountains to the modern city of Tehran; known as expert horsemen and archers, they were eventually defeated by the Persians.

megalith Literally, "great stone"; the word *megalith* is used when describing structures such as Stonehenge. These massive structures are the result of cooperative planning and work.

megarons Large buildings found in Troy (level II) that are the predecessors of the classic Greek temple.

Meiji Empire Empire created under the leadership of Mutsuhito, emperor of Japan from 1868 until 1912. During the Meiji period Japan became a world industrial and naval power.

Meiji Restoration (1868–1912) Reign of the Meiji Emperor, which was characterized by a new nationalist identity, economic advances, and political transformation.

Mencius Disciple of Confucius who lived from 372 to 289 BCE.

mercantilism Economic theory that drove European empire builders. In this economic system, the world had a fixed amount of wealth, which meant one country's wealth came at the expense of another's. Mercantilism assumed that colonies existed for the sole purpose of enriching the country that controlled the colony.

Mercosur Free-trade pact between the governments of Argentina, Brazil, Paraguay, and Uruguay.

meritocracy Rule by persons of talent.

Meroitic kingdom Thriving kingdom from the fourth century BCE to 300 CE. A successor to Kush, it was influenced by both Egyptian and Sudanic cultures.

Mestizos Mixed-blood offspring of Spanish settlers and Amerindians.

Métis Mixed-blood offspring of French settlers and Amerindians.

Mexican Revolution (1910–1920) Conflict fueled by the unequal distribution of land and by disgruntled workers; it erupted when political elites split over the succession of General Porfirio Díaz after decades of his rule. The fight lasted over ten years and cost 1 million lives, but it resulted in widespread reform and a new constitution.

Mfecane movement African political revolts in the first half of the nineteenth century that were caused by the expansionist methods of King Shaka of the Zulu people.

microsocieties Small-scale, fragmented communities that had little interaction with others. These communities were the norm for peoples living in the Americas and islanders in the Pacific and Aegean from 2000 to 1200 BCE.

Middle Kingdom Period of Egyptian history lasting from about 2055 to 1650 BCE, characterized by a consolidation of power and building activity in Upper Egypt.

migration Long-distance travel for the purpose of resettlement. In the case of early humans, the need to move was usually a response to an environmental shift, such as climate change during the Ice Age.

millenarian Believer (usually religious) in the cataclysmic destruction of a corrupt, fallen society and its replacement by an ideal, utopian future.

millenarian movement Believer (usually religious) in the cataclysmic destruction of a corrupt, fallen society and its replacement by an ideal, utopian future.

millets Minority religious communities of the Ottoman Empire.

minaret Slender tower within a mosque from which Muslims are called to prayer.

minbar Pulpit inside a mosque from which Muslim religious speakers broadcast their message to the faithful.

Ming dynasty Successor to the Mongol Yuan dynasty that reinstituted and reinforced Han Chinese ceremonies and ideals, including rule by an ethnically Han bureaucracy.

Minoans A people who built a large number of elaborate, independent palace centers on Crete, at Knossos, and elsewhere around 2000 BCE. Named after the legendary King Minos, said to have ruled Crete at the time, they sailed throughout the Mediterranean and by 1600 BCE had planted colonies on many Aegean islands, which in turn became trading and mining centers.

mission civilisatrice Term French colonizers used to refer to France's form of "rationalized" colonial rule, which attempted to bring "civilization" to the "uncivilized."

mitochondrial DNA Form of DNA found in mitochondria, structures located outside the nuclei of cells. Examining mitochondrial DNA enables researchers to measure the genetic variation among living organisms, including human beings. Only females pass mitochondrial DNA to their offspring.

Moche A people who extended their power and increased their wealth at the height of the Chimú Empire over several valleys in what is now Peru.

Model T Automobile manufactured by the Ford Motor Company, which was the first to be priced reasonably enough to be sold to the masses.

modernism In the arts, modernism refers to the effort to break with older conventions and seek new ways of seeing and describing the world.

Mohism School of thought in ancient China, named after Mo Di, or Mozi (c. 479–381 BCE). It emphasized one's obligation to society as a whole, not just to one's immediate family or social circle.

monarchy Political system in which one individual holds supreme power and passes that power on to his or her next of kin.

monasticism From the Greek word *monos* (meaning "alone"), the practice of living without the ties of marriage or family, forsaking earthly luxuries for a life of prayer and study. While Christian monasticism originated in Egypt, a variant of ascetic life had long been practiced in Buddhism.

monetization An economic shift from a barter-based economy to one dependent on currency.

Mongols Combination of nomadic forest and steppe peoples who lived by hunting and livestock herding and were expert horsemen. Beginning in 1206, the Mongols launched a series of conquests that brought far-flung parts of the world together under their rule. By incorporating conquered peoples and adapting some of their customs, the Mongols created a unified empire that stretched from the Pacific Ocean to the shores of the eastern Mediterranean and the southern steppes of Eurasia.

monotheism The belief in only one god; to be distinguished from polytheism (the belief in many gods) and henotheism (the belief that there may be many gods but one is superior to the others).

Moors Term employed by Europeans in the medieval period to refer to Muslim occupants of North Africa, the western Sahara, and the Iberian Peninsula.

mosque Place of worship for the people of Islam.

mound people Name for the people of Cahokia, since its landscape was dominated by earthen monuments in the shapes of mounds. The mounds were carefully maintained and were the loci from which Cahokians paid respect to spiritual forces. *See also* Cahokia.

Mu Chinese ruler (956–918 BCE) who put forth a formal bureaucratic system of governance, appointing officials, supervisors, and military captains to whom he was not related. He also instituted a formal legal code.

muckrakers Journalists who aimed to expose political and commercial corruption in late nineteenth- and early twentieth-century America.

Muftis Experts on Muslim religious law.

Mughal Empire One of Islam's greatest regimes. Established in 1526, it was a vigorous, centralized state whose political authority encompassed most of modern-day India. During the sixteenth century, it had a population of between 100 and 150 million.

Muhammad (570–632 ce) Prophet and founder of the Islamic faith. Born in Mecca in Saudi Arabia and orphaned when young, Muhammad lived under the protection of his uncle. His career as a prophet began around 610 CE, with his first experience of spiritual revelation.

Muhammad Ali (r. 1805–1848) Ruler of Egypt who initiated a set of modernizing reforms that sought to make it competitive with the great powers.

mullahs Religious leaders in Iran who in the 1970s led a movement opposing Shah Mohammad Reza Pahlavi and denounced American materialism and secularism.

multinational corporations Corporations based in many different countries that have global investment, trading, and distribution goals.

Muscovy The principality of Moscow. Originally a mixture of Slavs, Finnish tribes, Turkic speakers, and many others, Muscovy used territorial expansion and commercial networks to consolidate a powerful state and expanded to become the Russian Empire, a huge realm that spanned parts of Europe, much of northern Asia, numerous North Pacific islands, and even—for a time—a corner of North America (Alaska).

Muslim Brotherhood Egyptian organization founded in 1928 by Hassan al-Banna. It attacked liberal democracy as a cover for middle-class, business, and landowning interests and fought for a return to a purified Islam.

Muslim League National Muslim party of India.

Mussolini, Benito (1883–1945) Italian dictator and founder of the fascist movement in Italy. During World War II, he allied Italy with Germany and Japan.

Muwahhidin Literally, "unitarians"; followers of the Wahhabi movement that emerged in the Arabian Peninsula in the eighteenth century.

Mycenaeans Mainland competitors of the Minoans who took over Crete around 1400 BCE. Migrating to Greece from central Europe, they brought their Indo-European language, chariots, and metalworking skills, which they used to dominate until 1200 BCE.

Nagasaki Second Japanese city to be hit by an atomic bomb near the end of World War II.

Napoleon Bonaparte (1769–1821) General who rose to power in a postrevolutionary coup d'état, eventually proclaiming himself emperor of France. He placed security and order ahead of social reform and created a civil legal code. Napoleon expanded his empire through military action, but after his disastrous

Russian campaign, the united European powers defeated Napoleon and forced him into exile. He escaped and reassumed command of his army but was later defeated at the Battle of Waterloo.

Napoleonic Code Legal code drafted by Napoleon in 1804; it distilled different legal traditions to create one uniform law. The code confirmed the abolition of feudal privileges of all kinds and set the conditions for exercising property rights.

National Assembly of France Governing body of France that succeeded the Estates-General in 1789 during the French Revolution. It was composed of, and defined by, the delegates of the Third Estate.

National Association for the Advancement of Colored People (NAACP) A U.S. civil rights organization, founded in 1910, dedicated to ending inequality and segregation for Black Americans.

National Recovery Administration (NRA) U.S. New Deal agency created in 1933 to prepare codes of fair administration and to plan for public works. It was later declared unconstitutional.

nationalism The idea that members of a shared community called a nation should have sovereignty within the borders of their state.

nation-state Form of political organization that derived legitimacy from its inhabitants, often referred to as citizens, who in theory, if not always in practice, shared a common language, common culture, and common history.

native learning Japanese movement to promote nativist intellectual traditions and the celebration of Japanese texts.

native paramountcy British form of "rationalized" colonial rule, which attempted to bring "civilization" to the "uncivilized" by proclaiming that when the interests of European settlers in Africa clashed with those of the African population, the latter should take precedence.

natural rights Belief that emerged in eighteenth-century western Europe and North America that rights fundamental to human nature were discernible to reason and should be affirmed in human-made law.

natural selection Charles Darwin's theory that populations grew faster than the food supply, creating a "struggle for existence" among species. In later work he showed how the passing on of individual traits was also determined by what he called sexual selection—according to which the "best" mates are chosen for their strength, beauty, or talents. The outcome: the "fittest" survived to reproduce, while the less adaptable did not.

Nazis (National Socialist German Workers' Party) German organization dedicated to winning workers over from socialism to nationalism; the first Nazi Party platform combined nationalism with anticapitalism and anti-Semitism.

Neanderthals Members of an early wave of hominins from Africa who settled in western Afro-Eurasia, in an area reaching from present-day Uzbekistan and Iraq to Spain, approximately 150,000 years ago.

Negritos Hunting and gathering inhabitants of the East Asian coastal islands who migrated there around 28,000 BCE but by 2000 BCE had been replaced by new migrants.

Negritude The idea of a Black identity and culture different from, but not inferior to, European cultural forms; shaped by African and African American intellectuals like Senegal's first president, Léopold Sédar Senghor.

Nehemiah Jewish eunuch of the Persian court who was given permission to rebuild the fortification walls around the city of Jerusalem from 440 to 437 BCE.

Neo-Assyrian Empire Afro-Eurasian empire that dominated from 911 to 612 BCE. The Neo-Assyrians extended their control over resources and people beyond their own borders, and their empire lasted for three centuries.

neocolonialism Contemporary geopolitical policy or practice in which a politically, economically, and often militarily superior nation asserts control over a country that remains nominally sovereign.

Nestorian Christians Denomination of Christians whose beliefs about Christ differed from those of the official Byzantine church. Named after Nestorius, former bishop of Constantinople, they emphasized the human aspects of Jesus.

New Deal President Franklin Delano Roosevelt's package of government reforms that were enacted during the 1930s to provide jobs for the unemployed, social welfare programs for the poor, and security to the financial markets.

New Economic Policy Enacted decrees of the Bolsheviks between 1921 and 1927 that grudgingly sanctioned private trade and private property.

New Negro movement *See* Harlem Renaissance.

New World Term applied to the Americas that reflected the Europeans' view that anything previously unknown to them was "new," even if it had existed and supported societies long before European explorers arrived on its shores.

nirvana Literally, "nonexistence"; nirvana is the state of complete liberation from the concerns of worldly life, as in Buddhist thought.

Noble Eightfold Path Buddhist concept of a way of life by which people may rid themselves of individual desire to achieve nirvana. The path consists of wisdom, ethical behavior, and mental discipline.

Noh drama Masked theater favored by Japanese bureaucrats and regional lords during the Tokugawa period.

Nok culture Spectacular culture that arose in present-day Nigeria in the sixth century BCE. Iron smelting occurred there around 600 BCE. Thus the Nok people made the transition from stone to iron materials.

nomads People who move across vast distances without settling permanently in a particular place. Often pastoralists, nomads and transhumant herders introduced new forms of chariot-based warfare that transformed the Afro-Eurasian world.

nongovernmental organizations (NGOs) Term used to refer to private organizations like the Red Cross that play a large role in international affairs. *See also* supranational organizations.

nonviolent resistance Moral and political philosophy of resistance developed by Indian National Congress leader Mohandas Gandhi. Gandhi believed that if Indians pursued self-reliance and self-control in a nonviolent way, the British would eventually have to leave.

North American Free Trade Agreement (NAFTA) Treaty negotiated in the early 1990s to promote free trade between Canada, the United States, and Mexico.

North Atlantic Treaty Organization (NATO) International organization set up in 1949 to provide for the defense of western European countries and the United States from the perceived Soviet threat.

Northern Wei dynasty Regime founded in 386 CE by the Tuoba, a people originally from Inner Mongolia, that lasted one and a half centuries. The rulers of this dynasty adopted many practices of the earlier Chinese Han regime. At the same time, they struggled to consolidate authority over their own nomadic people. Ultimately, several decades of intense internal conflict led to the dynasty's downfall.

Northwest Passage Long-sought marine passageway between the Atlantic and Pacific Oceans along the northern coast of North America.

Oceania Collective name for Australia, New Zealand, and the islands of the southwest Pacific Ocean.

Odyssey An epic tale, composed in the eighth century BCE, of the journey of Odysseus, who traveled the Mediterranean back to his home in Ithaca after the siege of Troy.

oikos The word for "small family unit" in ancient Greece, similar to the *familia* in Rome. Its structure, with men as heads of household over women and children, embodied the fundamental power structure in Greek city-states.

oligarchy Clique of privileged rulers.

Olmecs Mesoamerican people, emerging around 1500 BCE, whose name means "inhabitants in the land of rubber," one of their major trade goods. Living in decentralized agrarian villages, this complex, stratified society shared language and religious ideas that were practiced at sacred ritual centers.

open-door policy Policy proposed by U.S. secretary of state John Hay that would give all foreign nations equal access to trade with China. As European imperial powers carved out spheres of influence in late nineteenth-century China, American leaders worried that the United States would be excluded from trade with China.

Opium Wars (1839–1842, 1856–1860) Wars fought between the British and Qing China over British trade in opium; the result was that China granted to the British the right to trade in five different ports and ceded Hong Kong to the British.

oracle bones Animal bones inscribed, heated, and interpreted by Shang ritual specialists to determine the will of the ancestors.

Organization of the Petroleum Exporting Countries (OPEC) International association established in 1960 to coordinate price and supply policies of oil-producing states.

Orientalism Genre of literature and painting that portrayed the nonwestern peoples of North Africa and Asia as exotic, sensuous, and economically backward with respect to Europeans.

Orientalists Western scholars who specialized in the study of Asia when Orientalism was at its peak.

Orrorin tugenensis Early hominid that first appeared 6 million years ago.

Ottoman Empire A Turkish warrior band that transformed itself into a vast, multicultural, bureaucratic empire that lasted from the early fourteenth century through the early twentieth century and encompassed Anatolia, the Arab world, and large swaths of southern and eastern Europe.

Pacific War (1879–1883) War between Chile and the alliance of Bolivia and Peru.

pagani Pejorative word used by Christians to designate pagans.

palace Official residence of the ruler, his family, and his entourage. The palace was both a social institution and a set of buildings. It first appeared around 2500 BCE, about a millennium later than the Mesopotamian temple, and quickly joined the temple as a defining landmark of city life. Eventually, it became a source of power rivaling the temple, and palace and temple life often blurred, as did the boundary between the sacred and the secular.

Palace of Versailles The palace complex, 11 miles away from the French capital of Paris, built by Louis XIV in the 1670s and 1680s to house and entertain his leading clergymen and nobles, with the hopes of diverting them from plotting against him.

Palmyra Roman trading depot located in modern-day Syria; part of a network of trading cities that connected various regions of Afro-Eurasia.

pan movements Groups that sought to link people across state boundaries in new communities based on ethnicity or, in some cases, religion (for example, pan-Germanism, pan-Islamism, and pan-Slavism).

pandemic An outbreak of disease occurring worldwide or over a great area spanning international boundaries and affecting a large number of people.

Pansophia Ideal republic of inquisitive Christians united in the search for knowledge of nature as a means of loving God.

papacy The institution of the pope, the Catholic spiritual leader in Rome.

papal Of, relating to, or issued by a pope.

Parthians Horse-riding people who pushed southward around the middle of the second century BCE and wiped out the Greek kingdoms in Iran. They then extended their power all the way to the Mediterranean, where they ran up against the Roman Empire in Anatolia and Mesopotamia.

pastoral nomads Peoples who move with their herds in perpetual motion across large areas, like the steppe lands of Inner Eurasia, and facilitate long-distance trade.

pastoralism A way of life in which humans herd domesticated animals and exploit their products (hides/fur, meat, and milk). Pastoralists include nomadic groups that range across vast distances, as well as transhumant herders who migrate seasonally in a more limited range.

paterfamilias Latin for "father of the family," the foundation of the Roman social order.

patria Latin, meaning "fatherland."

patrons In the Roman system of patronage, men and women of wealth and high social status who protected dependents or "clients" of a lower class.

Pax Mongolica The political and especially the commercial stability that the vast Mongol Empire provided for the travelers and merchants of Eurasia during the thirteenth and fourteenth centuries.

Pax Romana Latin term for "Roman Peace," referring to the period from 25 BCE to 235 CE, when conditions in the Roman Empire were relatively settled and peaceful, allowing trade and the economy to thrive.

Pax Sinica Modern term (paralleling the term *Pax Romana*) for the "Chinese Peace" that lasted from 149 to 87 BCE, a period when agriculture and commerce flourished, fueling the expansion of cities and the growth of the population of Han China.

Peace Preservation Law (1925) Act instituted in Japan that specified up to ten years' hard labor for any member of an organization advocating a basic change in the political system or the abolition of private property.

Pearl Harbor American naval base in Hawaii on which the Japanese launched a surprise attack on December 7, 1941, bringing the United States into World War II.

Peloponnesian War War fought between 431 and 404 BCE between two of Greece's most powerful city-states, Athens and Sparta.

Peninsular War (1808–1813) Conflict in which the Portuguese and Spanish populations, supported by the British, resisted an invasion of the Iberian Peninsula by the French under Napoleon.

Peninsulares Men and women born in Spain or Portugal who resided in the Americas. They regarded themselves as superior to Spaniards or Portuguese born in the colonies (Creoles).

People's Charter Document calling for universal suffrage for adult males, the secret ballot, electoral districts, and annual parliamentary elections. It was signed by over 3 million British between 1839 and 1842.

periplus "Sailing around" manual that preserved firsthand knowledge of navigation strategies and trading advice.

Persepolis Darius I's capital city in the highlands of Fars; a ceremonial center and expression of imperial identity as well as an important administrative hub of the Persian Empire.

Peterloo Massacre (1819) The killing of 11 and wounding of 460 following a peaceful demonstration for political reform by workers in Manchester, England.

Petra Literally, "rock"; city in modern-day Jordan that was the Nabatean capital. It profited greatly by supplying provisions and water to travelers and traders. Many of its houses and shrines were cut into the rocky mountains.

phalanx Military formation used by Philip II of Macedon, whereby heavily armored infantry were closely arrayed in battle.

Philip II of Macedon Father of Alexander the Great, under whose rule Macedonia developed into a large ethnic and territorial state. After unifying Macedonia, Philip went on to conquer neighboring states.

philosophes Enlightenment thinkers who applied scientific reasoning to human interaction and society as opposed to nature.

philosophia Literally, "love of wisdom"; a system of thought that originally included speculation on the nature of the cosmos, the environment, and human existence. It eventually came to include thought about the nature of humans and life in society.

Phoenicians An ethnic group in the Levant known for their ships, trading, and alphabet, and referred to in Hebrew scripture as the Canaanites. The term *Phoenician* (Greek for "purple people") derives from the major trade good they manufactured, a rare and expensive purple dye.

phonemes Primary and distinctive sounds that are characteristic of human language.

piety Strong sense of religious duty and devoutness, often inspiring extraordinary actions.

plant domestication The practice of growing plants, harvesting their seeds, and saving some of the seeds for planting in subsequent growing cycles, resulting in a steady food supply. Plant domestication was practiced as far back as 9000 BCE in the southern Levant and spread from there into the rest of Southwest Asia.

plantation slavery System whereby enslaved labor was used for the cultivation of crops wholly for the sake of producing surplus that was then used for profit; such plantations were a crucial part of the growth of the Mediterranean economy.

Plato (427–347 BCE) Disciple of the great philosopher Socrates; his works are the only record we have of Socrates's teaching. He was also the author of formative philosophical works on ethics and politics.

plebs The "common people" of Rome, whose interests were protected by officials called tribunes.

pochteca Archaic term for merchants of the Mexica.

polities Politically organized communities or states.

polyglot communities Societies composed of diverse linguistic and ethnic groups.

popular culture Affordable and accessible forms of art and entertainment available to people at all levels of society.

popular sovereignty The idea that the power of the state resides in the people.

populists Members of a political movement that supported U.S. farmers in late nineteenth-century America. The term is often used generically to refer to political groups who appeal to the majority of the population.

potassium-argon dating Major dating technique based on the decay of potassium into argon over time. This method makes possible the dating of objects up to a million years old.

potato famine (1840s) Severe famine in Ireland that led to the rise of radical political movements and the migration of large numbers of Irish to the United States.

potter's wheel Fast wheel that enabled people to mass-produce vessels in many different shapes. This advance, invented at the city of Uruk, enabled potters to make significant technical breakthroughs.

pottery Vessels made of mud and, later, clay used for storing and transporting food.

Prague Spring (1968) Program of liberalization by which communist authorities in Czechoslovakia strove to create a democratic and pluralist socialism; crushed by the Soviets, who branded it a "counterrevolutionary" movement.

predestination Belief of many sixteenth- and seventeenth-century Protestant groups that God had foreordained the lives of individuals, including their bad and good deeds.

primitivism Western art movement of the late nineteenth and early twentieth centuries that drew upon the so-called primitive art forms of Africa, Oceania, and pre-Columbian America.

printing press A machine used to print text or pictures from type or plates, dramatically increasing the speed at which information could be copied and disseminated. The spread of printing press technology in the 1450s created a revolution in communication around the world.

progressive reformers Members of the U.S. reform movement in the early twentieth century that aimed to eliminate political corruption, improve working conditions, and regulate the power of large industrial and financial enterprises.

proletarians Industrial wage workers.

prophets Charismatic freelance religious men of power who found themselves in opposition to the formal power of kings, bureaucrats, and priests.

Prophet's Town Indian village in present-day Indiana that was burned down by American forces in the early nineteenth century.

Protestant Reformation Religious movement initiated by sixteenth-century monk Martin Luther, who openly criticized the corruption in the Catholic Church and voiced his belief that Christians could speak directly to God. His doctrines gained wide support, and those who followed this new view of Christianity rejected the authority of the papacy and the Catholic clergy, broke away from the Catholic Church, and called themselves "Protestants."

Protestantism Division of Christianity that emerged in western Europe from the Protestant Reformation.

Proto-Indo-European The parent of all the languages in the Indo-European family, which includes, among many others, English, German, Norwegian, Portuguese, French, Russian, Persian, Hindi, and Bengali.

Pullman Strike (1894) American Railway Union strike in response to wage cuts and firings.

Punic Wars Series of three wars fought between Rome and Carthage from 264 to 146 BCE that resulted in the end of Carthaginian hegemony in the western Mediterranean, the growth of Roman military might (army and navy), and the beginning of Rome's aggressive foreign imperialism.

puppet states Governments with little power in the international arena that follow the dictates of their more powerful neighbors or patrons.

Puritans Seventeenth-century reform group of the Church of England; also known as dissenters or nonconformists.

Qadiriyya Sufi order that facilitated the spread of Islam into West Africa.

qadis Judges in the Ottoman Empire.

qanats Underground water channels, vital for irrigation, that were used in Persia. Little evaporation occurred when water was being moved through *qanats*.

Qing dynasty (1644–1911) Minority Manchu rule over China that incorporated new territories, experienced substantial population growth, and sustained significant economic growth.

Questions of King Milinda (Milindapunha) Name of a second-century BCE text espousing the teachings of Buddhism as set forth by Menander, a Yavana king. It featured a discussion between the king and a sophisticated Buddhist sage named Nagasena.

Quetzalcoatl Ancient deity and legendary ruler of Native American peoples living in Mexico.

Quran The scripture of the Islamic faith. Originally a verbal recitation, the Quran was eventually compiled into a book with its verses in the order in which we have them today. According to traditional Islamic interpretation, the Quran was revealed to Muhammad by the angel Gabriel over a period of twenty-three years.

radicalism The conviction that real change is possible only by going to the root (in Latin, *radix*) of the problem and promoting complete political and social reform. Tendencies toward radicalism can be found in every culture that develops a complex set of institutions and hierarchies, but have been found most frequently in the west since 1789.

radicals Widely used term in nineteenth-century Europe that referred to those individuals and political organizations that favored the total reconfiguration of Europe's old state system.

radiocarbon dating Dating technique using the isotope C^{14}, contained by all living organisms, which plants acquire directly from the atmosphere and animals acquire indirectly when they consume plants or other animals. When organisms die, the C^{14} they contain begins to decay into a stable nonradioactive isotope, C^{12}. The rate of decay is regular and measurable, making it possible to ascertain the ages of fossils that leave organic remains up to 40,000 years.

Raj British crown's administration of India following the end of the East India Company's rule after the Rebellion of 1857.

raja "King" in the Kshatriya period in South Asia; could also refer to the head of a family, but indicated the person who had control of land and resources in South Asian city-states.

Ramadan Ninth month of the Muslim year, during which all Muslims must fast during daylight hours.

rape of Nanjing Attack against the Chinese in which the Japanese slaughtered at least 100,000 civilians and raped thousands of women between December 1937 and February 1938.

Rashtriya Swayamsevak Sangh (RSS) **(1925)** Campaign to organize Hindus as a militant, modern community in India; translated in English as "National Volunteer Organization."

Rebellion of 1857 Indian uprising against the East India Company whose aims were religious purification, an egalitarian society, and local and communal solidarity without the interference of British rule.

rebus Probably originating in Uruk, a representation that transfers meaning from the name of a thing to the sound of that name. For example, a picture of a bee can represent the sound "b." Such pictures opened the door to writing: a technology of symbols that uses marks to represent specific discrete sounds.

Reconquista Spanish reconquest of territories lost to the Islamic empire, beginning with Toledo in 1061.

Red Guards Chinese students who were the shock troopers in the early phases of Mao Zedong's Great Proletarian Cultural Revolution in 1966–1976.

Red Lanterns Female supporters of the Chinese Boxers who dressed in red garments. Most were teenage girls and unmarried women.

Red Turban movement Diverse religious movement in China during the fourteenth century that spread the belief that the world was drawing to an end as Mongol rule was collapsing.

Reds Bolsheviks.

Reich German empire composed of Denmark, Austria, and parts of western France (1933–1945).

Reichstag The German parliament.

Reign of Terror Campaign at the height of the French Revolution in the early 1790s that used violence, including systematic execution of opponents of the revolution, to purge France of its enemies and to extend the revolution beyond its borders; radicals executed as many as 40,000 persons who were judged enemies of the state.

Renaissance Term meaning "rebirth" used by historians to characterize the cultural flourishing of European nations between 1430 and 1550, which emphasized a break from the church-centered medieval world and a new concept of humankind as the center of the world.

republican government Government in which power and rulership rest with representatives of the people, not with a king.

res publica Term (meaning "public thing") used by Romans to describe their Republic, which was advised by a Senate and was governed by popular assemblies of free adult males, who were arranged into voting units, based on wealth and social status, to elect officers and legislate.

Restoration (1815–1848) European movement after the defeat of Napoleon to restore Europe to its pre-French-revolutionary status and to quash radical movements.

Rift Valley Area of northeastern Africa where some of the most important early human archaeological discoveries of fossils were made, especially one of an intact skull that is 1.8 million years old.

river basin Area drained by a river, including all its tributaries. River basins were rich in fertile soil, water for irrigation, and plant and animal life, which made them attractive for human habitation. Cultivators were able to produce surplus agriculture to support the first cities.

Roman army Military force of the Roman Empire. The Romans devised a military draft that could draw from a huge population. In their encounter with Hannibal, they lost up to 80,000 men in three separate encounters and still won the war.

Roman Catholicism Western European Christianity, centered on the papacy in Rome, that emphasizes the atoning power of Jesus's death and aims to expand as far as possible.

Roman law The legal system of Rome, under which disputes were brought to public courts and decisions were made by judges and sometimes by large juries. Rome's legal system featured written law and institutions for settling legal disputes.

roving bandits Large bands of dispossessed and marginalized peasants who vented their anger at tax collectors in the waning years of the Ming dynasty.

Royal Road A 1,600-mile road from Sardis in Anatolia to Susa in Iran; used by messengers, traders, the army, and those taking tribute to the king in the fifth century BCE.

Russification Programs to assimilate people of over 146 dialects into the Russian Empire.

Sack of Constantinople Rampage in 1204 by the Frankish armies on the capital city of Constantinople.

sacred kingships Institutions that marked the centralized politics of West Africa. The inhabitants of these kingships believed that their kings were descendants of the gods.

Sahel The area of sub-Saharan Africa spanning the continent just south of the Sahara Desert.

St. Bartholomew's Day Massacre (1572) Roman Catholic massacre of French Protestants in Paris.

St. Patrick A formerly enslaved man brought to Ireland from Britain who later became a missionary, also called the "Apostle of Ireland." He died in 461 CE.

Salt March (1930) A 240-mile trek to the sea in India, led by Mohandas Gandhi, to gather salt for free, thus breaking the British colonial monopoly on salt.

samurai Japanese warriors who made up the private armies of Japanese daimyos.

Sandinista coalition Left-leaning Nicaraguan coalition of the 1970s and 1980s.

Sanskrit cosmopolis Cultural synthesis based on Hindu spiritual beliefs expressed in the Sanskrit language that unified South Asia in place of a centralized empire.

Santería African-based religion, blended with Christian influences, that was first practiced by enslaved people in Cuba.

Sargon the Great King of Akkad, a city-state located near present-day Baghdad. Reigning from 2334 to 2279 BCE, Sargon helped bring the competitive era of city-states to an end and sponsored monumental works of architecture, art, and literature.

Sasanian Empire Empire that succeeded the Parthians in the mid-220s CE in Inner Eurasia. The Sasanian Empire controlled the trade crossroads of Afro-Eurasia and possessed a strong armored cavalry, which made it a powerful rival to Rome. The Sasanians were also tolerant of Judaism and Christianity, which allowed Christians to flourish.

sati Hindu practice whereby a widow was burned to death on the pyre of her dead husband.

satrap Governor of a province in the Persian Empire. Each satrap was a relative or intimate associate of the king.

satrapy Province in the Persian empire, ruled over by a governor, called a satrap, who was usually a relative or associate of the king.

satyagraha See nonviolent resistance.

scientific method Method of inquiry based on experimentation in nature. Many of its principles were first laid out by the philosopher Sir Francis Bacon (1561–1626), who claimed that real science entailed the formulation of hypotheses that could be tested in carefully controlled experiments.

Scramble for Africa European rush to colonize parts of Africa at the end of the nineteenth century.

scribes Those who wield writing tools; from the very beginning they were at the top of the social ladder, under the major power brokers.

Scythian ethos Warrior ethos that embodied the extremes of aggressive horse-mounted culture. In part, the Scythian ethos was the result of the constant struggle between settlers, hunters and gatherers, and nomads on the northern frontier of Europe around 1000 BCE.

Sea Peoples Migrants from north of the Mediterranean who invaded cities of Egypt, Asia Minor, and the Levant in the second millennium BCE.

SEATO (Southeast Asia Treaty Organization) Military alliance of pro-American, anticommunist states in Southeast Asia from 1954 to 1977.

Second World Term invented during the Cold War to refer to the communist countries, as opposed to the west (or First World) and the former colonies (or Third World).

second-generation societies First-millennium BCE societies that innovated on their older political, religious, and cultural ideas by incorporating new aspects of cultures they encountered to reshape their way of life.

Seleucus Nikator Successor of Alexander the Great who lived from 358 to 281 BCE. He controlled Mesopotamia, Syria, Persia, and parts of the Punjab.

Self-Strengthening movement A movement of reformist Chinese bureaucrats in the latter half of the nineteenth century that attempted to adopt western elements of learning and technological skill while retaining their core Chinese culture.

Semu Term meaning "outsiders," or non-Chinese people—Mongols, Tanguts, Khitan, Jurchen, Muslims, Tibetans, Persians, Turks, Nestorians, Jews, and Armenians—who became a new ruling elite over a Han majority population in the late thirteenth century.

sepoys Hindu and Muslim recruits of the East India Company's military force.

serfs Peasants who farmed the land and paid fees to be protected and governed by lords under a system of rule called manorialism.

settled agriculture Humans' use of tools, animals, and their own labor to work the same plot of land for more than one growing cycle. It involves switching from a hunting and gathering lifestyle to one based on farming.

Seven Years' War (1756–1763) Also known as the French and Indian War; worldwide war that ended when Prussia defeated Austria, establishing itself as a European power, and when Britain gained control of India and many of France's colonies through the Treaty of Paris.

sexual revolution Increased freedom in sexual behavior, resulting in part from advances in contraception, notably the introduction of oral contraception in 1960, that allowed men and women to limit childbearing and to have sex with less fear of pregnancy.

shah Traditional title of Persian rulers.

shamans Certain humans whose powers supposedly enabled them to commune with the supernatural and to transform themselves wholly or partly into beasts.

shamisen Three-stringed instrument, often played by Japanese geisha.

Shandingdong Man A *Homo sapiens* whose fossil remains and relics can be dated to about 18,000 years ago. His physical characteristics were close to those of modern humans, and he had a similar brain size.

Shang state Dynasty in northeastern China that ruled from 1600 to 1046 BCE. Though not as well defined by borders as the territorial states in the southwest of Asia, it did have a ruling lineage. Four fundamental elements of the Shang state were a metal industry based on copper, pottery making, standardized architectural forms and walled towns, and divination using animal bones.

Shanghai School Late nineteenth-century style of painting characterized by an emphasis on spontaneous brushwork, feeling, and the incorporation of western influences into classical Chinese pieces.

sharecropping System of farming in which tenant farmers rented land and gave over a share of their crops to the land's owners. Sometimes seen as a cheap way for the state to conduct agricultural affairs, sharecropping often resulted in the impoverishment and marginalization of the underclass.

sharia Body of Islamic law that has developed over centuries, based on the Quran, the sayings of Muhammad (hadith), and the legal opinions of Muslim scholars (*ulama*).

Sharpeville Massacre (1960) Massacre of sixty-nine Black Africans when police fired upon a rally against the recently passed laws requiring non-White South Africans to carry identity papers.

Shawnees Native American tribe that inhabited the Ohio Valley during the eighteenth century.

Shays's Rebellion (1786) Uprising of armed farmers that broke out when the

Massachusetts state government refused to offer them economic relief.

Shi Huangdi Title taken by King Zheng in 221 BCE when he claimed the mandate of heaven and consolidated the Qin dynasty. He is known for his tight centralization of power, including standardizing weights, measures, and writing; constructing roads, canals, and the beginnings of the Great Wall; and preparing a massive tomb for himself filled with an army of terra-cotta warriors.

Shiism One of the two main branches of Islam, practiced in the Safavid Empire. Although always a minority sect in the Islamic world, Shiism contains several subsects, each of which has slightly different interpretations of theology and politics.

Shiites Minority tradition within modern Islam that traces political succession through the lineage of Muhammad and breaks with Sunni understandings of succession at the death of Ali (cousin and son-in-law of Muhammad and fourth caliph) in 661 CE.

Shinto Literally, "the way of the gods"; Japan's official religion, which promoted the state and the emperor's divinity.

Shiva The third of three Vedic deities, signifying destruction. *See also* Brahma *and* Vishnu.

shoguns Japanese military commanders. From 1185 to 1333, the Kamakura shoguns served as military "protectors" of the ruler in the city of Heian.

Shotoku (574–622 CE) Prince in the early Japanese Yamoto state who is credited with having introduced Buddhism to Japan.

Shudras Literally, "small ones"; workers and enslaved people from outside the Vedic lineage.

Siddhartha Gautama *See* Buddha.

Sikhism Islamic-inspired religion that calls on its followers to renounce the *varna* (caste) system and to treat all believers as equal before God.

Silicon Valley Valley between the California cities of San Francisco and San Jose, known for its innovative computer and high-technology industries.

silk Luxury textile that became a vastly popular export from China (via the Silk Roads) to the cities of the Roman world.

Silk Roads More than 5,000 miles of trade routes linking China, central Asia, and the Mediterranean. They were named for the silk famously traded along their land and sea routes, although ideas, people, and many other high-value commodities also moved along their lengths.

Silla One of three independent Korean states that may have emerged as early as the third century BCE. These states lasted until 668 CE, when Silla took control over the entire peninsula.

Silver Islands Term used by European merchants in the sixteenth century to refer to Japan because of its substantial trade in silver with China.

Sino-Japanese War (1894–1895) Conflict over the control of Korea in which China was forced to cede the province of Taiwan to Japan.

sipahi Urdu for "soldier."

small seal script Unified script that was used to the exclusion of other scripts under the Qin with the aim of centralizing administration; its use led to a less complicated style of clerical writing than had been in use under the Han.

social Darwinism Belief that Charles Darwin's theory of evolution was applicable to humans and justified the right of the ruling classes or countries to dominate the weak.

social hierarchies Distinctions between the privileged and the less privileged.

Social Security Act (1935) New Deal act that instituted old-age pensions and insurance for the unemployed.

socialism Political ideology that calls for a classless society with collective ownership of all property.

Socrates (469–399 BCE) Philosopher of Athens who encouraged people to reflect on ethics and morality. He stressed the importance of honor and integrity as opposed to wealth and power. Plato was his student.

Sogdians A people who lived in central Asia's commercial centers and maintained the stability and accessibility of the Silk Roads. They were crucial to the interconnectedness of the Afro-Eurasian landmass.

Solidarity The Soviet bloc's first independent trade union, established in Poland at the Gdańsk shipyard.

Song dynasty Chinese dynasty that took over the mandate of heaven for three centuries starting in 960 CE. It ruled in an era of many economic and political successes, but it eventually lost northern China to nomadic tribes.

Song porcelain Type of porcelain perfected during the Song dynasty that was light, durable, and quite beautiful.

South African War (1899–1902) *See* Anglo-Boer War.

Soviet bloc International alliance that included the eastern European countries of the Warsaw Pact as well as the Soviet Union, but also came to include Cuba.

Spanish-American War (1898) War between the United States and Spain in Cuba, Puerto Rico, and the Philippines. It ended with a treaty in which the United States took over the Philippines, Guam, and Puerto Rico; Cuba won partial independence.

speciation The formation of species.

specie Money in coin.

species A group of animals or plants sharing one or more distinctive characteristics.

spiritual ferment Process that occurred after 300 CE in which religion touched more areas of society and culture than before and in different, more demanding ways.

Spring and Autumn period Period between the eighth and fifth centuries BCE during which China was ruled by the feudal system. In this anarchic and turbulent time, there were 148 different tributary states.

SS (*Schutzstaffel*) Hitler's security police force.

Stalin, Joseph (1878–1953) Leader of the Communist Party and the Soviet Union; sought to create "socialism in one country." The name Stalin means "man of steel."

steel An alloy more malleable and stronger than iron that became essential for industries like shipbuilding and railways.

Stoicism Widespread philosophical movement initiated by Zeno (334–262 BCE). Zeno and his followers sought to understand the role of people in relation to the cosmos. For the Stoics, everything was grounded in nature. Being in love with nature and living a good life required being in control of one's passions and thus indifferent to pleasure or pain.

Strait of Malacca Seagoing gateway to Southeast and East Asia.

Strategic Defense Initiative Master plan, championed by U.S. president Ronald Reagan in the 1980s, that envisioned the deployment of satellites and space missiles to protect the United States from incoming nuclear bombs; nicknamed "Star Wars."

stupa Dome monument marking the burial site of relics of the Buddha.

Suez Canal Channel built in 1869 across the Isthmus of Suez to connect the Mediterranean Sea with the Red Sea in order to lower the costs of international trade.

Sufi brotherhoods Sufi religious orders that were responsible for the expansion of Islam into many regions of the world.

Sufis Islamic mystics who stressed contemplation and ecstasy through poetry, music, and dance.

Sufism Emotional and mystical form of Islam that appealed to the common people.

sultan Islamic political leader. In the Ottoman Empire, the sultan combined a warrior ethos with an unwavering devotion to Islam.

Sumerian King List Text that recounts the making of political dynasties. Recorded around 2000 BCE, it organizes the reigns of kings by dynasty, one city at a time.

Sumerian pantheon The Sumerian gods, each of whom had a home in a particular floodplain city. In the Sumerian belief system, both gods and the natural forces they controlled had to be revered.

Sumerian temples Homes of the gods and symbols of Sumerian imperial identity. Sumerian temples also represented the gods' ability to hoard wealth at sites where people exchanged goods and services. In addition, temples distinguished the urban from the rural world.

Sun Yat-sen (1866–1925) Chinese revolutionary and first provisional president of the Republic of China. Sun played an important role in the overthrow of the Qing dynasty and later founded the Guomindang, the Nationalist Party of China.

Sunnis Majority sect within modern Islam that follows a line of political succession from Muhammad, through the first four caliphs (Abu Bakr, Umar, Uthman, and Ali), to the Umayyads and beyond, with caliphs chosen by election from the *umma* (not from Muhammad's direct lineage).

superior man In the Confucian view, a person of perfected moral character, fit to be a leader.

superpowers Label applied to the United States and the Soviet Union after World War II because of their size, their possession of the atomic bomb, and the fact that each embodied a model of civilization (capitalism and communism, respectively) applicable to the whole world.

supranational organizations Organizations that transcend national boundaries, such as nongovernmental organizations (NGOs), the World Bank, and the International Monetary Fund (IMF). These can be distinguished from international organizations, which are intergovernmental projects in which national governments cooperate for common goals—for example, the United Nations, the World Health Organization, and NATO.

survival of the fittest Charles Darwin's belief that as animal populations grew and resources became scarce, a struggle for existence arose, the outcome of which was that only the "fittest" survived to reproduce.

Suryavansha The second lineage of two (the solar) in Vedic society. *See also* Chandravansha.

Swadeshi movement Voluntary organizations in India that championed the creation of indigenous manufacturing enterprises and schools of nationalist thought in order to gain autonomy from Britain.

syndicalists Advocates of syndicalism, a movement of workplace associations that included unskilled labor and sought a replacement for capitalism led by workers. They believed those associations, rather than traditional political parties and parliaments, should make basic decisions.

tabula rasa Term used by John Locke to describe the human mind before it begins to acquire ideas from experience; Latin for "clean slate."

Taiping Heavenly Kingdom (Heavenly Kingdom of Great Peace) Religious sect established by the Chinese prophet Hong Xiuquan in the mid-nineteenth century. Hong Xiuquan believed that he was Jesus's younger brother. The group struggled to rid the world of evil and "restore" the heavenly kingdom, imagined as a just and egalitarian order.

Taiping Rebellion (1850–1864) Rebellion by followers of Hong Xiuquan and the Taiping Heavenly Kingdom against the Qing government over the economic and social turmoil caused by the Opium Wars. Despite raising an army of 100,000 rebels, the rebellion was crushed.

Taj Mahal Royal palace of the Mughal Empire, built by Shah Jahan in the seventeenth century in homage to his wife, Mumtaz.

Tale of Genji Japanese work written in the early eleventh century by Lady Murasaki that gives vivid accounts of Heian court life; Japan's first novel.

talking cure Psychological practice developed by Sigmund Freud whereby the symptoms of neurotic and traumatized patients would decrease after regular periods of thoughtful discussion.

Talmud Huge volumes of oral commentary on Jewish law eventually compiled in two versions, the Palestinian and the Babylonian, in the fifth and sixth centuries BCE.

Talmud of Jerusalem Codified written volumes of the traditions of Judaism; produced by the rabbis of Galilee around 400 CE.

Tang dynasty (618–907 ce) Regime that promoted a cosmopolitan culture, turning China into the hub of East Asian cultural integration, while expanding the borders of its empire. In order to govern such a diverse empire, the Tang established a political culture and civil service based on Confucian teachings. Candidates for the civil service were required to take examinations, the first of their kind in the world.

Tanzimat Reorganization period of the Ottoman Empire in the mid-nineteenth century; its modernizing reforms affected the military, trade, foreign relations, and civilian life.

tappers Rubber harvesters in Brazil, most of whom were either Indian or mixed-blood people.

Tarascans Mesoamerican society of the fifteenth century; rivals to and sometimes subjects of the Aztecs.

Tecumseh (1768–1813) Shawnee who circulated Tenskwatawa's message of Indian renaissance among Indian villages from the Great Lakes to the Gulf Coast. He preached the need for Indian unity, insisting that Indians resist any American attempts to get them to sell more land. In response, thousands of followers renounced their ties to colonial ways and prepared to combat the expansion of the United States.

tekkes Schools that taught the devotional strategies and religious knowledge needed for students to enter Sufi orders and become masters of the brotherhood.

temple Building where believers worshipped their gods and goddesses and where some peoples believed the deities had their earthly residence.

Tenskwatawa (1775–1836) Shawnee prophet who urged disciples to abstain from alcohol and return to traditional customs, reducing dependence on European trade goods and severing connections to Christian missionaries. His message spread to other tribes, raising the specter of a pan-Indian confederacy.

Teotihuacán City-state in a large, mountainous valley in present-day Mexico; the first major community to emerge after the Olmecs.

territorial state A kingdom made up of city-states and hinterlands joined together by a shared identity, controlled through the centralized rule of a charismatic leader, and supported by a large bureaucracy, legal codes, and military expansion.

Third Estate The French people minus the clergy and the aristocracy; this term was popularized in the late eighteenth century and used to exalt the power of the bourgeoisie during the French Revolution.

Third Reich The German state from 1933 to 1945 under Adolf Hitler.

Third World A collective term used for nations of the world, mostly in Asia, Latin America, and Africa, that were not highly industrialized like First World nations or tied to the Soviet bloc (the Second World); it implies a revolutionary challenge to the existing (liberal, capitalist) order. Debate surrounding the best terminology to describe these nations is ongoing.

Thirty Years' War (1618–1648) Conflict begun between Protestants and Catholics in Germany that escalated into a general European war fought against the unity and power of the Holy Roman Empire.

Tiahuanaco Also called Tiwanaku; the first great Andean polity, on the shores of Lake Titicaca.

Tiananmen Square Largest public square in the world and site of the pro-democracy demonstrations in 1989 that ended with the killing of thousands of protesters by the Chinese army.

tiers monde Term meaning "Third World," coined by French intellectuals to describe countries seeking a "third way" between Soviet communism and western capitalism.

Tiglath Pileser III Neo-Assyrian ruler from 745 to 728 BCE who instituted reforms that changed the administrative and social structure of the empire to make it more efficient, and who introduced a standing army.

Tlaxcalans Mesoamerican society of the fifteenth century; these people were enemies of the powerful Aztec Empire.

Tokugawa shogunate Hereditary military administration founded in 1603 that ruled Japan while keeping the emperor as a figurehead; it was toppled in 1868 by reformers who felt that Japan should adopt, not reject, western influences.

Toltecs Mesoamerican peoples who filled the political vacuum left by Teotihuacán's decline; established a temple-filled capital and commercial hub at Tula.

Tomb Culture Warlike group from Northeast Asia who arrived by sea in the middle of the third century CE and imposed their military and social power on southern Japan. These conquerors are known today as the Tomb Culture because of their elevated necropolises near present-day Osaka.

Topkapi Palace Palace complex located in Istanbul that served as both the residence of the sultan, along with his harem and larger household, and the political headquarters of the Ottoman Empire.

total war All-out war involving civilian populations as well as military forces, often used in reference to World War II.

transhumant herders Pastoral peoples who move seasonally from lowlands to highlands in proximity to city-states, with which they trade the products of their flocks (milk, fur, hides) for urban products (manufactured goods, such as metals).

Trans-Siberian Railroad Railroad built over very difficult terrain between 1891 and 1904 and subsequently expanded; it created an overland bridge for troops, peasant settlers, and commodities to move between Europe and the Pacific.

Treaty of Brest-Litovsk (1918) Separate peace between imperial Germany and the new Bolshevik regime in Russia. The treaty acknowledged the German victory on the Eastern Front and withdrew Russia from the war.

Treaty of Nanjing (1842) Treaty between China and Britain following the Opium Wars; it called for indemnities, the opening of new ports, and the cession of Hong Kong to the British.

Treaty of Tordesillas (1494) Treaty in which the pope decreed that the non-European world would be divided into spheres of trade and missionary responsibility between Spain and Portugal.

trickle trade Method by which a good is passed from one village to another, as in the case of obsidian among farming villages; the practice began around 7000 BCE. Also called "down-the-line trade."

Tripartite Pact (1940) Pact that stated that Germany, Italy, and Japan would act together in all future military ventures.

Triple Entente Alliance developed before World War I that included Britain, France, and Russia.

Troy City founded around 3000 BCE in the far west of Anatolia. Troy is legendary as the site of the war that was launched by the Greeks (the Achaeans) and that was recounted by Homer in the *Iliad*.

Truman Doctrine (1947) Declaration promising U.S. economic and military intervention, whenever and wherever needed, for the sake of preventing communist expansion.

Truth and Reconciliation Commission Quasi-judicial body established after the overthrow of the apartheid system in South Africa and the election of Nelson Mandela as the country's first Black president in 1994. The commission was to gather evidence about crimes committed during the apartheid years. Those who showed remorse for their actions could appeal for clemency. The South African leaders believed that an airing of the grievances from this period would promote racial harmony and reconciliation.

truth commissions Commissions established to inquire into human rights abuses by previous regimes. In Argentina, El Salvador, Guatemala, and South Africa, these commissions were vital for creating a new aura of legitimacy for democracies and for promising to uphold the rights of individuals.

tsar Russian word derived from the Latin *Caesar* to refer to the Russian ruler of Kiev, and eventually to all rulers in Russia. Also spelled as *czar*.

Tula Toltec capital city; a commercial hub and political and ceremonial center.

Uitlanders Literally, "outsiders"; British populations living in Afrikaner republics, who were denied voting rights and subjected to other forms of discrimination in the late nineteenth century.

ulama Arabic word that means "learned ones" or "scholars"; used for those who devoted themselves to knowledge of Islamic sciences.

Umayyads Family who founded the first dynasty in Islam. They established family rule and dynastic succession to the role of caliph. The first Umayyad caliph established Damascus as his capital and was named Mu'awiya Ibn Abi Sufyan.

umma Arabic word for "community"; used to refer to the Islamic polity or Islamic community.

Universal Declaration of Human Rights (1948) U.N. declaration that laid out the rights to which all human beings are entitled.

universalizing religions Religions that appeal to diverse populations; are adaptable to new cultures and places; promote universal rules and principles; proselytize new believers, often through missionaries; foster community; and, in some cases, do all of this through the support of an empire.

universitas Term used from the end of the twelfth century to denote scholars who came together, first in Paris. The term is borrowed from the merchant communities, where it denoted the equivalent of the modern union.

untouchables People in the Indian *varna* (caste) system whose jobs, usually in the more unsanitary aspects of urban life, rendered them "ritually and spiritually" impure.

Upanishads First-millennium BCE Vedic wisdom literature, in the form of a dialogue between students and teacher; together with the Vedas, they brought a cultural and spiritual unity to much of South Asia.

urban-rural divide Division between those living in cities and those living in rural areas. One of history's most durable worldwide distinctions, the urban-rural divide eventually encompassed the globe. Where cities arose, communities adopted lifestyles based on the mass production of goods and on specialized labor. Those living in the countryside remained close to nature, cultivating the land or tending livestock. They diversified their labor and exchanged their grains and animal products for necessities available in urban centers.

utopian socialism The most visionary of all Restoration-era movements. Utopian socialists like Charles Fourier dreamed of transforming states, work-places, and human relations and pro-posed plans to do so.

Vaishyas Householders or lesser clan members in Vedic society who worked the land and tended livestock.

Vardhamana Mahavira Advocate of Jainism who lived from around 540 to 468 BCE; he emphasized interpretation of the Upanishads to govern and guide daily life.

varna Sanskrit for "color"; refers to the four ranked social groups within early Vedic society (priests, warriors, commoners, and laborers). The term *caste*, which derives from the term *casta* ("race/breed" in Spanish and Portu-guese) is a later, anachronistic term often used for these divisions.

vassal states Subordinate states that had to pay tribute in luxury goods, raw materials, and manpower as part of a broad confederation of polities under a king's protection.

Vedas Rhymes, hymns, and explana-tory texts composed and orally transmit-ted in Sanskrit by Brahman priests. They shaped the society and religious rituals of Vedic peoples and became central texts in Hinduism.

Vedic peoples Indo-European nomadic group who migrated from the steppes of Inner Asia around 1500 BCE into the Indus basin, on to the Ganges River valley, and then as far south as the Deccan plateau, bringing with them their distinctive religious ideas (Vedas), Sanskrit, and domesticated horses.

veiling Practice of modest dress required of respectable women in the Neo-Assyrian Empire, introduced by Middle Assyrian authorities in the thirteenth century BCE.

Venus figures Representations of the goddess of fertility drawn on the Chauvet Cave in southeastern France. Discovered in 1994, they are probably about 35,000 years old.

Versailles Conference (1919) Peace conference among the victors of World War I; resulted in the Treaty of Versailles, which forced Germany to pay reparations and to give up its colonies to the victors.

Viet Cong Vietnamese communist group committed to overthrowing the government of South Vietnam and reunifying North and South Vietnam.

Viet Minh (League for the Indepen-dence of Vietnam) Group founded in 1941 by Ho Chi Minh to oppose the Japanese occupation of Indochina; it later fought the French colonial forces for independence.

Vietnam War (1965–1975) Conflict that resulted from U.S. concern over the spread of communism in Southeast Asia. The United States intervened on the side of South Vietnam in its struggle against peasant-supported Viet Cong guerrilla forces, who wanted to reunite Vietnam under a communist regime. Faced with antiwar opposition at home and ferocious resistance from the Vietnamese, American troops withdrew in 1973; the puppet South Vietnamese government collapsed two years later.

Vikings Warrior group from Scandi-navia that used its fighting skills and sophisticated ships to raid and trade deep into eastern Europe, southward into the Mediterranean, and westward to Iceland, Greenland, and North America.

Vishnu The second of three Vedic deities, signifying existence. *See also* Brahma *and* Shiva.

viziers Bureaucrats of the Ottoman Empire.

vodun Mixed religion of African and Christian customs practiced by enslaved and free Blacks in the colony of Saint-Domingue.

Voting Rights Act (1965) Law that granted universal suffrage in the United States.

Wafd Nationalist party that came into existence during a rebellion in Egypt in 1919 and held power sporadically after Egypt was granted limited independence from Britain in 1922.

Wahhabism Early eighteenth-century reform movement organized by Muhammad Ibn Abd al-Wahhab, who preached the absolute oneness of Allah and a return to the pure Islam of Muhammad.

Wang Mang Han minister who usurped the throne in 9 CE because he believed that the Han had lost the mandate of heaven. He ruled until 23 CE.

war ethos Strong social commitment to a continuous state of war. The Roman army constantly drafted men and engaged in annual spring military campaigns. Soldiers were taught to embrace a sense of honor that did not allow them to accept defeat, and those who repeatedly threw themselves into battle were commended.

War of 1812 Conflict between Britain and the United States arising from U.S. grievances over oppressive British maritime practices in the Napoleonic wars.

War on Poverty U.S. president Lyndon Johnson's push for an increased range of social programs and increased spending on social security, health, education, and assistance for the disabled.

Warring States period Period extending from the late fifth century to 221 BCE, when China's regional warring states were unified by the Qin dynasty.

Warsaw Pact (1955–1991) Military alliance between the Soviet Union and other communist states that was established in response to the creation of the North Atlantic Treaty Organization (NATO).

Weimar Republic (1919–1933) Constitutional republic of Germany that was subverted by Hitler soon after he became chancellor.

Western Front Battlefront that stretched from the English Channel through Belgium and France to the Alps during World War I.

White and Blue Niles The two main branches of the Nile, rising out of central Africa and Ethiopia, respectively. They come together at the present-day capital city of Sudan, Khartoum.

White Lotus Rebellion Series of uprisings in northern China (1790–1800s) inspired by mystical beliefs in folk Buddhism and, at times, the idea of restoring the Ming dynasty.

White Wolf Mysterious militia leader, depicted in popular myth as a Chinese Robin Hood whose mission was to rid the country of the injustices of Yuan Shikai's government in the early years of the Chinese republic (1910s).

Whites "Counterrevolutionaries" of the Bolshevik Revolution (1917) who fought the Bolsheviks (the Reds); included former supporters of the tsar, Social Democrats, and large independent peasant armies.

witnessing Dying for one's faith, or becoming a martyr.

wokou Supposedly Japanese pirates, many of whom were actually Chinese subjects of the Ming dynasty.

Works Progress Administration (WPA) New Deal program instituted in 1935 that put nearly 3 million people to work building roads, bridges, airports, and post offices.

World Bank International agency established in 1944 to provide economic assistance to war-torn and poor countries. Its formal title is the International Bank for Reconstruction and Development.

World War I *See* Great War.

World War II (1939–1945) Worldwide war that began in September 1939 in Europe, and even earlier in Asia, and pitted Britain, the United States, and the Soviet Union (the Allies) against Nazi Germany, Japan, and Italy (the Axis).

Wu, Emperor (r. 141–87 BCE) Also known as Emperor Han Wudi, or the "Martial Emperor"; the ruler of the Han dynasty for more than fifty years, during which he expanded the empire through his extensive military campaigns.

Wu Zhao Chinese empress who reigned from 684 to 705 CE. She began as a concubine in the court of Li Shimin and became the mother of his son's child. She eventually gained power equal to that of the emperor, and she named herself regent when she finagled a place for one of her own sons after their father's death.

Xiongnu The most powerful and intrusive of the nomadic peoples of Inner Asia; originally pastoralists from the eastern part of the Asian steppe in what is modern-day Mongolia. They appeared along the frontier with China in the late Zhou dynasty and by the third century BCE had become the most powerful of all the pastoral communities in that area.

Xunzi (310–237 BCE) Confucian moralist whose ideas were influential to Qin rulers. He believed that rational statecraft was more reliable than fickle human nature and that strict laws and severe punishments could create stability in society.

Yalta Accords Results of a meeting between President Roosevelt, Prime Minister Churchill, and Premier Stalin held in the Crimea in 1945 to plan for the post–World War II order.

Yavana kings Sanskrit name for Greek rulers, derived from the Greek name for the area of western Asia Minor called Ionia, a term that was then extended to anyone who spoke Greek or came from the Mediterranean.

yellow press Newspapers that sought mass circulation by featuring sensationalist reporting.

Yellow Turbans Daoist millenarian Chinese religious movement that emerged during the Later (Eastern) Han period. The group was named for the yellow scarves adherents wore around their heads.

Yin City that became the capital of the Shang dynasty in 1350 BCE, ushering in a golden age.

Young Egypt Antiliberal, fascist group that gained a large following in Egypt during the 1930s.

Young Italy Nationalist organization founded in 1832, made up of young students and intellectuals devoted to the unification and renewal of the Italian state.

Yuan dynasty Dynasty established by the Mongols after the defeat of the Song. The Yuan dynasty was strong from 1279 to 1368; its capital was at Dadu, or modern-day Beijing.

Yuan Mongols Mongol rulers of China who were overthrown by the Ming dynasty in 1368.

Yuezhi A Turkic nomadic people who roamed pastoral lands to the west of the Xiongnu territory of central Mongolia. They had friendly relationships with the farming societies in China, but detested the Xiongnu and had frequent armed clashes with them.

zaibatsu Large-scale, family-owned corporations in Japan, consisting of factories, import-export businesses, and banks, that dominated the Japanese economy until 1945.

zamindars Archaic tax system of the Mughal Empire in which decentralized lords collected tribute for the emperor.

Zapatistas Group of indigenous rebels that rose up against the Mexican government in 1994 and drew inspiration from an earlier Mexican rebel, Emiliano Zapata.

Zheng *See* Shi Huangdi.

Zheng He Ming naval commander who, from 1405 to 1433, led seven massive naval expeditions to impress other peoples with Ming might and to establish tributary relations with Southeast Asia, Indian Ocean ports, the Persian Gulf, and the east coast of Africa.

Zhong Shang Administrative central complex of the Shang.

Zhongguo Term originating in the ancient period and subsequently used to emphasize the central cultural and geographic location of China in the world; means "the middle kingdom."

ziggurat Stepped platform that served as the base of a Sumerian temple, which had evolved from the earlier elevated platform base by the end of the third millennium BCE.

Zionism Political movement advocating the reestablishment of a Jewish homeland in Palestine.

Zoroaster Sometimes known as Zarathustra; thought to have been a teacher around 1000 BCE in eastern Iran and credited with having solidified the region's religious beliefs into a unified system that moved away from animistic nomadic beliefs. The main source for his teachings is a compilation called the Avesta.

Zoroastrianism Dualistic Persian religion, based on the teaching of Zoroaster, in which forces of light and truth battle with those of darkness and falsehood.

Zulus African tribe that, under Shaka, created a ruthless warrior state in southern Africa in the early nineteenth century.

Credits

Front endpaper: ixstudio/Alamy Stock Photo; frontispiece: Photo Josse/Bridgeman Images; rear endpaper: Arunas Gabalis/Alamy.

Chapter 1

Page 9: Robert Preston/Alamy; p. 13: John Reader/Science Source; p. 14: Sabena Jane Blackbird/Alamy Stock Photo; p. 16: Pascal Goetgheluck/Science Source; p. 17: Lionel Bret/Science Source; p. 25: Ariadne Van Zandbergen/Alamy Stock Photo; p. 26: Prisma by Dukas Presseagentur GmbH/Alamy Stock Photo; p. 28: Erich Lessing/Art Resource; p. 33: Kimbell Art Museum, Fort Worth Texas/Art Resource; p. 41: De Agostini Picture Library/Getty Images.

Chapter 2

Page 47: © artefacts-berlin.de; Material: German Archaeological Institute; p. 54: Granger Collection; p. 56: Peter Bull Art Studio; p. 57: World Religions Photo Library/Alamy Stock Photo; p. 58: Penn Museum, image #141592; p. 60: (top left) Alamy Stock Photo; (top right) Erich Lessing/Art Resource; (bottom left) Ancient Art and Architecture/Alamy Stock Photo; (bottom right) © The Trustees of the British Museum/Art Resource; p. 67: National Geographic Image Collection/Alamy Stock Photo; p. 68: The Picture Art Collection/Alamy Stock Photo; p. 69: (left) World History Archive/Alamy Stock Photo; (right) Heritage Image Partnership Ltd/Alamy Stock Photo; p. 74: robertharding/Alamy Stock Photo; p. 77: Asian Art & Archaeology Inc./CORBIS/via Getty Images; p. 78: HIP/Art Resource; p. 81: Image Hans Elbers/Getty Images.

Chapter 3

Page 91: (top left) Art Resource; (top right) Scala/Art Resource; (bottom right) Imaginechina Limited/Alamy Stock Photo; p. 96: John Beasley/Alamy Stock Photo;

p. 97: Jose Lucas/Alamy Stock Photo; p. 100: Album/Alamy Stock Photo; p. 101: (right) DEA/S. VANNINI/De Agostini/Getty Images; (left) Peter Horree/Alamy Stock Photo; p. 104: (left) bpk Bildagentur/Vorderasiatisches Museum, Staatliche Museen/Art Resource; (right) De Agostini Picture Library/Bridgeman Images; p. 106: PRISMA ARCHIVO/Alamy Stock Photo; p. 109: ephotocorp/Alamy Stock Photo; p. 111: Hobart and Edward Small Moore Memorial Collection, Gift of Mrs. William H. Moore, Yale University Art Gallery; p. 116: Lyndon Giffard Images/Alamy Stock Photo; p. 121: WaterFrame/Alamy Stock Photo; p. 122: Erich Lessing/Art Resource.

Chapter 4

Page 132: (left) A. Paul Jenkin/Animals Animals; (right) Alexander Frolov/Alamy Stock Photo; p. 135: The Trustees of the British Museum/Art Resource; p. 136: Heritage Image Partnership Ltd/Alamy Stock Photo; p. 141: EmmePi Travel/Alamy Stock Photo; p. 142: Lloyd Cluff/Getty Images; p. 143: Scala/Art Resource; p. 145: Courtesy of the Metropolitan Museum of Art; p. 148: (left) Dagli Orti/Shutterstock; (right) North Wind Picture Archives; p. 152: Dinodia Photos/Alamy Stock Photo; p. 153: (both) The Trustees of the British Museum/Art Resource; p. 156: Giraudon/Art Resource; p. 157: Freer Gallery of Art, Smithsonian Institution/Bridgeman Images.

Chapter 5

Page 167: Artokoloro Quint Lox Limited/Alamy Stock Photo; p. 172: Pictures from History/Bridgeman Images; p. 174: Courtesy of the Hunan Provincial Museum; p. 175: SSPL/Getty Images; p. 178: Paul Almasy/Corbis/VCG via Getty Images; p. 180: Borromeo/Art Resource; p. 184: gameover/Alamy Stock Photo; p. 185: World History Archive/Ann Ronan Collection/age fotostock; p. 186: Francis Farquhar/Bridgeman Images; p. 188: Scala/Art Resource; p. 191: Insights Images/Peter Langer/Media Bakery; p. 197: Eric Lafforgue/age footstock.

Chapter 6

Page 205: Luisa Ricciarini/Bridgeman Images; p. 208: Erich Lessing/Art Resource; p. 209: (left) Bridgeman Images; (right) A. Dagli Orti/De Agostini Picture Library/Bridgeman Images; p. 212: Vanni/Art Resource; p. 214: William Francis Warden Fund/Bridgeman Images; p. 215: DeA Picture Library/Art Resource, NY; p. 217: Werner Forman Archive/Bridgeman Images; p. 221: (left) Brian A. Vikander/Getty Images; (right) Bridgeman Images; p. 223: (top row) The Granger Collection; (middle row) Dilip Rajgor/Dinodia Photo/age fotostock; (bottom left) MCLA Collection/Alamy Stock Photo; (bottom right) Jonathan O'Rourke/Alamy Stock Photo; p. 225: Igor Dymov/Alamy Stock Photo; p. 226: Courtesy of The Cleveland Museum of Art; p. 227: (both) Courtesy of The Metropolitan Museum of Art; p. 229: (top row) Heritage Image Partnership Ltd/Alamy Stock Photo; (middle row) The History Collection/Alamy Stock Photo (bottom row) PjrStudio/Alamy Stock Photo; p. 233: DEA/G. DAGLI ORTI/Getty Images; p. 235: NASA/JPL.

Chapter 7

Page 245: Courtesy of The Art Institute of Chicago; p. 249: Snark/Art Resource; p. 250: (top) Patrick AVENTURIER/Gamma-Rapho via Getty Images; (bottom) Bridgeman Images; p. 251: British Museum/Art Resource; p. 252: DeAgostini/Getty Images; p. 254: (left) Artokoloro Quint Lox Limited/Alamy Stock Photo; (middle and right) Asian Art & Archaeology Inc./Getty Images; p. 260: Courtesy of the Museum of Fine Arts Boston; Museum purchase with funds donated by Mrs. Gardner Brewer and by contribution and the Benjamin Pierce Cheney Donation; p. 264: Vanni/Art Resource; p. 266: Atlantide Phototravel/Getty Images; p. 267: Album/Alamy Stock Photo; p. 268: (left) Cultura RM/Alamy Stock Photo; (right) Scala/Art Resource; p. 269: (left) Toño Labra/age fotostock; (right) The Print Collector/Alamy Stock Photo; p. 271: HIP/Art Resource; p. 275: Erich Lessing/Art Resource.

Chapter 8

Page 287: (left) Nir Alon/Alamy Stock Photo; (right) Granger Collection; p. 288: Scala/Art Resource; p. 291: The State Hermitage Museum, St. Petersburg/photo by Vladimir Terebenin; p. 292: Ozbalci/Getty Images; p. 296: INTERFOTO/Alamy Stock Photo; p. 297: (left) Art Resource; (right) Martin Lindsay/Alamy Stock Photo; p. 299: akg-images; p. 300: Heritage Image Partnership Ltd/Alamy Stock Photo; p. 302: ephotocorp/Alamy Stock Photo; p. 305: Art Collection 3/Alamy Stock Photo; p. 308: Historical Views/age fotostock; p. 311: EDU Vision/Alamy Stock Photo; p. 313: Angelo Hornak/Alamy Stock Photo; p. 314: Werner Forman/Art Resource; p. 315: Kumar Sriskandan/Alamy Stock Photo.

Chapter 9

Page 321: SUHAIB SALEM/REUTERS/Newscom; p. 330: (left) geogphotos/Alamy Stock Photo; (right) Patrick Ward/Getty Images; p. 335: (left) Michel Piccaya/Shutterstock; (right) B.O'Kane/Alamy Stock Photo; p. 339: (left) De Agostini Picture Library/Bridgeman Images; (right) CPA Media Pte Ltd/Alamy Stock Photo; p. 340: (left) Werner Forman/Art Resource; (right) Kurt Scholz/SuperStock; p. 342: Eye Ubiquitous/Alamy Stock Photo; p. 345: (left) CulturalEyes-AusGS/Alamy; (right) Paul Fearn/Alamy Stock Photo; p. 349: GoFrance/Neil Sutherland/Alamy Stock Photo; p. 350: Giraudon/Bridgeman Images; p. 351: (left) imageBROKER/Alamy Stock Photo; (right) robertharding/Alamy Stock Photo; p. 353: Heritage Image Partnership Ltd/Alamy Stock Photo; p. 354: INTERFOTO/Alamy Stock Photo.

Chapter 10

Page 360: Godong/Alamy Stock Photo; p. 363: Granger; p. 364: Lao Ma/Shutterstock; p. 367: British Library Board. All Rights Reserved/Bridgeman Images; p. 371: Keren Su/China Span/Alamy Stock Photo; p. 375: FLHC 16/Alamy Stock Photo; p. 376: Hemis/Alamy Stock Photo; p. 377: Granger; p. 381: GL Archive/Alamy Stock Photo; p. 382: British Library Board/Robana/Art Resource; p. 386: The Picture Art Collection/Alamy Stock Photo; p. 387: Hemis/Alamy Stock Photo; p. 388: Bridgeman

Art Library/Getty Images; p. 389: (top) Beren Patterson/Alamy Stock Photo; (bottom) INTERFOTO/Alamy Stock Photo; p. 399: akg-images.

Chapter 11

Page 408: Sarin Images/Granger; p. 412: DeAgostini/Getty Images; p. 416: Sonia Halliday Photo Library/Alamy Stock Photo; p. 417: Muhammed Enes Yldrm/Anadolu Agency/Getty Images; p. 418: The Stapleton Collection/Bridgeman Images; p. 421: volkerpreusser/Alamy Stock Photo; p. 424: incamerastock/Alamy Stock Photo; p. 426: Granger; p. 428: (left) Ian Dagnall/Alamy Stock Photo; (right) Classic Image/Alamy Stock Photo; p. 429: Everett Collection Historical/Alamy Stock Photo; p. 432: Granger; p. 434: RMN-Grand Palais/Art Resource; p. 437: (left) The Picture Art Collection/Alamy Stock Photo; (right) Gregory A. Harlin/National Geographic Image Collection/Bridgeman Images.

Chapter 12

Page 447: akg-images/Cameraphoto; p. 450: Photo Josse/Bridgeman Images; p. 451: G. Dagli Orti/De Agostini Picture Library via Getty Images; p. 453: bpk Bildagentur/Art Resource; p. 455: Sarin Images/Granger; p. 457: (left) Granger; (right) Pictures from History/Granger; p. 463: Sarin Images/Granger; p. 469: INTERFOTO/Alamy Stock Photo; p. 473: Reunion des Musees Nationaux/Art Resource; p. 475: Sarin Images/Granger; p. 477: Courtesy of Indiana University Library.

Chapter 13

Page 490: (top) Courtesy of the Rijksmuseum, Purchased with the support of the Vereniging Rembrandt; (bottom) The Picture Art Collection/Alamy Stock Photo; p. 494: (left) Peter Newark American Pictures/Bridgeman Images; (right) North Wind Picture Archives/Alamy Stock Photo; p. 496: Granger; p. 499: (right) HIP/Art Resource, NY; (left) North Wind Picture Archives; p. 502: Bridgeman Images; p. 503: Sarin Images/Granger; p. 507: Dagli Orti/REX/Shutterstock; p. 509: Album/Alamy Stock Photo; p. 510: Artokoloro Quint Lox Limited/Alamy Stock Photo; p. 514: The

Picture Art Collection/Alamy Stock Photo; p. 517: Dagli Orti/REX/Shutterstock; p. 521: INTERFOTO/Alamy Stock Photo; p. 524: Peter Willi/Bridgeman Images.

Chapter 14

Page 531: DeAgostini/Superstock; p. 534: (left) Christie's Images/Bridgeman Images; (right) Victoria & Albert Museum London/Art Resource; p. 536: Pictures Now/Alamy Stock Photo; p. 537: (left) Scala/Art Resource; (right) Granger; p. 538: ART Collection/Alamy Stock Photo; p. 541: (left) Underwood & Underwood/Library of Congress/Corbis/VCG via Getty Images; (right) Library of Congress; p. 544: Bridgeman Images; p. 546: Alan Tobey/Getty Images; p. 547: Courtesy of The Metropolitan Museum of Art, The Michael C. Rockefeller Memorial Collection, Bequest of Nelson A. Rockefeller, 1979; p. 551: Peter Willi/Superstock; p. 553: (top) Archives Charmet/Bridgeman Images; (bottom) Bridgeman Images; p. 555: The Getty/Science Source; p. 557: SPCOLLECTION/Alamy Stock Photo; p. 560: (left) Album/Art Resource; (right) Bridgeman Images; p. 562: Courtesy of Le Bulletin de l'Institut Français d'Études Andines; p. 565: (left) HIP/Art Resource; (right) Granger.

Chapter 15

Page 573: Antiqua Print Gallery/Alamy Stock Photo; p. 574: FALKENSTEIN-FOTO/Alamy Stock Photo; p. 578: Library of Congress; p. 581: Hulton Archive/Getty Images; p. 582: Dagli Orti/REX/Shutterstock; p. 583: Bridgeman Images; p. 584: Sarin Images/Granger; p. 590: Michael Graham-Stewart/Bridgeman Images; p. 593: North Wind Picture Archives/Alamy Stock Photo; p. 597: Sarin Images/Granger; p. 604: Bridgeman Images; p. 607: North Wind Picture Archives.

Chapter 16

Page 620: (left) GL Archive/Alamy Stock Photo; (right) Smith Archive/Alamy Stock Photo; p. 621: Bonhams LondonUK/Bridgeman Images; p. 624: Pictures from History/Bridgeman Images; p. 630: Granger; p. 635: (both) Granger; p. 637: Granger; p. 639: Witold Skrypczak/Alamy Stock Photo; p. 643:

Public Domain; p. 645: V&A Images London/Art Resource; p. 646: Artokoloro Quint Lox Limited/Alamy Stock Photo.

Chapter 17

Page 656: (both) Sarin Images/Granger; p. 659: (right) CPA Media Pte Ltd/Alamy Stock Photo; (left) Artokoloro Quint Lox Limited/Alamy Stock Photo; p. 660: Dmitri Kessel/The LIFE Images Collection/Getty Images; p. 665: History Archive/REX/Shutterstock; p. 669: Private Collection (uncredited photo) from "Through Indian Eyes" by Judith Gutman, Oxford University Press; p. 670: Chronicle/Alamy Stock Photo; p. 674: (left) Hulton Archive/Getty Images; (right) Bridgeman Images; p. 675: Dagli Orti/REX/Shutterstock; p. 676: DeA Picture Library/Granger; p. 678: Album/Alamy Stock Photo; p. 680: The Art Archive/REX/Shutterstock; p. 681: Granger; p. 685: Sovfoto/Universal Images Group/Shutterstock.

Chapter 18

Page 698: Library of Congress; p. 699: Chronicle/Alamy Stock Photo; p. 703: ullstein bild/Granger; p. 705: SuperStock; p. 708: Science History Images/Alamy Stock Photo; p. 710: Public Domain; p. 713: Sean Sprague/Mexicolore/Bridgeman Images/© 2020 Banco de México Diego Rivera Frida Kahlo Museums Trust, Mexico, D.F./Artists Rights Society (ARS), New York; p. 715: Art Library/Alamy Stock Photo/© 2020 Estate of Pablo Picasso/Artists Rights Society (ARS), New York; p. 716: (left) National Gallery London/Art Resource; (right) Erich Lessing/Art Resource; p. 717: Historic Collection/Alamy Stock Photo; p. 721: Schalkwijk/Art Resource NY/© 2020 Banco de México Diego Rivera Frida Kahlo Museums Trust, Mexico, D.F./Artists Rights Society (ARS), New York; p. 723: (left) SZ Photo/Bridgeman Images; (right) Granger; p. 724: E. O. Hoppe/Getty Images; p. 725: Dagli Orti/REX/Shutterstock.

Chapter 19

Page 735: Public Domain; p. 736: Heritage Image Partnership Ltd/Alamy Stock Photo; p. 737: Three Lions/Getty Images; p. 740: Everett Collection Historical/Alamy Stock Photo; p. 744: Performing Arts Images/ ArenaPA/TopFoto; p. 745: (left) Album/Alamy Stock Photo; (right) Library of Congress; p. 747: Chronicle/Alamy Stock Photo; p. 750: Library of Congress; p. 752: Granger; p. 754: Shawshots/Alamy Stock Photo; p. 760: Genevieve Naylor/Corbis via Getty Images; p. 763: (both) Bridgeman Images; p. 764: ullstein bild via Getty Images; p. 765: Sueddeutsche Zeitung Photo/Alamy Stock Photo.

Chapter 20

Page 775: Laski Diffusion/Getty Images; p. 776: Patrizia Wyss/Alamy Stock Photo; p. 779: Three Lions/Getty Images; p. 781: Everett Collection Historical/Alamy Stock Photo; p. 785: Bettmann/Getty Images; p. 791: Heritage Image Partnership Ltd/Alamy Stock Photo; p. 793: FPG/Getty Images; p. 795: The Print Collector/Alamy Stock Photo; p. 797: Associated Press; p. 803: Roger-Viollet/TopFoto; p. 804: Bettmann/Getty Images; p. 807: Rolls Press/Popperfoto/Getty Images; p. 808: CTK/Alamy Stock Photo.

Chapter 21

Page 819: Keystone/Getty Images; p. 822: Peter Turnley/Corbis/VCG via Getty Images; p. 825: david pearson/Alamy Stock Photo; p. 826: Dana Fradon via Cartoon Collections; p. 831: Uriel Sinai/Getty Images; p. 833: Michael Ochs Archives/Stringer/Getty Images; p. 834: JSK/Alamy Stock Photo; p. 841: Vanessa Vick/Redux; p. 846: Susan I. Cunningham/Panos Pictures; p. 850: Peter Turnley/Corbis/VCG via Getty Images; p. 853: AP Photo/Jeff Widener; p. 854: Clive Shirley/Panos Pictures.

Chapter 22

Page 861: AP Photo/Carmen Taylor; p. 863: AP Photo/Jason DeCrow; p. 865: Xinhua/Alamy Stock Photo; p. 867: Xinhua/Alamy Stock Photo; p. 868: Sipa USA/Alamy Stock Photo; p. 876: AP Photo/Andres Kudacki; p. 880: ullsteinbild/TopFoto; p. 881: Timothy O'Rourke/Bloomberg via Getty Images; p. 883: AP Photo/Channi Anand; p. 885: AP Photo/Nasser Nasser; p. 887: Khaled Akasha/Anadolu Agency/Getty Images; p. 889: Alamy Stock Photo; p. 900: SOPA Images Limited/Alamy Stock Photo; p. 901: Greg Gard/Alamy Stock Photo.

Index

trade across, 104–105, 203, 214–215,
   228, *230–231,* 293–294,
   361–364, *362,* 394, 400
universal religions in, 281, *286,* 315
western imperial fringes of,
   142–148, *146*
Age of Ideology, 626
age of universe, *7*
aging, 838–839
Agni (Vedic god), 152
agora (marketplace), 185, *186,* 213,
   222, 233
Agra, India, 445, 538, 604
agricultural diffusion in first millennium,
   333
agricultural villages, 27, 38–40, *45,*
   71, 73
agriculture. *see also* climate change;
   farmers; irrigation; peasants; planters,
   plantations; plows; *specific nations
   and empires*
      and 1200 BCE drought, 128
      in Africa, 331
      in Americas, 391, 657
      of Aztecs, 456
      between 1600–1750, 499, 507,
         514, 515, 522–523
      between 1750–1850, 591, 601, 605
      between 1850–1914, 657, 671, 675
      between 1910–1939, 751–752
      in China, 75–77, 113–114,
         173–174, 331, 372–373,
         432–433, 473
      and climate change, 365
      commercialization of, 522–523
      decline of subsistence, 71
      and decolonization, *795*
      diffusion of, *333,* 340–341
      and economy, 522–523, 591
      and engineering innovations,
         340–341
      and Enlightenment, 549
      and enslaved people, 214–215
      and enslaved people trade, 499
      in Europe, 81, 83, *333*
      and expansion and nation building,
         657
      as flood-dependent, 52–53, 63,
         70–71, 75, 95, 128
      and globalization, 836, 842–843
      and imperialism, 671, 675

importance of water in, 48
in India, 331
in Indus Valley, 151
and iron, 129
and Islamic world, 331
and land ownership, 257–258
Mayan, 312
and Morocco, 331
and Mughal Empire, 508
and new colonies in Americas, 491
origins of, 27–29, *30–31, 45*
and politics, 751–752
in Roman Empire, 270
in Southeast Asia, 331
in Soviet Union, 751–752
and Spain, 331
and three-world order, 797
in West Africa, 331
ahimsa (non-violence), 180, 372
Ahmosis, 99
Ahriman, 139
Ahura Mazda (Ahuramazda), 139
Aï Khanoum, Afghanistan, 211, 223
AIDS (Acquired Immunodeficiency
   Syndrome). *see* HIV/AIDS
air pollution, 271
Airavata, *109*
Aisha, 325
Akbar (Mughal ruler), 471, 508, *536,*
   536–537
Akhenaten, *106*
Akkadians, 55, 56, 59, 60–62, *87,* 104
Akragas, coinage, 185
al-Assad, Bashar, *834,* 865–866,
   886, 887
al-Assad, Hafez, 886
al-Azhar mosque, 334, *335*
al-Azhar (university), 368
al-Baghdadi, Abu Bakr, 889–890
Al Jazeera, 886
Al-Khayzurān Bint Atta, 328
al-Nahda, 886
al-Qaeda, 859, 860, 861, 877, 888–890
al-Qarawiyyin (university), 368
al-Shatir, Ibn, 368
al-Sisi, Abdel-Fattah, 886
Al-Umari, *386*
al-Zarqawi, Abu Musab, 888–889
al-Zawahiri, Ayman, 888
Alaça Hüyük, Anatolia, 80
Alalakh, 143

Buddhacarita (Aśvaghosa), 226

Buddhism, 179–181, *201*, 203, 276,
    286, 317
    and alternative visions of
        nineteenth century, 622
    art and architecture of, *178, 180,
        225*, 226–228
    of Aśoka, 220–221
    between 1750–1850, 606
    and Brahmans, 179–181, *180*
    in central Asia, 281, 296–297
    in China, 281, 296–297, 305–306,
        315, 319, 335, 337, 341–343,
        345, 606
    Confucianism *vs.*, 315
    and cosmopolitanism, 225–228,
        364
    and creation story, 4
    and culture, 541, 543–544
    Dunhuang cave temple, 341
    Eightfold Way of, 181
    ethics of, 180–181, 225–226,
        238, 281
    Four Truths of, 181
    Gandharan, *180*
    Hinayana, 300–301
    in India, 296, *297,* 345
    in Japan, 345, *345,* 543–544
    in Korea, 345
    libraries of, 306
    Madhyamika, 305–306
    Mahayana, 203, 225–226,
        300–301, 305–306, 377
    monasteries of, 224, 302, 306,
        341, *342*
    in Red Turban Movement, 408
    and reincarnation, 225
    scriptures of, *305,* 305–306
    in Southeast Asia, 377
    spread with trade, *230–231,*
        236–238, 282, 296–297, *297,*
        298, 345
    Tang persecution of, 342–343
    transformation of, 225–228, 238, *240*
    as universalizing religion, 281,
        301–302, 305–306, 315, 345
    and Vedic gods, *109*
Buddhists, 220

Buenos Aires, Argentina, 588, 595, 659,
    695, 715, 721, 893
    neighborhoods in, 699

Buffon, Georges Louis LeClerc, comte
    de, 554

Bukhari, al-, 330

bureaucracy. *see also* administration;
    specific nations and empires
    of Aegeans, 122
    and alternative visions of nineteenth
        century, 624–625, 644
    between 1600–1750, 509–511, 518
    between 1750–1850, 602
    between 1850–1914, 663,
        685–686, 687–688
    of Chinese empires, 158–159, 173,
        244–245, 246, 250–251, 276,
        432–433, 439
    and consolidation of nation-states
        in Europe, 663
    in early cities, 49, 58, 65, 70
    of Ottoman Empire, 414–415,
        416–419, 433
    of Persian Empire, 138
    in Russia, 518
    in Soviet Union, 685–686
    in territorial states, 95, 100

burials, ancient of Han empire, *245*

Burma (Myanmar), 399, 514, 668,
    695, 777

Burundi, 892

Bush, George W., 845
    and war on terror, 860–861

Buttigieg, Pete, 901

Buyid family, 365

Byblos, 97

Byzantine Empire, Byzantium, 292–293,
    295, *317,* 347, 366, 381, 398, 400,
    438–439
    and Arabia, *356*
    and Islam, 322, 324, *326–327*
    and Ottoman Empire, 416
    and Turks, 366

C

Cable News Network (CNN), 853

Cabral, Pedro Álvares, 453

Cabrera, Miguel, *531*

Caffa, 404

Cahokia, 391–393, *392, 402*

Cairo, Egypt, *335, 362,* 365, 368, 695,
    837, 885, *885*
    as maritime commercial center, 361
    as Umayyad capitol, 334

China, Chinese (*Continued*)
Christianity in, 281, *339*, 400, 542, 687, 703
civil wars of, 249, 259, 303–304
and climate change, 77, 511, 866
coins from, 174, *175*, 235, *251*, 252
and Cold War, 785
and colonization between 1450–1600, 445, 452, 464, 474–478
and commerce and trade, 445–446, 452, 464, 474–478, *477*, 532–533
communism in, 785
Communist Revolution in, 785–787, 794, 797, 809
and COVID-19 pandemic of 2020, 866–867, 868
and creation story, 4
cultural modernism, *717*
culture in, 540–542, 567, *569*, 717–718, 802–803
defensive walls in, 249, 250, 256, 297, *297*, 395
democracy in, 852
diversity in, 540–542
Eastern Zhou dynasty of, 166–175, *170, 201*
economic growth in, 878, 879–882
economy of, *175*, 245, 248–249, 252–253, 255–256, 340–341, 362–364, *373*, 436, 445–446, 509–511, 514, 706, 802–803
education in, 687, 840
elites in, 687, 722–723
emigration of, 695
and Enlightenment, 556–557
enslaved people in, 114, 254, 258, 275
expansion of, 483, 540–542
expansionism in, 679
farmers in, 445
feminism in, 711
first cities in, 75–79, 85
first emperor of (*see* Shi Huangdi ("First August Emperor"))
flag of, 722
footbinding in, *541*, 711
foreigners in, 621, 687, 703–706
founding of republic, 722–723
and globalization, 824–826, *825*, 838, 840, 852, 878, 879–882, 899

Great Leap Forward in, 802–803, *813*
and Great Recession of 2008–2009, 863
and Great Wall, 512
Han dynasty of, 242, 244–246, *247*, 249–250
health care in, 839
and Hellenism, 236
and HIV/AIDS, 839
and Hong Kong, 881–882
and imperialism, 668, 703–706
India's trade with, 341, 377, 378
innovations of, 234, 252–253
and Iranian Nuclear Deal, 891
and Islam, 400
and Japan, 335, *344*, 377, 445, 510, 513, 517, 542, 543–544, 683, 686–687, 703, *705*, 777, 785–787
Korea influenced by, 335, 343, *344*
and literacy, 556
and Little Ice Age, 489
Long March in, 785, *786*
maritime ventures in, 436–437
and mass politics, 760, 763–765
and migration, 695
Ming, 430–437, *435, 440*
modernism in, 717–718, 722–723
Mongol conquest of, 398–400, *399*, 407
nationalism in, 763–765
navigational innovations of, 360, *363*
"one-child family" policy, 837
"open door" policy in, 703
"opening" of, 606–609
and opium, 606–609, *607*, 621, 624
and Ottoman Empire, 445
and pan movements, 725
as People's Republic of China, 787, 881–882
and persistence and change in Eurasia, 600
popular protests in, 722
population changes in 14th century, 409
population of, 369, 407, 430, 445, 474, 512, 606, 622, 703, 838
populism in, 763–765

E

Ea (Sumerian god), 56
early humans. *see* hominids; hominins; *Homo sapiens*
East Africa, 331. *see also specific nations*
    between 1600–1750, 498
    between 1890–1914, 692, 702
    and commerce and colonization
        between 1450–1600, 445, 452
    and enslaved people trade, 498
    and imperialism, 702
    Islam in, 331
    and World War I, 733, 735
East Asia. *see also specific countries*
    agriculture in, 33–35, *34*
    between 200–600, *316–317*
    between 200 BCE–200 CE, 242–259
    between 221 BCE–200 CE, *247*
    between 300–600, 303–306
    between 300 BCE–300 CE, *278–279*
    between 400–200 BCE, *240–241*
    between 600–1000, *346–357*
    between 700–1300, *402–403*
    between 1300–1500, *440–441*
    between 1500–1780, 539–545
    between 1600–1750, 515–518
    between 1850–1914, 679, 687–688
    between 1910–1939, *758*
    and commerce and colonization
        between 1450–1600, 445–446
    culture in, 539–545
    first century BCE, *257*
    first cities of, 75–79, *76*
    and globalization, 824–826
    hominins' migration to, 15–17
    politics in, 539–545
    territorial states in, 110–115
    Zhou Empire of, 154–160, *155, 162–163*, 166–175, *170*
East Germany, 781
East India Company (English), 478, 594, 644, 645
    and Asia in seventeenth and
        eighteenth centuries, 504
    between 1600–1750, 504, 508
    between 1750–1850, 602–603, *603*, 606
    between 1850–1914, 669–670
    and Calcutta, 604
    and commerce and colonization
        between 1450–1600, 478

    and imperialism, 669–670
    and India, 602–603, *603,* 641, 643, 669–670
    and Mughal Empire, 508
    and Qing dynasty, 606
East India Railway, *670*
East Indies, 478
Easter (holiday), 288
Easter Island, 117
Eastern Europe. *see also specific nations*
    between 1910–1939, 737, 741, *742*
    and Cold War, 780–782
    and globalization, 816, 827
    Soviet client states in, *812*
    and tensions in world communism, 807–808
    and three-world order, 807–808
    and World War I, 737, 741, *742*
    and World War II, 790
Eastern Front in World War I, *734*
Eastern Han dynasty, 258–259
Eastern Mediterranean
    climate change in, 365
    marginal settlements of, 79, *82*
    territorial states of, *98*
Eastern Zhou China, 166–175, *170*
    administration of, 173
    economy of, 173–175
    philosophies of, 167, 171
    Spring and Autumn period of, 166, 173–175
    warfare of, 167, 173
    Warring States period of, 166–175, *170, 172,* 199, 242, 246, 249
Eastman Kodak, 679
Ebola, 859, 866
ecological crisis, in the Amazon, *846*
economic globalization, 878–884
economic inequality, 863–864, 893–899
economy. *see also* consumption; Great Depression (1930s); production; *specific nations and empires*
    and 1200 BCE drought, 128
    between 1600–1750, 506–507, 510–511, 514, 526
    between 1750–1850, 572, 601, 604–605
    between 1850–1914, 655–656, 658–660, 665, 666–667, 671, 675–676, 681

India (*Continued*)
    Swadeshi Movement in, 719, 724
    and three-world order, 800
    trade by, 363, 369
    Turks in, 369, 370, 371, 372
    varna system of, 151–152
    and World War I, 731, 737
    and World War II, 777
    and worldwide insecurities, 711
Indian National Congress Party, 724,
    728, 762, 763, 787, 850
Indian Ocean, 331, 388, 393, 533
    between 1600–1750, 498, 508
    and commerce and colonization
        between 1450–1600, 445,
        451–452, 461, 471, 479
    enslaved people trade of, 388, 498
    and expansion of Ottoman Empire,
        446
    and Mughal Empire, 508
    navigation of, 360
    opened to commerce, 224, 232,
        236–238
    and overland commerce, 446
    trade in, 446, 508
Indian Rebellion, *646*
Indian subcontinent. *see* India; Mughal
    Empire
Indians. *see* American Indians; *specific*
    tribe
Indica (Megasthenes), 220
"individual," rise of, 213, 214
Indo-European languages, 90,
    105, 109
"Indo-Greek" cities, 222
Indo-Iranian language, 137
Indochina, 777
Indonesia, 117, 800, 809
    imperialism in, 671
Indra (Vedic god), 109, *109,* 153
Indus River, 47, 85, *87,* 125, 218
Indus River valley, 71–75. *see also* India;
    South Asia; Vedic people
    agriculture in, 175
    first cities of, 71–75, *72*
    nomads in, 90, 107–110, 123, 129,
        130–131
    territorial states in, 107–110
    Vedic culture of, *150,* 151, 160
industrial revolution, 592, 596–597, *599,*
    655–656, 665–666

industrialization. *see also* production
    and alternative visions of
        nineteenth century, 613, 631
    in Americas, 655–656
    between 1750–1850, 596–597, 604
    between 1850–1914, 651, 652,
        655–656, 665–667
    between 1890–1914, 694, 713
    between 1910–1939, 752, 762
    and economy, 596–597
    in Egypt, 601
    and expansion and nation-building,
        651, 652, 655–656
    and globalization, 817, 827, 836
    in India, 604, 762
    and mass politics, 752
    and regulation, 713
    in Soviet Union, 752, 799–800
    and worldwide insecurities, 713
infectious diseases. *see also* Black Death
    (bubonic plague)
    and cities, 268
    and climate, 398
    and "Dark Ages," 346
    and expansionism, 229, 255, 293
inflation, in China, 375
Inner Eurasian steppes, nomads from, 90,
    92–93, 130–131
Inner Mongolia, 52
Inquisition, 425, *441,* 467, *469*
Institutes (of Roman law), 293
integration, colonization *vs.,* 62, 238
intellectuals
    and alternative visions of
        nineteenth century, 628
    and Americas, 561–562
    between 1500–1750, 533–534
    between 1500–1780, 531
    between 1890–1914, 714,
        715–717, 723–724
    between 1910–1939, 753
    in China, 474
    and culture, 531, 533–534, 536–539,
        561–562, 714, 715–717
    and Enlightenment, 549–552
    in Hungary, 799
    in India, 723–724
    and Islam, 533–534
    and mass politics, 753
    in Mughal Empire, 536–539
    and nationalism, 723–724

and pan movements, 725–726
in Soviet Union, 753
and three-world order, 794, 799–800
in Vietnam, 794
Intergovernmental Science-Policy
Platform on Biodiversity and
Ecosystem (IPBES), 865
International Committee of the Red
Cross, 848
international language, Greek as, 211–212
International Monetary Fund (IMF),
800, 815, 823, 847
Internet, 814, 824, 835–836. *see also*
social media
intoxicants, 83. *see also* alcohol
Ionia, 223
Iran, 616, 809, 851. *see also* Persia,
Persians; Safavid Empire; *specific cities*
and Iranian Nuclear Deal, 891–892
Ottoman Empire in, 446
Sasanian rule of, 294–295, *317*
Shiites repressed in, 334
Sogdians in, 294, 296
Iranian Nuclear Deal, 891–892, *905*
Iranian plateau, transhumant herders
from, 90
Iranian Revolution, 851
Iraq, 616, *743*, 809, *891*. *see also* Baghdad,
Iraq
agriculture in, 388
anti-colonialism in, 741–743
and climate change, 505
invasion of, 859, 860–861, *904*
invasion of Kuwait, 843–844
Islamic conquest of, 322
as part of Mesopotamia, 52
Shiites repressed in, 334
and World War I, 731, 735
Ireland, 349, *351*, 352, 598, 663, 664,
749
emigration from, 664
and Great Recession of
2008–2009, 862
and migration, 694, 695
potato famine, 598, *665*
and World War I, 736
Irish Potato Famine, 598, *665*
iron
bronze replaced by, 94, 129
in China, 252, 373
in Ganges River plain, 175, 177

in Indus Valley, 110
plows, 110, 129, 151, 156, 174
in sub-Saharan Africa, *195*, 197,
198, 307
Iron Age, 129
Iroquois people, 489
irrigation, 432
and empire, 156–157, 248, 256
and first cities, 48, 54–55, 57,
63–65, 70–71, 84
Isabel, princess, *659*
Isabella of Castile, queen of Spain, 425,
426, 453
Isfahan, 535, *568*
Ishtar (Sumerian goddess), 56
ISIS. *see* Islamic State in Iraq and Syria
(ISIS)
Isis (Egyptian goddess), 68, *68*, 214
Iskandariya, 209
Islam, 318–319, 350, 364–365, *366*,
383, 388, 400, 405, 413, 416, 422,
425, 888. *see also* Crusades; Mughal
Empire; Muslims; Ottoman Empire;
Safavid Empire; Shiites; Sufis, Sufism;
Sunnis
in Africa, 331, *332*, 365, 367, 384,
388
and agriculture, *333*, 340
and alternative visions of
nineteenth century, 647
and anti-colonialism, 766–767
anti-immigrant sentiments,
876–877
between 1500–1780, 533–535,
545, 552, 566–567
between 1600–1750, 505–509
between 1890–1914, 711, 719,
725–726
between 1910–1939, 766–767
and Byzantines, 322, 324, *326–327*
and China, 328, 400
and climate change, 505
and colonization between
1450–1600, 478
and commerce and trade, 478
conversion to, 322, 324
and Crusades, 383–384
cultural flowering of, 368–369
culture in, 533–535, 545, 552,
566–567
and decolonization, 791

Mars (Roman god), 261
Marshall, George C., 781
Marshall Plan, 781
Martí, José, 650
Martin, Trayvon, 900
Martínez, Pedro, 834
martyrs
    Christian, 273, 280–281, 283, *287*
    Muslim, 283
Marx, Karl, 631–632, 647, *648, 721*
Marxism, 631–632, 685
Mary (mother of Jesus), *292*
Mary of Orange, queen of England, 524
mass production, 57
Massachusetts, 578
Master Kong. *see* Confucius
Master Lao (Laozi), 171, 259
Master Xun (Xunzi), 171–172
Master Zhuang (Zhuangzi), 171
Matamba, *502*
mathematics
    in Abbasid period, 330
    Mayan, 313
    in South Asia, 302
    in Southwest Asia and
        Mediterranean, 189
"Mathuran style," 226, *227*
Matilda, Queen, *381*
Mattel, 901
Matthew (disciple), 272
Matthias, Monika, 868–869
Maues, king, *223*
Maulavi Ahmadullah Shah, 644
Mauritius, 667
Mauryan Empire, 203, *206–207,*
    219–222, 238, *241*
Mawangdui texts, *235*
Mayans, 281, *310,* 311–314, *313,* 315, *315,*
    316, 637–641, *639,* 713
    and archaeological discoveries, 312
    cultural practices of, 312–314
Mazu, *364*
Mbundu, *502*
McCarthy, Joseph, 797
Meat Inspection Act (U.S., 1906), 713
Mecca, 320, *321,* 323, 324, *386,* 387
Medes, Medians, 133
media, 715, 731, 744–746, 832–833.
    see also radio
Medici family, 427
medicine, 512, 517. *see also* health care

Medina, 321
Mediterranean region. *see also* Carthage;
    Greece, Greeks; Levant; Roman
    Empire
    and Assyrian Empire, *134*
    in Axial Age, *168–169*
    colonization of, *195*
    and commerce and colonization
        between 1450–1600, 445, 452,
        464, 478
    and expansion of Ottoman Empire,
        446–450
    Greek city states of, *183*
    Greek colonization of, *146, 163,*
        186–187
    Hellenism in, 204–218, *206–207*
    marauders from, 129
    marginal settlements in, *82*
    and overland commerce, 445–446
    Phoenician city states of, *183*
    Phoenician colonization of, *146,*
        186–187, 218
    and revival of trade, 445–446, 452
    Roman Empire in, 260–261,
        262–263, 273–275, *278–279*
    "second-generation" societies of,
        182–189, *183*
    trade in, 118–119, *122, 183*
megaliths, *81, 82*–83
Megasthenes, 219–220
Megiddo, Battle of, 101
Mehmed II, 447
Mehmed the Conqueror, 416, 442, *534,*
    535
Meiji Restoration, 679–681, *682, 687, 691*
Mein Kampf (Hitler), 755
Melaka (Malacca), 361, *362, 363,* 504
men. *see* gender
Menander, *223,* 223–224
Menelik II (Ethiopian ruler), 672, 674, *675*
menorah, *217*
mercantilism, 485–488, 522, 525–526,
    550–551
merchants. *see also* chartered royal
  companies
    and African trade, 465, 498, 503,
        591
    and alternative visions of
        nineteenth century, 629
    and American Revolution, 578
    in Americas, 488

Mosul, 890
Mount Fuji, *517*
Mount Vesuvius, *266*
Mozambique, 793, 821, 831, 893
Mu Wang, Zhou king, *156*
Mubarak, Gamal, 886
Mubarak, Hosni, 885, *885*
muckraking, 707, *708*
Mugabe, Robert, 821
Mughal Empire, 604, 615
    and alternative visions of
        nineteenth century,
        641–646
    authority in, 508
    between 1600–1750, 484, 485,
        504, 507–509, 515, 518, 527
    between 1750–1850, 604
    and colonial reordering in India,
        604
    and commerce and colonization
        between 1450–1600, 473
    and culture between 1500–1780,
        532, 536–539
    diversity in, 471
    economy in, 473, 484, 485,
        508–509
    elites in, 508, 539
    end of, 485
    expansion of, *472*, 473, *481*, 508,
        529
    and Indian rebellion of 1857,
        641–646
    and insurgencies against colonizing
        and centralizing states,
        641–646
    Islam in, 471
    population of, 471
    revenue system in, 471
    and Safavid Empire, 504
    Turkish warriors in, 414
    unrest in, 484, 485, 508, 527
    wealth of, 473
    women in, 537
    zenith and decline of, 508–509
Muhammad, prophet of Islam, 319, 325,
    334, 616, 618
    and Christian texts, 322–323
    and conflicting biographical data,
        322–323
    early biographies of, 322–323
    and Jewish texts, 322–323

and lack of 7th-century
    Arabic-Muslim sources,
    322–323
life of, 320–323, *356*
in Medina, 320–321
mulattoes, *560*
multinational corporations, 801, 810
Mumbai, India, *300*, 832, 884
Murad II, Ottoman emperor, 415
Murshidabad, 604
Muscovy, 518
music
    in Han China, 253, *254*
    of *Homo sapiens,* 26
Muslim ban, *876*, 877
Muslim Brotherhood, *769*, 791, 886
Muslim League, 762–763, 788
Muslims, 615–621, 888. *see also* Islam;
    Shiites; Sufis, Sufism; Sunnis; *specific*
    ethnicities, nations and regions
    in Africa, 893
    and alternative visions of nineteenth
        century, 643, 644, 647
    and anti-colonialism, 762–763,
        766–767
    anti-immigrant sentiments,
        876–877
    between 1600–1750, 498
    between 1750–1850, 603
    between 1850–1914, 672
    between 1890–1914, 722, 725
    between 1910–1939, 762–763,
        766–767
    and China, 722
    and commerce and colonization
        between 1450–1600, 452, 473
    creationism of, 4
    and culture between 1500–1780,
        533–535
    and enslaved people trade, 465, 498
    and Europe, 876–877
    Fulani people, 616, 618–619
    and globalization, 851
    and imperialism, 672
    in India, 603, 643, 644, 724–725,
        762–763, 787–788
    and insurgencies against colonizing
        and centralizing states, 643, 644
    and mass politics, 762–763,
        766–767
    and Mughal Empire, 471

New Netherland, 493
New Rome. *see* Constantinople
New Spain, 561
New World
  between 1600–1750, 485, 491,
    493, 498, 511, 518
  and commerce and colonization
    between 1450–1600, 443, 445,
    452, 461–465, 477, 478
  and culture between 1500–1780,
    532, 550, 558–563, 566
  and economy, 485, 505–506
  and enslaved people trade,
    498–503
  and new colonies in Americas,
    491, 493
  and silver, 483
New York City, 493, 575, 656, 659, 695,
  698, 823
  Occupy Wall Street, *863*, 864
  September 11, 2001, attacks,
    858–859, 860, *861*
New York Stock Exchange, 656
New Zealand, 563, 695, 710, 737
  in World War I, 731
Newton, Isaac, 548, *569*
NGO Forum, 842
NGOs. *see* non-governmental
  organizations (NGOs)
Nguni peoples, 619
Ngwale, Kinjikitile, 692
Nicaragua, 816
Nicene Creed, 288
Nicholas I, tsar of Russia, 600–601
Nicholas II, tsar of Russia, 737
Nietzsche, Friedrich, 717
Niger, 489
Niger Delta, 893
Niger River, early settlement along, 84
Nigeria, 616, 618–619, 672, 801, 823, 893
  Bantu origin in, 281, 307
  and Benin and Oyo Empire, 546
  between 1850–1914, 676
  civil war in, 801
  and globalization, 827, 830
  and imperialism, 676
  Nok culture in, 198
  and three-world order, 801, 809
  women in, 795–796
  and World War I, 733
Nika riots (Byzantium), 293

Nike (company), 833, 855
Nile River, 47, 85, 141, 601
  11th and 12th century CE drought
    and, 365
  and 1200 BCE drought, 128
  early settlement along, 63–65, 194,
    196
Nimrud, palace at, *135*
Nineveh
  as capital city, 133
  fall of, 137
Nippur, Mesopotamia, 55, 56
nirvana, 181, 225, 300
Nixon, Richard, 807, 823
Nkrumah, Kwame, 788, 800
nobility. *see* elites
Noh, 543
Nok, 166, *168–169,* 198, *201*
nomadic pastoralists, 28–29
nomads
  in Afro-Eurasia, 1200 BCE,
    128–129, *130–131,* 137
  Afro-Eurasian communities of, 52,
    79, *92–93*
  and climate change, 365–367
  from Inner Eurasian steppes, 90,
    92–93
  invasions of, 229, 232, 238–239
  and territorial states, 94–95, 101,
    107–108
  and trade, 90, 229, *230–231,* 232
Nomo, Hideo, 834
non-governmental organizations (NGOs),
  848
nonviolence
  in civil rights movement, 798
  espoused by Aśoka, 220
  and Jains, 180
nonviolent resistance, 761–762
Normandy, D-Day landing at, 775
North Africa, 319, 334, 386, 618. *see also*
  Carthage; Egypt, Egyptians
  Assyrian Empire in, *134*
  Berbers in, 367
  between 1910–1939, *742*
  and colonization between
    1450–1600, 443
  and commerce and trade, 443
  enslaved people in, 386
  Islam in, 329, 330, 334
  Ottoman Empire in, 446

Soviet Union (*Continued*)
and Second World, 797, 798–800,
807–809
and Stalin, 751–753, 770
and Suez crisis, 791–792
and tensions in world communism,
807–809
and three-world order, 770–771,
797, 799–800, 801, 804,
807–809
and Turkey, 766
and Warsaw Pact, *783,* 799, *808*
women in, 757
World War II and, *772,* 774–775,
780
Spain, 187, 319, 384, 422, 424–426, *481,*
586–589
and agriculture, 331
and alternative visions of
nineteenth century, 638
and Americas, *462, 492,* 494, 559,
586–589
and Asia in seventeenth and
eighteenth centuries, 504
and Aztec Empire, 456–457
bankruptcy of, 470
between 1600–1750, 483, 485, *492,*
494, 496, 504, 518, 522, 526
between 1750–1850, 571, 584
between 1850–1914, 650, 658, 677
between 1890–1914, 713, 720
Christianity in, 330, 425–426
colonies of, 483, 494
and colonization between 1450–
1600, *453,* 453–454, 461–465,
462, 463, 470
and commerce and trade, 453, *453,*
461–465, *462, 463,* 470, 477
Cortes in, 422
counter-caliphate in, 324
and culture, 550, 559, *560,* 561
and Dutch independence, 470
and economy, 485, 522
and globalization, 830
Granada taken by, 425, *426, 441*
and Great Recession of 2008–
2009, 862
and imperialism, 677
and insurgencies against colonizing
and centralizing states, 638
Islam in, 324, 330, *330,* 425

Judaism in, 330, 425
and Little Ice Age, 489
and mercantilism, 526
and Mexican independence, 588
monarchy in, 425–426
and Napoleonic Empire, 584
and nation-building, 655, 658
and Peninsular War, 584
population, 430
and race, 720
reconquering Iberian Peninsula, *402*
and religious wars, 470
and transformation of Europe, 518
tribute for, 461
and worldwide insecurities, 713
Spanish-American War (1898), 677, *691*
Spanish flu of 1918–1919, 859, 867
Sparta, 144, 182, 186
women in, 183–184
Spartacus, 215, 270
specialization of labor, rise of cities and,
49, 55–56, 58, 67, 73, 178–179
spheres of influence, 703, 771
Spice Road, 232, 237
spice trade, *230–231,* 232, 237
and Asia in seventeenth and
eighteenth centuries, 504
between 1600–1750, 483, 504, 512
and China, 512
and commerce and colonization
between 1450–1600, 444, 446
spies, as tool of empire, 139
Spring and Autumn period of Zhou
dynasty, 160, 166, 173–175, *201*
Spurius Lilgustinus, 261
Sputnik, 799, *813*
Sri Lanka (Ceylon), 670
St. Bartholomew's Day Massacre, 470
St. George, Fort, 478
Stalin, Joseph, 751–753, 770, 780, 782,
799, 808, *812*
Stalingrad, 774, *774*
Standard Oil, 655, 666, 707
standardization
Persian, 138–139
Qin, 248
Roman, 270
Stanley, Henry Morton, 672, *674*
statecraft, 173, 303–304. *see also*
diplomacy
Stateira, 208

and nationalism, 803–805
and nuclear age, 782
overview of, 796
and rebuilding of Europe, 780–782
and Second World, 799–800,
807–809
tensions in, 771, 805–810
and Third World, 800–805,
809–810
and Vietnam, 793–794
and World War II and its
aftermath, 772–780
Thucydides, 144
Thuku, Harry, 795
Thutmosis II, king of Egypt, 101
Thutmosis III, king of Egypt, *100,* 101,
197
Thysdrus, *268*
Tiananmen Square, 852, *853, 857*
Tianjin, China, 705
Tiberius Gracchus, 265, *278*
Tibet, 398, 514, 605, 722
China invaded by, 336
Chinese expansion into, 336
Tiglath Pileser III, king of Assyria, *135*
Tigris and Euphrates rivers, 47, 52–53,
295
Tigris River, 85
Tikal, 312, 314, *314*
Timbuktu, 387, 393, 489
Timor, 563
Tippecanoe River, 636
Tipu Sultan, *604*
Tiryns, 122
Tlaxcalans, 456
tobacco, 491, 503, 679
toilets, ancient Aegean, 121. *see also*
sanitation
Tokugawa Japan, 515–518, *516, 528,* 539,
543–545, 679
Tokyo, 515, *517, 544,* 695, 696, 698, *698,*
823, 836–837, 846
in World War II, 775
Tolstoy, Leo, 685
Toltecs, 391, *393, 402*
Tomb Culture, 343
tombs, royal, *58,* 65–67, *69, 97*
Tometi, Opal, 900
Topkapi Palace, 417–418, *418,* 431, 533,
535
Torah, 148

torture, in early empires, 140
Toumai skull *(Sahelanthropus tchadensis),*
8, 12
Tower of the Palace, *313*
towns, garrison, 222–224
trade. *see also* caravan trading; commerce;
mercantilism; merchants; overland
commerce; Silk Road
with Africa, 591, 675–676
in Afro-Eurasia, 203, 214–215,
224, 228
in Afro-Eurasia, c. 150 CE, *230–231*
and alternative visions of nineteenth
century, 622, 638–639
with Americas, 491, 495–497
and Asia in seventeenth and
eighteenth centuries, 510–511
between 1450–1600, 445–446
between 1600–1750, 488,
495–497, 503, 506, 510–511,
514, 517, 518, 522, 525–526
between 1750–1850, 572, 591,
601, 604, 606–609
between 1850–1914, 669, 681
between 1890–1914, 703
between 1910–1939, 759, 760
and Calcutta, 604
in central marketplace, 185
with China, 445–446, 510–511,
514, 606–609, 622, 703
and commerce and colonization
between 1450–1600, 445–446,
447, 461–465, 473
and COVID-19 pandemic of 2020,
868
and culture between 1500–1780,
531, 532–533, 548
and early empires, 128, 129, 139,
140
in eastern Mediterranean, *120*
and economy, 522, 591–592,
666–667
and Egypt, 601
and Enlightenment, 548
in enslaved people (*see* enslaved
people trade)
first cities as centers of, 49, *64, 72,*
74–75, 84
free, 591–592, 604, 669
and globalization, 824–826, 835
and imperialism, 669

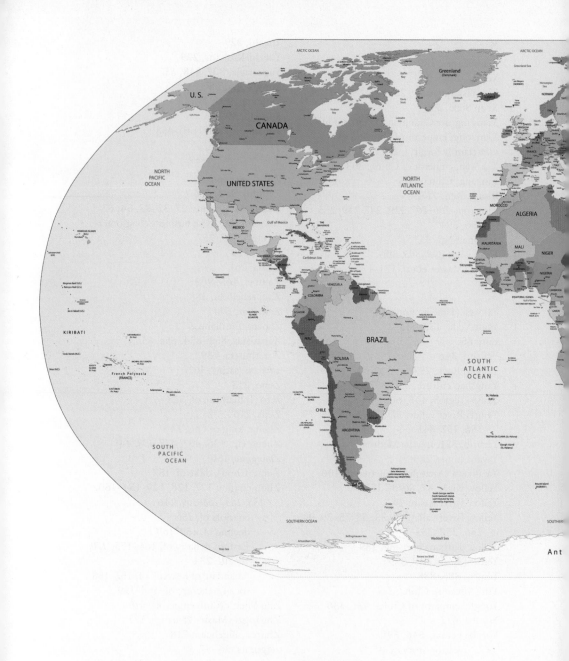

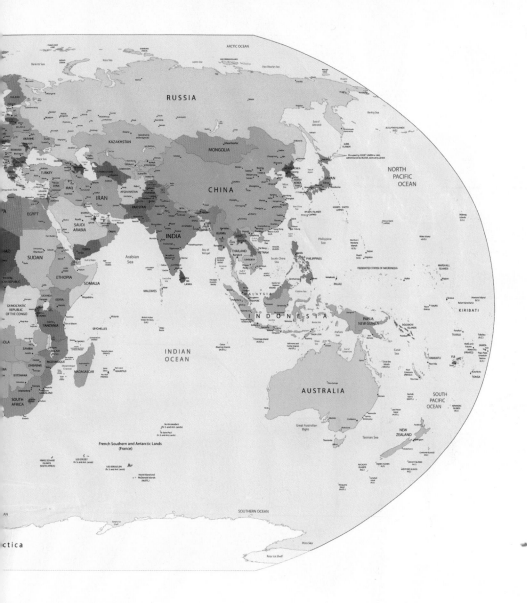